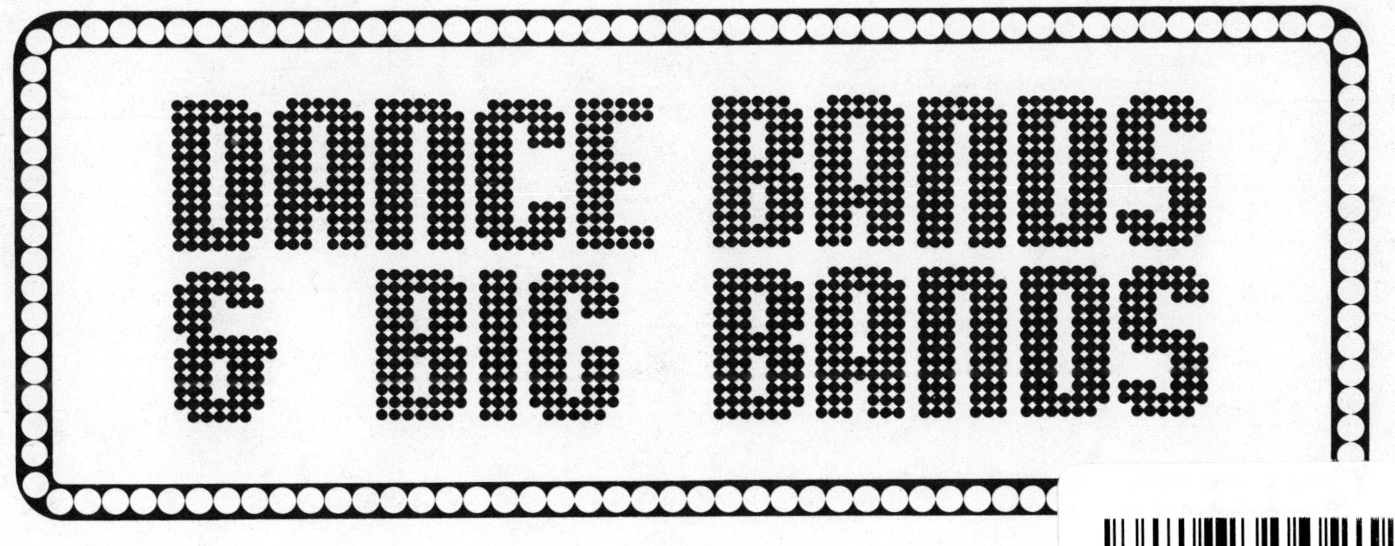

by

Alice Rogers

DOCUMENTING OVER 30,000 GOLDEN AGE DANCE & BIG BAND RECORDINGS – ALL ON 78rpm SINGLES.

ROGERS, Alice

"Dance Bands and Big Bands Buyers-Sellers Reference Book and Price Guide"

Printed in United States of America

First Edition — First Printing ISBN – 0-932117-01-5

AUTHOR'S INTRODUCTION

What a spendid time it was – the era of the great dance bands and big bands in the 1920s, '30s, and '40s – when life was slower, more simple, and even more carefree despite the Great Depression, until this country entered into the most far-flung war that the world had ever known. For a dollar or less, a guy could take this best girl out dancing to the music of their favorite orchestra, for a respite from harsh economic times or from war worries. Or, they could dance to their special phonograph records, or simply tune in the radio, when the music of a wide variety of great bands filled the air waves nightly.

And now for more than a decade, there has been a marked renewal of interest in the big bands, and people are again dancing to sweet and swing band music from coast to coast.

Artie Shaw, after 30 years' retirement, has formed a new orchestra; their first engagement was the re-opening of the famed Glen Island Casino, newly rebuilt at a cost of millions of dollars, on 26 acres of Long Island Sound. There are plans to bring in many more groups to play big band-type music, and it appears from the capacity crowds flocking to the Casino thus far, that it will shortly regain its legendary greatness of the big band era.

Tex Beneke and His Orchestra regularly play engagements nationwide, generally booked solid for a year or more in advance; Count Basie continued to appear with his orchestra until his death in April 1984 at the age of 79. Benny Goodman, now 76, remains active, playing in concerts, and was the winner of *Down Beat* magazine's poll for best clarinetist of 1983.

Many other groups, both from the big band era and newly-formed bands, are playing dance band music around the nation. A glance at your favorite band's listing in this book will tell you whether or not the group is still active.

This resurgence of interest in the big band does not appear to be limited to the over-50 crowd on a nostalgia trip. Many members of the younger generation have also discovered swing and cheek-to-cheek dancing, and a large number of high school and college bands are again playing the music of Glenn Miller, Tommy Dorsey and others from the big-band/dance band era, as well as traditional and modern jazz.

In view of the above and of the fact that there are a large number of record collectors specializing in dance band and big band records, this Dance Band and Big Band Guidebook has been added to Jerry Osborn's Buyers-Sellers Reference Book and Price Guide Series.

This first edition documents nearly 16,000 records from the 1890's into the 1950's, but primarily those great 78s from the 1920s, '30s and '40s are recalled, priced and arranged for examination. This book also includes a number of jazz as well as blues records because of the cross-overs practiced by many bands. Both sides of each release are listed alphabetically by the "A" (or first) side, and vocalists on each side are noted. Other information of sufficient interest which affects the value of the record on the collector's market is included.

In this edition we have noted the values only for records in "very good" condition, which is halfway between "good" and "near mint." A record is "good" condition – which should not be synonymous for "bad" – would be worth half the listed price, while records in "near mint" condition would be worth fifty per cent more than the value shown. However, "near mint" 78 rpm records are rarely found today; thus the noted prices, and below for the more common "good" condition, represent the average sale at this time.

You'll find, however, that this book is much more than simply a source for determining the values of the big band, dance band, some jazz and blues records in your collection, or of those which you are contemplating buying or selling.

For instance, many bands recorded extensively under a bewildering array of pseudonyms, particularly in the 1920s and early 1930s, and these pseudonyms have plagued record collectors and dealers since. Here, by means of cross-referencing, the identity of the recording band is easily discovered simply by looking up, alphabetically, the pseudeonyms credited on thousands of labels. As an example, the label on Okeh 8836 lists the *Harlem Footwarmers* as the performing band. Upon looking for the *Harlem Footwarmers*, you will find the cross reference: see *Ellington, Duke & His Orchestra.* In the Duke Ellington section will be found a caption which reads: *Ellington, Duke, & His Orchestra as The Harlem Footwarmers*, and it is there that Okeh 8836 is documented.

To add to the confusion, many bands even recorded under double pseudonyms on occasion. Thus, while the label of Claxtonola 40373 credits the *Dixie Boys*, a referral to the Dixie Boys in the alphabetical listing will indicate that the record will be found under the heading *California Ramblers, The, as The Vagabonds recorded under the name The Dixie Boys.* One artist alone recorded under 47 different band names and pseudonyms documented in this book, yet everything he did is listed together! This feature alone makes this book a must for collectors and dealers.

Much additional information will be found throughout this book. Most bandleaders' birth dates, and dates of death if deceased, are noted, and if the group continues to play engagements, this is also indicated.

To name just a few of the little known facts to be found all through this book: Ben Selvin was the most prolific of all the recording dance band leaders; Sam Lanin was second; The Coon-Sanders Original Nighthawk Orchestra was the first band to gain popularity through regular radio broadcasts; Candy Candido, string bassist and vocalist with Ted Fio Rito and His Orchestra, reportedly had the widest voice range in the world; Fred MacMurray of later motion picture and television fame, played tenor saxophone in the orchestras of George Olsen and Gus Arnheim in 1929 and 1930 respectively.

Did you know that the first "Gold Record" was awarded to Glenn Miller in 1942 for *"Chattanooga Choo Choo,"* which was the first million-selling record since 1927 due to the economic condition of the period? For a more complete explanation, see *I Know Why /Chattanooga Choo Choo"* under Glenn Miller and his Orchestra– a classic example of the "B" (or second) side of the record becoming the "hit" side.

And, did you know that there was a song titled *"Rock And Roll"* in 1934?! It was featured in an obscure motion picture musical, *"Transatlantic Merry-Go-Round,"* which starred the Boswell Sisters accompanied by Jimmie Grier and His Orchestra. In this instance, "rock and roll" simply referred to the rocking and rolling of the waves, or "ocean motion," and it is believed that this was the first time that the phrase "rock and roll" was used as a song title. For more details, see Joe Haymes & His Orchestra, Johnny Johnson & His Orchestra, and Harry Reser & His Orchestra.

And now, a few words about the alphabet, or how to find your favorite bands.

Individual names, whether genuine bandleaders or pseudonyms, are listed last name first in strict alphabetical order, without regard to punctuation or spaces between words. Names of groups are shown first name first (disregarding a, an, and the) and song titles are alphabetized in the same manner, by the "A" (or first) side.

Groups of pseudonyms used by and documented under authentic bands are set up somewhat differently. It is felt that pseudonymous names such as Frank Auburn and His Orchestra, which sound like genuine names of orchestra leaders, would be more easily located among a maze of pseudonyms if filed under the surname, *disregarding the first name and other extraneous words such as and, his, and the,* for alphabetical purposes.

For example, Fred Rich has 25 different bands and pseudonyms arranged for examination in this book; among them you will see *Rich, Fred, & His Orchestra as Richard Hampton & His Orchestra,* which precedes *Rich, Fred & His Orchestra as Lloyd Keating's Music.* On the other hand, pseudonyms which have group-sounding names are alphabetized under the first name, (again disregarding a, an, and the). As an example, *Rich, Fred, & His (La Palina) Orchestra as the New York Syncopators* is followed by *Rich, Fred, & His (La Palina) Orchestra as George Wells & His Orchestra.*

As always, comments and criticisms are welcome, and particularly we welcome direction and input to verify listings reflected herein, to amplify information known, or to correct errors.

Following are some of the things we'd appreciate from our collector-friends:

(1) Clear, glossy photos of any rare records not pictured in this book.

(2) Unpublished, or rare photos of any of the stars which you would be willing to lend us for reproduction in our second edition. We will take care of them and return them, of course.

(3) Substantiated dates of release on any that are missing from our listing.

(4) Information on a record or records which you feel should be included in the second edition of this book. Photocopies of both sides of the records are preferred, but if this is not possible, please give us all pertinent information, including the label and record number, and exact titles and credits, even including parentheses and punctuation, and any opinion you may have regarding its value.

(5) Correction of errors. This book has been proofread with excruciating care, but as errors have a way of occasionally eluding even the sharpest eye, your input will be appreciated.

Please address correspondence on any of the above directly to:

Alice Rogers
Route 1, Box 146A
Deming, New Mexico 88030

THE BIG BAND SCENE TODAY

Not long ago, bumper stickers along our highways were proclaiming: "The big bands are back!"

That statement, of course, didn't apply to my orchestra and a number of others which have continued to play the big band sound throughout the years, and fans from coast-to-coast and worldwide, have continued to come in the thousands to hear and/or dance to the music.

The enthusiastic response of audiences all over the world has not diminished, from the time I took over the leadership of the first postwar Glenn Miller Orchestra in 1946, through the more than thirty years of leading my own band. And the crowds *have* kept coming, year after year ... more than 10,000 in Cleveland, 7,000 in Duluth, and at the Hollywood Palladium, 6,500 paid admissions, the largest crowd ever to pack the famous ballroom, even in its big band heyday.

Today, most of our engagements are for conventions, music festivals, colleges, major amusement parks, country clubs, public dances and private parties. As of this writing in August 1984, my orchestra is booked through October 1985, and wherever we play, enthusiasm runs high, and the mixture of dancers and listeners frequently includes many young people who are discovering the fun of dancing together to a smooth, romantic ballad. All of this would seem to indicate that the big band scene is very much with us, and alive and well!

Probably among the reasons for the tremendous popularity of the big bands today, at least in the case of my own band, is the bringing together of yesterday and today. In addition to helping to keep alive memories of the incomparable sounds of Glenn Miller by the replaying of Miller favorites, for variety we present contemporary tunes, some with the Miller sound, and others with newer arrangements especially created for me by Alan Copeland and Billy May. At a typical engagement we treat audiences to a taste of almost every flavor on the popular music menu – sweet, swing, romantic and contemporary. Everything's there to whet the appetite – a musical feast that will please yesterday's teenagers and delight the youngsters of today.

Among others from the big bands of the 1930s and 1940s, as well as from the "new" big bands, I am on the Advisory Board of the Big Band Academy of America, an organization "dedicated to preserving the memory and future of the sound of the Big Bands."

Fans sometimes ask, "What would the popular music field have been like for the past forty years if Glenn Miller had returned from World War II?" In my opinion, the Miller band would have gone on to enjoy even greater prominence and prestige after the war. I believe that Glenn Miller would have advanced the Big Band Era, and that he would have made a difference in the direction that popular music took after the war, not only because of the innovations he had already introduced, but also because he knew – instinctively – what songstyles the American public most wanted to hear.

Tex Beneke

COLLECTIBLE VOCALISTS

Allen, Bob
Allen, Ed
Allen Stuart
Allen, Terry
Anderson, Ivie
Andrews, Patty
Andrews Sisters, The
Arlen, Harold
Arluck, Harold
Armstrong, Lillian (Lil)
Arnell, Amy
Astaire, Adele
Astaire, Fred
Austin, Gene

Babbitt, Harry
Baby Rose Marie
Bacon, Louis
Baird, Eugenie
Baker, Belle
Baker, Bonnie
Barksdale, Everett
Barrie, Gracie
Barris, Harry
Baur, Franklyn
Bennett, Lee
Bernard, Al
Blair, Janet
Blake, Jerry
Blanc, Mel
Blane, Ralph
Bloom, Rube
Bogue, Merwyn (Ishkabibble)
Bonney, Betty
Bose, Sterling
Boswell, Connee (Connie)
Boswell Sisters, The
Boyer, Anita
Bradley, Betty
Brito, Phil
Brown, Don
Brown, Jimmy
Bruce, Carol
Bullock, Chick
Bunn, Teddy
Burke, Clyde

Cantor, Eddie
Cara, Mancy
Carlisle, Una Mae
Carlyle, Russ
Carpenter, Thelma
Carpenter, Wingy
Carroll, Bob
Casey, Floyd
Charioteers, The
Christy, June
Churchill, Savannah
Claire, Dorothy
Clark, Buddy
Clooney, Rose Mary
Clooney Sisters, The
Collins, Dorothy
Colonna, Jerry
Como, Perry
Conlon, Jud as
Jud Conlon's Rhythmaires
Cool, Harry
Cooper, Jerry
Cornell, Don
Cotton, Larry
Courtney, Alan
Crumit, Frank
Crosby, Bing
Curtis, Ken

Dale, Carlotta
Dalhart, Vernon
Darnel (also spelled Darnell), Bill
Davies, Ramona
Day, Doris
Day (also spelled Daye), Irene
De Castro Sisters, The
DeHaven, Gloria
Le Leath, Vaughn
Delta Rhythm Boys, The
De Marco Sisters, The
Dennis, Clarke
Derwin, Hal
Desmond, Johnny
De Witt, Allan
Dillard, Bill
Dixon, Joe
Douglas, Billy
Douglas, Michael (Mike)
Dunn, Artie

Eberly (also spelled Eberle), Bob
Eckstine, Billy
Edwards, Joan
Eldridge, Jean
Etting, Ruth

Fain, Sammy
Faye, Alice
Forrest, Helen
Foster, Stuart
Four King Sisters, The
(also see King Sisters, The)
Four Modernaires, The
(also see Modernaires, The)
Froman, Jane
Fuller, Walter
Fulton, Jack

Gaines, Charlie
Gardner, Kenny
Garry, Sid
Gaylor, Ruth
Gibbs, Georgia
Gibbs, Parker
Gibson, Fredda
Gilmore, Patricia
Grable, Betty
Grace, Teddy
Greer, Sonny
Grissom, Dan

Haines, Connie
Hall, Adelaide
Hall, Wendell
Hannon, Bob
Hanshaw, Annette
Hare, Ernest
Harris, Joe
Harrison, Jimmy
Haskell, Jack
Haymes, Bob
Haymes, Dick
Heard, J. C.
Heilbron, Fritz
Herfurt, Skeets
Hilaire, Andrew
Hilliard, Harriet
Hodges, Joy
Holiday, Billie
Holland, Peanuts
Holman, Libby
Horne, Lena
Hughes, Marjorie
Humes, Helen
Hunt, Frances
Hunt, Mildred
Hurst, Lou
Hutton, Betty
Hutton, June
Hutton, Marian (Marion)

Ink Spots, The
Ishkabibble, (Bogue, Merwyn)

Jackson, Quentin
James, Lewis
Jeffries, Herb
Jenkins, Freddy
Johnson, Albert "Budd"
Johnson, Lem
Johnston, Johnny
Jolson, Al
Jones, Billy
Jordan, Taft

DANCE BANDS AND BIG BANDS
BUYERS-SELLERS REFERENCE BOOK & PRICE GUIDE

EXPLANATION OF FORMAT

Artists and/or Band Name — **Recording Title on Label**

SPITALNY, Phil, & His Hour Of Charm All-Girl Orchestra
(Phil Spitalny: 11/7/90 – 10-11/70) — **Artist's actual name, birthdate, date deceased**

WINTER, "Chic", & His Orchestra/ Chic Winter Orchestra — **Artist's name, nickname, band names**
also see ELLINGTON, Duke, & His Orchestra as The Washingtonians — **refer to this artist**

Song titles — **Vocalist or note** — **Record Label & number**

SING, YOU SINNERS (Vocal: Smith Ballew) /
IN MY LITTLE HOPE CHEST
(Vocal: Unknown female) .... *Odeon ONY-36051* 5-8 30

SING, YOU SINNERS (Vocal: Smith Ballew) /
IN MY LITTLE HOPE CHEST
(Vocal: Unknown female).................. *Okeh 41384* 5-8 30
(Simultaneously released on two labels)

Dollar value — **Year of issue**

If the vocalist(s) name is listed underneath the title/label/value/year, then the vocalist(s) appear on both sides. If the vocalist(s) name appears directly after a song title, that vocalist appears only on that side.

All records are 78 rpm. Additional information (notes on artist, band, or the record labels) are noted below the Artist/Band's title. Notes on individual records are noted beneath the record's title/label/value/year. Often, a record was released under several different labels simultaneously; note that values may differ.

Additional format notes in Alice Rogers author's introduction.

AARONSON, Irving, & His Commanders
(Irving Aaronson: 2/7/95 – 5/10/63)

COMMANDERISM (theme song) / JAZZEROO........................ *Columbia 3043-D* 5-8 35

CRAZY WORDS – CRAZY TUNE (Vocals: Irving Aaronson, Phil Saxe & Bob Leitner) / I NEVER SEE MAGGIE ALONE (Vocal: Phil Saxe) .... *Victor 20473* 3-5 27

GIVE ME A UKELELE & A UKELELE BABY (Vocals: Irving Aaronson, Phil Saxe, Harold Saliers) / EVERYTHING'S PEACHES (Vocal: Franklyn Baur) .... *Victor 20385* 2-4 27

HE AIN'T DONE RIGHT BY NELL / SPRING IS HERE.................... *Victor 20034* 3-5 26
(Vocals: Phil Saxe & Clifford "Red" Stanley)

IF I HAD YOU (Vocal: Scrappy Lambert as Burt Lorin)/ ALL BY YOURSELF IN THE MOONLIGHT (Vocals: Phil Saxe & Trio)................. *Victor 21867* 2-4 29

I'M JUST WILD ABOUT ANIMAL CRACKERS (Vocals: Aaronson, Phil Saxe, "Red" Stanley & Stanley Johnson) / WAFFLES (Vocals: Phil Saxe & Chorus) .... *Victor 20094* 2-4 26

LAND OF GOING-TO-BE (Vocal: Jack Armstrong) / LET'S DO IT, LET'S FALL IN LOVE (Vocals: Phil Saxe & Jack Armstrong) .... *Victor 21745* 4-6 28

LET'S MISBEHAVE (Vocals: Phil Saxe & chorus) / AN' FURTHERMORE (Vocals: Irving Aaronson, Phil Saxe & chorus)...................... *Victor 21260* 3-5 28

OH! YOU SWEET OLD WHATCHA-MAY-CALL-IT (Vocals: Charlie Trotta, Jimmy Taylor, Phil Saxe & Tony Pastor) / I'LL GET BY AS LONG AS I HAVE YOU (Vocals: J. Taylor, C. Trotta, T. Pastor & J. Armstrong)........................ *Victor 21778* 3-5 28

PUMP SONG, The (Vocal: Phil Saxe) / ANY ICE TODAY, LADY? (by Fred Waring & His Pennsylvanians, Vocal: Poley McClintock).................. *Victor 20083* 3-5 26

SNOWBALL / THAT'S HOW RHYTHM WAS BORN .... *Vocalion 2535* 5-8 33
(Vocals: Ernie Mathias)

WIMMIN – AAH! (Vocals: Phil Saxe & chorus) / POOR PAPA (He's Got Nothing At All) (Vocals: Irving Aaronson, Phil Saxe, & Frank Cornwell) .... *Victor 20002* 2-4 26

ABBOTT, Larry, & His Orchestra

I'M MORE THAN SATISFIED (Vocals: duet) / JUBILEE (by Frankie Trumbauer & Orchestra) .... *Okeh 41044* 25-30 28

ABRAMS, Irwin, & His Hotel Manager Orchestra

I AIN'T THAT KIND OF BABY / BYE-BYE, PRETTY BABY............. *Okeh 40864* 3-5 27
(Vocals: Unknown)

MY HEART STOOD STILL / I FEEL AT HOME WITH YOU................. *Okeh 40948* 2-4 28
(Vocals: Unknown)

SHAKING THE BLUES AWAY / IT ALL BELONGS TO ME .... *Okeh 40880* 3-5 27
(Vocals: Unknown)

WHEREVER YOU ARE / HEADIN' FOR HARLEM............... *Okeh 40918* 2-4 27
(Vocals: duet)

ABRAMS, Irwin, & His Orchestra

HEARTACHES & DREAMS / BABY FEET GO PITTER PATTER................ *Edison 52114* 3-5 27
(Vocals: Unknown)

LUCKY DAY / BIRTH OF THE BLUES........................ *Banner 1783* 3-5 26
(Vocals: Irving Kaufman)

LUCKY DAY / BIRTH OF THE BLUES........................ *Domino 3752* 3-5 26
(Vocals: Irving Kaufman)

LUCKY DAY / BIRTH OF THE BLUES.......................... *Regal 8092* 3-5 26
(Vocals: Irving Kaufman)
(Simultaneously released on three labels)

MUDDY WATER (Vocal: Les Reis) / A TREE IN THE PARK .... *Pathe Actuelle 36586* 3-5 27

MUDDY WATER (Vocal: Les Reis) / A TREE IN THE PARK............... *Perfect 14767* 2-4 27
(Simultaneously released on two labels)

ADRIAN & HIS ORCHESTRA:
see ROLLINI, Adrian

ADRIAN & HIS TAP ROOM GANG:
see ROLLINI, Adrian

ADRIAN'S RAMBLERS:
see ROLLINI, Adrian

ALABAMA RED PEPPERS, The:
see HARING, Bob, & His Orchestra

ALBERT, Don, & His Orchestra
(Don Albert: 8/5/08 –)

ON THE SUNNY SIDE OF THE STREET (Vocal: Billy Douglas) / DEEP BLUE MELODY...... *Vocalion 3423* 10-12 37

SHEIK OF ARABY, THE / YOU DON'T LOVE ME.............. *Vocalion 3411* 10-12 37
(Vocals: Merle Turner)

TRUE BLUE LOU (Vocal: Merle Turner) / ROCKIN' AND SWINGIN'............ *Vocalion 3401* 10-12 37

ALEXANDER, Van, & His Orchestra
(Van Alexander: 5/2/15 –)

ALEXANDER'S SWINGING (theme song) / I FOUND MY YELLOW BASKET (Vocal: Shirley Brown) .... *Bluebird B-10033* 2-4 38

DANCING IN THE DARK / DON'T LOOK NOW (Vocal: Butch Stone) .... *Bluebird B-10164* 2-4 39

DREAM CARAVAN (Vocal: Joel Livingstone) / DIGA DIGA DOO .... *Bluebird B-10102* 3-5 39

GIRL FRIEND OF THE WHIRLING DERVISH, THE (Vocal: Butch Stone) / F.D.R. JONES (Vocal: Jayne Dover) ... *Bluebird B-10092* 2-4 39

I CAN'T RESIST YOU / JUNGLE JIVE ... *Varsity 8335* 3-5 40

IF I DIDN'T CARE / NO REASON AT ALL .... *Bluebird B-10231* 2-4 39
(Vocals: Phyllis Kenny)

IN A GOOD-FOR-NOTHING MOOD / WE'LL NEVER KNOW .... *Bluebird B-10057* 2-4 39
(Vocals: Jayne Dover)

IN THE MIDDLE OF A DREAM / LET THERE BE LOVE .... *Bluebird B-10297* 2-4 39
(Vocals: Phyllis Kenny)

JUMPIN' JIVE, The (Vocal: Butch Stone) / RAGTIME COWBOY JOE.......... *Bluebird B-10330* 2-4 39

LA ROSITA / STUMBLING.......... *Bluebird B-10338* 2-4 39

MARY LOU / AY-AY-AY (Vocal: Butch Stone)....... *Bluebird B-10313* 2-4 39

MASQUERADE IS OVER, THE / HEAVEN CAN WAIT .... *Bluebird B-10118* 2-4 39
(Vocals: Jayne Dover)

MOON OF MANAKOORA / ANOTHER NIGHT ALONE (Vocal: Phyllis Kenny)........ *Bluebird B-10197* 2-4 39

NO STAR IS LOST / I CRIED FOR YOU .... *Bluebird B-10049* 2-4 39
(Vocals: Jayne Dover)

OH, I'M EVIL (Vocal: Butch Stone) / HONEY BUNNY BOO (Vocal: Jayne Dover).... *Bluebird B-10137* 3-5 39

ON BEHALF OF THE VISITING FIREMEN (Vocals: Van Alexander, Butch Stone)/ I WON'T GO HOME UNTIL YOU KISS ME (Vocal: Phyllis Kenny)...... *Varsity 8328* 2-4 40

ON THE ROAD TO MANDALAY / NIGHT AND DAY................ *Bluebird B-10073* 2-4 38

SIX LESSONS FROM MADAME LA ZONGA (Vocal: Phyllis Kenny) / PLEASE TAKE A LETTER, MISS BROWN (Vocal: Butch Stone) .... *Varsity 8312* 2-4 40

TONY'S WIFE / THOU SWELL...... *Bluebird B-10277* 2-4 39

'WAY DOWN YONDER IN NEW ORLEANS / ADIOS, MUCHACHOS .... *Bluebird B-10278* 2-4 39

WHERE HAS MY LITTLE DOG GONE? (Vocal: Shirley Brown) / GOTTA PEBBLE IN MY SHOE (Vocal: Butch Stone)....... *Bluebird B-10030* 2-4 38

YOU'RE GONNA SEE A LOT OF ME / YOUR EYES ARE BIGGER THAN YOUR HEART .... *Bluebird B-10063* 2-4 39
(Vocals: Butch Stone)

ALEXANDER, Van, & His Swingtime Band

EASY DOES IT (Vocal: Phyllis Kenny) / HO-SA-BONNIE (Vocal: Butch Stone)..... *Varsity 8177* 2-4 40

HONESTLY / SCATTERBRAIN .... *Varsity 8075* 2-4 39
(Vocals: Unknown)

IN THE MOOD/ANGRY (Vocal: Phyllis Kenny) *Varsity 8065* 2-4 39

I WANT TO WRAP YOU UP / OH! WHAT A LOVELY DREAM .... *Varsity 8126* 2-4 40
(Vocals: Phyllis Kenny)

I WONDER WHO'S KISSING HER NOW /-MARIE................. *Varsity 8112* 2-4 39
(Vocals: Unknown)

MANY DREAMS AGO (Vocal: Phyllis Kenny) / HOT DOG JOE (Vocal: Butch Stone)....... *Varsity 8082* 2-4 39

PINCH ME (Vocal: Phyllis Kenny) / PRELUDE TO A BUGHOUSE.......... *Varsity 8133* 2-4 40

SAY IT (Vocal: Phyllis Kenny) / MY! MY! (Vocal: Butch Stone).............. *Varsity 8172* 2-4 40

TEMPUS FUGIT / HEAR MY SONG, VIOLETTA (Vocal: Phyllis Kenny)......... *Varsity 8250* 2-4 40

YODELIN' JIVE (Vocal: Butch Stone) / THE LITTLE RED FOX (Vocal: Phyllis Kenny)........... *Varsity 8102* 2-4 39

ALLEN, Bob, & His Orchestra

KEEPIN' OUT OF TROUBLE (Vocal: Bob Allen) / SWEETHEART SERENADE............ *Beacon 103* 5-8 42

ALLEN, Henry "Red", & His Orchestra
(Henry Allen: 1/7/08 – 4/7/67)

EVERYBODY SHOUT/DANCING DAVE. *Victor V-38121* 45-50 30

FEELING DROWSY / SWING OUT..... *Victor V-38080* 50-60 29

FUNNY FEATHERS BLUES / HOW DO THEY DO IT THAT WAY?................. *Victor V-38088* 50-60 29
(Vocals: Victoria Spivey)

IT SHOULD BE YOU/BIFF'LY BLUES... *Victor V-38073* 45-50 29

I WISH I WERE TWINS / I NEVER SLEPT A WINK LAST NIGHT .... *Banner 33081* 10-12 34
(Vocals: Henry Allen)

I WISH I WERE TWINS / I NEVER SLEPT A WINK LAST NIGHT .... *Melotone M-13045* 10-12 34
(Vocals: Henry Allen)

I WISH I WERE TWINS / I NEVER SLEPT A WINK LAST NIGHT .... *Oriole 2915* 10-12 34
(Vocals: Henry Allen)

I WISH I WERE TWINS / I NEVER SLEPT A WINK LAST NIGHT........................ *Perfect 15948* 10-12 34
(Vocals: Henry Allen)

I WISH I WERE TWINS / I NEVER SLEPT A WINK LAST NIGHT......................... *Romeo 2289* 10-12 34
(Vocals: Henry Allen)
(Simultaneously released on five labels)

MAKE A COUNTRY BIRD FLY WILD (Vocals: The Four Wanderers) /PLEASIN' PAUL..... *Victor V-38107* 50-60 29

SUGAR HILL FUNCTION / YOU MIGHT GET BETTER, BUT YOU'LL NEVER GET WELL (Vocal: Will Johnson) .... *Victor V-38140* 45-50 30

ALLEN, Henry – Coleman Hawkins & Their Orchestra
(Coleman Hawkins: 11/21/04 – 5/19/69)

RIVER'S TAKIN' CARE OF ME / AIN'TCHA GOT MUSIC? .... *Banner 32840* 12-15 33
(Vocals: Henry Allen)

RIVER'S TAKIN' CARE OF ME / AIN'TCHA GOT MUSIC?.......... *Melotone M-12769* 12-15 33
(Vocals: Henry Allen)

RIVER'S TAKIN' CARE OF ME / AIN'TCHA GOT MUSIC?............... *Oriole 2746* 12-15 33
(Vocals: Henry Allen)

RIVER'S TAKIN' CARE OF ME / AIN'TCHA GOT MUSIC? .... *Perfect 15808* 12-15 33
(Vocals: Henry Allen)

RIVER'S TAKIN' CARE OF ME / AIN'TCHA GOT MUSIC? .... *Romeo 2119* 12-15 33
(Vocals: Henry Allen)
(Simultaneously released on five labels)

STRINGIN' ALONG ON A SHOE STRING / SHADOW ON THE SWANEE......... *Banner 32829* 10-12 33
(Vocals: Henry Allen)

STRINGIN' ALONG ON A SHOE STRING / SHADOW ON THE SWANEE..... *Melotone M-12759* 10-12 33
(Vocals: Henry Allen)

STRINGIN' ALONG ON A SHOE STRING / SHADOW ON THE SWANEE........... *Oriole 2739* 10-12 33
(Vocals: Henry Allen)

STRINGIN' ALONG ON A SHOE STRING / SHADOW ON THE SWANEE......... *Perfect 15802* 10-12 33
(Vocals: Henry Allen)

STRINGIN' ALONG ON A SHOE STRING / SHADOW ON THE SWANEE.......... *Romeo 2112* 10-12 33
(Vocals: Henry Allen)
(Simultaneously released on five labels)

ALL STAR BAND, The

BLUE LOU / THE BLUES............... *Victor 26144* 4-6 39

ALL STAR CALIFORNIANS, The

I'M PROUD OF YOU / NEVER SWAT A FLY............ *Melotone M-12002* 5-8 30
(Vocals: Irving Kaufman)

ALL STAR COLLEGIANS, The:
See LANIN, Sam, & His Orchestra

ALPERT, Micki, & His Orchestra:
See SELVIN, Ben, & His Orchestra

AMMONS, Albert, & His Rhythm Kings
(Albert Ammons: 1907 – 12/5/49)

Title	Label	Price	Year
EARLY MORNIN' BLUES / MILE-OR-MO BIRD RAG	*Decca 975*	5-8	36
NAGASAKI / BOOGIE WOOGIE STOMP	*Decca 749*	5-8	36

ANDRE MUSETTE ORCHESTRA, The

Title	Label	Price	Year
NOT TONIGHT, JOSEPHINE (Vocals: chorus) / PIG KNUCKLES	*Standard T-5000*	2-4	42

ANTHONY, Ray, & His Orchestra
(Ray Anthony: 1/20/22 –)
(Ray Anthony & His Orchestra continue to play engagements in various parts of the country.)

Title	Label	Price	Year
AT LAST (Vocal: Tommy Mercer) / I'LL SEE YOU IN MY DREAMS	*Capitol 1912*	2-4	53
DANCING IN THE DARK / DRAGNET	*Capitol 2562*	2-4	54
DC-7 / PETE KELLY'S BLUES	*Capitol 3176*	2-4	57

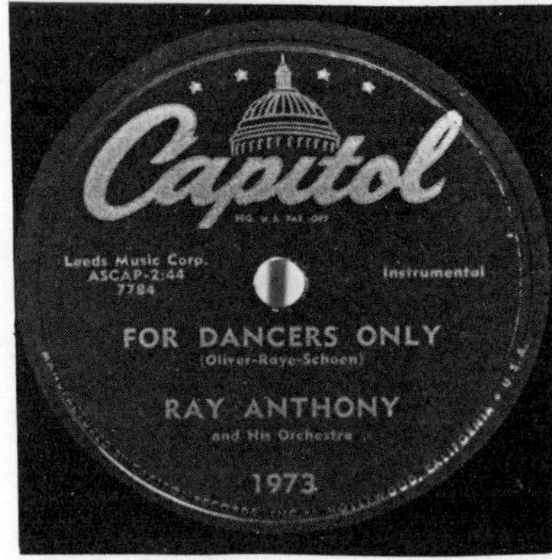

Title	Label	Price	Year
FOR DANCERS ONLY / I HEAR A RHAPSODY (Vocal: Tommy Mercer)	*Capitol 1973*	2-4	53
I'LL NEVER KNOW WHY / FAITHFULLY YOURS (Vocals: Tommy Mercer)	*Capitol 1490*	2-4	51
MAMA, TEACH ME TO DO THE CHARLESTON (Vocals: The Skyliners) / FRANCIE (Vocal: Ronnie Deauville)	*Capitol 1051*	2-4	50
MELANCHOLY RHAPSODY / VILIA	*Capitol 1556*	2-4	51
MY PRAYER / ELEANOR (Vocals: T. Mercer)	*Capitol 1438*	2-4	51
SAY HEY / SKOKIAAN	*Capitol 2896*	2-4	56
SKIP TO MY LOU / SCATTERED TOYS (Vocal: Ronnie Deauville)	*Capitol 1040*	2-4	50
SLUEFOOT / SOMETHING'S GOTTA GIVE (Vocals: The Skyliners)	*Capitol 3096*	2-4	56
THERE ARE SUCH THINGS (Vocal: Tommy Mercer) / MOONLIGHT SAVING TIME (Vocal: Marcie Miller)	*Capitol 2002*	2-4	53
TRUMPET BOOGIE / YOU'RE DRIVING ME CRAZY (Vocals: Marcie Miller)	*Capitol 2058*	2-4	53
TUXEDO JUNCTION / IN THE MOOD	*Capitol 2699*	2-4	54

ARABIAN KNIGHTS, The:
see ROYAL TROUBADOURS, The

ARDEN, Victor, – Phil Ohman & Their Orchestra
(Victor Arden: circa 1903 - , Philip Ohman: 10/7/96 – 8/8/54)

Title	Label	Price	Year
BLACK BOTTOM / LUCKY DAY (Vocals: Unknown)	*Brunswick 3242*	2-4	26
HALLELUJAH / SOMETIMES I'M HAPPY (Vocals: Unknown)	*Brunswick 3527*	2-4	27
I LOVE A PARADE / MUSIC IN MY FINGERS (Vocals: Frank Luther)	*Victor 22892*	2-4	32
I LOVE YOU SO MUCH / DANCING THE DEVIL AWAY (Vocals: Frank Luther)	*Victor 22383*	3-5	30
ME AND MY SHADOW / BROKEN HEARTED (Vocals: Unknown)	*Brunswick 3592*	2-4	27
OUT OF BREATH / I AM ONLY HUMAN AFTER ALL (Vocals: Frank Luther)	*Victor 22481*	3-5	30
YOU'RE MY EVERYTHING (Vocal: Frank Luther) / OOH! THAT KISS (Vocals: Sylvia Froos & Frank Luther)	*Victor 22818*	2-4	31

ARKANSAS / ARKANSAW TRAVELERS, The:
see LANIN, Sam

ARMSTRONG, Louis, & His Hot Five
(Louis Armstrong: 7/4/00 – 7/6/71)

Title	Label	Price	Year
BIG FAT MA & SKINNY PA (Vocal: Louis Armstrong) / SWEET LITTLE PAPA	*Okeh 8379*	40-45	26
DON'T FORGET TO MESS AROUND / I'M GONNA GITCHA (Vocals: Louis Armstrong)	*Okeh 8343*	40-45	26
DROPPING SHUCKS (Vocal: Louis Armstrong) / WHOSIT	*Okeh 8357*	40-45	26
MY HEART / CORNET CHOP SUEY	*Okeh 8320*	30-35	26
SKIP THE GUTTER / KNEE DROPS	*Okeh 8631*	40-45	28
YOU MADE ME LOVE YOU / IRISH BLACK BOTTOM (Vocals: Louis Armstrong)	*Okeh 8447*	40-45	26

ARMSTRONG, Louis, & His Hot Seven

Title	Label	Price	Year
WEARY BLUES / THAT'S WHEN I'LL COME BACK TO YOU (Vocals: Louis & Lil Armstrong)	*Okeh 8519*	40-45	27
WILLIE THE WEEPER / ALLIGATOR CRAWL	*Okeh 8482*	40-45	27

ARMSTRONG, Louis, & His Orchestra

Title	Label	Price	Year
AFTER YOU'VE GONE / ST. LOUIS BLUES (Vocal: Louis Armstrong)	*Okeh 41350*	15-20	30
AIN'T MISBEHAVIN' / (WHAT DID I DO TO BE SO) BLACK AND BLUE? (Vocals: Louis Armstrong)	*Okeh 8714*	15-20	29
ALEXANDER'S RAGTIME BAND / I'VE GOT A HEART FULL OF RHYTHM (Vocals: Louis Armstrong)	*Decca 1408*	5-8	37
AMONG MY SOUVENIRS / COQUETTE (Vocals: Louis Armstrong)	*Decca 4327*	3-5	42
BABY, WON'T YOU PLEASE COME HOME? / SHANTY BOAT ON THE MISSISSIPPI (Vocals: Louis Armstrong)	*Decca 2729*	3-5	39
BETWEEN THE DEVIL AND THE DEEP BLUE SEA / KICKIN' THE GONG AROUND (Vocals: Louis Armstrong)	*Okeh 41550*	15-20	32
BLUE AGAIN / WHEN YOUR LOVER HAS GONE (Vocals: Louis Armstrong)	*Okeh 41498*	15-20	31
CASH FOR YOUR TRASH / I NEVER KNEW (Vocals: Louis Armstrong)	*Decca 4229*	5-8	42
CHINATOWN, MY CHINATOWN / I GOT RHYTHM (Vocals: Louis Armstrong)	*Okeh 41534*	15-20	31
DALLAS BLUES / BESSIE COULDN'T HELP IT (Vocals: Louis Armstrong)	*Okeh 8774*	15-20	30
DINAH (Vocal: Louis Armstrong) / TIGER RAG	*Okeh 8800*	12-15	30
DUSKY STEVEDORE (Vocal: Louis Armstrong) / ST. LOUIS BLUES	*Victor 24320*	10-12	33
EVERYTHING'S BEEN DONE BEFORE / IN THE GLOAMING (Vocals: Louis Armstrong)	*Decca 3825*	3-5	41
HEAR ME TALKIN' TO YA / SAVE IT, PRETTY MAMA (Vocals: Louis Armstrong)	*Decca 2405*	3-5	39
HEP CATS' BALL / LAZY 'SIPPI STEAMER (Vocals: Louis Armstrong)	*Decca 3283*	3-5	40
HE'S A SON OF THE SOUTH / SOME SWEET DAY (Vocals: Louis Armstrong)	*Victor 24257*	10-12	33
HIGH SOCIETY (Vocal: Louis Armstong) / MAHOGANY HALL STOMP	*Victor 24232*	10-12	33
HOME / ALL OF ME (Vocals: Louis Armstrong)	*Okeh 41552*	15-20	32
HONEY, DON'T YOU LOVE ME ANYMORE? / THERE'S A CABIN IN THE PINES (Vocals: Louis Armstrong)	*Victor 24335*	10-12	33
HONEY, DO! / SNOWBALL (Vocals: Louis Armstrong)	*Victor 24369*	10-12	33
I AIN'T GOT NOBODY (Vocal: Louis Armstrong) / ROCKIN' CHAIR (Vocals: Louis Armstrong & Hogey Carmichael)	*Okeh 8756*	15-20	30
I CAN'T GIVE YOU ANYTHING BUT LOVE / AIN'T MISBEHAVIN' (Vocals: Louis Armstrong)	*Decca 2042*	3-5	38
I COME FROM A MUSICAL FAMILY / SOMEBODY STOLE MY BREAK (Vocals: Louis Armstrong)	*Decca 797*	5-8	36
I COVER THE WATERFRONT / LONG, LONG AGO (Vocals: Louis Armstrong)	*Decca 3700*	3-5	41
IF WE NEVER MEET AGAIN (Vocal: Louis Armstrong) / DIPPER MOUTH BLUES (By Louis Armstrong with Jimmy Dorsey & His Orchestra)	*Decca 906*	5-8	36
I GOTTA RIGHT TO SING THE BLUES / HUSTLIN' AND BUSTLIN' FOR BABY (Vocals: Louis Armstrong)	*Victor 24233*	10-12	33
I HATE TO LEAVE YOU NOW / YOU'LL WISH YOU'D NEVER BEEN BORN (Vocals: Louis Armstrong)	*Victor 24204*	10-12	33
I'LL GET MINE BYE AND BYE / YES SUH! (Vocals: Louis Armstrong)	*Decca 3900*	3-5	41
I'M IN THE MOOD FOR LOVE / GOT A BRAN' NEW SUIT (Vocals: Louis Armstrong)	*Decca 579*	5-8	35
I'M PUTTING ALL MY EGGS IN ONE BASKET / YES! YES! MY! MY! (Vocals: Louis Armstrong)	*Decca 698*	5-8	36
INDIAN CRADLE SONG / EXACTLY LIKE YOU (Vocals: Louis Armstrong)	*Okeh 41423*	15-20	30
I'VE GOT MY FINGERS CROSSED / I'M SHOOTING HIGH (Vocals: Louis Armstrong)	*Decca 623*	5-8	36
I'VE GOT THE WORLD ON A STRING / SITTIN' IN THE DARK (Vocals: Louis Armstrong)	*Victor 24245*	10-12	33
I WONDER WHO / DON'T PLAY ME CHEAP (Vocals: Louis Armstrong)	*Victor 24425*	10-12	33
JEEPERS CREEPERS / WHAT IS THIS THING CALLED SWING? (Vocals: Louis Armstrong)	*Decca 2267*	3-5	39
JUBILEE / TRUE CONFESSION (Vocals: Louis Armstrong)	*Decca 1635*	5-8	38
KEEPIN' OUT OF MISCHIEF NOW / LAWD, YOU MADE THE NIGHT TOO LONG (Vocals: Louis Armstrong)	*Okeh 41560*	15-20	32
LAUGHIN' LOUIE / TOMORROW NIGHT (Vocals: Louis Armstrong)	*Bluebird B-5363*	8-10	33
LAZY RIVER / GEORGIA ON MY MIND (Vocals: Louis Armstrong)	*Okeh 41541*	15-20	31

Title	Label	Price	Year
LEAP FROG / I USED TO LOVE YOU	*Decca 4106*	3-5	42
LITTLE JOE / THEM THERE EYES (Vocals: Louis Armstrong)	*Okeh 41501*	15-20	31
LOVE, YOU FUNNY THING / NEW TIGER RAG (Vocals: Louis Armstrong)	*Okeh 41557*	15-20	32
LYIN' TO MYSELF / EV'NTIDE (Vocals: Louis Armstrong)	*Decca 835*	5-8	36
MISSISSIPPI BASIN (Vocal: Louis Armstrong) / SWEET SUE, JUST YOU (Vocals: Louis Armstrong & Albert Johnson)	*Victor 24321*	10-12	33
MUSIC GOES 'ROUND AND AROUND / RHYTHM SAVED THE WORLD (Vocals: Louis Armstrong)	*Decca 685*	5-8	36
MY SWEET / I CAN'T BELIEVE THAT YOU'RE IN LOVE WITH ME (Vocals: Louis Armstrong)	*Okeh 41415*	15-20	30
NATURALLY / I'VE GOT A POCKETFUL OF DREAMS (Vocals: Louis Armstrong)	*Decca 1937*	3-5	38
NO / BASIN STREET BLUES (Vocals: Louis Armstrong, Earl Hines & Mancy Cara)	*Okeh 8690*	25-30	29
OLD MAN MOSE / FALLING IN LOVE WITH YOU (Vocals: Louis Armstrong)	*Decca 622*	5-8	36
ONCE IN A WHILE (Vocal: Louis Armstrong) / ON THE SUNNY SIDE OF THE STREET	*Decca 1560*	4-6	38
ON THE SENTIMENTAL SIDE / IT'S WONDERFUL (Vocals: Louis Armstrong)	*Decca 1841*	3-5	38
PERDIDO STREET BLUES / 2.19 BLUES (Vocal: Louis Armstrong)	*Decca 18090*	3-5	40
POOR OLD JOE / BYE AND BYE (Vocals: Louis Armstrong)	*Decca 3011*	4-6	40
PUBLIC MELODY NUMBER ONE / RED CAP (Vocals: Louis Armstrong)	*Decca 1347*	5-8	37
RED SAILS IN THE SUNSET / ON TREASURE ISLAND (Vocals: Louis Armstrong)	*Decca 648*	5-8	36
SATCHEL MOUTH SWING / I DOUBLE DARE YOU (Vocals: Louis Armstrong)	*Decca 1636*	5-8	38
SAVOY BLUES / ME AND BROTHER BILL (Vocal: Louis Armstrong)	*Decca 2538*	4-6	39
SHE'S THE DAUGHTER OF A PLANTER FROM HAVANA / CUBAN PETE (Vocals: Louis Armstrong)	*Decca 1353*	5-8	37
SHOE SHINE BOY / I HOPE GABRIEL LIKES MY MUSIC (Vocals: Louis Armstrong)	*Decca 672*	5-8	36
SO LITTLE TIME / MEXICAN SWING (Vocals: Louis Armstrong)	*Decca 1822*	4-6	38
SOME OF THESE DAYS / WHEN YOU'RE SMILING	*Okeh 8729*	15-20	29
SOMETHING TELLS ME / LOVE WALKED IN (Vocals: Louis Armstrong)	*Decca 1842*	3-5	38
SWING THAT MUSIC / THANKFUL (Vocals: Louis Armstrong)	*Decca 866*	5-8	36

THANKS A MILLION / SOLITUDE........ *Decca 666* 5-8 36
(Vocals: Louis Armstrong)

THAT RHYTHM MAN /
SWEET SAVANNAH SUE.............. *Okeh 8717* 15-20 29
(Vocals: Louis Armstrong)

THAT'S MY HOME / HOBO, YOU CAN'T
RIDE THIS TRAIN.................. *Victor 24200* 10-12 33
(Vocals: Louis Armstrong)

TRUMPET PLAYER'S LAMENT /
SWEET AS A SONG................... *Decca 1653* 5-8 38
(Vocals: Louis Armstrong)

WALKIN' MY BABY BACK HOME /
I SURRENDER DEAR................ *Okeh 41497* 15-20 31
(Vocals: Louis Armstrong)

WEST END BLUES / IF IT'S GOOD
THEN I WANT IT..................... *Decca 2480* 3-5 39
(Vocals: Louis Armstrong)

WHEN IT'S SLEEPY TIME DOWN SOUTH
(theme song) (with dialog between Louis & Charlie Alexander)/
I'LL BE GLAD WHEN YOU'RE DEAD, YOU RASCAL
YOU (Vocal: Louis Armstrong)............ *Okeh 41504* 15-20 31

WRAP YOUR TROUBLES IN DREAMS /
STAR DUST.......................... *Okeh 41530* 12-15 31
(Vocals: Louis Armstrong)

YOU ARE MY LUCKY STAR /
LA CUCARACHA...................... *Decca 580* 5-8 35
(Vocals: Louis Armstrong)

YOU CAN DEPEND ON ME (Vocal: Louis Armstrong) /
THE LONESOME ROAD (With dialog between
Louis, Zilmer Randolph, Mike McKendrick
& John Lindsay)........................ *Okeh 41538* 15-20 31
(Zilmer Randolph led his own big band in the 1930's, and Mike McKendrick also led a band in the 1930's. John Lindsay was with King Oliver and other jazz greats in the 1920's, and led a quartet in Chicago in the 1940's)

YOU'RE A LUCKY GUY / YOU'RE JUST
A NO ACCOUNT...................... *Decca 2934* 5-8 40
(Vocals: Louis Armstrong)

YOURS AND MINE / SUN SHOWERS..... *Decca 1369* 5-8 37
(Vocals: Louis Armstrong)

YOU RUN YOUR MOUTH, I'LL RUN MY BUSINESS /
CAIN AND ABEL..................... *Decca 3204* 3-5 40
(Vocals: Louis Armstrong)

YOU'VE GOT ME VOODOO'D /
HARLEM STOMP...................... *Decca 3092* 3-5 40
(Vocals: Louis Armstrong)

ARNHEIM, Gus, & His Ambassador Hotel Orchestra
(Gus Arnheim: 9/11/97 – 1/19/55)

I CAN'T DO WITHOUT YOU (Vocals: Unknown) /
FEELIN' GOOD....................... *Okeh 41057* 2-4 28

IF I CAN'T HAVE YOU (Vocals: by trio) /
BACK IN YOUR OWN BACK YARD..... *Okeh 41037* 3-5 28

ARNHEIM, Gus, & His Cocoanut Grove Orchestra
(Fred McMurray, of later motion picture & television fame, played clarinet and tenor sax with this orchestra in 1930/31.)

HO HUM! (Vocals: by Bing Crosby & Loyce Whiteman) / I'M
GONNA GET YOU (Vocal: Bing Crosby)... *Victor 22691* 5-8 31

IF YOU DON'T WANT TO BE
SWEETHEARTS (Vocal: Meri Bell) / LOVE IS
A DREAM (Vocal: Bud Struck)........... *Victor 24234* 2-4 33

I SURRENDER, DEAR (Vocal: Bing Crosby) /
LA ROSITA (Vocal: Samuel Pedrazza)...... *Victor 22618* 4-6 31

LOVE IN THE MOONLIGHT (Vocal: Loyce Whiteman) /
SUZANNE (Vocals: Three Rhythm Boys).... *Victor 24235* 2-4 33

THANKS TO YOU /
ONE MORE TIME.................... *Victor 22700* 5-8 31
(Vocals: Bing Crosby)

YOU'VE GOT ME IN THE PALM OF YOUR HAND
(Vocals: The Three Rhythm Rascals) /
EVENING (Vocal: Buddy Clark).......... *Victor 24061* 3-5 32

ARNHEIM, Gus, & His Orchestra

FOOL ME SOME MORE / IT MUST
BE TRUE........................... *Victor 22561* 5-8 30
(Vocals: Bing Crosby)

HAVE YOU GOT ANY CASTLES, BABY? /
ON WITH THE DANCE............ *Brunswick 7937* 4-6 37
(Vocals: Jimmy Farrell)

HIGH, WIDE AND HANDSOME / THE FOLKS
WHO LIVE ON THE HILL......... *Brunswick 7922* 4-6 37
(Vocals: Jimmy Farrell)

MY CABIN OF DREAMS / ALL YOU WANT
TO DO IS DANCE................ *Brunswick 7933* 4-6 37
(Vocals: Jimmy Farrell)

SO RARE / DANCING UNDER
THE STARS...................... *Brunswick 7919* 4-6 37
(Vocals: Jimmy Farrell)

THEM THERE EYES (Vocals: Bing Crosby, Al Rinker & Harry Barris) / THE LITTLE THINGS
IN LIFE (Vocal: Billy White)............. *Victor 22580* 5-8 31

ARTHUR, Zinn, & His Orchestra

DROP A NICKEL IN THE SLOT /
JOSEPH! JOSEPH! .... *Vocalion 4020* 4-6 38
(Vocals: Unknown)

LOVE IS GOOD FOR ANYTHING THAT
AILS YOU / WAS IT RAIN? .... *Variety 512* 4-6 37
(Vocals: Unknown)

ROMANCE IN THE DARK (Vocal: Zinn Arthur) / WHO
ARE WE TO SAY? (Vocals: Unknown).... *Vocalion 4033* 5-8 38

TWO SHADOWS / SHADOWS
ON THE MOON .... *Vocalion 4048* 3-5 38
(Vocals: Unknown)

ASH, Paul, & His Granada Orchestra
(Paul Ash: 2/11/91 – 7/13/58)

LA PALOMA /
ROSES OF PICARDY .... *Brunswick 2732* 2-4 24

OPEN YOUR HEART /
PESTICATIN' MAMA............. *Brunswick 2482* 4-6 23

PALE MOON / CAN'T YO' HEAR
ME CALLING, CAROLINE? .... *Brunswick 2684* 2-4 24

ASH, Paul, & His Orchestra

I AIN'T THAT KIND OF A BABY (Vocals: Unknown) /
AIN'T THAT A GRAND AND GLORIOUS FEELING?
(Vocal: Milton Watson).............. *Columbia 1066-D* 4-6 27

LET'S TALK ABOUT MY SWEETIE (Vocal: Harry Maxfield) / THANKS FOR THE BUGGY RIDE
(Vocal: Harry Barris)................ *Columbia 586-D* 4-6 26

YAAKA HULA HICKEY DULA /
RAGGIN' THE SCALE................ *Variety 649* 5-8 37

YOU DON'T LIKE IT – NOT MUCH /
SWEET SOMEONE.............. *Columbia 1034-D* 4-6 27
(Vocals: Unknown)

ASH, Paul, & His Pabst Blue Ribbon Casino Orchestra

LOUISVILLE LADY / FREE .... *Columbia 2798-D* 5-8 33
(Vocals: Unknown)

SHADOWS ON THE SWANEE /
BLUE ROSES.................... *Columbia 2796-D* 4-6 33
(Vocals: Unknown)

ASTORITES, The:
see RICH, Fred, & His Hotel Astor Orchestra

ATLANTIC DANCE ORCHESTRA, The

HUGO (I'LL GO WHERE YOU GO) /
LA ROSITA .... *Edison 51298* 2-4 24

I'VE GOT THE YES! WE HAVE NO
BANANAS BLUES / ACH! LOUIE!.... *Edison 51229* 3-5 23

JAKE THE SHEIK / THE FOX WALTZ.... *Edison 51077* 3-5 22

LAZY / THERE'S YES! YES! IN YOUR
EYES (by The Merry Sparklers) .... *Edison 51325* 3-5 24

LONELY LITTLE MELODY /
MY DREAM GIRL................... *Edison 51379* 3-5 24

MAH JONGG BLUES / FATE.......... *Edison 51102* 3-5 23

ROSES OF PICARDY / IN A TENT...... *Edison 51205* 2-4 23

SOME SUNNY DAY /
MEMORIES OF YOU................. *Edison 50973* 3-5 22

YOU ARE MY RAIN-BEAU /
BEES KNEES....................... *Edison 51094* 3-5 23

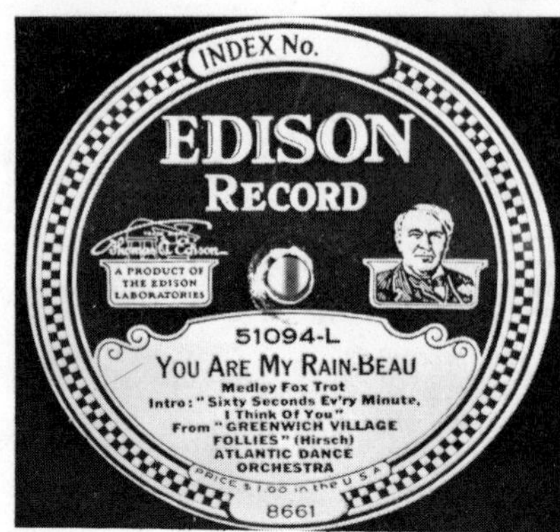

AUBURN, Frank, & His Orchestra:
see RICH, Fred, & His Orchestra, and
see SELVIN, Ben, & His Orchestra

AULD, George, & His Orchestra
(George Auld: 5/19/19 –)

ANGEL / I WANT MY MAMA.......... *Varsity 8152* 3-5 40
(Vocals: Kay Foster)

CHRISTMAS BALL, THE / IT AIN'T
SNOWIN' OUTSIDE................. *Coral 60558* 2-4 51
(Vocals: Bill Darnel)

JUST A-SITTIN' AND A-ROCKIN' /
COME TO BABY DO .... *Musicraft 15044* 2-4 45
(Vocals: Lynne Stevens)

MAN FROM MARS / LOVER, COME
BACK TO ME .... *Varsity 8163* 3-5 40

SHAKE DOWN THE STARS /
IMAGINATION...................... *Varsity 8199* 3-5 40
(Vocals: Kay Foster)

THIS IS ROMANCE (Vocal: Kay Foster) /
JUKE BOX JUMP.................... *Varsity 8159* 4-6 40

AYRES, Mitchell, & His Fashions In Music
(Mitchell Ayres: 12/24/10 – 9/5/69)

BARRELHOUSE BESSIE FROM BASIN STREET
(Vocals: Meredith Blake & Johnny Bond) /
OH, HOW I MISS YOU TONIGHT
(Vocal: Meredith Blake)............... *Bluebird B-11528* 3-5 42

BETWEEN YOU AND ME (Vocal: Mary Ann Mercer) /
PLAYMATES (Vocals: Mary Ann Mercer
& Tommy Taylor).................. *Bluebird B-10585* 2-4 40

BLAME IT ON MY LAST AFFAIR /
HEAVEN CAN WAIT............... *Vocalion 4699* 3-5 39
(Vocals: Mary Ann Mercer)

BOOGIE WOOGIE BUGLE BOY (Vocal: Tommy Taylor) /
YOU'RE A LUCKY FELLOW, MR. SMITH (Vocals: Mary Ann Mercer & Tommy Taylor)......... *Bluebird B-11046* 3-5 41

DINGBAT THE ACROBAT (Vocal: Mary Ann Mercer) /
ANGEL (Vocal: Tommy Taylor)....... *Bluebird B-10550* 2-4 40

DON'T FORGET TO SAY "NO", BABY
(Vocal: Meredith Blake) / THE WOLF SONG (Vocals: Meredith Blake & Johnny Bond)........ *Bluebird B-11563* 3-5 42

IF I HAD MY WAY / ON A BICYCLE
BUILT FOR TWO................... *Vocalion 4945* 3-5 39

I'M ON THE VERGE OF A MERGE (Vocal: Mary Ann Mercer) / PLEASE TAKE A LETTER, MISS BROWN
(Vocal: Tommy Taylor).............. *Bluebird B-10732* 2-4 40

I NEED A FRIEND / LITTLE CURLY HAIR
IN A HIGH CHAIR .... *Bluebird B-10641* 2-4 40
(Vocals: Tommy Taylor)

McNAMARA'S BAND (Vocal: Tommy Taylor) /
SCRATCHIN' THE SURFACE..... *Bluebird B-10929* 3-5 40

MAN ON THE FERRY, THE (Vocal: Tommy Taylor) / DO IT
AGAIN (Vocal: Mary Ann Mercer)..... *Bluebird B-10661* 2-4 40

ROW, ROW, ROW / MA! (HE'S MAKING
EYES AT ME).................... *Bluebird B-10541* 2-4 40
(Vocals: Mary Ann Mercer)

(GOTTA GET SOME) SHUT-EYE /
HEAVEN CAN WAIT.............. *Conqueror 9178* 2-4 39
(Vocals: Mary Ann Mercer)

WAITER AND THE PORTER AND THE
UPSTAIRS MAID, THE (Vocal: Johnny Bond) /
MISIRLOU....................... *Bluebird B-11295* 3-5 41

BADGERS, The:
see KATZMAN, Louis, as Katzman's Orchestra

BAILEY, Buster & His Sextet

BLUE ROOM / AM I BLUE .... *Varsity 8333* 4-6 40

PINETOP'S BOOGIE WOOGIE / ECCENTRIC RAG .... *Varsity 8365* 5-8 40

SEEMS LIKE A MONTH OF SUNDAYS / FABLE OF A ROSE .... *Varsity 8358* 4-6 40
(Vocals: Judy Ellington)

SHOULD I? / APRIL IN PARIS .... *Varsity 8337* 4-6 40

BAILEY, Buster, as the Buster Bailey Orchestra

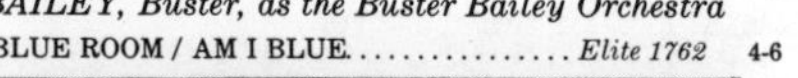

BLUE ROOM / AM I BLUE .... *Elite 1762* 4-6 40

BLUE ROOM / AM I BLUE .... *Philharmonic 84* 5-8 40

BAILEY, Mildred, & Her Alley Cats
(Mildred Bailey: 2/27/07 – 12/12/51)

SQUEEZE ME / DOWNHEARTED BLUES .... *Decca 18109* 5-8 41
(Vocals: Mildred Bailey)
(A 1935 recording first released in 1941)

WILLOW TREE/HONEYSUCKLE ROSE ... *Decca 18108* 5-8 41
(Vocals: Mildred Bailey)
(A 1935 recording first released in 1941)

BAILEY, Mildred, & Her Orchestra

BEWILDERED / AT YOUR BECK AND CALL .... *Vocalion 4036* 3-5 38
(Vocals: Mildred Bailey)

BLAME IT ON MY LAST AFFAIR / WHAT SHALL I SAY? .... *Vocalion 4632* 3-5 39
(Vocals: Mildred Bailey)

BOB WHITE (WATCHA GONNA SWING TONIGHT?) /JUST A STONE'S THROW FROM HEAVEN .... *Vocalion 3712* 5-8 37
(Vocals: Mildred Bailey)

FOR SENTIMENTAL REASONS / IT'S A LOVE I'M AFTER .... *Vocalion 3367* 5-8 37
(Vocals: Mildred Bailey)

FROM THE LAND OF SKY BLUE WATER / LOVER, COME BACK TO ME .... *Vocalion 3832* 4-6 38
(Vocals: Mildred Bailey)

GUESS I'LL GO BACK HOME / THE LITTLE MAN WHO WASN'T THERE .... *Vocalion 4966* 3-5 39
(Vocals: Mildred Bailey)

I CAN'T FACE THE MUSIC (WITHOUT SINGIN' THE BLUES) / DON'T BE THAT WAY ..... *Vocalion 4016* 5-8 38
(Vocals: Mildred Bailey)

I CRIED FOR YOU / BEGIN THE BEGUINE .... *Vocalion 4619* 4-6 39
(Vocals: Mildred Bailey)

IF YOU SHOULD EVER LEAVE / HEAVEN HELP THIS HEART OF MINE .... *Vocalion 3615* 5-8 37
(Vocals: Mildred Bailey)

I LET A SONG GO OUT OF MY HEART / ROCK IT FOR ME .... *Vocalion 4083* 5-8 38
(Vocals: Mildred Bailey)

I'M FOREVER BLOWING BUBBLES / A GHOST OF A CHANCE .... *Vocalion 5086* 4-6 39
(Vocals: Mildred Bailey)

I SEE YOUR FACE BEFORE ME / THANKS FOR THE MEMORY .... *Vocalion 3931* 5-8 38
(Vocals: Mildred Bailey)

IT SEEMS LIKE OLD TIMES / MOON LOVE .... *Vocalion 4939* 5-8 39
(Vocals: Mildred Bailey)

IT'S SUMMERTIME ALONG THE SWANEE / 'TAIN'T WHAT YOU DO (IT'S THE WAY THAT YOU DO IT) .... *Vocalion 4708* 5-8 39
(Vocals: Mildred Bailey)

'LONG ABOUT MIDNIGHT / MORE THAN YOU KNOW .... *Vocalion 3378* 5-8 37
(Vocals: Mildred Bailey)

LOVE IS WHERE YOU FIND IT / I USED TO BE COLOR BLIND ...... *Conqueror 9106* 3-5 38
(Vocals: Mildred Bailey)

LOVE IS WHERE YOU FIND IT / I USED TO BE COLOR BLIND .... *Vocalion 4345* 3-5 38
(Vocals: Mildred Bailey)
(Simultaneously released on two labels)

LOVING YOU / RIGHT OR WRONG .... *Vocalion 3758* 4-6 37
(Vocals: Mildred Bailey)

MOON GOT IN MY EYES, THE / IT'S THE NATURAL THING TO DO .... *Vocalion 3626* 5-8 37
(Vocals: Mildred Bailey)

MOONSHINE OVER KENTUCKY / IF YOU WERE IN MY PLACE .... *Vocalion 4109* 4-6 38
(Vocals: Mildred Bailey)

MY LAST AFFAIR / TRUST ME .... *Vocalion 3449* 4-6 37
(Vocals: Mildred Bailey)

MY MELANCHOLY BABY / THE LONESOME ROAD .... *Vocalion 4474* 5-8 38
(Vocals: Mildred Bailey)

MY REVERIE / WHAT HAVE YOU GOT THAT GETS ME? .... *Conqueror 9107* 5-8 38
(Vocals: Mildred Bailey)

MY REVERIE / WHAT HAVE YOU GOT THAT GETS ME? .... *Vocalion 4408* 5-8 38
(Vocals: Mildred Bailey)
(Simultaneously released on two labels)

NEVER IN A MILLION YEARS / THERE'S A LULL IN MY LIFE ...... *Vocalion 3508* 5-8 37
(Vocals: Mildred Bailey)

NOW IT CAN BE TOLD / I HAVEN'T CHANGED A THING ..... *Vocalion 4282* 4-6 38
(Vocals: Mildred Bailey)

OLD FOLKS / HAVE YOU FORGOTTEN SO SOON? .... *Vocalion 4432* 3-5 38
(Vocals: Mildred Bailey)

ROCKIN' CHAIR / LITTLE JOE .... *Vocalion 3553* 5-8 37
(Vocals: Mildred Bailey)

SMALL FRY / BORN TO SWING .... *Vocalion 4224* 5-8 38
(Vocals: Mildred Bailey)

SO HELP ME / AS LONG AS YOU LIVE YOU'LL BE DEAD IF YOU DIE ...... *Vocalion 4253* 4-6 38
(Vocals: Mildred Bailey)

THAT SLY OLD GENTLEMAN / AND THE ANGELS SING .... *Vocalion 4815* 5-8 39
(Vocals: Mildred Bailey)

THEY SAY / I GO FOR THAT .... *Vocalion 4548* 5-8 39
(Vocals: Mildred Bailey)

TIT WILLOW / THE LAMP IS LOW .... *Vocalion 4845* 4-6 39
(Vocals: Mildred Bailey)

WASHBOARD BLUES / ROUND THE OLD DESERTED FARM .... *Vocalion 4139* 5-8 38
(Vocals: Mildred Bailey)

WHERE ARE YOU? / YOU'RE LAUGHING AT ME .... *Vocalion 3456* 4-6 37
(Vocals: Mildred Bailey)

YOU'RE THE MOMENT IN MY LIFE / YOU AND YOUR LOVE .... *Vocalion 5006* 3-5 39
(Vocals: Mildred Bailey)

BAILEY, Mildred, & Her Oxford Greys

BARRELHOUSE MUSIC / YOU DON'T KNOW MY MIND BLUES .... *Vocalion 4802* 5-8 39
(Vocals: Mildred Bailey)

ST. LOUIS BLUES / ARKANSAS BLUES .... *Vocalion 4801* 5-8 39
(Vocals: Mildred Bailey)

THERE'LL BE SOME CHANGES MADE / PRISONER OF LOVE .... *Vocalion 5268* 5-8 39
(Vocals: Mildred Bailey)

BAILEY, Mildred, & Her Swing Band

I'D LOVE TO TAKE ORDERS FROM YOU / I'D RATHER LISTEN TO YOUR EYES ... *Vocalion 3056* 5-8 35
(Vocals: Mildred Bailey)

SOMEDAY, SWEETHEART / WHEN DAY IS DONE .... *Vocalion 3057* 5-8 35
(Vocals: Mildred Bailey)

BAILEY'S LUCKY SEVEN:
see LANIN, Sam

BAKER, Phil, as Phil Baker's Bad Boys
(Phil Baker: 8/24/96 – 11/30/63)

HOW CAN YOU LOOK SO GOOD (AND STILL BE SO DOG-GONE BAD?) / PRETTY LITTLE BABY .... *Edison 51645* 5-8 25

BALLEW, Smith, & His Orchestra
(Smith Ballew: 1/21/02 –)

ALONE WITH MY DREAMS / WHERE THE GOLDEN DAFFODILS GROW .... *Okeh 41394* 5-8 30
(Vocals: Smith Ballew)

ANIMAL CRACKERS IN MY SOUP (Vocal: Durelle Alexander) / THE SIMPLE THINGS IN LIFE (Vocal: Smith Ballew) .... *Melotone 35-09-16* 5-8 35

BEAT O' MY HEART, THE / MADEMOISELLE .... *Banner 33042* 5-8 34
(Vocals: Smith Ballew)

BEAT O' MY HEART, THE / MADEMOISELLE .... *Melotone 13004* 5-8 34
(Vocals: Smith Ballew)

BEAT O' MY HEART, THE / MADEMOISELLE .... *Perfect 15926* 5-8 34
(Vocals: Smith Ballew)
(Simultaneously released on three labels)

BE CAREFUL, YOUNG LADY / A LITTLE WHITE GARDENIA .... *Banner 33333* 5-8 35
(Vocals: Smith Ballew)

BE CAREFUL, YOUNG LADY / A LITTLE WHITE GARDENIA .... *Melotone M-13300* 5-8 35
(Vocals: Smith Ballew)

BE CAREFUL, YOUNG LADY / A LITTLE WHITE GARDENIA .... *Oriole 3083* 5-8 35
(Vocals: Smith Ballew)

BE CAREFUL, YOUNG LADY / A LITTLE WHITE GARDENIA .... *Perfect 16067* 5-8 35
(Vocals: Smith Ballew)

BE CAREFUL, YOUNG LADY / A LITTLE WHITE GARDENIA .... *Romeo 2457* 5-8 35
(Vocals: Smith Ballew)
(Simultaneously released on five labels)

CHAMPAGNE WALTZ (Vocal: Smith Ballew) / PLAY TO ME, GYPSY (Vocals: by trio) ..... *Melotone M-12968* 5-8 34

CHAMPAGNE WALTZ (Vocal: Smith Ballew) / PLAY TO ME, GYPSY (Vocals: by trio) .... *Perfect 15907* 5-8 34
(Simultaneously released on two labels)

DREAM LOVER / MY LOVE PARADE .... *Okeh 41341* 5-8 29
(Vocals: Smith Ballew)

DREAM LOVER / MY LOVE PARADE .... *Odeon ONY-36013* 5-8 29
(Vocals: Smith Ballew)
(Simultaneously released on two labels)

EV'RY SINGLE LITTLE TINGLE OF MY HEART / WHAT A LITTLE MOONLIGHT CAN DO .... *Melotone 35-09-01* 5-8 35
(Vocals: Smith Ballew)

FORBIDDEN LIPS (Vocal: Smith Ballew) / FOOLIN' WITH THE OTHER WOMAN'S MAN (Vocal: Kay Weber) .... *Banner 33065* 5-8 34

FORBIDDEN LIPS (Vocal: Smith Ballew) / FOOLIN' WITH THE OTHER WOMAN'S MAN (Vocal: Kay Weber) ... *Melotone 13029* 5-8 34

FORBIDDEN LIPS (Vocal: Smith Ballew) / FOOLIN' WITH THE OTHER WOMAN'S MAN (Vocal: Kay Weber) .... *Oriole 2904* 5-8 34

FORBIDDEN LIPS (Vocal: Smith Ballew) / FOOLIN' WITH THE OTHER WOMAN'S MAN (Vocal: Kay Weber) ..... *Perfect 15937* 5-8 34

FORBIDDEN LIPS (Vocal: Smith Ballew) / FOOLIN' WITH THE OTHER WOMAN'S MAN (Vocal: Kay Weber) ...... *Romeo 2278* 5-8 34
(Simultaneously released on five labels)

GIGOLETTE/THE WORLD IS MINE ... *Melotone 13224* 5-8 34
(Vocals: Smith Ballew)

GIGOLETTE / THE WORLD IS MINE ... *Perfect 16028* 5-8 34
(Vocals: Smith Ballew)
(Simultaneously released on two labels)

I'LL KEEP WARM ALL WINTER / ONE LITTLE KISS .... *Melotone 13258* 5-8 35
(Vocals: Smith Ballew)

I'LL KEEP WARM ALL WINTER / ONE LITTLE KISS .... *Perfect 16046* 5-8 35
(Vocals: Smith Ballew)
(Simultaneously released on two labels)

I LOVE YOU BEST OF ALL / CALL ME DARLING .... *Crown 3209* 8-10 31
(Vocals: Smith Ballew)

I'M THROWIN' MY LOVE AWAY (Vocal: Kay Weber) / LITTLE DID I DREAM (Vocal: Smith Ballew) .... *Melotone M-12970* 5-8 34

I'M THROWIN' MY LOVE AWAY (Vocal: Kay Weber) / LITTLE DID I DREAM (Vocal: Smith Ballew) .... *Perfect 15908* 5-8 34
(Simultaneously released on two labels)

IN THE MIDDLE OF A KISS / YOU'RE ALL I NEED .... *Melotone M-13422* 5-8 35
(Vocals: Smith Ballew)

IN THE MIDDLE OF A KISS / YOU'RE ALL I NEED .... *Perfect 16128* 5-8 35
(Vocals: Smith Ballew)

IN THE MIDDLE OF A KISS / YOU'RE ALL I NEED .... *Romeo 2531* 5-8 35
(Vocals: Smith Ballew)
(Simultaneously released on three labels)

I WON'T DANCE / LOVELY TO LOOK AT .... *Banner 33376* 5-8 35
(Vocals: Smith Ballew)

I WON'T DANCE / LOVELY TO LOOK AT .... *Melotone M-13343* 5-8 35
(Vocals: Smith Ballew)

I WON'T DANCE / LOVELY TO LOOK AT .... *Oriole 3108* 5-8 35
(Vocals: Smith Ballew)
(Simultaneously released on three labels)

JUST ANOTHER KISS / S'POSIN' .... *Okeh 41256* 5-8 29
(Vocals: Smith Ballew)

JUST YOU, JUST ME / BLONDY .... *Okeh 41282* 5-8 29
(Vocals: Smith Ballew)

LANGUAGE OF LOVE, THE / FUNNY, DEAR, WHAT LOVE CAN DO .... *Okeh 41265* 5-8 30
(Vocals: Smith Ballew)

LET'S TRY AGAIN / MOONLIGHT ON THE RIVER .... *Perfect 15630* 5-8 32
(Vocals: Smith Ballew)

LOVE AND KISSES / YOU SAVED MY LIFE .... *Melotone 35-09-17* 5-8 35
(Vocals: Smith Ballew)

MERRY WIDOW WALTZ, THE/ VILIA ... *Melotone 13200* 5-8 34
(Vocals: Smith Ballew)

MERRY WIDOW WALTZ, THE /VILIA ... *Perfect 16018* 5-8 34
(Vocals: Smith Ballew)
(Simultaneously released on two labels)

MY INTRODUCTION TO LOVE / LIFE IS A SONG .... *Banner 33408* 5-8 35
(Vocals: Smith Ballew)

MY INTRODUCTION TO LOVE / LIFE IS A SONG .... *Melotone M-13375* 5-8 35
(Vocals: Smith Ballew)

MY INTRODUCTION TO LOVE / LIFE IS A SONG .... *Oriole 3128* 5-8 35
(Vocals: Smith Ballew)

MY INTRODUCTION TO LOVE / LIFE IS A SONG .... *Perfect 16105* 5-8 35
(Vocals: Smith Ballew)

MY INTRODUCTION TO LOVE / LIFE IS A SONG .... *Romeo 2508* 5-8 35
(Vocals: Smith Ballew)
(Simultaneously released on five labels)

NIGHT IS YOUNG, THE / WHEN I GROW TOO OLD TO DREAM .... *Banner 33318* 5-8 35
(Vocals: Smith Ballew)

NIGHT IS YOUNG, THE / WHEN I GROW TOO OLD TO DREAM .... *Melotone M-13285* 5-8 35
(Vocals: Smith Ballew)

NIGHT IS YOUNG, THE / WHEN I GROW TOO OLD TO DREAM .... *Oriole 3075* 5-8 35
(Vocals: Smith Ballew)

NIGHT IS YOUNG, THE / WHEN I GROW TOO OLD TO DREAM .... *Perfect 16059* 5-8 35
(Vocals: Smith Ballew)

NIGHT IS YOUNG, THE / WHEN I GROW TOO OLD TO DREAM .... *Romeo 2469* 5-8 35
(Vocals: Smith Ballew)
(Simultaneously released on five labels)

OVERNIGHT / TO WHOM IT MAY CONCERN .... *Columbia 2373-D* 5-8 31
(Vocals: Smith Ballew)

PAINTING THE CLOUDS WITH SUNSHINE / TIP-TOE THROW THE TULIPS WITH ME .... *Okeh 41299* 5-8 29
(Vocals: Smith Ballew)

SAY A LITTLE PRAYER FOR ME / OUT OF NOWHERE .... *Columbia 2430-D* 5-8 31
(Vocals: Smith Ballew)

SHEPHERD'S SERENADE, THE / CHARMING .... *Odeon ONY-36022* 5-8 30
(Vocals: Smith Ballew)

SHEPHERD'S SERENADE, THE / CHARMING .... *Odeon ONY-36018* 4-6 30
(Alternate version with no vocals)

SHEPHERD'S SERENADE, THE / CHARMING .... *Okeh 41352* 5-8 30
(Vocals: Smith Ballew)
(Released on two labels)

SING, YOU SINNERS (Vocal: Smith Ballew) / IN MY LITTLE HOPE CHEST (Vocal: Unknown female) .... *Odeon ONY-36051* 5-8 30

SING, YOU SINNERS (Vocal: Smith Ballew) / IN MY LITTLE HOPE CHEST (Vocal: Unknown female) .... *Okeh 41384* 5-8 30
(Simultaneously released on two labels)

SNUGGLED ON YOUR SHOULDER / DANCING ON THE CEILING .... *Conqueror 7928* 5-8 32
(Vocals: Smith Ballew)

SNUGGLED ON YOUR SHOULDER / DANCING ON THE CEILING .... *Perfect 15566* 5-8 32
(Vocals: Smith Ballew)

SNUGGLED ON YOUR SHOULDER / DANCING ON THE CEILING .... *Romeo 1787* 5-8 32
(Vocals: Smith Ballew)
(Simultaneously released on three labels)

STARLIGHT / TELL TALES .... *Conqueror 7925* 5-8 32
(Vocals: Smith Ballew)

STARLIGHT / TELL TALES .... *Perfect 15564* 5-8 32
(Vocals: Smith Ballew)
(Simultaneously released on two labels)

TAKE THE ACHE FROM MY HEART / FOOTLOOSE AND FANCY FREE .... *Melotone M-13423* 5-8 35
(Vocals: Smith Ballew)

TAKE THE ACHE FROM MY HEART / FOOTLOOSE AND FANCY FREE .... *Perfect 16129* 5-8 35
(Vocals: Smith Ballew)

TAKE THE ACHE FROM MY HEART / FOOTLOOSE AND FANCY FREE .... *Romeo 2532* 5-8 35
(Vocals: Smith Ballew)
(Simultaneously released on three labels)

THERE'S SOMETHING MISSING IN YOUR EYES / NINE LITTLE MILES FROM TEN-TEN-TENNESSEE .... *Columbia 2350-D* 5-8 31
(Vocals: Smith Ballew)

THINGS THAT WERE MEANT FOR LOVE, THE / BLUE HAWAII .... *Okeh 41242* 5-8 29
(Vocals: Smith Ballew)

TIA JUANA / ISLE OF CAPRI .... *Banner 33273* 5-8 35
(Vocals: Smith Ballew)

TIA JUANA / ISLE OF CAPRI ...... *Melotone M-13240* 5-8 35
(Vocals: Smith Ballew)

TIA JUANA / ISLE OF CAPRI .... *Oriole 3047* 5-8 35
(Vocals: Smith Ballew)

TIA JUANA / ISLE OF CAPRI .... *Perfect 16037* 5-8 35
(Vocals: Smith Ballew)
(Simultaneously released on four labels)

WE CAN LIVE ON LOVE / I HATE MYSELF .... *Columbia 2406-D* 5-8 31
(Vocals: Smith Ballew)

WE'LL BUILD A LITTLE WORLD OF OUR OWN / WHERE THE GOLDEN DAFFODILS GROW .... *Odeon ONY-36059* 5-8 30

WHEN I GROW TOO OLD TO DREAM / A LITTLE WHITE GARDENIA ...... *Conqueror 8472* 5-8 35
(Vocals: Smith Ballew)

WHEN I WORE MY DADDY'S BROWN DERBY (AND YOU WORE YOUR MOTHER'S BLUE GOWN) / CUBAN LOVE SONG .... *Crown 3228* 5-8 31
(Vocals: Smith Ballew)

WHEN MY PRINCE CHARMING COMES ALONG (Vocal: Kay Weber) / THIS IS MY YEAR (Vocal: Smith Ballew) .... *Banner 33334* 5-8 35

WHEN MY PRINCE CHARMING COMES ALONG (Vocal: Kay Weber) / THIS IS MY YEAR (Vocal: Smith Ballew) .... *Melotone M-13301* 5-8 35

WHEN MY PRINCE CHARMING COMES ALONG (Vocal: Kay Weber) / THIS IS MY YEAR (Vocal: Smith Ballew) .... *Oriole 3084* 5-8 35

WHEN MY PRINCE CHARMING COMES ALONG (Vocal: Kay Weber) / THIS IS MY YEAR (Vocal: Smith Ballew) .... *Perfect 16068* 5-8 35

WHEN MY PRINCE CHARMING COMES ALONG (Vocal: Kay Weber) / THIS IS MY YEAR (Vocal: Smith Ballew) .... *Romeo 2458* 5-8 35
(Simultaneously released on five labels)

WHOLE DARNED THING'S FOR YOU / GIRL TROUBLE .... *Odeon ONY-36078* 5-8 30
(Vocals: Smith Ballew)

YOU TRY SOMEBODY ELSE / I'M FOR YOU A HUNDRED PER CENT .... *Crown 3227* 5-8 31
(Vocals: Smith Ballew)

YOU WERE ONLY PASSING TIME WITH ME / YOU'RE SIMPLY DELISH .... *Columbia 2320-D* 5-8 30
(Vocals: Smith Ballew)

BALLEW, Smith, & His Orchestra as Buddy Blue & His Texans

BODY AND SOUL / HERE COMES THE SUN .... *Crown 3008* 5-8 30
(Vocals: Smith Ballew)

CAN'T YOU READ BETWEEN THE LINES? / NEVERTHELESS .... *Crown 3132* 5-8 31
(Vocals: Smith Ballew)

HAVE YOU FORGOTTEN? / HOW TIME CAN FLY .... *Crown 3146* 5-8 31
(Vocals: Smith Ballew)

I FOUND A MILLION-DOLLAR BABY / ON THE BEACH WITH YOU .... *Crown 3149* 5-8 31
(Vocals: Smith Ballew)

I'LL BE BLUE / WHAT A FOOL I'VE BEEN .... *Crown 3021* 5-8 30
(Vocals: Smith Ballew)

I STILL GET A THRILL / GO HOME AND TELL YOUR MOTHER .... *Crown 3015* 5-8 30
(Vocals: Smith Ballew)

I'VE MADE UP MY MIND TO FALL FOR SOMEONE / SOMEWHERE .... *Romeo 1329* 4-6 30
(Vocals: Smith Ballew)

LET'S HAVE ANOTHER CUP OF COFFEE / SOFT LIGHTS AND SWEET MUSIC .... *Crown 3281* 4-6 31
(Vocals: Smith Ballew)

LITTLE JOE / OH, HOW I MISS YOU ..... *Crown 3108* 5-8 31
(Vocals: Smith Ballew)

MY SONG OF THE NILE / LONELY LITTLE CINDERELLA ...... *Banner 6438* 5-8 29
(Vocals: Smith Ballew)

MY SONG OF THE NILE / LONELY LITTLE CINDERELLA ...... *Domino 4367* 5-8 29
(Vocals: Smith Ballew)

MY SONG OF THE NILE / LONELY LITTLE CINDERELLA .... *Regal 8812* 5-8 29
(Vocals: Smith Ballew)
(Simultaneously released on three labels)

ROMANCE / MOLLY .... *Perfect 15278* 4-6 30
(Vocals: Smith Ballew)

RUNNING BETWEEN THE RAINDROPS / TIE A LITTLE STRING AROUND YOUR FINGER .... *Crown 3068* 5-8 31
(Vocals: Smith Ballew)

SAY A LITTLE PRAYER FOR ME / WHISTLING IN THE DARK .... *Crown 3104* 5-8 31
(Vocals: Smith Ballew)

SMILING IRISH EYES / LOVE IS A DREAMER .... *Regal 8830* 5-8 29
(Vocals: Smith Ballew)

SWEETHEART OF MY STUDENT DAYS / I'M YOURS .... *Crown 3022* 5-8 30
(Vocals: Smith Ballew)

BALLEW, Smith, & His Orchestra as Ted Raph & His Orchestra

EV'RYTHING THAT'S NICE BELONGS TO YOU / DREAM A LITTLE DREAM OF ME ... *Columbia 2450-D* 5-8 31
(Vocals: Smith Ballew)

WHEN I TAKE MY SUGAR TO TEA / PLEASE DON'T TALK ABOUT ME WHEN I'M GONE .... *Columbia 2440-D* 5-8 31
(Vocals: Smith Ballew)

BAL TABERIN JAZZ ORCHESTRA, The:

see RADERMAN, Harry

BANJOPATORS, The

BEAUTIFUL ANNABEL LEE / GRIEVING FOR YOU .... *Grey Gull L-1038* 2-4 20

CARESSES / I'VE GOT THE BLUES FOR MY OLD KENTUCKY HOME ...... *Grey Gull L-1034* 2-4 20

PALESTEENA / MY HOME-TOWN IS A ONE-HORSE TOWN .... *Grey Gull L-1040* 2-4 21
(Vocals: Ernest Hare)

ROSE / LOOK WHAT YOU'VE DONE WITH YOUR DOGGONE DANGEROUS EYES ... *Grey Gull L-1041* 2-4 21
(Vocals: Ernest Hare)

YOU OUGHTA SEE MY BABY / WHY DON'T YOU? .... *Grey Gull L-1042* 2-4 21
(Vocals: Ernest Hare)

BANNER DANCE ORCHESTRA, The:

see SAMUELS, Joseph, & His Orchestra

BARBER, Lloyd as Lloyd Barber's Green Mill Orchestra

CANADIAN CAPERS / LOVE DAYS ..... *Gennett 4852* 2-4 22

PICK ME UP AND LAY ME DOWN IN DEAR OLD DIXIE LAND / HONEYMOON BLUES .... *Gennett 4853* 3-5 22

WIGWAM BLUES / TEE PEE BLUES .... *Gennett 4851* 3-5 22

BARGY, Roy:

see BENSON ORCHESTRA OF CHICAGO, The

BAR HARBOR ORCHESTRA / BAR HARBOR SOCIETY ORCHESTRA, The,

see SELVIN, Ben

BARNET, Charlie, & His Orchestra

(Charlie Barnet: 10/26/13 –)

ASLEEP OR AWAKE / SPOSIN' ..... *Bluebird B-10206* 2-4 39
(Vocals: Judy Ellington)

BABY, TAKE A BOW / THIS IS OUR LAST NIGHT TOGETHER .... *Banner 33029* 4-6 34
(Vocals: Jackie Martin)

BABY, TAKE A BOW / THIS IS OUR LAST NIGHT TOGETHER .... *Melotone M-12988* 4-6 34
(Vocals: Jackie Martin)

BABY, TAKE A BOW / THIS IS OUR LAST NIGHT TOGETHER .... *Oriole 2880* 4-6 34
(Vocals: Jackie Martin)

BABY, TAKE A BOW / THIS IS OUR LAST NIGHT TOGETHER .... *Perfect 15919* 4-6 34
(Vocals: Jackie Martin)

BABY, TAKE A BOW / THIS IS OUR LAST NIGHT TOGETHER .... *Romeo 2254* 4-6 34
(Vocals: Jackie Martin)
(Simultaneously released on five labels)

BETWEEN 18TH & 19TH ON CHESTNUT STREET / SOMEBODY TOLD ME .... *Bluebird B-10543* 2-4 40
(Vocals: Mary Ann McCall)

BLUE JUICE / HARMONY HAVEN (Vocals: Bob Carroll & the Three Moaxes) .... *Bluebird B-11111* 3-5 41

BLUES IN THE NIGHT (Vocal: Bobby Canvin) / ISLE OF PINES (Vocal: Bob Carroll) .... *Bluebird B-11327* 2-4 41

BREEZE AND I, THE / THE FABLE OF THE ROSE .... *Bluebird B-10696* 2-4 40
(Vocals: Mary Ann McCall)

BUFFY BOY / HAUNTED TOWN (Vocal: Lena Horne) .... *Bluebird B-11093* 3-5 41

BUTTERFINGERS / INFATUATION .... *Banner 33015* 3-5 34
(Vocals: Helen Heath)

BUTTERFINGERS/ INFATUATION ... *Conqueror 8281* 3-5 34
(Vocals: Helen Heath)

BUTTERFINGERS/INFATUATION .... *Melotone M-12974* 3-5 34
(Vocals: Helen Heath)

BUTTERFINGERS / INFATUATION ...... *Oriole 2872* 3-5 34
(Vocals: Helen Heath)

BUTTERFINGERS / INFATUATION ..... *Perfect 15912* 3-5 34
(Vocals: Helen Heath)

BUTTERFINGERS / INFATUATION ...... *Romeo 2246* 3-5 34
(Vocals: Helen Heath)
(Simultaneously released on six labels)

CARAVAN / DARKTOWN STRUTTER'S BALL .... *Apollo 1070* 4-6 48
("Record of the Month" – Song Hits Magazine)

CHARLESTON ALLEY / — .... *V-Disc 266* 5-8 -
(This is an oversize 12-inch 78 rpm, A World War II release)

CHEROKEE (theme song) / POMPTON TURNPIKE .... *V-Disc 307* 4-6 -
(This is an oversize 12-inch 78 rpm.)
(A World War II release)

CHEROKEE (Theme Song) / THE ALL-NIGHT RECORD MAN (Vocals: Charlie Barnet & Judy Ellington) .... *Bluebird B-10373* 2-4 39

CLAP HANDS, HERE COMES CHARLIE / SOUTHLAND SHUFFLE.......... *Bluebird B-10602* 3-5 40

CLASS WILL TELL / SOME LIKE IT HOT.............. *Bluebird B-10182* 3-5 39
(Vocals: Judy Ellington)

CUBAN BOOGIE WOOGIE / TWO HEARTS ARE BETTER THAN ONE............. *Bluebird B-10479* 3-5 39
(Vocals: Judy Ellington)

DANGER IN THE DARK / IT MUST HAVE BEEN TWO OTHER PEOPLE............ *Bluebird B-10336* 2-4 39
(Vocals: Larry Taylor)

DROP ME OFF IN HARLEM / GULF COAST BLUES .... *Decca 18810* 2-4 46

DUKE'S IDEA, THE / THE COUNT'S IDEA .... *Bluebird B-10453* 3-5 39

EBONY RHAPSODY / LAMENT FOR A LOST LOVE ..... *Bluebird B-10341* 3-5 39

ECHOES OF HARLEM / SCOTCH & SODA................ *Bluebird B-10210* 3-5 39

FLYING HOME / TANGLEWEED 'ROUND MY HEART (Vocal: Larry Taylor)..... *Bluebird B-10794* 2-4 40

FOR TONIGHT / WHAT'S NEW? .... *Bluebird B-10361* 2-4 39
(Vocals: Larry Taylor)

GOOD FOR NOTHIN' JOE (Vocal: Lena Horne) / CHARLESTON ALLEY .... *Bluebird B-11037* 2-4 41

GROWLIN' / ON A HOLIDAY .... *Bluebird B-5816* 4-6 35

HARLEM SPEAKS / SWINGIN' ON NOTHIN' (Vocal: Ford Leary)..... *Bluebird B-11281* 2-4 41

HEART YOU STOLE FROM ME, THE (Vocal: Bob Carroll) MURDER AT PEYTON HALL..... *Bluebird B-11292* 2-4 41

I DON'T WANT ANYBODY AT ALL (Vocal: Huck Andrews) / THAT OLD BLACK MAGIC (Vocal: Frances Wayne)............ *Decca 18541* 2-4 42

I DON'T WANT TO CRY ANYMORE (Vocal: Larry Taylor) POMPTON TURNPIKE........... *Bluebird B-10825* 2-4 40

I GET ALONG WITHOUT YOU VERY WELL (Vocal: Judy Ellington) / I'M PRAYIN' HUMBLE.............. *Bluebird B-10119* 3-5 39

I LIKE TO RIFF (Vocal: Peanuts Holland) / SHADY LADY........................ *Decca 18378* 2-4 42

I LIKE TO RIFF (Vocal: Peanuts Holland) / SHADY LADY......................... *V-Disc 342* 5-8 -
(The V-Disc is a World War II release)
(Simultaneously released on two labels)

I'M AN OLD COWHAND / EMPTY SADDLES................ *Bluebird B-6448* 4-6 36
(Vocals: Joe Hostetter)

I'M COMING, VIGINIA (Vocal: Ford Leary) / I'LL REMEMBER APRIL (Vocal: Bob Carroll) .... *Bluebird B-11417* 2-4 41

I'M NO ANGEL (Vocal: Helen Heath) / I WANT YOU – I NEED YOU (Vocal: Harry Von Zell) ...... *Banner 32875* 4-6 33

I'M NO ANGEL (Vocal: Helen Heath) / I WANT YOU – I NEED YOU (Vocal: Harry Von Zell)... *Melotone M-12817* 4-6 33

I'M NO ANGEL (Vocal: Helen Heath) / I WANT YOU – I NEED YOU (Vocal: Harry Von Zell)......... *Oriole 2777* 4-6 33

I'M NO ANGEL (Vocal: Helen Heath) / I WANT YOU – I NEED YOU (Vocal: Harry Von Zell) .... *Perfect 15833* 4-6 33

I'M NO ANGEL (Vocal: Helen Heath) / I WANT YOU – I NEED YOU (Vocal: Harry Von Zell) .... *Romeo 2150* 4-6 33
(Simultaneously released on five labels)

IN A MIZZ (Vocal: Judy Ellington) / NIGHT SONG.................... *Bluebird B-10191* 2-4 39

IT'S A WONDERFUL WORLD / BUSY AS A BEE .... *Bluebird B-10610* 2-4 40
(Vocals: Mary Ann McCall)

JUBILEE JUMP / DEEP PURPLE .... *Apollo 1092* 3-5 48

JUMP SESSION / SWING STREET STRUT.......... *Bluebird B-10172* 3-5 39

LAMENT FOR MAY / SIX LESSONS FROM MADAME LA ZONGA (Vocal: Mary Ann McCall).... *Bluebird 10743* 2-4 40

LEAPIN' AT THE LINCOLN / DARK AVENUE (Vocal: Mary Ann McCall) ... *Bluebird B-10774* 2-4 40

LITTLE JOHN ORDINARY / CONSIDER YOURSELF KISSED (Vocal: Bob Carroll) .... *Bluebird B-11165* 2-4 41

LONG AGO AND FAR AWAY (Vocal: Charlie Barnet) /WHERE IS MY HEART? (Vocal: Joe Hostetter)................. *Bluebird B-6432* 4-6 36

LOVER IS BLUE, A (Vocal: Judy Ellington) / NIGHT GLOW.................... *Bluebird B-10511* 2-4 39

LOVER'S LULLABY, A / YOU'VE GOT ME VOODOO'D...... *Bluebird B-10662* 2-4 40
(Vocals: Mary Ann McCall)

MACUMBA / 50,000,000 NICKELS (Vocal: Ford Leary)........ *Bluebird B-11396* 2-4 41

MAKE-BELIEVE BALLROOM / BYE, BYE, BABY................. *Bluebird B-6504* 5-8 36

MIDWEEK FUNCTION / I NEVER KNEW .... *Bluebird B-10285* 2-4 39

MILKMAN'S MATINEE, THE (Vocals: The Barnet Modernaires) / SING, BABY, SING (Vocal: Charlie Barnet)................ *Bluebird B-6593* 4-6 36

MOON IS CRYIN' FOR ME, THE (Vocals: Larry Taylor) / I HEAR A RHAPSODY (Vocals: Bob Carroll)................ *Bluebird B-10934* 2-4 40

MY HEART KEEPS CRYING / TAKE A TIP FROM THE WHIPPOORWILL..... *Bluebird B-10426* 2-4 39
(Vocals: Judy Ellington)

NAGASAKI / FARE THEE WELL, ANNA-BELLE (Vocal: Marion Nichols)........ *Bluebird B-5815* 5-8 35

NO NAME JIVE / NO NAME JIVE, PART 2.......... *Bluebird B-10737* 2-4 40

NOWHERE / YOU'RE MY THRILL (Vocal: Lena Horne)......... *Bluebird B-11141* 2-4 41

NOW YOU KNOW / NIGHT AFTER NIGHT WITH YOU .... *Bluebird B-10549* 2-4 40
(Vocals: Mary Ann McCall)

OGOUN BADAGRIS / THE RIGHT IDEA................ *Bluebird B-10530* 3-5 39

PONCE DE LEON / LITTLE DIP .... *Bluebird B-11194* 2-4 41

RAINBOW ON THE RIVER (Vocal: Charlie Barnet) / I'VE GOT SOMETHING IN MY EYE (Amanda Randolph & Her Orchestra; Vocal: Amanda Randolph)..... *Bluebird B-6619* 4-6 36

REMINISCING (Vocal: Mary Ann McCall) / PEACEFUL VALLEY............. *Bluebird B-10846* 2-4 40

SAILBOAT IN THE MOONLIGHT (Vocals: Kurt Bloom) / HE WALKED RIGHT IN (Vocals: Kurt Bloom & Kathleen Lane)...................... *Bluebird B-6967* 4-6 37

SCRUB ME, MAMA, WITH A BOOGIE BEAT (Vocal: Ford Leary) / I CAN'T REMEMBER TO FORGET (Vocal: Bob Carroll)......... *Bluebird B-10975* 3-5 41

SERGEANT WAS SHY, THE / RING DEM BELLS .... *Bluebird B-10862* 2-4 40

720 IN THE BOOKS / SO FAR, SO GOOD................ *Bluebird B-10618* 2-4 40
(Vocals: Mary Ann McCall)

SHAME ON YOU (Vocal: Charlie Barnet) / IF YOU'RE EVER IN MY ARMS AGAIN (Vocals: The Four Stars)................... *Variety 627* 4-6 37

SOUTHERN FRIED / REDSKIN RHUMBA............. *Bluebird B-10944* 2-4 40

STAR FELL OUT OF HEAVEN, A / WHEN DID YOU LEAVE HEAVEN? .... *Bluebird B-6488* 4-6 36
(Vocals: Joe Hostetter)

STRANGE ENCHANTMENT (Vocal: Judy Ellington) / ONLY A ROSE.................. *Bluebird B-10227* 2-4 39

SURREALISM / OVERHEARD IN A COCKTAIL LOUNGE .... *Variety 633* 4-6 37

SWING WALTZ, THE (Vocal: Joe Hostetter) / CROSS PATCH (Vocal: Charlie Barnet)........ *Melotone 6-07-13* 4-6 36

TAPPIN' AT THE TAPPA / COMANCHE WAR DANCE........ *Bluebird B-10584* 3-5 40

THAT REAL ROMANCE (Vocal: Larry Taylor) / SMILES............................... *Decca 18363* 2-4 42

THINGS AIN'T WHAT THEY USED TO BE / THE VICTORY WALK.................. *Decca 18507* 3-5 42

THIS IS NO DREAM / THAT'S RIGHT – I'M WRONG...................... *Bluebird B-10273* 2-4 39
(Vocals: Judy Ellington)

TIN ROOF BLUES / KNOCKIN' AT THE FAMOUS DOOR............. *Bluebird B-10131* 3-5 39

UNTIL THE REAL THING COMES ALONG (Vocal: Charlie Barnet) / ALWAYS..... *Bluebird B-6487* 4-6 36

WANDERIN' BLUES (Vocal: Mary Ann McCall) / SHAKE, RATTLE 'N' ROLL....... *Bluebird B-10721* 3-5 40

WASHINGTON WHIRLIGIG / — .... *V-Disc 137* 5-8 -
(This is an oversize 12-inch 78 rpm, a World War II release)

WHATCHA KNOW JOE? (Vocals: Ford Leary & trio) / ISOLA BELLA (Vocal: Bob Carroll) ... *Bluebird B-10918* 2-4 40

WHAT IS SWEETER (THAN THE SWEETNESS OF "I LOVE YOU") (Vocal: Harry Von Zell) / BUCKIN' THE WIND (Vocal: Helen Heath) .... *Banner 32876* 4-6 33

WHAT IS SWEETER (THAN THE SWEETNESS OF "I LOVE YOU") (Vocal: Harry Von Zell) / BUCKIN' THE WIND (Vocal: Helen Heath)..... *Melotone M-12818* 4-6 33

WHAT IS SWEETER (THAN THE SWEETNESS OF "I LOVE YOU") (Vocal: Harry Von Zell) / BUCKIN' THE WIND (Vocal: Helen Heath) .... *Oriole 2778* 4-6 33

WHAT IS SWEETER (THAN THE SWEETNESS OF "I LOVE YOU") (Vocal: Harry Von Zell) / BUCKIN' THE WIND (Vocal: Helen Heath)......... *Perfect 15834* 4-6 33

WHAT IS SWEETER (THAN THE SWEETNESS OF "I LOVE YOU") (Vocal: Harry Von Zell) / BUCKIN' THE WIND (Vocal: Helen Heath).......... *Romeo 2151* 4-6 33
(Simultaneously released on five labels)

WHEN THE SPIRIT MOVES ME (Vocal: Mary Ann McCall) / YOU AND WHO ELSE? (Vocal: Larry Taylor) .... *Bluebird B-10734* 2-4 40

WHERE WAS I? / 'DEED I DO ...... *Bluebird B-10669* 2-4 40
(Vocals: Mary Ann McCall)

WRONG IDEA, THE (Vocal: Billy May) / FRIENDSHIP (by Tommy Dorsey & His Orchestra as the Dorsey Family; Vocals by the Pied Pipers)................. *Bluebird B-10804* 3-5 40

YOU DO THE DARNDEST THINGS, BABY / IT'S LOVE I'M AFTER............ *Bluebird B-6594* 4-6 36
(Vocals: Charlie Barnet)

BARRIE, Dick, & His Orchestra
(brother of singer Gracie Barrie)

DON'T CROSS YOUR FINGERS, CROSS YOUR HEART / LOVE IS WHERE YOU FIND IT ...... *Vocalion 4271* 3-5 38

HI-YO SILVER! / MY MARGARITA..... *Vocalion 4193* 4-6 38

MY REVERIE / SIXTY SECONDS GOT TOGETHER.................... *Vocalion 4366* 4-6 38

SUMMER SOUVENIRS (Vocal: Dick Barrie) / ALL ASHORE (Vocal: Eddie Metcalfe).... *Vocalion 4397* 4-6 38

TU-LI-TULIP TIME / COULD YOU PASS IN LOVE? .... *Vocalion 4285* 3-5 38

YOU'RE THE ONLY STAR IN MY BLUE HEAVEN / TEN PINS IN THE SKY............. *Vocalion 4348* 4-6 38

BARRON, Blue, & His Orchestra
(Blue Barron: 3/22/11 –)

ANGELS WITH DIRTY FACES / IT'S A LONELY TRAIL............ *Bluebird B-7856* 2-4 38
(Vocals: Russ Carlyle)

BABY, WHAT CAN I DO? (Vocal: Alan Holmes) / HERE COMES THE NIGHT (Vocal: Russ Carlyle) .... *Bluebird B-10452* 2-4 39

CONFUCIOUS SAY (Vocal: The Bluenotes) / I WANT MY MAMA (Vocal: Charlie Fischer) .... *Bluebird B-10548* 2-4 40

DADDY'S BOY / MOONLIGHT IN WAIKIKI......... *Bluebird B-7542* 2-4 38
(Vocals: Russ Carlyle)

DARN THAT DREAM (Vocal: Russ Carlyle) / PEACE, BROTHER! (Vocal: Charlie Fischer)... *Bluebird B-10525* 2-4 40

GARDEN OF THE MOON / BAMBINA .... *Bluebird B-7709* 2-4 38
(Vocals: Russ Carlyle)

HOW CAN YOU FORGET? (Vocal: Ernie Straub) / THERE'S A BOY IN HARLEM (Vocal: Charlie Fischer) .... *Bluebird B-7456* 2-4 38

IF IT WASN'T FOR THE MOON (Vocal: Alan Holmes) / THE SINGING HILLS (Vocal: Russ Carlyle) .... *Bluebird B-10552* 2-4 40

MEAN TO ME (Vocal: Charlie Fischer) / IN COPA-CABANA (Vocal: Russ Carlyle) .... *Bluebird B-11019* 2-4 40

RIVER HOME (Vocal: Alan Holmes) / THE BELLS OF MONTEREY (Vocal: Russ Carlyle) .... *Bluebird B-10905* 2-4 40

SOMETIMES I'M HAPPY (theme song) (Vocal: Russ Carlyle) / GET THE MOON OUT OF YOUR EYES (Vocals: The 3 Blue Notes) ..... *Bluebird B-10826* 2-4 40

WALKIN' THRU' MOCKIN' BIRD LANE (Vocals: The 3 Blue Notes) / MY MOTHER'S LULLABY (Vocal: Charlie Fischer) .... *Bluebird B-11052* 2-4 40

BARTH, Harry, as Harry Barth's Mississipians

CAROLINA MOON / A WALTZ IN THE MOONLIGHT AND YOU .... *Perfect 14382* 2-4 25

MELANCHOLY LOU / SUGAR PLUM ... *Perfect 14511* 2-4 25

BARTH, Harry, as Harry Barth's Novelty Orchestra

CLOVER BLOSSOMS / DREAM OF HEAVEN .... *Pathe Actuelle 036101* 3-5 24

CLOVER BLOSSOMS / DREAM OF HEAVEN .... *Perfect 14281* 2-4 24
(Simultaneously released on two labels)

THERE'S A BEND AT THE END OF THE SWANEE / ADORING YOU .... *Pathe Actuelle 036147* 3-5 24

THERE'S A BEND AT THE END OF THE SWANEE / ADORING YOU ... *Perfect 14328* 2-4 24
(Simultaneously released on two labels)

BARTH, Harry, as the Melody Waltz Orchestra

AH, SWEET MYSTERY OF LIFE / WAS IT A DREAM? .... *Harmony 620-H* 2-4 28

DREAMING / DIRTY FACE .... *Harmony 478-H* 2-4 27

HOME, SWEET HOME / LA GOLONDRINA .... *Harmony 398-H* 2-4 27

MISSOURI WALTZ / I DREAM OF A COTTAGE AND YOU .... *Harmony 453-H* 2-4 27

BASIE, Count, & His All-American Rhythm Section

(Count Basie: 8/21/04 – 4/26/84)
(Played engagements until his death in 1984; has been awarded a star in the "Walk of Fame" in Hollywood.)

BLUES BY BASIE (a 4-record set) ... *Columbia Set C-101* 12-20 45
(Individual records in the set listed numerically with value:

BUGLE BLUES / SUGAR BLUES ... *Columbia 36709* 3-5 -

HOW LONG BLUES / ROYAL GARDEN BLUES .... *Columbia 36710* 3-5 -

CAFE SOCIETY BLUES / ST. LOUIS BLUES .... *Columbia 36711* 3-5 -

FAREWELL BLUES / WAY BACK BLUES .... *Columbia 36712* 3-5 -

BASIE, Count, & His Orchestra

BASIE BLUES/ I'M GONNA MOVE TO THE OUTSKIRTS OF TOWN (Vocal: Jimmy Rushing) ..... *Columbia 36601* 2-4 42

BETWEEN THE DEVIL AND THE DEEP BLUE SEA (Vocal: Helen Humes) / HAM 'N' EGGS .... *Columbia 35357* 3-5 39

BLOW TOP / GONE WITH "WHAT" WIND .... *Okeh 5629* 3-5 40

EVENIN' (Vocal: Jimmy Rushing) / MOTEN SWING .... *Okeh 5732* 3-5 40

FEATHER MERCHANT / AIN'T IT THE TRUTH .... *Columbia 36845* 2-4 41

FIESTA IN BLUE / TAKE ME BACK, BABY (Vocal: Jimmy Rushing) .... *Okeh 6440* 3-5 41

FIVE O'CLOCK WHISTLE / MY WANDERIN' MAN (Vocal: Helen Humes) .... *Okeh 5922* 3-5 40

HOLLYWOOD JUMP / SOMEDAY, SWEET-HEART (Vocal: Helen Humes) .... *Columbia 35338* 3-5 39

IT'S SQUARE BUT IT ROCKS (Vocal: Helen Humes) / MUSIC MAKERS .... *Conqueror 9631* 3-5 41

IT'S SQUARE BUT IT ROCKS (Vocal: Helen Humes) / MUSIC MAKERS .... *Okeh 6047* 3-5 41
(Simultaneously released on two labels)

LET ME SEE / BASIE BOOGIE .... *Okeh 6330* 3-5 41

9:20 SPECIAL / GOIN' TO CHICAGO BLUES (Vocal: Jimmy Rushing) .... *Okeh 6244* 3-5 41

SUPER CHIEF / YOU CAN'T RUN AROUND (Vocal: Jimmy Rushing) .... *Okeh 5623* 3-5 40

VOLCANO / ROCKIN' THE BLUES .... *Okeh 6010* 3-5 40

WHAT'S YOUR NUMBER? / DRAFTIN' BLUES (Vocal: Jimmy Rushing) .... *Okeh 5897* 3-5 40

WIGGLE WOOGIE / JUMP THE BLUES AWAY .... *Okeh 6157* 3-5 41

BASIE, Count, as Count Basie's Kansas City Seven

DICKIE'S DREAM/LESTER LEAPS IN... *Vocalion 5118* 4-6 39

BASIE, Count, as Jones-Smith Incorporated

BOOGIE-WOOGIE (Vocal: Jimmy Rushing) / LADY BE GOOD .... *Vocalion 3459* 10-12 36

SHOE-SHINE BOY / EVENIN' (Vocal: Jimmy Rushing) .... *Vocalion 3441* 10-12 36

BAXTER, Phil, & His Orchestra

(Phil Baxter: 9/5/96 – 11/21/72)
(Phil Baster composed "Piccolo Pete", "I'm A Ding Dong Daddy" & other hit songs of the 1930s)

DOWN WHERE THE BLUE BONNETS GROW / I AIN'T GOT NO GAL NOW .... *Victor V-40160* 12-15 29
(Vocals: Phil Baxter)

I DON'T KNOW NOBODY BUT YOU (Vocal: Phil Baxter) / HONEY CHILD (Vocal: Jack Jones) ..... *Victor V-40204* 10-12 29

BEAGLE, Ray, & His Hounds of Music:
see RADERMAN, Lou, & His Orchestra

BEALE STREET FIVE, THE:
see HARING, Bob & His Velvet Tone Orchestra

BECHET, Sidney, & His New Orleans Feetwarmers
also see HAITIAN ORCHESTRA, The

(Sidney Bechet: 5/14/97 – 5/14/59)

INDIAN SUMMER / PREACHIN' BLUES (Vocal: Wilson Myers) .... *Bluebird B-10623* 5-8 40

I'VE FOUND A NEW BABY / SHAG (Vocal: Wilson Myers) ...... *Victor 24150* 50-60 32

I WANT YOU TONIGHT (Vocal: Wilson Myers) / LAY YOUR RACKET (Vocal: Billy Maxey) ...... *Victor 23358* 50-60 32

SWEETIE DEAR / MAPLE LEAF RAG... *Victor 23360* 45-50 32

SWING PARADE / I KNOW THAT YOU KNOW .... *Victor 27574* 5-8 41

WHEN IT'S SLEEPY TIME DOWN SOUTH / I AIN'T GONNA GIVE NOBODY NONE O' THIS JELLY-ROLL .... *Victor 27447* 5-8 41

BECHET, Sidney, & His Orchestra

HOLD TIGHT (Vocals: the Two Fishmongers) / JUNGLE DRUMS .... *Vocalion 4537* 5-8 39

WHAT A DREAM / CHANT IN THE NIGHT .... *Vocalion 4575* 5-8 39

BEIDERBECKE, Bix:
see Wolverine Orchestra, The

BELASCO, Leon, & His Hotel St. Moritz Orchestra

DON'T BLAME ME / TROUBLE IN PARADISE .... *Vocalion 25006* 2-4 33
(Vocals: Unknown)

DON'T CHANGE / SHAME ON YOU .... *Vocalion 2552* 3-5 33
(Vocals: Unknown)

SHANGHAI LIL / SITTIN' ON A BACKYARD FENCE .... *Vocalion 2548* 3-5 33
(Vocal: Chick Bullock)

BELASCO, Leon, & His Orchestra

THERE'S A LULL IN MY LIFE (Vocal: Patty Andrews) / WAKE UP AND LIVE (Vocals: The Andrews Sisters) .... *Brunswick 7872* 4-6 37

TURN OFF THE MOON / JAMMIN' (Vocals: Andrews Sisters)..... *Brunswick 7863* 4-6 37

BENEKE, Tex, & His Orchestra

(Tex Beneke: 2/12/14 –)

(also see *"THE BIG BAND SCENE TODAY"* [front of book], an informative article written by Tex Beneke for this book)

Beneke took over leadership of the first postwar Glenn Miller Orchestra in 1946, and has led his own very successful band for more than 30 years. Tex Beneke and His Orchestra continue to play engagements throughout the country, booked for a year or more in advance. In 1978, the author and husband spent a most enjoyable evening as guests of Tex at Knott's Berry Farm in Buena Park, Calif., where the orchestra was appearing. The guests had the honor of sitting with Mrs. Beneke and Tex's manager Dick Hecker and Mrs. Hecker, in the wings just offstage while Beneke and the orchestra gave an outstanding performance of sweet, swing, romantic and contemporary music, including replaying of many Miller favorites.

BLUES IN THE NIGHT MARCH / THE ONE WHO GETS YOU (Vocals: Tex Beneke & The Moonlight Serenaders) .... *RCA Victor 20-3513* 2-4 49

LONE STAR MOON / (GOTTA GET TO) OKLAHOMA CITY .... *RCA Victor 20-2566* 2-4 47
(Vocals: Tex Beneke)

LOVELY RAINY AFTERNOON, A (Vocal: Garry Stevens) / RAMBLIN' AROUND (Vocal: Tex Beneke) ...... *RCA Victor 20-2837* 2-4 48

MAKIN' LOVE MOUNTAIN STYLE (Vocal: Tex Beneke) / MEADOWLANDS .... *RCA Victor 20-2898* 2-4 48

MISSISSIPPI FLYER / LOOK UP .... *RCA Victor 20-3340* 2-4 49
(Vocals: Tex Beneke & The Moonlight Serenaders)

MY LOVE AN' MY MULE (Vocal: Tex Beneke) / PALLADIUM PATROL .... *MGM 10936* 2-4 51

OLD FASHIONED SONG (Vocal: Glenn Douglas) / TULSA (Vocal: Tex Beneke) .... *RCA Victor 20-3417* 2-4 49

ST. LOUIS BLUES MARCH / CHEROKEE CANYON (Vocal: Tex Beneke) ...... *RCA Victor 20-2722* 2-4 48

BENNETT, Ralph, & His Seven Aces:
see KARDOS, Gene, & His Orchestra

BENNETT, Ralph, as The Seven Aces

DON'T TAKE THAT BLACK BOTTOM AWAY / THAT'S MY GIRL (Vocal: Ralph Bennett) .... *Columbia 816-D* 3-5 26

I CAN'T BELIEVE THAT YOU'RE IN LOVE WITH ME (Vocal: Ralph Bennett) / THERE'S EVERYTHING NICE ABOUT YOU (Vocals: The Peabody Trio) .... *Columbia 1001-D* 2-4 27

THAT'S MY HAP-HAP-HAPPINESS / WHEN JENNY DOES THAT LOW DOWN DANCE... *Columbia 1046-D* 3-5 27

WHO'LL BE THE ONE? / HAVE YOU FORGOTTEN? .... *Columbia 863-D* 2-4 26

BENNETT, Ralph, as Warner's Seven Aces
also see WARNER, Byron H. as Warner's Seven Aces

GO GET 'EM, CAROLINE / TWEEDLE-DEE, TWEEDLE-DOO .... *Columbia 491-D* 3-5 25

HANGIN' AROUND / WHO'D BE BLUE? .... *Columbia 752-D* 3-5 26

YOU'VE GOT THOSE "WANNA GO BACK AGAIN" BLUES (Vocals: Ralph Bennett & Bob Pittman) / SO IS YOUR OLD LADY (Vocal: M. C. "Shucks" Park) .... *Columbia 656-D* 3-5 26

BENRUS RADIO ORCHESTRA, The:
see LANIN, Sam, as Sam Lanin's Dance Ensemble

BEN'S BAD BOYS:
see POLLACK, Ben, & His Park Central Orchestra

BENSON ORCHESTRA OF CHICAGO, The

(Directed by Roy Bargy: -/-/- – 1/15/74)

COPENHAGEN / KEEP ON DANCING... *Victor 19568* 2-4 24

DOODLE-UM BLUES, THE / PICKIN' 'EM UP AND LAYIN' 'EM DOWN .... *Victor 19386* 2-4 24

FORGETFUL BLUES / THAT LULLABY STRAIN .... *Victor 19235* 2-4 23

RIVERBOAT SHUFFLE / SWEET GEORGIA BROWN (by Oliver Naylor's Orchestra) .... *Victor 19688* 5-8 25

SAN / NA-JO .... *Victor 18779* 2-4 21

TEE PEE BLUES / BLACK-EYED BLUES .... *Victor 18874* 2-4 22

THOSE LONGING FOR YOU BLUES / STUTTERING .... *Victor 18948* 2-4 22

WABASH BLUES / TUCK ME TO SLEEP IN MY OLD 'TUCKY HOME .... *Victor 18820* 2-4 21

BERGE, William:
see HACKEL-BERGE ORCHESTRA, The

BERIGAN, Bunny, & His Blue Boys
(Bunny Berigan: 11/2/08 – 6/2/42)

BLUES / I'M COMING VIRGINIA .... *Decca 18116* 4-6 41
(A 1935 release recording first released in 1941)

YOU TOOK ADVANTAGE OF ME / CHICKEN AND WAFFLES .... *Decca 18117* 4-6 41
(A 1935 release recording first released in 1941)

BERIGAN, Bunny, & His Boys

I CAN'T GET STARTED (theme song) (Vocal: Bunny Berigan) / RHYTHM SAVED THE WORLD (Vocal: Chick Bullock) .... *Vocalion 3225* 5-8 36

I'D RATHER LEAD A BAND / LET YOURSELF GO .... *Vocalion 3178* 10-12 36
(Vocals: Chick Bullock)

IN A LITTLE SPANISH TOWN / I CAN'T GET STARTED (theme song) (Vocal: Bunny Berigan) .... *Special Editions 5004-S* 5-8 -

I NEARLY LET LOVE GO SLIPPING THRU' MY FINGERS / IF I HAD MY WAY .... *Vocalion 3254* 8-10 36
(Vocals: Chick Bullock)

IT'S BEEN SO LONG / SWING, MISTER CHARLIE .... *Vocalion 3179* 10-12 36
(Vocals: Chick Bullock)

MELODY FROM THE SKY / LITTLE BIT LATER ON .... *Vocalion 3224* 10-12 36
(Vocals: Chick Bullock)

BERIGAN, Bunny, & His Men

CANDLELIGHTS / IN THE DARK .... *Victor 26122* 4-6 39

FLASHES / DAVENPORT BLUES .... *Victor 26121* 4-6 39

IN A MIST / WALKIN' THE DOG .... *Victor 26123* 4-6 39

BERIGAN, Bunny, & His Orchestra

ALL GOD'S CHILLUN GOT RHYTHM / THE LADY FROM FIFTH AVENUE .... *Victor 25609* 4-6 37
(Vocals: Ruth Gaylor)

BLACK BOTTOM / TREES .... *Victor 26138* 2-4 39

BUNNY BERIGAN MEMORIAL ALBUM
(Swing Classics) (A 4-record album set; each individual record listed numerically with value of each.) .... *Victor P-134* 12-15 43
I CAN'T GET STARTED (theme song) FRANKIE AND JOHNNY.......... *Victor 20-1500* 2-4 -
TREES / RUSSIAN LULLABY .... *Victor 20-1501* 2-4 -
JELLY ROLL BLUES / BLACK BOTTOM......... *Victor 20-1502* 2-4 -
'DEED I DO / HIGH SOCIETY........ *Victor 20-1503* 2-4 -

BUTTON, BUTTON / ROCKIN' ROLLERS' JUBILEE................... *Victor 26077* 4-6 38
(Vocals: Jayne Dover)

CARAVAN / A STUDY IN BROWN....... *Victor 25653* 4-6 37

DIXIELAND SHUFFLE / LET'S DO IT .... *Brunswick 7858* 8-10 38

DOWN STREAM / SOPHISTICATED SWING .... *Victor 25811* 4-6 38
(Vocals: Gail Reese)

GEE, BUT IT'S GREAT TO MEET A FRIEND / EBB TIDE .... *Victor 25666* 4-6 37
(Vocals: Gail Reese)

GOONA GOO, THE (Vocal: Art Gentry) / BLUE LOU....................... *Brunswick 7832* 5-8 37

HAVE YOU EVER BEEN IN HEAVEN? (Vocal: Gail Reese) / MAMA, I WANNA MAKE RHYTHM (Vocal: Bunny Berigan) .... *Victor 25677* 4-6 37

I CAN'T GET STARTED (theme song) (Vocal: Bunny Berigan) / AT THE WOODCHOPPER'S BALL (by Woody Herman & His Orchestra) .... *V-Disc 29* 5-8 -
(A World War II Release)

I CAN'T GET STARTED (theme song) (Vocal: Bunny Berigan) / THE PRISONER'S SONG ..... *Victor 36208* 5-8 37
(This is an oversize 12 inch 78 rpm.)

I GOT IT BAD AND THAT AIN'T GOOD (Vocal: Lynne Richards) / SOMEBODY ELSE IS TAKING MY PLACE (Vocal: Nita Sharon) .... *Philharmonic 64* 4-6 42

I GOT IT BAD AND THAT AIN'T GOOD / THE WHITE CLIFFS OF DOVER .... *Elite 5006* 3-5 41
(Vocals: Lynne Richards)

IMAGE OF YOU, THE / I'M HAPPY, DARLING, DANCING WITH YOU................ *Victor 25587* 3-5 37
(Vocals: Sid Pearlmutter)

I'M GONNA KISS MYSELF GOODBYE / BIG BOY BLUE........ *Brunswick 7847* 5-8 37
(Vocals: Johnny Hauser)

IN A LITTLE SPANISH TOWN / CAN'T HELP LOVIN' DAT MAN................... *Victor 26152* 4-6 39

I'VE GOT A GUY / MOONSHINE OVER KENTUCKY................... *Victor 25833* 3-5 38
(Vocals: Ruth Gaylor)

JAZZ ME BLUES / THERE'LL BE SOME CHANGES MADE .... *Victor 26244* 4-6 39

JELLY ROLL BLUES / 'DEED I DO (Vocal: Kathleen Lane) .... *Victor 26113* 4-6 39

LET 'ER GO / TURN ON THAT RED-HOT HEAT .... *Victor 25646* 4-6 37
(Vocals: Ruth Gaylor)

LET'S HAVE ANOTHER CIGARETTE / ROSES IN DECEMBER .... *Victor 25613* 3-5 37
(Vocals: Ruth Gaylor)

LITTLE GATE'S SPECIAL / GANGBUSTER'S HOLIDAY............................ *Victor 26338* 4-6 39

LIVERY STABLE BLUES / HIGH SOCIETY............................ *Victor 26068* 4-6 38

LOVELIGHT IN THE STARLIGHT / AN OLD STRAW HAT......................... *Victor 25816* 3-5 38
(Vocals: Gail Reese)

MAHOGANY HALL STOMP / CHOPIN'S GHOST (by Bert Shefter & His Rhythm Octet)............. *Victor 25622* 5-8 37

MILES APART / A STRANGE LONELINESS.......................... *Victor 25690* 3-5 37
(Vocals: Gail Reese)

MOTHER GOOSE (Vocal: Ruth Gaylor) / FRANKIE AND JOHNNY .... *Victor 25616* 3-5 37

PATTY CAKE, PATTY CAKE / Y' HAD IT COMIN' TO YOU..................... *Victor 26196* 3-5 39
(Vocals: Kathleen Lane)

PEG O' MY HEART / NIGHT SONG...... *Victor 27258* 2-4 40

PIANO TUNER MAN / HEIGH-HO (THE DWARF'S MARCHING SONG) .... *Victor 25776* 5-8 38
(Vocals: Gail Reese)

PIED PIPER, THE / (HOW TO MAKE LOVE IN) TEN EASY LESSONS.................. *Victor 25881* 4-6 38
(Vocals: Ruth Gaylor)

SERENADE TO THE STARS, A / OUTSIDE OF PARADISE .... *Victor 25781* 3-5 38
(Vocals: Gail Reese)

SKYLARK (Vocal: Danny Richards) / MY LITTLE COUSIN (Vocal: Lynne Richards)........... *Elite 5020* 3-5 42

SKYLARK / ME AND MY MELINDA .... *Philharmonic 61* 4-6 42
(Vocals: Danny Richards)

SOBBIN' BLUES / I CRIED FOR YOU (Vocal: Kathleen Lane)......... *Victor 26116* 4-6 39

SOMEBODY ELSE IS TAKING MY PLACE (Vocal: Nita Sharon) / ME AND MY MELINDA (Vocal: Danny Richards).................. *Elite 5019* 3-5 42

THAT FOOLISH FEELING / WHERE ARE YOU? .... *Brunswick 7784* 5-8 37
(Vocals: Art Gentry)

'TIS AUTUMN / MY LITTLE COUSIN.................. *Philharmonic 63* 4-6 42
(Vocals: Lynne Richards)

WHITE CLIFFS OF DOVER, THE / TWO IN LOVE................... *Philharmonic 62* 4-6 41
(Vocals: Lynne Richards)

YOU CAN'T RUN AWAY FROM LOVE (Vocal: Gail Reese) / 'CAUSE MY BABY SAYS IT'S SO (Vocal: Bunny Berigan) .... *Victor 25562* 4-6 37

BERNIE, Ben, & All The Lads
(Ben Bernie: 5/30/91 – 10/20/43)

DUKE IS ON A BAT AGAIN, THE / AIN'T THAT MARVELOUS?....... *Columbia 2809-D* 5-8 33
(Vocals: Unknown)

MARCHING ALONG TOGETHER / WE WON'T HAVE TO SELL THE FARM....... *Columbia 2804-D* 5-8 33
(Vocals: Unknown)

MICKEY MOUSE AND MINNIE'S IN TOWN / SO THIS IS SUSIE?............... *Columbia 2836-D* 5-8 33
(Vocals: Unknown)

SHANGHAI LIL / WHO'S AFRAID OF THE BIG BAD WOLF?......... *Columbia 2824-D* 5-8 33
(Vocals: Unknown)

THIS IS ROMANCE / YOU GOTTA BE A FOOTBALL HERO......... *Columbia 2820-D* 5-8 33
(Vocals: Unknown)

BERNIE, Ben, & His Hotel Roosevelt Orchestra

ALL ABOARD FOR HEAVEN / CHEATIN' ON ME................ *Vocalion 15027* 3-5 25

AU REVOIR, PLEASANT DREAMS (Closing Theme) (Vocal: Ben Bernie) / IT'S A LONESOME OLD TOWN (Opening Theme) (Vocals: Unknown) ..... *Brunswick 4943* 4-6 31

BELL-HOPPIN' BLUES / THE ROSES BROUGHT ME YOU (Vocal: Arthur Fields) .... *Brunswick 3082* 4-6 26

BOTTOMS UP / BIGGER AND BETTER THAN EVER...................... *Brunswick 4516* 3-5 29
(Vocals: Unknown)

BUTTON YOUR OVERCOAT (Vocal: Dick Robertson) / I WANT TO BE BAD (Vocal: Zelma O'Neal)................. *Brunswick 4204* 4-6 29
(Zelma O'Neal was a star of stage & screen musical comedies in the 1920s & early 1930s)

COLLEGIATE (Vocals: Irving & Jack Kaufman, Lester O'Keefe) / YES SIR, THAT'S MY BABY................... *Vocalion 15080* 3-5 25

CRYING FOR YOU / SWINGING DOWN THE LANE .... *Vocalion 14537* 2-4 22

DID ANYONE CALL? (Vocal: Don Saxon) / HI' YA BUD (Vocals: Ben Bernie, The Bailey Sisters, & Don Saxon)............ *Okeh 5914* 2-4 40

DOODLE-DOO-DOO / JUNE NIGHT.... *Vocalion 14878* 4-6 24

DOWN BY THE O-HI-O / IT'S THE LAST TIME I'LL FALL IN LOVE .... *Okeh 5646* 2-4 40
(Vocals: The Bailey Sisters)

FLOWER OF ARABY / MY BUDDY.... *Vocalion 14494* 2-4 23

FOLLOWING YOU AROUND / I'M IN LOVE AGAIN .... *Brunswick 3496* 3-5 27
(Vocals: Scrappy Lambert & Billy Hillpot)

'FRAIDY CAT (Vocals: by chorus) / LI'L ABNER (Vocals: Ben Bernie & The Bailey Sisters)...... *Decca 3986* 4-6 41

GENTLEMAN NEEDS A SHAVE, THE (Vocals: Ben Bernie & The Bailey Sisters) / IT'S A WONDERFUL WORLD (Vocal: Don Saxon)............. *Vocalion 5615* 2-4 40

HEADIN' FOR LOUISVILLE / THE LONESOMEST GAL IN TOWN .... *Brunswick 2991* 3-5 26
(Vocals: Unknown)

HINDUSTAN/ CANNON BALL RAG... *Brunswick 4042* 5-8 28

I'M BRINGING A RED, RED ROSE / MAKIN' WHOOPEE........ *Brunswick 4142* 3-5 29
(Vocals: Scrappy Lambert)

IT'S A LONESOME OLD TOWN (opening theme) (Vocal: Don Saxon) / AU REVOIR, PLEASANT DREAMS (closing theme) (Vocal: Ben Bernie) .... *Decca 4158* 2-4 41

LET'S MISBEHAVE / CHANGES..... *Brunswick 3761* 3-5 28
(Vocals: Scrappy Lambert & Billy Hillpot)

LIFE IS JUST A BOWL OF CHERRIES (Vocals: Ben Bernie & Manny Prager) / THIS IS THE MISSUS (Vocal: Ben Bernie)................ *Brunswick 6165* 4-6 31

LITTLE BIT BAD, A / SLEEPY-TIME GAL................ *Brunswick 2992* 3-5 26
(Vocals: Arthur Fields)

LITTLE CURLY HAIR IN A HIGH CHAIR / TINY TOWN.............. *Conqueror 9461* 2-4 40
(Vocals: Ben Bernie & The Bailey Sisters)

LITTLE CURLY HAIR IN A HIGH CHAIR / TINY TOWN................ *Vocalion 5482* 2-4 40
(Vocals: Ben Bernie & The Bailey Sisters)
(Simultaneously released on two labels)

LONELY EYES / WHO'LL BE THE ONE? .... *Brunswick 3401* 3-5 27
(Vocals: Scrappy Lambert & Billy Hillpot)

LONG AGO AND FAR AWAY (Vocal: Ray Hendricks) / SAN FRANCISCO (Vocal: Billy Wilson)..... *Decca 874* 4-6 36

MY BUNDLE OF LOVE (Vocal: Ben Bernie) / JIG WALK........................ *Brunswick 3126* 3-5 26

MY SWEETIE WENT AWAY (Vocal: Ernest Hare) / LOVE TALES .... *Vocalion 14622* 2-4 23

NO, MAMA, NO / I'M TAKIN' MY TIME WITH YOU................ *Vocalion 5087* 2-4 39
(Vocals: The Bailey Sisters)

ONE LITTLE RAINDROP / 99 OUT OF A HUNDRED WANNA BE LOVED... *Brunswick 6062* 3-5 31
(Vocals: Frank Sylvano)

PRETTY LITTLE BABY (Vocal: Arthur Fields) / FALLEN ARCHES................. *Brunswick 3042* 3-5 26

SIDE STREET TROUBADOUR (Vocals: The Bailey Sisters) / LITTLE SHEPHERD OF MY DREAMS (Vocal: Don Saxon)...................... *Vocalion 5331* 2-4 40

SONG OF THE BAYOU (Vocals: Unknown) / BLACK EYES..................... *Brunswick 4725* 4-6 30

SONG OF THE METRONOME, THE (Vocals: Ben Bernie & The Bailey Sisters) / I'M SORRY FOR MYSELF (Vocals: Helen Daniels & Ben Bernie) .... *Vocalion 4916* 2-4 39

STAR FELL OUT OF HEAVEN, A / WHEN DID YOU LEAVE HEAVEN? .... *Decca 878* 4-6 36
(Vocals: Ray Hendricks)

TAKE YOUR UMBRELLA WHEN IT RAINS / PIERRE OF THE SASKATCHEWAN........ *Okeh 5889* 2-4 40
(Vocals: The Bailey Sisters)

TELL HER IN THE SPRINGTIME / OH! LADY BE GOOD........ *Vocalion 14955* 3-5 25

TOMORROW NIGHT / GOODNIGHT, MY BEAUTIFUL........ *Conqueror 9315* 2-4 39
(Vocals: Don Saxon)

TOMORROW NIGHT / GOODNIGHT, MY BEAUTIFUL........ *Vocalion 5072* 2-4 39
(Vocals: Don Saxon)
(Simultaneously released on two labels)

UP AND AT 'EM / SOMEBODY'S LONELY (Vocal: Paul Hagan)........ *Brunswick 3145* 3-5 26

WHAT! NO MICKEY MOUSE? / ALL-AMERICAN GIRL........ *Brunswick 6389* 10-12 32
(Vocals: Ben Bernie)

WHAT! NO MICKEY MOUSE? / ALL-AMERICAN GIRL........ *Vocalion 5151* 10-12 32
(Vocals: Ben Bernie)
(Simultaneously released on two labels)

WHERE WAS I? (Vocal: Don Saxon) / MY WONDERFUL ONE, LET'S DANCE........ *Vocalion 5492* 2-4 40

WILDFLOWER / WHO'S SORRY NOW?........ *Vocalion 14555* 3-5 23

YEARNING / SWEET GEORGIA BROWN........ *Vocalion 15002* 4-6 25

YOU BROUGHT A NEW KIND OF LOVE TO ME / LIVIN' IN THE SUNLIGHT, LOVIN' IN THE MOONLIGHT........ *Brunswick 4767* 4-6 30
(Vocals: Ben Bernie)

YOU KNOW I LOVE YOU / ONE O'CLOCK BABY........ *Brunswick 3531* 3-5 27
(Vocals: Scrappy Lambert & Billy Hillpot)

BERRY, Chu, & His Jazz Ensemble
(Chu Berry: 9/13/10 – 10/31/41)

BLOWING UP A BREEZE / MONDAY AT MINTON'S........ *Commodore 541* 4-6 41

ON THE SUNNY SIDE OF THE STREET / GEE, AIN'T I GOOD TO YOU? (Vocal: Hot Lips Page)........ *Commodore 1508* 5-8 41
(This is an oversize 12-inch 78 rpm)

BERRY, Chu, & His Little Jazz Ensemble

SITTIN' IN (with dialog between Roy Eldridge & Chu Berry) / FORTY-SIX WEST FIFTY-TWO........ *Commodore 516* 5-8 39

STARDUST / BODY AND SOUL........ *Commodore 1502* 5-8 39
(This is an oversize 12-inch 78 rpm)

BERRY, Chu, & His Stompy Stevedores

INDIANA / LIMEHOUSE BLUES........ *Variety 587* 8-10 37

NOW YOU'RE TALKING MY LANGUAGE / TOO MARVELOUS FOR WORDS........ *Variety 532* 8-10 37
(Vocal: Hot Lips Page)

BERTON, Vic, & His Orchestra
(Vic Berton: 5/7/96 – 12/26/51)

DEVIL'S KITCHEN / I'VE BEEN WAITING ALL WINTER (Vocal: Chick Bullock)........ *Columbia 3074-D* 5-8 35

IMITATIONS OF YOU / TWO RIVERS FLOW THROUGH HARLEM........ *Columbia 3092-D* 5-8 35
(Vocals: Chick Bullock)

JEALOUS (Vocal: Chick Bullock) / DARDANELLA........ *Vocalion 2915* 5-8 35

MARY LOU (Vocal: Chick Bullock) / LONESOME & SORRY........ *Vocalion 2944* 5-8 35

TABOO (Vocal: Chick Bullock) / BLUE........ *Vocalion 2974* 5-8 35

BESTOR, Don, & His Orchestra
(Don Bestor: 9/23/89 – 1/13/70)

ANIMAL CRACKERS IN MY SOUP / THE SIMPLE THINGS IN LIFE........ *Brunswick 7495* 3-5 35
(Vocals: Unknown)

DANCING ON A ROOFTOP (Vocal: Charles Yontz) / MOONGLOW (Vocal: Joy Lynne)........ *Victor 24658* 3-5 34

DEEP IN THE BLUES (Vocal: Florence Case) / TONIGHT MAY NEVER COME AGAIN (Vocal: Neil Buckley)........ *Victor 24422* 3-5 33

HOLD YOUR MAN / UNDER A BLANKET OF BLUE........ *Victor 24345* 3-5 33
(Vocals: Florence Case)

INKA DINKA DOO (Vocal: The Chanters) / MASQUERADING IN THE NAME OF LOVE (Vocal: Neil Buckley)........ *Victor 24503* 2-4 34

LIKE A BOLT FROM THE BLUE / I'M A HUNDRED PER CENT FOR YOU........ *Brunswick 7345* 3-5 35
(Vocals: Joy Lynne)

ON A SUNDAY AFTERNOON / YOU ARE MY LUCKY STAR........ *Brunswick 7516* 3-5 35
(Vocals: Unknown)

SHUFFLE OFF TO BUFFALO (Vocal: Maurice Cross) / FORTY-SECOND STREET (Vocal: Dudley Mecom)........ *Victor 24253* 3-5 33

SUMMER NIGHTS / CHARLESTON BABY OF MINE........ *Victor 19751* 2-4 25

SWEETHEART HOUR (Vocal: Neil Buckley) / CONTENTED........ *Victor 24135* 2-4 32

WHO'S AFRAID OF THE BIG BAD WOLF? / MICKEY MOUSE AND MINNIE'S IN TOWN........ *Victor 24410* 10-12 33
(Vocals: Florence Case, Charles Yontz, Frank Sherry, & The DeMarco Girls)

YOU'RE A SWEETHEART / A STRANGE LONELINESS........ *Bluebird B-7240* 3-5 37
(Vocals: Neil Buckley)

B. F. GOODRICH SILVERTOWN CORD Orchestra, The
(Directed by Joseph M. Knecht)

BROWN EYES, WHY ARE YOU BLUE? / A KISS IN THE MOONLIGHT........ *Victor 19793* 2-4 25
(Vocals: Joseph White, the "Silvermasked Tenor")

BURGUNDY (Vocal: Joseph White, the "Silvermasked Tenor") / CHERIE, I LOVE YOU (by Fred Waring's Pennsylvanians; Vocal: Tom Waring)........ *Victor 20074* 2-4 26

IF ALL THE STARS WERE PRETTY BABIES (Vocal: Joseph White, the "Silvermasked Tenor") / A LANE IN SPAIN (by Jean Goldkette & His Orchestra; Vocals: Lewis James, Charles Harrison, Elliott Shaw & Wilfred Glenn)........ *Victor 20491* 5-8 27

I WONDER WHERE WE'VE MET BEFORE? / CAROLINA SWEETHEART........ *Victor 19798* 2-4 25
(Vocals: Joseph White, the "Silvermasked Tenor")

NIGHT OF LOVE, A / REACHING FOR THE MOON........ *Victor 20016* 2-4 26
(Vocals: Joseph White, the "Silvermasked Tenor")

PETRUSHKA / MARY LOU........ *Victor 20204* 2-4 26
(Vocals: Joseph White, the "Silvermasked Tenor")

TRAIL OF DREAMS / FALLING IN LOVE WITH YOU........ *Victor 20238* 2-4 26
(Vocals: Joseph White, the "Silvermasked Tenor")

BIAGINI, Henry (Hank), & His Orchestra

I'M LOST FOR WORDS / LITTLE COLONEL........ *Banner 33396* 5-8 35
(Vocals: Bob Godet)

I'M LOST FOR WORDS / LITTLE COLONEL........ *Melotone M-13363* 5-8 35
(Vocals: Bob Godet)

I'M LOST FOR WORDS / LITTLE COLONEL........ *Oriole 3122* 5-8 35
(Vocals: Bob Godet)

I'M LOST FOR WORDS / LITTLE COLONEL........ *Perfect 16100* 5-8 35
(Vocals: Bob Godet)

I'M LOST FOR WORDS / LITTLE COLONEL........ *Romeo 2496* 5-8 35
(Vocals: Bob Godet)
(Simultaneously released on five labels)

LITTLE THINGS YOU USED TO DO, THE (Vocal: Bob Godet) / GO INTO YOUR DANCE (Vocal: Glenn Hughes)........ *Banner 33395* 5-8 35

LITTLE THINGS YOU USED TO DO, THE (Vocal: Bob Godet) / GO INTO YOUR DANCE (Vocal: Glenn Hughes)........ *Melotone M-13362* 5-8 35

LITTLE THINGS YOU USED TO DO, THE (Vocal: Bob Godet) / GO INTO YOUR DANCE (Vocal: Glenn Hughes)........ *Oriole 3121* 5-8 35

LITTLE THINGS YOU USED TO DO, THE (Vocal: Bob Godet) / GO INTO YOUR DANCE (Vocal: Glenn Hughes)........ *Perfect 16099* 5-8 35

LITTLE THINGS YOU USED TO DO, THE (Vocal: Bob Godet) / GO INTO YOUR DANCE (Vocal: Glenn Hughes)........ *Romeo 2495* 5-8 35
(Simultaneously released on five labels)

BIG CITY SIX ORCHESTRA, The:
see CALIFORNIA RAMBLERS, The

BINNEY, Jack, & His Orchestra:
see PETTIS, Jack, & His Orchestra

BLACK, Ben, & His Orchestra

BLINKY MOON BAY (Vocals: Nina Hinds & Pearl Leonard) / HERE COMES EMALINE........ *Victor 20050* 3-5 26

LAY MY HEAD BENEATH A ROSE (Vocal: Drury Lennington) / THE PRISONER'S SONG (Vocals: Unknown)........ *Victor 20049* 3-5 26

SAILIN' ON (Vocal: Dudley B. Chambers) / MOONLIT WATERS (Vocal: Lewis James)........ *Victor 20690* 3-5 27

BLACK, Ted, & His Orchestra

BORN TO BE TRUE / MAKIN' TIME WITH YOU........ *Champion 16174* 3-5 30
(Vocals: Ted Black)

GIVE ME YOUR AFFECTION, HONEY / I LOVE YOU IN THE SAME SWEET WAY........ *Victor 22762* 3-5 31
(Vocals: Tom Brown)

I KNEW YOU WHEN / WITHOUT THAT CERTAIN THING........ *Bluebird B-5370* 4-6 34
(Vocals: Edith Caldwell)

I KNEW YOU WHEN / WITHOUT THAT CERTAIN THING........ *Sunrise S-3451* 12-15 34
(Vocals: Edith Caldwell)
(Simultaneously released on two labels)

LOVE LETTERS IN THE SAND / IT'S A LONG TIME BETWEEN KISSES........ *Victor 22799* 3-5 31
(Vocals: Tom Brown)

MASQUERADE / BANKING ON THE WEATHER........ *Victor 24046* 2-4 32
(Vocals: Dick Robertson)

ONE MORE KISS (Vocal: Frank Munn) / PAGAN MOON (Vocal: Chick Bullock)........ *Victor 22878* 2-4 32

RAIN, RAIN, GO AWAY (Vocal: Dick Robertson) / IN A SHANTY IN OLD SHANTY TOWN (Vocal: Chick Bullock)........ *Victor 24050* 2-4 32

TRUE / DO YOU MISS ME TONIGHT?........ *Bluebird B-5375* 4-6 34
(Vocals: Edith Caldwell)

TRUE / DO YOU MISS ME TONIGHT?........ *Sunrise S-3456* 12-15 34
(Vocals: Edith Caldwell)
(Simultaneously released on two labels)

BLAINE, Jerry, & His Streamline Rhythm

ALWAYS AND ALWAYS / SAIL ALONG, SILVERY MOON........ *Bluebird B-7357* 3-5 38
(Vocals: Phyllis Kenny)

BEI MIR BIST DU SCHOEN (Vocal: Phyllis Kenny) / THE BIG DIPPER........ *Bluebird B-7344* 4-6 38

DIPSY DOODLE, THE (Vocal: Phyllis Kenny) / THE SNAKE CHARMER........ *Bluebird B-7228* 4-6 37

DOWN WITH LOVE (Vocal: Johnny McKeever) / MOANIN' IN THE MORNING (Vocal: Phyllis Kenny)........ *Bluebird B-7244* 4-6 37

I DOUBLE DARE YOU (Vocals: Phyllis Kenny & Jerry Blaine) / YOU'RE OUT OF THIS WORLD (Vocal: Jerry Blaine)........ *Bluebird B-7354* 3-5 38

ROMANCE IN THE DARK / LET'S SAIL TO DREAMLAND........ *Bluebird B-7455* 3-5 38
(Vocals: Phyllis Kenny)

TI-PI-TIN / PROVE IT........ *Bluebird B-7443* 3-5 38
(Vocals: Phyllis Kenny)

BLAINE, Rex, & His Orchestra:
see KARDOS, Gene, & His Orchestra

BLAKE, Eubie, & His Orchestra
(Eubie Blake: 2/7/1883 – 2/12/1983)

BLUES IN MY HEART / SWEET GEORGIA BROWN .... *Crown 3197* 10-12 31
(Vocals: Dick Robertson)

CUTIE / BROKEN TOY (by Erdody & His Famous Orchestra) .... *Regal 9198* 4-6 22

NOBODY'S SWEETHEART / ST. LOUIS BLUES .... *Crown 3130* 12-15 31
(Vocals: Dick Robertson)

PLEASE DON'T TALK ABOUT ME WHEM I'M GONE / I'M NO ACCOUNT ANY MORE .... *Crown 3090* 10-12 31
(Vocals: Dick Robertson)

BLAKE, Eubie, & His Shuffle Along Orchestra

BALITMORE BUZZ / BANDANA DAYS .... *Victor 18791* 3-5 21

BLEYER, Archie, & His Orchestra

BROADWAY RHYTHM / YOU ARE MY LUCKY STAR .... *Melotone 35-10-23* 3-5 35
(Vocals: Unknown)

DON'T LET ME STAND IN YOUR WAY / THE NIGHT YOU SAID GOODBYE .... *Joe Davis 7621* 2-4 46
(Vocals: Armen Camp)

ISN'T THIS A LOVELY DAY? / TOP HAT, WHITE TIE AND TAILS .... *Melotone 35-09-19* 2-4 35
(Vocals: Unknown)

OBJECT OF MY AFFECTION, THE / I'VE GOT AN INVITATION TO THE DANCE .... *Vocalion 2835* 3-5 34
(Vocals: Unknown)

ON A SUNDAY AFTERNOON / I'VE GOT A FEELIN' YOU'RE FOOLIN' .... *Melotone 35-10-22* 2-4 35
(Vocals: Unknown)

PICCOLINO, THE / CHEEK TO CHEEK .... *Melotone 35-09-18* 3-5 35
(Vocals: Unknown)

WILD HONEY / IRRESISTIBLE (Vocals: Unknown) .... *Vocalion 2823* 3-5 34

WINTER WONDERLAND / I'M GROWING FONDER OF YOU .... *Vocalion 2836* 3-5 34
(Vocals: Unknown)

WORLD IS MINE, THE / STAY AS SWEET AS YOU ARE .... *Vocalion 2822* 3-5 34
(Vocals: Unknown)

BLOCK, Bert, & His Bell Music

(I CAN DREAM) CAN'T I? / THIS IS MY NIGHT TO DREAM .... *Vocalion 3969* 2-4 38
(Vocals: Unknown)

DANCING TAMBOURINE / TOY TRUMPET .... *Vocalion 4087* 3-5 38

GLOW-WORM / ALEXANDER'S RAGTIME BAND .... *Vocalion 4166* 3-5 38

IN MY LITTLE RED BOOK / A SHACK IN THE BACK OF THE HILLS .... *Vocalion 3994* 2-4 38
(Vocals: Unknown)

VIENI, VIENI / ONCE IN A WHILE .... *Perfect 7-12-04* 3-5 37
(Vocals: Bill Johnson)

VIENI, VIENI / ONCE IN A WHILE .... *Vocalion 3747* 3-5 37
(Vocals: Bill Johnson)
(Simultaneously released on two labels)

WHISTLE WHILE YOU WORK / A LITTLE WHITE LIGHTHOUSE .... *Conqueror 8989* 4-6 38
(Vocals: Unknown)

WHISTLE WHILE YOU WORK / A LITTLE WHITE LIGHTHOUSE .... *Vocalion 3958* 4-6 38
(Vocals: Unknown)
(Simultaneously released on two labels)

YOU COULDN'T BE CUTER / JUST LET ME LOOK AT YOU .... *Conqueror 9017* 2-4 38
(Vocals: Unknown)

YOU COULDN'T BE CUTER / JUST LET ME LOOK AT YOU .... *Vocalion 4006* 2-4 38
(Vocals: Unknown)
(Simultaneously released on two labels)

BLUE BEAVER ORCHESTRA, The

SOMEDAY WE'LL MEET AGAIN / WHEN EYES OF BLUE ARE FOOLING YOU .... *Gennett 3080* 3-5 25

TIA JUANA TROT, THE / HAWAIIAN MOON .... *Champion 15022* 4-6 25

BLUE, Bud, & His Orchestra
see RICH, Fred, & His (La Palina) Orchestra

BLUE, Buddy, & His Texans:
see BALLEW, Smith, & His Orchestra

BLUE DIAMOND DANCE ORCHESTRA, The

BLUE DANUBE BLUES / KA-LU-A .... *Okeh 4497* 2-4 22

LONESOME LIPS / HAWAIIAN SIGHS .... *Okeh 4581* 2-4 22

SMILIN' / AIN'T YOU COMIN' OUT, MALINDA? .... *Okeh 4516* 2-4 21

BLUEJEANS, The

BIDIN' MY TIME (Vocals: Phil Crow, Frank Luther, & Carson Robinson) / SAM AND DELILAH (by Duke Ellington & His Cotton Club Orchestra; Vocal: Chick Bullock) .... *Victor 23036* 15-20 31

BLUE RHYTHM ORCHESTRA, The

KEEP YOUR TEMPER / HOLD 'ER, DEACON .... *Perfect 14545* 20-25 25

BLUE RIBBON TRIO, The

CHILDHOOD DAYS / WHO LOVES YOU MOST, AFTER ALL? .... *Okeh 4710* 2-4 22

SWEET ANABEL / GOOD-NIGHT .... *Okeh 4900* 2-4 23

THAT DA DA STRAIN / AGGRAVATIN' PAPA .... *Okeh 4824* 3-5 23

BOHN, Tommy & His Penn-Sirens Orchestra

AMOS 'N' ANDY / THE PERFECT SONG ... *Okeh 41372* 8-10 30
(Vocals: Unknown)

BONANO, Sharkey, as Sharkey & His Sharks of Rhythm
(Sharkey Bonano: 4/9/04 – 3/27/72)

MISTER BROWN GOES TO TOWN / WHEN YOU'RE SMILING .... *Vocalion 3400* 8-10 37
(Vocals: Sharkey Bonano)

MUDHOLE BLUES / SWING IN, SWING OUT .... *Vocalion 3353* 8-10 36

OLD FASHIONED SWING / BIG BOY BLUE .... *Vocalion 3450* 5-8 37
(Vocals: Sharkey Bonano)

SWINGIN' ON THE SWANEE SHORE / SWING LIKE A RUSTY GATE .... *Vocalion 3470* 5-8 37
(Vocals: Sharkey Bonano)

BON BON & HIS BUDDIES:
see TUNNELL, Bon Bon

BOOTS & HIS BUDDIES:
see DOUGLAS, Boots

BOSTONIANS, The:
see RESER, Harry &
see RYAN, Joe, & His Orchestra

BOULANGER, Charles, as the Georgia Melodians

GIVE US THE CHARLESTON / YES SIR! THAT'S MY BABY .... *Edison 51588* 10-12 25

HOW YOU GONNA KEEP KOOL? / IN SPITE OF IT ALL .... *Edison 51359* 8-10 24

RED-HOT MAMA (Vocal: Vernon Dalhart) / CHARLEY, MY BOY .... *Edison 51394* 10-12 24

RHYTHM OF THE DAY / EV'RYBODY'S CHARLESTON CRAZY .... *Edison 51730* 10-12 26

SHE'S DRIVIN' ME WILD / RED-HOT HENRY BROWN (Vocal: Vernon Dalhart) .... *Edison 51598* 10-12 25

SPANISH SHAWL / CHARLESTON BALL .... *Edison 51678* 8-10 26

BOWLLY, Al, & His Orchestra
(Al Bowlly: 1/7/98 – 4/17/41)

EVERY DAY'S A HOLIDAY / OUTSIDE OF PARADISE .... *Bluebird B-7319* 5-8 38
(Vocals: Al Bowlly)

HALF MOON ON THE HUDSON / SWEET AS A SONG .... *Bluebird B-7317* 5-8 38
(Vocals: Al Bowlly)

I CAN DREAM, CAN'T I / SWEET STRANGER .... *Bluebird B-7332* 5-8 38
(Vocals: Al Bowlly)

BRACKEN, Jimmy, as Jimmy Bracken's Toe Ticklers:
see MILLS, Irving, & His Hotsy Totsy Gang, and
see MILLS, Irving, as Mills Merry Makers

BRADLEY, Will, & His Boogie Woogie Boys
(Will Bradley: 7/12/12 –)

JINGLE BELLS BOOGIE WOOGIE / CRYIN' THE BOOGIE BLUES .... *Joe Davis 7013* 3-5 46

LIGHTNING BOOGIE / SUGAR HILL BOOGIE WOOGIE .... *Joe Davis 7014* 3-5 46

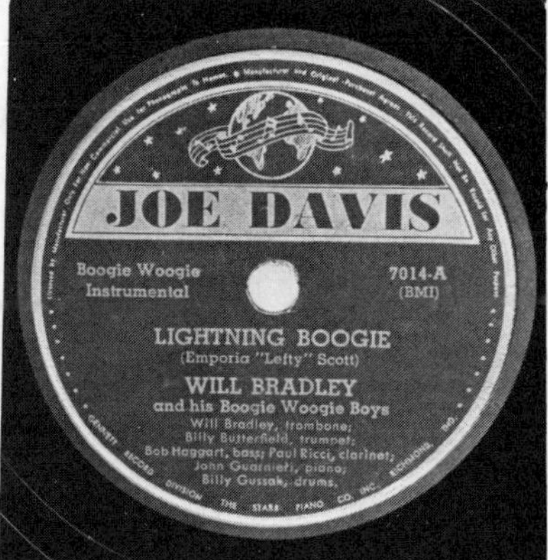

BRADLEY, Will, & His Orchestra

APRIL IN PARIS / STOP! AND ASK SOMEBODY (Vocal: Terry Allen) ...... *Columbia 36401* 2-4 41

AS LONG AS I LIVE / IN A LITTLE SPANISH TOWN .... *Columbia 35566* 2-4 40

BEAT ME, DADDY, EIGHT TO THE BAR / BEAT ME, DADDY, EIGHT TO THE BAR, PART II .... *Columbia 35530* 2-4 40

BOOGIE WOOGIE CONGA (Vocal: Ray McKinley) / I NEED SOMEBODY TO LOVE (Vocal: Terry Allen) .... *Columbia 35994* 2-4 41

BOOGLIE WOOGLIE PIGGY (Vocal: Ray McKinley) / LOVE ME A LITTLE (Vocal: Lynn Gardner) .... *Columbia 36231* 2-4 41

CHICKEN GUMBOOGIE (Vocal: Ray McKinley) / STARDUST (Vocal: Jimmy Valentine) ... *Columbia 35939* 2-4 41

DEAREST, DAREST I? (Vocal: Ray McKinley) / FIVE O'CLOCK WHISTLE .... *Columbia 35793* 2-4 40

DON'T LET JULIA FOOL YA (Vocal: Terry Allen) / JACK AND JILL (Vocals: Lynn Gardner & Terry Allen) .... *Columbia 36372* 2-4 41

ETUDE BRUTUS / IF I'M LUCKY (Vocal: Phil Hanna) .... *Signature 15048* 2-4 46

FLYIN' HOME / SO FAR, SO GOOD (Vocal: Carlotta Dale) .... *Columbia 35542* 2-4 40

FOREVER MORE / MEAN TO ME (Vocal: Carlotta Dale) .... *Vocalion 5237* 3-5 39

FRY ME, COOKIE, WITH A CAN OF LARD (Vocal: Ray McKinley) / REQUEST TO A RHUMBA .... *Columbia 36719* 2-4 42

GET THEE BEHIND ME, SATAN (Vocal: Terry Allen) / ALL THAT MEAT AND NO POTATOES (Vocal: Ray McKinley) .... *Columbia 36248* 2-4 41

HIGH ON A WINDY HILL / LOVE OF MY LIFE .... *Columbia 35912* 2-4 41
(Vocals: Jimmy Valentine)

I BOOGIED WHEN I SHOULD HAVE WOOGIED (Vocal: Ray McKinley) / THAT'S HER MASON DIXON LINE (Vocals: Lynn Gardner & Ray McKinley) .... *Columbia 36044* 2-4 41

I COULD MAKE YOU CARE / ONCE IN A LOVETIME .... *Columbia 35645* 2-4 40
(Vocals: Jimmy Valentine)

I DON'T STAND A GHOST OF A CHANCE (Vocal: Charlotta Dale) / JIMTOWN BLUES ... *Columbia 35376* 3-5 40

I GET A KICK OUTA CORN (Vocal: Ray McKinley) / GOTTA GET HOME (Vocal: Carlotta Dale) .... *Columbia 35399* 2-4 40

I GUESS I'LL BE ON MY WAY / SEEING YOU AGAIN DID ME NO GOOD .... *Columbia 36547* 2-4 42
(Vocals: Terry Allen)

IN THE HALL OF THE MOUNTAIN KING / FROM THE LAND OF SKY BLUE WATER ..... *Columbia 36286* 2-4 41

I THINK OF YOU (Vocal: Terry Allen) / THE THREE B'S (BARRELHOUSE, BOOGIE AND BLUES) (Vocal: Ray McKinley) .... *Columbia 36444* 3-5 41

I THOUGHT ABOUT YOU (Vocal: Carlotta Dale) / SPEAKING OF HEAVEN (Vocal: Larry Southern) .... *Vocalion 5182* 3-5 39

IT'S A WONDERFUL WORLD / WATCH THE CLOCK .... *Columbia 35414* 3-5 40
(Vocals: Carlotta Dale)

IT'S SQUARE, BUT IT ROCKS (Vocal: Ray McKinley) / PRAIRIELAND LULLABY (Vocal: Terry Allen) .... *Columbia 36014* 2-4 41

JOHNSON RAG / HALLELUJAH ..... *Columbia 35333* 3-5 40

LOVE LIES / ORCHIDS FOR REMEMBERANCE .... *Columbia 35597* 2-4 40
(Vocals: Jimmy Valentine)

LOVE NEST / I'M COMIN' VIRGINIA ... *Columbia 35354* 2-4 39

MAKE WITH THE KISSES / FIT TO BE TIED .... *Vocalion 5210* 3-5 39
(Vocals: Carlotta Dale)

MEMPHIS BLUES / OLD DOC YAK (Vocal: Ray McKinley) .... *Vocalion 5130* 3-5 39

MOON FELL IN THE RIVER, THE / SOMEWHERE ...... *Columbia 35764* 2-4 40
(Vocals: Jimmy Valentine)

SCRAMBLE TWO / ROCK-A-BYE THE BOOGIE .... *Columbia 35732* 3-5 40
(Vocals: Ray McKinley)

SCRUB ME, MAMA WITH A BOOGIE BEAT (Vocal: Ray McKinley) / — .... *V-Disc 173* 5-8 -
(A World War II release)

SCRUB ME, MAMA, WITH A BOOGIE BEAT (Vocal: Ray McKinley) / THERE I GO (Vocal: Jimmy Valentine) .... *Columbia 35743* 3-5 40

SECRETS IN THE MOONLIGHT / POLKA DOTS AND MOONBEAMS .... *Columbia 35470* 2-4 40
(Vocals: Jimmy Valentine)

SHADOWS IN THE NIGHT (Vocal: Terry Allen) / CALL ME A TAXI (Vocal: Ray McKinley)..... *Columbia 36082* 2-4 41

SLEEPY-TIME GAL / WHO CAN I TURN TO? .... *Columbia 36470* 2-4 41
(Vocals: Terry Allen)

SOUTHPAW SERENADE / BOUNCE ME, BROTHER, WITH A SOLID FOUR .... *Columbia 35963* 3-5 41
(Vocals: Ray McKinley)

STRANGE CARGO (theme song) / WHERE DO YOU KEEP YOUR HEART (Vocal: Jimmy Valentine) .... *Columbia 35545* 2-4 40

SWINGIN' A DREAM (Vocal: Ray McKinley) / THIS CHANGING WORLD (Vocal: Carlotta Dale) .... *Vocalion 5262* 3-5 40

SWINGIN' DOWN THE LANE / FLAMINGO (Vocal: Terry Allen) ...... *Columbia 36147* 2-4 41

THIS IS THE BEGINNING OF THE END (Vocal: Carlotta Dale) / RHUMBOOGIE (Vocal: Ray McKinley) ... *Columbia 35464* 2-4 40

THIS LITTLE ICKY WENT TO TOWN / BREAK IT TO ME GENTLY (Vocal: Ray McKinley) ... *Columbia 35922* 3-5 41

THREE RING RAGOUT / I SHOULD HAVE KNOWN YOU YEARS AGO (Vocal: Phyllis Miles). *Columbia 35871* 3-5 41

WHAT D'YA HEAR FROM YOUR HEART? (Vocal: Lynn Gardner) / TALKING TO THE WIND (Vocal: Terry Allen)....... *Columbia 36052* 2-4 41

WHEN YOU AND I WERE YOUNG, MAGGIE / I'M MISUNDERSTOOD (Vocal: Terry Allen).................. *Columbia 36182* 2-4 41

YOU'RE LUCKY TO ME / THE LONESOME ROAD........... *Columbia 35849* 2-4 40

BRADSHAW, Tiny, & His Orchestra
(Tiny Bradshaw: 1905 – 12/58)

DARKTOWN STRUTTERS' BALL, THE / THE SHEIK OF ARABY................. *Decca 194* 5-8 34
(Vocals: Tiny Bradshaw)

MISTER, WILL YOU SEREDADE? / SHE'LL BE COMING 'ROUND THE MOUNTAIN...... *Decca 317* 5-8 34
(Vocals: Tiny Bradshaw)

OL'MAN RIVER / I'M A DING DONG DADDY .... *Decca 236* 5-8 34
(Vocals: Tiny Bradshaw)

ONE, TWO THREE, KICK BLUES (Vocal: Dorena Deene) / WALK THAT MESS (Vocal: Tiny Bradshaw)... *King 4427* 3-5 -

SHOUT, SISTER, SHOUT / I AIN'T GOT NOBODY......................... *Decca 456* 5-8 34
(Vocals: Tiny Bradshaw)

BRANDWYNNE, Nat, & His Orchestra
(Nat Brandwynne: : 7/23/10 – 3/8/78)

BABALU / IN-CHI-CHI-CASTENANGO ... *Decca 18182* 2-4 42
(Vocals: Bernice Parks)

FRENESI / NOCHE AZUL .... *Decca 3912* 2-4 41

IF WE NEVER MEET AGAIN / BYE, BYE, BABY (Vocal: Buddy Clark ...... *Brunswick 7714* 3-5 36

IN THE CHAPEL IN THE MOONLIGHT / NEVER SHOULD HAVE TOLD YOU........ *Brunswick 7772* 3-5 36
(Vocals: Barry McKinley)

IT'S YOU I'M TALKING ABOUT / THERE'S ALWAYS A HAPPY ENDING................ *Brunswick 7655* 3-5 36
(Vocals: Buddy Clark)

LAZY WEATHER / THE GLORY OF LOVE......................... *Brunswick 7660* 3-5 36
(Vocals: Buddy Clark)

LONG AGO AND FAR AWAY / WHERE IS MY HEART? .... *Brunswick 7678* 3-5 36
(Vocals: Buddy Clark)

SPEAK TO ME OF LOVE (Vocal: Jerry Wayne) / I NEED NEW WORDS (Vocal: Lois Wynne)......... *Decca 3947* 2-4 41

TAKE MY HEART / THESE FOOLISH THINGS .... *Brunswick 7676* 3-5 36
(Vocals: Buddy Clark)

UNDER A ROOF IN PAREE (Vocal: Jerry Wayne) / FOR YOU (Vocal: Lois Wynne)............. *Decca 3950* 2-4 41

UNTIL TODAY / WITHOUT A SHADOW OF A DOUBT........... *Brunswick 7712* 3-5 36
(Vocals: Buddy Clark)

BREED, Perley, as Perley Breed's Shepard Colonial Orchestra

TELL ME, DREAMY EYES (Vocal: Frank Cornwell) / WHERE'S MY SWEETIE HIDING?.... *Gennett 5608* 5-8 24

BREESE, Lou, & His Orchestra

HOW LONG DID I DREAM? (Vocal: Jean Williams) / HUMPTY DUMPTY HEART (Vocal: Skip Morr)....................... *Decca 4107* 2-4 42

LORETTA / SWEETHEART, WAIT FOR ME .... *Decca 4269* 2-4 42
(Vocals: Unknown)

PLEASANT DREAMS (Vocal: Jean Williams) / CHIQUITA (Vocals: Barry Warren & Skip Morr) .... *Decca 4127* 2-4 42

SEVEN DAYS A WEEK / SOMEBODY NOBODY LOVES...................... *Decca 4255* 2-4 42
(Vocals: Unknown)

BREGMAN, Buddy, & His Orchestra:
see FRITZGERALD, Ella, accompanied by Buddy Bregman & His Orchestra

BRIGODE, Ace, & His Fourteen Virginians
(Ace Brigode: — – 2/3/60)

ALABAMY BOUND / A SUN-KIST COTTAGE IN CALIFORNIA................. *Columbia 282-D* 4-6 24

ALONE AT LAST / I'M TIRED OF EVERYTHING BUT YOU .... *Columbia 426-D* 3-5 25

BYE, BYE, BABY / A SUN-KIST COTTAGE IN CALIFORNIA...................... *Okeh 40223* 3-5 24

DON'T TAKE YOUR TROUBLES TO BED / ONLY YOU! .... *Okeh 40152* 3-5 24

FOOLING / WHEN I THINK OF YOU ... *Edison 51533* 4-6 25

MY SUGAR / CHEATIN' ON ME (by The California Ramblers as The Varsity Eight)...................... *Cameo 725* 4-6 25

NEVER AGAIN/DON'T MIND THE RAIN... *Okeh 40088* 3-5 24

NORMANDY / WHY AREN'T YEZ EATIN' MORE ORANGES? (Vocals: Eddie Allen & Fred Brohez) ..... *Columbia 477-D* 3-5 25

TOKIO BLUES / I'LL SEE YOU IN MY DREAMS.................... *Edison 51511* 4-6 25

WAIT'LL IT'S MOONLIGHT / MAKE THOSE NAUGHTY EYES BEHAVE .... *Columbia 401-D* 4-6 25

BRIGODE, Ace, & His Orchestra

WHY SHOULD I CRY OVER YOU? / YOU KNOW YOU BELONG TO SOMEBODY ELSE..... *Conqueror 9452* 3-5 40
(Vocals: Buddy Curran)

WHY SHOULD I CRY OVER YOU? / YOU KNOW YOU BELONG TO SOMEBODY ELSE ...... *Vocalion 5446* 3-5 40
(Vocals: Buddy Curran)
(Simultaneously released on two labels)

BRILLHARDT'S ORCHESTRA

GIRL FRIEND, THE (Vocal: Lester O'Keefe) / — .... *Pathe Actuelle 36430* 5-8 26

GIRL FRIEND, THE (Vocal: Lester O'Keefe) / — .... *Perfect 14611* 5-8 26
(Simultaneously released on two labels)

HELLO, ALOHA! HOW ARE YOU? (Vocal: Lester O'Keefe) / — .... *Pathe Actuelle 36438* 5-8 26

HELLO, ALOHA! HOW ARE YOU? (Vocal: Lester O'Keefe) / — .... *Perfect 14619* 4-6 26
(Simultaneously released on two labels)

STATE STREET SHUFFLE / —... *Pathe Actuelle 36450* 5-8 26

STATE STREET SHUFFLE / —......... *Perfect 14631* 4-6 26
(Simultaneously released on two labels)

BRITT, Mart, & His Orchestra

LEARNING (Vocal: Mart Britt) / MAMA DON'T WANT NO PEAS AN' RICE AN' COCONUT OIL (Vocals: by Orchestra)................ *Victor 22933* 5-8 32

ONLY AN ANGEL (Vocal: Mart Britt) / GOOSE CREEK STOMP................ *Victor 21760* 10-12 28

SADNESS WILL BE GLADNESS (Vocal: Matt Britt) / TELL ME, SWEET ROSE............ *Victor V-40012* 8-10 28

WHO PLAYED POKER WITH POCAHONTAS (Vocal: Sue Miller) / DOWN THE OLD BACK ROAD (Vocal: Bill Robertson)............. *Victor 22956* 5-8 32

BROADWAY BELL-HOPS, The:
see LANIN, Sam

BROADWAY BROADCASTERS, The:
see LANIN, Sam

BROADWAY DANCE ORCHESTRA, The

BEALE STREET MAMA / DEAREST.... *Edison 51069* 4-6 23

BRING BACK MY BLUSHING ROSE / SECOND HAND ROSE.............. *Edison 50832* 3-5 21

CAROLINA IN THE MORNING / AGGRAVATIN' PAPA................ *Edison 51176* 4-6 23

DOODLE-DOO-DOO / OH PETER (YOU'RE SO NICE).................. *Edison 51421* 4-6 24

HEADIN' HOME / THAT BRAN' NEW GAL O' MINE............. *Edison 51282* 4-6 24

LITTLE DEVIL / LADY OF THE NILE.... *Edison 51513* 4-6 25

MY SUNNY TENNESSEE / WHEN THE HONEYMOON WAS OVER .... *Edison 50827* 3-5 21

NO, NO, NORA / CANNIBOLA............ *Edison 51233* 3-5 23

ROSE-MARIE / MY TWILIGHT ROSE... *Edison 51411* 3-5 24

RUNNIN' WILD / ROSE OF THE RIO GRANDE .... *Edison 51066* 4-6 23

SAL-O-MAY (SALOME) / WABASH BLUES.................... *Edison 50874* 4-6 21

SWANEE BUTTERFLY / ORIENTAL MOON.................. *Edison 51543* 3-5 25

TELL ME GYPSY / WHO'S SORRY NOW?................ *Edison 51173* 3-5 23

TWO LITTLE WOODEN SHOES / DIXIE HIGHWAY.................... *Edison 51022* 3-5 22

YANKEE DOODLE BLUES, THE / NOBODY LIED............... *Edison 51004* 4-6 22

YOU KNOW YOU BELONG TO SOMEONE ELSE / MARCH OF THE MANNIKINS......... *Edison 51142* 3-5 23

BROADWAY NITELIGHTS, The:
see SELVIN, Ben, & His Orchestra

BROADWAY SYNCOPATORS, The:
see SELVIN, Ben

BRODSKY, Irving, & His Orchestra

IF YOU BELIEVE IN ME / I MAY BE WRONG, BUT I THINK YOU'RE WONDERFUL.... *Harmony 1021-H* 8-10 29
(Vocals: Irving Kaufman as Robert Wood)

BROOKS, Randy, & His Orchestra
(Randy Brooks: 3/28/17 – 3/21/67)

HARLEM NOCTURNE / A NIGHT AT THE THREE DEUCES .... *Decca 23935* 2-4 47

IN THE MOON MIST / DON'T LET ME DREAM............... *Decca 18752* 2-4 46

LAMPLIGHT (Vocal: Harry Prime) / TENDERLY.......................... *Decca 24161* 2-4 47

LAND OF THE LOON / I'D DO IT ALL OVER AGAIN .... *Decca 18697* 2-4 46

SURRENDER / ONE LOVE.............. *Decca 18897* 2-4 46

TIPPIN' IN / AFTER HOURS .... *Decca 23869* 2-4 47

TO BEAT OR NOT TO BEAT / — .... *V-Disc 523* 5-8 45
(A World War II release)

BROOKS, Sunny, & His Hollywood Stars:
see LANE, Eddie, & His Hotel McAlpin Orchestra

BROWN, Les, & His Duke University Blue Devils
(Les Brown: 3/14/12 –)
(Les Brown & His Orchestra regularly play engagements in the west coast area as "Les Brown & His Band of Renown" and provide musical accompaniment for Bob Hope's TV specials.)

DANCE OF THE BLUE-DEVILS (early theme song) / SWAMP FIRE .... *Decca 1231* 5-8 37

DON'T YOU CARE WHAT ANYONE SAYS? (Vocal: Herb Muse) / RAMONA .... *Decca 1296* 4-6 37

DON'T YOU GO WORRYIN' ABOUT JUDGMENT DAY (Vocal: Herb Muse) / RIGMAROLE.... *Decca 1238* 5-8 37

FEATHER YOUR NEST / LAZY RIVER (Vocal: Herb Muse) .... *Decca 1323* 4-6 37

MUTINY ON THE BANDSTAND (Vocal: Herb Muse) / WHEN YOU WORE A TULIP............ *Decca 2045* 3-5 37

PAPA TREETOP TALL / SWING FOR SALE .... *Decca 991* 5-8 36
(Vocals: Herb Muse)

BROWN, Les, & His Orchestra

ALEXANDER THE SWOOSE / KEEP COOL, FOOL.......................... *Okeh 6167* 2-4 41
(Vocals: Doris Day)

AMAPLOA / EASY AS PIE............... *Okeh 6062* 2-4 41
(Vocals: Doris Day)

AS IF YOU DIDN'T KNOW (Vocal: Ralph Young) / ALL THAT MEAT AND NO POTATOES (Vocal: Betty Bonney)........... *Okeh 6323* 2-4 41

BABY MINE / HE'S 1-A IN THE ARMY AND HE'S A-1 IN MY HEART............... *Okeh 6500* 2-4 41
(Vocals: Betty Bonney)

BETWEEN FRIENDS (Vocal: Doris Day) / ANVIL CHORUS........................ *Okeh 6011* 2-4 41

BIZET HAS HIS DAY / A GOOD MAN IS HARD TO FIND (Vocal: Henry Stone)............ *Columbia 36688* 2-4 42

BREATHLESS (Vocal: Betty Bonney) / DON'T SIT UNDER THE APPLE TREE (Vocal: Henry Stone) .... *Okeh 6653* 3-5 42

BROOMSTREET / BARBARA ALLEN...... *Okeh 6049* 2-4 41
(Vocals: Doris Day)

CELERY STALKS AT MIDNIGHT / BEAU NIGHT IN HOTCHKISS CORNERS............. *Okeh 6098* 2-4 41
(Vocals: Doris Day)

CHICO'S LOVE SONG (Vocal: Herb Muse) / I LOVE TO SING THE WORDS WHILE WE'RE DANCING (Vocal: Mirian Shaw)...... *Bluebird B-10457* 2-4 39

COMANCHE WAR DANCE / A MELLOW BIT OF RHYTHM .... *Decca 3155* 3-5 40

DARLING NELLIE GRAY (Vocal: Miriam Shaw) / LIGHTLY AND POLITELY........ *Bluebird B-10114* 2-4 39

DAY BY DAY (Vocal: Doris Day) / DOCTOR, LAWYER, INDIAN CHIEF (Vocal: Butch Stone)... *Columbia 36945* 2-4 46

DIG IT / WHILE THE MUSIC PLAYS ON... *Okeh 5964* 2-4 40
(Vocals: Doris Day)

DUCK FOOT WADDLE / PLUMBER'S REVENGE.......... *Bluebird B-10174* 3-5 39

EVERYBODY'S MAKING MONEY BUT TCHAIKOVSKY (Vocal: Betty Bonney) / HEREAFTER (Vocal: Ralph Young)......... *Okeh 6573* 2-4 42

FROM NOW ON / GET OUT OF TOWN .... *Bluebird B-10009* 2-4 38
(Vocals: Herb Muse)

GRAVEDIGGER'S HOLIDAY / BLUE DIVEL JAZZ.......... *Bluebird B-10827* 3-5 39

HAVE YOU FORGOTTEN SO SOON? (Vocal: Miriam Shaw) / LIKE A MONKEY LIKES COCONUTS (Vocal: Herb Muse).......... *Bluebird B-7869* 3-5 38

IF IT'S GOOD THEN I WANT IT / STICKS AND STONES.......... *Bluebird B-10203* 2-4 39
(Vocals: Herb Muse)

I GUESS I'LL HAVE TO DREAM THE REST / BE FAIR.......... *Okeh 6308* 2-4 41
(Vocals: Ralph Young)

IT'S YOU AGAIN / CITY CALLED HEAVEN .... *Okeh 6367* 2-4 41
(Vocals: Ralph Young)

I'VE GOT MY EYES ON YOU (Vocal: Herb Muse) / I CONCENTRATE ON YOU (Vocal: Shirley Howard).......... *Bluebird B-10551* 2-4 40

I'VE GOT MY LOVE TO KEEP ME WARM / I'M A-TELLIN' YOU SAM (Vocal: Doris Day).......... *Columbia 38324* 2-4 48

LET'S BE BUDDIES / THREE AT A TABLE FOR TWO .... *Okeh 5937* 2-4 40
(Vocals: Doris Day)

LITTLE MISS IRISH (Vocal: Ronnie Chase) / BOOGLIE WOOGLIE PIGGY (Vocal: Doris Day)........ *Okeh 6085* 2-4 41

LOVE FOR SALE / OUT OF THE NIGHT (Vocal: Mirian Shaw) .... *Bluebird B-10211* 2-4 39

LOVE, YOUR MAGIC SPELL IS EVERYWHERE / SHANGRI-LA.......... *Bluebird B-10226* 2-4 39

MAKE WITH THE MUSIC (Vocal: Herb Muse) / YOU BRING ME DOWN (Vocal: Miriam Shaw)......... *Bluebird B-10480* 2-4 39

MEXICAN HAT DANCE / WHEN THE LIGHTS GO ON AGAIN (Vocal: Jack Carroll)......... *Okeh 6696* 3-5 42

MY DREAMS ARE GETTING BETTER ALL THE TIME / HE'S HOME FOR A LITTLE WHILE.......... *Columbia 36779* 2-4 44
(Vocals: Doris Day)

MY NUMBER ONE DREAM CAME TRUE / YOU SHOULD HAVE TOLD ME.... *Columbia 37208* 2-4 47
(Vocals: Doris Day)

NICKEL SERENADE, THE (Vocal: Betty Bonney) / JOLTIN' JOE DI MAGGIO .... *Okeh 6377* 2-4 41

NOTHIN' / I GOT IT BAD AND THAT AIN'T GOOD .... *Conqueror 9909* 3-5 41
(Vocals: Betty Bonney)

NOTHIN' / I GOT IT BAD AND THAT AIN'T GOOD.......... *Okeh 6414* 3-5 41
(Vocals: Betty Bonney)
(Simultaneously released on two labels)

OH MARIE! (Vocal: Herb Muse) / CIRIBIRIBIN .... *Bluebird B-10421* 2-4 39

PERISPHERE SHUFFLE / TRYLON STOMP.......... *Bluebird B-10314* 3-5 39

PROCESSION OF THE SARDAR / FUNICULI, FINUCULA .... *Okeh 6293* 2-4 41

ROCKET SHIP TO MARS / PAPOOSE.......... *Bluebird B-10787* 3-5 39

SCISSORS AND KNIVES TO GRIND (Vocal: Herb Muse) / MAKIN' WHOOPEE.......... *Bluebird B-10381* 2-4 39

SENTIMENTAL JOURNEY (theme song) (Vocal: Doris Day)/ TWILIGHT TIME........ *Columbia 36769* 2-4 44

SOONER OR LATER (Vocal: Doris Day) / YEARS AND YEARS AGO (Vocal: Jack Haskell) ..... *Columbia 37153* 2-4 47

STAR DUST (Vocal: Mirian Shaw) / BOOGIE WOOGIE.......... *Bluebird B-7858* 4-6 38

STOP BEATIN' 'ROUND THE MULBERRY BUSH / PEELIN' THE PEACH ..... *Bluebird B-7796* 3-5 38
(Vocals: Herb Muse)

SUNDAY (Vocals: Butch Stone) / OUT OF NOWHERE .... *Columbia 36724* 2-4 44

SWEET ELOISE (Vocals: Marie Greene & the Merry Men) / HERE YOU ARE (Vocal: Ralph Young)... *Columbia 36602* 2-4 42

'TAIN'T ME / I'LL ALWAYS BE WITH YOU .... *Columbia 36804* 2-4 45
(Vocals: Doris Day)

THAT OLD GANG OF MINE / THE MAN WHO COMES AROUND.......... *Bluebird B-10558* 2-4 40
(Vocals: Herb Muse)

THERE'S GOOD BLUES TONIGHT (Vocal: Doris Day) / IN LOVE IN VAIN (Vocal: Jack Haskell).......... *Columbia 36972* 2-4 46

THIS CAN'T BE LOVE / SING FOR YOUR SUPPER.......... *Bluebird B-10017* 2-4 38
(Vocals: Miriam Shaw)

TILL THE END OF TIME / HE'LL HAVE TO CROSS THE ATLANTIC .... *Columbia 36828* 2-4 45
(Vocals: Doris Day)

TWO FOOLS IN LOVE / ONLY WHEN YOU'RE IN MY ARMS.......... *Bluebird B-10166* 2-4 39
(Vocals: Herb Muse)

WHAT GOES UP MUST COME DOWN / DON'T WORRY 'BOUT ME.......... *Bluebird B-10161* 2-4 39
(Vocals: Herb Muse)

WHEN DAY IS DONE (Vocal: Miriam Shaw) / SOBBIN' BLUES.......... *Bluebird B-10026* 3-5 38

WITH YOU ON MY MIND / WHY DOESN'T SOMEBODY TELL ME THESE THINGS?........ *Bluebird B-7812* 3-5 38
(Vocals: Wendy Bishop)

YOU, YOU, YOU / HARLEM WOOGIE.......... *Bluebird B-10105* 3-5 39
(Vocals: Herb Muse)

BROWN-MORRIS ORCHESTRA, The

HEADIN' FOR HARLEM / I LEFT MY SUGAR STANDING IN THE RAIN .... *Harmony 521-H* 5-8 27
(Vocals: Irving Kaufman)

BROWN, Pete, & His Jump Six:
see FEATHER, Leonard, as Leonard Feather's All-star Jam Band

BROWN, Tom:
see SIX BROWN BROTHERS, The

BROWN, Walter, & Orchestra:
see HASTON, Gus, & Orchestra

BRUNIS, George, as the Mills Cavalcade Orchestra
(George Brunis: 2/6/00 –)

LOVELY LIZA LEE / RHYTHM LULLABY .... *Columbia 3066-D* 10-12 35

BRYANT, Willie, & His Orchestra
(Willie Bryant: 8/30/08 – 2/9/64)

GLORY OF LOVE, THE / RIDE, RED, RIDE.......... *Bluebird B-6374* 5-8 36
(Vocals: Willie Bryant)

I LIKE BANANAS / I'M GRATEFUL TO YOU.......... *Bluebird B-6436* 4-6 36
(Vocals: Willie Bryant)

IS IT TRUE WHAT THEY SAY ABOUT DIXIE? / MOONRISE ON THE LOWLANDS ... *Bluebird B-6362* 4-6 36
(Vocals: Willie Bryant)

IT'S OVER BECAUSE WE'RE THROUGH (theme song) / A VIPER'S MOAN .... *Victor 24858* 5-8 35
(Vocals: Willie Bryant)

'LONG ABOUT MIDNIGHT / JERRY THE JUNKER.......... *Victor 25045* 5-8 35
(Vocals: Willie Bryant)

ON THE ALAMO / NEGLECTED.......... *Decca 1772* 3-5 38
(Vocals: Willie Bryant)

RIGAMAROLE / THE SHEIK.......... *Victor 25038* 5-8 35

STEAK AND POTATOES (Vocal: Willie Bryant) / LIZA.......... *Victor 25160* 5-8 35

THROWIN' STONES AT THE SUN / CHIMES AT THE MEETIN' (Vocals: Willie Bryant).......... *Victor 24847* 5-8 35

YOU'LL NEVER REMEMBER AND I'LL NEVER FORGET / YOU'RE GONNA LOSE YOUR GAL.......... *Decca 1881* 3-5 38
(Vocals: Willie Bryant)

BUFFALODIANS, The

HERE COMES EMALINE / DEEP HENDERSON .... *Columbia 665-D* 4-6 26

WOULDJA?/SHE'S STILL MY BABY... *Columbia 723-D* 4-6 26

BUFFALODIANS, The, as The Yankee Ten
(with Harold Arlen, famed composer as well as pianist and vocalist.)

BABY FACE / HOW MANY TIMES?... *Broadway 1027* 4-6 26
(Vocals: Harold Arlen)

BABY FACE / HOW MANY TIMES?.......... *Paramount 20469* 5-8 26
(Vocals: Harold Arlen)

BABY FACE / HOW MANY TIMES? .... *Puritan 11469* 4-6 26
(Vocals: Harold Arlen)
(Simultaneously released on three labels)

BULLOCK, Chick, & His Levee Loungers:
see KARDOS, Gene, & His Orchestra, and see ROLLINS, Todd, & His Orchestra

BUNCH, Billy, & His Smoky Rhythm:
see REDMAN, Don, & His Orchestra

BURKE, Sonny, & His Orchestra
(Sonny Burke: 3/22/14 – 1979)

CAN I BE SURE? (Vocal: Lynne Sherman) / CARRY ME BACK TO OLD VIRGINNY (Vocal: Ken Meisel).......... *Okeh 5873* 2-4 40

COUNT BASICALLY, THE / MORE THAN YOU KNOW .... *Okeh 5955* 3-5 40

IF IT WASN'T FOR THE MOON (Vocal: Lynne Sherman) / EASY DOES IT.......... *Vocalion 5397* 3-5 40

I MAY BE WRONG / LAMENT (Vocal: Paul Petrilla).......... *Vocalion 5356* 3-5 39

JIMMIE MEETS THE COUNT / BLUE SONATA (theme song).......... *Okeh 5813* 3-5 40

JUMPIN' SALTY / MINOR DE LUXE....... *Okeh 5989* 3-5 40

LAST JAM SESSION, THE (Vocal: Sonny Burke) / TEA FOR TWO.......... *Vocalion 5139* 3-5 39

MEMORIES OF YOU / ENCHANTED APRIL.......... *Decca 24891* 2-4 50
(Vocals: Dave Howard)

PICK-A-RIB / I NEVER PURPOSELY HURT YOU (Vocal: Paul Petrilla) .... *Vocalion 5459* 3-5 40

TEA FOR TWO / CARRY ME BACK TO OLD VIRGINNY (Vocal: Ken Meisel).... *Conqueror 9640* 3-5 40

BURNS, Allen, & His Orchestra:
see MARTIN, Freddy, & His Orchestra

BURRIS, Johnny, & His Orchestra

I'LL NEVER FORGET (Vocals: Unknown) / SO COMFY.......... *Gennett 6850* 15-20 29

BURROWES, Ben, & His Orchestra

GOIN' TO TOWN / WHEN WE'RE ALONE ... *Brunswick private recording, un-numbered* 15-20 32

BURTNETT, Earl, & His Drake Hotel Orchestra
(Earl Burtnett: 2/7/96 – 1/2/36)

RIDIN' AROUND IN THE RAIN / WAITIN' AT THE GATE FOR KATY .... *Columbia 2921-D* 4-6 34
(Vocals: by trio)

SHE REMINDS ME OF YOU / NEIGHBORS.......... *Columbia 2922-D* 4-6 34
(Vocals: Stanley Hickman)

BURTNETT, Earl, & His Los Angeles / Biltmore Hotel Orchestra

AT LAST I'M IN LOVE / RED HOT RHYTHM.......... *Brunswick 4607* 4-6 29
(Vocals: Unknown)

COURTIN' TIME / 'LEVEN-THIRTY SATURDAY NIGHT.......... *Brunswick 4754* 3-5 30
(Vocals: Unknown)

GO HOME AND TELL YOUR MOTHER / I'M DOIN' THAT THING.......... *Brunswick 4872* 3-5 30
(Vocals: the Biltmore Trio)

GOT A FEELIN' FOR YOU (Vocal: Paul Gibbons) / LOW DOWN RHYTHM (Vocal: June Pursell)... *Brunswick 4376* 3-5 29

MY LITTLE HOME / WHEN ERASTUS PLAYS HIS OLD KAZOO (By The Garden Dancing Palace Orchestra).......... *Columbia 1599-D* 3-5 28

ORANGE BLOSSOM TIME (Vocals: The Biltmore Trio) /SINGIN' IN THE RAIN (Vocal: Paul Gibbons).......... *Brunswick 4375* 2-4 29

PARADE OF THE BLUES / REACH OUT FOR A RAINBOW .... *Brunswick 4634* 4-6 30

PLODDIN' ALONG / DO YOU EVER THINK OF ME? .... *Brunswick 4217* 3-5 29
(Vocals: The Biltmore Trio)

RICKETTS / WHY DO YA ROLL THOSE EYES?.......... *Columbia 825-D* 3-5 26

SONG OF THE WANDERER / ON THE ROAD TO MANDALAY.......... *Columbia 787-D* 3-5 26

TREES / IF I SHOULD LOSE YOU... *Columbia 1190-D* 3-5 27

BUSSE'S BUZZARDS:
see BUSSE, Henry

BUSSE, Henry, & His Orchestra
(Henry Busse: 5/19/94 – 4/23/55)

ALEXANDER'S RAGTIME BAND / MY MELANCHOLY BABY.......... *Decca 1015* 3-5 36

BEER BARREL POLKA (Vocals: by trio) / HOT PRETZELS (Vocals: Dick Wharton & Trio).... *Decca 2453* 2-4 39

CHANGES / AUNT HAGAR'S BLUES ..... *Decca 1207* 4-6 37

HAUNTING BLUES (Vocals: Unknown) / BE YOURSELF.......... *Decca 3443* 3-5 40

HE'S JUST A HORN-TOOTIN' FOOL / IDA, SWEET AS APPLE CIDER .... *Decca 789* 4-6 36

HOT LIPS (opening theme) / JEALOUS.......... *Columbia 2937-D* 5-8 34

IF THE MOON TURNS GREEN (Vocal: Steve Bowers) / TWO SEATS IN THE BALCONY (Vocal: Carl Grayson).......... *Decca 398* 4-6 35

IT SERVES ME RIGHT (Vocal: Billy Sherman) / NOTHING BUT .... *Decca 3407* 2-4 40

MAMA'S GONE, GOODBYE (Vocals: by quartet) / TISHOMINGO BLUES .... *Decca 4325* 2-4 41

ONE STEP TO HEAVEN (Vocals: The Four Recorders) / HOW ABOUT IT? .... *Victor 21674* 2-4 28

RAINBOW 'ROUND THE MOON (Vocal: Skip Morr) / HAVE YOU FORGOTTEN SO SOON? (Vocal: Don Huston) .... *Decca 2126* 2-4 38

SMOOTH SAILING (Vocal: Carl Grayson) / WHOSE HONEY ARE YOU? .... *Decca 399* 4-6 35

STOMPING ROOM ONLY / THE LADY IN RED .... *Decca 3975* 3-5 41

THRILL ME / I SURRENDER, DEAR .... *Victor 22658* 2-4 31 (Vocals: Richard Barry)

WANG-WANG BLUES / HOT LIPS .... *Decca 198* 3-5 34

'WAY DOWN YONDER IN NEW ORLEANS / THE DARKTOWN STRUTTER'S BALL ... *Decca 440* 4-6 34

WEARY BLUES / DOWN HOME RAG ..... *Decca 2976* 3-5 40

WHEN DAY IS DONE (closing theme) / ON THE ALAMO .... *Decca 774* 3-5 36

WHO BLEW OUT THE FLAME? (Vocal: Don Huston) / MY HEART IS UNEMPOYED (Vocal: Skip Morr) .... *Decca 2106* 2-4 38

BUSSE, Henry, as Busse's Buzzards

DEEP ELM (YOU TELL 'EM I'M BLUE) / — .... *Victor 19727* 4-6 25

MONKEY DOODLE-DOO / — .... *Victor 19934* 4-6 26

RED-HOT HENRY BROWN / MILENBERG JOYS .... *Victor 19782* 4-6 25

BUTTERFIELD, Billy, & His Orchestra

(Billy Butterfield: 1/14/17 –)

AFTERNOON IN AUGUST / MALAGUENA .... *Capitol 15127* 2-4 48

HOW AM I TO KNOW? / MORE THAN YOU KNOW .... *Capitol 815* 2-4 50

MOONLIGHT IN VERMONT / THERE GOES THAT SONG AGAIN .... *Capitol 182* 2-4 45

NARCISSUS / BUGLE CALL RAG .... *Capitol 475* 3-5 47

SOONER OR LATER (Vocal: Pat O'Connor) / STARDUST .... *Capitol 305* 2-4 46

STEAMROLLER (Vocal: Billy Butterfield) / JALOUSIE .... *Capitol 335* 2-4 46

STELLA BY STARLIGHT / MAYBE YOU'LL BE THERE .... *Capitol 397* 2-4 47

WE COULD MAKE SUCH BEAUTIFUL MUSIC (Vocal: Pat Flaherty) / AIN'T MISBEHAVIN' (Vocal: Billy Butterfield) .... *Capitol 371* 2-4 47

WHAT'S NEW (theme song) / WILD OATS .... *Capitol 15186* 2-4 48

BYERS, Hale, & His Orchestra

ROSES / WHEN THE RED, RED ROBIN COMES BOB, BOB, BOBBIN' ALONG .... *Vocalion 15370* 5-8 26

SEA LEGS / CLAP HANDS! HERE COMES CHARLEY .... *Brunswick 3092* 5-8 26

SO DOES YOUR OLD MANDARIN / TENTIN' DOWN IN TENNESEE .... *Brunswick 3108* 5-8 26

BYRNE, Bobby, & His Orchestra

(Bobby Byrne: 10/10/18 –)

(Jimmy Palmer or De Palma, vocalist on several of the following releases, led his own very successful dance band through the 1960s, and singer Stuart Wade became an actor.)

ANGELUS RINGS AGAIN, THE / NOW AND FOREVER .... *Decca 4306* 2-4 42 (Vocals: Jimmy Palmer)

BRAZILIAN NUTS / BOBBY'S TROMBONE BLUES .... *Decca 3648* 3-5 41 (Vocals: Kay Little)

CAN'T WE BE FRIENDS? (Vocal: Jimmy De Palma) / TWO LITTLE DOODLE BUGS (Vocal: Dorothy Claire) .... *Decca 2956* 2-4 40

DANNY BOY (theme song) / MARIA ELENA (Vocal: Jimmy Palmer) .... *Decca 3442* 2-4 40

HOW CAN YOU PRETEND? (Vocal: Jimmy Palmer) / EASY DOES IT (Vocal: Dorothy Claire) .... *Decca 3020* 2-4 40

HOW MANY TIMES? (Vocal: Dorothy Claire) / BARNYARD CAKEWALK .... *Decca 3108* 2-4 40

IF I COULD BE THE DUMMY ON YOUR KNEE / SLOW FREIGHT .... *Decca 3123* 2-4 40 (Vocals: Dorothy Claire)

I FOUND A MILLION-DOLLAR BABY (Vocal: Dorothy Claire) / ON THE BEACH AT WAIKIKI ... *Decca 3771* 2-4 41

I'LL PRAY FOR YOU / BLUE TAHITIAN MOON .... *Decca 4302* 2-4 42 (Vocals: Jimmy Palmer)

IT'S YOU AGAIN (Vocal: Dorothy Claire) / I WENT OUT OF MY WAY (Vocal: Stuart Wade) .... *Decca 3969* 2-4 41

MUSIC MAKERS / WHEN YOU AND I WERE YOUNG, MAGGIE .... *Decca 3739* 3-5 41

NIGHTY NIGHT (Vocal: Dorothy Claire) / DO I WORRY? (Vocal: Stuart Wade) .... *Decca 3773* 2-4 41

SPEAKING OF HEAVEN / MAKE WITH THE KISSES .... *Decca 2815* 2-4 39 (Vocals: Jimmy De Palma)

THAT'S FOR ME (Vocal: Dorothy Claire) / ONLY FOREVER (Vocal: Jimmy Palmer) .... *Decca 3313* 2-4 40

THESE THINGS YOU LEFT ME / TWO HEARTS THAT PASS IN THE NIGHT .... *Decca 3774* 2-4 41 (Vocals: Stuart Wade)

THINKING OF YOU (Vocal: Jimmy Palmer) / 'DEED I DO (Vocal: Dorothy Claire) .... *Decca 3170* 2-4 40

'WAY BACK IN 1939 A. D. (Vocal: Jimmy Palmer) / BUSY AS A BEE (Vocal: Dorothy Claire) .... *Decca 3028* 2-4 40

WHAT WORD IS SWEETER THAN SWEETHEART? / I GUESS I'LL HAVE TO DREAM THE REST .... *Decca 3906* 2-4 41 (Vocals: Stuart Wade)

WHEN THE SWALLOWS COME BACK TO CAPISTRANO (Vocal: Jimmy Palmer) / STOP PRETENDING (Vocal: Dorothy Claire) ...... *Decca 3278* 2-4 40

YOU WALK BY / CHAPEL IN THE VALLEY .... *Decca 3613* 2-4 41 (Vocals: Jerry Wayne)

CALIFORNIA COLLEGIANS, The:
see HALL, Fred, as Fred Hall's Jazz Band

CALIFORNIA RAMBLERS, The
(Managed/directed by Wallace T. "Ed" Kirkeby: 10/10/91 – 6/78)
(Some of the best music of the 1920s was produced by the California Ramblers, whose membership included, at various times, the Dorsey Brothers, Jimmy and Tommy, Glenn Miller, Sylvester Ahola, Sterling Boze, and Red Nichols.)

BEES KNEES / TEDDY BEAR BLUES .... *Paramount 21074* 4-6 23
BEES KNEES / TOOT-TOOT-TOOTSIE .... *Bell P-191* 3-5 23
BIG BOY / CHARLEY, MY BOY ...... *Columbia 179-D* 2-4 24
BY THE SAPPHIRE SEA / LONESOME HOURS .... *Bell P-143* 4-6 22

CALIFORNIA / PICK ME UP AND LAY ME DOWN IN DEAR OLD DIXIELAND (by Brown's Dixieland Orchestra, a pseudonym ofr an unidentified band; Vocal: Arthur Hall) .... *Famous 3110* 3-5 22
CASEY JONES / STEAMBOAT BILL .... *Pathe Actuelle 36650* 4-6 27
(Vocals: The Collegiate Rockers)
CASEY JONES / STEAMBOAT BILL .... *Perfect 14831* 3-5 27
(Vocals: The Collegiate Rockers)
(Simultaneously released on two labels)
COPENHAGEN / GOTTA GETTA GIRL .... *Columbia 236-D* 3-5 24
DANCING FOOL / PHAROAH LAND .... *Perfect 14035* 2-4 22
DELIRIUM / FAREWELL BLUES ...... *Domino 4014* 4-6 27
DELIRIUM / FAREWELL BLUES .... *Regal 8376* 4-6 27
(Simultaneously released on two labels)
DOWN SOUTH CAMP MEETING / TAKE MY WORD .... *Variety 577* 3-5 37
EDDIE LEONARD BLUES / MY MAMMY KNOWS .... *Vocalion 14300* 2-4 22
GEE, BUT I HATE TO GO HOME ALONE / COW BELLS .... *Perfect 14075* 2-4 22
GONE AGAIN GAL (Vocal: Ernest Hare) / SHE KNOWS HER ONIONS (Vocal: Ed Kirkeby) .... *Columbia 758-D* 3-5 26
HEART-BREAKIN' BABY (Vocal: Ed Kirkeby) / — .... *Pathe Actuelle 366* 4-6 27
HEART-BREAKIN' BABY (Vocal: Ed Kirkeby) / — .... *Perfect 14874* 3-5 27
(Simultaneously released on two labels)
HOT LIPS / NOBODY LIED .... *Bell P-159* 3-5 22
I'D CLIMB THE HIGHEST MOUNTAIN / UNDER THE UKULELE TREE .... *Columbia 610-D* 3-5 26
I LOVE ME (I'M WILD ABOUT MYSELF) / WHO'S SORRY NOW? .... *Broadway 11233* 3-5 23
I LOVE ME (I'M WILD ABOUT MYSELF) / WHO'S SORRY NOW? .... *Paramount 20227* 4-6 23
(Simultaneously released on two labels)
I LOVE THE COLLEGE GIRLS / IF I DIDN'T KNOW YOUR HUSBAND .... *Pathe Actuelle 36592* 3-5 27
(Vocals: Ernest Hare & Irving Kaufman)
I LOVE THE COLLEGE GIRLS / IF I DIDN'T KNOW YOUR HUSBAND .... *Perfect 14773* 2-4 27
(Vocals: Ernest Hare & Irving Kaufman)
(Simultaneously released on two labels)
I LOVE YOU SO MUCH / F'R INSTANCE .... *Columbia 2231-D* 4-6 30
(Vocals: Smith Ballew)
I'M NEEDIN' YOU / WASHIN' THE BLUES FROM MY SOUL .... *Columbia 2208-D* 4-6 30
(Vocals: Smith Ballew)
JUST A LITTLE DRINK / DROMEDARY .... *Columbia 340-D* 5-8 25
KEEP IT UNDER YOUR HAT / LONG-LOST MAMA .... *Paramount 20232* 5-8 23
LADY LUCK / (I'M A DREAMER) AREN'T WE ALL? .... *Edison 14083* 12-15 29
(Vocals: The Smith Ballew Trio)
(A rare lateral-cut thin Edison disc)
LAZY WEATHER / VO-DO-DO-DE-O BLUES .... *Columbia 1038-D* 4-6 27
(Vocals: Ed Kirkeby)
LONESOME MAMA BLUES / I WISH I COULD SHIMMY LIKE MY SISTER KATE ... *Vocalion 14486* 3-5 22
LOOK-A WHAT I GOT NOW / TESSIE, STOP TEASING ME .... *Broadway 11421* 4-6 24
(Vocals: Arthur Hall)
LOOK-A WHAT I GOT NOW / TESSIE, STOP TEASING ME .... *Carnival 11421* 5-8 24
(Vocals: Arthur Hall)
LOOK-A WHAT I GOT NOW / TESSIE, STOP TEASING ME .... *Hudson 11421* 5-8 24
(Vocals: Arthur Hall)
LOOK-A WHAT I GOT NOW / TESSIE, STOP TEASING ME .... *Lyraphone 11421* 4-6 24
(Vocals: Arthur Hall)
LOOK-A WHAT I GOT NOW / TESSIE, STOP TEASING ME .... *Puretone 11421* 5-8 24
(Vocals: Arthur Hall)
LOOK-A WHAT I GOT NOW / TESSIE, STOP TEASING ME .... *Triangle 11421* 4-6 24
(Vocals: Arthur Hall)
(Simultaneously released on six labels)
LOUISVILLE / THAT BIG BLONDE MAMA .... *Columbia A-3979* 3-5 23
MAMA LOVES PAPA, PAPA LOVES MAMA / YOU DARLING YOU .... *Perfect 14182* 3-5 23
MY HONEY LOVIN' ARMS / WHO ..... *Vocalion 14329* 3-5 22
MY MAMMY KNOWS / WHILE MIAMI DREAMS .... *Okeh 4547* 3-5 22
MY SWEETIE WENT AWAY / I LOVE ME (I'M WILD ABOUT MYSELF) ...... *Columbia A-3956* 2-4 23
OH! LADY, BE GOOD / SWANEE BUTTERFLY .... *Columbia 293-D* 3-5 25
PEANUT VENDOR / TWENTY SWEDES RAN THROUGH THE WEEDS (CHASING ONE NORWEGIAN) .... *Columbia 2351-D* 4-6 31
(Vocals: by chorus)
PLEASE / CHARLESTON CABIN .... *Columbia 171-D* 2-4 24
RHYTHM AND ROMANCE / THE SIMPLE THINGS IN LIFE .... *Bluebird B-6076* 4-6 35
(Vocals: Ed Kirkeby as Ted Wallace)
ROAMIN' TO WYOMIN'/KAINTUCKY ... *Columbia 39-D* 3-5 24
SAY IT WHILE DANCING / PARADE OF THE WOODEN SOLDIERS .... *Cameo 252* 2-4 22
SHEIK, THE / GEORGIA ROSE .... *Vocalion 14275* 3-5 22
SHINE / IT HAD TO BE YOU .... *Columbia 127-D* 3-5 24
SMILIN' / BOW WOW BLUES .... *Columbia A-3554* 3-5 22
SONYA (Vocal: Billy Jones) / I'M GONNA CHARLESTON BACK TO CHARLESTON .... *Columbia 419-D* 5-8 25
SWANEE BLUE BIRD / NO USE CRYING .... *Columbia A-3635* 2-4 22
SWINGIN' DOWN TO RIO / CHRIS AND HIS GANG .... *Variety 603* 5-8 37
TAKE A LITTLE ONE-STEP / ON SUCH A NIGHT .... *Columbia 91-D* 2-4 24
TELL ALL THE FOLKS IN KENTUCKY / SITTIN' IN A CORNER (Vocal: Arthur Hill as Arthur Grant) .... *Perfect 14172* 3-5 23
WHEN YOU'RE COUNTING THE STARS ALONE / PRETTY LITTLE YOU ...... *Edison 14072* 12-15 29
(A rare lateral-cut thin Edison disc)
WHEN YOU'RE NEAR / YOU GAVE ME YOUR HEART .... *Perfect 14060* 2-4 22
WHO COULD BE MORE WONDERFUL THAN YOU? (Vocal: Irving Kaufman) / WHAT-CHA-MA-CALL-IT ...... *Pathe Actuelle 36509* 3-5 26
WHY SHOULD I CRY OVER YOU / SWEET INDIANA HOME .... *Perfect 14057* 2-4 22
YA GOTTA KNOW HOW TO LOVE (Vocal: Arthur Fields) / I'M JUST WILD ABOUT ANIMAL CRACKERS (Vocal: Frank Harris) .... *Columbia 669-D* 3-5 26
YOU DARLING YOU / MELANCHOLY .... *Columbia 9-D* 2-4 23
YOU KNOW ME, ALABAM' / WHERE THE DREAMY WABASH FLOWS .... *Columbia 153-D* 2-4 24
YOU'VE SIMPLY GOT ME CUCKOO / IF I CAN'T GET THE SWEETIE I WANT .... *Columbia A-3986* 2-4 23

CALIFORNIA RAMBLERS, The, as The Big City Six Orchestra

LOOK-A WHAT I GOT NOW / TESSIE, STOP TEASING ME .... *Grey Gull 1234* 4-6 24
(Vocals: Arthur Hall)
LOOK-A WHAT I GOT NOW / TESSIE, STOP TEASING ME .... *Radiex 1234* 4-6 24
(Vocals: Arthur Hall)
(Simultaneously released on two labels)

CALIFORNIA RAMBLERS, The, as The Golden Gate Orchestra

BEALE STREET BLUES / FAREWELL BLUES .... *Banner 6048* 5-8 27
BUTTON UP YOUR OVERCOAT / I WANT TO BE BAD .... *Edison 52513* 8-10 29
(Vocals: Jack Parker)
CHEATIN' ON ME (Vocal: Vernon Dalhart) / WHEN THE MOON SHINES IN CORAL GABLES (Vocal: Charles Hart) .... *Edison 51562* 10-12 25
COULD I? – I CERTAINLY COULD (Vocal: Johnny Ryan) / STATIC STRUT .... *Edison 51746* 5-8 26
CROSS ROADS / ME AND THE MAN IN THE MOON .... *Harmony 778-H* 5-8 28
(Vocals: Billy Murray)
EV'RYTHING IS HOTSY-TOTSY NOW (Vocal: Vernon Dalhart) / THE FLAPPER WIFE (Vocal: Arthur Hall) .... *Edison 51551* 10-12 25
HONEY (Vocal: Ed Kirkeby) / MY SIN ..... *Edison 52580* 5-8 29
I AIN'T GOT NOBODY / THIRD RAIL ... *Edison 52206* 8-10 28
I'M ON THE CREST OF A WAVE / OUT OF THE DAWN .... *Edison 52371* 5-8 28
(Vocals: Unknown)
JELLY ROLL BLUES / I AIN'T GOT NOBODY (Vocal: Ed Kirkeby) .... *Banner 6082* 5-8 27
JUST ANOTHER DAY WASTED AWAY (Vocal: Ed Kirkeby) / ZULU WAIL .... *Banner 6007* 5-8 27

JUST YOU, JUST ME / MARIANNE (by Sam Lanin and His Orchestra) .... *Velvet Tone 1984-V* 4-6 29
(Vocals: Irving Kaufman as Robert Wood)
KEEP SMILING AT TROUBLE / OH! MABEL .... *Edison 51491* 5-8 25
LUCKY ME – LOVABLE YOU / THERE WILL NEVER BE ANOTHER MARY .... *Harmony 1057-H* 5-8 30
(Vocals: Unknown)
MISS ANNABELLE LEE / WHEN ERASTUS PLAYS HIS OLD KAZOO .... *Edison 52075* 5-8 27
MY GAL DON'T LOVE ME ANY MORE / I LIKE PIE, I LIKE CAKE .... *Banner 1502* 4-6 25
(Vocals: Vernon Dalhart)
MY GAL DON'T LOVE ME ANY MORE / I LIKE PIE, I LIKE CAKE .... *Regal 9799* 4-6 25
(Vocals: Vernon Dalhart)
(Simultaneously released on two labels)
MY SUPPRESSED DESIRE (Vocal: Ed Kirkeby) / CRADLE OF LOVE .... *Edison 52550* 4-6 29
MY SWEETER THAN SWEET / ALMA MAMMY .... *Harmony 1045-H* 5-8 29
(Vocals: Irving Kaufman)
PAINTING THE CLOUDS WITH SUNSHINE / TIP-TOE THRU' THE TULIPS .... *Harmony 947-H* 3-5 29
(Vocals: Unknown)
READY FOR THE RIVER (Vocal: Ed Kirkeby) / 'CAUSE I FEEL LOW-DOWN .... *Harmony 704-H* 4-6 28
RIGHT KIND OF MAN, THE / CHANT OF THE JUNGLE .... *Harmony 1016-H* 5-8 29
(Vocals: Jim Andrews)
SHOO SHOO BOOGIE BOO / DO I KNOW WHAT I'M DOIN? .... *Harmony 995-H* 3-5 29
(Vocals: Irving Kaufman)
SONG OF THE BLUES (Vocal: Phil Dewey) / BROKEN IDOL .... *Edison 52638* 5-8 29
STOCKHOLM STOMP / SIDEWALK BLUES .... *Edison 51897* 10-12 27
SWEET MAN / BROWN EYES, WHY ARE YOU BLUE? .... *Edison 51622* 5-8 25
THERE'S A RAINBOW 'ROUND MY SHOULDER (Vocal: Jack Parker) / FOREVER .... *Edison 52437* 4-6 28
WHAT A MAN! / SHAKE .... *Edison 51737* 5-8 26
WHO WOULDN'T BE JEALOUS OF YOU / WEARY RIVER .... *Harmony 839-H* 5-8 29
(Vocals: John Ryan)
YES SHE DO (NO SHE DON'T) (Vocal: Jack Kaufman) / Hallelujah (Vocal: Arthur Fields) .... *Edison 52014* 4-6 27
YOU WILL COME BACK TO ME / YOU CAN'T STOP ME FROM FALLING IN LOVE WITH YOU .... *Harmony 1123-H* 4-6 30
(Vocals: Arthur Fields)

CALIFORNIA RAMBLERS, The, as The Golden Gate Syncopators

LIMEHOUSE BLUES / TIN ROOF BLUES .... *Bell P-278* 5-8 24

CALIFORNIA RAMBLERS, The, as The Goofus Five & Their Orchestra

I CAN'T GIVE YOU ANYTHING BUT LOVE / READY FOR THE RIVER .... *Okeh 41069* 5-8 28
(Vocals: Scrappy Lambert)
MAMA'S GROWN YOUNG, PAPA'S GROWN OLD / RIGHT OR WRONG .... *Okeh 41110* 5-8 28
(Vocals: Scrappy Lambert)
MY BLACKBIRDS ARE BLUEBIRDS NOW / SONNY BOY .... *Okeh 41138* 4-6 28
(Vocals: Irving Kaufman)
RAMBLING WRECK FROM GEORGIA TECH / ALMA MATER GEORGIA TECH .... *Okeh 41177* 5-8 29
(Vocals: by trio)
VANITEASER / ALL OF THE TIME ...... *Okeh 41113* 4-6 28
(Vocals: Ed Kirkeby as Ted Wallace)

CALIFORNIA RAMBLERS, The, as The Little Ramblers

CROSS WORDS BETWEEN MY SWEETIE AND ME / DON'T BRING LULU .... *Columbia 346-D* 5-8 25
(Vocals: Billy Jones)
DEEP BLUE SEA BLUES / I'M SATISFIED BESIDE THAT SWEETIE O' MINE .... *Columbia 217-D* 5-8 24
I'M ON A SEE-SAW (Vocal: Ward Pinkett) / I'M PAINTING THE TOWN RED .... *Bluebird B-6130* 8-10 35

LOOK WHO'S HERE! / GOT NO TIME... *Columbia 403-D* 5-8 25
MELANCHOLY LOU / DEEP ELM.... *Columbia 423-D* 5-8 25
PLAY IT, RED / SWAMP BLUES.... *Columbia 1103-D* 5-8 27
STREAMLINED GRETNA GREEN / LOVELESS LOVE................ *Bluebird B-6043* 5-8 35
(Vocals: Fred McElmurry)
THOSE PANAMA MAMAS / PRINCE OF WAILS....................... *Columbia 248-D* 5-8 25

CALIFORNIA RAMBLERS, The, as The McAlpineers

RHAPSODY IN RHYTHM / RED HOT... *Edison 52266* 10-12 28

CALIFORNIA RAMBLERS, The, as The Paramounteers

MY SWEETER THAN SWEET / ALMA MAMMY..................... *Publix 1055-P* 10-12 29
(Vocals: Irving Kaufman)

CALIFORNIA RAMBLERS, The, as The Rockaway Ramblers

WHO COULD ME MORE WONDERFUL THAN YOU? (Vocal: Irving Kaufman) / WHAT-CHA-MA-CALL-IT............ *Perfect 14690* 3-5 26

CALIFORNIA RAMBLERS, The, as The Seven Blue Babies

COLLEGIATE SAM / I'M KEEPING COMPANY NOW.................... *Edison 14081* 15-20 29
(Vocals: Jack Kaufman as Jack Dalton)
(A rare lateral-cut Edison thin disc)
HEAVEN HELP A SAILOR ON A NIGHT LIKE THIS / OUTSIDE.............. *Edison 52528* 5-8 29
(Vocals: Jack Kaufman as Jack Dalton)
I'M CUCKOO AGAIN / I DON'T WORK FOR A LIVING............... *Edison 14030* 12-15 29
(Vocals: Jack Kaufman as Jack Dalton)
(A rare lateral-cut Edison thin disc)
I'M CUCKOO AGAIN / I DON'T WORK FOR A LIVING............... *Edison 52621* 5-8 29
(Vocals: Jack Kaufman as Jack Dalton)
I'M WILD ABOUT HORNS ON AUTOMOBILES / I LOVE TO BUMPITY BUMP ON A BUMPY ROAD WITH YOU.......................... *Edison 52508* 8-10 29
(Vocals: Jack Kaufman)
IT GOES LIKE THIS (THAT FUNNY MELODY) / NAGASAKI...... *Edison 52405* 8-10 28
(Vocals: Jack Kaufman)
MY WIFE IS ON A DIET / BESSIE COULDN'T HELP IT................ *Edison 14047* 15-20 29
(Vocals: Jack Kaufman as Jack Dalton)
(A rare lateral-cut Edison thin disc)
PLEASE DON'T CUT OUT MY SAUERKRAUT / IF I GIVE UP THE SAXOPHONE.......... *Edison 52556* 5-8 29
(Vocals: Jack Kaufman as Jack Dalton)
PLEASE DON'T CUT OUT MY SAUERKRAUT / IF I GIVE UP THE SAXOPHONE.......... *Edison 14011* 15-20 29
(Vocals: Jack Kaufman as Jack Dalton)
(A rare lateral-cut Edison thin disc)
SHE'S A GOOD GIRL / THE WHOOPEE HAT BRIGADE...................... *Edison 52583* 5-8 29
(Vocals: Jack Kaufman as Jack Dalton)
SINCE SHE LEARNED TO RIDE A HORSE / MAMA'S GROWN YOUNG – PAPA'S GROWN OLD...................... *Edison 52323* 5-8 28
(Vocals: Jack Kaufman)
THAT'S MY WEAKNESS NOW / BUTTERNUT....................... *Edison 52364* 5-8 28
(Vocals. Jack Kaufman)
THERE OUGHT TO BE A LAW AGAINST THAT / THE GRASS GROWS GREENER.......... *Edison 52209* 5-8 28
(Vocals: Jack Kaufman)
TINKER, TAILOR, SOLDIER, SAILOR / WHAT'S THE COLOR OF A "YELLOW" HORSE? .... *Edison 52298* 5-8 28
(Vocals: Jack Kaufman)

CALIFORNIA RAMBERS, The, as The Six Black Diamonds

AM I TO BLAME / YOU KNOW YOU BELONG TO SOMEONE ELSE........ *Banner 1166* 3-5 23

CALIFORNIA RAMBERS, The, as The University Six

(The University Six was a small, "hot" dance unit with members from the California Ramblers)

BLESS HER LITTLE HEART / AIN'T THAT A GRAND & GLORIOUS FEELING?.......... *Harmony 444-H* 3-5 27
(Vocals: Arthur Fields)
CAMEL WALK / SHE WAS JUST A SAILOR'S SWEETHEART .... *Harmony 36-H* 4-6 25
(Vocals: Arthur Hall)
GRASS GROWS GREENER, THE / LET A SMILE BE YOUR UMBRELLA................ *Harmony 581-H* 3-5 28
(Vocals: Dolly Kaye)
IN YOUR GREEN HAT (Vocals: by orchestra) / I LOVE MY BABY .... *Harmony 73-H* 3-5 26
IS SHE MY GIRL FRIEND? / THE BEGGAR.................. *Harmony 534-H* 3-5 27
(Vocals: Arthur Fields)
I WISH I COULD SHIMMY LIKE MY SISTER KATE / BEALE STREET BLUES.......... *Harmony 414-H* 5-8 27
MY BABY KNOWS HOW (Vocal: Arthur Fields) / LONELY EYES.................. *Harmony 296-H* 5-8 26
NOBODY BUT / IT'S O.K., KATY, WITH ME..................... *Harmony 382-H* 4-6 27
(Vocals: Hal White)
OH! IF I ONLY HAD YOU / I AIN'T GOT NOBODY.................... *Harmony 230-H* 5-8 26
OH LIZZIE (Vocal: Hal White) / THE CAT......................... *Harmony 367-H* 4-6 27
ROAM ON MY LITTLE GYPSY SWEETHEART (Vocals: Unknown) / SWANEE SHORE .... *Harmony 466-H* 3-5 27
SLOW RIVER / LAZY WEATHER .... *Harmony 433-H* 5-8 27
(Vocals: Arthur Fields)
SMILE A LITTLE BIT / THEN I'LL BE HAPPY .... *Harmony 71-H* 4-6 26
SO LONG, PAL (Vocals: Athur Fields) / ROSY CHEEKS (Vocals: Hal White)..................... *Harmony 399-H* 3-5 27
SPEEDY BOY / SHE'S THE SWEETHEART OF SIX OTHER GUYS................ *Harmony 619-H* 4-6 28
(Vocals: Jack Kaufman)
STAY OUT OF THE SOUTH / LILA... *Harmony 617-H* 4-6 28
(Vocals: Arthur Fields)
THAT'S A GOOD GIRL / GIVE ME A UKULELE AND A UKULELE BABY .... *Harmony 262-H* 5-8 26
THERE'S SOMETHING SPANISH IN YOUR EYES / CHANGES.......... *Harmony 551-H* 3-5 28
(Vocals: Arthur Fields)
TIGER RAG / SAN................. *Harmony 224-H* 5-8 26
WAIT'LL YOU SEE (MY BRAND NEW MAMA) / IT TAKES A GOOD WOMAN (Vocal: Arthur Fields)................. *Harmony 316-H* 5-8 26
WHAT A MAN! (Vocal: Arthur Fields) / SITTIN' AROUND................. *Harmony 160-H* 4-6 26
WHAT DO YOU SAY? / YOU GOTTA BE GOOD TO ME................. *Harmony 591-H* 3-5 28
(Vocals: Jane Gray)
WHEN YOU'RE WITH SOMEBODY ELSE / MINE – ALL MINE .... *Harmony 565-H* 3-5 28
(Vocals: Arthur Fields)
WHO'S THAT KNOCKIN' AT MY DOOR? / OH DORIS! WHERE DO YOU LIVE? .... *Harmony 489-H* 3-5 27
(Vocals: Arthur Fields)
YES SHE DO – NO SHE DON'T (Vocal: Hal White) / SHE'S GOT "IT" (Vocal: Arthur Fields) .... *Harmony 425-H* 4-6 27

CALIFORNIA RAMBERS, The, as The Vagabonds

AFTER MY LAUGHTER CAME TEARS / DOLORES .... *Silvertone 8063* 4-6 28
(Vocals: Jerry White)
AFTER MY LAUGHTER CAME TEARS / DOLORES .... *Supertone 9000* 4-6 28
(Vocals: Jerry White)
(Simultaneously released on two labels)
COVER ME UP WITH THE SUNSHINE OF VIRGINIA / CALIFORNIA HERE I COME............................ *Gennett 5362* 5-8 24
DID YOU MEAN IT? (Vocals: Al King & Joe Griffith) / GIRL OF MY DREAMS (Vocal: Joe Griffith) ... *Silvertone 8053* 3-5 28
DID YOU MEAN IT? (Vocals: Al King & Joe Griffith) / GIRL OF MY DREAMS (Vocal: Joe Griffith) ... *Supertone 9004* 3-5 28
(Simultaneously released on two labels)
FROM ONE TILL TWO (Vocals: Vernon Dalhart) / DON'T MIND THE RAIN............ *Gennett 5448* 5-8 24
GIMME A LI'L KISS, WILL YA, HUH? / COULD I? I CERTAINLY COULD............... *Gennett 3282* 5-8 26
(Vocals: Arthur Fields)
I WANT TO BE HAPPY / DREARY WEATHER................ *Gennett 5539* 5-8 24
I WONDER WHAT'S BECOME OF SALLY? / NOBODY'S CHILD .... *Gennett 5501* 5-8 24
JEALOUS / SHINE.................... *Gennett 5447* 5-8 24
KNOCK AT THE DOOR / LOUISE .... *Gennett 5502* 5-8 24
NANCY / I DON'T KNOW WHY .... *Gennett 5568* 4-6 24
OH! BABY (Vocal: Jerry White) / HE'S WORTH HIS WEIGHT IN GOLD (Vocal: Al Lynch) ... *Silvertone 8068* 4-6 28
ON THE RIVIERA (Vocal: Arthur Fields) / THE BIRTH OF THE BLUES....................... *Gennett 3361* 5-8 26

ROSE MARIE / COLD MAMAS (BURN ME UP) (by Sam Lanin as Bailey's Lucky Seven) .... *Gennett 5540* 5-8 24
SOMEBODY LIKE YOU / I CAN'T STOP BABYING YOU................ *Gennett 5630* 5-8 25
SWEET BUTTER / SITTIN' IN A CORNER....................... *Gennett 5291* 5-8 23
SWEET MAN / MY SWEETIE TURNED ME DOWN .... *Gennett 3137* 5-8 25
SWEET MAN / MY SWEETIE TURNED ME DOWN .... *Silvertone 4004* 4-6 25
(Simultaneously released on two labels)
WHERE THE DREAMY WABASH FLOWS / PLEASE.................... *Gennett 5485* 4-6 24

CALIFORNIA RAMBERS, The, as The Vagabonds recorded under the name The Dixie Boys

I WANT TO BE HAPPY / DREARY WEATHER............. *Claxtonola 40373* 5-8 24
KNOCK AT THE DOOR / LOUISE ... *Claxtonola 40342* 5-8 24
SOMEBODY LIKE YOU / I CAN'T STOP BABYING YOU.................. *Claxtonola 40412* 5-8 25
SWEET MAN / MY SWEETIE TURNED ME DOWN............. *Champion 15021* 5-8 25

CALIFORNIA RAMBERS, The, as The Vagabonds recorded under the name The Memphis Melody Boys

LOOKING AT THE WORLD THRU' ROSE-COLORED GLASSES / ON THE RIVIERA .... *Buddy 8068* 15-20 26
(Vocals: Arthur Fields)

CALIFORNIA RAMBERS, The, as The Varsity Eight

(The Varsity Eight was a small, "hot" dance unit with members from the California Ramblers)

AIN'T MY BABY GRAND? / I AIN'T GOT NOBODY TO LOVE............... *Cameo 680* 4-6 25

CHEATIN' ON ME / MY SUGAR (by Ace Bigode & His Fourteen Virginians)...................... *Cameo 725* 4-6 25
CHICKEN REEL / FAREWELL BLUES... *Cameo 8141* 5-8 28
CHICKEN REEL / FAREWELL BLUES.... *Romeo 564* 5-8 28
(Simultaneously released on two labels)
DON'T BRING LULU / NOBODY KNOWS WHAT A RED HEAD MAMA CAN DO................ *Cameo 714* 8-10 25
DOO WACKA DOO / HAPPY............. *Cameo 641* 4-6 25
IS SHE MY GIRL FRIEND? (Vocal: Arthur Fields) / I WISH I COULD SHIMMY LIKE MY SISTER KATE.......................... *Cameo 1280* 5-8 28
IS SHE MY GIRL FRIEND? (Vocal: Arthur Fields) / I WISH I COULD SHIMMY LIKE MY SISTER KATE.......................... *Romeo 514* 5-8 28
(Simultaneously released on two labels)
MICKEY MOUSE (YOU CUTE LITTLE FELLER) / POPEYE (THE SAILOR MAN)......... *Perfect 15473* 10-12 31
(Vocals: Unknown)
OH! JOE / SITTIN' IN A CORNER (by Bob Haring & His Velvetone Orchestra) .... *Cameo 420* 2-4 23
OH SAY! CAN I SEE YOU TONIGHT? / I WANT TO SEE A LITTLE MORE OF WHAT I SAW IN ARKANSAS........... *Cameo 772* 5-8 25
STATIC STRUT / YA GOTTA KNOW HOW TO LOVE................. *Cameo 975* 5-8 26

SWEET GEORGIA BROWN /
LADY OF THE NILE .... *Cameo 730* 5-8 25

THOSE PANAMA MAMAS (ARE RUINING ME) /
HOW I LOVE THAT GIRL .... *Cameo 635* 5-8 24

T. N. T. / IN MY
GONDOLA (Vocals: Unknown) .... *Cameo 870* 5-8 26

TOODLE-OO / YOU'RE DRIVING
ME CRAZY .... *Domino 4679* 4-6 30

WHO'S CALLING YOU SWEETHEART TONIGHT? /
WHEN KENTUCKY BIDS THE WORLD
"GOOD MORNING" .... *Domino 4680* 3-5 30
(Vocals: Unknown)

YOU KNOW ME, ALABAM' / I CAN'T GET
THE ONE I WANT .... *Cameo 567* 4-6 24

CALIFORNIA RAMBERS, The, as Ted Wallace & His Campus Boys

ABSENCE MAKES THE HEART GROW FONDER /
HERE COMES THE SUN .... *Columbia 2236-D* 3-5 30
(Vocals: by trio)

BOTTOMS UP / BIGGER AND BETTER
THAN EVER .... *Columbia 1970-D* 5-8 29
(Vocals: Smith Ballew)

CAMPUS CAPERS / COLLEGE
DAYS .... *Columbia 1984-D* 4-6 29
(Vocals: Smith Ballew)

JERICHO / I'VE GOT A
FEELING I'M FALLING .... *Columbia 1833-D* 5-8 29
(Vocals: Smith Ballew)

LUCKY ME – LOVABLE YOU / LOVE AIN'T
NOTHING BUT THE BLUES ...... *Columbia 2046-D* 5-8 29
(Vocals: Smith Ballew)

MEAN TO ME / THE ONE THAT I
LOVE LOVES ME .... *Columbia 1756-D* 3-5 29
(Vocals: Smith Ballew)

MOONLIGHT MARCH /
SWEETNESS .... *Columbia 1908-D* 3-5 29
(Vocals: Smith Ballew)

MY BABY JUST CARES FOR ME /
SWEET JENNIE LEE .... *Columbia 2301-D* 4-6 30
(Vocals: by trio)

MY KINDA LOVE / SWEET
SEVENTEEN .... *Columbia 1791-D* 3-5 29
(Vocals: Smith Ballew)

SITTIN' ON A DOORSTEP / YOU CAME,
I SAW, YOU CONQUERED ME .... *Columbia 2057-D* 5-8 30
(Vocals: Smith Ballew)

SWEETHEARTS' HOLIDAY / HUGGABLE,
KISSABLE YOU .... *Columbia 1938-D* 3-5 29
(Vocals: Smith Ballew)

TOMORROW IS ANOTHER DAY /
DON'T TELL HER .... *Columbia 2275-D* 5-8 30
(Vocals: by trio)

CALIFORNIA RAMBLERS, The, as Ted Wallace & His Orchestra

CHANGES (Vocals: by duet) / FOR MY BABY
(Vocal : Russell Douglas as Les Reis) .... *Okeh 40961* 3-5 28

CORNFED / ZULU WAIL .... *Okeh 40915* 4-6 27

IF ALL THE STARS WERE PRETTY BABIES
(Vocal: Irving Kaufman) / WHEN I FIRST
MET MARY (Vocal: Ed Kirkeby) .... *Okeh 40749* 3-5 27

OH! LIZZIE / THE CAT .... *Okeh 40778* 4-6 27
(Vocals: Russell Douglas as Les Reis)

PLEADING / LOVE AND KISSES .... *Okeh 40850* 3-5 27
(Vocals: Russell Douglas as Les Reis)

SHE'S FUNNY THAT WAY / ALL BY YOURSELF
IN THE MOONLIGHT .... *Domino 4250* 2-4 29
(Vocals: The Radio Imps)

SHE'S FUNNY THAT WAY / ALL BY YOURSELF
IN THE MOONLIGHT .... *Regal 8691* 2-4 29
(Vocals: The Radio Imps)
(Simultaneously released on two labels)

CALIFORNIA RAMBERS, The, as Ted Wallace His Orchestra recorded under the name Ed Loyd & His Orchestra

DIXIANA / MY ONE
AMBITION IS YOU .... *Odeon ONY-36124* 5-8 30
(Vocals: Unknown)

HE'S MY SECRET PASSION / LADY, PLAY
YOUR MANDOLIN .... *Odeon ONY-36177* 5-8 31
(Vocals: Unknown)

LOVABLE AND SWEET / WAITING AT
THE END OF THE ROAD .... *Okeh 41294* 3-5 29
(Vocals: Unknown)

NOBODY CARES IF I'M BLUE /
MYSTERIOUS MOSE .... *Odeon ONY-36081* 8-10 30
(Vocals: Unknown)

ONE IN THE WORLD, THE (Vocals: Unknown) /
AM I BLUE? (by the Dorsey Brothers' Orchestra as the
Travelers; Vocal: Irving Kaufman) .... *Okeh 41259* 5-8 29

PAGAN LOVE SONG / I GET THE BLUES
WHEN IT RAINS .... *Okeh 41250* 3-5 29
(Vocals: Unknown)

SINGING A VAGABOND SONG / THERE'S DANGER
IN YOUR EYES, CHERIE .... *Odeon ONY-36026* 5-8 30
(Vocals: Smith Ballew)

SINGING A VAGABOND SONG / THERE'S DANGER
IN YOUR EYES, CHERIE .... *Okeh 41367* 5-8 30
(Vocals: Smith Ballew)
(Simultaneously released on two labels)

SING SONG GIRL / WALKIN'
MY BABY BACK HOME .... *Odeon ONY-36185* 5-8 31
(Vocals: Unknown)

WOULDN'T IT BE WONDERFUL? / I MAY BE WRONG,
BUT I THINK YOU'RE WONDERFUL ... *Okeh 41312* 5-8 29
(Vocals: Smith Ballew)

WRAPPED IN A RED, RED ROSE /
PUT A LITTLE SALT ON THE
BLUEBIRD'S TAIL .... *Odeon ONY-36023* 5-8 30
(Vocals: Smith Ballew)

WRAPPED IN A RED, RED ROSE /
PUT A LITTLE SALT ON THE
BLUEBIRD'S TAIL .... *Okeh 41354* 5-8 30
(Vocals: Smith Ballew)
(Simultaneously released on two labels)

YOU BROUGHT A NEW KIND OF LOVE TO ME /
LIVING IN THE SUNLIGHT, LOVING IN
THE MOONLIGHT .... *Odeon ONY-36065* 4-6 30
(Vocals: Unknown)

YOU BROUGHT A NEW KIND OF LOVE TO ME /
LIVING IN THE SUNLIGHT, LOVING IN
THE MOONLIGHT .... *Okeh 41407* 4-6 30
(Vocals: Unknown)
(Simultaneously released on two labels)

CALIFORNIA RAMBERS, The, as Ted Wallace & His Orchestra recorded under the name The New York Syncopators

BLESS HER LITTLE HEART / WHO-OO? YOU-OO, THAT'S WHO! .... *Okeh 40860* 4-6 27
(Vocals: Russell Douglas as Les Reis)

MARY (WHAT ARE YOU WAITING FOR?) (Vocal:
Russell Douglas as Les Reis) / COBBLE-STONES
(Vocals: Sammy Fain & Artie Dunn) .... *Okeh 40965* 3-5 28

THERE AIN'T NO MAYBE IN MY BABY'S EYES /
CRAZY WORDS – CRAZY TUNE .... *Okeh 40757* 4-6 27
(Vocals: Ed Kirkeby)

CALLENDER, George "Red" as The Red Callender Sextette

(George "Red" Callender: 3/16/18 –)

Callender is a fine string bassist who performed with many of the best bands, including Luis Russell and His Orchestra, fronted by Louis Armstrong, in 1937-38. Though still in his teens when he joined that group, Red replaced the legendary George "Pops" Foster as bassman during Foster's illness. Callender also plays excellent Tuba, and reportedly was the first to play melody on that horn, rather than using it strictly as a rhythm instrument. In a 1978 interview in the author's home, Callender was questioned in this regard and his reply was, "I've always considered the tuba to be just a fat trumpet, so why not use it to play melody?"

TILL I WALTZ AGAIN WITH YOU / PAPA
(Vocal: Scat Man Crothers) ... *Recorded in Hollywood 142* 10-12 -
(45 rpm)

YES! I KNEW (WHAT YOU'RE PUTTING DOWN)
(Vocal: Linda Hayes) / SISTER ANNE
(music by Que Martyn) .... *Recorded in Hollywood 244* 8-10 -

CALLENDER, George "Red" as The Red Callender Trio

RED BOOGIE / BY THE RIVER
SAINTE MARIE .... *Black & White 782* 5-8 46

RED LIGHT / BE HAPPY
PAPPY .... *Black & White 781* 5-8 46
(Vocals: Unknown)

CALLOWAY, Blanche, & Her Band

(circa 1904 –)

LOUISIANA LIZA / I GOTTA SWING ... *Vocalion 3112* 8-10 36

YOU AIN'T LIVIN' RIGHT (Vocal:
Blanche Calloway) / LINE-A-JIVE ...... *Vocalion 3113* 8-10 36

CALLOWAY, Blanche, & Her Joy Boys

BLUE MEMORIES (Vocal: Blanche Calloway) / SITTIN'
ON A RUBBISH CAN (by Snooks & His Memphis Ramblers
with Julia Gerity; recorded under the name Julia Gerity & Her
Play Boys; vocals: Ken Herlin, Walter Ashby, Elly Bellare, &
Julia Gerity) .... *Victor 22896* 10-12 32

CONCENTRATIN' ON YOU /
LAST DOLLAR .... *Victor 22862* 10-12 32
(Vocals: Blanche Calloway)

I GOT WHAT IT TAKES /
GROWLIN' DAN .... *Victor 22866* 10-12 32
(Vocals: Blanche Calloway)

I'M GETTIN' MYSELF READY
FOR YOU / LOVELESS LOVE .... *Victor 22659* 10-12 31
(Vocals: Blanche Calloway)

I NEED LOVIN' / WHAT'S A POOR
GIRL GONNA DO? .... *Banner 33224* 8-10 34
(Vocals: Blanche Calloway)

I NEED LOVIN' / WHAT'S A POOR
GIRL GONNA DO? .... *Melotone M-13191* 8-10 34
(Vocals: Blanche Calloway)

I NEED LOVIN' / WHAT'S A POOR
GIRL GONNA DO? .... *Oriole 3018* 8-10 34
(Vocals: Blanche Calloway)

I NEED LOVIN' / WHAT'S A POOR
GIRL GONNA DO? .... *Perfect 16010* 8-10 34
(Vocals: Blanche Calloway)

I NEED LOVIN' / WHAT'S A POOR
GIRL GONNA DO? .... *Romeo 2382* 8-10 34
(Vocals: Blanche Calloway)
(Simultaneously released on five labels)

IT LOOKS LIKE SUSIE / WITHOUT
THAT GAL! .... *Victor 22733* 10-12 31
(Vocals: Blanche Calloway)

JUST A CRAZY SONG (Vocal: Blanche Calloway) /
SUGAR BLUES (Vocal: Billy Massey) .... *Victor 22661* 10-12 31

MISERY / IT'S RIGHT
HERE FOR YOU .... *Victor 22717* 10-12 31
(Vocals: Blanche Calloway)

THERE'S RHYTHM IN THE
RIVER / I NEED LOVIN' .... *Victor 22641* 10-12 31
(Vocals: Blanche Calloway)

CALLOWAY, Cab, & His Cotton Club Orchestra

(Cab Calloway: 12/25/07 –)

(Cab Calloway & His Orchestra still play engagements throughout the country)

EVENIN' / HARLEM HOSPITALITY .... *Victor 24414* 5-8 33
(Vocals: Cab Calloway)

LADY WITH THE FAN, THE / FATHER'S GOT
HIS GLASSES ON .... *Victor 24451* 5-8 33
(Vocals: Cab Calloway)

LITTLE TOWN GAL / HARLEM
CAMP MEETING .... *Victor 24494* 5-8 34
(Vocals: Cab Calloway)

'LONG ABOUT MIDNIGHT /
JITTER BUG .... *Victor 24592* 5-8 33
(Vocals: Cab Calloway)

MARGIE / EMALINE .... *Victor 24659* 5-8 33
(Vocals: Cab Calloway)

MOONGLOW / HOTCHA
RAZZ-MA-TAZZ .... *Victor 24690* 5-8 34
(Vocals: Cab Calloway)

SCAT SONG, THE / THERE'S A
CABIN IN THE COTTON .... *Victor 24511* 5-8 34
(Vocals: Cab Calloway)

ZAZ ZUH ZAZ / I LEARNED ABOUT
LOVE FROM HER .... *Victor 24557* 5-8 33
(Vocals: Cab Calloway)

CALLOWAY, Cab, & His Orchestra

AIN'T NO GAL IN THIS
TOWN / TRICKERATION .... *Brunswick 6214* 5-8 31
(Vocals: Cab Calloway)

AT THE CLAMBAKE CARNIVAL / JIVE (PAGE ONE
OF THE HEPSTER'S DICTIONARY)
(Vocal: Cab Calloway) .... *Vocalion 4437* 5-8 38

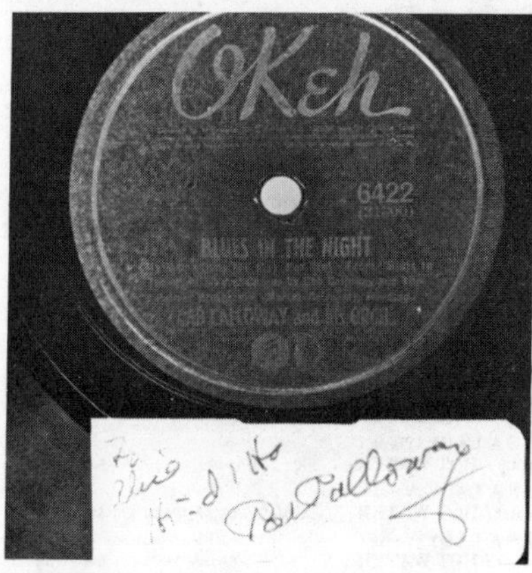

AZURE / PECK-A-DOODLE-DO
(Vocal: Cab Calloway) .... *Vocalion 4100* 5-8 38

BETWEEN THE DEVIL AND THE DEEP BLUE SEA /
KICKIN' THE GONG AROUND .... *Brunswick 6209* 5-8 31
(Vocals: Cab Calloway)

BLACK RHYTHM / SIX OR SEVEN TIMES
(Vocal: Cab Calloway) .... *Brunswick 6141* 5-8 31

BLUE INTERLUDE / TEE-UM, TEE-UM,
TEE-I, TAHITI (Vocal: Cab Calloway) ... *Vocalion 4538* 5-8 38

BLUES IN THE NIGHT / SAYS WHO?
SAYS YOU, SAYS I! .... *Okeh 6422* 5-8 41
(Vocals: Cab Calloway)

BOOGIE-WOOGIE / SHOUT, SHOUT,
SHOUT (Vocal: Cab Calloway) .... *Conqueror 9091* 5-8 38

BUGLE BLUES / FOOLIN'
WITH YOU (Vocal: Cab Calloway) ..... *Conqueror 9090* 5-8 38

BUGLE BLUES / FOOLIN'
WITH YOU (Vocal: Cab Calloway) ...... *Vocalion 4019* 5-8 38
(Simultaneously released on two labels)

BUGLE CALL RAG / YOU RASCAL,
YOU (Vocal: Cab Calloway) .... *Brunswick 6196* 8-10 31

BYE-BYE BLUES / RUN,
LITTLE RABBIT .... *Okeh 6084* 5-8 41
(Vocals: Cab Calloway)

CHICKEN AIN'T NOTHIN' BUT A BIRD /
MAKE YOURSELF AT HOME .... *Okeh 5847* 5-8 40
(Vocals: Cab Calloway)

CHILI CON CONGA (Vocal:
Cab Calloway) / VUELVA .... *Vocalion 5315* 4-6 39

CHINESE RHYTHM / WEAKNESS ... *Brunswick 6992* 5-8 34
(Vocals: Cab Calloway)

CHOP, CHOP, CHARLIE
CHAN / BOOG IT .... *Vocalion 5444* 5-8 40
(Vocals: Cab Calloway)

COME ON WITH THE "COME ON" /
A GHOST OF A CHANCE .... *Okeh 5687* 5-8 40

CONGO-CONGA / THERE'S A SUNNY SIDE TO EVERYTHING.................. *Vocalion 4411* 4-6 38
(Vocals: Cab Calloway)

COPPER-COLORED GAL / THE WEDDING OF MR. AND MRS. SWING............... *Brunswick 7748* 5-8 36
(Vocals: Cab Calloway)

CUPID'S NIGHTMARE / ARE YOU ALL REET? (Vocal: Cab Calloway)........ *Okeh 6035* 5-8 40

DINAH / I'M NOW PREPARED TO TELL THE WORLD IT'S YOU............ *Banner 32483* 5-8 32
(Vocals: Cab Calloway)

DINAH / I'M NOW PREPARED TO TELL THE WORLD IT'S YOU.......... *Melotone M-12489* 5-8 32
(Vocals: Cab Calloway)

DINAH / I'M NOW PREPARED TO TELL THE WORLD IT'S YOU.............. *Oriole 2495* 5-8 32
(Vocals: Cab Calloway)

DINAH / I'M NOW PREPARED TO TELL THE WORLD IT'S YOU............. *Perfect 15623* 5-8 32
(Vocals: Cab Calloway)

DINAH / I'M NOW PREPARED TO TELL THE WORLD IT'S YOU.............. *Romeo 1868* 5-8 32
(Vocals: Cab Calloway)
(Simultaneously released on five labels)

DIXIE DOORWAY / WAH-DEE-DAH ... *Banner 32812* 5-8 32
(Vocals: Cab Calloway)

DIXIE DOORWAY/WAH-DEE-DAH... *Brunswick 6435* 8-10 32
(Vocals: Cab Calloway)

DIXIE DOORWAY / WAH-DEE-DAH..... *Oriole 2727* 5-8 32
(Vocals: Cab Calloway)

DIXIE DOORWAY / WAH-DEE-DAH ... *Perfect 15791* 5-8 32
(Vocals: Cab Calloway)

DIXIE DOORWAY / WAH-DEE-DAH .... *Romeo 2100* 5-8 32
(Vocals: Cab Calloway)
(Simultaneously released on five labels)

DIXIE VAGABOND / SO SWEET....... *Banner 32116* 5-8 31
(Vocals: Cab Calloway)

DIXIE VAGABOND / SO SWEET......... *Jewel 6224* 5-8 31
(Vocals: Cab Calloway)

DIXIE VAGABOND / SO SWEET......... *Oriole 2224* 5-8 31
(Vocals: Cab Calloway)

DIXIE VAGABOND / SO SWEET....... *Perfect 15442* 5-8 31
(Vocals: Cab Calloway)

DIXIE VAGABOND / SO SWEET........ *Regal 10279* 5-8 31
(Vocals: Cab Calloway)

DIXIE VAGABOND / SO SWEET........ *Romeo 1587* 5-8 31
(Vocals: Cab Calloway)
(Simultaneously released on six labels)

DO I CARE? NO, NO / HI-DE-HO SERENADE....................... *Vocalion 5591* 4-6 40
(Vocals: Cab Calloway)

DON'T KNOW IF I'M COMIN' OR GOIN' / WAKE UP AND LIVE................ *Variety 535* 5-8 37
(Vocals: Cab Calloway)

DOWN-HEARTED BLUES / CORINNE CORINNA......................... *Banner 32340* 8-10 32
(Vocals: Cab Calloway)

DOWN-HEARTED BLUES / CORINNE CORINNA........................... *Oriole 2396* 8-10 32
(Vocals: Cab Calloway)

DOWN-HEARTED BLUES / CORINNE CORINNA.......................... *Perfect 15551* 8-10 32
(Vocals: Cab Calloway)

DOWN-HEARTED BLUES / CORINNE CORINNA........................... *Romeo 1766* 8-10 32
(Vocals: Cab Calloway)
(Simultaneously released on four labels)

DO YOU WANNA JUMP, CHILDREN? / APRIL IN MY HEART..................... *Vocalion 4477* 5-8 38
(Vocals: Cab Calloway)

EADIE WAS A LADY (Vocal: Cab Calloway) / HOT WATER.......... *Banner 32647* 5-8 33

EADIE WAS A LADY (Vocal: Cab Calloway) / HOT WATER...... *Melotone M-12583* 5-8 33

EADIE WAS A LADY (Vocal: Cab Calloway) / HOT WATER........... *Oriole 2626* 5-8 33

EADIE WAS A LADY (Vocal: Cab Calloway) / HOT WATER.......... *Perfect 15715* 5-8 33

EADIE WAS A LADY (Vocal: Cab Calloway) / HOT WATER........... *Romeo 1997* 5-8 33
(Simultaneously released on five labels)

EBONY SILHOUETTE / HEP CAT LOVE SONG.......................... *Okeh 6192* 5-8 41
(Vocals: Cab Calloway)

EVERY DAY'S A HOLIDAY / JUBILEE......................... *Vocalion 3896* 4-6 38
(Vocals: Cab Calloway)

F. D. R. JONES (Vocal: Cab Calloway) / ANGELS WITH DIRTY FACES (Vocal: June Richmond).... *Vocalion 4498* 5-8 38

FIFTEEN MINUTE INTERMISSION (Vocal: Cab Calloway) / RHAPSODY IN RHUMBA..... *Okeh 5664* 5-8 40

FOR THE LAST TIME I CRIED OVER YOU (Vocal: Cab Calloway) / TWEE-TWEE-TWEET (Vocals: Unknown)..................... *Vocalion 5126* 4-6 39

FRISCO FLO / THE HI-DE-HO MIRACLE MAN.................. *Brunswick 7756* 5-8 36
(Vocals: Cab Calloway)

GEECHY JOE (Vocal: Cab Calloway) / SPECIAL DELIVERY.................. *Okeh 6147* 5-8 41

GEECHY JOE / ST. JAMES INFIRMARY.......................... *V-Disc 259* 8-10 -
(Vocals: Cab Calloway)
(A World War II release)

GHOST OF SMOKY JOE, THE / FLOOGIE WALK..................... *Vocalion 4807* 5-8 39
(Vocals: Cab Calloway)

GOIN' CONGA / NORTH OF THE MOHAWK TRAIL................ *Okeh 5911* 4-6 40
(Vocals: Cab Calloway)

GOOD SAUCE FROM THE GRAVY BOWL / KEEP THAT HI-DE-HI IN YOUR SOUL... *Brunswick 7386* 5-8 35
(Vocals: Cab Calloway)

GO SOUTH, YOUNG MAN / MAMA, I WANNA MAKE RHYTHM..................... *Variety 644* 5-8 37
(Vocals: Cab Calloway)

HARD TIMES / WHO'S YEHOODI (Vocal: Cab Calloway).................. *Vocalion 5566* 5-8 40

HEY DOC (Vocals: Tyree Glenn & Cab Calloway) / CONCHITA (Vocal: Cab Calloway).......... *Okeh 6354* 4-6 41
(Tyree Glenn was better known for excellent performances at the vibraphone and on trombone. He toured with Ma Rainey, the legendary blues singer, Ethel Waters, and with numerous bands. Also led own groups from time to time.

HOW COME YOU DO ME LIKE YOU DO? / SWANEE LULLABY..... *Banner 32540* 5-8 32
(Vocals: Cab Calloway)

HOW COME YOU DO ME LIKE YOU DO? / SWANEE LULLABY... *Melotone M-12488* 5-8 32
(Vocals: Cab Calloway)

HOW COME YOU DO ME LIKE YOU DO? / SWANEE LULLABY...... *Perfect 15659* 5-8 32
(Vocals: Cab Calloway)
(Simultaneously released on three labels)

I AIN'T GETTIN' NOWHERE FAST / JIVE FORMATION, PLEASE .... *Vocalion 5195* 5-8 39
(Vocals: Cab Calloway)

I AIN'T GOT NOBODY / BABY, WON'T YOU PLEASE COME HOME?........... *Brunswick 7530* 5-8 35
(Vocals: Cab Calloway)

I LOVE TO SING-A / SAVE ME, SISTER............... *Brunswick 7638* 5-8 36
(Vocals: Cab Calloway)

I'M ALWAYS IN THE MOOD FOR YOU / SHE'S TALL, SHE'S TAN, SHE'S TERRIFIC......... *Variety 643* 5-8 37
(Vocals: Cab Calloway)

I'M CRAZY 'BOUT MY BABY / CREOLE LOVE SONG........................ *Perfect 15474* 8-10 31
(Vocals: Cab Calloway)

I'M MADLY IN LOVE WITH YOU (Vocal: Cab Calloway) /DEEP IN A DREAM (Vocal: June Richmond)............... *Conqueror 9127* 5-8 38

I'M MADLY IN LOVE WITH YOU (Vocal: Cab Calloway) / DEEP IN A DREAM (Vocal: June Richmond)................ *Vocalion 4511* 5-8 38

IN AN OLD ENGLISH VILLAGE / ERROR IN THE NEWS.................... *Vocalion 3912* 4-6 38
(Vocals: Cab Calloway)

IS THAT RELIGION? / SOME OF THESE DAYS................... *Brunswick 6020* 5-8 31
(Vocals: Cab Calloway)

IT LOOKS LIKE SUSIE / BASIN STREET BLUES.................. *Banner 32237* 5-8 31
(Vocals: Cab Calloway)

IT LOOKS LIKE SUSIE / BASIN STREET BLUES.................. *Mel-O-Dee 305* 10-12 31
(Vocals: Cab Calloway)

IT LOOKS LIKE SUSIE / BASIN STREET BLUES...................... *Oriole 2317* 5-8 31
(Vocals: Cab Calloway)

IT LOOKS LIKE SUSIE / BASIN STREET BLUES .... *Perfect 15500* 5-8 31
(Vocals: Cab Calloway)

IT LOOKS LIKE SUSIE / BASIN STREET BLUES .... *Romeo 1685* 5-8 31
(Vocals: Cab Calloway)
(Simultaneously released on five labels)

I 'VE GOT THE WORLD ON A STRING / HARLEM HOLIDAYS............ *Brunswick 6424* 5-8 32
(Vocals: Cab Calloway)

I WANT TO ROCK / 'TAIN'T NO GOOD.... *Okeh 6616* 5-8 42
(Vocals: Cab Calloway)

LEEVEE LOW-DOWN / BLUES IN MY HEART..................... *Banner 32221* 5-8 31
(Vocals: Cab Calloway)

LEEVEE LOW-DOWN / BLUES IN MY HEART...................... *Romeo 1671* 5-8 31
(Vocals: Cab Calloway)
(Simultaneously released on two labels)

LEVEE LULLABY / HOT AIR........... *Okeh 5950* 5-8 40

LONG, LONG AGO / AFRAID OF LOVE.......................... *Vocalion 4905* 4-6 39
(Vocals: Cab Calloway)

LOVE IS THE REASON / JES' NATCH'ULLY LAZY......... *Brunswick 7677* 5-8 36
(Vocals: Cab Calloway)

MAN FROM HARLEM, THE / MY SUNDAY GAL................ *Brunswick 6450* 5-8 33
(Vocals: Cab Calloway)

MERMAID SONG, THE / WHO CALLS? ... *Okeh 6501* 4-6 41
(Vocals: Cab Calloway)

MINNIE THE MOOCHER (theme song) / DOIN' THE RHUMBA............. *Brunswick 6074* 5-8 31
(Vocals: Cab Calloway)

MINNIE THE MOOCHER'S WEDDING DAY / ANGELINE.............. *Brunswick 6321* 5-8 32
(Vocals: Cab Calloway)

MISS HALLELUJAH BROWN (Vocal: Cab Calloway) / THE BOOGIE-WOOGIE .... *Vocalion 4400* 5-8 38

MISS OTIS REGRETS / NAGASAKI ... *Brunswick 7504* 5-8 35
(Vocals: Cab Calloway)

MOOD INDIGO / FAREWELL BLUES (Vocal: Cab Calloway) .... *Banner 32152* 5-8 31

MOOD INDIGO / FAREWELL BLUES (Vocal: Cab Calloway) .... *Jewel 6243* 5-8 31

MOOD INDIGO / FAREWELL BLUES (Vocal: Cab Calloway) .... *Melotone 91117* 5-8 31

MOOD INDIGO / FAREWELL BLUES (Vocal: Cab Calloway)............ *Oriole 2243* 5-8 31

MOOD INDIGO / FAREWELL BLUES (Vocal: Cab Calloway) .... *Perfect 15457* 5-8 31

MOOD INDIGO / FAREWELL BLUES (Vocal: Cab Calloway) .... *Regal 10327* 5-8 31

MOOD INDIGO / FAREWELL BLUES (Vocal: Cab Calloway) .... *Romeo 1609* 5-8 31
(Simultaneously released on seven labels)

MOON AT SEA / HI-DE-HO ROMEO.... *Variety 651* 5-8 37
(Vocals: Cab Calloway)

MOONLIGHT RHAPSODY/AVALON... *Brunswick 7411* 5-8 34
(Vocals: Cab Calloway)

MRS. FINNIGAN / MY COO-COO BIRD.... *Okeh 6459* 5-8 41
(Vocals: Cab Calloway)

MY GAL MEZZANINE / CONGO......... *Variety 593* 5-8 37
(Vocals: Cab Calloway)

MY HONEY'S LOVIN' ARMS / THE NIGHTMARE .... *Banner 32227* 5-8 31

MY HONEY'S LOVIN' ARMS / THE NIGHTMARE.................... *Oriole 2302* 5-8 31

MY HONEY'S LOVIN' ARMS / THE NIGHTMARE.................. *Perfect 15494* 5-8 31

MY HONEY'S LOVIN' ARMS / THE NIGHTMARE.................. *Romeo 1677* 5-8 31
(Simultaneously released on four labels)

NAIN, NAIN (Vocal: Cab Calloway) / TAPPIN' OFF.......................... *Okeh 6547* 5-8 41

NEW MOON AND OLD SERENADE, A / ONE LOOK AT YOU............. *Conqueror 9199* 4-6 39
(Vocals: Cab Calloway)

NEW MOON AND OLD SERENADE, A / ONE LOOK AT YOU .... *Vocalion 4767* 4-6 39
(Vocals: Cab Calloway)
(Simultaneously released on two labels)

NOBODY'S SWEETHEART / ST. JAMES' INFIRMARY..................... *Brunswick 6105* 5-8 31
(Vocals: Cab Calloway)

OLD YAZOO (Vocal: Cab Calloway) / HOT TODDY........... *Brunswick 6400* 5-8 32

ONE BIG UNION FOR TWO / DOING THE REACTIONARY............... *Vocalion 3970* 5-8 38
(Vocals: Cab Calloway)

PAPA'S IN BED WITH HIS BRITCHES ON (Vocal: Cab Calloway) / CALLING ALL BARS..... *Okeh 5731* 5-8 40

PECKIN' (Vocal: Cab Calloway) / MANHATTAN JAM................... *Variety 612* 5-8 37

PICKIN' THE CABBAGE (Vocal: Cab Calloway) / PARADIDDLE .... *Vocalion 5467* 5-8 40

PLUCKIN' THE BASS / GIVE, BABY, GIVE (Vocal: Cab Calloway) .... *Conqueror 9465* 5-8 40

PLUCKIN' THE BASS / GIVE, BABY, GIVE (Vocal: Cab Calloway)...... *Vocalion 5406* 5-8 40
(Simultaneously released on two labels)

QUEEN ISABELLA / SAVAGE RHYTHM.................. *Variety 662* 5-8 37

RATAMACUE / AD-DE-DEY (Vocal: Cab Calloway).................. *Vocalion 4700* 5-8 39

REEFER MAN / YOU GOTTA HO-DE-HO .... *Brunswick 6340* 5-8 32
(Vocals: Cab Calloway)

REEFER MAN / YOU GOTTA HO-DE-HO .... *Romeo 2196* 5-8 32
(Vocals: Cab Calloway)
(Simultaneously released on two labels)

RUSTLE OF SWING / HOY-HOY (Vocal: Cab Calloway)........ *Vocalion 4144* 5-8 38

SCAT SONG, THE / THE CABIN IN THE COTTON................ *Brunswick 6272* 5-8 32
(Vocals: Cab Calloway)

SHOUT, SHOUT, SHOUT / MISTER PAGANINI, SWING FOR MINNIE............... *Vocalion 4369* 5-8 38
(Vocals: Cab Calloway)

SILLY OLD MOON (Vocal: Cab Calloway) / BOO-WAH BOO-WAH................. *Okeh 5774* 5-8 40

SINCERE LOVE / DO IT AGAIN....... *Vocalion 5364* 5-8 40
(Vocals: Cab Calloway)

SKRONTCH / WE'RE BREAKIN' UP A LOVELY AFFAIR............ *Vocalion 4045* 5-8 38
(Vocals: Cab Calloway)

SMO-O-OTH ONE, A / LET'S GO, JOE ..... *Okeh 6720* 4-6 42
(Vocals: Cab Calloway)

STARDUST / YOU CAN'T STOP ME FROM LOVIN' YOU (Vocal: Cab Calloway)...... *Banner 32295* 5-8 31

STARDUST / YOU CAN'T STOP ME FROM LOVIN' YOU (Vocal: Cab Calloway)........ *Oriole 2361* 5-8 31

STARDUST / YOU CAN'T STOP ME FROM LOVIN' YOU (Vocal: Cab Calloway) ...... *Perfect 15531* 5-8 31

STARDUST / YOU CAN'T STOP ME FROM LOVIN' YOU (Vocal: Cab Calloway) .... *Romeo 1731* 5-8 31
(Simultaneously released on four labels)

STRANGE AS IT SEEMS / BEALE STREET MAMA..................... *Banner 32624* 8-10 33
(Vocals: Cab Calloway)

STRANGE AS IT SEEMS / BEALE STREET MAMA................ *Melotone M-12554* 8-10 33
(Vocals: Cab Calloway)

STRANGE AS IT SEEMS / BEALE STREET MAMA...................... *Oriole 2607* 8-10 33
(Vocals: Cab Calloway)

STRANGE AS IT SEEMS / BEALE STREET MAMA..................... *Perfect 15704* 8-10 33
(Vocals: Cab Calloway)

STRANGE AS IT SEEMS / BEALE STREET MAMA..................... *Romeo 1980* 8-10 33
(Vocals: Cab Calloway)
(Simultaneously released on five labels)

STRICTLY CULLUD AFFAIR / AW YOU DAWG.................. *Brunswick 6292* 5-8 32

SUNSET / ARE YOU HEP TO THE JIVE?.... *Okeh 5804* 5-8 40
(Vocals: Cab Calloway)

SWEET RHYTHM / GOTTA GO PLACES AND DO THINGS........ *Brunswick 6473* 5-8 33
(Vocals: Cab Calloway)

TAKE THE 'A' TRAIN / CHATTANOOGA CHOO-CHOO (Vocal: Cab Calloway).... *Conqueror 9914* 5-8 41

TAKE THE 'A' TRAIN / CHATTANOOGA CHOO-CHOO (Vocal: Cab Calloway) .... *Okeh 6305* 5-8 41
(Simultaneously released on two labels)

TARZAN OF HARLEM / A BEE GEZINDT.................. *Vocalion 5267* 5-8 40
(Vocals: Cab Calloway)

THAT MAN IS HERE AGAIN / SWING, SWING, SWING .... *Variety 501* 5-8 33
(Vocals: Cab Calloway)

THAT'S WHAT I HATE ABOUT LOVE / I GOTTA RIGHT TO SING THE BLUES...... *Brunswick 6460* 5-8 33
(Vocals: Cab Calloway)

THERE'S A SUNNY SIDE TO EVERYTHING / MISTER PAGANINI, SWING FOR MINNIE............. *Conqueror 9088* 5-8 38
(Vocals: Cab Calloway)

THREE SWINGS AND OUT / I LIKE MUSIC (WITH A SWING LIKE THAT)
(Vocal: Cab Calloway).................. *Vocalion 3995* 5-8 38

TRYLON SWING / JUMPIN' JIVE
(Vocal: Cab Calloway)................ *Conqueror 9300* 5-8 39

TRYLON SWING / JUMPIN' JIVE (Vocal: Cab Calloway).............. *Vocalion 5005* 5-8 39
(Simultaneously released on two labels)

UTT-DA-ZAY (Vocal: Cab Calloway) / CRESCENDO IN DRUMS......................... *Vocalion 5062* 5-8 39

VIRGINIA, GEORGIA AND CAROLINE / I'LL BE AROUND..................... *Okeh 6717* 4-6 42
(Vocals: Cab Calloway)

WE GO WELL TOGETHER / I SEE A MILLION PEOPLE..................... *Okeh 6341* 4-6 41
(Vocals: Cab Calloway)

WHEN YOU'RE SMILING / ARE YOU IN LOVE WITH ME AGAIN?................ *Brunswick 7685* 4-6 36
(Vocals: Cab Calloway)

WILLOW, WEEP FOR ME / JONAH JOINS THE CAB (Vocal: Cab Calloway)..... *Okeh 6109* 4-6 41

WITHOUT RHYTHM / STACK O'LEE BLUES............................ *Banner 32378* 5-8 32
(Vocals: Cab Calloway)

WITHOUT RHYTHM / STACK O'LEE BLUES.............................. *Oriole 2421* 5-8 32
(Vocals: Cab Calloway)

WITHOUT RHYTHM / STACK O'LEE BLUES.............................. *Perfect 15572* 5-8 32
(Vocals: Cab Calloway)

WITHOUT RHYTHM / STACK O'LEE BLUES.............................. *Romeo 1794* 5-8 32
(Vocals: Cab Calloway)
(Simultaneously released on four labels)

YALLER (Vocal: Cab Calloway) / THE VIPER'S DRAG................ *Domino 4686* 5-8 31

YALLER (Vocal: Cab Calloway) / THE VIPER'S DRAG.................... *Jewel 6285* 5-8 31

YALLER (Vocal: Cab Calloway) / THE VIPER'S DRAG.................. *Oriole 2185* 5-8 31

YALLER (Vocal: Cab Calloway) / THE VIPER'S DRAG................ *Perfect 15412* 5-8 31

YALLER (Vocal: Cab Calloway) / THE VIPER'S DRAG................ *Regal 10230* 5-8 31

YALLER (Vocal: Cab Calloway) / THE VIPER'S DRAG.................. *Romeo 1548* 5-8 31
(Simultaneously released on six labels)

YO ETA CANSA / LONESOME NIGHTS... *Okeh 5827* 4-6 40

YOU ARE THE ONE IN MY HEART / ST. JAMES' INFIRMARY............... *Okeh 6391* 4-6 41
(Vocals: Cab Calloway)

YOU DOG / SOMEBODY STOLE MY GAL.................... *Banner 32323* 5-8 32
(Vocals: Cab Calloway)

YOU DOG / SOMEBODY STOLE MY GAL...................... *Oriole 2382* 5-8 32
(Vocals: Cab Calloway)

YOU DOG / SOMEBODY STOLE MY GAL..................... *Perfect 15541* 5-8 32
(Vocals: Cab Calloway)

YOU DOG / SOMEBODY STOLE MY GAL...................... *Romeo 1751* 5-8 32
(Vocals: Cab Calloway)
(Simultaneously released on four labels)

CALLOWAY, Cab, & His Orchestra as The Caroliners

SWEET JENNIE LEE / HAPPY FEET... *Domino 4656* 5-8 30
(Vocals: Cab Calloway)

CALLOWAY, Cab, & His Orchestra as The Jungle Band

GOTTA DARN GOOD REASON NOW / ST. LOUIS BLUES................. *Brunswick 4936* 8-10 30
(Vocals: Cab Calloway)

CALLOWAY, Jean, & His Orchestra:
see KARDOS, Gene, & His Orchestra

CAMPBELL, Buddy, & His Orchestra:
see SELVIN, Ben, & His Orchestra

CANDIDO, "Candy", & His Candy Kids
(Candy Candido: Circa 1905 –)
(Candido was promoted as having the widest vocal range of any singer in the world)

MA! (HE'S MAKING EYES AT ME) / THE BIG BASS FIDDLE............... *Decca 1590* 10-12 37
(Vocals: "Candy" Candido)

CANDULLO, Joe, & His Everglades Orchestra

BASS ALE BLUES / MEASLY BLUES... *Edison 51826* 8-10 26

BLACK BOTTOM / MESSIN' AROUND ... *Banner 1796* 4-6 26

BLACK BOTTOM/MESSIN' AROUND... *Domino 3772* 4-6 26
(Simultaneously released on two labels)

BLACK BOTTOM / MESSIN' AROUND (Vocals: Unknown)........... *Challenge 127* 10-12 26

BLACK BOTTOM / MESSIN' AROUND (Vocals: Unknown)............ *Herwin 55004* 25-30 26
(Simultaneously released on two labels)

BLACK BOTTOM / THE ST. LOUIS HOP.......................... *Gennett 3358* 5-8 26

BLOWIN' OFF STEAM / BROWN SUGAR................. *Harmony 286-H* 5-8 26

CHANT, THE / WINDY CITY STOMP... *Edison 51912* 10-12 27

'DEED I DO / IT TAKES A GOOD WOMAN (TO KEEP A GOOD MAN AT HOME)... *Cameo 1061* 5-8 27

DEEP HENDERSON / JACKASS BLUES.................... *Banner 1784* 5-8 26

DEEP HENDERSON / JACKASS BLUES.................... *Domino 3751* 5-8 26

DEEP HENDERSON / JACKASS BLUES..................... *Regal 8089* 5-8 26
(Simultaneously released on three labels)

HOBO'S PRAYER, THE / BASS ALE BLUES.......................... *Harmony 150-H* 4-6 26

NIGHTMARE, THE / SPANISH MAMA.................... *Gennett 3316* 5-8 26

ST. LOUIS HOP, THE / MESSIN' AROUND (Vocals: Unknown) .... *Buddy 8070* 20-25 26

CANDULLO, Joe, & His Orchestra

S-L-U-E FOOT / A JAZZ HOLIDAY....... *Banner 7169* 8-10 28
(Vocals: Joe Candullo)

S-L-U-E FOOT / A JAZZ HOLIDAY ..... *Domino 4167* 8-10 28
(Vocals: Joe Candullo)

S-L-U-E FOOT / A JAZZ HOLIDAY .... *Jewel 5335* 8-10 28
(Vocals: Joe Candullo)

S-L-U-E FOOT / A JAZZ HOLIDAY .... *Regal 8595* 8-10 28
(Vocals: Joe Candullo)
(Simultaneously released on four labels)

CANDULLO, Joe, & His Orchestra asThe Dixie Jazz Band

S-L-U-E FOOT / A JAZZ HOLIDAY........ *Oriole 1287* 8-10 28
(Vocals: Joe Candullo)

CARLE, Frankie, & His Orchestra
(Frankie Carle: 3/25/03 –)
(Frankie Carle & His Orchestra continue to play occasionally in the Phoenix area, now his home. Marjorie Hughes, vocalist on numerous Carle records, is his daughter. Marjorie's change-of-name was at the insistence of her father, in order for her to make the grade as vocalist on her own talent rather than capitalizing on the Carle name.)

AROUND THE WORLD (Vocal: Donald Maddox) / WHERE THE RED ROSES GROW
(Vocal: Joan House) .... *RCA Victor 20-4075* 2-4 50

CARLEBOOGIE, THE / THE RHYTHM OF THE RAINDROPS.......... *RCA Victor 20-5319* 2-4 52

COUNTING THE DAYS (Vocal: Paul Allen) / MISSOURI WALTZ............. *Columbia 36805* 2-4 45

CRAZY HEARTS / SILVER AND GOLD........... *RCA Victor 20-4545* 2-4 51
(Vocals: Johnny Prophet)

I'D BE LOST WITHOUT YOU / CYNTHIA'S IN LOVE............. *Columbia 36994* 2-4 46
(Vocals: Marjorie Hughes)

I'M GLAD I WAITED FOR YOU (Vocal: Paul Allen) / NO, BABY, NOBODY BUT YOU
(Vocal: Marjorie Hughes).............. *Columbia 36906* 2-4 46

IT'S ALL OVER NOW / EITHER IT'S LOVE OR IT ISN'T...................... *Columbia 37146* 2-4 46
(Vocals: Marjorie Hughes)

I WAS HERE WHEN YOU LEFT ME (Vocal: Phyllis Lynne) / I'D RATHER BE ME
(Vocal: Paul Allen)................... *Columbia 36826* 2-4 45

LAZY MOOD (Vocal: Gregg Lawrence) / THERE'S THAT LONELY FEELING AGAIN
(Vocal: Marjorie Hughes).............. *Columbia 37481* 2-4 47

MAN WHO PAINTS THE RAINBOW IN THE SKY, THE / UNLESS IT CAN HAPPEN WITH YOU............. *Columbia 37311* 2-4 47

MY ROSE GARDEN / THE BLOSSOMS ON THE BOUGH .... *Columbia 38646* 2-4 48
(Vocals: Marjorie Hughes)

OH! WHAT IT SEEMED TO BE (Vocal: Marjorie Hughes) / AS LONG AS I LIVE
(Vocal: Paul Allen)............. *Columbia 36892* 2-4 45

PENGUIN AT THE WALDORF / THE GLOW-WORM.................... *Columbia 37567* 2-4 47

ROSES IN THE RAIN (Vocal: Marjorie Hughes) / YOU ARE THERE (Vocal: Gregg Lawrence).... *Columbia 37252* 2-4 47

SATURDAY NIGHT (Vocal: Phyllis Lynne) / CARLE BOOGIE.................... *Columbia 36777* 2-4 44

SUNRISE SERENADE (theme song) / CARLE BOOGIE.................. *Columbia 37269* 2-4 47
(Frankie Carle was the composer of Sunrise Serenade)

WHAT'VE YOU GOT TO LOSE (Vocal: Marjorie Hughes) / EASY PICKIN'S .... *Columbia 37194* 2-4 46

WHO WERE YOU KISSING (Vocal: Marjorie Hughes) / CORABELLE
(Vocal: Gregg Lawrence)............... *Columbia 37972* 2-4 47

CARLE, Frankie, & His Sunrise Serenaders

BLUE FANTASY / NIGHT GLOW
(Vocal: Virginia LeAhn) .... *Vocalion 5241* 3-5 39

CHICO'S LOVE SONG / IT'S A WHOLE NEW THING.............. *Vocalion 5155* 3-5 39
(Vocals: The LeAhn Sisters)

CARLE, Frankie, at the piano with rhythm section

CARLE COMES CALLING
(a 4-record album set).............. *Columbia Set C-129* 8-10 45
Individual records in the set, listed numerically (with value of each):

STARDUST/CANADIAN CAPERS... *Columbia 37315* 2-4 –
I'LL GET BY / DEEP PURPLE...... *Columbia 37316* 2-4 –
PENTHOUSE SERENADE / I WANT A GIRL........................ *Columbia 37317* 2-4 –
CHOPIN'S POLONAISE IN BOOGIE / IF YOU WERE THE ONLY GIRL ... *Columbia 37318* 2-4 –

FRANKIE CARLE AND HIS GIRL FRIENDS
(a 4-record album set).............. *Columbia Set C-97* 8-10 44
Individual records in the set, listed numerically (with value of each):

IDA / LIZA......................... *Columbia 36689* 2-4 -
CHARMAINE / DIANE .... *Columbia 36690* 2-4 -
MARGIE / ROSE MARIE........... *Columbia 36691* 2-4 –
LOUISE / JOSEPHINE.............. *Columbia 36692* 2-4 –

CARLSON, Bill, & His Orchestra

BABY, WON'T YOU PLEASE COME HOME? / ALONE WITH MY DREAMS........ *Broadway 1365* 10-12 30
(Vocals: Jack Teter)

CLARINET MARMALADE / MILENBERG JOYS............... *Broadway 1359* 12-15 30

CLARINET MARMALADE / MILENBERG JOYS.............. *Paramount 20797* 15-20 30
(Simultaneously released on two labels)

HOW COME YOU DO ME LIKE YOU DO? / A GOOD MAN IS HARD TO FIND............ *Vocalion 5466* 4-6 40

"O" / MY MAN.................... *Conqueror 9462* 3-5 40

"O" / MY MAN....................... *Vocalion 5506* 3-5 40
(Simultaneously released on two labels)

ONE I LOVE BELONGS TO SOMEBODY ELSE, THE / BLACK-EYED SUSAN BROWN......... *Okeh 5763* 3-5 40

CARLSON, Roy, as Roy Carlson's Dance Orchestra:
see SCHUBERT, Adrian, & His Salon Orchestra

CARLSON, Russ, & His Orchestra

IT'S THE GIRL! / HIKIN' DOWN THE HIGHWAY ... *Crown 3163* 4-6 31
(Vocals: Unknown)

MINNIE THE MOOCHER / WRAP YOUR TROUBLES IN DREAMS ... *Crown 3147* 5-8 31
(Vocals: Unknown)

WE JUST COULDN'T SAY GOODBYE / I CAN'T BELIEVE IT'S TRUE ... *Crown 3360* 4-6 32
(Vocals: Unknown)

CARMICHAEL, Hoagy, accompanied by a small recording group

(Hoagy Carmichael: 11/22/99 – 12/27/81)

MR. MUSIC MASTER / JUDY ... *Decca 18396* 2-4 42
(Vocals: Hoagy Carmichael)

OLD MAN HARLEM / DON'T FORGET TO SAY NO, BABY ... *Decca 18397* 2-4 42
(Vocals: Hoagy Carmichael)

STAR DUST / HONG KONG BLUES ... *Decca 18395* 2-4 42
(Vocals: Hoagy Carmichael)

HONG KONG BLUES / RIVERBOAT SHUFFLE ... *Brunswick 8255* 5-8 38
(Vocals: Hoagy Carmichael)

TWO SLEEPY PEOPLE / NEW ORLEANS ... *Brunswick 8250* 5-8 38
(Vocals: Hoagy Carmichael & Ella Logan. Ella was a stage, screen & vaudeville actress, best known for her starring role in the hit musical, Finian's Rainbow on Broadway.)

CARMICHAEL, Hoagy, accompanied by Glen Grey & The Casa Loma Orchestra

WASHBOARD BLUES / LITTLE OLD LADY ... *Decca 2394* 3-5 39
(Vocals: Hoagy Carmichael)

CARMICHAEL, Hoagy, & His Orchestra

GEORGIA ON MY MIND / ONE NIGHT IN HAVANA ... *Victor 23013* 15-20 30
(Vocals: Hoagy Carmichael)

JUDY / MOON COUNTRY ... *Victor 24627* 5-8 34
(Vocals: Hoagy Carmichael)

LAZY RIVER / JUST FORGET ... *Victor 23034* 10-12 31
(Vocals: Hoagy Carmichael)

MIGHTY RIVER (Vocal: Dick Robertson) / HOT JAZZ PIE (by Joe Haymes & His Orchestra; Vocals: Joe Haymes & Mike Doty) ... *Victor 24123* 5-8 32

ROCKIN' CHAIR (Vocals: Hoagy Carmichael & Irving Brodsky) / BARNACLE BILL THE SAILOR (Vocals: Carmichael, Carson Robison, & Joe Venuti) ... *Victor V-38139* 15-20 30

SING IT WAY DOWN LOW (Vocal: Hoagy Carmichael) / THANKSGIVIN' (Vocal: Dick Robertson) ... *Victor 24182* 3-5 32

CARMICHAEL, Hoagy & His Pals

ONE NIGHT IN HAVANA / STARDUST ... *Gennett 6311* 10-12 27

CARMICHAEL, Hoagy as Carmichael's Collegians

MARCH OF THE HOODLUMS / WALKIN' THE DOG ... *Champion 16453* 12-15 28

MARCH OF THE HOODLUMS / WALKIN' THE DOG ... *Gennett 6474* 15-20 28
(Simultaneously released on two labels)

CAROLINA CLUB ORCHESTRA, The:
see KEMP, Hall, and
see SPECHT, Paul & His Orchestra

CAROLINA COTTON PICKERS, The:
see DENMAN, Hal, and
see SMALL, Abe

CAROLINA DANDIES, The:
see CLAPP, Sunny, & His Band O'Sunshine

CAROLINERS, The:
see CALLOWAY, Cab, & His Orchestra
see HARING, Bob, & His Orchestra
see HARING, Bob, & His Velvetone Orchestra
see LANIN, Sam, & His Orchestra, and
see LANIN, Sam, as Sam Lanin's Troubadours

CARROLL, Irv, & His Orchestra

BARTENDER SONG, THE (Vocals: Al Jennings & The Carrolleers) / THERE AIN'T ANY CHORUS (TO THIS SONG) (Vocals: The Carrolleers) ... *Bluebird B-11346* 4-6 41

GO HOME, LITTLE GIRL, GO HOME (Vocal: Don Rogers) / FIVE GUYS NAMED MOE (Vocal: Irv Carroll & Al Jennings) ... *Bluebird B-11390* 4-6 41

OH! DEM GOLDEN SLIPPERS (Vocals: Al Jennings & chorus) / LET'S ALL SNORE (Vocals: Johnny Russell & Al Jennings) ... *Bluebird B-11505* 3-5 42

WE'RE IN IT (Vocal: Johnny Russell) / MY BONNIE LIES OVER THE OCEAN (Vocal: Al Jennings) ... *Bluebird B-11470* 4-6 42

CARROLL, Roy, & His Sands Point Orchestra:
see GRAY, Glen, & The Casa Loma Orchestra
see LANIN, Sam, & His Famous Players & Singers, and
see SELVIN, Ben, & His Orchestra

CARSON, Bud, & His Collegians:
see HALL, Fred, as the Tin Pan Paraders

CARTER, Benny, & His Orchestra
(Benny Carter: 8/8/07 –)

ALL OF ME / THE VERY THOUGHT OF YOU (Vocal: Roy Felton) ... *Bluebird B-10962* 3-5 41

AMONG MY SOUVENIRS (Vocal: Roy Felton) / FISH FRY ... *Okeh 5458* 3-5 40

AMONG MY SOUVENIRS (Vocal: Roy Felton) / FISH FRY ... *Vocalion 5458* 3-5 40
(Simultaneously released on two labels)

BABALU / THERE, I'VE SAID IT AGAIN (Vocal: Roy Felton) ... *Bluebird B-11090* 3-5 41

BIG BEN BLUES (Vocal: Benny Carter) / WHEN DAY IS DONE ... *Brunswick 7786* 4-6 36

BY THE WATERMELON VINE, LINDY LOU (Vocals: Roy Felton & The Mills Brothers) / I'VE BEEN IN LOVE BEFORE (Vocals: Roy Felton) ... *Decca 3545* 3-5 40

COCKTAILS FOR TWO / TAKIN' MY TIME ... *Bluebird B-10998* 3-5 41

CUDDLE UP, HUDDLE UP / WHAT A DIFFERENCE A DAY MADE (Vocal: Maxine Sullivan) ... *Bluebird B-11197* 4-6 41

DEVIL'S HOLIDAY / SYMPHONY IN RIFFS ... *Columbia 2898-D* 12-15 33
(This record was pressed in blue shellac)

EVERYBODY SHUFFLE / SYNTHETIC LOVE (Vocal: Charles Holland) ... *Vocalion 2870* 8-10 35

FAVOR OF A FOOL, THE / RIFF ROMP ... *Vocalion 5294* 5-8 39

HURRY! HURRY! (Vocal: Savannah Churchill) / POINCIANA ... *Capitol 144* 3-5 43

JOE TURNER BLUES / BEALE STREET BLUES ... *Okeh 6001* 4-6 40

LAST KISS YOU GAVE ME, THE (Vocal: Roy Felton) / BOOGIE WOOGIE SUGAR BLUES ... *Decca 3588* 4-6 40

LONESOME NIGHTS / BLUE LOU ... *Okeh 41567* 12-15 33

MIDNIGHT (Vocal: Maxine Sullivan) / MY FAVORITE BLUES ... *Bluebird B-11288* 4-6 41

NIGHT HOP / O.K. FOR BABY ... *Decca 3294* 3-5 40

POM POM / SERENADE TO A SARONG ... *Decca 3262* 3-5 40

PLYMOUTH ROCK / MELANCHOLY LULLABY ... *Vocalion 4984* 5-8 39

SAVOY STAMPEDE / SCANDAL IN A FLAT ... *Vocalion 5112* 5-8 39

SHOOT THE WORKS / DREAM LULLABY ... *Vocalion 2898* 8-10 35

SHUFFLEBUG SHUFFLE / MORE THAN YOU KNOW (Vocal: Roy Felton) ... *Vocalion 5508* 5-8 39

SLEEP / SLOW FREIGHT ... *Vocalion 5399* 5-8 40

SUNDAY / BACK BAY BOOGIE ... *Bluebird B-11341* 4-6 41

VAGABOND DREAMS / LOVE'S GOT ME DOWN AGAIN ... *Vocalion 5224* 4-6 39
(Vocals: Roy Felton)

CASA LOMA ORCHESTRA, The:
see GRAY, Glen, & The Casa Loma Orchestra

CASINO DANCE ORCHESTRA, The:
see HARING, Bob, & His Orchestra

CASTLE-BY-THE-SEA ORCHESTRA, The:
see SAMUELS, Joseph, & His Orchestra

CASTLEWOOD MARIMBA BAND, The

CLOSE YOUR EYES / GARLAND OF OLD-FASHIONED ROSES ... *Brunswick 2953* 2-4 25

DRIFTING AND DREAMING (Vocals: by quartet) / SONG OF THE ISLANDS (Vocals: by trio) ... *Brunswick 4955* 3-5 30

I MISS YOU MOST AT GLOAMING / MEXICALI ROSE (Vocals: Billy Jones & Earnest Hare) ... *Brunswick 2649* 2-4 24

MELANCHOLY MOON / SPRINGTIME, LOVETIME, YOU ... *Brunswick 4791* 3-5 30

MISSISSIPPI RIPPLES / STEAL A LITTLE KISS WHILE DANCING ... *Brunswick 2511* 2-4 23

MY CRADLE SWEETHEART / ROCK ME IN A CRADLE OF KALUA ... *Brunswick 6121* 4-6 31
(Vocals: Smith Ballew)

CATS AND THE FIDDLE, THE

PUBLIC JITTERBUG NO. 1 / I MISS YOU SO ... *Bluebird B-8429* 5-8 38
(Vocals: Austin Powell)

CAUSER, Bob, & His Cornellians:
see HARLAN, Earl, & His Orchestra
see MARTIN, Freddy, & His Orchestra
see MORGAN, Russ, & His Orchestra, and
see REDMAN, Don, & His Orchestra

CAVALIERS, The:
see SELVIN, Ben, & His Orchestra

CAVALLARO, Carmen, & His Orchestra
(Carmen Cavallaro: 5/6/13 –)

AIN'TCHA EVER COMIN' BACK / I HAVE BUT ONE HEART ... *Decca 24154* 2-4 47
(Vocals: Bob Allen)

CARIOCA / BRAZIL ... *Decca 23847* 2-4 47

IT'S DREAMTIME / MIDNIGHT MASQUERADE ... *Decca 23852* 2-4 47
(Vocals: Bob Allen)

MALAGUENA / NOSTALGIAS ... *Decca 24257* 2-4 47

SONATA / THROUGH A THOUSAND DREAMS ... *Decca 23747* 2-4 47
(Vocals: Frank Gallagher)

CHERWIN, Dick, & His Orchestra:
see RING, Justin, & His Dance Orchestra

CHESTER, Bob, & His Orchestra
(Bob Chester: 3/20/08 –)

AUNT HAGAR'S BLUES / 57TH STREET RAG ... *Bluebird B-10513* 3-5 39

BILLY / I CAN'T TELL WHY I LOVE YOU BUT I DO ... *Bluebird B-10427* 2-4 39
(Vocals: Kathleen Lane)

BUZZ BUZZ BUZZ / MAY I NEVER LOVE AGAIN (Vocal: Dolores O'Neill) ... *Bluebird B-10904* 2-4 40

CHESTER'S CHOICE / RIVER, STAY 'WAY FROM MY DOOR (Vocal: Al Stuart) ... *Bluebird B-10780* 2-4 40

CHILLY AND COLD (Vocal: Betty Bradley) / TILL THE LIGHTS OF LONDON SHINE AGAIN (Vocal: Bill Darnell) ... *Bluebird B-10972* 3-5 41

CLOCK IS FAST, THE (Vocal: Betty Bradley) / HARLEM CONFUSION ... *Bluebird B-11384* 2-4 41

EASY DOES IT / MAKE LOVE WITH A GUITAR (Vocal: Dolores O'Neill) ... *Bluebird B-10576* 2-4 40

FLINGING A WHING-DING / I'M IN A LOVABLE MOOD TONIGHT (Vocal: Dolores O'Neill) ... *Bluebird B-10964* 2-4 40

I THOUGHT ABOUT YOU / DON'T MAKE ME LAUGH ... *Bluebird B-10489* 2-4 39
(Vocals: Dolores O'Neill)

I'VE GOT NO STRINGS (Vocal: Dolores O'Neill) / TURN ON THE OLD MUSIC BOX ... *Bluebird B-10566* 2-4 40

JOLTIN' JOE DIMAGGIO (Vocals: Betty Bradley, Bob Chester & Bob Haymes) / THIS LOVE OF MINE (Vocal: Betty Bradley) ... *Bluebird B-11316* 2-4 41
(Bob Haymes is younger brother to singer Dick Haymes.)

JUST FOR A THRILL (Vocal: Kathleen Lane) / HOY! HOY! (Vocal: Al Stuart) ... *Bluebird B-10375* 2-4 39

LOVE NEVER WENT TO COLLEGE / AFTER ALL ... *Bluebird B-10470* 2-4 41
(Vocals: Dolores O'Neill)

MAGIC OF MAGNOLIAS (Vocal: Bob Haymes) / FROM MAINE TO CALIFORNIA ... *Bluebird B-11313* 2-4 41
(Bob Haymes is younger brother to singer Dick Haymes)

MAYBE (Vocal: Dolores O'Neill) / PUSHIN' THE CONVERSATION ALONG (Vocals: Dolores O'Neill & Al Stuart) ... *Bluebird B-10752* 2-4 40

MOONLIGHT BAY (Vocals: Bob Chester, Gene Howard & The Four Notes) / TANNING DR. JEKYLL'S HYDE ... *Bluebird B-11521* 2-4 42

MOON WON'T TALK, THE / ORCHIDS FOR REMEMBERANCE ... *Bluebird B-10735* 2-4 40
(Vocals: Dolores O'Neill)

OCTAVE JUMP, THE / YOU LITTLE HEART-BREAKER YOU (Vocal: Al Stuart) ... *Bluebird B-10649* 2-4 40

OFF THE RECORD / WE THREE (Vocal: Dolores O'Neill) ... *Bluebird B-10865* 3-5 40

OH LOOK AT ME NOW / DOLORES .... *Bluebird B-11054* 2-4 41
(Vocals: Bill Darnell)

ONE LOOK AT YOU / THERE SHALL BE NO NIGHT .... *Bluebird B-10842* 2-4 40
(Vocals: Dolores O'Neill)

RHUMBOOGIE / RHYTHM ON THE RIVER .... *Bluebird B-10800* 2-4 40
(Vocals: Al Stuart)

SHOOT THE SHERBET TO ME, HERBERT / YOU TELL ME YOUR DREAM ... *Bluebird B-10396* 2-4 39
(Vocals: Kathleen Lane)

SONG OF OLD HAWAII, A / TAKE CARE .... *Bluebird B-10849* 2-4 40
(Vocals: Dolores O'Neill)

STRICTLY INSTRUMENTAL / KEEP THE HOME FIRES BURNING
(Vocals: The Rhythmaires) .... *Bluebird B-11548* 3-5 42

THERE GOES THAT SONG AGAIN / IT'S SO PEACEFUL IN THE COUNTRY ... *Bluebird B-11227* 2-4 41
(Vocals: Betty Bradley)

THEY OUGHT TO WRITE A BOOK ABOUT YOU / SECRETS IN THE MOONLIGHT .... *Bluebird B-10699* 2-4 40
(Vocals: Dolores O'Neill)

TOMORROW'S SUNRISE (Vocal: Gene Howard) / SUNBURST (theme song) .... *Bluebird B-11478* 2-4 42

WHY GO ON PRETENDING? / IN THE HEART OF THE DARK .... *Bluebird B-10524* 2-4 40
(Vocals: Dolores O'Neill)

WINTER WEATHER / HAWAIIAN WAR CHANT .... *Bluebird B-11405* 2-4 42
(Vocals: Betty Bradley)

WITH THE WIND AND THE RAIN IN YOUR HAIR (Vocal: Dolores O'Neill) / I WALK WITH MUSIC .... *Bluebird B-10614* 2-4 40

YESTERDAY'S GARDENIAS (Vocal: Gene Howard) / ISABELLA KISSED A FELLA (Vocal: Betty Bradley) .... *Bluebird B-11565* 2-4 42

YOU'RE BREAKING MY HEART ALL OVER AGAIN / ARISE MY LOVE .... *Bluebird B-10890* 2-4 40
(Vocals: Dolores O'Neill)

YOU WERE MEANT FOR ME / A NEW SHADE OF BLUE .... *Bluebird B-11259* 2-4 41
(Vocals: Betty Bradley)

CHILDS, Reggie, & His Hotel Roosevelt Orchestra

DID YOU EVER SEE A DREAM WALKING? (Vocal: Don Howard) / MANY MOONS AGO (Vocal: Duke Durbin) .... *Bluebird B-5269* 5-8 34

DID YOU EVER SEE A DREAM WALKING? (Vocal: Don Howard) / MANY MOONS AGO (Vocal: Duke Durbin) .... *Electradisk 2144* 15-20 34

DID YOU EVER SEE A DREAM WALKING? (Vocal: Don Howard) / MANY MOONS AGO (Vocal: Duke Durbin) .... *Sunrise S-3350* 15-20 34
(Simultaneously released on three labels)

OUR BIG LOVE SCENE (Vocal: Don Howard) / AFTER SUNDOWN (Vocal: Duke Durbin) ..... *Bluebird B-5279* 5-8 34

OUR BIG LOVE SCENE (Vocal: Don Howard) / AFTER SUNDOWN (Vocal: Duke Durbin) ..... *Electradisk 2153* 15-20 34

OUR BIG LOVE SCENE (Vocal: Don Howard) / AFTER SUNDOWN (Vocal: Duke Durbin) ...... *Sunrise S-3360* 15-20 34
(Simultaneously released on three labels)

CHILDS, Reggie, & His Orchestra

AT A CARNIVAL IN VENICE (Vocal: Joe Fitzpatrick) / HONEY BUNCH (Vocal: Pops Carroll) ...... *Decca 1269* 4-6 37

DID YOU MEAN IT? (Vocal: Stephanie Dale) / CLOSE TO ME (Vocal: Billy Pritchard) .... *Decca 978* 4-6 36

GOODNIGHT, ANGEL (Vocal: Jimmy De Palma) / THERE'S A NEW MOON OVER THE OLD HILL (Vocal: Unknown) .... *Decca 1673* 3-5 38

LULU'S BACK IN TOWN (Vocal: Rocky Jordan) / YOU CAN BE KISSED (Vocal: Unknown) .... *Bluebird B-5985* 5-8 35

NO MORE TEARS (Vocal: Joe Fitzpatrick) / MAYBE (Vocal: Pops Carroll) .... *Decca 1262* 4-6 37

ON A TYPICAL TROPICAL NIGHT (Vocal: Stephanie Dale) / I WAS SAYING TO THE MOON (Vocal: Pops Carroll) .... *Decca 987* 4-6 36

SWEET STRANGER / I'M THE ONE WHO LOVES YOU .... *Decca 1582* 3-5 38
(Vocals: Pops Carroll)

CHRISTIAN, Tommy, & His Orchestra

'DEED I DO / SONG OF THE WANDERER .... *Harmony 348-H* 3-5 27
(Vocals: Unknown)

HEAVEN HELP A SAILOR (ON A NIGHT LIKE THIS) (Vocal: Unknown) / BEEDLE-UM-BO ... *Harmony 394-H* 2-4 27

THAT CERTAIN PARTY / SHOW ME THE WAY TO GO .... *Harmony 74-H* 3-5 26
(Vocals: orchestra)

CHUBB-STEINBERG ORCHESTRA, The, directed by Art Hicks

BECAUSE THEY ALL LOVE YOU / — ... *Gennett 5663* 10-12 25

BLUE EVENING BLUES / HORSEY, KEEP YOUR TAIL UP (Vocal: Art Hicks) .... *Okeh 40107* 12-15 24

MANDY, MAKE UP YOUR MIND / STEPPIN' IN SOCIETY (Vocal: Art Hicks) .... *Gennett 3058* 12-15 25

WALKING TALKING DOLLY / FROM ONE TILL TWO .... *Okeh 40106* 12-15 24

CIBELLI, Antonio:
see PAN-AMERICAN MARIMBA BAND, The

CLAPP, Sunny, & His Band O' Sunshine

DOWN ON BISCAYNE BAY / WE CAN'T USE EACH OTHER ANY MORE .... *Victor V-40152* 5-8 29
(Vocals: Bob Hutchingson)

TREAT ME LIKE A BABY (Vocals: Jeanne Geddes, Tom Howell, Lee Howell, & S. Anderson) / LEARN TO CROON (Vocal: Jeanne Geddes) .... *Victor 22682* 5-8 31

CLAPP, Sunny, & His Band O' Sunshine as The Carolina Dandies

COME EASY, GO EASY (Vocal: Hoagy Carmichael) / WHEN I CAN'T BE WITH YOU (Vocal: George Marks) .... *Victor 22776* 5-8 31

CLARK, Dick, & His Orchestra:
see HAYMES, Joe, & His Orchestra

CLARK, Don, & His La Monica Ballroom Orchestra

BIG BAD BILL / CHEATIN' ON ME ..... *Victor 19622* 3-5 25

LONESOME TRAIL / IT'S TOO GOOD TO BE TRUE .... *Victor 19736* 3-5 25

CLARK, Don, & His Los Angeles Biltmore Hotel Orchestra

IDOLIZING (Vocals: Unknown) / I'VE GOT THE GIRL (Vocals: Bing Crosby & Al Rinker) .... *Columbia 824-D* 15-20 26
(This is Bing Crosby's first record)

CLARKE, Buddy, & His Orchestra
(This is not the Buddy Clark of vocal fame)

SWEET DREAMS (Vocal: Joan Brooks) / WHY IS MY LITTLE RED-HEAD BLUE? (Vocal: Happy Jim Parsons) .... *Beacon 105* 5-8 42

CLEVELANDERS, The;
see RESER, Harry

CLICQUOT CLUB ESKIMOS, The:
see RESER, Harry

CLINTON, Larry, & His Orchestra
(8/17/09 –)

(Larry Clinton's theme song was 'The Dipsey Doodle', which he wrote and arranged while a member of the Tommy Dorsey Orchestra, and Dorsey recorded it for Victor. When Clinton formed his own orchestra, also under contract to RCA Victor, the Victor executives and Dorsey saw no need for a second, competetive recording of the tune. As a result, although 'The Dipsey Doodle' was his own composition and remained his theme song, Clinton's Orchestra never had the opportunity to record it.)

ABBA DABBA / THE CAMPBELLS ARE SWINGIN' .... *Victor 25707* 3-5 37

AFTER LOOKING AT YOU / I KISSED YOU IN A DREAM LAST NIGHT .... *Victor 26083* 2-4 38
(Vocals: Bea Wain)

ARE YOU IN THE MOOD FOR MISCHIEF? (Vocal: Bea Wain) / FOR MEN ONLY .... *Victor 26118* 2-4 39

AT LEAST YOU COULD SAY HELLO (Vocal: Terry Allen) / HOW LONG HAS THIS BEEN GOING ON? (Vocal: Mary Dugan) .... *Victor 26374* 2-4 39

BACH TO BOOGIE / NARCISSUS .... *Victor 27510* 2-4 41

BIG DIPPER, THE / MIDNIGHT IN THE MADHOUSE .... *Victor 25697* 3-5 37

BREAD AND BUTTER / HOW HIGH THE MOON (Vocal: Terry Allen) .... *Victor 26521* 2-4 40

CHANGE PARTNERS / THE YAM ...... *Victor 26010* 3-5 38
(Vocals: Bea Wain)

COLLEGE HUMOR (Vocals: Bea Wain & Larry Clinton) / STOP! AND RECONSIDER (Vocal: Bea Wain) .... *Victor 25825* 2-4 38

COMES LOVE (Vocal: Ford Leary) / A BOY NAMED LEM (Vocal: Mary Dugan) .... *Victor 26277* 2-4 39

CRY, BABY, CRY / YOU'LL BE REMINDED OF ME .... *Victor 25819* 2-4 38
(Vocals: Bea Wain)

DANCING ON A DIME / I HEAR MUSIC .... *Victor 26766* 2-4 40
(Vocals: Terry Allen)

DEEP PURPLE (Vocal: Bea Wain) / A STUDY IN RED .... *Victor 26141* 2-4 39

DESIGN FOR DANCING / CHANT OF THE JUNGLE .... *Victor 26076* 3-5 38

DOCTOR RHYTHM / ALWAYS AND ALWAYS .... *Victor 25768* 3-5 38
(Vocals: Bea Wain)

DODGIN' THE DEAN / HEART AND SOUL (Vocal: Bea Wain) .... *Victor 26046* 3-5 38

FOO TO YOU (Vocals: by orchestra) / HARMONICA HOP .... *Victor 25882* 2-4 38

FROM ANOTHER WORLD / IT NEVER ENTERED MY MIND .... *Victor 26534* 2-4 40
(Vocals: Terry Allen)

GAVOTTE (Vocal: Bea Wain) / DANCE OF THE HOURS .... *Victor 25805* 2-4 38

HEZEKIAH / ROCKIN' CHAIR .... *Victor 26319* 2-4 39
(Vocals: Ford Leary)

HOW CAN IF EVER BE ALONE? (Vocal: Terry Allen) / BLUE LOVEBIRD (Vocal: Helen Southern) .... *Victor 26626* 2-4 40

HOW'DJA LIKE TO LOVE ME? / I FALL IN LOVE WITH YOU EVERY DAY .... *Victor 25775* 2-4 38
(Vocals: Bea Wain)

HOW TO WIN FRIENDS AND INFLUENCE PEOPLE / I MARRIED AN ANGEL .... *Victor 25837* 2-4 38
(Vocals: Bea Wain)

I CASH CLO'ES / SWING LIGHTLY ..... *Victor 25704* 3-5 37

I DREAM OF JEANIE WITH THE LIGHT BROWN HAIR (Vocal: Terry Allen) / THE OLD FOLKS AT HOME .... *Victor 26468* 2-4 40

I DOUBLE DARE YOU / TWO DREAMS GOT TOGETHER .... *Victor 25740* 3-5 38
(Vocals: Bea Wain)

IF IT RAINS, WHO CARES! / FERDINAND THE BULL .... *Victor 25841* 4-6 38
(Vocals: Bea Wain)

I GET ALONG WITHOUT YOU VERY WELL (Vocals: Bea Wain & Ford Leary) / THE MASQUERADE IS OVER (Vocal: Bea Wain) .... *Victor 26151* 2-4 39

IT'S A LONELY TRAIL (Vocal: Bea Wain) / I GO FOR THAT (Vocal: Ford Leary) .... *Victor 26131* 2-4 39

I'VE GOT MY HEART SET ON YOU / TRUE CONFESSION .... *Victor 25706* 3-5 37
(Vocals: Bea Wain)

I WANT MY SHARE OF LOVE / DON'T LOOK NOW .... *Victor 26158* 2-4 39
(Vocals: Bea Wain)

I WAS DOING ALL RIGHT / LOVE IS HERE TO STAY .... *Victor 25761* 2-4 38
(Vocals: Bea Wain)

JEEPERS CREEPERS / DEVIL WITH THE DEVIL .... *Victor 26108* 2-4 39
(Vocals: Ford Leary)

JITTERBUG, THE (Vocal: Ford Leary) / OVER THE RAINBOW (Vocal: Bea Wain) .... *Victor 26174* 3-5 39

JOHNSON RAG / DOWN HOME RAG ... *Victor 26414* 3-5 39

JUBILEE / SCRAPIN' THE TOAST ..... *Victor 225721* 3-5 38
(Vocals: Bea Wain)

KISS FOR YOU, A / LIMEHOUSE BLUES .... *Victor 26523* 3-5 40

LADY SAID "YES", THE (Vocal: Ford Leary) / TEN MILE HOP .... *Victor 26575* 2-4 40

LAST TWO WEEKS IN JULY, THE / TWILIGHT INTERLUDE .... *Victor 26351* 2-4 39
(Vocals: Terry Allen)

LOOK / YOU'RE AN EDUCATION ...... *Victor 25794* 2-4 38
(Vocals: Bea Wain)

LULLABY (Vocal: Bea Wain) / THE KERRY DANCERS (Vocal: Ford Leary) .... *Victor 26127* 2-4 39

MARTHA / I DREAMT I DWELT IN MARBLE HALLS .... *Victor 25789* 2-4 38

MILENBERG JOYS / DIPPERMOUTH BLUES .... *Victor 26018* 3-5 38

MILITARY MADCAPS / SHADES OF HADES.......................... *Victor 25755* 3-5 38

MY HEART BELONGS TO DADDY / MOST GENTLEMEN DON'T LIKE LOVE .... *Victor 26100* 2-4 39
(Vocals: Bea Wain)

MY REVERIE (Vocal: Bea Wain) / BOOGIE WOOGIE BLUES........... *Victor 26006* 3-5 38

MY SILENT MOOD (Vocal: Terry Allen) / TOSELLI'S SERENADE.............. *Victor 26417* 2-4 39

NEARNESS TO YOU, THE (Vocal: Helen Southern) / WHEN THE SWALLOWS COME BACK TO CAPISTANO .... *Victor 26634* 2-4 40

ONE ROSE, THE (Vocal: Bea Wain) / OH! LADY BE GOOD .... *Victor 25724* 3-5 38

PARADE OF THE WOODEN SOLDIERS / THE LITTLE MAN WHO WASN'T THERE... *Victor 26308* 2-4 39
(Vocals: Ford leary)

POOR LITTLE RICH GIRL / IN A PERSIAN MARKET .... *Victor 26283* 2-4 39

ROMANCE IN THE DARK / A GYPSY TOLD ME.................. *Victor 25800* 2-4 38
(Vocals: Bea Wain)

SATAN IN SATIN / GOLDEN BANTAM.................. *Victor 26354* 2-4 39

'S GOOD ENOUGH FOR ME (Vocal: Carol Bruce) / HOW AM I TO KNOW? .... *Victor 25870* 2-4 38

SHADRACH (Vocal: Ford Leary) / OLD FOLKS (Vocal: Bea Wain) .... *Victor 26056* 2-4 38

STILL THE BLUEBIRD SINGS (Vocal: Mary Dugan) / AN APPLE FOR THE TEACHER (Vocal: Ford Leary).................... *Victor 26332* 2-4 39

STOLEN HEAVEN / WHO DO YOU THINK I SAW LAST NIGHT? .... *Victor 25829* 2-4 38
(Vocals: Bean Wain)

STUDY IN BLUE, A / NIGHT SHADES (Vocal: Bea Wain) .... *Victor 25897* 2-4 38

STUDY IN GREEN, A / PLEASE COME OUT OF YOUR DREAM (Vocal: Bea Wain)........ *Victor 26137* 2-4 39

STUDY IN MODERNISM / MISSOURI SCRAMBLER....................... *Victor 26582* 3-5 40

STUDY IN SCARLET, A / THIS IS MY SONG (LONDONERRY AIR) (Vocal: Terry Allen).................... *Victor 26435* 2-4 39

STUDY IN SURREALISM / SUNDAY.... *Victor 26481* 2-4 40

SUNNY SIDE OF THINGS (Vocal: Dick Todd) / PUT YOUR HEART INTO A SONG (Vocal: Bea Wain).............. *Victor 25892* 2-4 38

SWEET LITTLE BUTTERCUP (Vocal: Ford Leary) / I'VE GOT A LITTLE LIST (Vocal: Bea Wain) .... *Victor 26161* 2-4 39

'S WONDERFUL / THE MOON IS LOW.... *Victor 26341* 2-4 39
(Vocals: Terry Allen)

TABLE IN THE CORNER, A / CAN I HELP IT? .... *Victor 26392* 2-4 39
(Vocals: Terry Allen)

THERE'S A BRAND-NEW PICTURE IN MY PICTURE-FRAME / I'M GONNA LOCK MY HEART AND THROW AWAY THE KEY....... *Victor 25885* 2-4 38
(Vocals: Bea Wain)

TINY OLD TOWN / YOU OUGHTA HANG YOUR HEART IN SHAME (Vocal: Terry Allen)............. *Victor 26541* 2-4 40

TOWN TATTLER / TEMPUS FUGIT..... *Victor 27446* 2-4 41

VARIETY IS THE SPICE OF LIFE (Vocals: Bea Wain & Ford Leary) / TEMPTATION .... *Victor 26112* 2-4 39

VICTORY MARCH / FIGHT ON .... *Victor 26034* 2-4 38

WANNA HAT WITH CHERRIES / I'LL REMEMBER.................... *Victor 26303* 2-4 39
(Vocals: Mary Dugan)

WHEN THE HEATHER IS IN BLOOM / AT THE PERFUME COUNTER................ *Victor 25778* 2-4 38
(Vocals: Bea Wain)

WHO BLEW OUT THE FLAME? / IT TOOK A MILLION YEARS.................... *Victor 26073* 2-4 38
(Vocals: Bea Wain)

WILL YOU REMEMBER TONIGHT TOMORROW? (Vocal: Jack Chesleigh) / MY BEST WISHES (Vocal: Carol Bruce)................ *Victor 25875* 2-4 38

WOLVERINE BLUES / STRICTLY FOR THE PERSIANS .... *Victor 25863* 3-5 38

YOU GO TO MY HEAD / I CAN'T FACE THE MUSIC (WITHOUT SINGIN' THE BLUES)..... *Victor 25849* 2-4 38
(Vocals: Bea Wain)

YOU NEVER KNOW / AT LONG LAST LOVE......................... *Victor 26014* 2-4 38
(Vocals: Bea Wain)

YOU, YOU, YOU / CRYING IN THE CHAPEL.................. *Bell Record 1008* 4-6 -
(Vocals: Snooky Lanson)
(A seven-inch 78 rpm record with microgrooves, containing 0the same amount of music as the usual ten-inch records.)

ZIG ZAG / SUMMER SOUVENIRS (Vocal: Bea Wain).......... *Victor 26042* 2-4 38

CLINTON, Larry, as Larry Clinton's Bluebird Orchestra

ARAB DANCE / DANCE OF THE REED FLUTES............. *Bluebird B-10927* 2-4 40

BLIND DATE (Vocal: Terry Allen) / ISN'T IT TIME TO FALL IN LOVE (Vocal: Peggy Mann)................ *Bluebird B-11076* 2-4 41

BOO-WA BOO-WA (Vocal: Jack Palmer) / HALF-WAY DOWN THE STREET (Vocal: Terry Allen) .... *Bluebird B-10820* 2-4 40

BROWN BIRD SINGING, A (Vocal: Terry Allen) / DANCE OF THE CANDY FAIRY.......... *Bluebird B-10850* 2-4 40

CAMPTOWN RACES / ABERCROMBIE HAD A ZOMBIE (Vocal: Butch Stone) .... *Bluebird B-11048* 2-4 41

CARNIVAL OF VENICE / CIELITO LINDO..................... *Bluebird B-10999* 2-4 41

CIELITO LINDO; SAHARA (Vocal: Peggy Mann) / DRUM BOOGIE (Vocals: Irene Day & chorus) ; THAT DRUMMER'S BAND .... *V-Disc 279* 5-8 -
(The third & fourth titles are by Gene Krupa & His Orchestra)
(A World War II release)

COMIN' THRO' THE RYE / TENEMENT SYMPHONY (Vocals: Peggy Mann & Butch Stone)... *Bluebird B-11224* 2-4 41

ESSENTIAL TO ME (Vocals: Peggy Mann & Butch Stone) / ESTRELLITA.................. *Bluebird B-11140* 2-4 41

I CAN'T CHANGE MY HEART (Vocal: Peggy Mann) / WHAT'S THE GOOD OF MOONLIGHT? (Vocals: Peggy Mann & Butch Stone) .... *Bluebird B-11208* 2-4 41

I MAY BE WRONG, BUT I THINK YOU'RE WONDERFUL / LOVE LIES (Vocal: Terry Allen) .... *Bluebird B-10801* 2-4 40

JAZZ ME BLUES / LET ME OFF UPTOWN (Vocal: Butch Stone) ... *Bluebird B-11240* 3-5 41

JUMP JOE / I WANT TO ROCK..... *Bluebird B-10961* 3-5 40

MOONLIGHT AND TEARS (Vocal: Peggy Mann) / YOU FORGOT ABOUT ME (Vocal: Terry Allen) .... *Bluebird B-10984* 2-4 41

MY BUDDY / DIG ME, HONEY..... *Bluebird B-10868* 3-5 40

MY GREATEST MISTAKE (Vocal: Terry Allen) / FEELING LIKE A DREAM....... *Bluebird B-10784* 2-4 40

NIGHT WE MET IN HONOLULU (Vocal: Peggy Mann) / SMILES (Vocal: Butch Stone)........... *Bluebird B-11130* 2-4 41

NOBODY KNOWS THE TROUBLE I'VE SEEN (Vocal: Peggy Mann) / ROCKIN' CHAIR (Vocals: Peggy Mann & Butch Stone)... *Bluebird B-11018* 2-4 41

SAHARA / BECAUSE OF YOU..... *Bluebird B-11094* 2-4 41
(Vocals: Peggy Mann)

SEMPER FIDELIS / DANCE OF THE FLOWERS................. *Bluebird B-10911* 2-4 40

SHADES OF TWILIGHT / BOLERO IN BLUE .... *Bluebird B-10836* 2-4 41
(Vocals: Terry Allen)

TABOO / DO YOU CALL THAT A BUDDY (Vocal: Butch Stone)...... *Bluebird B- 1058* 2-4 41

WORRIED MIND / THAT SOLID OLD MAN .... *Bluebird B-11343* 2-4 41
(Vocals: Butch Stone)

YOU'LL NEVER KNOW / YOUR WORDS AND MY MUSIC................ *Bluebird B-11318* 2-4 41
(Vocals: Peggy Mann)

YOU STARTED SOMETHING / LOVELINESS AND LOVE .... *Bluebird B-11166* 2-4 41
(Vocals: Peggy Mann)

CLOVERDALE COUNTRY CLUB ORCHESTRA, The:
see SELVIN, Ben, & His Orchestra

CLOVER GARDENS ORCHESTRA, The:
see POLLA, W. C.

CLYDE, Billy, & His Orchestra:
see McCOY, Clyde, & His Orchestra

COAKLEY, Tom, & His Orchestra

I'M JUST AN ORDINARY HUMAN / RAINBOW .... *Victor 25058* 2-4 35
(Vocals: Carl Ravazza)

RHYTHM IS OUR BUSINESS (Vocal: Dudley Nix) / SIMPLY GRAND (Vocal: Armand Camgros)................ *Victor 25062* 3-5 35

COAKLEY, Tom, & His Palace Hotel Orchestra

I'LL STRING ALONG WITH YOU / FAIR AND WARMER............. *Victor 24600* 2-4 34
(Vocals: Carl Ravazza)

TAKE A NUMBER FROM ONE TO TEN (Vocal: Kay Thompson) / LET'S GIVE THREE CHEERS FOR LOVE (Vocal: Frank Barton) .... *Victor 24744* 2-4 34

COBURN, Jolly & His Orchestra

AM I DREAMING? (Vocal: Harold van Emburgh) / HAVE YOU GOT ANY CASTLES, BABY? (Vocal: Joan Brooks).................. *Bluebird B-7081* 3-5 37

COLLEGE RHYTHM (Vocals: by orchestra) / STAY AS SWEET AS YOU ARE (Vocal: Roy Strom) ... *Victor 24743* 4-6 34

GONE WITH THE DAWN (Vocal: Bill Hawley) / HAVING WONDERFUL TIME (Vocal: Harold Kolb).................. *Bluebird B-7049* 3-5 37

LOVELINESS OF YOU, THE / AFRAID TO DREAM .... *Bluebird B-7083* 3-5 37
(Vocals: Joan Brooks)

REMEMBER ME? (Vocal: Harold Kolb) / AM I IN LOVE? (Vocal: Harold van Emburgh)........... *Bluebird B-7100* 2-4 37

COLEMAN, Emil, & His Club Trocadero Orchestra
(Emil Coleman: 6/19/94 –)

JUST ONE MORE NIGHT IN YOUR ARMS / FROM ONE TILL TWO............. *Vocalion 14793* 2-4 24

LIMEHOUSE BLUES / VIRGINIA (DON'T GO TOO FAR)...................... *Vocalion 14772* 2-4 24

TIA JUANA / IN A LITTLE RENDEVOUS.............. *Vocalion 14879* 2-4 24

COLEMAN, Emil, & His Hotel Ambassador Orchestra

LINGER AWHILE / THE ONLY GIRL... *Vocalion 14712* 2-4 24

COLEMAN, Emil, & His Montmartre Orchestra

BEES KNEES/ TEDDY BEAR BLUES.... *Vocalion 14458* 2-4 22

BLUE-EYED BLUES / DEEDLE DEEDLE DUM .... *Vocalion 14356* 2-4 22

I'VE GOT THE WONDER WHERE HE WENT AND WHEN HE'S COMING BACK BLUES / ON THE ALAMO .... *Vocalion 14319* 2-4 22

PACK UP YOUR SINS (AND GO TO THE DEVIL) / PORCELAIN MAID .... *Vocalion 14462* 2-4 22

THAT RED HEAD GAL/SNAKE HIPS ... *Vocalion 14565* 3-5 23

COLEMAN, Emil, & His Orchestra

CLOUDS / BE CAREFUL, YOUNG LADY ... *Decca 366* 2-4 35
(Vocals: Unknown)

DAWN (Vocal: Jerry Cooper) / DAWN ..... *Columbia private recording, un-numbered* 15-20 34

I'VE GOT FIVE DOLLARS / WE'LL BE THE SAME............ *Brunswick 6036* 3-5 31
(Vocals: Unknown)

LITTLE MAN, YOU'VE HAD A BUSY DAY / SO HELP ME........ *Columbia 2930-D* 4-6 34
(Vocals: Unknown)

COLEMAN, Emil, & His Palais Royal Orchestra

ONE MORNING IN MAY / ON THE WRONG SIDE OF THE FENCE .... *Columbia 2877-D* 5-8 34
(Vocals: Unknown)

WITHOUT THAT CERTAIN THING / I WAS IN THE MOOD............ *Columbia 2882-D* 5-8 34
(Vocals: Unknown)

COLEMAN, Emil, & His Riviera Orchestra

I'LL BE HARD TO HANDLE (Vocals: The Harmonians) / YOU'RE DEVASTATING (Vocal: Jerry Cooper) .... *Columbia 2847-D* 5-8 34
(This record was pressed in blue shellac.)

SMOKE GETS IN YOUR EYES / LET'S BEGIN .... *Columbia 2846-D* 5-8 34
(Vocals: Unknown)

COLLINS, Artie, & His Orchestra

I NEVER DREAMT YOU'D FALL IN LOVE WITH ME / WASN'T IT BEAUTIFUL WHILE IT LASTED? .... *Broadway 1376* 3-5 30

IT HAPPENED IN MONTEREY / KISS ME WITH YOUR EYES (Vocal: Artie Collins)...... *Broadway 1371* 3-5 30

RED HOT AND BLUE RHYTHM / WHY? .... *Broadway 1375* 4-6 30
(Vocals: Artie Collins)

COLLINS, Roy, as Roy Collins' Orchestra:
see GLANTZ, Nathan, & His Orchestra, and see SAMUELS, Joseph, & His Orchestra

COLOMBO, Al, as Al Colombo's Golden Glades Orchestra

NESTING TIME/JABBERWOCKY... *Paramount 20060* 3-5 21

YOO-HOO / SAY IT WITH MUSIC ... *Paramount 20072* 3-5 21

YOO-HOO / SAY IT WITH MUSIC ...... *Puritan 11072* 2-4 21
(Simultaneously released on two labels)

COLONIAL CLUB ORCHESTRA, The:
see HARING, Bob, & His Orchestra, and see KATZMAN, Louis, & His Orchestra

COLUMBIA DANCE ORCHESTRA, The,
directed by Charles A. Prince
also see Prince's Band / Orchestra)

I'M DRIFTING BACK TO DREAMLAND / JUST A GIRL THAT MEN FORGET .... *Columbia 1-D* 3-5 23

MY DREAM GIRL / SAN' MAN....... *Columbia 181-D* 2-4 24

ROLL ALONG, MISSOURI / ABANDONADO .... *Columbia A-3982* 2-4 23

WONDERFUL ONE / RED MOON ... *Columbia A-3859* 2-4 23

COLUMBIA NOVELTY ORCHESTRA, The

OH! HOW I LOVE MY DARLING / WHO WANTS A BAD LITTLE BOY? .... *Columbia 247-D* 2-4 24
(Vocals: Billy Jones)

WHY DID I KISS THAT GIRL? / OH, BABY! .... *Columbia 131-D* 2-4 24
(Vocals: Billy Jones)

COLUMBIANS, The (a studio band)
also see SELVIN, Ben, & His Orchestra

CAROLINA MAMMY / THAT RED-HEAD GAL .... *Columbia A-3935* 2-4 23

DEAR OLD SOUTHLAND / VIRGINIA BLUES .... *Columbia A-3570* 2-4 22

PACK UP YOUR SINS AND GO TO THE DEVIL/ CRINOLINE DAYS.... *Columbia A-3761* 2-4 22

TUCK ME TO SLEEP (IN MY OLD KENTUCKY HOME) / WABASH BLUES .... *Columbia A-3497* 2-4 21

COLUMBIA PHOTO PLAYERS, The:
see SELVIN, Ben, & His Orchestra

COMSTOCK, Frank, & His Orchestra
(Frank Comstock: 9/20/22 –)

SHOELESS JOE FROM HANNIBAL, MO / THIS IS THE NIGHT .... *Starlite 1369* 3-5 -
(Vocals: by The Hi-Lo's)

CONCERT TABERIN JAZZ ORCHESTRA, The;
see RADERMAN, Harry, as Raderman's Bal Taberin Jazz Orchestra

CONFREY, Zez, & His Orchestra
(Zez Confrey: 4/3/95 – 1972)

CHARLESTON CHUCKLES / HUMORESTLESS.................... *Victor 19606* 2-4 25

KITTEN ON THE KEYS / DIZZY FINGERS..................... *Victor 20777* 3-5 27

NEW HAMPSHIRE / MARCHETA (by the Great White Way Orchestra) .... *Victor 19046* 2-4 23

NICKEL IN THE SLOT / MISSISSIPPI SHIVERS .... *Victor 19430* 3-5 24

CONNIE'S INN ORCHESTRA, The:
see HENDERSON, Fletcher, & His Orchestra

CONN, Irving, & His Orchestra

AND I STILL DO! / THE PRIZE WALTZ .... *Melotone M-13079* 2-4 34
(Vocals: Unknown)

AND I STILL DO! / THE PRIZE WALTZ............................. *Perfect 15963* 2-4 34
(Vocals: Unknown)
(Simultaneously released on two labels)

VERY THOUGHT OF YOU, THE / AS FAR AS I'M CONCERNED............ *Melotone M-13069* 3-5 34
(Vocals: Unknown)

VERY THOUGHT OF YOU, THE / AS FAR AS I'M CONCERNED................ *Perfect 15959* 3-5 34
(Vocals: Unknown)
(Simultaneously released on two labels)

CONNOR, Lou, as Lou Connor's Collegians:
see MILLS, Irving, & His Hotsy Totsy Gang

CONSOLIDATED CLUB ORCHESTRA, The:
see SPECHT, Paul, & His Orchestra

CONWAY, Patrick, as Conway's Band

EYES THAT SAY "I LOVE YOU" / THE MUSIC OF WEDDING CHIMES .... *Okeh 1241* 2-4 19

HAVE A SMILE / OUT OF THE EAST ..... *Okeh 1248* 2-4 19

TENTS OF ARABS / NOBODY EVER ...... *Okeh 4071* 2-4 20

COOK, Doc, & His Dreamland Orchestra
(Doc Cook: 9/3/91 – 12/15/58)

BROWN SUGAR / HIGH FEVER..... *Columbia 813-D* 20-25 26

HERE COMES THE HOT TAMALE MAN! / SPANISH MAMA .... *Columbia 727-D* 20-25 26
(Vocals: Unknown)

COOK, Doc, & His 14 Doctors of Syncopation

ALLIGATOR CRAWL / BRAINSTORM .... *Columbia 1298-D* 15-20 27

HUM AND STRUM (Vocals: by trio) / I GOT WORRY (Vocal: Andrew Hilaire) .... *Columbia 1430-D* 15-20 28

WILLIE THE WEEPER (Vocal: Andrew Hilaire) / SLUE FOOT....................... *Columbia 1070-D* 20-25 27

COOK, Doc, as Cookie's Gingersnaps

HIGH FEVER / HERE COMES THE HOT TAMALE MAN .... *Okeh 8369* 25-30 26

COOK, Doc, as Cook's Dreamland Orchestra

LONELY LITTLE WALLFLOWER / MOANFUL MAN .... *Gennett 5373* 25-30 24

LONELY LITTLE WALLFLOWER / MOANFUL MAN.................. *Silvertone 4045* 20-25 24
(Simultaneously released on two labels)

SCISSOR-GRINDER JOE / THE MEMPHIS MAYBE MAN........................ *Gennett 5374* 35-40 24

SCISSOR-GRINDER JOE / THE MEMPHIS MAYBE MAN...................... *Silvertone 4044* 30-35 24
(Simultaneously released on two labels)

SO THIS IS VENICE / THE ONE I LOVE BELONGS TO SOMEBODY ELSE .... *Gennett 5360* 20-25 24

COON-SANDERS ORCHESTRA, The
(directed by Carleton Coon: 2/5/94 – 5/4/32, and Joe Sanders: 10/15/96 – 5/15/65)
also see SANDERS, Joe, & His Orchestra

AFTER YOU'VE GONE (Vocals: Carleton Coon & Joe Sanders) / DARKTOWN STRUTTERS' BALL (Vocal: Carleton Coon) .... *Victor 22342* 5-8 30

AND ESPECIALLY YOU (Vocal: Joe Sanders) / BIRMINGHAM BERTHA (by Jean Goldkette & His Orchestra; Vocal: Kay Palmer)........ *Victor 22077* 5-8 29

GOT A GREAT BIG DATE WITH A LITTLE BITTA GIRL (Vocal: Joe Sanders) / OLD ITALIAN LOVE SONG (by Jean Goldkette & His Orchestra) .... *Victor 22123* 3-5 29

HARLEM MADNESS (Vocal: Joe Sanders) / THERE WILL NEVER BE ANOTHER MARY (by Ted Fio Rito & His Orchestra; Vocal: Pedro Espino) .... *Victor 22300* 10-12 30

HERE COMES MY BALL AND CHAIN / WHO WOULDN'T BE JEALOUS OF YOU? ... *Victor 21812* 5-8 29
(Vocals: Joe Sanders)

HIGH FEVER / YOU'RE THE ONE FOR ME (Ben Pollack & His Californians; Vocal: Ilomay Bailey)............ *Victor 20461* 15-20 27

I NEED LOVIN' (Vocal: Joe Sanders) / 'DEED I DO (by Ben Pollack & His Orchestra)........... *Victor 20408* 5-8 27

KEEPIN' OUT OF MISCHIEF NOW / I KNOW YOU'RE LIVING, BUT I LOVE IT .... *Victor 22969* 5-8 32
(Vocals: Joe Sanders)

LET THAT BE A LESSON TO YOU / WHAT A LIFE! .... *Victor 22950* 5-8 32
(Vocals: Joe Sanders)

LITTLE ORPHAN ANNIE (Vocal: Joe Sanders) / BLESS YOU, SISTER (Vocal: Carleton Coon)...... *Victor 21895* 8-10 29

LO AND BEHOLD / SING A NEW SONG... *Victor 22951* 5-8 32
(Vocals: Joe Sanders)

LOUDER AND FUNNIER / SMILIN' SKIES (Vocals: Carleton Coon)......... *Victor V-38083* 8-10 29

MINE-ALL MINE (Vocals: Carleton Coon & Joe Sanders) / IS SHE MY GIRL FRIEND? (Vocal: Joe Sanders) .... *Victor 21148* 4-6 28

MOANIN' FOR YOU (Vocal: Joe Sanders) / SOMEBODY MIGHTY LIKE YOU (by Wayne King & His Orchestra) .... *Victor 22278* 5-8 30

MY BABY KNOWS HOW (Vocal: Joe Sanders) / BRAINSTORM.......................... *Victor 20390* 5-8 27

MY SUPPRESSED DESIRE (Vocal: Carleton Coon) / WHAT A GIRL! WHAT A NIGHT! (Vocal: Joe Sanders)................... *Victor 21803* 4-6 29

READY FOR THE RIVER (Vocal: Joe Sanders) / OH! YOU HAVE NO IDEA (Vocals: Carleton Coon & Joe Sanders)......................... *Victor 21501* 4-6 28

RHYTHM KING (Vocal: Carleton Coon) / MISSISSIPPI, HERE I AM (Vocals: Carleton Coon & Joe Sanders) .... *Victor 21891* 4-6 29

'ROUND MY HEART / I WANT TO GO HOME .... *Victor 22972* 5-8 32
(Vocals: Joe Sanders)

SLUEFOOT (Vocals: Carleton Coon & Joe Sanders) / THE WAIL .... *Victor 21305* 5-8 28

STAY OUT OF THE SOUTH (Vocals: Carleton Coon & Joe Sanders) / WHO'S BLUE NOW? (by Fred Waring & His Pennsylvanians; Vocals: by orchestra)....... *Victor 21258* 4-6 28

TENNESSEE LAZY (some copies show TENNESSEE LADY) / KANSAS CITY KITTY................ *Victor 21939* 5-8 29
(Vocals: Joe Sanders)

TOO BUSY! (Vocal: Carleton Coon) / DOWN WHERE THE SUN GOES DOWN (Vocal: Joe Sanders).... *Victor 21546* 5-8 28

COON-SANDERS ORIGINAL NIGHTHAWK ORCHESTRA, The
directed by Carleton Coon & Joe Sanders
(The Coon-Sanders Nighthawk Orchestra in Kansas City in the early 1920's was the first band to gain popularity through regular radio broadcasts.)

DEEP HENDERSON / ACE IN THE HOLE (by Al Katz & His Kittens) .... *Victor 20081* 5-8 26
FLAMIN' MAMIE (Vocal: Joe Sanders) / – ... *Victor 19922* 5-8 26
HONGKONG DREAM GIRL (Vocals: Carleton Coon & Joe Sanders) / WHO WOULDN'T LOVE YOU? (Vocal: Joe Sanders) .... *Victor 19754* 4-6 25
I'M GONNA CHARLESTON BACK TO CHARLESTON (Vocals: Joe Sanders & Carleton Coon) / ALONE AT LAST (Vocal: Joe Sanders) .... *Victor 19727* 4-6 25
MOONLIGHT AND YOU / SHOW ME THE WAY .... *Victor 19525* 4-6 25
(Vocals: Joe Sanders & Carleton Coon)
NIGHT HAWK BLUES / RED-HOT MAMA .... *Victor 19316* 5-8 24
(Vocals: Joe Sanders & Carleton Coon)
ORIENTAL LOVE-DREAMS / MY DADDY'S DREAM-TIME .... *Victor 19325* 3-5 24
(Vocals: Joe Sanders & Carleton Coon)
THAT'S ALL THERE IS (THERE AIN'T NO MORE) (Vocal: Carleton Coon) / EVERYTHING IS HOTSY-TOTSY NOW (Vocal: Joe Sanders) ... *Victor 19750* 4-6 25
THERE'S NO-ONE JUST LIKE YOU / WHY DON'T MY DREAMS COME TRUE? (Vocals: Joe Sanders & Carleton Coon) .... *Victor 19357* 3-5 24

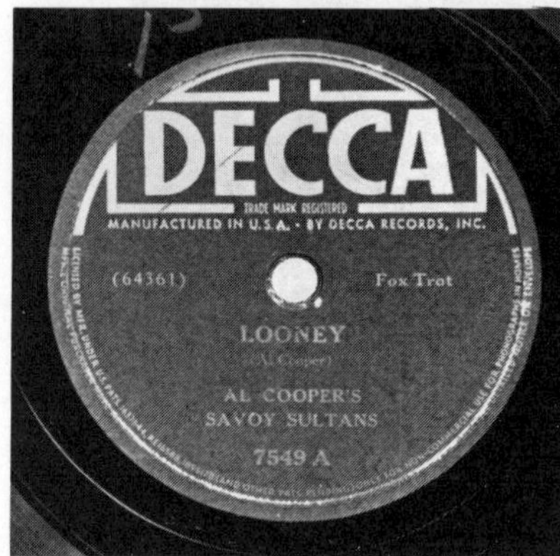

COOPER, Al, & His Savoy Sultans

'AT'S IN THERE (Vocal: Betty Roche) / LET YOUR CONSCIENCE BY YOUR GUIDE (Vocal: George Kelley) .... *Decca 8615* 5-8 42
BOATS / FISH FOR YOUR SUPPER (Vocals: by chorus) .... *Decca 8598* 5-8 42
FRENZY / STOP AND ASK SOMEBODY (Vocal: Paul Chapman) .... *Decca 3142* 5-8 40
JEEPS BLUES / YOU'LL NEVER MISS THE WATER (Vocal: Helen Proctor) .... *Decca 7502* 5-8 38
JUMPIN' AT THE SAVOY (Vocals: by chorus) / WE'D RATHER JUMP THAN SWING (Vocal: Pat Jenkins) .... *Decca 2526* 5-8 39
JUMP STEADY / RHYTHM DOCTOR MAN ... *Decca 7499* 5-8 38
LITTLE SALLY WATER (Vocals: by chorus) / LOVE GAVE ME YOU (Vocal: Paul Chapman) .... *Decca 2819* 4-6 39
LOONEY / SOMEONE OUTSIDE IS TAKING YOUR MIND OFF ME (Vocal: Helen Proctor) .... *Decca 7549* 5-8 38
NORFOLK FERRY / SEE WHAT I MEAN? ... *Decca 8540* 4-6 41
SECOND BALCONY JUMP / JACKIE BOY ... *Decca 8545* 5-8 41
STITCHES / DRAGGIN' MY HEART AROUND (Vocal: Evelyn White) .... *Decca 2608* 4-6 39
THING, THE / GETTIN' IN THE GROOVE ... *Decca 7525* 5-8 38
WISHING AND CRYING FOR YOU (Vocal: Evelyn White) / SOPHISTICATED JUMP .... *Decca 3274* 5-8 40

CORDES, John, as Cordes' Society Orchestra

ALL THE QUAKERS ARE SHOULDER SHAKERS (Vocal: Billy de Rex) / HAPPY DAYS ...... *Gennett 9022* 2-4 20
OH, WHAT A PAL WAS MARY (Vocals: Unknown) / HONEYMOON .... *Gennett 9014* 2-4 19
PEGGY (Vocal: Billy de Rex) / FOLLIES MEDLEY .... *Gennett 9010* 2-4 19

CORNELIUS, Paul, & His Orchestra

I'VE FOUND A NEW BABY / I'M STILL DREAMING OF YOU (Vocal: Clyde Kissinger) .... *Champion 16734* 3-5 34
PLEASE HANDLE WITH CARE / SAY IT ISN'T SO .... *Champion 16523* 2-4 32
(Vocals: Jim Hartley)
SMOKE GETS IN YOUR EYES (Vocal: Clyde Kissinger) / ORCHIDS IN THE MOONLIGHT ... *Champion 16727* 2-4 34
WERE YOU SINCERE? / BUBBLING OVER WITH LOVE .... *Superior 2685* 2-4 31
(Vocals: Jim Hartley)
WERE YOU SINCERE? (Vocal: Jim Hartley) / HO HUM! (Vocal: Bud Surtace) .... *Champion 16282* 2-4 31

CORNELL, & His Orchestra:
see SMELSER, Cornell

CORNWELL, Frank, & His Orchestra

DAWN / – .... *Edison 52166* 5-8 28
HERE OR THERE / SINCE I FOUND YOU (Vocal: Frank Cornwell) .... *Harmony 320-H* 5-8 26
VOOM VOOM (Vocals: by orchestra) / CRAZY WORDS– CRAZY TUNE (Vocals: Gus Gudarian & Forrest "Fuzzy" Knight) .... *Harmony 341-H* 8-10 27

COURTNEY, Del, & His Orchestra
(Del Courtney: 1910 –)

ALL THIS AND HEAVEN TOO (Vocal: Sherman Hayes) / YOU THINK OF EV'RYTHING (Vocal: Joe Martin) .... *Vocalion 5608* 2-4 40
AN APPLE FOR THE TEACHER (Vocal: Sherman Hayes) / STILL THE BLUEBIRD SINGS (Vocal: Dick Dildine) .... *Conqueror 9301* 2-4 39
AN APPLE FOR THE TEACHER (Vocal: Sherman Hayes) / STILL THE BLUEBIRD SINGS (Vocal: Dick Dildine) .... *Vocalion 4985* 2-4 39
(Simultaneously released on two labels)
BASKET WEAVER (Vocal: Sherman Hayes) / NOW I LAY ME DOWN TO DREAM (Vocal: Joe Martin) .... *Okeh 5720* 2-4 40
HAWAIIAN WAR CHANT (Vocals: by orchestra) / THE SINGING HILLS (Vocal: Joe Martin) .... *Conqueror 9468* 2-4 40
HAWAIIAN WAR CHANT (Vocals: by orchestra) / THE SINGING HILLS (Vocal: Joe Martin) .... *Vocalion 5354* 2-4 40
(Simultaneously released on two labels)
HOW LOVELY YOU ARE (Vocal: Joe Martin) / OVER THE RAINBOW (Vocal: Sherman Hayes) ...... *Vocalion 4992* 3-5 39
LAMP IS LOW, THE (Vocals: Sherman Hayes) / SOMEBODY TOLD ME THEY LOVED ME (Vocal: Joe Martin) .... *Vocalion 4864* 3-5 39
OUT OF SPACE (Vocal: Sherman Hayes) / BLUE RAIN (Vocal: Joe Martin) .... *Vocalion 5279* 2-4 39
STOP KICKING MY HEART AROUND (Vocal: Sherman Hayes) / OCEANS APART (Vocal: Dick Dildine) .... *Vocalion 5088* 2-4 39
TO YOU, SWEETHEART, ALOHA / PUT THAT DOWN IN WRITING .... *Vocalion 5046* 2-4 39
(Vocals: Joe Martin)
WHEN LOVE BECKONED (Vocal: Joe Martin) / IT WAS WRITTEN IN THE STARS (Vocal: Sherman Hayes) .... *Vocalion 5291* 3-5 40

COWAN, Lynn, as Lynn Cowan's Boulevard Theatre Orchestra
see LANIN, Sam, & His Orchestra

COY, Dick, & His Racketeers

'LEVEN-THIRTY SATURDAY NIGHT (Vocal: Jimmy McPoland) / BARNACLE BILL THE SAILOR (Vocals: by orchestra) .... *Gennett 7175* 10-15 30

CRAIG, Francis, & His Orchestra
(Francis Craig: 9/10/00 –)

DREAM RIVER / ALL DAY LONG ... *Columbia 1440-D* 3-5 28
HARD-TO-GET GERTIE / DO YOU BELIEVE IN DREAMS? .... *Columbia 709-D* 4-6 26
MARBLE HALLS / STEADY ROLL BLUES .... *Columbia 567-D* 4-6 25
RED ROSE / COON-TAIL .... *Columbia 1544-D* 3-5 28
THAT FLORIDA LOW-DOWN / MOONLIGHT IN MANDALAY .... *Columbia 1266-D* 4-6 26

CRAWFORD, Jack, & His Boys:
see SEIDEL, Emil, & His Orchestra

CRAWFORD, Jesse, & His Orchestra
(Jesse Crawford 12/2/95 – 5/28/62)

IT'S THE NATURAL THING TO DO / AFTER YOU .... *Bluebird B-7107* 3-5 37
(Vocals: Bob Murray)
ME, MYSELF AND I / DANCING UNDER THE STARS .... *Bluebird B-7105* 3-5 37
(Vocals: Bob Murray)
ON WITH THE DANCE / LOVE IS ON THE AIR TONIGHT .... *Bluebird B-7117* 3-5 37
(Vocals: Bob Murray)

CREAGER, Willie, & His Orchestra

BYGONES (Vocal: Arthur Hall) / INDIAN LOVE CALL .... *Gennett 5668* 3-5 25
CLIMBING UP THE LADDER OF LOVE / HUGS AND KISSES .... *Pathe Actuelle 36532* 3-5 26
(Vocals: Irving Kaufman)
CLIMBING UP THE LADDER OF LOVE / HUGS AND KISSES .... *Perfect 14713* 2-4 26
(Vocals: Irving Kaufman)
(Simultaneously released on two labels)
GOTTA GETTA GIRL / EVERYTHING YOU DO .... *Gennett 5599* 3-5 25
I'LL ALWAYS BE IN LOVE WITH YOU / LOVE IS IN THE AIR .... *Gennett 6893* 3-5 29
(Vocals: Jerry White)
IT MADE YOU HAPPY WHEN YOU MADE ME CRY / LONELY EYES .... *Banner 1890* 2-4 27
(Vocals: Irving Kaufman)
IT MADE YOU HAPPY WHEN YOU MADE ME CRY / LONELY EYES .... *Domino 3854* 2-4 27
(Vocals: Irving Kaufman)
(Simultaneously released on two labels)
JUST A LITTLE LONGER / DON'T SING ALOHA WHEN I GO .... *Gennett 3404* 3-5 26
(Vocals: The Keller Sisters & Lynch)
THINKING ABOUT MY BABY (Vocal: Unknown) / DADDY, WON'T YOU PLEASE COME HOME? .... *Harmony 922-H* 2-4 29
WHEN MY DREAMS COME TRUE / LOVE IS IN THE AIR .... *Champion 15757* 2-4 29
(Vocals: Jerry White)
WHY DO YOU ROLL THOSE EYES / LUCKY DAY .... *Gennett 3374* 3-5 26
(Vocals: Leroy Montesanto)

CROSBY, Bob, & His Orchestra
(Bob Crosby: 8/23/13 –)
(Bob Crosby & His Orchestra regularly play engagements all over the nation. Nappy Lamare and Eddie Miller, who sing on some of the following sides, are noted for guitar and tenor saxophone performances respectively. Both are original members of the Crosby band formed in 1935, and are still active with the group.)

AIN'T GOIN' NOWHERE / DRUMMER BOY (Vocals: The Bob-O-Links) ... *Decca 3451* 2-4 40
AIR MAIL STOMP / OH! WHAT YOU SAID (Vocal: Marion Mann) .... *Decca 2992* 3-5 40
ALWAYS AND ALWAYS (Vocal: Kay Weber) / MORE THAN EVER (Vocal: Bob Crosby) .... *Decca 1657* 2-4 38
ANCHORS AWEIGH / THE CAISSONS GO ROLLING ALONG .... *Decca 4395* 3-5 42
AT A LITTLE HOT-DOG STAND (Vocals: Bob Crosby & Marion Mann) / IF I DIDN'T CARE (Vocal: Bob Crosby) .... *Decca 2401* 2-4 39
BE A GOOD SPORT (Vocal: Bob Crosby) / SWEET SOMEONE (Vocal: Kay Weber) ..... *Decca 1576* 4-6 38
BELIEVING (Vocal: Marion McCann) / THIS IS THE BEGINNING OF THE END (Vocal: Bob Crosby) .... *Decca 3103* 2-4 40
BETWEEN 18TH AND 19TH ON CHESTNUT STREET (Vocals: Nappy Lamare & Eddie Miller) / I WANNA WRAP YOU UP (Vocal: Teddy Grace) .... *Decca 2935* 2-4 40
BIG NOISE FROM WINNETKA, THE / SUNSET AT SEA .... *Decca 3611* 2-4 40
(Vocals: Bob Crosby)
BIG TOM / 'WAY DOWN YONDER IN NEW ORLEANS (Vocals: Eddie Miller & Nappy Lamare) .... *Decca 4403* 2-4 42
BLACK ZEPHYR / BLUE SURREAL .... *Decca 4415* 2-4 42
BLUE ORCHIDS (Vocal: Teddy Grace) / THE WORLD IS WAITING FOR THE SUNRISE .... *Decca 2734* 3-5 39
BOOGIE WOOGIE MAXIXE / HIGH SOCIETY .... *Decca 2848* 3-5 39
BRASS BOOGIE / BRASS BOOGIE, PART II .... *Decca 18359* 3-5 42
CAN I HELP IT? (Vocal: Bob Crosby) / THE LITTLE MAN WHO WASN'T THERE (Vocal: Teddy Grace) .... *Decca 2776* 2-4 39
CHAIN GANG / EC-STACY .... *Decca 15064* 4-6 42
(This is an oversize 12-inch 78 rpm)
CHERRY (Vocal: Nappy Lamare) / DAY IN, DAY OUT (Vocal: Helen Ward) .... *Decca 2703* 2-4 39
CHICK-EE-CHICK (Vocal: Bonnie King) / BLUE ECHOES (Vocals: Bob Crosby & The Bob-O-Links) ...... *Decca 3605* 2-4 41
CHRISTOPHER COLUMBUS / IT'S GREAT TO BE IN LOVE AGAIN (Vocal: Bob Crosby) .... *Decca 753* 4-6 36
COMPLAININ' / JA DA .... *Decca 3233* 2-4 40

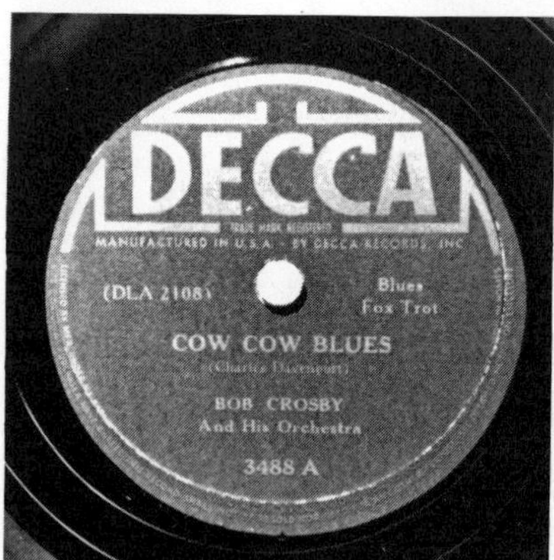

COW COW BLUES / DRY BONES (Vocals: Nappy Lamare & The Bob-O-Links) .... *Decca 3488* 3-5 40
CROSS PATCH (Vocal: Bob Crosby) / BIG CHIEF DE SOTO .... *Decca 841* 3-5 36
DIGA DIGA DOO / DIGA DIGA DOO, PART II .... *Decca 2275* 2-4 38
DIXIELAND BAND, THE (Vocal: Bob Crosby) / BEALE STREET BLUES (Vocal: Joe Harris) .... *Decca 479* 5-8 35
DON'T WORRY 'BOUT ME (Vocal: Marion Mann) / WHAT GOES UP MUST COME DOWN (Vocal: Bob Crosby) .... *Decca 2402* 2-4 39
DO YOU CARE? (Vocals: Bob Crosby & The Bob-O-Links) / WILL YOU STILL BE MINE? .... *Decca 3860* 2-4 41
DO YOU KNOW WHY? (Vocal: Bonnie King) / ISN'T THAT JUST LIKE LOVE? (Vocal: Bob Crosby) ..... *Decca 3445* 2-4 40
EAST OF THE SUN (Vocal: Frank Tennille) / AND THEN SOME (Vocal: Bob Crosby) ...... *Decca 502* 5-8 35
ELMER'S TUNE / THE ANGELS CAME THRU (Vocals: Bob Crosby & The Bob-O-Links) ...... *Decca 3929* 2-4 41
FAR AWAY MUSIC (Vocal: Bonnie King) / FLAMINGO .... *Decca 3752* 2-4 41
FLOWERS FOR MADAME / IN A LITTLE GYPSY TEA ROOM .... *Decca 478* 4-6 35
(Vocals: Frank Tennille)
FOOLS RUSH IN (Vocal: Marion Mann) / SYMPATHY .... *Decca 3154* 2-4 40

FOR DANCERS ONLY / WHERE THE BLUE OF THE NIGHT MEETS THE GOLD OF THE DAY (Vocal: Bob Crosby) ..... *Decca 3138* 3-5 40

FROM ANOTHER WORLD (Vocal: Marion Mann) / OVER THE WAVES .... *Decca 3091* 2-4 40

GAY RANCHERO, A (Vocal: Liz Tilton) / SOMETHING NEW (Vocals: Bob Crosby & Liz Tilton)....... *Decca 4028* 2-4 41

GIN MILL BLUES / IF I HAD YOU (Vocal: Bob Crosby)............ *Decca 1170* 4-6 37

GIVE A BROKEN HEART A BREAK (Vocal: Bob Crosby) / IT'S BETTER TO BE BY YOURSELF (Vocal: Gordon Polk) .... *Decca 18915* 2-4 42

GOODY GOODY / WHAT'S THE NAME OF THAT SONG?........................ *Decca 727* 5-8 38 (Vocals: Bob Crosby)

GRAND TERRACE RHYTHM / DO YE KEN JOHN PEEL?......................... *Decca 1725* 3-5 38 (Vocals: Nappy Lamare)

GUESS WHO / MARY HAD A LITTLE LAMB........................ *Decca 836* 4-6 36 (Vocals: Bob Crosby)

HAPPY BIRTHDAY TO LOVE (Vocal: Teddy Grace) / THE ANSWER IS LOVE (Vocal: Bob Crosby)..... *Decca 2824* 2-4 39

HERE'S TO ROMANCE / I FOUND A DREAM.............................. *Decca 615* 5-8 35 (Vocals: Frank Tennille)

HOW CAN YOU FORGET? (Vocal: Bob Crosby) / THERE'S A BOY IN HARLEM (Vocal: Nappy Lamare) .... *Decca 1732* 2-4 38

HURRY HOME (Vocal: Bob Crosby) / DEEP IN A DREAM (Vocal: Marion Mann).... *Decca 2151* 2-4 38

I'D KNOW YOU ANYWHERE (Vocal: Bonnie King) / I'VE GOT A ONE-TRACK MIND (Vocal: Bob Crosby) .... *Decca 3434* 2-4 40

IF I WERE SURE OF YOU (Vocal: Marion Mann) / THE LADY'S IN LOVE WITH YOU (Vocal: Bob Crosby)...................... *Decca 2465* 2-4 39

I'LL BE TRUE TO THE ONE I LOVE / WHEN YOU THINK OF LOVIN', BABY THINK OF ME................. *Decca 4357* 2-4 42 (Vocals: Bob Crosby)

I'LL CAPTURE YOUR HEART (Vocals: Bing Crosby & Fred Astaire) / LAZY (Vocal: Bing Crosby) .... *Decca 18427* 4-6 42

I'LL KEEP THE LOVELIGHT BURNING / DON'T SIT UNDER THE APPLE TREE............ *Decca 4290* 2-4 42 (Vocals: Bob Crosby)

I'M IN THE MOOD FOR LOVE / TWO TOGETHER....................... *Decca 508* 5-8 35

I'M NOBODY'S BABY (Vocal: Marion Mann) / SPEAK EASY......................... *Decca 3179* 2-4 40

I'M TRUSTING IN YOU / FROM ONE LOVE TO ANOTHER................. *Decca 4027* 2-4 41 (Vocals: Bob Crosby)

I NEVER KNEW HEAVEN COULD SPEAK (Vocal: Marion Mann) / ROSE OF WASHINGTON SQUARE (Vocal: Bob Crosby).............. *Decca 2464* 2-4 39

IN THE SHADE OF THE OLD APPLE TREE / IT'S EASIER SAID THAN DONE........ *Decca 1658* 2-4 38 (Vocals: Bob Crosby)

IT'S A WHOLE NEW THING / ANGRY .... *Decca 2839* 2-4 39 (Vocals: Teddy Grace)

IT WAS ONLY A DREAM (Vocal: Eddie Miller) / TAKE IT EASY........................ *Decca 4137* 3-5 41

I'VE GOT A STRANGE NEW RHYTHM IN MY HEART / WHY SHOULD I CARE?.... *Decca 1555* 4-6 37 (Vocals: Bob Crosby)

I'VE GOT MY EYES ON YOU (Vocal: Marion Mann) / GOTTA GET HOME (Vocal: Bob Crosby) .... *Decca 2991* 2-4 40

I'VE HITCHED MY WAGON TO A STAR / SILHOUETTED IN THE MOONLIGHT... *Decca 1556* 4-6 37 (Vocals: Bob Crosby)

I, YI, YI, YI, YI (I LIKE YOU VERY MUCH) / CHICA-CHICA-BOOM-CHIC.... *Decca 3623* 2-4 41 (Vocals: Bonnie King)

JUST STROLLING / IT'S WONDERFUL (Vocal: Kay Weber) .... *Decca 1670* 3-5 38

LAST NIGHT (Vocal: Bob Crosby) / I THOUGHT ABOUT YOU (Vocal: Teddy Grace).......... *Decca 2812* 2-4 39

LITTLE BIT INDEPENDENT, A / NO OTHER ONE........................ *Decca 629* 5-8 36 (Vocals: Bob Crosby)

LITTLE ROCK GETAWAY / VIENI, VIENI........................ *Decca 1552* 5-8 37

LOVELINESS OF YOU, THE (Vocal: Bob Crosby) / YOU CAN'T HAVE EVERYTHING (Vocal: Kay Weber) .... *Decca 1370* 4-6 37

MARINES' HYMN, THE / WHERE DO WE GO FROM HERE?...................... *Decca 4385* 3-5 42 (Vocals: Bob Crosby)

MARK HOP, THE / BURNIN' THE CANDLE AT BOTH ENDS........................ *Decca 3694* 2-4 41

MELANCHOLY MOOD / OH, YOU CRAZY MOON........................ *Decca 2652* 2-4 39 (Vocals: Bob Crosby)

MILK COW BLUES (Vocal: Nappy Lamare) / SQUEEZE ME........................ *Decca 1962* 3-5 38

MOMENTS IN THE MOONLIGHT / AN ANGEL IN DISGUISE......................... *Decca 3070* 2-4 40 (Vocals: Marion Mann)

MUCH MORE LOVELY (Vocal: Bonnie King) / WELL, WELL (Vocals: Bob Crosby & The Bob-O-Links)........................ *Decca 3762* 2-4 41

MUSKRAT RAMBLE / DIXIELAND SHUFFLE........................ *Decca 825* 5-8 36

MY IMAGINARY LOVE (Vocal: Bob Crosby) / WEEKEND IN HAVANA (Vocal: Liz Tilton)............ *Decca 4049* 2-4 41

MY INSPIRATION / LOOPIN' THE LOOP (by The Bobcats) .... *Decca 2209* 2-4 38

MY KINGDOM FOR A KISS / THROUGH THE COURTESY OF LOVE .... *Decca 903* 4-6 36 (Vocals: Bob Crosby)

MY! MY! (Vocals: Bob Crosby & Marion Mann) / SAY IT (Vocal: Bob Crosby)............ *Decca 3079* 2-4 40

NICE WORK IF YOU CAN GET IT (Vocal: Bob Crosby) / A FOGGY DAY (Vocal: Kay Weber).......... *Decca 1539* 3-5 37

OLD FOLKS / MY REVERIE............. *Decca 2123* 4-6 38 (Vocals: Bing Crosby)

OLD SPINNING WHEEL / BETWEEN THE DEVIL AND THE DEEP BLUE SEA.............. *Decca 1196* 5-8 37

ONE NIGHT IN MONTE CARLO / EENY MEENY MINEY MO..................... *Decca 633* 4-6 36 (Vocals: Bob Crosby)

ONLY WHEN YOU'RE IN MY ARMS (Vocal: Bob Crosby) / PENTHOUSE SERENADE (Vocal: Marion Mann)...................... *Decca 2452* 2-4 39

ON TREASURE ISLAND / AT YOUR SERVICE, MADAME.................... *Decca 614* 4-6 35 (Vocals: Bob Crosby)

OOH! LOOK-A THERE! AIN'T SHE PRETTY? / YOU'RE TOOTS TO ME................... *Decca 759* 5-8 36 (Vocals: Bob Crosby)

OVER THERE / (PACK UP YOUR TROUBLES IN YOUR OLD KIT BAG AND) SMILE, SMILE, SMILE................ *Decca 4368* 2-4 42

PAGAN LOVE SONG / COME BACK, SWEET PAPA (Vocal: Nappy Lamare) .... *Decca 896* 5-8 36

PANAMA / BIG APPLE CALLS (Vocal: Nappy Lamare).............. *Decca 1615* 4-6 38

PETER PIPER (Vocal: Bob Crosby) / WOMAN ON MY WEARY MIND...................... *Decca 930* 4-6 36

PINCH ME (Vocal: Bob Crosby) / THE LITTLE RED FOX (Vocal: Teddy Grace)............. *Decca 2924* 2-4 40

PLEASE BE KIND (Vocal: Kay Weber) / I SIMPLY ADORE YOU (Vocal: Bob Crosby) .... *Decca 1693* 2-4 38

POOR YOU / LAST CALL FOR LOVE...... *Decca 4316* 2-4 42 (Vocals: Bob Crosby)

REMINISCING TIME / TIT WILLOW (Vocal: Marion Mann) .... *Decca 3054* 2-4 40

ROYAL GARDEN BLUES / TEA FOR TWO...................... *Decca 1850* 3-5 38

SAN ANTONIO ROSE / IT MAKES NO DIFFERENCE NOW................ *Decca 3590* 4-6 40 (Vocals: Bing Crosby)

SEMPER PARATUS / ARMY AIR CORPS (Vocal: Bob Crosby)............... *Decca 4374* 3-5 42

SHAKE DOWN THE STARS / LEANIN' ON THE OLD TOP RAIL.................... *Decca 3027* 2-4 40 (Vocals: Bob Crosby)

SHANGHAI / THAT NAUGHTY WALTZ... *Capitol 1525* 2-4 50

SHORT'NIN' BREAD (Vocal: Eddie Miller) / EMBRACEABLE YOU (Vocal: Bob Crosby)... *Decca 3271* 2-4 40

SINNER KISSED AN ANGEL, A / TWO IN LOVE......................... *Decca 4009* 2-4 41 (Vocals: Bob Crosby)

SKATERS WALTZ (IN SWINGTIME) / EYE OPENER............................. *Decca 2282* 2-4 39

SOMETHING I DREAMED, NO DOUBT / CALL IT ANYTHING (IT'S LOVE)................ *Decca 3815* 2-4 41 (Vocals: Bob Crosby & The Bob-O-Links)

SO THIS IS HEAVEN / I DON'T WANT TO MAKE HISTORY..................... *Decca 728* 5-8 36 (Vocals: Bob Crosby)

SOUTH RAMPART STREET PARADE / DOGTOWN BLUES.......................... *Decca 15038* 4-6 38 (This is an oversize 12-inch 78 rpm)

SOUTH RAMPART STREET PARADE / SMOKEY MARY........................ *Decca 2569* 2-4 39

STARLIT HOUR, THE / ANGEL.......... *Decca 2978* 2-4 40 (Vocals: Bob Crosby)

STOMP OFF, LET'S GO (Vocal: Nappy Lamare) / SONG OF THE WANDERER............ *Decca 2379* 2-4 39

STRANGE ENCHANTMENT (Vocal: Marion Mann) / THAT SENTIMENTAL SANDWICH (Vocal: Bob Crosby)........................ *Decca 2415* 2-4 39

SUGAR FOOT STOMP / KING PORTER STOMP............................... *Decca 4390* 2-4 42

SUGAR FOOT STRUT / SAVOY BLUES.... *Decca 1094* 5-8 36

SUMMERTIME; SHORT'NIN' BREAD (Vocal: Eddie Miller) / STRICTLY INSTRUMENTAL (by Harry James & His Orchestra)............ *V-Disc 311* 5-8 - (A World War II release)

SWEET GENEVIEVE / UNTIL YOU FALL IN LOVE....................... *Decca 3668* 2-4 40 (Vocals: Bob Crosby)

SWINGIN' AT THE SUGAR BOWL (Vocal: Nappy Lamare) / I'M PRAYIN' HUMBLE... *Decca 2210* 3-5 38

TENDER IS THE NIGHT (Vocal: Frank Tennille) / ROLL ALONG, PRAIRIE MOON (Vocal: Bob Crosby)........................ *Decca 544* 5-8 35

THEY OUGHT TO WRITE A BOOK ABOUT YOU / CECILIA .... *Decca 3090* 2-4 40 (Vocals: Bob Crosby)

THIS NEVER HAPPENED BEFORE / LET'S GIVE LOVE ANOTHER CHANCE .... *Decca 1566* 5-8 38 (Vocals: Kay Weber)

THRILL OF A LIFETIME, THE (Vocal: Kay Weber) / EVERY DAY'S A HOLIDAY (Vocal: Bob Crosby)...................... *Decca 1580* 5-8 37

TWO DREAMS MET / DOWN ARGENTINE WAY..................... *Decca 3404* 2-4 40 (Vocals: Bonnie King)

TWO SLEEPY PEOPLE (Vocals: Bob Crosby & Marion Mann) / WAIT TILL MY HEART FINDS OUT (Vocal: Bob Crosby) .... *Decca 2150* 2-4 38

UP THE CHIMNEY GO MY DREAMS / RUN, RABBIT, RUN.................... *Decca 3039* 2-4 40 (Vocals: Marion Mann)

VULTEE SPECIAL / RUSSIAN SAILORS' DANCE .... *Decca 4397* 2-4 42

WHAT HAVE YOU GOT THAT GETS ME? (Vocal: Marion Mann) / YOU'RE LOVELY, MADAME (Vocal: Bob Crosby)............ *Decca 2142* 2-4 38

WHAT'S NEW? / SUMMERTIME (theme song).............. *Decca 2205* 2-4 38

WHAT USED TO WAS USED TO WAS (NOW IT AIN'T) (Vocal: Teddy Grace) / LILACS IN THE RAIN (Vocal: Bob Crosby)...................... *Decca 2763* 2-4 39

WHEN THE RED, RED ROBIN COMES BOB, BOB, BOBBIN' ALONG / THEM THERE EYES... *Decca 2537* 2-4 39

WHISPERS IN THE DARK (Vocal: Kay Weber) / STOP, YOU'RE BREAKING MY HEART (Vocal: Bob Crosby)................... *Decca 1346* 5-8 37

WOLVERINE BLUES / LOUISE, LOUISE (Vocal: Eddie Miller) ..... *Decca 2032* 3-5 38

YANCEY SPECIAL / AT THE JAZZ BAND BALL.......................... *Decca 1747* 3-5 38

YOU AND YOUR LOVE / OVER THE RAINBOW .... *Decca 2657* 2-4 39 (Vocals: Teddy Grace)

YOU FORGOT ABOUT ME (Vocals: Bob Crosby & The Bob-O-Links) / GONE, BUT NOT FOGOTTEN (Vocal: Bonnie King) .... *Decca 3417* 2-4 40

YOU'RE A DARLIN' DEVIL / DEAR OLD DONEGAL (Vocal: Muriel Lane)............ *Decca 4305* 2-4 42

YOU'RE AN EDUCATION / JEZEBEL..... *Decca 1713* 2-4 38 (Vocals: Bob Crosby)

YOU, YOU DARLIN' / WITH THE WIND AND THE RAIN IN YOUR HAIR................... *Decca 3018* 2-4 40 (Vocals: Marion Mann)

ZOOT SUIT, A (Vocal: Nappy Lamare) / BARRELHOUSE BESSIE FROM BASIN STREET (Vocal: Eddie Miller).............. *Decca 4169* 3-5 42

CROSBY, Bob, as Bob Crosby's Bobcats

BEGIN THE BEGUINE / LONG TIME NO SEE............................ *Decca 2290* 2-4 39 (Vocals: The Andrews Sisters)

BIG FOOT JUMP / FIVE POINT BLUES.... *Decca 2108* 3-5 38

BLOW, BLOW, THOU WINTER WIND / SIGH NO MORE, LADIES........................ *Decca 2663* 2-4 39 (Vocals: Marion Mann)

COQUETTE / THE BIG CRASH FROM CHINA .... *Decca 1756* 2-4 38

DON'T CALL ME BOY / YOU'RE BOUND TO LOOK LIKE A MONKEY (WHEN YOU GROW OLD) .... *Decca 3431* 2-4 40
(Vocals: Nappy Lamare)

DO YOU EVER THINK OF ME? (Vocal: Nappy Lamare) / JAZZ ME BLUES .... *Decca 3040* 3-5 40

HANG YOUR HEART ON A HICKORY LIMB / SING A SONG OF SUNBEAMS .... *Decca 2416* 2-4 39
(Vocals: Marion Mann)

HINDUSTAN / MOURNIN' BLUES .... *Decca 2482* 3-5 39

I HEAR YOU TALKING / CALL ME A TAXI .... *Decca 2207* 3-5 38

IT'S ALL OVER NOW (Vocal: Bob Crosby) / ADIOS AMERICANO (Vocal: Marion Mann) .... *Decca 3104* 2-4 39

IT WAS A LOVER AND HIS LASS / OH, MISTRESS MINE .... *Decca 2662* 2-4 39
(Vocals: Marion Mann)

LOOPIN' THE LOOP / MY INSPIRATION (by Bob Crosby & His Orchestra) .... *Decca 2209* 2-4 38

MAMA'S GONE, GOODBYE / A VOUS TOUT DE VEY, VOUS .... *Decca 3056* 2-4 40
(Vocals: Marion Mann)

PALESTEENA (Vocal: Nappy Lamare) / SLOW MOOD .... *Decca 2011* 3-5 38

SO FAR, SO GOOD / YOU OUGHTA HANG YOUR HEAD IN SHAME .... *Decca 3055* 2-4 40
(Vocals: Marion Mann)

SPAIN / ALL BY MYSELF (Vocal: Marion Mann) .... *Decca 3248* 2-4 40

SPEAK TO ME OF LOVE / BIG BASS VIOL .... *Decca 2206* 2-4 38
(Vocals: Marion Mann)

STUMBLING / FIDGETY FEET .... *Decca 1593* 5-8 38

SWEETHEARTS ON PARADE / IT'S A LONG, LONG WAY TO TIPPERARY .... *Decca 18355* 2-4 42

TEA FOR TWO / YES INDEED .... *Decca 3689* 4-6 41
(Vocals: Bing Crosby & Connee Boswell)

THOSE THINGS I CAN'T FORGET / A PRECIOUS MEMORY .... *Decca 4398* 2-4 41
(Vocals: Bob Crosby)

TILL WE MEET AGAIN / THE LOVE NEST .... *Decca 2825* 2-4 39

WASHINGTON AND LEE SWING / PERUNA .... *Decca 2789* 3-5 39

WHEN MY DREAM BOAT COMES HOME / WALKIN' THE FLOOR OVER YOU .... *Decca 18371* 3-5 42
(Vocals: Bing Crosby)

WHO'S SORRY NOW / MARCH OF THE BOB CATS .... *Decca 1865* 2-4 38

YOU'RE DRIVING ME CRAZY / CAN'T WE BE FRIENDS? .... *Decca 1680* 3-5 38

CUGAT, Xavier, & His Waldorf-Astoria Orchestra

(Xavier Cugat: 1/1/00 –)

ADIOS, MUCHACHO (Vocal: Joseph de Soiza) / THE LADY IN RED (Vocal: Don Reid) .... *Victor 25012* 2-4 35

CIELITO LINDO / LA PALOMA .... *Victor 25826* 2-4 38
(Vocals: Chacha Aguilar & Carmen Castillo)

COCONITO (LITTLE TURKEY) / JARAPE TAPATIO (MEXICAN HAT DANCE) .... *Columbia 36697* 2-4 42

GYPSY AIRS TANGO / RANCHO GRANDE (Vocals: by orchestra) .... *Victor 24673* 3-5 33

MINNIE FROM TRINIDAD / AURORA .... *Columbia 36139* 2-4 41
(Vocals: Machito)

MY SHAWL (theme song) / SILENCIO (Vocal: Carmen Castillo) .... *Victor 24508* 3-5 33

PEANUT VENDOR, THE / MAMA INEZ .... *Columbia 35799* 2-4 40

QUIEREME MUCHO (YOURS) (Vocal: Dinah Shore) / ONE-TWO-THREE KICK
(Vocal: Catalino Rolon) .... *Victor 26384* 2-4 39

SIBONEY / I WANT MY MAMA (Vocal: Carmen Castillo) .... *Victor 26522* 2-4 40

WHEN THE SWALLOWS COME BACK TO CAPISTRANO / THE BREEZE AND I .... *Victor 26641* 2-4 40
(Vocals: Dinah Shore)

CUMMINS, Bernie, & His Hotel New Yorker Orchestra

(For many years, Wally Smith was a reed man and violinist with the Cummins Orchestras. As a young man, already a master of the violin, Smith fell victim to the 1918 influenza epidemic which claimed tens fo thousands of lives. While his condition remained a touch-and-go situation, his physcian told Smith's mother that if she could get the boy to play a wind instrument, thereby strengthening his lungs, he might have a chance for recovery. Mrs. Smith purchased a saxophone, brought it home and placed it on the coffee table near a sofa where Wally was resting.

When the family questioned the mother's plans regarding the saxophone, she replied, "I'm going to learn to play it." After a few days the young violinist began practicing on the sax and a full recovery from influenza ensued. Wally Smith became a proficient reed instrumentalist, and played saxophone and clarinet regularly, as well as violin from time to time, throughout his dance band career.)

DEEP SEA LOW DOWN (Vocal: Bernie Cummins) / PLAY THAT HOT GUITAR (by Ted Weems & His Orchestra; Vocal: Parker Gibbs) .... *Victor 24053* 5-8 30

MINNIE THE MERMAID (Vocals: by orchestra) / YOU WILL COME BACK TO ME
(Vocal: Walter Cummins) .... *Victor 22355* 4-6 30

ON THE SUNNY SIDE OF THE STREET / EXACTLY LIKE YOU .... *Victor 22354* 4-6 30
(Vocals: Bernie Cummins)

CUMMINS, Bernie, & His New York Biltmore Orchestra

DON'T HANG YOUR DREAMS ON A RAINBOW (Vocal: Bernie Cummins) / THE WORLD'S GREATEST SWEETHEART IS YOU (Vocals: Bernie Cummins, Walter Cummins, & Paul Roberts) .... *Victor 22110* 3-5 29

LITTLE BY LITTLE / EV'RY DAY AWAY FROM YOU .... *Victor 22088* 3-5 29
(Vocals: Bernie Cummins)

CUMMINS, Bernie, & His Orchestra

GOODBYE, JONAH (Vocals: Bernie Cummins & The Sophisticates) / DREAMS FOR SALE
(Vocal: Walter Cummins) .... *Vocalion 3749* 4-6 37

HAVE YOU EVER BEEN IN HEAVEN? (Vocal: Walter Cummins) / MAMA, I WANNA MAKE RHYTHM (Vocal: Bernie Cummins) ..... *Conqueror 8967* 4-6 37

(I LIKE PIE, I LIKE CAKE, BUT) I LIKE YOU BEST OF ALL / POPLAR STREET BLUES ...... *Gennett 5641* 5-8 25

JIMINY GEE / WHEN THE WIND BLOWS NORTH .... *Gennett 5468* 5-8 24

LADY IS A TRAMP (Vocal: Connie Barleau) / GETTING SOME FUN OUT OF LIFE
(Vocal: Bernie Cummins) .... *Conqueror 8959* 3-5 37

LADY IS A TRAMP (Vocal: Connie Barleau) / GETTING SOME FUN OUT OF LIFE
(Vocal: Bernie Cummins) .... *Vocalion 3714* 3-5 37
(Simultaneously released on two labels)

MAKE MY COT WHERE THE COT-COT-COTTON GROWS (Vocals: by trio) / EV'RYBODY LOVES MY GIRL (Vocal: Bernie Cummins) ..... *Brunswick 3722* 3-5 28

SAILING HOME / IN THE MISSION BY THE SEA .... *Vocalion 3759* 3-5 37
(Vocals: Walter Cummins)

SEEMS LIKE A MONTH OF SUNDAYS (Vocal: Bernie Cummins) / I'M LOSING MY MIND (BECAUSE OF YOU)
(Vocal: Connie Barleau) .... *Bluebird B-10777* 4-6 40

SO DEEP IS THE NIGHT (Vocal: Walter Cummins) / RAGTIME COWBOY JOE (Vocals: Connie Barleau, Chet James, & chorus) .... *Bluebird B-10815* 4-6 40

THERE'LL BE SOME CHANGES MADE / BASIN STREET BLUES .... *Vocalion 4181* 4-6 37
(Vocals: Bernie Cummins)

WHEN / ST. LOUIS BLUES .... *Gennett 5466* 5-8 24

WORDS / KEEP ON DANCING .... *Gennett 5546* 4-6 24

YOU'RE MY DISH (Vocal: Connie Barleau) / MORE POWER TO YOU (Vocal: Jerry Lang) ..... *Vocalion 3889* 3-5 37

CUMMINS, Bernie, & His Toadstool Inn Orchestra

HOME FOLKS BLUES / IDA .... *Gennett 5395* 5-8 24

DAILEY, Frank, & His Meadowbrook Orchestra
(Frank Dailey: circa 1901 – 2/27/56)

DOUBLE TROUBLE (Vocal: Nancy Flake) / I WISHED ON THE MOON (Vocal: Howard Dulany) ... *Bluebird B-6028* 3-5 35

I'LL NEVER SAY "NEVER AGAIN" AGAIN (Vocal: Nancy Flake) / GYPSY VIOLIN (Vocal: Howard Dulany) .... *Bluebird B-5954* 3-5 35

TIME WILL TELL (Vocal: Nancy Flake) / RHYTHM IS OUR BUSINESS (Vocal: Al Fish) .... *Bluebird B-5955* 3-5 35

DAILEY, Frank, & His Orchestra

CAN'T YOU HEAR THAT MOUNTAIN MUSIC? / GOOD MORNIN' .... *Variety 568* 5-8 37

SCATTIN' AT THE KIT KAT / SOUTHLAND SERENADE .... *Variety 573* 5-8 37
(Vocals: Louise Wallace)

SOMETHING TO SING ABOUT / EVERYTHNG YOU SAID CAME TRUE .... *Vocalion 3798* 3-5 37
(Vocals: Unknown)

DAILEY, Frank, & His Stop-And-Go Orchestra

FOOL AND HIS HONEY ARE SOON PARTED, A (Vocal: Barbara Bush) / IT'S AN OLD-FASHIONED LOCKET (Vocal: Howard Dulany) .... *Bluebird B-10212* 2-4 39

HAVE MERCY / LET'S TIE THE OLD FORGET-ME-NOT ...... *Bluebird B-10204* 2-4 39
(Vocals: Howard Dulany)

IN BAD WITH SINBAD (Vocal: Curly Barron) / TOY TRUMPET (Vocals: by trio) .... *Bluebird B-7479* 3-5 38

I WISH I WAS THE WILLOW (Vocal: Howard Dulany) / GREAT CAMP MEETIN' GROUND (Vocals: by trio) .... *Bluebird B-7646* 3-5 38

LITTLE KISS AT TWILIGHT (Vocal: Howard Dulany) / WHAT GOES ON HERE IN MY HEART? (Vocals: by trio) .... *Bluebird B-7648* 3-5 38

WHILE A CIGARETTE WAS BURNING / APRIL IN MY HEART .... *Bluebird B-10004* 2-4 38
(Vocals: Howard Dulany)

WHY CAN'T THIS NIGHT LAST FOREVER? / I HAVE ROOM IN MY HEART .... *Bluebird B-10011* 2-4 38
(Vocals: Howard Dulany)

DAILEY, Frank, as Frank Dailey's Meadowbrooks

PETER PAN / SHOW ME THE WAY .... *Bell 324* 4-6 25

DALE'S DANCE ORCHESTRA:
see HARING, Bob, & His Velvetone Orchestra

DANDRIDGE, Putney, & His Orchestra
(Putney Dandridge 1900 – 1946)

CHASING SHADOWS / WHEN I GROW TOO OLD TO DREAM .... *Vocalion 2982* 8-10 35
(Vocals: Putney Dandridge)

DINNER FOR ONE, PLEASE JAMES / A BEAUTIFUL LADY IN BLUE .... *Vocalion 3189* 4-6 36
(Vocals: Putney Dandridge)

EASY TO LOVE / YOU DO THE DARNDEST THINGS BABY .... *Vocalion 3351* 5-8 36
(Vocals: Putney Dandridge)

EENY MEENY MINEY MO / SANTA CLAUS CAME IN THE SPRING .... *Vocalion 3083* 5-8 35
(Vocals: Putney Dandridge)

HERE COMES YOUR PAPPY / IF WE NEVER MEET AGAIN .... *Vocalion 3291* 8-10 36
(Vocals: Putney Dandridge)

HIGH HAT, A PICCOLO AND A CANE, A / THE SKELETON IN THE CLOSET.... *Vocalion 3352* 5-8 36
(Vocals: Putney Dandridge)

I'M IN A DANCING MOOD / WITH PLENTY OF MONEY AND YOU .... *Vocalion 3399* 8-10 37
(Vocals: Putney Dandridge)

I'M IN THE MOOD FOR LOVE / THAT'S WHAT YOU THINK .... *Vocalion 3007* 5-8 35
(Vocals: Putney Dandridge)

I'M ON A SEE-SAW / DOUBLE TROUBLE .... *Vocalion 3082* 5-8 35
(Vocals: Putney Dandridge)

ISN'T THIS A LOVELY DAY? / CHEEK TO CHEEK .... *Vocalion 3006* 5-8 35
(Vocals: Putney Dandridge)

IT'S A SIN TO TELL A LIE / ALL MY LIFE .... *Vocalion 3252* 5-8 36
(Vocals: Putney Dandridge)

IT'S THE GYPSY IN ME / WHEN A LADY MEETS A GENTLEMAN DOWN SOUTH .... *Vocalion 3315* 5-8 36
(Vocals: Putney Dandridge)

NAGASAKI / SHINE .... *Vocalion 3024* 8-10 35
(Vocals: Putney Dandridge)

NO OTHER ONE / A LITTLE BIT INDEPENDENT .... *Vocalion 3122* 5-8 36
(Vocals: Putney Dandridge)

OL'MAN RIVER / WHY WAS I BORN? .... *Vocalion 3269* 5-8 36
(Vocals: Putney Dandridge)

SING, BABY, SING / YOU TURNED THE TABLES ON ME .... *Vocalion 3304* 5-8 36
(Vocals: Putnev Dandridge)

STAR FELL OUR OF HEAVEN, A / MARY HAD A LITTLE LAMB .... *Vocalion 3287* 5-8 36
(Vocals: Putney Dandridge)

SWEET VIOLETS / HONEYSUCKLE ROSE .... *Vocalion 3190* 5-8 36
(Vocals: Putney Dandridge)

THAT FOOLISH FEELING / GEE! BUT YOU'RE SWELL .... *Vocalion 3409* 5-8 37
(Vocals: Putney Dandridge)

YOU HIT THE SPOT / YOU TOOK MY BREATH AWAY .... *Vocalion 3123* 5-8 36
(Vocals: Putney Dandridge)

YOU'RE A HEAVENLY THING / MR. BLUEBIRD .... *Vocalion 2935* 3-5 35
(Vocals: Putney Dandridge)

DAUGHERTY, Doc, & His Orchestra

BECAUSE YOU LOVE ME, BABY / BABY GIRL .... *Victor V-40119* 5-8 29
(Vocals: Frank Luther)

NINETY IN THE SHADE / ALCOHOLIC BLUES .... *Victor V-40111* 12-15 29

TIE A LITTLE STRING AROUND YOUR FINGER / SHE'S A GORGEOUS THING! .... *Victor 23040* 5-8 31
(Vocals: Frank Luther)

DAVIS, Charles K., & His Orchestra
(The value of the following records is determined by their rarity)

KIDLETS / IRISH MEDLEY ..... *Famous Singers 5053* 25-30 21

LOVE'S APPEAL / MOONLIGHT ... *Famous Singers 5051* 25-30 21

MADELINE / OHIO .... *Famous Singers 5055* 30-35 21

PAGAN / DREAMING .... *Famous Singers 5050* 25-30 21

ROZALIA / SUNSHINE .... *Famous Singers 5052* 30-35 21

WHERE SWEET DADDIES GROW / IRISH MOTHER OF MINE .... *Famous Singers 5054* 25-30 21

DAVIS, Charlie, & His Orchestra

I'VE GOT A WARM SPOT IN MY HEART FOR YOU (Vocal: Clarence Morrison) / SO HELP ME (Vocal: Frank Parrish) .... *Melotone M-13022* 2-4 34

I'VE GOT A WARM SPOT IN MY HEART FOR YOU (Vocal: Clarence Morrison) / SO HELP ME (Vocal: Frank Parrish) .... *Oriole 2902* 2-4 34

I'VE GOT A WARM SPOT IN MY HEART FOR YOU (Vocal: Clarence Morrison) / SO HELP ME (Vocal: Frank Parrish) .... *Perfect 15935* 2-4 34

I'VE GOT A WARM SPOT IN MY HEART FOR YOU (Vocal: Clarence Morrison) / SO HELP ME (Vocal: Frank Parrish) .... *Romeo 2276* 2-4 34
(Simultaneously released on four labels)

JUST LIKE A MELODY OUT OF THE SKY (Vocal: Harry Williford) / YOU'RE A REAL SWEETHEART (Vocal: Dick Powell..... *Vocalion 15702* 4-6 28

MEAN TO ME (Vocal: Louis Lowe) / ON THE ROAD TO MANDALAY...... *Gennett 20353* 4-6 29

ROLLIN' HOME / I NEVER HAD A CHANCE .... *Banner 33089* 3-5 34
(Vocals: Frank Parrish)

ROLLIN' HOME / I NEVER HAD A CHANCE .... *Melotone M-13053* 3-5 34
(Vocals: Frank Parrish)

ROLLIN' HOME / I NEVER HAD A CHANCE .... *Oriole 2919* 3-5 34
(Vocals: Frank Parrish)

ROLLIN' HOME / I NEVER HAD A CHANCE .... *Perfect 15952* 3-5 34
(Vocals: Frank Parrish)

ROLLIN' HOME / I NEVER HAD A CHANCE .... *Romeo 2?93* 3-5 34
(Vocals: Frank Parrish)
(Simultaneously released on five labels)

SWEETEST MUSIC THIS SIDE OF HEAVEN, THE (Vocal: Frank Parrish) / FARE THEE WELL (Vocal: Clarence Morrison) .... *Banner 33067* 2-4 34

SWEETEST MUSIC THIS SIDE OF HEAVEN, THE (Vocal: Frank Parrish) / FARE THEE WELL (Vocal: Clarence Morrison) .... *Melotone M-13041* 2-4 34

SWEETEST MUSIC THIS SIDE OF HEAVEN, THE (Vocal: Frank Parrish) / FARE THEE WELL (Vocal: Clarence Morrison) .... *Oriole 2911* 2-4 34

SWEETEST MUSIC THIS SIDE OF HEAVEN, THE (Vocal: Frank Parrish) / FARE THEE WELL (Vocal: Clarence Morrison) .... *Perfect 15944* 2-4 34

SWEETEST MUSIC THIS SIDE OF HEAVEN, THE (Vocal: Frank Parrish) / FARE THEE WELL (Vocal: Clarence Morrison) .... *Romeo 2285* 2-4 34
(Simultaneously released on five labels)

WHEN (Vocal: Harry Williford) / THE DRAG .... *Vocalion 15701* 3-5 28

DAVIS, Eddie, & His Orchestra

HOT LIPS / LONESOME MAMA BLUES .... *Grey Gull 1120* 5-8 22

I GAVE YOU UP JUST BEFORE YOU THREW ME DOWN / IVY .... *Broadway 11210* 3-5 23

DAVIS, Johnny "Scat", & His Orchestra
(Johnny "Scat" Davis: circa 1915 –)

COLLEGE RHYTHM / TAKE A NUMBER FROM ONE TO TEN .... *Decca 272* 8-10 34
0(Vocals: Johnny Davis)

DON'T STOP ME IF YOU'VE HEARD IT BEFORE / WERE YOU FOOLIN' .... *Decca 256* 8-10 34
(Vocals: Johnny Davis)

HUNDRED TO ONE IT'S YOU, A / CONGRATULATE ME .... *Decca 257* 8-10 34
(Vocals: Johnny Davis)

I FEEL A SONG COMIN' ON / EVERYTHING IS OKEY-DOKEY .... *Decca 583* 5-8 35
(Vocals: Johnny Davis)

TRUCKIN' / LOAFIN' TIME .... *Decca 573* 5-8 35
(Vocals: Johnny Davis)

YOU GOTTA GIVE CREDIT TO LOVE / BETWEEN SHOWERS .... *Decca 271* 8-10 34
(Vocals: Johnny Davis)

YOURS AND MINE / THE WEDDING OF THE BIRDS .... *Broadway 1422* 4-6 30
(Vocals: Johnny Davis)

DAVIS, Marlon, & His Orchestra

LONESOMEST GIRL IN TOWN, THE / SWEET HAWAIIAN DREAMS .... *Gennett 3201* 3-5 26

DAVIS, Meyer, & His Orchestra
(Meyer Davis: circa 1895 –)

DID YOU EVER SEE A DREAM WALKING? / MANY MOONS AGO .... *Columbia 2852-D* 5-8 34
(Vocals: Unknown)
(This record was pressed in blue shellac.)

I KNOW THAT YOU KNOW / I WANT TO BE HAPPY .... *Columbia 36427* 2-4 41

LONELY HEART (Vocals: Unknown) / HEAT WAVE (Vocal: Charlotte Murray) ...... *Columbia 2821-D* 5-8 33
(This record was pressed in blue shellac.)

TIME ON MY HANDS / CARIOCA .... *Columbia 36426* 2-4 41

WITHOUT A SONG / GREAT DAY .... *Columbia 36428* 2-4 41

DAVIS, Meyer, as Meyer Davis' Le Paradis Band

ALL ABOARD FOR HEAVEN / LET IT RAIN, LET IT POUR .... *Victor 19630* 3-5 25
(Vocals: Billy Murray)

NOBODY LOVES YOU LIKE I DO / WASHINGTON AND LEE SWING .... *Victor 19526* 3-5 25

DAVIS, Meyer, as Meyer Davis' Swanee Syncopators

HAPPY DAYS AND LONELY NIGHTS / WHEN SUMMER IS GONE .... *Brunswick 4134* 5-8 28
(Vocals: Smith Ballew)

IN THE EVENING (Vocal: Ernest Charles) / I CAN'T GIVE YOU ANYTHING BUT LOVE (Vocal: Al Shayne) .... *Brunswick 3938* 3-5 28

DAVISON, Walter, as Walter Davison's Louisville Loons

GIVE ME A LITTLE BIT O' SUNSHINE (Vocals: by quartet) / WHERE THE WILD, WILD FLOWERS GROW (by Earl Gresh and His Gangplank Orchestra; Vocal: Irving Kaufman) .... *Columbia 1031-D* 5-8 27

KNOWING YOU THE WAY I DO / —..... *Lincoln 2438* 5-8 26

MY SMALL TOWN GAL / — .... *Cameo 834* 5-8 26

MY SMALL TOWN GAL / — .... *Lincoln 2435* 5-8 26
(Simultaneously released on two labels)

SOUTH WIND (Vocal: by quartet) / WHEN THE PUSSY WILLOW WHISPERS TO THE CATNIP (Vocals: by the band) .... *Columbia 989-D* 5-8 27

DAVIS SAXOPHONE OCTET, The

HELLO, ALOHA! HOW ARE YOU? / AS LONG AS I HAVE YOU .... *Cameo 936* 2-4 26

HELLO, ALOHA! HOW ARE YOU? / MY DREAM OF THE BIG PARADE .... *Lincoln 2553* 2-4 26

JIG WALK / WHOSE WHO ARE YOU? ..... *Cameo 906* 3-5 26

JIG WALK / WHOSE WHO ARE YOU? ... *Lincoln 2490* 3-5 26
(Simultaneously released on two labels)

SOMEBODY'S LONELY / I'D CLIMB THE HIGHEST MOUNTAIN IF I KNEW I'D FIND YOU .... *Cameo 923* 3-5 26

DAWN, Dolly, & Her Dawn Patrol
also see HALL, George, & His Orchestra
(Dolly Dawn: 2/3/19 –)

ALIBI BABY / THE YOU AND ME THAT USED TO BE .... *Vocalion 3770* 2-4 37
(Vocals: Dolly Dawn)

BETTER GET OFF YOUR HIGH HORSE / THERE'S FROST ON THE MOON .... *Bluebird B-6699* 3-5 37
(Vocals: Dolly Dawn)

CABIN IN THE SKY / YOU CAN'T PULL THE WOOL OVER MY EYES .... *Bluebird B-6382* 3-5 36
(Vocals: Dolly Dawn)

GAY RANCHERO/ HALLELUJAH!... *Bluebird B-11345* 2-4 41
(Vocals: Dolly Dawn)

I CAN'T BREAK THE HABIT OF YOU / WHAT WILL I TELL MY HEART? .... *Bluebird B-6796* 3-5 37
(Vocals: Dolly Dawn)

I FOUND MY YELLOW BASKET / WHERE HAS MY LITTLE DOG GONE? .... *Vocalion 4509* 2-4 39
(Vocals: Dolly Dawn)

I'M GONNA CLAP MY HANDS / WAKE ME UR AND SING .... *Bluebird B-6268* 3-5 36
(Vocals: Dolly Dawn)

I PROMISE YOU / BEETHOVEN WROTE IT BUT IT SWINGS..................... *Vocalion 4682* 3-5 39
(Vocals: Dolly Dawn)

IT'S FUNNY TO EVERYONE BUT ME / LOVE GROWS ON THE WHITE-OAK TREE .... *Vocalion 5045* 2-4 39
(Vocals: Dolly Dawn)

I'VE GOT RAIN IN MY EYES / THE MOOD THAT I'M IN...................... *Bluebird B-6861* 3-5 37
(Vocals: Dolly Dawn)

LET'S PITCH A LITTLE WOO (Vocals: Unknown) / YOU'RE A SWEETHEART
(Vocal: Dolly Dawn) .... *Vocalion 3874* 2-4 38

MEANEST THING YOU EVER DID WAS KISS ME, THE / HOW COULD YOU? ..... *Bluebird B-6797* 3-5 37
(Vocals: Dolly Dawn)

ON THE SENTIMENTAL SIDE / MY HEART IS TAKING LESSONS.................. *Vocalion 3968* 2-4 38
(Vocals: Dolly Dawn)

QUICKER THAN YOU CAN SAY JACK ROBINSON / THE BROKEN RECORD .... *Bluebird B-6217* 3-5 36
(Vocals: Dolly Dawn)

SHINE / TWENTY-FOUR HOURS A DAY .... *Bluebird B-6170* 3-5 36
(Vocals: Dolly Dawn)

SING A SONG OF NONSENSE / COPPER-COLORED GAL.......... *Bluebird B-6576* 3-5 36
(Vocals: Dolly Dawn)

SO YOU'RE THE ONE / HEP-TEE-HOOTIE (JUKE BOX JIVE)....................... *Okeh 5842* 2-4 40
(Vocals: Dolly Dawn)

PIG FOOT PETE / THERE GOES MY DREAM...................... *Bluebird B-11402* 3-5 41
(Vocals: Dolly Dawn)

TWO DREAMS GOT TOGETHER / BEI MIR BIST DU SCHOEN................... *Vocalion 3908* 2-4 38
(Vocals: Dolly Dawn)

WHO BLEW OUT THE FLAME (Vocals: Unknown) / THE GIRL FRIEND OF THE WHIRLING DERVISH
(Vocal: Dolly Dawn)................... *Conqueror 9137* 2-4 38

WHO BLEW OUT THE FLAME (Vocals: Unknown) / THE GIRL FRIEND OF THE WHIRLING DERVISH
(Vocal: Dolly Dawn) .... *Vocalion 4383* 2-4 38
(Simultaneously released on two labels)

YANKEE DOODLE BAND / LET'S HAVE ANOTHER CIGARETTE .... *Vocalion 3776* 2-4 37
(Vocals: Dolly Dawn)

YANKEE DOODLE NEVER WENT TO TOWN / GEORGIA ROCKIN' CHAIR .... *Bluebird B-6171* 3-5 36
(Vocals: Dolly Dawn)

DEAN & HIS KIDS, The:
see POLLACK, Ben

DEAUVILLE DOZEN, The

DREAMING OF TOMORROW / PEP .... *Pathe Actuelle 36338* 8-10 25

DREAMING OF TOMORROW / PEP................... *Perfect 14519* 5-8 25
(Simultaneously released on two labels)

DEAUVILLE SYNCOPATORS, The:
see RICH, Fred, & His (La Palina) Orchestra, and see RICH, Fred, & His Orchestra

DEEP RIVER ORCHESTRA, The:
see ROBISON, Willard, & His Orchestra

DEIKMAN, Bob, & His Orchestra

CAMEL WALK, THE / MAMA LET ROSIE ALONE...................... *Gennett 3161* 4-6 25

COBBLE-STONES / AMONG MY SOUVENIRS......................... *Gennett 6325* 3-5 28
(Vocals: Kermit Simmons)

EVERYBODY LOVES MY GIRL (Vocal: Kermit Simmons) / ROLL UP THE CARPETS............. *Gennett 6339* 3-5 28

I'LL THINK OF YOU / DANCING TAMBOURINE .... *Gennett 6310* 3-5 28
(Vocals: Kermit Simmons)

SOME OTHER BIRD WHISTLED A TUNE / SPANISH MELODY (by Henry Thies & His Castle Farm Orchestra)................... *Gennett 3142* 5-8 25

SPANISH SHAWL / HELLO SANDY..... *Gennett 3196* 5-8 26
(The legendary jazz drummer George Wettling states that 0this was his first recording session)

DEIRO, Pietro, as Pietro & His Blue Horse Tavern Orchestra

HAWAIIAN LOVE BIRD (whistling by Carson Robinson; Vocal: Frank Luther) / ONCE IN A BLUE MOON
(Vocal: Frank Luther)..................... *Victor 22216* 5-8 30

DE LANGE, Eddie, & His Orchestra
also see HUDSON-DE LANGE ORCHESTRA, The
(Eddie De Lange: 1/12/04 – 7/13/49)

BEER BARREL POLKA (Vocal: Elisse Cooper) / SERENADE TO A WILDCAT...... *Bluebird B-10199* 3-5 39

BROOM DANCE (Vocal: Elisse Cooper) / WPA POLKA..................... *Bluebird B-10356* 4-6 39

BUTTON, BUTTON / JUMP JUMP'S HERE .... *Bluebird B-7837* 4-6 38
(Vocals: Elisse Cooper)

COPENHAGEN / YOU CAN'T KISS A FRIGIDAIRE (Vocal: Eddie DeLange)... *Bluebird B-10027* 3-5 38

EAGLE EYE FINKLE / MRS. MOSE HAS A MILLION BEAUS.............. *Bluebird B-10213* 2-4 39
(Vocals: Elisse Cooper)

JELLY ROLL POLKA (Vocal: Elisse Cooper) / THE MERRY OLD LAND OF OZ
(Vocal: Eddie DeLange) .... *Bluebird B-10368* 2-4 39

LIVERY STABLE BLUES (Vocal: Phil Sillman) / THE COCK-EYED MAYOR OF KAUNAKAKAI
(Vocal: Elisse Cooper)................ *Bluebird B-10094* 3-5 39

POP CORN MAN / WILLIE THE WEEPER........... *Bluebird B-7841* 5-8 38
(Vocals: Elisse Cooper)

STOP! IT'S WONDERFUL (Vocal: Eddie DeLange) / JIMINY CRICKET (Vocals: Elisse Cooper & Eddie DeLange) .... *Bluebird B-10441* 4-6 39

WHAT ARE LITTLE GIRLS MADE OF? (Vocal: Elisse Cooper) / NEW SHOES BLUES ...... *Bluebird B-7855* 4-6 38

DENMAN, Hal, & His Carolina Cotton Pickers

I CAN'T GET ENOUGH OF YOU / WHEN I TAKE MY SUGAR TO TEA...................... *Superior 2674* 3-5 31
(Vocals: Hal Denman)

IT LOOKS LIKE LOVE / I CAN'T GET ENOUGH OF YOU........... *Champion 16266* 3-5 31
(Vocals: Hal Denman)

DENMAN, Hal, & His Orchestra

I DON'T KNOW WHY I LOVE YOU LIKE I DO / HOW'S YOUR UNCLE?............ *Champion 16355* 3-5 32
(Vocals: Hal Denman)

I DON'T KNOW WHY I LOVE YOU LIKE I DO / HOW'S YOUR UNCLE? .... *Superior 2768* 3-5 32
(Vocals: Hal Denman)
(Simultaneously released on two labels)

WOODEN SOLDIER AND THE CHINA DOLL, THE / SNUGGLED ON YOUR SHOULDER... *Superior 2800* 2-4 32
(Vocals: Unknown)

WOODEN SOLDIER AND THE CHINA DOLL, THE / WAS THAT THE HUMAN THING TO DO? .... *Champion 16397* 2-4 32
(Vocals: Unknown)
(Simultaneously released on two labels)

DENNY, Jack, & His Orchestra
(Jack Denny: circa 1894 – 9/15/50)

EASY GOIN' MAMA / —................... *Cameo 646* 4-6 24

EASY GOIN' MAMA / — .... *Lincoln 2351* 4-6 24
(Simultaneously released on two labels)

NEAPOLITAN NIGHTS / JUST A COTTAGE SMALL................. *Brunswick 3129* 2-4 26

DENNY, Jack, & His Waldorf-Astoria Orchestra

I'VE TOLD EV'RY LITTLE STAR / THE SONG IS YOU .... *Victor 24183* 3-5 33
(Vocals: Paul Small)

MY RIVER HOME (Vocal: Robert Royce) / THAT'S ALL THAT MATTERS TO ME
(Vocal: Paul Small)...................... *Victor 24185* 3-5 33

DEUTSCH, Emery, & His Orchestra
(Emery Deutsch: 9/10/07 –)

BONNIE WITH THE BIG BLUE EYES (Vocal: Mildred Craig) / IF I KNEW THEN
(Vocal: Jack Starr) .... *Bluebird B-10440* 2-4 39

HUNGARIAN DANCE NO. 1 / VAS VILST DE GAILY STAR (Vocal: Mildred Craig).......... *Bluebird B-10340* 2-4 39

JOSEPH! JOSEPH! / WHO'LL BUY MY BUBLITCHKI?................ *Brunswick 8109* 2-4 38
(Vocals: Nan Wynn)

LONG HAIR SWING / ON THE ISLE OF BONG BONG (Vocal: Mildred Craig)... *Bluebird B-10571* 3-5 39

SAILBOAT IN THE MOONLIGHT, A (Vocal: Barry McKinley) / MOONLIGHT ON THE HIGHWAY
(Vocal: Frank Parrish) .... *Brunswick 7905* 3-5 37

STARDUST ON THE MOON / HARBOR LIGHTS................. *Brunswick 7961* 3-5 37
(Vocals: Frank Parrish)

DEVINE'S WISCONSIN ROOF ORCHESTRA

DREAM TRAIN / THAT'S WHY I'M CRYING FOR YOU................. *Broadway 1249* 3-5 29
(Vocals: Edwin Taylor)

DREAM TRAIN / THAT'S WHY I'M CRYING FOR YOU .... *Paramount 20690* 4-6 29
(Vocals: Edwin Taylor)

DICKSON'S HARLEM ORCHESTRA:
see KARDOS, Gene, & His Orchestra

DIGGS, Duke, & His Orchestra:
see TRENT, Alphonse, & His Orchestra

DIXIE BOYS, The:
see CALIFORNIA RAMBLERS, The, as the Vagabonds

DIXIE DAISIES, The:
see HARING, Bob, & His Velvetone Orchestra, and
see MILLS, Irving as Goody's Good Timers

DIXIE JAZZ BAND, The:
see CANDULLO, Joe, & His Orchestra
see ELLINGTON, Duke, & His Cotton Club Orchestra as The Whoopee Makers
see HALL, Fred, as Fred Hall's Jazz Band
see MILLS, Irving, as Mill's Merry Makers, and
see PETTIS, Jack, & His Band

DIXIE MARIMBA PLAYERS,
directed by Celso Hurtado

JEANNINE (Vocal: Scrappy Lambert) / SOMEDAY, SOMEWHERE........... *Domino 4196* 2-4 28

JEANNINE (Vocal: Scrappy Lambert) / SOMEDAY, SOMEWHERE............. *Regal 8632* 2-4 28
(Simultaneously released on two labels)

MY HEART BELONGS TO THE GIRL WHO BELONGS TO SOMEBODY ELSE / DANCING WITH TEARS IN MY EYES.......................... *Perfect 15315* 3-5 30
(Vocals: Smith Ballew)

SOMEWHERE IN OLD WYOMING / MOONLIGHT ON THE COLORADO.................... *Perfect 15338* 2-4 30
(Vocals: Scrappy Lambert)

THERE'LL NEVER BE ANOTHER YOU / KING FOR A DAY................... *Domino 4183* 2-4 28
(Vocals: Scrappy Lambert)

THERE'LL NEVER BE ANOTHER YOU / KING FOR A DAY...................... *Regal 8609* 2-4 28
(Vocals: Scrappy Lambert)
(Simultaneously released on two labels)

DIXIE STOMPERS, The:
see HENDERSON, Fletcher, & His Orchestra

DOCTOR SAUSAGE & HIS FIVE PORK CHOPS:
see TYSON, "Dr. Sausage"

DOERR, Clyde, & His Orchestra

HERE AM I, BROKEN HEARTED / (WHAT DO WE DO) ON A DEW-DEW-DEWY DAY?........ *Edison 52065* 3-5 27

JUST ACROSS THE STREET FROM HEAVEN / BLUEBERRY LANE................. *Edison 52297* 3-5 28
(Vocals: Unknown duet)

SON OF THE SHEIK / JUST A LITTLE LONGER................... *Edison 51873* 3-5 26

DOERR, Clyde, as Clyde Doerr's Saxophone Orchestra

MIAMI / SOMEONE'S STOLEN MY SWEET, SWEET BABY........... *Columbia 507-D* 2-4 25

REMEMBER / JUST A COTTAGE SMALL......................... *Columbia 578-D* 2-4 26

DOERR, Clyde, as Doerr's Saxophone Octette

NIGHTMARE, THE / DOWN HOME RAG... *Cameo 1120* 3-5 27

DONAHUE, Al, & His Orchestra
(Al Donahue: 6/12/04 –)

ALONE / THE WINTER WALTZ.......... *Decca 626* 3-5 36
(Vocals: Barry McKinley)

A-TISKET, A-TASKET / STOP BEATIN' ROUND THE MULBERRY BUSH................ *Conqueror 9042* 2-4 38
(Vocals: Paula Kelly)

BE HONEST WITH ME (Vocal: Phil Brito) / HI, NEIGHBOR (Vocals: Phil Brito & ensemble)........................ *Conqueror 9908* 2-4 41

BESIDE A MOONLIT STREAM (Vocal: Barry McKinley) / NATURALLY (Vocal: Paula Kelly)....... *Vocalion 4195* 2-4 38

BURNING THE MIDNIGHT OIL / THE BLUE JUMP...................... *Okeh 5828* 3-5 40

BUTTON, BUTTON / WHEN PAW WAS COURTIN' MAW.................. *Vocalion 4476* 2-4 38
(Vocals: Paula Kelly)

CAN I HELP IT? / IN THE MOOD...... *Vocalion 5238* 2-4 39
(Vocals: Paula Kelly)

CHAPEL IN THE VALLEY (Vocal: Phil Brito) / JAVA JIVE (Vocal: Dee Keating).......... *Okeh 6086* 2-4 41

HOW DO IT RATE WITH YOU? / YOU TOOK MY BREATH AWAY.................... *Decca 630* 4-6 36
(Vocals: Barry McKinley)

I HEAR A RHAPSODY (Vocal: Phil Brito) / FRENESI............................. *Okeh 5888* 3-5 40

I LIVE FOR LOVE / MINE ALONE......... *Decca 604* 4-6 35
(Vocals: Dick Robertson)

I'M STEPPING OUT WITH A MEMORY TONIGHT / FOOLS RUSH IN.................... *Vocalion 5519* 2-4 40
(Vocals: Phil Brito)

JEEPERS CREEPERS / HURRY HOME..................... *Vocalion 4513* 2-4 39
(Vocals: Paula Kelly)

LAMBETH WALK / HEART AND SOUL....................... *Conqueror 9095* 2-4 38
(Vocals: Paula Kelly)

LAST NIGHT'S GARDENIAS (Vocal: Paula Kelly) / THE SKY FELL DOWN (Vocal: Phil Brito).... *Vocalion 5396* 2-4 40

LET THERE BE LOVE (Vocal: Phil Brito) / IMAGINATION (Vocal: Paula Kelly).... *Conqueror 9453* 2-4 40

LET THERE BE LOVE (Vocal: Phil Brito) / IMAGINATION (Vocal: Paula Kelly)..... *Vocalion 5454* 2-4 40
(Simultaneously released on two labels)

LOW DOWN RHYTHM IN A TOP HAT (theme song) (Vocal: Phil Brito) / COPENHAGEN........... *Vocalion 5314* 3-5 40

MOON LOVE / TO YOU............... *Vocalion 4888* 2-4 39
(Vocals: Paula Kelly)

MY DISPOSITION (Vocal: Phil Brito) / OHIO BREAKAWAY.................. *Okeh 5925* 3-5 40

MY PRAYER (Vocal: Phil Brito) / I WANNA HAT WITH CHERRIES (Vocal: Paula Kelly)......... *Vocalion 5047* 2-4 39

MY SILENT MOOD / ON A LITTLE STREET IN SINGAPORE............ *Vocalion 5211* 2-4 39
(Vocals: Phil Brito)

OUR LOVE / LITTLE SKIPPER........ *Vocalion 4736* 2-4 39
(Vocals: Paula Kelly)

PERSIAN RUG / WHITE SAILS (Vocal: Paula Kelly).............. *Vocalion 4956* 2-4 39

ROUTE 23 / SOUTHERN FRIED........... *Okeh 5660* 2-4 40

SKY FELL DOWN, THE (Vocal: Phil Brito) / TUXEDO JUNCTION.............. *Conqueror 9456* 2-4 40

STAIRWAY TO THE STARS / CINDERELLA...................... *Vocalion 4846* 2-4 39
(Vocals: Paula Kelly)

STOP BEATIN' ROUND THE MULBERRY BUSH / LAMBETH WALK........... *Vocalion 4318* 2-4 38
(Vocals: Paula Kelly)

TABU / JUMPIN' AT THE JUKE BOX (Vocal: Dee Keating)............ *Okeh 6136* 3-5 41

TATTOOED LADY, THE (Vocal: Paula Kelly) / ALEXANDER'S SWINGIN'........... *Vocalion 4562* 3-5 39

TEMPTATION / PINCH ME (Vocal: Paula Kelly).......... *Vocalion 5351* 2-4 39

THIS HEART OF MINE / OH! YOU CRAZY MOON....................... *Vocalion 4993* 2-4 39
(Vocals: Paula Kelly)

TUXEDO JUNCTION / BEETHOVEN BOUNCE........................... *Vocalion 5384* 3-5 40

TWENTY-FOUR HOURS A DAY (Vocal: Dick Robertson) / LOVE MAKES THE WORLD GO ROUND (Vocal: Tommy Norato)..................... *Decca 599* 4-6 35

WAITER AND THE PORTER AND THE UPSTAIRS MAID, THE / HOW DEEP IS THE OCEAN?......................... *Okeh 6432* 2-4 41
(Vocals: Phil Brito)

WHEN YOU WISH UPON A STAR (Vocal: Phil Brito) / TURN ON THE OLD MUSIC BOX (Vocal: Paula Kelly).............. *Vocalion 5327* 3-5 40

DONAHUE, Sam, & His Orchestra
(Sam Donahue: 3/8/18 – 3/22/74)

AU REET (Vocal: Mitchell Paull) / THEY STILL MAKE LOVE IN LONDON (Vocal: Frances Claire)............... *Bluebird B-11131* 3-5 41

COFFEE AND CAKES (Vocal: Frances Claire) / HALF A HEART (Vocal: Andy Blaine)......... *Bluebird B-11377* 2-4 42

DO YOU CARE? (Vocal: Irene Day) / SIX MILE STRETCH............. *Bluebird B-11198* 3-5 41

FLO FLO / I'LL NEVER TIRE OF YOU (Vocal: Andy Blaine)...... *Bluebird B-11479* 2-4 42

FOUR OR FIVE TIMES (Vocal: Ken Meisel) / SKOOTER............................. *Okeh 6358* 3-5 41

I'M OLD-FASHIONED / MANHATTAN SERENADE............................. *Hit 7016* 2-4 42
(Vocals: Bob Matthews)

IT COUNTS A LOT / LONESOME.......... *Okeh 6334* 2-4 41

JUST AS THOUGH YOU WERE HERE / PENNSYLVANIA POLKA.............. *Hit 7015* 2-5 42
(Vocals: Bob Matthews)

LOAFIN' ON A LAZY DAY (Vocal: Frances Claire) / SAXOPHONE SAM (Vocal: Ken Meisel)............... *Bluebird B-11169* 2-4 41

RAINY NIGHT IN RIO, A (Vocal: Sam Donahue) / ANYBODY'S LOVE SONG (Vocal: Bill Lockwood).................... *Capitol 325* 2-4 47

DORNBERGER, Charles, & His Orchestra

BIT BY BIT YOU'RE BREAKING MY HEART / SUNSHINE OF MINE................. *Victor 19184* 2-4 23

I'M ON MY WAY BACK HOME (Vocal: Carson Robinson) / JUST ONE NIGHT IN YOUR ARMS.... *Victor 19354* 3-5 24

JINGLE BELLS (Vocals: by chorus) / I'LL BE THE MEANEST MAN IN TOWN (Vocal: Charles Dornberger)............... *Victor 24198* 3-5 33

SHE'LL BE COMIN' AROUND THE MOUNTAIN / OLD MacDONALD HAD A FARM...... *Victor 24199* 3-5 33
(Vocals: by chorus)

D'ORSAY DANCE ORCHESTRA, The:
see SELVIN, Ben, & His Orchestra

DORSEY BROTHERS & THEIR CONCERT ORCHESTRA, The
directed by Justin Ring

LOVER, COME BACK TO ME (Vocal: Smith Ballew) / LOVER, COME BACK TO ME, PART II.... *Okeh 41223* 10-12 29

DORSEY BROTHERS' CONCERT ORCHESTRA, The:
directed by Dr. Eugene Ormandy

WAS IT A DREAM? / WAS IT A DREAM, PART II (Vocals: Smith Ballew, Hal Kemp, Nye Mayhew, Saxie Dowell, and Skinnay Ennis)........... *Okeh 41083* 12-15 28

DORSEY BROTHERS' ORCHESTRA, The
(directed by Jimmy Dorsey (2/29/04 – 6/12/57) and Tommy Dorsey (11/19/05 – 11/26/56)

AN EARFUL OF MUSIC / YOUR HEAD ON MY SHOULDER.................... *Decca 258* 5-8 34
(Vocals: Kay Weber)

ANNIE'S COUSIN FANNY / DR. HECKLE AND MR. JIBE......................... *Decca 117* 5-8 34
(Vocals: Don Mattison, Skeets Herfurt, & Roc Hillman)

ANYTHING GOES (Vocals: Don Mattison, Skeets Herfurt, & Roc Hillman) / ALL THROUGH THE NIGHT (Vocal: Kay Weber)..................... *Decca 318* 4-6 35

APACHE (Vocal: Kay Weber) / IT'S DARK ON OBSERVATORY HILL (Vocal: Bob Crosby).. *Decca 314* 4-6 35

AU REVOIR L'MOUR (Vocal: Bob Crosby) / SINGING A HAPPY SONG (Vocals: Don Mattison, Skeets Herfurt, Roc Hillman).......................... *Decca 357* 4-6 35

BLAME IT ON MY YOUTH (Vocal: Bob Crosby) / YOU DIDN'T KNOW ME FROM ADAM (Vocal: Kay Weber)....................... *Decca 320* 4-6 35

BLUE ROOM / FIDGETY............ *Brunswick 6722* 10-12 33

BY HECK / BASIN STREET BLUES........ *Decca 118* 5-8 34

BY THE SYCAMORE TREE / OOH! THAT KISS............... *Columbia 2581-D* 10-12 32
(Vocals: Wes Vaughn)

CHASING SHADOWS (Vocal: Bob Eberle) / EV'RY SINGLE LITTLE TINGLE OF MY HEART (Vocal: Kay Weber)............ *Decca 476* 5-8 35

CONGRATULATIONS / BESIDE AN OPEN FIREPLACE............... *Conqueror 7476* 5-8 30
(Vocals: Scappy Lambert as Rodman Lewis)

CONGRATULATIONS / BESIDE AN OPEN FIREPLACE.................. *Domino 4486* 5-8 30
(Vocals: Scappy Lambert as Rodman Lewis)

CONGRATULATIONS / BESIDE AN OPEN FIREPLACE........... *Pathe Actuelle 37088* 5-8 30
(Vocals: Scappy Lambert as Rodman Lewis)

CONGRATULATIONS / BESIDE AN OPEN FIREPLACE.................. *Perfect 15269* 5-8 30
(Vocals: Scappy Lambert as Rodman Lewis)

CONGRATULATIONS / BESIDE AN OPEN FIREPLACE........................ *Regal 8931* 5-8 30
(Vocals: Scappy Lambert as Rodman Lewis)
(Simultaneously released on five labels)

COQUETTE / YALE BLUES............. *Okeh 41007* 5-8 28
(Vocals: Bill Dutton)

DIPPER MOUTH / THE GENTLEMAN OBVIOUSLY DOESN'T BELIEVE (Vocal: Kay Weber)..... *Decca 561* 5-8 35

DON'T BE AFRAID TO TELL YOUR MOTHER / I'M GOIN' SHOPPIN' WITH YOU......... *Decca 371* 4-6 35
(Vocals: Bob Crosby)

DORSEY BROTHERS ORCHESTRA (a 4-record set)
Individual records in the set listed numerically with (value of each):.............. *Columbia C-51 Set* 15-20 42

PRAYIN' THE BLUES / OODLES OF NOODLES................... *Columbia 36063* 3-5

ANYTHING / JAZZ ME BLUES (with the Original Memphis Five).............. *Columbia 36064* 3-5

I'M GETTING SENTIMENTAL OVER YOU / BY HECK................. *Columbia 36065* 3-5

SHIM SHAM SHIMMY / MOOD HOLLYWOOD............ *Columbia 36066* 3-5

DREAM MAN (Vocal: Bob Crosby) / HANDS ACROSS THE TABLE (Vocal: Kay Weber) .... *Decca 291* 4-6 34

EVENING STAR / FORGETTING YOU .... *Okeh 41065* 5-8 28
(Vocals: Scrappy Lambert)

EVERY LITTLE MOMENT (Vocal: Kay Weber) / I'LL NEVER SAY "NEVER AGAIN" AGAIN (Vocals: Don Mattison, Skeets Herfurt, & Roc Hillman) .... *Decca 480* 5-8 35

FOOTLOOSE AND FANCY FREE (Vocals: Don Mattison, Skeets Herfurt, & Roc Hillman) / YOU'RE ALL I NEED (Vocal: Bob Eberle) .... *Decca 482* 5-8 35

HAVE A LITTLE FAITH IN ME / CRYIN' FOR THE CAROLINES (by Harry Reser as the Clicquot Club Eskimos)................. *Perfect 15265* 5-8 30
(Vocals: Scrappy Lambert as Rodman Lewis)

HEAT WAVE / STOP, LOOK & LISTEN..... *Decca 208* 5-8 34

HOME TIES (Vocal: Bob Crosby) / THE CHURCH BELLS TOLLED (Vocal: Kay Weber) .... *Decca 340* 3-5 35

HONEYSUCKLE ROSE / HONEYSUCKLE ROSE, PART II .... *Decca 296* 5-8 34
(Vocals: Don Mattison, Skeets Herfurt, & Roc Hillman)

HOW CAN YOU FACE ME? (Vocal: Bob Crosby) / THE MOON WAS YELLOW (Vocal: Kay Weber) ... *Decca 196* 4-6 34

I AIN'T GONNA SIN NO MORE / I CAN'T DANCE (I GOT ANTS IN MY PANTS)............. *Decca 116* 5-8 34
(Vocals: Bob Crosby)

I BELIEVE IN MIRACLES (Vocal: Bob Crosby) / DANCING WITH MY SHADOW (Vocal: Kay Weber) .... *Decca 335* 4-6 35

I'D LIKE TO DUNK YOU IN MY COFFEE / IF IT'S LOVE .... *Decca 321* 4-6 35
(Vocals: Bob Crosby)

I'M GETTING SENTIMENTAL OVER YOU / SING................. *Brunswick 6409* 5-8 32
(Vocals: Jean Bowes)

I'M GETTING SENTIMENTAL OVER YOU (Vocal: Bob Crosby) / LONG MAY WE LOVE (Vocal: Kay Weber) .... *Decca 115* 4-6 34

I'M JUST A LITTLE BOY BLUE (Vocal: Kay Weber) / NEW DEAL IN LOVE (Vocal: Bob Crosby)......... *Decca 348* 4-6 35

INDIAN CRADLE SONG / MY MELANCHOLY BABY................................ *Okeh 41032* 5-8 28
(Vocals: Seger Ellis)

I THREW A BEAN BAG AT THE MOON (Vocal: Bob Crosby) / THE FARMER TAKES A WIFE .... *Decca 368* 3-5 35

I'VE GOT YOUR NUMBER / TOMORROW'S ANOTHER DAY (Vocal: Kay Weber) .... *Decca 515* 5-8 35

JUDY / ANNIE'S COUSIN FANNY (Vocals: Glenn Miller & Chorus)... *Brunswick 6938* 8-10 34

LET'S TAKE A WALK AROUND THE BLOCK (Vocal: Kay Weber) / FUN TO BE FOOLED (Vocal: Bob Crosby)......................... *Decca 260* 4-6 34

LOST IN A FOG / I COULDN'T BE MEAN TO YOU...................... *Decca 195* 4-6 34
(Vocals: Bob Crosby)

LOVE IS JUST AROUND THE CORNER / HERE IS MY HEART................... *Decca 311* 4-6 34
(Vocals: Bob Crosby)

LULLABY OF BROADWAY (Vocal: Bob Crosby) / THE WORDS ARE IN MY HEART (Vocal: Kay Weber) .... *Decca 370* 5-8 35

MARY ANN (Vocal: Irving Kaufman as Noel Taylor) / PERSIAN RUG........................ *Okeh 40995* 8-10 28

MAY I? / LOVE THY NEIGHBOR....... *Vocalion 2707* 5-8 34
(Vocals: Chick Bullock)

MEAN TO ME / BUTTON UP YOUR OVERCOAT..................... *Okeh 41210* 10-12 29
(Vocals: Smith Ballew)

MILENBERG JOYS / ST. LOUIS BLUES .... *Decca 119* 5-8 34

MISSOURI MISERY (Vocal: Bob Crosby) / SANDMAN (Vocal: Kay Weber) .... *Decca 297* 4-6 35

MOOD HOLLYWOOD / SHIM SHAM SHIMMY .... *Brunswick 6537* 8-10 33

MY VERY GOOD FRIEND THE MILKMAN (Vocals: Kay Weber, Bob Eberle, Don Mattison, Skeets Herfurt, & Roc Hillman) / I COULDN'T BELIEVE MY EYES (theme song) (Vocal: Kay Weber)............. *Decca 519* 4-6 35

NO STRINGS / TOP HAT, WHITE TIE, AND TAILS .... *Decca 516* 4-6 35
(Vocals: Don Mattison, Skeets Herfurt, & Roc Hillman)

OKAY, TOOTS (Vocals: Don Mattison, Skeets Herfurt, & Roc Hillman) / WHEN MY SHIP COMES IN (Vocal: Bob Crosby)............................ *Decca 259* 4-6 34

OLD MAN HARLEM / BY HECK ..... *Brunswick 6624* 5-8 33

ON A SUNDAY AFTERNOON (Vocal: Kay Weber) / YOU ARE MY LUCKY STAR (Vocal: Bob Eberle) .... *Decca 559* 4-6 35

OUT IN THE COLD AGAIN / DAY DREAMS......................... *Decca 206* 4-6 34
(Vocals: Bob Crosby)

RHYTHM OF THE RAIN (Vocal: Kay Weber) / I WAS LUCKY (Vocal: Bob Crosby)........... *Decca 358* 5-8 35

'ROUND EVENING / OUT OF THE DAWN... *Okeh 41124* 8-10 28
(Vocals: Smith Ballew)

SALLY OF MY DREAMS / CROSS ROADS.... *Okeh 41151* 8-10 29
(Vocals: Smith Ballew)

SHE'S FUNNY THAT WAY (Vocal: Jerry Cooper) / BUT I CAN'T MAKE A MAN (Vocal: Mildred Bailey) .... *Brunswick 7542* 8-10 33

SINGIN' IN THE RAIN / YOU MOTHER AND MINE .... *Okeh 41272* 8-10 29
(Vocals: Irving Kaufman)

SO HELP ME / EASY COME, EASY GO.... *Vocalion 2721* 5-8 34
(Vocals: Chick Bullock)

SOLITUDE (Vocal: Kay Weber) / WEARY BLUES .... *Decca 15013* 5-8 35
(This is an oversize 12 inch 78 rpm)

TAILSPIN / I'VE GOT A FEELIN' YOU'RE FOOLIN' (Vocal: Bob Eberle) .... *Decca 560* 5-8 35

THAT'S MY MAMMY / DIXIE DAWN ..... *Okeh 41050* 5-8 28
(Vocals: Bill Dutton)

TINY LITTLE FINGERPRINTS (Vocal: Kay Weber) / I'M FACING THE MUSIC (Vocal: Bob Crosby).... *Decca 367* 3-5 35

WEARY BLUES / DESE DEM DOSE .... *Decca 469* 5-8 35

WHAT A DIFF'RENCE A DAY MADE (Vocal: Bob Crosby) / WHAT CAN YOU SAY IN A LOVE SONG? (Vocal: Kay Weber) .... *Decca 283* 4-6 34

WHY DID IT HAVE TO BE ME? (Vocals: Wes Vaughn) / WOLF WOBBLE (by Joe Venuti's Rhythm Boys)...................... *Columbia 2589-D* 10-12 32

YOU'RE O.K. / ECCENTRIC .... *Decca 1304* 5-8 35

YOU'RE SO DARN CHARMING (Vocal: Don Mattison) / YOU SAVED MY LIFE (Vocal: Kay Weber)... *Decca 520* 4-6 35

YOU'RE THE TOP (Vocal: Roc Hillman) / I GET A KICK OUT OF YOU (Vocal: Kay Weber) .... *Decca 319* 4-6 35

DORSEY BROTHERS' ORCHESTRA, The, as The Musical Voyagers

CAN THIS BE LOVE? (Vocal: Scrappy Lambert) / I CAN MAKE MOST ANYTHING, BUT I CAN'T MAKE A MAN (Vocal: Wes Vaughn) ...... *Parlophone PNY-34152* 12-15 30

DORSEY BROTHERS' ORCHESTRA, The, as Bob Snyder & His Orchestra

HOLD MY HAND / MY DOG LOVES YOUR DOG .... *Vocalion 2660* 8-10 34
(Vocals: Kay Weber)

SWEET AND SIMPLE / NASTY MAN... *Vocalion 2661* 10-12 34
(Vocals: Kay Weber)

DORSEY BROTHERS' ORCHESTRA, The, as The Travelers

AM I BLUE? (Vocal: Irving Kaufman) / THE ONE IN THE WORLD (by The California Ramblers as Ted Wallace & His Orchestra, recorded under the name Ed Loyd & His Orchestra, with an unknown vocalist)................. *Okeh 41259* 5-8 29

BABY, OH! WHERE CAN YOU BE (Vocal: Irving Kaufman) / BREAKAWAY.... *Okeh 41260* 8-10 29

CAN THIS BE LOVE? / FINE AND DANDY.............. *Odeon ONY-36160* 10-12 30
(Vocals: Scrappy Lambert)

FINE AND DANDY (Vocal: Scrappy Lambert) / I CAN MAKE MOST ANYTHING, BUT I CAN'T MAKE A MAN (Vocal: Wes Vaughn) .... *Okeh 41471* 10-12 30

I APOLOGIZE / BEGGING FOR LOVE.......................... *Melotone M-12227* 8-10 31
(Vocals: Scrappy Lambert)

I'VE GOT A SWEET SOMEBODY / DREAM A LITTLE DREAM OF ME.................. *Melotone M-12148* 10-12 31
(Vocals: Scrappy Lambert)

YOU SAID IT / SWEET AND HOT... *Melotone M-12113* 10-12 31
(Vocals: Scrappy Lambert)

DORSEY, Jimmy, accompanied by a recording group

(Jimmy Dorsey: 2/29/04 – 6/12/57)

BEEBE / PRAYING THE BLUES......... *Okeh 41245* 8-10 29

DORSEY, Jimmy, & His Orchestra

ABSENT-MINDED MOON (Vocal: Bob Eberly) / ME AND MY MALINDA (Vocal: Phil Washburn) ...... *Decca 4263* 2-4 42

AFTER YOU / IT'S THE NATURAL THING TO DO.......................... *Decca 1378* 3-5 37
(Vocals: Don Mattison)

AH-WOO! AH-WOO! TO YOU / THERE'S NO SUBSTITUTE FOR YOU .... *Decca 873* 3-5 36
(Vocals: Toots Camarata, Bobby Byrne, Roc Hillman)

ALL GOD'S CHILDREN GOT RHYTHM (Vocal: Vicki Joyce) / MUTINY IN THE BRASS SECTION .... *Decca 1256* 4-6 37

ALL I REMEMBER IS YOU (Vocal: Helen O'Connell) / SHOW YOUR LINEN, MISS RICHARDSON (Vocal: Ray McKinley) .... *Decca 2523* 2-4 39

ALL OR NOTHING AT ALL (Vocal: Bob Eberly) / IN THE MIDDLE OF A DREAM (Vocal: Helen O'Connell) .... *Decca 2580* 2-4 39

ARE YOU HAVIN' ANY FUN? / MELANCHOLY LULLABY............... *Decca 2761* 2-4 39
(Vocals: Helen O'Connell)

ARKANSAW TRAVELER / YOU'RE SO DESIRABLE (Vocal: Bob Eberly)........... *Decca 2363* 3-5 39

AT A PERFUME COUNTER / LOVE WALKED IN .... *Decca 1724* 2-4 38
(Vocals: Bob Eberly)

AT THE CROSS-ROADS / MANHATTAN SERENADE............ *Decca 18467* 2-4 42
(Vocals: Bob Eberly)

AT YOUR BECK AND CALL (Vocal: Bob Eberly) / WHO DO YOU THINK I SAW LAST NIGHT? (Vocal: Don Mattison) .... *Decca 1784* 2-4 38

AU REET / MAN, THAT'S GROOVY .... *Decca 3721* 2-4 41
(Vocals: Helen O'Connell)

AURORA (Vocal: Helen O'Connell) / BAR BABBLE .... *Decca 3772* 2-4 41

BACK TO BACK / ESPECIALLY FOR YOU... *Decca 2554* 2-4 39
(Vocals: Helen O'Connell)

BLUE CHAMPAGNE / ALL ALONE AND LONELY........................ *Decca 3775* 2-4 41
(Vocals: Bob Eberly)

BLUE SKIES / SOMEDAY, SWEETHEART (Vocal: Helen O'Connell) ... *Decca 18385* 2-4 42

BODY AND SOUL (Vocal: Bob Eberly) / DIXIELAND DETOUR .... *Decca 2735* 3-5 39

BRAZIL (Vocals: Bob Eberly & Helen O'Connell) / DAYBREAK (Vocal: Bob Eberly).......... *Decca 18460* 2-4 42

CHANGE PARTNERS (Vocal: Bob Eberly) / THE YAM (Vocals: Bobby Byrne, Don Mattison, & Roc Hillman) .... *Decca 2002* 2-4 38

CHARLESTON ALLEY / THE SPIRIT'S GOT ME (Vocal: Bob Eberly)............... *Decca 4075* 2-4 41

CONTRASTS (theme song) / TONIGHT (PERFIDIA) .... *Decca 3198* 2-4 40

DARKTOWN STRUTTERS' BALL, THE (Vocal: June Richardson) / DUSK IN UPPER SANDUSKY.................... *Decca 1939* 3-5 38

DEEP PURPLE / FATE .... *Decca 2295* 2-4 39
(Vocals: Bob Eberly)

DOCTOR RHYTHM (Vocals: Don Mattison, Roc Hillman, & Bob Eberly) / ON THE SENTIMENTAL SIDE (Vocal: Bob Eberly) .... *Decca 1651* 3-5 38

DROP ME A LINE (Vocal: Helen O'Connell) / WHEN THE ROSES BLOOM AGAIN (Vocal: Bob Eberly) .... *Decca 4165* 3-5 42

EASY TO LOVE / SWINGIN' THE JINX AWAY............................ *Decca 940* 4-6 36
(Vocals: Frances Langford)

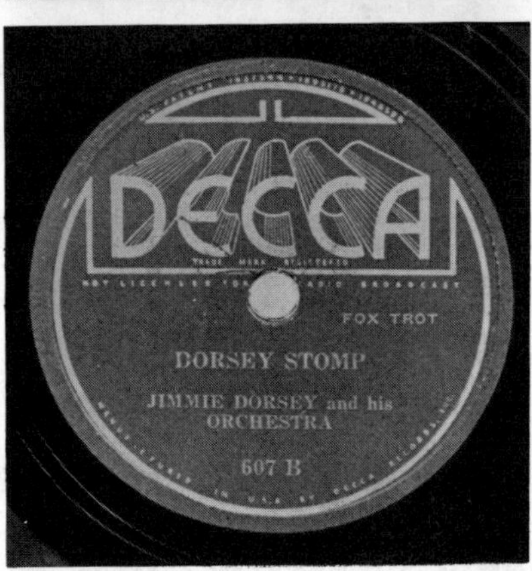

EMBRACEABLE YOU (Vocal: Bob Eberly) / FINGERBUSTIN' .... *Decca 3928* 2-4 41

FUNICULI, FUNICULA / CHICKEN REEL... *Decca 1086* 3-5 36

GIVE ME THE SIMPLE LIFE / IT'S THE TALK OF THE TOWN .... *Decca 23469* 2-4 46
(Vocals: Bing Crosby)

GOOD FOR NOTHIN' (BUT LOVE) (Vocal: Bob Eberly) / ROMANCE RUNS IN THE FAMILY (Vocal: Helen O'Connell) .... *Decca 2294* 2-4 39

HANDFUL OF STARS, A / FALLING LEAVES.................... *Decca 3446* 2-4 40
(Vocals: Bob Eberly)

HEAR MY SONG, VIOLETTA / DEVIL MAY CARE .... *Decca 3255* 2-4 40
(Vocals: Bob Eberly)

HEP-TEE-HOOTIE (JOOK BOX JIVE) (Vocal: Helen O'Connell) / DOLIMITE .... *Decca 3312* 2-4 40

HOLD TIGHT (Vocals: The Andrews Sisters) / BILLY BOY (Vocals: Ray McKinley & the Andrews Sisters)..... *Decca 2214* 2-4 39

HOME IN THE CLOUDS, A (Vocal: Helen O'Connell) / MY LOVE FOR YOU (Vocal: Bob Eberly)......... *Decca 2522* 2-4 39

HOW CAN I EVER BE ALONE? (Vocal: Bob Eberly) / TENNESSEE FISH-FRY (Vocal: Helen O'Connell) .... *Decca 3197* 2-4 40

HOW'DJA LIKE TO LOVE ME? (Vocal: Don Mattison) / I FALL IN LOVE WITH YOU EVERY DAY (Vocal: Bob Eberly) .... *Decca 1671* 2-4 38

I BOUGHT A WOODEN WHISTLE (Vocal: Helen O'Connell) / BLUE (Vocals: Helen O'Connell & Bob Eberly) .... *Decca 3280* 2-4 40

I CAN'T FACE THE MUSIC (WITHOUT SINGIN' THE BLUES (Vocal: June Richmond) / LOST AND FOUND (Vocal: Bob Eberly) .... *Decca 1746* 3-5 38

I CAN'T RESIST YOU (Vocal: Bob Eberly) / I LOVE TO WATCH THE MOONLIGHT (Vocal: Helen O'Connell) .... *Decca 3215* 2-4 40

I CRIED FOR YOU / SONG OF THE VOLGA BOATMAN.................... *Decca 15041* 3-5 38
(This is an oversize 12-inch 78 rpm)

IF I FORGET YOU / ALL THIS AND HEAVEN TOO.......................... *Decca 3259* 2-4 40
(Vocals: Bob Eberly)

IF I HAD YOU / A TABLE IN THE CORNER...................... *Decca 2814* 2-4 39
(Vocals: Bob Eberly)

IF YOU ARE BUT A DREAM / FULL MOON .... *Decca 4312* 2-4 42
(Vocals: Bob Eberly)

IF YOU WERE IN MY PLACE / I LET A SONG GO OUT OF MY HEART .... *Decca 1809* 2-4 38
(Vocals: June Richmond)

I GET ALONG WITHOUT YOU VERY WELL / IT'S ANYBODY'S MOON................ *Decca 2322* 2-4 39
(Vocals: Bob Eberly)

I GOT RHYTHM / FLIGHT
OF THE BUMBLE-BEE .... *Decca 1508* 4-6 37

I HADN'T ANYONE TILL YOU / THERE'S A
FARAWAY LOOK IN YOUR EYE .... *Decca 1834* 2-4 38
(Vocals: Bob Eberly)

I HAVEN'T CHANGED A THING (Vocal: June Richmond) /
KILLY-KA-LEE (Vocal: Ray McKinley) ..... *Decca 1961* 3-5 38

I HEAR A RHAPSODY / THE MEM'RY OF
A ROSE .... *Decca 3570* 2-4 41
(Vocals: Bob Eberly)

I LOVE YOU IN TECHNICOLOR (Vocal: Bob Eberly) /
ANY OLD TIME AT ALL (Vocal: Vi Mele) ..... *Decca 1921* 3-5 38

I'M A GAMBLER (Vocal: Bob Eberly) /
DORSEY STOMP .... *Decca 607* 4-6 35

I'M GLAD THERE IS YOU /
TOMORROW'S SUNRISE .... *Decca 4197* 2-4 42
(Vocals: Bob Eberly)

I'M IN LOVE WITH SOMEONE /
IT'S A CRYING SHAME .... *Decca 18611* 2-4 42
(Vocals: Gladys Tell)

IN A LITTLE HULA HEAVEN / NEVER IN A
MILLION YEARS .... *Decca 1210* 5-8 37
(Vocals: Bing Crosby)

IN A SENTIMENTAL MOOD /
STOMPIN' AT THE SAVOY .... *Decca 882* 4-6 36

I POURED MY HEART INTO A SONG (Vocal:
Bob Eberly) / AN OLD-FASHIONED TUNE IS
ALWAYS NEW (Vocal: Don Mattison) .... *Decca 2553* 2-4 39

I REMEMBER YOU (Vocal: Bob Eberly) / IF YOU BUILD A
BETTER MOUSETRAP (Vocals: Bob Eberly
& Helen O'Connell) .... *Decca 4132* 2-4 42

ISLE OF PINES (Vocal: Bob Eberly) / TIME WAS
(Vocals: Bob Eberly & Helen O'Connell) .... *Decca 3859* 2-4 41

IT AIN'T RIGHT (Vocal: Don Mattison) / THE BOSTON
TEA PARTY (Vocals: Toots Camarata, Bobby Byrne,
Don Mattison, & Roc Hillman) .... *Decca 901* 4-6 36

IT HAPPENED IN HAWAII (Vocals: Bob Eberly
& Helen O'Connell) / TROPICAL MAGIC
(Vocal: Bob Eberly) .... *Decca 4034* 2-4 41

IT'S ALL YOURS (Vocal: Helen O'Connell) /
THIS IS IT (Vocal: Bob Eberly) .... *Decca 2332* 2-4 39

IT'S NO FUN / MOONRISE
ON THE LOWLANDS .... *Decca 782* 4-6 36
(Vocals: Seger Ellis)

IT'S THE DREAMER IN ME (Vocal: Bob Eberly) /
DON'T BE THAT WAY .... *Decca 1733* 2-4 38

I UNDERSTAND / HIGH ON A
WINDY HILL .... *Decca 3585* 2-4 41
(Vocals: Bob Eberly)

JAMBOREE (Vocal: Bob Eberly) /
HOLLYWOOD PASTIME .... *Decca 1200* 4-6 37

JIM (Vocals: Bob Eberly & Helen O'Connell) / A NEW SHADE
OF BLUE (Vocal: Bob Eberly) .... *Decca 3963* 2-4 41

JOHN SILVER / THAT FEELING
IS GONE (Vocal: Don Mattison) .... *Decca 1860* 2-4 38

LAMP IS LOW, THE (Vocal: Bob Eberly) /
BEGONE (Vocal: Helen O'Connell) .... *Decca 2579* 2-4 39

LA ROSITA / MINNIE FROM
TRINIDAD (Vocal: Helen O'Connell) .... *Decca 3711* 2-4 41

LAST NIGHT I SAID A PRAYER / ALWAYS IN
MY HEART .... *Decca 4277* 2-4 42
(Vocals: Bob Eberly)

LATINS KNOW HOW / FOOLS FALL
IN LOVE (Vocal: Bob Eberly) .... *Decca 3176* 2-4 40

LET ME DREAM / AND SO DO I .... *Decca 3311* 2-4 40
(Vocals: Bob Eberly)

LET'S MAKE MEMORIES TONIGHT (Vocal: Bob Eberly) /
COMES LOVE (Vocal: Helen O'Connell) .... *Decca 2745* 2-4 39

LET'S STOP THE CLOCK / THE MASQUERADE
IS OVER .... *Decca 2293* 2-4 39
(Vocals: Bob Eberly)

LISTEN TO THE MOCKING-BIRD / THE LOVE BUG
WILL BITE YOU (Vocal: Ray McKinley) ..... *Decca 1187* 3-5 37

LITTLE CURLY HAIR IN A HIGH CHAIR
(Vocal: Helen O'Connell) / THE BREEZE AND I
(Vocal: Bob Eberly) .... *Decca 3150* 2-4 40

LOVE IS HERE TO STAY / I WAS DOING
ALL RIGHT (Vocal: Bob Eberly) .... *Decca 1660* 2-4 38

LOVE IS WHERE YOU FIND IT /
GARDEN OF THE MOON .... *Decca 1970* 2-4 38
(Vocals: Bob Eberly)

LOVE NEVER WENT TO COLLEGE
(Vocal: Helen O'Connell) / I DIDN'T KNOW
WHAT TIME IT WAS (Vocal: Bob Eberly) ... *Decca 2813* 2-4 39

MAGIC OF MAGNOLIAS / DAY-DREAM ... *Decca 4047* 2-4 41
(Vocals: Bob Eberly)

MAJOR AND MINOR STOMP / KEEP A-KNOCKIN'
(Vocals: Helen O'Connell & chorus) .... *Decca 2980* 3-5 40

MAN AND HIS DREAM, A (Vocal: Bob Eberly) / GO FLY A
KITE (Vocal: Helen O'Connell) .... *Decca 2650* 2-4 39

MAN AND HIS DRUM, A / CHEROKEE ... *Decca 2961* 3-5 40

MOON GOT IN MY EYES, THE / ALL YOU
WANT TO DO IS DANCE .... *Decca 1377* 3-5 37
(Vocals: Bob Eberly)

MOONLIGHT MASQUERADE /
WASN'T IT YOU? .... *Decca 3991* 2-4 41
(Vocals: Bob Eberly)

MURDER! HE SAYS (Vocal: Helen O'Connell) / LET'S GET
LOST (Vocal: Bob Eberly) .... *Decca 18532* 2-4 42

MY DEVOTION (Vocal: Bob Eberly) /
SORGHUM SWITCH .... *Decca 18372* 2-4 42

MY LITTLE COUSIN (Vocal: Helen O'Connell) /
JERSEY BOUNCE .... *Decca 4288* 2-4 42

MY PRAYER (Vocal: Bob Eberly) /
YOU'RE THE GREATEST DISCOVERY
(SINCE 1492) (Vocal: Helen O'Connell) .... *Decca 2810* 2-4 39

MY SISTER AND I (Vocal: Bob Eberly) / IN THE HUSH
OF THE NIGHT (Vocals: Bob Eberly
& Helen O'Connell) .... *Decca 3710* 2-4 41

NOT MINE (Vocals: Bob Eberly & Helen O'Connell) /
ARTHUR MURRAY TAUGHT ME DANCING IN A
HURRY (Vocal: Helen O'Connell) .... *Decca 4122* 2-4 42

NOW YOU KNOW (Vocal: Bob Eberly) / DO IT AGAIN
(Vocals: Helen O'Connell & Bob Eberly) .... *Decca 2925* 2-4 40

ON A LITTLE STREET IN SINGAPORE /
MY SILENT MOOD .... *Decca 2838* 2-4 39
(Vocals: Bob Eberly)

ONCE AND FOR ALL / THE THINGS
I LOVE .... *Decca 3737* 2-4
(Vocals: Bob Eberly)

ONCE IN A LOVETIME (Vocal: Bob Eberly) / WHILE THE
MUSIC PLAYS ON (Vocal: Helen O'Connell) ... *Decca 3322* 2-4 40

ON ECHO HILL (Vocal: Bob Eberly) /
WONDER WHEN MY BABY'S COMING HOME?
(Vocal: Helen O'Connell) .... *Decca 18362* 2-4 42

ONE SWEET LETTER FROM YOU
(Vocal: Helen O'Connell) / IT'S FUNNY TO
EVERYONE BUT ME (Vocal: Bob Eberly) ... *Decca 2702* 2-4 39

ONE, TWO, BUTTON YOUR SHOE /
PENNIES FROM HEAVEN .... *Decca 951* 3-5 36
(Vocals: Bob Eberly)

ONLY A ROSE / I'LL FIND YOU .... *Decca 18545* 2-4 42
(Vocals: Bob Eberly)

OUR LOVE (Vocal: Bob Eberly) /
ALL OF ME (Vocal: Helen O'Connell) .... *Decca 2352* 2-4 39

PARADE OF THE MILK BOTTLE CAPS /
DON'T LOOK NOW (Vocals: Toots Camarata,
Bobby Byrne, & Roc Hillman) .... *Decca 941* 4-6 36

PECKIN' (Vocal: Bing Crosby) / JUST LATELY
(Vocal: Vicki Joyce) .... *Decca 1301* 4-6 37

PICTURE OF ME WITHOUT YOU, A (Vocals: Kay Weber
& Bob Eberly) / WHY SHOULDN'T I
(Vocal: Kay Weber) .... *Decca 571* 3-5 35

POOR BALLERINA / LET THERE
BE LOVE .... *Decca 3166* 2-4 40
(Vocals: Bob Eberly)

POPCORN MAN / COWBOY
FROM BROOKLYN .... *Decca 1799* 3-5 38
(Vocals: Ray McKinley)

RAP TAP ON WOOD / I'VE GOT
YOU UNDER MY SKIN .... *Decca 939* 4-6 36
(Vocals: Frances Langford)

RENDEVOUS TIME IN PAREE (Vocal: Bob Eberly) /
IS IT POSSIBLE? (Vocal: Helen O'Connell) ... *Decca 2577* 2-4 39

RIGMAROLE / SWAMP FIRE .... *Decca 2918* 3-5 40

ROBINS AND ROSES (Vocal: Kay Weber) /
SING, SING SING (Vocals: Toots Camarata,
Bobby Byrne, Roc Hillman) .... *Decca 776* 4-6 36

ROMANCE / THIS IS
NO DREAM (Vocal: Bob Eberly) .... *Decca 2546* 2-4 39

ROOM WITH A VIEW, A (Vocal: Bob Eberly) /
KINDA LONESOME
(Vocal: Lee Leighton) .... *Decca 2213* 2-4 39

SERENADE TO NOBODY IN PARTICULAR /
DORSEY DERVISH (WADDLIN' AT
THE WALDORF) .... *Decca 1040* 3-5 36

SHOOT THE MEAT BALLS TO ME, DOMINICK
BOY! (Vocal: Ray McKinley) / THE JUMPIN' JIVE
(Vocal: Helen O'Connell) .... *Decca 2612* 3-5 39

SINNER KISSED AN ANGEL (Vocal: Bob Eberly) /
YOU MADE ME LOVE YOU
(Vocal: Helen O'Connell) .... *Decca 4142* 2-4 42

SIX LESSONS FROM MADAME
LA ZONGA / BOOG IT .... *Decca 3152* 2-4 40
(Vocals: Helen O'Connell)

SLEEPY LAGOON (Vocal: Bob Eberly) / I THREW A KISS
IN THE OCEAN (Vocal: Helen O'Connell) .... *Decca 4304* 2-4 42

SMOKE FROM A CHIMNEY (Vocal: Bob Eberly) /
MY FIRST IMPRESSION OF YOU
(Vocal: Don Mattison) .... *Decca 1652* 2-4 38

SO DO I / LET'S CALL
A HEART A HEART .... *Decca 950* 3-5 36
(Vocals: Bob Eberly)

SO MANY TIMES (Vocal: Bob Eberly) /
TAKE A TIP FROM THE WHIPPOORWILL
(Vocals: Helen O'Connell) .... *Decca 2727* 2-4 39

'TAIN'T NO GOOD (Vocal: Phil Washburn) /
'TAIN'T NO GOOD, PART II (Vocals: Phil Washburn
& Helen O'Connell) .... *Decca 4262* 2-4 42

'TAIN'T NO USE (Vocals: Toots Camarata,
Bobby Byrne, & Roc Hillman) / I LOVE TO SING-A
(Vocal: Don Mattison) .... *Decca 808* 3-5 36

TAKE ME (Vocal: Helen O'Connell) / THIS IS WORTH
FIGHTING FOR (Vocal: Bob Eberly) .... *Decca 18376* 3-5 42

THEY ALL LAUGHED / LET'S CALL THE
WHOLE THING OFF .... *Decca 1204* 3-5 37
(Vocals: Don Mattison)

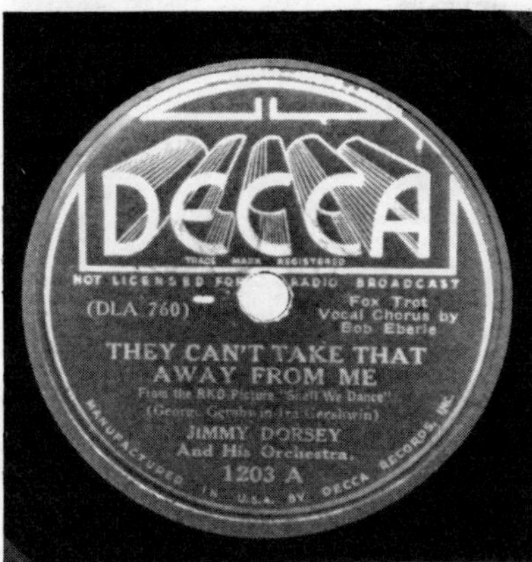

THEY CAN'T TAKE THAT AWAY
FROM ME / SLAP THAT BASS .... *Decca 1203* 3-5 37
(Vocals: Bob Eberly)

TU-LI-TULIP TIME / SHA-SHA .... *Decca 1974* 2-4 38
(Vocals: The Andrews Sisters)

TURN LEFT / TURN RIGHT .... *Decca 3647* 2-4 41

TWO BOUQUETS (Vocal: Bob Eberly) /
JOSEPH! JOSEPH! (Vocal: June Richmond) ... *Decca 1723* 2-4 38

WAH-HOO! (Vocals: Toots Camarata, Bobby Byrne,
& Roc Hillman) / WHAT'S THE REASON (I'M
NOT PLEASIN' YOU) .... *Decca 762* 3-5 36

WASHINGTON GRAYS / TAP DANCER'S
NIGHTMARE .... *Decca 655* 3-5 35

WEEK-END OF A PRIVATE SECRETARY, THE (Vocal:
June Richmond) / STOP! AND RECONSIDER (Vocals:
Bobby Byrne, Don Mattison, & Roc Hillman) .... *Decca 1745* 2-4 38

WELCOME STRANGER (Vocal: Kay Weber) / IS IT TRUE
WHAT THEY SAY ABOUT DIXIE?
(Vocal: Bob Eberly) .... *Decca 768* 3-5 36

WHEN LOVE COMES YOUR WAY (Vocal: Kay Weber) /
ME AND MARIE (Vocal: Bob Eberly) .... *Decca 570* 3-5 35

WHEN THE SUN COMES OUT
(Vocal: Helen O'Connell) / YOURS
(Vocals: Bob Eberly & Helen O'Connell) .... *Decca 3657* 2-4 41

WHERE AM I? (Vocal: Kay Weber) /
YOU LET ME DOWN (Vocal: Bob Eberly) .... *Decca 602* 3-5 35

WHERE DO YOU KEEP YOU HEART? /
SHADES OF TWILIGHT .... *Decca 3270* 2-4 40
(Vocals: Bob Eberly)

WHISPER WHILE WE DANCE / STAIRWAY TO
THE STARS .... *Decca 2567* 2-4 39
(Vocals: Bob Eberly)

WHITE CLIFFS OF DOVER, THE / I GOT IT
BAD (AND THAT AIN'T GOOD)
(Vocal: Helen O'Connell) .... *Decca 4103* 3-5 42

YESTERTHOUGHTS (Vocal: Bob Eberly) /
ON THE TRAIL .... *Decca 3395* 2-4 40

YOU NEVER LOOKED
SO BEAUTIFUL / YOU .... *Decca 764* 3-5 36
(Vocals: Bob Eberly)

YOU'RE A LUCKY GUY (Vocal: Helen O'Connell) /
TOMORROW NIGHT (Vocal: Bob Eberly) ... *Decca 2837* 2-4 39

YOU'VE GOT ME THIS WAY / THE BAD
HUMOR MAN .... *Decca 3435* 2-4 40
(Vocals: Helen O'Connell)

DORSEY, Tommy, accompanied by a recording group
(Tommy Dorsey: 11/9/05 – 11/26/56)

IT'S RIGHT HERE FOR YOU /
TIGER RAG .... *Okeh 41198* 10-12 29
(Tommy Dorsey solos on trumpet rather than trombone on this release, one of the rare occasions he does so)

DORSEY, Tommy, & His Clambake Seven

ALL YOU WANT TO DO IS
DANCE / AFTER YOU .... *Victor 25647* 2-4 37
(Vocals: Edythe Wright)

A-TISKET, A-TASKET / AS LONG AS
YOU LIVE .... *Victor 25899* 3-5 38
(Vocals: Edythe Wright)

BUT I DO MIND IF YA DON'T / THAT'S LIFE,
I GUESS .... *Victor 20-2302* 2-4 47
(Vocals: Hannah Williams)

CHINATOWN, MY CHINATOWN /
THE SHEIK OF ARABY .... *Victor 26023* 3-5 38

DON'T EVER CHANGE / OUR LOVE WAS
MEANT TO BE .... *Victor 25607* 2-4 37
(Vocals: Edythe Wright)

DO YOU REMEMBER LAST NIGHT? / THANKS FOR
EVERYTHING .... *Victor 26119* 2-4 39
(Vocals: Edythe Wright)

GOTTA GO TO WORK AGAIN (Vocals: by trio) /
EVERY MINUTE OF EVERY HOUR
(Vocal: Edythe Wright) .... *Victor 25256* 3-5 35

HAVING WONDERFUL TIME (WISH YOU WERE
HERE) / STARDUST ON THE MOON ... *Victor 25630* 2-4 37
(Vocals: Edythe Wright)

HE'S A GYPSY FROM POUGHKEEPSIE /
ALIBI BABY .... *Victor 25577* 2-4 37
(Vocals: Edythe Wright)

IF YOU EVER SHOULD LEAVE/POSIN' ... *Victor 25605* 3-5 37
(Vocals: Edythe Wright)

IS THIS GONNA BE MY LUCKY SUMMER? / WHO'LL
BE THE ONE THIS SUMMER? .... *Victor 25610* 2-4 37
(Vocals: Edythe Wright)

IT'S A HUNDRED TO ONE (Vocal: Edythe Wright) /
VOL VISTU GAILY STAR (Vocals: Hughie Prince
& Tommy Dorsey) .... *Victor 26363* 2-4 39

JOSEPHINE / IF THE MAN IN
THE MOON WERE A COON .... *Victor 25676* 2-4 37
(Vocals: Jack Leonard)

LADY IS A TRAMP, THE /
TEARS IN MY HEART .... *Victor 25673* 2-4 37
(Vocals: Edythe Wright)

LITTLE RENDEVOUS IN HONOLULU / THAT
LOVELY NIGHT IN BUDAPEST .... *Victor 25246* 3-5 35
(Vocals: Jack Leonard)

LOVE WILL LIVE ON (Vocal: Buddy Gately) /
THEN I SHAN'T LOVE YOU ANY MORE
(Vocal: Edythe Wright) .... *Victor 25214* 3-5 35

MILKMAN'S MATINEE, THE (Vocal: Edythe Wright) /
TWILIGHT IN TURKEY .... *Victor 25568* 2-4 37

MUSIC GOES 'ROUND AND AROUND (Vocals: Tommy
Dorsey & Edythe Wright) / RHYTHM IN MY NURSERY
RHYMES (Vocal: Edythe Wright) .... *Victor 25201* 3-5 36

MY CABIN OF DREAMS /
AM I DREAMING? .... *Victor 25620* 2-4 37
(Vocals: Edythe Wright)

NICE WORK IF YOU CAN GET IT / YOU'RE
A SWEETHEART .... *Victor 25695* 2-4 37
(Vocals: Edythe Wright)

ONE NIGHT IN MONTE CARLO / THE DAY I LET YOU GET AWAY .... *Victor 25220* 3-5 36
(Vocals: Edythe Wright)

RHYTHM SAVED THE WORLD / AT THE CODFISH BALL .... *Victor 25314* 3-5 36

SAILING AT MIDNIGHT / YOU MUST HAVE BEEN A BEAUTIFUL BABY .... *Victor 26066* 2-4 38
(Vocals: Edythe Wright)

SHOOT THE SHERBET TO ME, HERBERT (Vocals: Edythe Wright & Tommy Dorsey) / ALLA EN EL RANCHO GRANDE (Vocal: Hughie Prince) .... *Victor 26370* 2-4 39

STOP KICKING MY HEART AROUND / ALL IN FAVOR OF SWING SAY "AYE" (by Tommy Dorsey & His Orchestra) .... *Victor 26356* 2-4 39
(Vocals: Edythe Wright)

TOMMY DORSEY'S CLAMBAKE SEVEN (a 4-record album set) .... *RCA Victor P 220* 10-12 -
Individual records in the set, listed numerically (with value of each):
- MUSIC GOES 'ROUND AND 'ROUND, THE / SAILING AT MIDNIGHT .... *Victor 20-3030* 2-4
(Vocals: Edythe Wright)
- AT THE CODFISH BALL (Vocal: Edythe Wright) / JOSEPHINE (Vocal: Jack Leonard) .... *Victor 20-3031* 2-4
- LADY IS A TRAMP, THE (Vocal: Edythe Wright) / THE SHEIK OF ARABY .... *Victor 20-3032* 2-4
- ALLA EN EL RANCHO GRANDE (Vocal: Hughie Prince) CHINATOWN, MY CHINATOWN .... *Victor 20-3033* 2-4

WHEN THE MIDNIGHT CHOO-CHOO LEAVES FOR ALABAM' / EVERYBODY'S DOING IT .... *Victor 25821* 2-4 38
(Vocals: Edythe Wright)

DORSEY, Tommy, & His Novelty Orchestra

DADDY, CHANGE YOUR MIND / YOU CAN'T CHEAT A CHEATER .... *Okeh 41422* 10-15 29
(Tommy Dorsey plays trumpet on this release)

DORSEY, Tommy, & His Orchestra

AFTER ALL / BLUE RAIN .... *Victor 26418* 2-4 39
(Vocals: Jack Leonard)

AFTER I SAY I'M SORRY (Vocals: The Pied Pipers) / THE SKY FELL DOWN (Vocal: Frank Sinatra) .... *Victor 26518* 2-4 40

ALL IN FAVOR OR SWING SAY "AYE" / STOP KICKING MY HEART AROUND (by Tommy Dorsey & His Clambake Seven) .... *Victor 26356* 2-4 39
(Vocals: Edythe Wright)

ALL IN FUN / HEAVEN IN MY ARMS .... *Victor 26406* 2-4 39
(Vocals: Anita Boyer)

ALL THIS AND HEAVEN TOO / WHERE DO YOU KEEP YOUR HEART? .... *Victor 26653* 2-4 40
(Vocals: Frank Sinatra)

AM I PROUD? (Vocal: Anita Boyer) / EASY DOES IT .... *Victor 26429* 2-4 39

AND SO DO I (Vocal: Connie Haines) / THE ONE I LOVE BELONGS TO SOMEBODY ELSE (Vocal: Frank Sinatra) .... *Victor 26660* 2-4 40

ANGEL (Vocal: Allan De Witt) / IT'S A BLUE WORLD (Vocals: Anita Boyer) .... *Victor 26465* 2-4 40

ANGELS WITH DIRTY FACES / BETWEEN A KISS AND A SIGH .... *Victor 26115* 2-4 39
(Vocal: Edythe Wright)

APRIL PLAYED THE FIDDLE / I HAVEN'T TIME TO BE A MILLIONAIRE .... *Victor 26606* 2-4 40
(Vocals: Frank Sinatra)

ARE YOU HAVING ANY FUN? (Vocal: Edythe Wright) / GOODNIGHT, MY BEAUTIFUL (Vocal: Jack Leonard) .... *Victor 26335* 2-4 39

ASLEEP OR AWAKE (Vocal: Jack Leonard) / IF YOU EVER CHANGE YOUR MIND (Vocal: Edythe Wright) .... *Victor 26210* 2-4 39

BACK STAGE AT THE BALLET / BLUE SKIES (Vocal: Frank Sinatra) .... *Victor 27566* 2-4 41

BEWILDERED / JEZEBEL .... *Victor 25795* 2-4 38
(Vocals: Jack Leonard)

BIRDS OF A FEATHER (Vocal: Connie Haines) / IT'S ALWAYS YOU (Vocal: Frank Sinatra) .... *Victor 27345* 2-4 41

BLAME THE WEATHER (Vocal: Jack Leonard) / DAVENPORT BLUES .... *Victor 26135* 3-5 39

BLUE DANUBE / DARK EYES .... *Victor 25556* 3-5 37

BLUE SKIES (Vocal: Frank Sinatra) / — .... *V-Disc 1* 5-8 -
(A World War II release)

BOOGIE WOOGIE / — .... *V-Disc 18* 4-6 -
(A World War II release)

BOOGIE WOOGIE / WEARY BLUES .... *Victor 26054* 2-4 38

BY THE RIVER SAINTE MARIE / MARCH OF THE TOYS .... *Victor 26346* 2-4 39

BY THE SLEEPY LAGOON / MELODY .... *Victor 10-1045* 5-8 42
(A Red Seal Victor release)

CALL OF THE CANYON, THE / LOVE LIES .... *Victor 26678* 2-4 40
(Vocals: Frank Sinatra)

CARELESS (Vocal: Allan De Witt) / DARN THAT DREAM (Vocal: Anita Boyer) .... *Victor 26433* 2-4 40

CHARMING LITTLE FAKER (Vocals: The Pied Pipers) / IMAGINATION (Vocal: Frank Sinatra) .... *Victor 26581* 2-4 40

COWBOY FROM BROOKLYN (Vocal: Skeets Herfurt) / I'LL DREAM TONIGHT (Vocal: Jack Leonard) .... *Victor 25832* 2-4 38

DAWN ON THE DESERT / WHY BEGIN AGAIN? (Vocal: Jack Leonard) .... *Victor 26246* 2-4 39

DAY IN, DAY OUT / BLUE ORCHIDS .... *Victor 26339* 2-4 39
(Vocals: Jack Leonard)

'DEED I DO (Vocal: Edythe Wright) / YEARNING (Vocal: Jack Leonard) .... *Victor 25815* 2-4 38

DEEP RIVER / — .... *V-Disc 509* 5-8 -
(A World War II release)

DO I WORRY? (Vocals: Frank Sinatra & The Pied Pipers) / LITTLE MAN WITH A CANDY CIGAR (Vocal: Jo Stafford) .... *Victor 27338* 2-4 41

DON'T GIVE UP THE SHIP / AT A LITTLE CHURCH AFFAIR .... *Victor 25183* 3-5 35
(Vocals: Cliff Weston)

ELI, ELI / NONE BUT THE LONELY HEART .... *Victor 27597* 2-4 41

FABLE OF THE ROSE, THE / THIS IS THE BEGINNING OF THE END .... *Victor 26555* 2-4 40
(Vocals: Frank Sinatra)

FAITHFUL TO YOU (Vocal: Anita Boyer) / LOSERS WEEPERS .... *Victor 26439* 2-4 40

FIFTY MILLION SWEETHEARTS CAN'T BE WRONG / THAT SOLID OLD MAN IS HERE AGAIN .... *Victor 27617* 2-4 41
(Vocals: Connie Haines)

FOOLS RUSH IN / DEVIL MAY CARE .... *Victor 26593* 2-4 40
(Vocals: Frank Sinatra)

FOR SENTIMENTAL REASONS / ANOTHER PERFECT NIGHT IS ENDING .... *Victor 25446* 3-5 36
(Vocals: Jack Leonard)

FOR YOU (Vocal: Jo Stafford); WITHOUT A SONG (Vocal: Frank Sinatra) / GOOD ENOUGH TO KEEP (by Benny Goodman & His Sextet) .... *V-Disc 33* 5-8 -
(A World War II release)

FREE FOR ALL / YOU AND I .... *Victor 27532* 2-4 41
(Vocals: Frank Sinatra)

GETTING SOME FUN OUT OF LIFE (Vocal: Edythe Wright) / IN THE MISSION BY THE SEA (Vocal: Jack Leonard) .... *Victor 25694* 2-4 37

GOODNIGHT, SWEET DREAMS / MOONLIGHT ON THE PURPLE SAGE .... *Victor 25803* 2-4 38
(Vocals: Jack Leonard)

GOT A BRAN' NEW SUIT / THAT'S NOT CRICKET .... *Victor 25173* 3-5 35
(Vocals: Eleanor Powell)

GOT NO TIME (Vocal: Edythe Wright) / LITTLE SKIPPER (Vocal: Jack Leonard) .... *Victor 26195* 2-4 39

HAPPY BIRTHDAY TO LOVE / STRANGERS IN THE DARK .... *Victor 25596* 2-4 37
(Vocals: Jack Leonard)

HAVE YOU GOT ANY CASTLES, BABY? (Vocal: Jack Leonard) / YOU'VE GOT SOMETHING THERE (Vocal: Edythe Wright) .... *Victor 25638* 2-4 37

HEAD OVER HEELS IN LOVE (Vocal: Edythe Wright) / MAY I HAVE THE NEXT ROMANCE WITH YOU? (Vocal: Jack Leonard) .... *Victor 25487* 3-5 37

HEAR MY SONG, VIOLETTA / YOURS IS MY HEART ALONE .... *Victor 26616* 3-5 40
(Vocals: Frank Sinatra)

HEAVEN CAN WAIT / YOU TAUGHT ME TO LOVE AGAIN .... *Victor 26154* 2-4 39
(Vocals: Jack Leonard)

HE'S MY GUY (Vocal: Jo Stafford) / LIGHT A CANDLE IN THE CHAPEL (Vocal: Frank Sinatra) .... *Victor 27941* 3-5 42

HIGH HAT, A PICCOLO AND A CANE (Vocals: by trio) / CLOSE TO ME (Vocal: Jack Leonard) .... *Victor 25447* 3-5 36

HONG KONG BLUES (Vocal: Skeets Herfurt) / YOU THINK OF EVERYTHING (Vocal: Connie Haines) .... *Victor 26636* 2-4 40

HOW AM I TO KNOW? / GUESS I'LL GO BACK HOME .... *Victor 26294* 2-4 39
(Vocals: Jack Leonard)

HOW CAN YOU FORGET? / THERE'S A BOY IN HARLEM .... *Victor 25799* 2-4 38
(Vocals: Edythe Wright)

HOW DO YOU DO WITHOUT ME? (Vocal: Frank Sinatra) / IT ISN'T A DREAM ANYMORE (Vocal: Jo Stafford) .... *Victor 27710* 2-4 41

HULA HULA BOOGIE, THE / YOU BLEW OUT THE FLAME IN MY HEART .... *Decca 27723* 2-4 50
(Vocals: Frances Irvin)

HUMORESQUE / ROLLIN' HOME .... *Victor 25600* 2-4 37

I CAN DREAM, CAN'T I? / THE ONE I LOVE .... *Victor 25741* 2-4 38
(Vocals: Jack Leonard)

I COULD MAKE YOU CARE / THE WORLD IS IN MY ARMS .... *Victor 26717* 2-4 40
(Vocals: Frank Sinatra)

I DREAM OF YOU (Vocal: Freddie Stewart) / OPUS NO. 1 .... *Victor 20-1608* 2-4 45

I GUESS I'LL HAVE TO DREAM THE REST (Vocals: Frank Sinatra & The Pied Pipers) / LOOSE LID SPECIAL .... *Victor 27526* 3-5 41

I'LL BE SEEING YOU / POLKA DOTS AND MOONBEAMS .... *Victor 26539* 2-4 40
(Vocals: Frank Sinatra)

I'LL DREAM MY WAY TO HEAVEN (Vocals: The Three Esquires) / THANKS FOR EVERYTHING (Vocal: Jack Leonard) .... *Victor 25534* 2-4 37

I'LL TAKE TALLULAH (narrated by Tommy Dorsey; Vocals: Frank Sinatra & The Pied Pipers) / NOT SO QUIET, PLEASE .... *Victor 27869* 3-5 42

I'M GETTING SENTIMENTAL OVER YOU (theme song) / I'VE GOT A NOTE (Vocal: Cliff Weston) .... *Victor 25236* 2-4 35

I'M NOBODY'S BABY / BUDS WON'T BUD .... *Victor 26609* 2-4 40
(Vocals: Connie Haines)

I'M SO WEARY OF IT ALL / NEVER AGAIN .... *Victor 26148* 2-4 39
(Vocals: Jack Leonard)

INDIAN SUMMER / A LOVER IS BLUE .... *Victor 26390* 2-4 39
(Vocals: Jack Leonard)

I NEVER KNEW / COMIN' THRO' THE RYE .... *Victor 25813* 2-4 38
(Vocals: Edythe Wright)

IN THE BLUE OF THE EVENING (Vocal: Frank Sinatra) / A BOY IN KHAKI, A GIRL IN LACE (Vocal: Jo Stafford) .... *Victor 27947* 2-4 42

IN THE MIDDLE OF A DREAM / YOU GROW SWEETER AS THE YEARS GO BY .... *Victor 26226* 2-4 39
(Vocals: Jack Leonard)

IN THE STILL OF THE NIGHT / WHO KNOWS? .... *Victor 25663* 2-4 37
(Vocals: Jack Leonard)

I PICKED A FLOWER THE COLOR OF YOUR EYES (Vocal: Edythe Wright) / PLEASE BELIEVE ME (Vocal: Buddy Gately) .... *Victor 25217* 3-5 36

I POURED MY HEART INTO A SONG (Vocal: Jack Leonard) / BACK TO BACK (Vocal: Edythe Wright) .... *Victor 26271* 2-4 39

I THINK OF YOU (Vocal: Frank Sinatra) / WHO CAN I TURN TO? (Vocal: Jo Stafford) .... *Victor 27701* 2-4 41

I TRIED (Vocal: Frank Sinatra) / DOLORES (Vocals: Frank Sinatra & The Pied Pipers) .... *Victor 27317* 2-4 41

IT STARTED ALL OVER AGAIN (Vocals: Frank Sinatra & The Pied Pipers) / MANDY, MAKE UP YOUR MIND .... *Victor 20-1522* 2-4 42

IT'S WRITTEN IN THE STARS (Vocal: Edythe Wright) / ONE UMBRELLA FOR TWO (Vocal: Cliff Weston) .... *Victor 25172* 3-5 35

IT'S YOU I'M TALKING ABOUT / WILL I EVER KNOW IT? .... *Victor 25292* 3-5 36
(Vocals: Edythe Wright)

I'VE GOT MY EYES ON YOU (Vocal: Allan De Witt) / I CONCENTRATE ON YOU (Vocal: Anita Boyer) .... *Victor 26470* 2-4 40

I'VE GOT RAIN IN MY EYES (Vocal: Edythe Wright) / THEY CAN'T TAKE THAT AWAY FROM ME (Vocal: Jack Leonard) .... *Victor 25549* 2-4 37

I WOULDN'T TAKE A MILLION (Vocal: Connie Haines) / LOOKING FOR YESTERDAY (Vocal: Frank Sinatra) .... *Victor 26738* 2-4 40

JUST A SIMPLE MELODY / LITTLE WHITE LIES .... *Victor 25750* 2-4 38

JUST AS THOUGH YOU WERE HERE / STREET OF DREAMS .... *Victor 27903* 2-4 42
(Vocals: Frank Sinatra)

KISS THE BOYS GOODBYE (Vocal: Connie Haines) / I'LL NEVER LET A DAY PASS BY (Vocal: Frank Sinatra) .... *Victor 27461* 2-4 41

LA ROSITA / LET'S DISAPPEAR (Vocal: Jack Leonard) .... *Victor 26333* 2-4 39

LET'S GET AWAY FROM IT ALL (Vocals: The Pied Pipers) / LET'S GET AWAY FROM IT ALL, PART II (Vocals: Frank Sinatra, Connie Haines, & The Pied Pipers) .... *Victor 27377* 2-4 41

LIGHTLY AND POLITELY / WASHBOARD BLUES .... *Victor 26085* 3-5 38

LITTLE WHITE LIGHTHOUSE, A / I'M THE ONE WHO LOVES YOU .... *Victor 25733* 2-4 38
(Vocals: Jack Leonard)

LONESOME ROAD, THE / THE LONESOME ROAD, PART II .... *Victor 26508* 2-4 40

LOSERS WEEPERS / — .... *V-Disc 220* 5-8 -
(A World War II release)

LOVE IS NEVER OUT OF SEASON / OUR PENTHOUSE ON THIRD AVENUE .... *Victor 25591* 2-4 37
(Vocals: Jack Leonard)

LOVELY LADY (Vocal: Buddy Gately) / I'M SHOOTING HIGH (Vocal: Edythe Wright) .... *Victor 25216* 3-5 36

LOVE SENDS A LITTLE GIFT OF ROSES (Vocals: Ken Curtis & The Pied Pipers) / WHAT IS THIS THING CALLED LOVE? (Vocal: Connie Haines) .... *Victor 27782* 2-4 42

MAKE ME KNOW IT / WHEN I SAW YOU .... *Victor 26786* 2-4 40
(Vocals: Connie Haines)

MAN AND HIS DREAM, A (Vocal: Jack Leonard) / GO FLY A KITE (Vocal: Edythe Wright) .... *Victor 26313* 2-4 39

MANHATTAN SERENADE (Vocal: Jo Stafford) / BLUE BLAZES .... *Victor 27962* 3-5 42

MAPLE LEAF RAG / JAMBOREE (Vocals: Edythe Wright & The Three Esquires) .... *Victor 25496* 3-5 37

MARCHETA / I'LL NEVER SMILE AGAIN (Vocals: Frank Sinatra & The Pied Pipers) .... *Victor 26628* 2-4 40

MARCHING ALONG WITH TIME (Vocal: Edythe Wright) / THIS TIME IT'S REAL (Vocal: Jack Leonard) .... *Victor 25862* 2-4 38

MARIE (Vocal: Gordon Polk) / GREEN EYES (Vocals: Johnny Amoroso & Lynn Roberts) .... *Bell Record 1028* 4-6 -
(This is a seven-inch 78 rpm record with microgrooves, containing the same amount of music as the usual ten-inch records.)

MENDLESSOHN'S SPRING SONG / LIEBESTRAUM .... *Victor 25539* 3-5 37

MIDNIGHT ON THE TRAIL (Vocal: Jack Leonard) / HAWAIIAN WAR CHANT .... *Victor 26126* 2-4 39

MILENBERG JOYS / MILENBERG JOYS, PART II .... *Victor 26437* 3-5 39

MOANIN' IN THE MORNIN' / DOWN WITH LOVE .... *Victor 25692* 3-5 37
(Vocals: Edythe Wright)

MORE AND MORE (Vocal: Bonnie Lou Williams) / YOU'RE DRIVIN' ME CRAZY (Vocals: The Sentimentalists) .... *Victor 20-1614* 2-4 44

MORE THAN EVER (Vocal: Jack Leonard) / ANNIE LAURIE .... *Victor 25774* 2-4 38

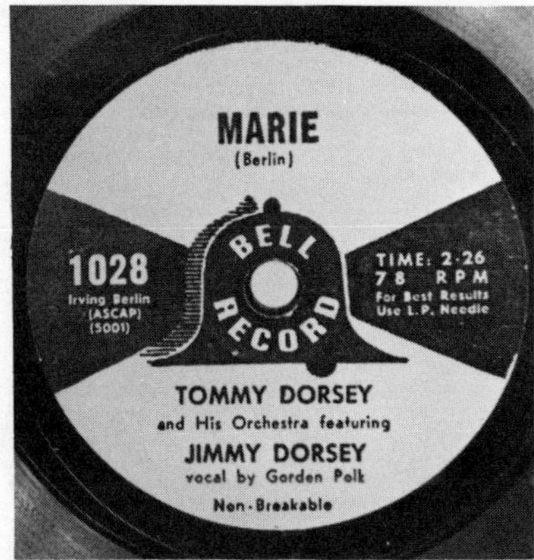

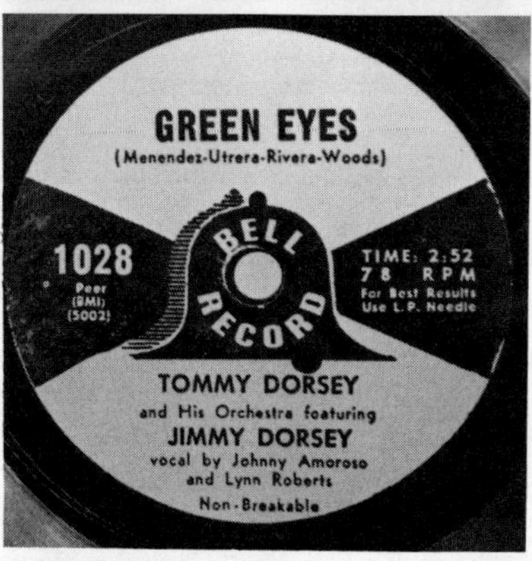

MOUNTAIN MUSIC / GOOD MORNIN' ... *Victor 25581* 3-5 37
(Vocals: Edythe Wright)

MR. GHOST GOES TO TOWN / LOOKIN' AROUND CORNERS FOR YOU (Vocals: The Three Esquires) .... *Victor 25509* 2-4 37

MUSIC, MAESTRO, PLEASE / ALL THROUGH THE NIGHT........................ *Victor 25866* 2-4 38
(Vocals: Edythe Wright)

NEVADA (Vocals: Stuart Foster & The Sentimentalists) / THAT'S IT......................... *Victor 20-1710* 2-4 46

NEW MOON AND AN OLD SERENADE, A (Vocal: Jack Leonard) / PECKIN' WITH THE PENGUINS.................... *Victor 26181* 3-5 39

NIGHT AND DAY / SMOKE GETS IN YOUR EYES........................ *Victor 25657* 2-4 37

NINE OLD MEN (Vocals: The Pied Pipers) / LOVE ME AS I AM (Vocal: Frank Sinatra) .... *Victor 27483* 2-4 41

NOLA / SATAN TAKES A HOLIDAY..... *Victor 25570* 2-4 37

OH! HOW I HATE TO GET UP IN THE MORNING! / WHAT'LL I DO?...................... *Victor 25824* 3-5 38

OH! LOOK AT ME NOW / YOU MIGHT HAVE BELONGED TO ANOTHER............ *Victor 27274* 2-4 41
(Vocals: Frank Sinatra, Connie Haines, & The Pied Pipers)

OH, PROMISE ME / SHINE ON, HARVEST MOON.................... *Victor 25780* 2-4 38

OLD FLAME NEVER DIES (Vocal: Jack Leonard) / IF YOU WERE SOMEONE ELSE (Vocal: Edythe Wright) .... *Victor 25649* 2-4 37

ON A LITTLE BAMBOO BRIDGE / HOW COULD YOU?..................... *Victor 25513* 2-4 37
(Vocals: Edythe Wright)

ONLY WHEN YOU'RE IN MY ARMS (Vocal: Edythe Wright) / OUR LOVE (Vocal: Jack Leonard) .... *Victor 26202* 2-4 39

ON THE BEACH AT BALI-BALI (Vocal: Edythe Wright) / NO REGRETS (Vocal: Jack Leonard) ...... *Victor 25349* 3-5 36

PAGAN STAR / WEARY (Vocal: Buddy Gately)............ *Victor 25206* 3-5 36

PALE MOON (Vocal: Frank Sinatra) / HALLELUJAH! .... *Victor 27591* 2-4 41

PANAMA / BLUE MOON (Vocal: Jack Leonard) .... *Victor 26185* 3-5 39

POOR YOU (Vocal: Frank Sinatra) / THE LAST CALL FOR LOVE (Vocals: Frank Sinatra & The Pied Pipers) .... *Victor 27849* 2-4 42

RAINBOW 'ROUND THE MOON (Vocal: Edythe Wright) / STOMPIN' AT THE STADIUM (Vocals: Edythe Wright & Skeets Herfurt) .... *Victor 26062* 2-4 38

RENDEVOUS TIME IN PAREE (Vocal: Jack Leonard) / IS IT POSSIBLE? (Vocal: Edythe Wright)..... *Victor 26264* 2-4 39

ROBINS AND ROSES (Vocal: Edythe Wright) / YOU STARTED ME DREAMING (Vocal: Joe Dixon)...................... *Victor 25284* 3-5 36

ROOM WITH A VIEW (Vocal: Jack Leonard) / DOWN HOME RAG.................. *Victor 26097* 2-4 38

ROYAL GARDEN BLUES / JA-DA....... *Victor 25326* 3-5 36

SAY IT (Vocal: Frank Sinatra) / MY! MY! (Vocals: The Pied Pipers)......... *Victor 26535* 2-4 40

SAYS MY HEART (Vocal: Edythe Wright) / YOU LEAVE ME BREATHLESS (Vocal: Jack Leonard) ... *Victor 25828* 2-4 38

SHADOWS ON THE SAND / YOU'RE BREAKING MY HEART ALL OVER AGAIN........... *Victor 26761* 2-4 40
(Vocals: Frank Sinatra)

SHAKE DOWN THE STARS / MOMENTS IN THE MOONLIGHT................... *Victor 26525* 2-4 40
(Vocals: Frank Sinatra)

SKUNK SONG, THE / THE SKUNK SONG, PART II...................... *Victor 27621* 3-5 41
(narrations by Tommy Dorsey; Vocals: Charlie Peterson.)

SMOKE FROM A CHIMNEY (Vocal: Jack Leonard) / THE BIG DIPPER (Vocal: Edythe Wright) ... *Victor 25763* 2-4 38

SMOKE GETS IN YOUR EYES / — .... *V-Disc 391* 5-8 -
(A World War II release)

SNOOTIE LITTLE CUTIE (Vocals: Frank Sinatra, Connie Haines, & The Pied Pipers) / MOONLIGHT ON THE GANGES....................... *Victor 27876* 2-4 42

SO MANY TIMES (Vocal: Jack Leonard) / BABY, WHAT ELSE CAN IT DO? (Vocal: Anita Boyer) ... *Victor 26386* 2-4 39

SOME BODY LOVES ME (Vocals: The Pied Pipers) / — .... *V-Disc 282* 5-8 -
(A World War II release)

SOMEWHERE A VOICE IS CALLING (Vocal: Frank Sinatra) / WELL, GIT IT! .... *Victor 27887* 2-4 42

STOMP IT OFF / NIGHT GLOW.......... *Victor 26376* 3-5 39

STOP BEATIN' AROUND THE MULBERRY BUSH (Vocal: Edythe Wright) / I'LL SEE YOU IN MY DREAMS (Vocal: Jack Leonard) .... *Victor 26012* 2-4 38

STOP, LOOK AND LISTEN / BEALE STREET BLUES .... *Victor 36207* 3-5 37
(This is an oversize 12-inch 78 rpm)

SUNSHINE OF YOUR SMILE, THE (Vocal: Frank Sinatra) / EMBRACEABLE YOU (Vocals: Jo Stafford & The Pied Pipers)............... *Victor 27638* 2-4 41

SWANEE RIVER / STAR DUST (Vocals: Frank Sinatra & The Pied Pipers) .... *Victor 27233* 2-4 41

SWEETHEART OF SIGMA CHI (Vocals: The Three Esquires) / COPENHAGEN .... *Victor 26016* 3-5 38

SWEET IS THE WORD FOR YOU (Vocal: Jack Leonard) / IN A LITTLE HULA HEAVEN (Vocal: Edythe Wright) .... *Victor 25532* 2-4 37

SWEET POTATO PIPER (Vocals: The Pied Pipers) / TOO ROMANTIC (Vocal: Frank Sinatra) ... *Victor 26500* 2-4 40

SWINGIN' ON NOTHIN' (Vocals: Jo Stafford & Sy Oliver) / ON THE ALAMO .... *Victor 27578* 2-4 41

SWING TIME UP IN HARLEM (Vocal: Connie Haines) / SWING HIGH .... *Victor 27249* 3-5 40

TAKE ME BACK TO MY BOOTS AND SADDLE (Vocal: Cliff Weston) / ON TREASURE ISLAND (Vocal: Edythe Wright) .... *Victor 25144* 3-5 35

TAKE ME / BE CAREFUL, IT'S MY HEART .... *Victor 27923* 2-4 42
(Vocals: Frank Sinatra)

TEA FOR TWO / NIGHT IN SUDAN...... *Victor 26321* 2-4 39

TEA ON THE TERRACE (Vocal: Edythe Wright) / I'M IN A DANCING MOOD (Vocal: Jack Leonard) ... *Victor 25476* 2-4 37

TELL ME AT MIDNIGHT / WE THREE .... *Victor 26747* 2-4 40
(Vocals: Frank Sinatra)

THAT LUCKY FELLOW / ALL THINGS YOU ARE............................ *Victor 26401* 2-4 39
(Vocals: Jack Leonard)

THAT'S FOR ME (Vocal: Connie Haines) / OUR LOVE AFFAIR (Vocal: Frank Sinatra) .... *Victor 26736* 2-4 40

THAT'S MY HOME / GOTTA GET ME SOMEBODY TO LOVE............... *Victor 20-1958* 2-4 46
(Vocals: Stuart Foster)

THERE ARE SUCH THINGS (Vocals: Frank Sinatra & The Pied Pipers) / DAYBREAK (Vocal: Frank Sinatra)....................... *Victor 27974* 2-4 42

THERE'S FROST ON THE MOON (Vocal: Edythe Wright) / KEEPIN' OUT OF MISCHIEF NOW (Vocal: Jack Leonard) .... *Victor 25482* 3-5 37

THINGS I WANT, THE (Vocal: Bud Freeman) / ALLEGHENY AL (Vocal: Edythe Wright)... *Victor 25623* 3-5 37

THIS LOVE OF MINE / NEIANI .... *Victor 27508* 2-4 41
(Vocals: Frank Sinatra)

THIS NIGHT (Vocal: Jack Leonard) / HONOLULU (Vocal: Edythe Wright)....... *Victor 26172* 2-4 39

TIN ROOF BLUES / SWEET SUE (Vocal: Jack Leonard)........ *Victor 26105* 3-5 38

TRADE WINDS (Vocal: Frank Sinatra) / ONLY FOREVER (Vocal: Alton Storr) .... *Victor 26666* 2-4 40

TURN OFF THE MOON (Vocal: Jack Leonard) / JAMMIN' (Vocal: Edythe Wright)........ *Victor 25553* 3-5 37

TWO HEARTS CARVED ON A LONESOME PINE / ALONE........... *Victor 25191* 3-5 35
(Vocals: Cliff Weston)

TWO IN LOVE / A SINNER KISSED AN ANGEL.................. *Victor 27611* 2-4 41
(Vocals: Frank Sinatra)

VIOLETS FOR YOUR FURS (Vocal: Frank Sinatra) / SOMBODY LOVES ME (Vocals: The Pied Pipers)............................ *Victor 27690* 2-4 41

WEARY BLUES / NOW YOU'VE GOT ME DOIN' IT (Vocal: Edythe Wright).......... *Victor 25159* 3-5 35

WELL, ALL RIGHT (Vocal: Edythe Wright) / ALL I REMEMBER IS YOU (Vocal: Jack Leonard) ... *Victor 26281* 2-4 39

WELL, GIT IT! / — .... *V-Disc 86* 5-8 -
(A World War II release)

WHATCHA KNOW, JOE? (Vocals: The Pied Pipers) / EVERYTHING HAPPENS TO ME (Vocal: Frank Sinatra).................... *Victor 27359* 2-4 41

WHEN YOU AWAKE (Vocal: Frank Sinatra) / TWO DREAMS MET (Vocal: Connie Haines)..... *Victor 26764* 2-4 40

WHERE ARE YOU? (Vocal: Jack Leonard) / THAT FOOLISH FEELING (Vocal: Edythe Wright).................... *Victor 25474* 2-4 37

WHERE IS MY HEART? / LONG AGO AND FAR AWAY.................... *Victor 25335* 2-4 36
(Vocals: Jack Leonard)

WHO? (Vocal: Jack Leonard) / THE DIPSY DOODLE (Vocal: Edythe Wright).......... *Victor 25693* 2-4 37

WHO'LL BUY MY VIOLETS? / MELODY IN F....................... *Victor 25519* 3-5 37

WILL YOU STILL BE MINE? (Vocal: Connie Haines) / YES INDEED (Vocals: Sy Oliver & Jo Stafford) .... *Victor 27421* 2-4 41

WINTER WEATHER (Vocals: The Pied Pipers) / HOW ABOUT YOU? (Vocal: Frank Sinatra) ...... *Victor 27749* 2-4 42

WITHOUT A SONG (Vocal: Frank Sinatra) / DEEP RIVER.................................. *Victor 36396* 3-6 -
(This is an oversize 12-inch 78 rpm.)

YA GOT ME / THERE'S NO PLACE LIKE YOUR ARMS .... *Victor 26030* 2-4 38
(Vocals: Edythe Wright)

YOU AND I KNOW / GOODBYE, JONAH ... *Victor 25648* 2-4 37
(Vocals: Edythe Wright)

YOU ARE MY LUCKY STAR / I'VE GOT A FEELIN' YOU'RE FOOLIN'............ *Victor 25158* 4-6 35
(Vocals: Eleanor Powell)

YOU BETCHA MY LIFE (Vocal: Connie Haines) / I LOVE IT SO (Vocals: Paul Mason & The Pied Pipers) .... *Victor 27392* 2-4 41

YOU COULDN'T BE CUTER (Vocal: Edythe Wright) / JUST LET ME LOOK AT YOU (Vocal: Jack Leonard) .... *Victor 25768* 2-4 38

YOU DON'T KNOW HOW MUCH YOU CAN SUFFER / OH, YOU CRAZY MOON............ *Victor 26287* 2-4 39
(Vocals: Jack Leonard)

YOU LUCKY PEOPLE (Vocal: Frank Sinatra) / YOU'RE DANGEROUS (Vocal: Connie Haines)...... *Victor 27350* 2-4 41

YOU'RE HERE, YOU'RE THERE, YOU'RE EVERYWHERE/DEDICATED TO YOU... *Victor 25516* 2-4 37
(Vocals: Jack Leonard)

YOU'RE LONELY AND I'M LONELY / IT'S A LOVELY DAY TOMORROW .... *Victor 26596* 2-4 40
(Vocals: Frank Sinatra)

YOU'RE PRECIOUS TO ME (Vocal: Jack Leonard) / THAT STOLEN MELODY .... *Victor 25603* 2-4 37

YOU SAY THE SWEETEST THINGS (Vocals: Connie Haines & The Pied Pipers) / NOT SO LONG AGO (Vocal: Frank Sinatra)..................... *Victor 27219* 2-4 41

YOU TOOK MY LOVE (Vocal: Jo Stafford) / DIG DOWN DEEP (Vocals: Frank Sinatra & The Pied Pipers).................... *Victor 20-1539* 3-5 42

YOU'VE GOT ME THIS WAY (Vocals: The Pied Pipers) / I'D KNOW YOU ANYWHERE (Vocal: Frank Sinatra)................... *Victor 26770* 2-4 40

YOU'VE GOTTA EAT YOUR SPINACH, BABY / SAN FRANCISCO... *Victor 25352* 3-5 36
(Vocals: Edythe Wright)

DORSEY, Tommy, & His Orchestra as The Dorsey Family (Mountain Branch)

FRIENDSHIP (Vocals: The Pied Pipers) / THE WRONG IDEA (by Charlie Barnet and His Orchestra; Vocal: Billy May).... *Bluebird B-10804* 3-5 40

DORSEY, Tommy, as Tommy Dorsey's Sentimentalists

EAST OF THE SUN / HEAD ON MY PILLOW .... *Bluebird B-10726* 2-4 40
(Vocals: Frank Sinatra)

FUNNY THING PEDRO (Vocals: The Pied Pipers) / WHISPERING (Vocals: Frank Sinatra & The Pied Pipers).................... *Bluebird B-10771* 2-4 40

QUIET, PLEASE / SO WHAT! .... *Bluebird B-10810* 3-5 40

DOTY, Mike, & His Orchestra:

see HAYMES, Joe, & His Orchestra

DOUGLAS, Boots, as Boots & His Buddies

AIN'T MISBEHAVIN' (Vocal: Cora Woods) / LADY, BE GOOD (by Frankie Reynolds & His Orchestra; Vocal: Barbara Lane).............. *Bluebird B-7241* 5-8 37

BLUES OF AVALON / THE RAGGLE TAGGLE............................ *Bluebird B-7187* 8-10 37

EAST COMMERCE STOMP / CARELESS LOVE................ *Bluebird B-10036* 8-10 38

GOO, THE (Vocal: Celeste Allen) / THE WEEP......................... *Bluebird B-7217* 8-10 37

HOW LONG (Vocal: Celeste Allen) / ANYTIME.......................... *Bluebird B-6132* 5-8 35

HOW LONG – PART II (Vocal: Celeste Allen) / GEORGIA........................ *Bluebird B-6301* 5-8 36

I DON'T STAND A GHOST OF A CHANCE WITH YOU / BOOTS STOMP....... *Bluebird B-10106* 5-8 38

LONESOME ROAD STOMP / REMEMBER...................... *Bluebird B-10113* 5-8 38

MARIE / COQUETTE................ *Bluebird B-6307* 5-8 36

RHYTHMIC RHAPSODY / SWANEE RIVER BLUES.................... *Bluebird B-6921* 5-8 37

RIFFS / I LOVE YOU TRULY (Vocal: Celeste Allen)..... *Bluebird B-6081* 5-8 35

ROSE ROOM / WILD CHERRY (theme song) .... *Bluebird B-6063* 5-8 35

SALUTE TO HARLEM, A / DO-RE-MI .... *Bluebird B-7944* 5-8 38
(Vocals: Cora Woods)

SWEET GIRL (Vocal: Celeste Allen) / SWING, MR. CHARLIE (by Louis "King" Garcia and His Swing Band; Vocal: Dan Darcy) .... *Bluebird B-6357* 5-8 36

VAMP, THE / THE SWING .... *Bluebird B-6333* 8-10 36

DREAMLAND HARMONISTS, The:
see McKAY, Marion, & His Orchestra

DREW, George, & His Orchestra:
see MILLS, Floyd, & His Marylanders

DUCHIN, Eddy, & His Central Park Casino Orchestra
(Eddy Duchin: 4/10/10 – 2/9/51)

NIGHT AND DAY / AFTER YOU – WHO? (Vocal: Lew Sherwood) .... *Brunswick 6445* 3-5 33

SNUGGLED ON YOUR SHOULDER / CAN'T WE TALK IT OVER? .... *Columbia 2625-D* 5-8 32
(Vocals: Lew Sherwood)

SOFT LIGHTS AND SWEET MUSIC / BY THE FIRESIDE .... *Columbia 2626-D* 5-8 32
(Vocals: Lew Sherwood)

SONG IS YOU, THE (Vocal: Frank Munn) / I'VE TOLD EV'RY LITTLE STAR (Vocal: Lew Sherwood) .... *Brunswick 6425* 3-5 33

DUCHIN, Eddy, & His Orchestra

ALL IN FUN / ALL THE THINGS YOU ARE .... *Columbia 35302* 2-4 39
(Vocals: Stanley Worth)

ANNIVERSARY WALTZ, THE (Vocal: Tony Leonard) / AROUND AND AROUND SHE GOES (Vocals: Lew Sherwood & The Earbenders) .... *Columbia 36442* 2-4 41

CAMERA DOESN'T LIE, THE / HEAVEN HELP THIS HEART OF MINE .... *Victor 25595* 2-4 37
(Vocals: Buddy Clark)

CARELESS / IN AN OLD DUTCH GARDEN .... *Columbia 35329* 2-4 40
(Vocals: Stanley Worth)

EV'RY TIME (Vocals: June Robbins and Bill Heathcock) / THIS TIME THE DREAM'S ON ME (Vocal: June Robbins) .... *Columbia 36423* 2-4 41

FROM NOW ON / GET OUT OF TOWN .... *Brunswick 8252* 2-4 38

HANDS ACROSS THE TABLE / LIFE BEGINS WITH LOVE .... *Victor 24805* 2-4 34
(Vocals: Lew Sherwood)

HEART AND SOUL / IT'S A LONELY TRAIL .... *Brunswick 8238* 2-4 38
(Vocals: Stanley Worth)

HOW CAN WE BE WRONG? / MY REVERIE .... *Brunswick 8224* 2-4 38
(Vocals: Stanley Worth)

HOW DO I RATE WITH YOU? / YOU TOOK MY BREATH AWAY .... *Victor 25178* 2-4 35
(Vocals: Lew Sherwood)

I CONCENTRATE ON YOU (Vocal: Stanley Worth) / I HAPPEN TO BE IN LOVE (Vocal: Johnny McAfee) .... *Columbia 35369* 2-4 40

I COVER THE WATERFRONT / ISN'T IT HEAVENLY? .... *Victor 24325* 2-4 33
(Vocals: Lew Sherwood)

ILL WIND / AS LONG AS I LIVE .... *Victor 24579* 3-5 34
(Vocals: Harold Arlen)

I'M AN OLD COWHAND / I CAN'T ESCAPE FROM YOU .... *Victor 25347* 2-4 36
(Vocals: Jerry Cooper)

IN OLD BRAZIL (Vocal: Tony Leonard) / AT THE CROSSROADS .... *Columbia 36537* 2-4 42

ISN'T THIS A LOVELY DAY? / CHEEK TO CHEEK .... *Victor 25093* 2-4 35
(Vocals: Lew Sherwood)

IT'S THE TALK OF THE TOWN / TROUBLE IN PARADISE .... *Victor 24377* 2-4 33
(Vocals: Lew Sherwood)

I'VE GOT YOU UNDER MY SKIN / EASY TO LOVE .... *Columbia 36542* 2-4 42

LET'S CALL THE WHOLE THING OFF / WITHOUT YOUR LOVE .... *Victor 25569* 2-4 37
(Vocals: Jerry Cooper)

MERRY-GO-ROUND BROKE DOWN, THE / SOUTH WIND .... *Victor 25585* 2-4 37
(Vocals: Lew Sherwood)

MOONBURN (Vocal: Lew Sherwood) / HYPNOTIZED (by Rudy Vallee & His Connecticut Yankees; Vocal: Rudy Vallee) .... *Victor 25231* 3-5 36

MOONLIGHT AND SHADOWS / LOVE IS GOOD FOR ANYTHING THAT AILS YOU .... *Victor 25514* 2-4 37
(Vocals: Lew Sherwood)

MOON OVER MIAMI / LIGHTS OUT .... *Victor 25212* 3-5 36
(Vocals: Lew Sherwood)

MY HEART BELONGS TO DADDY / MOST GENTLEMEN DON'T LIKE LOVE ... *Brunswick 8282* 5-8 39
(Vocals: Mary Martin)

OOH! WHAT YOU SAID / THE GAUCHO SERENADE .... *Columbia 35360* 2-4 40
(Vocals: Johnny McAfee)

OL' MAN MOSE / BETWEEN THE DEVIL AND THE DEEP BLUE SEA .... *Brunswick 8155* 10-12 38
(Vocals: Patricia Norman)

ONLY FOREVER (Vocal: June Robbins) / WHO ARE YOU? (Vocal: Tony Leonard) .... *Columbia 35624* 2-4 40

ON THE ALAMO / MOANIN' LOW .... *Columbia 35491* 2-4 40

SO DO I / PENNIES FROM HEAVEN .... *Victor 25431* 2-4 36
(Vocals: Lew Sherwood)

SPEAKING OF HEAVEN (Vocal: Johnny McAfee) / EL RANCHO GRANDE (Vocal: Lew Sherwood) .... *Columbia 35296* 2-4 39

STARLIGHT, STARBRIGHT (Vocal: Tony Leonard) / TIME WAS (Vocals: by orchestra) ...... *Columbia 36221* 2-4 41

STORMY WEATHER / STARDUST ... *Brunswick 8367* 3-5 39

TIME AND TIME AGAIN (Vocal: June Robbins) / MARIA ELENA (Vocal: Tony Leonard) .... *Columbia 36089* 2-4 41

TOO MARVELOUS FOR WORDS / JUST A QUIET EVENING .... *Victor 25517* 2-4 37
(Vocals: Jerry Cooper)

WHEN A WOMAN LOVES A MAN / EASY COME, EASY GO .... *Victor 24611* 3-5 34
(Vocals: DeMarco Sisters)

YOU ARE MY LUCKY STAR / I'VE GOT A FEELIN' YOU'RE FOOLIN' .... *Victor 25125* 3-5 35
(Vocals: Lew Sherwood)

DUNHAM, Sonny, accompanied by a recording group
(Sonny Dunham: 11/16/14 –)

JUST A MEMORY / ESTRELLITA .... *Varsity 8205* 3-5 40

LITTLE WHITE LIES / DARK EYES .... *Varsity 8227* 3-5 40

MEMORIES OF YOU / BLUE SKIES ... *Bluebird B-18234* 3-5 40

DUNHAM, Sonny, & His Orchestra

BAR BABBLE / THROWING PEBBLES IN THE MILLSTREAM (Vocal: Ray Kellogg) ... *Bluebird B-11148* 3-5 41

DELIVER ME TO TENNESSEE / HEAVENLY HIDEAWAY .... *Bluebird B-11504* 2-4 42
(Vocals: Ray Kellogg)

LAMENT TO LOVE (Vocal: Ray Kellogg) / DOWN, DOWN, DOWN (Vocal: Harriet Clark) .... *Bluebird B-11214* 2-4 41

MEMORIES OF YOU (theme song) / AS WE WALK INTO THE SUNSET (Vocal: Ray Kellogg) ... *Bluebird B-11239* 2-4 41

MIGHTY LAK' A ROSE / I UNDERSTAND (Vocal: Ray Kellogg) .... *Bluebird B-11124* 3-5 41

MY FOOLISH HEART AND I (Vocal: Ray Kellogg) / NOTHIN' (Vocal: Harriet Clark) ...... *Bluebird B-11305* 2-4 41

NICKEL SERENADE, THE (Vocal: Diana Mitchell) / HI NEIGHBOR (Vocal: Ray Kellogg) ..... *Bluebird B-11253* 2-4 41

SAND IN MY SHOES / EASY STREET .... *Bluebird B-11200* 2-4 41
(Vocals: Ray Kellogg)

SWEET TALK (Vocal: Ray Kellogg) / YOU'RE BLASE .... *Bluebird B-11514* 2-4 42

WHEN I GROW TOO OLD TO DREAM (Vocals: by orchestra) / WATCH THE BIRDIE (Vocals: Harriet Clark & orchestra) .... *Bluebird B-11337* 2-4 41

YOU GAVE ME THE RUNAROUND / WHEN SUMMER COMES .... *Embassy P-1009* 4-6 48
(Vocals: Pete Hanley)

DURHAM, Dave, & The Dixieland Swingsters

FERDINAND THE BULL / THE WIDOW'S DAUGHTER .... *Bluebird B-7857* 5-8 38
(Vocals: Unknown)

DURHAM, Eddy, & His Band
(Eddy Durham: 8/19/06 –)

FARE THEE HONEY, FARE THEE WELL (Vocal: Lem Johnson) / MAGIC CARPET .... *Decca 8529* 5-8 40

I WANT A LITTLE GIRL / MOTEN'S SWING .... *Decca 18126* 5-8 40

EBERLE, Ray, & His Orchestra
(Ray Eberle: 7/24/16 – 8/79)

SERENADE IN BLUE (theme song) (Vocals: Ray Eberle) / EASY RIDE ... *Signature 15214* 5-8 48

EDWARDS, Wally, & His Orchestra:
see SELVIN, Ben, & His Orchestra

ELDRIDGE, Roy, & His Orchestra
(Roy Eldridge: 1/30/11 –)

BASIN STREET / I REMEMBER HARLEM ... *Mercury 8962* 4-6 49
HECKLER'S HOP / THAT THING ... *Vocalion 3577* 8-10 37
HIGH SOCIETY / MUSKRAT RAMBLE ... *Varsity 8154* 5-8 40
IT'S MY TURN NOW (Vocal: Laurel Watson) / YOU'RE A LUCKY GUY (Vocal: Roy Eldridge) ... *Varsity 8084* 5-8 39
LITTLE JAZZ BOOGIE / EMBRACEABLE YOU ... *Decca 23471* 3-5 45
PLUCKIN' THE BASS / I'M GETTIN' SENTIMENTAL OVER YOU (Vocal: Laurel Watson) ... *Varsity 8107* 5-8 39
WABASH STOMP / FLORIDA STOMP ... *Vocalion 3479* 8-10 37
WHERE THE LAZY RIVER GOES BY / AFTER YOU'VE GONE ... *Vocalion 3458* 5-8 37
(Vocals: Gladys Palmer)
WHO TOLD YOU I CARED? / DOES YOUR HEART BEAT FOR ME? ... *Varsity 8144* 5-8 40
(Vocals: Laurel Watson)

ELKINS, Eddie, & His Orchestra

BLUE / WHO CARES? ... *Columbia A-3751* 3-5 22
CAROLINA IN THE MORNING / SILVER SWANEE ... *Columbia A-3737* 2-4 22
CHARLESTON CABIN / PUT AWAY A LITTLE RAY OF GOLDEN SUNSHINE ... *Okeh 41076* 2-4 24
COAL BLACK MAMMY / TEMPTING ... *Columbia A-3697* 2-4 22
HOODOO MAN, THE / JEALOUS ... *Okeh 40125* 2-4 24
OTHER LIPS / STELLA ... *Gennett 5155* 3-5 23
TAKE A LITTLE ONE-STEP / SAY IT AGAIN ... *Okeh 40058* 2-4 24
WHEN YOU WALKED OUT, SOMEONE ELSE WALKED RIGHT IN / ALA MOANA ... *Pathe Actuelle 021018* 3-5 23
WHEN YOU WALKED OUT, SOMEONE ELSE WALKED RIGHT IN / ALA MOANA ... *Perfect 14143* 2-4 23
(Simultaneously released on two labels)
WHO? / SUNNY ... *Columbia 493-D* 4-6 25

ELKINS, Eddie, as The Knickerbocker Orchestra

BLUE DANUBE BLUES / KA-LU-A ... *Columbia A-3516* 2-4 22
CHO-CHO-SAN / TEA CUP GIRL ... *Columbia A-3509* 2-4 21

ELLINGTON, Duke
(Duke Ellington: 4/29/99 – 5/24/74)
(Vocals: The Duke Ellington Orchestra continues to perform under the leadership of Mercer Ellington, the Duke's son. The group recently appeared at the newly-opened, legendary Glen Island Casino in New Rochelle, New York.)

SOUVENIR OF DUKE ELLINGTON, A ... *Oriole, no #* 30-35 33
(Accompanying himself on the piano, Ellington talks with Percy M. Brooks, editor of **Melody Maker Magazine**. This one-sided record was given free to customers of Messrs. Levy's of Aldgate, London, with the purchase of any six Duke Ellington records.)

ELLINGTON, Duke, & His Cotton Club Orchestra

BANDANNA BABIES (Vocal: Ozie Ware) / I MUST HAVE THAT MAN ... *Victor V-38007* 15-20 29
BLUES WITH A FEELING / MISTY MORNIN' ... *Okeh 8662* 15-20 29
BREAKFAST DANCE / MARCH OF THE HOODLUMS ... *Victor V-38115* 20-25 30
COTTON CLUB STOMP / ARABIAN LOVER ... *Victor V-38079* 20-25 29
DICTY GLIDE, THE / STEVEDORE STOMP ... *Victor V-38053* 20-25 29
DUKE STEPS OUT, THE / HAUNTED NIGHTS ... *Victor V-38092* 20-25 29
FLAMING YOUTH / DOIN' THE VOOM VOOM ... *Victor V-38035* 20-25 29
HOT FEET (Vocal: Cootie Williams) / SLOPPY JOE (Vocal: Sonny Greer) ... *Victor V-38065* 20-25 29
I CAN'T GIVE YOU ANYTHING BUT LOVE (Vocals: Baby Cox & Irving Mills) / DIGA DIGA DOO (Vocals: Irving Mills & Ozie Ware) ... *Victor V-38008* 15-20 29
JAPANESE DREAM / HARLEMANIA ... *Victor V-38045* 20-25 29
JAZZ LIPS (ZONKY BLUES) / DOUBLE CHECK STOMP ... *Victor V-38129* 20-25 30
JOLLY WOG / JAZZ CONVULSIONS ... *Brunswick 4705* 15-20 29
JUNGLE NIGHTS IN HARLEM / OLD MAN BLUES (by Duke Ellington & His Orchestra) ... *Victor 23022* 20-25 30
LOUISIANA / AWFUL SAD ... *Brunswick 4110* 15-20 28
MISSISSIPPI / SWANEE SHUFFLE ... *Victor V-38089* 20-25 29
MISTY MORNIN' / SARATOGA SWING ... *Victor V-38058* 20-25 29

MOOD INDIGO / — ... *V-Disc 67* 5-8 -
(A World War II release)
MY GAL IS GOOD FOR NOTHING BUT LOVE / I WAS MADE TO LOVE YOU ... *Victor V-38130* 15-20 30
(Vocals: Frank Marvin)
NINE LITTLE MILES FROM TEN-TEN-TENNESSEE (Vocal: Smith Ballew as Billy Smith) / WHAT GOOD AM I WITHOUT YOU? (Vocal: Dick Robertson) ... *Victor 22586* 15-20 31
RED HOT BAND / DOIN' THE FROG ... *Vocalion 1153* 40-50 28
SAM AND DELILAH (Vocal: Chick Bullock) / BIDIN' MY TIME (by The Bluejeans; Vocals: Phil Crow, Frank Luther, & Carson Robison) ... *Victor 23036* 15 31
SATURDAY NIGHT FUNCTION / HIGH LIFE ... *Victor V-38036* 20-25 29
SHOUT 'EM, AUNT TILLIE / I'M SO IN LOVE WITH YOU (Vocal: Smith Ballew as Billy Smith) ... *Victor 23041* 25-30 30
SWEET DREAMS OF LOVE / SWEET JAZZ O' MINE ... *Victor V-38143* 20-25 30
WHEN A BLACK MAN'S BLUE (Vocal: Benny Paine) / MOOD INDIGO ... *Victor 22587* 12-15 31

ELLINGTON, Duke, & His Cotton Club Orchestra as Mills' Ten Black Berries
also see ELLINGTON, Duke, & His Cotton Club Orchestra as The Ten Black Berries

HOT AND BOTHERED / BLACK AND TAN FANTASY ... *Clarion 5331-C* 15-20 30
HOT AND BOTHERED / BLACK AND TAN FANTASY ... *Diva 6056-G* 15-20 30
HOT AND BOTHERED / BLACK AND TAN FANTASY ... *Velvet Tone 7082-V* 15-20 30
(Simultaneously released on three labels)
MOOCHE, THE / EAST ST. LOUIS TOODLE-OO ... *Diva 6046-G* 15-20 30
MOOCHE, THE / EAST ST. LOUIS TOODLE-OO ... *Velvet Tone 7072-V* 15-20 30
(Simultaneously released on two labels)
SWEET MAMA / DOUBLE CHECK STOMP ... *Clarion 5332-C* 20-25 30
SWEET MAMA / DOUBLE CHECK STOMP ... *Diva 6062-G* 20-25 30
SWEET MAMA / DOUBLE CHECK STOMP ... *Velvet Tone 7088-V* 20-25 30
(Simultaneously released on three labels)

ELLINGTON, Duke, & His Cotton Club Orchestra as The Ten Black Berries
also see ELLINGTON, Duke, & His Cotton Club Orchestra as Mills' Ten Black Berries

ST. JAMES' INFIRMARY (Vocal: Irving Mills as Sunny Smith) / RENT PARTY BLUES ... *Banner 0594* 10-12 30
ST. JAMES' INFIRMARY (Vocal: Irving Mills as Sunny Smith) / RENT PARTY BLUES ... *Cameo 0194* 10-12 30
ST. JAMES' INFIRMARY (Vocal: Irving Mills as Sunny Smith) / RENT PARTY BLUES ... *Challenge 867* 10-12 30
ST. JAMES' INFIRMARY (Vocal: Irving Mills as Sunny Smith) / RENT PARTY BLUES ... *Jewel 5849* 10-12 30
ST. JAMES' INFIRMARY (Vocal: Irving Mills as Sunny Smith) / RENT PARTY BLUES ... *Romeo 1209* 10-12 30
(Simultaneously released on five labels)
ST. JAMES' INFIRMARY / WHEN YOU'RE SMILING ... *Conqueror 7486* 10-12 30
(Vocals: Irving Mills as Sunny Smith)
ST. JAMES' INFIRMARY / WHEN YOU'RE SMILING ... *Domino 4498* 10-12 30
(Vocals: Irving Mills as Sunny Smith)
ST. JAMES' INFIRMARY / WHEN YOU'RE SMILING ... *Perfect 15272* 10-12 30
(Vocals: Irving Mills as Sunny Smith)
ST. JAMES' INFIRMARY / WHEN YOU'RE SMILING ... *Regal 8941* 10-12 30
(Vocals: Irving Mills as Sunny Smith)
(Simultaneously released on four labels)

ELLINGTON, Duke, & His Cotton Club Orchestra as The Whoopee Makers
also see ELLINGTON, Duke, & His Orchestra as The Whoopee Makers

DOIN' THE VOOM VOOM / FLAMING YOUTH ... *Pathe Actuelle 37059* 15-20 29
DOIN' THE VOOM VOOM / FLAMING YOUTH ... *Perfect 15240* 15-20 29
(Simultaneously released on two labels)
DOIN' THE VOOM VOOM / SATURDAY NIGHT FUNCTION ... *Banner 6548* 15-20 29
DOIN' THE VOOM VOOM / SATURDAY NIGHT FUNCTION ... *Cameo 9306* 15-20 29
DOIN' THE VOOM VOOM / SATURDAY NIGHT FUNCTION ... *Lincoln 3330* 15-20 29
(Simultaneously released on three labels)
HOTTENTOT / MISTY MORNIN' ... *Pathe Actuelle 36923* 20-25 29
HOTTENTOT / MISTY MORNIN' ... *Perfect 15104* 15-20 29
HOTTENTOT / MISTY MORNIN' ... *Romeo 840* 15-20 29
(Simultaneously released on three labels)

ELLINGTON, Duke, & His Cotton Club Orchestra as The Whoopee Makers recorded under the name The Dixie Jazz Band

DOIN' THE VOOM VOOM / FLAMING YOUTH ... *Regal 8874* 15-20 29
DOIN' THE VOOM VOOM / SATURDAY NIGHT FUNCTION ... *Oriole 1730* 15-20 29

ELLINGTON, Duke, & His Famous Orchestra

ACROSS THE TRACK BLUES / CHLOE ... *Victor 27235* 4-6 40
ALL GOD'S CHILDREN GOT RHYTHM / ALABAMY HOME (Vocal: Ivie Anderson) ... *Master 137* 5-8 37
ANY TIME, ANY DAY, ANYWHERE / EERIE MOAN ... *Brunswick 6467* 8-10 33
ARE YOU STICKING? / I DON'T KNOW WHAT KIND OF BLUES I GOT (Vocal: Herb Jeffries) ... *Victor 27804* 3-5 41
AT A DIXIE ROADSIDE DINER (Vocal: Ivie Anderson) / MY GREATEST MISTAKE ... *Victor 26719* 3-5 40
BAKIFF / GIDDYBUG GALLOP ... *Victor 27502* 3-5 41
BLACKBIRDS MEDLEY, PART I: I CAN'T GIVE YOU ANYTHING BUT LOVE; DOIN' THE NEW LOWDOWN; I MUST HAVE THAT MAN; BABY / BLACKBIRDS MEDLEY, PART II: DIXIE, DIGA DIGA DOO; PORGY; I CAN'T GIVE YOU ANYTHING BUT LOVE ... *Brunswick 6516* 8-10 33
BLACK BUTTERFLY / HARMONY IN HARLEM ... *Brunswick 8044* 5-8 37
BLUE HARLEM / BEST WISHES ... *Brunswick 6374* 8-10 32
BLUE LIGHT (TRANSBLUCENCY) / SLAP HAPPY ... *Brunswick 8297* 5-8 39
BLUE MOOD / DELTA BOUND (Vocal: Ivie Anderson) ... *Columbia 37298* 5-8 47
(A 1932 recording first released in 1947)
BLUES SERENADE, A / HIP CHIC ... *Brunswick 8221* 5-8 38
BOJANGLES / A PORTRAIT OF BERT WILLIAMS ... *Victor 26644* 4-6 40
BRAGGIN' IN BRASS / CARNIVAL IN CAROLINE (Vocal: Ivie Anderson) ... *Brunswick 8099* 5-8 38
BROWN SKIN GAL / JUMP FOR JOY ... *Victor 27517* 3-5 41
(Vocals: Herb Jeffries)
BUFFET FLAT / MIGHTY LIKE THE BLUES ... *Brunswick 8231* 5-8 38
CARAVAN / AZURE ... *Master 131* 5-8 37
CHATTER BOX / DUSK IN THE DESERT ... *Brunswick 8029* 5-8 37
CHELSEA BRIDGE / WHAT GOOD WOULD IT DO? (Vocal: Herb Jeffries) ... *Victor 27740* 3-5 42
CHOCOLATE SHAKE / I GOT IT BAD ... *Victor 27531* 2-4 41
(Vocals: Ivie Anderson)
'C' JAM BLUES / MOON MIST ... *Victor 27856* 2-4 42
CLARINET LAMENT (BARNEY'S CONCERTO) / ECHOES OF HARLEM (COOTIE'S CONCERTO) ... *Brunswick 7650* 5-8 36
CLEMENTINE / FIVE O'CLOCK DRAG ... *Victor 27700* 3-5 41
CONCERTO FOR COOTIE (DO NOTHIN' TILL YOU HEAR FROM ME) / ME AND YOU (Vocal: Ivie Anderson) ... *Victor 26598* 2-4 40
COTTON CLUB STOMP / IN A MIZZ (Vocal: Ivie Anderson) ... *Brunswick 8405* 5-8 39
COTTON TAIL (SHUCKIN' AND STIFFIN') / NEVER NO LAMENT (DON'T GET AROUND MUCH ANYMORE) ... *Victor 26610* 2-4 40
CREOLE RHAPSODY / CREOLE RHAPSODY, PART II ... *Brunswick 6093* 12-15 31
DIMINUENDO IN BLUE / CRESCENDO IN BLUE ... *Brunswick 8004* 5-8 37
DIMINUENDO IN BLUE / CRESCENDO IN BLUE ... *Columbia 36125* 2-4 41
(The Columbia release is a reissue)
DINAH (Vocals: Ivie Anderson & Sonny Greer) / BUGLE CALL RAG ... *Victor 22938* 10-12 32
DINAH'S IN A JAM / YOU GAVE ME THE GATE (AND I'M SWINGIN') (Vocal: Ivie Anderson) ... *Brunswick 8169* 5-8 38
DOIN' THE VOOM VOOM / I'M CHECKIN' OUT, GOO'M BYE (Vocal: Ivie Anderson) ... *Columbia 35208* 3-5 39
DUCKY WUCKY / SWING LOW ... *Brunswick 6432* 8-10 32
DUCKY WUCKY / SWING LOW ... *Columbia 35683* 3-5 41
(The Columbia release is a reissue)

DUKE ELLINGTON & HIS FAMOUS ORCHESTRA AT CARNEGIE HALL (A 4-record album set) ... *Musicraft S-6* 20-25 48
Individual records in the set listed numerically (with value of each):
OVERTURE TO A JAM SESSION / OVERTURE TO A JAM SESSION, PART II ... *Musicraft 463* 5-8 -
BEAUTIFUL INDIANS / BEAUTIFUL INDIANS, PART II ... *Musicraft 464* 5-8 -
FLIPPANT FLURRY / GOLDEN FEATHER ... *Musicraft 465* 5-8 -
SULTRY SUNSET / JAM-A-DITTY ... *Musicraft 466* 5-8 -

DUKE ELLINGTON PANORAMA, A (A 4-record album set) ... *Victor P 138* 10-12 43
Individual records in the set listed numerically (with value of each):
EAST ST. LOUIS TOODLE-OO / THE MOOCHE ... *Victor 20-1531* 2-4 -
RING DEM BELLS / MOOD INDIGO ... *Victor 20-1532* 2-4 -
STOMPY JONES / DELTA SERENADE ... *Victor 20-1533* 2-4 -
DUSK / WARM VALLEY ... *Victor 20-1534* 2-4 -

DUKE ELLINGTON PLAYS THE BLUES (A 45 rpm 4-record album set) ... *RCA Victor (M) WP 182* 8-10 -
Individual records in the set listed numerically (with value of each):
ROYAL GARDEN BLUES / FRANKIE AND JOHNNY ... *RCA Victor (M) 47-3033* 2-4 -
ST. LOUIS BLUES / DRAWING ROOM BLUES ... *RCA Victor (M) 47-3034* 2-4 -
BEALE STREET BLUES / PRETTY WOMAN ... *RCA Victor (M) 47-3035* 2-4 -
MEMPHIS BLUES / TRANSBUCENCY ... *RCA Victor (M) 47-3036* 2-4 -

DUKE, THE (HOT JAZZ CLASSICS (A 4-record album set of 1932 recordings released in 1948) ... *Columbia Set C-38* 15-20 48
Individual records in the set listed numerically (with value of each):
LAZY RHAPSODY (Vocal: Cootie Williams) / BLUE RAMBLE ... *Columbia 35834* 3-5 -
BABY, WHEN YOU AIN'T THERE (Vocal: Cootie Williams) / LIGHTNIN' ... *Columbia 35835* 3-5 -
BEST WISHES / BUNDLE OF BLUES ... *Columbia 35836* 3-5 -
DROP ME OFF AT HARLEM / MERRY-GO-ROUND ... *Columbia 35837* 3-5 -

DUSK / BLUE GOOSE ... *Victor 26677* 3-5 40
FLAMINGO (Vocal: Herb Jeffries) / TAKE THE "A" TRAIN ... *V-Disc 212* 5-8 -
(A World War II release)
GAL FROM JOE'S, THE / I LET A SONG GO OUT OF MY HEART ... *Brunswick 8108* 5-8 38

GET YOURSELF A NEW BROOM (AND SWEEP THE BLUES AWAY) (Vocal: Ivie Anderson) / BUNDLE OF BLUES (DRAGON BLUES) ... *Brunswick 6607* 5-8 33
GRIEVIN' / TOOTIN' THROUGH THE ROOF ... *Columbia 35310* 3-5 39
HAPPY AS THE DAY IS LONG / RAISIN' THE RENT ... *Brunswick 6571* 5-8 33
(Vocals: Ivie Anderson)
HARLEM AIR-SHAFT / SEPIA PANORAMA ... *Victor 26731* 3-5 40
HARLEM SPEAKS / IN THE SHADE OF THE OLD APPLE TREE ... *Brunswick 6646* 8-10 33
HAYFOOT, STRAWFOOT (Vocal: Ivie Anderson) / SHERMAN SHUFFLE (FUSSY PUSS) ... *Victor 20-1505* 3-5 42
I DON'T KNOW WHY I LOVE YOU SO / T. T. ON TOAST ... *Columbia 37296* 5-8 47
(Two recordings from 1936 and 1938, first released in 1947)
IF YOU WERE IN MY PLACE / SCROUNCH ... *Brunswick 8093* 5-8 38
(Vocals: Ivie Anderson)
I'M CHECKIN' OUT, GOO'M BYE (Vocal: Ivie Anderson) / TOOTIN' THROUGH THE ROOF ... *V-Disc 723* 5-8 -
(A World War II release)
I'M SATISFIED (Vocal: Ivie Anderson) / JIVE STOMP ... *Brunswick 6638* 8-10 33
IN A SENTIMENTAL MOOD / SHOWBOAT SHUFFLE ... *Brunswick 7461* 5-8 35
I NEVER FELT THIS WAY BEFORE / WEELY (A PORTRAIT OF BILLY STRAYHORN) ... *Columbia 35353* 5-8 39
ISN'T LOVE THE STRANGEST THING? / NO GREATER LOVE ... *Brunswick 7625* 5-8 36
(Vocals: Ivie Anderson)

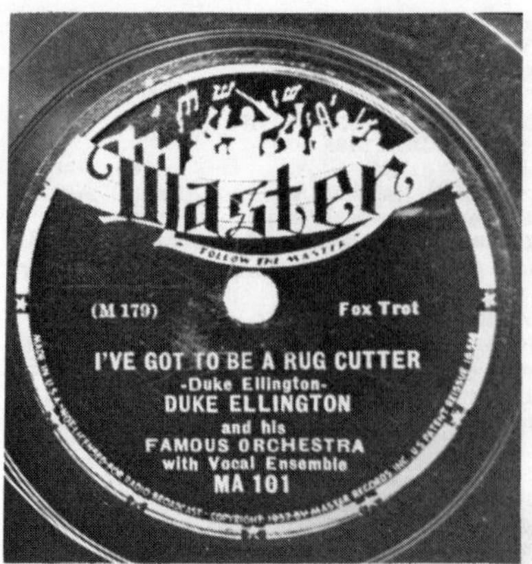

I'VE GOT TO BE A RUG-CUTTER (Vocals: Ivie Anderson, Rex Stewart, Harry Carney, & Hayes Alvis) / NEW EAST ST. LOUIS TOODLE-OO ... *Master 101* 5-8 37
JACK THE BEAR / MORNING GLORY ... *Victor 26536* 5-8 40
JAZZ COCKTAIL / LIGHTNIN' ... *Brunswick 6404* 10-12 32
JAZZ POTPOURRI (MYRTLE AVENUE STOMP) / BATTLE OF SWING (LE HOT JAZZ) ... *Brunswick 8293* 5-8 39
JOHN HARDY'S WIFE / AFTER ALL ... *Victor 27434* 3-5 41
JUMPIN' PUNKINS / BLUE SERGE ... *Victor 27356* 3-5 41
JUST A-SETTIN' AND A-ROCKIN' / MOON OVER CUBA ... *Victor 27587* 2-4 41
KILLIN' MYSELF (Vocals: Ivie Anderson & Billy Strayhorn) / YOUR LOVE HAS FADED (Vocal: Ivie Anderson) ... *Columbia 35640* 3-5 39
KO-KO / CONGA BRAVA ... *Victor 26577* 3-5 40
LADY IN BLUE / LITTLE POSEY ... *Columbia 35291* 3-5 39
LAMBETH WALK / PRELUDE TO A KISS ... *Brunswick 8204* 5-8 38
LAZY RHAPSODY (SWANEE RHAPSODY) / BLUE TUNE ... *Brunswick 6288* 8-10 32
LONELY CO-ED, A (Vocal: Ivie Anderson) / BOUNCING BUOYANCY ... *Columbia 35240* 4-6 39
LOVE IS LIKE A CIGARETTE / KISSIN' MY BABY GOODNIGHT ... *Brunswick 7627* 5-8 36
(Vocals: Ivie Anderson)
MAGENTA HAZE / TULIP OR TURNIP (Vocals: Ray Nance) ... *Musicraft 483* 4-6 48
MAIN STEM / JOHNNY COME LATELY ... *Victor 20-1556* 3-5 42
MARGIE / COTTON (Vocal: Ivie Anderson) ... *Brunswick 7526* 6-8 35
MERRY-GO-ROUND / ADMIRATION ... *Brunswick 7440* 5-8 35
MERRY-GO-ROUND / DROP ME OFF IN HARLEM ... *Columbia 35837* 3-5 41
(The first side is not a reissue of the Brunswick above, but uses an arrangement from a 1933 session. First released in 1941.)
MINOR GOES MUGGIN' / TONIGHT I SHALL SLEEP ... *Victor 45-0002* 3-5 -
(This is a double feature record, with Duke Ellington and His Famous Orchestra on the first side, and Tommy Dorsey and His Orchestra on the reverse.)
MOON OVER DIXIE (Vocal: Sonny Greer) / BABY, WHEN YOU AIN'T THERE (Vocal: Cootie Williams) ... *Brunswick 6317* 8-10 32
MY HEART SINGS (Vocal: Joya Sherrill) / CARNEGIE BLUES ... *Victor 20-1644* 3-5 44
NEW BIRMINGHAM BREAKDOWN / SCATTIN' AT THE KIT-KAT ... *Master 123* 5-8 37
OLD KING DOOJI / BOY MEETS HORN (TWITS AND TWERPS) ... *Brunswick 8306* 5-8 39
OLD KING DOOJI / BOY MEETS HORN (TWITS AND TWERPS) ... *Columbia 36123* 2-4 41
(The Columbia release is a reissue)
PORTRAIT OF THE LION / SOMETHING TO LIVE FOR (Vocal: Jean Elridge) ... *Brunswick 8365* 5-8 39
PROLOGUE TO BLACK AND TAN FANTASY / PLEASE FORGIVE ME ... *Brunswick 8256* 5-8 38

PUSSY WILLOW / SUBTLE LAMENT ... *Brunswick 8344* 5-8 39
PYRAMID / WHEN MY SUGAR WALKS DOWN THE STREET (Vocal: Ivie Anderson) ... *Brunswick 8168* 5-8 38
RAINCHECK / PERDIDO ... *Victor 27880* 2-4 42
REMINISCING IN TEMPO, PART I / REMINISCING IN TEMPO, PART II ... *Brunswick 7546* 8-10 35
REMINISCING IN TEMPO, PART III / REMINISCING IN TEMPO, PART IV ... *Brunswick 7547* 8-10 35
RIDING ON A BLUE NOTE / LOST IN MEDITATION ... *Brunswick 8083* 5-8 38
ROCKS IN MY BED (Vocal: Ivie Anderson) / BLI-BLIP (Vocal: Ray Nance) ... *Victor 27639* 3-5 41
ROSE OF THE RIO GRANDE (Vocal: Ivie Anderson) / A GYPSY WITHOUT A SONG ... *Brunswick 8186* 5-8 38
RUMPUS IN RICHMOND (BRASSIERE) / IN A MELLOTONE ... *Victor 26788* 4-6 40
SERENADE TO SWEDEN / THE SERGEANT WAS SHY ... *Columbia 35214* 4-6 39
SHEIK OF ARABY, THE / BLUE RAMBLE ... *Brunswick 6336* 8-10 32
SLIPPERY HORN / CLOUDS IN MY HEART (HARLEM ROMANCE) ... *Columbia 37299* 4-6 47
(A 1932 recording first released in 1947)
SLIPPERY HORN / DROP ME OFF AT HARLEM ... *Brunswick 6527* 8-10 33
SMORGASBORD AND SCHNAPPS / SOLID OLD MAN ... *Brunswick 8380* 5-8 39
SOMEONE / MY LITTLE BROWN BOOK (Vocal: Herb Jeffries) ... *Victor 20-1584* 2-4 42
SOPHISTICATED LADY / — ... *V-Disc 183* 5-8 -
(A World War II release)
SOPHISTICATED LADY / STORMY WEATHER ... *Brunswick 6600* 5-8 33
STEPPIN' INTO SWING SOCIETY / THE NEW BLACK AND TAN FANTASY ... *Brunswick 8063* 5-8 38
STEVEDORE'S SERENADE, THE / LA DE DOODY DO (Vocal: Ivie Anderson) ... *Brunswick 8174* 5-8 38
ST. LOUIS BLUES (Vocal: Bing Crosby) / CREOLE LOVE CALL ... *Brunswick 20105* 12-15 32
(This is an oversize 12-inch 78 rpm)
STORMY WEATHER (Vocal: Ivie Anderson) / SOPHISTICATED LADY ... *Columbia 35556* 2-4 40
SWAMPY RIVER / FAST AND FURIOUS ... *Brunswick 6355* 10-12 32
SWINGTIME IN HONOLULU (Vocal: Ivie Anderson) / I'M SLAPPIN' SEVENTH AVENUE (WITH THE SOLE OF MY SHOE) ... *Brunswick 8131* 5-8 38
TAKE THE "A" TRAIN (theme song) / SIDEWALKS OF NEW YORK ... *Victor 27380* 2-4 41
THERE'S A LULL IN MY LIFE / IT'S SWELL OF YOU ... *Master 117* 5-8 37
(Vocals: Ivie Anderson)
THERE SHALL BE NO NIGHT (Vocal: Herb Jeffries) / FIVE O'CLOCK WHISTLE (Vocal: Ivie Anderson) ... *Victor 26748* 3-5 40
TRUCKIN' (Vocal: Ivie Anderson) / ACCENT ON YOUTH ... *Brunswick 7514* 5-8 35
WARM VALLEY / — ... *V-Disc 10* 4-6 -
(A World War II release)
WARM VALLEY / THE FLAMING SWORD ... *Victor 26796* 3-5 40
WATERMELON MAN (Vocal: Ivie Anderson) / LOVE IN SWINGTIME (Vocal: Scat Powell) ... *Brunswick 8200* 5-8 38
WAY LOW / YOU CAN COUNT ON ME (Vocal: Ivie Anderson) ... *Brunswick 8411* 5-8 39
WHAT AM I HERE FOR? / I DON'T MIND (Vocal: Ivie Anderson) ... *Victor 20-1598* 2-4 42
YOU CAN'T RUN AWAY FROM LOVE TONIGHT (Vocal: Ivie Anderson) / THE LADY WHO COULDN'T BE KISSED ... *Master 124* 5-8 37
YOU, YOU DARLIN' (Vocal: Herb Jeffries) / SO FAR, SO GOOD (Vocal: Ivie Anderson) ... *Victor 26537* 3-5 40

ELLINGTON, Duke, & His Famous Orchestra as Earl Jackson & His Musical Champions

PEANUT VENDOR, THE / IS THAT RELIGION? (Vocal: Frank Martin) ... *Melotone M-12080* 12-15 31

ELLINGTON, Duke, & His Kentucky Club Orchestra

BIRMINGHAM BREAKDOWN / EAST ST. LOUIS TOODLE-OO ... *Brunswick 3480* 20-25 27
EAST ST. LOUIS TOODLE-OO (early theme song) / BIRMINGHAM BREAKDOWN ... *Vocalion 1064* 25-30 27
IMMIGRATION BLUES / THE CREEPER ... *Vocalion 1077* 40-50 27
NEW ORLEANS LOW-DOWN / SONG OF THE COTTON FIELD ... *Vocalion 1086* 40-50 27

ELLINGTON, Duke, & His Orchestra

BLACK BEAUTY / JUBILEE STOMP ... *Victor 21580* 15-20 28
BLUES I LOVE TO SING, THE (Vocal: Adelaide Hall) / BLUE BUBBLES ... *Victor 21490* 20-25 27
COCKTAILS FOR TWO / LIVE AND LOVE TONIGHT ... *Victor 24617* 5-8 34
CREOLE LOVE CALL (Vocal: Adelaide Hall) / BLACK AND TAN FANTASIE ... *Victor 21137* 12-15 27
CREOLE RHAPSODY / CREOLE RHAPSODY, PART II ... *Victor 36049* 15-20 31
(This is an oversize 12-inch 78 rpm.)
DEAR OLD SOUTHLAND (Vocal: Louis Bacon) / DAYBREAK EXPRESS ... *Victor 24501* 5-8 33
DIGA DIGA DOO / DOIN' THE NEW LOW-DOWN ... *Okeh 8602* 15-20 28
(Vocals: Irving Mills)
EBONY RHAPSODY (Vocal: Ivie Anderson) / I MET MY WATERLOO ... *Victor 24622* 8-10 34

HITTIN' THE BOTTLE / THAT LINDY HOP.................... *Victor 23016* 25-30 30
(Vocals: Dick Robertson)

IN A JAM / UPTOWN DOWNBEAT... *Brunswick 7734* 8-10 36

IT DON'T MEAN A THING (IF IT AIN'T GOT THAT SWING) (Vocal: Ivie Anderson) / ROSE ROOM...................... *Brunswick 6265* 5-8 32

LIMEHOUSE BLUES / ECHOES OF THE JUNGLE........................ *Victor 22743* 8-10 31

MOOCHE, THE / HOT AND BOTHERED... *Okeh 8623* 12-15 28
(Vocals: Baby Cox)

OLD MAN BLUES / JUNGLE NIGHTS IN HARLEM (by Duke Ellington & His Cotton Club Orchestra).................. *Victor 23022* 20-25 30

ROCKIN' IN RHYTHM / TWELFTH STREET RAG..................... *Brunswick 6038* 10-12 31

RING DEM BELLS (Vocal: Cootie Williams) / THREE LITTLE WORDS (Vocals: The Rhythm Boys, Bing Crosby, Al Rinker, and Harry Barris)........ *Victor 22528* 10-12 30

RUDE INTERLUDE (Vocal: Louis Bacon) / DALLAS DOINGS.................... *Victor 24431* 10-12 33

SADDEST TALE / SUMPN' 'BOUT RHYTHM.................. *Brunswick 7310* 12-15 34

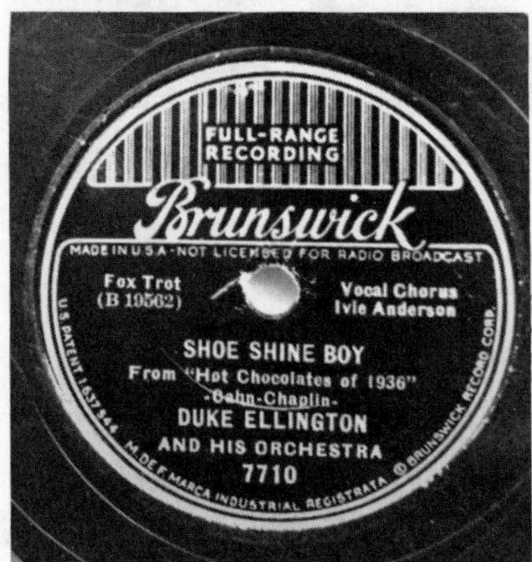

SHOE SHINE BOY / IT WAS A SAD NIGHT IN HARLEM............... *Brunswick 7710* 8-10 36
(Vocals: Ivie Anderson)

SOLITUDE / DELTA SERENADE....... *Victor 24755* 8-10 34

SOLITUDE / MOONGLOW........... *Brunswick 6987* 8-10 34

STOMPY JONES / BLUE FEELING...... *Victor 24521* 12-15 34

TAKE IT EASY / JUBILEE STOMP....... *Okeh 41013* 15-20 28

TROUBLED WATERS/MY OLD FLAME... *Victor 24651* 10-12 34
(Vocals: Ivie Anderson)

TRUMPET IN SPADES (REX'S CONCERTO) / YEARNING FOR LOVE (LAWRENCE'S CONCERTO)................ *Brunswick 7752* 8-10 36

(YOU'VE GOT THOSE) WANNA-GO-BACK-AGAIN BLUES / IF YOU CAN'T HOLD THE MAN YOU LOVE.................... *Gennett 3291* 40-45 26
(Vocals: Jimmy Harrison)

WASHINGTON WOBBLE / HARLEM RIVER QUIVER...................... *Victor 21284* 15-20 28

WHAT CAN A POOR FELLOW DO? / BLACK AND TAN FANTASY.................. *Okeh 8521* 15-20 27

YELLOW DOG BLUES / TISHOMINGO BLUES............. *Brunswick 3987* 15-20 28

YOU'RE LUCKY TO ME / MEMORIES OF YOU................. *Victor 23017* 25-30 30
(Vocals: Dick Robertson)

ELLINGTON, Duke, & His Orchestra as The Harlem Footwarmers

BIG HOUSE BLUES / ROCKY MOUNTAIN BLUES............................... *Okeh 8836* 30-35 30

BLUES OF THE VAGABOND / SYNCOPATED SHUFFLE............... *Okeh 8746* 30-35 30

I CAN'T REALIZE YOU LOVE ME / I'M SO IN LOVE WITH YOU........... *Parlophone PNY-34183* 20-25 30
(Vocals: Sid Garry)

JUNGLE JAMBOREE / SHAKE HIP DANCE........................... *Okeh 8720* 30-35 29

OLD MAN BLUES / ROCKING IN RHYTHM.......................... *Okeh 8869* 30-35 30

SWEET CHARIOT (Vocal: Cootie Williams) / MOOD INDIGO.......................... *Okeh 8840* 25-30 30

ELLINGTON, Duke, & His Orchestra as The Harlem Footwarmers recorded under the name The Harlem Music Masters

RING DEM BELLS (Vocal: Cootie Williams) / THREE LITTLE WORDS......... *Odeon ONY-36166* 25-30 30

ELLINGTON, Duke, & His Orchestra as The Harlem Footwarmers recorded under the name The Memphis Hot Shots

I CAN'T REALIZE YOU LOVE ME / I'M SO IN LOVE WITH YOU........................ *Clarion 5391-C* 15-20 30
(Vocals: Sid Garry)

I CAN'T REALIZE YOU LOVE ME / I'M SO IN LOVE WITH YOU...................... *Harmony 1377-H* 15-20 30
(Vocals: Sid Garry)

I CAN'T REALIZE YOU LOVE ME / I'M SO IN LOVE WITH YOU..................... *Velvet Tone 2455-V* 15-20 30
(Vocals: Sid Garry)
(Simultaneously released on three labels)

ELLINGTON, Duke, & His Orchestra as The Harlem Hot Chocolates

SING, YOU SINNERS (Vocal: Irving Mills)............. *Hit Of The Week 1045* 15-20 30

ST. JAMES' INFIRMARY (Vocal: Irving Mills).............. *Hit Of The Week 1046* 15-20 30
(Hit Of The Week records are one-sided paper discs)

ELLINGTON, Duke, & His Orchestra as The Jungle Band

BLACK AND BLUE / JUNGLE JAMBOREE.............. *Brunswick 4492* 15-20 29

DOIN' THE VOOM VOOM / RENT PARTY BLUES.................... *Brunswick 4345* 15-20 29

DOUBLE CHECK STOMP / ACCORDION JOE (Vocal: Dick Robertson)........... *Brunswick 4783* 15-20 30

HOME AGAIN BLUES (Vocal: Irving Mills) / WANG WANG BLUES (Vocals: Benny Paine & Irving Mills)....................... *Brunswick 6003* 10-12 30

MAORI / ADMIRATION.............. *Brunswick 4776* 10-12 30

PADUCAH / HARLEM FLAT BLUES... *Brunswick 4309* 15-20 29

RUNNIN' WILD (Vocal: Dick Robertson) / MOOD INDIGO................... *Brunswick 4952* 10-12 30

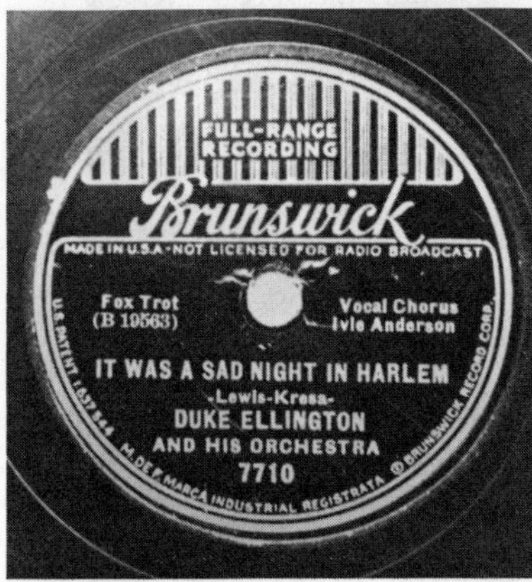

SWEET MAMA / WHEN YOU'RE SMILING (Vocal: Irving Mills)......... *Brunswick 4760* 12-15 30

TIGER RAG / TIGER RAG, PART II... *Brunswick 4238* 15-20 29

WALL STREET WAIL / COTTON CLUB STOMP..................... *Brunswick 4887* 15-20 30

ELLINGTON, Duke, & His Orchestra as The Washingtonians

also see ELLINGTON, Duke, & His Washingtonians and see ELLINGTON, Duke, as Duke Ellington's Washingtonians

BLACK AND TAN FANTASY / SOLILOQUY....................... *Brunswick 3526* 10-12 27

CHOO CHOO / RAINY NIGHTS...... *Blue-Disc T-1002* 125-150 24
(Blue-Disc is one of the rarest American records)

DOIN' THE VOOM VOOM / SATURDAY NIGHT FUNCTION................... *Romeo 1101* 15-20 29

EAST ST. LOUIS TOODLE-OO (early theme song) / JUBILEE STOMP...................... *Cameo 8182* 15-20 28

EAST ST. LOUIS TOODLE-OO (early theme song) / JUBILEE STOMP..................... *Lincoln 2837* 15-20 28
(Simultaneously released on two labels)

I'M GONNA HANG AROUND MY SUGAR / TROMBONE BLUES....................... *Pathe Actuelle 36333* 25-30 25

I'M GONNA HANG AROUND MY SUGAR / TROMBONE BLUES.............................. *Perfect 14514* 20-25 25
(Simultaneously released on two labels)

SARATOGA SWING / WHO SAID "IT'S TIGHT LIKE THAT"? (Vocal: Cootie Williams)........... *Romeo 977* 15-20 29

SWEET MAMA / BUGLE CALL RAG........................ *Harmony 577-H* 15-20 28

TAKE IT EASY / BLACK SUNDAY... *Brunswick 4009* 15-20 28

ELLINGTON, Duke, & His Orchestra as The Washingtonians recorded under the name The Traymore Orchestra

BLACK AND TAN FANTASY / SOLILOQUY....................... *Vocalion 15556* 10-12 27

ELLINGTON, Duke, & His Orchestra as The Washingtonians recorded under the name The Chick Winters Orchestra

CHOO CHOO / RAINY NIGHTS...... *Pennington 1437* 70-80 24
(Pennington records are extremely rare)

ELLINGTON, Duke, & His Orchestra as The Whoopee Makers

also see ELLINGTON, Duke, & His Cotton Club Orchestra as The Whoopee Makers

MOOCHE, THE / MOVE OVER... *Pathe Actuelle 36899* 15-20 28

MOOCHE, THE / MOVE OVER.......... *Perfect 15080* 12-15 28
(Simultaneously released on two labels)

THEM THERE EYES / ROCKIN' CHAIR... *Banner 32070* 15-20 31
(Vocals: Chick Bullock)

THEM THERE EYES / ROCKIN' CHAIR.... *Oriole 2191* 15-20 31
(Vocals: Chick Bullock)

THEM THERE EYES / ROCKIN' CHAIR... *Perfect 15418* 15-20 31
(Vocals: Chick Bullock)

THEM THERE EYES / ROCKIN' CHAIR.... *Romeo 1556* 15-20 31
(Vocals: Chick Bullock)
(Simultaneously released on four labels)

ELLINGTON, Duke, & His Washingtonians

also see ELLINGTON, Duke, as Duke Ellington's Washingtonians and see ELLINGTON, Duke, & His Orchestra as the Washingtonians

ANIMAL CRACKERS / LI'L FARINA..... *Buddy 8063* 50-60 26

ANIMAL CRACKERS / LI'L FARINA.... *Gennett 3342* 40-50 26
(Simultaneously released on two labels)

EAST ST. LOUIS TOODLE-OO (early theme song) / HOP HEAD...................... *Columbia 953-D* 15-20 27

ELLINGTON, Duke, as The Duke Ellington Sextet

TOUGH TRUCKIN' / INDIGO ECHOES... *Columbia 37297* 10-12 47
(A 1935 recording first released in 1947)

ELLINGTON, Duke, as Duke Ellington's Washingtonians

also see ELLINGTON, Duke, & His Orchestra as the Washingtonians and see ELLINGTON, Duke, & His Washingtonians

GEORGIA GRIND / PARLOR SOCIAL STOMP................. *Pathe Actuelle 7504* 40-45 26

GEORGIA GRIND / PARLOR SOCIAL STOMP......................... *Perfect 104* 40-45 26
(Simultaneously released on two labels)

ELLINGTON, Duke, as The Six Jolly Jesters

SIX OR SEVEN TIMES (Vocals: Freddy Jenkins & Sonny Greer) / GOIN' NUTS (Vocal: Harold Randolph)... *Vocalion 15853* 40-45 29

ELLINGTON, Duke – Jimmy Blanton piano & string bass duets

BLUES / PLUCKED AGAIN.......... *Columbia 35322* 5-8 40

BODY AND SOUL / MR. J. B. BLUES..... *Victor 27406* 5-8 40

PITTER PANTHER PATTER / SOPHISTICATED LADY.............. *Victor 27221* 5-8 40

ELLIOTT, Baron, & His Stardust Melodies Orchestra

VOS ZOKT EER (Vocals: the Stardust Trio) / STARDUST (Vocal: Babe Rhodes)........... *Musicraft* 3-5 43

ELLIS, Frank, & His St. Francis Hotel Orchestra

BABY FEET GO PITTER PATTER / SONG OF THE ISLANDS.................. *Columbia 1165-D* 2-4 27

HEADIN' HOME / WAITIN' FOR THE SPRINGTIME.......... *Columbia 1181-D* 3-5 27

PERSIAN RUG / MIDNIGHT MOONLIGHT..................... *Columbia 964-D* 2-4 27

WHO'LL BUY MY VIOLETS? / HOP SKIP........................ *Columbia 930-D* 3-5 27

ELLIS, Seger & His "Choir of Brass"

(Seger Ellis: 7/4/04 –)

IF EVER A HEART WAS IN THE RIGHT PLACE / MY HEART RAN AWAY WITH MY HEAD.................. *Brunswick 8371* 3-5 39
(Vocals: Seger Ellis)

ME AND MY CANDID CAMERA / I'M A LUCKY DEVIL.............. *Brunswick 8362* 3-5 39

PIED PIPER OF HAMLIN, THE (Vocal: Irene Taylor) / PLEASE COME OUT OF YOUR DREAMS (Vocal: Seger Ellis).................. *Brunswick 8275* 3-5 38

ROOM WITH A VIEW, A (Vocal: Seger Ellis) / YOUR EYES ARE BIGGER THAN YOUR HEART (Vocal: Irene Taylor).................. *Brunswick 8290* 3-5 39

SOME RAINY DAY (Vocal: Irene Taylor) / KISS ME WITH YOUR EYES (Vocal: Seger Ellis)....... *Brunswick 8325* 2-4 39

WE SPEAK OF YOU OFTEN (Vocal: Irene Taylor) / THE MOON IS A SILVER DOLLAR (Vocal: Seger Ellis).................. *Brunswick 8321* 3-5 39

WHAT DO YOU KNOW ABOUT LOVE? (Vocal: Irene Taylor) / I WISH I HAD YOU (Vocal: Seger Ellis).................. *Brunswick 8261* 2-4 38

ELLIS, Seger, & His Choirs of Brass Orchestra

BEES KNEES / SOMETIMES I'M HAPPY (Vocal: Seger Ellis)............. *Decca 1350* 3-5 37

PRETTY GIRL IS LIKE A MELODY, A / I KNOW THAT YOU KNOW..................... *Decca 1322* 4-6 37

THREE LITTLE WORDS (Vocal: Seger Ellis) / SHIVERY STOMP...................... *Decca 1275* 4-6 37

ELLIS, Seger, & His Orchestra

HAPPY TRAVELIN' / CUDDLE UP A LITTLE CLOSER...................... *Okeh 5721* 3-5 40

HAPPY TRAVELIN' / CUDDLE UP A LITTLE CLOSER.............. *Vocalion 5721* 3-5 40
(Simultaneously released on two labels)

MELLOW STUFF / JITTERBUG'S JUMP.... *Okeh 6051* 4-6 40

TOO LAZY FOR LOVE / BYE BYE BLUES.................. *Vocalion 5534* 3-5 40
(Vocals: Irene Taylor)

WHEN IT'S SLEEPY TIME DOWN SOUTH (Vocal: Irene Taylor) / NO JUG, NO JAZZ.......... *Okeh 5966* 3-5 40

WHEN IT'S SLEEPY TIME DOWN SOUTH (Vocal: Irene Taylor) / NO JUG, NO JAZZ....... *Vocalion 5966* 3-5 40
(Simultaneously released on two labels)

ELMAN, Ziggy, & His Orchestra
(Ziggy Elman: 5/26/14 – 6/26/68)

AM I BLUE? / I HAVE EVERYTHING TO LIVE FOR.................... *Bluebird B-10490* 3-5 39
AM I BLUE? / I HAVE EVERYTHING TO LIVE FOR........... *Montgomery Ward M-8652* 3-5 39
(Simultaneously released on two labels)
BYE 'N' BYE / DEEP NIGHT........ *Bluebird B-10855* 3-5 40
FRALICH IN SWING (AND THE ANGELS SING) / BUBLITCHKI.................... *Bluebird B-10103* 3-5 39
I'M THROUGH WITH LOVE / SOMETHING TO REMEMBER YOU BY............. *Bluebird B-10663* 2-4 40
IRRESISTABLE YOU / ME AND MY SHADOW............................ *MGM 10543* 2-4 49
LET'S FALL IN LOVE / I'LL NEVER BE THE SAME.................. *Bluebird B-10342* 3-5 39
LET'S FALL IN LOVE / I'LL NEVER BE THE SAME........... *Montgomery Ward M-8333* 3-5 39
(Simultaneously released on two labels)
LOVE IS THE SWEETEST THING / FORGIVE MY HEART.................... *Bluebird B-10741* 2-4 40
29TH AND DEARBORN / SUGAR ... *Bluebird B-10096* 4-6 39
WHAT USED TO WAS USED TO WAS (NOW IT AIN'T) / TOOTIN' MY BABY BACK HOME.............. *Bluebird B-10563* 3-5 40
YOU'RE MINE, YOU / ZAGGIN' WITH ZIG.......................... *Bluebird B-10316* 2-4 39
YOU'RE MINE, YOU / ZAGGIN' WITH ZIG............... *Montgomery Ward M-8334* 2-4 39
(Simultaneously released on two labels)
YOU TOOK ADVANTAGE OF ME / I'M YOURS...................... *Bluebird B-10413* 3-5 39
YOU TOOK ADVANTAGE OF ME / I'M YOURS................. *Montgomery Ward 8332* 3-5 39
(Simultaneously released on two labels)

EMBASSY DANCE ORCHESTRA, The

I'LL NEVER BE THE SAME / THREE KISSES....................... *Crown 3363* 4-6 32
(Vocals: Unknown)
LOVE LETTERS IN THE SAND / WHILE HEARTS ARE SINGING........................ *Crown 3183* 5-8 31
(Vocals: Unknown)
REACHING FOR THE MOON / SING-SONG GIRL......................... *Crown 3049* 4-6 31
(Vocals: Unknown)
YOURS AND MINE / SOMETHING TO REMEMBER YOU BY............. *Crown 3037* 5-8 31
(Vocals: Unknown)

EMERSON DANCE ORCHESTRA, THE

CAROLINA MAMMY (Vocal: Vernon Dalhart) / SWINGING DOWN THE LANE...... *Emerson 10643* 3-5 23
DARKTOWN STRUTTERS' BALL / HONEY-MOON (by the Emerson Military Band)........... *Emerson 7212* 2-4 17
SOMEBODY LOVES ME / DOODLE DOO DOO............................ *Emerson 10785* 2-4 24
THEM DOGGON'D TRIFLIN' BLUES / INDIANA (by the Emerson Military Band)... *Emerson 7211* 3-5 17
WHEN THE SUN GOES DOWN IN DIXIE / SHIM-ME-SHA-WABBLE .... *Emerson 7211* 3-5 17

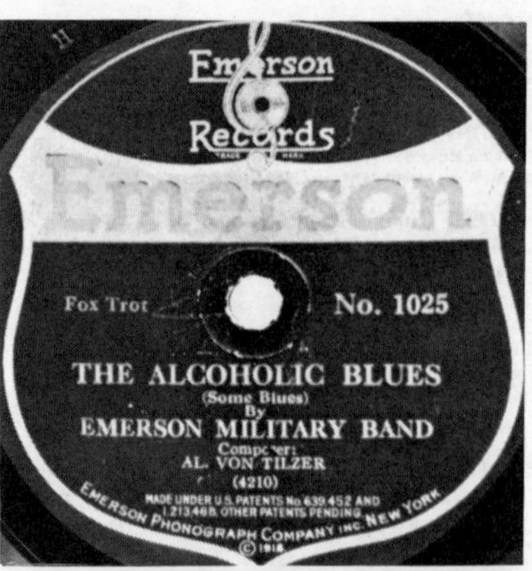

EMERSON MILITARY BAND, THE (a dance band)

ALCOHOLIC BLUES, THE / WESTERN LAND.................. *Emerson 1025* 2-4 19
BABY'S PRAYER AT TWILIGHT FOR HER DADDY OVER THERE, A / GATE CITY....... *Emerson 7341* 2-4 18
HONEYMOON / DARKTOWN STRUTTERS' BALL (by the Emerson Dance Orchestra)... *Emerson 7212* 2-4 17
INDIANA / THEM DOGGON'D TRIFLIN' BLUES (by the Emerson Dance Orchestra).............. *Emerson 7224* 2-4 17
LI'L LIZA JANE / 'A FRANGESA ...... *Emerson 7343* 2-4 18
PLEASE / MY BABY'S ARMS......... *Emerson 10142* 2-4 20
SAND DUNES / SHUTTLE FOX TROT... *Emerson 992* 2-4 18
SINGAPORE / RINGTAIL BLUES...... *Emerson 7461* 2-4 19
TELL ME, TELL ME WHY / MAMMY O' MINE.................. *Emerson 1034* 2-4 19
THERE'LL BE A HOT TIME FOR THE OLD MEN WHILE THE YOUNG MEN ARE AWAY / THE HANDICAP....... *Emerson 7360* 3-5 18
WHAT'S THAT? / HOW YA GONNA KEEP 'EM DOWN ON THE FARM? .... *Emerson 7492* 3-5 19
WILD, WILD WOMEN ARE MAKING A WILD MAN OF ME / THE TICKLE TOE .... *Emerson 7322* 2-4 18

EMPIRE DANCE ORCHESTRA, THE:
see ORLANDO, Nicholas as Nicholas Orlando's Orchestra, and see SAMUELS, Joseph, & His Orchestra

ENNIS, Skinnay, & His Orchestra
(Skinnay Ennis: 8/13/09 – 6/3/63)

AROUND AND AROUND SHE GOES (Vocals: Skinnay Ennis & Carmen Calhoun) / DREAMSVILLE, OHIO (Vocal: Skinnay Ennis) .... *Victor 27735* 3-5 42
DEEP IN A DREAM / GARDENIAS...... *Victor 26094* 4-6 38
(Vocals: Skinnay Ennis)
DON'T LET JULIA FOOL YA / I DON'T WANT TO SET THE WORLD ON FIRE........... *Victor 27586* 3-5 41
(Vocals: Skinnay Ennis)
GARDEN OF THE MOON / THE GIRL FRIEND OF THE SHIRLING DERVISH .... *Victor 26047* 3-5 38
(Vocals: Skinnay Ennis)
SLEIGH RIDE IN JULY (Vocal: Carmene Calhoun) / JUMPIN' JIMINY .... *ARA 110* 2-4 45
STRANGE ENCHANTMENT / THAT SENTIMENTAL SANDWICH.......... *Victor 26207* 3-5 39
(Vocals: Skinnay Ennis)
WISHING / HOORAY FOR SPINACH..... *Victor 26212* 3-5 39
(Vocals: Skinnay Ennis)
YOU ARE THE LYRIC (Vocal: Carmene Calhoun) / I FOUND YOU IN THE RAIN (Vocal: Skinnay Ennis) .... *Victor 27747* 3-5 42
YOU MEAN SO MUCH TO ME (Vocal: Carmene Calhoun) / THE WHISTLER'S MOTHER-IN-LAW (Vocal: Skinnay Ennis) .... *Victor 27599* 3-5 41

EPP'S HOTEL ASTOR ORCHESTRA
(Directed by Al Epstein)

FROM ONE TILL TWO / THERE'S YES, YES IN YOUR EYES.................. *Emerson 10751* 2-4 24
HOME IN PASADENA / SAY IT AGAIN .... *Emerson 10730* 2-4 23
HULA LOU / TOODLE-OO.............. *Emerson 10735* 2-4 24
I'M GOING SOUTH / WHEN LIGHTS ARE LOW .... *Emerson 10707* 2-4 23

EQUINOX ORCHESTRA OF PRINCETON, NEW JERSEY, The:
see Princeton Triangle Club Jazz Band, The

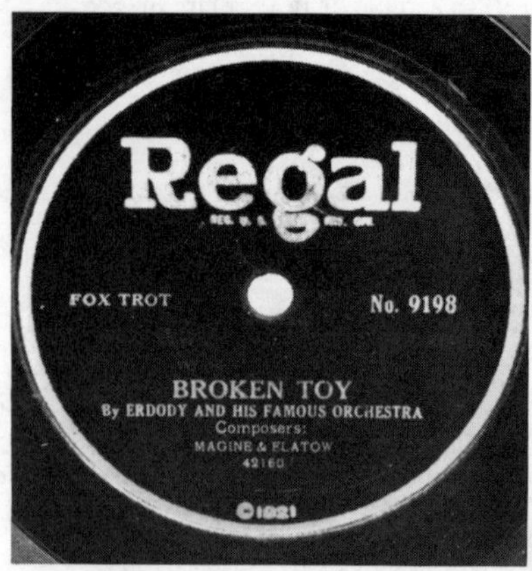

ERDODY, Leo, as Erdody & His Famous Orchestra

BROKEN TOY / CUTIE (by Eubie Blake and His Orchestra)........................... *Regal 9198* 4-6 22
BROKEN TOY / LONESOME HOURS...... *Okeh 4568* 2-4 22
RIGOLETTO QUARTETTE / MIGHTY LAK' A ROSE....................... *Puritan 11132* 2-4 22

ERDODY, Leo, as Erdody's Hotel Pennsylvania Orchestra

AIN'T WE GOT FUN? / ALL FOR YOU..... *Okeh 4368* 2-4 21
ALL FOR YOU / MELLO 'CELLO..... *Brunswick 2118* 2-4 21
MY DREAM ROSE / ABSENCE............ *Okeh 4300* 2-4 21
MY TEA CUP GIRL / I WONDER WHERE MY SWEET, SWEET DADDY'S GONE........... *Vocalion 14195* 2-4 21

ERICKSON, Wally, as Wally Erickson's Coliseum Orchestra

HONG KONG DREAM GIRL / THE CALL OF THE SOUTH....................... *Gennett 3069* 5-8 25
I GET THE BLUES WHEN IT RAINS / HARD LUCK............ *Vocalion 15778* 4-6 21
MEANEST KIND OF BLUES / GOT NO TIME .... *Gennett 3068* 8-10 25

ESSIG, Abe, & His Ritz-Carlton Casa Valencia Orchestra

I NEVER KNEW WHAT THE MOONLIGHT COULD DO / CLIMBING UP THE LADDER OF LOVE.................... *Okeh 40680* 4-6 26
(Vocals: Paul Hagen)

EUROPE, James Reese, as Europe's Society Orchestra
(James Reese Europe: 2/22/81 – 5/19/19)
(The first three releases are oversize 12-inch 78 rpm records)

AMAPA-MAXIXE BRESILIEN / EL IRRESISTIBLE........................ *Victor 35360* 2-4 13
CASTLE HOUSE RAG / CONGRATULATIONS WALTZ............................. *Victor 35372* 3-5 14
(Recorded under the personal supervision of Vernon & Irene Castle, the dance team who popularized the tango and fox trot.)
TOO MUCH MUSTARD / DOWN HOME RAG.......................... *Victor 35359* 4-6 13
YOU'RE HERE AND I'M THERE / CASTLE WALK .... *Victor 17553* 2-4 14

EUROPE, James Reese as Lt. Jim Europe's 369th Infantry "Hellfighters" Band

ALL OF NO-MAN'S-LAND IS OURS / JAZZOLA............................. *Pathe 22104* 3-5 19
(Vocals: Noble Sissle)
BROADWAY HIT MEDLEY / JA DA...... *Pathe 22082* 3-5 19
DANCING DEACON / CLARINET MARMALADE........................ *Pathe 22167* 5-8 19
HESITATING BLUES / PLANTATION ECHOES .... *Pathe 22086* 5-8 19
(Vocals: Noble Sissle)
HOW YA GONNA KEEP 'EM DOWN ON THE FARM? / ARABIAN NIGHTS.... *Pathe 22080* 3-5 19
INDIANOLA / DARKTOWN STRUTTERS' BALL.................. *Pathe 22081* 5-8 19
JAZZ BABY (Vocal: Creighton Thompson) / WHEN THE BEES MAKE HONEY ..... *Pathe 22103* 4-6 19
MIRANDY / ON PATROL IN NO-MANS-LAND .... *Pathe 22089* 4-6 19
(Vocals: Noble Sissle)
MISSOURI BLUES / MY CHOC'LATE SOLDIER SAMMY BOY (Vocal: Noble Sissle)......... *Pathe 22147* 5-8 19
RUSSIAN RAG / CLARINET MARMALADE...................... *Perfect 14110* 5-8 19
ST. LOUIS BLUES / RUSSIAN RAG ...... *Pathe 22087* 5-8 19
THAT MOANING TROMBONE / MEMPHIS BLUES.................... *Pathe 22085* 5-8 19
THAT MOANING TROMBONE / MEMPHIS BLUES................... *Perfect 14111* 4-6 19
(Simultaneously released on two labels)
THAT'S GOT 'EM / DIXIE IS DIXIE ONCE MORE (Vocal: Noble Sissle)......... *Pathe 22146* 3-5 19

EVERETT, Elliott, & His Orchestra:
see KARDOS, Gene, & His Orchestra and see PELTYNS, Sid, & His Orchestra

FALLON, Owen, & His Californians:
see MARTIN, Freddy, & His Orchestra, and
see ROLLINI, Adrian, & His Orchestra

FAMOUS ROSEMONT DANCE ORCHESTRA, THE:
see SMALL, Abe, as Small's Melodian Men

FARBERMAN, Hymie, as the Farberman Instrumental Quartet

MOONBEAM! KISS HER FOR ME / RUSSIAN LULLABY .... *Gennett 6100* 4-6 27
(Vocals: Elliott Stewart)

FARLEY, Eddie, & His Orchestra
also see RILEY, Mike – Eddie Farley & Their Onyx Club Boys)
(Eddie Farley: 7/14/05 –)

I CAN'T BREAK THE HABIT OF YOU (Vocal: Al Rose) / NERO .... *Decca 1165* 5-8 37

I'M BUBBLING OVER (Vocal: Larry Norman) / I HUM A WALTZ (Vocal: Al Rose) ...... *Decca 1250* 5-8 37

THERE'S NO TWO WAYS ABOUT IT (Vocal: Al Rose) / TO A SWEET PRETTY THING (Vocal: Larry Norman) .... *Decca 1237* 5-8 37

YOU'RE EVERYTHING SWEET / THE MOOD THAT I'M IN .... *Decca 1168* 5-8 37
(Vocals: Al Rose)

FARMER, Willie, & His Orchestra

CURFEW TIME IN HARLEM (Vocal: Scat Powell) / KILLY-KA-LEE (Vocal: Burt Shaw) ... *Bluebird B-7735* 4-6 38

IF I LOVED YOU MORE / IS THAT THE WAY TO TREAT A SWEETHEART? ...... *Bluebird B-7795* 3-5 38
(Vocals: Burt Shaw)

LAUGHING BOY BLUES / A-TISKET A-TASKET .... *Bluebird B-7687* 5-8 37
(Vocals: Burt Shaw)

MAMA, I WANNA MAKE RHYTHM / HAVE YOU EVER BEEN IN HEAVEN? .... *Bluebird B-7183* 4-6 37
(Vocals: Shirley Brown)

MIDNIGHT IN THE MADHOUSE / THE LADY IS A TRAMP (Vocal: Shirley Brown) .... *Bluebird B-7170* 4-6 37

MORE POWER TO YOU / YOU'RE MY DISH .... *Bluebird B-7181* 3-5 37
(Vocals: Shirley Brown)

MUSKRAT RAMBLE / TIN ROOF BLUES (Vocal: Scat Powell) .... *Bluebird B-7724* 5-8 38

SCATTIN' AT THE KIT-KAT / RIDING HOBBY-HORSES IN THE PARK (Vocal: Nat Brown) .... *Bluebird B-7026* 4-6 37

SKRONTCH / WHO DO YOU THINK I SAW LAST NIGHT? (Vocal: Burt Shaw) ..... *Bluebird B-7519* 4-6 38

STOP! YOU'RE BREAKING MY HEART (Vocal: Ann Seaton) / WHISPERS IN THE DARK (Vocal: Billy Pritchard) .... *Bluebird B-7036* 3-5 38

SUGAR BABE (Vocal: Scat Powell) / DOWN HOME RAG .... *Bluebird B-7813* 4-6 38

SUN SHOWERS (Vocal: Ann Seaton) / YOUR BROADWAY AND MY BROADWAY .... *Bluebird B-7024* 3-5 37

TEARS IN MY HEART (Vocal: Shirley Brown) / ALLIGATOR CRAWL .... *Bluebird B-7171* 4-6 37

THIS MAY BE THE NIGHT / I'VE GOT A DATE WITH A DREAM .... *Bluebird B-7698* 3-5 38
(Vocals: Burt Shaw)

TU-LI-TU-LIP TIME (Vocal: Burt Shaw) / TARZAN (Vocal: Scat Powell) .... *Bluebird B-7722* 4-6 38

FARMER, Willie, & His Simplon Club Orchestra

LET'S FALL IN LOVE / LOVE IS LOVE ANYWHERE .... *Banner 32938* 4-6 34
(Vocals: Pete Cantor)

LET'S FALL IN LOVE / LOVE IS LOVE ANYWHERE .... *Melotone M-12881* 4-6 34
(Vocals: Pete Cantor)

LET'S FALL IN LOVE / LOVE IS LOVE ANYWHERE .... *Oriole 2819* 4-6 34
(Vocals: Pete Cantor)

LET'S FALL IN LOVE / LOVE IS LOVE ANYWHERE .... *Perfect 15868* 4-6 34
(Vocals: Pete Cantor)

LET'S FALL IN LOVE / LOVE IS LOVE ANYWHERE .... *Romeo 2192* 4-6 34
(Vocals: Pete Cantor)
(Simultaneously released on five labels)

YOU ALONE / ROOF TOP SERENADE .... *Melotone M-12868* 4-6 34
(Vocals: Pete Cantor)

YOU ALONE / ROOF TOP SERENADE .... *Oriole 2813* 4-6 34
(Vocals: Pete Cantor)

YOU ALONE / ROOF TOP SERENADE .... *Perfect 15863* 4-6 34
(Vocals: Pete Cantor)

YOU ALONE / ROOF TOP SERENADE ... *Romeo 2186* 4-6 34
(Vocals: Pete Cantor)
(Simultaneously released on four labels)

FARRELL, Frank, & His Greenwich Village Inn Orchestra

ARE YOU HAPPY? / CHEERIE-BEERIE-BE .... *Harmony 471-H* 3-5 27

CHARMAINE! (Vocal: Arthur Fields) / A LITTLE GIRL – A LITTLE BOY – A LITTLE MOON (by Lou Gold & His Orchestra; Vocal: Jimmy Kern) .... *Harmony 445-H* 2-4 27

JUST ANOTHER DAY WASTED AWAY / GORGEOUS .... *Harmony 434-H* 4-6 27
(Vocals: Unknown)

OOH! MAYBE IT'S YOU / SHAKING THE BLUES AWAY .... *Harmony 483-H* 4-6 27
(Vocals: Unknown)

SOUTH WIND / — .... *Harmony 371-H* 5-8 27

WHAT DO YOU SAY? / BACK IN YOUR OWN BACK YARD .... *Harmony 584-H* 3-5 28
(Vocals: Unknown)

WHO KNOWS? / THE SONG IS ENDED .... *Harmony 537-H* 3-5 27
(Vocals: Unknown)

ZULU WAIL / — .... *Cameo 1195* 4-6 27

ZULU WAIL / — .... *Lincoln 2658* 4-6 27

ZULU WAIL / — .... *Romeo 423* 4-6 27
(Simultaneously released on three labels)

FAZOLA, Irving, & The Musical Maniacs
(Irving Fazola: 12/10/12 – 3/20/49)

DOWN BY THE OLD MILL STREAM / AM I BLUE? .... *Vocalion 3691* 5-8 37

PAGAN LOVE SONG (Vocal: Bud Johnson) / SOMEBODY STOLE MY GAL .... *Vocalion 3655* 5-8 37

FEATHER, Leonard, as Leonard Feather's All-Star Jam Band
recorded under the name Pete Brown & His Jump Six

MEN OF HARLEM / OCEAN MOTION.... *Decca 18118* 5-8 41
(A 1939 recording first released in 1941.)

FEATHER, Leonard, as Leonard Feather's All-Star Jam Band
recorded under the name Joe Marsala & His Delta Six

TWELVE BAR STAMPEDE / FEATHER BED LAMENT .... *Decca 18111* 5-8 41
(Another 1939 recording first released in 1941.)

FEATHER, Leonard, Piano
accompanied by various recording groups

FOR HE'S A JOLLY GOOD FELLOW (Vocals: Leo Watson) / LET'S GET HAPPY .... *Commodore 528* 5-8 38

JAMMIN' THE WALTZ / CLEMENTINE ... *Vocalion 4062* 5-8 38

FELDKAMP, Elmer, & His Orchestra
(Elmer Feldkamp: — – 9/27/38)

CHEWING GUM / IT WAS A NIGHT IN JUNE .... *Crown 3492* 5-8 33
(Vocals: Elmer Feldkamp)

I'LL NEVER HAVE TO DREAM AGAIN / WHEN MOTHER PLAYED THE ORGAN .... *Crown 3391* 4-6 32
(Vocals: Elmer Feldkamp)

IT ISN'T FAIR / LET'S MAKE UP .... *Crown 3521* 4-6 33
(Vocals: Elmer Feldkamp)

MORNING, NOON AND NIGHT / UNDER A BLANKET OF BLUE .... *Crown 3510* 5-8 33
(Vocals: Elmer Feldkamp)

STORMY WEATHER / ME AND THAT OLD GANG OF MINE .... *Crown 3481* 5-8 33
(Vocals: Elmer Feldkamp)

THREE'S A CROWD / SWEETHEARTS FOREVER .... *Crown 3374* 4-6 32
(Vocals: Elmer Feldkamp)

FELDKAMP, Walter, & His Manor Orchestra

HOLD ME / THE GRASS IS GETTIN' GREENER ALL THE TIME .... *Crown 3482* 4-6 33
(Vocals: Unknown)

I COVER THE WATERFRONT / AN OLD, OLD MAN WITH AN OLD, OLD PIPE .... *Crown 3494* 5-8 33
(Vocals: Unknown)

IN THE PARK IN PAREE / LOOK WHAT I'VE GOT .... *Crown 3480* 4-6 33
(Vocals: Unknown)

REFLECTIONS IN THE WATER / WHEN THE SWEET MAGNOLIAS BLOOM AGAIN .... *Crown 3511* 4-6 33
(Vocals: Unknown)

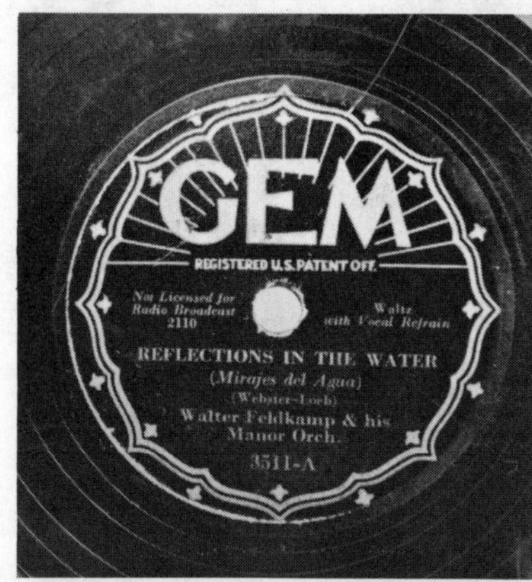

REFLECTIONS IN THE WATER / WHEN THE SWEET MAGNOLIAS BLOOM AGAIN .... *Gem 3511* 5-8 33
(Vocals: Unknown)
(Simultaneously released on two labels)

TAKE ME IN YOUR ARMS / SOMEDAY WE'LL MEET AGAIN .... *Crown 3405* 5-8 30
(Vocals: Unknown)

FELL, Max, as Max Fell's Della Robbia Orchestra

ARABIAN YOGI MAN / CALLING ...... *Edison 50758* 3-5 21

BRAZIL / GOODBYE .... *Pathe 22485* 3-5 20

I'M NOBODY'S BABY / DOWN AROUND THE 'SIP 'SIP 'SIPPI SHORE .... *Paramount 20057* 4-6 21

I'M NOBODY'S BABY / DOWN AROUND THE 'SIP 'SIP 'SIPPI SHORE .... *Broadway 11057* 3-5 21
(Simultaneously released on two labels)

I'M NOBOBY'S BABY / PAPER DOLL .... *Pathe Actuelle 020555* 3-5 21

JUNE / CARESSES .... *Pathe 22471* 2-4 20

MELLO 'CELLO / BRAZIL .... *Edison 50794* 3-5 21

MON HOMME / CHERIE .... *Paramount 20056* 3-5 21

MOONLIGHT / I'LL KEEP ON LOVING YOU .... *Edison 50777* 3-5 21

ROSE OF WASHINGTON SQUARE / ORIENTAL STARS .... *Pathe 22347* 2-4 20

SUNRISE AND YOU / ROSES OF LOVE ... *Edison 51332* 3-5 24

FELTON, Happy, & His Orchestra

ALLEGHENY AL (Vocal: Happy Felton) / MOON AT SEA (Vocal: Ken Nealy) ...... *Vocalion 3702* 4-6 37

LET ME WHISPER (Vocals: The Three Reasons) / YOU HAD AN EV'NING TO SPARE (Vocal: Happy Felton) .... *Vocalion 4060* 5-8 38

ROLLIN' PLAINS / PATCH UP MY HEART .... *Vocalion 3761* 4-6 37
(Vocals: Ken Nealy)

TWO BOUQUETS (Vocal: Armand Camgros) / THE WEEK-END OF A PRIVATE SECRETARY (Vocal: Happy Felton) .... *Vocalion 4034* 5-8 38

FENTON, Carl, & His Orchestra

BEGINNER'S LUCK / THEY CAN'T TAKE THAT AWAY FROM ME .... *Variety 529* 4-6 37
(Vocals: Unknown)

DOLL DANCE / DELIRIUM .... *Brunswick 3519* 5-8 27

GEORGIA / BLACK-EYED BLUES .... *Brunswick 2259* 2-4 22

GO 'LONG, MULE / THE ANIMAL FAIR .... *Brunswick 2683* 3-5 24
(Vocals: Billy Jones & Ernest Hare)

GOODBYE SHANGHAI! / WHILE MIAMI DREAMS .... *Brunswick 2190* 2-4 22

I DON'T WANT TO GET MARRIED / PLEASE BE GOOD TO MY OLD GIRL .... *Brunswick 2834* 3-5 25
(Vocals: Billy Jones & Ernest Hare)

I'M SITTING ON TOP OF THE WORLD / YOU FLEW AWAY FROM THE NEST .... *Brunswick 3014* 8-10 25
(Vocals: Al Jolson)

IT'S YOU / TUCK ME TO SLEEP IN MY OLD 'TUCKY HOME . ..... *Brunswick 2158* 2-4 21

KA-LU-A / BLUE DANUBE BLUES ... *Brunswick 2170* 2-4 21

KARAVAN / ROMANCE .... *Brunswick 2011* 2-4 19

KING ISN'T KING ANY MORE, THE / THE FARMER TOOK ANOTHER LOAD AWAY, HAY, HAY! .... *Brunswick 2965* 3-5 25
(Vocals: Billy Jones & Ernest Hare)

KISS IN THE DARK, A / DREAMY MELODY (by Russo & Fio Rito's Oriole Orchestra) .... *Brunswick 2428* 2-4 23

KITTEN ON THE KEYS / NOLA ...... *Brunswick 2261* 2-4 22

LAST NIGHT ON THE BACK PORCH (Vocals: Billy Jones & Ernest Hare) / CHICK-A-DEE .... *Brunswick 2499* 3-5 23

LEAVE ME WITH A SMILE / WEEP NO MORE, MY MAMMY .... *Brunswick 2177* 2-4 21

LIMEHOUSE BLUES / WORRIED .... *Brunswick 2603* 3-5 24

LOVEY DOVE / YOU WON'T BE SORRY .... *Brunswick 2277* 2-4 22

OH! LADY BE GOOD / FASCINATING RHYTHM .... *Brunswick 2790* 3-5 25

OH, YOU CAN'T FOOL AN OLD HOSS-FLY / OH! HOW I LOVE MY DARLING .... *Brunswick 2757* 3-5 25
(Vocals: Billy Jones & Ernest Hare)

OL' MAN RIVER (Vocal: Emil Cote) / SENTIMENTAL BABY (Vocal: Al Lynch) ..... *Bell 597* 3-5 28

PACK UP YOUR SINS AND GO TO THE DEVIL / LADY OF THE EVENING .... *Brunswick 2353* 3-5 22

SEND BACK MY HONEY MAN / COUNT THE DAYS .... *Brunswick 2295* 2-4 22

ST. JAMES' INFIRMARY / SHAKE IT DOWN .... *QRS Q-1023* 15-20 30
(Vocals: Unknown)

THAT NAUGHTY WALTZ / GLOAMING TIME .... *Brunswick 2097* 2-4 21

THREE O'CLOCK IN THE MORNING / INDIANA LULLABY .... *Brunswick 2193* 2-4 22

WEARY RIVER / MISSISSIPPI, HERE I AM .... *Gennett 6753* 4-6 29
(Vocals: Elmer Russell)

WEARY RIVER / MISSISSIPPI, HERE I AM .... *Supertone 9360* 3-5 29
(Vocals: Elmer Russell)
(Simultaneously released on two labels)

WHAT A DAY! (Vocal: Eddy Thomas) / MAYBE - WHO KNOWS? (Vocal: Dick Robertson) ...... *Brunswick 4421* 8-10 29

WHAT HAS BECOME OF HINKEY DINKEY PARLAY VOO? / A THOUSAND MILES FROM HERE .... *Brunswick 2618* 3-5 24
(Vocals: Billy Jones & Ernest Hare)

WHOSE IZZY IS HE? (Vocal: Billy Jones) / IT AIN'T GONNA RAIN NO MO' (Vocals: Billy Jones & Ernest Hare) .... *Brunswick 2568* 3-5 24

WRECK OF THE SOUTHERN OLD 97 / THE OLD GREY MARE .... *Brunswick 2857* 3-5 25
(Vocals: Billy Jones & Ernest Hare)

YOO-HOO / SECOND-HAND ROSE ... *Brunswick 2137* 2-4 21

YOU DO SOMETHING TO ME / WHAT IS THIS THING CALLED LOVE? .... *Gennett 7104* 5-8 30
(Vocals: Norman Wallace)

YOU DO SOMETHING TO ME / WHAT IS THIS THING CALLED LOVE? .... *Supertone 9604* 4-6 30
(Vocals: Norman Wallace)
(Simultaneously released on two labels)

FENTON, Carl, & His Orchestra as Ruby Green's Manhattan Madcaps

SENTIMENTAL BABY (Vocal: Al Lynch) / OL' MAN RIVER (by Carl Fenton & His Orchestra as the New Yorkers; Vocal: Emil Cote) .... *Gennett 6428* 3-5 28

FENTON, Carl, & His Orchestra as The Manhattan Madcaps

ROSES OF YESTERDAY / TALKIN' TO MYSELF (by Carl Fenton & His Orchestra as The New Yorkers) ... *Gennett 6609* 3-5 28
(Vocals: Norman Wallace)

FENTON, Carl, & His Orchestra as the New Yorkers

OL' MAN RIVER (Vocals: Emil Cote) / SENTIMENTAL BABY (by Carl Fenton & His Orchestra as Ruby Green's Manhattan Madcaps; Vocal: Al Lynch) .... *Gennett 6428* 3-5 28

TALKIN' TO MYSELF / ROSES OF YESTERDAY (by Carl Fenton and His Orchestra as The Manhattan Madcaps) .... *Gennett 6609* 3-5 28
(Vocals: Norman Wallace)

YOU'RE THE CREAM IN MY COFFEE / ORANGE BLOSSOM HOME .... *Herwin 8312* 15-20 28
(Vocals: Ray Strom)

YOU'RE THE CREAM IN MY COFFEE / ORANGE BLOSSOM HOME .... *Supertone 9273* 3-5 28
(Vocals: Ray Strom)
(Simultaneously released on two labels)

FENTON, Carl, as The Rhythmodic Orchestra

HUNGARIA / EGYPTIAN ECHOES ... *Brunswick 2828* 2-4 25

RIGOLETTO RIGGLES / CARMEN CAPERS .... *Vocalion 15113* 2-4 25

THISTLES AND HEATHER / DIXIE DITTIES .... *Vocalion 15163* 2-4 25

FENWYCK, Jerry, & His Orchestra:
see SELVIN, Ben, & His Orchestra

FERDINANDO, Angelo, & His Hotel Great Northern Orchestra

ALL I DO IS DREAM OF YOU / HEAVEN ON EARTH .... *Bluebird B-5458* 3-5 34

BLUE SKY AVENUE / THE CONTINENTAL .... *Bluebird B-5640* 3-5 34
(Vocals: Dick Robertson)

JUST SAY THE WORD / TALKIN' TO MYSELF .... *Bluebird B-5646* 3-5 34
(Vocals: Dick Robertson)

TWO CIGARETTES IN THE DARK / LOST IN A FOG .... *Bluebird B-5639* 3-5 34
(Vocals: Dick Robertson)

FERDINANDO, Felix, & His Orchestra

BABY / IT'S WINTER AGAIN .... *Crown 3421* 3-5 32
(Vocals: Unknown)

CORONADO NIGHTS / SMILE .... *Gennett 6066* 3-5 27
(Vocals: Elliott Stewart)

IN A LITTLE SPANISH TOWN / MY BABY KNOWS HOW (Vocals: Unknown) .... *Gennett 3409* 4-6 26

JUST AN ECHO IN THE VALLEY / 'TILL TOMORROW .... *Crown 3422* 3-5 32
(Vocals: Tommy Foster)

WILLOW, WEEP FOR ME / WALTZING IN A DREAM .... *Crown 3424* 3-5 32
(Vocals: Unknown)

FIELDING, Allan, & His Tic-Toc Music

BY THE CAMP FIRE'S GLOW / WHY'D YOU MAKE ME FALL IN LOVE? .... *Vocalion 4155* 3-5 38

SAME SWEET YOU, THE / BYE-BYE, MISTER DREAM MAN .... *Vocalion 4179* 3-5 38

FIELDS, Arthur, & His Assassinators
(Arthur Fields: 8/6/88 – 3/29/53)

PICCOLO PETE / I CAN'T SLEEP IN THE MOVIES ANYMORE .... *Edison 14075* 12-15 29
(Vocals: Arthur Fields)
(A rare, lateral-cut thin Edison disc)

PLENTY OF SUNSHINE / LOOK IN THE MIRROR (AND SEE JUST WHO I LOVE) .... *Edison 52180* 8-10 28
(Vocals: Arthur Fields)

SHE'S A GREAT, GREAT GIRL / HELLO, MONTREAL .... *Edison 52264* 10-12 28
(Vocals: Arthur Fields)

FIELDS, Arthur, & His Orchestra

HO-HO-HO-HOGAN / WHEN SWEET SUSIE GOES STEPPIN' BY .... *Pathe Actuelle 36874* 5-8 28
(Vocals: Arthur Fields)

HO-HO-HO-HOGAN / WHEN SWEET SUSIE GOES STEPPIN' BY .... *Perfect 15055* 4-6 28
(Vocals: Arthur Fields)
(Simultaneously released on two labels)

FIELDS, Ernie, & His Orchestra

BLUES AT MIDNIGHT (Vocal: Lenora Davis) / BLUES IN YOUR HEART (Vocal: Melvin Moore) ..... *Vocalion 5344* 5-8 39

JUST LET ME ALONE (Vocal: Melvin Moore) / HIGH JIVIN' .... *Vocalion 5157* 5-8 39

T-TOWN BLUES (Vocal: Melvin Moore) / LARD STOMP .... *Vocalion 5073* 5-8 39

YOU GAVE ME EVERYTHING BUT LOVE / I'M LIVING IN A GREAT BIG WAY .... *Vocalion 5240* 5-8 39
(Vocals: Lenora Davis)

FIELDS, Herbie, & His Orchestra
(Herbie Fields: 5/24/19 – 9/17/58)

I GUESS I'LL GET THE PAPERS (Vocal: Herbie Fields) / THERE'S NOTHING THE MATTER WITH ME (THAT A KISS CAN'T CURE) (Vocal: Marianne Dunne) .... *RCA Victor 20-1962* 3-5 46

FIELDS, Herbie, as the Herbie Fields Quintet

I WANNA (Vocals: Herbie Fields & chorus) / SOPRANO BOOGIE .... *RCA Victor 20-2179* 3-5 47

FIELDS, Shep, & His New Music
(Shep Fields: 9/12/10 – 2/81)

BLUE PRELUDE / YOU'RE DRIVING ME CRAZY .... *Bluebird B-11312* 3-5 41

(AT THE) CROSS-ROADS / I CAME HERE TO TALK FOR JOE (Vocal: Ralph Young) .... *Bluebird B-11578* 2-4 42

DEAR OLD PAL OF MINE / THE CAISSONS GO ROLLING ALONG .... *Bluebird B-11477* 3-5 42
(Vocals: Ken Carter)

DON'T BLAME ME / HUNGARIAN DANCE NO. 5 .... *Bluebird B-11225* 2-4 41

LONG MAY WE LOVE (Vocal: Ken Carter) / JERSEY BOUNCE .... *Bluebird B-11490* 2-4 42

LOST CHORD, THE / SOMEONE'S ROCKING MY DREAMBOAT ...... *Bluebird B-11424* 2-4 42
(Vocals: Ken Carter)

MARCHE SLAVE / I FOUND A MILLION-DOLLAR BABY (Vocals: Dorothy Allen & Larry Neill) .... *Bluebird B-11150* 2-4 41

PLEASE THINK OF ME (Vocal: Ralph Young) / TAKE IT SLOW .... *Bluebird 30-0807* 2-4 42

WHEN THE LIGHTS GO ON AGAIN / BETTER NOT ROLL THOSE BLUE, BLUE EYES ... *Bluebird B-11583* 3-5 42
(Vocals: Ralph Young)

WHO CAN I TURN TO? (Vocal: Ann Perry) / AUTUMN NOCTURNE .... *Bluebird B-11325* 2-4 41

WONDER WHEN MY BABY'S COMING HOME / THIS IS WORTH FIGHTING FOR .... *Bluebird B-11537* 3-5 42
(Vocals: Ken Carter)

FIELDS, Shep, & His Rippling Rhythm

ALEXANDER'S RAGTIME BAND / BOB WHITE (Vocal: Bob Goday) ...... *Bluebird B-7345* 3-5 37

BASIN STREET BLUES (Vocal: Bob Goday) / RIPPLING RHYTHM (theme song) .... *Bluebird B-6759* 3-5 37

CARAVAN / SATAN TAKES A HOLIDAY .... *Bluebird B-7138* 3-5 37

DO YOU OR DON'T YOU LOVE ME? / ON THE BEACH AT BALI-BALI .... *Bluebird B-6417* 3-5 36
(Vocals: Charles Chester)

GOODNIGHT MY LOVE / ONE NEVER KNOWS – DOES ONE? .... *Bluebird B-6685* 3-5 37
(Vocals: Bob Goday)

HAVIN' MYSELF A TIME (Vocal: Hal Derwin) / I'VE GOT A POCKETFUL OF DREAMS (Vocal: Phyllis Kenny) .... *Bluebird B-7581* 2-4 38

IN A LITTLE CAROLINA TOWN / WORRIED OVER YOU .... *Bluebird B-7142* 2-4 37
(Vocals: Bob Goday)

I'VE GOT YOU UNDER MY SKIN / EASY TO LOVE .... *Bluebird B-6592* 3-5 36
(Vocals: Dick Robertson)

LA CUCARACHA / GOTTA SEE A DREAM ABOUT A GIRL (Vocal: Sonny Washburn) ..... *Bluebird B-11064* 2-4 41

MAY I HAVE THE NEXT ROMANCE WITH YOU? / HEAD OVER HEELS IN LOVE ..... *Bluebird B-6689* 3-5 37
(Vocals: Bob Goday)

MERRY-GO-ROUND BROKE DOWN, THE / THAT'S WHEN YOUR HEARTACHES BEGIN .... *Bluebird B-7015* 3-5 37
(Vocals: Bob Goday)

MOON AT SEA / THE SHAG .... *Bluebird B-7068* 3-5 37
(Vocals: Bob Goday)

MOONLIGHT AND SHADOWS / DEDICATED TO YOU .... *Bluebird B-6803* 2-4 37
(Vocals: Bob Goday)

NERO / 12TH STREET RAG .... *Bluebird B-6817* 3-5 37

NOW THAT SUMMER IS GONE (Vocal: Bob Goday) / SWAMP FIRE .... *Bluebird B-6662* 3-5 36

SEPTEMBER IN THE RAIN / MELODY FOR TWO .... *Bluebird B-6805* 2-4 37
(Vocals: Bob Goday)

SOUTH OF THE BORDER (Vocal: Hal Derwin) / IT'S ALL OVER TOWN (Vocal: Jerry Stewart) ... *Bluebird B-10376* 2-4 39

SUCH STUFF AS DREAMS ARE MADE OF / LET'S BE BUDDIES .... *Bluebird B-10923* 2-4 40
(Vocals: Larry Neill)

THAT'S A PLENTY / A BLUES SERENADE (Vocal: Hal Derwin) ...... *Bluebird B-7785* 3-5 38

WAY YOU LOOK TO-NIGHT, THE / NEVER GONNA DANCE .... *Bluebird B-6505* 3-5 36
(Vocals: Charles Chester)

FINNEY, Chick:

see Original St. Louis Crackerjacks, The

FINZEL, William, as Finzel's Arcadia Orchestra of Detroit

BIG BAD BILL IS SWEET WILLIAM NOW / WEEPIN' THE BLUES .... *Okeh 40301* 5-8 25

CALLING (FOR YOU) / STEALING TO VIRGINIA .... *Okeh 4985* 3-5 23

DICTY BLUES / AFRICA (by Markel's Orchestra) .... *Okeh 40161* 2-4 25

I CAN'T STOP BABYING YOU / LISTENING .... *Okeh 40304* 2-4 25

I'M GOING TO WANDER / KEEP A-GOIN' ... *Okeh 40043* 3-5 23

LAFF IT OFF (Vocal: Charlotte Meyers) / AIN'T MY BABY GRAND? .... *Okeh 40298* 5-8 25
(The first side was recorded at the Arcadia Ballroom in Detroit with several thousand dancers in attendance.
It is described as the first public recording to be made and issued in the United States)

LOTS O' MAMA / MANDALAY .... *Okeh 40148* 4-6 24

WHO'S SORRY NOW? / LITTLE ROVER ... *Okeh 4858* 3-5 23

FIO RITO, Ted, & His Orchestra

(Ted Fio Rito: 12/20/00 / 7/22/71)
also see RUSSO & Fio Rito's Oriole Orchestra / Oriole Terrace Orchestra

BABY, WON'T YOU PLEASE COME HOME? (Vocal: Candy Candido) / ALABAMY BOUND (Vocal: Frank Flynn) .... *Bluebird B-10753* 3-5 40

CHARLEY, MY BOY (Vocal: Maureen O'Connor) / I NEVER KNEW (Vocal: Bob Carroll) .... *Decca 4334* 2-4 42

DONKEY SERENADE, THE (Vocals: Muzzy Marcellino & The Debutantes) / CIELITO LINDO (Vocals: The Debutantes) .... *Decca 1614* 3-5 38

EVENING STAR / MY HEART AT THY SWEET VOICE .... *Decca 1829* 2-4 38

FAIR AND WARMER (Vocal: Dick Powell) / I'LL STRING ALONG WITH YOU (Vocal: Muzzy Marcellino) .... *Brunswick 6859* 4-6 34

FOLLOW YOUR HEART / MAGNOLIAS IN THE MOONLIGHT .... *Decca 910* 4-6 36
(Vocals: Stanley Hickman)

GLORY OF LOVE, THE / CABIN IN THE SKY .... *Decca 793* 4-6 36
(Vocals: Muzzy Marcellino)

IT'S BEEN SO LONG (Vocal: Muzzy Marcellino) / LET'S FACE THE MUSIC AND DANCE (Vocal: Stanley Hickman) .... *Decca 697* 4-6 36

JUST ONE OF THOSE THINGS / I'M GONNA SIT RIGHT DOWN AND WRITE MYSELF A LETTER .... *Decca 678* 4-6 36
(Vocals: Muzzy Marcellino)

KING FOR A DAY / NO! NO! NORA .... *Decca 3936* 2-4 42
(Vocals: Bob Carroll)

LA ESTRELLITA / LA PALOMA .... *Decca 1866* 2-4 38

MICKEY MOUSE'S BIRTHDAY PARTY / THERE'S "YOO-HOO" IN YOUR EYES .... *Decca 954* 5-8 36
(Vocals: Muzzy Marcellino and The Debutantes)

MY BABY JUST CARES FOR ME (Vocals: Unknown) / — ... *Hit of the Week 1104* 5-8 30
(Hit of the Week records are one-sided paper discs)

NEVER GONNA DANCE (Vocal: Muzzy Marcellino) / THE NIGHT IS YOUNG AND YOU'RE SO BEAUTIFUL (Vocal: Stanley Hickman) .... *Decca 894* 4-6 36

ONE MORE WALTZ / UNTIL WE MEET AGAIN, SWEETHEART .... *Victor 22521* 4-6 30
(Vocals: Stan Jacobsen)

RIO RITA (theme song) / LILY OF LAGUNA ... *Decca 4258* 2-4 42
(Vocals: Bob Carroll)

ROSE MARIE / INDIAN LOVE CALL ...... *Decca 694* 4-6 36
(Vocals: Stanley Hickman)

SWEET LEILANI (Vocals: Muzzy Marcellino & The Debutantes) / HAWAIIAN HOSPITALITY (Vocals: The Debutantes) .... *Decca 1176* 4-6 37

THERE WILL NEVER BE ANOTHER MARY (Vocal: Pedro Espino) / HARLEM MADNESS (by The Coon-Sanders Orchestra; Vocal: Joe Sanders) ...... *Victor 22300* 10-12 30

WILLOW WEEP FOR ME / MORE BEAUTIFUL THAN EVER .... *Brunswick 6422* 4-6 32
(Vocals: Muzzy Marcellino)

YOU ARE TOO BEAUTIFUL / HALLELUJAH, I'M A BUM .... *Brunswick 6503* 4-6 33
(Vocals: Muzzy Marcellino)

YOU CAN BE KISSED / LULU'S BACK IN TOWN .... *Brunswick 7452* 4-6 35
(Vocals: Unknown)

YOURS TRULY IS TRULY YOURS / HONEY .... *Decca 746* 4-6 36
(Vocals: Muzzy Marcellino)

FISHER, Freddy "Schnickelfritz", & His Orchestra

(Freddy Fisher: 1904 –   )

CUCKOO WALTZ / MUZIKY, MUZIKY .... *Decca 45063* 2-4 48

HOT TIME IN THE OLD TOWN TONIGHT / SOME OF THESE DAYS .... *Decca 2168* 2-4 38

WHEN MY BABY SMILES AT ME / NOBODY'S GOT THE BLUES BUT ME .... *Decca 1501* 4-6 37

WILD WILD WOMEN, THE (Vocal: Stan Fritts) / COLONEL CORN (Vocal: Freddie Fisher) .... *Decca 1771* 2-4 38

FISHER, Mark, & His Edgewater Beach Hotel Orchestra

BLACK-EYED SUSAN BROWN / LOVEY .... *Columbia 2749-D* 5-8 33
(Vocals: Mark Fisher)
(This record was pressed in blue shellac)

TREE WAS A TREE, A / WHY CAN'T THIS NIGHT GO ON FOREVER? .... *Columbia 2754-D* 5-8 33
(Vocals: Mark Fisher)
(This record was pressed in blue shellac)

FISHER, "Schnickelfritz", & His Orchestra:

see FISHER, Freddy "Schnickelfritz", & His Orchestra

FISHER, Scott, & His Orchestra

DON'T WORRY, SWEETHEART / ONCE UPON A MIDNIGHT .... *Banner 33424* 3-5 35
(Vocals: Lee Johnson)

DON'T WORRY, SWEETHEART / ONCE UPON A MIDNIGHT .... *Melotone 13391* 3-5 35
(Vocals: Lee Johnson)

DON'T WORRY, SWEETHEART / ONCE UPON A MIDNIGHT .... *Oriole 3137* 3-5 35
(Vocals: Lee Johnson)

DON'T WORRY, SWEETHEART / ONCE UPON A MIDNIGHT .... *Perfect 16113* 3-5 35
(Vocals: Lee Johnson)

DON'T WORRY, SWEETHEART / ONCE UPON A MIDNIGHT .... *Romeo 2511* 3-5 35
(Vocals: Lee Johnson)
(Simultaneously released on five labels)

JUST A FAIR-WEATHER FRIEND / HAUNTING ME .... *Vocalion 2878* 4-6 35
(Vocals: Lee Johnson)

TINY LITTLE FINGER PRINTS (Vocal: Durelle Alexander) / IN A BLUE AND PENSIVE MOOD (Vocal: Lee Johnson) .... *Vocalion 2879* 4-6 35

YOU'RE AN ANGEL (Vocal: Russ Morgan) / I'M IN LOVE ALL OVER AGAIN (Vocal: Lee Johnson) .... *Banner 33440* 3-5 35

YOU'RE AN ANGEL (Vocal: Russ Morgan) / I'M IN LOVE ALL OVER AGAIN (Vocal: Lee Johnson) .... *Melotone 13407* 3-5 35

YOU'RE AN ANGEL (Vocal: Russ Morgan) / I'M IN LOVE ALL OVER AGAIN (Vocal: Lee Johnson) .... *Oriole 3148* 3-5 35

YOU'RE AN ANGEL (Vocal: Russ Morgan) / I'M IN LOVE ALL OVER AGAIN (Vocal: Lee Johnson) .... *Perfect 16124* 3-5 35

YOU'RE AN ANGEL (Vocal: Russ Morgan) / I'M IN LOVE ALL OVER AGAIN (Vocal: Lee Johnson) .... *Romeo 2522* 3-5 35
(Simultaneously released on five labels)

FISK, Charlie, & His Orchestra

HIS KISSES MADE A MISSUS OUT OF ME / MOUNTAIN HIGH, VALLEY LOW ... *Radio Artist 222* 4-6 48
(Vocals: Unknown)

FITZGERALD, Ella, & Her Famous Orchestra

(Ella Fitzgerald: 4/25/18 –   )

AFTER I SAY I'M SORRY / BABY, WHAT ELSE CAN I DO? .... *Decca 2826* 2-4 39
(Vocals: Ella Fitzgerald)

BETCHA NICKEL / MOON RAY .... *Decca 2904* 2-4 39
(Vocals: Ella Fitzgerald)

BILLY / PLEASE TELL ME THE TRUTH .... *Decca 2769* 2-4 39
(Vocals: Ella Fitzgerald)

COW-COW BOOGIE (Vocals: Ella Fitzgerald & the Ink Spots) / WHEN MY SUGAR WALKS DOWN THE STREET (Vocal: Ella Fitzgerald) .... *Decca 18587* 3-5 41

DEEDLE-DE-DUM / GULF COAST BLUES ... *Decca 3324* 2-4 40
(Vocals: Ella Fitzgerald)

FIVE O'CLOCK WHISTLE / SO LONG ..... *Decca 3420* 2-4 40
(Vocals: Ella Fitzgerald)

HELLO MA! I DONE IT AGAIN / WISHFUL THINKING .... *Decca 3612* 2-4 41
(Vocals: Ella Fitzgerald)

I CAN'T BELIEVE THAT YOU'RE IN LOVE WITH ME / CAN'T HELP LOVIN' DAT MAN .... *Decca 18421* 2-4 41
(Vocals: Ella Fitzgerald)

IF IT WEREN'T FOR YOU / SING SONG SWING .... *Decca 3126* 2-4 40
(Vocals: Ella Fitzgerald)

I GOT IT BAD (AND THAT AIN'T GOOD) / MELINDA THE MOUSIE .... *Decca 3968* 2-4 41
(Vocals: Ella Fitzgerald)

I'M NOT COMPLAININ' / WHAT'S THE MATTER WITH ME? .... *Decca 3005* 2-4 40
(Vocals: Ella Fitzgerald)

I'M THE LONESOMEST GAL IN TOWN / THE MUFFIN MAN .... *Decca 3666* 2-4 41
(Vocals: Ella Fitzgerald)

IS THERE SOMEBODY ELSE? / THE STARLIT HOUR .... *Decca 2988* 2-4 40
(Vocals: Ella Fitzgerald)

I WANT THE WAITER (WITH THE WATER) / THAT'S ALL, BROTHER .... *Decca 2628* 2-4 39
(Vocals: Ella Fitzgerald)

KEEP COOL, FOOL / NO NOTHING .... *Decca 3754* 2-4 41
(Vocals: Ella Fitzgerald)

LINDY HOPPERS' DELIGHT / BABY, WON'T YOU PLEASE COME HOME? (Vocal: Ella Fitzgerald) .... *Decca 3186* 3-5 40

MY MAN / WHO ARE YOU? .... *Decca 4291* 2-4 41
(Vocals: Ella Fitzgerald)

SHAKE DOWN THE STARS / I FELL IN LOVE WITH A DREAM .... *Decca 3199* 2-4 40
(Vocals: Ella Fitzgerald)

STAIRWAY TO THE STARS / OUT OF NOWHERE .... *Decca 2598* 3-5 39
(Vocals: Ella Fitzgerald)

SUGAR BLUES / IMAGINATION .... *Decca 3078* 3-5 40
(Vocals: Ella Fitzgerald)

TAKE IT FROM THE TOP / JUBILEE SWING .... *Decca 3236* 4-6 40
(Vocals: Ella Fitzgerald)

TAKING A CHANCE ON LOVE / CABIN IN THE SKY .... *Decca 3490* 3-5 40
(Vocals: Ella Fitzgerald)

TEA DANCE / LOUISVILLE, K–Y .... *Decca 3441* 2-4 40
(Vocals: Ella Fitzgerald)

THREE LITTLE WORDS / THE ONE I LOVE .... *Decca 3608* 2-4 41
(Vocals: Ella Fitzgerald)

YOU'RE GONNA LOSE YOUR GAL / MY WUBBA DOLLY .... *Decca 2816* 2-4 39
(Vocals: Ella Fitzgerald)

FITZGERALD, Ella, & Her Savoy Eight

ALL OR NOTHING AT ALL / DEEP IN THE HEART OF THE SOUTH .... *Decca 1339* 5-8 37
(Vocals: Ella Fitzgerald)

BEI MIR BIST DU SCHOEN / IT'S MY TURN NOW .... *Decca 1596* 5-8 38
(Vocals: Ella Fitzgerald)

IF ANYTHING HAPPENED TO YOU / IF YOU EVER CHANGE YOUR MIND .... *Decca 2481* 2-4 39
(Vocals: Ella Fitzgerald)

IF YOU SHOULD EVER LEAVE / EVERYONE'S WRONG BUT ME .... *Decca 1302* 5-8 37
(Vocals: Ella Fitzgerald)

I HAD TO LIVE AND LEARN / IF THAT'S WHAT YOU'RE THINKING .... *Decca 2581* 2-4 39
(Vocals: Ella Fitzgerald)

IT'S WONDERFUL / I WAS DOING ALL RIGHT .... *Decca 1669* 4-6 38
(Vocals: Ella Fitzgerald)

MY LAST AFFAIR / DARKTOWN STRUTTERS' BALL .... *Decca 1061* 5-8 37
(Vocals: Ella Fitzgerald)

ONCE IS ENOUGH FOR ME / DON'T WORRY 'BOUT ME .... *Decca 2451* 2-4 39
(Vocals: Ella Fitzgerald)

ORGAN GRINDER'S SWING / SHINE ..... *Decca 1062* 5-8 37
(Vocals: Ella Fitzgerald)

STRICTLY FROM DIXIE / WOE IS ME ..... *Decca 2202* 3-5 38
(Vocals: Ella Fitzgerald)

THIS TIME IT'S REAL / YOU CAN'T BE MINE (AND SOMEBODY ELSE'S TOO) .... *Decca 1806* 3-5 38
(Vocals: Ella Fitzgerald)

WE CAN'T GO ON THIS WAY / SAVING MYSELF FOR YOU .... *Decca 1846* 2-4 39
(Vocals: Ella Fitzgerald)

WHAT DO YOU KNOW ABOUT LOVE? / IF YOU ONLY KNEW .... *Decca 1967* 2-4 38
(Vocals: Ella Fitzgerald)

FITZPATRICK, Ed, & His Orchestra

GENTLEMAN AWAITS, THE / TO A SWEET PRETTY THING .... *Vocalion 3535* 3-5 37
(Vocals: Unknown)

I DREAM OF SAN MARINO / SWEET HEARTACHE .... *Vocalion 3510* 3-5 37
(Vocals: Unknown)

FLANAGAN, Ralph, & His Orchestra
(Ralph Flanagan: 4/7/19 –)

ANGELA MIA (Vocals: Buddy Victor & The Singing Winds) / ROO, ROO, ROO KANGAROO .... *RCA Victor 20-5676* 2-4 53

BLUES FROM AN AMERICAN IN PARIS, THE / LOVE IS HERE TO STAY (Vocals: Harry Prime & The Singing Winds) .... *RCA Victor 20-4247* 2-4 51

HALLS OF IVY (Vocal: Harry Prime) / OH BABE! (Vocal: Steve Benoric) ... *RCA Victor 20-3954* 2-4 50

HONEST AND TRULY (Vocals: Harry Prime & The Singing Winds) / SINGING WINDS (theme song) .... *RCA Victor 20-4656* 2-4 52

HOT TODDY / SERENADE .... *RCA Victor 20-5095* 2-4 53

I'LL WALK ALONE / JUST A LITTLE LOVIN' .... *RCA Victor 20-4703* 2-4 52

I SHOULD CARE (Vocals: Harry Prime & The Singing Winds) / TIPPIN' IN .... *RCA Victor 20-4885* 2-4 52

LITTLE BROWN JUG MAMBO, THE / THE AMERICAN PATROL MAMBO .... *RCA Victor 20-5908* 2-4 54
(An early high fidelity recording)

ON MY WAY NOW (Vocals: The Cincinnati Shouters & the audience) / ONE ALONE ...... *RCA Victor 20-4487* 2-4 51

RED WE WANT IS THE RED WE'VE GOT, THE / NEVERTHELESS (Vocal: Harry Prime) .... *RCA Victor 20-3904* 2-4 50

SOMETHING SPECIAL / PETER PIPER BOOGIE (Vocals: Buddy Victor & The Young Sisters) .... *RCA Victor 20-5451* 2-4 53

STRANGER IN PARADISE / THE TYPEWRITER .... *RCA Victor 20-5505* 2-4 53

VERY GOOD ADVICE (Vocal: Pegge King) / TWILIGHT RHAPSODY (Vocals: Harry Prime & The Singing Winds) .... *RCA Victor 20-4133* 2-4 50

WAY BACK HOME (Vocal: Harry Prime) / THE TRAIL OF THE LONESOME PINE .... *RCA Victor 30-0017* 3-5 49
(A turquoise label RCA Victor Bluebird Series release.)

FLORIDA CLUBMEN, THE:
see HUDSON, Dean

FLORIDA FOUR, THE

I'M TIRED OF EVERYTHING BUT YOU / NOBODY BUT FANNY .... *Edison 51630* 4-6 25

MY KENTUCKY KINFOLKS / NO FOOLIN' .... *Edison 51747* 4-6 26

ROLL 'EM, GIRLS (Vocal: Arthur Hall) / MIAMI (Vocal: Vernon Dalhart) .... *Edison 51650* 5-8 25

WHEN YOU'RE WITH SOMEBODY ELSE / RAMONA .... *Edison 52231* 3-5 28
(Vocals: Unknown)

YOU WENT AWAY TOO FAR / WHEN I FIRST MET MARY .... *Edison 51921* 4-6 27

FLOYD, Troy, & His Plaza Hotel Orchestra

SHADOWLAND BLUES / SHADOWLAND BLUES, PART II .... *Okeh 8571* 25-30 28

FLOYD, Troy, & His Shadowland Orchestra

DREAMLAND BLUES / DREAMLAND BLUES, PART II .... *Okeh 8719* 25-30 29

FOLEY, Bill, As Bill Foley's Keystone Serenaders
directed by Ray McConnell

LONESOME ME / I'M KNEE-DEEP IN DAISIES .... *Vocalion 15123* 3-5 25

NORMANDY / THE CO-ED .... *Vocalion 15124* 3-5 26
(Vocals: Unknown)

WHERE CAN I FIND YOU? / EVERYTHING IS HOTSY-TOTSY NOW (Vocals: Unknown) .... *Vocalion 15122* 5-8 25

FOMEEN, Basil, & His Orchestra

SONG HITS OF 1928
(A 4-record album set) .... *Decca A-1928 Set* 8-10 42
Individual records in the set, listed numerically (with value of each):

SONNY BOY; ANGELA MIA; WHERE THE SHY LITTLE VIOLETS GROW / CAROLINA MOON; JEANNINE; CHIQUITA .... *Decca 24044* 2-4 -
(Vocals: Don Saxon)

LOVER, COME BACK TO ME!; BUTTON UP YOUR OVERCOAT; YOU'RE THE CREAM IN MY COFFEE / LET'S DO IT; SWEETHEARTS ON PARADE; YOU TOOK ADVANTAGE OF ME .... *Decca 24045* 2-4
(Vocals: Don Saxon)

LAUGH, CLOWN, LAUGH; I CAN'T GIVE YOU ANYTHING BUT LOVE; I AIN'T GOT NOBODY / DIGA, DIGA DOO; NAGASAKI; I FAW DOWN AN' GO 'BOOM'! .... *Decca 24046* 2-4
(Vocals: Don Saxon)

BACK IN YOUR OWN BACK YARD; I'LL GET BY; MARIE / HONEY; SWEET SUE – JUST YOU; THAT'S MY WEAKNESS NOW .... *Decca 24047* 2-4
(Vocals: Don Saxon)

SONG HITS OF 1925
(A 4-record album set) .... *Decca A-1925 Set* 8-10 42
Individual records in the set, listed numerically (with value of each):

DINAH; DON'T BRING LULU; IF I HAD A GIRL LIKE YOU (Vocal: James Murphy) / BROWN EYES, WHY ARE YOU BLUE?; DRIFTING AND DREAMING; ONLY A ROSE (Vocals: by trio) .... *Decca 24032* 2-4 -

COLLEGIATE; SAVE YOUR SORROW FOR TOMORROW; ALABAMY BOUND (Vocals: by trio) / FIVE FOOT TWO, EYES OF BLUE; MOONLIGHT AND ROSES; I'M SITTING ON TOP OF THE WORLD .... *Decca 24033* 2-4 -

WHO?; JUST A COTTAGE SMALL; HERE IN MY ARMS (Vocal: James Murphy) / REMEMBER; ALWAYS (Vocal: Don Saxon) .... *Decca 24034* 2-4 -

VAGABOND KING WALTZ; NEOPOLITAN NIGHTS; DOWN BY THE WINEGAR WOIKS (Vocal: James Murphy) / YES, SIR! THAT'S MY BABY; YEARNING (Vocal: Don Saxon) .... *Decca 24035* 2-4 -

FOOR-ROBINSON CAROLINA CLUB ORCHESTRA, The
directed by William Truesdale

COLLEGIATE (Vocals: by trio) / ROSE OF THE NILE .... *Okeh 40466* 4-6 25

FORBSTEIN, Louis, as Louis Forbstein's Royal Syncopators

DEEP ELM (Vocal: Rex Newman) / TWILIGHT, THE STARS AND YOU .... *Okeh 40379* 5-8 25

DOWN AND OUT BLUES / THAT'S ALL THERE IS, THERE AIN'T NO MORE (Vocal: Rex Newman) .... *Okeh 40417* 8-10 25

SOMEDAY WE'LL MEET AGAIN (Vocal: Rex Newman) / THE WORLD IS SUCH A LONESOME PLACE .... *Okeh 40392* 5-8 25

FORESYTHE, Reginald, as The New Music Of Reginald Foresythe
(Reginald Foresythe: 5/28/07 –)
(The following records were pressed in blue shellac.)

LULLABY / DODGING A DIVORCEE .... *Columbia 3012-D* 10-12 35

MELANCHOLY CLOWN / GREENER THE GRASS .... *Columbia 3060-D* 10-12 35

FOSDICK, Gene, as Gene Fosdiek's Hoosiers

FAREWELL BLUES / AUNT HAGAR'S BLUES .... *Vocalion 14535* 4-6 23

ONE NIGHT IN JUNE / LOST .... *Vocalion 14473* 2-4 22

PEGGY DEAR / APPLE SAUCE .... *Vocalion 14503* 2-4 23

YOU'VE GOT TO SEE MAMA EV'RY NIGHT / 'WAY DOWN YONDER IN NEW ORLEANS .... *Vocalion 14496* 4-6 23

FOSTER, Chuck, & His Orchestra
(Chuck Foster: 8/26/12 –)

ALL I DESIRE (Vocal: Dorothy Brandon) / SPRING FEVER .... *Okeh 6003* 4-6 40

IF IT'S YOU / JUST ONCE AGAIN .... *Okeh 6333* 3-5 41
(Vocals: Unknown)

I'VE BEEN DRAFTED (NOW I'M DRAFTING YOU) / THE KISS POLKA .... *Okeh 6304* 3-5 41
(Vocals: Unknown)

SLEEPY TIME GAL (Vocal: Chuck Foster) / OH, YOU BEAUTIFUL DOLL (theme song) (Vocal: Jimmy Castle) .... *Okeh 5915* 3-5 40

FOSTER, Deacon, & His Boys:
see TRENT, Alphonse, & His Orchestra

FOTINE, Larry, & His Orchestra

BEAUTIFUL EYES / "A" – YOU'RE ADORABLE (Vocals: Maralyn Marsh & Johnny Goodfellow) .... *Decca 24579* 2-4 49

LITTLE JUG (Vocals: Maralyn Marsh & Johnny Goodfellow) / RAIN (Vocal: Maralyn Marsh) .... *Decca 24950* 2-4 50

FOX, Roy, & His Montmartre Orchestra
(Roy Fox: circa 1902 –)

MASQUERADE / CUDDLE UP A LITTLE CLOSER................ *Vocalion 15746* 3-5 28
(Vocals: Art Cripper)

MY MELODY MAN (Vocals: Unknown) / NOBODY'S FAULT BUT YOUR OWN (Vocals: Art Cripper & quartet).......... *Brunswick 4384* 2-4 29

PAINTING THE CLOUDS WITH SUNSHINE (Vocal: Art Cripper) / TIP-TOE THROUGH THE TULIPS (Vocals: Unknown)...... *Brunswick 4419* 2-4 29

SWEETHEART OF ALL MY DREAMS / MAKIN' WHOOPEE .... *Vocalion 15770* 3-5 29
(Vocals: Unknown)

WHEN I SEE MY SUGAR / OO-LA-LA-LA-LA–............... *Brunswick 4505* 2-4 29
(Vocals: Unknown)

FRANK, Arnold, & His Orchestra

HOW COULD ANYTHING SO GOOD BE BAD? / YOU'RE A REAL SWEETHEART....... *Okeh 41086* 5-8 28
(Vocals: Bud Cunningham)

FRANK, Arnold, & His Roger's Cafe Orchestra

RAIN (Vocal: Stan Thompson) / BLACK MARIA........................ *Okeh 40896* 5-8 27

FRANKIE AND JOHNNIE ORCHESTRA, The:

FRANKIE AND JOHNIE SWING (Vocals: Bill Morgan) / I DON'T CARE (Vocal: John Gilliland).... *Bluebird B-6760* 10-12 36

STOMPIN' / DON'T KNOW WHY..... *Bluebird B-6499* 10-12 36

SWING FEVER (Vocal: John Gilliland) / GUESS WHO? (Vocal: Frank Strange)........ *Okeh 6470* 10-12 36

FRANKLIN, Buddy, & His Orchestra

INNOCENT ME, SOPHISTICATED YOU (Vocal: Harriet Collins) / THERE'S NO YOU (Vocal: Eddie Allyn) .... *Musicraft 15039* 2-4 46

FRANKLIN, Joseph, as Joseph Franklin's Orchestra:
see SAMUELS, Joseph, & His Orchestra

FRANKLIN, Sam, as Sam Franklin's Orchestra:
see SAMUELS, Joseph, & His Orchestra

FRAZIER, Eddie, & His Plantation Orchestra

CHEATIN' ON ME / EVERYTHING IS HOTSY-TOTSY NOW.................. *Sunset 1100* 15-20 25

FREEMAN, Jerry / Jay, & His Orchestra

DARK CLOUDS / HUSH MY MOUTH (IF I AIN'T GOIN' SOUTH).................... *Bluebird B-5233* 4-6 33
(Vocals: Frank Sylvano)

DARK CLOUDS / HUSH MY MOUTH (IF I AIN'T GOIN' SOUTH)................... *Electradisk 2116* 12-15 33
(Vocals: Frank Sylvano)

DARK CLOUDS / HUSH MY MOUTH (IF I AIN'T GOIN' SOUTH)..................... *Sunrise S-3316* 12-15 33
(Vocals: Frank Sylvano)
(Simultaneously released on three labels)

GOODNIGHT, LITTLE GIRL OF MY DREAMS / LULLABY LAND................. *Bluebird B-5231* 3-5 33
(Vocals: Frank Sylvano)

GOODNIGHT, LITTLE GIRL OF MY DREAMS / LULLABY LAND .... *Electradisk 2114* 8-10 33
(Vocals: Frank Sylvano)

GOODNIGHT, LITTLE GIRL OF MY DREAMS / LULLABY LAND.................. *Sunrise S-3314* 8-10 33
(Vocals: Frank Sylvano)
(Simultaneously released on three labels)

I'M AT THE MERCY OF LOVE / COPPER COLORED GAL.................. *Melotone 6-12-17* 4-6 36
(Vocals: Unknown)

I'M AT THE MERCY OF LOVE / COPPER COLORED GAL.................... *Perfect 6-12-17* 4-6 36
(Vocals: Unknown)
(Simultaneously released on two labels)

I'M DANCIN' ON A RAINBOW / EVERYTHING I HAVE IS YOURS................. *Bluebird B-5232* 4-6 33
(Vocals: Frank Sylvano)

I'M DANCIN' ON A RAINBOW / EVERYTHING I HAVE IS YOURS .... *Electradisk 2115* 12-15 33
(Vocals: Frank Sylvano)

I'M DANCIN' ON A RAINBOW / EVERYTHING I HAVE IS YOURS................. *Sunrise S-3315* 12-15 33
(Vocals: Frank Sylvano)
(Simultaneously released on three labels)

MOMENT IN THE DARK, A / MY NEWEST EXCITEMENT....... *Melotone 7-03-07* 4-6 37
(Vocals: Unknown)

MR. GHOST GOES TO TOWN / GETTING AWAY WITH MURDER .... *Melotone 7-02-08* 5-8 37

POOR ROBINSON CRUSOE / GOODNIGHT, MY LUCKY DAY .... *Variety 511* 5-8 37

SUGAR FOOT STOMP / THE NIGHT RIDE .... *Melotone 7-08-09* 5-8 37

THAT'S WHAT YOU MEAN TO ME / ALABAMA BARBECUE... *Melotone 6-12-05* 4-6 36
(Vocals: Unknown)

FREY, Fran, & His Orchestra:
see SELVIN, Ben, & His Orchestra

FREY, Hugo:
see GREAT WHITE WAY ORCHESTRA, The

FRIEDMAN, Al, & His Yoeng's Orchestra

EVENING SHADOWS / FLORA ("HAPPY JACK")............ *Edison 52352* 3-5 28

FOUR WALLS / HE LOVES AND SHE LOVES.................... *Edison 52190* 3-5 28
(Vocals: The Rollickers)

GOOD BOY / DON'T WAIT UNTIL THE LIGHTS ARE LOW............. *Edison 52444* 4-6 28

HAPPY DAYS AND LONELY NIGHTS / ME AND THE MAN IN THE MOON................. *Edison 52484* 4-6 29
(Vocals: Tommy Weir)

HONEYSUCKLE LANE / SOMEBODY ELSE................... *Edison 52053* 3-5 27
(Vocals: Leroy Montesanto)

SPELL OF THE BLUES, THE / GUESS WHO'S IN TOWN.......................... *Edison 52529* 5-8 29
(Vocals: Tommy Weir)

TWO LIPS (Vocal: Theo Alban) / JUST A NIGHT FOR MEDITATION.... *Edison 52365* 3-5 28

FRIEDMAN, Joe, as Joe Friedman's Monte Carlo Orchestra

COLLEGIATE (Vocal: Billy Jones) / ON A NIGHT LIKE THIS .... *Harmony 11-H* 4-6 25

OH! BOY, WHAT A GIRL (Vocals: by Orchestra) / — .... *Harmony 19-H* 5-8 25

SPEECH! (Vocal: Billy Jones) / BREEZIN' ALONG TO GEORGIA.... *Harmony 30-H* 4-6 25

FRIEDMAN, Snooks, as Snooks & His Memphis Ramblers / Stompers

CUTEST KID IN TOWN / KISSABLE BABY.......................... *Victor 22813* 5-8 31
(Vocals: Ken Herlin, Walter Ashby, & Elly Bellare)

DIP YOUR BRUSH IN THE SUNSHINE / LET A LITTLE PLEASURE INTERFERE WITH BUSINESS.................... *Victor 22720* 5-8 31
(Vocals: Walter Ashby)

GOODNIGHT, SWEETHEART / GUILTY......................... *Melotone M-12245* 5-8 31
(Vocals: Walter Ashby)

HELLO, BEAUTIFUL! (Vocals: Ken Herlin, Walter Ashby, & Elly Bellare) / WHA'D JA DO TO ME? (Vocals: Ken Herlin, Walter Ashby, Elly Bellare, & Pat McCarthy).... *Victor 23038* 8-10 31

I'M HAPPY WHEN YOU'RE HAPPY / LOVE IS LIKE THAT (WHAT CAN YOU DO?)......... *Victor 22629* 5-8 31
(Vocals: Ken Herlin, Walter Ashby, & Elly Bellare)

JUST ONE MORE CHANCE (Vocal: Walter Ashby) / THAT'S THE TIME A FELLOW NEEDS A GIRL FRIEND (Vocal: Pat McCarthy) ...... *Melotone M-12210* 5-8 31

NOTHIN' TO DO BUT LOVE (Vocals: Ken Herlin, Walter Ashby, & Elly Bellare) / WHY DID IT HAVE TO BE ME? (Vocal: Walter Ashby)............................ *Victor 22895* 5-8 32

SMILE, DARN YA, SMILE (Vocals: Ken Herlin, Walter Ashby, & Elly Bellare) / I'M CRAZY 'BOUT MY BABY (Vocals: Walter Ashby).................. *Victor 22662* 5-8 31

SOME OTHER TIME (Vocals: Elly Bellare) / SWEET GEORGIA BROWN (Vocal: Estes Monasco)... *Victor 22779* 5-8 31

THAT'S MY DESIRE (Vocals: Ken Herlin, Walter Ashby, & Elly Bellare) / MAKIN' FACES AT THE MAN IN THE MOON (Vocal: Elly Bellare) .... *Melotone M-12203* 5-8 31

THAT'S MY DESIRE (Vocals: Ken Herlin, Walter Ashby, & Elly Bellare) / ONE MORE TIME (Vocals: Unknown) .... *Banner 32190* 5-8 31

THAT'S MY DESIRE (Vocals: Ken Herlin, Walter Ashby, & Elly Bellare) / ONE MORE TIME (Vocals: Unknown) .... *Oriole 2279* 5-8 31

THAT'S MY DESIRE (Vocals: Ken Herlin, Walter Ashby, & Elly Bellare) / ONE MORE TIME (Vocals: Unknown)....................... *Perfect 15479* 5-8 31

THAT'S MY DESIRE (Vocals: Ken Herlin, Walter Ashby, & Elly Bellare) / ONE MORE TIME (Vocals: Unknown)........................ *Romeo 1647* 5-8 31
(Simultaneously released on four labels)

WHEN A PAL BIDS A PAL GOODBYE (Vocal: Oscar Grogan) / 'NEATH THE SILVERY MOON (Vocal: Elly Bellare)............... *Victor 22988* 5-8 32

WHEN IT'S SLEEPY TIME DOWN SOUTH (Vocal: Pat McCarthy) / WAS IT WRONG? (Vocal: Walter Ashby) .... *Melotone M-12259* 5-8 31

FRIEDMAN, Snooks, as Snooks & His Memphis Ramblers / Stompers with Julia Gerity recorded under the name Julia Gerity & Her Play Boys

GOOD MAN IS HARD TO FIND, A (Vocals: Ken Herlin, Walter Ashby, Elly Bellare, & Julia Gerity) / WATERLOO (by Boyd Senter & His Senterpedes; Vocal: Ray Stilwell)...................... *Victor 22812* 8-10 31

SITTIN' ON A RUBBISH CAN (Vocals: Ken Herlin, Walter Ashby, Elly Bellare, & Julia Gerity) / BLUE MEMORIES (by Blanche Calloway & Her Joy Boys; Vocal: Blanche Calloway) .... *Victor 22896* 10-12 32

FRISCO SYNCOPATORS, The:
see KATZMAN, Louis, as Louis Katzman's Dance Orchestra, see SELVIN, Ben, as The Moulin Rouge Orchestra, and see STRAIGHT, Charley, & His Orchestra

FRIVOLITY CLUB ORCHESTRA, The

ADORABLE / LONESOME AND SORRY....................... *Vocalion 15316* 2-4 26

CHINKY BUTTERFLY / ALWAYS..... *Vocalion 15261* 2-4 26

DO YOU BELIEVE IN DREAMS? / SOMEBODY'S LONELY................ *Vocalion 15329* 2-4 26

FOREVER AND EVER WITH YOU / SMILE A LITTLE BIT (Vocals: Unknown)...... *Vocalion 15203* 2-4 26

I LOST MY HEART IN MONTEREY / SHE BELONGS TO ME .... *Vocalion 15459* 2-4 26

I NEVER KNEW WHAT THE MOONLIGHT COULD DO / SOME DAY............ *Vocalion 15489* 2-4 27

I'VE GOT THE GIRL / JUST A BIRD'S-EYE VIEW OF MY OLD KENTUCKY HOME .... *Vocalion 15465* 2-4 26

SHORT AN' SWEET / HELLO BLUEBIRD................. *Vocalion 15480* 2-4 27

WATERS OF THE PERKIOMEN / A COAL MINER'S DREAM.................. *Vocalion 15313* 2-4 26

FROEBA, Frank, & His Orchestra
(Frank Froeba: 8/07 –)

BIG APPLE, THE (Vocals: Al Rinker Trio) / JOSEPHINE (Vocal: Kurt Bloom)........... *Decca 1401* 5-8 37

DANGER, LOVE AT WORK (Vocals: Al Rinker Trio) / MILES APART (Vocal: Bill Darnell) .... *Decca 1525* 5-8 37

GOBLINS IN THE STEEPLE / WHO? (Vocal: Jack Wilmot)................ *Decca 1545* 5-8 37

MY SWISS HILLY BILLY (Vocals: Al Rinker Trio) / TEARS IN MY HEART (Vocal: Bill Darnell)......... *Decca 1500* 5-8 37

NOTHING CAN STOP ME NOW / DON'T SAVE YOUR LOVE (FOR A RAINY DAY)............. *Decca 1418* 4-6 37
(Vocals: Kurt Bloom)

FROEBA, Frank, & His Swing Band

JUST TO BE IN CAROLINE / 'TAIN'T NOBODY'S BIZ'NESS WHAT I DO............ *Columbia 3131-D* 12-15 36
(This record was pressed in blue shellac.)

MUSIC GOES 'ROUND AND AROUND, THE (Vocal: Jack Purvis) / THERE'LL BE A GREAT DAY IN THE MORNING............... *Columbia 3110-D* 8-10 36

ORGAN GRINDER'S SWING / RHYTHM LULLABY....................... *Columbia 3151-D* 12-15 36
(Vocals: Midge Williams)

WHATCHA GONNA DO WHEN THERE AIN'T NO SWING? / IT ALL BEGINS AND ENDS WITH YOU...................... *Columbia 3152-D* 12-15 36
(Vocals: Midge Williams)

FRY, Charlie, & His Million-Dollar Pier Orchestra

COPENHAGEN / BLUE EVENING BLUES.............................. *Edison 51406* 5-8 24

GOTTA GETTA GIRL / BYE BYE BABY... *Edison 51469* 5-8 25

HONOLULU / SHANGHAI SHUFFLE... *Edison 51416* 5-8 24

I'M GONNA CHARLESTON BACK TO CHARLESTON / DEEP ELM (YOU TELL 'EM I'M BLUE)........... *Edison 51574* 5-8 25

LOUISVILLE LOU / MY VIRGINIA................ *Pathe Actuelle 020997* 4-6 23

LOUISVILLE LOU / MY VIRGINIA...... *Perfect 14140* 3-5 23
(Simultaneously released on two labels)

MY SATURDAY EVENING GIRL / IF I STAY AWAY TOO LONG FROM CAROLINA... *Pathe Actuelle 036078* 3-5 24

MY SATURDAY EVENING GIRL / IF I STAY AWAY TOO LONG FROM CAROLINA......... *Perfect 14259* 2-4 24
(Simultaneously released on two labels)

MY WIFE'S IN EUROPE TODAY (Vocal: Johnny Marvin) A LITTLE GIRL, A LITTLE BOY, A LITTLE MOON..................... *Victor 20726* 2-4 27

SORRY FOR ME (Vocal: Lewis James) / LOOK WHAT YOU'VE DONE.......... *Victor 21496* 2-4 28

TESSIE (STOP TEASING ME) / DEAR ONE .... *Edison 51435* 5-8 25

THERE'S YES! YES! IN YOUR EYES / SOUVENIR.................. *Pathe Actuelle 036070* 3-5 24

THERE'S YES! YES! IN YOUR EYES / SOUVENIR.......................... *Perfect 14251* 2-4 24
(Simultaneously released on two labels)

UNDERNEATH THE YUM YUM TREE / WHY IS LOVE?...................... *Edison 51599* 3-5 25

FULCHER, Charles, & His Orchestra

ESKIMO SONG, THE / BLACK CAT BLUES .... *Okeh 4889* 10-12 23

GEORGIA STOMP, THE / HOME SWEET HOME BLUES .... *Columbia 316-D* 5-8 25

HEY! HEY! (Vocal: Charles Fulcher) / MAMA'S GONE, GOODBYE (by Thelma Terry & Her Play Boys) .... *Columbia 1706-D* 5-8 28

I FAW DOWN AND GO 'BOOM'! / ATLANTA GAL .... *Columbia 1734-D* 4-6 29
(Vocals: Unknown)

MY PRETTY GIRL / BLUE FOR YOU .... *Columbia 551-D* 4-6 25

SINCE WE PARTED (Vocal: Charles Fulcher) / BLUE GEORGIA MOON .... *Columbia 726-D* 4-6 26

FULCHER, Charles, as Fulcher's Dance Trio

AFTER THAT / DAYLIGHT'S BREAKING BLUES .... *Columbia 1267-D* 5-8 25

FULLER, Earl, as Earl Fuller's Famous Jazz Band

COON BAND CONTEST, A / LI'L LIZA JANE (Vocal effects by the band) .... *Victor 18394* 3-5 17

JAZORIENT / JAZOLOGY .... *Arto 9009* 4-6 20

JAZORIENT / JAZOLOGY .... *Fuller 1001* 35-40 20

JAZORIENT / JAZOLOGY .... *Meteor 1205* 35-40 20
(The Fuller and Meteor releases are extremely rare.)
(Simultaneously released on three labels)

JAZZ DE LUXE / JAZZBO JAZZ .... *Emerson 952* 3-5 18

OLD GREY MARE, THE / BEALE STREET BLUES .... *Victor 18369* 4-6 17

SLIPPERY HANK / YAH-DE-DAH .... *Victor 18321* 2-4 17

FULLER, Earl, as Earl Fuller's New York Orchestra

AIN'T WE GOT FUN? / JUST BECAUSE .... *Olympic 15116* 5-8 21

JUST BECAUSE / I WONDER WHERE MY SWEET DADDY'S GONE .... *Edison 50824* 4-6 21

FULLER, Earl, as Earl Fuller's Rector Novelty Orchestra

COLD TURKEY / 12TH STREET RAG .... *Columbia A-2298* 3-5 17

EGYPTLAND / MUMMY MINE .... *Columbia A-2722* 2-4 19

GRAVEYARD BLUES / SWEET EMALINA, MY GAL .... *Columbia A-2523* 3-5 18

HOWDY! / RUSSIAN RAG .... *Columbia A-2649* 2-4 18

I AIN'T GOT NOBODY MUCH / DOWN HOME RAG .... *Columbia A-2547* 3-5 18

MICKEY / HERE COMES AMERICA .... *Columbia A-2595* 3-5 18

MORE CANDY / IDA! SWEET AS APPLE CIDER .... *Columbia A-2403* 3-5 17

ONE FLEETING HOUR / CASTLE VALSE CLASSIQUE .... *Columbia A-5989* 2-4 17

RUSPANA / SWEET SIAMESE .... *Columbia A-2712* 2-4 19

SAND DUNES / SPANIOLA .... *Columbia A-2697* 2-4 19

SINGAPORE / OUT OF THE EAST ... *Columbia A-2686* 2-4 19

WE'LL DO OUR SHARE (WHILE YOU'RE OVER THERE) / I WANT HIM BACK AGAIN .... *Columbia A-2566* 3-5 18

FUNK, Larry, & His Band Of A Thousand Melodies

RAIN / I'M LONESOME FOR YOU, CAROLINE .... *Banner 33219* 5-8 34
(Vocals: Vaughn Monroe)

RAIN / I'M LONESOME FOR YOU, CAROLINE .... *Conqueror 8410* 5-8 34
(Vocals: Vaughn Monroe)

RAIN / I'M LONESOME FOR YOU, CAROLINE .... *Melotone 13186* 5-8 34
(Vocals: Vaughn Monroe)

RAIN / I'M LONESOME FOR YOU, CAROLINE .... *Oriole 3014* 5-8 34
(Vocals: Vaughn Monroe)

RAIN / I'M LONESOME FOR YOU, CAROLINE .... *Perfect 16005* 5-8 34
(Vocals: Vaughn Monroe)

RAIN / I'M LONESOME FOR YOU, CAROLINE .... *Romeo 2388* 5-8 34
(Vocals: Vaughn Monroe)
(Simultaneously released on six labels)

TOO BEAUTIFUL FOR WORDS / WHEN YOU'RE IN LOVE .... *Banner 33237* 4-6 34
(Vocals: Vaughn Monroe)

TOO BEAUTIFUL FOR WORDS / WHEN YOU'RE IN LOVE .... *Melotone 13204* 4-6 34
(Vocals: Vaughn Monroe)

TOO BEAUTIFUL FOR WORDS / WHEN YOU'RE IN LOVE .... *Oriole 3014* 4-6 34
(Vocals: Vaughn Monroe)

TOO BEAUTIFUL FOR WORDS / WHEN YOU'RE IN LOVE .... *Perfect 16022* 4-6 34
(Vocals: Vaughn Monroe)

TOO BEAUTIFUL FOR WORDS / WHEN YOU'RE IN LOVE .... *Romeo 2399* 4-6 34
(Vocals: Vaughn Monroe)
(Simultaneously released on five labels)

FURST, Joe, & His Orchestra

AT THE BABY PARADE / DID YOU MEAN WHAT YOU SAID LAST NIGHT? .... *Banner 32649* 5-8 33
(Vocals: Paul Small)

AT THE BABY PARADE / DID YOU MEAN WHAT YOU SAID LAST NIGHT? .... *Melotone M-12580* 5-8 33
(Vocals: Paul Small)

AT THE BABY PARADE / DID YOU MEAN WHAT YOU SAID LAST NIGHT? .... *Oriole 2624* 5-8 33
(Vocals: Paul Small)

AT THE BABY PARADE / DID YOU MEAN WHAT YOU SAID LAST NIGHT? .... *Perfect 15717* 5-8 33
(Vocals: Paul Small)

AT THE BABY PARADE / DID YOU MEAN WHAT YOU SAID LAST NIGHT? .... *Romeo 1999* 5-8 33
(Vocals: Paul Small)
(Simultaneously released on five labels)

GAILLARD, Slim, & His Flat Foot Floogie Boys
(Slim Gaillard: 1/14/16 –)

AH NOW / BASSOLOGY .... *Okeh 6295* 3-5 41

A-WELL-A-TAKE-UM-A-JOE (CRAPSHOOTER'S JIVE) / CHICKEN RHYTHM.......... *Vocalion 5138* 4-6 39

BABY BE MINE / SPLOGHM........... *Vocalion 5619* 3-5 40

BEATIN' THE BOARD / LOOK OUT .... *Vocalion 5483* 3-5 39

BINGIE-BINGIE-SCOOTIE / CHAMPAGNE LULLABY .... *Okeh 6382* 3-5 41

CHITTLIN' SWITCH BLUES / HUH! OH HUH! .... *Vocalion 5341* 5-8 39

DON'T LET US SAY GOODBYE / BROADWAY JUMP .... *Okeh 5792* 4-6 40

•IT'S YOU, ONLY YOU / MATZOH BALLS.................... *Vocalion 5301* 3-5 39

LOOKIN' FOR A PLACE TO PARK / HIT THAT MESS .... *Okeh 6260* 4-6 40

PUT YOUR ARMS AROUND ME, BABY / HEY! CHIEF .... *Okeh 6088* 4-6 40

RHYTHM MAD / BONGO .... *Okeh 6015* 4-6 40

SWINGIN' IN THE KEY OF C / BOOT–TA–LA–ZA .... *Vocalion 5388* 4-6 39

THAT'S A BRINGER, THAT'S A HANGER / EARLY IN THE MORNING.................... *Vocalion 5220* 4-6 39

TIP ON THE NUMBERS, A / SLIM SLAM BOOGIE.................. *Okeh 6135* 5-8 41

WINDY CITY HOP / FITZWATER STREET............................ *Vocalion 5557* 4-6 40

GAILLARD, Slim, as Slim & Slam

DANCING ON THE BEACH / FERDINAND THE BULL.......................... *Vocalion 4110* 5-8 38

DOPEY JOE / BUCK DANCE RHYTHM... *Vocalion 4521* 5-8 38

8, 9 AND 10 / OH, LADY BE GOOD...... *Vocalion 4163* 5-8 38

FLAT FOOT FLOOGIE, THE / CHINATOWN, MY CHINATOWN .... *Vocalion 4021* 5-8 38

HUMPTY DUMPTY / LAUGHIN' IN RHYTHM....................... *Vocalion 4461* 4-6 38

JUMP SESSION / VOL VIST DU GAILY STAR.................... *Vocalion 4346* 5-8 38

SWEET SAFRONIA / IT'S GETTIN' KINDA CHILLY..................... *Vocalion 4594* 4-6 39

THAT'S WHAT YOU CALL ROMANCE / TI–PI–TIN .... *Vocalion 3981* 4-6 38

TUTTI FRUTTI / LOOK-A THERE...... *Vocalion 4225* 4-6 38

GARBER, Jan, & His Greater Columbia Recording Orchestra
(Jan Garber: 11/5/97 – 10/5/77)
(The Jan Garber Orchestra continues to play engagements under the leadership of Dick Whitman.)

PUTTIN' ON THE RITZ / WHEN A WOMAN LOVES A MAN.................. *Columbia 2115-D* 10-12 30
(Vocals: Unknown)

GARBER, Jan, & His Orchestra

ALL I DO IS DREAM OF YOU (Vocal: Fritz Heilbron) / GRANDFATHER'S CLOCK
(Vocal: Lee Bennett) .... *Victor 24629* 2-4 34

AVALON / STARDUST .... *Brunswick 8039* 3-5 37

BOULEVARD OF BROKEN DREAMS / TEMPTATION........................ *Victor 24498* 2-4 34
(Vocals: Lee Bennett)

BRIGHT LIGHTS AND BLONDE-HAIRED WOMEN (Vocal: Roy Cordell) / WHERE THE RED ROSES GROW
(Vocals: Roy Cordell & Joy Conley).......... *Capitol 1483* 2-4 51

BROWN BIRD SINGING, A / CHLOE ... *Vocalion 5196* 2-4 39

BUT WHERE ARE YOU? (Vocal: Lee Bennett) / I'M PUTTING ALL MY EGGS IN ONE BASKET
(Vocal: Fritz Heilbron)...................... *Decca 699* 4-6 36

DOING WHAT COMES NATUR'LLY (Vocals: June Arthur & The Foursome) / THE GYPSY
(Vocal: Tommy Traynor)............ *Black & White 774* 2-4 46

DOROTHY (Vocal: Jack Gifford) / THERE'S A BLUE RIDGE IN MY HEART, VIRGINIA ..... *Victor 20114* 2-4 26

EVERYTHING YOU SAID CAME TRUE / I'VE HITCHED MY WAGON TO A STAR... *Brunswick 8018* 2-4 38
(Vocals: Unknown)

GAZING AT A BLAZING FIRE / MY SUGAR TAKES ME WITH A GRAIN OF SALT.......... *Brunswick 7820* 3-5 37
(Vocals: Unknown)

HOT CANARY, THE (Vocals: The Ewing Sisters) / THAT'S HOW OUR LOVE WILL GROW
(Vocal: Roy Cordell) .... *Capitol 1430* 2-4 51

I'LL SEE YOU IN MY DREAMS / SOMEBODY LOVES ME (Vocal: Lee Bennett) .... *Okeh 5319* 2-4 39

I WANT THE WAITER (WITH THE WATER) (Vocal: Fritz Heilbron) / WORLD'S FAIR WALTZ (Vocal: Lee Bennett) .... *Vocalion 5012* 2-4 39

I WANT TO BE HAPPY / I NEVER CARE 'BOUT TOMORROW................... *Victor 19404* 3-5 24

LAZY LOU'SIANA MOON (Vocals: Unknown) / — .... *Hit Of The Week 1043* 4-6 30
(Hit Of The Week records are one-sided paper discs)

LOVE CAME OUT OF THE NIGHT / A LITTLE RENDEZVOUS IN HONOLULU .... *Decca 693* 4-6 36
(Vocals: Lee Bennett)

MY WONDERFUL ONE (Vocal: Russell Brown) / MY BUDDY (Vocal: Lew Palmer)........... *Decca 1008* 4-6 36

OBJECT OF MY AFFECTION, THE / BLAME IT ON MY YOUTH...................... *Victor 24809* 3-5 35
(Vocals: Lee Bennett)

ON THE SENTIMENTAL SIDE / MY HEART IS TAKING LESSONS................ *Brunswick 8065* 2-4 38
(Vocals: Russell Brown)

POSITIVELY-ABSOLUTELY (Vocal: Harry Goldfield) / YOU DON'T LIKE IT – NOT MUCH
(Vocals: Harry Goldfield & Webb Hahne) ..... *Victor 20676* 4-6 27

RHYTHM SAVED THE WORLD (Vocal: Fritz Heilbron) / BASIN STREET BLUES
(Vocal: Lee Bennett)............................ *Decca 803* 4-6 36

ROMANCE IN THE DARK (Vocal: Russ Brown) / I LOVE TO WHISTLE (Vocal: Fritz Heilbron) ... *Brunswick 8102* 3-5 38

SHINE ON HARVEST MOON / AMONG MY SOUVENIRS...................... *Decca 1007* 3-5 36
(Vocals: Lew Palmer)

SINCE MY BEST GIRL TURNED ME DOWN (Vocal: Harry Goldfield) / I WISH I COULD SHIMMY LIKE MY SISTER KATE............... *Columbia 1306-D* 5-8 28

SOMEBODY LOVES ME (Vocal: Lee Bennett) / I'LL SEE YOU IN MY DREAMS..... *Conqueror 9497* 2-4 39

SOMEBODY LOVES ME (Vocal: Lee Bennett) / I'LL SEE YOU IN MY DREAMS....... *Vocalion 5319* 2-4 39
(Simultaneously released on two labels)

SWEET MARIE / BYE-BYE, PRETTY BABY...................... *Victor 20833* 2-4 27
(Vocals: Johnny Marvin)

TOUCH OF YOUR LIPS, THE / LOST....... *Decca 739* 3-5 36
(Vocals: Lee Bennett)

UNTIL THE REAL THING COMES ALONG / YOU TURNED THE TABLES ON ME.......... *Decca 891* 3-5 36
(Vocals: Russell Brown)

WAITIN' FOR THE MOON / DON'T BRING LULU.................. *Victor 19661* 3-5 25

WASHINGTON AND LEE SWING / V.M.I. SPIRIT .... *Columbia 1452-D* 3-5 28
(Vocals: by chorus)

WAS IT A DREAM? (Vocal: Sonny Faircloth) / SHE'S A GREAT, GREAT GIRL (Vocal: Harry Goldfield as Goldie) .... *Columbia 1372-D* 5-8 29

'WAY DOWN YONDER IN NEW ORLEANS / THAT'S WHY I'M HAPPY................ *Columbia 1823-D* 3-5 29
(Vocals: Unknown)

WEARY RIVER / CARESSING YOU ... *Columbia 1724-D* 3-5 29
(Vocals: Unknown)

WE'LL REST AT THE END OF THE TRAIL / MEXICALI ROSE .... *Decca 792* 3-5 36
(Vocals: Lee Bennett)

WHISTLIN' COWBOY / ON THE WRONG SIDE OF THE FENCE................ *Victor 24507* 2-4 34
(Vocals: Lee Bennett)

WHO LOVED YOU BEST? (Vocal: Jack Gifford) / CROSS WORDS BETWEEN SWEETIE AND ME............................ *Victor 19708* 2-4 25

ZITHER BLUES / HONKY TONK BLUES (Vocal: Roy Cordell) .... *Capitol 2068* 2-4 53

GARBER, Jan, as The Garber-Davis Orchestra

DEEP IN YOUR EYES / HONEYMOON BAY............... *Columbia A-3683* 2-4 22

HAUNTING BLUES / IF YOU DON'T THINK SO, YOU'RE CRAZY .... *Columbia A-3781* 3-5 22

LIST'NING ON SOME RADIO / YOU'RE THE GIRL (I'M CRAZY ABOUT) .... *Columbia A-3782* 2-4 22

TEASIN' / IN MY HEART, ON MY MIND ALL DAY........... *Columbia A-3600* 3-5 22

TEE PEE BLUES / I'VE GOT MY HABITS ON .... *Columbia A-3675* 3-5 22

THAT BRAN' NEW GAL OF MINE / YOU'RE IN KENTUCKY SURE AS YOU'RE BORN ...... *Victor 19216* 3-5 24

GARCIA, Louis "King", & His Swing Band
(Louis "King" Garcia: 8/25/05 –)

CHRISTOPHER COLUMBUS / SWING, MR. CHARLIE .... *Montgomery Ward M-4891* 5-8 36
(Vocals: Dan Darcy)

CHRISTOPHER COLUMBUS / THERE IS NO GREATER LOVE................ *Bluebird B-6303* 5-8 36
(Vocals: Dan Darcy)

IT'S GREAT TO BE IN LOVE AGAIN / LOVE IS LIKE A CIGARETTE....................... *Bluebird B-6302* 5-8 36
(Vocals: Dan Darcy)

IT'S GREAT TO BE IN LOVE AGAIN / LOVE IS LIKE A CIGARETTE.......... *Montgomery Ward M-4996* 5-8 36
(Vocals: Dan Darcy)
(Simultaneously released on two labels)

SWING, MR. CHARLIE (Vocal: Dan Darcy) / SWEET GIRL (by Boots Douglas as Boots & His Buddies; Vocal: Celeste Allen) .... *Bluebird B-6357* 5-8 36

GARDEN DANCING PALACE ORCHESTRA, The

NIGHT TIME IN PICARDY / MY WILD IRISH ROSE .... *Columbia 1147-D* 2-4 27

ROSE ROOM / DEEP HOLLOW...... *Columbia 1501-D* 3-5 28

SUNSHINE / I'M AFRAID YOU SING THAT SONG TO SOMEBODY ELSE...... *Columbia 1171-D* 2-4 27
(Vocals: Unknown)

WHEN ERASTUS PLAYS HIS OLD KAZOO / MY LITTLE HOME (by Earl Burtnett & His Los Angeles Biltmore Hotel Orchestra)............ *Columbia 1599-D* 3-5 28

GARDNER, Fred, as Fred Gardner's Texas University Troubadours

LOVELESS LOVE / PAPA'S GONE........ *Okeh 41440* 12-15 30
(Vocals: Jay "Bird" Thomas)

LOVELESS LOVE / PAPA'S GONE... *Odeon ONY-36135* 12-15 30
(Vocals: Jay "Bird" Thomas)
(Simultaneously released on two labels)

NO TRUMPS / DANIEL'S BLUES (Vocal: Jay "Bird" Thomas) .... *Okeh 41458* 12-15 30

GARDNER, Jack, as Jack Gardner's Orchestra
(Jack Gardner: 8/14/03 – 11/26/57)

BY THE RIVER NILE / HITCH UP THE HORSES (Vocal: Stanton Crocker) ..... *Okeh 40495* 5-8 24

GIVE ME JUST A LITTLE BIT / JAPP-A-JAZZ.......................... *Okeh 40555* 5-8 25

HOT AIRE / THE CAMEL WALK.......... *Okeh 40518* 5-8 25

IDA, I DO / WHEN A BLONDE MAKES UP HER MIND TO DO YOU GOOD (Vocal: Stanton Crocker) ... *Okeh 40501* 5-8 25

PONJOLA / I KNOW SHE DOES (Vocal: Stanton Crocker) .... *Okeh 40245* 4-6 24

TOO LATE NOW / BLACKIN' BLUES (Vocal: Stanton Crocker)............ *Okeh 40265* 5-8 24

WHO? YOU! (Vocal: Dillon White) / WHO'D A THUNK IT?................... *Okeh 40339* 4-6 24

YOU'LL NEVER KNOW THE DIFFERENCE (A HUNDRED YEARS FROM NOW) (Vocals: Belcanto Quartet) / I'M A LITTLE PRAIRIE FLOWER (I'M WILD, I'M WILD) (Vocal: Stanton Crocker).... *Okeh 40572* 4-6 25

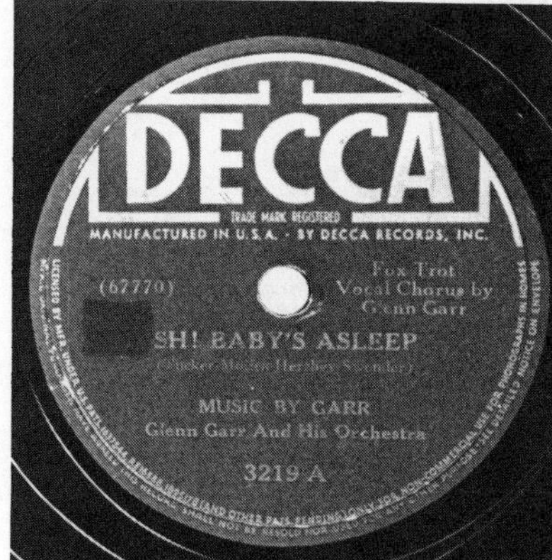

GARR, Glenn, & His Orchestra

SH! BABY'S ASLEEP / IT'S THE LAST TIME I'LL FALL IN LOVE.................... *Decca 3219* 4-6 40
(Vocals: Glenn Garr)

GERITY, Julia, & Her Play Boys:
see FRIEDMAN, Snooks, as Snooks & His Memphis Ramblers / Stompers

GERUNOVITCH, Tom, & His Roof Garden Orchestra
(also see GERUN, Tom, & His Orchestra)
(Tom Gerunovitch subsequently used the name Tom Gerun.)

I GOTTA TELL SOMEONE / OLD MAN SUNSHINE............. *Brunswick 4115* 5-8 28
(Vocals: Biff Hoffman)

I'M TELLING YOU (Vocal: Jimmy Davis) / I FOUND YOU OUT WHEN I FOUND YOU IN SOMEBODY ELSE'S ARMS (Vocal: Steve Bowers)........... *Brunswick 4179* 5-8 29

STAIRWAY OF DREAMS (Vocal: Steve Bowers) / THAT'S THE GOOD OLD SUNNY SOUTH (Vocals: by trio)........ *Brunswick 4277* 5-8 29

THERE'S A RAINBOW 'ROUND MY SHOULDER (Vocal: Steve Bowers) / MY GAL SAL........ *Brunswick 4050* 5-8 28

YOU TELL ME YOUR DREAM AND I'LL TELL YOU MINE (Vocals: by chorus) / SINCERELY I DO........ *Brunswick 4047* 4-6 28

GERUN, Tom, & His Orchestra
(also see GERUNOVITCH, Tom, & His Roof Garden Orchestra
(Tom Gerun's real name was Tom Gerunovitch and he also made records under that name)

AM I BLUE? (Vocal: Jimmy Davis) / LET ME HAVE MY DREAMS (Vocal: Steve Bowers)........ *Brunswick 4429* 4-6 29

AROUND THE CORNER / ABSENCE MAKES THE HEART GROW FONDER (FOR SOMEBODY ELSE)........ *Brunswick 4829* 3-5 30
(Vocals: Unknown)

BOOGIE MAN IS HERE, THE (Vocal: Steve Bowers) / THERE'S SUGAR CANE AROUND MY DOOR (Vocal: Jimmy Davis)........ *Brunswick 4430* 5-8 29

IN MY LITTLE HOPE CHEST / SING, YOU SINNERS........ *Brunswick 4727* 4-6 30
(Vocals: Unknown)

LADY I LOVE, THE / IN A SHANTY IN OLD SHANTY TOWN........ *Brunswick 6353* 5-8 32
(Vocals: Smith Ballew)

MEMORIES OF YOU / YOU'RE LUCKY TO ME........ *Brunswick 4916* 4-6 30
(Vocals: Unknown)

MY HEART'S AT EASE (Vocal: Jean Wakefield) / LONESOME ME (Vocal: Woody Herman)........ *Brunswick 6364* 5-8 32

ONE SWEET KISS / SOME DAY SOON........ *Brunswick 4521* 4-6 29
(Vocals: by chorus)

GENE'S MERRYMAKERS:
see KARDOS, Gene, & His Orchestra

GENTILE, Al, & The Americans

BLOWIN' THE BLUES AWAY / SUNNY DISPOSISH........ *Gennett 3379* 4-6 26
(Vocals: Jack Kaufman)

GENTILE, Al, as A. Gentile's Dance Orchestra

WEEP NO MORE, MY MAMMY / I WANT MY MAMMY........ *Gennett 4808* 3-5 22

GEORGIA MELODIANS, The:
see BOULANGER, Charles

GEORGIANS, The:
see SPECHT, Paul

GERBRECHT, Edward, "Pinkie", as Pinkie's Birmingham Five

HEADIN' FOR LOUISVILLE / CAROLINA STOMP........ *Gennett 3208* 12-15 26

SENTIMENTAL GENTLEMAN FROM GEORGIA (Vocal: Woody Herman) / WE WERE ONLY WALKING IN THE MOONLIGHT (Vocals: Jean Wakefield & Steve Bowers)........ *Brunswick 6371* 4-6 32

SWEETHEARTS FOREVER / THREE'S A CROWD........ *Brunswick 6365* 4-6 32
(Vocals: Smith Ballew)

WEB OF LOVE, THE / THE NEW STEP........ *Brunswick 4519* 4-6 29
(Vocals: by chorus)

WHEN WE'RE ALONE (PENTHOUSE SERENADE) / ALL OF ME........ *Brunswick 6236* 4-6 32
(Vocals: Scappy Lambert)

GILL, Emerson, & His Bamboo Garden Orchestra

WILL YOU BE SORRY? / THAT'S WHAT I CALL KEEN........ *Columbia 1396-D* 4-6 28
(Vocals: Pinkey Hunter)

YALE BLUES, THE / DANCE OF THE BLUE DANUBE........ *Columbia 1355-D* 4-6 28
(Vocals: Pinkey Hunter)

GILL, Emerson, & His Castle of Paris Orchestra

MY BUNDLE OF LOVE (Vocal: Pinkey Hunter) / THE RHYTHM RAG........ *Okeh 40594* 5-8 26

WEARY / LO-NAH........ *Okeh 40615* 5-8 26

GILL, Emerson, & His Orchestra

HOME IN PASADENA / DAYS OF YESTERDAY........ *Okeh 40066* 4-6 24

ON SATURDAY NIGHT / MOBILE BLUES... *Okeh 40065* 5-8 24

GILLETTE, Mickey, & His Romanciers

WILL YOU REMEMBER, SWEETHEART? / MOONLIGHT ON THE DANUBE (Vocal: Lee Lykins)........ *Victor 21385* 5-8 28

GLANTZ, Nathan, & His Orchestra

BENAMOR / IT AIN'T GONNA RAIN NO MO'........ *Gennett 5591* 3-5 24

HOT ROASTED PEANUTS / TWO-TIME DAN........ *Pathe Actuelle 021051* 3-5 23

HOT ROASTED PEANUTS / TWO-TIME DAN........ *Perfect 14169* 2-4 23
(Simultaneously released on two labels)

LOOSE FEET / RUNNING WILD........ *Pathe Actuelle 020883* 3-5 23

LOOSE FEET / RUNNING WILD........ *Perfect 14-76* 2-4 23
(Simultaneously released on two labels)

MY OLD PLANTATION HOME / LOVIN' SAM........ *Emerson 10554* 2-4 22

OH, SARAH! WON'T YOU PLEASE PULL DOWN THAT SHADE? / SORRY FOR YOU........ *Okeh 40154* 2-4 24

STARS (Vocal: Arthur Hall) / WHEN BUDDHA SMILES........ *Paramount 20089* 4-6 22

STARS (Vocal: Arthur Hall) / WHEN BUDDHA SMILES........ *Puritan 11089* 2-4 22
(Simultaneously released on two labels)

STARS / SONG OF INDIA........ *Gennett 4810* 2-4 22

STATE STREET BLUES / SUEZ........ *Gennett 4875* 3-5 22

WHEN LIGHTS ARE LOW / DREAM BOAT........ *Federal 5372* 3-5 24

YES, SIR, THAT'S MY BABY / LINDEY........ *Everybody's 1058* 10-12 25

GLANTZ, Nathan, & His Orchestra as Ray Collins' Orchestra

AGGRAVATIN' PAPA / PEGGY DEAR... *Banner 1168* 3-5 23

GLANTZ, Nathan, & His Orchestra as The Majestic Dance Orchestra

AGGRAVATIN' PAPA / PEGGY DEAR..... *Regal 9440* 3-5 23

ARE YOU LONESOME TONIGHT? / TIRED HANDS........ *Banner 6103* 2-4 27
(Vocals: Unknown)

TRICKS / COAL BLACK MAMMY... *Pathe Actuelle 020820* 3-5 22

TRICKS / COAL BLACK MAMMY........ *Perfect 14046* 2-4 22
(Simultaneously released on two labels)

GLANTZ, Nathan, & His Orchestra as Straun's Pullman Porters

CASEY JONES (Vocal: Chick Straun) / A HOT TIME IN THE OLD TOWN........ *Gennett 3005* 3-5 25

GLANTZ, Nathan, & His Orchestra as the Texas Ten

SWEET GEORGIA BROWN / CHARLESTON........ *Banner 1540* 3-5 25

SWEET GEORGIA BROWN / CHARLESTON........ *Domino 3510* 3-5 25

SWEET GEORGIA BROWN / CHARLESTON........ *Regal 9835* 3-5 25
(Simultaneously released on three labels)

GLOBE MUSIC MASTERS, The:
see SELVIN, Ben, & His Orchestra

GLORIA PALACE ORCHESTRA, The:
see KARDOS, Gene, & His Orchestra

GLUSKIN, Lud, & His (Continental) Orchestra
(Lud Gluskin: 1901 –)

CONTINENTAL, THE (Vocal: Joe Host) / LA CUCARACHA (Vocal: "Chiquito")..... *Columbia 2952-D* 5-8 34
(This record was pressed in blue shellac)

HERE'S TO ROMANCE / MIDNIGHT IN PARIS........ *Brunswick 7536* 3-5 35
(Vocals: Buddy Clark)

MAY I HAVE THE NEXT ROMANCE WITH YOU? / HEAD OVER HEELS IN LOVE..... *Brunswick 7788* 3-5 37
(Vocals: Buddy Clark)

MOON OVER MIAMI (Vocal: Buddy Clark) / THE GHOST OF THE RUMBA...... *Brunswick 7590* 3-5 36

MY FIRST THRILL / SHE SHALL HAVE MUSIC........ *Brunswick 7658* 3-5 36
(Vocals: Buddy Clark)

ON THE AIR / SUNSHINE AT MIDNIGHT........ *Brunswick 7664* 3-5 36
(Vocals: Buddy Clark)

RAINBOW ON THE RIVER / YOU'RE TOO GOOD TO BE TRUE........ *Brunswick 7779* 3-5 37
(Vocals: Buddy Clark)

RHYTHM AND ROMANCE / RED SAILS IN THE SUNSET........ *Brunswick 7535* 4-6 35
(Vocals: Buddy Clark)

SPEAK TO ME WITH YOUR EYES / HANDS ACROSS THE TABLE........ *Columbia 2970-D* 5-8 34
(Vocals: Buddy Clark)

SWEET MUSIC / JUST MENTION JOE........ *Columbia 2987-D* 5-8 35
(Vocals: Buddy Clark)

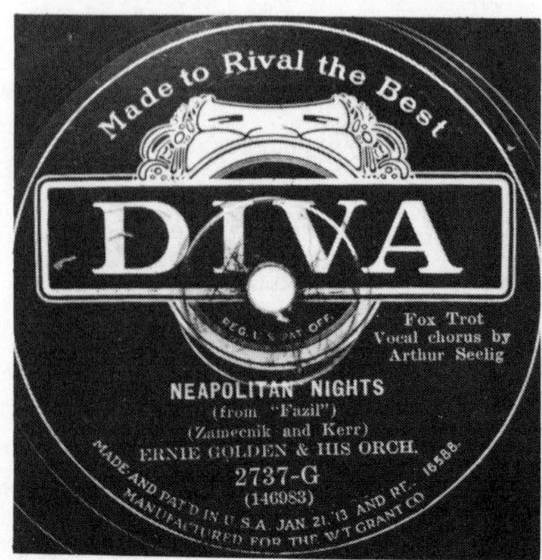

GOLDEN, Ernie & His Orchestra

ALWAYS / ALWAYS (Vocal: Irving Kaufman with orchestral accompaniment)......... Harmony 110-H 2-4 26

DOIN' THE RACCOON / COME ON BABY......................... Conqueror 7219 3-5 29
(Vocals: Irving Kaufman)

HELLO BEAUTIFUL / PLEASE DON'T TALK ABOUT ME WHEN I'M GONE............ Champion 16217 3-5 31
(Vocals: Tommy Weir)

MY LITTLE BUTTERFLY (Vocals: Tom and Roy) / LITTLE WHITE LIES (by Harry Reser as The Clicquot Club Eskimos; Vocal: Speed Young)..................... Banner 0755 3-5 30

ON THE SUNNY SIDE OF THE STREET / DANCING WITH TEARS IN MY EYES........... Gennett 7212 3-5 30
(Vocals: Tommy Weir)

SONNY BOY / NEOPOLITAN NIGHTS........................... Harmony 737-H 3-5 28
(Vocals: Arthur Seelig)

SONNY BOY / NEOPOLITAN NIGHTS... Diva 2737-G 3-5 28
(Vocals: Arthur Seelig)
(Simultaneously released on two labels)

TILL WE MEET (Vocal: Jack Kerr) / MEAN TO ME (Vocals: by trio)........... Gennett 6802 3-5 29

GOLDEN GATE ORCHESTRA, The:
see California Ramblers, The

GOLDEN GATE SYNCOPATORS, The:
see California Ramblers, The

GOLDEN TERRACE ORCHESTRA, The:
see SELVIN, Ben, & His Orchestra

GOLDKETTE, Jean, & His Orchestra
(Jean Goldkette: 3/18/99 – 3/24-62)

AFTER I SAY I'M SORRY (Vocals: Frank Bessinger) / DINAH.............................. Victor 19947 5-8 26

BIRMINGHAM BERTHA (Vocals: Kay Palmer, male vocalist) AND ESPECIALLY YOU! (by The Coon-Sanders Orchestra; Vocal: Joe Sanders)............. Victor 22077 5-8 29

BLUE RIVER (Vocal: Lewis James) / WHEN MORNING GLORIES WAKE UP IN THE MORNING (by Jacques Renard & His Cocoanut Grove Orchestra; Vocal: Johnny Marvin)..................... Victor 20981 5-8 27

COVER ME UP WITH SUNSHINE (Vocal: Frank Bessinger) / MY PRETTY GIRL............................... Victor 20588 8-10 27

GIMME A LITTLE KISS, WILL YOU? HUH? (Vocals: by orchestra) / LONESOME AND SORRY (Vocals: Carl Mathieu & James Stanley)............. Victor 20031 5-8 26

HOOSIER SWEETHEART (Vocal: Ray Muerer) / WHAT DOES IT MATTER (by Nat Shilkret & The Victor Orchestra; Vocal: Elliot Shaw)...................... Victor 20471 5-8 27

IDOLIZING / HUSH-A-BYE............ Victor 20270 5-8 27
(Vocals: Frank Bessinger)

I'D RATHER BE THE GIRL IN YOUR ARMS (Vocal: Frank Bessinger) / SUNDAY (Vocals: The Keller Sisters & Al Lynch)...... Victor 20273 4-6 26

I'M GONNA MEET MY SWEETIE NOW / SLOW RIVER....... Victor 25354 8-10 36
(A 1927 recording first released in 1936.)

I'M LOOKING OVER A FOUR LEAF CLOVER (Vocal: Billy Murray) / YANKEE ROSE (Vocals: Roger Wolfe Kahn & His Orchestra)......... Victor 20466 8-10 27

IN MY MERRY OLDSMOBILE (in waltz tempo) / IN MY MERRY OLDSMOBILE (in fox trot tempo; vocals: Ray Lodwig, Doc Ryker, & Howdy Quicksell).... Victor Special 125-150 27
(A promotional release, un-numbered, and extremely rare.)

IN THE EVENING / WHERE THE LAZY DAISIES GROW...................... Victor 19308 5-8 24

I WANT TO SEE MY TENNESEE / REMEMBER (Vocals: Seymour Simons).... Victor 19548 4-6 25

LANE IN SPAIN, A (Vocals: Lewis James, Charles Harrison, Elliott Shaw and Wilfred Glenn) / IF ALL THE STARS WERE PRETTY BABIES (by the B. F. Goodrich Silvertown Cord Orchestra; Vocals: Joseph White, the "Silver-Masked Tenor")......... Victor 20491 5-8 27

MY BLACKBIRDS ARE BLUEBIRDS NOW (Vocals: Van Fleming) / DON'T BE LIKE THAT (Vocals: Harold Stokes)............. Victor 21805 8-10 29

MY OHIO HOME (Vocal: Hoagy Carmichael) / HERE COMES THE SHOWBOAT (Vocals: Myron Schultz, Ray Porter, & Harold Stokes)............. Victor 21166 4-6 28

OLD ITALIAN LOVE SONG / GOTTA GREAT BIG DATE WITH A LITTLE BITTA GIRL (by The Coon-Sanders Orchestra)..................... Victor 22123 3-5 29

PAINTING THE CLOUDS WITH SUNSHINE / TIP-TOE THROUGH THE TULIPS WITH ME.... Victor 22027 3-5 29
(Vocals: Frank Munn)

PLAY ME SLOW / WHAT'S THE USE OF DREAMING?...................... Victor 19664 5-8 25

ROSETTE / FOR OLD TIMES' SAKE..... Victor 21527 3-5 28
(Vocals: Frank Wilson)

SO TIRED (Vocal: Hoagy Carmichael) / JUST A LITTLE KISS FROM A LITTLE MISS (Vocals: Lorin Schulz, Myron Schulz, & Ray Porter)........................... 21150 3-5 28

SUNNY DISPOSISH (Vocals: Lewis James, Charles Harrison, Elliot Shaw, & Wilfred Glenn) / A LITTLE BIRDIE TOLD ME SO (by Roger Wolfe Kahn & His Orchestra; Vocal: Johnny Marvin)................... Victor 20493 8-10 27

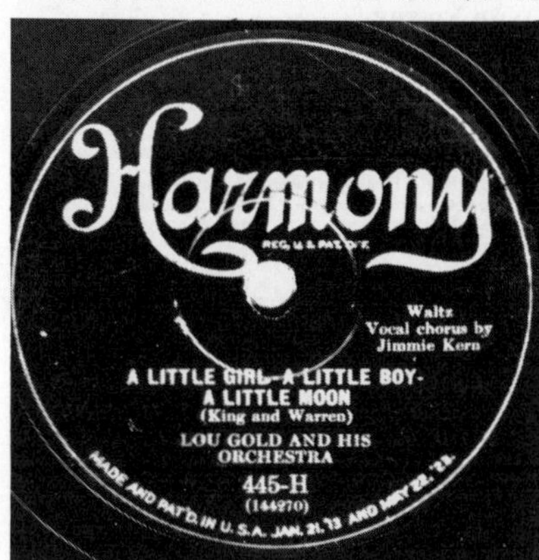

SWEETHEARTS ON PARADE (Vocal: Van Fleming) / THAT'S WHAT PUTS THE "SWEET" IN HOME, SWEET HOME (Vocal: Harold Stokes)..... Victor 21800 3-5 29

TAKE A GOOD LOOK AT MINE (Vocal: Harold Stokes) /YA COMIN' UP TONIGHT, HUH? (Vocals: Wynken-Blynken-Nod)............. Victor 21889 5-8 29

GOLDKETTE, Jean, as Goldkette's Book-Cadillac Orchestra

I'D LOVE TO CALL YOU MY SWEETHEART / KENTUCKY LULLABY.................. Victor 20257 3-5 26

THERE'S A LITTLE WHITE HOUSE ON A LITTLE GREEN HILL / JUST A BIRD'S EYE VIEW OF MY OLD KENTUCKY HOME.............. Victor 20268 3-5 26

GOLD, Lou, & His Orchestra

BREAKAWAY / THAT'S YOU, BABY (Vocals: Unknown)............. Harmony 924-H 3-5 29

FLAPPER WIFE, THE / —................ Cameo 735 5-8 25

I'M SOMEBODY NOBODY LOVES / DON'T MIND THE RAIN............................ Cameo 542 2-4 24

IT'S TIGHT LIKE THAT (Vocal: Irving Kaufman as Robert Wood) / ALL I WANT IS 'ITTLE OOTSIE OO (Vocals: Unknown)........ Harmony 851-H 3-5 29

KEEP YOUR SKIRTS DOWN, MARY ANN / JUST AROUND THE CORNER.......... Cameo 860 5-8 26
(Vocals: Unknown)

LITTLE GIRL – A LITTLE BOY – A LITTLE MOON, A (Vocal: Jimmie Kern) / CHARMAINE! (by Frank Farrell & His Greenwich Village Inn Orchestra; Vocal: Arthur Fields)..... Harmony 445-H 2-4 27

PLENTY OF SUNSHINE / WHO GIVES YOU ALL YOUR KISSES?............. Perfect 14914 3-5 28
(Vocals: Annette Hanshaw)

PRECIOUS LITTLE THING CALLED LOVE / BUY, BUY FOR BABY (OR BABY WILL BYE-BYE YOU).................. Harmony 814-H 2-4 29
(Vocals: Irving Kaufman as Tom Frawley)

PRECIOUS LITTLE THING CALLED LOVE / BUY, BUY FOR BABY (OR BABY WILL BYE-BYE YOU).................. Puritone 1037-S 10-12 29
(Vocals: Irving Kaufman as Tom Frawley)
(Simultaneously released on two labels)

SHOO SHOO BOOGIE BOO / CHANT OF THE JUNGLE....................... Gennett 7029 4-6 30
(Vocals: Sid Garry)

GOLD, Lou, & His Orchestra as The Miami Melodists

SINCE I FOUND YOU / BLAME IT ON THE WALTZ (by Lou Gold & His Orchestra as The Virginia Creepers)............ Pathe Actuelle 36588 5-8 27
(Vocals: Harry Jockin)
(A rare marbled wax disc, forerunner of the multi-colored vinyl records which would become so popular fifty years later.)

GOLD, Lou, & His Orchestra as Barney Trimble & His Oklahomans

BLUE, TURNING GREY OVER YOU / NOBODY'S USING IT NOW................. Harmony 1093-H 4-6 30
(Vocals: Unknown)

GOLD, Lou, & His Orchestra as Rex King & His Sovereigns

LOVE VOWS (Vocal: Chick Bullock as Rex King) / SOMEWHERE IN OLD WYOMING (by Ben Selvin as The Bar Harbor Society Orchestra; Vocal: Irving Kaufman as Robert Wood)..................... Clarion 5089-C 4-6 30

GOLD, Lou, & His Orchestra as The Virginia Creepers

PLENTY OF SUNSHINE / WHO GIVES YOU ALL YOUR KISSES?............... Pathe Actuelle 36733 4-6 28
(Vocals: Annette Hanshaw)

BLAME IT ON THE WALTZ / SINCE I FOUND YOU (by Lou Gold & His Orchestra as The Miami Melodists)............ Pathe Actuelle 36588 5-8 27
(Vocals: Harry Jockin)
(A rare marbled wax disc, forerunner of the multi-colored vinyl records which would become so popular fifty years later.)

GOODMAN, Al, & His Orchestra

LOVABLE AND SWEET / MY DREAM MEMORY......................... Brunswick 4488 4-6 29
(Vocals: Unknown)

NOLA / BEAUTIFUL OHIO........... Victor 46-0007 2-4 -
(An oversize 12-inch 78 rpm)

TICO TICO / SOFTLY AS IN A MORNING SUNRISE.......... Victor 28-0403 2-4 -
(An oversize 12-inch 78 rpm)

GOODMAN, Benny, & His Music Hall Orchestra
(Benny Goodman: 5/30/09 –)
(Benny Goodman is known as the "King of Swing," and is credited with setting the big band era into motion in 1935, at the Palomar Ballroom in Hollywood, California. Now 76, Goodman remains active, appearing in concerts, and was the winner of Down Beat Magazine's poll for best clarinetist in 1983.)

COKEY / MUSIC HALL RAG........ *Columbia 3011-D* 10-12 35

I'M A HUNDRED PER CENT FOR YOU (Vocal: Helen Ward) / LIKE A BOLT FROM THE BLUE (Vocal: Buddy Clark) ..... *Columbia 2988-D* 12-15 35
(This record was pressed in blue shellac.)

NITWIT SERENADE / BUGLE CALL RAG............... *Columbia 2958-D* 15-20 34
(This record was pressed in blue shellac.)

TAKE MY WORD / IT HAPPENS TO THE BEST OF FRIENDS (Vocal: Ann Graham)....... *Columbia 2947-D* 15-20 34
(This record was pressed in blue shellac.)

GOODMAN, Benny, & His Music Hall Orchestra as The Modernists

SOLITUDE / I'M GETTING SENTIMENTAL OVER YOU (Vocal: Tony Sacco).......... *Banner 33192* 12-15 34

SOLITUDE / I'M GETTING SENTIMENTAL OVER YOU (Vocal: Tony Sacco)........... *Oriole 2990* 12-15 34

SOLITUDE / I'M GETTING SENTIMENTAL OVER YOU (Vocal: Tony Sacco).......... *Perfect 16002* 12-15 34

SOLITUDE / I'M GETTING SENTIMENTAL OVER YOU (Vocal: Tony Sacco).......... *Romeo 2364* 12-15 34
(Simultaneously released on four labels)

GOODMAN, Benny, & His Music Hall Orchestra as Vincent Rose & His Orchestra

LEARNING / STARS FELL ON ALABAMA...................... *Banner 33191* 12-15 34
(Vocals: Tony Sacco)

LEARNING / STARS FELL ON ALABAMA.................. *Melotone M-13158* 12-15 34
(Vocals: Tony Sacco)

LEARNING / STARS FELL ON ALABAMA........................ *Oriole 2989* 12-15 34
(Vocals: Tony Sacco)

LEARNING / STARS FELL ON ALABAMA....................... *Perfect 16001* 12-15 34
(Vocals: Tony Sacco)

LEARNING / STARS FELL ON ALABAMA....................... *Romeo 2363* 12-15 34
(Vocals: Tony Sacco)
(Simultaneously released on five labels)

SOLITUDE / I'M GETTING SENTIMENTAL OVER YOU (Vocal: Tony Sacco)...... *Melotone M-13159* 12-15 34

GOODMAN, Benny, & His Orchestra

AIR MAIL SPECIAL / TUESDAY AT TEN .... *Columbia 36254* 2-4 41

ALL I NEED IS YOU / ON THE SUNNY SIDE OF THE STREET (by The Benny Goodman Sextet)..................... *Columbia 36617* 2-4 42
(Vocals: Peggy Lee)

AMAPOLA (Vocal: Helen Foster) / INTERMEZZO..................... *Columbia 36050* 2-4 41

AND THE ANGELS SING (Vocal: Martha Tilton) / SENT FOR YOU YESTERDAY AND HERE YOU COME TODAY (Vocal: Johnny Mercer)..... *Victor 26170* 2-4 39

AT THE DARKTOWN STRUTTERS'S BALL / AFTER YOU'VE GONE............ *Columbia 36699* 2-4 42

AT THE DARKTOWN STRUTTERS' BALL; THE EARL / JUMPIN' AT THE WOODSIDE; DOWN BY THE OLD MILL STREAM .... *V-Disc 205* 5-8 -
(A World War II release)

BASIN STREET BLUES (Vocal: Joe Harris) / WHEN BUDDHA SMILES.................. *Victor 25258* 3-5 36

BEFORE (RACHMANINOFF SPECIAL) / WE'LL MEET AGAIN (Vocal: Peggy Lee)........... *Okeh 6644* 2-4 42

BENNY RIDES AGAIN (a 4-record album set) .... *Capitol BD 57 Set* 10-12 47
Individual records in the set, listed numerically (with value of each):
LAZY RIVER (by The Benny Goodman Duo) / NO, BABY, NO (by The Benny Goodman Orchestra).... *Capitol B20124* -4 -
PUTTIN' ON THE RITZ (by The Benny Goodman Trio) / CHICAGO (by The Benny Goodman Orchestra)......................... *Capitol B20125* 2-4 -
BENNY'S BOOGIE (by The Benny Goodman Quartet) / HOW HIGH THE MOON (by The Benny Goodman Septet).................... *Capitol B20126* 2-4 -
BANNISTER SLIDE, THE (by The Benny Goodman Sextet) MUSIC MAESTRO PLEASE (by The Benny Goodman Quintet)................... *Capitol B20127* 2-4 -

BIG JOHN SPECIAL / FLAT FOOT FLOOGEE (Vocals: by orchestra).......... *Victor 25871* 2-4 38

BIRDS OF A FEATHER / YOU'RE DANGEROUS..................... *Columbia 35977* 2-4 41
(Vocals: Helen Forrest)

BLUE INTERLUDE / WHEN I GO A-DREAMIN'..................... *Victor 26021* 3-5 38
(Vocals: Martha Tilton)

BLUE MOON / THROWIN' STONES AT THE SUN .... *Columbia 3003-D* 15-20 35
(Vocals: Helen Ward)

BLUE ORCHIDS / WHAT'S NEW? .... *Columbia 35211* 2-4 39
(Vocals: Louise Tobin)

BLUE SKIES/DEAR OLD SOUTHLAND... *Victor 25136* 3-5 35

BOARD MEETING / LET'S ALL SING TOGETHER (Vocal: Helen Forrest)..... *Columbia 35396* 2-4 40

BOB WHITE (Vocal: Martha Tilton) / MINNIE THE MOOCHER'S WEDDIN' DAY .... *Victor 25683* 3-5 37

BUCKLE DOWN, WINSOCKI (an alternate take; Vocal: Tommy Taylor) / ON THE ALAMO (by the Benny Goodman Sextet).............. *V-Disc 55* 5-8 -
(This take of the first title was not released on any other label.)
(A World War II release.)

BUMBLE BEE STOMP / CIRIBIRIBIN.... *Victor 26087* 3-5 38

BUSY AS A BEE (Vocal: Helen Forrest) / ZAGGIN' WITH ZIG................ *Columbia 35356* 2-4 40

CAN'T TEACH MY HEART NEW TRICKS / SILHOUETTED IN THE MOONLIGHT (by The Benny Goodman Trio)............. *Victor 25711* 2-4 37
(Vocals: Martha Tilton)

CAN'T YOU TELL? / ONCE MORE (Vocal: Helen Forrest).... *Columbia 35543* 2-4 40

CAPRICE XXIV PAGANINI / I'M HERE......................... *Columbia 36411* 2-4 41

CLARINET A LA KING / HOW LONG HAS THIS BEEN GOING ON? (Vocal: Peggy Lee)............. *Okeh 6544* 2-4 42

CLOUDS (Vocal: Ray Hendricks) / NIGHT WIND (Vocal: Helen Ward)........... *Columbia 3015-D* 12-15 35
(This record was pressed in blue shellac.)

COCOANUT GROVE / THE HOUR OF PARTING..................... *Columbia 35527* 2-4 40

CORN SILK / THE MEM'RY OF A ROSE .... *Columbia 35992* 2-4 41
(Vocals: Helen Forrest)

COUNT, THE / I SEE A MILLION PEOPLE (Vocal: Peggy Lee)........... *Columbia 36379* 2-4 41

CRAZY RHYTHM / MISTER MEADOWLARK (Vocal: Helen Forrest)................. *Columbia 35497* 2-4 40

CUCKOO IN THE CLOCK (Vocal: Johnny Mercer) / A HOME IN THE CLOUDS (Vocal: Martha Tilton).................... *Victor 26175* 2-4 39

DARN THAT DREAM / PEACE, BROTHER........................ *Columbia 35331* 3-5 40
(Vocals: Mildred Bailey)

DEARLY BELOVED / I'M OLD-FASHIONED................ *Columbia 36641* 2-4 42
(Vocals: Buzz Alston)

DEVIL AND THE DEEP BLUE SEA, THE (Vocal: Helen Ward) / MADHOUSE........ *Victor 25268* 3-5 35

DEVIL MAY CARE (Vocal: Helen Forrest) / EV'RY SUNDAY AFTERNOON ..... *Columbia 35461* 2-4 40

DIXIELAND BAND, THE (Vocal: Helen Ward) / DOWN HOME RAG.............. *Columbia 3033-D* 10-12 35

DON'T WAKE UP MY HEART / I'VE BEEN SAVING MYSELF FOR YOU .... *Victor 25867* 2-4 38
(Vocals: Martha Tilton)

DOWN BY THE OLD MILL STREAM / YOURS IS MY HEART ALONE (Vocal: Helen Forrest)... *Columbia 35445* 2-4 40

DR. HECKLE AND MR. JIBE (Vocals: Dick McDonough, Charlie Teagarden, & Jack Teagarden) / TEXAS TEA PARTY (Vocal: Jack Teagarden)....... *Columbia 2845-D* 20-25 33
(This record was pressed in blue shellac.)

EARL, THE / LET'S DO IT (Vocal: Peggy Lee) .... *Okeh 6474* 2-4 41

ELMER'S TUNE (Vocal: Peggy Lee) / THE BIRTH OF THE BLUES.................. *Columbia 36359* 2-4 41

FAITHFUL FOREVER / BLUEBIRDS IN THE MOONLIGHT................ *Columbia 35289* 3-5 39
(Vocals: Mildred Bailey)

FALLING IN LOVE AGAIN / IF YOU HAVEN'T GOT A GIRL.................... *Melotone M-12079* 12-15 31
(Vocals: Unknown)

FEELIN' HIGH AND HAPPY / I LET A SONG GO OUT OF MY HEART...................... *Victor 25840* 2-4 38
(Vocals: Martha Tilton)

FRENESI / HARD TO GET (Vocal: Helen Forrest)...................... *Columbia 35863* 2-4 41

FROM ONE LOVE TO ANOTHER / ANYTHING...................... *Columbia 36305* 2-4 37
(Vocals: Tommy Taylor)

GEE, BUT YOU'RE SWELL / SMOKE DREAMS .... *Victor 25486* 3-5 37
(Vocals: Helen Ward)

GEORGIA JUBILEE / EMALINE (Vocal: Mildred Bailey) .... *Columbia 2907-D* 12-15 34

GET HAPPY / CHRISTOPHER COLUMBUS......................... *Victor 25279* 3-5 36

GET RHYTHM IN YOUR FEET (Vocal: Helen Ward) / BALLAD IN BLUE .... *Victor 25081* 4-6 35

GOOD-BYE (closing theme) / SANDMAN.... *Victor 25215* 3-5 36

GOOD EVENIN', GOOD LOOKIN'! / I FOUND A MILLION-DOLLAR BABY........ *Columbia 36136* 2-4 41
(Vocals: Helen Forrest)

GOOD FOR NOTHIN' BUT LOVE / (GOTTA GET SOME) SHUT-EYE.......................... *Victor 26159* 2-4 39
(Vocals: Martha Tilton)

GOODNIGHT, MY LOVE / TAKE ANOTHER GUESS.................... *Victor 25461* 15-20 36
(Vocals: Ella Fitzgerald)
(Rare. Victor withdrew this record shortly after its release because of a dispute over the use of Ella Fitzgerald, a Decca artist.

GOTTA BE THIS OR THAT (Vocal: Benny Goodman) / GOTTA BE THIS OR THAT, PART II... *Columbia 36813* 2-4 45

HE AIN'T GOT RHYTHM (Vocal: Jimmy Rushing) / THIS YEAR'S KISSES (Vocal: Margaret McCrea) ... *Victor 25505* 4-6 37

HEAVEN IN MY ARMS / THAT LUCKY FELLOW.................. *Columbia 35308* 3-5 39
(Vocals: Mildred Bailey)

HE'S NOT WORTH YOUR TEARS / AND THEN YOUR LIPS MET MINE................. *Melotone M-12023* 15-20 30
(Vocals: Unknown)

HORA STACCATO / MAN HERE PLAYS FINE PIANO (Vocal: Eve Young) ...... *Columbia 37207* 2-4 47

HOUSE HOP / (I WOULD DO) ANYTHING FOR YOU .... *Victor 25350* 4-6 36

HOW HIGH THE MOON / THE FABLE OF THE ROSE................... *Columbia 35391* 2-4 35

HUNKADOLA / THE DIXIELAND BAND (Vocal: Helen Ward)............... *Victor 25009* 5-8 35

I AIN'T LAZY – I'M JUST DREAMIN' / AS LONG AS I LIVE.............. *Columbia 2923-D* 15-20 34
(Vocals: Jack Teagarden)

I CAN'T RESIST YOU / DREAMING OUT LOUD........................ *Columbia 35574* 2-4 40
(Vocals: Helen Forrest)

I DIDN'T KNOW WHAT TIME IT WAS / LOVE NEVER WENT TO COLLEGE .... *Columbia 35230* 2-4 39
(Vocals: Louise Tobin)

IF I COULD BE WITH YOU / I KNOW THAT YOU KNOW.......................... *Victor 25290* 3-5 36

I GOTTA RIGHT TO SING THE BLUES / AIN'TCHA GLAD?................ *Columbia 2835-D* 15-20 33
(Vocals: Jack Teagarden)

I GOTTA RIGHT TO SING THE BLUES / AIN'TCHA GLAD?............. *Hot Jazz Clubs of America HC-96* 5-8 -
(Vocals: Jack Teagarden)
(The Columbia release was pressed in blue shellac. The Hot Jazz Clubs of Amer. is a release of undetermined date, a reissue of the Columbia.)

I LEFT MY HEART IN YOUR HAND / I HEAR A RHAPSODY..................... *Columbia 35937* 2-4 41
(Vocals: Helen Forrest)

I'LL ALWAYS BE IN LOVE WITH YOU / ESTRELLITA............ *Victor 26187* 2-4 39

I'M ALWAYS CHASING RAINBOWS (Vocal: Helen Forrest) / SOMEBODY STOLE MY GAL............................ *Columbia 35916* 2-4 41

I'M LIVIN' IN A GREAT BIG WAY (Vocal: Buddy Clark) / HOORAY FOR LOVE (Vocal: Helen Ward).... *Victor 25011* 4-6 35

I'M NOT COMPLAININ' / MY SISTER AND I (Vocal: Helen Forrest) .... *Columbia 36022* 2-4 41

I MUST SEE ANNIE TONIGHT / KINDA LONESOME .... *Victor 26110* 2-4 39
(Vocals: Martha Tilton)

I NEVER KNEW / SWEET SUE – JUST YOU........................... *Victor 26089* 2-4 38

IT HAD TO BE YOU / LOUISE........... *Victor 26125* 2-4 39

I THREW A KISS IN THE OCEAN / FULL MOON.......................... *Okeh 6652* 2-4 42
(Vocals: Peggy Lee)

IT'S ALWAYS YOU / YOU LUCKY PEOPLE, YOU.................... *Columbia 36002* 2-4 41
(Vocals: Helen Forrest)

IT'S BEEN SO LONG / GOODY-GOODY... *Victor 25245* 3-5 36
(Vocals: Helen Ward)

IT'S THE DREAMER IN ME / WHY'D YA MAKE ME FALL IN LOVE?...................... *Victor 25846* 2-4 38
(Vocals: Martha Tilton)

IT'S THE TALK OF THE TOWN (Vocal: Art Lund) / SWING ANGEL .... *Columbia 36955* 2-4 46

IT'S WONDERFUL / THANKS FOR THE MEMORY....................... *Victor 25727* 2-4 38
(Vocals: Martha Tilton)

I'VE FOUND A NEW BABY / SWINGTIME IN THE ROCKIES .... *Victor 25355* 2-4 36

I'VE GOT A DATE WITH A DREAM / COULD YOU PASS IN LOVE?...................... *Victor 26000* 3-5 38
(Vocals: Martha Tilton)

I'VE GOT A GAL IN KALAMAZOO / SERENADE IN BLUE .... *Columbia 36622* 2-4 42
(Vocals: Dick Haymes)

JAPANESE SANDMAN / ALWAYS...... *Victor 25024* 4-6 35

JERSEY BOUNCE / A STRING OF PEARLS.......................... *Okeh 6590* 3-5 42

JERSEY BOUNCE (an alternate version) / A STRING OF PEARLS................. *V-Disc 409* 5-8 -
(A World War II release.)

JUNK MAN / OL' PAPPY .... *Columbia 2892-D* 15-20 34
(Vocals: Mildred Bailey)
(This record was pressed in blue shellac)

KEEP ON DOIN' WHAT YOU'RE DOIN' (Vocal: Jack Teagarden) / RIFFIN' THE SCOTCH (Vocal: Billie Holiday)............... *Columbia 2867-D* 15-20 34
(This record was pressed in blue shellac)

KING PORTER / SOMETIMES I'M HAPPY........................... *Victor 25090* 2-4 35

LAMP OF MEMORY, THE (Vocal: Peggy Lee) / WHEN THE ROSES BLOOM AGAIN (Vocal: Art Lund) .... *Okeh 6580* 2-4 42

LAZY RIVER / OH! LOOK AT ME NOW .... *Columbia 36012* 2-4 41
(Vocals: Helen Forrest)

LET'S DANCE (opening theme) / BOY MEETS HORN................ *Columbia 35301* 2-4 39

LET THAT BE A LESSON TO YOU / I'VE HITCHED MY WAGON TO A STAR.................. *Victor 25708* 3-5 37
(Vocals: Martha Tilton)

LET THE DOOR KNOB HITCHA (Vocal: Cootie Williams) / PERFIDIA (Vocal: Helen Forrest) ...... *Columbia 35962* 3-5 41

LI'L BOY LOVE (Vocal: Helen Forrest) / NOSTALGIA .... *Columbia 35594* 2-4 40

LINDA (Vocal: Harold Arlen) / OVERNIGHT (Vocal: Unknown).................. *Melotone M-12024* 15-20 30

LITTLE JOE (Vocal: Dick Robertson) / IT LOOKS LIKE LOVE (Vocal: Paul Small) .... *Melotone M-12149* 15-20 31

LOCH LOMOND (Vocals: Martha Tilton & Benny Goodman) / CAMEL HOP .... *Victor 25717* 3-5 38

LOVE ME OR LEAVE ME / WHY COULDN'T IT BE POOR LITTLE ME? .... *Columbia 2871-D* 15-20 34
(This record was pressed in blue shellac.)

LULLABY IN RHYTHM / THAT FEELING IS GONE .... *Victor 25827* 3-5 38

MAKE BELIEVE / THE BLUE ROOM .... *Victor 26088* 3-5 38

MAKE WITH THE KISSES / I THOUGHT ABOUT YOU .... *Columbia 35313* 3-5 39
(Vocals: Mildred Bailey)

MAN I LOVE, THE (Vocal: Helen Forrest) / BENNY RIDES AGAIN .... *Columbia 55001* 4-6 41
(This is an oversize 12-inch rpm)

MARGIE / RUSSIAN LULLABY .... *Victor 26060* 2-4 38

MOONGLOW / BREAKFAST BALL ... *Columbia 2927-D* 15-20 34
(This record was pressed in blue shellac.)

MOON WON'T TALK, THE / I CAN'T LOVE YOU ANYMORE (ANY MORE THAN I DO) .... *Columbia 35487* 2-4 40
(Vocals: Helen Forrest)

MY HONEY'S LOVIN' ARMS / FAREWELL BLUES .... *Victor 26095* 3-5 39

MY MELANCHOLY BABY / WRAPPIN' IT UP .... *Victor 25880* 4-6 38

NEVER SHOULD HAVE TOLD YOU / YOU CAN TELL SHE COMES FROM DIXIE .... *Victor 25500* 3-5 37
(Vocals: Margaret McCrea)

NIGHT AND DAY / BEYOND THE MOON .... *Columbia 35410* 3-5 39

99 OUT OF A HUNDRED WANNA BE LOVED / MINE YESTERDAY, HIS TODAY .... *Melotone M-12100* 15-20 31
(Vocals: Paul Small)

NOBODY (Vocal: Helen Forrest) / HENDERSON STOMP .... *Columbia 35820* 3-5 41

NOT MINE (Vocal: Peggy Lee) / IF YOU BUILD A BETTER MOUSETRAP (Vocals: Peggy Lee & Art Lund) .... *Columbia Columbia 36580* 2-4 42

NOT THAT I CARE / HELP YOURSELF TO HAPPINESS .... *Columbia 2542-D* 12-15 31
(Vocals: Smith Ballew)

ONE SWEET LETTER FROM YOU / SCATTER-BRAIN ..... *Columbia 35241* 2-4 39
(Vocals: Louise Tobin)

ON THE ALAMO (Vocal: Art Lund) / RATTLE AND ROLL .... *Columbia 35241* 2-4 46

OOOOO-OH BOOM! (Vocals: Benny Goodman & Martha Tilton) / ALWAYS AND ALWAYS (Vocal: Martha Tilton) .... *Victor 25808* 4-6 38
(This was the second issue of Victor 25808. See "Pop-corn Man.")

ORGAN GRINDER'S SWING / PETER PIPER (Vocal: Helen Ward) .... *Victor 25442* 4-6 36

PARDON ME, PRETTY BABY / WHAT AM I GONNA DO FOR LOVIN' .... *Melotone M-12208* 15-20 31
(Vocals: Unknown)

PECKIN' / CAN'T WE BE FRIENDS? .... *Victor 25621* 3-5 37

PERFIDA (Vocal: Helen Forrest) / WHY DON'T YOU DO RIGHT? (Vocal: Peggy Lee) .... *V-Disc 13* 5-8 -
(A World War II Release)

PICK YOURSELF UP / DOWN SOUTH CAMP MEETING .... *Victor 25387* 3-5 36

PLEASE BE KIND (Vocal: Martha Tilton) / TI-PI-TIN .... *Victor 25814* 3-5 38

POP-CORN MAN (Vocal: Martha Tilton) / OOOO-OH BOOM! (Vocals: Martha Tilton & Benny Goodman) .... *Victor 25808* 500-750 39
(Of all the multiple millions of commercially-released dance band and big band records in existence today, the original recording of "Pop-Corn Man" by Benny Goodman & His Orchestra is perhaps the most sought after, and can certainly be counted among the rarest of them all. Only about ten copies have been accounted for. The enormous rarity resulted from the recall of the record just one week after release, when an infinitesimal number of records had passed from RCA to distributors to retail stores, thence to the buying public. Upon recall, masters of all takes and even the labels were destroyed. Another tune, "Always And Always" was substituted for "Pop-Corn Man" and hastily released with the same catalog number. See "O-ooo-Oh Boom!"
RCA executives have offered no explanation, and Goodman apparently doesn't know the reason for the precipitous recall. Listening to the record reveals no objectionable lyrics; seemingly, withdrawal of the tune is destined to remain one of the mysteries of the record-collecting world.
Although reissued on LP in 1960, the quest for the original recording of "Pop-Corn Man" by Benny Goodman & His Orchestra continues strongly among collectors.)

POUND RIDGE / I GOT IT BAD (AND THAT AIN'T GOOD) (Vocal: Peggy Lee) .... *Columbia 36421* 2-4 41

PUT THAT KISS BACK WHERE YOU FOUND IT / MY BLUE HEAVEN ... *Columbia 37091* 2-4 47
(Vocals: Art Lund)

REMEMBER / WALK, JENNIE, WALK .. *Victor 25329* 4-6 36

RENDEZVOUS TIME IN PAREE / COMES LOVE .... *Columbia 35201* 2-4 39
(Vocals: Louise Tobin)

ROLL 'EM / AFRAID TO DREAM (Vocal: Betty Van) .... *Victor 25627* 4-6 37

ROSE OF WASHINGTON SQUARE / THE SIREN'S SONG .... *Victor 26230* 2-4 39

SANTA CLAUS CAME IN THE SPRING (Vocal: Joe Harris) / EENY MEENY MINEY MO (Vocal: Helen Ward) .... *Victor 25195* 3-5 35

SCARECROW / — .... *V-Disc 849* 5-8 -
(A release of undetermined date.)

SHADY LADY BIRD (Vocal: Peggy Lee) / BUCKLE DOWN WINSOCKI (Vocal: Tommy Dix) .... *Columbia 36429* 2-4 41

SHAKE DOWN THE STARS / BE SURE .... *Columbia 35426* 2-4 40
(Vocals: Helen Forrest)

SHOW YOUR LINEN, MISS RICHARDSON (Vocal: Johnny Mercer) / THE LADY'S IN LOVE WITH YOU (Vocal: Martha Tilton) .... *Victor 26211* 2-4 39

SINGING A HAPPY SONG / I WAS LUCKY .... *Columbia 3018-D* 12-15 35
(Vocals: Helen Ward)
(This record was pressed in blue shellac.)

SING, SING, SING / SING, SING, SING, PART II .... *Victor 36205* 3-5 37
(This is an oversize 12-inch 78 rpm)

SIX FLATS UNFURNISHED / WHY DON'T YOU DO RIGHT? (Vocal: Peggy Lee) .... *Columbia 36652* 2-4 42

SKY FELL DOWN, THE / IT NEVER ENTERED MY MIND .... *Columbia 35420* 2-4 40
(Vocals: Helen Forrest)

SLOW BUT SURE / YOU CAN'T STOP ME FROM LOVIN' YOU .... *Melotone M-12205* 15-20 31
(Vocals: Unknown)

SMOKE GETS IN YOUR EYES (Vocal: Helen Forrest) / LA ROSITA .... *Columbia 36284* 2-4 41

SOFT AS SPRING / DOWN, DOWN .... *Columbia 36219* 2-4 41
(Vocals: Helen Forrest)

SOLO FLIGHT / THE WORLD IS WAITING FOR THE SUNRISE (by The Benny Goodman Quartet) .... *Columbia 36684* 2-4 42

SOMEBODY ELSE IS TAKING MY PLACE / THAT DID IT, MARIE .... *Okeh 6497* 2-4 42
(Vocals: Peggy Lee)

SOMEBODY LOVES ME / JAM SESSION ... *Victor 25497* 3-5 36

SOMEBODY NOBODY LOVES (Vocal: Peggy Lee) / LET'S GIVE LOVE A CHANCE (Vocal: Art Lund) .... *Okeh 6562* 2-4 42

SOMEONE'S ROCKING MY DREAMBOAT / YOU DON'T KNOW WHAT LOVE IS ...... *Okeh 6534* 2-4 42
(Vocals: Art Lund)

SOMETHING NEW / WHEN THE SUN COMES OUT (Vocal: Helen Forrest) .... *Columbia 36209* 2-4 41

SOMETIMES I'M HAPPY / BUBLE CALL RAG .... *V-Disc 38* 5-8 -
(A World War II release)

SPRING SONG / HONEYSUCKLE ROSE .... *Columbia 35319* 2-4 39

STEALIN' APPLES / OPUS LOCAL 802 .... *Columbia 35362* 2-4 40

STOMPIN' AT THE SAVOY / BREAKIN' IN A PAIR OF SHOES .... *Victor 25247* 2-4 36

SUGAR FOOT STOMP / I CAN'T GIVE YOU ANYTHING BUT LOVE, BABY (Vocal: Martha Tilton) .... *Victor 25678* 3-5 37

SUPERMAN / MORE THAN YOU KNOW (Vocal: Helen Forrest) ..... *Columbia 55002* 10-12 41
(This is an oversize 12-inch 78 rpm.)

SUPERMAN / — .... *V-Disc 79* 12-15 -
(A World War II release)

SWEETHEART OF ALL MY DREAMS (Vocal: Bob Hayden) / EV'RY TIME (Vocal: June Harvey) .... *Columbia 36790* 2-4 45

'TAIN'T NO USE (Vocal: Benny Goodman) / DID YOU MEAN IT? (Vocal: Ella Fitzgerald) .... *Victor 25469* 15-20 36
(Rare. Victor withdrew this record shortly after its release because of a dispute over the use of Ella Fitzgerald, a Decca artist.)

'TAIN'T NO USE (Vocal: Benny Goodman) / GOODNIGHT, MY LOVE (Vocal: Frances Hunt) .... *Victor 25461* 8-10 36
(After the call-back of "Goodnight, My Love", Victor issued this record with the same number, 25461.)

TAKE ME / IDAHO .... *Columbia 36613* 2-4 42
(Vocals: Dick Haymes)

TAKING A CHANCE ON LOVE / CABIN IN THE SKY .... *Columbia 35869* 2-4 41
(Vocals: Helen Forrest)

TANGERINE (Vocal: Art Lund) / RAMONA .... *Columbia 20323* 8-10 42
(Argentine release - the only issue of "Tangerine")

THERE'LL BE SOME CHANGES MADE (Vocal: Louise Tobin) / JUMPIN' AT THE WOODSIDE .... *Columbia 36210* 2-4 39

THESE FOOLISH THINGS REMIND ME OF YOU (Vocal: Helen Ward) / IN A SENTIMENTAL MOOD .... *Victor 25351* 3-5 36

THESE THINGS YOU LEFT ME / YES, MY DARLING DAUGHTER .... *Columbia 35910* 2-4 41
(Vocals: Helen Forrest)

THIS IS NEW / BEWITCHED .... *Columbia 35944* 2-4 41
(Vocals: Helen Forrest)

TIME ON MY HANDS / SCARECROW .... *Columbia 36180* 2-4 41

TOPSY / SMOKE HOUSE RHYTHM ...... *Victor 26107* 3-5 39

UNDECIDED / WE'LL NEVER KNOW (Vocal: Martha Tilton) .... *Victor 26134* 3-5 39

WE CAN LIVE ON LOVE / WHEN YOUR LOVER HAS GONE .... *Melotone M-121120* 15-20 31
(Vocals: Paul Small)

WHAT HAVE WE GOT TO DO TONIGHT / I WANNA BE AROUND MY BABY .... *Melotone M-12138* 15-20 31
(Vocals: Paul Small)

WHAT'S THE MATTER WITH ME? / WHAT'LL THEY THINK OF NEXT? .... *Columbia 35374* 2-4 40
(Vocals: Helen Forrest)

WHEN A LADY MEETS A GENTLEMAN DOWN SOUTH / YOU'RE GIVING ME A SONG AND A DANCE .... *Victor 25434* 3-5 36
(Vocals: Helen Ward)

WHEN IT'S SLEEPY-TIME DOWN SOUTH / CHANGES .... *Victor 25634* 4-6 37

WHEN YOU AND I WERE YOUNG, MAGGIE / SWING LOW, SWEET CHARIOT .... *Victor 25492* 4-6 37

WHISPERING / BACH GOES TO TOWN .... *Victor 26130* 3-5 39

WINTER WEATHER (Vocals: Peggy Lee & Art Lund) / EV'RYTHING I LOVE (Vocal: Peggy Lee) .... *Okeh 6516* 2-4 42

YOU AND YOUR LOVE (Vocal: Martha Tilton) / WHO'LL BUY MY BUBLITCHKI? ...... *Victor 26263* 2-4 39

YOU CAN'T PULL THE WOOL OVER MY EYES / THE GLORY OF LOVE .... *Victor 25316* 3-5 36
(Vocals: Helen Ward)

YOU'RE A HEAVENLY THING / RESTLESS .... *Victor 25021* 3-5 35
(Vocals: Helen Ward)

YOU'RE A SWEET LITTLE HEADACHE / I HAVE EYES .... *Victor 26071* 2-4 38
(Vocals: Martha Tilton)

YOUR MOTHER'S SON-IN-LAW (Vocal: Billie Holiday) / TAPPIN' THE BARREL (Vocal: Jack Teagarden) .... *Columbia 2856-D* 15-20 34
(This record was pressed in blue shellac. The release was Billie Holiday's first record at age 17.)

YOURS (Vocal: Helen Forrest) / TAKE IT (Vocals: by chorus) .... *Columbia 36067* 2-4 41

YOU TOOK THE WORDS RIGHT OUT OF MY HEART / MAMA, THAT MOON IS HERE AGAIN ... *Victor 25720* 3-5 38
(Vocals: Martha Tilton)

YOU TURNED THE TABLES ON ME (Vocal: Helen Ward) / HERE'S LOVE IN YOUR EYES .... *Victor 25391* 2-4 36

ZOOT SUIT, A (Vocal: Art Lund) / MY LITTLE COUSIN (Vocal: Peggy Lee) .... *Okeh 6606* 3-5 42

GOODMAN, Benny, & His Orchestra as Art Kahn & His Orchestra

I'M HAPPY WHEN YOU'RE HAPPY / YOU DIDN'T HAVE TO TELL ME .... *Melotone M-12090* 12-15 31
(Vocals: Small Paul)

GOODMAN, Benny, & His Orchestra as the Radiolites

LOVE LETTERS IN THE SAND / I DON'T KNOW WHY .... *Columbia 2540-D* 12-15 31
(Vocals: Smith Ballew)

GOODMAN, Benny, as Benny Goodman's Boys

AFTER A WHILE / MUSKRAT SCRAMBLE .... *Brunswick 4968* 15-20 29

BLUE / SHIRT TAIL STOMP .... *Brunswick 3975* 10-12 28

JUNGLE BLUES / ROOM 1411 .... *Brunswick 4014* 10-12 28

GOODMAN, Benny, as Benny Goodman's Boys with Jim & Glenn

JAZZ HOLIDAY, A / WOLVERINE BLUES .... *Vocalion 15656* 35-40 28

GOODMAN, Benny, as The Benny Goodman Quartet

AVALON / THE MAN I LOVE .... *Victor 25644* 3-5 37
BEI MIR BIST DU SCHOEN / BEI MIR BIST DU SCHOEN, PART II .... *Victor 25751* 4-6 38
(Vocals: Martha Tilton)
BLUES IN YOUR FLAT, THE / THE BLUES IN MY FLAT (Vocal: Lionel Hampton) .... *Victor 26044* 4-6 38
DIZZY SPELLS / SWEET LORRAINE (by The Benny Goodman Trio) .... *Victor 25822* 2-4 38
HANDFUL OF KEYS / VIENI, VIENI .... *Victor 25705* 3-5 37
I KNOW THAT YOU KNOW / I CRIED FOR YOU (by The Benny Goodman Quintet) .... *Victor 26139* 3-5 39
I'M A DING-DONG DADDY (FROM DUMAS) / WHERE OR WHEN (by The Benny Goodman Trio) .... *Victor 25725* 3-5 38
MOONGLOW / DINAH .... *Victor 25398* 4-6 36
OPUS ½ / — .... *V-Disc 180* 5-8 -
(A World War II release)
OPUS ½ / SWEET GEORGIA BROWN .... *Victor 26091* 3-5 38
SMILES / LIZA .... *Victor 25660* 4-6 37
SUGAR / OPUS THREE-QUARTERS .... *Victor 26240* 3-5 39
SWEET SUE - JUST YOU / MY MELANCHOLY BABY .... *Victor 25473* 4-6 37
'S WONDERFUL / I MUST HAVE THAT MAN (by The Benny Goodman Trio) .... *Victor 26090* 3-5 38
TEA FOR TWO / RUNNIN' WILD .... *Victor 25529* 3-5 37
WORLD IS WAITING FOR THE SUNRISE, THE / SOLO FLIGHT (by Benny Goodman & His Orchestra) .... *Columbia 36684* 2-4 42

GOODMAN, Benny, as the Benny Goodman Quintet

I CRIED FOR YOU / I KNOW THAT YOU KNOW (by The Benny Goodman Quartet) .... *Victor 26139* 3-5 39
PICK-A-RIB / PICK-A-RIB, PART II .... *Victor 26166* 4-6 39

GOODMAN, Benny, as The Benny Goodman Sextet

AS LONG AS I LIVE / BENNY'S BUGLE .... *Columbia 35901* 3-5 41
(This release features Count Basie at the piano)
BLUES IN THE NIGHT (Vocals: Peggy Lee & Lou McGarity) / WHERE OR WHEN (Vocal: Peggy Lee) .... *Okeh 6553* 3-5 42
BREAKFAST FEUD / I FOUND A NEW BABY .... *Columbia 36039* 3-5 41
(This release also features Count Basie at the piano)
DON'T BE A BABY, BABY (Vocal: Art Lund) / ALL THE CATS JOIN IN (Vocals: Liza Morrow & Benny Goodman) .... *Columbia 36967* 2-4 46
FLYING HOME / ROSE ROOM .... *Columbia 35254* 2-4 39
GOOD ENOUGH TO KEEP / FOR YOU (Vocal: Jo Stafford) / WITHOUT A SONG (Vocal: Frank Sinatra .... *V-Disc 33* 5-8 -
(The 2nd & 3rd titles are by Tommy Dorsey & His Orchestra.)
(A World War II Release)
IF I HAD YOU / LIMEHOUSE BLUES .... *Okeh 6486* 3-5 41
MEMORIES OF YOU / SOFT WINDS .... *Columbia 35320* 2-4 40
ON THE ALAMO / BUCKLE DOWN, WINSOCKI (an alternate take - by Benny Goodman & His Orchestra; Vocal: Tommy Taylor) .... *V-Disc 55* 5-8 -
(This take of the 2nd title was not released on any other label)
(A World War II release)
ON THE ALAMO / GONE WITH WHAT DRAFT .... *Columbia 35938* 3-5 41
(This release features Count Basie at the piano)
ON THE SUNNY SIDE OF THE STREET / ALL I NEED IS YOU (by Benny Goodman & His Orchestra) .... *Columbia 36617* 2-4 42
SEVEN COME ELEVEN / SHIVERS .... *Columbia 35349* 3-5 40
SHEIK, THE / POOR BUTTERFLY .... *Columbia 35466* 3-5 40
SIX APPEAL / THESE FOOLISH THINGS .... *Columbia 35553* 3-5 40
SLIPPED DISC / OOMPH FAH FAH .... *Columbia 36817* 2-4 45
SMO-O-O-OTH ONE, A / AIR MAIL SPECIAL .... *Columbia 36099* 2-4 41
TILL TOM SPECIAL / GONE WITH "WHAT" WIND .... *Columbia 35404* 2-4 40
WANG-WANG BLUES, THE / THE WAY YOU LOOK TONIGHT (Vocal: Peggy Lee) .... *Columbia 36594* 2-4 42
WHOLLY CATS / ROYAL GARDEN BLUES .... *Columbia 35810* 3-5 40
(This release features Count Basie at the piano)

GOODMAN, Benny, as the Benny Goodman Trio

ALL MY LIFE / TOO GOOD TO BE TRUE .... *Victor 25324* 4-6 36
(Vocals: Helen Ward)
BODY AND SOUL / AFTER YOU'VE GONE .... *Victor 25115* 3-5 35
CHINA BOY / OH, LADY BE GOOD! .... *Victor 25333* 3-5 36
I MUST HAVE THAT MAN / 'S WONDERFUL (by The Benny Goodman Quartet) .... *Victor 26090* 3-5 38
(Vocals: Martha Tipton)
SILHOUETTED IN THE MOONLIGHT / CAN'T TEACH MY HEART NEW TRICKS (by Benny Goodman & His Orchestra) .... *Victor 25711* 2-4 37
(Vocals: Martha Tilton)
SWEET LORRAINE / DIZZY SPELLS (by The Benny Goodman Quartet) .... *Victor 25822* 2-4 38
WHERE OR WHEN / I'M A DING-DONG DADDY (FROM DUMAS) (by The Benny Goodman Quartet) .... *Victor 25725* 3-5 38
WHO? / SOMEDAY, SWEETHEART .... *Victor 25181* 4-6 35

GOODMAN, Benny, as the Benny Goodman Trio / Quartet

HOT JAZZ (a 4-record album set with an enclosed booklet containing biographical sketch of Benny Goodman and an analysis of his works by Charles E. Smith, co-author of "The Jazz Record Book") .... *RCA Victor HJ 2 Set* 12-15 -
Biographical Sketch of Benny Goodman .... *Enclosed booklet* 2-4 -
BODY AND SOUL / TIGER RAG .... *RCA Victor 40-0106* 2-4 -
AFTER YOU'VE GONE / OH, LADY BE GOOD .... *RCA Victor 40-0107* 2-4 -
DINAH / VIBRAPHONE BLUES .... *RCA Victor 40-0108* 2-4 -
STOMPIN' AT THE SAVOY / RUNNIN' WILD .... *RCA Victor 40-0109* 2-4 -

GOODRICH, B. F. Silvertown Cord Orchestra, The:
see B. F. GOODRICH Silvertown Cord Orchestra, The

GOODY'S GOOD TIMERS:
see MILLS, Irving

GOOFUS FIVE & Their Orchestra, The:
see CALIFORNIA RAMBLERS, The

GORDON, Gray, & His Tic-Toc Rhythm
(Gray Gordon: – 7/76)

BLACKOUT-HOLD ME TIGHT / I LOVE TO WATCH THE MOONLIGHT .... *Bluebird B-10718* 2-4 40
(Vocals: Meredith Blake)
BLUE IN THE BLACK OF THE NIGHT / THERE'S SOMETHING ABOUT AN OLD LOVE .... *Bluebird B-7838* 3-5 38
(Vocals: Cliff Grass)
CHOPSTICKS / IT'S NEVER TOO LATE (Vocal: Betty Bradley) .... *Victor 26184* 2-4 39
DANCING ON A DIME (Vocal: Art Perry) / I HEAR MUSIC (Vocal: Meredith Blake) .... *Bluebird B-10873* 2-4 40
GONE WITH THE WIND / WAY BACK IN 1939 A.D. .... *Bluebird B-10575* 2-4 40
(Vocals: Cliff Grass)
I COULD MAKE YOU CARE (Vocal: Art Perry) / FERRY BOAT SERENADE (Vocal: Meredith Blake) .... *Bluebird B-10819* 2-4 40
IF I DIDN'T CARE (Vocal: Cliff Grass) / WHY DON'T YOU TRY YOUR LOVE ON ME? (Vocal: Betty Bradley) .... *Victor 26253* 2-4 39
I KISSED YOU IN A DREAM LAST NIGHT / AFTER LOOKING AT YOU .... *Bluebird B-10020* 2-4 38
(Vocals: Cliff Grass)
I LOVE ME / AIN'T YOU ASHAMED? .... *Bluebird B-10591* 2-4 40
(Vocals: Rita Ray)
KEEP AN EYE ON YOUR HEART (Vocal: Chet Bruce) / SAN ANTONIO ROSE (Vocal: Art Perry) .... *Bluebird B-10988* 2-4 41
LING'RING ON YOUR DOORSTEP / IT'S FUNNY TO EVERYONE BUT ME .... *Victor 26350* 2-4 39
(Vocals: Cliff Grass)
MAKE BELIEVE (Vocal: Art Perry) / WHY DO I LOVE YOU? (Vocal: Meredith Blake) .... *Bluebird B-11138* 2-4 41
OH! THEY'RE MAKING ME ALL OVER IN THE ARMY (Vocals: by orchestra) / I'LL TAKE YOU HOME AGAIN, KATHLEEN (Vocals: Art Perry & orchestra) .... *Bluebird B-10925* 2-4 40
YOU WAITED TOO LONG (Vocal: Meredith Blake) / GRANADA (Vocal: Art Perry) .... *Bluebird B-11077* 2-4 41

GORDON, Herb, & His Orchestra

GOODBYE LOVE (Vocal: Rose Blane) / TONIGHT MAY NEVER COME AGAIN (Vocal: Dick Dickson) .... *Banner 32877* 3-5 33
GOODBYE LOVE (Vocal: Rose Blane) / TONIGHT MAY NEVER COME AGAIN (Vocal: Dick Dickson) .... *Melotone M-12819* 3-5 33
GOODBYE LOVE (Vocal: Rose Blane) / TONIGHT MAY NEVER COME AGAIN (Vocal: Dick Dickson) .... *Oriole 2779* 3-5 33
GOODBYE LOVE (Vocal: Rose Blane) / TONIGHT MAY NEVER COME AGAIN (Vocal: Dick Dickson) .... *Perfect 15835* 3-5 33
GOODBYE LOVE (Vocal: Rose Blane) / TONIGHT MAY NEVER COME AGAIN (Vocal: Dick Dickson) .... *Romeo 2152* 3-5 33
(Simultaneously released on five labels)
NIGHT OWL (Vocal: Dick Dickson) / IT'S ONLY A PAPER MOON (Vocal: Rose Blane) .... *Melotone M-12806* 4-6 33
NIGHT OWL (Vocal: Dick Dickson) / IT'S ONLY A PAPER MOON (Vocal: Rose Blane) .... *Oriole 2770* 4-6 33
NIGHT OWL (Vocal: Dick Dickson) / IT'S ONLY A PAPER MOON (Vocal: Rose Blane) .... *Perfect 15829* 4-6 33
NIGHT OWL (Vocal: Dick Dickson) / IT'S ONLY A PAPER MOON (Vocal: Rose Blane) .... *Romeo 2143* 4-6 33
(Simultaneously released on four labels)

GORDON, Herb, as Herb Gordon's Hotel Adelphia Whispering Orchestra

COQUETTE / MY RAINBOW .... *Brunswick 3862* 3-5 28
(Vocals: Dick Robertson & Ed Smalle.)
SUNRISE, THE / THOU SWELL .... *Brunswick 3827* 3-5 28
(Vocals: Scappy Lambert)

GORDON, Ralph, & His Orchestra

FUN IN A BOILER FACTORY / TWO LEFT FEET .... *Victor 26033* 5-8 38
TWELVE O'CLOCK IN JOLOPI / ARABIAN NIGHTMARE .... *Victor 26041* 5-8 38

GORMAN, Ross, & His Earl Carroll Orchestra
also see WHITEMAN, Paul, & His Orchestra as The Virginians, directed by Ross Gorman)
(Ross Gorman: circa 1890 – 2/28/53)

HUGO, I'LL GO WHERE YOU GO (Vocal: Arthur Fields) / WANT A LITTLE LOVIN' (Vocals: Harry & Charles Warren) .... *Columbia 460-D* 4-6 25
I'M SITTING ON TOP OF THE WORLD / RHYTHM OF THE DAY .... *Columbia 498-D* 5-8 25
I NEVER KNEW / SLEEPY-TIME GAL .... *Columbia 516-D* 5-8 26
I WANT SOMEBODY TO CHEER ME UP (Vocal: Billy Jones) / LO-NAH .... *Columbia 576-D* 4-6 26
KISS IN THE MOONLIGHT, A / SOMEBODY'S CRAZY ABOUT YOU .... *Columbia 495-D* 5-8 25
NO MORE WORRYIN' / I'D RATHER BE THE GIRL IN YOUR ARMS .... *Columbia 615-D* 5-8 26
SOMEBODY'S EYES / THE PRISONER'S SONG (Vocal: Vernon Dalhart) .... *Columbia 563-D* 4-6 26
VALENCIA (Vocal: Elliott Shaw) / CHERIE, I LOVE YOU .... *Columbia 631-D* 3-5 26
YOU FORGOT TO REMEMBER / OH, BOY! WHAT A GIRL .... *Columbia 435-D* 5-8 25

GORDON, Ross, & His Fire Eaters

KICKAPOO TRAIL (Vocals: Al Shayne) / PHANTOM BLUES .... *Gennett 6118* 5-8 27
PARDON THE GLOVE / MY WIFE'S IN EUROPE TODAY (Vocal: Al Shayne) .... *Gennett 6132* 5-8 27
SHE LOOKS LIKE HELEN BROWN / COME DAY, GO DAY .... *Challenge 258* 4-6 27
(Vocals: Jimmy Kern)
SHE LOOKS LIKE HELEN BROWN / COME DAY, GO DAY .... *Gennett 6057* 5-8 27
(Vocals: Jimmy Kern)
(Simultaneously released on two labels)

GORMAN, Ross, & His Orchestra

SPHINX, THE / COME DAY, GO DAY .... *Edison 51905* 5-8 27
YOU'RE BURNING ME UP / HAWAIIAN ROSE .... *Edison 51896* 5-8 27

GORMAN, Ross, as Ross Gorman's Virginians

COME DAY, GO DAY / SIDEWALK BLUES .... *Harmony 322-H* 4-6 27
SHE LOOKS LIKE HELEN BROWN / OH! BABY, DON'T WE GET ALONG? .... *Harmony 372-H* 3-5 27
(Vocals: Arthur Fields)

GRANT, Bob, & His Orchestra

SONG HITS OF 1924 (a 4-record album set) .... *Decca A-1924 Set* 8-10 42
Individual records in the set, listed numerically (with value of each):
WHAT'LL I DO; ALL ALONE / EVERYBODY LOVES MY BABY; CHARLEY, MY BOY; S-H-I-N-E .... *Decca 24028* 2-4 -
(Vocals: Tony Sacco)
TEA FOR TWO; FOLLOW THE SWALLOW; LIMEHOUSE BLUES / THE MAN I LOVE; JUNE BROUGHT THE ROSES .... *Decca 24029* 2-4 -
(Vocals: Tony Sacco)
ROSE MARIE; CALIFORNIA HERE I COME; OH KATHARINA / I WONDER WHAT'S BECOME OF SALLY?; WHEN YOU AND I WERE SEVENTEEN .... *Decca 24030* 2-4 -
(Vocals: Tony Sacco)
JEALOUS; KEEP SMILING AT TROUBLE; AMAPOLA / THE PRISONER'S SONG; WEST OF THE GREAT DIVIDE .... *Decca 24031* 2-4 -
(Vocals: Tony Sacco)

GRAY, Glen, & The Casa Loma Orchestra
(Glen Gray: 6/7/06 – 8/23/63)
(The Orange Blossoms, one of Jean Goldkette's many bands, became the nucleus of the Casa Loma Orchestra. Mel Jenssen fronted the early Casa Loma while handsome Glen Gray (Knoblaugh), the titular head, sat in the saxophone section. Gray eventually took over.)

AFTER TONIGHT / ONE LITTLE WORD LED TO ANOTHER .... *Brunswick 6397* 8-10 32
(Vocals: Kenny Sargent)

AIN'T IT JUST TOO BAD? (Vocal: Pee Wee Hunt) / THINGS MIGHT HAVE BEEN SO DIFF'RENT (Vocal: Kenny Sargent) .... *Decca 375* 5-8 35

ALEXANDER'S RAGTIME BAND (Vocal: Jack Richmond) / PUT ON YOUR OLD GREY BONNET (Vocal: Pee Wee Hunt) .... *Brunswick 6100* 5-8 31

ALEXANDER'S RAGTIME BAND / PUT ON YOUR OLD GREY BONNET .... *Odeon ONY-36171* 5-8 31
(Vocals: Pee Wee Hunt)

ALEXANDER'S RAGTIME BAND / PUT ON YOUR OLD GREY BONNET .... *Okeh 41476* 5-8 31
(Vocals: Pee Wee Hunt)
(Simultaneously released on two labels)

AVALON / CHINA GIRL .... *Brunswick 7532* 5-8 34

AY AY AY / IF I HAD MY WAY (Vocal: Kenny Sargent) .... *Decca 2437* 3-5 39

BEAUTIFUL LOVE (Vocal: Kenny Sargent) / SHADOWS .... *Decca 2748* 3-5 39

BLACK JAZZ / MANIAC'S BALL ..... *Brunswick 6242* 8-10 32

BLOW THE SMOKE AWAY / I'D RATHER DREAM .... *Decca 3610* 3-5 40
(Vocals: Kenny Sargent)

BLUE JAZZ / DON'T TELL A SOUL (Vocal: Kenny Sargent) .... *Brunswick 6358* 5-8 32

BLUE KENTUCKY MOON / CAN'T YOU SEE? .... *Brunswick 6187* 5-8 31
(Vocals: Kenny Sargent)

BLUE RAIN / OUT OF SPACE .... *Decca 2802* 3-5 39
(Vocals: Kenny Sargent)

BONEYARD SHUFFLE / GEORGIA ON MY MIND .... *Decca 2399* 4-6 39

BOOGIE WOOGIE PIANO MAN (Vocal: Pee Wee Hunt) / AS IF YOU DIDN'T KNOW (Vocal: Kenny Sargent) .... *Decca 3845* 3-5 41

BOTTOM MAN ON THE TOTEM POLE / BOTTOM MAN ON THE TOTEM POLE, PART II .... *Decca 4156* 3-5 42
(Vocals: Pee Wee Hunt)

CARRY ME BACK TO THE LONE PRAIRIE (Vocal: Pee Wee Hunt) / TALL GROWS THE TIMBER (Vocal: Kenny Sargent) .... *Decca 18525* 2-4 42

CASA LOMA STOMP / CONSTANTLY (Vocal: Kenny Sargent) ...... *Brunswick* 40-45 32
(This is a seven-inch publicity record without a catalog number, featuring a picture of the orchestra on one side, and advertising on the reverse. Extremely rare.)

CASA LOMA STOMP / FOR YOU (Vocal: Kenny Sargent) .... *Decca 1412* 4-6 37

CASA LOMA STOMP / JUNK MAN (by Jack Teagarden & His Orchestra) .... *Brunswick 7652* 8-10 33

CHAMPAGNE WALTZ, THE / THE HOUSE IS HAUNTED .... *Brunswick 6858* 5-8 34
(Vocals: Kenny Sargent)

CHARMING LITTLE FAKER (Vocal: Pee Wee Hunt) / POLKA DOTS AND MOONBEAMS (Vocal: Kenny Sargent) .... *Decca 3121* 3-5 40

CHINA GIRL / SAN SUE STRUT .... *Okeh 41403* 5-8 30

CITY CALLED HEAVEN / I FOUND YOU IN THE RAIN .... *Decca 4048* 3-5 41
(Vocals: Kenny Sargent)

CLEAR OUT OF THIS WORLD (Vocals: Kenny Sargent) / A LATIN TUNE, A MANHATTAN MOON AND YOU (Vocal: Pee Wee Hunt) .... *Decca 3216* 3-5 40

COME AND GET IT / MIRAGE .... *Decca 3348* 4-6 40

COPENHAGEN / JUNGLE JITTERS .... *Decca 1048* 5-8 36

CORINNE CORINNA / SAN SUE STRUT .... *Brunswick 7427* 5-8 34

COTTON (Vocal: Pee Wee Hunt) / CHANT OF THE JUNGLE .... *Decca 463* 5-8 35

COULD BE (Vocal: Pee Wee Hunt) / I WON'T BELIEVE IT (Vocal: Clyde Burke) .... *Decca 2292* 3-5 39

DADDY'S BOY / YOU GO TO MY HEAD ... *Decca 1783* 4-6 38
(Vocals: Kenny Sargent)

DANCE OF THE LAME DUCK, THE / BLUE PRELUDE .... *Brunswick 6513* 8-10 33

DARDANELLA / CASA LOMA STOMP ... *Victor 24256* 5-8 33

DARLING, HOW YOU LIED / I'LL NEVER FORGET .... *Decca 4166* 3-5 42
(Vocals: Kenny Sargent)

DON'T GET AROUND MUCH ANYMORE (Vocals: Kenny Sargent & The LeBrun Sisters) / DON'T DO IT, DARLING (Vocals: Pee Wee Hunt, Kenny Sargent, & The Boresome Foursome) .... *Decca 18479* 2-4 42

DUST / LEAVE IT THAT WAY ..... *Odeon ONY-36079* 5-8 30
(Vocals: Jack Richmond)

FABLE OF THE ROSE, THE (Vocal: Kenny Sargent) / SAVE YOUR SORROW FOR TOMORROW (Vocal: Pee Wee Hunt) .... *Decca 3068* 3-5 40

FARE THEE WELL, ANNABELE (Vocal: Pee Wee Hunt) / IN A BLUE AND PENSIVE MOOD .... *Decca 352* 5-8 35

FOR YOU / I LOVE YOU TRULY ...... *Brunswick 6606* 5-8 33
(Vocals: Kenny Sargent)

GIRL OF MY DREAMS / DID AN ANGEL KISS YOU THE DAY YOU WERE BORN? .... *Decca 1634* 3-5 38
(Vocals: Kenny Sargent)

GOBLIN BAND, THE / ZIG-ZAG .... *Decca 1312* 5-8 37

GOING, GOING, GONE / BLACK-EYED SUSAN BROWN .... *Victor 24254* 8-10 33
(Vocals: Pee Wee Hunt)

GOODBYE, LOVE / AND SO, GOODBYE .... *Brunswick 6666* 5-8 33
(Vocals: Kenny Sargent)

HAPPY-GO-LUCKY YOU / ALL OF A SUDDEN .... *Brunswick 6318* 8-10 32
(Vocals: Kenny Sargent)

HAPPY MOOD / LULLABY OF THE RAIN (Vocals: The LeBrun Sisters) .... *Decca 18471* 2-4 42

HAVE YOU MET MISS JONES? / I'D RATHER BE RIGHT .... *Decca 1520* 4-6 37
(Vocals: Kenny Sargent)

HEAD ON MY PILLOW (Vocal: Kenny Sargent) / COTTONWOOD CORNERS (Vocal: Pee Wee Hunt) .... *Decca 3471* 3-5 40

HEAT WAVE (Vocal: Mildred Bailey) / NOT FOR ALL THE RICE IN CHINA (Vocal: Pee Wee Hunt) .... *Brunswick 6679* 8-10 33

HELP YOURSELF TO HAPPINESS (Vocal: Kenny Sargent) / DO THE NEW YORK (Vocals: by chorus) .... *Brunswick 6150* 8-10 31

HERE COME THE BRITISH (Vocal: Pee Wee Hunt) / TWO CIGARETTES IN THE DARK (Vocal: Kenny Sargent) .... *Brunswick 6954* 5-8 34

HERE YOU ARE (Vocal: Kenny Sargent) / OH, THE PITY OF IT ALL (Vocal: Pee Wee Hunt) .... *Decca 4298* 2-4 42

HOBOKEN BUCKET / LAST NIGHT A MIRACLE HAPPENED (Vocal: Kenny Sargent) .... *Decca 2281* 4-6 39

HUNDRED YEARS FROM TODAY, A (Vocal: Lee Wiley) / CAROLINA (Vocal: Connee Boswell) .... *Brunswick 6775* 8-10 34

I CAME HERE TO TALK TO JOE (Vocals: Kenny Sargent & The LeBrun Sisters) / YOU'RE IN LOVE WITH SOMEONE ELSE (Vocal: Kenny Sargent) ... *Decca 18468* 2-4 42

I CAN DREAM, CAN'T I? / TWO DREAMS GOT TOGETHER .... *Decca 1607* 4-6 38
(Vocals: Kenny Sargent)

I CONCENTRATE ON YOU / LAST NIGHT'S GARDENIAS .... *Decca 3006* 2-4 40
(Vocals: Kenny Sargent)

I'D BE A FOOL AGAIN / YOU'RE HERE, YOU'RE THERE .... *Decca 1179* 4-6 37
(Vocals: Kenny Sargent)

I DREAM OF JEANIE WITH THE LIGHT BROWN HAIR / BEAUTIFUL DREAMER .... *Decca 3201* 3-5 40
(Vocals: Kenny Sargent)

I HAVEN'T TIME TO BE A MILLIONAIRE / APRIL PLAYED THE FIDDLE .... *Decca 3163* 3-5 40
(Vocals: Kenny Sargent)

I'M CRAZY 'BOUT MY BABY (Vocal: Jack Richmond) / WHITE JAZZ .... *Brunswick 6092* 5-8 31

I NEVER KNEW (Vocals: Pee Wee Hunt, Clarence Hutchinrider, & Stanley Dennis) / INDIANA .... *Brunswick 6337* 8-10 32

I NEVER SLEPT A WINK LAST NIGHT (Vocal: Pee Wee Hunt) / JUNGLE FEVER .... *Brunswick 6932* 8-10 34

IN THE MISSION BY THE SEA / FAREWELL, MY LOVE .... *Decca 1519* 4-6 37
(Vocals: Kenny Sargent)

IN THE STILL OF THE NIGHT / SMOKE RINGS (theme song) .... *Brunswick 6289* 4-6 32

I PROMISE YOU (Vocal: Clyde Burke) / (GOTTA GET SOME) SHUT-EYE (Vocal: Pee Wee Hunt) ... *Decca 2307* 3-5 39

I REMEMBER / I'VE GOT MY HEART SET ON YOU .... *Decca 1530* 4-6 37
(Vocals: Kenny Sargent)

I SEE YOUR FACE BEFORE ME (Vocal: Kenny Sargent) / YOU HAVE EVERYTHING (Vocal: Pee Wee Hunt) ...... *Decca 1608* 4-6 38

IT'S THE TALK OF THE TOWN (Vocal: Kenny Sargent) / THAT'S HOW RHYTHM WAS BORN (Vocal: Pee Wee Hunt) .... *Brunswick 6626* 8-10 33

I'VE GOT AN INVITATION TO A DANCE / MAYBE I'M WRONG AGAIN .... *Decca 287* 5-8 34
(Vocals: Kenny Sargent)

I WANNA SING ABOUT YOU (Vocal: Kenny Sargent) / JUST A BLUE-EYED BLONDE (Vocal: Pee Wee Hunt) .... *Brunswick 6124* 8-10 31

I WISH I WERE ALADDIN (Vocal: Kenny Sargent) / THE DEVIL IS AFRAID OF MUSIC (Vocal: Pee Wee Hunt) .... *Decca 553* 5-8 35

JIMTOWN BLUES / BIG BAD BILL (Vocal: Pee Wee Hunt) .... *Decca 3303* 3-5 40

JUST A FAIR-WEATHER FRIEND (Vocal: Kenny Sargent) / IN MY COUNTRY THAT MEANS LOVE (Vocal: Pee Wee Hunt) .... *Decca 339* 5-8 35

JUST AN OLD MANUSCRIPT / BLUE RHAPSODY .... *Decca 18918* 2-4 46

JUST FRIENDS / I'M THRU' WITH LOVE ... *Decca 18546* 2-4 41
(Vocals: Kenny Sargent)

KISS BY KISS / ONE OF US WAS WRONG .... *Brunswick 6256* 5-8 32
(Vocals: Kenny Sargent)

LADY FROM ST. PAUL, THE (Vocal: Pee Wee Hunt) / NEW ORLEANS (Vocal: Clarence Hutchinrider) .... *Brunswick 6486* 8-10 33

LAZYBONES (Vocal: Pee Wee Hunt) / SOPHISTICATED LADY .... *Victor 24338* 5-8 33

LAZY DAY / EVENING .... *Brunswick 6311* 8-10 32
(Vocals: Kenny Sargent)

LAZY RIVER / MOON COUNTRY .... *Decca 2397* 3-5 39
(Vocals: by The Merry Mass)

LET 'ER GO / SWING LOW, SWEET CHARIOT .... *Decca 1396* 5-8 37

LET'S MAKE IT A LIFE-TIME (Vocal: Kenny Sargent) / BEI MIR BIST DU SCHOEN (Vocal: Pee Wee Hunt) .... *Decca 1575* 4-6 38

LET YOURSELF GO / I'D RATHER LEAD A BAND .... *Decca 696* 5-8 36
(Vocals: Pee Wee Hunt)

LIMEHOUSE BLUES .... *Brunswick* 15-20 32
(A promotional record, un-numbered.)

LIMEHOUSE BLUES / DALLAS BLUES .... *Brunswick 6886* 8-10 34

LINGER AWHILE / PANAMA .... *Brunswick 7325* 8-10 34

LITTLE MAN WITH THE HAMMER, THE (Vocal: Pee Wee Hunt) / WHO'S SORRY NOW? .... *Decca 379* 5-8 35

LONG MAY WE LOVE / I NEVER HAD A CHANCE .... *Brunswick 6927* 5-8 34
(Vocals: Kenny Sargent)

LOOKIE, LOOKIE, LOOKIE, HERE COMES COOKIE (Vocal: Pee Wee Hunt) / MY HEART IS AN OPEN BOOK (Vocal: Kenny Sargent) .... *Decca 386* 5-8 35

LOVELY LADY / WITH ALL MY HEART ... *Decca 652* 5-8 36
(Vocals: Kenny Sargent)

LUCKY ME, LOVABLE YOU / HAPPY DAYS ARE HERE AGAIN .... *Okeh 41339* 8-10 29
(Vocals: Jack Richmond)

LULLABY IN BLUE / THAT'S LOVE ... *Brunswick 6764* 5-8 34
(Vocals: Kenny Sargent)

MALADY IN F MINOR / MY BONNIE LIES OVER THE OCEAN (Vocal: Pee Wee Hunt) .... *Decca 1755* 3-5 38

MARGIE / BYE-BYE BLUES (Vocal: Kenny Sargent) .... *Decca 3639* 3-5 40

ME FOR YOU FOREVER / SWEET MADNESS .... *Brunswick 6660* 5-8 33
(Vocals: Kenny Sargent)

MEMORIES OF YOU / NUTTY NURSEY RHYMES .... *Decca 1672* 4-6 38
(Vocals: Pee Wee Hunt)

MEMORY LANE / THE BELLS OF SAN RAQUEL .... *Decca 4067* 2-4 41
(Vocals: Kenny Sargent)

MEM'RY OF THIS DANCE, THE (Vocal: Kenny Sargent) / ONE DOZEN ROSES (Vocal: Pee Wee Hunt) .... *Decca 4299* 2-4 42

MIGHTY RIVER (Vocal: Pee Wee Hunt) / WHY CAN'T I FIND SOMEBODY TO LOVE? (Vocal: Kenny Sargent) .... *Brunswick 6409* 8-10 32

MILENBERG JOYS / OUT OF SPACE ... *Brunswick 6922* 8-10 34

MISSISSIPPI BASIN (Vocal: Clarence Hutchinrider) / LOU'SIANA LULLABY (Vocal: Pee Wee Hunt) .... *Brunswick 6618* 8-10 33

MOONBURN (Vocal: Pee Wee Hunt) / MY HEART AND I (Vocal: Kenny Sargent) .... *Decca 688* 5-8 36

MOONLIGHT COCKTAIL / AUTUMN NOCTURNE .... *Decca 4114* 3-5 42

MOONLIGHT MOOD / PURPLE MOONLIGHT .... *Decca 18508* 2-4 42
(Vocals: Kenny Sargent)

MUSIC FROM ACROSS THE SEA / THE MOMENT I LOOKED INTO YOUR EYES .... *Brunswick 6628* 5-8 33
(Vocals: Kenny Sargent)

MY DANCE (Vocal: Kenny Sargent) / LOVE AND A DIME; EAST OF THE SUN .... *Decca 387* 5-8 35

MY HEART IS TAKING LESSONS (Vocal: Pee Wee Hunt) / THIS IS MY NIGHT TO DREAM (Vocal: Kenny Sargent) .... *Decca 1650* 3-5 38

MY IMAGINARY SWEETHEART / THE NIGHT WE MET .... *Victor 24340* 5-8 33
(Vocals: Kenny Sargent)

MY LOVE / THIS IS ROMANCE ...... *Brunswick 6642* 5-8 33
(Vocals: Kenny Sargent)

MY WILD IRISH ROSE / WHEN IRISH EYES ARE SMILING .... *Decca 2968* 2-4 39
(Vocals: Kenny Sargent)

NAGASAKI / P.S. I LOVE YOU (Vocal: Kenny Sargent) .... *Decca 200* 5-8 34

NARCISSUS / NOCTURNE .... *Brunswick 7321* 8-10 34

NEW MOON IS OVER MY SHOULDER, A / I'M IN LOVE .... *Decca 192* 5-8 34
(Vocals: Kenny Sargent)

NO NAME JIVE / NO NAME JIVE, PART II .... *Decca 3089* 2-4 40

NOT SO LONG AGO / MAGIC MOUNTAIN ... *Decca 3573* 3-5 41
(Vocals: Kenny Sargent)

ONCE UPON A MIDNIGHT / TWO HEADS AGAINST THE MOON .... *Decca 430* 5-8 35
(Vocals: Kenny Sargent)

ONE MORE TOMORROW (Vocal: Eugenie Baird) / IF I LOVE AGAIN .... *Decca 18843* 2-4 46

ONE, TWO, THREE LITTLE HOURS / WOULD YOU LIKE TO BUY A DREAM? .... *Decca 1246* 5-8 37
(Vocals: Kenny Sargent)

OUT IN THE COLD AGAIN / LEARNING .... *Brunswick 6964* 5-8 34
(Vocals: Kenny Sargent)

OVERNIGHT / LITTLE DID I KNOW .... *Odeon ONY-36173* 8-10 31
(Vocals: Jack Richmond)

OVERNIGHT / LITTLE DID I KNOW...... *Okeh 41477* 8-10 31
(Vocals: Jack Richmond)
(Simultaneously released on two labels)

PARAMOUR / I MAY BE WRONG, BUT I THINK YOU'RE WONDERFUL (Vocal: P. W. Hunt)... *Decca 15035* 5-8 37
(This is an oversize 12-inch 78 rpm.)

PARDON MY SOUTHERN ACCENT (Vocal: Pee Wee Hunt) / SAY IT (Vocal: Kenny Sargent).... *Brunswick 6945* 5-8 34

PESSIMISTIC CHARACTER (WITH THE CRAB APPLE FACE) / MEET THE SUN HALF-WAY... *Decca 3164* 3-5 40
(Vocals: Pee Wee Hunt)

PRELUDE IN C SHARP MINOR / LOVE GROWS ON THE WHITE-OAK TREE (Vocal: Pee Wee Hunt).............. *Decca 2709* 3-5 39

RIDIN' AROUND IN THE RAIN / MOON COUNTRY .... *Brunswick 6870* 5-8 34
(Vocals: Pee Wee Hunt)

RIVER'S TAKIN' CARE OF ME, THE (Vocal: Pee Wee Hunt) / TROUBLE IN PARADISE (Vocal: Kenny Sargent)..... *Brunswick 6602* 5-8 33

ROCK-A-BYE BAY / I'M OLD-FASHIONED (Vocal: Kenny Sargent) ...... *Decca 18481* 3-5 42

ROCKIN' CHAIR / LAZYBONES .... *Decca 2395* 5-8 39
(Vocals: Pee Wee Hunt & Louis Armstrong)

ROSE OF THE RIO GRANDE / BUGLE CALL RAG......................... *Decca 869* 5-8 36

SAN SUE STRUT / ROYAL GARDEN BLUES........................... *Columbia 2884-D* 8-10 31

SHADES OF HADES / ROYAL GARDEN BLUES................................ *Decca 986* 5-8 36

SHINE ON, HARVEST MOON (Vocal: Kenny Sargent) / MIDNIGHT LULLABY................. *Decca 2903* 3-5 39

SIERRA SUE (Vocal: Kenny Sargent) / SOFT WINDS.......................... *Decca 3122* 3-5 40

SITTIN' BY THE FIRE WITH YOU / WHERE ARE YOU TONIGHT?...................... *Victor 24224* 8-10 33
(Vocals: Kenny Sargent)

SLEEPY TIME GAL / DRIFTING APART... *Decca 15042* 5-8 38
(This is an oversize 12-inch 78 rpm.)

SMOKE RINGS (theme song) / ALWAYS..... *Decca 1473* 4-6 37

SONG OF INDIA / MINDIN' MY BUSINESS......................... *Decca 2031* 3-5 38

SPELLBOUND / DON'T LET IT HAPPEN AGAIN .... *Brunswick 6910* 5-8 34
(Vocals: Kenny Sargent)

STAR DUST / ONE MORNING IN MAY.... *Decca 2396* 3-5 39
(Vocals: Kenny Sargent)

STARLIGHT / RAIN ON THE ROOF.... *Brunswick 6252* 8-10 32
(Vocals: Kenny Sargent)

STOMPIN' AROUND / IRRESISTIBLE (Vocal: Kenny Sargent) ...... *Decca 286* 5-8 34

STUDY IN BROWN, A / WHOA, BABE! (Vocal: Pee Wee Hunt) ...... *Decca 1159* 5-8 37

SUNRISE SERENADE / HEAVEN CAN WAIT (Vocal: Clyde Burke) .... *Decca 2321* 3-5 39

SWEEPING THE CLOUDS AWAY / ANY TIME'S THE TIME TO FALL IN LOVE....... *Odeon ONY-36046* 8-10 30
(Vocals: Jack Richmond)

SWEEPING THE CLOUDS AWAY / ANY TIME'S THE TIME TO FALL IN LOVE.............. *Okeh 41373* 8-10 30
(Vocals: Jack Richmond)
(Simultaneously released on two labels)

SWEET AS A SONG / I COULD USE A DREAM...................... *Decca 1597* 4-6 38
(Vocals: Kenny Sargent)

SWING HIGH, SWING LOW (Vocal: Pee Wee Hunt) / PLEASE KEEP ME IN YOUR DREAMS (Vocal: Kenny Sargent)......................... *Decca 1129* 5-8 37

TAKE IT FROM ME (Vocal: Pee Wee Hunt) / IT'S THE GIRL (Vocals: Joe Hostetter, Pee Wee Hunt & Kenny Sargent) .... *Brunswick 6153* 8-10 31

TEMPTATION / I TOUCHED A STAR ..... *Decca 3232* 3-5 40
(Vocals: Kenny Sargent)

THANKS FOR THE MEMORY (Vocal: Kenny Sargent) / MAMA, THAT MOON IS HERE AGAIN (Vocal: Pee Wee Hunt)..................... *Decca 1541* 5-8 38

THANKSGIVIN' / RHYTHM MAN .... *Brunswick 6463* 8-10 33
(Vocals: Pee Wee Hunt)

THERE'S A LULL IN MY LIFE / NEVER IN A MILLION YEARS.................... *Decca 1211* 4-6 37
(Vocals: Kenny Sargent)

THIS NIGHT (Vocal: Clyde Burke) / HONOLULU (Vocal: Pee Wee Hunt)......... *Decca 2308* 2-4 39

TILL WE MEET AGAIN / DEAR OLD PAL OF MINE........................ *Decca 18322* 2-4 42
(Vocals: Kenny Sargent)

TIME ON MY HANDS / I CRIED FOR YOU (Vocal: Kenny Sargent)........... *Decca 1864* 4-6 38

TIME ON MY HANDS (Vocal: Kenny Sargent) / IF I DIDN'T HAVE YOU (Vocal: Pee Wee Hunt)..... *Brunswick 6201* 8-10 31

TIRED OF IT ALL (Vocal: Kenny Sargent) / DIXIE LEE (Vocal: Pee Wee Hunt)..... *Brunswick 6726* 5-8 34

TOO MARVELOUS FOR WORDS / SENTIMENTAL AND MELANCHOLY.................. *Decca 1158* 4-6 37
(Vocals: Kenny Sargent)

TUMBLING TUMBLEWEEDS/THROUGH... *Decca 2777* 2-4 39
(Vocals: Kenny Sargent)

TWO IN A DREAM (Vocal: Kenny Sargent) / THE OBJECT OF MY AFFECTION (Vocal: Pee Wee Hunt) .... *Decca 298* 5-8 35

UNDER A BLANKET OF BLUE / LOVE IS THE THING .... *Brunswick 6584* 5-8 33
(Vocals: Kenny Sargent)

UNDER A BLANKET OF BLUE (Vocal: Kenny Sargent) / ROSK ISLAND FLAG STOP............. *Decca 3193* 3-5 40

UNTIL THE STARS FALL DOWN / IT'S THE TALK OF THE TOWN .... *Decca 4292* 2-4 42
(Vocals: Kenny Sargent)

WASHBOARD BLUES (Vocal: Connee Boswell) / FOUR INDIAN LOVE LYRICS..... *Brunswick 20108* 8-10 32
(This is an oversize 12-inch 78 rpm)

WASHBOARD BLUES / LITTLE OLD LADY........................... *Decca 2394* 3-5 39
(Vocals: Hoagy Carmichael)

WAS IT RAIN? (Vocal: Kenny Sargent) / LOVE IS GOOD FOR ANYTHING THAT AILS YOU (Vocal: Pee Wee Hunt).................... *Decca 1180* 5-8 37

WATCHING THE CLOCK (Vocals: Kenny Sargent) / WOULDN'ST COULD I BUT KISS THY HAND, OH BABE (Vocal: Pee Wee Hunt)........... *Decca 3016* 3-5 40

WEEP NO MORE, MY BABY (Vocal: Kenny Sargent) / SAVAGE SERENADE (Vocal: Pee Wee Hunt) .... *Brunswick 6647* 8-10 33

WE THREE / OUR LOVE AFFAIR .... *Decca 3416* 3-5 40
(Vocals: Kenny Sargent)

WHAT IS THIS THING CALLED LOVE? / YOURS, ALL YOURS (Vocal: Pee Wee Hunt) .... *Decca 2144* 3-5 38

WHEN BUDDHA SMILES / CORAL SEA.... *Decca 3261* 3-5 40

WHEN I GROW TOO OLD TO DREAM / THE NIGHT IS YOUNG.............................. *Decca 349* 5-8 35
(Vocals: Kenny Sargent)

WHEN I TAKE MY SUGAR TO TEA (Vocal: Pee Wee Hunt) / I WANNA BE AROUND MY BABY ALL THE TIME (Vocal: Jack Richmond)................ *Brunswick 6085* 8-10 31

WHEN WILL I KNOW? (Vocal: Kenny Sargent) / CHINATOWN, MY CHINATOWN......... *Decca 199* 5-8 34

WHEN YOU AWAKE / MOON OVER BURMA................................. *Decca 3426* 3-5 40
(Vocals: Kenny Sargent)

WHERE THERE'S SMOKE THERE'S FIRE / BLUE MOON .... *Decca 312* 5-8 35
(Vocals: Kenny Sargent)

WHY CAN'T THIS NIGHT GO ON FOREVER? / IF YOU DON'T WANT TO BE SWEETHEARTS..... *Brunswick 6494* 5-8 33
(Vocals: Kenny Sargent)

WILD GOOSE CHASE / BUJI......... *Brunswick 6588* 8-10 33

WILL LOVE FIND A WAY? (Vocal: Kenny Sargent) / YANKEE DOODLE NEVER WENT TO TOWN (Vocal: Pee Wee Hunt)............ *Decca 603* 5-8 35

WITHOUT A WORD OF WARNING (Vocal: Kenny Sargent) / TAKES TWO TO MAKE A BARGAIN (Vocal: Pee Wee Hunt)... *Decca 552* 5-8 35

WOODLAND SYMPHONY/SWING TONIC... *Decca 3875* 3-5 41

WORLD IS WAITING FOR THE SUNRISE, THE / I'D LOVE TO LIVE IN LOVELAND .... *Decca 3667* 3-5 40
(Vocals: Kenny Sargent)

YESTERDAY'S GARDENIAS / SOUTH WIND .... *Decca 18465* 2-4 42
(Vocals: Kenny Sargent)

YOU AIN'T BEEN LIVING RIGHT (Vocal: Pee Wee Hunt) / MOONGLOW (Vocal: Kenny Sargent)... *Brunswick 6937* 8-10 34

YOU BETTER CHANGE YOUR TUNE / THE OLD APPLE TREE......................... *Decca 1679* 4-6 38
(Vocals: Pee Wee Hunt)

YOU GROW SWEETER AS THE YEARS GO BY / TEARS FROM MY INKWELL... *Decca 2388* 3-5 39
(Vocals: Kenny Sargent)

YOU HAVE TAKEN MY HEART / SHADOWS OF LOVE .... *Brunswick 6738* 5-8 34
(Vocals: Kenny Sargent)

YOU NEVER KNOW / AT LONG LAST LOVE........................... *Decca 2010* 3-5 38
(Vocals: Kenny Sargent)

YOU'RE A BUILDER-UPPER / JUDY....... *Decca 193* 5-8 34
(Vocals: Pee Wee Hunt)

YOU'RE GONNA LOSE YOUR GAL (Vocal: Pee Wee Hunt) / WE WERE THE BEST OF FRIENDS (Vocal: Kenny Sargent)... *Brunswick 6708* 8-10 34

YOU'RE LAUGHING AT ME / I'VE GOT MY LOVE TO KEEP ME WARM...................... *Decca 1126* 4-6 37
(Vocals: Kenny Sargent)

YOU'RE STILL IN MY HEART / FALLING IN LOVE WITH YOU (early theme song)......... *Brunswick 6263* 5-8 32
(Vocals: Kenny Sargent)

YOU'RE WALKING IN MY SLEEP / LOVE PASSES BY .... *Decca 405* 5-8 35
(Vocals: Kenny Sargent)

YOURS AND MINE (Vocal: Kenny Sargent) / I'M FEELIN' LIKE A MILLION (Vocal: Pee Wee Hunt).... *Decca 1368* 4-6 37

YOURS IS MY HEART ALONE (Vocal: Kenny Sargent) / A LOVER'S LULLABY................. *Decca 3053* 3-5 40

YOU SAY THE SWEETEST THINGS (Vocal: Pee Wee Hunt) / I DO, DO YOU? (Vocal: Kenny Sargent)........... *Decca 3572* 2-4 41

YOU TOOK ADVANTAGE OF ME (Vocal: Pee Wee Hunt) / I WOKE UP TOO SOON (Vocal: Kenny Sargent) .... *Decca 334* 5-8 35

YOU TOOK THE WORDS RIGHT OUT OF MY HEART / THE WALTZ LIVES ON ... *Decca 1540* 4-6 38
(Vocals: Kenny Sargent)

YOU'VE GOT ME OUT ON A LIMB / CASTLE OF DREAMS................. *Decca 3082* 3-5 40
(Vocals: Kenny Sargent)

GRAY, Glen, & The Casa Loma Orchestra accompanying Hoagy Carmichael:

see CARMICHAEL, Hoagy, accompanied by Glen Gray & The Casa Loma Orchestra

GRAY, Glen, & The Casa Loma Orchestra as Roy Carroll & His Sands Point Orchestra

CASA LOMA STOMP / ROYAL GARDEN BLUES .... *Harmony 1271-H* 5-8 31

GRAY, Jerry, & His Orchestra

(Jerry Gray: 7/3/15 – 8/9/76)

ANCHORS AWEIGH / ON, BRAVE OLD ARMY TEAM......................... *Decca 28383* 2-4 52
(Vocals: The Skylarks)

CHAMPAGNE BOOGIE / $500 REWARD (Vocal: Linda Lee)......... *Decca 29231* 2-4 53

CORONADO CRUISE / STOP THAT DANCING (Vocal: Linda Lee)....... *Decca 29038* 2-4 53

CREEP, THE (Vocal: Linda Lee) / OOMP-CHUCK....................... *Decca 28986* 2-4 53

CRY (Vocal: Lynn Franklin) / ADIOS......... *Decca 27966* 2-4 51

DREAMY MELODY / DARLING, HOW COULD YOU.......................... *Decca 27756* 2-4 51
(Vocals: Tommy Traynor)

FAREWELL BLUES / JOHNSON RAG.... *Decca 27570* 2-4 51

GARDEN IN THE RAIN, A (Vocal: Tommy Traynor) / UNFORGETTABLE (Vocal: Lynn Franklin)... *Decca 27976* 2-4 51

HOME COOKIN' (Vocals: The Crew Chiefs) / CRAZY SHE CALLS ME (Vocal: Tommy Traynor) .... *Decca 27010* 2-4 50

I DON'T CARE IF THE SUN DON'T SHINE / VAGABOND SHOES.................. *Decca 27179* 2-4 50
(Vocals: The Crew Chiefs)

I NEVER WAS LOVED BY ANYONE ELSE (Vocals: Tommy Traynor & The Skylarks) / TURN BACK THE HANDS OF TIME (Vocals: Tommy Traynor, Gilda, & The Skylarks)...................... *Decca 27839* 2-4 51

NO MOON AT ALL / MY HEART BELONGS TO ONLY YOU .... *Decca 28561* 2-4 52
(Vocals: Jo Ann Greer)

PAIR OF TRUMPETS, A / ONE STOP BOOGIE......................... *Decca 28782* 2-4 52

PALE MOON (Vocal: Thurl Ravenscroft) / OFF THE WALL..................... *Decca 28718* 2-4 52

RE-STRINGING THE PEARLS / TELL ME (Vocal: Tommy Traynor)......... *Decca 27621* 2-4 51

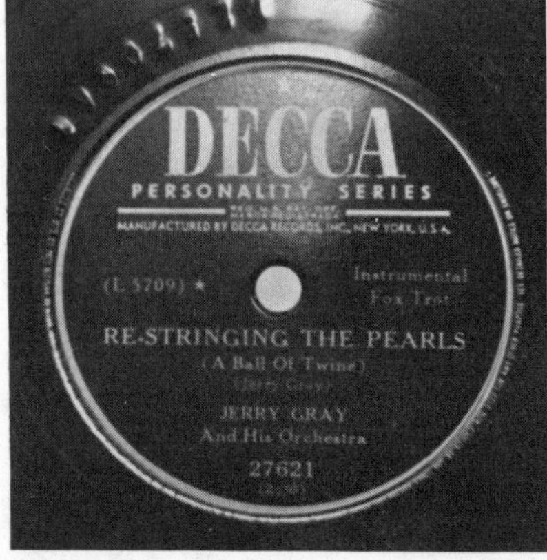

SHINE ON HARVEST MOON / FLAG WAVER .... *Decca 27868* 2-4 51

STORMY WEATHER MARCH / THE CARIOCA .... *Decca 24912* 2-4 50

TEXAS AND PACIFIC (Vocal: Frankie Laine) / ANVIL CHORUS .... *Mercury 5015* 3-5 47

WHERE DO I GO FROM YOU (Vocal: Tommy Traynor) / THE SPIRIT IS WILLING .... *Decca 27311* 2-4 50

YEAH! YEAH! YEAH! (Vocals: Tony Gray & Kitty White) / GOSPEL TRAIN (Vocals: Tony Gray & ensemble) .... *Decca 27476* 2-4 50

GRAY, Kitty, & Her Wampus Cats

DOING THE DOOGA / I'M YOURS TO COMMAND .... *Vocalion 04629* 8-10 39
(Vocals: Kitty Gray)

I CAN'T DANCE (GOT ANTS IN MY PANTS) / ROUND AND ROUND .... *Vocalion 03992* 10-12 37
(Vocals: Kitty Gray)

MY BABY'S WAYS (Vocal: Kitty Gray) / GETTIN' AWAY .... *Vocalion 04121* 10-12 37

SWINGOLOGY / POSIN' .... *Vocalion 03869* 8-10 37
(Vocals: Kitty Gray)

YOU'RE STANDING ON THE OUTSIDE NOW / WEEPING WILLOW SWING .... *Vocalion 04014* 8-10 37
(Vocals: Kitty Gray)

GREAT WESTERN SERENADERS, The:

see SAMUELS, Joseph, & His Orchestra

GREAT WHITE WAY ORCHESTRA, The:

directed by Hugo Frey

BESIDE A BABBLING BROOK (whistling by Master Billee Osborn) / SWINGIN' DOWN THE LANE ... *Victor 19058* 2-4 23

BORN AND BRED IN BROOKLYN / WHEN JUNE COMES ALONG WITH A SONG (whistling by Billy Murray) .... *Victor 19091* 3-5 23

MARCHETA / NEW HAMPSHIRE (by Zee Confrey & His Orchestra) .... *Victor 19046* 2-4 23

STELLA / CAROLINA MAMMY .... *Victor 19087* 2-4 23

TOMORROW / YOU GAVE ME YOUR HEART .... *Victor 18964* 2-4 22

WILDFLOWER (whistling by Billy Murray) / DREAMY MELODY .... *Victor 19077* 3-5 23

GREEN BROTHERS' NOVELTY BAND, The

directed by George Hamilton Green & Joe Green

AS LONG AS I HAVE YOU (Vocal: Arthur Fields) / LOUISE, YOU TEASE! .... *Edison 51753* 4-6 26

DO YOU EVER THINK OF ME? / MAZIE .... *Pathe Actuelle 020494* 3-5 21

FASCINATING RHYTHM / OH, LADY BE GOOD! .... *Edison 51497* 4-6 25

GREAT BIG HEAP MUCH BULL / CAROLINA ROLLING STONE .... *Okeh 4534* 2-4 22

HOP, SKIP AND JUMP / ALABAMA MOON .... *Lyric 4239* 5-8 20

IN SWEET SEPTEMBER / EV'RYBODY CALLS ME HONEY .... *Brunswick 2043* 2-4 20

LAST NIGHT ON THE BACK PORCH / POLLY-OLLY-OO .... *Edison 51212* 4-6 23

LOVE NEST / ALABAMA MOON .... *Mandel 4009* 20-25 20
(Mandel is a rare record)

MISSISSIPPI CRADLE / CANADIAN CAPERS .... *Cardinal 2047* 5-8 22

MONASTERY BELLS / WHEN FRANCIS DANCES WITH ME (by Markel's Orchestra) .... *Okeh 4467* 2-4 22

NEW ORLEANS WIGGLE / GLAD .... *Edison 51321* 5-8 24

SHE LOVES ME (Vocal: Billy Jones) / GO, EMMALINE (Vocal: Vernon Dalhart) ... *Edison 51385* 5-8 24

STARS OF NORMANDY / JAZZIN' THE CHIMES .... *Okeh 4311* 2-4 21

STOP IT / I'M A JAZZ VAMPIRE .... *Emerson 10217* 2-4 20

SWEET MAMA, PAPA'S GETTING MAD / ARABIA .... *Emerson 10348* 2-4 21

GREEN BROTHERS' XYLOPHONE ORCHESTRA, The

directed by George Hamilton Green & Joe Green

IDA, SWEET AS APPLE CIDER / TACKIN' 'EM DOWN .... *Pathe 22067* 3-5 19

MY BABY'S ARMS / JERRY .... *Paramount 33026* 4-6 19

MY CAIRO LOVE / THE VAMP .... *Edison 50554* 3-5 19

SHAKE YOUR SHOULDERS / THE VAMP ... *Okeh 1209* 3-5 19

TURKO / 'ROUND THE CORNER (by Fred Van Eps as The Van Eps Quartette) .... *Okeh 4048* 5-8 20
(This release has the "Indian head" label.)

WHO'S SORRY NOW? / THAT RED-HEAD GAL .... *Gennett 5122* 4-6 23

GREEN, George Hamilton as George Green's Novelty Orchestra

ARIZONA MONA / GREASED LIGHTNING .... *Emerson 1095* 2-4 19

FROM ONE TILL TWO / DON'T MIND THE RAIN .... *Paramount 20323* 3-5 24

HOP, SKIP AND JUMP / SHOW ME HOW .... *Lyric 4235* 5-8 20

THAT NAUGHTY WALTZ / LITTLE BLUE DEVIL .... *Emerson 10117* 2-4 20

VALSE CLASSIQUE / STOP TIME .... *Empire 506* 4-6 20

YOUNG MAN'S FANCY / KISMET .... *Concert 1061* 25-30 20
(Concert is a very rare record.)

GREEN, George Hamilton as George Hamilton Green's Star Trio

SWEET YVETTE / HAVANA .... *Edison 52071* 3-5 27

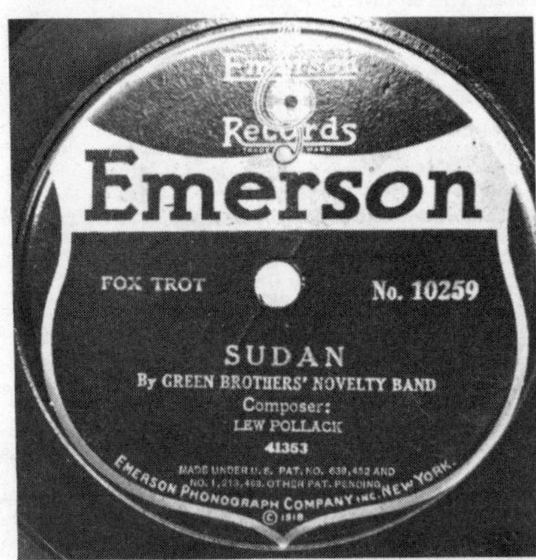

GREEN, Joe, & His Novelty Orchestra

AN OLD-FASHIONED HOME IN NEW HAMPSHIRE / TWO LOVES (HAVE I) .... *Crown 3253* 4-6 32
(Vocals: Smith Ballew)

DOLL DANCE, THE / THE WEDDING OF THE PAINTED DOLL .... *Romeo 255* 4-6 34
(This is a 7-inch 78 rpm record for children)

PARADE OF THE WOODEN SOLDIERS / TOM THUMB'S DRUM .... *Romeo 257* 4-6 34
(This is a 7-inch 78 rpm record for children)

SINGING A HAPPY SONG / RHYTHM OF THE RAIN .... *Vocalion 2886* 2-4 35
(Vocals: Chick Bullock)

TWO CIGARETTES IN THE DARK / I'M JUST THAT WAY .... *Vocalion 2777* 2-4 34
(Vocals: Jack Parker)

WATER UNDER THE BRIDGE / RAIN .... *Vocalion 2813* 2-4 34
(Vocals: Jack Parker)

WOMAN IN THE SHOE, THE / PARADE OF THE DUCKS .... *Romeo 254* 4-6 34
(This is a 7-inch 78 rpm record for children)

GREEN, Joe, & His Orchestra

DON'T FORGET ME IN YOUR DREAMS / THE RIVER AND ME .... *Perfect 15423* 3-5 31
(Vocals: William Robyn)

PALS OF THE LITTLE RED SCHOOL / WHEN IT'S SPRINGTIME IN THE BLUE RIDGE MOUNTAINS .... *Melotone M-12313* 3-5 32
(Vocals: Dick Robertson)

SIBONY / MAMA INEZ .... *Crown 3067* 3-5 31

SONG OF THE BIG TRAIL / I'M ALONE BECAUSE I LOVE YOU .... *Brunswick 4978* 3-5 31
(Vocals: Unknown)

WABASH MOON / BLUE PACIFIC MOONLIGHT .... *Crown 3061* 4-6 31
(Vocals: Unknown)

WHEN YOU AND I WERE SEVENTEEN / YOU'RE MY EVERYTHING (Vocals: Unknown) .... *Crown 3195* 4-6 31

GREEN, Joe, as Joe Green's Ambassadors

BENEATH MONTANA SKIES / AFTER THE DANCE .... *Melotone M-12166* 3-5 31
(Vocals: Dick Robertson)

SAME OLD MOON (Vocal: Dick Robertson) / WE'RE DANCING TOGETHER AGAIN (Vocal: Harold van Emburgh) .... *Melotone M-12420* 3-5 32

SONG THAT BROKE MY HEART, THE (Vocal: Dick Robertson) / CAN LOVE LIKE OURS BE WRONG (Vocal: Harold van Emburgh) .... *Melotone M-12421* 3-5 32

GREEN, Joe, as Joe Green's Novelty Marimba Band

ANITA / TWELVE O'CLOCK WALTZ ... *Brunswick 4023* 2-4 28
(Vocals: Jack Parker)

ONE NIGHT OF LOVE / THERE'LL NEVER BE ANOTHER YOU .... *Brunswick 3939* 3-5 28
(Vocals: Frank Munn)

SPRING, BEAUTIFUL SPRING / DANUBE WAVES .... *Edison 52068* 3-5 27

GREEN, Joe, as Joe Green's Vibraphone Dance Orchestra

I ALWAYS THINK OF YOU / SINCE YOU CALLED ME SWEETHEART .... *Cameo 822* 2-4 25

IF LOVE WERE ALL / WON'T YOU GIVE ME ONE MORE WALTZ? .... *Cameo 796* 2-4 25

IF LOVE WERE ALL / WON'T YOU GIVE ME ONE MORE WALTZ? .... *Lincoln 2402* 2-4 25
(Simultaneously released on two labels)

ONLY A BROKEN STRING OF PEARLS / TOO MANY PARTIES AND TOO MANY PALS .... *Lincoln 2468* 3-5 26

GREEN, Johnny, & His Orchestra

(Johnny Green: 10/10/08 –)

AN EARFUL OF MUSIC / YOU'RE A BUILDER-UPPER .... *Brunswick 6995* 5-8 34
(Vocals: Ethel Merman)

BEYOND THE SHADOW OF A DOUBT (Vocal: Marjory Logan) / LIVING ON VELVET (Vocal: Jimmy Farrell) .... *Columbia 3024-D* 3-5 35

EASY COME, EASY GO / REPEAL THE BLUES .... *Brunswick 6855* 8-10 34
(Vocals: Lee Wiley)

FROM OUT OF NOWHERE (Vocal: Ralph Blane) / THE STREAM IS ON THE BEAM (Vocal: Kay Thompson & Her Singers) .... *Decca 23435* 2-4 46

GO INTO YOUR DANCE / THE LITTLE THINGS YOU USED TO DO .... *Columbia 3028-D* 3-5 35
(Vocals: Marjory Logan)

ISN'T THIS A LOVELY DAY? / TOP HAT, WHITE TIE AND TAILS .... *Brunswick 7487* 5-8 35
(Vocals: Fred Astaire)

LIVE AND LOVE TONIGHT / COCKTAILS FOR TWO .... *Brunswick 6797* 5-8 34
(Vocals: Howard Phillips)

LOVELY TO LOOK AT (Vocal: Jimmy Farrell) / I WON'T DANCE (Vocals: Marjory Logan & Jimmy Farrell) .... *Columbia 3022-D* 4-6 35

NEW MOON IS OVER MY SHOULDER, A (Vocal: Bernice Park) / BY THE TAJ MAHAL (Vocal: George Bouler) .... *Columbia 2940-D* 4-6 34

RENDEZVOUS WITH A DREAM / WE'LL REST AT THE TRAIL .... *Brunswick 7662* 3-5 36
(Vocals: Unknown)

SHE'S A LATIN FROM MANHATTAN / ABOUT A QUARER TO NINE .... *Columbia 3029-D* 4-6 35
(Vocals: Jimmy Farrell)

TWO CIGARETTES IN THE DARK (Vocal: George Bouler) / THE FORTUNE TELLER (Vocal: Peg La Centra) .... *Columbia 2943-D* 4-6 34

WERE YOU FOOLIN'? (Vocal: Allen Curtis) / THE WORLD IS MINE (Vocal: George Bouler) .... *Columbia 2959-D* 4-6 34

WHY SHOULDN'T I? / WHEN LOVES COMES YOUR WAY .... *Brunswick 7522* 3-5 35
(Vocals: Unknown)

GREEN, Larry, & His Orchestra

BEG YOUR PARDON / CAN I EVER BE THE SAME? (Vocal: Don Grady) .... *RCA Victor 20-2647* 2-4 48

HOW HIGH THE MOON / FAR AWAY ISLAND .... *RCA Victor 20-2119* 2-4 47
(Vocals: Gil Phelan)

MY COUSIN LOUELLA / MY PROMISE TO YOU (Vocal: Don Grady) ... *RCA Victor 20-2582* 2-4 47

NEAR YOU / PIC-A-NIC-IN (Vocal: June Robbins) .... *RCA Victor 20-2421* 2-4 47

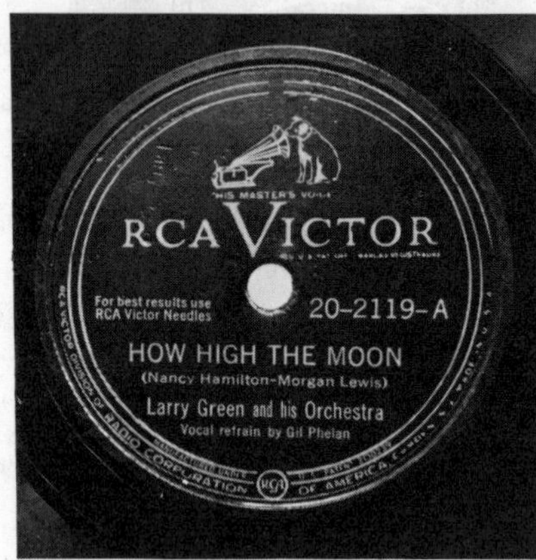

GREEN, Ruby, as Ruby Green's Manhattan Madcaps:
see FENTON, Carl, & His Orchestra

GRESH, Earl, & His Gangplank Orchestra

ACE IN THE HOLE / THE PUMP SONG (Vocals: by orchestra)........... *Columbia 672-D* 5-8 26
FRESHIE / HELP! .... *Columbia 469-D* 4-6 25
(Vocals: by orchestra)
ROW, ROW, ROSIE / SHE WAS JUST A SAILOR'S SWEETHEART .... *Columbia 424-D* 5-8 25
(Vocals: by orchestra)
TENDERLY / SCATTER YOUR SMILES .... *Columbia 693-D* 4-6 26
WHERE THE WILD, WILD FLOWERS GROW (Vocal: Irving Kaufman) / GIVE ME A LITTLE BIT O'SUNSHINE (by Walter Davison's Louisville Loons; Vocals: by quartet) .... *Columbia 1031-D* 5-8 27

GRIER, Jimmy, & His Cocoanut Grove Orchestra
(Jimmy Grier: 3/17/02 – 6/4/59)

HERE LIES LOVE / I CANNOT TELL YOU WHY...................... *Victor 24174* 5-8 32
(Vocals: Ray Hendricks)
MOONSTRUCK / LEARN TO CROON... *Brunswick 6597* 3-5 33
(Vocals: Unknown)
ONE HOUR WITH YOU / MUSIC IN THE MOONLIGHT (theme song)......... *Victor 22971* 3-5 32
(Vocals: Donald Novis)
SECOND-HAND HEART (Vocal: Gogo Delys) / I CAN DEPEND ON YOU (Vocal: Dick Webster).... *Victor 24175* 5-8 32

GRIER, Jimmy, & His Orchestra

COLLEGE RHYTHM / LET'S GIVE THREE CHEERS FOR LOVE............... *Brunswick 7306* 4-6 34
(Vocals: Unknown)
DAYDREAMING / I WANNA GO BACK TO BALI .... *Decca 1813* 3-5 38
(Vocals: Dick Webster)
DON'T BE AFRAID TO TELL YOUR MOTHER (Vocal: Pinky Tomlin) / WHAT'S THE REASON (I'M NOT PLEASIN' YOU) (Vocals: Unknown) .... *Brunswick 7355* 4-6 35
(Pinky Tomlin composed both tunes on this release, as well as numerous other pop songs.)

IN AN IVY-COVERED ARBOR / RIVER MAN...................... *Brunswick 7683* 4-6 36
(Vocals: Dick Webster)
OLD-FASHIONED LOVE (Vocal: Joy Hodges) / BUGLE CALL RAG................ *Brunswick 7528* 5-8 35
SOMETHING TO SING ABOUT (Vocal: Julie Gibson) / OUT OF THE BLUE (Vocal: Dick Webster) .... *Decca 1474* 4-6 37
STRANGER IN PAREE, A (Vocal: Dick Webster) / ISLE OF CAPRI........................ *Decca 1812* 4-6 37
YANKEE DOODLE (Vocals: The Rhythm Rascals) / BOB WHITE (WHATCHA GONNA SWING TONIGHT?)........................... *Decca 1497* 5-8 37
YOU LEAVE ME BREATHLESS / SAYS MY HEART .... *Decca 1797* 4-6 37
(Vocals: Julie Gibson)

GROFE, Ferdie, & His Orchestra
(Ferdie Grofe: 3/27/92 – 4/3/72)

CINDERELLA'S FELLA (Vocals: The Rhythm Boys) / TEMPTATION (Vocals: Unknown).... *Columbia 2851-D* 5-8 34
INKA DINKA DOO (Vocals: The Rhythm Boys) / COUNT YOUR BLESSINGS (Vocal: Unknown)... *Columbia 2858-D* 5-8 34

GROSS, Carl:
see ROANE'S PENNSYLVANIANS

GROSSO, Elmer, & His Grennwich Village Orchestra

ANGEL EYES / THINKING OF YOU... *Silvertone 5031* 3-5 27
MAYBE SOMETIME / NESTING TIME... *Gennett 6093* 2-4 27
(Vocals: Grosso Brothers)
WANDERING IN DREAMLAND / IN A SHADY NOOK BY A BABBLING BROOK............. *Gennett 6158* 2-4 27
(Vocals: Irving Edwards)

GROSSO, Elmer, as Elmer Grosso's Mount Royal Orchestra

BYE BYE BLUES / JUST A LITTLE CLOSER..................... *Gennett 7253* 4-6 30
(Vocals: Claude Reese)
BYE BYE BLUES / JUST A LITTLE CLOSER................... *Supertone 9743* 3-5 30
(Vocals: Claude Reese)
(Simultaneously released on two labels)
CHEERFUL LITTLE EARFUL / TO MAKE A LONG STORY SHORT .... *Champion 16176* 3-5 31
(Vocals: Claude Reese)
C.O.N.S.T.A.N.T.I.N.O.P.L.E. (Vocal: Carl Mathieu) / JUST A NIGHT FOR MEDITATION (Vocal: Elmer Russell) .... *Gennett 6521* 3-5 28
DANCE OF THE WOODEN SHOES / BLUE IS THE NIGHT................ *Gennett 7103* 4-6 30
(Vocals: Tommy Weir as Jack Wilson)
DANCE OF THE WOODEN SHOES / BLUE IS THE NIGHT............... *Supertone 9603* 3-5 30
(Vocals: Tommy Weir as Jack Wilson)
(Simultaneously released on two labels)
I'M WHISTLING IN THE DARK / LOVELIGHT, KEEP SHINING FOR ME................ *Champion 16252* 3-5 31
(Vocals: Elmer Grosso)
MISS YOU / FOR SOMEONE I LOVE..... *Gennett 6935* 4-6 29
(Vocals: Jerry White)
MISS YOU / THE MOONLIGHT MARCH .... *Supertone 9460* 3-5 29
(Vocals: Jerry White)
MONTANA CALL / THE MOON IS LOW.............................. *Gennett 7134* 4-6 30
(Vocals: Frank Luther)
MONTANA CALL / THE MOON IS LOW............................ *Supertone 9618* 3-5 30
(Vocals: Frank Luther)
(Simultaneously released on two labels)
MY BLACKBIRDS ARE BLUEBIRDS NOW / PRETTY, PETITE AND SWEET .... *Herwin 8314* 15-20 28
(Vocals: Elmer Russell)
MY SWEETER THAN SWEET / I MAY BE WRONG, BUT I THINK YOU'RE WONDERFUL... *Gennett 7044* 4-6 30
(Vocals: Elmer Grosso)
MY SWEETER THAN SWEET / I MAY BE WRONG, BUT I THINK YOU'RE WONDERFUL... *Supertone 9582* 3-5 30
(Vocals: Elmer Grosso)
(Simultaneously released on two labels)
OLD MAN SUNSHINE / C.O.N.S.T.A.N.T.I.N.O.P.L.E .... *Supertone 9041* 3-5 28
(Vocals: Carl Mathieu)
SONNY BOY / WHY?................. *Supertone 9058* 2-4 28
(Vocals: Elmer Russell)

GUARENTE, Frank:
see SPECHT, Paul, as the Georgians

GUARNIERI, Johnny, & His All Star Orchestra
(Johnny Guarnieri: 3/23/17 – 1/85)

BASIE ENGLISH / EXERCISE IN SWING.... *Savoy 509* 4-6 44

GUMIN, Joe, & His Orchestra

BLUE AGAIN (Vocal: Sammy Sievert) / TIE A LITTLE STRING AROUND YOUR FINGER (Vocals: by trio)...................... *Broadway 1430* 4-6 31
JINGLE BELLS (sung in five languages) / I'LL THINK OF YOU.............. *Columbia 2571-D* 5-8 31
(Vocals: Unknown)
LOVE IS LIKE THAT / MY CRADLE SWEETHEART.................... *Broadway 1468* 3-5 31
(Vocals: Unknown)

GUNN, Jimmie, & His Orchestra

MY BLUE HEAVEN (Vocal: Sam Jennings) / STAR DUST (Vocal: David Pugh) ...... *Bluebird B-6469* 5-8 36
SLAT'S SHUFFLE / MADHOUSE (by Bob Pope & His Hotel Charlotte Orchestra)........ *Bluebird B-6508* 5-8 36
TO MY LEVEE HOME (Vocal: David Pugh) / I'VE FOUND A NEW BABY........ *Bluebird B-6500* 5-8 36

GUY, Mickey, & His Rose-Tree Orchestra

ROSE-TREE STRUT / SO THAT'S THE KIND OF A GIRL YOU ARE................. *Okeh 40462* 5-8 25

GUY, Mickey, as Mickey Guy's Hottentots

IN YOUR GREEN HAT / IN MY GONDOLA............................ *Okeh 40588* 4-6 26
RHYTHM RAG/PHILADELPHIA... *Pathe Actuelle 36433* 5-8 26
RHYTHM RAG / PHILADELPHIA....... *Perfect 14614* 4-6 26
(Simultaneously released on two labels)
TWO-TON TESSIE / —........... *Pathe Actuelle 36478* 5-8 26
TWO-TON TESSIE / — .... *Perfect 14659* 4-6 26
(Simultaneously released on two labels)

GUYON'S PARADISE ORCHESTRA
directed by Jules R. Herbuveaux

HENPECKED BLUES / LOUISVILLE LOU... *Okeh 4862* 4-6 23
ISLE OF SWEETHEARTS / HAWAII....... *Okeh 4742* 2-4 23
I'VE GOT THE AIN'T GOT NOTHIN', NEVER HAD NOTHIN' BLUES / —...... *Okeh 4866* 3-5 23
JUST FOR TONIGHT / ABANDONADO..... *Okeh 4865* 2-4 23
LAND OF COTTON BLUES / —............ *Okeh 4999* 3-5 23
LOST / I'M THROUGH.................... *Okeh 4737* 3-5 23
SILVER SWANEE / LOVIN' SAM (THE SHEIK OF ALABAM')................... *Okeh 4732* 4-6 23

HACKEL, Alexander:
see HACKEL-BERGE Orchestra, The

HACKEL-BERGE ORCHESTRA, The
directed by Alexander Hackel and William Berge

DON'T FORGET TO REMEMBER / I'M ALL BROKEN UP OVER YOU .... *Federal 5385* 3-5 24

JUST AS LONG AS YOU HAVE ME / WHEN ALL YOUR CASTLES COME TUMBLING DOWN ..... *Pathe Actuelle 020843* 3-5 22

JUST AS LONG AS YOU HAVE ME / WHEN ALL YOUR CASTLES COME TUMBLING DOWN .... *Perfect 14062* 2-4 22
(Simultaneously released on two labels)

NELLIE KELLY, I LOVE YOU / DOWN OLD VIRGINIA WAY .... *Federal 5218* 2-4 22

RAGGEDY ANN / A LOVE SONG .... *Federal 5373* 3-5 24

HACKEL-BERGE TRIO, The

HOLY NIGHT / SILENT NIGHT, HOLY NIGHT .... *Blue Bird 33069* 30-35 21
(An exceptionally rare release produced by the Blue Bird Talking Machine Company in Los Angeles, California.)

HACKETT, Bobby, & His Orchestra
(Bobby Hackett: 1/31/15 – 6/7/76)

AIN'T MISBEHAVIN' / EMBRACEABLE YOU (theme song) .... *Vocalion 4877* 4-6 39

BLUE AND SENTIMENTAL (Vocal: Linda Keene) / POOR BUTTERFLY .... *Vocalion 4499* 4-6 38

BUGLE CALL RAG / DARDANELLA ... *Vocalion 5375* 3-5 39

CLARINET MARMALADE / SINGIN' THE BLUES .... *Vocalion 5493* 3-5 40

IF DREAMS COME TRUE (Vocal: Lola Bard) / AT THE JAZZ BAND BALL .... *Vocalion 4047* 4-6 38

JA DA / I SURRENDER, DEAR (Vocal: Claire Martin) .... *Vocalion 5198* 3-5 39

THAT OLD GANG OF MINE / AFTER I SAY I'M SORRY .... *Vocalion 5620* 3-5 40
(Vocals: The Tempo Twisters)

THAT'S HOW DREAMS SHOULD END / SUNRISE SERENADE .... *Vocalion 4806* 3-5 39

HAGAN, Cass, & His Hotel Manger Orchestra
(Cass Hagan: 1904 –)

HALLELUJAH! / SOMETIMES I'M HAPPY .... *Columbia 966-D* 5-8 27
(Vocals: Franklyn Baur)

MELANCHOLY CHARLIE / VARIETY STOMP .... *Columbia 1033-D* 5-8 27

HAGAN, Cass, & His Orchestra

I ADORE YOU / LILY .... *Edison 52012* 5-8 27

KINKAJOU, THE / IT ALL DEPENDS ON YOU (Vocal: Arthur Fields) .... *Edison 51959* 5-8 27

HAGAN, Cass, & His Park Central Hotel Orchestra

BROADWAY (Vocal: Lewis James) / MANHATTAN MARY (Vocals: Lewis James, Frank Luther, & Elliot Shaw) .... *Columbia 1138-D* 3-5 27

HAVANA / HERE AM I – BROKEN-HEARTED .... *Columbia 1089-D* 5-8 27
(Vocals: Franklyn Baur)

MY OHIO HOME (Vocal: Irving Kaufman as Frank Harris) / I STILL LOVE YOU (by Ben Selvin as the Radiolites, with an unknown vocalist) .... *Columbia 1301-D* 3-5 28

VARSITY DRAG, THE (Vocals: Franklyn Baur, Lewis James & Elliot Shaw) / DANCING TAMBOURINE (by Ben Selvin as the Radiolites) .... *Columbia 1114-D* 5-8 27

HAID, Bill, & His Cubs

BLUE GRASS / HOLD EVERYTHING, HERE COMES MY GIRL .... *Broadway 1200* 4-6 28
(Vocals: Frank Wells)

BLUE GRASS / HOLD EVERYTHING, HERE COMES MY GIRL .... *Paramount 20644* 5-8 28
(Vocals: Frank Wells)
(Simultaneously released on two labels)

BLUE SHADOWS / THAT'S MY WAY OF FORGETTING YOU .... *Broadway 1207* 4-6 28
(Vocals: J. Allen)

BLUE SHADOWS / THAT'S MY WAY OF FORGETTING YOU .... *Paramount 20648* 5-8 28
(Vocals: J. Allen)
(Simultaneously released on two labels)

ETIQUETTE / PICKIN' COTTON ...... *Broadway 1205* 4-6 28
(Vocals: J. Allen)

ETIQUETTE / PICKIN' COTTON ...... *Paramount 20646* 5-8 28
(Vocals: J. Allen)
(Simultaneously released on two labels)

I AIN'T GOT NOBODY / A GOOD MAN IS HARD TO FIND .... *Broadway 1217* 4-6 28
(Vocals: Diana Dell)

I AIN'T GOT NOBODY / A GOOD MAN IS HARD TO FIND .... *Paramount 20658* 5-8 28
(Vocals: Diana Dell)
(Simultaneously released on two labels)

I CAN'T GIVE YOU ANYTHING BUT LOVE / CRAZY RHYTHM .... *Broadway 1206* 4-6 28
(Vocals: J. Allen)

I CAN'T GIVE YOU ANYTHING BUT LOVE / CRAZY RHYTHM .... *Paramount 20647* 5-8 28
(Vocals: J. Allen)
(Simultaneously released on two labels)

IF YOU DON'T LOVE ME / JEANNINE .... *Broadway 1201* 3-5 28
(Vocals: Frank Wells)

IF YOU DON'T LOVE ME / JEANNINE .... *Paramount 20643* 4-6 28
(Vocals: Frank Wells)
(Simultaneously released on two labels)

ME AND THE MAN IN THE MOON / DOIN' THE RACCOON .... *Broadway 1235* 4-6 29
(Vocals: Edwin Taylor)

ME AND THE MAN IN THE MOON / DOIN' THE RACCOON .... *Paramount 20676* 5-8 29
(Vocals: Edwin Taylor)
(Simultaneously released on two labels)

SHAKE IT DOWN (Vocal: Frank Wells) / WEARY WEASEL .... *Broadway 1220* 5-8 28

SHAKE IT DOWN (Vocal: Frank Wells) / WEARY WEASEL .... *Paramount 20661* 8-10 28
(Simultaneously released on two labels)

THAT OLD SWEETHEART OF MINE / MARIE .... *Broadway 1229* 4-6 28
(Vocals: Frank Wells)

THAT OLD SWEETHEART OF MINE / MARIE .... *Paramount 20660* 5-8 28
(Vocals: Frank Wells)
(Simultaneously released on two labels)

HAID, Bill, & His Thieves of Sleep

SLUE FOOT / LONELY LITTLE BLUEBIRD (Vocal: George Moore) ...... *Broadway 1187* 4-6 28

SLUE FOOT / LONELY LITTLE BLUEBIRD (Vocal: George Moore) .... *Paramount 20628* 5-8 28
(Simultaneously released on two labels)

WAITING / I'M WALKING BETWEEN THE RAINDROPS ...... *Broadway 1188* 4-6 28
(Vocals: George Moore)

WAITING / I'M WALKING BETWEEN THE RAINDROPS ..... *Paramount 20630* 5-8 28
(Vocals: George Moore)
(Simultaneously released on two labels)

HAITIAN ORCHESTRA, The
star performers: Sidney Bechet (5/14/97 – 5/14/59)
Kenneth Roane (circa 1902 –)
Willie "the Lion" Smith (11/25/97 – 4/18/73)

DIANE / NANA .... *Baldwin 1013* 10-12 40

MAYOTTE / MAGIC ISLANDS .... *Varsity 8399* 4-6 40

ORIGINAL HAITIAN MUSIC / ORIGINAL HAITIAN MUSIC, PART II .... *Varsity 8363* 4-6 40

ORIGINAL HAITIAN MUSIC, PART III / ORIGINAL HAITIAN MUSIC, PART IV .... *Varsity 8364* 4-6 40

ROSE RHUMBA / SOUS LES PALMIERS ... *Varsity 8405* 4-6 40

TI RALPH / MERENGUE D'AMOUR .... *Baldwin 1012* 10-12 40

TROPICAL MOON / BABA .... *Varsity 8360* 4-6 40

HALL, Al:
see PEERLES SERENADERS of Al Tearney's Town Club, The

HALLETT, Mal, & His Orchestra
(Mal Hallett: circa 1893 – 11/20/52)

ALIBI BABY (Vocal: Teddy Grace) / YOU'RE LOOKING FOR ROMANCE (Vocal: Clark Yocum) ...... *Decca 1282* 4-6 37

BOSTON TEA PARTY (theme song) (Vocal: Buddy Welcome) / SWEET MISERY OF LOVE .... *Vocalion 3278* 4-6 36

DOES SHE LOVE ME? POSITIVELY – ABSOLUTELY / MY IDEA OF HEAVEN .... *Columbia 967-D* 5-8 27
(Vocals: Tess Gardelle as Aunt Jemima)

EARFUL OF MUSIC (Vocal: Clarke Yocum) / OKAY, TOOTS (Vocal: Charles Blake) ..... *Banner 33235* 4-6 34

EARFUL OF MUSIC (Vocal: Clarke Yocum) / OKAY, TOOTS (Vocal: Charles Blake) ... *Melotone M-13202* 4-6 34

EARFUL OF MUSIC (Vocal: Clarke Yocum) / OKAY, TOOTS (Vocal: Charles Blake) .... *Oriole 3023* 4-6 34

EARFUL OF MUSIC (Vocal: Clarke Yocum) / OKAY, TOOTS (Vocal: Charles Blake) ..... *Perfect 16020* 4-6 34

EARFUL OF MUSIC (Vocal: Clarke Yocum) / OKAY, TOOTS (Vocal: Charles Blake) ...... *Romeo 2397* 4-6 34
(Simultaneously released on five labels)

I CAN'T LOSE THAT LONGING FOR YOU (Vocal: Jerry Perkins) / OH, SAY, CAN YOU SWING? (Vocal: Buddy Welcome) .... *Decca 1111* 4-6 37

I'D LOVE TO PLAY A LOVE SCENE (OPPOSITE YOU) (Vocal: Jerry Perkins) / I WANT A NEW ROMANCE (Vocal: Teddy Grace) ...... *Decca 1532* 3-5 37

I'VE GOT RAIN IN MY EYES / THE TROUBLE WITH ME IS YOU .... *Decca 1167* 4-6 37
(Vocals: Teddy Grace)

LET ME SING IN ECHO VALLEY / IN THE CHAPEL IN THE MOONLIGHT .... *Decca 1033* 4-6 36
(Vocals: Jerry Perkins)

LET'S HAVE ANOTHER CIGARETTE (Vocal: Jerry Perkins) / THE LIFE OF THE PARTY (Vocal: Teddy Grace) .... *Decca 1403* 4-6 37

LET'S SING AGAIN / THE GLORY OF LOVE .... *Vocalion 3235* 4-6 36
(Vocals: Unknown)

LOONEY LITTLE TOONEY / IF I WERE YOU .... *Decca 2043* 3-5 38
(Vocals: Buddy Welcome)

MARY LOU / SWING FEVER (Vocal: Buddy Welcome) .... *Vocalion 3236* 5-8 36

MOONLIGHT ON THE HIGHWAY (Vocal: Jerry Perkins) / TURN ON THAT RED HOT HEAT (BURN YOUR BLUES AWAY) (Vocal: Teddy Grace) .... *Decca 1384* 4-6 37

OH LIZZIE (Vocal: Sam Sherman) / IT'S O.K., KATY, WITH ME (Vocals: Bill Carlin & Sam Sherman) .... *Columbia 917-D* 3-5 27

ONLY YOU AND LONELY ME / WHAT GOOD IS "GOOD MORNING"? .... *Harmony 161-H* 4-6 26

RIDIN' HIGH / BIG BOY BLUE (Vocal: Buddy Welcome) .... *Decca 1163* 4-6 37

ROCKIN' CHAIR SWING (Vocal: Teddy Grace) / HUMORESQUE .... *Decca 1190* 4-6 37

TURN OFF THE MOON (Vocal: Teddy Grace) / EASY ON THE EYES (Vocal: Buddy Welcome) .... *Decca 1270* 4-6 37

WHEN THE BUTTERFLIES KISS THE BUTTERCUP / BOOMERANG .... *Edison 14080* 10-12 29
(A rare lateral-cut thin Edison disc.)

WHOSE WHO ARE YOU / LONESOME ME .... *Okeh 40573* 4-6 26

WHY DO I LIE TO MYSELF ABOUT YOU? / I'M AN OLD COWHAND .... *Vocalion 3268* 3-5 36
(Vocals: Unknown)

YANKEE DOODLE BAND (Vocal: Buddy Welcome) / ROSES IN DECEMBER (Vocal: Jerry Perkins) ... *Decca 1402* 4-6 37

YOU AND ME / IT'S THE LITTLE THINGS THAT COUNT .... *Decca 1863* 3-5 38
(Vocals: Jerry Perkins)

YOU AND ME THAT USED TO BE, THE (Vocal: Teddy Grace) / 'CAUSE MY BABY SAYS IT'S SO (Vocal: Buddy Welcome) .... *Decca 1281* 4-6 37

YOU'RE OUT OF THIS WORLD TO ME (Vocal: Teddy Grace) / TRUE CONFESSION (Vocal: Jerry Perkins) .... *Decca 1533* 3-5 37

YOUR HEAD ON MY SHOULDER (Vocal: Clark Yocum) / WHEN MY SHIP COMES IN .... *Banner 33234* 3-5 34

YOUR HEAD ON MY SHOULDER (Vocal: Clark Yocum) / WHEN MY SHIP COMES IN ...... *Melotone M-13201* 3-5 34

YOUR HEAD ON MY SHOULDER (Vocal: Clark Yocum) / WHEN MY SHIP COMES IN .... *Oriole 3022* 3-5 34

YOUR HEAD ON MY SHOULDER (Vocal: Clark Yocum) / WHEN MY SHIP COMES IN .... *Perfect 16019* 3-5 34

YOUR HEAD ON MY SHOULDER (Vocal: Clark Yocum) / WHEN MY SHIP COMES IN .... *Romeo 2396* 3-5 34
(Simultaneously released on five labels)

HALL, Fred "Sugar", & His Sugar Babies
(Fred "Sugar" Hall: 4/10/98 – 10/8/64)

COME ON, BABY / I'M WILD ABOUT HORNS ON AUTOMOBILES............ *Okeh 41152* 4-6 29
(Vocals: Arthur Fields)

C.O.N.S.T.A.N.T.I.N.O.P.L.E. (Vocal: Arthur Fields) / CHILLY-POM-POM-PEE.............. *Okeh 41055* 4-6 28

GRASS GROWS GREENER, THE / (NO MATTER HOW YOU SLICE IT) IT'S BOLOGNEY......... *Okeh 41008* 4-6 28
(Vocals: Arthur Fields)

HARMONICA HARRY / 'TAIN'T NO SIN (TO TAKE OFF YOUR SKIN AND DANCE AROUND IN YOUR BONES)...... *Odeon ONY-36041* 5-8 30
(Vocals: Arthur Fields)

HARMONICA HARRY / 'TAIN'T NO SIN (TO TAKE OFF YOUR SKIN AND DANCE AROUND IN YOUR BONES)............ *Okeh 41369* 5-8 30
(Vocals: Arthur Fields)
(Simultaneously released on two labels)

HERE'S THAT PARTY NOW IN PERSON / I GOT A "CODE" IN MY "DOZE"............... *Okeh41239* 4-6 29
(Vocals: Arthur Fields)

I AIN'T GOT NOBODY / I'M GONNA HANG AROUND MY SUGAR.................. *Okeh 40496* 5-8 25

I LIFT UP MY FINGER AND I SAY "TWEET TWEET" / SOPHOMORE PROM......... *Okeh 41310* 4-6 29
(Vocals: Arthur Fields)

IS IT POSSIBLE? / SOMEDAY YOU'LL SAY "O. K."........................... *Okeh 40891* 4-6 27
(Vocals: Arthur Fields)

IT GOES LIKE THIS / EVERYTHING WE LIKE WE LIKE ALIKE................ *Okeh 41123* 4-6 28
(Vocals: Arthur Fields)

LOOK WHO'S HERE! / MY SUGAR....... *Okeh 40410* 5-8 25

MELANCHOLY LOU / CHARLESTON BABY O' MINE........................ *Okeh 40482* 5-8 25

ON THE NIGHT WE DID THE BOOM-BOOM BY THE SEA / BUTTERNUT........... *Okeh 41112* 4-6 28
(Vocals: Arthur Fields)

PICCOLO PETE / SERGEANT FLAGG AND SERGEANT QUIRT.................... *Okeh 41317* 5-8 29
(Vocals: Arthur Fields & Fred Hall)

PLENTY OF SUNSHINE / LOOK IN THE MIRROR.......................... *Okeh 40986* 3-5 27
(Vocals: Arthur Fields)

SHE ONLY LAUGHS AT ME / I FAW DOWN AND GO 'BOOM'!.................. *Okeh 41183* 5-8 29
(Vocals: Arthur Fields)

SHE'S THE SWEETHEART OF SIX OTHER GUYS / WAITIN' FOR KATY................. *Okeh 41026* 4-6 28
(Vocals: Arthur Fields)

SOBBIN' BLUES / DALLAS BLUES...... *Okeh 40437* 5-8 25

THERE'S A FOUR-LEAF CLOVER IN MY POCKET / IT AIN'T NO FAULT OF MINE........... *Okeh 41269* 4-6 29
(Vocals: Arthur Fields)

HALL, Fred, as Fred Hall's Jazz Band

WEST END BLUES / MISSOURI SQUABBLE.......................... *Domino 4214* 5-8 28

WEST END BLUES / MISSOURI SQUABBLE.......................... *Regal 8655* 5-8 28
(Simultaneously released on two labels)

HALL, Fred, as Fred Hall's Jazz Band recorded under the name The California Collegians

WEST END BLUES / MISSOURI SQUABBLE........................ *Challenge 952* 5-8 28

HALL, Fred, as Fred Hall's Jazz Band recorded under the name The Dixie Jazz Band

LOUDER AND FUNNIER / MISSOURI SQUABBLE.......................... *Oriole 1416* 5-8 28

HALL, Fred, as The Honey Swamp Stompers

WIPIN' THE PAN / BETTY.......... *Harmony 856-H* 5-8 29
(Vocals: Arthur Fields & Fred Hall)

HALL, Fred, as The Tin Tan Paraders

CHINNIN' AND CHATTIN' WITH MAY (Vocal: Arthur Fields) / AMOS 'N ANDY (Vocal: Arthur Fields & Fred Hall).......... *Gennett 7174* 4-6 30

IF I WERE YOU I'D FALL IN LOVE WITH ME / I LIFT UP MY FINGER AND I SAY "TWEET TWEET"............. *Gennett 6965* 3-5 29
(Vocals: Arthur Fields)

I GOT A "CODE" IN MY "DOZE" / SHE ONLY LAUGHS AT ME..................... *Gennett 6849* 5-8 29
(Vocals: Arthur Fields)

I GOT A "CODE" IN MY "DOZE" / SHE ONLY LAUGHS AT ME.................. *Supertone 9416* 4-6 29
(Vocals: Arthur Fields)
(Simultaneously released on two labels)

I GOTTA HAVE YOU / CLOWNING........ *Gennett 7012* 5-8 29
(Vocals: Arthur Fields)

I GOTTA HAVE YOU / CLOWNING.... *Supertone 9544* 4-6 29
(Vocals: Arthur Fields)
(Simultaneously released on two labels)

MAMA'S GROWN YOUNG, PAPA'S GROWN OLD / WHO WOULDN'T BE BLUE?.......... *Herwin 8069* 15-20 28
(Vocals: Arthur Fields)

MAMA'S GROWN YOUNG, PAPA'S GROWN OLD / WHO WOULDN'T BE BLUE?........ *Supertone 9013* 4-6 28
(Vocals: Arthur Fields)
(Simultaneously released on two labels)

MAN FROM THE SOUTH / HARMONICA HARRY................... *Gennett 7132* 5-8 30
(Vocals: Arthur Fields)

MAN FROM THE SOUTH / HARMONICA HARRY.............. *Supertone 9616* 4-6 30
(Vocals: Arthur Fields)
(Simultaneously released on two labels)

MY PET / AN' FURTHERMORE........ *Gennett 6456* 4-6 28
(Vocals: Arthur Fields)

MY PET / AN' FURTHERMORE......... *Herwin 8067* 15-20 28
(Vocals: Arthur Fields)
(Simultaneously released on two labels)

NOW I'M IN LOVE / BELIEVE IT OR NOT........................... *Gennett 6921* 3-5 29
(Vocals: Arthur Fields)

NOW I'M IN LOVE / BELIEVE IT OR NOT.......................... *Supertone 9464* 2-4 29
(Vocals: Arthur Fields)
(Simultaneously released on two labels)

'S BEEN A LONG TIME BETWEEN TIME / I LIFT UP MY FINGER AND I SAY "TWEET TWEET"........... *Supertone 9477* 3-5 29
(Vocals: Arthur Fields)

WOMAN IN THE SHOE, THE / WAKE UP YOUR FEET........................ *Gennett 7072* 4-6 30
(Vocals: Arthur Fields)

WOMAN IN THE SHOE, THE / WAKE UP YOUR FEET...................... *Supertone 9586* 3-5 30
(Vocals: Arthur Fields)
(Simultaneously released on two labels)

YOU'VE GOT THAT THING / THE ONE I LOVE JUST CAN'T BE BOTHERED WITH ME..... *Gennett 7146* 5-8 30
(Vocals: Arthur Fields)

YOU'VE GOT THAT THING / THE ONE I LOVE JUST CAN'T BE BOTHERED WITH ME... *Supertone 9620* 4-6 30
(Vocals: Arthur Fields)
(Simultaneously released on two labels)

HALL, Fred, as The Tin Pan Paraders recorded under the name Bud Carson & His Collegians

CHINNIN' AND CHATTIN' WITH MAY / THE FREE AND EASY...................... *Champion 15976* 3-5 30
(Vocals: Arthur Fields)

IF I WERE YOU I'D FALL IN LOVE WITH ME / I'M FINDING THE LONG WAY HOME... *Champion 15843* 3-5 29

I GOT A "CODE" IN MY "DOZE" / SHE ONLY LAUGHS AT ME................. *Champion 15728* 4-6 29
(Vocals: Arthur Fields)

I GOTTA HAVE YOU / CLOWNING... *Champion 15838* 4-6 29
(Vocals: Arthur Fields)

MAMA'S GROWN YOUNG, PAPA'S GROWN OLD / WHO WOULDN'T BE BLUE? ...... *Champion 15514* 4-6 28
(Vocals: Arthur Fields)

MAN FROM THE SOUTH / KICKIN' A HOLE IN THE SKY..................... *Champion 15918* 4-6 30
(Vocals: Arthur Fields)

MY PET / WHEN SWEET SUSIE GOES STEPPIN' BY........ *Champion 15535* 4-6 28
(Vocals: Arthur Fields)

PUTTIN' ON THE RITZ / HARMONICA HARRY............ *Champion 15934* 4-6 30
(Vocals: Arthur Fields)

YOU'RE RESPONSIBLE / THE WOMAN IN THE SHOE................... *Champion 15887* 3-5 30
(Vocals: Arthur Fields)

YOU'VE GOT THAT THING / THE ONE I LOVE JUST CAN'T BE BOTHERED WITH ME ... *Champion 15954* 4-6 30
(Vocals: Arthur Fields)

HALL, George, & His Hotel Taft Orchestra

BLUE IN LOVE / I COULDN'T BE MEAN TO YOU.................. *Bluebird B-5643* 3-5 34
(Vocals: Allen Church)

BUT WHERE ARE YOU? (Vocal: Johnny McKeever) / I'M PUTTING ALL MY EGGS IN ONE BASKET (Vocal: Dolly Dawn)............... *Bluebird B-6266* 3-5 36

DID MY HEART BEAT? (Vocals: Loretta Lee & Barry Wells) / I MAY BE DANCING WITH SOMEONE ELSE (Vocal: Barry Wells).................. *Bluebird B-5117* 3-5 33

DID MY HEART BEAT? (Vocals: Loretta Lee & Barry Wells) / I MAY BE DANCING WITH SOMEONE ELSE (Vocal: Barry Wells).................. *Electradisk 2027* 10-12 33

DID MY HEART BEAT? (Vocals: Loretta Lee & Barry Wells) / I MAY BE DANCING WITH SOMEONE ELSE (Vocal: Barry Wells).................. *Sunrise S-3198* 10-12 33
(Simultaneously released on three labels)

DOWN A CAROLINA LANE / MY DIXIE HIDEE-HIDEAWAY.............. *Bluebird B-5023* 3-5 33
(Vocals: Loretta Lee)

DOWN A CAROLINA LANE / MY DIXIE HIDEE-HIDEAWAY .... *Electradisk 1950* 10-12 33
(Vocals: Loretta Lee)
(Simultaneously released on two labels)

EVERY NOW AND THEN (Vocal: Sonny Schuyler) / ACCENT ON YOUTH (Vocal: Dolly Dawn).................. *Bluebird B-6099* 3-5 35

EV'RY MINUTE OF THE HOUR (Vocal: Dolly Dawn) / SUNDOWN IN PEACEFUL VALLEY (Vocal: Johnny McKeever)............ *Bluebird B-6282* 3-5 36

FLIRTATION WALK (Vocal: Sonny Schuyler) / MR. AND MRS. IS THE NAME (Vocals: Loretta Lee & Sonny Schuyler).................. *Bluebird B-5709* 3-5 34

GOOD MORNING, GLORY / YOU'RE SUCH A COMFORT TO ME................ *Bluebird B-5312* 3-5 34
(Vocals: Loretta Lee)

GOOD MORNING, GLORY / YOU'RE SUCH A COMFORT TO ME.................. *Sunrise S-3393* 8-10 34
(Vocals: Loretta Lee)
(Simultaneously released on two labels)

I DREAM TOO MUCH / LIGHTS OUT......................... *Bluebird B-6215* 4-6 36
(Vocals: Johnny McKeever)

I'M MISUNDERSTOOD (Vocal: Loretta Lee) / OH SUSANNAH (DUST OFF THAT OLD PIANNA) (Vocals: Loretta Lee & Sonny Schuyler)... *Bluebird B-5864* 4-6 35

IN A LITTLE GYPSY TEA ROOM / 'WAY BACK HOME............... *Bluebird B-5934* 4-6 35
(Vocals: Sonny Schuyler)

IN THE VALLEY OF THE MOON / HAVE YOU EVER BEEN LONELY?................ *Bluebird B-5021* 4-6 33
(Vocals: Glenn Cross)

IN THE VALLEY OF THE MOON / HAVE YOU EVER BEEN LONELY?................. *Electradisk 1951* 12-15 33
(Vocals: Glenn Cross)

IN THE VALLEY OF THE MOON / HAVE YOU EVER BEEN LONELY?.................. *Sunrise S-3102* 12-15 33
(Vocals: Glenn Cross)
(Simultaneously released on three labels)

IT'S AN OLD SOUTHERN CUSTOM (Vocal: Loretta Lee) / ACCORDING TO THE MOONLIGHT (Vocal: Sonny Schuyler).............. *Bluebird B-5865* 3-5 35

MY BLUE-EYED SUE / IN THE VALLEY OF YESTERDAY................. *Bluebird B-5313* 3-5 34
(Vocals: Barry Wells)

MY BLUE-EYED SUE / IN THE VALLEY OF YESTERDAY.................. *Sunrise S-3394* 10-12 34
(Vocals: Barry Wells)
(Simultaneously released on two labels)

MY VERY GOOD FRIEND THE MILKMAN (Vocals: Dolly Dawn & Sonny Schuyler) / YOUNG IDEAS (Vocal: Dolly Dawn)................... *Bluebird B-6015* 3-5 35

NIGHT IS YOUNG AND YOU'RE SO BEAUTIFUL, THE / I'M IN A DANCING MOOD... *Bluebird B-6702* 2-4 37
(Vocals: Johnny McKeever)

ONE NIGHT IN MONTE CARLO (Vocal: Johnny McKeever) / MOON OVER MIAMI (Vocal: Dolly Dawn).................... *Bluebird B-6214* 3-5 36

PICTURE OF ME WITHOUT YOU, A (Vocals: Dolly Dawn & Sonny Schuyler) / GOT A BRAN' NEW SUIT (Vocal: Dolly Dawn)................. *Bluebird B-6127* 3-5 35

RAINBOW / GIVE A BROKEN HEART A BREAK................ *Bluebird B-5937* 3-5 35
(Vocals: Sonny Schuyler)

SANTA, BRING MY MOMMY BACK TO ME (Vocal: Dolly Dawn) / ALONE (Vocal: Johnny McKeever)...... *Bluebird B-6172* 4-6 35

THAT'S WHAT MAKES THE WORLD GO 'ROUND / INFATUATION...... *Bluebird B-5400* 3-5 34
(Vocals: Barry Wells)

THERE'S ALWAYS A HAPPY ENDING (Vocal: Johnny McKeever) / LOVE CAME OUT OF THE NIGHT (Vocal: Dolly Dawn)... *Bluebird B-6379* 3-5 36

TIRED OF IT ALL / LET'S FALL IN LOVE.................. *Bluebird B-5314* 3-5 34
(Vocals: Barry Wells)

TIRED OF IT ALL / LET'S FALL IN LOVE..................... *Sunrise S-3395* 8-10 34
(Vocals: Barry Wells)
(Simultaneously released on two labels)

UNDER A BLANKET OF BLUE (Vocal: Barry Wells) / BLUE PRELUDE (Vocal: Loretta Lee).................. *Bluebird B-5112* 4-6 33

UNDER A BLANKET OF BLUE (Vocal: Barry Wells) / BLUE PRELUDE (Vocal: Loretta Lee).................. *Electradisk 2016* 12-15 33

UNDER A BLANKET OF BLUE (Vocal: Barry Wells) / BLUE PRELUDE (Vocal: Loretta Lee).................. *Sunrise S-3182* 12-15 33
(Simultaneously released on three labels)

WHEEL OF THE WAGON IS BROKEN, THE / MISTY ISLANDS OF THE HIGHLANDS.... *Bluebird B-6267* 3-5 36
(Vocals: Johnny McKeever)

WOULD YOU? (Vocal: Johnny McKeever) / IT'S A SIN TO TELL A LIE (Vocal: Dolly Dawn)...... *Bluebird B-6378* 3-5 36

HALL, George, & His Orchestra

AM I IN LOVE / REMEMBER ME...... *Vocalion 3781* 3-5 37
(Vocals: Unknown)

AT SUNDOWN / FAITHFUL TO YOU... *Vocalion 5343* 2-4 40
(Vocals: Unknown)

CHOPSTICKS / STICKS AND STONES.... *Vocalion4683* 2-4 39
(Vocals: Unknown)

DID AN ANGEL KISS YOU (THE DAY YOU WERE BORN) / SMOKE FROM A CHIMNEY... *Vocalion3944* 3-5 38
(Vocals: Unknown)

GYPSY TOLD ME, A / TI-PI-TIN....... *Vocalion 3991* 2-4 38
(Vocals: Unknown)

IT'S SAD BUT TRUE / HOW DID HE LOOK?.............................. *Okeh 5954* 2-4 41
(Vocals: Dolly Dawn)

MY CABIN OF DREAMS / LOVELY ONE...................... *Vocalion 3775* 3-5 37
(Vocals: Unknown)

ONLY WHEN YOU'RE IN MY ARMS / AT A LITTLE HOT DOG STAND.................. *Vocalion 4766* 2-4 39
(Vocals: Unknown)

SOUTH OF THE BORDER / DING-DONG! THE WITCH IS DEAD........................ *Vocalion 5019* 5-8 39
(Vocals: Unknown)

SWEET AS A SONG / HALF-MOON ON THE HUDSON.................. *Vocalion 3919* 2-4 38
(Vocals: Unknown)

TAKE CARE / MAY I NEVER LOVE AGAIN.......................... *Okeh 5863* 2-4 40
(Vocals: Dolly Dawn)

THANKS FOR EV'RYTHING / SAY IT WITH A KISS..................... *Vocalion 4510* 2-4 39
(Vocals: Unknown)

YOU'RE MY DISH / MORE POWER TO YOU....................... *Variety 663* 4-6 37
(Vocals: Unknown)

YOUR EYES ARE BIGGER THAN YOUR HEART / THEY SAY.......... *Vocalion 4523* 3-5 39
(Vocals: Dolly Dawn)

HALL, George, as George Hall's Arcadians

DOLORES / TRES JOLIE.............. *Cameo 8264* 2-4 28

DOLORES / TRES JOLIE.............. *Lincoln 2912* 2-4 28

DOLORES / TRES JOLIE.............. *Romeo 687* 2-4 28
(Simultaneously released on three labels)

SLOW RIVER / POSITIVELY-ABSOLUTELY................ *Pathe Actuelle 36627* 4-6 27
(Vocals: Scrappy Lambert)

SLOW RIVER / POSITIVELY-ABSOLUTELY....................... *Perfect 14808* 3-5 27
(Vocals: Scrappy Lambert)
(Simultaneously released on two labels)

HALL, Sleepy, & His Collegians

Title	Label	Price	Year
GOODNIGHT VIENNA / LIVING IN CLOVER (Vocals: Smith Ballew)	*Melotone 12466*	5-8	32
SLEEPY-TIME GAL (theme song) / THAT OLD OAKEN BUCKET	*Variety 583*	5-8	37

HALSTEAD, Henry, & His Orchestra

Title	Label	Price	Year
GIVE ME TODAY / THE ROSES BROUGHT ME YOU (Vocal: Craig Leitch)	*Victor 20061*	5-8	26
I DON'T KNOW WHY / THAT'S MY GIRL	*Victor 19482*	3-5	24
IF I WERE KING / DREAM OF LOVE AND YOU (Vocals: Craig Leitch)	*Victor 20062*	5-8	24
ROSY CHEEKS / AIN'T THAT TOO BAD?	*Victor 20691*	3-5	27
TEAR DROPS / ONE MOMENT MORE WITH YOU (Vocal: Buster Dees)	*Victor 22000*	2-4	29

HAMM, Fred, & His Orchestra

Title	Label	Price	Year
STOMP OFF, LET'S GO / FLAG THAT TRAIN (TO ALABAM') (Vocal: Fred Hamm)	*Victor 19672*	4-6	25
SUGAR FOOT STOMP / SLIPPERY ELM (by Art Landry and His Orchestra)	*Victor 20023*	4-6	26

HAMP, Johnny, & His Orchestra

Title	Label	Price	Year
ALL ON ACCOUNT OF YOUR KISSES / ROCKIN' CHAIR (Vocals: Andrew Freeman)	*Victor 22636*	3-5	31
CABIN IN THE COTTON (Vocal: Charles Socci) / BY A RIPPLING STREAM (Vocals: Cliff Gamet, Charles Socci, & Carl Graub)	*Victor 22999*	3-5	32
GOONA GOO, THE (Vocal: Jayne Whitney) / MR. GHOST GOES TO TOWN	*Bluebird B-6746*	4-6	37
LOVE IS GOOD FOR ANYTHING THAT AILS YOU (Vocal: Millicent Hope) / WAS IT RAIN? (Vocal: Jack Campbell)	*Bluebird B-6848*	3-5	37
NEVERTHELESS (Vocals: by trio) / LOOK IN THE LOOKING GLASS (Vocal: Andrew Freeman)	*Victor 22722*	3-5	31
SMOKE DREAMS (Vocal: Johnny McAfee) / WHO'S THAT KNOCKIN' AT MY HEART? (Vocal: Jayne Whitney)	*Bluebird B-6745*	3-5	37
TOMORROW IS ANOTHER DAY / BLUE VENETIAN WATERS (Vocals: Jack Campbell)	*Bluebird B-6836*	3-5	37
WHISTLE AND BLOW YOUR BLUES AWAY (Vocals: Cliff Gamet, Charles Socci & Carl Graub) / HUMMIN' TO MYSELF (Vocal: Carl Graub)	*Victor 24000*	3-5	32

HAMP, Johnny, as Johnny Hamp's Kentucky Serenaders

Title	Label	Price	Year
ANRGY / OH SAY! CAN I SEE YOU TO-NIGHT (Vocals: Charles Buckwalter, Frank Masterson, & Elwood Groff)	*Victor 19786*	2-4	25
BLUE SHADOWS (Vocal: Frank Munn) / WHAT D'YA SAY? (Vocal: Johnny Marvin)	*Victor 21632*	2-4	28
CECILIA (Vocals: Charles Buckwalter, Frank Masterson, & Elwood Groff) / THE PROMENADE WALK	*Victor 19756*	3-5	25
I CAN'T GET OVER A GIRL LIKE YOU (Vocal: Billy Murray) / TENDERLY (Vocals: Charles Buckwalter, Frank Masterson, & Elwood Groff)	*Victor 20119*	3-5	26
IT ALL BELONGS TO ME / SOMEDAY YOU'LL SAY "O.K." (Vocals: Franklyn Baur)	*Victor 20900*	2-4	27
NOBODY BUT FANNY / WHEN THE DEAR OLD SUMMER GOES (Vocals: Charles Buckwalter, & Frank Masterson)	*Victor 19807*	2-4	25
ONE O'CLOCK BABY (Vocal: Franklyn Baur) / THE WHISPER SONG (by Art Landry & His Orchestra; Vocals: Bill Van Dusen, Denny Curtis, & Red Thomas)	*Victor 20644*	3-5	27

HAMPTON, Lionel, & His Orchestra
(Lionel Hampton: 4/12/09 –)

(Lionel Hampton and His Orchestra still play engagements all over the country, and on June 5th, 1982, Lionel Hampton was awarded a star in the "Walk of Fame" in Hollywood. The Lionel and Gladys Hampton Foundation awards scholarships to eligible young musicians for further music studies.)

Title	Label	Price	Year
AIN'TCHA COMIN' HOME? / 12TH STREET RAG	*Victor 26362*	2-4	39
BABY, WON'T YOU PLEASE COME HOME? / AFTER YOU'VE GONE (Vocals: Lionel Hampton)	*Victor 25674*	3-5	37
BUZZIN' 'ROUND WITH THE BEE / WHOA BABE (Vocals: Lionel Hampton)	*Victor 25575*	4-6	37
CHINA STOMP / RHYTHM, RHYTHM	*Victor 25586*	3-5	37
CONFESSIN' (Vocal: Lionel Hampton) / DRUM STOMP	*Victor 25658*	3-5	37
DINAH / SINGIN' THE BLUES	*Victor 26557*	3-5	40
DON'T BE THAT WAY / FIDDLE DIDDLE (Vocal: Lionel Hampton)	*Victor 26173*	3-5	38
DOUGH-RA-ME (Vocals: The Hampton Rhythm Boys) / I DON'T STAND A GHOST OF A CHANCE (Vocal: Helen Forrest)	*Victor 26696*	3-5	40
DOWN HOME JUMP / ROCK HILL SPECIAL	*Victor 26114*	3-5	38
EVERYBODY LOVES MY BABY / I JUST COULDN'T TAKE IT, BABY (Vocals: Lionel Hampton)	*Victor 25682*	4-6	37
FLYING HOME (theme song) / IN THE BAG	*Decca 18394*	2-4	42
FLYING HOME (theme song) / SAVE IT, PRETTY MAMA	*Victor 26595*	2-4	40
HAMP'S BOOGIE WOOGIE / CHOP-CHOP	*Decca 18613*	2-4	45
HEEBIE JEEBIES ARE ROCKIN' THE TOWN (Vocal: Lionel Hampton) / GIN FOR CHRISTMAS	*Victor 26423*	3-5	39
HIGH SOCIETY / SWEETHEARTS ON PARADE (Vocal: Lionel Hampton)	*Victor 26209*	2-4	39
HOUSE OF MORGAN / I'D BE LOST WITHOUT YOU (Vocal: Helen Forrest)	*Victor 26751*	2-4	40
I'M IN THE MOOD FOR SWING / SHOE SHINER'S DRAG	*Victor 26011*	3-5	38
I'M ON MY WAY FROM YOU (Vocal: Lionel Hampton) / HAVEN'T NAMED IT YET	*Victor 26476*	4-6	39

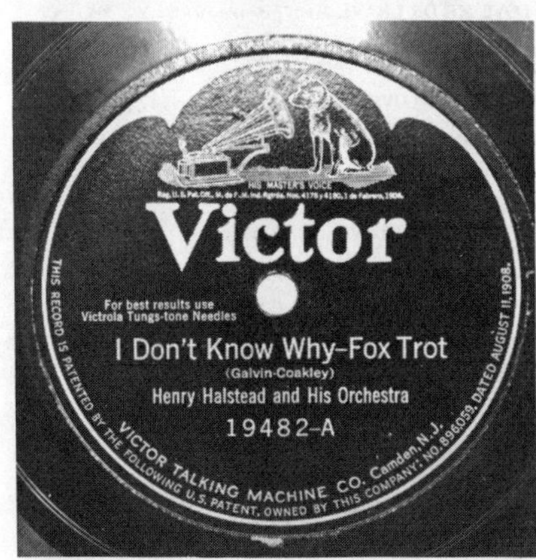

Title	Label	Price	Year
I SURRENDER, DEAR / PIANO STOMP	*Victor 25666*	3-5	37
IT DON'T MEAN A THING (IF IT AIN'T GOT THAT SWING) (Vocal: Lionel Hampton) / SHUFFLIN' AT THE HOLLYWOOD	*Victor 26254*	3-5	39
I'VE FOUND A NEW BABY / FOUR OR FIVE TIMES (Vocal: Lionel Hampton)	*Victor 26447*	3-5	39
JACK THE BELLBOY / CENTRAL AVENUE BREAKDOWN	*Victor 26652*	2-4	40
JIVIN' THE VIBRES / STOMP	*Victor 25535*	3-5	37
JIVIN' WITH JARVIS (Vocals: Hampton Rhythm Boys) / BLUE	*Victor 26724*	3-5	40
JUST FOR LAFFS / PIG FOOT SONATA	*Victor 26793*	3-5	40
JUST FOR YOU / MY WISH (Vocals: Rubel Blakey)	*Decca 18265*	2-4	42
LOOSE WIG / OVERTIME	*Decca 18669*	2-4	45
MARTIN ON EVERY BLOCK / CHARLIE WAS A SAILOR (Vocal: Doug Daniels)	*Victor 26739*	2-4	40
MEMORIES OF YOU / THE JUMPIN' JIVE (Vocal: Lionel Hampton)	*Victor 26304*	3-5	39
MIDNIGHT SUN / AIRMAIL SPECIAL	*Clef 89153*	2-4	-
MUNSON STREET BREAKDOWN / I CAN'T GET STARTED	*Victor 26453*	3-5	39
MY BUDDY / TEMPO AND SWING	*Victor 26608*	2-4	40
MY LAST AFFAIR / THE MOOD THAT I'M IN (Vocals: Lionel Hampton)	*Victor 25527*	2-4	37
OBJECT OF MY AFFECTION, THE / JUDY (Vocals: Lionel Hampton)	*Victor 25699*	3-5	37
ONE SWEET LETTER FROM YOU (Vocal: Lionel Hampton) / EARLY SESSION HOP	*Victor 26393*	2-4	39
ON THE SUNNY SIDE OF THE STREET (Vocal: Lionel Hampton) / I KNOW THAT YOU KNOW	*Victor 25592*	3-5	37
PENCIL BROKE, THE (Vocal: Lionel Hampton) / TEMPO'S BIRTHDAY	*Decca 23696*	2-4	46
RED TOP / GIDDY-UP	*Decca 24281*	2-4	48
RING DEM BELLS (Vocal: Lionel Hampton) / MUSKRAT RAMBLE (Side One is a reissue)	*Victor 26017*	2-4	38
RING DEM BELLS (Vocal: Lionel Hampton) / PICK THE WINNER (anonymous artists) (Side Two is a rare multi-track "puzzle" record.)	*Victor 25889*	10-12	38
SHADES OF JADE / TILL TOM SPECIAL	*Victor 26604*	3-5	40
SOUTHERN ECHOES (Vocal: Lionel Hampton) / NOLA	*Decca 18285*	2-4	42
STAND BY! FOR FURTHER ANNOUNCEMENTS (AND MORE GOOD NEWS) (Vocal: Lionel Hampton) / BIG-WIG IN THE WIGWAM	*Victor 26296*	3-5	39
WHEN LIGHTS ARE LOW / HOT MALLETS	*Victor 26371*	3-5	39
WIZZIN' THE WIZZ / DENISON SWING	*Victor 26233*	3-5	39

HAMPTON, Lionel, & His Quartet

Title	Label	Price	Year
HAMP'S SALTY BLUES (Vocal: Lionel Hampton) / CHORD-A-RE-BOP	*Decca 18830*	3-5	46

HAMPTON, Lionel, & His Sextette

BOGO JO / OPEN HOUSE .... *Victor 27341* 2-4 41

FIDDLE-DEE-DEE / BOUNCING AT THE BEACON .... *Victor 27364* 2-4 41

GIVE ME SOME SKIN (Vocal: Lionel Hampton) / THREE-QUARTER BOOGIE .... *Victor 27409* 2-4 41

I NEARLY LOST MY MIND (Vocal: Evelyn Myers) / ALTITUDE .... *Victor 27316* 2-4 41

LOST LOVE (Vocals: Lee Young & The Rhythm Girls) / SMART ALEC .... *Victor 27278* 2-4 41
(Lee Young is a jazz drummer, younger brother to tenor saxophone great Lester Young. Lee led his own group in the 1940s, and later was with VeeJay records)

NOW THAT YOU'RE MINE (Vocal: Rubel Blakey) / CHASIN' WITH CHASE .... *Victor 27529* 2-4 41

HAMPTON, Richard, & His Orchestra:
seeRICH, Fred, & His Orchestra

HANDLER, Al, & His Alamo Cafe Orchestra

CRYIN' FOR THE MOON / MANDY ... *Columbia 713-D* 3-5 26

HAVIN' LOTS OF FUN / OH! HOW SHE COULD PLAY A UKELELE .... *Columbia 866-D* 3-5 27

PRETTY LIPS (Vocals: Unknown) / LONELY EYES .... *Columbia 833-D* 2-4 27

HANDLER, Al, & His Hotel Davis Orchestra

THAT'S WHAT I THINK OF YOU (Vocals: Frank Sylvano) / RAIN (by Don Voorhees & His Orchestra: Vocal: Billy Day) .... *Columbia 1126-D* 5-8 27

THERE'S A TRICK IN PICKIN' A CHICK-CHICK-CHICKEN (Vocal: Frank Sylvano) / MAGNOLIA (Vocal: Eddie Clifford) .... *Columbia 1047-D* 2-4 27

HANNAFORD, Ephraim, as Eph Hannaford's Broadway Orchestra:
see SAMUELS, Joseph

HANNON, Leo, & His Broadway Bellhops

UNDERNEATH THE HARLEM MOON / LET'S PUT OUT THE LIGHTS (AND GO TO SLEEP) .... *Crown 3387* 5-8 32
(Vocals: Unknown)

HANSON, Ted, & His Normandie Orchestra

I MET MY WATERLOO / MY OLD FLAME .... *Bluebird B-5494* 5-8 34
(Vocals: Helen Young)

IN A LITTLE RED BARN / NIGHT OF THE DESERT .... *Bluebird B-5493* 5-8 34
(Vocals: William Wolfson)

WITH MY EYES WIDE OPEN, I'M DREAMING / TAKE A LESSON FROM THE LARK ...... *Bluebird B-5492* 5-8 34
(Vocals: George Gould)

HAPPINESS ORCHESTRA, The:
see KAPLAN, Dave

HAPPY HOUR ORCHESTRA, The:
see RICH, Fred, & His Hotel Astor Orchestra

HAPPY SIX, The:
see YERKES, Harry A.

HARING, Bob, & His Orchestra

ALL THROUGH THE NIGHT / SWINGIN' IN A HAMMOCK .... *Brunswick 4851* 3-5 30
(Vocals: Unknown)

BETTY CO-ED / I LOVE YOU SO MUCH .... *Brunswick 4852* 4-6 30
(Vocals: Unknown)

CHIMES OF SPRING (Vocals: Unknown) / TWO HEARTS IN WALTZ TIME (Vocal: Smith Ballew) .... *Brunswick 6031* 3-5 31

HO HUM! / LET'S GET FRIENDLY ..... *Banner 32162* 4-6 31
(Vocals: Chick Bullock)

HO HUM! / LET'S GET FRIENDLY ...... *Perfect 15462* 4-6 31
(Vocals: Chick Bullock)

HO HUM! / LET'S GET FRIENDLY .... *Romeo 1618* 4-6 31
(Vocals: Chick Bullock)
(Simultaneously released on three labels)

SOME SWEET DAY / WEARY RIVER ... *Brunswick 4273* 3-5 29
(Vocals: Unknown)

WHEN I TAKE MY SUGAR TO TEA / I SURRENDER, DEAR .... *Perfect 15444* 3-5 31
(Vocals: Jack Parker)

WRAP YOUR TROUBLES IN DREAMS / JUNE TIME IS LOVE TIME .... *Perfect 15487* 2-4 31
(Vocals: Chick Bullock)

HARING, Bob, & His Orchestra as The Alabama Red Peppers

RED HEAD BLUES / THE DRAG .... *Perfect 15022* 5-8 28

HARING, Bob, & His Orchestra as the Caroliners

HIGHWAYS ARE HAPPY WAYS / THE WINDING TRAIL (by Bob Haring and His Orchestra as the Society Night Club Orchestra) .... *Cameo 1233* 2-4 27

HIGHWAYS ARE HAPPY WAYS / THE WINDING TRAIL (by Bob Haring and His Orchestra as the Society Night Club Orchestra) .... *Lincoln 2698* 2-4 27

HIGHWAYS ARE HAPPY WAYS / THE WINDING TRAIL (by Bob Haring and His Orchestra as the Society Night Club Orchestra) .... *Romeo 461* 2-4 27
(Simultaneously released on three labels)

HARING, Bob, & His Orchestra, as The Casino Dance Orchestra

DANCE OF THE BLUE DANUBE / YOU'RE A REAL SWEETHEART .... *Cameo 8276* 2-4 28
(Vocals: Scrappy Lambert as Chester Hale)

DANCE OF THE BLUE DANUBE / YOU'RE A REAL SWEETHEART .... *Lincoln 2924* 2-4 28
(Vocals: Scrappy Lambert as Chester Hale)

DANCE OF THE BLUE DANUBE / YOU'RE A REAL SWEETHEART .... *Romeo 699* 2-4 28
(Vocals: Scrappy Lambert as Chester Hale)
(Simultaneously released on three labels)

HARING, Bob & His Orchestra as The Caroliners

YOUR DISPOSITION IS MINE (Vocal: Unknown) / DO SOMETHING (by Sam Lanin as The Broadway Broadcasters; Vocal: Scrappy Lambert) .... *Romeo 960* 4-6 29

HARING, Bob, & His Orchestra as The Colonial Club Orchestra

ARE YOU LONESOME TONIGHT? (Vocal: Vaughn de Leath) / AN OLD GUITAR AND AN OLD REFRAIN (Vocal: Irving Kaufman) .... *Brunswick 3673* 2-4 27

CHLOE (Vocal: Irving Kaufman) / SOMEBODY LIED ABOUT ME (Vocal: Frank Munn) .... *Brunswick 3700* 2-4 28

HITTIN' THE BOTTLE / OUT OF A CLEAR BLUE SKY .... *Brunswick 4858* 3-5 30
(Vocals: Irving Kaufman)

MY MAN IS ON THE MAKE (Vocal: Libby Holman) / WHY DO YOU SUPPOSE? (Vocal: Unknown) ... *Brunswick 4554* 4-6 29

MY SIN / LOVE ME OR LEAVE ME ... *Brunswick 4342* 2-4 29
(Vocals: Unknown)

SONNY BOY / BLUE NIGHT .... *Brunswick 4082* 2-4 28
(Vocals: Oliver Smith)

TO KNOW YOU IS TO LOVE YOU (Vocal: Eddy Thomas) / YOU'RE THE CREAM IN MY COFFEE (Vocal: Scrappy Lambert) .... *Brunswick 4118* 2-4 28

WOULDJA / AIN'T WE CARRYIN' ON? .... *Brunswick 3280* 4-6 26
(Vocals: Irving Kaufman)

YOU'VE GOT THAT THING (Vocal: Unknown) / FIND ME A PRIMITIVE MAN (Vocal: Libby Holman) .... *Brunswick 4666* 4-6 30

HARING, Bob, & His Orchestra as The Majestic Dance Orchestra

BY MY SIDE / OUT OF NOWHERE ...... *Perfect 15453* 3-5 31
(Vocals: Smith Ballew as Buddy Blue)

WHO WOULDN'T BE JEALOUS OF YOU? / I FAW DOWN AND GO BOOM! .... *Pathe Actuelle 36931* 3-5 29
(Vocals: Irving Kaufman)

WHO WOULDN'T BE JEALOUS OF YOU? / I FAW DOWN AND GO BOOM! .... *Perfect 15112* 2-4 29
(Vocals: Irving Kaufman)
(Simultaneously released on two labels)

HARING, Bob, & His Orchestra as Oppenheim's Benjamin Franklin Hotel Orchestra

ALL BY YOURSELF IN THE MOONLIGHT / BUY, BUY FOR BABY .... *Pathe Actuelle 36919* 3-5 29
(Vocals: Billy Murray)

ALL BY YOURSELF IN THE MOONLIGHT / BUY, BUY FOR BABY .... *Perfect 15100* 2-4 29
(Vocals: Billy Murray)
(Simultaneously released on two labels)

HARING, Bob, & His Orchestra as The Society Night Club Orchestra

WINDING TRAIL, THE / HIGHWAYS ARE HAPPY WAYS (by Bob Haring and His Orchestra as The Caroliners) .... *Cameo 1233* 2-4 27

WINDING TRAIL, THE / HIGHWAYS ARE HAPPY WAYS (by Bob Haring and His Orchestra as The Caroliners) .... *Lincoln 2698* 2-4 27

WINDING TRAIL, THE / HIGHWAYS ARE HAPPY WAYS (by Bob Haring and His Orchestra as The Caroliners) .... *Romeo 461* 2-4 27
(Simultaneously released on three labels)

HARING, Bob, & His Velvetone Orchestra

CLIMBING UP THE LADDER OF LOVE / WHILE THE YEARS GO DRIFTING BY .... *Cameo 1014* 2-4 26
(Vocals: Unknown)

COAL BLACK MAMMY / I GAVE UP JUST BEFORE YOU THREW ME DOWN .... *Cameo 272* 2-4 22

DOWN AMONG THE SLEEPY HILLS OF TENNESSEE / SWINGIN' DOWN THE LANE .... *Cameo 338* 2-4 23

DRIFTING AND DREAMING / IN THE MIDDLE OF THE NIGHT .... *Cameo 897* 2-4 26

HOMESICK / IN MY HOME TOWN .... *Cameo 266* 2-4 22

I'LL SEE YOU IN MY DREAMS / ORIENTAL MOON .... *Cameo 685* 2-4 25

NOBODY LIED / JUST BECAUSE YOU'RE YOU .... *Cameo 247* 2-4 22

PRINCE OF WAILS / LAFF IT OFF (Vocals: Al Weston & Irene Young) .... *Cameo 643* 3-5 25

ROSES / A NIGHT OF LOVE (Vocals: Unknown) .... *Cameo 890* 2-4 26

SAY IT AGAIN / LONESOME AND BLUE (by Henry Santrey & His Cameo Record Orchestra) .... *Cameo 501* 2-4 24

SITTIN' IN A CORNER / OH! JOE (by The California Ramblers as The Varsity Eight) ...... *Cameo 420* 2-4 23

VALENCIA / LUCKY MOON .... *Cameo 947* 2-4 26

HARING, Bob, & His Velvetone Orchestra as The Beale Street Five

G'WAN WITH IT / RED HOT MAMA (by Bob Haring & His Velvetone Orchestra as The Caroliners) ...... *Lincoln 2215* 3-6 24

HARING, Bob, & His Velvetone Orchestra as The Caroliners

OH SISTER! AIN'T THAT HOT? / MAMA GOES WHERE PAPA GOES (OR PAPA DON'T GO OUT TONIGHT) .... *Lincoln 2108* 3-5 23

RED HOT MAMA / G'WAN WITH IT (by Bob Haring & His Velvetone Orchestra as The Beale Street Five) ... *Lincoln 2215* 3-5 24

HARING, Bob, & His Velvetone Orchestra as Dale's Dance Orchestra

FOOTLOOSE / CECILIA .... *Lincoln 2391* 2-4 25

HARING, Bob, & His Velvetone Orchestra as The Dixie Daisies

OH, SISTER! AIN'T THAT HOT? / MAMA GOES WHERE PAPA GOES (OR PAPA DON'T GO OUT TONIGHT) .... *Cameo 418* 3-5 23

HARING, Bob, & His Velvetone Orchestra as The Lincoln Dance Orchestra

DRIFTING AND DREAMING / AFRAID ... *Lincoln 2479* 2-4 26

JUST A COTTAGE SMALL / IN THE SPRING .... *Lincoln 2475* 4-6 26
(Vocals: Unknown)

KATINKA / ARE YOU LONESOME? ..... *Lincoln 2540* 2-4 26

TIE ME TO YOUR APRON STRINGS AGAIN (Vocals: Unknown) / ROSES ...... *Lincoln 2480* 3-5 26

VALENCIA / LUCKY MOON .... *Lincoln 2508* 2-4 26

HARING, Bob, as Haring's Happy Harmonizers

OH LIZZIE / GO WASH AN ELEPHANT ... *Gennett 6115* 3-5 27
(Vocals: Jerry Macy)

HARING, Bob, as Haring's Happy Harmonizers recorded under the name Bill Williams & His Gang

ZULU WAIL / OH LIZZIE .... *Champion 15253* 3-5 27
(Vocals: Jerry Macy)

HARKINS, Jim, & His Orchestra:
see PELTYN, Sid, & His Orchestra

HARKNESS, Eddie, & His Hotel Mark Hopkins Orchestra

HAUNTING WALTZ (Vocal: Dudley B. Chambers) / CONSOLATION .... *Victor 20631* 2-4 27

HARKNESS, Eddie, & His Orchestra

EITHER YOU DO OR YOU DON'T / I'M WONDERIN' WHO .... *Victor 21764* 2-4 28
(Vocals: Van Fleming)

TREES (Vocal: Harold Dana) / PERSIAN RUG (by Herman Kenin & His Multnomah Hotel Orchestra; Vocal: Van Fleming) .... *Victor 21313* 3-5 28

HARLAN, Earl, & His Orchestra:
see REDMAN, Don, & His Orchestra

HARLEM FOOTWARMERS, The:
see ELLINGTON, Duke, & His Orchestra

HARLEM HOT CHOCOLATES, The:
see ELLINGTON, Duke, & His Orchestra

HARLEM MUSIC MASTERS, The:
see ELLINGTON, Duke, & His Orchestra as The Harlem Footwarmers

HARMAN, Dave, & His Orchestra

COCKTAILS FOR TWO / LIVE AND LOVE TONIGHT (Vocal: George Marks) ...... *Bluebird B-5437* 3-5 34

EILEEN / ARE YOU LONELY? .... *Columbia 90-D* 3-5 24

HOT-HOT-HOTTENTOT / SOMEBODY LIKE YOU .... *Edison 51479* 5-8 25

I'LL STRING ALONG WITH YOU (Vocals: Dave Harman & Paul Fraser) / MARAHUANA (Vocal: Dave Harman) .... *Bluebird B-5438* 4-6 34

PRINCE OF WAILS / NANCY .... *Edison 51458* 5-8 25

SOB SISTER SADIE (Vocal: Dave Harman) / TWILIGHT .... *Edison 51510* 5-8 25

WE'RE OUT OF THE RED / BROADWAY'S GONE HILL BILLY................ *Bluebird B-5436* 3-5 34
(Vocals: George Marks)

HARMOGRAPH DANCE ORCHESTRA, The:
see STRAIGHT, Charley, & His Orchestra

HARMONIANS, The:
see SELVIN, Ben, & His Orchestra

HARMONY DANCE ORCHESTRA, The:
see SELVIN, Ben, & His Orchestra

HARRIS, Ace, & His Sunset Royal Orchestra

RHYTHM 'BOUT TOWN / ONE LITTLE WORD LED TO ANOTHER........... *Vocalion 3835* 5-8 37

WHO? (Vocal: Ace Harris) / HURLY BURLY.................... *Vocalion 3864* 5-8 37

HARRISON, Frank, as Frank Harrison's Banjo Orchestra:
see RESER, Harry, & His Orchestra

HARRIS, Phil, & His Cocoanut Grove Orchestra
also see LOFNER-HARRIS St. Francis Hotel Orchestra, The
(Phil Harris: 1/16/04 –)

HOW'S ABOUT IT? / WAS MY FACE RED?..................... *Columbia 2766-D* 5-8 33
(Vocals: Phil Harris)

YOU'VE GOT ME CRYING AGAIN / WHAT HAVE WE GOT TO LOSE?.................. *Columbia 2761-D* 5-8 33
(Vocals: Phil Harris)
(This record was pressed in blue shellac)

HARRIS, Phil, & His Orchestra

DARK TOWN POKER CLUB, THE / JELLY BEAN .... *ARA RM116* 3-5 44
(Vocals: Phil Harris)

DARKTOWN STRUTTERS' BALL / BETWEEN THE DEVIL AND THE DEEP BLUE SEA.... *Vocalion 3565* 5-8 37
(Vocals: Phil Harris)

GOODNIGHT, MY LOVE / SWING HIGH, SWING LOW.............................. *Vocalion 3447* 5-8 37
(Vocals: Phil Harris)

JAMMIN' / THAT'S SOUTHERN HOSPITALITY....................... *Vocalion 3533* 5-8 37
(Vocals: Phil Harris)

JELLY BEAN / NOBODY.............. *Vocalion 3430* 5-8 37
(Vocals: Phil Harris)

LOADED PISTOLS, LOADED DICE / NOW YOU'VE GONE AND HURT MY SOUTHERN PRIDE......... *RCA Victor 20-2575* 2-4 47
(Vocals: Phil Harris)

PREACHER AND THE BEAR, THE / WHERE DOES IT GET YOU IN THE END?........ *RCA Victor 20-2143* 2-4 47
(Vocals: Phil Harris)

SMOKE, SMOKE, SMOKE / CRAWDAD SONG.............. *RCA Victor 20-2370* 2-4 47
(Vocals: Phil Harris)

SWINGIN' FOR THE KING / WOODMAN, WOODMAN, SPARE THAT TREE................. *Vocalion 3466* 5-8 37
(Vocals: Phil Harris)

THAT'S WHAT I LIKE ABOUT THE SOUTH / CONSTANTLY .... *Vocalion 3583* 4-6 37
(Vocals: Phil Harris)

TOO MARVELOUS FOR WORDS / SENTIMENTAL AND MELANCHOLY................ *Vocalion 3488* 5-8 37
(Vocals: Phil Harris)

WHERE THE LAZY RIVER GOES BY / YOU CAN SEE SHE COMES FROM DIXIE .... *Vocalion 3419* 4-6 37
(Vocals: Phil Harris)

HARTY, Bill, as Bill Harty Presents

GEORGE VAN EPS MUSICALE: A DUCKY DISH / JIM TAFT MUSICALE: THE 'VARSITY DRAG.................... *Vocalion 4183* 5-8 38

GEORGE VAN EPS MUSICALE: SQUATTIN' AT THE GROTTO / GEORGE VAN EPS MUSICALE: LOCK IT UP...................... *Columbia 35694* 5-8 40
(A 1938 recording first released in 1940.)

HASTON, Gus, & His Orchestra

KICKING THE GONG AROUND / RIVER, STAY 'WAY FROM MY DOOR .... *Victor 22898* 5-8 32
(Vocals: Gus Haston)

HASTON, Gus, & His Orchestra as Walter Brown & Orchestra

OH MO 'NAH! / I DON'T KNOW WHY.... *Victor 23314* 8-10 32
(Vocals: Gus Haston)

HASTY, Harlan, & His Orchestra:
see PALMQUIST, Ernie, & His Carolina Collegians

HAUER, Michael, & His Orchestra

LET THAT BE A LESSON TO YOU / WHISTLE AND BLOW YOUR BLUES AWAY....... *Champion 16405* 4-6 32
(Vocals: Unknown)

YOU DARLIN' / YOU'RE THE SWEETEST GIRL THIS SIDE OF HEAVEN..... *Champion 16085* 3-5 30
(Vocals: Hall Runkle)

YOU DARLIN' / YOU'RE THE SWEETEST GIRL THIS SIDE OF HEAVEN .... *Gennett 7299* 4-6 30
(Vocals: Hall Runkle)
(Simultaneously released on two labels)

HAVANA NOVELTY ORCHESTRA, The:
see SHILKRET, Nat

HAWAIIAN NOVELTY ORCHESTRA, The

MOON RIVER / HAWAIIAN NIGHTINGALE .... *Brunswick 2276* 2-4 22

RED MOON / AFTER EVERY PARTY... *Brunswick 2429* 2-4 22

HAWKINS, Coleman, & His All American Five
(Coleman Hawkins: 11/21/04 – 5/19/69)

SHANTY IN OLD SHANTY TOWN / BEYOND THE BLUE HORIZON.................. *Keynote K-622* 4-6 46

HAWKINS, Coleman, & His Orchestra

FINE DINNER / BODY AND SOUL (theme song)........................ *Bluebird B-10523* 3-5 39

MEET DOCTOR FOO / SHE'S FUNNY THAT WAY (Vocal: Thelma Carpenter)....... *Bluebird B-10477* 4-6 39

PASSIN' IT AROUND / ROCKY COMFORT... *Okeh 6284* 4-6 40

WOODYN' YOU / RAINBOW MIST......... *Apollo 751* 4-6 45

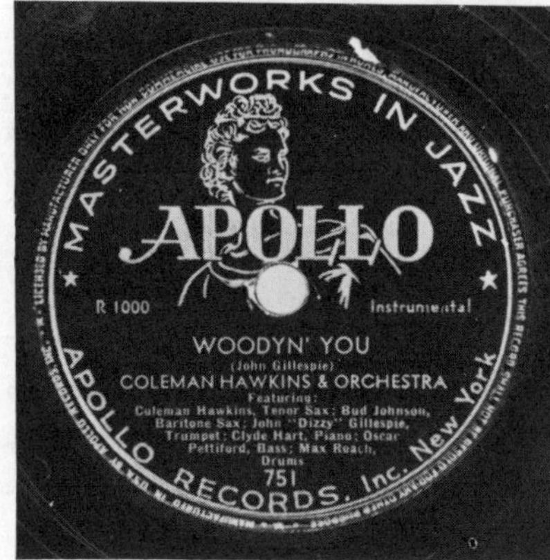

HAWKINS, Coleman, & His Rhythm

DEDICATION / — .... *Commodore 533* 4-6 40

HAWKINS, Coleman, as Coleman Hawkins' All-Star Octet

SHEIK OF ARABY, THE / MY BLUE HEAVEN................ *Bluebird B-10770* 4-6 40

WHEN DAY IS DONE / BOUNCING WITH BEAN.................... *Bluebird B-10693* 4-6 40

HAWKINS, Erskine, & His 'Bama State Collegians
(Erskine Hawkins: 7/26/14 –)

CARRY ME BACK TO OLD VIRGINIA / WHO'S SORRY NOW?............................ *Vocalion 4072* 5-8 38

COQUETTE (Vocal: Billy Daniels) / BIG JOHN'S SPECIAL .... *Vocalion 3318* 5-8 36

I'LL SEE YOU IN MY DREAMS / I'LL GET ALONG SOMEHOW (Vocal: Jimmy Mitchelle)...... *Vocalion 3689* 5-8 37

IT WAS A SAD NIGHT IN HARLEM / WITHOUT A SHADOW OF A DOUBT.............. *Vocalion 3289* 5-8 36
(Vocals: Jimmy Mitchelle)

LET ME DAY DREAM / LOST IN THE SHUFFLE .... *Vocalion 4007* 5-8 38

RED CAP (Vocal: Jimmy Mitchelle) / I FOUND A NEW BABY............. *Vocalion 3668* 5-8 37

SWINGING IN HARLEM / A SWINGY LITTLE RHYTHM.................. *Vocalion 3336* 8-10 36

UNTIL THE REAL THING COMES ALONG / I CAN'T ESCAPE FROM YOU................ *Vocalion 3280* 5-8 36
(Vocals: Billy Daniels)

UPROAR SHOUT / IF YOU LEAVE ME (Vocal: Jimmy Mitchelle) ..... *Vocalion 3545* 5-8 37

'WAY DOWN UPON THE SWANEE RIVER / DEAR OLD SOUTHLAND............ *Vocalion 3567* 5-8 37

HAWKINS, Erskine, & His Orchestra

BIG WIG IN THE WIGWAM (Vocal: Ida James) / POLKA DOTTY (Vocal: Jimmy Michelle)....... *Bluebird B-10287* 3-5 39

BLUE SEA / I LOVE YOU TRULY (Vocals: Jimmy Mitchelle & Ida James)........................ *Bluebird B-11419* 2-4 41

CHERRY / YOU CAN'T ESCAPE FROM ME............... *Bluebird B-10540* 2-4 39
(Vocals: Jimmy Mitchelle)

DON'T CRY BABY (Vocal: Jimmy Mitchelle) / —.... *V-Disc 314* 4-6
(A World War II release)

DON'T CRY BABY (Vocal: Jimmy Mitchelle) / BEAR MASH BLUES............. *Bluebird 30-0813* 3-5 42

DO YOU WANNA JUMP, CHILDREN? / BECAUSE OF YOU .... *Bluebird B-10019* 3-5 38
(Vocals: Jimmy Mitchelle)

FINE AND MELLOW (Vocal: Dolores Brown) / MIDNIGHT STROLL............. *Bluebird B-10709* 3-5 40

GIN MILL SPECIAL / TUXEDO JUNCTION (theme song)............ *Bluebird B-10409* 4-6 39

GIN MILL SPECIAL / TUXEDO JUNCTION (theme song).... *Montgomery Ward M-8340* 4-6 39
(Simultaneously released on two labels)

HEY DOC / SOMEONE'S ROCKING MY DREAM BOAT .... *Bluebird B-11277* 2-4 41
(Vocals: Jimmy Mitchelle)

HOT PLATTER / WEDDIN' BLUES... *Bluebird B-10364* 4-6 39

HOT PLATTER / WEDDIN' BLUES .... *Montgomery Ward M-8341* 4-6 39
(Simultaneously released on two labels)

I GUESS I'LL HAVE TO GET ALONG WITHOUT YOU (Vocal: Dolores Brown) / HOLIDAY FOR SWING .... *RCA Victor 20-1794* 2-4 46

I HADN'T ANYONE 'TILL YOU (Vocal: Dolores Brown) / BALTIMORE BOUNCE .... *Bluebird B-10565* 2-4 40

I'M MADLY IN LOVE WITH YOU (Vocal: Merle Turner) / MISS HALLELUJAH BROWN...... *Bluebird B-7810* 3-5 38

JUMPIN' IN A JULEP JOINT (Vocal: Ida James) / BICYCLE BOUNCE............... *Bluebird B-11547* 3-5 42

JUNCTION BLUES / ASHES IN THE TRAY (Vocal: Dolores Brown).... *Bluebird B-10790* 3-5 40

KEEP COOL, FOOL (Vocal: Jimmy Mitchelle) / NO USE SQUAWKIN'............ *Bluebird B-11049* 2-4 41

KNOCK ME A KISS (Vocal: Ida James) / 'TAIN'T NO GOOD (Vocal: Jimmy Mitchelle).... *Bluebird B-11564* 2-4 42

MORE THAN YOU KNOW (Vocal: Dolores Brown) / UPTOWN SHUFFLE............. *Bluebird B-10504* 3-5 39

NONA / I KNOW A SECRET (Vocal: Jimmy Mitchelle)... *Bluebird B-10979* 2-4 41

NO SOAP / SWINGIN' ON LENOX AVENUE............ *Bluebird B-10292* 3-5 39

PROVE IT BY THE THINGS YOU DO (Vocal: Carol Tucker) / DRIFTING ALONG.................. *Victor 20-1723* 2-4 45

PUT YOURSELF IN MY PLACE (Vocal: Dolores Brown) / NORFOLK FERRY .... *Bluebird B-10932* 2-4 40

RIFF TIME / TONIGHT YOU BELONG TO ME (Vocal: Jimmy Mitchelle)....... *Bluebird B-11161* 2-4 41

ROCKIN' ROLLERS' JUBILEE / LET THIS BE A WARNING TO YOU (Vocal: Jimmy Mitchelle)............ *Bluebird B-7826* 4-6 38

SHIPYARD RAMBLE / NIGHT AFTER NIGHT (Vocal: Ida James) .... *Bluebird B-11218* 2-4 41

SOFT WINDS / S'POSIN' (Vocal: Dolores Brown)...... *Bluebird B-11001* 2-4 41

SO LONG, SHORTY (Vocal: Ida James) / WRAP YOUR TROUBLES IN DREAMS (Vocal: Jimmy Mitchelle)............... *Bluebird B-11485* 2-4 42

SOMETIMES / I DON'T WANT TO WALK WITHOUT YOU .... *Bluebird B-11439* 3-5 42
(Vocals: Jimmy Mitchelle)

SONG OF THE WANDERER (Vocal: Jimmy Mitchelle) / AFTER HOURS .... *Bluebird B-10879* 2-4 40

STRICTLY SWING / WHAT DO YOU KNOW ABOUT LOVE? (Vocal: Ida James).... *Bluebird B-10012* 3-5 38

STUDY IN BLUE, A / EASY RIDER ... *Bluebird B-10029* 3-5 38

SWEET GEORGIA BROWN / FIVE O'CLOCK WHISTLE......... *Bluebird B-10854* 3-5 40

SWING OUT / RAID THE JOINT .... *Bluebird B-10224* 3-5 39

UNCLE BUD / I'M IN A LOW-DOWN GROOVE (Vocal: Jimmy Mitchelle)..... *Bluebird B-11372* 3-5 41

WEARY BLUES / KING PORTER STOMP.......................... *Bluebird B-7839* 4-6 38

WHISPERING GRASS (Vocal: Jimmy Mitchelle) / GABRIEL MEETS THE DUKE..... *Bluebird B-10671* 3-5 40

WHO'S BEATIN' MY TIME WITH YOU? (Vocal: Ida James) / BLACKOUT ..... *Bluebird B-11192* 3-5 41

HAYES, Bobby, & His Orchestra

DEDICATED TO YOU / GOODNIGHT, MY LUCKY DAY..................... *Melotone 7-04-20* 3-5 37
(Vocals: Lou Valero)

MAY I HAVE THE NEXT ROMANCE WITH YOU? / HEAD OVER HEELS IN LOVE..... *Melotone 7-03-08* 3-5 37
(Vocals: Billy Mure)

SOMEONE TO CARE FOR ME / WINTERTIME DREAMS.......... *Melotone 7-02-02* 3-5 37
(Vocals: Unknown)

TRUST IN ME / LOOKIN' AROUND CORNERS FOR YOU......................... *Melotone 7-03-09* 3-5 37
(Vocals: Billy Mure)

WHEN LOVE IS YOUNG / DID ANYONE EVER TELL YOU?................ *Melotone 7-04-19* 3-5 37
(Vocals: Lou Valero)

YOU'RE TOO GOOD TO BE TRUE / I STUMBLED OVER LOVE..................... *Melotone 7-02-03* 3-5 37
(Vocals: Unknown)

HAYES, Edgar, & His Orchestra
(Edgar Hayes: 5/23/04 –)

CARAVAN / EDGAR STEPS OUT......... *Decca 1338* 4-6 37

FUGITIVE FROM A HAREM / SOPHISTICATED SWING.............................. *Decca 1748* 3-5 38

HIGH, WIDE AND HANDSOME (Vocal: Ruth Ellington) / SATAN TAKES A HOLIDAY............ *Decca 1382* 4-6 37

LET'S LOVE (Vocal: Bill Darnell) / SWINGIN' IN THE PROMISED LAND... *Decca 1665* 3-5 38

MEET THE BAND / BARBARY COAST BLUES (Vocal: Earlene Howell)............ *Decca 1940* 3-5 38

QUEEN ISABELLA / OLD KING COLE (Vocal: Bill Darnell)................. *Decca 1527* 4-6 37

SHINDIG (Vocal: Bill Darnell) / YOU'RE MY FIRST THOUGHT EVERY MORNING (Vocal: James Anderson)......... *Decca 2048* 3-5 38

STARDUST (theme song) / IN THE MOOD... *Decca 1882* 3-5 38

STOMPING AT THE RENNY / LAUGHING AT LIFE (Vocal: Bernie Flood)............ *Decca 1416* 4-6 37

HAYES, Edgar, as The Edgar Hayes Quintet

BLUE SKIES / SWEETHEART........... *Decca 1684* 3-5 37

I KNOW NOW / WHEN YOU AND I WERE YOUNG, MAGGIE.............. *Decca 1509* 3-5 37
(Vocals: Bill Darnell)

LOVE ME OR LEAVE ME / SO RARE ..... *Decca 1444* 3-5 37
(Vocals: Bill Darnell)

HAYMES, Joe, & His Orchestra
(Joe Haymes: 1908 –)

(I WENT HUNTING) AND THE BIG BAD WOLF WAS DEAD (Vocal: Cliff Weston) / DILLY DALLY (Vocal: Gene Traxler)..... *Banner 33111* 5-8 34

(I WENT HUNTING) AND THE BIG BAD WOLF WAS DEAD (Vocal: Cliff Weston) / DILLY DALLY (Vocal: Gene Traxler)... *Melotone M-13078* 5-8 34

(I WENT HUNTING) AND THE BIG BAD WOLF WAS DEAD (Vocal: Cliff Weston) / DILLY DALLY (Vocal: Gene Traxler)....... *Oriole 2932* 5-8 34

(I WENT HUNTING) AND THE BIG BAD WOLF WAS DEAD (Vocal: Cliff Weston) / DILLY DALLY (Vocal: Gene Traxler) ..... *Perfect 15962* 5-8 34

(I WENT HUNTING) AND THE BIG BAD WOLF WAS DEAD (Vocal: Cliff Weston) / DILLY DALLY (Vocal: Gene Traxler) ...... *Romeo 2306* 5-8 34
(Simultaneously released on five labels)

BATHTUB RAN OVER AGAIN, THE (Vocal: Cliff Weston) / HAVE A LITTLE DREAM ON ME (Vocal: Gene Traxler).... *Banner 33141* 5-8 34

BATHTUB RAN OVER AGAIN, THE (Vocal: Cliff Weston) / HAVE A LITTLE DREAM ON ME (Vocal: Gene Traxler)........ *Melotone M-13108* 5-8 34

BATHTUB RAN OVER AGAIN, THE (Vocal: Cliff Weston) / HAVE A LITTLE DREAM ON ME (Vocal: Gene Traxler)...... *Oriole 2948* 5-8 34

BATHTUB RAN OVER AGAIN, THE (Vocal: Cliff Weston) / HAVE A LITTLE DREAM ON ME (Vocal: Gene Traxler).... *Perfect 15974* 5-8 34

BATHTUB RAN OVER AGAIN, THE (Vocal: Cliff Weston) / HAVE A LITTLE DREAM ON ME (Vocal: Gene Traxler)...... *Romeo 2322* 5-8 34
(Simultaneously released on five labels)

BREEZE, THE (Vocal: Cliff Weston) / UNDER A BEACH UMBRELLA WITH YOU (Vocal: Gene Traxler) .... *Banner 33100* 4-6 34

BREEZE, THE (Vocal: Cliff Weston) / UNDER A BEACH UMBRELLA WITH YOU (Vocal: Gene Traxler)............... *Melotone M-13068* 4-6 34

BREEZE, THE (Vocal: Cliff Weston) / UNDER A BEACH UMBRELLA WITH YOU (Vocal: Gene Traxler).................... *Oriole 2927* 4-6 34

BREEZE, THE (Vocal: Cliff Weston) / UNDER A BEACH UMBRELLA WITH YOU (Vocal: Gene Traxler).................... *Perfect 15958* 4-6 34

BREEZE, THE (Vocal: Cliff Weston) / UNDER A BEACH UMBRELLA WITH YOU (Vocal: Gene Traxler).................... *Romeo 2301* 4-6 34
(Simultaneously released on five labels)

CAN'T DO WITHOUT HIS LOVE / THE YES HABIT...................... *Victor 24060* 4-6 32
(Vocals: Phil Dooley and orchestra)

DAMES / ROLLING IN LOVE.......... *Banner 33099* 5-8 34
(Vocals: Cliff Weston)

DAMES / ROLLING IN LOVE....... *Melotone M-13067* 5-8 34
(Vocals: Cliff Weston)

DAMES / ROLLING IN LOVE .... *Oriole 2926* 5-8 34
(Vocals: Cliff Weston)

DAMES / ROLLING IN LOVE........... *Perfect 15957* 5-8 34
(Vocals: Cliff Weston)

DAMES / ROLLING IN LOVE............ *Romeo 2300* 5-8 34
(Vocals: Cliff Weston)
(Simultaneously released on five labels)

DOIN' THE SUZY-Q / THE WEDDING OF MR. AND MRS. SWING .... *Vocalion 3335* 5-8 36
(Vocals: Cliff Weston)

FROM THE TOP OF YOUR HEAD (Vocal: Cliff Weston); WITHOUT A WORD OF WARNING; RHYTHM AND ROMANCE (Vocals: Ed Kirkeby as Skippy Carlstrom); I'M ON A SEE-SAW (Vocal: Cliff Weston) / ISN'T IT A LOVELY DAY; NO STRINGS; CHEEK TO CHEEK (Vocals: Unknown); THE PICCOLINO ... *Thesaurus 166* 15-20 35
(An electical transcription produced for radio broadcast, not for commercial release.)

GENTLEMAN OBVIOUSLY DOESN'T BELIEVE, THE / I'M ON A SEE SAW .... *Conqueror 8552* 4-6 35
(Vocals: Cliff Weston)

GENTLEMAN OBVIOUSLY DOESN'T BELIEVE, THE / I'M ON A SEE SAW .... *Melotone 35-10-25* 4-6 35
(Vocals: Cliff Weston)
(Simultaneously released on two labels)

GOTTA GO! (Vocal: Mike Doty) / LOUISVILLE LADY (Vocal: Ward Silloway)............ *Banner 32816* 5-8 33

GOTTA GO! (Vocal: Mike Doty) / LOUISVILLE LADY (Vocal: Ward Silloway)........ *Melotone M-12744* 5-8 33

GOTTA GO! (Vocal: Mike Doty) / LOUISVILLE LADY (Vocal: Ward Silloway)............ *Oriole 2731* 5-8 33

GOTTA GO! (Vocal: Mike Doty) / LOUISVILLE LADY (Vocal: Ward Silloway) .... *Perfect 15795* 5-8 33

GOTTA GO! (Vocal: Mike Doty) / LOUISVILLE LADY (Vocal: Ward Silloway).............. *Romeo 2104* 5-8 33
(Simultaneously released on five labels)

HOT JAZZ PIE (Vocals: Joe Haymes & Mike Doty) / MIGHTY RIVER (by Hoagy Carmichael & His Orchestra. Vocals: Dick Robertson).......... *Victor 24123* 5-8 32

I AIN'T GONNA GRIEVE NO MORE (Vocals: by orchestra) / JUST GIVE ME THE GIRL (Vocal: Ward Silloway)............... *Columbia 2784-D* 8-10 33

I COULDN'T BE MEAN TO YOU (Vocal: Gene Traxler) / I SAW STARS (Vocal: Cliff Weston) ...... *Banner 33142* 4-6 34

I COULDN'T BE MEAN TO YOU (Vocal: Gene Traxler) / I SAW STARS (Vocal: Cliff Weston)... *Melotone M-13109* 4-6 34

I COULDN'T BE MEAN TO YOU (Vocal: Gene Traxler) / I SAW STARS (Vocal: Cliff Weston) .... *Oriole 2949* 4-6 34

I COULDN'T BE MEAN TO YOU (Vocal: Gene Traxler) / I SAW STARS (Vocal: Cliff Weston)....... *Perfect 15975* 4-6 34

I COULDN'T BE MEAN TO YOU (Vocal: Gene Traxler) / I SAW STARS (Vocal: Cliff Weston) .... *Romeo 2323* 4-6 34
(Simultaneously released on five labels)

I SAW STARS (Vocal: Cliff Weston) / IF I HAD A MILLION DOLLARS (Vocal: Gene Traxler)........ *Conqueror 8414* 4-6 34

I'SE A MUGGIN' (Vocals: Cliff Weston & The Headliners) / CHRISTOPHER COLUMBUS....... *Melotone 6-05-09* 5-8 36

IT'S ABOUT TIME (Vocal: Larry Murphy) / EVERY LITTLE BIT OF ME (Vocal: Jimmy Underwood)................ *Victor 24038* 5-8 32

IT'S ALL FORGOTTEN NOW (Vocal: Gene Traxler) / DAY DREAMS (Vocal: Cliff Weston)...... *Banner 33175* 3-5 34

IT'S ALL FORGOTTEN NOW (Vocal: Gene Traxler) / DAY DREAMS (Vocal: Cliff Weston) ... *Melotone M-13142* 3-5 34

IT'S ALL FORGOTTEN NOW (Vocal: Gene Traxler) / DAY DREAMS (Vocal: Cliff Weston)........ *Oriole 2977* 3-5 34

IT'S ALL FORGOTTEN NOW (Vocal: Gene Traxler) / DAY DREAMS (Vocal: Cliff Weston) ...... *Perfect 15991* 3-5 34

IT'S ALL FORGOTTEN NOW (Vocal: Gene Traxler) / DAY DREAMS (Vocal: Cliff Weston) .... *Romeo 2351* 3-5 34
(Simultaneously released on five labels)

I WANNA WOO / POLLY-WOLLY-DOODLE.......... *Melotone 6-02-11* 5-8 36
(Vocals: The Headliners)

JAZZ PIE (Vocals: Joe Haymes & Mike Doty) / ONE-NOTE TRUMPET PLAYER (Vocals: Joe Haymes & orchestra)....... *Columbia 2739-D* 8-10 32
(This record was pressed in blue shellac)

LADY IN RED, THE (Vocal: Cliff Weston) / MY MELANCHOLY BABY (Vocal: Skeeter Palmer) .... *Bluebird B-5918* 5-8 35

LADY IN RED, THE (Vocal: Cliff Weston) / TO CALL YOU MY OWN (Vocal: Skeeter Palmer) .... *Banner 33439* 4-6 35

LADY IN RED, THE (Vocal: Cliff Weston) / TO CALL YOU MY OWN (Vocal: Skeeter Palmer)..... *Melotone M-13406* 4-6 35

LADY IN RED, THE (Vocal: Cliff Weston) / TO CALL YOU MY OWN (Vocal: Skeeter Palmer)........... *Oriole 3147* 4-6 35

LADY IN RED, THE (Vocal: Cliff Weston) / TO CALL YOU MY OWN (Vocal: Skeeter Palmer)......... *Perfect 16121* 4-6 35

LADY IN RED, THE (Vocal: Cliff Weston) / TO CALL YOU MY OWN (Vocal: Skeeter Palmer).......... *Romeo 2521* 4-6 35
(Simultaneously released on five labels)

LAZYBONES (Vocal: Roy Wager) / HAPPY AS THE DAY IS LONG (Vocal: Mike Doty)........ *Banner 32807* 5-8 33

LAZYBONES (Vocal: Roy Wager) / HAPPY AS THE DAY IS LONG (Vocal: Mike Doty)...... *Conqueror 8188* 5-8 33

LAZYBONES (Vocal: Roy Wager) / HAPPY AS THE DAY IS LONG (Vocal: Mike Doty).... *Melotone M-12740* 5-8 33

LAZYBONES (Vocal: Roy Wager) / HAPPY AS THE DAY IS LONG (Vocal: Mike Doty).......... *Oriole 2725* 5-8 33

LAZYBONES (Vocal: Roy Wager) / HAPPY AS THE DAY IS LONG (Vocal: Mike Doty) .... *Perfect 15790* 5-8 33

LAZYBONES (Vocal: Roy Wager) / HAPPY AS THE DAY IS LONG (Vocal: Mike Doty) .... *Romeo 2098* 5-8 33
(Simultaneously released on six labels)

LET'S CALL THE WHOLE THING OFF / SLAP THAT BASS .... *Melotone 7-05-14* 4-6 37
(Vocals: Cliff Weston)

LET'S HAVE A PARTY (Vocals: Joe Haymes, John Scott, & orchestra) / THE OLD MAN OF THE MOUNTAIN (Vocal: Larry Murphy) .... *Columbia 2704-D* 8-10 32

LET'S HAVE A PARTY (Vocals: by orchestra) / WHY LITTLE BOY BLUE WAS BLUE (Vocal: Larry Murphy) .... *Victor 24055* 5-8 32

LIFE IS A SONG / SEEING IS BELIEVING...................... *Bluebird B-5916* 4-6 35
(Vocals: Skeeter Palmer)

LIMEHOUSE BLUES / SHINE ON, HARVEST MOON .... *Bluebird B-5133* 5-8 33

LIMEHOUSE BLUES / SHINE ON, HARVEST MOON................. *Electradisk 2039* 15-20 33

LIMEHOUSE BLUES / SHINE ON, HARVEST MOON .... *Sunrise S-3214* 15-20 33
(Simultaneously released on three labels)

LOST IN MY DREAMS (Vocal: Ronnie Chase) / SITTING ON THE MOON (Vocal: Cliff Weston)................. *Hollywood H-506* 10-12 36

LOST IN MY DREAMS (Vocal: Ronnie Chase) / SITTING ON THE MOON (Vocal: Cliff Weston) .... *Melotone 6-11-12* 4-6 36
(Simultaneously released on two labels)

LOUISVILLE LADY (Vocal: Ward Silloway) / GOTTA GO! (Vocal: Mike Doty)........ *Bluebird B-5116* 5-8 33

LOUISVILLE LADY (Vocal: Ward Silloway) / GOTTA GO! (Vocal: Mike Doty) .... *Electradisk 2026* 15-20 33

LOUISVILLE LADY (Vocal: Ward Silloway) / GOTTA GO! (Vocal: Mike Doty)......... *Sunrise S-3197* 15-20 33
(Simultaneously released on three labels)

LOVE BUG WILL BITE YOU, THE (Vocal: Cliff Weston) / MY LITTLE BUCKAROO (Vocal: Clyde Rogers)...... *Conqueror 8804* 4-6 37

LOVE BUG WILL BITE YOU, THE (Vocal: Cliff Weston) / MY LITTLE BUCKAROO (Vocal: Clyde Rogers)..... *Melotone 7-05-13* 4-6 37
(Simultaneously released on two labels)

MANDY / IF I HAD A MILLION DOLLARS.............. *Banner 33222* 4-6 34
(Vocals: Gene Traxler)

MANDY / IF I HAD A MILLION DOLLARS........... *Melotone M-13189* 4-6 34
(Vocals: Gene Traxler)

MANDY / IF I HAD A MILLION DOLLARS................ *Oriole 3016* 4-6 34
(Vocals: Gene Traxler)

MANDY / IF I HAD A MILLION DOLLARS .... *Perfect 16008* 4-6 34
(Vocals: Gene Traxler)

MANDY / IF I HAD A MILLION DOLLARS................. *Romeo 2390* 4-6 34
(Vocals: Gene Traxler)
(Simultaneously released on five labels)

MARTINIQUE, THE / I WAS TAKEN BY STORM......................... *Banner 33426* 4-6 35
(Vocals: Skeeter Palmer)

MARTINIQUE, THE / I WAS TAKEN BY STORM..................... *Melotone M-13393* 4-6 35
(Vocals: Skeeter Palmer)

MARTINIQUE, THE / I WAS TAKEN BY STORM........................... *Oriole 3139* 4-6 35
(Vocals: Skeeter Palmer)

MARTINIQUE, THE / I WAS TAKEN BY STORM .... *Perfect 16115* 4-6 35
(Vocals: Skeeter Palmer)

MARTINIQUE, THE / I WAS TAKEN BY STORM .... *Romeo 2513* 4-6 35
(Vocals: Skeeter Palmer)
(Simultaneously released on five labels)

MODERN MELODY / JUST GIVE ME THE GIRL (Vocal: Ward Silloway) ..... *Bluebird B-5119* 4-6 33

MODERN MELODY / JUST GIVE ME THE GIRL (Vocal: Ward Silloway) ..... *Electradisk 2029* 12-15 33

MODERN MELODY / JUST GIVE ME THE GIRL (Vocal: Ward Silloway) ...... *Sunrise S-3200* 12-15 33
(Simultaneously released on three labels)

MUSIC GOES' ROUND AND AROUND, THE / RHYTHM IN MY NURSERY RHYMES........ *Conqueror 8619* 4-6 36
(Vocals: Cliff Weston & The Headliners)

MUSIC GOES' ROUND AND AROUND, THE / RHYTHM IN MY NURSERY RHYMES........ *Melotone 6-02-07* 4-6 36
(Vocals: Cliff Weston & The Headliners)
(Simultaneously released on two labels)

MY HEART'S IN THE RIGHT PLACE / I GOT A NEW DEAL IN LOVE..................... *Banner 33320* 5-8 35
(Vocals: Chick Bullock)

MY HEART'S IN THE RIGHT PLACE / I GOT A NEW DEAL IN LOVE.................. *Melotone M-13287* 5-8 35
(Vocals: Chick Bullock)

MY HEART'S IN THE RIGHT PLACE / I GOT A NEW DEAL IN LOVE .... *Oriole 3077* 5-8 35
(Vocals: Chick Bullock)

MY HEART'S IN THE RIGHT PLACE / I GOT A NEW DEAL IN LOVE...................... *Perfect 16061* 5-8 35
(Vocals: Chick Bullock)

MY HEART'S IN THE RIGHT PLACE / I GOT A NEW DEAL IN LOVE....................... *Romeo 2451* 5-8 35
(Vocals: Chick Bullock)
(Simultaneously released on five labels)

NANA / OH! YOU SWEET THING... *Melotone 35-10-07* 5-8 35
(Vocals: Cliff Weston)

NOTHING LIVES LONGER THAN LOVE (Vocal: Ed Kirkeby as Skippy Carlstrom) / TRUCKIN' (Vocal: Cliff Weston) .... *Melotone 35-10-26* 5-8 35

NOW I'M A LADY (Vocal: Skeeter Palmer) / HONEYSUCKLE ROSE............ *Bluebird B-5920* 5-8 35

ORGAN GRINDER'S SWING / PAPA TREE-TOP TALL........... *Melotone 6-11-05* 5-8 36
(Vocals: Cliff Weston)

POLLY-WOLLY-DOODLE (Vocals: The Headliners) / I LOVE TO RIDE THE HORSES (ON A MERRY-GO-ROUND (Vocal: Cliff Weston)...... *Fox-Movietone F-129* 10-12 35

PRAY FOR THE LIGHTS TO GO OUT (Vocals: Joe Haymes & Orchestra) / WHEN I PUT ON MY LONG WHITE ROBE (Vocals: Jimmy Underwood & orchestra) .... *Victor 24040* 5-8 32

ROCK AND ROLL / OH! LEO (IT'S LOVE)........................ *Banner 33250* 5-8 34
(Vocals: Cliff Weston)

ROCK AND ROLL / OH! LEO (IT'S LOVE) .... *Melotone M-13217* 5-8 34
(Vocals: Cliff Weston)

ROCK AND ROLL / OH! LEO (IT'S LOVE) .... *Oriole 3031* 5-8 34
(Vocals: Cliff Weston)

ROCK AND ROLL / OH! LEO (IT'S LOVE)............................. *Perfect 16025* 5-8 34
(Vocals: Cliff Weston)

ROCK AND ROLL / OH! LEO (IT'S LOVE).......................... *Romeo 2408* 5-8 34
(Vocals: Cliff Weston)
(Simultaneously released on five labels)
(One of the first occasions when the phrase "Rock and roll" was used as a song title. From the 1934 motion picture "Transatlantic Merry-Go-Round", a musical starring the Boswell Sisters and Jimmie Grier & His Orchestra. Composed by Richard Whiting (Margaret's father); lyrics by Sidney Clare.)

SINGING BETWEEN KISSES / WILD HONEY...................... *Banner 33258* 4-6 34
(Vocals: Cliff Weston)

SINGING BETWEEN KISSES / WILD HONEY.................... *Melotone M-13225* 4-6 34
(Vocals: Cliff Weston)

SINGING BETWEEN KISSES / WILD HONEY........................ *Oriole 3038* 4-6 34
(Vocals: Cliff Weston)

SINGING BETWEEN KISSES / WILD HONEY .... *Perfect 16029* 4-6 34
(Vocals: Cliff Weston)

SINGING BETWEEN KISSES / WILD HONEY .... *Romeo 2412* 4-6 34
(Vocals: Cliff Weston)
(Simultaneously released on five labels)

SISTER KATE / THAT'S A PLENTY.... *Vocalion 3307* 5-8 36

SQUEEZE ME / GOBLIN MARKET..... *Banner 33338* 5-8 34

SQUEEZE ME / GOBLIN MARKET... *Melotone M-13305* 5-8 34

SQUEEZE ME / GOBLIN MARKET....... *Oriole 3088* 5-8 34

SQUEEZE ME / GOBLIN MARKET...... *Perfect 16072* 5-8 34

SQUEEZE ME / GOBLIN MARKET....... *Romeo 2462* 5-8 34
(Simultaneously released on five labels)

ST. LOUIS BLUES / SHOULD I?........ *Vocalion 3369* 5-8 36

SWINGIN' FOR THE KING (Vocal: Toots Mondello) / LOST MOTION..................... *Banner 33484* 5-8 34

SWINGIN' FOR THE KING (Vocal: Toots Mondello) / LOST MOTION.................. *Melotone M-13451* 5-8 34

SWINGIN' FOR THE KING (Vocal: Toots Mondello) / LOST MOTION .... *Oriole 3173* 5-8 34

SWINGIN' FOR THE KING (Vocal: Toots Mondello) / LOST MOTION....................... *Perfect 16143* 5-8 34

SWINGIN' FOR THE KING (Vocal: Toots Mondello) / LOST MOTION........................ *Romeo 2547* 5-8 34
(Simultaneously released on five labels)

THERE'S GONNA BE A WEDDING IN THE BAND / CROSS-EYED KELLY... *Banner 33223* 5-8 34
(Vocals: Cliff Weston)

THERE'S GONNA BE A WEDDING IN THE BAND / CROSS-EYED KELLY........... *Melotone M-13190* 5-8 34
(Vocals: Cliff Weston)

THERE'S GONNA BE A WEDDING IN THE BAND / CROSS-EYED KELLY..... *Oriole 3017* 5-8 34
(Vocals: Cliff Weston)

THERE'S GONNA BE A WEDDING IN THE BAND / CROSS-EYED KELLY ... *Perfect 16009* 5-8 34
(Vocals: Cliff Weston)

THERE'S GONNA BE A WEDDING IN THE BAND / CROSS-EYED KELLY..... *Romeo 2391* 5-8 34
(Vocals: Cliff Weston)
(Simultaneously released on five labels)

THROWIN' STONES AT THE SUN / IN MY COUNTRY THAT MEANS LOVE............... *Banner 33319* 4-6 35
(Vocals: Cliff Weston)

THROWIN' STONES AT THE SUN / IN MY COUNTRY THAT MEANS LOVE............ *Melotone M-13286* 4-6 35
(Vocals: Cliff Weston)

THROWIN' STONES AT THE SUN / IN MY COUNTRY THAT MEANS LOVE .... *Oriole 3076* 4-6 35
(Vocals: Cliff Weston)

THROWIN' STONES AT THE SUN / IN MY COUNTRY THAT MEANS LOVE................ *Perfect 16060* 4-6 35
(Vocals: Cliff Weston)

THROWIN' STONES AT THE SUN / IN MY COUNTRY THAT MEANS LOVE.................. *Romeo 2450* 4-6 35
(Vocals: Cliff Weston)
(Simultaneously released on five labels)

TWENTY-FOUR HOURS IN GEORGIA / TEN YARDS TO GO............................. *Banner 33193* 5-8 34
(Vocals: Cliff Weston)

TWENTY-FOUR HOURS IN GEORGIA / TEN YARDS TO GO.......................... *Melotone M-13160* 5-8 34
(Vocals: Cliff Weston)

TWENTY-FOUR HOURS IN GEORGIA / TEN YARDS TO GO .... *Oriole 2991* 5-8 34
(Vocals: Cliff Weston)

TWENTY-FOUR HOURS IN GEORGIA / TEN YARDS TO GO.............................. *Perfect 16003* 5-8 34
(Vocals: Cliff Weston)

TWENTY-FOUR HOURS IN GEORGIA / TEN YARDS TO GO.............................. *Romeo 2365* 5-8 34
(Vocals: Cliff Weston)
(Simultaneously released on five labels)

UNCLE JOE'S MUSIC STORE (Vocal: Joe Haymes) / I COVER THE WATERFRONT (Vocal: Unknown).................. *Columbia 2781-D* 8-10 33
(This record was pressed in blue shellac)

WHEN I PUT ON MY LONG WHITE ROBE (Vocal: John Scott) / AIN'T GONNA PAY NO TOLL (Vocals: John Scott & Orchestra) ... *Columbia 2716-D* 5-8 32

HAYMES, Joe, & His Orchestra as Dick Clark & His Orchestra

IF IT AIN'T LOVE / WITH SUMMER COMING ON...................... *Electradisk 2509* 20-25 32
(Vocals: Larry Murphy)

HAYMES, Joe, & His Orchestra as Mike Doty & His Orchestra

LENOX AVENUE (Vocal: Roy Wager) / LONELY LANE (Vocal: Ward Silloway) .... *Bluebird B-5252* 5-8 34

LENOX AVENUE (Vocal: Roy Wager) / LONELY LANE (Vocal: Ward Silloway) .... *Electradisk 2132* 15-20 34

LENOX AVENUE (Vocal: Roy Wager) / LONELY LANE (Vocal: Ward Silloway) .... *Sunrise S-3335* 15-20 34
(Simultaneously released on three labels)

MY GALVESTON GAL (Vocal: Mike Doty) / CAN THIS BE THE END OF LOVE? (Vocal: Ward Silloway)........................ *Bluebird B-5253* 5-8 34

MY GALVESTON GAL (Vocal: Mike Doty) / CAN THIS BE THE END OF LOVE? (Vocal: Ward Silloway)............... *Electradisk 2133* 15-20 34

MY GALVESTON GAL (Vocal: Mike Doty) / CAN THIS BE THE END OF LOVE? (Vocal: Ward Silloway)................ *Sunrise S-3336* 15-20 34
(Simultaneously released on three labels)

PUDDIN' HEAD JONES (Vocal: Mike Doty) / ANNIE DOESN'T LIVE HERE ANY MORE (Vocal: Ward Silloway)................ *Bluebird B-5251* 5-8 33

PUDDIN' HEAD JONES (Vocal: Mike Doty) / ANNIE DOESN'T LIVE HERE ANY MORE (Vocal: Ward Silloway)............... *Electradisk 2131* 15-20 33

PUDDIN' HEAD JONES (Vocal: Mike Doty) / ANNIE DOESN'T LIVE HERE ANY MORE (Vocal: Ward Silloway)................. *Sunrise S-3334* 15-20 33
(Simultaneously released on three labels)

SHARING / I BEG YOUR PARDON, MADEMOISELLE....... *Electradisk 2508* 15-20 32
(Vocals: Larry Murphy)

YOU'RE MY THRILL (Vocal: Ward Silloway) / IT'S THE IRISH IN ME (Vocal: Mike Doty)...... *Bluebird B-5277* 4-6 34

YOU'RE MY THRILL (Vocal: Ward Silloway) / IT'S THE IRISH IN ME (Vocal: Mike Doty)...... *Electradisk 2151* 12-25 34

YOU'RE MY THRILL (Vocal: Ward Silloway) / IT'S THE IRISH IN ME (Vocal: Mike Doty) .... *Sunrise S-3358* 15-20 34
(Simultaneously released on three labels)

HAYMES, Joe, & His Orchestra as Carl Snyder & His Orchestra

LULLABY OF THE LEAVES / THERE'S OCEANS OF LOVE BY THE BEAUTIFUL SEA.... *Electradisk 2502* 15-20 32
(Vocals: Larry Murphy)

HAYMES, Joe, & His Orchestra as Jimmy Underwood & His Orchestra

HUMMIN' TO MYSELF / IS I IN LOVE? I IS....................... *Electradisk 2506* 15-20 32
(Vocals: Jimmy Underwood)

HAYMES, Joe, & His Orchestra as Roy Wager & His Orchestra

NIGHT WILL BE FILLED WITH MUSIC, THE (Vocal: Larry Murphy) / AM I WASTING MY TIME? (Vocal: Roy Wager) .... *Electradisk 2504* 15-20 32

HAYMES, Joe, & His Orchestra as Duke Wilson & His Ten Black Berries

PRAY FOR THE LIGHTS TO GO OUT / WHEN I PUT ON MY LONG WHITE ROBE .... *Conqueror 8024* 5-8 32
(Vocals: Jimmy Underwood & orchestra)

PRAY FOR THE LIGHTS TO GO OUT / WHEN I PUT ON MY LONG WHITE ROBE .... *Perfect 15662* 5-8 32
(Vocals: Jimmy Underwood & orchestra)
(Simultaneously released on two labels)

HAYS, Billy, & His Orchestra

BAY RUM SONG, THE (Vocal: Billy Hays) / SITTIN' AND WHITTLIN' (Vocals: Frank Luther & Peter Moore) .... *Victor V-40087* 5-8 29

I'VE GOT TO HAVE A MAMA NOW (Vocal: Andrew T. Stanton) / DO YOU BELIEVE? (Vocal: Billy Hays) .... *Victor V-40113* 5-8 29

MY SUGAR AND ME (Vocal: Billy Hays) / SWEET VIRGINIA ROSE (Vocal: Andrew T. Stanton)................ *Victor V-40056* 5-8 29

HAYS, Billy, as Billy Hays' Cathay Orchestra

DOIN' THE RACOON / I CAN'T GET ENOUGH OF YOU........................ *Okeh 41137* 5-8 28
(Vocals: Unknown)

PRETTY FACE / ALL BY YOURSELF IN THE MOONLIGHT................. *Okeh 41193* 5-8 29
(Vocals: Unknown)

HAYTON, Lenny, & His Orchestra

(Lenny Hayton: 2/13/08 – 4/24/71)

AC-DC CURRENT / TIMES SQUARE SCUTTLE.......................... *Vocalion 5471* 5-8 40

AT THE BALALAIKA / THE STARLIT HOUR................................ *Varsity 8125* 3-5 40

CABIN IN THE COTTON / WITH SUMMER COMING ON .... *Brunswick 6329* 8-10 32
(Vocals: Bing Crosby)

CARELESSLY / IT LOOKS LIKE RAIN IN CHERRY BLOSSOM LANE .... *Decca 1248* 3-5 37
(Vocals: Paul Barry)

GONE WITH THE WIND / WHAT A BEAUTIFUL BEGINNING.............. *Decca 1341* 3-5 37
(Vocals: Paul Barry)

I KNOW NOW / YOU CAN'T RUN AWAY FROM LOVE TONIGHT................ *Decca 1267* 3-5 37
(Vocals: Paul Barry)

I LOVE YOU MUCH TOO MUCH / ONE CIGARETTE FOR TWO ....Vocalion 5421 5-8 40
(Vocals: Linda Keene)

LADY WHO COULDN'T BE KISSED, THE / NIGHT OVER SHANGHAI .... *Decca 1268* 4-6 37
(Vocals: Paul Barry)

LOVE ME TONIGHT / SOME OF THESE DAYS..................... *Brunswick 6351* 8-10 32
(Vocals: Bing Crosby)

ONCE IN A WHILE / THE MORNING AFTER.............................. *Decca 1443* 4-6 37
(Vocals: Paul Barry)

PEG O' MY HEART / AS LONG AS I LIVE .... *Varsity 8134* 3-5 40

THAT OLD FEELING / LOVELY ONE..... *Decca 1354* 3-5 37
(Vocals: Paul Barry)

HEIDT, Horace, & His Brigadiers

(Horace Heidt: 5/21/01 –)

DARDANELLA (Vocals: The Four Jacks & The Four Kings) / IN THE GOOD OLD SUMMER TIME... *Brunswick 8248* 2-4 38

GONE WITH THE WIND (Vocal: Larry Cotton) / THE MILLER'S DAUGHTER, MARIANNE (Vocals: Bob McCoy & The Glee Club) .... *Brunswick 7913* 3-5 37

HOT LIPS (Vocals: The King Sisters) / THE BELLS OF ST. MARY'S.................. *Brunswick 7916* 3-5 37

Title	Label / No.	Price	Year
I'LL LOVE YOU IN MY DREAMS (theme song) (Vocal: Larry Cotton) / BUGLE CALL RAG	Brunswick 7981	4-6	37
I'LL TAKE YOU HOME AGAIN, KATHLEEN (Vocal: Larry Cotton) / HEIGH-HO! (DWARFS' MARCHING SONG) (Vocals: The King Sisters & The Glee Club)	Brunswick 8074	4-6	38
IT'S THE NATURAL THING TO DO (Vocals: The King Sisters) / THE MOON GOT IN MY EYES (Vocal: Larry Cotton)	Brunswick 7927	3-5	37
MY MARGARITA (Vocals: Larry Cotton, Bob McCoy, & The Charioteers) / DUST (Vocal: Larry Cotton and The Charioteers) (This release features a picture of Horace Heidt on the label)	Brunswick 8129	5-8	38
OH! MA-MA (THE BUTCHER BOY) (Vocals: Red Farrington & Frank DeVol) / FERDINAND THE BULL (Vocals: The Three Kings)	Brunswick 8138	3-5	38
ONCE IN A WHILE (Vocal: Larry Cotton) / SWEET VARSITY SUE (Vocal: Jerry Bowne)	Brunswick 7977	3-5	37
PRETTY GIRL IS LIKE A MELODY, A (Vocal: Larry Cotton) / DANCE OF THE BLUE DANUBE	Brunswick 8203	2-4	38
SUGAR BLUES / RIDIN' TO GLORY ON A TRUMPET (Vocals: The Three Kings)	Brunswick 8162	3-5	38
SWEET AS A SONG (Vocal: Larry Cotton) / HALF MOON ON THE HUDSON (Vocals: The King Sisters)	Brunswick 8043	2-4	38
THIS CAN'T BE LOVE (Vocal: Larry Cotton) / SING FOR YOUR SUPPER (Vocals: Charles Goodwin)	Brunswick 8257	2-4	38
TOY TRUMPET, THE / THE HISTORY OF SWEET SWING (Vocals: The King Sisters & The Glee Club)	Brunswick 8048	3-5	38

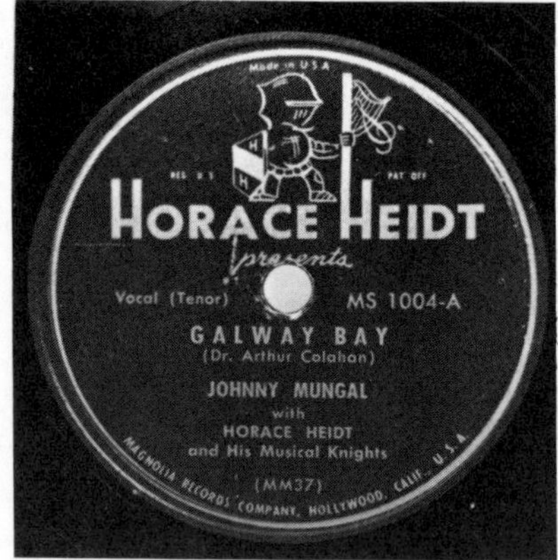

HEIDT, Horace, & His Musical Knights

Title	Label / No.	Price	Year
AMERICA THE BEAUTIFUL (Vocals: Ruth Davis & Henry Russell) / COLUMBIA, THE GEM OF THE OCEAN (Vocals: Ruth Davis & Larry Cotton)	*Columbia 35575*	2-4	40
BOY IN KHAKI – A GIRL IN LACE, A / I MET HER ON MONDAY (Vocals: Donna & Her Don Juans & Charles Goodman)	Columbia 36636	3-5	42
BREEZE AND I, THE / HEAR MY SONG, VIOLETTA (Vocals: Larry Cotton)	Columbia 35498	2-4	40
CAISSONS GO ROLLING ALONG, THE (Vocals: by chorus) / THE LAMPLIGHTER'S SERENADE (Vocals: Unknown)	Columbia 36536	3-5	42
CARNIVAL OF VENICE, THE / THE GREEN GRASS GREW ALL ROUND (Vocals: Horace Heidt & Glee Club)	Brunswick 8305	2-4	39
CLARINET POLKA / WHERE HAS MY LITTLE DOG GONE?	Brunswick 8299	2-4	39
DAWN OF A NEW DAY (SONG OF THE NEW YORK WORLD'S FAIR) (Vocal: Charles Goodwin) / PENNY SERENADE (Vocal: Larry Cotton)	Brunswick 8313	3-5	39
GALWAY BAY / YOU'RE IRISH AND YOU'RE BEAUTIFUL (Vocals: Johnny Mungal)	Horace Heidt MS-1004	4-6	49
GOD BLESS AMERICA / STARS AND STRIPES FOREVER (Vocals: Ruth Davis, Larry Cotton, Henry Russell, & chorus)	Columbia 35637	2-4	40
GOOD MORNING (Vocals: The Heidt-Lights) / GOD'S COUNTRY (Vocal: Larry Cotton)	Columbia 35239	2-4	39
HOW STRANGE / THE MASQUERADE IS OVER (Vocals: Larry Cotton)	Brunswick 8329	2-4	39
HOW WARM IT IS THE WEATHER (HOW COLD IT IS YOUR HEART) / SUNRISE SERENADE (Vocals: Larry Cotton)	Brunswick 8372	3-5	39
IF I CARED A LITTLE BIT LESS / THAT OLD BLACK MAGIC (Vocals: Unknown)	Columbia 36670	2-4	42
I'LL GET BY (Vocals: The Heidt-Lights) / S'POSIN' (Vocal: Larry Cotton)	Brunswick 8368	2-4	39
I POURED MY HEART INTO A SONG (Vocals: Larry Cotton & The Heidt-Lights) / BACK TO BACK (Vocals: The Heidt-Lights)	Brunswick 8393	3-5	39
I PROMISE YOU (Vocals: Bob Matthews, The Sweetswingsters, & The Glee Club) / DON'T FENCE ME IN (Vocals: Gene Walsh, The Sweetswingsters, & The Glee Club)	Columbia 36761	2-4	45
LET'S MAKE MEMORIES TONIGHT (Vocal: Larry Cotton) / MOON LOVE (Vocals: Larry Cotton & The Heidt-Lights)	Brunswick 8414	2-4	39
LITTLE CURLY HAIR IN A HIGH CHAIR / A LOVER'S LULLABY (Vocals: Larry Cotton)	Columbia 35446	2-4	40
LITTLE SIR ECHO (Vocals: Emily Stevenson & Larry Cotton) / LET'S STOP THE CLOCK (Vocal: Larry Cotton)	Brunswick 8309	2-4	39
LORETTA / DEEP IN THE HEART OF TEXAS (Vocals: Unknown)	Columbia 36525	2-4	42
MAMA / I DON'T WANT TO SET THE WORLD ON FIRE (Vocals: Larry Cotton, & Donna & Her Don Juans)	Columbia 36295	2-4	41
MARY (Vocals: Larry Cotton, Donna & Her Don Juans) / THREE LITTLE SISTERS (Vocals: Sailor Ollie O'Toole, Marine Red Farrington, & Soldier Charles Goodman)	Columbia 36576	3-5	42
MISSOURI WALTZ (Vocal: Larry Cotton) / THAT NAUGHTY WALTZ	Columbia 35425	2-4	40
MOONLIGHT COCKTAIL (Vocals: Unknown) / THE WHISTLING COWBOY (whistling by Fred Lowery)	Columbia 36512	2-4	42
NEW MOON AND AN OLD SERENADE, A / THE CHESTNUT TREE (Vocals: The Heidt-Lights)	Brunswick 8360	2-4	39
OVER THE RAINBOW / ADDRESS UNKNOWN (Vocals: Larry Cotton)	Brunswick 8441	2-4	39
PAGAN LOVE SONG / TO YOU, SWEETHEART, ALOHA (Vocal: Larry Cotton)	Columbia 35309	2-4	39
THIS IS NO DREAM (Vocal: Larry Cotton) / WISHING (Vocals: Larry Cotton & The Heidt-Lights)	Brunswick 8382	2-4	39
THIS IS THE ARMY MISTER JONES / WHERE THE MOUNTAINS MEET THE SKY (Vocals: Unknown)	Columbia 36667	3-5	42
WALKIN' 'ROUND IN CIRCLES / THE HUT SUT SONG (Vocals: Donna & Her Don Juans)	Columbia 36138	2-4	41
WHAT GOES UP MUST COME DOWN (Vocal: Tony Russell) / DON'T WORRY 'BOUT ME (Vocal: Larry Cotton)	Brunswick 8334	2-4	39
WHEN YOU WISH UPON A STAR (Vocal: Larry Cotton) / GIVE A LITTLE WHISTLE (Vocal: Henry Russell)	Columbia 35351	4-6	40

HEIDT, Horace, & His Orchestra

Title	Label / No.	Price	Year
CUDDLE UP A LITTLE CLOSER, LOVEY MINE (Vocal: Lee Lykins) / I LOVE YOU TRULY	Victor 21335	2-4	28
GOLDEN GATE / WHAT A WONDERFUL WEDDING THAT WILL BE (Vocals: Jerry Bowne, Warren Lewis, & Charles Bradshaw)	Victor 21310	2-4	28
I'M KA-RAZY FOR YOU (Vocal: Jerry Bowne) / WEDDING OF THE PAINTED DOLL	Victor 21957	2-4	29
I STILL LOVE YOU / EVERY EVENING (Vocals: Lee Lykins)	Victor 21312	2-4	28
MINE / HELLO CUTIE! (Vocals: Lee Lykins)	Victor 20608	2-4	27
PLODDIN' ALONG (Vocal: Harold Moore) / STAIRWAY OF DREAMS (Vocal: Lee Lykins)	Victor 21956	2-4	29

HENDERSON, Fletcher, & His Orchestra

(Fletcher Henderson: 12/18/98 – 12/29/52)

Title	Label / No.	Price	Year
AFTER YOU'VE GONE (Vocals: Unknown) / STARDUST	Crown 3093	12-15	31
ALL GOD'S CHILLUN GOT RHYTHM (Vocal: Jerry Blake) / CHRIS AND HIS GANG	Vocalion 3641	8-10	37
BACK IN YOUR OWN BACKYARD / ROSE ROOM	Vocalion 3511	8-10	37
BEALE STREET MAMA / DON'T THINK YOU'LL BE MISSED	Broadway 11247	15-20	23
BEALE STREET MAMA / DON'T THINK YOU'LL BE MISSED	Claxtonola 40226	20-25	23
BEALE STREET MAMA / DON'T THINK YOU'LL BE MISSED	Famous 3220	15-20	23
BEALE STREET MAMA / DON'T THINK YOU'LL BE MISSED	Harmograph 803	20-25	23
BEALE STREET MAMA / DON'T THINK YOU'LL BE MISSED	Paramount 20226	20-25	23
BEALE STREET MAMA / DON'T THINK YOU'LL BE MISSED	Puritan 11247	15-20	23
BEALE STREET MAMA / DON'T THINK YOU'LL BE MISSED (Simultaneously released on seven labels)	Triangle 11247	15-20	23
BLUES IN MY HEART / SUGAR (Vocals: Les Reis)	Columbia 2559-D	15-20	31
CHATTANOOGA (DOWN IN TENNESSEE)) / GHOST OF THE BLUES	Emerson 10744	15-20	24
CHRISTOPHER COLUMBUS (theme song) / BLUE LOU	Vocalion 3211	8-10	36
COME ON BABY! (Vocal: Benny Carter) / EASY MONEY	Columbia 14392-D	15-20	29
COTTON PICKER'S BALL / LOT'S O' MAMA	Vocalion 14759	10-12	24
DON'T LET THE RHYTHM GO TO YOUR HEAD (Vocal: Chuck Richards) / MOTEN STOMP	Vocalion 4180	8-10	38
GRAND TERRACE SWING / STEALIN' APPLES	Vocalion 3213	8-10	36
HARD HEARTED HANNAH / CHARLEY, MY BOY	Banner 1383	8-10	24
HE'S THE HOTTEST MAN IN TOWN / I NEVER CARE 'BOUT TOMORROW	Columbia 209-D	10-12	24
HOCUS POCUS / TIDAL WAVE	Bluebird B-5682	8-10	34
HOUSE RENT BALL / DARKTOWN HAS A GAY WHITE WAY	Ajax 17023	25-30	24
IF YOU SHOULD EVER LEAVE / POSIN' (Vocals: Chuck Richards)	Vocalion 3627	5-8	37
IT'S THE TALK OF THE TOWN / NAGASAKI (Vocal: Henry Allen)	Columbia 2825-D	15-20	33
I'VE FOUND WHAT I WANTED IN YOU (Vocal: Lois Deppe) / SWEET AND HOT (Vocal: Jimmy Harrison)	Columbia 2414-D	15-20	31
I WANT TO SEE A LITTLE MORE OF WHAT I SAW IN ARKANSAS / LET ME INTRODUCE YOU TO MY ROSIE	Vocalion 15205	20-25	26
I WISH I COULD MAKE YOU CRY / SAY SAY SADIE	Pathe Actuelle 036084	10-12	24
I WISH I COULD MAKE YOU CRY / SAY SAY SADIE (Simultaneously released on two labels)	Perfect 14265	8-10	24
JUST HOT / DOWN SOUTH BLUES	Vocalion 14691	10-12	28
KING PORTER STOMP / "D" NATURAL BLUES	Columbia 1543-D	12-15	28
LET'S GO HOME / I LIKE MY SUGAR SWEET (Vocal: Helen Young)	Columbia 36214	3-5	41
LIMEHOUSE BLUES / WRAPPIN' IT UP	Decca 157	5-8	34
MANDA / GO 'LONG, MULE	Columbia 228-D	15-20	24
MEANEST KIND OF BLUES, THE / NAUGHTY MAN	Columbia 249-D	15-20	25
OH! SISTER, AIN'T THAT HOT? / MAMA'S GONNA SLOW YOU DOWN	Emerson 10713	15-20	24
PEACEFUL VALLEY / HAY FOOT, STRAW FOOT	Vocalion 15174	20-25	26
PHANTOM FANTASIE / HARLEM MADNESS (Vocal: Charles Holland)	Victor 24699	12-15	34
PIXIE FROM DIXIE / WE GO WELL TOGETHER (Vocal: Helen Young)	Columbia 36289	3-5	41
SAVING MYSELF FOR YOU / IT'S THE LITTLE THINGS THAT COUNT (Vocals: Chuck Richards)	Vocalion 4154	5-8	38
SAY THAT YOU WERE TEASING ME / TAKE A PICTURE OF THE MOON (Vocals: Baby Rose Marie)	Victor 22960	15-20	32
SHANGHAI SHUFFLE / NAUGHTY MAN	Vocalion 14935	15-20	25
SHOE SHINE BOY (Vocal: Roy Eldridge) / SING, SING, SING (Vocal: Arthur Lee "Georgia Boy" Simpkins)	Victor 25375	5-8	36
STAMPEDE / GREAT CAESAR'S GHOST	Vocalion 3534	8-10	37
STOCKHOLM STOMP / HAVE IT READY	Brunswick 3460	12-15	27
STOCKHOLM STOMP / HAVE IT READY (Simultaneously released on two labels)	Vocalion 15532	10-12	27
TELL ME, DREAMY EYES / SHANGHAI SHUFFLE	Harmograph 982	20-25	24
TELL ME, DREAMY EYES / SHANGHAI SHUFFLE	Pathe Actuelle 036157	15-20	24
TELL ME, DREAMY EYES / SHANGHAI SHUFFLE (Simultaneously released on three labels)	Perfect 14338	12-15	24
THAT'S GEORGIA / YOU'LL NEVER GET TO HEAVEN WITH THOSE EYES	Columbia 202-D	15-20	24
WHAT'S YOUR STORY (WHAT'S YOUR JIVE) (Vocal: Jerry Blake) / TREES (Vocal: Chuck Richards)	Vocalion 3760	5-8	37
WHAT WILL I TELL MY HEART? (Vocal: Dorothy Derrick) / SLUMMING ON PARK AVENUE (Vocal: Jerry Blake)	Vocalion 3485	5-8	37
WHERE THE DREAMY WABASH FLOWS / THE GRASS IS GREENER (IN THE OTHER FELLOW'S YARD)	Banner 1388	8-10	24
WILD PARTY / RUG CUTTER'S SWING	Decca 342	5-8	34
YOU'VE GOT TO GET HOT / CHARLESTON CRAZY	Silvertone 3021	10-12	23
YOU'VE GOT TO GET HOT / CHARLESTON CRAZY (Simultaneously released on two labels)	Vocalion 14726	10-12	23

HENDERSON, Fletcher, & His Orchestra as Connie's Inn Orchestra

Title	Label / No.	Price	Year
CASA LOMA STOMP / GOODBYE BLUES	Melotone M-12340	15-20	32
HOUSE OF DAVID BLUES, THE / YOU RASCAL, YOU (Vocal: Rex Stewart)	Melotone M-12216	15-20	31
I'M CRAZY 'BOUT MY BABY (Vocal: George Bias) / SINGIN' THE BLUES	Melotone M-12145	15-20	31
SUGAR FOOT STOMP / JUST BLUES	Melotone M-12239	12-15	31
SUGAR FOOT STOMP / LOW DOWN ON THE BAYOU	Crown 3194	15-20	31
TWELFTH STREET RAG / MILENBERG JOYS	Crown 3212	15-20	31
YOU RASCAL, YOU (Vocal: Claude Jones) / BLUE RHYTHM	Crown 3180	15-20	31

HENDERSON, Fletcher, & His Orchestra as The Dixie Stompers

AIN'T SHE SWEET? / SNAG IT....... *Harmony 353-H* 8-10 27
BLACK MARIA / BALTIMORE....... *Harmony 526-H* 12-15 27
CHINESE BLUES / PANAMA......... *Harmony 92-H* 10-12 26
CORNFED! / GOOSE PIMPLES....... *Harmony 545-H* 12-15 27
FLORIDA STOMP / GET IT FIXED (Vocal: Don Redman)........... *Harmony 88-H* 12-15 25
NERVOUS CHARLIE STOMP / BLACK HORSE STOMP.......... *Harmony 153-H* 12-15 26
OFF TO BUFFALO / BROTHERLY LOVE.......... *Harmony 299-H* 12-15 26
OH, BABY / FEELIN' GOOD........ *Harmony 636-H* 10-12 28
SPANISH SHAWL / CLAP HANDS, HERE COMES CHARLIE.......... *Harmony 70-H* 8-10 25
VARIETY STOMP / THE ST. LOUIS BLUES.......... *Harmony 451-H* 12-15 27

HENDERSON, Fletcher, as Fletcher Henderson's Dance Orchestra

FEELING THE WAY I DO / RED HOT MAMA.......... *Banner 1364* 18-10 24
FEELING THE WAY I DO / RED HOT MAMA.......... *Regal 9658* 8-10 24
(Simultaneously released on two labels)

HENDERSON, Fletcher as Henderson's Dance Orchestra

BAMBOO ISLE / BLUE.......... *Black Swan 2079* 15-20 22
CHICAGO BLUES / WHY PUT THE BLAME ON YOU?........ *Pathe Actuelle 036069* 10-12 24
CHICAGO BLUES / WHY PUT THE BLAME ON YOU?.......... *Perfect 14250* 8-10 24
(Simultaneously released on two labels)
LOVE DAYS / SAY IT WHILE DANCING.......... *Black Swan 2076* 15-20 22
SHAKE YOUR FEET / SWANEE RIVER BLUES.......... *Pathe Actuelle 036027* 10-12 24
SHAKE YOUR FEET / SWANEE RIVER BLUES.......... *Perfect 14208* 8-10 24
(Simultaneously released on two labels)

HENDERSON, Fletcher, as Henderson's Dance Players

DOWN BY THE RIVER / TROT ALONG... *Olympic 1442* 10-12 23
FAREWELL BLUES / WET YO' THUMB... *Olympic 1435* 10-12 23

HENDERSON, Fletcher as Henderson's Dance Players recorded under the name Sammy Swift's Jazz Band

FAREWELL BLUES / WET YO' THUMB.......... *Black Swan 2125* 15-20 23

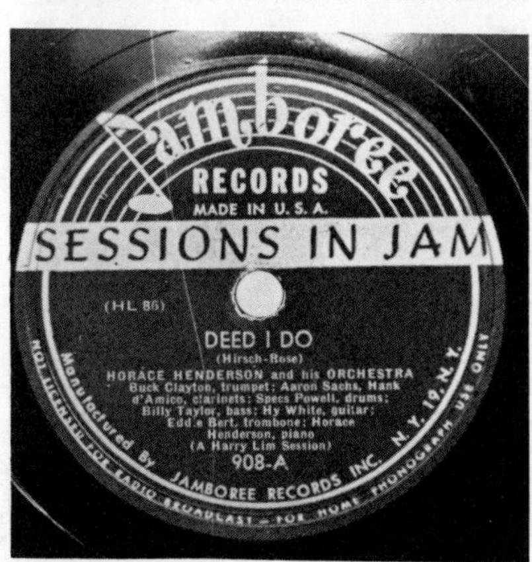

HENDERSON, Horace, & His Orchestra
(Horace Henderson: 11/22/04 –)

CHLOE / CHLOE (by John Kirby & His Orchestra)... *Okeh 5632* 4-6 40
DEED I DO / SMACK'S BLUES.......... *Jamboree 908* 3-5 46
HONEYSUCKLE ROSE (Vocal: Rose Jefferson) / THEY JITTERED ALL THE TIME (Vocal: Ray Nance).......... *Vocalion 5579* 5-8 40
I STILL HAVE MY DREAMS / COQUETTE... *Okeh 5841* 4-6 40
OH BOY, I'M IN THE GROOVE (Vocal: Viola Jefferson) / KITTY ON TOAST........ *Conqueror 9477* 4-6 40
OH BOY, I'M IN THE GROOVE (Vocal: Viola Jefferson) / KITTY ON TOAST......... *Vocalion 5433* 4-6 40
(Simultaneously released on two labels)
SHUFFLIN' JOE / I GOT RHYTHM (Vocal: Viola Jefferson).......... *Vocalion 5518* 4-6 40
SMOOTH SAILING / AIN'T MISBEHAVIN'... *Okeh 5900* 4-6 40
WHEN DREAMS COME TRUE / FLINGING A WHING DING.......... *Okeh 5748* 4-6 40
YOU DON'T MEAN ME NO GOOD (Vocal: Debo Mills) / I'LL ALWAYS BE IN LOVE WITH YOU (Vocal: Harold Johnson).......... *Okeh 5953* 4-6 40
YOU'RE MINE, YOU! (Vocal: Viola Jefferson) / SWINGIN' AND JUMPIN'.......... *Vocalion 5606* 5-8 40

HENDERSON'S DANCE ORCHESTRA:
see HENDERSON, Fletcher, and see LANIN, Sam, as Lanin's Southern Serenaders

HENDERSON'S DANCE PLAYERS:
see HENDERSON, Fletcher

HENRY, Tal, & His North Carolinians

CARIOCA / I CAN'T GO ON LIKE THIS (Vocal: Taz Wolter)........ *Bluebird B-5366* 4-6 34
CARIOCA / I CAN'T GO ON LIKE THIS (Vocal: Taz Wolter)......... *Sunrise S-3477* 12-15 34
(Simultaneously released on two labels)
DON'T SAY GOODNIGHT (Vocal: Chester Shaw) / GOIN' TO HEAVEN ON A MULE (Vocals: Unknown)....... *Bluebird B-5364* 4-6 34
DON'T SAY GOODNIGHT (Vocal: Chester Shaw) / GOIN' TO HEAVEN ON A MULE (Vocals: Unknown)........ *Sunrise S-3445* 12-15 34
(Simultaneously released on two labels)
I'D TRADE MY AIR CASTLES FOR A LOVE NEST AND YOU / LONESOME.......... *Victor 21471* 5-8 28
MY SONG OF SONGS TO YOU (Vocal: Chester Shaw) / SOME LITTLE SOMEONE (Vocals: Walter Brown, Ivan Morris, & Chester Shaw).......... *Victor 21404* 5-8 28
WHY DO YOU MAKE ME LONESOME? (Vocal: Chester Shaw) / LOUISE, I LOVE YOU.......... *Victor 21573* 5-8 28

HENRY, Tal, & His Orchestra

I KNOW WHY I THINK OF YOU (Vocal: Harold Madsen) / SHAME ON YOU (Vocals: Walter Fellman, Walter Brown, & Ivan Morris)........... *Victor V-40133* 5-8 29
JUST YOU AND I (Vocal: Harold Madsen) / FOUND MY GAL (Vocals: Walter Fellman, Walter Brown, & Ivan Morris)........... *Victor V-40035* 5-8 29
WHEN SHADOWS FALL / MY LITTLE OLD HOME DOWN IN NEW ORLEANS.......... *Victor V-40034* 5-8 29

HERBECK, Ray, & His Music With Romance
(Ray Herbeck (Circa 1915 –)

BREAKFAST FOR TWO (Vocal: Ray Olsen) / IT'S SAD BUT TRUE (Vocals: The Glee Club).......... *Okeh 6063* 2-4 41
DANCE WITH A DOLLY (WITH A HOLE IN HER STOCKIN') (Vocal: George Van) / ANGEL IN DISGUISE (Vocal: Ray Olsen).......... *Vocalion 5470* 3-5 40
HIGHWAYS ARE HAPPY WAYS (Vocals: The Glee Club) / IN OLD HAWAII (Vocal: George Van).... *Vocalion 5544* 2-4 40
I JUST GOT A LETTER (Vocal: Betty Bronson) / HERE COMES THE NIGHT (Vocal: Kirby Brooks).......... *Vocalion 5143* 2-4 39
IT'S EIGHT O'CLOCK (Vocal: George Van) / SHADOWS ON THE SAND (Vocal: Ray Olsen).......... *Okeh 5818* 2-4 40
LI'L BOY LOVE (Vocal: Betty Bronson) / ONE LOOK AT YOU (Vocal: Ray Olsen).......... *Okeh 5675* 2-4 40
MOON OVER MADISON SQUARE, THE / THE CALL OF THE CANYON.......... *Okeh 5706* 2-4 40
(Vocals: Ray Olsen)
MY HEART KEEPS CRYING (Vocal: Betty Bronson) / GOOD MORNING (Vocal: Kirby Brooks).... *Vocalion 5115* 2-4 39
NEARNESS OF YOU, THE / WHEN THE SWALLOWS COME BACK TO CAPISTRANO.......... *Okeh 5568* 2-4 40
(Vocals: Ray Olsen)
NOW AND THEN / BLUE TAHITIAN MOONLIGHT.......... *Vocalion 5089* 2-4 39
(Vocals: Kirby Brooks)
NOW AND THEN / GOOD MORNING... *Conqueror 9292* 2-4 39
(Vocals: Kirby Brooks)
OH JOHNNY, OH JOHNNY, OH! (Vocal: Betty Bronson) / CHATTERBOX (Vocal: Kirby Brooks)... *Conqueror 9393* 2-4 40
OH JOHNNY, OH JOHNNY, OH! (Vocal: Betty Bronson) / CHATTERBOX (Vocal: Kirby Brooks).... *Vocalion 5250* 2-4 40
(Simultaneously released on two labels)
PLAYMATES (Vocal: Betty Benson) / APPLE BLOSSOMS AND CHAPEL BELLS (Vocals: Unknown).......... *Vocalion 5386* 3-5 40
ROMANCE (theme song) (Vocal: Kirby Brooks) / OH, DEAR! WHAT CAN THE MATTER BE? (Vocal: Betty Bronson).......... *Vocalion 5197* 2-4 39
SENTIMENTAL ME / THE MOON FELL IN THE RIVER.......... *Okeh 5840* 2-4 40
(Vocals: Ray Olsen)
SEPTEMBER SONG / IT NEVER WAS YOU.......... *Vocalion 4551* 2-4 39
(Vocals: Kirby Brooks)
THERE'S A HOLE IN THE OLD OAKEN BUCKET (Vocals: Kirby Brooks & George Winslow) / ROMANCE RUNS IN THE FAMILY (Vocal: Kirby Brooks).......... *Vocalion 4635* 2-4 39
TIME STOOD STILL (Vocal: Ray Olsen) / TISS ME OR YA DOTTA DET OUT (Vocal: Betty Benson)..... *Okeh 6111* 2-4 41
YESTERTHOUGHTS (Vocal: Ray Olsen) / I JUST WANNA PLAY WITH YOU (Vocal: Betty Benson).......... *Okeh 5790* 2-4 40

YOU'VE GOT ME CRYING AGAIN (Vocal: Kirby Brooks) / THE LAST TRIP ON THE OLD SHIP (Vocals: Kirby Brooks & The Glee Club).......... *Vocalion 4955* 2-4 39

HERBUVEAUX, Jules R.:
see GUYON'S PARADISE ORCHESTRA

HERLIHY, Joe, & His Orchestra

BYE-BYE, PRETTY BABY / —.......... *Edison 52098* 12-15 27
(Vocals: by trio)
CORNFED / —.......... *Edison 52059* 8-10 27
ROLLING AROUND IN ROSES / —..... *Edison 52100* 12-15 27
STATE AND MADISON / LIGHTHOUSE BLUES.......... *Edison 52076* 15-20 27

HERMAN, Len, & His Orchestra:
see NORVO, Red, & His Orchestra

HERMAN, Lenny, & His Hotel Astor Orchestra

ENGAGEMENT WALTZ / MY MUCHACHA.......... *Manor 1103* 2-4 45
(Vocals: Lenny Herman)

HERMAN, Woody, & His Four Chips
(Woody Herman: 5/16/13 –)
(Woody Herman and His Orchestra continue to play engagements all over the country.)

ELSIE / YARDBIRD SHUFFLE........... *Decca 4353* 3-5 41

HERMAN, Woody, & His Orchestra

AT THE WOODCHOPPER'S BALL / BIG WIG IN THE WIGWAM (Vocal: Mary Ann McCall).......... *Decca 2440* 2-4 39
AT THE WOODCHOPPER'S BALL / I CAN'T GET STARTED (by Bunny Berigan & His Orchestra; Vocal: Bunny Berigan).......... *V-Disc 29* 5-8
(A World War II release)
BESSIE'S BLUES (Vocals: Woody Herman & Steady Nelson) / MUSIC BY THE MOON (Vocal: Woody Herman).......... *Decca 3380* 3-5 40
BISHOP'S BLUES / WOODSHEDDIN' WITH WOODY.......... *Decca 3972* 3-5 41
BLUE FLAME / —.......... *V-Disc 297* 5-8
(A World War II release)
BLUE FLAME (theme song) / FUR TRAPPERS' BALL.......... *Decca 3643* 2-4 41
BLUE UPSTAIRS (Vocal: Woody Herman) / BLUES DOWNSTAIRS.......... *Decca 2508* 4-6 39
BOOGIE WOOGIE BUGLE BOY (Vocal: Woody Herman) / BOUNCE ME BROTHER, WITH A SOLID FOUR (Vocal: Muriel Lane).......... *Decca 3617* 3-5 41
CALDONIA (Vocal: Woody Herman) / HAPPINESS IS A THING CALLED JOE (Vocal: Frances Wayne).......... *Columbia 36789* 2-4 45
CALLIOPE BLUES / THE FLAT FOOT FLOOGIE.......... *Decca 1879* 4-6 38
(Vocals: Woody Herman)
CAN THIS BE LOVE? (Vocal: Mary Ann McCall) / BLUE INK.......... *Decca 3081* 2-4 40
CAROLINA IN THE MORNING / I'M SAVING MYSELF FOR YOU.......... *Decca 1839* 4-6 38
(Vocals: Woody Herman)
CASBAH BLUES / FAREWELL BLUES... *Decca 2582* 3-5 39
DALLAS BLUES / RIVER BED BLUES (by Woody Herman & His Woodchoppers; Vocal: Woody Herman)... *Decca 2629* 3-5 39
DEEP NIGHT / WHISTLE STOP.......... *Decca 3332* 3-5 40
DON'T YOU KNOW OR DON'T YOU CARE? / DOUBLE OR NOTHING.......... *Decca 1397* 5-8 37
(Vocals: Woody Herman)
DUPREE BLUES / IT HAPPENED DOWN IN DIXIELAND.......... *Decca 1288* 8-10 37
(Vocals: Woody Herman)
EAST SIDE KICK / ON THE ISLE OF MAY (Vocal: Woody Herman).......... *Decca 2993* 2-4 40
EVEN STEVEN (Vocal: Billie Rogers) / THE LAMPLIGHTER'S SERENADE (Vocal: Woody Herman).......... *Decca 4253* 2-4 42
FRENESI / SONG OF OLD HAWAII....... *Decca 3427* 2-4 40
(Vocals: Woody Herman)
G'BYE NOW (Vocal: Muriel Lane) / UNTIL TOMORROW (Vocal: Woody Herman).......... *Decca 3745* 2-4 41
GIVE A LITTLE WHISTLE / PEACH TREE STREET.......... *Decca 3008* 2-4 40
(Vocals: Woody Herman)
GOOD EARTH, THE / SURRENDER (Vocals: Woody Herman & The Blue Flames)...... *Columbia 36985* 2-4 46
HERMAN AT THE SHERMAN / JUKIN'... *Decca 3272* 3-5 40
HOT CHESTNUTS / FOUR OR FIVE TIMES (Vocals: Woody Herman & orchestra)... *Decca 18526* 2-4 42

I DOUBLE DARE YOU / WHY TALK
ABOUT LOVE? .... *Decca 1523* 5-8 37
(Vocals: Woody Herman)

IF I KNEW THEN / BLUE DAWN......... *Decca 2772* 2-4 39
(Vocals: Woody Herman)

I LOVE YOU MORE, MORE EVERY DAY (Vocal: Woody Herman) / CONCERTO NO. 1 IN B-FLAT MINOR
FOR PIANO AND ORCHESTRA......... *Decca 3973* 3-5 41

INDIAN BOOGIE WOOGIE / BLUE
EVENING............................. *Decca 2250* 2-4 39
(Vocals: Woody Herman)

I WANNA BE IN WINCHELL'S COLUMN /
BROADWAY'S GONE HAWAII.......... *Decca 1583* 5-8 38
(Vocals: Woody Herman)

JUMPIN' BLUES / BIG MORNING......... *Decca 2664* 3-5 39
(Vocals: Woody Herman)

LAS CHIAPANECAS / A STRING
OF PEARLS........................... *Decca 4176* 2-4 42

LAZY RHAPSODY / YOU'LL NEVER
KNOW (Vocal: Woody Herman)............ *Decca 3813* 2-4 41

LET ME LOVE YOU TONIGHT
(Vocal: Billie Rogers) / WHO DAT
UP DERE? (Vocal: Woody Herman)........ *Decca 18619* 2-4 42

LET'S GET AWAY FROM IT ALL (Vocal: Muriel Lane) /
CHLOE (Vocal: Woody Herman)........... *Decca 3712* 2-4 41

LET'S PITCH A LITTLE WOO /
LOCH LOMOND...................... *Decca 1570* 5-8 38
(Vocals: Woody Herman)

LINGER IN MY ARMS A LITTLE LONGER, BABY
(Vocal: Lynne Stevens) / MABEL! MABEL!
(Vocal: Woody Herman)............... *Columbia 36995* 2-4 46

LOVE'S GOT ME DOWN AGAIN (Vocal: Carol Kay) /
BLUES ON PARADE................... *Decca 2933* 2-4 40

LULLABY IN RHYTHM / DON'T WAKE
UP MY HEART....................... *Decca 1900* 5-8 38
(Vocals: Woody Herman)

MIDNIGHT ECHOES / I'M COMIN'
VIRGINIA (Vocal: Steady Nelson)........... *Decca 2817* 3-5 39

MR. GHOST GOES TO TOWN / BETTER GET OFF YOUR
HIGH HORSE (Vocal: Woody Herman)...... *Decca 1079* 5-8 37

MY FINE FEATHERED FRIEND / YOU'RE
A SWEETHEART..................... *Decca 1535* 5-8 37
(Vocals: Woody Herman)

NIGHT WATCHMAN /
HEY DOC! (Vocal: Muriel Lane)........... *Decca 3889* 3-5 41

NOW THAT SUMMER IS GONE /
OLD-FASHIONED SWING............. *Decca 1064* 5-8 36
(Vocals: Woody Herman)

PALEFACE / THE SHEIK OF ARABY..... *Decca 2539* 3-5 39

PICK-A-RIB (Vocals: by orchestra) /
SAY "SI SI"........................... *Decca 2979* 3-5 40

RHUMBA JUMPS, THE /
PEACE, BROTHER!.................... *Decca 2939* 2-4 40
(Vocals: Woody Herman)

SHE'LL ALWAYS REMEMBER
(Vocal: Carolyn Grey) / A SOLDIER DREAMS
(Vocal: Woody Herman)................. *Decca 18315* 3-5 42

SKY FELL DOWN, THE /
BLUE PRELUDE...................... *Decca 3017* 2-4 40
(Vocals: Woody Herman)

SLEEPY SERENADE / EVERYTHING HAPPENS
TO ME (Vocal: Woody Herman)............ *Decca 3693* 2-4 41

SOMEONE TO CARE FOR ME /
I CAN'T PRETEND.................... *Decca 1057* 5-8 36
(Vocals: Woody Herman)

SORRENTO / BISHOP'S BLUES........... *V-Disc 293* 4-6 -
(A World War II release)

SORRENTO / OH! LOOK AT ME NOW..... *Decca 3630* 2-4 41
(Vocals: Woody Herman)

STARDUST ON THE MOON / THE LADY
FROM FIFTH AVENUE................ *Decca 1385* 5-8 37
(Vocals: Woody Herman)

STORY OF A STARRY NIGHT, THE / JUST
PLAIN LONESOME.................... *Decca 18356* 2-4 42
(Vocals: Woody Herman)

THERE ARE RIVERS TO CROSS
(Vocal: Woody Herman) / WE'LL MEET AGAIN
(Vocal: Billie Rogers).................... *Decca 18314* 2-4 42

THERE I GO / BEAT ME DADDY,
EIGHT TO A BAR..................... *Decca 3454* 3-5 40
(Vocals: Woody Herman)

THERE WILL NEVER BE ANOTHER YOU (Vocal: Woody Herman) / PLEASE BE THERE ... *Decca 18469* 2-4 42

THIS TIME THE DREAM'S ON ME / BLUES
IN THE NIGHT....................... *Decca 4030* 3-5 41
(Vocals: Woody Herman)

TIME CHANGES EVERYTHING / DANCING
IN THE DARK........................ *Decca 3751* 2-4 41
(Vocals: Woody Herman)

'TIS AUTUMN (Vocals: Woody Herman & Carolyn Grey) / I GUESS I'LL BE
ON MY WAY (Vocal: Woody Herman)....... *Decca 4095* 2-4 42

TROUBLE IN MIND / DOCTOR JAZZ...... *Decca 1307* 5-8 37
(Vocals: Woody Herman)

TWIN CITY BLUES / LAUGHING BOY
BLUES (Vocals: Woody Herman & Sonny Skylar)... *Decca 1801* 5-8 38

WHO'LL BUY MY VIOLETS? / LISTEN TO
THE MOCKINGBIRD................... *Decca 2362* 4-6 39
(Vocals: Mary Martin)

WILD ROOT / ATLANTA, G.A. (Vocal: Woody Herman)........................ *Columbia 36949* 2-4 46

WINTERTIME DREAMS / THE GOOSE
HANGS HIGH........................ *Decca 1056* 5-8 36
(Vocals: Woody Herman)

HERMAN, Woody, & His Woodchoppers

RIVER BED BLUES (Vocal: Woody Herman) /
DALLAS BLUES (by Woody Herman & His Orchestra)......................... *Decca 2629* 3-5 39

SOUTH / FAN IT........................ *Decca 3761* 3-5 41
(Vocals: Woody Herman)

TOO LATE / FT. WORTH JAIL........... *Decca 4293* 3-5 41
(Vocals: Woody Herman)

HERMAN, Woody, & The New Third Herd

EARLY AUTUMN (Vocal: Woody Herman) /
CELESTIAL BLUES.................. *Mars M-300* 3-5 -

JUMP IN THE LINE (Vocal: Woody Herman) /
STOMPIN' AT THE SAVOY............ *Mars M-200* 3-5 -

MESS AROUND (Vocal: Woody Herman) /
CASTLE ROCK...................... *Mars M-1005* 4-6 46
(An early high fidelity recording.)

HERTH, Milt, as The Milt Herth Quartet
(Milt Herth: birthdate unknown – 6/18/69)

FLAT FOOT FLOOGIE (Vocals: O'Neil Spencer & Teddy Bunn) / LOONEY LITTLE TOONEY (by the Milt Herth Trio; Vocal: O'Neil Spencer)........ *Decca 1800* 3-5 38

JUMP JUMP'S HERE (Vocal: O'Neil Spencer) / GOBLINS IN
THE STEEPLE (by the Milt Herth Trio)..... *Decca 2227* 3-5 39

SHOOT THE LIKKER TO ME, JOHN BOY
(Vocals: O'Neil Spencer & Teddy Bunn) / EGYPTIAN-ELLA
(Vocal: O'Neil Spencer).................. *Decca 1868* 3-5 38

SPIDER AND THE FLY, THE / EVERYBODY LOVES
MY BABY (by The Milt Herth Trio).......... *Decca 2632* 3-5 39
(Vocals: O'Neil Spencer)

HERTH, Milt, as The Milt Herth Trio

ANNABELLA (Vocal: Terry Shand) /
THE WHISTLER AND HIS DOG......... *Decca 2336* 2-4 39

AT A GEORGIA CAMP MEETING /
THE MONKEY'S HAVE NO TAILS IN
PAGO-PAGO (Vocal: O'Neil Spencer)........ *Decca 2964* 3-5 39

BEI MIR BIST DU SCHOEN /
THE BIG DIPPER...................... *Decca 1612* 3-5 38

BLUE DANUBE SWING /
HEZEKIAH (Vocal: O'Neil Spencer)......... *Decca 3032* 3-5 39

BOY SCOUT IN SWITZERLAND / PEACH TREE
STREET (Vocal: O'Neil Spencer)............ *Decca 2907* 3-5 39

CAMPBELLS ARE SWINGING, THE /
POP-CORN MAN (Vocal: O'Neil Spencer).... *Decca 1736* 4-6 38

CHURCH MOUSE ON A SPREE /
SCATTER-BRAIN (Vocal: O'Neil Spencer)... *Decca 2818* 3-5 39

CREOLE LOVE CALL / BLACK AND
TAN FANTASY....................... *Decca 3393* 3-5 40

DARDANELLA / DOWN
SOUTH (Vocal: Teddy Grace).............. *Decca 3284* 2-4 40

DIPSY DOODLE, THE (Vocal: O'Neil Spencer) /
THAT'S A PLENTY.................. *Decca 1553* 4-6 37

EVERYBODY LOVES MY BABY / THE SPIDER AND
THE FLY (by The Milt Herth Quartet)....... *Decca 2632* 3-5 39
(Vocals: O'Neil Spencer)

GOBLINS IN THE STEEPLE / JUMP JUMP'S HERE (by the Milt Herth Quartet; Vocal: O'Neil Spencer).... *Decca 2227* 3-5 39

GOOFUS / JOLLY PETER................ *Decca 3251* 3-5 40

HONKY-TONK TRAIN BLUES / THE GIRL WITH THE
LIGHT BLUE HAIR................... *Decca 3158* 3-5 40

IN AN 18TH-CENTURY DRAWING-ROOM /
THE SHOEMAKER'S HOLIDAY......... *Decca 2572* 3-5 39

LAMBETH WALK, THE (Vocal: O'Neil Spencer) /
ROCKIN' IN RHYTHM................ *Decca 2046* 3-5 38

LOONEY LITTLE TOONEY (Vocal: O'Neil Spencer) /
FLAT FOOT FLOOGIE (by The Milt Herth Quartet;
Vocals: O'Neil Spencer & Teddy Bunn)........ *Decca 1800* 3-5 38

LOST IN THE SHUFFLE /
JOSEPHINE (Vocal: O'Neil Spencer)........ *Decca 1699* 3-5 38

MINUET IN JAZZ / HOME-COOKIN' MAMA WITH THE
FRYIN' PAN (Vocal: O'Neil Spencer)........ *Decca 2087* 4-6 38

SISSY (Vocal: O'Neil Spencer) /
JAZZ ME BLUES.................... *Decca 1727* 3-5 38

SLOW FREIGHT / EPE-IPE (WANNA PIECE
OF PIE) (Vocals: Teddy Grace)............ *Decca 3171* 3-5 40

TOY TRUMPET, THE / THE THREE
BLIND MICE (Vocal: O'Neil Spencer)....... *Decca 1816* 3-5 38

HICKMAN, Art, & His Orchestra
(Art Hickman: 6/13/86 – 1/16/30)

(Art Hickman is believed to have originated the standard instrumentation of reed, brass, & rhythm sections used during the dance band and big band eras.)

CAIRO / ROSE ROOM (theme song).... *Columbia A-2858* 2-4 19

CUBAN MOON / IN OLD
MANILA (Vocal: Frank Crumit)....... *Columbia A-2982* 2-4 20

DANCE IT AGAIN WITH ME /
HOLD ME...................... *Columbia A-2899* 2-4 19

HOLD ME IN YOUR ARMS AGAIN
(Vocal: John Preston) / DOWN THE LANE
WITH YOU AGAIN................... *Victor 20687* 2-4 27

IN THE GLOAMING / A YOUNG
MAN'S FANCY................... *Columbia A-2970* 2-4 20

I SPOILED YOU / NESTLE IN YOUR
DADDY'S ARMS.................. *Columbia A-3391* 2-4 21

JAPANESE SANDMAN / AVALON ... *Columbia A-3322* 2-4 20

ON THE STREETS OF CAIRO /
MY BABY'S ARMS................ *Columbia A-2811* 2-4 19

PATSY / G'WAN WITH IT.............. *Victor 19399* 2-4 24

PEGGY / TELL ME WHY .... *Columbia A-2812* 2-4 19

SHIPS THAT PASS IN
THE NIGHT / LITTLE DEVIL......... *Victor 19732* 2-4 25

SWEET AND LOW / PATCHES...... *Columbia A-2814* 2-4 19

THIS TIME IS THE LAST TIME (YOU'RE
EVER GOIN' TO TWO-TIME ME) /
YOU'RE THE ONLY ONE.............. *Victor 19734* 2-4 25

THOSE DRAFTIN' BLUES / HESITATING
BLUES.......................... *Columbia A-2813* 3-5 19

WHEN WE ARE TOGETHER / I WANT YOUR
LOVE (Vocal: Leonard M. Van Berg)........ *Victor 19618* 2-4 25

WHISPERING / IF A WISH COULD
MAKE IT SO..................... *Columbia A-3301* 2-4 20

WONDERFUL PAL / NOBODY
KNOWS......................... *Columbia A-2839* 2-4 19

YOU AND I / ANYTIME,
ANYDAY, ANYWHERE........... *Columbia A-3325* 2-4 19

HICKS, Art:
see CHUBB-STEINBERG Orchestra, The

HIGH HATTERS, The, directed by Leonard Joy
see also JOY, Leonard, & His String Dance Orchestra

DADDY, WON'T YOU PLEASE COME HOME?
(Vocal: Belle Mann) / TAKES YOU
(Vocal: Frank Luther).................. *Victor 22046* 3-5 29

IN MY LITTLE HOPE CHEST
(Vocal: Olga M. Albani) / SING, YOU SINNERS
(Vocal: Frank Luther).................. *Victor 22322* 2-4 30

IT'S THE DARNDEST THING / SINGIN'
THE BLUES....................... *Victor 22809* 3-5 31
(Vocals: Chick Bullock)

LOW-DOWN RHYTHM / GOTTA FEELING
FOR YOU.......................... *Victor 22041* 3-5 29
(Vocals: Frank Luther)

MUG SONG, THE / ANCHORS AWEIGH ... *Victor 22424* 2-4 30
(Vocals: The American Singers)

PLUCKY LINDY'S LUCKY DAY (Vocals: Frank Luther, Len Stokes, Randolph Weyant) / GOOD LITTLE, BAD LITTLE
YOU (Vocal: Frank Luther).............. *Victor 21909* 3-5 29

SEND FOR ME (Vocal: Frank Luther) / TEN CENTS A
DANCE (Vocal: Welcome Lewis)........... *Victor 22353* 2-4 30

SOME SWEET SOMEONE / I WANNA BE
LOVED BY YOU.................... *Victor 21682* 3-5 28
(Vocals: Sam Coslow)

YOU SAID IT / SWEET AND HOT....... *Victor 22607* 3-5 31
(Vocals: Frank Luther)

HIGH HATTERS, The, directed by Ken McComber

LOVE IS JUST AROUND THE CORNER /
THE DEBUTANTE WALTZ .... *Bluebird B-5767* 4-6 35

OBJECT OF MY AFFECTION, THE /
HAUNTING ME.................. *Bluebird B-5769* 4-6 35

HILLMAN, Roc, as The Roc Hillman Trio

THERE WAS A TIME / YOU SENT
A DREAM MY WAY................ *Hallmark 505* 3-5 -
(This record was pressed on transparent red vinyl)

HILL, Teddy, & His NBC Orchestra
(Teddy Hill: 12/07/06 –)

BIG BOY BLUE (Vocals: Bill Dillard & Teddy Hill) /
THE HARLEM TWISTER.......... *Bluebird B-6908* 10-12 37

I KNOW NOW / THE LADY WHO
COULDN'T BE KISSED........... *Bluebird B-6954* 10-12 37
(Vocals: Bill Dillard)

I'M HAPPY DARLING, DANCING WITH YOU / BLUE
RHYTHM FANTASY.............. *Bluebird B-6989* 8-10 37

LOVE BUG WILL BITE YOU, THE (Vocals: by orchestra) /
WOULDN'T YOU LIKE TO BUY A DREAM?
(Vocal: Beatrice Douglas).............. *Bluebird B-6897* 10-12 37

SAN ANTON' (Vocal: Bill Dillard) /
KING PORTER STOMP .... *Bluebird B-6988* 12-15 37

STUDY IN BROWN, A / TWILIGHT
IN TURKEY..................... *Bluebird B-6943* 8-10 37

WHERE IS THE SUN? (Vocal: Bill Dillard) /
MY MARIE...................... *Bluebird B-6898* 8-10 37

YOURS AND MINE / I'M FEELING
LIKE A MILLION................ *Bluebird B-7013* 10-12 37
(Vocals: Bill Dillard)

HILL, Teddy, & His Orchestra

AT THE RUG CUTTER'S BALL / BLUE RHYTHM FANTASY.... *Vocalion 3247* 12-15 36

(LOOKIE, LOOKIE, LOOKIE) HERE COMES COOKIE / GOT ME DOIN' THINGS (Vocal: Bill Dillard).... *Banner 33384* 10-12 35

(LOOKIE, LOOKIE, LOOKIE) HERE COMES COOKIE / GOT ME DOIN' THINGS (Vocal: Bill Dillard).... *Melotone M-13351* 10-12 35

(LOOKIE, LOOKIE, LOOKIE) HERE COMES COOKIE / GOT ME DOIN' THINGS (Vocal: Bill Dillard).... *Oriole 3114* 10-12 35

(LOOKIE, LOOKIE, LOOKIE) HERE COMES COOKIE / GOT ME DOIN' THINGS (Vocal: Bill Dillard).... *Perfect 16093* 10-12 35

(LOOKIE, LOOKIE, LOOKIE) HERE COMES COOKIE / GOT ME DOIN' THINGS (Vocal: Bill Dillard).... *Romeo 2488* 10-12 35
(Simultaneously released on five labels)

UPTOWN RHAPSODY (theme song) / PASSIONETTE.... *Vocalion 3294* 10-12 36

HILL, Tiny, & His Orchestra
(Tiny Hill: 7/19/06 – 1972)

DANCE AND STAY YOUNG (Vocals: Unknown) / SWEET AS HONEY (Vocal: Tiny Hill).... *Okeh 6269* 2-4 41

DOIN' THE CHAMBERLAIN / AIN'T CHA COMIN' OUT?.... *Vocalion 4919* 3-5 39
(Vocals: Allan DeWitt)

DON'T LET JULIA FOOL YA / TIME CHANGES EVERYTHING.... *Conqueror 9912* 2-4 41
(Vocals: Unknown)

DON'T LET JULIA FOOL YA / TIME CHANGES EVERYTHING.... *Okeh 6343* 2-4 41
(Vocals: Unknown)
(Simultaneously released on two labels)

DOODLE DOO DOO / MAMA'S GONE, GOODBYE.... *Conqueror 9346* 2-4 39

DREAM GIRL / DOODLE DOO DOO.... *Vocalion 5060* 2-4 39

EVERY LITTLE MOVEMENT (Vocal: Ervin Bendel) / MAMA'S GONE, GOODBYE.... *Vocalion 5128* 3-5 39

I'M KNEE-DEEP IN DAISIES / FIVE FOOT TWO, EYES OF BLUE.... *Okeh 5635* 2-4 40
(Vocals: Tiny Hill)

I'M LOOKING OVER A FOUR-LEAF CLOVER / I HEAR YOU KNOCKIN' (BUT YOU CAN'T COME IN).... *Okeh 6537* 2-4 41
(Vocals: Unknown)

IN LOVE WITH LOVE (Vocal: Allan DeWitt) / ANGRY (theme song) (Vocal: Tiny Hill).... *Vocalion 4957* 2-4 39

I WISH I COULD SHIMMY LIKE MY SISTER KATE / SHOW ME THE WAY TO GO HOME.... *Okeh 5875* 2-4 40
(Vocals: Tiny Hill)

MY BEST GIRL / YOU'VE GOT TO SEE MAMA EV'RY NIGHT.... *Conqueror 9523* 2-4 40
(Vocals: Tiny Hill)

MY BEST GIRL / YOU'VE GOT TO SEE MAMA EV'RY NIGHT.... *Vocalion 5387* 2-4 40
(Vocals: Tiny Hill)
(Simultaneously released on two labels)

PLEASE DON'T TALK ABOUT ME WHEN I'M GONE (Vocal: Tiny Hill) / MICKEY (Vocal: Erwin Bendel).... *Conqueror 9521* 2-4 40

PLEASE DON'T TALK ABOUT ME WHEN I'M GONE (Vocal: Tiny Hill) / MICKEY (Vocal: Erwin Bendel).... *Vocalion 5445* 2-4 40
(Simultaneously released on two labels)

SKIRTS / I GET THE BLUES WHEN IT RAINS.... *Conqueror 9520* 2-4 40
(Vocals: Tiny Hill)

SKIRTS / I GET THE BLUES WHEN IT RAINS.... *Vocalion 5340* 2-4 40
(Vocals: Tiny Hill)
(Simultaneously released on two labels)

THAT'S MY WEAKNESS NOW (Vocal: Tiny Hill) / LADY OF THE EVENING (Vocal: Erwin Bendel).... *Okeh 6073* 2-4 40

TWO-TON TESSIE / I'M ALONE BECAUSE I LOVE YOU.... *Okeh 5674* 2-4 40
(Vocals: Tiny Hill)

YES SIR, THAT'S MY BABY / HE'S A CURBSTONE CUTIE.... *Vocalion 5567* 2-4 40
(Vocals: Tiny Hill)

YOU GOTTA QUIT CHEATIN' ON ME / THE FACE ON THE BARROOM FLOOR.... *Okeh 5775* 3-5 40
(Vocals: Tiny Hill)

HILL TOP INN ORCHESTRA, The:
see ROYAL TROUBADOURS, The

HILO HAWAIIAN ORCHESTRA, The:
see SHILKRET, Nat

HIMBER, Richard, & His Essex House Orchestra
(Richard Himber: 2/20/07 – 12/11/66)

DOIN' THE UPTOWN LOWDOWN (Vocal: Johnny Mercer) / YOU'RE MY PAST, PRESENT AND FUTURE (Vocal: Joey Nash).... *Vocalion 2572* 5-8 33

IT ISN'T FAIR (theme song) / IT MIGHT HAVE BEEN A DIFF'RENT STORY.... *Vocalion 25008* 5-8 33
(Vocals: Joey Nash)

LAST ROUND-UP, THE (Vocal: Joey Nash) / WHO'S AFRAID OF THE BIG BAD WOLF? (Vocals: by chorus).... *Vocalion 2551* 5-8 33

LOVE IS THE THING / LOVE IS THE SWEETEST THING.... *Vocalion 2526* 5-8 33
(Vocals: Joey Nash)

PARADE OF THE BANDS, PART I / PARADE OF THE BANDS, Part II (Vocal: Stuart Allen).... *Victor 25754* 4-6 38

PARADE OF THE BANDS PART III / PARADE OF THE BANDS PART IV.... *Victor 26007* 3-5 38

PARADE OF THE BANDS PART V / PARADE OF THE BANDS PART VI.... *Victor 26164* 4-6 39

SMOKE RINGS (Vocal: Joey Nash) / SOPHISTICATED LADY.... *Vocalion 2537* 5-8 33

THRILL OF A LIFETIME / I LIVE THE LIFE I LOVE.... *Victor 25742* 4-6 38
(Vocals: Stuart Allen)

WAR DANCE FOR WOODEN INDIAN / MINUET IN JAZZ.... *Victor 26101* 3-5 38

WHOSE THEME SONG? / WHOSE THEME SONG? PART II.... *Royale 1795* 5-8 40

HIMBER, Richard, & His Essex House Orchestra as Richard Himber's Rhythmic Pyramids Orchestra

SWEET AND HIGH / JEANNINE SWINGS OUT (Vocal: Stuart Allen).... *Victor 26146* 3-5 39

YOU CALL IT MADNESS (Vocal: Stuart Allen) / PYRAMIDING "THE SWAN".... *Victor 26142* 3-5 39

DAYDREAMING / DARLING, JE VOUS AIME BEAUCOUP.... *Decca 4036* 2-4 41
(Vocals: Johnny Johnston)

(WAS I TO BLAME FOR) FALLING IN LOVE WITH YOU? (The Studebaker theme song) / BLUE MOON.... *Decca 3618* 2-4 41

I KNOW WHY (Vocal: Johnny Johnston) / THE KISS POLKA (Vocals: The Joseph Lilley Ensemble).... *Decca 3896* 2-4 41

HIMBER, Richard, & His Ritz-Carlton Orchestra

BROADWAY RHYTHM / ON A SUNDAY AFTERNOON.... *Victor 25124* 3-5 35
(Vocals: Stuart Allen)

CLING TO ME / SO THIS IS HEAVEN.... *Victor 25235* 4-6 36
(Vocals: Stuart Allen)

I'D RATHER LEAD A BAND / GET THEE BEHIND ME, SATAN.... *Victor 25243* 5-8 36
(Vocals: Stuart Allen)

IN A BLUE AND PENSIVE MOOD / I WOKE UP TOO SOON.... *Victor 24824* 4-6 35
(Vocals: Joey Nash)

IN THE CHAPEL IN THE MOONLIGHT / YOU'RE EV'RYTHING SWEET.... *Victor 25441* 4-6 36
(Vocals: Stuart Allen)

LIFE BEGINS WHEN YOU'RE IN LOVE / SUZANNAH (Vocal: Stuart Allen).... *Victor 25239* 5-8 36

LOVE MAKES THE WORLD GO ROUND / TAKE THIS RING.... *Victor 25132* 3-5 35
(Vocals: Stuart Allen)

LULLABY OF BROADWAY / ZING! WENT THE STRINGS OF MY HEART.... *Victor 24868* 4-6 35
(Vocals: Joey Nash)

MIDNIGHT BLUE / ME AND THE MOON.... *Victor 25365* 5-8 36
(Vocals: Stuart Allen)

STARS FELL ON ALABAMA / IF I HAD A MILLION DOLLARS.... *Victor 24745* 4-6 34
(Vocals: Joey Nash)

TILL THE CLOCK STRIKES THREE / SO MANY MEMORIES.... *Victor 25645* 3-5 37
(Vocals: Stuart Allen)

WERE YOU FOOLIN'? / WINTER WONDERLAND.... *Victor 24757* 4-6 34
(Vocals: Joey Nash)

WHAT A WONDERFUL WORLD / FAREWELL, MY LOVELY.... *Victor 25122* 4-6 35
(Vocals: Stuart Allen)

WHEN LOVE COMES SWINGIN' ALONG / SAY WHEN.... *Victor 24764* 4-6 34
(Vocals: Joey Nash)

HINES, Earl "Fatha", & His Orchestra
(Earl Hines: 12/28/05 – 4/23/83)

ANN (Vocal: Billy Eckstine) / TOPSY-TURVY (Vocal: Walter Fuller).... *Bluebird B-10870* 3-5 40

BLUE (Vocal: Herb Jeffries) / JULIA (Vocal: Walter Fuller).... *Brunswick 6872* 10-12 34

BOOGIE WOOGIE ON ST. LOUIS BLUES (dialog by George Dixon) / NUMBER 19.... *Bluebird B-10674* 2-4 40

BUBBLING OVER / I WANT A LOT OF LOVE.... *Brunswick 6710* 10-12 33

CALL ME HAPPY / BLUE BECAUSE OF YOU (Vocal: Leroy Harris).... *Bluebird B-10835* 3-5 40

COMIN' IN HOME / JULIA (Vocal: Billy Eckstine).... *Bluebird B-11199* 3-5 41

DISAPPOINTED IN LOVE / RHYTHM LULLABY.... *Decca 389* 8-10 35
(Vocals: Palmer Brothers)

DOMINICK SWING / JEZEBEL (Vocal: Leroy Harris).... *Vocalion 4032* 8-10 38

EVERYBODY LOVES MY BABY (Vocal: Earl Hines) / CHICAGO RHYTHM.... *Victor V-38042* 25-30 29

FAT BABES / MAPLE LEAF RAG.... *Decca 218* 8-10 34

FATHER JUMPS, THE / THE JITNEY MAN (Vocal: Billy Eckstine).... *Bluebird B-11535* 2-4 42

FATHER STEPS IN / PIANO MAN (Vocal: Walter Fuller).... *Bluebird B-10377* 3-5 39

'GATOR SWING / MY HEART BEATS FOR YOU (Vocal: Billy Eckstine).... *Bluebird B-10763* 3-5 40

GOOD LITTLE, BAD LITTLE YOU (Vocal: William Franklin) / BEAU-KOO JACK.... *Victor V-38043* 25-30 29

GRAND PIANO BLUES / BLUE NIGHTS.... *Victor V-38096* 35-40 29

I LOVE YOU BECAUSE I LOVE YOU (Vocal: Walter Fuller) / SENSATIONAL MOOD.... *Brunswick 6379* 10-12 32

I'M FALLING FOR YOU / JELLY, JELLY.... *Bluebird B-11065* 3-5 41
(Vocals: Billy Eckstine)

INDIANA / G.T. STOMP.... *Bluebird B-10391* 5-8 39

IN SWAMP LANDS / EVERYTHING DEPENDS ON YOU (Vocals: Madeline Greene & The Three Varieties).... *Bluebird B-11036* 3-5 41

IT HAD TO BE YOU (Vocals: Madeline Greene & The Three Varieties) / YELLOW FIRE.... *Bluebird B-11308* 3-5 41

JUST TO BE IN CAROLINE (Vocal: Herb Jeffries) / WE FOUND ROMANCE (Vocal: Walter Fuller).... *Brunswick 6960* 8-10 34

LIGHTLY AND POLITELY / DEEP FOREST (theme song).... *Bluebird B-10727* 3-5 40

MADHOUSE / DARKNESS.... *Vocalion 3379* 8-10 34

ME AND COLUMBUS (Vocal: Laura Rucker) / AFTER ALL I'VE BEEN TO YOU (Vocal: Walter Fuller).... *Bluebird B-10467* 4-6 39

OH! YOU SWEET THING / BLUE DRAG.... *Brunswick 6345* 10-12 32

PLEASE BE KIND (Vocal: Ida Mae James) / GOODNIGHT, SWEET DREAMS, GOODNIGHT.... *Vocalion 4008* 5-8 38

RHYTHM SUNDAE / I CAN'T BELIEVE THAT YOU'RE IN LOVE WITH ME (Vocal: I. M. James).... *Vocalion 3467* 8-10 37

RIDIN' AND JIVIN' / GRAND TERRACE SHUFFLE.... *Bluebird B-10351* 5-8 39

RIFF MEDLEY / XYZ.... *Bluebird B-10531* 5-8 39

ROSETTA / CAVERNISM.... *Brunswick 6541* 10-12 33

ROSETTA (Vocal: Walter Fuller) / COPENHAGEN.... *Decca 337* 8-10 34

SALLY, WON'T YOU COME BACK (Vocals: Madeline Greene & The Three Varieties) / JERSEY BOUNCE.... *Bluebird B-11126* 3-5 41

SECOND BALCONY JUMP / STORMY MONDAY BLUES (Vocal: Billy Eckstine).... *Bluebird B-11567* 3-5 42

SHE'LL ALWAYS REMEMBER (Vocals: Madeline Greene & The Three Varieties) / SKYLARK (Vocal: Billy Eckstine).... *Bluebird B-11512* 3-5 42

SOLID MAMA / TIPPIN' AT THE TERRACE.... *Vocalion 4143* 8-10 38

SOMEHOW (Vocal: Billy Eckstine) / THE EARL.... *Bluebird B-11432* 2-4 42

STRAIGHT TO LOVE (Vocal: Leroy Harris) / I GOT IT BAD AND THAT AIN'T GOOD (Vocals: Billy Eckstine, Madeline Greene, & The Three Varieties).... *Bluebird B-11374* 2-4 41

SWINGIN' ON C / I NEVER DREAMT (Vocals: Madeline Greene & The Three Varieties).... *Bluebird B-11465* 3-5 41

TAKE IT EASY / HARLEM LAMENT.... *Brunswick 6771* 10-12 33

THAT'S A PLENTY / SWEET GEORGIA BROWN.... *Decca 182* 8-10 34

UP JUMPED THE DEVIL / SOUTH SIDE.... *Bluebird B-11237* 3-5 41

WAIT 'TIL IT HAPPENS TO YOU (Vocal: Billy Eckstine) / EASY RHYTHM.... *Bluebird B-10985* 3-5 41

WINDY CITY JIVE / WATER BOY (Vocal: Billy Eckstine).... *Bluebird B-11329* 3-5 41

WOLVERINE BLUES / ROCK AND RYE.... *Decca 577* 8-10 34

YOU CAN DEPEND ON ME (Vocal: Walter Fuller) / TANTALIZING A CUBAN.... *Bluebird B-10792* 3-5 40

YOU'RE THE ONE OF MY DREAMS (Vocal: Walter Fuller) / SWINGIN' DOWN.... *Vocalion 3392* 8-10 34

HIRSCH, Bert, & The Hit Of The Week Orchestra
(Hit Of The Week records are one-sided paper discs)

CRYING MYSELF TO SLEEP.... *Hit Of The Week 1124* 4-6 31
(Vocal: Dick Robertson)

DANCING WITH TEARS IN MY EYES.... *Hit Of The Week 1075* 3-5 30
(Vocal: Frank Munn)

IF I COULD BE WITH YOU ONE HOUR TONIGHT.... *Hit Of The Week 1111* 4-6 30
(Vocal: Dick Robertson)

I'M KEEPIN' COMPANY .... *Hit Of The Week 1159* 5-8 31
(Vocal: Scrappy Lambert)

I WANNA SING ABOUT YOU.... *Hit Of The Week 1152* 5-8 31
(Vocal: Smith Ballew)

JUST A LITTLE CLOSER........ *Hit Of The Week 1084* 4-6 30
(Vocal: Frank Munn)

JUST ONE MORE CHANCE ..... *Hit Of The Week 1158* 5-8 31
(Vocal: Scrappy Lambert)

LITTLE THINGS IN LIFE, THE.... *Hit Of The Week 1118* 4-6 31
(Vocal: Dick Robertson)

RO-RO-ROLLIN' ALONG........ *Hit Of The Week 1074* 4-6 30
(Vocal: Irving Kaufman)

SOMEWHERE IN
OLD WYOMING.............. *Hit Of The Week 1101* 4-6 30

YOU'LL BE MINE
IN APPLE BLOSSOM TIME.... *Hit Of The Week 1143* 3-5 31
(Vocal: Dick Robertson)

HITE, Les, & His Orchestra
(Les Hite: 2/13/03 – 2/6/62)

BOARD MEETING / THE WORLD IS WAITING FOR
THE SUNRISE...................... *Varsity 8373* 5-8 40

I REMEMBER YOU / JERSEY BOUNCE..... *Hit 7001* 5-8 42

T-BONE BLUES (Vocal: T-Bone Walker) / IT MUST HAVE
A DREAM (theme song)................. *Varsity 8391* 5-8 40

THAT'S THE LICK / T-BONE
BLUES............................ *Bluebird B-11210* 5-8 41

WAITING FOR YOU / THAT'S
THE LICK.......................... *Varsity 8396* 4-6 40

WORLD IS WAITING FOR THE SUNRISE, THE /
BOARD MEETIN' .... *Bluebird B-11109* 5-8 41

HIT OF THE WEEK ORCHESTRA, The:
see HIRSCH, Bert

HOAGLAND, Everett, & His Orchestra

BLESS YOU / IT'S ALL OVER TOWN...... *Decca 2773* 2-4 39
(Vocals: Don Burke)

EACH TIME YOU SAY "GOODBYE" (I DIE A LITTLE)
(Vocal: Homer Rhodes) / STOP KICKING MY HEART
AROUND (Vocal: Don Burke).............. *Decca 2766* 2-4 39

MOON AND THE WILLOW TREE, THE
(Vocal: Don Burke) / I'M TOO ROMANTIC
(Vocal: Homer Rhodes) .... *Decca 3009* 2-4 40

MY SON, MY SON (Vocal: Don Burke) /
APPLE BLOSSOMS AND CHAPEL BELLS
(Vocal: Homer Rhodes) .... *Decca 2983* 2-4 40

SONG OF THE METRONOME, THE / DRIFTING DOWN
THE RIVER OF DREAMS............. *Decca 2659* 2-4 39
(Vocals: Homer Rhodes)

THIS HEART OF MINE / LITTLE OLD
BAND OF GOLD...................... *Decca 2668* 2-4 39
(Vocals: Don Burke)

HOFF, Carl, & His Orchestra
(Carl Hoff: circa 1905 –)

I KNOW WHY (Vocal: Tony Russell) /
KENTUCKY BABE (Vocals: The Murphy Sisters
& Tony Russell)........................... *Okeh 6478* 3-5 41

MISS YOU (Vocal: Al Nobel) / THE SON-OF-A-GUN
WHO PICKS ON UNCLE SAM (Vocals: Al Nobel
& The Murphy Sisters) .... *Okeh 6609* 4-6 42

PALE MOON (Vocal: Tony Russell) /
THE MARRIAGE BROKER'S DAUGHTER
(Vocals: The Murphy Sisters) .... *Okeh 6538* 3-5 41

SWING LOW, SWEET CHARIOT (Vocals: The Murphy
Sisters) / WHEN JOHNNY COMES
MARCHING HOME..................... *Okeh 6450* 4-6 41

WE DID IT BEFORE (AND WE CAN DO IT AGAIN) /
YOU'RE A SAP, MR. JAP.................. *Okeh 6556* 4-6 42
(Vocals: The Murphy Sisters)

HOLDEN, Lou, & His Disciples of Rhythm

FERRYBOAT SERENADE / THE MAID WITH THE
SLIGHT SWISS ACCENT .... *Decca 3260* 3-5 40

LION AND THE MOUSE, THE / A WINDY DAY ON THE
OUTER DRIVE .... *Decca 3281* 4-6 40

RED WAGON (Vocal: Teddy Grace) / IT'S THE END OF MY
WORLD (Vocal: Lou Holden).............. *Decca 3444* 5-8 40

HOLLYWOOD DANCE ORCHESTRA, The:
see SAMUELS, Joseph, & His Orchestra and
see SCHUBERT, Adrian, & His Salon Orchestra

HOLMES, Herbie, & His Orchestra

LITTLE LOVE IS A DANGEROUS THING, A /
SAY, MISTER! HAVE YOU MET
ROSIE'S SISTER? .... *Okeh 6249* 4-6 41
(Vocals: Herbie Holmes)

LOVE ME A LITTLE LITTLE (Vocal: Laverne) /
IDA, SWEET AT APPLE CIDER (Vocals: Herbie
Holmes & The Cromwell Sisters).............. *Okeh 6133* 4-6 41

HOLST, Ernie, & His Central Park Casino Orchestra

FOR ALL WE KNOW (Vocal: Norman Moon) /
AND I STILL DO (Vocal: Ernie Holst).... *Bluebird B-5576* 4-6 34

THERE'S A NEW MOON OVER MY SHOULDER
(Vocal: Norman Moon) / FROM NOW ON
(Vocal: Ernie Holst) .... *Bluebird B-5584* 4-6 34

THERE'S NOTHING ELSE TO DO IN
MA-LA-KA-MO-KA-LU (Vocal: Ernie Holst) / LOVE IN
BLOOM (Vocal: Norman Moon) .... *Bluebird B-5577* 4-6 34

HOLST, Ernie, & His Hotel Lexington Orchestra

DINNER AT EIGHT (Vocal: Ernie Holst) / BLESS YOUR
HEART (Vocal: Edith Caldwell)........ *Bluebird B-5206* 4-6 33

DINNER AT EIGHT (Vocal: Ernie Holst) / BLESS YOUR
HEART (Vocal: Edith Caldwell)........ *Electradisk 2092* 12-15 33

DINNER AT EIGHT (Vocal: Ernie Holst) / BLESS YOUR
HEART (Vocal: Edith Caldwell)......... *Sunrise S-3287* 12-15 33
(Simultaneously released on three labels)

WE'LL MAKE HAY WHILE THE SUN SHINES
(Vocal: Ernie Holst) / ANSWER MY HEART
(Vocal: Chris Fletcher) .... *Bluebird B-5209* 4-6 33

WE'LL MAKE HAY WHILE THE SUN SHINES
(Vocal: Ernie Holst) / ANSWER MY HEART
(Vocal: Chris Fletcher)................ *Electradisk 2095* 12-15 33

WE'LL MAKE HAY WHILE THE SUN SHINES
(Vocal: Ernie Holst) / ANSWER MY HEART
(Vocal: Chris Fletcher) .... *Sunrise S-3290* 12-15 33
(Simultaneously released on three labels)

YOU'RE MY PAST, PRESENT AND
FUTURE / AIN'T CHA GLAD?...... *Bluebird B-5207* 4-6 33
(Vocals: Ernie Holst)

YOU'RE MY PAST, PRESENT AND
FUTURE / AIN'T CHA GLAD? ..... *Electradisk 2093* 12-15 33
(Vocals: Ernie Holst)

YOU'RE MY PAST, PRESENT AND
FUTURE / AIN'T CHA GLAD?....... *Sunrise S-3288* 12-15 33
(Vocals: Ernie Holst)
(Simultaneously released on three labels)

HONEY SWAMP STOMPERS, The:
see HALL, Fred

HOPKINS, Claude, & His Orchestra
(Claude Hopkins: 8/24/03 –)

AIN'T MISBEHAVIN' (Vocals: Orlando Roberson) /
HARLEM RHYTHM DANCE ...... *Columbia 2880-D* 10-12 34
(This record was pressed in blue shellac)

(I WOULD DO) ANYTHING FOR YOU /
MAD MOMENTS .... *Columbia 2665-D* 10-12
(This record was pressed in blue shellac)

CHASING ALL THE BLUES AWAY
(Vocal: Ovie Alston) / JUNE IN
JANUARY (Vocal: Orlando Roberson) .... *Decca 441* 5-8 35

DON'T LET YOUR LOVE GO WRONG (Vocal: Ovie
Alston) / I CAN'T DANCE
(Vocal: Fred Norman)................ *Brunswick 6891* 8-10 34

EVERYBODY SHUFFLE (Vocals: Ovie Alston) /
MARGIE (Vocal: Orlando Roberson) .... *Brunswick 6916* 8-10 34

HE'S A SON OF THE SOUTH / -- .... *Columbia 2747-D* 10-12
(This record was pressed in blue shellac)

HONEY / MY KINDA LOVE .... *Decca 1316* 5-8 37
(Vocals: Beverley White)

JUNE NIGHT (Vocal: Beverley White) /
CHURCH STREET SOBBIN' BLUES..... *Decca 1286* 8-10 37

JUST YOU, JUST ME / WHO? .... *Decca 185* 5-8 34
(Vocals: Orlando Roberson)

KING PORTER STOMP / IN THE SHADE OF
THE OLD APPLE TREE.................. *Decca 184* 8-10 34

LITTLE RAIN MUST FALL, A (Vocal: Orlando Roberson) /
YACHT CLUB SWING .... *Ammor 116* 5-8 40

LOOK WHO'S HERE (Vocal: Ovie Alston) / CALIFORNIA,
HERE I COME .... *Columbia 2741-D* 10-12 33
(This record was pressed in blue shellac)

MUSH MOUTH / HOW'M
I DOIN'? (Vocal: Ovie Alston)........ *Columbia 2674-D* 10-12 32

MANDY / DO YOU EVER THINK OF ME?..... *Decca 353* 8-10 34
(Vocals: Orlando Roberson)

MONKEY BUSINESS / ZOZOI............. *Decca 674* 8-10 34
(This record was pressed in blue shellac)

MY GAL SAL (Vocal: Ovie Alston) /
THREE LITTLE WORDS........... *Brunswick 6864* 8-10 34

OUT TO LUNCH / WHAT'S THE MATTER
WITH ME? (Vocal: Orlando Robertson)...... *Ammor 115* 5-8 40

SUNDAY / SWINGIN' DOWN THE LANE ... *Decca 1153* 8-10 37
(Vocals: Beverley White)

TREES / LOVE IN BLOOM .... *Decca 374* 5-8 35
(Vocals: Orlando Roberson)

WALKIN' THE DOG (Vocal: Ovie Alston) / SWEETHEART
O'MINE (Vocal: Orlando Roberson)........... *Decca 270* 8-10 34

WASHINTON SQUABBLE /
MYSTIC MOAN.................. *Brunswick 6750* 8-10 34

HOTCHA TRIO, The:
see ROSE, Dave

HOTEL ASTOR ORCHESTRA, The:
see RICH, Fred

HOTEL BOSSERT ORCHESTRA, The:
see MARTIN, Freddy, & His Orchestra

HOT SPRINGS NOVELTY ORCHESTRA, The:
see ORLANDO, Nicholas, as Nicholas Orlando's Orchestra

HOTSY TOTSY GANG, The:
see MILLS, Irving, & His Hotsy Totsy Gang

HOTTENTOTS, The:
see MILLS, Floyd, & His Marylanders

HOWARD, Bob, & His Orchestra

MUCH TOO MUCH / GARBO GREEN....... *Decca 722* 5-8 36
(Vocals: Bob Howard)

HOWARD, Eddy, & His Orchestra
(Eddy Howard: 9/12/14 – 5/23/63)

AMERICAN BEAUTY ROSE / SEEMS LIKE
YESTERDAY........................ *Mercury 5433* 2-4 50
(Vocals: Eddy Howard)

CARELESS (theme song) / TO EACH
HIS OWN .... *Majestic 1070* 2-4 46
(Vocals: Eddy Howard)

EXACTLY LIKE YOU / WRAP YOUR TROUBLES
IN DREAMS .... *Columbia 35915* 4-6 40
(Vocals: Eddy Howard)

GIRL THAT I MARRY, THE /
BROTHER BILL..................... *Mercury 5394* 2-4 49
(Vocals: Eddy Howard)

GOODBYE GIRLS, I'M THROUGH / TILL WE MEET
AGAIN............................. *Majestic 1109* 2-4 47
(Vocals: Eddy Howard)

I CAN'T BELIEVE IT WAS ALL MAKE-BELIEVE /
MAYBE YOU'LL BE THERE.......... *Majestic 1120* 2-4 47
(Vocals: Eddy Howard)

LASSUS TROMBONE / PUT YOUR ARMS AROUND
ME, HONEY (Vocals: by chorus)......... *Mercury 5439* 2-4 50

MY ADOBE HACIENDA / MIDNIGHT
MASQUERADE...................... *Majestic 1117* 2-4 47
(Vocals: Eddy Howard)

OLD FASHIONED LOVE /
STAR DUST...................... *Columbia 35771* 4-6 40
(Vocals: Eddy Howard)

REMEMBER PEARL HARBOR (Vocals: Eddy Howard) /
WE DID IT BEFORE AND WE CAN DO
IT AGAIN (Vocals: The Glee Club)...... *Columbia 36497* 3-5 42

SHE'S FUNNY THAT WAY / THE RICKETY
RICKSHAW MAN.................... *Majestic 7192* 2-4 47
(Vocals: Eddy Howard)

SOMEONE CARES / ALL DRESSED UP WITH
A BROKEN HEART................. *Majestic 1236* 2-4 47
(Vocals: Eddy Howard)

HOWARD, Gordon, & His Multnomah Chieftains

GOLDEN GATE (Vocals: The Four Bachelors) / IF I CAN'T
HAVE YOU (Vocal: Jerry Macy) .... *Superior 337* 8-10 28

WOB-A-LY WALK (Vocals: The Four Bachelors) / IF I CAN'T
HAVE YOU (Vocal: Jerry Macy) .... *Gennett 6381* 10-12 28

HOWARD, Gordon, & His Multnomah Chieftains as Chuck Sawyer & His Syncopators

WOB-A-LY WALK / GOLDEN GATE......... *Bell 582* 8-10 28
(Vocals: The Four Bachelors)

HOWARD, Tex, & His Orchestra

LET'S HONEYMOON AGAIN / SOMEBODY'S
BIRTHDAY............................. *Decca 417* 4-6 35
(Vocals: Wyatt Howard)

LOVE DROPPED IN FOR TEA / PUT ON
A PAIR OF SHOES..................... *Decca 416* 4-6 35
(Vocals: Wyatt Howard)

HUBER, Justin, as Justin Huber's Hotel Gibson Dance Orchestra

SWEET PAPA JOE / SHE'S GOT
THAT TOO.......................... *Gennett 5253* 5-8 23

HUDSON, Dean, & The Florida Clubmen
(Dean Hudson: circa 1906 –)

ANNIE LAURIE (Vocal: Frances Colwell) / MIAMI
DREAMS (Vocal: Dean Hudson) .... *Bluebird B-7422* 3-5 38

WASHINGTON AND LEE SWING /
ALMA MATER................... *Bluebird B-7458* 3-5 38
(Vocals: by chorus)

HUDSON, Dean, & His Orchestra

CARAVAN / PARADISE (Vocal: Frances
Colwell)......................... *Musicraft 15026* 2-4 45

LET'S TRY AGAIN (Vocal: Sam Latimer) /
I'LL TAKE YOU HOME AGAIN,
KATHLEEN (Vocal: Sonny Stockton) .... *Okeh 6171* 3-5 41

MA, I MISS YOUR APPLE PIE (Vocals: The Dixie Debs) /
HOLLY HOP .... *Okeh 6355* 4-6 41

RED RIVER VALLEY / CAN'T
YOU TELL? (Vocal: Ruth Dale)............ *Okeh 6148* 3-5 41

YOU'RE GONE (Vocals: Dean Hudson & The Dixie Debs) /
BLITZKRIEG........................... *Okeh 6460* 4-6 41

HUDSON - DE LANGE ORCHESTRA, The,
directed by Will Hudson & Eddie De Lange
also see DE LANGE, Eddie, & His Orchestra and see HUDSON, Will, & His Orchestra
(Will Hudson: 3/8/08 –) (Eddie De Lange: 1/12/04 – 7/13/49)

DOIN' THE REACTIONARY / SUNDAY IN THE PARK .... *Brunswick 8077* 3-5 38
(Vocals: Mary McHugh)

GRAB YOUR PARTNER AND SWING / CROSS COUNTRY HOP .... *Brunswick 7743* 5-8 36

HOBO ON PARK AVENUE / EIGHT BARS IN SEARCH OF A MELODY (theme song) .... *Brunswick 7618* 5-8 36

HOW WAS I TO KNOW? (Vocal: Eddie De Lange) / AM I INTRUDING? .... *Brunswick 7809* 3-5 37

IF WE NEVER MEET AGAIN (Vocal: Fredda Gibson) / MIDNIGHT AT THE ONYX......... *Brunswick 7795* 4-6 37
(Fredda Gibson was later known as Georgia Gibbs)

I KNOW THAT YOU KNOW / I NEVER KNEW.............................. *Brunswick 8090* 4-6 37

I NEVER KNEW / WHEN IT'S SLEEPY-TIME DOWN SOUTH...... *Brunswick 7708* 4-6 36

IT'S A LOT OF IDLE GOSSIP / TORMENTED............ *Brunswick 7598* 3-5 36
(Vocals: Ruth Gaylor)

LOOKING DOWN AT THE STARS / WHAT THE HEART BELIEVES (THE HEART WILL SEE) .... *Brunswick 7727* 3-5 36
(Vocals: Ruth Gaylor)

MAGNOLIA / IF I COULD BE WITH YOU (ONE HOUR TONIGHT)....... *Brunswick 8016* 4-6 37

MAID'S NIGHT OFF, THE / SOPHISTICATED SWING............... *Master 103* 5-8 37

MOON IS GRINNING AT ME, THE (Vocal: Ruth Gaylor) / IT SEEMS I'VE DONE SOMETHING WRONG AGAIN (Vocal: Eddie De Lange).............. *Brunswick 7700* 3-5 36

MR. GHOST GOES TO TOWN / MINT JULEP...................... *Brunswick 7715* 5-8 36

MR. SWEENEY'S LEARNED TO SWING / AT YOUR BECK AND CALL (Vocal: Mary McHugh)...................... *Brunswick 8081* 4-6 38

OFF AGAIN, ON AGAIN (Vocal: Betty Allen) / DEFINITION OF SWING (Vocal: Elyse Cooper) .... *Brunswick 8071* 4-6 38

ONE I LOVE BELONGS TO SOMEBODY ELSE, THE / ON THE ALAMO ..... *Brunswick 8156* 4-6 38

ORGAN GRINDER'S SWING / YOU'RE NOT THE KIND (Vocal: Ruth Gaylor)....... *Brunswick 7656* 4-6 36

POPCORN MAN (Vocal: Nan Wynn) / GOIN' HAYWIRE................. *Brunswick 8007* 5-8 37

REMEMBER WHEN (Vocal: Eddie De Lange) / I'LL NEVER TELL YOU I LOVE YOU (Vocal: Fredda Gibson) .... *Brunswick 7785* 3-5 37
(Fredda Gibson was later known as Georgia Gibbs)

ROCKIN' THE TOWN / MY HEAVEN ON EARTH .... *Brunswick 8023* 4-6 38
(Vocals: Betty Allen)

STARDUST / BUGLE CALL RAG.......... *Master 125* 5-8 37

WAKE UP AND LIVE / NEVER IN A MILLION YEARS.................... *Master 112* 4-6 37
(Vocals: Ruth Gaylor)

WHY PRETEND? (Vocal: Jane Dover) / CHINA CLIPPER................. *Brunswick 8147* 4-6 38

YOU'RE MY DESIRE (Vocal: Ruth Gaylor) / BACK IN YOUR ARMS (Vocal: Eddie De Lange)....... *Master 132* 4-6 37

HUDSON, Will, & His Orchestra
also see HUDSON-DE LANGE ORCHESTRA, The
(Will Hudson: 3/8/08 –)

BLACK VELVET / EASY ROCKER........ *Decca 3702* 3-5 41

BREAK IT DOWN / BREAK IT UP.... *Brunswick 8222* 4-6 38

FLAT FOOT FLOOGEE (Vocals: by chorus) / THERE'S SOMETHING ABOUT AN OLD LOVE (Vocal: Jane Dover)........ *Brunswick 8164* 4-6 38

NIGHT IS FILLED WITH MUSIC, THE / MAY I HAVE MY HEART BACK?............... *Brunswick 8191* 3-5 38
(Vocals: Jane Dover)

ON THE VERGE / HI YA, MR. CHIPS...... *Decca 3473* 3-5 40

THREE AT A TABLE FOR TWO (Vocal: Kay Kenny) / START JUMPIN'....................... *Decca 3579* 3-5 41

WORLD WITHOUT YOU, THE (Vocal: Kay Kenny) / PEEKIN' AT THE DEACON .... *Decca 3429* 3-5 40

HUDSON, Will, & His Seven Swingsters

CORRIGAN HOP, THE / MIRACLE AT MIDNIGHT.................... *Brunswick 8195* 4-6 38

LADY OF THE NIGHT / HANGOVER IN HONGKONG.................. *Brunswick 8177* 4-6 38

HUGHES, Phil, & His High Hatters:
see LANIN, Sam, & His Famous Players & Singers see RESER, Harry, as the Seven Little Polar Bears and see SELVIN, Ben, & His Orchestra

HUNTLEY, Lloyd, & His Isle O' Blues Orchestra

ALONE IN THE RAIN (Vocals: by trio) / MOANIN' FOR YOU (Vocal: Floyd Rock).............. *Brunswick 4703* 4-6 29

LONELY / GEE, BUT I'D LIKE TO MAKE YOU HAPPY .... *Brunswick 4937* 3-5 30
(Vocals: Unknown)

MOLLY (Vocal: Floyd Rock) / THERE WILL NEVER BE ANOTHER MARY (Vocal: Elmo Tanner)........... *Brunswick 4704* 4-6 29

ON A BLUE AND MOONLESS NIGHT / PROMISES.............. *Brunswick 4784* 3-5 30
(Vocals: Frank Sylvano)

SAME OLD MOON (Vocal: Floyd Rock) / HEAD LOW (Vocals: Unknown) .... *Brunswick 4643* 4-6 29

TAKE ME / JUST ANOTHER NIGHT WITH YOU .... *Brunswick 4797* 3-5 30
(Vocals: Unknown)

WOND'RING / THE SONG OF THE FOOL........................ *Brunswick 4970* 3-5 30
(Vocals: Unknown)

HURTADO, Celso:
see DIXIE MARIMBA PLAYERS, The

HUTTON, Ina Ray, & Her Melodears
(Ina Ray Hutton: 3/13/16 – 2/19/84)
(Ina Ray Hutton & Her Melodears was an all-girl orchestra.)

GEORGIA'S GORGEOUS GAL (Vocal: Ruth Bradley) / TWENTY-FOUR HOURS IN GEORGIA (Vocal: Ina Ray Hutton) .... *Vocalion 2801* 5-8 34

HOW'S ABOUT TOMORROW NIGHT? (Vocal: Ina Ray Hutton) / AND I STILL DO (Vocal: Ruth Bradley)................... *Victor 24692* 5-8 34

WILD PARTY / WITCH DOCTOR....... *Vocalion 2816* 5-8 34

HUTTON, Ina Ray, & Her Orchestra

EV'RYTHING I LOVE (Vocal: Stuart Foster) / YOU MADE ME LOVE YOU (Vocals: Ina Ray Hutton)..... *Elite 5008* 3-5 41

FIVE O'CLOCK WHISTLE (Vocal: Ina Ray Hutton) / MAKE ME KNOW IT .... *Okeh 5852* 4-6 40

GOTTA HAVE YOUR LOVE (theme song) / A HANDFUL OF STARS (Vocal: Stuart Foster)............ *Okeh 5830* 4-6 40

NOBODY'S SWEETHEART (Vocal: Ina Ray Hutton) / BACK IN YOUR OWN BACK YARD...... *Okeh 6380* 3-5 41

SINNER KISSED AN ANGEL / MADELAINE .... *Elite 5007* 3-5 41
(Vocals: Unknown)

WHAT'S THE GOOD OF MOONLIGHT (WHEN YOU HAVEN'T GOT A GIRL TO LOVE) (Vocal: Ina Ray Hutton) / AT LAST (Vocal: Stewart Foster) .... *Okeh 6335* 4-6 41

IMPERIAL DANCE ORCHESTRA, The:
see SAMUELS, Joseph, & His Orchestra and
see SCHUBERT, Adrian, & His Salon Orchestra

IMPERIAL MARIMBA BAND, The

CLOVER CLUB / NONA................ *Edison 50508* 3-5 18

SOMEONE IS THINKING OF YOU / THE HAUNTING WALTZ............................ *Edison 51195* 3-5 23

INGRAHAM, Roy, & His Orchestra

CHANT OF THE JUNGLE / THAT WONDERFUL SOMETHING...................... *Brunswick 4586* 4-6 29
(Vocals: Unknown)

LIKE A BREATH OF SPRINGTIME / DEEP IN THE ARMS OF LOVE.................. *Brunswick 4544* 3-5 29
(Vocals: Unknown)

THAT'S LIVING / ME AND THE CLOCK...................... *Brunswick 4366* 3-5 29
(Vocals: Unknown)

INTERNATIONAL NOVELTY ORCHESTRA, The:
see SHILKRET, Nat

IONA, Andy, & His Orchestra

ALOHA HAWAII (A 4-record album set)........................ *Columbia Set C-39* 8-10 40
Individual records in the set, listed numerically (with value of each):
IN AN OLD HAWAIIAN VILLAGE (Vocal: Gary "Naihe" Speare) / BEAUTIFUL KAHANA (Vocals: Miulan & Dan Stewart)......... *Columbia 35843* 2-4 -
ISLAND SERENADE / SWEET GARDENIA LEI (Vocal: Gary "Naihe" Speare)....... *Columbia 35844* 2-4 -
HOI MAI (Vocal: George Piltz) / LOVELY HAWAIIAN MADONNA (Vocal: Danny Stewart).... *Columbia 35845* 2-4 -
HOW'D YA DO / WHISPERING LULLABY........................ *Columbia 35846* 2-4 -

IPANA TROUBADOURS, The:
see LANIN, Sam

IRVING, Rex, & The Boys:
see RISKIN, Irving

IRWIN, Vic, & His Orchestra

LIFE IS JUST A BOWL OF CHERRIES / THIS IS THE MISSUS........................ *Perfect 15516* 3-5 31
(Vocals: Paul Small)

NOW'S THE TIME TO FALL IN LOVE / SHE'S SO NICE..................... *Banner 32327* 5-8 31
(Vocals: The Eton Boys)

NOW'S THE TIME TO FALL IN LOVE / SHE'S SO NICE....................... *Oriole 2387* 5-8 31
(Vocals: The Eton Boys)

NOW'S THE TIME TO FALL IN LOVE / SHE'S SO NICE...................... *Romeo 1760* 5-8 31
(Vocals: The Eton Boys)
(Simultaneously released on three labels)

RHAPSODY IN BLUE / RHAPSODY IN BLUE, PART II.................. *Harmony 422-H* 3-5 27

WHO'S YOUR LITTLE WHO-ZIS? / I DON'T BLAME YOU............................... *Banner 32331* 5-8 31
(Vocals: The Eton Boys)

WHO'S YOUR LITTLE WHO-ZIS? / I DON'T BLAME YOU................................. *Oriole 2386* 5-8 31
(Vocals: The Eton Boys)

WHO'S YOUR LITTLE WHO-ZIS? / I DON'T BLAME YOU............................... *Perfect 15547* 5-8 31
(Vocals: The Eton Boys)

WHO'S YOUR LITTLE WHO-ZIS? / I DON'T BLAME YOU................................. *Romeo 1747* 5-8 31
(Vocals: The Eton Boys)
(Simultaneously released on four labels)

ISRAEL, Howard:
see PEERLES SERENADERS of Al Tearney's Town Club, The

JACKSON, Earl, & His Musical Champions:
see ELLINGTON, Duke, & His Famous Orchestra

JACKSON, Eddie, & His Orchestra:
see MARTIN, Freddy, & His Orchestra

JAMES, Harry, & His Orchestra
(Harry James: 3/15/16 – 7/5/83)

ALL FOR LOVE (Vocal: Jimmy Saunders) / BLUES IN THE NIGHT .... *Columbia 36500* 3-5 42

ALL OF MY LIFE (Vocal: Buddy Di Vito) / YAH-TA-TA, TAH-TA-TA (Vocal: Kitty Kallen) ...... *Columbia 36788* 2-4 45

ALL OR NOTHING AT ALL (Vocal: Frank Sinatra) / FLASH .... *Columbia 35587* 3-5 39

AND THE ANGELS SING / GOT NO TIME.................... *Brunswick 8355* 5-8 39
(Vocals: Bernice Byers)

B-19 / — .... *V-Disc 493* 5-8 -
(A World War II release)

BALME IT ON MY LAST AFFAIR / LOVE'S A NECESSARY THING .... *Brunswick 8326* 5-8 39
(Vocals: Bernice Byers)

BRAGGIN' / FOR WANT OF A STAR.... *Columbia 36081* 2-4 41
(Vocals: Dick Haymes)

BOOG-IT (Vocal: Jack Palmer) / THE SHEIK OF ARABY .... *Varsity 8270* 3-5 40

BUT NOT FOR ME (Vocal: Helen Forrest) / —..... *V-Disc 380* 5-8 -
(A World War II release)

BY THE SLEEPY LAGOON / TRUMPET BLUES AND CANTABILE...................... *Columbia 36549* 2-4 42

CHERRY / JUMP TOWN .... *Columbia 36683* 2-4 42

CIRIBIRIBIN (theme song) / SWEET GEORGIA BROWN .... *Brunswick 8327* 4-6 39

COMES LOVE / I CAN'T AFFORD TO DREAM............. *Brunswick 8395* 5-8 39
(Vocals: Connie Haines)

CONCERTO FOR TRUMPET / I'M IN THE MARKET FOR YOU .... *Columbia 35340* 3-5 40

CROSS COUNTRY JUMP / EVERY DAY OF MY LIFE (Vocal: Frank Sinatra)........ *Columbia 35531* 3-5 39

DADDY (Vocal: Helen Ward) / AURORA (Vocal: (Dick Haymes) .... *Columbia 36171* 2-4 41

DODGERS' FAN DANCE / — .... *V-Disc 512* 5-8 -
(A World War II release)

DO YOU LOVE ME (Vocal: Ginnie Powell) / AS IF I DIDN'T HAVE ENOUGH ON MY MIND (Vocal: Buddy Di Vito) .... *Columbia 36985* 2-4 46

EAST COAST BLUES / I UNDERSTAND (Vocal: Buddy Di Vito) .... *Columbia 38059* 2-4 48

EASTER PARADE / CRAZY RHYTHM .... *Columbia 36545* 2-4 42

FLIGHT OF THE BUMBLE BEE / FOUR OR FIVE TIMES (Vocals: by orchestra)............. *Varsity 8298* 3-5 40

FOOLS RUSH IN / SECRETS IN THE MOONLIGHT .... *Varsity 8264* 2-4 40
(Vocals: Dick Haymes)

FRIAR ROCK / EASY................ *Columbia 36996* 2-4 46

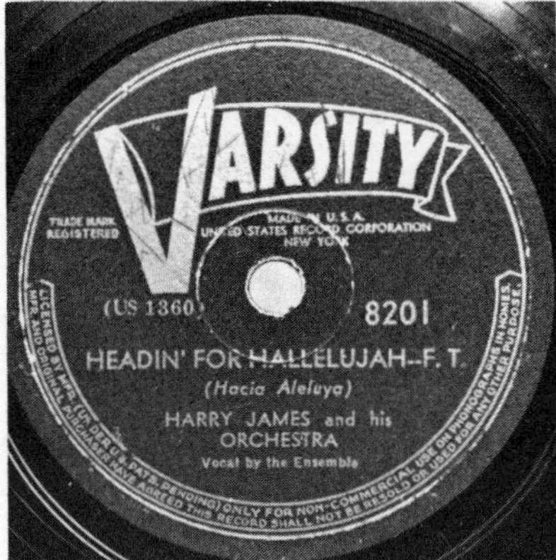

FROM THE BOTTOM OF MY HEART / MELANCHOLY MOOD.............................. *Brunswick 8443* 5-8 39
(Vocals: Frank Sinatra)

HEADIN' FOR HALLELUJAH (Vocals: by orchestra) / ALICE BLUE GOWN .... *Varsity 8201* 3-5 40

HERE COMES THE NIGHT (Vocal: Frank Sinatra) / FEET DRAGGIN' BLUES........... *Columbia 35227* 5-8 39

HE'S 1-A IN THE ARMY (Vocal: Helen Forrest) / DAY DREAMING (Vocal: Dick Haymes) ..... *Columbia 36455* 2-4 41

HODGE PODGE / FOUR OR FIVE TIMES (Vocals: by orchestra).......... *Elite 5028* 4-6 40

HODGE PODGE / FOUR OR FIVE TIMES (Vocals: by orchestra) .... *Philharmonic 71* 4-6 40
(Simultaneously released on two labels)

I CRIED FOR YOU (Vocal: Helen Forrest) / LET ME UP....................... *Columbia 36623* 2-4 42

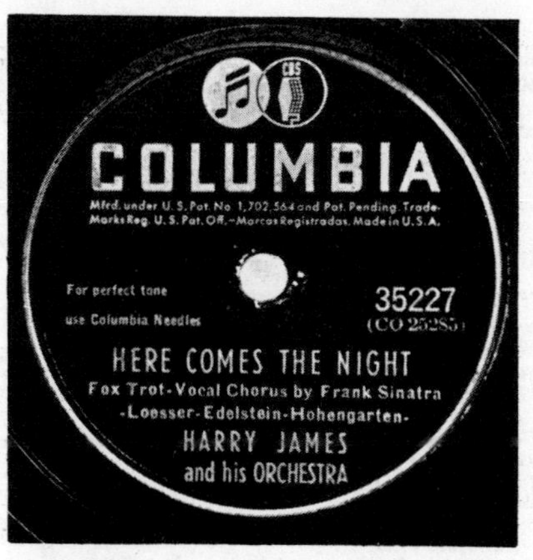

I DON'T WANT TO WALK WITHOUT YOU (Vocal: Helen Forrest) / B-19........... *Columbia 36478* 3-5 42

I FOUND A NEW BABY / FANNY MAY .... *Brunswick 8406* 5-8 39

I GUESS I'LL HAVE TO DREAM THE REST / I'LL NEVER LET A DAY PASS BY...... *Columbia 36255* 2-4 41
(Vocals: Dick Haymes)

INDIANA / KING PORTER STOMP.... *Brunswick 8366* 5-8 39

I NEVER PURPOSELY HURT YOU (Vocal: Dick Haymes) / FLATBUSH FLANAGAN........... *Columbia 35947* 2-4 41

I REMEMBER YOU (Vocal: Helen Forrest) / LAST NIGHT I SAID A PRAYER (Vocal: Jimmy Saunders).................... *Columbia 36518* 2-4 42

IT'S BEEN A LONG, LONG TIME (Vocal: Kitty Kallen) / AUTUMN SERENADE............. *Columbia 36838* 2-4 44

IT'S THE DREAMER IN ME (Vocal: Helen Humes) / ONE O'CLOCK JUMP .... *Brunswick 8055* 8-10 38

JAMES SESSION / I HEARD YOU CRIED LAST NIGHT (Vocal: Helen Forrest).......... *Columbia 36677* 2-4 42

JEFFRIES' BLUES / SHARP AS A TACK .... *Columbia 36190* 3-5 42

JUBILEE / (I CAN DREAM) CAN'T I?... *Brunswick 8038* 8-10 38
(Vocals: Helen Humes)

LAMENT TO LOVE / DODGERS' FAN DANCE..................... *Columbia 36222* 2-4 41

LITTLE BIT OF HEAVEN, A / ELI-ELI .... *Columbia 35979* 3-5 41

MANHATTAN SERENADE (Vocal: Helen Forrest) / DAYBREAK (Vocal: Jimmy Saunders) ... *Columbia 36644* 2-4 42

MEMPHIS BLUES / — .... *V-Disc 299* 5-8 -
(A World War II release)

MINKA (Vocal: Dick Haymes) / MISIRLOU....................... *Columbia 36390* 2-4 41

MISTER MEADOWLARK / THE NEARNESS OF YOU .... *Varsity 8293* 3-5 40
(Vocals: Dick Haymes)

MOLE, THE / — .... *V-Disc 419* 5-8 -
(A World War II release)

MOONLIGHT BECOMES YOU (Vocal: Johnny McAfee) / I'VE HEARD THAT SONG BEFORE (Vocal: Helen Forrest)................ *Columbia 36668* 2-4 42

MOON WON'T TALK, THE / MY GREATEST MISTAKE.......................... *Varsity 8389* 3-5 40
(Vocals: Dick Haymes)

MONTEVIDEO (Vocal: Dick Haymes) / MUSIC MAKERS .... *Columbia 35932* 2-4 41

MY BUDDY (Vocal: Frank Sinatra) / WILLOW, WEEP FOR ME.......... *Columbia 35242* 5-8 39

MY SILENT LOVE (Vocal: Dick Haymes) / MY MELANCHOLY BABY.......... *Columbia 36434* 2-4 41

NIGHT SPECIAL / BACK BEAT BOOGIE .... *Columbia 35456* 3-5 40

NOBODY KNOWS THE TROUBLE I'VE SEEN / YOU'VE CHANGED (Vocal: Dick Haymes) ...... *Columbia 36412* 2-4 41

OH, BUT I DO (Vocal: Buddy Di Vito) / LIFE CAN BE BEAUTIFUL (Vocal: Marion Morgan)... *Columbia 37156* 2-4 46

OL' MAN RIVER (Vocal: Dick Haymes) / ANSWER MAN...................... *Columbia 36023* 2-4 41

ON A LITTLE STREET IN SINGAPORE / WHO TOLD YOU I CARED?.................. *Columbia 35261* 5-8 39
(Vocals: Frank Sinatra)

ONE DOZEN ROSES (Vocal: Jimmy Saunders) / YOU'RE TOO GOOD FOR GOOD-FOR-NOTHING ME (Vocal: Helen Forrest)................ *Columbia 36566* 2-4 42

OUT OF NOWHERE / LULLABY IN RHYTHM..................... *Brunswick 8136* 5-8 38

POEM SET TO MUSIC, A (Vocal: Johnny McAfee) / I HAD THE CRAZIEST DREAM (Vocal: Helen Forrest)................ *Columbia 36659* 2-4 42

PRINCE CHARMING / VELVET MOON .... *Columbia 36672* 2-4 42

SHEIK OF ARABY, THE / EXACTLY LIKE YOU .... *Elite 5036* 3-5 40

SKYLARK (Vocal: Helen Forrest) / THE CLIPPER .... *Columbia 36533* 2-4 42

STRICTLY INSTRUMENTAL / SUMMERTIME; SHORT'NIN' BREAD (Vocal: Eddie Miller) ... *V-Disc 311* 5-8 -
(The second and third titles are by Bob Crosby & His Orchestra. A World War II release)

STRICTLY INSTRUMENTAL / WHEN YOU'RE A LONG, LONG WAY FROM HOME (Vocal: Jimmy Saunders)................ *Columbia 36579* 3-5 42

'TAIN'T WHAT YOU DO (Vocal: Jack Palmer) / TWO O'CLOCK JUMP .... *Brunswick 8337* 5-8 39

TEMPO DE LUXE / EXACTLY LIKE YOU.......................... *Varsity 8411* 3-5 40

TEXAS CHATTER / SONG OF THE WANDERER (Vocal: Helen Humes).... *Brunswick 8067* 8-10 38

THAT SOLDIER OF MINE / MISTER FIVE-BY-FIVE .... *Columbia 36650* 3-5 42
(Vocals: Helen Forrest)

THIS IS ALWAYS (Vocal: Buddy Di Vito) / I'VE NEVER FORGOTTEN (Vocal: Ginnie Powell).... *Columbia 37052* 2-4 46

TRUMPET RHAPSODY / TRUMPET RHAPSODY, PART II.............. *Columbia 36160* 3-5 41

TUXEDO JUNCTION / PALMS OF PARADISE (Vocal: Fran Heines).......... *Montgomery Ward 10006* 3-5 40

TUXEDO JUNCTION / PALMS OF PARADISE (Vocal: Fran Heines) .... *Varsity 8194* 3-5 40
(Simultaneously released on two labels)

VELVET MOON / —....................... *V-Disc 57* 5-8 -
(A World War II release)

VOL VISTU GAILY STAR (Vocal: Jack Palmer) / IT'S FUNNY TO EVERYONE BUT ME (Vocal: Frank Sinatra)................. *Columbia 35209* 5-8 39

WAITIN' FOR THE TRAIN TO COME IN (Vocal: Kitty Kallen) / I CAN'T BEGIN TO TELL YOU (Vocal: Betty Grable as Ruth Haag) ...... *Columbia 36867* 3-5 45

WALKIN' BY THE RIVER/DOLORES... *Columbia 36069* 2-4 41
(Vocals: Dick Haymes)

WHEN WE'RE ALONE / LIFE GOES TO A PARTY...................... *Brunswick 8035* 5-8 38

WRAP YOUR TROUBLES IN DREAMS / LITTLE WHITE LIES.......................... *Brunswick 8178* 5-8 38

YES INDEED! / IT'S SO PEACEFUL IN THE COUNTRY .... *Columbia 36246* 2-4 41
(Vocals: Dick Haymes)

YOU MADE ME LOVE YOU / A SINNER KISSED AN ANGEL (Vocal: Dick Haymes)...... *Columbia 36296* 2-4 41

YOU MADE ME LOVE YOU / CHERRY.... *V-Disc 193* 3-5 -
(A World War II release.)

YOU'RE IN LOVE WITH SOMEONE ELSE / HE'S MY GUY............... *Columbia 36614* 2-4 42
(Vocals: Helen Forrest)

JARRETT, Art, accompanied by a recording group
(Art Jarrett: 1909 –)

GOODBYE BLUES / THIS TIME IT'S LOVE .... *Columbia 2672-D* 5-8 32
(Vocals: Art Jarrett)

MUSIC, MUSIC EVERYWHERE / LOVE ME TONIGHT.................. *Columbia 2691-D* 5-8 32
(Vocals: Art Jarrett)

JARRETT, Art, & His Orchestra

ALL ALONE AND LONELY (Vocal: Babe Stuart) / GREEN EYES (Vocals: Art Jarrett & The Smoothies) .... *Victor 27501* 3-5 41

BELLS OF SAN RAQUEL (Vocal: Art Jarrett) / MA-MA-MARIA (Vocals: The Smoothies) ... *Victor 27612* 3-5 41

COWBOY SERENADE, THE (Vocal: Art Jarrett) / CALL IT ANYTHING, IT'S LOVE (Vocal: Gale Robbins) .... *Victor 27534* 3-5 41

IT MUST BE TRUE / EVERYTHING'S BEEN DONE BEFORE (theme song) .... *Victor 27590* 2-4 41
(Vocals: Art Jarrett)

I WOULD IF I COULD (Vocal: Brad Henry) / WE'VE GOT TO DO A JOB ON THE JAPS, BABY (Vocals: Art Jarrett, Gale Robbins, & quartet)................ *Victor 27781* 4-6 42

JIM (Vocal: Gale Robbins) / YOU CAN DEPEND ON ME (Vocal: Art Jarrett).............. *Victor 27580* 2-4 41

LOVELINESS AND LOVE (Vocal: Art Jarrett) / YOU STARTED SOMETHING (Vocals: The Smoothies) .... *Victor 27474* 3-5 41

NICKEL SERENADE, THE (Vocals: The Smoothies) / DELILAH (Vocal: Art Jarrett)........... *Victor 27571* 2-4 41

THREE LITTLE SISTERS (Vocals: by quartet) / HEAVENLY HIDEAWAY (Vocal: Betty Barrett)...................... *Victor 27857* 3-5 42

WHO DO YOU THINK I AM? (Vocals: Gale Robbins & Art Jarrett) / BUCKLE DOWN, WINSOCKI (Vocals: Art Jarrett & chorus).................. *Victor 27665* 2-4 41

WOULD IT MAKE ANY DIFFERENCE TO YOU? (Vocal: Gale Robbins) / GOODBYE, MAMA (I'M OFF TO YOKOHAMA) (Vocals: Art Jarrett & orchestra) .... *Victor 27758* 4-6 42

YOU CAN'T HOLD A MEMORY IN YOUR ARMS (Vocal: Brad Henry) / DON'T SIT UNDER THE APPLE TREE (Vocals: by quartet)...................... *Victor 27851* 4-6 42

JAUDAS' SOCIETY ORCHESTRA

BEAUTIFUL OHIO / CITY OF DREAMS... *Edison 50511* 3-5 18
BROKEN DOLL / GO GET 'EM........ *Edison 50409* 3-5 16
LI'L LIZA JANE / THE DARKTOWN STRUTTERS' BALL........ *Edison 50469* 5-8 18
MISSOURI WALTZ/POOR BUTTERFLY... *Edison 50428* 3-5 17
OH JOHNNY, OH JOHNNY, OH! / THAT CREEPY WEEPY FEELING........ *Edison 50441* 4-6 17
STEP WITH PEP / THERE'S A LITTLE BIT OF BAD IN EVERY GOOD LITTLE GIRL .... *Edison 50412* 4-6 17

JAZZ HARMONISTS, The:
see WOLVERINE ORCHESTRA, The

JAZZ-O-HARMONISTS, The

DARKTOWN REVEILLE / SALT YOUR SUGAR........ *Edison 51247* 10-12 23

JAZZ PILOTS, The:
see RESER, Harry

JENNEY, Jack, & His Orchestra
(Jack Jenney: 5/12/10 – 12/16/45)

IF YOU KNEW SUSIE (Vocal: Kirby Walker) / SINCE YOU CAME INTO MY DREAMS (Vocal: Frank Bond)........ *Vocalion 5545* 4-6 40
I'LL GET BY (Vocal: Frank Bond) / (WHAT CAN I SAY) AFTER I SAY I'M SORRY? (Vocal: Meredith Blake)........ *Conqueror 9494* 3-5 40
I'LL GET BY (Vocal: Frank Bond) / (WHAT CAN I SAY) AFTER I SAY I'M SORRY? (Vocal: Meredith Blake)........ *Vocalion 5494* 3-5 40
(Simultaneously released on two labels)
I'VE GONE ROMANTIC ON YOU / IN THE SHADE OF THE NEW APPLE TREE........ *Vocalion 3972* 3-5 38
(Vocals: Adelaide Moffatt)
I WALK ALONE (Vocal: Meredith Blake) / CITY NIGHT (theme song) (Vocal: Frank Sherman)........ *Vocalion 5535* 4-6 40
MOON RAY (Vocal: Meredith Blake) / HIGH SOCIETY........ *Vocalion 5223* 5-8 39
SWINGIN' THE APACH' / THE NIGHT IS BLUE........ *Vocalion 4130* 5-8 38
STAR DUST / CUBAN BOOGIE WOOGIE........ *Vocalion 5304* 4-6 40
STAR DUST / THE WORLD IS WAITING FOR THE SUNRISE........ *Conqueror 9493* 4-6 39
WHAT IS THERE TO SAY? / THE WORLD IS WAITING FOR THE SUNRISE........ *Vocalion 5407* 4-6 40
WHAT MORE CAN I GIVE YOU? / GOT NO TIME (Vocal: Louise Tobin)........ *Vocalion 4803* 3-5 39

JESSUP, Red, & His Melody Makers

BLUE ROOM, THE (Vocals: Unknown) / LADY BE GOOD (Vocal: Jimmy Lewis)........ *Melotone 7-07-15* 5-8 37
TOODLE-OO (Vocal: Mert Curtis) / (CAN'T YOU HEAR THAT) MOUNTAIN MUSIC (Vocal: Chick Bullock)........ *Melotone 7-07-01* 5-8 37

JETER-PILLARS CLUB PLANTATION ORCHESTRA
directed by James Jeter and Charles Pillars

I LIKE PIE, I LIKE CAKE (Vocal: Hayes Pillars) / LAZY RHYTHM........ *Vocalion 3715* 8-10 37
MAKE BELIEVE / I'LL ALWAYS BE IN LOVE WITH YOU........ *Vocalion 3973* 8-10 37
(Vocals: Ted Smith)

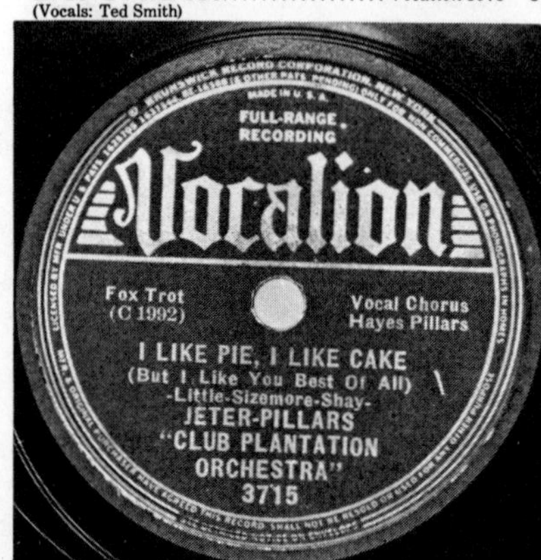

JOCKERS, Al, as Al Jockers' Dance Orchestra

BRIGHT EYES / NA–JO........ *Vocalion 14153* 2-4 21
EMALINE / IN MY TIPPY CANOE........ *Vocalion 14232* 2-4 21
EVERYBODY STEP / HOW MANY TIMES?........ *Vocalion 14255* 2-4 21
I NEVER KNEW / LOOK FOR THE SILVER LINING........ *Vocalion 14156* 3-5 21
MA! / JUST LIKE A RAINBOW........ *Vocalion 14241* 3-5 21
ROSIE / WHY DON'T YOU?........ *Vocalion 14146* 2-4 21
'SIPPI SHORE / PINING........ *Vocalion 14165* 2-4 21

JOCKERS, Al, as Al Jockers' Woodmansten Orchestra

MY HOME TOWN / I'M JUST WILD ABOUT HARRY........ *Cameo 224* 3-5 22
WHO'LL TAKE MY PLACE WHEN I'M GONE? / BLUE........ *Cameo 261* 2-4 22

JOHNS, Brooke, & His Orchestra

I WANT A PRETTY GIRL / DON'T CRY, SWANEE........ *Victor 19051* 2-4 23
(Vocals: Brooke Johns)
LONESOME / NOT YET, SUZETTE!........ *Victor 19285* 2-4 24
(Vocals: Brooke Johns)
WHEN YOU WALKED OUT, SOMEONE ELSE WALKED RIGHT IN / BEBE........ *Victor 19092* 2-4 23
(Vocals: Brooke Johns)

JOHNSON, Arnold, & His Orchestra
(Arnold Johnson: 3/23/93 –)

AWAY DOWN EAST IN MAINE / CRINOLINE DAYS........ *Brunswick 2377* 2-4 23
CHINA BOY / ONE NIGHT IN JUNE........ *Brunswick 2355* 3-5 22
KISS ME / SWEET LOVIN' MAMA........ *Brunswick 2411* 3-5 23
WHAT'S THE REASON? / GET YOUR MAN........ *Brunswick 3914* 4-6 28
(Vocals: Roy Strom, Roy Ingram, & Harold Arluck, later known as Harold Arlen, the famed composer.)

JOHNSON, Arnold, & His Paramount Hotel Orchestra

BREAKAWAY / BIG CITY BLUES........ *Brunswick 4348* 3-5 29
(Vocals: Unknown)
I'LL NEVER ASK FOR MORE / WHEN THE WORLD IS AT REST........ *Brunswick 4203* 2-4 29
(Vocals: Roy Strom)
ME AND THE MAN IN THE MOON / EV'RYBODY LOVES YOU........ *Brunswick 4125* 2-4 29
(Vocals: Unknown)

JOHNSON, Haven, & His Orchestra

BEFORE WE PART / THERE IS NO MOON........ *Vocalion 3457* 10-12 37
(Vocals: Haven Johnson)

JOHNSON, James P. / Jimmy, & His Orchestra
(James P. Johnson: 2/1/91 – 11/17/55)

BACK WATER BLUES / HE'S MINE, ALL MINE........ *Vocalion 4903* 10-12 39
(Vocals: Ruby Smith)
(Ruby Smith is the niece of the legendary blues artist, Bessie Smith.)
CHICAGO BLUES (dialog by Perry Bradford) / MOURNFUL THO'TS........ *Columbia 14334-D* 15-20 28
GO HARLEM (Vocal: Andy Razaf) / JUST A CRAZY SONG (Vocals: Andy Razaf, Ward Pinkett, & chorus)........ *Columbia 2448-D* 12-15 31
HARLEM WOOGIE (Vocal: Anna Robinson) / AFTER TONIGHT........ *Vocalion 4768* 10-12 39
YOU DON'T UNDERSTAND / YOU'VE GOT TO BE MODERNISTIC........ *Victor V-38099* 35-40 29
(Vocals: by the "Keep Shufflin' Trio")

JOHNSON, Johnny, & His Orchestra
(Johnny Johnson: circa 1902 –)

ALL MY LIFE / LAUGHING IRISH EYES........ *Melotone 6-05-04* 2-4 36
(Vocals: Unknown)
BROKEN RECORD, THE / A BEAUTIFUL LADY IN BLUE........ *Melotone 6-03-01* 2-4 36
(Vocals: Unknown)
COTTAGE BY THE MOON / IT'S THE GYPSY IN ME........ *Melotone 6-11-14* 2-4 36
(Vocals: Unknown)
EV'RY TIME I LOOK AT YOU / DANCING FEET........ *Melotone 6-03-11* 2-4 36
(Vocals: Unknown)
GOODY-GOODY / THE WHEEL OF THE WAGON IS BROKEN........ *Melotone 6-05-01* 2-4 36
(Vocals: Unknown)
HOW COULD YOU? / SEPTEMBER IN THE RAIN........ *Melotone 7-04-11* 3-5 37
(Vocals: Lee Johnson)
I'M KEEPING THOSE KEEPSAKES YOU GAVE ME (Vocal: Walter Botsford) / LULLABY OF BROADWAY (Vocal: Bob Treaster)........ *Banner 33353* 2-4 35
I'M KEEPING THOSE KEEPSAKES YOU GAVE ME (Vocal: Walter Botsford) / LULLABY OF BROADWAY (Vocal: Bob Treaster)........ *Melotone M-13320* 2-4 35
I'M KEEPING THOSE KEEPSAKES YOU GAVE ME (Vocal: Walter Botsford) / LULLABY OF BROADWAY (Vocal: Bob Treaster)........ *Oriole 3095* 2-4 35
I'M KEEPING THOSE KEEPSAKES YOU GAVE ME (Vocal: Walter Botsford) / LULLABY OF BROADWAY (Vocal: Bob Treaster)........ *Perfect 16078* 2-4 35
I'M KEEPING THOSE KEEPSAKES YOU GAVE ME (Vocal: Walter Botsford) / LULLABY OF BROADWAY (Vocal: Bob Treaster)........ *Romeo 2469* 2-4 35
(Simultaneously released on five labels)
JUST A QUIET EVENING / TOO MARVELOUS FOR WORDS........ *Melotone 7-04-10* 3-5 37
(Vocals: Lee Johnson)
LITTLE OLD-FASHIONED MUSIC BOX / HEAVEN HELP THIS HEART OF MINE........ *Melotone 7-08-08* 3-5 37
(Vocals: Lee Johnson)
OH! LEO (Vocal: Harry McDaniel) / ROCK AND ROLL (Vocal: Lee Johnson)........ *Vocalion 2811* 4-6 34
(One of the first occasions when the phrase "Rock and roll" was used as a song title. From the 1934 motion picture "Transatlantic Merry-Go-Round", a musical starring the Boswell Sisters and Jimmie Grier & His Orchestra. Composed by Richard Whiting (Margaret's father); lyrics by Sidney Clare.)
PUT ON AN OLD PAIR OF SHOES (Vocal: Walter Botsford) / ROLL ALONG, COVERED WAGON (Vocal: Al Jennings)........ *Banner 33392* 2-4 35
PUT ON AN OLD PAIR OF SHOES (Vocal: Walter Botsford) / ROLL ALONG, COVERED WAGON (Vocal: Al Jennings)........ *Conqueror 8506* 2-4 35
PUT ON AN OLD PAIR OF SHOES (Vocal: Walter Botsford) / ROLL ALONG, COVERED WAGON (Vocal: Al Jennings)........ *Melotone M-13359* 2-4 35
PUT ON AN OLD PAIR OF SHOES (Vocal: Walter Botsford) / ROLL ALONG, COVERED WAGON (Vocal: Al Jennings)........ *Oriole 3118* 2-4 35
PUT ON AN OLD PAIR OF SHOES (Vocal: Walter Botsford) / ROLL ALONG, COVERED WAGON (Vocal: Al Jennings)........ *Perfect 16096* 2-4 35
PUT ON AN OLD PAIR OF SHOES (Vocal: Walter Botsford) / ROLL ALONG, COVERED WAGON (Vocal: Al Jennings)........ *Romeo 2492* 2-4 35
(Simultaneously released on six labels)
SHORT'NIN' BREAD (Vocal: Al Jennings) / DING DONG DADDY (Vocal: Harry McDaniel)........ *Vocalion 2847* 3-5 34
WOP BLUES / STAY HOME, LITTLE GIRL, STAY HOME........ *Cameo 477* 5-8 24

JOHNSON, Johnny, & His Statler Pennsylvanians

GIVE ME A NIGHT IN JUNE (Vocals: Bob Treaster, Charles Murray, & Sam Browne) / TOGETHER, WE TWO (Vocal: Franklyn Baur)........ *Victor 21016* 2-4 27
MAKE BELIEVE YOU'RE HAPPY / LOVELY LADY........ *Victor 21101* 2-4 28
(Vocals: Bob Treaster, Charles Murray, & Sam Browne)
MY ONE AND ONLY / THOU SWELL........ *Victor 21113* 5-8 28
(Vocals: Charles Murray, Sam Browne, & Bob Treaster)
ONCE IN A LIFETIME / SUNBEAMS........ *Victor 21677* 2-4 28
(Vocals: Franklyn Baur)

JOHNSON, Lem, & His Washboard Band:
see PRICE, Sam, & His Texas Blusicians

JOHNSTON, Jimmy, as Jimmy Johnston's Rebels:
see RESER, Harry

JOHNSTON, Merle, & His Ceco Couriers

EXACTLY LIKE YOU / SO SYMPATHETIC........ *Columbia 2160-D* 5-8 30
IF I HAD MY WAY / WHERE THE SWEET FORGET-ME-NOTS REMEMBER........ *Columbia 1968-D* 5-8 29
WATCHING MY DREAMS GO BY / SWEET NOTHINGS OF LOVE........ *Columbia 2114-D* 4-6 30
YOU'RE RESPONSIBLE / WITH YOU – WITH ME........ *Columbia 2005-D* 4-6 29

JOHNSTON, Merle, & His Orchestra

CALL ME DARLING / TIME ON MY HANDS........ *Perfect 15528* 3-5 31
(Vocals: Tom Brown)
I'M FOR YOU A HUNDRED PER CENT / IT'S LOVE........ *Perfect 15543* 4-6 32
(Vocals: Smith Ballew)

JOHNSTON, Merle, as Merle Johnston's Saxophone Quartet

ALWAYS IN ALL WAYS / IT'S A GREAT LIFE (IF YOU DON'T WEAKEN)........ *Columbia 2313-D* 3-5 30
(Vocals: Smith Ballew)
BABY – OH WHERE CAN YOU BE? / DO SOMETHING........ *Columbia 1923-D* 3-5 29

JONES, Bobby, & His Orchestra:
see SYLVESTER, Johnny, & His Playmates

JONES, Isham, & His Orchestra
(Isham Jones: 1/31/94 – 10/19/56)

AFTER THE RAIN / THOSE LONGING FOR YOU BLUES........ *Brunswick 2243* 3-5 22
AND STILL I CARE (Vocal: Charles French) / MUSIC, MUSIC EVERYWHERE (Vocal: Eddie Stone)........ *Victor 24098* 5-8 32
AUNT HAGAR'S CHILDREN BLUES / BURNING SANDS........ *Brunswick 5178* 4-6 22
BIRDIE/YANKEE DOODLE BLUES... *Brunswick 5144* 3-5 22
BLUE HOOSIER BLUES / WHEN YOU WALKED OUT, SOMEONE ELSE WALKED RIGHT IN........ *Brunswick 2456* 3-5 23
BLUE PRELUDE / JUST BORN TO BE LONESOME (Vocal: Joe Martin)........ *Victor 24298* 4-6 33
BLUE ROOM / BLACK MAGIC........ *Decca 493* 5-8 34
BLUE ROOM / GEORGIA JUBILEE........ *Victor 24701* 5-8 34
CHINA BOY / DALLAS BLUES........ *Victor 24649* 5-8 34
CRYIN' FOR YOU / AGGRAVATIN' PAPA........ *Brunswick 2400* 4-6 23
DOIN' THE UPTOWN LOWDOWN / YOU'RE MY PAST, PRESENT AND FUTURE........ *Victor 24409* 5-8 33
(Vocals: Joe Martin)
EVERY TIME I SEE YOU (Vocal: Marilyn Thorne) / SHE PICKED IT UP IN MEXICO (Vocal: Bob Allen)........ *Bantam D-9001* 10-12 -
(Bantom records are rare.)

EV'RY TIME I LOOK AT YOU (Vocal: Woody Herman) / SADDLE YOUR BLUES TO A WILD MUSTANG (Vocal: Eddie Stone) .... *Decca 695* 4-6 36

FORGETFUL BLUES / 'NEATH EGYPTIAN SKIES .... *Brunswick 2531* 3-5 23

FOUR OR FIVE TIMES / JIMTOWN BLUES .... *Decca 300* 5-8 34

FRANKIE AND JOHNNIE / JAPANESE SANDMAN (Vocal: Eddie Thomas) ..... *Brunswick 3695* 3-5 27

FRANKIE AND JOHNNIE / MEMPHIS BLUES .... *Brunswick 2423* 4-6 23

HENPECKED BLUES/OH! HAROLD ... *Brunswick 2479* 3-5 23

HERE COME THE BRITISH (Vocal: Eddie Stone) / I ONLY HAVE EYES FOR YOU (Vocal: Joe Martin) .... *Decca 168* 4-6 34

HONEST AND TRULY / DOO WACKA DOO .... *Brunswick 2767* 3-5 25

I DOUBLE DARE YOU (Vocal: Eddie Stone) / MORE THAN EVER (Vocal: Joe Martin) ... *Vocalion 3920* 3-5 38

INDIAN LOVE CALL / ALABAMY BOUND .... *Brunswick 2789* 3-5 25

I'VE FOUND A NEW BABY / TIGER RAG ..... *Decca 262* 5-8 34

I'VE GOT A NEW LEASE ON LOVE (Vocal: Eddie Stone) / TWILIGHT IN TURKEY .... *Melotone 7-06-12* 3-5 37

I'VE GOT A NEW LEASE ON LOVE (Vocal: Eddie Stone) / TWILIGHT IN TURKEY .... *Vocalion 3544* 3-5 37
(Simultaneously released on two labels)

I WONDER WHERE MY BABY IS TONIGHT? (Vocals: Billy Jones & Ernest Hare) / I'M SITTING ON TOP OF THE WORLD .... *Brunswick 3022* 2-4 26

JUNK MAN (Vocal: Eddie Stone) / THERE GOES MY HEART (Vocal: Joe Martin) .... *Victor 24519* 5-8 34

MA / WABASH BLUES .... *Brunswick 5065* 4-6 21

MISS HANNAH (Vocals: Unknown) / THERE'S A WAH-WAH GIRL IN AGUA CALIENTE ... *Brunswick 4868* 4-6 30

MY MELANCHOLY BABY / STOMPING AT THE SAVOY .... *Decca 754* 5-8 36

MY SWEETIE'S SWEETER THAN THAT / COTTON PICKER'S BALL .... *Brunswick 2548* 3-5 23

NOBODY LIED / MY HONEY'S LOVIN' ARMS .... *Brunswick 2301* 3-5 22

NOBODY'S SWEETHEART / BLUE EVENING BLUES .... *Brunswick 2578* 3-5 24

ONE LITTLE WORD LED TO ANOTHER (Vocal: Charles French) / SENTIMENTAL GENTLEMAN FROM GEORGIA (Vocal: Eddie Stone) .... *Victor 24099* 5-8 32

OUT OF SPACE / BLUE LAMENT .... *Victor 24695* 5-8 34

OUT OF SPACE / FOR ALL WE KNOW (Vocal: Joe Martin) .... *Decca 170* 5-8 34

PANAMA / ROCK YOUR BLUES AWAY .... *Decca 662* 5-8 34

PARDON MY SOUTHERN ACCENT (Vocal: Eddie Stone) / I NEVER HAD A CHANCE (Vocal: Joe Martin) .... *Decca 169* 4-6 34

PLAY THE FUNNY BLUES / THINK OF ME .... *Brunswick 2374* 4-6 22

POPLAR STREET BLUES / PANGO PANGO MAID .... *Brunswick 2877* 3-5 25

SAMSON AND DELILAH / PILGRIM'S BLUES .... *Brunswick 2244* 3-5 22

SOMEBODY'S WRONG / EASY MELODY .... *Brunswick 2500* 3-5 23

SOMEONE IS KEEPING ME OUT OF YOUR DREAMS / IT'S THE BLUES .... *Brunswick 3027* 4-6 26

SOME OTHER DAY, SOME OTHER GIRL (Vocals: Unknown) / GET LUCKY ...... *Brunswick 2678* 3-5 24

STEALING TO VIRGINIA / MAMA LOVES PAPA .... *Brunswick 2506* 2-4 23

SUN GOD / HIGH BROWN BLUES .... *Brunswick 5137* 3-5 22

SWANEE BUTTERFLY / RIVERBOAT SHUFFLE .... *Brunswick 2854* 3-5 25

SWEET GEORGIA BROWN / LET'S TRY AGAIN .... *Brunswick 6320* 8-10 32
(Vocals: Bing Crosby)

SWEET MAN / THE ORIGINAL CHARLESTON .... *Brunswick 2970* 3-5 25

SWEET SOMEONE (Vocal: Joe Martin) / I WANNA BE IN WINCHELL'S COLUMN (Vocal: Eddie Stone) .... *Vocalion 3862* 3-5 37

SWEET SUE / CHINA BOY .... *Decca 443* 5-8 34

SWINGIN' DOWN THE LANE / WHO'S SORRY NOW .... *Brunswick 2438* 3-5 23

THANKS FOR THE MEMORY (Vocal: Eddie Stone) / THERE'S A GOLD MINE IN THE SKY (Vocal: Joe Martin) .... *Vocalion 3910* 3-5 38

THREE-THIRTY BLUES / TELL ME YOU LOVE ME .... *Brunswick 3204* 3-5 26

UNFORTUNATE BLUES / NEVER AGAIN .... *Brunswick 2577* 3-5 24

WEEPIN' THE BLUES / PICKIN' 'EM UP AND LAYIN' 'EM DOWN .... *Brunswick 2615* 3-5 24

YOU'RE IN KENTUCKY SURE AS YOU'RE BORN / HULA LOU .... *Brunswick 2557* 3-5 24

YOU'RE O.K. / WHEN YOU CLIMB THOSE GOLDEN STAIRS .... *Decca 220* 5-8 34
(Vocals: Eddie Stone)

YOU'RE ONLY A BABY / VIRGINIA BLUES .... *Brunswick 2195* 3-5 22

YOU TOOK THE WORDS RIGHT OUT OF MY HEART (Vocal: Joe Martin) / MAMA, THAT MOON IS HERE AGAIN (Vocal: Eddie Stone) .... *Vocalion 3872* 3-5 37

YOU'VE GOT ME CRYING AGAIN / HONESTLY .... *Victor 24255* 4-6 33
(Vocals: Joe Martin)

JONES, Isham, & His Rainbo Orchestra

ROSE / MY MAMMY .... *Brunswick 5046* 2-4 21

SWEET WOMAN / DREAMY PARADISE .... *Brunswick 5028* 2-4 20

WHISPERING / AVALON .... *Brunswick 5027* 2-4 20

JONES, Isham, as Isham Jones' Juniors

I'VE HAD THE BLUES SO LONG / TORMENTED .... *Decca 770* 5-8 36
(Vocals: Woody Herman)

NOLA / FAN IT (Vocal: Woody Herman) .... *Decca 834* 5-8 36

JONES, Isham, as Isham Jones' Juniors recorded under the name The Swanee Swingers

SLAPPIN' THE BASS (Vocal: Virginia Verrell) / TAKE IT EASY (Vocal: Woody Herman) .... *Decca 1022* 5-8 36

JONES-SMITH, Incorporated:

see BASIE, Count

JONES, Spike, & His City Slickers

(Spike Jones: 12/14/11 – 5/1/64)

ALL I WANT FOR CHRISTMAS (Vocal: George Rock) / HAPPY NEW YEAR (Vocals: Sir Frederick Gas, George Rock, Doodles Weaver, & Spike Jones) .... *RCA Victor 20-3177* 4-6 48

BARSTOOL COWBOY FROM OLD BARSTOW / THE COVERED WAGON ROLLED RIGHT ALONG .... *Bluebird B-11364* 5-8 41
(Vocals: Del Porter)

CLINK, CLINK, ANOTHER DRINK (Vocal: Del Porter with sound effects by Mel Blanc) / PACK UP YOUR TROUBLES IN YOUR OLD KIT BAG (Vocals: The City Slickers) .... *Bluebird B-11466* 5-8 42

DANCE OF THE HOURS (Vocal: Doodles Weaver) / NONE BUT THE LONELY HEART (Vocals: Helen Grayco & Spike Jones) .... *RCA Victor 20-3516* 4-6 49

DER FUEHER'S FACE (Vocal: Carl Grayson) / I WANNA GO BACK TO WEST VIRGINIA (Vocals: Del Porter & The Boys In The Back Room) .... *Bluebird B-11586* 5-8 42

GLOW-WORM, THE (Vocals: Red Ingle & Aileen Carlisle) / HAWAIIAN WAR CHANT .... *Victor 20-1893* 4-6 46

I SAW MOMMY KISSING SANTA CLAUS (Vocal: George Rock) / WINTER (Vocals: The Mello Men) ... *RCA Victor 20-5067* 4-6 51

LITTLE BO-PEEP HAS LOST HER JEEP / PASS THE BISCUITS, MIRANDY .... *Bluebird B-11530* 5-8 42
(Vocals: Del Porter)

OH! BY JINGO (Vocals: Del Porter & The Boys In The Back Room) / SHEIK OF ARABY (Vocals: Del Porter & Carl Grayson) .... *Bluebird 30-0812* 5-8 42

RED WING / BEHIND THOSE SWINGING DOORS .... *Bluebird B-11282* 5-8 41
(Vocals: Del Porter)

SIAM (Vocals: King Jackson, Del Porter, & Carl Grayson) / COME, JOSEPHINE, IN MY FLYING MACHINE (Vocals: King Jackson & The Boys In The Back Room) .... *Bluebird B-11560* 5-8 42

TENNESSEE WALTZ (Vocals: Sara Berner assisted by Sir Frederick Gas) / I HAVEN'T BEEN HOME FOR THREE WHOLE NIGHTS (Vocal: Dick Morgan) .... *RCA Victor 20-4011* 4-6 50

WILD, WILD WOMEN, THE (Vocal: Del Porter) / HOTCHA CORNIA (sound effects by Willie Spicer) .... *Bluebird B-0818* 5-8 42

WILLIAM TELL OVERTURE / THE MAN ON THE FLYING TRAPEZE .... *RCA Victor 20-2861* 5-8 48
(Vocals: Doodles Weaver)

JONES, Spike & His Other Orchestra

LAURA (Vocals: Jimmy Cassidy, Red Ingle, & Dr. Horatio Q. Birdbath) / WHEN YUBA PLAYS THE RHUMBA ON THE TUBA .... *RCA Victor 20-2118* 5-8 47

MINKA / LASSUS TROMBONE ... *RCA Victor 20-1983* 5-8 47

JORDAN, Louis, & His Tympany Five

(Louis Jordan: 7/8/08 – 2/4/75)

BEWARE / DON'T LET THE SUN CATCH YOU CRYIN' .... *Decca 18818* 3-5 46
(Vocals: Louis Jordan)

BOUNCE THE BALL / DON'T COME CRYIN' ON MY SHOULDER .... *Decca 3253* 3-5 40
(Vocals: Louis Jordan)

CALDONIA / SOMEBODY DONE CHANGED THE LOCK ON THE DOOR .... *Decca 8670* 4-6 42
(Vocals: Louis Jordan)

CHICKEN AIN'T NOTHIN' BUT A BIRD, A / I KNOW YOU (I KNOW WHAT YOU WANNA DO) ... *Decca 8501* 5-8 40
(Vocals: Louis Jordan)

FLAT FACE / DOUG THE JITTERBUG (Vocal: Louis Jordan) .... *Decca 7590* 5-8 39

'FORE DAY BLUES / YOU AIN'T NOWHERE .... *Decca 7693* 5-8 40
(Vocals: Louis Jordan)

HAVE YOU GOT THE GUMPTION / ROAMIN' BLUES .... *Decca 24571* 3-5 49
(Vocals: Louis Jordan)

HONEYSUCKLE ROSE / BUT I'LL BE BACK .... *Decca 7675* 5-8 40
(Vocals: Louis Jordan)

HOW 'BOUT THAT? / THE GREEN GRASS GREW ALL AROUND .... *Decca 8605* 5-8 42
(Vocals: Louis Jordan)

I KNOW WHAT YOU'RE PUTTIN' DOWN / JACK, YOU'RE DEAD .... *Decca 23901* 3-5 47
(Vocals: Louis Jordan)

I'M GONNA LEAVE YOU ON THE OUTSKIRTS OF TOWN / IT'S A LOW-DOWN DIRTY SHAME .... *Decca 8638* 5-8 42
(Vocals: Louis Jordan)

JAKE, WHAT A SNAKE / YOU'RE MY MEAT (Vocal: Louis Jordan) .... *Decca 7719* 5-8 40

JUNE TENTH JAMBOREE / I'M ALABAMA BOUND .... *Decca 7723* 5-8 40
(Vocals: Louis Jordan)

KEEP A-KNOCKIN' / AT THE SWING CATS' BALL .... *Decca 7609* 5-8 39
(Vocals: Louis Jordan)

KNOCK ME A KISS / I'M GONNA MOVE TO THE OUTSKIRTS OF TOWN .... *Decca 8593* 5-8 42
(Vocals: Louis Jordan)

LOVIE JOE (Vocal: Mabel Robinson) / SOMEBODY DONE HOODOOED THE HOODOO MAN (Vocal: Louis Jordan) .... *Decca 7745* 5-8 40

MAMA MAMA BLUES / SMALL TOWN BOY .... *Decca 8627* 5-8 42
(Vocals: Louis Jordan)

OH BOY, I'M IN THE GROOVE / WAITIN' FOR THE ROBERT E. LEE .... *Decca 3360* 4-6 40
(Vocals: Louis Jordan)

PENTHOUSE IN THE BASEMENT / NEVER LET YOUR LEFT HAND KNOW WHAT YOUR RIGHT HAND'S DOIN' .... *Decca 7777* 5-8 40
(Vocals: Louis Jordan)

PINETOP'S BOOGIE WOOGIE / T-BONE BLUES (Vocal: Louis Jordan) .... *Decca 8525* 5-8 41

POMPTON TURNPIKE (Vocal: Louis Jordan) / DO YOU CALL THAT A BUDDY? (Vocals: Louis Jordan, & The Tympany Five) .... *Decca 8500* 5-8 40

RATION BLUES / DEACON JONES .... *Decca 8654* 5-8 42
(Vocals: Louis Jordan)

RECONVERSION BLUES / SALT PORK, WEST VIRGINIA .... *Decca 18762* 4-6 46
(Vocals: Louis Jordan)

RUN JOE / ALL FOR THE LOVE OF LIL .... *Decca 24448* 2-4 48
(Vocals: Louis Jordan)

SAM JONES DONE SNAGGED HIS BRITCHES (Vocal: Louis Jordan) / SWINGIN' IN THE COCOANUT TREES .... *Decca 7623* 5-8 39

SATURDAY NIGHT FISH FRY / SATURDAY NIGHT FISH FRY, PART II .... *Decca 24725* 4-6 49
(Vocals: Louis Jordan)

SAXA-WOOGIE (Vocals: The Tympany Five) / BROTHERLY LOVE (Vocal: Louis Jordan) .... *Decca 8560* 5-8 41

STONE COLD DEAD IN THE MARKET / PETOOTIE PIE .... *Decca 23546* 3-5 46
(Vocals: Ella Fitzgerald & Louis Jordan)

ST. VITUS DANCE / BOOGIE WOOGIE CAME TO TOWN .... *Decca 8581* 5-8 41
(Vocals: Louis Jordan)

THAT CHICK'S TOO YOUNG TO FRY / CHOO CHOO CH'BOOGIE .... *Decca 23610* 3-5 46
(Vocals: Louis Jordan)

THAT'LL JUST 'BOUT KNOCK ME OUT / FIVE GUYS NAMED MOE .... *Decca 8653* 4-6 42
(Vocals: Louis Jordan)

TWO LITTLE SQUIRRELS (NUTS TO YOU) / PAN-PAN .... *Decca 8537* 5-8 41
(Vocals: Louis Jordan)

WHAT'S THE USE OF GETTING SOBER / THE CHICKS I PICK ARE SLENDER AND TENDER AND TALL .... *Decca 8645* 4-6 42
(Vocals: Louis Jordan)

YEAH, YEAH, BABY / PUT SOME MONEY IN THE POT, BOY 'CAUSE THE JUICE IS RUNNING LOW.................. *Aladdin 3264* 5-8 48
(Vocals: Louis Jordan)

YOU CAN'T GET THAT NO MORE / MOP! MOP!.................... *Decca 8668* 4-6 42
(Vocals: Louis Jordan)

YOU GOT TO GO WHEN THE WAGON COMES (Vocal: Daisy Winchester) / AFTER SCHOOL SWING SESSION...................... *Decca 7729* 5-8 40

YOU RUN YOUR MOUTH AND I'LL RUN MY BUSINESS (Vocal: Louis Jordan) / HARD LOVIN' BLUES (Vocal: Yack Taylor)............... *Decca 7705* 5-8 40

JORDAN, Louis, as Louis Jordan's Elks Rendezvous Band

HONEY IN THE BEE BALL / BARNACLE BILL THE SAILOR.......................... *Decca 7556* 5-8 39
(Vocals: Louis Jordan)

JORDAN, Taft, & The Mob
(Taft Jordan: 2/15/15 –)

DEVIL IN THE MOON / LOUISIANA FAIRY TALE....................... *Banner 33398* 8-10 35

DEVIL IN THE MOON / LOUISIANA FAIRY TALE.................... *Melotone M-13365* 8-10 35

DEVIL IN THE MOON / LOUISIANA FAIRY TALE.......................... *Oriole 3124* 8-10 35

DEVIL IN THE MOON / LOUISIANA FAIRY TALE........................ *Perfect 16102* 8-10 35

DEVIL IN THE MOON / LOUISIANA FAIRY TALE.......................... *Romeo 2498* 8-10 35
(Simultaneously released on five labels)

NIGHT WIND / IF THE MOON TURNS GREEN..................... *Banner 33385* 8-10 35

NIGHT WIND / IF THE MOON TURNS GREEN................. *Melotone M-13352* 8-10 35

NIGHT WIND / IF THE MOON TURNS GREEN....................... *Oriole 3115* 8-10 35

NIGHT WIND / IF THE MOON TURNS GREEN....................... *Perfect 16094* 8-10 35

NIGHT WIND / IF THE MOON TURNS GREEN...................... *Romeo 2489* 8-10 35
(Simultaneously released on five labels)

JOYCE, Teddy, & His Penn State Recorders

COLLEGIATE SAM / GOTTA FEELIN' FOR YOU............... *Harmony 1009-H* 8-10 29
(Vocals: Teddy Joyce)

JOY, Jimmy, as Jimmie's Joys
(Jimmy Joy's surname was Maloney. In the 1920s, there was a comic strip, "Joy And Gloom," that he liked so much that Jimmy adopted the name Joy as his professional name.)

BUGLE CALL RAG / ST. LOUIS BLUES............................ *Golden B-1865* 15-20 23

NO NO NORA / TIGER RAG........... *Golden B-1858* 15-20 23

JOY, Jimmy, as Jimmy Joy's Baker Hotel Orchestra

BE YOURSELF / WILD JAZZ............. *Okeh 40420* 10-12 25

HAY FOOT, STRAW FOOT / EVERYBODY STOMP.................................. *Okeh 40504* 8-10 25

INDIAN DAWN / CHINA GIRL........... *Okeh 40381* 8-10 25

MEMPHIS BOUND / RIVERBOAT SHUFFLE............................. *Okeh 40388* 12-15 25

MY SWEET GAL / ST. LOUIS BLUES..... *Okeh 40539* 10-12 25

RED HOT HENRY BROWN / FALLIN' DOWN......................... *Okeh 40494* 10-12 25

JOY, Jimmy, as Jimmy Joy's Orchestra

FROM MONDAY ON (Vocal: Orville Andrews) / THE YALE BLUES (Vocals: by trio) ... *Brunswick 3905* 8-10 28

HARMONICA HARRY / CAN'T YOU UNDERSTAND?.................. *Brunswick 4640* 12-15 29
(Vocals: Unkown)

YOU'RE THE FIRST THING I THINK OF IN THE MORNING / I GOT WORRY.... *Brunswick 3959* 8-10 28
(Vocals: by trio)

JOY, Jimmy, as Jimmy Joy's St. Anthony's Hotel Orchestra

CLARINET MARMALADE BLUES / COMMON STREET BLUES (by the Scranton Sirens Orchestra)......................... *Okeh 40329* 10-12 25

MILENBERG JOYS / MAMA WILL BE GONE....................... *Okeh 40251* 10-12 24

JOY, Leonard, & His String Dance Orchestra
also see HIGH HATTERS, The

I'M NEEDIN' YOU / WHERE CAN YOU BE?........................ *Victor 22467* 2-4 30
(Vocals: Frank Luther)

US AND COMPANY / I'LL STILL BELONG TO YOU.................... *Victor 22569* 2-4 30
(Vocals: Chester Gaylord)

JUNGLE BAND, The:
see CALLOWAY, Cab, & His Orchestra and see ELLINGTON, Duke, & His Orchestra

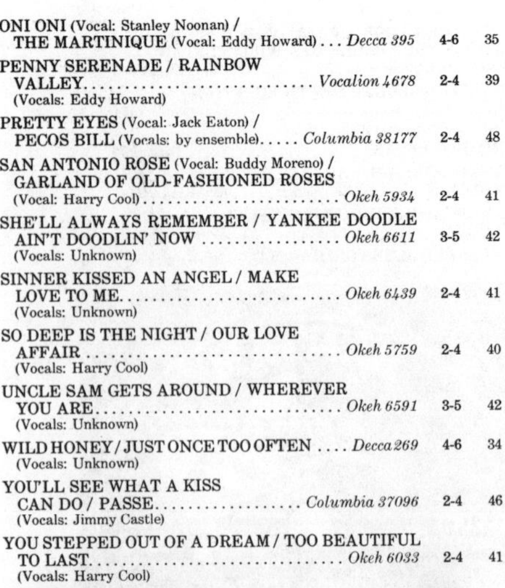

JURGENS, Dick, & His Orchestra
(Dick Jurgens: 1/9/10 –)

ALL I REMEMBER IS YOU / RAGTIME COWBOY JOE....................... *Vocalion 4901* 2-4 39
(Vocals: Eddy Howard)

ALONG THE SANTA FE TRAIL / SWEET MOLLY MALONE.............................. *Okeh 5858* 2-4 40
(Vocals: Harry Cool)

BESSIE COULDN'T HELP IT (Vocal: Ronnie Kemper) / HER NAME WAS ROSITA (Vocal: Harry Cool)........................... *Okeh 5552* 3-5 40

BESSIE COULDN'T HELP IT (Vocal: Ronnie Kemper) / HER NAME WAS ROSITA (Vocal: Harry Cool)..................... *Vocalion 5552* 3-5 40
(Simultaneously released on two labels)

BLUEBIRDS IN THE MOONLIGHT / FAITHFUL FOREVER............. *Conqueror 9339* 2-4 39
(Vocals: Eddy Howard)

BLUEBIRDS IN THE MOONLIGHT / FAITHFUL FOREVER............... *Vocalion 5181* 2-4 39
(Vocals: Eddy Howard)
(Simultaneously released on two labels)

CECILIA (Vocal: Ronnie Kemper) / LOVE SONG OF RENALDO (Vocals: Eddy Howard, Ronnie Kemper, & Carl Brandt)................... *Okeh 5405* 2-4 40

CECILIA (Vocal: Ronnie Kemper) / LOVE SONG OF RENALDO (Vocals: Eddy Howard, Ronnie Kemper, & Carl Brandt)................ *Vocalion 5405* 2-4 40
(Simultaneously released on two labels)

DAY DREAMS COME TRUE AT NIGHT (theme song) / MISSOURI WALTZ............ *Vocalion 5313* 2-4 39
(Vocals: Eddy Howard)

EASY TO LOVE / I'VE GOT YOU UNDER MY SKIN................. *Melotone 6-12-04* 3-5 36
(Vocals: Unknown)

ELMER'S TUNE / A SINNER KISSED AN ANGEL (Vocals: Unknown)........ *Conqueror 9890* 2-4 41

ELMER'S TUNE / YOU'RE THE SUNSHINE OF MY HEART (Vocal: Harry Cool)............... *Okeh 6209* 2-4 41

GARDEN OF THE MOON / BAMBINA.... *Vocalion 4321* 3-5 38
(Vocals: Eddy Howard)

GOODBYE, LITTLE DARLIN', GOODBYE / DANCING ON A DIME........................... *Okeh 5801* 2-4 40
(Vocals: Harry Cool)

IN AN OLD DUTCH GARDEN / I CONCENTRATE ON YOU......... *Conqueror 9476* 2-4 40
(Vocals: Eddy Howard)

IN THE QUIET OF THE NIGHT / STRANGE..................... *Decca 268* 4-6 34
(Vocals: Unknown)

I ONLY WANT A BUDDY — NOT A SWEETHEART / CARELESS....................... *Conqueror 9340* 2-4 39
(Vocals: Eddy Howard)

I ONLY WANT A BUDDY — NOT A SWEETHEART / CARELESS........................ *Vocalion 5235* 2-4 39
(Vocals: Eddy Howard)
(Simultaneously released on two labels)

IT'S LOVE I'M AFTER / YOU'RE SLIGHTLY TERRIFIC....................... *Melotone 6-12-08* 3-5 36
(Vocals: Unknown)

LILACS IN THE RAIN / IF I KNEW THEN..................... *Conqueror 9393* 3-5 39
(Vocals: Eddy Howard)

LILACS IN THE RAIN / IF I KNEW THEN...................... *Vocalion 5074* 3-5 39
(Vocals: Eddy Howard)
(Simultaneously released on two labels)

LITTLE SIR ECHO / PENNY SERENADE....................... *Conqueror 9176* 2-4 39
(Vocals: Eddy Howard)

LITTLE SIR ECHO / RED SKIES IN THE NIGHT..................... *Vocalion 4677* 2-4 39
(Vocals: Eddy Howard)

MAMA'S GONE, GOODBYE / SIDE BY SIDE (Vocals: Jimmy Castle & the band).... *Columbia 38107* 2-4 48

NIGHT AND DAY / MY SILENT LOVE..... *Okeh 6022* 2-4 41
(Vocals: Harry Cool)

ONI ONI (Vocal: Stanley Noonan) / THE MARTINIQUE (Vocal: Eddy Howard)... *Decca 395* 4-6 35

PENNY SERENADE / RAINBOW VALLEY............................ *Vocalion 4678* 2-4 39
(Vocals: Eddy Howard)

PRETTY EYES (Vocal: Jack Eaton) / PECOS BILL (Vocals: by ensemble)..... *Columbia 38177* 2-4 48

SAN ANTONIO ROSE (Vocal: Buddy Moreno) / GARLAND OF OLD-FASHIONED ROSES (Vocal: Harry Cool)........................ *Okeh 5934* 2-4 41

SHE'LL ALWAYS REMEMBER / YANKEE DOODLE AIN'T DOODLIN' NOW................. *Okeh 6611* 3-5 42
(Vocals: Unknown)

SINNER KISSED AN ANGEL / MAKE LOVE TO ME.......................... *Okeh 6439* 2-4 41
(Vocals: Unknown)

SO DEEP IS THE NIGHT / OUR LOVE AFFAIR................................ *Okeh 5759* 2-4 40
(Vocals: Harry Cool)

UNCLE SAM GETS AROUND / WHEREVER YOU ARE.............................. *Okeh 6591* 3-5 42
(Vocals: Unknown)

WILD HONEY / JUST ONCE TOO OFTEN.... *Decca 269* 4-6 34
(Vocals: Unknown)

YOU'LL SEE WHAT A KISS CAN DO / PASSE.................. *Columbia 37096* 2-4 46
(Vocals: Jimmy Castle)

YOU STEPPED OUT OF A DREAM / TOO BEAUTIFUL TO LAST.............................. *Okeh 6033* 2-4 41
(Vocals: Harry Cool)

KAHN, Art, & His Orchestra

BAHAMA / SHANGHAI LULLABY.... *Columbia 45-D* 3-5 24

BIT BY BIT, YOU'RE BREAKING MY HEART / SOBBIN' BLUES.................. *Columbia 16-D* 3-5 23

BLUE EVENING BLUES / ALL BROKEN UP OVER YOU (by Paul Specht & His Hotel Alamac Orchestra).................. *Columbia 104-D* 3-5 24

BY THE WATERS OF MINNETONKA / PEACEFUL VALLEY.............. *Columbia 490-D* 2-4 25

CO-ED, THE / BACK HOME IN ILLINOIS...................... *Columbia 468-D* 2-4 25
(Vocals: Marty Livingston)

DON'T MIND THE RAIN / THERE'S YES! YES! IN YOUR EYES...................... *Columbia 109-D* 2-4 24

FOLLOW THE SWALLOW / THE LITTLE OLD CLOCK ON THE MANTEL................ *Columbia 212-D* 2-4 24

GILDA / OFF AND GONE........... *Columbia 221-D* 3-5 24

GLAD / THERE'S NOBODY ELSE BUT YOU.................. *Columbia 111-D* 2-4 24

HELLO BABY (Vocal: Ruth Etting) / WHILE THE YEARS GO DRIFTING BY................. *Columbia 716-D* 4-6 26

HE'S THE LAST WORD / HELLO! SWANEE, HELLO!........ *Columbia 830-D* 2-4 27
(Vocals: Unknown)

HOBO'S PRAYER / WHAT A MAN!... *Columbia 624-D* 3-5 26

I AIN'T GOT NOBODY / HOODLE-DEE-DOO-DEE-DOO-DOO (Vocals: Unknown).... *Columbia 769-D* 3-5 26

INSUFFICIENT SWEETIE / YOU SHOULD HAVE TOLD ME.................. *Columbia 294-D* 2-4 25

MORNING / PATSY (by Paul Specht & His Hotel Alamac Orchestra)........... *Columbia 215-D* 3-5 24

SOME OF THESE DAYS / LUCKY KENTUCKY......................... *Columbia 310-D* 3-5 25

TIE ME TO YOUR APRON STRINGS AGAIN (Vocal: Ned Miller) / TALKING TO THE MOON... *Columbia 582-D* 3-5 26

KAHN, Art, & His Orchestra or as Art Kahn's Orchestra:
see GOODMAN, Benny, & His Orchestra
see KARDOS, Gene, & His Orchestra
see MAYHEW, Nye, & His Orchestra, and
see PAYNE, Art, & His Orchestra

KAHN, Roger Wolfe, & His Hotel Biltmore Orchestra
(Roger Wolfe Kahn: 10/19/07 – 7/12/62)

HOT-HOT-HOTTENTOT / YEARNING (Vocal: Elliott Shaw)......... *Victor 19616* 3-5 25

I'M SITTING ON TOP OF THE WORLD / I NEVER KNEW.............. *Victor 19845* 4-6 26

LITTLE BUNGALOW, A / LUCKY BOY... *Victor 19860* 3-5 26

LOOK WHO'S HERE! / BAM-BAM-BAMMY SHORE........... *Victor 19808* 3-5 25

KAHN, Roger Wolfe, & His Orchestra

ADORABLE (Vocals: Gladys Rice & Carl Mathieu) / YOU NEED SOMEONE TO LOVE (by George Olsen & His Music; Vocals: Fran Frey, Bob Borger, & Bob Rice)... *Victor 20106* 3-5 26

ANOTHER NIGHT ALONE (Vocal: Del Porter) / SHELTERED BY THE STARS, CRADLED BY THE MOON (Vocals: The Kahn-A-Sirs)...... *Columbia 2697-D* 5-8 32

AT PEACE WITH THE WORLD (Vocal: Henry Burr) / I'D CLIMB THE HIGHEST MOUNTAIN..... *Victor 20045* 3-5 26

BABY (Vocal: Billy Jones) / LANTERN OF LOVE................. *Victor 19942* 3-5 26

BIRDIE (whistling by Sibyl Sanderson Fagan) / TAMIAMI TRAIL (by Whitey Kaufman & His Orchestra)... *Victor 19996* 3-5 26

CLAP YO' HANDS / DO-DO-DO (by George Olsen & His Music; Vocals: Fran Frey, Bob Berger, & Bob Rice)............................ *Victor 20327* 4-6 27

COOKING BREAKFAST FOR THE ONE I LOVE / WHEN A WOMAN LOVES A MAN.... *Brunswick 4699* 5-8 30
(Vocals: Libby Holman)

CROSS YOUR HEART (Vocal: Henry Burr) / MOUNTAIN GREENERY............. *Victor 20071* 3-5 26

CUP OF COFFEE, A SANDWICH AND YOU, A / SONG OF THE FLAME.................... *Victor 19935* 4-6 26

DARK NIGHT / INTO MY HEART.... *Brunswick 4811* 5-8 30
(Vocals: Scrappy Lambert)

DO WHAT YOU DO / LIZA........... *Brunswick 4479* 5-8 29
(Vocals: Unknown)

EXACTLY LIKE YOU / ON THE SUNNY SIDE OF THE STREET........... *Brunswick 4742* 5-8 30
(Vocals: Libby Holman)

FIT AS A FIDDLE (Vocals: The Kahn-A-Sirs) / JUST A LITTLE HOME FOR THE OLD FOLKS (Vocal: Del Porter)...... *Columbia 2726-D* 5-8 32

GREAT DAY / WITHOUT A SONG.... *Brunswick 4600* 5-8 29
(Vocals: William C. Elkins Jubilee Singers)

IMAGINATION / CRAZY RHYTHM...... *Victor 21368* 5-8 28
(Vocals: Franklyn Baur)

IN A BAMBOO GARDEN (Vocal: Frank Munn) / ANYTHING YOU SAY (Vocal: Johnny Marvin).................. *Victor 21675* 5-8 28

JERSEY WALK / HALF A MOON (by Nat Shilkret & The Victor Orchestra; Vocal: Johnny Marvin)...... *Victor 20231* 4-6 26

LAZY DAY (Vocal: Dick Robertson) / MY SILENT LOVE (Vocal: Elmer Feldkamp)....... *Columbia 2653-D* 5-8 32

LITTLE BIRDIE TOLD ME SO, A (Vocal: Johnny Marvin) / SUNNY DISPOSISH (by Gene Goldkette & His Orchestra; Vocals: Lewis James, Charles Harrison, Elliot Shaw & Wilfred Glenn).................. *Victor 20493* 8-10 27

MONTANA CALL / THE MOON IS LOW.......................... *Brunswick 4750* 5-8 30
(Vocals: Unknown)

PRETTY LITTLE THING / HEIGH-HO, EVERYBODY, HEIGH-HO....................... *Brunswick 4374* 5-8 29
(Vocals: Frank Munn)

ROOM WITH A VIEW / DANCE, LITTLE LADY...................... *Victor 21801* 5-8 29
(Vocals: Franklyn Baur)

SHADY LADY (Vocal: Scrappy Lambert as Burt Lorin) / YOU'RE THE ONLY ONE FOR ME..... *Victor 21897* 5-8 29

SHINE ON YOUR SHOES (Vocals: Unknown) / IT DON'T MEAN A THING (IF IT AIN'T GOT THAT SWING) (Vocals: The Kahn-A-Sirs)........... *Columbia 2722-D* 8-10 32

THEN YOU'VE NEVER BEEN BLUE / THROUGH!............... *Brunswick 4571* 5-8 29
(Vocals: Unknown)

THERE I GO DREAMING AGAIN (Vocal: Dick Robertson) / TELL ME WHY YOU SMILE, MONA LISA (Vocal: Elmer Feldkamp)............ *Columbia 2662-D* 5-8 32

TING-A-LING, THE BELLS'LL RING / WHY DO YOU WANT TO KNOW WHY? (by George Olsen & His Music; Vocals: Fran Frey, Bob Borger, & Bob Rice)... *Victor 20116* 3-5 26

TONIGHT YOU BELONG TO ME (Vocal: Franklyn Baur) / I'VE GOT THE GIRL (by George Olsen & His Music; Vocal: Fran Frey)...................... *Victor 20359* 4-6 27

'TWAS NOT SO LONG AGO / DON'T EVER LEAVE ME...................... *Brunswick 4614* 5-8 29
(Vocals: Unknown)

WHY WAS I BORN? / HERE AM I.... *Brunswick 4583* 5-8 29
(Vocals: Unknown)

YANKEE ROSE / I'M LOOKING OVER A FOUR LEAF CLOVER (by Jean Goldkette & His Orchestra; Vocal: Billy Murray)....... *Victor 20466* 8-10 27

YOU'RE A REAL SWEETHEART (Vocal: Frank Munn) / LONELY LITTLE BLUEBIRD (Vocal: Franklyn Baur.................. *Victor 21510* 4-6 28

YOU'VE GOT ME IN THE PALM OF YOUR HAND (Vocals: The Kahn-A-Sirs) / I CAN'T BELIEVE IT'S TRUE (Vocals: Unknown)........ *Columbia 2695-D* 5-8 32

KAPLAN, Dave, as The Happiness Orchestra

BARBARA / COQUETTE............ *Herwin 8060* 12-15 28
(Vocals: Billy Jones)

IN THE EVENING / PERSIAN RUG..... *Herwin 8075* 12-15 28
(Vocals: Ernest Hare)

SWEET ELLA MAY / ONE STEP TO HEAVEN......................... *Gennett 6538* 4-6 28
(Vocals: Billy Jones)

KARDOS, Gene, & His Orchestra

ALEXANDER'S RAGTIME BAND / GLORY........................... *Victor 22920* 3-5 32
(Vocals: Dick Robertson)

BREEZE (THAT'S BRINGIN' MY HONEY BACK TO ME) / FRECKLE FACE, YOU'RE BEAUTIFUL......................... *Vocalion 2746* 3-5 34
(Vocals: Joe Hostetter)

BUSINESS IN F (Vocals: Gene Kardos & orchestra) / CORN-FED GAL (Vocal: Joel Shaw)....... *Victor 22899* 5-8 32

DON'T LET YOUR LOVE GO WRONG / MOON COUNTRY...... *Vocalion 2717* 3-5 34
(Vocals: Dick Robertson)

DOWN ON THE FARM (Vocals: Gene Kardos & Dick Robertson) / SWEET VIOLETS (Vocal: Dick Robertson).................. *Victor 22863* 3-5 32

EARFUL OF MUSIC, AN (Vocal: Bea Wain) / O. K. TOOTS (Vocal: Chick Bullock)....... *Vocalion 2815* 3-5 34

FREDDY THE FRESHMAN / NOW'S THE TIME TO FALL IN LOVE...................... *Victor 22865* 4-6 32
(Vocals: Dick Robertson)

HOT DOG, A BLANKET AND YOU, A (Vocals: by orchestra) / WHAT ARE YOU THINKIN' ABOUT, BABY? (Vocal: Dick Robertson)... *Victor 22840* 4-6 31

IN OTHER WORDS, WE'RE THROUGH / LOVE LOCKED OUT...................... *Banner 32962* 3-5 34
(Vocals: Chick Bullock)

IN OTHER WORDS, WE'RE THROUGH / LOVE LOCKED OUT.................. *Melotone M-12912* 3-5 34
(Vocals: Chick Bullock)

IN OTHER WORDS, WE'RE THROUGH / LOVE LOCKED OUT.......................... *Oriole 2818* 3-5 34
(Vocals: Chick Bullock)

IN OTHER WORDS, WE'RE THROUGH / LOVE LOCKED OUT....................... *Perfect 15882* 3-5 34
(Vocals: Chick Bullock)

IN OTHER WORDS, WE'RE THROUGH / LOVE LOCKED OUT........................ *Romeo 2211* 3-5 34
(Vocals: Chick Bullock)
(Simultaneously released on five labels)

LEARNING / STARS FELL ON ALABAMA...................... *Vocalion 2794* 3-5 34
(Vocals: Paul Small)

LOVE IS HERE TO STAY (Vocal: Lee Russell) / LOVE WALKED IN (Vocal: Pat Henry)....... *Conqueror 8994* 3-5 38

MEAN MUSIC (Vocal: Dick Robertson) / CHINA BOY........................... *Victor 22790* 5-8 31

MY EXTRAORDINARY GAL / WHEN NOBODY ELSE IS AROUND......................... *Victor 22986* 3-5 32
(Vocals: Dick Robertson)

PETER AND PAUL (Vocals: by orchestra) / YOU'VE GOT TO SELL IT (Vocals: Gene Kardos & orchestra)................. *Victor 22843* 5-8 31

SADDLE YOUR BLUES TO A WILD MUSTANG (Vocal: Al Lane) / WEST WIND (Vocal: Bea Wain).................... *Conqueror 8648* 4-6 36

SAILIN' ON THE ROBERT E. LEE / THE SUN'S IN MY HEART...................... *Victor 22957* 4-6 32
(Vocals: Dick Robertson)

SPELLBOUND / I NEVER HAD A CHANCE.................... Vocalion 2745 3-5 34
(Vocals: Joe Hostetter)

SWEET OF YOU (Vocal: Bea Wain) / IF I HAD A MILLION DOLLARS (Vocal: Chick Bullock)......... *Vocalion 2814* 3-5 34

TALKIN' TO MYSELF (Vocal: Paul Small) / THE CONTINENTAL................ *Vocalion 2795* 3-5 34

TELL TALES / YOU'RE FOOLIN' YOURSELF .... *Victor 22897* 4-6 32
(Vocals: Dick Robertson)

WAITING FOR THE MOON / RED-HEADED BABY........................... *Victor 22792* 4-6 31
(Vocals: Dick Robertson)

WHAT WILL I TELL MY HEART? / BOO-HOO............... *Conqueror 8797* 3-5 37
(Vocals: Dick Robertson)

WHAT WILL I TELL MY HEART? / BOO-HOO.............. *Melotone 7-04-03* 3-5 37
(Vocals: Dick Robertson)
(Simultaneously released on two labels)

WITH MY EYES WIDE OPEN I'M DREAMING / ALL I DO IS DREAM OF YOU.............. *Vocalion 2722* 3-5 34
(Vocals: Dick Robertson)

KARDOS, Gene, & His Orchestra as Ralph Bennett & His Seven Aces

HIGH SOCIETY / SING (IT'S GOOD FOR YA) (Vocal: Chick Bullock)....... *Melotone M-12491* 4-6 32

LOVE ME TONIGHT / ISN'T IT ROMANTIC?................. *Melotone M-12479* 3-5 32
(Vocals: Ralph Kirberry)

KARDOS, Gene, & His Orchestra as Rex Blaine & His Orchestra

IS I IN LOVE? I IS / I GOT THE POTATOES – I GOT THE TOMATOES (BUT SOMEONE ELSE HAS GOT MY GIRL).................... *Electradisk 1802* 20-25 32
(Vocals: Rex Blaine)
(An early 8-inch Electradisk, exceptionally rare.)

KARDOS, Gene, & His Orchestra as Chick Bullock & His Levee Loungers

FORTY-SECOND STREET / SHUFFLE OFF TO BUFFALO................... *Perfect 15729* 4-6 33
(Vocals: Dick Robertson)

HERE IT IS MONDAY AND I'VE STILL GOT A DOLLAR / MY RIVER HOME....... *Banner 32625* 3-5 33
(Vocals: Chick Bullock)

HERE IT IS MONDAY AND I'VE STILL GOT A DOLLAR / MY RIVER HOME... *Melotone M-12558* 3-5 33
(Vocals: Chick Bullock)

HERE IT IS MONDAY AND I'VE STILL GOT A DOLLAR / MY RIVER HOME......... *Oriole 2609* 3-5 33
(Vocals: Chick Bullock)

HERE IT IS MONDAY AND I'VE STILL GOT A DOLLAR / MY RIVER HOME....... *Perfect 15707* 3-5 33
(Vocals: Chick Bullock)

HERE IT IS MONDAY AND I'VE STILL GOT A DOLLAR / MY RIVER HOME........ *Romeo 1983* 3-5 33
(Vocals: Chick Bullock)
(Simultaneously released on five labels)

IS I IN LOVE? / WHY DON'T YOU GET LOST?..................... *Perfect 15607* 3-5 32
(Vocals: Chick Bullock)

KARDOS, Gene, & His Orchestra as Jean Calloway & Orchestra

SADIE THE SHAKER / THERE OUGHT TO BE A LAW AGAINST THAT...................... *Victor 22959* 4-6 32
(Vocals: Dick Robertson)

KARDOS, Gene, & His Orchestra as Dickson's Harlem Orchestra

JAM MAN (Vocal: Dick Robertson) / JAZZ RONDO......................... *Victor 23377* 8-10 32

KARDOS, Gene, & His Orchestra as Elliot Everett & His Orchestra

HE'S IN THE JAILHOUSE NOW / CHARLIE THE CHISELLER .... *Victor 22987* 4-6 32
(Vocals: Dick Robertson)

KARDOS, Gene, & His Orchestra, as Gene's Merrymakers

HONEYMOON HOTEL / SHANGHAI LIL..................... *Banner 32862* 4-6 33
(Vocals: Dick Robertson)

HONEYMOON HOTEL / SHANGHAI LIL .... *Conqueror 8248* 4-6 33
(Vocals: Dick Robertson)

HONEYMOON HOTEL / SHANGHAI LIL .... *Melotone M-12789* 4-6 33
(Vocals: Dick Robertson)

HONEYMOON HOTEL / SHANGHAI LIL....................... *Oriole 2758* 4-6 33
(Vocals: Dick Robertson)

HONEYMOON HOTEL / SHANGHAI LIL..................... *Perfect 15818* 4-6 33
(Vocals: Dick Robertson)

HONEYMOON HOTEL / SHANGHAI LIL .... *Romeo 2131* 4-6 33
(Vocals: Dick Robertson)
(Simultaneously released on six labels)

I BEG YOUR PARDON, MADEMOISELLE / GOOFUS .... *Perfect 15609* 3-5 32
(Vocals: Dick Robertson)

LET'S ALL SING LIKE THE BIRDIES SING / I LIKE MOUNTAIN MUSIC .... *Banner 32717* 2-4 33
(Vocals: Dick Robertson)

LET'S ALL SING LIKE THE BIRDIES SING / I LIKE MOUNTAIN MUSIC .... *Melotone M-12646* 2-4 33
(Vocals: Dick Robertson)

LET'S ALL SING LIKE THE BIRDIES SING / I LIKE MOUNTAIN MUSIC .... *Perfect 15744* 2-4 33
(Vocals: Dick Robertson)

LET'S ALL SING LIKE THE BIRDIES SING / I LIKE MOUNTAIN MUSIC .... *Romeo 2039* 2-4 33
(Vocals: Dick Robertson)
(Simultaneously released on four labels)

OLD FASHIONED LOVE / MILENBERG JOYS .... *Perfect 15693* 4-6 32

PINK ELEPHANTS (Vocal: Harry Goldfield as "Goldie") / LISTEN TO THE GERMAN BAND (Vocal: Dick Robertson) .... *Banner 32618* 3-5 33

PINK ELEPHANTS (Vocal: Harry Goldfield as "Goldie") / LISTEN TO THE GERMAN BAND (Vocal: Dick Robertson) .... *Conqueror 8082* 3-5 33

PINK ELEPHANTS (Vocal: Harry Goldfield as "Goldie") / LISTEN TO THE GERMAN BAND (Vocal: Dick Robertson) .... *Melotone M-12535* 3-5 33

PINK ELEPHANTS (Vocal: Harry Goldfield as "Goldie") / LISTEN TO THE GERMAN BAND (Vocal: Dick Robertson) .... *Oriole 2604* 3-5 33

PINK ELEPHANTS (Vocal: Harry Goldfield as "Goldie") / LISTEN TO THE GERMAN BAND (Vocal: Dick Robertson) .... *Perfect 15698* 3-5 33
(Simultaneously released on five labels)

SHAME ON YOU / THERE'S A NEW MOON OVER MY SHOULDER .... *Banner 32852* 3-5 33
(Vocals: Dick Robertson)

SHAME ON YOU / THERE'S A NEW MOON OVER MY SHOULDER .... *Melotone M-12779* 3-5 33
(Vocals: Dick Robertson)

SHAME ON YOU / THERE'S A NEW MOON OVER MY SHOULDER .... *Oriole 2753* 3-5 33
(Vocals: Dick Robertson)

SHAME ON YOU / THERE'S A NEW MOON OVER MY SHOULDER .... *Perfect 15813* 3-5 33
(Vocals: Dick Robertson)

SHAME ON YOU / THERE'S A NEW MOON OVER MY SHOULDER .... *Romeo 2126* 3-5 33
(Vocals: Dick Robertson)
(Simultaneously released on five labels)

KARDOS, Gene, & His Orchestra as The Gloria Palace Orchestra

(These releases are early eight-inch Electradisks, exceptionally rare)

LULLABY OF THE LEAVES / I'M SO ALONE WITH THE CROWD .... *Electradisk 1807* 20-25 32
(Vocals: Rex Blaine)

REMEMBER, CHERIE / MY SILENT LOVE .... *Electradisk 1803* 20-25 32
(Vocals: Rex Blaine)

KARDOS, Gene, & His Orchestra as Art Kahn's Orchestra

FORTY-SECOND STREET / SHUFFLE OFF TO BUFFALO .... *Banner 32676* 4-6 33
(Vocals: Dick Robertson)

FORTY-SECOND STREET / SHUFFLE OFF TO BUFFALO .... *Conqueror 8115* 4-6 33
(Vocals: Dick Robertson)

FORTY-SECOND STREET / SHUFFLE OFF TO BUFFALO .... *Melotone M-12605* 4-6 33
(Vocals: Dick Robertson)

FORTY-SECOND STREET / SHUFFLE OFF TO BUFFALO .... *Oriole 2643* 4-6 33
(Vocals: Dick Robertson)

FORTY-SECOND STREET / SHUFFLE OFF TO BUFFALO .... *Romeo 2016* 4-6 33
(Vocals: Dick Robertson)
(Simultaneously released on five labels)

GOLD DIGGERS' SONG / PETTIN' IN THE PARK .... *Banner 32763* 5-8 33
(Vocals: Chick Bullock)

GOLD DIGGERS' SONG / PETTIN' IN THE PARK .... *Melotone M-12692* 5-8 33
(Vocals: Chick Bullock)

GOLD DIGGERS' SONG / PETTIN' IN THE PARK .... *Oriole 2696* 5-8 33
(Vocals: Chick Bullock)

GOLD DIGGERS' SONG / PETTIN' IN THE PARK .... *Perfect 15768* 5-8 33
(Vocals: Chick Bullock)

GOLD DIGGERS' SONG / PETTIN' IN THE PARK .... *Romeo 2069* 5-8 33
(Vocals: Chick Bullock)
(Simultaneously released on five labels)

KARDOS, Gene, & His Orchestra as Ralph Kirberry & His Orchestra

LOVE ME TONIGHT / ISN'T IT ROMANTIC? .... *Conqueror 8020* 3-5 32
(Vocals: Ralph Kirberry)

LOVE ME TONIGHT / ISN'T IT ROMANTIC? .... *Perfect 15672* 3-5 32
(Vocals: Ralph Kirberry)
(Simultaneously released on two labels)

NIGHTFALL / THREE KISSES .... *Perfect 15661* 3-5 32
(Vocals: Ralph Kirberry)

KARDOS, Gene, & His Orchestra as Ed Loyd & His Orchestra

FIT AS A FIDDLE / AH! BUT I'VE LEARNED .... *Banner 32622* 3-5 32
(Vocals: Chick Bullock)

FIT AS A FIDDLE / AH! BUT I'VE LEARNED .... *Melotone M-12534* 3-5 32
(Vocals: Chick Bullock)

FIT AS A FIDDLE / AH! BUT I'VE LEARNED .... *Oriole 2601* 3-5 32
(Vocals: Chick Bullock)

FIT AS A FIDDLE / AH! BUT I'VE LEARNED .... *Perfect 15702* 3-5 32
(Vocals: Chick Bullock)

FIT AS A FIDDLE / AH! BUT I'VE LEARNED .... *Romeo 1978* 3-5 32
(Vocals: Chick Bullock)
(Simultaneously released on five labels)

WILLOW, WEEP FOR ME / LONESOME AND BLUE .... *Banner 32640* 4-6 33
(Vocals: Dick Robertson)

WILLOW, WEEP FOR ME / LONESOME AND BLUE .... *Melotone M-12566* 4-6 33
(Vocals: Dick Robertson)

WILLOW, WEEP FOR ME / LONESOME AND BLUE .... *Oriole 2617* 4-6 33
(Vocals: Dick Robertson)

WILLOW, WEEP FOR ME / LONESOME AND BLUE .... *Perfect 15713* 4-6 33
(Vocals: Dick Robertson)

WILLOW, WEEP FOR ME / LONESOME AND BLUE .... *Romeo 1993* 4-6 33
(Vocals: Dick Robertson)
(Simultaneously released on five labels)

YOUNG AND HEALTHY / YOU'RE GETTING TO BE A HABIT WITH ME .... *Banner 32675* 4-6 33
(Vocals: Dick Robertson)

YOUNG AND HEALTHY / YOU'RE GETTING TO BE A HABIT WITH ME .... *Melotone M-12606* 4-6 33
(Vocals: Dick Robertson)

YOUNG AND HEALTHY / YOU'RE GETTING TO BE A HABIT WITH ME .... *Oriole 2642* 4-6 33
(Vocals: Dick Robertson)

YOUNG AND HEALTHY / YOU'RE GETTING TO BE A HABIT WITH ME .... *Romeo 2015* 4-6 33
(Vocals: Dick Robertson)
(Simultaneously released on four labels)

KARDOS, Gene, & His Orchestra as The New Yorkers

(The Electradisk releases are early eight-inch records, exceptionally rare.)

BANKING ON THE WEATHER / HAVING A GOOD TIME – WISH YOU WERE HERE ... *Electradisk 1808* 20-25 32
(Vocals: Rex Blaine)

WHEN THE LIGHTS ARE SOFT AND LOW / EV'RY LITTLE BIT OF ME .... *Electradisk 1800* 20-25 32
(Vocals: Rex Blaine)

WHO, BESIDES ME / CRAZY PEOPLE ... *Victor 24009* 4-6 32
(Vocals: Dick Robertson)

KARDOS, Gene, & His Orchestra as The Pennsylvania Collegians

BANKING ON THE WEATHER / IN A SHANTY IN OLD SHANTY TOWN .... *Electradisk 2503* 15-20 32
(Vocals: Rex Blaine)
(This ten-inch Electradisk release is rare)

KASSEL, Art, & His Kassels-In-The-Air

(Art Kassel: 1/18/96 – 2/3/65)

ALEXANDER THE SWOOSE (Vocal: Marion Holmes) / LITTLE SLEEPY HEAD (Vocal: Harvey Crawford) .... *Bluebird B-10990* 2-4 41

CHANT OF THE SWAMP / RAGGIN' THE SCALE (by The Joe Venuti-Eddie Lang Blue Five) ... *Columbia 2765-D* 10-12 33
(This record was pressed in blue shellac)

DOODLE-DOO-DOO (early theme song) (Vocals: by trio) / THE ONE ROSE (Vocal: Billy Leach) ... *Bluebird B-7184* 3-5 37

HELL'S BELLS (later theme song) / O. K. AMERICA .... *Columbia 2682-D* 5-8 32
(Vocals: Ralph Morris, Ding Johnson, & Floyd Townes)

(WHERE WILL YOU BE) IN 1933? (official song of the Chicago World's Fair, composed by Art Kassel; Vocals: Unknown) / CENTURY OF PROGRESS MARCH .... *Columbia 2745-D* 5-8 33

JUNE IN JANUARY / WITH EVERY BREATH I TAKE .... *Bluebird B-5727* 3-5 34
(Vocals: Norm Ruvell)

KNOCKING AT YOUR DOOR (Vocals: The Kassel Trio) / DO I WORRY? (Vocals: Harvey Crawford & The Kassel Trio) .... *Bluebird B-11073* 2-4 41

MUSIC, MAESTRO, PLEASE / CABIN IN THE CAROLINES .... *Bluebird B-7619* 3-5 38
(Vocals: Billy Leach)

MY HEART'S AT EASE / RAIN, RAIN, GO AWAY .... *Columbia 2687-D* 4-6 32
(Vocals: Unknown)

NO OTHER ONE (Vocal: Art Kassel) / IT'S DANGEROUS TO LOVE LIKE THIS (Vocal: Grace Dunn) .... *Bluebird B-6154* 3-5 35

WE'RE HAVING A BABY (Vocals: The Kassel Trio) / ZOOT SUIT (Vocals: Gloria Hart & orchestra) ... *Bluebird B-11455* 3-5 42

YOU AIN'T GOT NO ROMANCE / RING THE BELL FOR UNCLE SAM .... *Bluebird B-11534* 3-5 42
(Vocals: by orchestra)

YOU MADE ME LOVE YOU (Vocals: Marion Holmes & Trio) / DON'T BE A WORRYBIRD (THE FLOOGIE-BOO SONG) (Vocals: by trio) .... *Bluebird B-11395* 2-4 42

KATZ, Al, & His Kittens

ACE IN THE HOLE / DEEP HENDERSON (by The Coon-Sanders Original Nighthawk Orchestra) ...... *Victor 20081* 5-8 26

KATZ, Al, & His Orchestra

I LIFT UP MY FINGER AND SAY "TWEET TWEET" / MY WIFE IS ON A DIET .... *Columbia 1997-D* 4-6 29
(Vocals: Unknown)

I MAY BE WRONG, BUT I THINK YOU'RE WONDERFUL / A YEAR FROM TODAY ..... *Columbia 1971-D* 4-6 29
(Vocals: Unknown)

KATZMAN, Louis, & The Brunswick Orchestra

MY MAN (Vocal: Vaughn de Leath) / I'D RATHER BE BLUE (Vocal: Dick Robertson) .... *Brunswick 4213* 3-5 29

REDSKIN (Vocal: Vaughn de Leath) / DARDANELLA .... *Brunswick 4218* 3-5 29

KATZMAN, Louis, & His Orchestra

CARIOCA / BESAME .... *Decca 111* 3-5 34

CONTINENTAL, THE / FASCINATION ..... *Decca 109* 4-6 34

DUST ON THE MOON / WINE SONG .... *Decca 221* 4-6 34
(Vocals: Walter Preston)

HAVE YOU FORGOTTEN? / COME TO ME .... *Perfect 15496* 3-5 3
(Vocals: Frank Munn)

LA CUCARACHA / INCA TANGO .... *Decca 110* 3-5 34

LOVE GOES ON JUST THE SAME (Vocal: Paul Small) / WHY DID IT HAVE TO BE ME? (Vocal: Chick Bullock) .... *Perfect 15546* 3-5 32

ORCHIDS IN THE MOONLIGHT / TANGO DREAMS .... *Decca 201* 3-5 34

PEANUT VENDOR, THE / FIESTA .... *Decca 202* 3-5 34

KATZMAN, Louis, & His Orchestra as The Colonial Club Orchestra

I DARE NOT LOVE YOU / THE ROAD OF DREAMS .... *Brunswick 3034* 3-5 26

WHEN YUBA PLAYS THE RHUMBA ON THE TUBA / PARDON ME, PRETTY BABY .... *Perfect 15497* 3-5 31
(Vocals: Dick Robertson)

KATZMAN, Louis, as Katzman's Orchestra recorded under the name The Badgers

SNAKE HIPS / BARNEY GOOGLE .... *Paramount 20211* 10-12 23

KATZMAN, Louis, as Katzman's Orchestra recorded under the name The Melody Dance Players

SNAKES HIPS / BARNEY GOOGLE ... *Harmograph 795* 8-10 23

KATZ, Mickey, & His Kosher-Jammers

HAIM AFEN RANGE (HOME ON THE RANGE) / YIDDISH SQUARE DANCE ... . *Victor 25-5081* 4-6 45

KAUFMAN, Whitey, & His Orchestra

DEEP RIVER BLUES / TINY TOWN ..... *Victor 20125* 4-6 26

TAMIAMI TRAIL / BIRDIE (by Roger Wolfe Kahn & His Orchestra; whistling: Sibyl Sanderson Fagan) ... *Victor 19996* 3-5 26

KAUFMAN, Whitey, as Whitey Kaufman's Original Pennsylvania Serenaders

COME ON, RED / UNFORTUNATE BLUES .... *Victor 19384* 4-6 24

HURRY BACK, OLD SWEETHEART OF MINE / MY GIRL .... *Victor 19673* 3-5 25

IN A CHARLESTON CABIN / FROM ONE TILL TWO (Vocal: Elliott Shaw) .... *Victor 19304* 3-5 24

KAVELIN, Al, & His Blackstone Hotel Orchestra

SWEETEST LITTLE BROWN EYES (Vocal: Don Pedro) / CARIBBEAN STAR .... *Decca 1358* 3-5 37

UNDERNEATH A PALM BEACH MOON (Vocal: Don Pedro) / RENITA BONITA ..... *Decca 1191* 3-5 37

KAVELIN, Al, & His Cascading Chords

PRACTICE MAKES PERFECT (Vocal: Bill Darnell) / THE SWISS BELLRINGER (Vocals: Marlyn Stuart & Bill Darnell) .... *Okeh 5746* 2-4 40

SOME RAINY DAY (Vocal: Patti Morgan) / LOVE, I'D GIVE MY LIFE FOR YOU (Vocal: Al Shelladay) .... *Vocalion 4634* 3-5 39

WHATEVER HAPPENED TO YOU? / WHO DREAMED YOU UP? .... *Okeh 5829* 2-4 40
(Vocals: Bill Darnell)

KAVELIN, Al, & His Orchestra

BLUE MOON (Vocal: Jerry Ray) / I THRILL WHEN THEY MENTION YOUR NAME (Vocal: Cole Coleman) ...... *Vocalion 2868* 3-5 35

DANCING WITH MY SHADOW (Vocal: Cole Coleman) / THE CHURCH BELLS TOLD (Vocal: Jerry Ray) .... *Vocalion 2869* 3-5 35

IT'S YOU / TANGO ORIENTAL .... *Decca 1113* 3-5 37

JUNE IN JANUARY / WITH EVERY BREATH I TAKE .... *Vocalion 2845* 3-5 34
(Vocals: Cole Coleman)

LOVE HAS GONE (theme song) (Vocal: Brooks Temple) / 'WAY DOWN SOUTH IN NORTH CAROLINA (Vocal: Nancy White) .... *Vocalion 2824* 3-5 34

KAYE, Sammy, as Swing And Sway With Sammy Kaye
(Sammy Kaye: 3/13/10 –)
(Sammy Kaye had the most hit singles of all the big bands. Kaye is now 76, and he and his band continue to play better spots coast to coast.)

ALIBI BABY (Vocal: Jimmy Brown) / WHY DO YOU PASS ME BY? (Vocal: Tommy Ryan) .... *Vocalion 3556* 3-5 37

BLUEBERRY HILL / MAYBE .... *Victor 26643* 2-4 40
(Vocals: Tommy Ryan)

DADDY (Vocals: The Kaye Choir) / TWO HEARTS THAT PASS IN THE NIGHT (Vocal: Arthur Wright) .... *Victor 27391* 2-4 41

DEAR MOM (Vocal: Allan Foster) / REMEMBER PEARL HARBOR (Vocals: The Glee Club) .... *Victor 27738* 3-5 42

DREAM VALLEY / A NIGHTINGALE SANG IN BERKELEY SQUARE .... *Victor 26795* 2-4 40
(Vocals: Tommy Ryan)

GOOD MORNIN' (Vocals: The Three Barons) / STRANGERS IN THE DARK (Vocal: Charlie Wilson) .... *Vocalion 3618* 3-5 37

I CAN'T AFFORD TO DREAM / LET'S MAKE MEMORIES TONIGHT .... *Victor 26285* 2-4 39
(Vocals: Clyde Burke)

I CAN'T BEGIN TO TELL YOU (Vocal: Nancy Norman) / WHAT MAKES THE SUNSET? (Vocals: Billy Williams) .... *Victor 20-1720* 2-4 45

I LEFT MY HEART AT THE STAGE DOOR CANTEEN (Vocal: Don Cornell) / SOUTH WIND (Vocal: Allan Foster) .... *Victor 27932* 3-5 42

I'VE GOT A POCKETFUL OF DREAMS (Vocals: The Three Barons) / DON'T LET THAT MOON GET AWAY (Vocal: Charlie Wilson) .... *Vocalion 4226* 3-5 38

I'VE NEVER FORGOTTEN (Vocal: Betty Barclay) / LAUGHING ON THE OUTSIDE, CRYING ON THE INSIDE (Vocal: Billy Williams)..... *RCA Victor 20-1856* 2-4 46

JOSEPHINE / AVALON (Vocal: Jimmy Brown) .... *Vocalion 3681* 2-4 37

MISS AMERICANA (Vocal: Don Cornell) / YOU CAN'T SAY NO TO A SOLDIER (Vocals: Three Kadets) .... *Victor 27952* 3-5 42

MOON LOVE (Vocal: Clyde Burke) / SHAVE AND A HAIRCUT SHAMPOO (Vocals: Sammy Kaye & chorus) .... *Victor 26279* 2-4 39

PLEASE TAKE A LETTER, MISS BROWN (Vocal: Clyde Burke) / SIERRA SUE (Vocal: Tommy Ryan) .... *Victor 26540* 2-4 40

SEEING YOU AGAIN DID ME NO GOOD (Vocal: Tommy Ryan) / SOMEBODY ELSE IS TAKING MY PLACE (Vocal: Allan Foster) .... *Victor 27757* 2-4 42

SHABBY OLD CABBY (Vocals: The Three Barons) / COUNTERPOINT A LA MODE .... *Victor 26298* 2-4 39

SWING AND SWAY (Vocals: The Three Barons) / MY BUDDY (Vocals: Tommy Ryan & The Glee Club) .... *Vocalion 3669* 3-5 37

SWING IS HERE TO SWAY / THE DIPSY DOODLE .... *Vocalion 3849* 3-5 37
(Vocals: Jimmy Brown)

TABOO (Vocals: Tommy Ryan, Don Cornell & The Glee Club) / IF I CARED A LITTLE BIT LESS (Vocal: Don Cornell) .... *Victor 27972* 2-4 42

THERE WILL NEVER BE ANOTHER YOU (Vocal: Nancy Norman) / LET'S BRING NEW GLORY TO OLD GLORY (Vocals: Tommy Ryan & octet) ... *Victor 27949* 3-5 42

THREE BELLS, THE (Vocal: Tony Russo) / I ONLY HAVE ONE LIFE TO LIVE (Vocals: The Kaydets & The Kaye Choir) .... *Columbia 39602* 2-4 51

TOMORROW NIGHT (Vocal: Clyde Burke) / SCATTER-BRAIN (Vocal: Charlie Wilson) .... *Victor 26387* 2-4 39

WHEN YOU WISH UPON A STAR (Vocal: Tommy Ryan) / TURN ON THE OLD MUSIC BOX (Vocal: Clyde Burke) .... *Victor 26455* 3-5 40

WHITE CLIFFS OF DOVER (Vocal: Arthur Wright) / MADELAINE (Vocal: Allan Foster) .... *Victor 27704* 3-5 42

WHITE SAILS (Vocal: Clyde Burke) / STAIRWAY TO THE STARS (Vocal: Jimmy Brown) .... *Victor 26267* 2-4 39

YOU'RE GONNA SEE A LOT OF ME (Vocal: Charlie Wilson) / THE UMBRELLA MAN (Vocals: The Three Barons) .... *Victor 26117* 2-4 39

ZIP-A-DEE DOO-DAH (Vocals: The Three Kaydets) / SOONER OR LATER (Vocal: Betty Barclay) .... *RCA Victor 20-1976* 2-4 46

KAY, Herbie, & His Orchestra
(Herbie Kay: circa 1904 – 5/11/44)

GLORIANNA (Vocals: Unknown) / IT'S ALL SO NEW TO ME (Vocal: King Harvey) .... *Vocalion 4752* 4-6 39

PETER, PETER, PUMPKIN EATER / VIOLETS AND FRIENDS (theme song) (Vocals: The Kay Kwire) .... *Columbia 36135* 4-6 39

Y'HAD IT COMIN' TO YOU (Vocal: Wynne Fair) / BY CANDLELIGHT (Vocals: King Harvey & The Kay Kwire) .... *Vocalion 4820* 5-8 39

KEATING, Lloyd, & His Music / Lloyd Keating's Music:
see LANIN, Sam, & His Famous Players & Singers
see RICH, Fred, & His (La Palina) orchestra
see RICH, Fred, & His Orchestra and
see SELVIN, Ben, & His Orchestra

KELLY, George, & The Original Six

ANGEL CHILD / SHE'S A MEAN JOB ..... *Okeh 4546* 3-5 22

DON'T FORGET / EYES .... *Okeh 4574* 2-4 22

HE MAY BE YOUR MAN, BUT HE COMES TO SEE ME SOMETIMES / WHOA, TILLIE, TAKE YOUR TIME! .... *Okeh 4774* 3-5 23

JUMP STEADY BLUES / SING-SONG MAN ... *Okeh 4655* 3-5 22

'WAY DOWN YONDER IN NEW ORLEANS / THE THIEF .... *Okeh 4778* 3-5 23

KEMP, Hal, & His Orchestra
(Hal Kemp: 3/27/05 – 12/21/40)

BLUE EVENING / YOURS FOR A SONG ... *Victor 26247* 2-4 39
(Vocals: Bob Allen)

BOOM! (Vocal: Maxine Gray) / S'POSIN' (Vocals: Bob Allen) .... *Victor 26241* 2-4 39

BRIDE COMES HOME, THE / I'M GONNA SIT RIGHT DOWN AND WRITE MYSELF A LETTER .... *Brunswick 7601* 4-6 36
(Vocals: Skinnay Ennis)

BY SPECIAL PERMISSION OF THE COPYRIGHT OWNERS (I LOVE YOU) (Vocal: Skinnay Ennis) / WOULD YOU LIKE TO TAKE A WALK? (Vocals: Hal Kemp, Saxie Dowell, & Skinnay Ennis) .... *Brunswick 6055* 5-8 31

CAN'T GET INDIANA OFF MY MIND / I JUST COULDN'T TAKE IT, BABY .... *Victor 26655* 2-4 40
(Vocals: Bob Allen)

DON'T WORRY 'BOUT ME / WHAT GOES UP MUST COME DOWN (AND BABY, YOU'VE BEEN FLYIN' TOO HIGH) .... *Victor 26188* 2-4 39
(Vocals: Bob Allen)

FOGGY DAY IN LONDON, A (Vocal: Skinnay Ennis) / THINGS ARE LOOKING UP (Vocal: Bob Allen) .... *Victor 25685* 2-4 37

FORTY-SECOND STREET (Vocals: Unknown) / SHUFFLE OFF TO BUFFALO (Vocal: Skinnay Ennis) .... *Brunswick 6471* 4-6 33

GET OUT AND GET UNDER THE MOON (Vocals: Hal Kemp, Saxie Dowell & Skinnay Ennis) / OH, BABY! (Vocal: Skinnay Ennis) .... *Brunswick 3954* 4-6 28

GIVE YOURSELF A PAT ON THE BACK / IF I HAD A GIRL LIKE YOU .... *Brunswick 4807* 5-8 30
(Vocals: Unknown)

GLOOMY SUNDAY / DESIRE .... *Brunswick 7630* 4-6 36
(Vocals: Bob Allen)

GOODNIGHT, ANGEL (Vocal: Bob Allen) / SWINGIN' IN THE CORN (Vocal: Saxie Dowell) .... *Victor 25722* 3-5 38

GOT A DATE WITH AN ANGEL / LAMPLIGHT .... *Victor 25651* 2-4 37

GOT TO DANCE MY WAY TO HEAVEN (Vocal: Bob Allen) / I NEARLY LET LOVE GO SLIPPING THROUGH MY FINGERS (Vocal: Skinnay Ennis) ...... *Brunswick 7668* 4-6 36

HEART OF STONE / YOU'VE GOT ME CRYING AGAIN .... *Victor 26165* 2-4 39
(Vocals: Bob Allen)

HURT / THEM THERE EYES .... *Brunswick 4992* 4-6 30
(Vocals: Unknown)

I DIDN'T KNOW WHAT TIME IT WAS (Vocal: Bob Allen) / LOVER NEVER WENT TO COLLEGE (Vocals: The Smoothies) .... *Victor 26368* 2-4 39

IF I CAN'T HAVE YOU / MARY ANN ... *Brunswick 3792* 4-6 28
(Vocals: Hal Kemp, Saxie Dowell, & Skinnay Ennis)

IT IT'S GOOD (THEN I WANT IT) (Vocal: Fredda Gibson) / SUNRISE SERENADE .... *Victor 26215* 2-4 39
(Fredda Gibson was later known as Georgia Gibbs)

I'M KEEPIN' COMPANY / UNDER YOUR WINDOW TONIGHT .... *Brunswick 6130* 4-6 31
(Vocals: Skinnay Ennis)

I'SE A MUGGIN' (Vocals: Unknown) / I DON'T WANT TO MAKE HISTORY (Vocal: Maxine Gray) ... *Brunswick 7636* 4-6 36

IT ALL COMES BACK TO ME NOW (Vocal: Bob Allen) / TALKIN' TO MY HEART (Vocal: Janet Blair) .... *Victor 27255* 2-4 41
(Janet Blair later became a motion picture star)

IT'S ONLY A PAPER MOON / NIGHT OWL .... *Brunswick 6648* 4-6 33
(Vocals: Skinnay Ennis)

I'VE GOT A POCKETFUL OF DREAMS (Vocal: Judy Starr) / DON'T LET THAT MOON GET AWAY (Vocal: Bob Allen) ..... *Victor 25896* 2-4 38

I'VE GOT NO STRINGS (Vocal: Janet Blair) / GIVE A LITTLE WHISTLE (Vocals: The Smoothies) ... *Victor 26466* 2-4 40

I'VE GOT YOU UNDER MY SKIN (Vocal: Skinnay Ennis) / EASY TO LOVE (Vocals: Unknown) .... *Brunswick 7745* 3-5 36

I WOKE UP TOO SOON / IN A BLUE AND PENSIVE MOOD .... *Brunswick 7351* 4-6 35
(Vocals: Bob Allen)

JAZZ ME BLUES / DODGING A DIVORCEE .... *Brunswick 7458* 5-8 35

JUST A LITTLE FLOWER SHOP AROUND THE CORNER / YOU'VE GOT ME CRYING AGAIN .... *Brunswick 6528* 4-6 33
(Vocals: Unknown)

LILACS IN THE RAIN (Vocal: Nan Wynn) / THE GIRL WITH THE PIGTAILS IN HER HAIR (Vocals: The Smoothies) .... *Victor 26385* 2-4 39

LITTLE KISS EACH MORNING / I LOVE YOU, BELIEVE ME, I LOVE YOU .... *Brunswick 4612* 5-8 30
(Vocals: Unknown)

LOVE FOR SALE (Vocals: The Smoothies) / PARADISE (Vocal: Nan Wynn) .... *Victor 26278* 2-4 39

LOVE IN BLOOM / STRAIGHT FROM THE SHOULDER .... *Brunswick 6943* 4-6 34
(Vocals: Skinnay Ennis)

LOVEY / LOW DOWN UPON THE HARLEM RIVER .... *Brunswick 6532* 5-8 33
(Vocals: Unknown)

LULLABY OF BROADWAY / THE WORDS ARE IN MY HEART .... *Brunswick 7369* 4-6 35
(Vocals: Bob Allen)

MARY DEAR / GO, JOE, GO .... *Brunswick 3536* 5-8 27

MY OLD MAN (Vocal: Skinnay Ennis) / PUDDIN' HEAD JONES (Vocal: Deane Janis) .... *Brunswick 6703* 4-6 34

NIGHT IS FILLED WITH MUSIC / I USED TO BE COLOR BLIND .... *Victor 26009* 2-4 38
(Vocals: Bob Allen)

OOH! WHAT YOU SAID (Vocals: The Smoothies) / 'WAY BACK IN 1939 A. D. (Vocal: Bob Allen) .... *Victor 26449* 2-4 40

ORGAN GRINDER, THE / HELL'S BELLS .... *Brunswick 6436* 5-8 33
(Vocals: Unknown)

PEG LEG STOMP / BLUE RHYTHM .... *Columbia 671-D* 5-8 26

PETTIN' IN THE PARK / THE GOLD DIGGER'S SONG .... *Brunswick 6582* 4-6 33
(Vocals: Skinnay Ennis)

POWERHOUSE / IN DUTCH WITH THE DUCHESS .... *Victor 25718* 3-5 38

PURSUIN' THE BLUES / B'WANGA ... *Brunswick 7730* 4-6 36

SERENADE FOR A WEALTHY WIDOW / GOT A DATE WITH AN ANGEL (Vocal: Skinnay Ennis) .... *Brunswick 7319* 3-5 34

SHE LOVES ME JUST THE SAME / FRATERNITY BLUES ..... *Brunswick 4988* 4-6 30
(Vocals: Unknown)

SNOWBALL / LOVE IS THE SWEETEST THING .... *Brunswick 6636* 4-6 33
(Vocals: Skinnay Ennis)

SO DO IT (Vocal: Skinnay Ennis) / PENNIES FROM HEAVEN (Vocal: Maxine Gray) .... *Brunswick 7749* 3-5 36

STOP! YOU'RE BREAKING MY HEART (Vocal: Skinnay Ennis) / WHISPERS IN THE DARK (Vocal: Bob Allen) .... *Victor 25598* 2-4 37

THANK YOUR STARS (Vocal: Bob Allen) / PLAYMATES (Vocals: The Smoothies) ..... *Victor 26469* 2-4 40

THAT MOMENT OF MOMENTS (Vocal: Bob Allen) / I CAN'T GET STARTED (Vocal: Skinnay Ennis) .... *Brunswick 7600* 3-5 36

THERE'S A SMALL HOTEL / IT'S GOT TO BE LOVE .... *Brunswick 7634* 3-5 36
(Vocals: Unknown)

THREE LITTLE FISHIES (Vocals: The Smoothies) / THE CHESTNUT TREE (Vocal: Saxie Dowell) .... *Victor 26204* 2-4 39

TIME ON MY HANDS (Vocal: Nan Wynn) / LET'S DO IT (Vocals: by trio) .... *Victor 26300* 2-4 39

TOUCH OF YOUR LIPS, THE (Vocal: Skinnay Ennis) / LOST (Vocal: Bob Allen) .... *Brunswick 7626* 3-5 36

WALKIN' BY THE RIVER / SO YOU'RE THE ONE .... *Victor 27222* 2-4 40
(Vocals: Janet Blair ... who later became a motion picture star)

WASHINGTON AND LEE SWING / HIGH UP ON A HILL-TOP .... *Brunswick 4078* 4-6 28
(Vocals: Hal Kemp, Saxie Dowell & Gus Mayhew)

WASHIN' THE BLUES FROM MY SOUL / I REMEMBER YOU FROM SOMEWHERE .... *Brunswick 4805* 5-8 30
(Vocals: Unknown)

WHEN I'M WITH YOU (Vocal: Skinnay Ennis) / BUT DEFINITELY (Vocal: Maxine Gray) .... *Brunswick 7681* 3-5 36

WHO'S BLUE NOW? (Vocals: Hal Kemp, Saxie McDowell, & Skinnay Ennis) / DIDN'T I TELL YOU (Vocal: Skinnay Ennis) .... *Brunswick 3841* 4-6 28

WORKOUT / THE BRIDE COMES HOME (Vocal: Bob Allen) .... *Victor 26662* 3-5 40

WOULDJA MIND? (Vocal: Claire Martin) / CONFUCIUS SAY (Vocals: The Smoothies) .... *Victor 26452* 2-4 40

KEMP, Hal, as The Carolina Club Orchestra

ALLAH'S HOLIDAY / SHINE ON, HARVEST MOON (Vocal: Saxie Dowell) .... *Melotone M-12202* 3-5 31

BYE-BYE BABY / EVERYBODY LOVES MY BABY .... *Pathe Actuelle 036181* 4-6 25

BYE-BYE BABY / EVERYBODY LOVES MY BABY .... *Perfect 14362* 3-5 25
(Simultaneously released on two labels)

CAROLINA (Vocals: Unknown) / HOW I'LL MISS YOU (WHEN SUMMER IS GONE) .... *Okeh 41337* 5-8 29

CONSTANTLY (Vocal: Gus Mayhew) / IF YOU HAVEN'T GOT LOVE (Vocal: Skinnay Ennis) .... *Melotone M-12167* 3-5 31

I FOUND A MILLION-DOLLAR BABY (Vocal: Skinnay Ennis) / SING A LITTLE JINGLE (Vocals: Unknown) .... *Melotone M-12177* 4-6 31

I'M ALWAYS CHASING RAINBOWS / ALLAH'S HOLIDAY .... *Okeh 41409* 4-6 29

I'M ALWAYS THINKING OF SOMEONE / HURRY BACK, OLD SWEETHEART OF MINE ..... *Pathe Actuelle 036245* 4-6 25

I'M ALWAYS THINKING OF SOMEONE / HURRY BACK, OLD SWEETHEART OF MINE ... *Perfect 14426* 3-5 25
(Simultaneously released on two labels)

MEMORIES / GLORY TO GEORGIA (Vocals: Unknown) .... *Okeh 41336* 5-8 29

SOMEBODY MIGHTY LIKE YOU / MISS WONDERFUL .... *Okeh 41309* 5-8 29
(Vocals: Unknown)

WALKING WITH SUSIE (Vocal: Saxie Dowell) / THAT'S YOU, BABY (Vocals: by quartet) .... *Okeh 41237* 4-6 29

KENDIS, Sonny, & His Stork Club Orchestra

DIGA DIGA DOO / A PRETTY GIRL IS LIKE A MELODY (Vocal: Sonny Schuyler as Sonny Saunders) .... *Columbia 36396* 3-5 41

STAR DUST / IF I HAD YOU (Vocal: Sonny Schuyler as Sonny Saunders) .... *Columbia 36395* 3-5 41

STUMBLING / MY BLUE HEAVEN (Vocal: Sonny Schuyler as Sonny Saunders) .... *Columbia 36397* 3-5 41

YOU'RE THE CREAM IN MY COFFEE / MY BUDDY (Vocal: Sonny Schuyler as Sonny Saunders) .... *Columbia 36398* 3-5 41

KENIN, Herman, & His Ambassador Hotel Orchestra
(Herman Kenin: circa 1901 – 7/21/70)

HE'S A GOOD MAN TO HAVE AROUND / I'M THE LAST OF THE RED HOT MAMA'S ..... *Victor 22005* 4-6 29

THERE'S A PLACE IN THE SUN FOR YOU (Vocal: Ken Allen) / THAT'S WHAT I CALL SWEET MUSIC (Vocal: Ted O'Hara ...... *Victor 22006* 3-5 29

WALKIN' AROUND IN A DREAM (Vocal: Ted O'Hara) / AFTER THINKING IT OVER (Vocal: Ken Allen) .... *Victor 21980* 3-5 29

KENIN, Herman, & His Multnomah Hotel Orchestra

ALL I WANT IS YOU / PRETTY LITTLE THING .... *Victor 20725* 3-5 27
(Vocals: Van Fleming)

CANOE AND YOU, A (Vocals: Vernon Leathers, Van Fleming, & Gene Dahlgren) / WHEN LOVE COMES STEALING (Vocal: Van Fleming) .... *Victor 21336* 2-4 28

PERSIAN RUG (Vocal: Van Fleming) / TREES (by Eddie Harkness & His Orchestra; Vocal: Harold Dana) .... *Victor 21313* 3-5 28

ROSE OF MONTEREY (Vocal: Van Fleming) / ROSE ROOM .... *Victor 21314* 3-5 28

SOME OTHER DAY (Vocals: Press Watkins & Van Fleming) / SAD 'N' BLUE (Vocal: Van Fleming) .... *Victor 20782* 3-5 27

KENNY, Ken, & His Orchestra:
see NORVO, Red, & His Orchestra

KENSINGTON SERENADERS, The:
see SELVIN, Ben, & His Orchestra

KENT, Larry, & His Orchestra

GOODNIGHT MY LOVE (Vocal: Arvon Dale) / ONE NEVER KNOWS, DOES ONE? (Vocal: Harriet Kaye) .... *Melotone 7-02-10* 3-5 37

KENTON, Stan, & His Orchestra
(Stan Kenton: 2/19/12 – 8/25/79)

BUT THEN YOU KISSED ME (Vocal: Jay Johnson) / EASY GO .... *Capitol 1191* 2-4 50

CURIOSITY (Vocal: June Christy) / THEME TO THE WEST .... *Capitol 15005* 2-4 46

EV'RY TIME WE SAY GOODBYE (Vocal: Gene Howard) / ARE YOU LIVIN' OLD MAN (Vocal: Anita O'Day) .... *Capitol 187* 2-4 45

HIS FEET TOO BIG FOR DE BED (Vocals: June Christy & The Pastels) / AFTER YOU (Vocals: The Pastels) .... *Capitol 361* 2-4 47

HOW AM I TO KNOW / HE WAS A GOOD MAN AS GOOD MEN GO (Vocal: June Christy) .... *Capitol 15327* 2-4 49

LADY IN RED, THE / UNDER A BLANKET OF BLUE .... *Capitol 2822* 2-4 52

SHOO FLY PIE (AND APPLE PAN DOWDY) (Vocal: June Christy) / I BEEN DOWN IN TEXAS (Vocals: June Christy, Gene Howard, Ray Wetzel, & Stan Kenton) .... *Capitol 235* 2-4 46

TAMPICO (Vocal: June Christy) / SOUTHERN SCANDAL .... *Capitol 202* 2-4 46

KENTUCKY GRASSHOPPERS, The:
see MILLS, Irving, & His Hotsy Totsy Gang

KENTUCKY SERENADERS, The:
see LANIN, Sam, as Lanin's Southern Serenaders

KERR, Charlie, as Charlie Kerr's Orchestra

GOOD MORNING, DEARIE / A SILVER CANOE .... *Edison 51070* 5-8 23

IN A CARAVAN / GONE (BUT STILL IN MY HEART) .... *Edison 51147* 5-8 23

MY SWEETIE WENT AWAY / OPHELIA ... *Edison 51194* 5-8 23

KERR, Charlie, as Kerr's Famous Players

WHAT DID I TELL YA? / GOODBYE .... *Gennett 3219* 5-8 25

KEYES, Frank, & His Orchestra:
see LANIN, Sam, & His Orchestra

KING, Henry, & His Orchestra

BREEZE, THE / DANCING AND DREAMING .... *Victor 24656* 3-5 34
(Vocals: Joe Sudy)

BUY A KISS / ROOF TOP SERENADE ... *Victor 24466* 3-5 34
(Vocals: Joe Sudy)

DANCING WITH MY SHADOW / I WOKE UP TOO SOON .... *Columbia 2992-D* 5-8 35
(Vocals: Joe Sudy)
(This record was pressed in blue shellac.)

EASTER PARADE / NOT FOR ALL THE RICE IN CHINA .... *Vocalion 2579* 3-5 33
(Vocals: Joe Sudy)

ENDING WITH A KISS / CALL OF LOVE ... *Victor 24608* 2-4 34
(Vocals: Joe Sudy)

FUNNY OLD HILLS / I HAVE EYES ...... *Decca 2198* 2-4 38
(Vocals: Don Raymond)

HEAR MY SONG VIOLETTA / I HEAR BLUEBIRDS .... *Decca 3093* 2-4 40
(Vocals: Tony Russell)

I'LL BE SEEING YOU / PALMS OF PARADISE .... *Decca 3072* 2-4 40
(Vocals: Bob Carroll)

IMAGE OF YOU, THE / WHERE OR WHEN .... *Decca 1319* 3-5 37
(Vocals: Joe Sudy)

LITTLE WHITE GARDENIA / BE CAREFUL, YOUNG LADY .... *Columbia 3005-D* 4-6 35
(Vocals: Joe Sudy)

LONELY FEET / JUST A FAIR WEATHER FRIEND .... *Columbia 2991-D* 5-8 35
(Vocals: Joe Sudy)

MAKE BELIEVE / OL' MAN RIVER .... *Decca 801* 3-5 36
(Vocals: Joe Sudy)

MARTINIQUE, THE / TELL ME THAT YOU LOVE ME .... *Columbia 3036-D* 5-8 35
(Vocals: Joe Sudy)

MY DAY BEGINS AND ENDS WITH YOU / A BLUES SERENADE (theme song) .... *Decca 1063* 3-5 36
(Vocals: Joe Sudy)

MY ROMANCE / LOVE IS LIKE A CIGARETTE .... *Decca 745* 3-5 36
(Vocals: Joe Sudy)

NEEDLE IN A HAYSTACK / DON'T LET IT BOTHER YOU .... *Columbia 2949-D* 5-8 34
(Vocals: Joe Sudy)
(This record was pressed in blue shellac.)

NIGHT OWL / IT'S ONLY A PAPER MOON .... *Vocalion 2550* 4-6 33
(Vocals: Dick Robertson)

OH, YOU BEAUTIFUL DOLL (Vocal: Siggy Lane) / DAY DREAMS COME TRUE AT NIGHT (Vocal: Tony Russell) .... *Decca 3057* 2-4 40

SAILBOAT IN THE MOONLIGHT / WHO'LL BE THE ONE THIS SUMMER? .... *Decca 1320* 3-5 37
(Vocals: Joe Sudy)

SOMEDAY I'LL FIND YOU / MY HEART STOOD STILL .... *Decca 1009* 3-5 36
(Vocals: Joe Sudy)

SO RARE / WHEN TWO LOVE EACH OTHER .... *Decca 1332* 3-5 37
(Vocals: Joe Sudy)

SWEET IS THE WORD FOR YOU / BLUE HAWAII .... *Decca 1177* 3-5 37
(Vocals: Joe Sudy)

SWEET MADNESS / ME FOR YOU FOREVER .... *Vocalion 2561* 4-6 33
(Vocals: Howard Phillips)

TEN FAMOUS RHUMBAS (a5-record album set) ... *Decca 16* 12-15 40
Individual records in the set, listed numerically (with value of each):
SIBONEY / HAVANA IS CALLING ME .... *Decca 2068* 2-4 -
PEANUT VENDOR, THE / JUNGLE DRUMS .... *Decca 2069* 2-4 -
SAY SI SI / TABU .... *Decca 2070* 2-4 -
MAMA INEZ / MARIA LA O .... *Decca 2071* 2-4 -
CACHITA / MY SHAWL .... *Decca 2072* 2-4 -

THERE'S A SMALL HOTEL / IT'S GOT TO BE LOVE .... *Decca 763* 3-5 36

WALTZ WAS BORN IN VIENNA, A / GLOOMY SUNDAY .... *Decca 743* 3-5 36
(Vocals: Joe Sudy)

WAY YOU LOOK TONIGHT, THE / A FINE ROMANCE .... *Decca 890* 3-5 36
(Vocals: Joe Sudy)

WHAT IS SWEETER? / TONIGHT MAY NEVER COME AGAIN .... *Vocalion 2573* 3-5 33
(Vocals: Joe Sudy)

WHEN I GROW TOO OLD TO DREAM (Vocal: Joe Sudy) / THE NIGHT IS YOUNG (Vocal: Don Reid) .... *Columbia 2998-D* 4-6 35
(This record was pressed in blue shellac.)

WHEN I'M WITH YOU / BUT DEFINITELY .... *Decca 804* 4-6 36
(Vocals: Joe Sudy)

YOU'VE GOT EVERYTHING / I'D BE TELLING A LIE .... *Vocalion 2562* 3-5 33
(Vocals: Joe Sudy)

KING, Henry, & His Orchestra as Don Walker & His Orchestra

AND I STILL DO! / FOR ALL WE KNOW .... *Vocalion 2766* 3-5 34
(Vocals: Joe Sudy)

LOVE IN BLOOM / STRAIGHT FROM THE SHOULDER .... *Vocalion 2767* 3-5 34
(Vocals: Joe Sudy)

ONE MINUTE TO ONE (Vocal: Ray Hunkel) / COUNT YOUR BLESSINGS (Vocal: Joe Sudy) .... *Vocalion 2599* 3-5 33

SMOKE GETS IN YOUR EYES / WHAT IS THERE TO SAY? .... *Vocalion 2607* 3-5 33
(Vocals: Joe Sudy)

KING, Rex, & His Sovereigns
see GOLD, Lou & His Orchestra

KING, Wayne, & His Orchestra
(Wayne King: 2/16/01 –)
(Wayne King regularly tours the country with his orchestra. The last living member of the original orchestra, violinist Herb Miska, and vocalist Nancy Evans are still featured.)

ANNIVERSARY WALTZ / SAILBOAT IN THE SKY (Vocals: Wayne King & Trio) .... *Victor 27741* 2-4 42

BROKEN MELODY (Vocals: Unknown) / WORRIED MIND (Vocals: Wayne King & Trio) .... *Victor 27373* 2-4 41

CORPORAL TAKES COMMAND, THE / TIME WAS (Vocals: Unknown) .... *Victor 27535* 2-4 41

DON'T TELL A LIE ABOUT ME, DEAR (AND I WON'T TELL THE TRUTH ABOUT YOU) / BE BRAVE, BELOVED .... *Victor 27871* 3-5 42
(Vocals: Linda Barrie)

ECHO SAYS NO, THE (Vocal: Wayne King) / RUSSIAN ROSE .... *Victor 27752* 2-4 42

GOBELUES (theme from the George Gobel Show) / RED PETTICOATS (Vocal: Nancy Evans) .... *Decca 29550* 2-4 -

I DON'T KNOW WHY (Vocals: Ernie Birchill, Andy Hansen, & Bill Egner) / GUILTY (Vocal: Ernie Birchill) ... *Victor 22817* 3-5 31

I SHOULD HAVE KNOWN YOU YEARS AGO / HE'S MY UNCLE .... *Victor 27201* 3-5 40
(Vocals: Buddy Clark)

I WONDER WHO'S KISSING HER NOW? (Vocal: Wayne King) / SMOKE GETS IN YOUR EYES ... *Victor 26329* 2-4 39

JUMPIN' JUPITER / DARLING, HOW YOU LIED (Vocals: Unknown) .... *Victor 27575* 2-4 41

LAMP OF MEMORY / DEEP IN THE HEART OF TEXAS (Vocals: Wayne King & Trio) .... *Victor 27808* 2-4 42

LONESOME, THAT'S ALL (Vocal: Wayne King) / 'TILL THE SANDS OF THE DESERT GROW COLD .... *Victor 26180* 2-4 39

MELODY OF LOVE (Franklyn McCormack recites 'Why I Love You" from Tony Wons' "Scrapbook") / NONE BUT THE LONELY HEART (Franklyn McCormack recites "Alone" by Robert J. Burdett) .... *Victor 27713* 3-5 41

MOON IS A SILVER DOLLAR, THE / KISS ME WITH YOUR EYES .... *Victor 26160* 3-5 39
(Vocals: Charles Farrell)

NONCHALANT / 'TAIN'T NO USE .... *Victor 25427* 3-5 36

ONE MORNING IN MAY / SONG OF SURRENDER (Vocals: Unknown) .... *Brunswick 6735* 3-5 34

PRINCE CHARMING / THE EVENING STAR .... *Brunswick 6540* 3-5 33

SALLY (Vocal: Tony Hillis) / IF I'M DREAMING (Vocal: Elmo Tanner) .... *Victor 22240* 3-5 30

SINGING HILLS, THE / ONE CIGARETTE FOR TWO .... *Victor 26475* 2-4 40
(Vocals: Wayne King)

SOMEBODY MIGHTY LIKE YOU / MOANIN' FOR YOU (by The Coon-Sanders Orchestra; Vocal: Joe Sanders) .... *Victor 22278* 5-8 30

SWAMP GHOSTS (Vocal: Burke Bivens) / GOOFUS .... *Victor 22600* 3-5 30

'TILL REVEILLE (Vocals: Unknown) / DAWN .... *Victor 27511* 2-4 41

TIME AND TIME AGAIN (Vocal: Unknown) / BLUE DANUBE .... *Victor 27516* 2-4 41

TIME CHANGES EVERYTHING (Vocals: Wayne King & Trio) / MISIRLOU .... *Victor 27694* 2-4 41

WABASH MOON (Vocals: Ernie Birchill, Andy Hansen, Bill Egner, & Johnny Kozel) / DREAM A LITTLE DREAM OF ME (Vocal: Ernie Birchill) .... *Victor 22643* 3-5 31

WALTZ YOU SAVED FOR ME, THE (theme song) / SONG OF THE ISLANDS .... *Victor 27224* 2-4 40

WHEN I LOST YOU (Vocal: Wayne King) / (I'LL BE WITH YOU) IN APPLE BLOSSOM TIME .... *Victor 27336* 2-4 41

WRAPPED IN A RED, RED ROSE / PUT A LITTLE SALT ON THE BLUEBIRD'S TAIL .... *Victor 22256* 3-5 30
(Vocals: Ernie Birchill)

KINNEY, Ray, & His Hawaiians

HONOLULU HARBOR / LEIMANA .... *Victor 27971* 2-4 41
(Vocals: Ray Kinney)

PAGAN LOVE SONG / SWEET HAWAIIAN MOONLIGHT .... *Decca 3402* 2-4 41

KIRBERRY, Ralph, & His Orchestra:
see KARDOS, Gene, & His Orchestra

KIRBY, John, & His Onyx Club Boys
(John Kirby: 12/31/08 – 6/14/52)

FROM A FLAT TO C / UNDECIDED .... *Decca 2216* 5-8 38

REHEARSIN' FOR A NERVOUS BREAKDOWN / PASTEL BLUE (Vocal: O'Neil Spencer) .... *Decca 2367* 5-8 38

KIRBY, John, & His Orchestra

ANITRA'S DANCE / DRINK TO ME ONLY WITH THINE EYES .... *Vocalion 4890* 4-6 39

BLUES PETITE / ANDIOLOGY .... *Okeh 5805* 5-8 40

BOUNCE OF THE SUGAR PLUM FAIRY / DOUBLE TALK .... *Columbia 35998* 4-6 41

CHLOE / CHLOE (by Horace Henderson & His Orchestra) .... *Okeh 5632* 4-6 40

CLOSE SHAVE / BUGLER'S DILEMMA ... *Victor 27568* 4-6 41

FRASQUITA SERENADE / SEXTET FROM "LUCIA" .... *Okeh 5705* 4-6 40

FRONT AND CENTER / NOCTURNE .... *Vocalion 5520* 5-8 39

I LOVE YOU TRULY / CUTTIN' THE CAMPUS .... *Columbia 36165* 4-6 41

IMPROMPTU / LITTLE BROWN JUG .... *Vocalion 5570* 5-8 39

IT FEELS GOOD / EFFERVESCENT BLUES .... *Vocalion 4624* 5-8 39

IT'S ONLY A PAPER MOON / FIFI'S RHAPSODY .... *Victor 27598* 4-6 41

JUMPIN' IN THE PUMP ROOM / TEMPTATION .... *Okeh 5661* 5-8 40

KEEP SMILIN' (Vocals: Charlie Shavers, Buster Bailey, & Russell Procope) / COMIN' BACK .... *Victor 27890* 3-5 42

MINUTE WALTZ / YOU GO YOUR WAY .... *Vocalion 5542* 4-6 39

MOVE OVER / WONDERING WHERE .... *Victor 27712* 3-5 41

NIGHT WHISPERS / TWEED ME .... *Victor 27667* 3-5 41

NO BLUES AT ALL / ST. LOUIS BLUES .... *Victor 27926* 4-6 41

ON A LITTLE STREET IN SINGAPORE / ZOOMING AT THE ZOMBIE .... *Okeh 5761* 5-8 40

ONE ALONE / HUMORESQUE .... *Vocalion 5605* 4-6 39

OPUS 5 / I MAY BE WRONG .... *Conqueror 9504* 4-6 39

OPUS 5 / I MAY BE WRONG .... *Vocalion 5048* 4-6 39
(Simultaneously released on two labels)

ROSE ROOM / 20TH CENTURY CLOSET .... *Columbia 36000* 3-5 39

ROYAL GARDEN BLUES / BLUE SKIES .... *Conqueror 9505* 4-6 39

ROYAL GARDEN BLUES / BLUE SKIES .... *Vocalion 5187* 4-6 39
(Simultaneously released on two labels)

ROYAL GARDEN BLUES / COQUETTE .... *V-Disc 237* 5-8 -
(A World War II release.)

SWEET GEORGIA BROWN / SERENADE .... *Columbia 36001* 3-5 39

THEN I'LL BE HAPPY / COQUETTE .... *Columbia 35999* 3-5 40

TURF, THE / DAWN ON THE DESERT .... *Vocalion 4653* 5-8 39

KIRK, Andy, & His Twelve Clouds Of Joy
(Andy Kirk: 5/28/98 –)

ALL THE JIVE IS GONE (Vocal: Pha Terrell) / I'SE A-MUGGIN' (Vocal: Ben Thigpen) .... *Decca 744* 5-8 36

BETTER LUCK NEXT TIME / I WANT TO BE A GYPSY .... *Decca 1422* 5-8 37
(Vocals: Pha Terrell)

BIG DIPPER, THE / BEAR DOWN .... *Decca 1606* 5-8 38

BIG TIME CRIP (Vocals: by orchestra) / 47TH STREET JIVE (Vocal: June Richmond) .... *Decca 4042* 4-6 41

BLESS YOU, MY DEAR (Vocal: Pha Terrell) / MESS-A STOMP .... *Decca 2204* 4-6 38

BOOGIE WOOGIE COCKTAIL / WORRIED LIFE BLUES (Vocal: Floyd Smith) .... *Decca 4381* 4-6 42

BREEZE / SITTIN' AROUND AND DREAMIN' .... *Decca 2261* 3-5 38
(Vocals: Pha Terrell)

CLOSE TO FIVE / I'LL NEVER FAIL YOU (Vocal: Pha Terrell) .... *Decca 2407* 4-6 39

CLOUDS / GOODBYE .... *Decca 2570* 3-5 39
(Vocals: Pha Terrell)

CLOUDY / CASEY JONES SPECIAL .... *Brunswick 4653* 15-20 30

CORKY / BLUE ILLUSION (Vocal: Pha Terrell) .... *Decca 772* 5-8 36

CORKY STOMP / FROGGY BOTTOM .... *Brunswick 4893* 15-20 30

COUNT, THE / TWELFTH STREET RAG ... *Decca 18123* 3-5 41

CUBAN BOOGIE WOOGIE (Vocal: June Richmond) / RING DEM BELLS .... *Decca 3663* 4-6 41

DOWNSTREAM / I'M GLAD FOR YOUR SAKE .... *Decca 1531* 4-6 37
(Vocals: Pha Terrell)

DREAM DROPPED IN, A / IS IT A SIN (LOVING YOU) ? .... *Decca 3619* 3-5 41
(Vocals: Henry Wells)

DUNKIN' A DOUGHNUT / THEN I'LL BE HAPPY (Vocal: June Richmond) .... *Decca 2723* 4-6 39

FINE AND MELLOW / FIFTEEN MINUTE INTERMISSION .... *Decca 3282* 5-8 40
(Vocals: June Richmond)

FROGGY BOTTOM (Vocal: Ben Thigpen) / CHRISTOPHER COLUMBUS .... *Decca 729* 5-8 36

GIT (Vocal: Ben Thigpen) / STEPPIN' PRETTY .... *Decca 931* 5-8 36

HEY LAWDY MAMA (Vocal: June Richmond) / McGHEE SPECIAL .... *Decca 4405* 4-6 42

HONEY (Vocal: Pha Terrell) / MARY'S IDEA ... *Decca 2326* 4-6 39

HOW CAN WE BE WRONG? / HOW MUCH DO YOU MEAN TO ME? .... *Decca 2081* 3-5 38
(Vocals: Pha Terrell)

I DON'T STAND A GHOST OF A CHANCE (Vocal: Pha Terrell) / BIG JIM BLUES .... *Decca 2915* 4-6 40

IF I FEEL THIS WAY TOMORROW / OR HAVE I? .... *Decca 3582* 3-5 41
(Vocals: Henry Wells)

I'LL NEVER LEARN / S'POSIN' .... *Decca 2510* 3-5 39
(Vocals: Pha Terrell)

I LOST MY GAL FROM MEMPHIS / LOOSE ANKLES .... *Brunswick 4803* 15-20 30
(Vocals: Billy Massey)

I'M GETTING NOWHERE WITH YOU (Vocal: Pha Terrell) / IT ALWAYS WILL BE YOU (Vocal: June Richmond) .... *Decca 2957* 3-5 40

I'M MISUNDERSTOOD / NO ANSWER .... *Decca 4141* 3-5 41
(Vocals: Henry Wells)

IN THE GROOVE / FOOLIN' MYSELF (Vocal: Pha Terrell) .... *Decca 1261* 5-8 37

I SURRENDER, DEAR (Vocal: Pha Terrell) / I'LL GET BY (Vocal: Henry Wells) .... *Decca 1916* 3-5 38

JULIUS CAESAR (Vocal: O'Neil Spencer) / YOU SET ME ON FIRE (Vocal: Pha Terrell) .... *Decca 2383* 3-5 39

JUMP JACK JUMP / GHOST OF LOVE (Vocal: Pha Terrell) .... *Decca 2226* 4-6 38

KEY TO MY HEART, THE (Vocal: Pha Terrell) / LITTLE JOE FROM CHICAGO (Vocals: by orchestra) ... *Decca 1710* 4-6 38

LADY WHO SWINGS THE BAND, THE (Vocal: Harry Mills) / WHAT WILL I TELL MY HEART? (Vocal: Pha Terrell) .... *Decca 1085* 5-8 37

LITTLE MISS / WHEN I SAW YOU (Vocal: Henry Wells) .... *Decca 3491* 3-5 40

LOTTA SAX APPEAL / BEARCAT SHUFFLE .... *Decca 1046* 5-8 36

LOVER, COME BACK TO ME / POOR BUTTERFLY .... *Decca 1663* 3-5 38
(Vocals: Pha Terrell)

MARY'S IDEA / ONCE OR TWICE (Vocal: Billy Massey) .... *Brunswick 4863* 12-15 30

MELLOW BIT OF RHYTHM, A / IN MY WILDEST DREAMS (Vocal: Pha Terrell) .... *Decca 1579* 5-8 37

MESS-A-STOMP / BLUE CLARINET STOMP (Vocal: Harry Lawson) .... *Brunswick 4694* 15-20 30

MOTEN SWING / GIVE HER A PINT (AND SHE'LL TELL IT ALL) (Vocal: Pha Terrell) .... *Decca 853* 5-8 36

NO GREATER LOVE (Vocal: Pha Terrell) / MIDNIGHT STROLL (Vocal: June Richmond) .... *Decca 3350* 3-5 40

PLEASE DON'T TALK ABOUT ME WHEN I'M GONE (Vocal: June Richmond) / WHY GO ON PRETENDING? (Vocal: Pha Terrell) .... *Decca 3033* 3-5 40

RIDE ON, RIDE ON / UNLUCKY BLUES .... *Decca 4436* 5-8 42
(Vocals: June Richmond)

SATURDAY / SOPHOMORE .... *Brunswick 6027* 12-15 31
(Vocals: Dick Robertson)

SCRATCHING IN THE GRAVEL / TAKE THOSE BLUES AWAY (Vocal: June Richmond) .... *Decca 3293* 5-8 40

SKIES ARE BLUE / I'LL GET ALONG SOMEHOW .... *Decca 1349* 4-6 37
(Vocals: Pha Terrell)

SNAG IT / SWEET AND HOT .... *Brunswick 4878* 15-20 30

TAKE IT AND GIT (Vocals: by orchestra) / HIP HIP HOORAY (Vocal: June Richmond) .... *Decca 4366* 4-6 42

TOADIE TODDLE (Vocal: Ben Thigpen) / I WON'T TELL A SOUL (Vocal: Pha Terrell) .... *Decca 2127* 4-6 38

TRAVELIN' THAT ROCKY ROAD / HONEY, JUST FOR YOU (Vocal: Billy Massey) .... *Brunswick 4981* 15-20 30

TWINKLIN' / FLOYD'S GUITAR BLUES .... *Decca 2483* 4-6 39
(Floyd's Guitar Blues was written by Floyd Smith, guitarist in the Kirk band. Smith was a pioneer in the use of amplified guitar in jazz.)

WALKIN' AND SWINGIN' / UNTIL THE REAL THING COMES ALONG (Vocal: Pha Terrell) .... *Decca 809* 5-8 36

WEDNESDAY NIGHT HOP / WORRIED
OVER YOU (Vocal: Pha Terrell) .... *Decca 1303* 5-8 37

WHAM (WHAM-RE-BOP-BOOM-BAM)
(Vocal: June Richmond) / LOVE IS
THE THING (Vocal: Pha Terrell) .... *Decca 2962* 4-6 40

WHAT A LIFE / SEPTEMBER
IN THE RAIN .... *Decca 2617* 3-5 39
(Vocals: Pha Terrell)

WHAT'S MINE IS YOURS /
IT MUST BE TRUE.................... *Decca 1827* 3-5 38
(Vocals: Pha Terrell)

WHAT WOULD PEOPLE SAY? / BUT IT DIDN'T MEAN
A THING.............................. *Decca 2277* 3-5 39
(Vocals: Pha Terrell)

WITH LOVE IN MY HEART (Vocal: Pha Terrell) /
WHY CAN'T WE DO IT AGAIN?
(Vocal: Henry Wells) .... *Decca 1477* 5-8 37

KIRK, Andy, as The Seven Little Clouds Of Joy

GETTIN' OFF A MESS / YOU RASCAL,
YOU (Vocal: Billy Massey)............ *Brunswick 7180* 15-20 30

KIRKEBY, Ed:
see CALIFORNIA RAMBLERS, The

KLEIN, Mannie, & His Orchestra
(Mannie Klein: 2/4/08 –)

AT SUNDOWN / BEI MIR BIST
DU SCHOEN .... *Keynote K-631* 5-8 46

HOT SPELL (Vocals: Bea Wain & The Bachelors) /
JUBA.......................... *Brunswick 7606* 10-12 36

RINGSIDE TABLE FOR TWO (Vocal: Bob Carter) / I'M IN
LOVE (Vocal: Bea Wain)............. *Brunswick 7605* 8-10 36

KNAPP, Orville, & His Orchestra
(Orville Knapp (circa 1908 – 7/16/36)

ACCENT ON YOUTH / THE GIRL
I LEFT BEHIND ME .... *Decca 554* 5-8 35
(Vocals: Norman Ruvell)

BLUE SKY AVENUE (Vocal: Virginia Verrell) /
TOO BEAUTIFUL FOR WORDS (Vocal:
Don Raymond)........................... *Decca 128* 5-8 34

I'M JUST BEGINNING TO CARE / THE STATE
OF MY HEART................... *Brunswick 7675* 4-6 36
(Vocals: Unknown)

LITTLE ANGEL TOLD ME SO, A /
ME WITHOUT YOU .... *Decca 316* 4-6 35
(Vocals: Edith Caldwell)

SMALL TOWN GIRL / YOU CAN'T JUDGE A BOOK BY
ITS COVER .... *Brunswick 7654* 4-6 36
(Vocals: Unknown)

SPEAKING CONFIDENTIALLY /
TAKE IT EASY......................... *Decca 539* 4-6 35
(Vocals: Edith Caldwell)

TALKIN' TO MYSELF (Vocal: Virginia Verrell) /
BELIEVE ME (Vocal: Don Raymond) .... *Decca 224* 5-8 34

TONIGHT'S THE NIGHT (Vocal: Larry Johnson) /
IT'S HIGH TIME I GOT THE LOW-DOWN ON YOU
(Vocal: Edith Caldwell)............... *Brunswick 7671* 5-8 36

YOU'RE A HEAVENLY THING (Vocal: Edith Caldwell) /
I WAS TAKEN BY STORM
(Vocal: Dave Marshall).................... *Decca 413* 4-6 35

KNECHT, Joseph M.:
see B. F. GOODRICH Silvertown Cord Orchestra, The

KNICKERBOCKER ORCHESTRA, The:
see ELKINS, Eddie

KNICKERBOCKERS, The:
see SELVIN, Ben, & His Orchestra

KNIGHT, Gaye, & His Orchestra

MOONGLOW / THE VERY
THOUGHT OF YOU................. *Vocalion 2757* 5-8 34
(Vocals: Ruth Dalmar)

(WE'RE JUST POOR FOLKS) ROLLING
IN LOVE / TONIGHT IS MINE........ *Vocalion 2756* 4-6 34
(Vocals: Ruth Dalmar)

KOLSTER DANCE ORCHESTRA, The:
see SELVIN, Ben, & His Orchestra

KORN KOBBLERS, The

LET'S GO OUT TO THE MOVIES (Vocals: The Kuartet) /
WANG WANG BLUES................ *MGM 10803* 2-4 -

KRENZ, Bill, & His Ragtimers

GOOFUS / THIS OLD PIANO .... *Deed 1007* 4-6 -

KRUEGER, Bennie, & His Orchestra
(Bennie Krueger: 1899 – 4/29/67)

ALL BY MYSELF / WHY, DEAR ...... *Olympic 15120* 3-5 21

BEALE STREET BLUES / ST. LOUIS
BLUES (Vocal: Al Bernard) .... *Connorized 3009* 5-8 21

BEALE STREET BLUES / ST. LOUIS
BLUES (Vocal: Al Bernard) .... *Gennett 4751* 5-8 21
(Simultaneously released on two labels)

BIMINI BAY / I'VE GOT THE JOYS.... *Vocalion 14253* 2-4 21

BLUE / HAUNTING BLUES .... *Brunswick 2315* 3-5 22

BOARDWALK BLUES / MR. GALLAGHER
AND MR. SHEAN .... *Brunswick 2327* 3-5 22

CAROLINA BLUES / ON THE 'GIN
'GIN 'GINNY SHORE .... *Brunswick 2192* 2-4 22

CHARLEY, MY BOY (Vocal: Billy Jones) /
PLEASURE MAD.................. *Brunswick 2667* 3-5 24

CRAZY BLUES (Vocal: Al Bernard) /
ROYAL GARDEN BLUES.......... *Brunswick 2077* 4-6 21

DANGEROUS BLUES / AIN'T WE
GOT FUN? .... *Brunswick 2109* 3-5 21

DO IT AGAIN / TEASIN'....... .... *Brunswick 2260* 3-5 22

DUMBELL / THE THIEF .... *Brunswick 2354* 2-4 22

GONE AGAIN GAL / NO-ONE BUT YOU KNOWS HOW
TO LOVE .... *Brunswick 3323* 2-4 26
(Vocals: Unknown)

GOODBYE TO LOVE / SAME
OLD MOON .... *Brunswick 6359* 3-5 32
(Vocals: Paul Small)

GOODNIGHT LOVELY LITTLE LADY / ONCE IN A
BLUE MOON.................... *Columbia 2918-D* 5-8 34
(Vocals: Unknown)
(This record was pressed in blue shellac.)

GRANNY / DOO DAH BLUES........ *Brunswick 2194* 2-4 22

HOW CAN YOU SAY "NO" / AS YOU
DESIRE ME...................... *Brunswick 6387* 2-4 32
(Vocals: Paul Small)

HOW MANY TIMES? / LEAVE ME
SOMETHING TO REMEMBER...... *Brunswick 3237* 2-4 26

I DON'T KNOW WHY / I IDOLIZE
MY BABY'S EYES................ *Brunswick 6185* 4-6 31
(Vocals: Smith Ballew)

I'M CUCKOO OVER YOU /
BOW WOW BLUES .... *Brunswick 2174* 3-5 22

IS I IN LOVE? I IS (Vocal: Fran Frey) / HUMMIN' TO
MYSELF (Vocal: Scrappy Lambert)..... *Brunswick 6331* 2-4 32

I'VE GOT THE JOYS / MY SUNNY
TENNESSEE .... *Gennett 4793* 3-5 21

LANTERN OF LOVE / TUCK ME TO SLEEP (IN MY
OLD 'TUCKY HOME) .... *Emerson 10452* 2-4 21

LONG-LOST MAMA / YES! WE HAVE
NO BANANAS (Vocal: Billy Jones)..... *Brunswick 2445* 3-5 23

NOTHING BUT / OPEN YOUR
ARMS, MY ALABAMY .... *Brunswick 2376* 2-4 23

O-HI-O / LEARNING........... *Pathe Actuelle 022499* 2-4 21

PICK ME UP AND LAY ME DOWN
IN DEAR OLD DIXIELAND /
LITTLE TIN SOLDIER............ *Brunswick 2258* 2-4 22

POOR LITTLE ME / DON'T LEAVE
ME, MAMMY..................... *Brunswick 2246* 2-4 22

SALLY, WON'T YOU COME BACK? /
SATURDAY................. *Pathe Actuelle 020596* 2-4 21

SATANIC BLUES / I WONDER WHERE MY SWEET
DADDY'S GONE.................. *Brunswick 2105* 2-4 21

SAY IT WITH A UKELELE / SO THIS
IS VENICE! (Vocal: Billy Jones) .... *Brunswick 2549* 2-4 24

SCHOOL HOUSE BLUES / I'VE GOT
MY HABITS ON.................. *Brunswick 2181* 2-4 22

SOME OF THESE DAYS / IT'S GETTING DARK ON
OLD BROADWAY .... *Brunswick 2340* 2-4 22

SPREAD YO' STUFF /
WANG-WANG BLUES............ *Brunswick 2083* 3-5 21

STARS / WEEP NO
MORE, MY MAMMY .... *Pathe Actuelle 020662* 2-4 21

STRUTTIN' AT THE STRUTTERS' BALL / WHO'LL
TAKE MY PLACE? .... *Brunswick 2303* 2-4 22

STUMBLING / I'M JUST
WILD ABOUT HARRY............ *Brunswick 2272* 2-4 22

SWEETHEART HOUR / MOON....... *Brunswick 6386* 2-4 32
(Vocals: Paul Small)

TELL ME, RADIO / SAVANNAH (THE
GEORGIANNA BLUES)........... *Brunswick 2619* 2-4 24

31ST STREET BLUES / THERE'S NOBODY ELSE BUT
YOU (Vocals: Billy Jones & Ernest Hare) ... *Brunswick 2571* 3-5 24

THOUSAND GOODNIGHTS, A /
RIPTIDE .... *Columbia 2919-D* 5-8 34
(Vocals: Unknown)

WAIT'LL YOU SEE MY GAL /
EASY GOIN' MAN................ *Brunswick 2634* 2-4 24

WANG-WANG BLUES / GET HOT ...... *Gennett 4722* 4-6 21
(Vocals: Al Bernard)

WANG-WANG BLUES / SOME
LITTLE BIRD..................... *Olympic 15106* 3-5 21

WET YO' THUMB / YOU KNOW YOU BELONG
TO SOMEBODY ELSE .... *Brunswick 2403* 3-5 23

WHY DID I KISS THAT GIRL? (Vocals: Billy Jones
& Ernest Hare) / I WONDER WHO'S DANCING
WITH YOU TONIGHT?............ *Brunswick 2576* 2-4 24

YEARNING / DON'T BRING
LULU (Vocal: Billy Jones)............ *Brunswick 2859* 3-5 25

YES, SIR, THAT'S MY BABY / IF I HAD
A GIRL LIKE YOU.............. *Brunswick 2936* 3-5 25

KRUEGER, Benny, as Bennie Krueger's Melody Syncopators

CROCODILE, THE / — .... *Gennett 9038* 3-5 20

SPREAD YO' STUFF / HOME
AGAIN BLUES................. *Grey Gull L-1046* 3-5 21

KRUPA, Gene, & His Orchestra
(Gene Krupa: 1/15/09 – 10/16/73)

AFTER ALL / VAGABOND DREAMS... *Columbia 35304* 2-4 39
(Vocals: Irene Day)

ALL THROUGH THE NIGHT (Vocal: Johnny Desmond) /
BALL OF FIRE........................ *Okeh 6563* 3-5 42

ALREET / GEORGIA ON MY MIND........ *Okeh 6118* 3-5 41
(Vocals: Anita O'Day)

AMOUR (Vocals: Anita O'Day & Howard Dulaney) / WATCH
THE BIRDIE (Vocal: Anita O'Day)........ *Okeh 6400* 2-4 41

AND SO DO I (Vocal: Howard Dulaney) /
I AM AN AMERICAN (Vocals:
Irene Day & Howard Dulaney) .... *Okeh 5701* 2-4 40

ANNIVERSARY WALTZ, THE / I THINK
OF YOU.............................. *Okeh 6465* 2-4 41
(Vocals: Johhny Desmond)

BIG DO, THE / BOOGIE WOOGIE
BUGLE BOY .... *Okeh 6034* 3-5 41
(Vocals: Irene Day)

BLUE RHYTHM FANTASY / BLUE RHYTHM
FANTASY, PART II.................... *Okeh 5627* 2-4 40

BLUES KRIEG / YES, MY
DARLING DAUGHTER .... *Okeh 5909* 2-4 40
(Vocals: Irene Day)

BOLERO AT THE SAVOY (Vocal: Irene Day) /
MURDY PURDY.................. *Brunswick 8284* 4-6 39

BOOGIE BLUES (Vocal: Anita O'Day) /
LOVER .... *Columbia 36986* 2-4 46

BYE-BYE BLUES / AFTER
LOOKING AT YOU .... *Brunswick 8249* 5-8 38
(Vocals: Irene Day)

CAISSONS GO ROLLING ALONG /
THE MARINES' HYMN .... *Okeh 6582* 3-5 42
(Vocals: Johnny Desmond)

CHALLENGER CHOP / DON'T
BE SURPRISED.................. *Brunswick 8412* 4-6 39

CHOP CHOP CHARLIE CHAN (Vocal: Irene Day) /
LOVE IN MY HEART .... *Columbia 35490* 2-4 40

COME BE MY LOVE (Vocal: Howard Dulaney) /
THE WALLS KEEP TALKING (Vocals: Anita
O'Day & Roy Eldridge)..................... *Okeh 6438* 2-4 41

DAY DREAMING / TROPICAL MAGIC..... *Okeh 6517* 2-4 42
(Vocals: Johnny Desmond)

DEEP IN THE BLUES (Vocal: Howard Dulaney) /
YOU FORGOT ABOUT ME (Vocals: Irene Day
& Howard Dulaney) .... *Okeh 5961* 3-5 41

DISC JOCKEY JUMP / GENE'S
BOOGIE (Vocal: Carolyn Grey)......... *Columbia 37589* 2-4 47

DOWN BY THE OLD MILL STREAM / SWEET
GEORGIA BROWN..................... *Okeh 6070* 2-4 40

DRACULA / FOO FOR TWO.......... *Brunswick 8361* 4-6 39

DRUM BOOGIE (Vocals: Irene Day & chorus) ; THAT
DRUMMER'S BAND / CIELITO LINDO;
SAHARA (Vocal: Peggy Mann)............ *V-Disc 279* 5-8 -
(The third & fourth titles are by Larry Clinton's Bluebird
Orchestra. A World War II release)

DRUMMIN' MAN (Vocal: Irene Day) / I'D LOVE TO CALL
YOU SWEETHEART.............. *Columbia 35324* 2-4 39

FEELIN' FANCY / WASHINGTON
AND LEE SWING .... *Okeh 5921* 3-5 40

FOOL AM I / SLOW DOWN.......... ...... *Okeh 6154* 2-4 41
(Vocals: Anita O'Day)

GEORGIA ON MY MIND (Vocal: Anita O'Day) /
THE THINGS I LOVE (Vocal:
Howard Dulaney).................... *Conqueror 9616* 2-4 41

GRANDFATHER'S CLOCK / I KNOW
THAT YOU KNOW................ *Brunswick 8124* 5-8 38

GUESS I'LL GO BACK HOME / WHISPER
WHILE WE DANCE.............. *Brunswick 8451* 3-5 39
(Vocals: Irene Day)

HE'S GONE / THE SARGEANT WAS SHY.... *Okeh 5985* 2-4 40

HIGH ON A WINDY HILL / IT ALL COMES
BACK TO ME NOW..................... *Okeh 5883* 2-4 40
(Vocals: Howard Dulaney)

HODGE PODGE / ON THE BEAM .... *Columbia 35262* 3-5 39

HOW 'BOUT THAT MESS? /
DRUM BOOGIE........................ *Okeh 6046* 2-4 41
(Vocals: Irene Day)

IF IT RAINS, WHO CARES? / THERE'S HONEY ON
THE MOON TONIGHT............. *Brunswick 8161* 5-8 38
(Vocals: Irene Day)

I LIKE TO RECOGNIZE THE TUNE / ALL DRESSED
UP SPIC AND SPANISH .... *Columbia 35237* 2-4 39
(Vocals: Irene Day)

I TAKE TO YOU (Vocal: Anita O'Day) /
WHERE YOU ARE (Vocal: Howard Dulaney)... *Okeh 6187* 2-4 41

IT HAPPENED IN KALOHA / I LOVE YOU MUCH TOO MUCH................. *Columbia 35429* 2-4 40
(Vocals: Irene Day)

I'VE GOT NO STRINGS / THE RHUMBA JUMPS............. *Columbia 35366* 2-4 40
(Vocals: Irene Day)

I WON'T BELIEVE IT / AN OLD CURIOUSITY SHOP................ *Brunswick 8292* 3-5 39
(Vocals: Irene Day)

JAM ON TOAST / TUTTI FRUTTI (Vocal: Leo Watson).......... *Brunswick 8211* 5-8 38

JEEPERS CREEPERS / SAY IT WITH A KISS..................... *Brunswick 8280* 4-6 39
(Vocals: Irene Day)

JUST A LITTLE FOND AFFECTION (Vocal: Buddy Steward) / CHICKERY CHICK (Vocal: Anita O'Day)........... *Columbia 36877* 2-4 46

KICK IT (Vocal: Anita O'Day) / AFTER YOU'VE GONE..................... *Okeh 6278* 2-4 41

KNOCK ME A KISS (Vocal: Roy Eldridge) / DELIVER ME TO TENNESSEE (Vocal: Anita O'Day)... *Columbia 36591* 2-4 42

LADY'S IN LOVE WITH YOU, THE / SOME LIKE IT HOT............... *Brunswick 8340* 4-6 39
(Vocals: Irene Day)

LET ME OFF UPTOWN (Vocals: Anita O'Day & Roy Eldridge) / FLAMINGO (Vocal: Howard Dulaney)........ *Okeh 6210* 2-4 41

LET'S GET AWAY FROM IT ALL / JUST A LITTLE BIT SOUTH OF NORTH CAROLINA.......... *Okeh 6130* 2-4 41
(Vocals: Anita O'Day)

LIKE THE FELLA ONCE SAID / I'D KNOW YOU ANYWHERE...................... *Okeh 5836* 2-4 40
(Vocals: Irene Day)

LOOKING FOR YESTERDAY (Vocal: Howard Dulaney) / DRUMMER BOY (Vocal: Irene Day)......... *Okeh 5747* 2-4 40

LOVER IS BLUE, A / I'VE GOT MY EYES ON YOU................. *Columbia 35361* 2-4 40
(Vocals: Irene Day)

LOVER'S LULLABY, A / BOOG IT (Vocal: Irene Day)........... *Columbia 35415* 2-4 40

MARIA ELENA / A RENDEZVOUS IN RIO... *Okeh 6165* 2-4 41
(Vocals: Howard Dulaney)

MASSACHUSETTS / MURDER, HE SAYS.... *Okeh 6685* 2-4 42
(Vocals: Anita O'Day)

MAYBE (Vocal: Irene Day) / I'LL NEVER SMILE AGAIN (Vocal: Howard Dulaney)................... *Okeh 5643* 2-4 40

MEET THE BEAT OF MY HEART (Vocal: Irene Day) / NAGASAKI (Vocal: Leo Watson)....... *Brunswick 8188* 5-8 38

MOMENTS IN THE MOONLIGHT (Vocal: Howard Dulaney) / MANHATTAN TRANSFER... *Columbia 35444* 2-4 40

MY HANDS ARE TIED / VARIETY IS THE SPICE OF LIFE.............. *Brunswick 8346* 3-5 39
(Vocals: Irene Day)

MY OWN / ANY TIME AT ALL....... *Brunswick 8205* 4-6 38
(Vocals: Irene Day)

MY WONDERFUL ONE, LET'S DANCE (Vocal: Irene Day) / MAKE BELIEVE ISLAND (Vocal: Howard Dulaney)................ *Columbia 35474* 2-4 40

NEVER FELT BETTER, NEVER HAD LESS (Vocal: Irene Day) / DO YOU WANNA JUMP, CHILDREN? (Vocal: Leo Watson)....... *Brunswick 8289* 5-8 39

NEVER TOOK A LESSON IN MY LIFE (Vocal: Irene Day) / TONIGHT (PERFIDIA) (Vocal: Howard Dulaney)............................ *Okeh 5715* 2-4 40

NIGHTINGALE SANG IN BERKELEY SQUARE, A (Vocal: Howard Delaney) / I HEAR MUSIC (Vocal: Irene Day)........................ *Okeh 5802* 2-4 40

NIGHT OF NIGHTS (Vocal: Johnny Desmond) / FIGHTIN' DOUG MacARTHUR (Vocal: Anita O'Day)... *Okeh 6635* 3-5 42

NO NAME JIVE / SIX LESSONS FROM MADAME LAZONGA (Vocal: Irene Day)......... *Columbia 35508* 3-5 40

OLD BLACK JOE / MY OLD KENTUCKY HOME................ *Columbia 35205* 2-4 39

OLD, OLD CASTLE IN SCOTLAND (Vocal: Howard Dulaney) / RHUMBOOGIE (Vocal: Irene Day)... *Okeh 5788* 2-4 40

ONE MORE DREAM / FEELIN' HIGH AND HAPPY...................... *Brunswick 8123* 5-8 38
(Vocals: Helen Ward)

OPUS NO. 1 (Vocal: Anita O'Day) / VALSE TRISTE......................... *Columbia 37224* 2-4 47

ORCHIDS FOR REMEMBRANCE / BLUEBERRY HILL..................... *Okeh 5672* 3-5 40
(Vocals: Howard Dulaney)

PASS THE BOUNCE (Vocal: Anita O'Day) / ME AND MY MELINDA (Vocal: Johnny Desmond)............ *Okeh 6619* 2-4 42

PRELUDE TO A STOMP / FARE THEE WELL, ANNIE LAURIE (Vocal: Jerry Kruger)......... *Brunswick 8139* 5-8 38

QUIET AND ROLL 'EM / THE MADAM SWINGS IT.......................... *Brunswick 8335* 5-8 39

SIERRA SUE (Vocal: Howard Dulaney) / TIGER RAG........................ *Columbia 35454* 3-5 40

SIREN SERENADE / DON'T CRY, CHERIE (Vocal: Howard Dulaney)........... *Okeh 6198* 2-4 41

SKYLARK / HARLEM ON PARADE....... *Okeh 6607* 3-5 42
(Vocals: Anita O'Day)

SO LONG (Vocal: Irene Day) / TUXEDO JUNCTION.............. *Columbia 35423* 3-5 40

SOMEWHERE / YOU DANCED WITH DYNAMITE...................... *Okeh 5859* 2-4 40
(Vocals: Howard Dulaney)

STOP! THE RED LIGHT'S ON (Vocal: Anita O'Day) / WHO CAN I TURN TO? (Vocal: Howard Dulaney).... *Okeh 6411* 2-4 41

SWANEE RIVER / I DREAM OF JEANIE WITH THE LIGHT BROWN HAIR............. *Brunswick 8387* 3-5 39

SWEETHEART, HONEY, DARLIN', DEAR / TAKE YOUR LOVE..................... *Columbia 35218* 2-4 39
(Vocals: Irene Day)

SYMPHONY IN RIFFS / MARCHETA... *Columbia 35387* 2-4 40

TA-RA-RA-BOOM-DER-E / APURKSODY (early theme song)...... *Brunswick 8296* 2-4 39

TELL ME WITH YOUR KISSES / LOVE DOESN'T GROW ON TREES............... *Brunswick 8246* 5-8 38
(Vocals: Irene Day)

THANKS FOR THE BOOGIE RIDE (Vocals: Anita O'Day & Roy Elridge) / KEEP 'EM FLYING (Vocal: Johnny Desmond).......................... *Okeh 6506* 3-5 42

THAT DRUMMER'S BAND (later theme song) / WHAT'S THIS? (Vocals: David Lambert & Buddy Stewart).................... *Columbia 36819* 2-4 42

THAT'S WHAT YOU THINK (Vocal: Anita O'Day) / ALL THOSE WONDERFUL YEARS (Vocal: Johnny Desmond).............. *Columbia 36621* 2-4 42

THERE'LL BE SOME CHANGES MADE (Vocal: Irene Day) / THESE THINGS YOU LEFT ME (Vocal: Howard Dulaney).......... *Okeh 6021* 2-4 41

THINGS I LOVE, THE / LITTLE MAN WITH THE CANDY CIGAR.............. *Okeh 6143* 2-4 41
(Vocals: Howard Dulaney)

THROWING PEBBLES IN THE MILLSTREAM (Vocal: Howard Dulaney) / GREEN EYES (Vocals: Anita O'Day & Howard Dulaney)............. *Okeh 6222* 2-4 41

'TILL REVEILLE / THE COWBOY SERENADE..................... *Conqueror 9896* 2-4 41
(Vocals: Howard Dulaney)

'TILL REVEILLE / THE COWBOY SERENADE........................... *Okeh 6266* 2-4 41
(Vocals: Howard Dulaney)
(Simultaneously released on two labels)

TUNIN' UP / ROCKIN' CHAIR............. *Okeh 6352* 3-5 41

TWO DREAMS MET (Vocal: Howard Dulaney) / DOWN ARGENTINA WAY (Vocal: Irene Day)...... *Okeh 5826* 2-4 40

TWO IN LOVE (Vocals: Anita O'Day & Johnny Desmond) / THIS TIME THE DREAM'S ON ME (Vocal: Johnny Desmond)........................ *Okeh 6447* 2-4 41

VIOLETS FOR YOUR FURS (Vocal: Johnny Desmond) / COPPIN' A PLEA (Vocal: Anita O'Day)...... *Okeh 6498* 2-4 41

WAIT UNTIL MY HEART FINDS OUT (Vocal: Irene Day) / LIGHTLY AND POLITELY......... *Brunswick 8274* 4-6 39

WALKIN' AND SWINGIN' / SINCE MY BEST GAL TURNED ME DOWN.......... *Brunswick 8253* 5-8 38

WHEN THE SWALLOWS COME BACK TO CAPISTRANO / ALL THIS AND HEAVEN TOO.............. *Columbia 35520* 2-4 40
(Vocals: Howard Dulaney)

WHEN YOU AWAKE / OH! THEY'RE MAKING ME ALL OVER IN THE ARMY.............. *Okeh 5872* 2-4 40
(Vocals: Howard Dulaney)

WHO? / FULL DRESS HOP................ *Okeh 6009* 3-5 40

WIRE BRUSH STOMP / WHAT GOES ON HERE IN MY HEART? (Vocal: Irene Day)... *Brunswick 8166* 4-6 38

WOODPECKER SONG, THE (Vocal: Irene Day) / SAY "SI SI"....................... *Columbia 35408* 2-4 40

WORLD IS IN MY ARMS, THE / I'M WAITING FOR SHIPS THAT NEVER COME IN.......... *Okeh 5760* 2-4 40
(Vocals: Howard Dulaney)

YOU AND YOUR LOVE / MOONLIGHT SERENADE...................... *Brunswick 8448* 3-5 39
(Vocals: Irene Day)

YOU ARE THE ONE (Vocal: Howard Dulaney) / ISN'T THAT JUST LIKE LOVE? (Vocal: Irene Day)....................... *Okeh 5935* 2-4 41

YOU'RE A LUCKY GUY (Vocal: Irene Day) / THREE LITTLE WORDS........... *Columbia 35336* 2-4 40

YOU'RE AS PRETTY AS A PICTURE (Vocal: Irene Day) / RHYTHM JAM................... *Brunswick 8198* 4-6 38

YOU'RE BREAKING MY HEART ALL OVER AGAIN (Vocal: Howard Dulaney) / MOON OVER BURMA (Vocal: Irene Day)................ *Okeh 5814* 2-4 40

YOU TAUGHT ME TO LOVE AGAIN (Vocal: Irene Day) / JUNGLE MADNESS............... *Brunswick 8400* 4-6 39

KRUPA, Gene, as The Gene Krupa Sextet

PAYIN' THEM DUES BLUES / JUNGLE DRUMS................................ *Clef 89082* 4-6 -

WINDY / MEDDLE MY MINOR........... *Clef 89119* 4-6 -

KRUPA, Gene, as Gene Krupa's Swing Band

I HOPE GABRIEL LIKES MY MUSIC / SWING IS HERE........................ *Victor 25276* 5-8 36

MUTINY IN THE PARLOR / I'M GONNA CLAP MY HANDS..................... *Victor 25263* 5-8 36
(Vocals: Helen Ward)

KYLE, Billy, & His Swing Club Band

(Billy Kyle: 7/17/14 – 2/23/66)

BIG BOY BLUE (Vocals: The Palmer Brothers) / MARGIE................................ *Variety 531* 10-12 37

CAN I FORGET YOU? / ALL YOU WANT TO DO IS DANCE....................... *Variety 617* 8-10 37
(Vocals: Leon Lafell)

HANDLE MY HEART WITH CARE / GIRL OF MY DREAMS............. *Variety 659* 8-10 37
(Vocals: Leon Lafell)

SUNDAYS ARE RESERVED (Vocals: The Palmer Brothers) / HAVIN' A BALL...................... *Variety 574* 10-12 37

KYSER, Kay, & His Orchestra

(Kay Kyser: 6/18/06 – 7/23/85)

ANGEL CHILD (Vocal: Harry Babbitt) / ROSE OF THE RIO GRANDE........................ *Columbia 35584* 2-4 40

ARMS FOR THE LOVE OF AMERICA (written by Irving Berlin for the Army Ordnance) / ANY BONDS TODAY? (written by Irving Berlin for the Secretary of the Treasury)....................... *Columbia 36228* 3-5 41

AS LONG AS I LIVE (Vocal: Jane Russell) / POSSUM SONG (Vocals: The Campus Kids)............. *Columbia 37292* 3-5 47
(Jane Russell gained fame as a motion picture star.)

AT LONG LAST LOVE (Vocal: Ginny Simms) / FOR NO RHYME OR REASON (Vocals: Ginny Simms & Harry Babbitt).......... *Brunswick 8209* 3-5 38

BLUEBERRY HILL (Vocal: Harry Babbitt) / WHO'S YEHUDI? (Vocals: Kay Kyser, Sully Mason & Harry Babbitt)...................... *Columbia 35554* 2-4 40

BLUE LOVE BIRD (Vocal: Ginny Simms) / THE NEARNESS OF YOU (Vocal: Harry Babbitt)................ *Columbia 35488* 2-4 40

BLUES (MY NAUGHTY SWEETIE GIVES TO ME)) / WHO? (Vocals: by trio)............. *Brunswick 7846* 3-5 37

BROKEN DREAMS OF YESTERDAY / TELL HER (YOU REALLY LOVE HER)......... *Victor V-40028* 4-6 29

CAFE CONTINENTAL (Vocal: Bill Stoker) / A HORSE AIN'T GOT MUCH SENSE (Vocals: Unknown)........... *Brunswick 7826* 3-5 37

CALL OF THE CANYON (Vocal: Ginny Simms) / FERRYBOAT SERENADE (Vocals: Harry Babbitt & chorus)..................... *Columbia 35627* 2-4 40

CAN'T GET OUT OF THIS MOOD / MOONLIGHT MOOD............... *Columbia 36657* 2-4 42
(Vocals: Unknown)

'CAUSE MY BABY SAYS IT'S SO / (HAVE YOU FORGOTTEN) THE YOU AND ME THAT USED TO BE?................. *Brunswick 7891* 3-5 37
(Vocals: Unknown)

CHARMING LITTLE FAKER (Vocal: Harry Babbitt) / HAZY AND BLUE .... *Columbia 35451* 2-4 40

CHATTER BOX (Vocals: Ginny Simms & Harry Babbitt) / THIS CHANGING WORLD (Vocal: Ginny Simms) .... *Columbia 35307* 2-4 39

COFFEE TIME (Vocals: Lucy Ann Polk & Michael Douglas) / ANGEL (Vocals: Michael Douglas & The Campus Kids) .... *Columbia 36882* 2-4 42
(Michael Douglas is now known as Mike Douglas, former star and host of the long-running Mike Douglas Show on television.)

COLLEGIATE FANNY (Vocal: Sully Mason) / HARK THE SOUND OF TAR HEEL VOICES (Vocals: by orchestra) .... *Victor V-40258* 5-8 30

CONCERT IN THE PARK (Vocals: Ginny Simms & Harry Babbitt) / ALL I REMEMBER IS YOU (Vocal: Harry Babbitt) .... *Brunswick 8385* 3-5 39

COWBOY SERENADE (Vocal: Harry Babbitt) / YOU AND I (Vocals: Giny Simms, Max Williams, Harry Babbitt, & Jack Martin) .... *Columbia 36244* 2-4 41

DEEP IN A DREAM (Vocal: Ginny Simms) / WHEN PAW WAS COURTIN' MAW (Vocals: Sully Mason, Ginny Simms, & Harry Babbitt) .... *Brunswick 8267* 3-5 38

DO I LOVE YOU? / INDIAN SUMMER... *Columbia 35337* 2-4 40
(Vocals: Ginny Simms)

DON'T DROP A SLUG IN THE SLOT (Vocals: Ginny Simms, Merwyn Bogue, & Harry Babbitt) / SUNRISE IN SIAM.......................... *Brunswick 8143* 3-5 38

DON'T SIT UNDER THE APPLE TREE / THERE WON'T BE A SHORTAGE OF LOVE... *Columbia 36567* 3-5 42
(Vocals: Unknown)

EGG-A BREAD (Vocals: Unknown) / WONDER WHEN MY BABY'S COMING HOME? (Vocal: Dorothy Dunn) .... *Columbia 36615* 2-4 42

EVERYTHING HAPPENS TO ME (Vocal: Harry Babbitt) / I KNOW A SECRET (Vocals: Sully Mason & trio) .... *Columbia 35993* 2-4 41

FIT TO BE TIED (Vocal: Ginny Simms) / THE LITTLE RED FOX (Vocals: Kay Kyser, Harry Babbitt, Little Audrey & Pokey Carriere) .... *Columbia 35295* 2-4 39

FOOLS RUSH IN (Vocal: Ginny Simms) / LET THERE BE LOVE (Vocal: Harry Babbitt) .... *Columbia 35439* 2-4 40

GO FLY A KITE / A MAN AND HIS DREAM .... *Brunswick 8439* 3-5 39
(Vocals: Harry Babbitt)

GONE (Vocal: Ginny Simms) / I LOVE YOU FROM COAST TO COAST (Vocal: Bill Stoker) .... *Brunswick 7793* 3-5 37

HEADLESS HORSEMAN, THE (Vocals: The Campus Kids & Freddie Froghammer) / KATRINA (Vocal: Harry Babbitt) .... *Columbia 38540* 3-5 48

HER NAME WAS ROSITA (Vocal: Harry Babbitt) / I'M STEPPING OUT WITH A MEMORY TONIGHT (Vocal: Ginny Simms) .... *Columbia 35483* 2-4 40

HE'S A DEVIL IN HIS OWN HOME TOWN / DON'T BRING LULU .... *Brunswick 7555* 4-6 35
(Vocals: Unknown)

HE WEARS A PAIR OF SILVER WINGS (Vocal: Harry Babbitt) / JINGLE JANGLE JINGLE (Vocals: Julie Conway, Harry Babbitt & the group) ..... *Columbia 36604* 3-5 42

I CAME HERE TO TALK FOR JOE (Vocals: Harry Babbitt) / PRAISE THE LORD AND PASS THE AMMUNITION (Vocals: The Glee Club) .... *Columbia 36640* 3-5 42

I'D KNOW YOU ANYWHERE (Vocal: Ginny Simms) / THE BAD HUMOR MAN (Vocals: Merwyn Bogue, Sully Mason, & Harry Babbitt) .... *Columbia 35761* 2-4 40

IF I ONLY HAD A BRAIN (Vocal: Harry Babbitt) / THE MERRY OLD LAND OF OZ (Vocals: Ginny Simms, Sully Mason, & Harry Babbitt) .... *Brunswick 8440* 3-5 39

I GET ALONG WITHOUT YOU VERY WELL (Vocal: Harry Babbitt) / CHOPSTICKS (Vocal: Sully Mason) .... *Brunswick 8308* 3-5 39

I PROMISE YOU / HEAVEN CAN WAIT....................... *Brunswick 8317* 3-5 39
(Vocals: Harry Babbitt)

IT MUST HAVE BEEN TWO OTHER PEOPLE (Vocals: Ginny Simms & Harry Babbitt) / OH! YOU CRAZY MOON (Vocal: Ginny Simms) .... *Brunswick 8446* 3-5 39

IT'S KIND OF LONESOME OUT TONIGHT / NAUGHTY ANGELINE...................... *Columbia 37561* 2-4 47
(Vocals: Harry Babbitt & The Campus Kids)

IT'S LOVE I'M AFTER / YOU DO THE DARNDEST THINGS, BABY .... *Brunswick 7755* 3-5 36
(Vocals: Unknown)

I'VE BEEN DRAFTED (Vocals: Unknown) / WHY DON'T WE DO THIS MORE OFTEN? (Vocals: Ginny Simms & Harry Babbitt) .... *Columbia 36253* 3-5 41

I WANT MY MAMA (Vocals: Harry Babbitt & Jack Martin) / ANGEL (Vocal: Harry Babbitt)......... *Columbia 35358* 2-4 40

JUST A HAVEN (Vocals: Frank Fleming, Sully Mason & Benny Cash) / RAINY WEATHER (Vocal: Benny Cash) .... *Victor V-40222* 5-8 30

LIKE SOMEONE IN LOVE (Vocals: Linda Stevens & Dolly Mitchell) / AC-CENT-TCHU-ATE THE POSITIVE (Vocal: Dolly Mitchell)................ *Columbia 36771* 2-4 45

LOST AND FOUND (Vocal: Harry Babbitt) / TWO SHADOWS (Vocal: Ginny Simms)... *Brunswick 8120* 3-5 38

MA! (SHE'S MAKING EYES AT ME) (Vocals: Unknown) / WHO'S SORRY NOW?............. *Brunswick 7836* 3-5 37

MEET THE SUN HALF-WAY (Vocal: Harry Babbitt) / APRIL PLAYED THE FIDDLE (Vocal: Ginny Simms) .... *Columbia 35467* 2-4 40

MIGHTY LAK' A ROSE (Vocal: Ginny Simms) / ALL GOD'S CHILLUN GOT RHYTHM (Vocals: Ginny Simms, Sully Mason, & Harry Babbitt) .... *Brunswick 8295* 3-5 39

ON A SLOW BOAT TO CHINA (Vocals: Harry Babbitt & Gloria Wood) / IN THE MARKET PLACE OF OLD MONTEREY (Vocal: Harry Babbitt) .... *Columbia 38301* 2-4 48

ONE IN A MILLION (Vocals: Sully Mason) / THE GIRL ON THE LITTLE BLUE PLATE (Vocals: Ginny Simms) .... *Brunswick 7470* 3-5 35

ON THE ISLE OF MAY (Vocals: Ginny Simms & Harry Babbitt) / PLAYMATES (Vocals: Sully Mason & chorus) .... *Columbia 35375* 2-4 40

ON THE WRONG SIDE OF YOU (Vocal: Lucy Ann Polk) / OL' BUTTERMILK SKY (Vocals: Michael Douglas & The Campus Kids) .... *Columbia 37073* 2-4 46
(Michael Douglas is now known as Mike Douglas, former star and host of the long-running Mike Douglas Show on television.)

PUSHIN' SAND / YOU'RE SO GOOD TO ME (Vocals: Harry Babbitt, Trudy, Julie Conway, Dorothy Dunn, Jack Martin, & Max Williams) .... *Columbia 36676* 2-4 42

PUT THAT DOWN IN WRITING (Vocal: Sully Mason) / DAY IN – DAY OUT (Vocal: Harry Babbitt) .... *Columbia 35202* 2-4 39

ROMANCE RUNS IN THE FAMILY (Vocal: Sully Mason) / DEEP PURPLE (Vocal: Ginny Simms) ... *Brunswick 8301* 3-5 39

ROSEMARY (Vocal: Michael Douglas) / HORSES DON'T BET ON PEOPLE (Vocal: Clyde Rogers)... *Columbia 36824* 2-4 45

SHOW YOUR LINEN, MISS RICHARDSON (Vocal: Sully Mason) / THREE LITTLE FISHIES (Vocals: Ginny Simms, Merwyn Bogue, & Harry Babbitt)....... *Brunswick 8358* 3-5 39

(GOTTA GET SOME) SHUT EYE (Vocal: Harry Babbitt) / CUCKOO IN THE CLOCK (Vocal: Sully Mason) .... *Brunswick 8312* 3-5 39

SMALL FRY (Vocal: Sully Mason) / YOU GO TO MY HEAD (Vocal: Ginny Simms) .... *Brunswick 8185* 3-5 38

SOMETHING TELLS ME / CRY, BABY, CRY................. *Brunswick 8114* 3-5 38
(Vocals: Sully Mason)

SO YOU LEFT ME FOR THE LEADER OF A SWING BAND (Vocals: Merwyn Bogue & Sully Mason) / MUSIC, MAESTRO, PLEASE! (Vocal: Ginny Simms) .... *Brunswick 8149* 3-5 38

STAIRWAY TO THE STARS (Vocal: Harry Babbitt) / YOU DON'T KNOW HOW MUCH YOU CAN SUFFER (Vocal: Ginny Simms)......... *Brunswick 8381* 3-5 39

STAR GAZING / A SUNBONNET BLUE (Vocals: Unknown) .... *Brunswick 7465* 3-5 35

STARLIT HOUR, THE (Vocal: Ginny Simms) / CONFUCIOUS SAY (Vocal: Sully Mason) .... *Columbia 35343* 2-4 40

STUTTERING IN THE STARLIGHT (Vocal: Ginny Simms & Harry Babbitt) / LOVE WITH A CAPITAL "YOU" (Vocal: Harry Babbitt) .... *Brunswick 8456* 3-5 39

SWAN SONG TO A DYIN' DUCK (Vocal: Sully Mason) / ST. LOUIS BLUES.................. *Columbia 35563* 3-5 40

TAKE YOUR GIRLIE TO THE MOVIES (Vocals: Unknown) / ISCH-KA-BIBBLE (I SHOULD WORRY) (Vocal: Merwyn Bogue)............... *Brunswick 7453* 4-6 35

TENNESSEE FISH FRY (Vocal: Sully Mason) / HOW CAN I EVER BE ALONE? (Vocal: Ginny Simms) .... *Columbia 35518* 2-4 40

(I'VE GROWN SO LONESOME) THINKING OF YOU (theme song) / IF MY LOVE COULD TALK.................... *Brunswick 7449* 3-5 35
(Vocals: Unknown)

(LIGHTS OUT) 'TILL REVEILLE (Vocals: Ginny Simms, Max Williams, Harry Babbitt & Jack Martin) / SAY WHEN...................... *Columbia 36137* 2-4 41

TINKLE SONG / THE LAMP IS LOW ... *Brunswick 8377* 3-5 39

TOO BEAUTIFUL TO LAST (Vocal: Ginny Simms) / YOU STEPPED OUT OF A DREAM (Vocal: Harry Babbitt) .... *Columbia 35946* 2-4 41

TWO SLEEPY PEOPLE (Vocals: Ginny Simms & Harry Babbitt) / HAVE YOU FORGOTTEN TO SOON? (Vocal: Ginny Simms) .... *Brunswick 8244* 3-5 38

UMBRELLA MAN, THE (Vocals: Ginny Simms & Harry Babbitt) / SIXTY SECONDS GOT TOGETHER (Vocal: Harry Babbitt) .... *Brunswick 8225* 3-5 38

WHAT'S NEW? (Vocal: Ginny Simms) / HELLO, MR. KRINGLE (Vocals: Ginny Simms, Merwyn Bogue, Sully Mason, & Harry Babbitt) .... *Columbia 35248* 2-4 39

WHEN THE ROSES BLOOM AGAIN / A ZOOT SUIT............ *Columbia 36517* 2-4 42
(Vocals: Unknown)

LALLY, Howard, & His Orchestra
(Below are rare dark green & gold labelled Melotone releases.)

FIRST YOU HAVE ME HIGH (THEN YOU HAVE ME LOW) / SHAKE IT OFF (WITH RHYTHM) .... *Melotone 6-03-15* 5-8 36
(Vocals: Unknown)

LITTLE RENDEZVOUS IN HONOLULU, A / PLEASE BELIEVE ME..................... *Melotone 6-03-14* 4-6 36
(Vocals: Allen Ray)

LAMAR, Slim, & His Orchestra / Slim Lamar's Orchestra

BETTER THAN NOTHIN' / MEMPHIS KICK-UP .... *Victor V-40146* 10-12 29
(Vocals: Slim Lamar)

JUNE DAYS (Vocals: MacLeod & H. Lamar) / YOU NEVER DID THAT BEFORE (Vocals: The Ryan Sisters & H. Lamar) .... *Victor V-40130* 10-12 29

LAMAR, Slim, & His Southerners

HAPPY (Vocal: Bob Nolan) / GOOFUS (Vocals: Tony Almerico, Jim Rush, Dick Wilson, Jack Cohen) .... *Victor 21710* 8-10 28

I'M CRAZY OVER DAISY (Vocals: Jim Rush, Dick Wilson, & Jack Cohen) / MY CASTLE OF NEVER-CAN-BE (Vocal: Bob Noland) .... *Victor V-40005* 5-8 28

I'M GLAD IT WAS SOMEBODY ELSE (Vocal: Bob Nolan) / ORIENTAL ILLUSIONS.............. *Victor V-40049* 8-10 28

NANCY (Vocal: MacLeod) / I'VE GOT A BRAND-NEW GIRL.................... *Victor V-40093* 10-12 29

LAMAR, Slim, as Slim & His Hot Boys

THAT'S A PLENTY / MISSISSIPPI STOMP................ *Victor V-38044* 15-20 29

LAMAR, Slim, as Slim Lamar's Orchestra:
see LAMAR, Slim & His Orchestra

WHITE CLIFFS OF DOVER (Vocals: Harry Babbitt & chorus) / THE NADOCKY (Vocals: Dorothy Crawford, Max Williams, Jack Martin, & Trudy) .... *Columbia 36445* 3-5 41

WHY CRY, BABY, (Vocal: Sully Mason) / ALEXANDER THE SWOOSE (HALF SWAN, HALF GOOSE) (Vocals: Unknown) .... *Columbia 36040* 2-4 41

WISE OLD OWL / TELL IT TO THE MARINES.................. *Columbia 36051* 3-5 41
(Vocals: Unknown)

WITH THE WIND AND THE RAIN IN YOUR HAIR (Vocal: Ginny Simms) / 'WAY BACK IN 1939 A. D. (Vocals: Ginny Simms & Harry Babbitt) ... *Columbia 35350* 2-4 40

YOU'RE THE GREATEST DISCOVERY (SINCE 1492) (Vocal: Sully Mason) / BLUE RAIN (Vocal: Harry Babbitt) .... *Columbia 35264* 2-4 39

YOU SAY THE SWEETEST THINGS (BABY) (Vocal: Harry Babbitt) / WE'LL MEET AGAIN (Vocal: Ginny Simms & Harry Babbitt).............. *Columbia 35870* 2-4 41

YOU'VE GOT ME THIS WAY (Vocal: Harry Babbitt) / I'VE GOT A ONE-TRACK MIND (Vocal: Ginny Simms) .... *Columbia 35762* 2-4 40

LAMPE, Del, & His Orchestra

DARKNESS ON THE DELTA / A TREE WAS A TREE........................ *Crown 3441* 5-8 33
(Vocals: Unknown)

MY RIVER HOME / I CALLED TO SAY "GOODNIGHT"............... *Crown 3426* 5-8 32
(Vocals: Unknown)

SCATTIN' THE SKEETER SKOOT / PARADISE................. *Victor 24010* 5-8 32
(Vocals: Dick Robertson as Rob Roy)

STREET OF DREAMS / IT'S WITHIN YOUR POWER .... *Crown 3409* 5-8 32
(Vocals: Unknown)

WHEN YOU'RE GETTIN' ALONG WITH YOUR GAL / SPRING IS HERE AGAIN .... *Victor 24005* 5-8 32
(Vocals: Dick Robertson as Rob Roy)

LAMPE, Del, as Lampe's Orchestra from The Trianon Ballroom
(Autograph records are very rare)

ALL ALONE (Vocal: Al Dodson) / PRINCE OF WAILS .... *Autograph 604* 30-35 24

BROKEN DOWN HORN / CANDIED SWEETS................ *Autograph 629* 25-30 25

LADY OF THE NILE / THE MIDNIGHT WALTZ............ *Autograph 628* 20-25 25

TRIANON (A NEW DANCE) / TRIANON CHICAGO TANGO.................. *Autograph un-numbered* 20-25 25

LAMPE'S ORCHESTRA from The Trianon Ballroom:
see LAMPE, Del

LANDAU, Mike, & His Oakland Terrace Orchestra

DEEP NIGHT / SUGAR IS BACK IN TOWN .... *Edison 52538* 8-10 29
(Vocals: Unknown)

LANDRY, Art, & His Orchestra

CAMEL WALK / EVERYBODY STOMP ... *Victor 19858* 3-5 26

FIVE FOOT TWO, EYES OF BLUE (Vocal: Dinty Curtis) / DON'T WAIT TOO LONG .... *Victor 19850* 3-5 26

IT'LL GET YOU / LAZY BLUES .... *Victor 19488* 3-5 24

SLEEPY-TIME GAL (Vocal: Henry Burr) / WHAT COULD BE SWEETER THAN YOU? .... *Victor 19843* 2-4 26

SLIPPERY ELM / SUGAR FOOT STOMP (by Fred Hamm & His Orchestra) .... *Victor 20023* 4-6 26

TELL ME YOU LOVE ME / BREEZIN' ALONG WITH THE BREEZE (by The Seattle Harmony Kings) ... *Victor 20142* 3-5 26

WHISPER SONG (Vocals: Bil Van Dusen, Denny Curtis, & Red Thomas) / ONE O'CLOCK BABY (by Johnny Hamp's Kentucky Serenaders; Vocal: Franklyn Baur) ... *Victor 20644* 3-5 27

LANDRY, Art, as Art Landry's Call Of The North Orchestra

BARCAROLLE / MELODY IN F .... *Gennett 5170* 3-5 23

POPPIES / IN A COVERED WAGON ..... *Gennett 5222* 3-5 23

YOU TELL HER – I STUTTER / RIP SAW BLUES .... *Gennett 5171* 3-5 23

LANE, Eddie, & His Hotel McAlpin Orchestra

I SEND MY LOVE WITH THESE ROSES (Vocal: George Beuchler) / SHARING (MY LOVE WITH YOU) (Vocal: Eddie Lane) .... *Melotone M-12401* 3-5 32

LET'S GET FRIENDLY (Vocal: Eddie Lane) / CAN'T YOU READ BETWEEN THE LINES? (Vocal: Cliff Lowery) .... *Melotone M-12153* 4-6 31

SHARING (MY LOVE WITH YOU) / A GREAT BIG BUNCH OF YOU .... *Perfect 15604* 3-5 32
(Vocals: George Beuchler)

THRILL ME / WHAT HAVE WE GOT TO DO TONIGHT BUT DANCE? .... *Perfect 15456* 4-6 31
(Vocals: Scrappy Lambert as Chester Hale)

LANE, Eddie & His Hotel McAlpin Orchestra as Sunny Brooks & His Hollywood Stars

NEVERTHELESS / SINCE AN ANGEL LIKE MARY LOVES A DEVIL LIKE ME .... *Melotone M-12157* 4-6 31
(Vocals: Eddie Lane)

LANGE, Arthur, as Arthur Lange's Orchestra

SING SONG MAN / ROSY POSY (by The Harmograph Dance Orchestra, a pseudonym for a band whose identity is not known) .... *Harmograph 726* 8-10 22
(Harmograph records are rare.)

WHO CARES? / AWAY DOWN EAST IN MAINE (by the Dixie Daisies, believed to be a pseudonym for Arthur Lange's Orchestra) .... *Muse 302* 4-6 23

LANIN, Howard, & His Benjamin Franklin Hotel Orchestra

GIGOLETTE / FLORIDA .... *Columbia 333-D* 3-5 25

MELANCHOLY LOU / DON'T WAKE ME UP, LET ME DREAM .... *Victor 19797* 5-8 25

WHEN I THINK OF YOU / LADY OF THE NILE .... *Victor 19652* 3-5 25

LANIN, Howard, & His Orchestra

CROSS YOUR HEART / THE LITTLE WHITE HOUSE .... *Columbia 762-D* 2-4 26

GORGEOUS / I'M JUST DRIFTING ALONG .... *Columbia 1029-D* 3-5 27
(Vocals: Unknown)

KATJA THE DANCER / LEANDER ...... *Columbia 804-D* 2-4 26

LUCKY DAY (Vocal: Irving Kaufman as Frank Harris) / BLACK BOTTOM .... *Columbia 689-D* 3-5 26

MOONBEAM! KISS HER FOR ME / FORGIVE ME .... *Columbia 882-D* 2-4 27
(Vocals: Unknown)

LANIN, Howard, as Howard Lanin's Arcadia Orchestra

MIDNIGHT ROSE / LOVE TALES .... *Gennett 5202* 2-4 23

MY SWEETIE WENT AWAY / I CRIED FOR YOU .... *Gennett 5167* 3-5 23

YOU KNOW ME, ALABAM' / YOU'LL NEVER GET TO HEAVEN WITH THOSE EYES .... *Gennett 5484* 3-5 24

LANIN, Joe, as Joe Lanin's Waltz Kings

SO BLUE / THE MICHIGAN WALTZ .... *Gennett 6086* 4-6 27
(Vocals: Marcus Roth)

LANIN MELODY ORCHESTRA, The:
see LANIN, Sam

LANIN ORCHESTRA, The:
see LANIN, Sam, & His Orchestra

LANIN, Sam

(Sam Lanin was among the most prolific of the recording bandleaders, having directed approximately 400 sessions in a recording career which spanned the years 1920 through the major portion of 1931, for almost every label in existence in New York during the period. This large contribution of dance records was exceeded only by Ben Selvin.)

LANIN, Sam, & His Famous Players

IN A LITTLE SPANISH TOWN / MOONLIGHT ON THE GANGES .... *Okeh 40740* 5-8 27
(Vocals: Irving Kaufman)

IT MADE YOU HAPPY WHEN YOU MADE ME CRY / I GOTTA GET MYSELF SOMEBODY TO LOVE .... *Okeh 40738* 5-8 27
(Vocals: Russell Douglas)

IT'S A HAPPY OLD WORLD AFTER ALL / SIDE BY SIDE .... *Okeh 40810* 5-8 27
(Vocals: Johnny Marvin)

JUST A LITTLE LOVE SONG / THE SHEIK (OF ARABY) .... *Gennett 4820* 4-6 22

LEAVE ME WITH A SMILE / WABASH BLUES .... *Gennett 4796* 4-6 22

MY NEW YORK / WHERE HAVE YOU BEEN ALL MY LIFE? .... *Okeh 40937* 4-6 27
(Vocals: Unknown)

RITZI-MITZI / SWINGIN' DOWN THE LANE .... *Gennett 5143* 3-5 23

SHE'S GOT "IT" / SA-LU-TA! .... *Okeh 40833* 4-6 27
(Vocals: Unknown)

STEALING / AFTER THE RAIN .... *Gennett 4826* 3-5 22

TOGETHER, WE TWO / WHAT'LL YOU DO? .... *Okeh 40919* 4-6 27
(Vocals: Seger Ellis)

LANIN, Sam, & His Famous Players as Benny Meroff & His Orchestra

WHEN YOU'RE WITH SOMEBODY ELSE (Vocals: by duet) / LONELY MELODY (by Sam Lanin & His Orchestra as Benny Meroff & His Orchestra) .... *Okeh 40967* 5-8 28

LANIN, Sam, & His Famous Players & Singers

I'M CRAZY OVER YOU / SUSIANNA .... *Odeon ONY-41228* 15-20 29
(Vocals: Bing Crosby)

I'M CRAZY OVER YOU / SUSIANNA ...... *Okeh 41228* 15-20 29
(Vocals: Bing Crosby)
(Simultaneously released on two labels)

LIVE AND LOVE TODAY / SEEMS TO ME .... *Odeon ONY-36112* 8-10 30
(Vocals: Scrappy Lambert)

ONE THAT I LOVE LOVES ME, THE / NOW I'M IN LOVE .... *Odeon ONY-41264* 5-8 29
(Vocals: Smith Ballew)

ROSES OF YESTERDAY (Vocal: Unknown) / JUMPING JACK .... *Okeh 41121* 5-8 28

SWEETHEARTS ON PARADE / EV'RYBODY LOVES YOU .... *Okeh 41159* 5-8 29
(Vocals: Unknown)

TEA FOR TWO / I WANT TO BE HAPPY .... *Odeon ONY-36036* 5-8 30

TEN LITTLE MILES FROM TOWN / IF YOU DON'T LOVE ME .... *Okeh 41097* 5-8 28
(Vocals: The Three Star Singers)

WHEN I'M LOOKING AT YOU (Vocal: Smith Ballew) / COOKING BREAKFAST FOR THE ONE I LOVE (Vocal: Annette Hanshaw) .... *Okeh 41383* 5-8 30

WHEN I'M LOOKING AT YOU / MONA .... *Odeon ONY-36050* 5-8 30
(Vocals: Smith Ballew)

WHEN MY DREAMS COME TRUE / THIS IS HEAVEN .... *Okeh 41257* 5-8 29
(Vocals: Smith Ballew)

WHEN YOUR LOVER HAS GONE / YOU DIDN'T HAVE TO TELL ME .... *Okeh 41483* 5-8 31
(Vocals: Paul Small)

LANIN, Sam, & His Famous Players & Singers as Roy Carroll & His Sands Point Orchestra

WHEN YOUR LOVER HAS GONE / YOU DIDN'T HAVE TO TELL ME .... *Harmony 1297-H* 4-6 31
(Vocals: Paul Small)

LANIN, Sam, & His Famous Players & Singers as Phil Hughes & His High Hatters

WHISTLING IN THE DARK (Vocals: Unknown) / JUST A CRAZY SONG (Vocal: Dick Robertson) ... *Harmony 1313-H* 5-8 31

LANIN, Sam, & His Famous Players & Singers as Lloyd Keating & His Music

JUST A GIGOLO / KEEP A SONG IN YOUR SOUL .... *Harmony 1274-H* 5-8 31
(Vocals: Unknown)

LANIN, Sam, & His Famous Players & Singers as Albert Mason's Orchestra

BLUE IS THE NIGHT / I WANT TO BE HAPPY .... *Parlophone PNY-34030* 5-8 30

I WONDER HOW IT FEELS (TO BE HEAD OVER HEELS IN LOVE) / UNDER THE MOON IT'S YOU .... *Parlophone PNY-34114* 10-12 30
(Vocals: Scrappy Lambert)

LIVE AND LOVE TODAY / ROLLIN' DOWN THE RIVER .... *Parlophone PNY-34104* 10-12 30
(Vocals: Scrappy Lambert)

LANIN, Sam, & His Famous Players & Singers as Benny Meroff & His Orchestra

TOO BUSY! (Vocals: The Three Star Singers) / DARLING (Vocals: Unknown) .... *Okeh 41079* 5-8 28

LANIN, Sam, & His Famous Players & Singers as The New York Syncopators

I'M PROUD OF YOU (Vocal: Smith Ballew) / SATAN'S HOLIDAY .... *Odeon ONY-36152* 10-12 30

LANIN, Sam, & His Orchestra / The Lanin Orchestra / Sam Lanin's Orchestra

AFTER I SAY I'M SORRY (Vocal: Arthur Hall) / SONG OF THE FLAME.................. *Pathe Actuelle 36374* 5-8 26

AFTER I SAY I'M SORRY (Vocal: Arthur Hall) / SONG OF THE FLAME.................. *Perfect 14556* 4-6 26
(Simultaneously released on two labels)

AIN'T WE GOT FUN? / JUST LIKE A RAINBOW.......................... *Gennett 4732* 3-5 21

AVALON TOWN / I STILL BELONG TO YOU............. *Pathe Actuelle 36879* 4-6 28
(Vocals: William Smith)

AVALON TOWN / I STILL BELONG TO YOU.................... *Perfect 15060* 3-5 28
(Vocals: William Smith)
(Simultaneously released on two labels)

BYE BYE BLACKBIRD / LONESOME AND SORRY................. *Bell 412* 3-5 26

CARRY ME BACK TO MY CAROLINA HOME / LOST – A WONDERFUL GIRL................... *Federal 5239* 3-5 22

CLAP HANDS, HERE COMES CHARLEY! (Vocal: Arthur Hall) / NO MAN'S MAMA................. *Pathe Actuelle 36363* 5-8 26

CLAP HANDS, HERE COMES CHARLEY! (Vocal: Arthur Hall) / NO MAN'S MAMA............................. *Perfect 14544* 4-6 26
(Simultaneously released on two labels)

CLAP YO' HANDS / I KNOW THAT YOU KNOW............. *Pathe Actuelle 36570* 5-8 27
(Vocals: Arthur Hart)

CLAP YO' HANDS / I KNOW THAT YOU KNOW................... *Perfect 14751* 4-6 27
(Vocals: Arthur Hart)
(Simultaneously released on two labels)

DESDEMONA / THE PROMENADE WALK............................ *Columbia 447-D* 4-6 25

HELLO, CUTIE / RED LIPS, KISS MY BLUES AWAY................. *Broadway 1068* 4-6 27
(Vocals: Arthur Fields)

HELLO, CUTIE / RED LIPS, KISS MY BLUES AWAY............... *Paramount 20510* 5-8 27
(Vocals: Arthur Fields)

HELLO, CUTIE / RED LIPS, KISS MY BLUES AWAY................. *Puritan 11510* 4-6 27
(Vocals: Arthur Fields)
(Simultaneously released on three labels)

HONEY, I'M IN LOVE WITH YOU (Vocal: Billy Jones) / NO OTHER................ *Pathe Actuelle 036258* 5-8 25

HONEY, I'M IN LOVE WITH YOU (Vocal: Billy Jones) / NO OTHER.......................... *Perfect 11439* 4-6 25
(Simultaneously released on two labels)

HOOSIER HOP / I'M FOLLOWING YOU........... *Harmony 1065-H* 5-8 30
(Vocals: Irving Kaufman as Tom Frawley)

HUGO, I GO WHERE YOU GO / BAM BAM BAMMY SHORE...................... *Banner 1619* 5-8 25
(Vocals: Arthur Fields)

HUGO, I GO WHERE YOU GO / BAM BAM BAMMY SHORE..................... *Domino 3586* 5-8 25
(Vocals: Arthur Fields)
(Simultaneously released on two labels)

I APOLOGIZE (Vocal: Tom Brown) / ME! (Vocal: Paul Small)................. *Perfect 15508* 4-6 31

IF I'D ONLY BELIEVED IN YOU / LONELY EYES..................... *Perfect 14733* 4-6 26
(Vocals: Charles Kaley)

I FOUND A MILLION-DOLLAR BABY / LITTLE GIRL............... *Banner 32219* 5-8 31
(Vocals: Paul Small)

I FOUND A MILLION-DOLLAR BABY / LITTLE GIRL............... *Perfect 15486* 5-8 31
(Vocals: Paul Small)
(Simultaneously released on two labels)

I KNOW THAT YOU KNOW / ONE ALONE (Vocals: Unknown)......... *Banner 1913* 5-8 27

I KNOW THAT YOU KNOW / ONE ALONE (Vocals: Unknown)......... *Domino 3881* 5-8 27

I KNOW THAT YOU KNOW / ONE ALONE (Vocals: Unknown)........... *Regal 8228* 5-8 27
(Simultaneously released on three labels)

IN A BOAT FOR TWO / LUCKY DOG BLUES........................ *Edison 50779* 4-6 21

IT HAD TO BE YOU / INNOCENT EYES..... *Okeh 40084* 3-5 24

IVY (CLING TO ME) / RAILROAD MAN.... *Banner 1152* 3-5 23

IVY (CLING TO ME) / RAILROAD MAN.... *Regal 9422* 3-5 23
(Simultaneously released on two labels)

I WANT TO BE BAD / BUTTON UP YOUR OVERCOAT (by Sam Lanin and His Orchestra as The Majestic Dance Orchestra).... *Pathe Actuelle 36941* 5-8 29
(Vocals: Scrappy Lambert)

I WANT TO BE BAD / BUTTON UP YOUR OVERCOAT (by Sam Lanin and His Orchestra as The Majestic Dance Orchestra).......... *Perfect 15122* 4-6 29
(Vocals: Scrappy Lambert)
(Simultaneously released on two labels)

I WONDER WHAT'S BECOME OF SALLY? / THAT'S GEORGIA........ *Regal 9691* 3-5 24

JUNE MOON / SAY IT WITH MUSIC.... *Edison 50865* 3-5 21

LAST NIGHT ON THE BACK PORCH / ROAMIN' TO WYOMIN'.................. *Okeh 4986* 3-5 23

MARIANNE / JUST YOU, JUST ME (by The California Ramblers as the Golden Gate Orchestra)... *Velvet Tone 1984-V* 4-6 29

OH BABY / A BIG BOY................. *Okeh 40111* 5-8 24
(Vocals: Billy Jones)

ORANGE BLOSSOM TIME / IF I HAD MY WAY.................... *Domino 4402* 4-6 29
(Vocals: Scrappy Lambert as Rodman Lewis)

SAY IT WITH A UKULELE / SHE WOULDN'T DO WHAT I ASKED HER TO........... *Regal 9600* 5-8 24
(Vocals: Arthur Hall)

SHEIK, THE / DA DA MY DARLING..................... *Pathe Actuelle 020663* 4-6 22

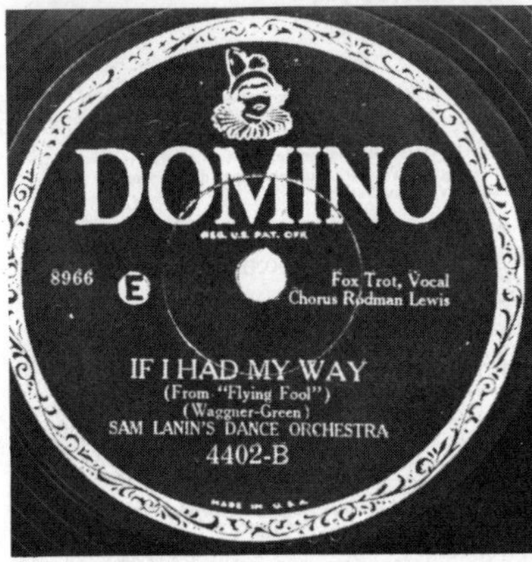

SMILE / SORRY................ *Pathe Actuelle 36931* 4-6 28

SMILE / SORRY...................... *Perfect 14902* 3-5 28
(Simultaneously released on two labels)

SOMEBODY LOVES ME / BAGDAD....... *Okeh 40170* 4-6 24

SONG OF THE MOONBEAMS / SONG OF THE BLUES.................. *Pathe Actuelle 37016* 5-8 29
(Vocals: Scrappy Lambert as Rodman Lewis)

SONG OF THE MOONBEAMS / SONG OF THE BLUES......................... *Perfect 15205* 4-6 29
(Vocals: Scrappy Lambert as Rodman Lewis)
(Simultaneously released on two labels)

STOP FLIRTING / CECILIA.......... *Columbia 438-D* 5-8 25

'S WONDERFUL / MY ONE AND ONLY.................. *Pathe Actuelle 36734* 5-8 27
(Vocals: Scrappy Lambert)

'S WONDERFUL / MY ONE AND ONLY......................... *Perfect 14915* 4-6 27
(Vocals: Scrappy Lambert)
(Simultaneously released on two labels)

TAKE, OH TAKE THOSE LIPS AWAY / SWANEE RIVER BLUES...................... *Banner 1283* 3-5 23

TAKE, OH TAKE THOSE LIPS AWAY / SWANEE RIVER BLUES........................ *Regal 9570* 3-5 23
(Simultaneously released on two labels)

TENDERLY / DEEP HENDERSON (by Sam Lanin & His Orchestra as The Caroliners)........... *Lincoln 2525* 5-8 26

THERE MUST BE SOMEBODY ELSE (Vocals: Unknown) / SUGAR............................. *Domino 4043* 5-8 27

THERE MUST BE SOMEBODY ELSE (Vocals: Unknown) / SUGAR............................... *Regal 8420* 5-8 27
(Simultaneously released on two labels)

TOO MANY PARTIES AND TOO MANY PALS / DON'T BE AFRAID TO COME HOME (by Ben Selvin as The Bar Harbor Orchestra)....... *Pathe Actuelle 36376* 5-8 26
(Vocals: Arthur Hall)

TOO MANY PARTIES AND TOO MANY PALS / DON'T BE AFRAID TO COME HOME (by Ben Selvin as The Bar Harbor Orchestra)............ *Perfect 14557* 4-6 26
(Vocals: Arthur Hall)
(Simultaneously released on two labels. The Perfect record was pressed in brown shellac.)

WHO WOULDN'T BE BLUE? (Vocal: John Ryan) / LOTS O' MAMA (by Sam Lanin as The Broadway Broadcasters).............. *Cameo 8228* 5-8 28

WHO WOULDN'T BE BLUE? (Vocal: John Ryan) / LOTS O' MAMA (by Sam Lanin as The Broadway Broadcasters)............. *Lincoln 2876* 5-8 28

WHO WOULDN'T BE BLUE? (Vocal: John Ryan) / LOTS O' MAMA (by Sam Lanin as The Broadway Broadcasters)................ *Romeo 605* 5-8 28
(Simultaneously released on three labels)

WORRYIN' / BARBARA................. *Cameo 1219* 3-5 27
(Vocals: Unknown)

WORRYIN' / BARBARA................. *Lincoln 2684* 3-5 27
(Vocals: Unknown)
(Simultaneously released on two labels)

YOU KNOW YOU BELONG TO SOMEBODY ELSE / CRYING FOR YOU............. *Columbia A-3850* 3-5 23

YOU'RE MY ONLY SWEETHEART / WHEN IT'S SLEEPY-TIME DOWN SOUTH .... *Columbia 2541-D* 3-5 31
(Vocals: Unknown)

YOU'RE THE ONE FOR ME / SUNNY DISPOSISH............ *Pathe Actuelle 36621* 5-8 27
(Vocals: Frank McGrath)

YOU'RE THE ONE FOR ME / SUNNY DISPOSISH.................. *Perfect 14802* 4-6 27
(Vocals: Frank McGrath)
(Simultaneously released on two labels)

YOU WERE MEANT FOR ME (Vocal: Scrappy Lambert) / BROADWAY MELODY (Vocal: William Robyn)... *Pathe Actuelle 36947* 5-8 29

YOU WERE MEANT FOR ME (Vocal: Scrappy Lambert) / BROADWAY MELODY (Vocal: William Robyn)......... *Perfect 15128* 4-6 29
(Simultaneously released on two labels)

LANIN, Sam, & His Orchestra as The All Star Collegians

LAZY RIVER / CHARLIE CADET....... *Perfect 15535* 3-5 31
(Vocals: The Eton Boys)

LANIN, Sam, & His Orchestra as The Caroliners

DEEP HENDERSON / TENDERLY (by Sam Lanin & His Orchestra)......................... *Lincoln 2525* 5-8 26

LANIN, Sam, & His Orchestra as Lynn Cowan's Boulevard Theatre Orchestra

JUST LIKE A BUTTERFLY / HALLELUJAH! (by Sam Lanin & His Orchestra as The Troubadors)..... *Romeo 398* 4-6 27

LANIN, Sam, & His Orchestra as Frank Keyes & His Orchestra

I GET THE BLUES WHEN IT RAINS / HONEY (by Sam Lanin & His Orchestra as Mills' Merry Makers).............. *Pathe Actuelle 36961* 5-8 29
(Vocals: Scrappy Lambert)

I GET THE BLUES WHEN IT RAINS / HONEY (by Sam Lanin & His Orchestra as Mills' Merry Makers).................... *Perfect 15142* 4-6 29
(Vocals: Scrappy Lambert)
(Simultaneously released on two labels)

LANIN, Sam, & His Orchestra as The Majestic Dance Orchestra

BUTTON UP YOUR OVERCOAT / I WANT TO BE BAD (by Sam Lanin & His Orchestra)..... *Pathe Actuelle 36941* 5-8 29
(Vocals: Scrappy Lambert)

BUTTON UP YOUR OVERCOAT / I WANT TO BE BAD (by Sam Lanin & His Orchestra)... *Perfect 15122* 4-6 29
(Vocals: Scrappy Lambert)
(Simultaneously released on two labels)

LANIN, Sam, & His Orchestra as Benny Meroff & His Orchestra

LONELY MELODY / WHEN YOU'RE WITH SOMEBODY ELSE (by Sam Lanin & His Famous Players as Benny Meroff & His Orchestra; Vocals: by duet)...... *Okeh 40967* 5-8 27

LANIN, Sam, & His Orchestra as Mills' Merry Makers

HONEY / I GET THE BLUES WHEN IT RAINS (by Sam Lanin & His Orchestra as Frank Keyes & His Orchestra)....... *Pathe Actuelle 36961* 5-8 29
(Vocals: Scrappy Lambert)

HONEY / I GET THE BLUES WHEN IT RAINS (by Sam Lanin & His Orchestra as Frank Keyes & His Orchestra)............ *Perfect 15142* 4-6 29
(Vocals: Scrappy Lambert)
(Simultaneously released on two labels)

LANIN, Sam, & His Orchestra as The Troubadours

HALLELUJAH! / JUST LIKE A BUTTERFLY (by Sam Lanin & His Orchestra as Lynn Cowan's Boulevard Theatre Orchestra)... *Romeo 398* 4-6 27

LANIN, Sam, & His Orchestra as Wilson's Novelty Ten

SHEIK, THE / DA DA MY DARLING.... *Perfect 14009* 3-5 22

LANIN, Sam, & His Roseland Orchestra / Lanin's Roseland Orchestra

APRIL SHOWERS / JUST A LITTLE LOVE SONG........................ *Arto 9125* 3-5 22

EGYPTIAN ECHOES / HUNGARIA... *Columbia 325-D* 3-5 25

I CAN'T STOP BABYING YOU / NO ONE.................... *Columbia 285-D* 4-6 25

IN A BOAT FOR TWO / CHERRY BLOSSOMS................ *Cardinal 2039* 4-6 21

MY MAN / FRANKIE AND JOHNNY....... *Arto 9077* 4-6 21

NA-JO / HAPPINESS........... *Pathe Actuelle 020498* 2-4 21

NO WONDER I'M BLUE / HUMMING... *Emerson 10321* 2-4 21

OH! BY JINGO / ROSE OF CHILE.... *Columbia A-2943* 2-4 20

SAY IT WITH MUSIC / IT'S YOU........... *Arto 9100* 3-5 21

SHANGHAI LULLABY / FORGETFUL BLUES................. *Federal 5371* 5-8 24

SUMMER NIGHTS / IF I HAD A GIRL LIKE YOU .... *Columbia 414-D* 5-8 25

TELL HER IN THE SPRINGTIME / AT THE END OF THE ROAD....................... *Columbia 324-D* 5-8 25

THAT RED-HEAD GAL / SNAKES HIPS... *Federal 5299* 5-8 23

THAT RED-HEAD GAL / SNAKES HIPS.... *Resona 75299* 5-8 23
(Simultaneously released on two labels)

TOODLE-OO / CHILE-BOM-BOM (Vocal: Vernon Dalhart)........ *Federal 5363* 4-6 24

WAITING FOR THE MOON / SUITE 16.... *Columbia 360-D* 5-8 25

LANIN, Sam, as The Arkansas / Arkansaw Travelers

BIRMINGHAM BREAKDOWN / I AIN'T GOT NOBODY..................... *Harmony 505-H* 8-10 27

BREEZIN' ALONG WITH THE BREEZE / WHEN THE RED, RED ROBIN COMES BOB, BOB, BOBBIN' ALONG.................. *Okeh 40640* 5-8 26

COPENHAGEN / THOSE PANAMA MAMAS.............................. *Okeh 40236* 5-8 25

GEORGIA BLUES / LOST MY BABY BLUES......................... *Okeh 40124* 5-8 24

HOW I LOVE THAT GIRL / I'LL SEE YOU IN MY DREAMS.................. *Okeh 40277* 5-8 25

I CAN'T GET OVER A GIRL LIKE YOU LOVING A BOY LIKE ME (Vocal: Lem Cleg) / BROWN SUGAR............................ *Okeh 40727* 5-8 27

JA DA / SENSATION................ *Harmony 421-H* 8-10 27

SHE LOVES ME / ANY WAY THE WIND BLOWS..................... *Okeh 40183* 4-6 24
(Vocals: Vernon Dalhart)

TING-A-LING, THE BELLS'LL RING / MY MAMA'S IN TOWN (by Lloyd Turner & His Villa Venice Orchestra)................ *Okeh 40674* 4-6 26

WASHBOARD BLUES / BONEYARD SHUFFLE........................ *Harmony 332-H* 8-10 27

LANIN, Sam, as Bailey's Lucky Seven

AFTER THE STORM / THERE'S YES! YES! IN YOUR EYES...................... *Gennett 5433* 4-6 24

AFTER THE STORM / THERE'S YES! YES! IN YOUR EYES....................... *Starr 9539* 4-6 24
(Simultaneously released on 2 labels, one Canadian [Starr])

BEBE / YES! WE HAVE NO BANANAS (Vocal: Irving Kaufman)... *Gennett 5154* 4-6 23

BEBE / YES! WE HAVE NO BANANAS (Vocal: Irving Kaufman)..... *Starr 9395* 4-6 23
(Simultaneously released on 2 labels, one Canadian [Starr])

BECAUSE OF YOU / COLLEGIATE...... *Gennett 3088* 5-8 25

BEES KNEES / WHERE THE BAMBOO BABIES GROW...................... *Gennett 5004* 4-6 23

COLD MAMAS (BURN ME UP) / ROSE MARIE (by The California Ramblers as The Vagabonds)...... *Gennett 5540* 5-8 24

COVERED WAGON DAYS / EASY MELODY (Vocal: Lewis James)..... *Gennett 5290* 4-6 23

DEAR ONE / WON'T YOU COME BACK TO MY ARMS?................ *Gennett 5637* 4-6 25

DINAH / (WHAT CAN I SAY) AFTER I SAY I'M SORRY?..................... *Gennett 3243* 5-8 26
(Vocals: The Tremaine Brothers)

DO IT AGAIN / SOME SUNNY DAY..... *Gennett 4872* 3-5 22

EVERYTHING IS K.O. IN K.Y. / CAROLINA MAMMY................. *Gennett 5078* 4-6 23
(Vocals: Ernest Hare)

EVERYTHING IS K.O. IN K.Y. / CAROLINA MAMMY.............. *Operaphone 9379* 4-6 23
(Vocals: Ernest Hare)

EVERYTHING IS K.O. IN K.Y. / CAROLINA MAMMY................... *Starr 9379* 4-6 23
(Vocals: Ernest Hare)
(Simultaneously released on 3 labels, one Canadian [Starr])

GEE, BUT I HATE TO GO HOME ALONE / TOMORROW MORNING..... *Gennett 5001* 4-6 22

GEE, BUT I HATE TO GO HOME ALONE / TOMORROW MORNING....... *Starr 9317* 4-6 22
(Simultaneously released on 2 labels, one Canadian [Starr])

GO, EMMALINE / LUCILLE............. *Gennett 5532* 8-10 24

GYPSY LADY / PAY DAY BLUES....... *Gennett 5057* 4-6 23

GYPSY LADY / PAY DAY BLUES......... *Starr 9369* 4-6 23
(Simultaneously released on 2 labels, one Canadian [Starr])

HOMESICK / CAROLINA IN THE MORNING........................... *Gennett 4979* 4-6 22

HOME / THAT BIG BLONDE MAMA.... *Gennett 5243* 5-8 23

HOW MANY TIMES? / WIMMIN......... *Gennett 4795* 3-5 21

IF YOU KNEW SUSIE LIKE I KNOW SUSIE / FLAG THAT TRAIN (TO ALABAM')......... *Gennett 5710* 5-8 25

I'VE GOT MY HABITS ON / IN MY HEART, ON MY MIND ALL DAY LONG............ *Connorized 3045* 5-8 22

I'VE GOT MY HABITS ON / IN MY HEART, ON MY MIND ALL DAY LONG.............. *Gennett 4815* 4-6 22
(Simultaneously released on two labels)

I WONDER BLUES / PICK ME UP AND LAY ME DOWN IN DEAR OLD DIXIELAND........... *Connorized 3065* 5-8 22

I WONDER BLUES / PICK ME UP AND LAY ME DOWN IN DEAR OLD DIXIELAND............... *Gennett 4855* 4-6 22

I WONDER BLUES / PICK ME UP AND LAY ME DOWN IN DEAR OLD DIXIELAND............. *Starr 9232* 4-6 22
(Simultaneously released on 3 labels, one Canadian [Starr])

I WONDER WHERE MY BABY IS TONIGHT? / DON'T WAIT TOO LONG (Vocal: Arthur Fields)... *Gennett 3191* 5-8 26

KICKY-KOO / THOSE LONGING FOR YOU BLUES..................... *Gennett 4887* 3-5 22

LOVEY COME BACK / HULA LOU...... *Gennett 5363* 4-6 24

MINDIN' MY BUSINESS / IF YOU'LL COME BACK......................... *Gennett 5364* 4-6 24

OH! MABEL / LUCKY KENTUCKY...... *Gennett 5625* 5-8 25

ON A NIGHT LIKE THIS (Vocal: Arthur Fields) / KINKY KIDS' PARADE.................. *Gennett 3125* 4-6 25

ROAMIN' TO WYOMIN' / NOT HERE – NOT THERE......................... *Gennett 5301* 3-5 23

SNAKES HIPS / DOWN AMONG THE SLEEPY HILLS OF TEN-TEN-TENNESSEE........... *Gennett 5110* 4-6 23

SNAKES HIPS / DOWN AMONG THE SLEEPY HILLS OF TEN-TEN-TENNESSEE.............. *Starr 9377* 4-6 23
(Simultaneously released on 2 labels, one Canadian [Starr])

STATIC / LET'S TALK ABOUT MY SWEETIE..................... *Gennett 3249* 5-8 26
(Vocals: The Trimble Boys)

STEPPIN' OUT / MAYBE.................. *Gennett 5349* 5-8 24

SUMMER NIGHTS / MARGUERITE..... *Gennett 3094* 5-8 25

THAT BRAN' NEW GAL OF MINE / LINGER AWHILE......... *Gennett 5300* 4-6 23

TIE ME TO YOUR APRON STRINGS AGAIN / SOMEBODY'S EYES......... *Gennett 3216* 5-8 26
(Vocals: Arthur Fields)

WHY COULDN'T IT BE POOR LITTLE ME? / NO-ONE.............. *Gennett 5645* 5-8 25

YEARNING / WHEN I THINK OF YOU.... *Gennett 5676* 5-8 25

YOU KNOW YOU BELONG TO SOMEBODY ELSE / APPLE SAUCE... *Gennett 5030* 3-5 23

LANIN, Sam, as The Broadway Bell-Hops

BUT I DO – YOU KNOW I DO / LET'S TALK ABOUT MY SWEETIE............ *Harmony 120-H* 5-8 26
(Vocals: Billy Jones)

BUT I DO – YOU KNOW I DO / LET'S TALK ABOUT MY SWEETIE.......... *Silvertone 3216* 5-8 26
(Vocals: Billy Jones)
(Simultaneously released on two labels)

COLLETTE / IF YOU SEE SALLY.... *Harmony 338-H* 5-8 27

COQUETTE / IN THE SWEET BYE AND BYE.................. *Harmony 605-H* 4-6 28

FOR MY BABY / SUMMERTIME SWEETHEARTS................... *Harmony 546-H* 3-5 28

HELLO BLUEBIRD (Vocal: Jimmy Flynn) / LONELY ACRES IN THE WEST..... *Harmony 272-H* 4-6 26

HELLO BLUEBIRD (Vocal: Jimmy Flynn) / LONELY ACRES IN THE WEST..... *Silvertone 3240* 4-6 26
(Simultaneously released on two labels)

I'D RATHER CRY OVER YOU / GET OUT AND GET UNDER THE MOON.............. *Harmony 644-H* 3-5 28
(Vocals: Unknown)

I FOUND A ROUNDABOUT WAY TO HEAVEN / SHOW THAT FELLOW THE DOOR (Vocal: Arthur Fields)..... *Harmony 159-H* 5-8 26

IN THE EVENING / HAPPY-GO-LUCKY LANE........................... *Harmony 630-H* 3-5 28

LEONORA / I'M IN LOVE AGAIN.... *Harmony 450-H* 4-6 27

MY OHIO HOME / LET A SMILE BE YOUR UMBRELLA ON A RAINY DAY............... *Harmony 564-H* 3-5 28
(Vocals: Lewis James)

OH! YOU LULU BELLE / GOODNIGHT............ *Harmony 140-H* 5-8 26
(Vocals: The Harmony Brothers)

SA-LU-TA! / UNDER THE MOON.... *Harmony 429-H* 5-8 27

SEVILLA / MY BARCELONA........ *Harmony 202-H* 5-8 26

SIDE BY SIDE / DON'T SOMEBODY WANT SOMEBODY TO LOVE?.............. *Harmony 390-H* 5-8 27

SOMEDAY YOU'LL SAY "O.K." / IT WAS ONLY A SUN SHOWER........... *Harmony 479-H* 5-8 27

SOMEONE IS LOSIN' SUSAN / BARCELONA........... *Harmony 223-H* 5-8 26

SUNDAY / DON'T TAKE THAT BLACK BOTTOM AWAY..... *Harmony 288-H* 5-8 26
(Vocals: Irving Kaufman)

THAT'S JUST MY WAY OF FORGETTING YOU / OLD MAN SUNSHINE............... *Harmony 661-H* 3-5 28

THAT'S MY HAP-HAP-HAPPINESS / NESTING TIME.................. *Harmony 365-H* 5-8 27

THERE AIN'T NO LAND LIKE DIXIELAND / THERE'S A CRADLE IN CAROLINE......... *Harmony 504-H* 20-25 27
(Vocals: Irving Kaufman)

TONIGHT'S MY NIGHT WITH BABY / HI-HO THE MERRIO!............. *Harmony 176-H* 5-8 26
(Vocals: Irving Kaufman)

UP IN THE CLOUDS / THINKING OF YOU............... *Harmony 523-H* 3-5 27
(Vocals: Irving Kaufman)

WHO COULD BE MORE WONDERFUL THAN YOU? / DON'T BE ANGRY WITH ME...... *Harmony 253-H* 5-8 26

LANIN, Sam, as The Broadway Broadcasters

BLACK BOTTOM / THE BIRTH OF THE BLUES........................ *Cameo 985* 5-8 26

BY THE LIGHT OF THE STARS / JUST A LITTLE DRINK........................ *Cameo 775* 4-6 25

HOT HENRY! / POOR PAPA............. *Cameo 939* 5-8 26

LOT'S O' MAMA / WHO WOULDN'T BE BLUE? (by Sam Lanin & His Orchestra; Vocal: John Ryan)..... *Cameo 8228* 5-8 28

LOT'S O' MAMA / WHO WOULDN'T BE BLUE? (by Sam Lanin & His Orchestra; Vocal: John Ryan).... *Lincoln 2876* 5-8 28

LOT'S O' MAMA / WHO WOULDN'T BE BLUE? (by Sam Lanin & His Orchestra; Vocal: John Ryan)...... *Romeo 650* 5-8 28
(Simultaneously released on three labels)

NO MAN'S MAMA / THAT CERTAIN PARTY.................................. *Cameo 836* 5-8 26

ROSES BROUGHT ME YOU / AFTER I SAY I'M SORRY (Vocals: Unknown)........... *Lincoln 2464* 4-6 26

SO SOMETHING (Vocal: Scrappy Lambert) / YOUR DISPOSITION IS MINE (by Bob Haring & His Orchestra as The Caroliners; Vocals: Unknown)... *Romeo 960* 4-6 29

LANIN, Sam, as The Broadway Broadcasters recorded under the name The Senators

ANY WAY THE WIND BLOWS / MY BEST GIRL...................... *Tremont 0506* 5-8 24

LANIN, Sam, as The Ipana Troubadours

ALONE IN THE RAIN / MOLLY..... *Columbia 2052-D* 4-6 30
(Vocals: Smith Ballew)

BLUE IS THE NIGHT / WHIPPOORWILL................. *Columbia 2174-D* 4-6 30
(Vocals: Unknown)

BUTTON UP YOUR HEART / BLUE AGAIN.................. *Columbia 2340-D* 5-8 31
(Vocals: Unknown)

COOKING BREAKFAST FOR THE ONE I LOVE / KICKIN' A HOLE IN THE SKY.... *Columbia 2117-D* 8-10 30
(Vocals: Unknown)

DO WHAT YOU DO / LIZA.......... *Columbia 1903-D* 5-8 29
(Vocals: Smith Ballew)

DREAM KISSES (Vocal: Harold Lambert) / AMONG MY SOUVENIRS (by Ben Selvin & His Orchestra; Vocal: Cyril Pitts)........ *Columbia 1188-D* 3-5 27

GLORIANNA / DO YOU? – THAT'S ALL I WANT TO KNOW.............. *Columbia 1638-D* 10-12 28
(Vocals: Unknown)

I CAN'T MAKE HER HAPPY / HEARTBROKEN AND LONELY....................... *Columbia 1586-D* 8-10 28
(Vocals: Smith Ballew)

I KNOW THAT YOU KNOW / SWEETER THAN YOU.............. *Columbia 829-D* 5-8 27

I'LL GET BY / ROSE OF MANDALAY... *Columbia 1994-D* 15-20 28
(Vocals: Bing Crosby)

I NEVER DREAMT / HANGIN' ON THE GARDEN GATE............ *Columbia 2147-D* 5-8 30
(Vocals: Smith Ballew)

JIG WALK / MYSTERIOUS EYES..... *Columbia 528-D* 5-8 26

JUST YOU – JUST ME / HANG ON TO ME....................... *Columbia 1920-D* 5-8 29
(Vocals: Smith Ballew)

MY STRONGEST WEAKNESS IS YOU / MY SWEETER THAN SWEET................. *Columbia 2006-D* 5-8 29
(Vocals: Smith Ballew)

NAGASAKI (Vocals: Unknown) / DOWN WHERE THE SUN GOES DOWN.............. *Columbia 1463-D* 10-12 28

ON THE BEACH WITH YOU / MANY HAPPY RETURNS OF THE DAY.......... *Columbia 2486-D* 4-6 31
(Vocals: Dick Robertson)

PADDLIN' MADELIN' HOME / SAY! WHO IS THAT BABY DOLL? ..... Columbia 503-D 5-8 25
(Vocals: Billy Jones)

SING / PROMISES ..... Columbia 2220-D 5-8 30
(Vocals: The Mariners)

SOME SWEET DAY / DEEP NIGHT ... Columbia 1747-D 5-8 29
(Vocals: Smith Ballew)

STEP ON THE BLUES / KITTY'S KISSES ..... Columbia 680-D 5-8 26

THAT LITTLE BOY OF MINE / IF YOU SHOULD EVER NEED ME ..... Columbia 2437-D 4-6 31
(Vocals: Chick Bullock)

THAT'S LIVING / TO BE IN LOVE ... Columbia 1840-D 5-8 29
(Vocals: Smith Ballew)

TRUE BLUE LOU / THERE'S TOO MANY EYES THAT WANNA MAKE EYES AT TWO PRETTY EYES I LOVE ..... Columbia 1982-D 5-8 29
(Vocals: Smith Ballew)

LANIN, Sam, as The Lanin Melody Orchestra

MINE / SO BLUE ..... Emerson 3135 3-5 27

LANIN, Sam, as Lanin's Arcadians

ALABAMY BOUND / I'LL SEE YOU IN MY DREAMS ..... Pathe Actuelle 036203 5-8 25

ALABAMY BOUND / I'LL SEE YOU IN MY DREAMS ..... Perfect 14384 4-6 25
(Simultaneously released on two labels)

LANIN, Sam, as Lanin's Jazz Band

UNFORTUNATE BLUES / NOBODY'S SWEETHEART NOW ..... Pathe Actuelle 036075 5-8 24

UNFORTUNATE BLUES / NOBODY'S SWEETHEART NOW ..... Perfect 14256 4-6 24
(Simultaneously released on two labels)

LANIN, Sam, as Lanin's Red Heads

IF YOU HADN'T GONE AWAY / FLAG THAT TRAIN ..... Columbia 376-D 8-10 25

I'M GONNA HANG AROUND MY SUGAR / FIVE FOOT TWO, EYES OF BLUE (Vocal: Art Gilham) ..... Columbia 483-D 5-8 25

JIMTOWN BLUES / KING PORTER STOMP ..... Columbia 327-D 10-12 25

LANIN, Sam, as Lanin's Southern Serenaders

ARKANSAS BLUES / LONESOME LOVESICK BLUES ..... Emerson 10496 5-8 22

ARKANSAS BLUES / LONESOME LOVESICK BLUES ..... Regal 9164 4-6 22
(Simultaneously released on two labels)

AUNT HAGAR'S CHILDREN BLUES / SHAKE IT AND BREAK IT (Vocal: Sam Lanin) ..... Blue Bird 20068 40-45 21

AUNT HAGAR'S CHILDREN BLUES / SHAKE IT AND BREAK IT (Vocal: Sam Lanin) ..... Claxtonola 40068 10-12 21

AUNT HAGAR'S CHILDREN BLUES / SHAKE IT AND BREAK IT (Vocal: Sam Lanin) ..... Famous 3062 8-10 21

AUNT HAGAR'S CHILDREN BLUES / SHAKE IT AND BREAK IT (Vocal: Sam Lanin) ..... Paramount 20068 10-12 21

AUNT HAGAR'S CHILDREN BLUES / SHAKE IT AND BREAK IT (Vocal: Sam Lanin) ..... Puritan 11068 8-10 21

AUNT HAGAR'S CHILDREN BLUES / SHAKE IT AND BREAK IT (Vocal: Sam Lanin) ..... Triangle 11068 8-10 21
(Simultaneously released on six labels. The Blue Bird release is exceptionally rare, produced by the Blue Bird Talking Machine Company in Los Angeles, California.)

EDDIE LEONARD BLUES / SATANIC BLUES ..... Emerson 10508 5-8 22

EDDIE LEONARD BLUES / SATANIC BLUES ..... Regal 9191 4-6 22
(Simultaneously released on two labels)

GOOD MORNIN' / I'M JUST WILD ABOUT HARRY ..... Banner 1100 5-8 22

GOOD MORNIN' / I'M JUST WILD ABOUT HARRY ..... Regal 9355 5-8 22
(Simultaneously released on two labels)

GYPSY BLUES / MY SUNNY TENNESSEE ..... Emerson 10467 3-5 21

I'VE GOT THE JOYS / MANDY 'N' ME ..... Pathe Actuelle 020649 3-5 21

MEMPHIS BLUES / ST. LOUIS BLUES ..... Arto 9097 8-10 21

MEMPHIS BLUES / ST. LOUIS BLUES ..... Bell P-97 8-10 21

MEMPHIS BLUES / ST. LOUIS BLUES ... Hy-Tone K-97 8-10 21
(Simultaneously released on three labels)

SHAKE IT AND BREAK IT (Vocal: Sam Lanin) / AUNT HAGAR'S CHILDREN BLUES ..... Emerson 10439 8-10 21

VIRGINIA BLUES / DOO DAH BLUES ..... Regal 9200 4-6 22

LANIN, Sam, as Lanin's Southern Serenaders recorded under the name Henderson's Dance Orchestra

AUNT HAGAR'S CHILDREN BLUES / SHAKE IT AND BREAK IT (Vocal: Sam Lanin) ..... Black Swan 2034 10-12 21

LANIN, Sam, as Lanin's Southern Serenaders recorded under The Kentucky Serenaders

SHAKE IT AND BREAK IT (Vocal: Sam Lanin) / AUNT HAGAR'S CHILDREN BLUES ..... Regal 9134 8-10 21

LANIN, Sam, as The Melody Sheiks

ALL ABOARD FOR HEAVEN / LADY OF THE NILE ..... Okeh 40341 3-5 25

FIVE FOOT TWO, EYES OF BLUE (Vocal: Billy Jones) / TOMORROW MORNING ..... Okeh 40529 4-6 26

FLORIDA / STEPPIN' IN SOCIETY ..... Okeh 40387 5-8 25

GIRLFRIEND, THE / THE BLUE ROOM ..... Okeh 40603 5-8 26

ISN'T SHE THE SWEETEST THING? / MOONLIGHT AND ROSES ..... Okeh 40358 4-6 25

MY BABY KNOWS HOW / I DON'T MIND BEING ALL ALONE (WHEN I'M ALL ALONE WITH YOU) ..... Okeh 40716 5-8 26
(Vocals: Lem Cleg)

SOB SISTER SADIE / CHEATIN' ON ME ..... Okeh 40326 5-8 25

SO DOES YOU OLD MANDARIN / OH! YOU LULU BELLE ..... Okeh 40580 5-8 26
(Vocals: Billy Jones)

TELL HER IN THE SPRINGTIME / TOKIO BLUESkeh 40279 5-8 25

TELL ME TONIGHT / IDOLIZING ..... Okeh 40744 5-8 27
(Vocals: Paul Hagan)

WHAT CAN I SAY AFTER I SAY I'M SORRY? / PRETTY LITTLE BABY ..... Okeh 40550 5-8 26

YOU NEED SOMEONE TO LOVE / ROSES REMIND ME OF YOU ..... Okeh 40632 4-6 26

LANIN, Sam, as The Okeh Melodians

MY BLUE HEAVEN / THERE AIN'T NO LAND LIKE DIXIELAND ..... Okeh 40898 4-6 27
(Vocals: Vaughn de Leath)

LANIN, Sam, as Sam Lanin's Dance Ensemble
(Hit of the Week records are one-sided paper discs)

BLUE AGAIN (Vocal: Paul Small) ..... Hit Of The Week 1126 5-8 31

BY MY SIDE (Vocal: Dick Robertson) ..... Hit Of The Week 1150 5-8 31

HELLO, BEAUTIFUL (Vocal: Paul Small) ..... Hit Of The Week 1136 3-5 31

I SURRENDER, DEAR (Vocal: Paul Small) ..... Hit Of The Week 1145 4-6 31

MAYBE IT'S LOVE (Vocal: Paul Small) ..... Hit Of The Week 1116 4-6 30

99 OUT OF A HUNDRED WANNA BE LOVED (Vocal: Paul Small) ... Hit Of The Week 1137 4-6 31

PARDON ME, PRETTY BABY (Vocal: Paul Small) ..... Hit Of The Week 1156 5-8 31

REACHING FOR THE MOON (Vocal: Scrappy Lambert) ..... Hit Of The Week 1133 3-5 31

SOMETHING TO REMEMBER YOU BY (Vocal: Paul Small) ..... Hit Of The Week 1125 5-8 31

THREE LITTLE WORDS (Vocal: Paul Small) ..... Hit Of The Week 1112 5-8 30

WHEN THE MOON COMES OVER THE MOUNTAIN (Vocal: Paul Small) ..... Hit Of The Week 1157 3-5 31

WHISTLING IN THE DARK (Vocal: Paul Small) ..... Hit Of The Week 1144 5-8 31

LANIN, Sam, as Sam Lanin's Dance Ensemble recorded under the name The Benrus Radio Orchestra

I'M YOURS (Vocal: Paul Small) ..... Hit Of The Week 1113 4-6 30

LANIN, Sam, as Sam Lanin's Dance Ensemble recorded under the name Phil Spitalny's Music

WHEN YOUR HAIR HAS TURNED TO SILVER (Vocal: Scrappy Lambert) ..... Hit Of The Week 1132 3-5 31

LANIN, Sam, as Sam Lanin's Orchestra:
see LANIN, Sam, & His Orchestra

LANIN, Sam, as Sam Lanin's Troubadours

EV'RYTHING'S GONNA BE ALL RIGHT / COULD I? I CERTAINLY COULD (Vocal: Billy Jones) ... Regal 8025 5-8 26

IN THE SWEET BYE-AND-BYE / AND THEN YOU CAME ALONG ..... Pathe Actuelle 36779 5-8 28
(Vocals: Jason Hawkes)

IN THE SWEET BYE-AND-BYE / AND THEN YOU CAME ALONG ..... Perfect 149660 4-6 28
(Vocals: Jason Hawkes)
(Simultaneously released on two labels)

NO FOOLIN' / THE GIRL FRIEND (Vocal: Irving Kaufman) ..... Banner 1753 4-6 26

NO FOOLIN' / THE GIRL FRIEND (Vocal: Irving Kaufman) ..... Domino 3724 4-6 26

NO FOOLIN' / THE GIRL FRIEND (Vocal: Irving Kaufman) ..... Regal 8057 4-6 26
(Simultaneously released on three labels)

PLENTY OF SUNSHINE (Vocals: Unknown) / EILEEN (by Sam Lanin's Troubadours as The Caroliners) ... Cameo 1283 4-6 28

PLENTY OF SUNSHINE (Vocals: Unknown) / EILEEN (by Sam Lanin's Troubadours as The Caroliners) ... Lincoln 2748 4-6 28

PLENTY OF SUNSHINE (Vocals: Unknown) / EILEEN (by Sam Lanin's Troubadours as The Caroliners) ..... Romeo 517 4-6 28
(Simultaneously released on three labels)

READY FOR THE RIVER / MY PET ..... Pathe Actuelle 36797 5-8 28
(Vocals: Scrappy Lambert)

READY FOR THE RIVER / MY PET ..... Perfect 14978 4-6 28
(Vocals: Scrappy Lambert)
(Simultaneously released on two labels)

SHE'S STILL MY BABY / WHO COULD BE MORE WONDERFUL THAN YOU? ..... Banner 1813 4-6 26

SHE'S STILL MY BABY / WHO COULD BE MORE WONDERFUL THAN YOU? ..... Domino 3789 4-6 26
(Simultaneously released on two labels)

LANIN, Sam, as Sam Lanin's Troubadours recorded under the name The Caroliners

EILEEN / PLENTY OF SUNSHINE (by Sam Lanin's Troubadours; Vocals: Unknown) ..... Cameo 1283 5-8 28

EILEEN / PLENTY OF SUNSHINE (by Sam Lanin's Troubadours; Vocals: Unknown) ..... Lincoln 2748 5-8 28

EILEEN / PLENTY OF SUNSHINE (by Sam Lanin's Troubadours; Vocals: Unknown) ..... Romeo 517 5-8 28
(Simultaneously released on two labels)

LANIN, Sam, as The University Orchestra

AFTER ALL, YOU'RE ALL I'M AFTER / I'M SO AFRAID OF YOU ..... Champion 16196 4-6 31
(Vocals: Paul Small)

AIN'T MISBEHAVIN' / HANG ON TO ME ..... Supertone 9550 5-8 29
(Vocals: Irving Kaufman)

ALONE WITH MY DREAMS / THANK YOUR FATHER ..... Gennett 7160 4-6 30
(Vocals: Tommy Weir)

ALONE WITH MY DREAMS / THANK YOUR FATHER ..... Supertone 9629 3-5 30
(Vocals: Tommy Weir)
(Simultaneously released on two labels)

AM I BLUE? / SINGIN' IN THE RAIN ... Gennett 6892 5-8 29
(Vocals: Arthur Fields)

BUTTON UP YOUR OVERCOAT / LOVER, COME BACK ..... Gennett 6815 5-8 29
(Vocals: Irving Kaufman)

HAPPY DAYS ARE HERE AGAIN / THERE'S DANGER IN YOUR EYES, CHERIE ... Gennett 7117 5-8 30
(Vocals: Irving Kaufman)

HAPPY DAYS ARE HERE AGAIN / THERE'S DANGER IN YOUR EYES, CHERIE ... Supertone 9615 4-6 30
(Vocals: Irving Kaufman)

HAPPY DAYS ARE HERE AGAIN / WHEN I'M LOOKING AT YOU ..... Champion 15930 4-6 30
(Vocals: Irving Kaufman)

HERE COMES THE SUN / HULLABALOO ..... Champion 16039 8-10 30
(Vocals: Claude Reese)

HERE COMES THE SUN / SWINGIN' IN A HAMMOCK ..... Gennett 7234 5-8 30
(Vocals: Claude Reese)

HULLABALOO (Vocal: Claude Reese) / LONELY (Vocal: Scrappy Lambert) ..... Gennett 7257 10-12 30

I'M YOURS / TOMORROW IS ANOTHER DAY ..... Gennett 7277 4-6 30
(Vocals: Scrappy Lambert)

I'M YOURS / TOMORROW IS ANOTHER DAY ..... Supertone 9742 3-5 30
(Vocals: Scrappy Lambert)
(Simultaneously released on two labels)

I NEVER DREAMT (Vocals: The Crooners) / SWINGIN' IN A HAMMOCK (Vocal: Claude Reese) ... Champion 16042 5-8 30

I NEVER DREAMT / TELLING IT TO THE DAISIES ..... Gennett 7193 6-8 30
(Vocals: The Crooners)

LITTLE KISS EACH MORNING, A / LADY LUCK ..... Champion 15861 5-8 30
(Vocals: Irving Kaufman)

LONESOME AND BLUE / GET A LITTLE CLOSER ..... Champion 16334 4-6 31
(Vocals: Paul Small)

LONESOME LOVER / WHEN KENTUCKY BIDS THE WORLD GOOD MORNING ... Champion 16177 3-5 31
(Vocals: Paul Small)

MISS WONDERFUL / SOMEBODY MIGHTY LIKE YOU ..... Gennett 7011 4-6 29
(Vocals: Irving Kaufman)

MISS WONDERFUL / SOMEBODY MIGHTY LIKE YOU ..... Supertone 9576 3-5 29
(Vocals: Irving Kaufman)
(Simultaneously released on two labels)

MY SUGAR AND ME / LOVER, COME BACK TO ME ..... Supertone 9381 4-6 29
(Vocals: Irving Kaufman)

OH, WHY? / SOMETHING TO REMEMBER YOU BY ..... Champion 16130 4-6 29
(Vocals: Paul Small)

ONE IN THE WORLD, THE / I'VE GOT A FEELING I'M FALLING ..... Gennett 6862 5-8 29
(Vocals: Irving Kaufman)

OR WHAT HAVE YOU? / HANG ON TO ME ..... Gennett 6980 5-8 29
(Vocals: Irving Kaufman)

SINGIN' IN THE RAIN / THAT'S YOU, BABY ..... Supertone 9444 4-6 29
(Vocals: Arthur Fields)

TOMORROW IS ANOTHER DAY / LONELY ..... Champion 16064 4-6 30
(Vocals: Scrappy Lambert)

USED TO YOU / I'M IN SEVENTH HEAVEN ..... Gennett 6920 5-8 29
(Vocals: Smith Ballew as Arthur Leroy)

USED TO YOU / I'M IN SEVENTH HEAVEN ..... Supertone 9458 4-6 29
(Vocals: Smith Ballew as Arthur Leroy)
(Simultaneously released on two labels)

WHAT A DAY! / I'VE GOT A FEELING I'M FALLING ..... Supertone 9437 4-6 29
(Vocals: Irving Kaufman)

WHY? / SWEET NOTHINGS
OF LOVE........................ *Champion 15884* 4-6 30
(Vocals: Scrappy Lambert as Norman Wallace)

WHY WAS I BORN? / LADY LUCK...... *Gennett 7042* 5-8 30
(Vocals: Irving Kaufman)

WHY WAS I BORN? / LADY LUCK.... *Supertone 9580* 4-6 30
(Vocals: Irving Kaufman)
(Simultaneously released on two labels)

YEAR FROM TODAY, A / SWEET NOTHINGS
OF LOVE........................... *Gennett 7087* 5-8 30
(Vocals: Scrappy Lambert as Norman Wallace)

YEAR FROM TODAY, A / SWEET NOTHINGS
OF LOVE......................... *Supertone 9590* 4-6 30
(Vocals: Scrappy Lambert as Norman Wallace)
(Simultaneously released on two labels)

LANIN, Sam, as The University Orchestra recorded under the name Al Morris & His Playmates

LONESOME LOVER / LONESOME
AND BLUE........................ *Superior 2578* 4-6 31
(Vocals: Paul Small)

WHEN KENTUCKY BIDS THE
WORLD GOOD MORNING / IT REALLY
DOESN'T MATTER................. *Superior 2576* 3-5 31
(Vocals: Paul Small)

LANIN, Sam, as The University Orchestra recorded under the name Joe Morris & His Orchestra

BUTTON UP YOUR OVERCOAT /
MY SUGAR AND ME.............. *Champion 15717* 5-8 29
(Vocals: Irving Kaufman)

HANG ON TO ME / SOMEBODY MIGHTY
LIKE YOU...................... *Champion 15842* 4-6 29
(Vocals: Irving Kaufman)

MISS WONDERFUL / WHEN THE REAL THING
COMES ALONG.................. *Champion 15839* 4-6 29
(Vocals: Irving Kaufman)

ONE IN THE WORLD, THE / I'VE GOT
A FEELING I'M FALLING......... *Champion 15738* 4-6 29
(Vocals: Irving Kaufman)

OR WHAT HAVE YOU? /
AIN'T MISBEHAVIN' .... *Champion 15803* 5-8 29
(Vocals: Irving Kaufman)

SINGIN' IN THE RAIN /
THAT'S YOU, BABY.............. *Champion 15758* 4-6 29
(Vocals: Arthur Fields)

USED TO YOU / I'M IN
SEVENTH HEAVEN.............. *Champion 15777* 4-6 29
(Vocals: Smith Ballew as Arthur Leroy)

LANIN'S ARCADIANS:
see LANIN, Sam

LANIN'S FAMOUS PLAYERS
see LANIN, Sam, & His Famous Players

LANIN'S JAZZ BAND:
see LANIN, Sam

LANIN'S RED HEADS:
see LANIN, SAM

LANIN'S ROSELAND ORCHESTRA:
see LANIN, Sam, & His Roseland Orchestra

LANIN'S SOUTHERN SERENADERS:
see LANIN, Sam

LA PALINA BROADCASTERS, The:
see RICH, Fred, & His Orchestra

LEARY, Ford, & His Orchestra
(Ford Leary: 9/5/08 – 6/4/49)

MUDDY WATER / I GET A KICK
OUT OF CORN.................. *Bluebird B-11031* 12-15 40
(Vocals: Ford Leary)
(A Canadian release, not issued in the United States)

ON REVIVAL DAY /
HONG KONG BLUES............ *Bluebird B-10652* 10-12 40
(Vocals: Ford Leary)

LEASH, Paul, as The Sophisticats

I'LL SAY / HAROLD HAWKINS'
HOBBLE.................................... *Decca 3351* 5-8 40

LOUISIANA PURCHASE / THE KITTEN WITH THE
BIG EYES............................ *Decca 3307* 4-6 40
(Vocals: Unknown)

LEIGHTON, Chester, & His Sophomores:
see RICH, Fred, & His (La Palina) Orchestra
see RICH, Fred, & His Orchestra, and
see SELVIN, Ben, & His Orchestra

LEM, Harold, & His Orchestra:
see RICH, Fred, & His (La Palina) Orchestra

LENTZ, Al, & His Orchestra

IF YOU CAN'T TELL THE WORLD SHE'S A GOOD
LITTLE GIRL, JUST SAY NOTHING AT ALL / SAM,
THE OLD ACCORDION MAN....... *Columbia 867-D* 3-5 27
(Vocals: Al Lentz)

I NEVER SEE MAGGIE ALONE / IF I DIDN'T
KNOW YOUR HUSBAND AND YOU
DIDN'T KNOW MY WIFE.......... *Columbia 856-D* 3-5 27
(Vocals: Al Lentz)

SUSIE'S FELLER / SWEET THING .... *Regal 8130* 3-5 26
(Vocals: Al Lentz)

WHO-OO? YOU-OO, THAT'S WHO! /
ZULU WAIL...................... *Columbia 1072-D* 4-6 27
(Vocals: Al Lentz)

LENZBERG, Julius, as Lenzberg's Riverside Orchestra

CHERIE / VAMPING ROSE................ *Arto 9064* 2-4 21

LASSIE / A YOUNG MAN'S FANCY..... *Edison 50679* 3-5 20

MA! (Vocal: Arthur Hall) / — .... *Paramount 20071* 4-6 21

MA! (Vocal: Arthur Hall) / — .... *Puritan 11071* 3-5 21
(Simultaneously released on two labels)

TEN LITTLE FINGERS AND TEN LITTLE
TOES / WABASH BLUES .... *Claxtonola 40081* 5-8 22

TEN LITTLE FINGERS AND TEN LITTLE
TOES / WABASH BLUES......... *Paramount 20081* 4-6 22

TEN LITTLE FINGERS AND TEN LITTLE
TOES / WABASH BLUES............ *Puritan 11081* 3-5 22
(Simultaneously released on three labels)

LEONARD, Harlan, & His Rockets
(Harlan Leonard: 7/2/05 –)

400 SWING / MY POP GAVE ME
A NICKEL (Vocal: Ernie Williams) .... *Bluebird B-10823* 4-6 40

HAIRY JOE JUMP / MY GAL SAL ... *Bluebird B-10625* 4-6 40

KEEP ROCKIN' /
DIG IT (Vocal: Myra Taylor).......... *Bluebird B-11302* 4-6 41

MISTREATED (Vocal: Ernie Williams) /
TOO MUCH .... *Bluebird B-11544* 3-5 41

RIDE MY BLUES AWAY (Vocal: Ernie Williams) /
MY DREAM (Vocal: Darwin Jones).... *Bluebird B-11032* 4-6 40

ROCKIN' WITH THE
ROCKETS / CONTACT............ *Bluebird B-10586* 4-6 40

SKEE / I DIDN'T WANT TO SET THE WORLD
ON FIRE (Vocal: Myra Taylor)........ *Bluebird B-10919* 3-5 40

SNAKY FEELING (Vocal: James Ross) /
ROCK AND RIDE .... *Bluebird B-10883* 5-8 40

LEONARD, Harold, & His Red Jackets

AIN'T GOT NOTHIN' NEVER HAD NOTHIN' /
THE CAT'S WHISKERS.............. *Gennett 5138* 3-5 23

LIMEHOUSE BLUES / WHERE THE LAZY
DAISIES GROW .... *Okeh 40083* 3-5 24

RED JACKET BLUES /
YOU KNOW WHY.................... *Gennett 5026* 3-5 23

SOME LONESOME NIGHT /
CHINA BOY .... *Gennett 5137* 3-5 23

UNFORTUNATE BLUES /
GOODNIGHT, SLEEP TIGHT........... *Okeh 40091* 3-5 24

LEONARD, Harold, & His Waldorf-Astoria Orchestra

DINAH / KENTUCKY'S WAY OF
SAYIN' "GOOD MORNIN'".......... *Brunswick 3000* 3-5 26

JUST A MEMORY / JOY BELLS..... *Columbia 1105-D* 2-4 27
(Vocals: Unknown)

LONESOME AND SORRY / I'M FLIRTING
WITH YOU...................... *Brunswick 3173* 2-4 26

MUDDY WATERS / ANGEL EYES.... *Brunswick 3402* 3-5 27
(Vocals: Lester O'Keefe)

WHILE THE YEARS GO
DRIFTING BY (Vocals: by orchestra) /
FLAPPERETTE.......................... *Brunswick 3255* 2-4 26

LE PETIT SALON ORCHESTRA

MY HAWAIIAN EVENING STAR /
GOLDEN MEMORIES (OF HAWAII)..... *Okeh 40483* 2-4 25

OH, HOW I MISS YOU TONIGHT / ROSE OF
THE EVENING (Vocals: Unknown) .... *Okeh 40409* 2-4 25

LEWIS, Ted, & His Band
(Ted Lewis: 6/6/92 – 8/25/71)
(Certain Columbia releases have silver and black picture labels, showing Ted Lewis with top hat held aloft. Those known issues are noted and priced accordingly, and any other releases with the picture labels would have similar values.)

ANGRY / SAY, ARABELLA.......... *Columbia 416-D* 3-5 25

AT LAST I'M HAPPY (Vocal: Ted Lewis) / TRULY (I LOVE
YOU (Vocals: by quintet)............ *Columbia 2408-D* 8-10 31

AUNT HAGAR'S BLUES /
WET YO' THUMB................. *Columbia A-3879* 3-5 23

AWAY DOWN SOUTH IN HEAVEN (Vocal: Ted Lewis) /
KEEP SWEEPING THE COBWEBS OFF
THE MOON (Vocal: Ruth Etting) ..... *Columbia 1242-D* 4-6 28

BAM-BAM-BAMY SHORE /
THE CAMEL WALK.............. *Columbia 478-D* 3-5 25

BARNYARD BLUES / THERE'LL BE SOME
CHANGES MADE .... *Columbia 170-D* 3-5 24

BEALE STREET BLUES /
TWELFTH STREET RAG .... *Columbia A-3972* 4-6 23

BEALE STREET MAMA /
LOUISVILLE LOU................ *Columbia A-3892* 3-5 23

BEES KNEES / LOVIN' SAM (THE
SHEIK OF ALABAM')............. *Columbia A-3730* 2-4 22

BUGLE CALL RAG / SOME OF
THESE DAYS (Vocal: Sophie Tucker)... *Columbia 826-D* 5-8 27

BUY AMERICAN! (AND GOOD TIMES
WILL COME THROUGH) / TRY A
LITTLE TENDERNESS........... *Columbia 2748-D* 5-8 33
(Vocals: Ted Lewis)

CLASSIC JAZZ (a 4-record album set) .... *Columbia C-207* 12-15 51
(Individual records in the set, listed numerically (with value of each):
AUNT HAGAR'S BLUES / ROYAL
GARDEN BLUES................. *Columbia 38840* 3-5
CLARINET MARMARLADE / DALLAS
BLUES (Vocal: Fats Waller)........... *Columbia 38841* 3-5
YELLOW DOG BLUES, THE /
SOBBIN' BLUES.................. *Columbia 38842* 3-5
DIP YOUR BRUSH IN THE SUNSHINE /
WHEN MY BABY SMILES AT
ME (Vocal: Ted Lewis)................ *Columbia 38843* 2-4

DALLAS BLUES / ROYAL
GARDEN BLUES................ *Columbia 2527-D* 12-15 31
(Vocals: Fats Waller)

DARKTOWN STRUTTERS' BALL / ALEXANDER'S
RAGTIME BAND................ *Columbia 1084-D* 4-6 27
(Vocals: Ted Lewis)

DON'T WAKE ME UP (LET ME DREAM) / THAT
CERTAIN PARTY (Vocal: Ted Lewis) ... *Columbia 551-D* 3-5 26

DOWN THE OLD CHURCH AISLE / IS EVERYBODY
HAPPY NOW? .... *Columbia 1207-D* 3-5 28
(Vocals: Ted Lewis)

DOWN THE OLD CHURCH
AISLE / MARIE.................. *Columbia A-3538* 2-4 21

DREAM DADDY / MR. RADIO MAN... *Columbia 82-D* 3-5 24

DRIFTING AND DREAMING / THE MONKEY
DOODLE-DOO .... *Columbia 620-D* 3-5 26

EGYPTIAN-ELLA (Vocal: Ted Lewis) / I'M CRAZY 'BOUT
MY BABY (Vocal: Fats Waller) .... *Columbia 2428-D* 10-12 31

FAREWELL BLUES /
WABASH BLUES .... *Columbia 2029-D* 5-8 29

FIFTY MILLION FRENCHMEN CAN'T BE WRONG /
ONE SWEET LETTER FROM YOU... *Columbia 988-D* 3-5 27
(Vocals: Ted Lewis)

GEORGETTE / SEND BACK
MY HONEYMAN .... *Columbia A-3662* 2-4 22

GOLD DIGGERS' SONG, THE / IT'S SUNDAY
DOWN IN CAROLINE .... *Columbia 2775-D* 10-12 33
(Vocals: Ted Lewis)

GOOD MAN IS HARD TO FIND, A /
I AIN'T GOT NOBODY........... *Columbia 1428-D* 4-6 28
(Vocals: Ted Lewis)

HEADIN' FOR BETTER TIMES /
JUST A GIGOLO................. *Columbia 2378-D* 10-12 31
(Vocals: Ted Lewis)

HOME-MADE SUNSHINE / LAUGHING
AT LIFE......................... *Columbia 2311-D* 8-10 30
(Vocals: Ted Lewis. This release has a silver and black picture label, showing Ted Lewis with top hat held aloft.)

HOMESICK (Vocal: Ted Lewis) / TOMORROW (I'LL BE IN
MY DIXIE HOME AGAIN)......... *Columbia A-3709* 2-4 22

HOT LIPS / I LOVE YOU,
SWEET ANGELINE.............. *Columbia A-3676* 2-4 22

I AIN'T GOT NOBODY TO LOVE / I LIKE
YOU BEST OF ALL............... *Columbia 274-D* 3-5 25

IF I HAD A MILLION DOLLARS / THERE'S GONNA BE A WEDDING IN THE BAND .... *Decca 242* 3-5 34
(Vocals: Ted Lewis)

I'M THE MEDICINE MAN FOR THE BLUES / WOULDN'T IT BE WONDERFUL? ... *Columbia 1882-D* 5-8 29
(Vocals: Ted Lewis. This release has a silver and black picture label, showing Ted Lewis with top hat held aloft.)

I'M WALKING AROUND IN A DREAM / MAYBE — WHO KNOWS .... *Columbia 1854-D* 5-8 29
(Vocals: Ted Lewis. This release has a silver and black picture label, showing Ted Lewis with top hat held aloft.)

IN A GARDEN IN OLD KALUA / AN OLD, OLD MAN WITH AN OLD, OLD PIPE (AND AN OLD, OLD LADY BESIDE HIM) .... *Columbia 2777-D* 3-5 33
(Vocals: Ted Lewis)

IN THE VINE-COVERED CURCH WAY BACK HOME / HERE YOU COME WITH LOVE ... *Columbia 2799-D* 3-5 33
(Vocals: Ted Lewis)

JAZZ HOLIDAY, A / JUNGLE BLUES ... *Columbia 1525-D* 4-6 28

JAZZNOCRACY / WHITE HEAT .... *Decca 107* 5-8 34

JUNE NIGHT / I WONDER WHAT'S BECOME OF SALLY .... *Columbia 157-D* 3-5 24

JUST AROUND THE CORNER / DOWN THE OLD CHURCH AISLE .... *Decca 3846* 2-4 41
(Vocals: Ted Lewis)

LAZY BONES (Vocal: Ted Lewis) / RHYTHM .... *Columbia 2786-D* 10-12 33

LEWISADA BLUES / I LOVE YOU (MY LOVE SONG) (Vocal: Ted Lewis) ..... *Columbia 1916-D* 8-10 29
(This release has a silver and black picture label, showing Ted Lewis with top hat aloft.)

LIMEHOUSE BLUES / ROSES OF PICARDY .... *Columbia 1789-D* 8-10 29
(Vocals: Ted Lewis. This release has a silver and black picture label, showing Ted Lewis with top hat aloft.)

LONESOME ROAD, THE/DINAH ... *Columbia 2181-D* 10-12 30
(Vocals: Ted Lewis & The Four Dusty Travelers)

MA! / BIMINI BAY .... *Columbia A-3473* 2-4 21

MEMPHIS BLUES, THE / BEALE STREET BLUES .... *Columbia 1050-D* 5-8 27

MEMPHIS BLUES / TIGER RAG ..... *Columbia A-3813* 3-5 23

MILENBERG JOYS / TIN ROOF BLUES .... *Columbia 439-D* 5-8 25

MOONLIGHT MADNESS / KING FOR A DAY .... *Columbia 1485-D* 3-5 28
(Vocals: Ted Lewis)

MOONLIGHT MILLIONAIRES (Vocal: Ted Lewis) / STORMY WEATHER (Vocal: Shirley Jay) .... *Columbia 2774-D* 5-8 33

MY LITTLE DREAM BOAT / LADY LUCK .... *Columbia 1999-D* 5-8 29
(Vocals: Ted Lewis. This release has a silver and black picture label, showing Ted Lewis with top hat aloft.)

MY MAMA'S IN TOWN (Vocal: Ted Lewis) / THE NEW ST. LOUIS BLUES ...... *Columbia 697-D* 4-6 26
(Vocals: Ted Lewis.)

MY OLD FLAME / ISN'T IT A SHAME? ..... *Decca 241* 3-5 34
(Vocals: Ted Lewis)

MY WOMAN! / SOMEBODY LOVES YOU .... *Columbia 2635-D* 10-12 32
(Vocals: Ted Lewis)

OLD PLAYMATE / AN EV'NING IN CAROLINE .... *Columbia 2560-D* 10-12 31
(Vocals: Ted Lewis. This release has a silver and black picture label, showing Ted Lewis with top hat aloft.)

OLD ST. LOUIS BLUES, THE / I'M THE MEDICINE MAN FOR THE BLUES .... *Decca 2033* 4-6 38
(Vocals: Ted Lewis)

ONE MORE TIME / HO HUM! .... *Columbia 2452-D* 12-15 31
(Vocals: Ted Lewis. This release has a silver and black picture label, showing Ted Lewis with top hat aloft.)

POP GOES YOUR HEART / HAPPINESS AHEAD .... *Decca 239* 4-6 34
(Vocals: Ted Lewis)

PRETTY LITTLE BABY / I WISH'T I WAS IN PEORIA (Vocal: Ted Lewis) .... *Columbia 543-D* 3-5 26

RUNNIN' WILD / ST. LOUIS BLUES .... *Columbia A-3790* 3-5 23

SAN / AUNT HAGAR'S BLUES (Vocal: Ted Lewis) .... *Columbia 2113-D* 10-12 30
(This release has a silver and black picture label, showing Ted Lewis with top hat aloft.)

SAN / SHE'S EVERYBODY'S SWEETHEART (Vocal: Ted Lewis) .... *Columbia 122-D* 3-5 24

SHANTY IN OLD SHANTY TOWN, A / SWEET SUE – JUST YOU .... *Columbia 2652-D* 10-12 32
(Vocals: Ted Lewis)

SHE LOVES ME (Vocal: Ted Lewis) / TOO TIRED .... *Columbia 227-D* 3-5 24

SHIM-ME-SHA-WABBLE / CLARINET MARMALADE .... *Columbia 1573-D* 4-6 28

SHOW ME THE WAY / NOBODY LOVES YOU LIKE I DO .... *Columbia 241-D* 3-5 24

SOMEBODY STOLE MY GAL / SOMEDAY, SWEETHEART .... *Columbia 2336-D* 8-10 30
(Vocals: Ted Lewis. This release has a silver and black picture label, showing Ted Lewis with top hat aloft.)

START THE BAND / OH BABY! ..... *Columbia 1391-D* 3-5 28
(Vocals: Ted Lewis)

STEPPIN' OUT / UNFORTUNATE BLUES .... *Columbia 48-D* 4-6 24

SUNNY SIDE OF THE STREET; JUST AROUND THE CORNER / ME AND MY SHADOW .... *Universal UPC 206/207* 10-12 40
(Vocals: Ted Lewis. This is a Universal Pictures record for promotion of the film "Oh Charlie". These arrangements were not issued commercially. This is one record.)

SWEETIE PIE / I'LL CLOSE MY EYES TO EVERYONE ELSE .... *Decca 240* 3-5 34
(Vocals: Ted Lewis)

SWEET LITTLE YOU / ECCENTRIC ... *Columbia 195-D* 3-5 24

TED LEWIS AND HIS ORCHESTRA (a 4-record album set) .... *Decca Album A-353* 8-10 40
(Individual records in the set, listed numerically (with value of each):

WHEN MY BABY SMILES AT ME / SHE'S FUNNY THAT WAY .... *Decca 23916* 2-4
(Vocals: Ted Lewis)

OLD ST. LOUIS BLUES, THE / I'M THE MEDICINE MAN FOR THE BLUES (Vocal: Ted Lewis) ... *Decca 23917* 2-4

WEAR A HAT WITH A SILVER LINING / JUST AROUND THE CORNER .... *Decca 23918* 2-4
(Vocals: Ted Lewis)

GOOD NIGHT / THE SWEETHEART OF SIGMA CHI .... *Decca 23919* 2-4
(Vocals: Ted Lewis)

TED LEWIS POPULAR FAVORITES / SHUBERT SERENADE (by The Columbia Symphony Orchestra) .... *Columbia 1 S* 3-5 23
(A promotional record)

TEN THOUSAND YEARS AGO / LITTLE LOCKET OF LONG AGO .... *Columbia 2807-D* 8-10 33
(Vocals: Ted Lewis)

THAT'S WHY I LOVE YOU / WHERE'D YOU GET THOSE EYES? .... *Columbia 667-D* 3-5 26
(Vocals: Ted Lewis)

THERE'S A NEW DAY COMING / HAVE YOU EVER BEEN LONELY .... *Columbia 2753-D* 8-10 33
(Vocals: Ted Lewis)

THERE'S A RING AROUND MY RAINBOW / ALL ABOARD FOR DREAMLAND, BABY .... *Columbia 2758-D* 10-12 33
(Vocals: Ted Lewis.) (This record was pressed in blue shellac.)

TIGER RAG / BLUES (MY NAUGHTY SWEETIE GIVES TO ME) .... *Columbia 770-D* 4-6 26

TIGER RAG / JAZZ ME BLUES .... *Decca 4272* 2-4 41

TWELVE O'CLOCK AT NIGHT / THE ONE I LOVE BELONGS TO SOMEBODY ELSE .... *Columbia 52-D* 4-6 24

TWO CIGARETTES IN THE DARK / TONIGHT IS MINE .... *Decca 106* 3-5 34
(Vocals: Ted Lewis)

WAH! WAH! / FRANKIE AND JOHNNY (Vocal: Ted Lewis) .... *Columbia 1017-D* 3-5 27

WEAR A HAT WITH A SILVER LINING / SHE'S FUNNY THAT WAY .... *Columbia 1656-D* 8-10 29
(Vocals: Ted Lewis. This release has a silver and black picture label, showing Ted Lewis with top hat aloft.)

WHEN MY BABY SMILES AT ME (theme song) / KEEP A LITTLE SUNSHINE IN YOUR HEART .... *Columbia 922-D* 3-5 27
(Vocals: Ted Lewis)

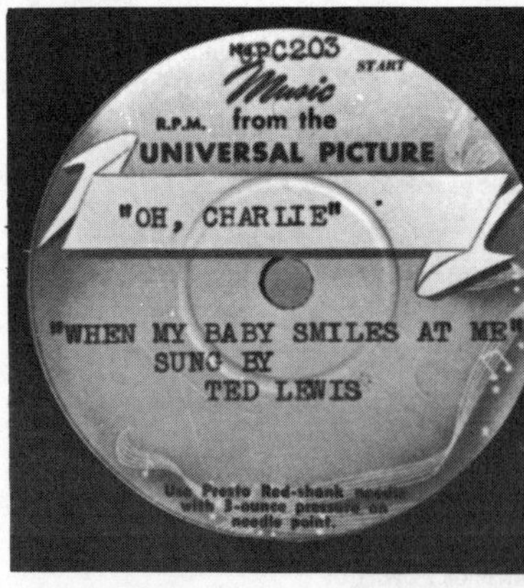

WHEN MY BABY SMILES AT ME (theme song) / LEADER OF THE BAND .... *Universal UPC 203/205* 10-12 40
(Vocals: Ted Lewis.) (This is a Universal Pictures record for promotion of the film "Oh Charlie". These arrangements were not issued commercially.)

WHEN MY BABY SMILES AT ME (theme song) / SHE'S FUNNY THAT WAY .... *Decca 2054* 4-6 38
(Vocals: Ted Lewis)

WHEN THE CURTAIN COMES DOWN / GLAD RAG DOLL .... *Columbia 1709-D* 4-6 29
(Vocals: Ted Lewis)

WHILE WE DANCED TILL DAWN / JUST AROUND THE CORNER .... *Columbia 504-D* 3-5 25
(Vocals: Ted Lewis)

WILL YOU REMEMBER ME? (Vocal: Ted Lewis) / O! KATHARINA .... *Columbia 295-D* 3-5 25

WORLD IS WAITING FOR THE SUNRISE, THE (whistling by Ted Lewis) / THREE O'CLOCK IN THE MORNING (Vocal: Ted Lewis) .... *Columbia 2246-D* 5-8 30

YELLOW DOG BLUES / SOBBIN' BLUES .... *Columbia 2217-D* 10-12 30
(This release has a silver and black picture label, showing Ted Lewis with top hat aloft.)

YOU'VE GOT THAT THING / HARMONICA HARRY .... *Columbia 2088-D* 10-12 30
(Vocals: Ted Lewis. This release has a silver and black picture label, showing Ted Lewis with top hat aloft.)

LEWIS, Ted, as The Ted Lewis Jazz Band

BROADWAY ROSE / MARGIE .... *Columbia A-3351* 2-4 20

FAIR ONE / GYPSY MOON .... *Columbia A-2998* 2-4 20

I'LL SEE YOU IN C-U-B-A / THE MOON SHINES ON THE MOON-SHINE (Vocal: Ted Lewis) .... *Columbia A-2927* 2-4 20

I LOVE YOU SUNDAY / THE HULA BLUES .... *Columbia A-3306* 2-4 20

QUEEN OF SHEBA / WHERE IS MY DADDY NOW BLUES .... *Columbia A-3421* 2-4 21

SALLY, WON'T YOU COME BACK? / SECOND-HAND ROSE .... *Columbia A-3453* 2-4 21

TIRED OF ME / THAT RIGA-LIGA-LEE .... *Columbia A-3329* 2-4 20

UNDERNEATH THE PALMS / LOVE ME .... *Columbia A-3411* 2-4 21

WANG-WANG BLUES / HOME AGAIN BLUES .... *Columbia A-3464* 2-4 21

LICHTER, Joie, as Joie Lichter's Strand Symphonists

AFTER I SAID I'M SORRY / SLIPPERY ELM .... *Paramount 20439* 8-10 26

AFTER I SAID I'M SORRY / SLIPPERY ELM .... *Puritan 11439* 5-8 26

AFTER I SAID I'M SORRY / SLIPPERY ELM .... *Silvertone 3507* 5-8 26
(Simultaneously released on three labels)

LINGER AWHILE / I'M ALL BROKE OUT WITH THE BLUES .... *Harmograph 887* 12-15 24

LINGER AWHILE / I'M ALL BROKE OUT WITH THE BLUES .... *Paramount 20289* 8-10 24
(Simultaneously released on two labels)

PATRICIA MINE / MOTHER'S BOY ..... *Gennett 5423* 3-5 24

SPANISH SHAWL / SANDY .... *Paramount 20428* 8-10 26

SPANISH SHAWL / SANDY .... *Puritan 11428* 5-8 26

SPANISH SHAWL / SANDY .... *Silvertone 3502* 5-8 26
(Simultaneously released on three labels)

LIDO VENICE DANCE ORCHESTRA, The:

see SMITH, Harl

LIGHT, Enoch, & His Hotel Governor Clinton Orchestra

(Enoch Light: 8/18/07 – 7/31/78)

IF I DIDN'T CARE (Vocal: Enoch Light) / NOTHING BUT THE BEST (Vocal: Jerry Baker) .... *Bluebird B-5348* 3-5 34

IF I DIDN'T CARE (Vocal: Enoch Light) / NOTHING BUT THE BEST (Vocal: Jerry Baker) .... *Sunrise S-3439* 10-12 34
(Simultaneously released on two labels)

NIGHT ON THE WATER (Vocal: Enoch Light) / WHEN TOMORROW COMES .... *Bluebird B-5347* 3-5 34

NIGHT ON THE WATER (Vocal: Enoch Light) / WHEN TOMORROW COMES .... *Sunrise S-3438* 10-12 34
(Simultaneously released on two labels)

THROW ANOTHER LOG ON THE FIRE / YOU HAVE TAKEN MY HEART .... *Bluebird B-5346* 3-5 34
(Vocals: Jerry Baker)

THROW ANOTHER LOG ON THE FIRE / YOU HAVE TAKEN MY HEART .... *Sunrise S-3437* 10-12 34
(Vocals: Jerry Baker)
(Simultaneously released on two labels)

LIGHT, Enoch, & His Hotel Taft Orchestra

AMONG THOSE SAILING (Vocal: Peggy Mann) / IT TOOK A MILLION YEARS (Vocal: George Hines) .... *Vocalion 4623* 3-5 39

LIGHT, Enoch, & His Orchestra

HERE IN MY HEART (Vocal: Loren Becker) / KISS OF FIRE (Vocal: Sally Sweetland) ...... *Prom 1016* 2-4 48

LITTLE HOUSE THAT LOVE BUILT, THE / SUMMER NIGHT .... *Melotone 7-03-06* 3-5 37
(Vocals: Johnny Muldowney)

LITTLE HOUSE THAT LOVE BUILT, THE / SUMMER NIGHT ...... *Vocalion 3421* 3-5 37
(Vocals: Johnny Muldowney)
(Simultaneously released on two labels)

RUN, RABBIT, RUN! (Vocal: Bunny O'Dare) / SOMEDAY YOU'LL FIND YOUR BLUEBIRD (Vocal: Peggy Mann) .... *Bluebird B-10597* 2-4 40

YOU'RE THE FIRST ON SECOND AVENUE (Vocal: Peggy Mann) / TINY OLD TOWN (Vocal: George Hines) .... *Bluebird B-10611* 2-4 40

LINCOLN DANCE ORCHESTRA, The:

see HARING, Bob, & His Velvetone Orchestra

LITTLE, Little Jack, & His Orchestra

(Little Jack Little: 5/28/00 – 4/9/56)

ADORABLE / HIAWATHA'S LULLABY .... *Bluebird B-5065* 4-6 33
(Vocals: Little Jack Little)

ADORABLE / HIAWATHA'S LULLABY .... *Electradisk 1988* 12-15 33
(Vocals: Little Jack Little)
(Simultaneously released on two labels)

BROADWAY CINDERELLA / WHERE AM I? (AM I IN HEAVEN?) .... *Columbia 3096-D* 3-5 35
(Vocals: Little Jack Little)

DON'T BE AFRAID TO TELL YOUR MOTHER / I BELIEVE IN MIRACLES .... *Columbia 3006-D* 5-8 35
(Vocals: Little Jack Little)

I DON'T WANT TO BE PRESIDENT / I'D LIKE TO DUNK YOU IN MY COFFEE....... *Columbia 2993-D* 5-8 35
(Vocals: Little Jack Little)

I'M SHOOTING HIGH / LIGHTS OUT... *Columbia 3108-D* 5-8 36
(Vocals: Little Jack Little)

IT'S SWELL OF YOU / OOH, BUT I'M HAPPY............. *Melotone 7-05-19* 4-6 37
(Vocals: Little Jack Little)

IT'S SWELL OF YOU / OOH, BUT I'M HAPPY.............................. *Vocalion 3498* 4-6 37
(Vocals: Little Jack Little)

I WISHED ON THE MOON / WHY DREAM?.................... *Columbia 3068-D* 5-8 35
(Vocals: Little Jack Little) (This record was pressed in blue shellac)

LET'S GIVE THREE CHEERS FOR LOVE / STAY AS SWEET AS YOU ARE............ *Columbia 2969-D* 5-8 34
(Vocals: Little Jack Little)

LOVE IS JUST AROUND THE CORNER / I'M JUST A LITTLE BOY BLUE............... *Columbia 2984-D* 4-6 35
(Vocals: Little Jack Little)

LULLABY OF BROADWAY / I'M GOIN' STOMPIN' WITH YOU.................... *Columbia 3009-D* 5-8 35
(Vocals: Little Jack Little) (This record was pressed in blue shellac)

MY HEART AND I / MOONBURN... *Columbia 3107-D* 4-6 36
(Vocals: Little Jack Little)

NO OTHER ONE / ON TREASURE ISLAND.............................. *Columbia 3095-D* 4-6 35
(Vocals: Little Jack Little)

NOTHING BUT THE BEST / YOU OUGHTA BE IN PICTURES................ *Columbia 2895-D* 5-8 34
(Vocals: Little Jack Little) (This record was pressed in blue shellac)

OLD ROSES / LIKE TWO LITTLE FLIES ON A LUMP OF SUGAR........... *Columbia 2900-D* 5-8 34
(Vocals: Little Jack Little) (This record was pressed in blue shellac)

ON THE ISLE OF KITCHY-MI-BOKO / TURN OFF THE MOON.............. *Vocalion 3521* 4-6 37
(Vocals: Little Jack Little)

SPEAKING CONFIDENTIALLY / I'M IN THE MOOD FOR LOVE...................... *Columbia 3069-D* 4-6 35
(Vocals: Little Jack Little)

STAY OUT OF MY DREAMS / WE'RE TOGETHER AGAIN........ *Bluebird B-5056* 4-6 33
(Vocals: Little Jack Little)

STAY OUT OF MY DREAMS / WE'RE TOGETHER AGAIN........ *Electradisk 1982* 12-15 33
(Vocals: Little Jack Little)
(Simultaneously released on two labels)

WITH EVERY BREATH I TAKE / JUNE IN JANUARY.............. *Columbia 2978-D* 5-8 34
(Vocals: Little Jack Little)

LITTLE RAMBLERS, The:
see CALIFORNIA RAMBLERS, The

LITZKE, Glen, as Glen Litzke's Midnight Serenaders

BETTY CO-ED / SO BEATS MY HEART FOR YOU................. *Broadway 1399* 4-6 30
(Vocals: Unknown)

MAYBE IT'S LOVE / STARS.......... *Broadway 1398* 4-6 30
(Vocals: Unknown)

LIVINGSTON, Jimmie, & His Orchestra

HEIGH-HO (Vocals: by orchestra) / ONE SONG (Vocal: Jack Crawley)...... *Bluebird B-7407* 5-8 38

JUST A SIMPLE MELODY / CLOVER BLOSSOMS.............. *Bluebird B-7431* 4-6 38

SOMEBODY'S THINKING OF YOU TONIGHT / SKATING DOWN THE OLD MILL STREAM.......... *Bluebird B-7421* 3-5 38
(Vocals: Jack Crawley)

LOFNER, Carol, & His Orchestra
(also see LOFNER-HARRIS St. Francis Hotel Orchestra, The)

I'M JUST AN ORDINARY HUMAN (Vocal: Betty Jane Rhodes) / GIVE A BROKEN HEART A BREAK (Vocal: Billy McDonald)................ *Banner 33437* 5-8 35

I'M JUST AN ORDINARY HUMAN (Vocal: Betty Jane Rhodes) / GIVE A BROKEN HEART A BREAK (Vocal: Billy McDonald)............. *Melotone M-13404* 5-8 35

I'M JUST AN ORDINARY HUMAN (Vocal: Betty Jane Rhodes) / GIVE A BROKEN HEART A BREAK (Vocal: Billy McDonald)..................... *Oriole 3145* 5-8 35

I'M JUST AN ORDINARY HUMAN (Vocal: Betty Jane Rhodes) / GIVE A BROKEN HEART A BREAK (Vocal: Billy McDonald).................. *Perfect 16119* 5-8 35

I'M JUST AN ORDINARY HUMAN (Vocal: Betty Jane Rhodes) / GIVE A BROKEN HEART A BREAK (Vocal: Billy McDonald).................. *Romeo 2519* 5-8 35
(Simultaneously released on five labels)

SOMEONE I LOVE (Vocal: Billy McDonald) / NINON (Vocal: Betty Jane Rhodes)....... *Banner 33438* 4-6 35

SOMEONE I LOVE (Vocal: Billy McDonald) / NINON (Vocal: Betty Jane Rhodes).... *Melotone M-13405* 4-6 35

SOMEONE I LOVE (Vocal: Billy McDonald) / NINON (Vocal: Betty Jane Rhodes)......... *Oriole 3146* 4-6 35

SOMEONE I LOVE (Vocal: Billy McDonald) / NINON (Vocal: Betty Jane Rhodes)........ *Perfect 16120* 4-6 35

SOMEONE I LOVE (Vocal: Billy McDonald) / NINON (Vocal: Betty Jane Rhodes)......... *Romeo 2520* 4-6 35
(Simultaneously released on two labels)

LOFNER-HARRIS ST. FRANCIS HOTEL ORCHESTRA, The, directed by Carol Lofner & Phil Harris
also see LOFNER, Carol, & His Orchestra, see HARRIS, Phil, & His Cocoanut Grove Orchestra, and see HARRIS, Phil, & His Orchestra

(Phil Harris: 1/16/04 –)

(BIG C (UNIVERSITY OF CALIFORNIA SONG) / HAIL TO CALIFORNIA (UNIVERSITY OF CALIFORNIA SONG)........................... *Victor 22832* 5-8 32
(Vocals: The Brick Morse Collegians)

I GOT THE RITZ FROM THE ONE I LOVE (GOT THE BIG GO-BY) (Vocal: Phil Harris) / I'M SORRY, DEAR (Vocal: Hal Schaer).......................... *Victor 22830* 5-8 31

WAS IT WRONG? (Vocal: Muzzy Marcellino) / RIVER, STAY 'WAY FROM MY DOOR (Vocal: Phil Harris)...................... *Victor 22831* 5-8 31

LOMBARDO, Guy, & His Royal Canadians

(Guy Lombardo: 6/19/02 – 11/5/77)

(Perhaps the most successful of all the dance bands, having appeared in better spots nationwide for more than fifty years. The orchestra continues to play engagements coast-to-coast under the leadership of Bill Lombardo, a nephew. On December 31, 1983, an old tradition was renewed; the Lombardo band again brought in the New Year, in the Grand Ballroom at the Waldorf-Astoria in New York City. A capacity crowd filled the ballroom as fans all over the country watched via television.)

AFTER YOU'VE GONE / NOBODY'S SWEETHEART........................ *Decca 3753* 2-4 41
(Vocals: Kenny Gardner)

ANNIVERSARY SONG (Vocal: Kenny Gardner) / UNCLE REMUS SAID (Vocals: Don Rodney & trio).... *Decca 23799* 3-5 46

ANSWER SHE IS "YES!" NO? / PLAY, HURDY-GURDY, PLAY................ *Decca 24999* 2-4 50
(Vocals: Kenny Gardner & trio)

ANYTHING THAT'S PART OF YOU (Vocals: by trio) / LOVE, CAN'T YOU HEAR ME CALLING? (Vocal: Liebert Lombardo)................... *Brunswick 6949* 3-5 34

AT LEAST YOU COULD SAY HELLO (Vocal: Carmen Lombardo) / SCATTER-BRAIN (Vocals: Carmen Lombardo, Larry Owen, & Fred Henry)............... *Decca 2767* 2-4 39

BAND PLAYED ON, THE (Vocal: Kenny Gardner) / YOU STEPPED OUT OF A DREAM (Vocal: Carmen Lombardo)................ *Decca 3675* 2-4 41

BEALE STREET BLUES (Vocals: Unknown) / FOR ME AND MY GAL (Vocal: Kenny Gardner)........ *Decca 4371* 2-4 42

BLESS 'EM ALL / JOHNNY DOUGHBOY FOUND A ROSE IN IRELAND.............. *Decca 4278* 3-5 42
(Vocals: Unknown)

BLUE LOVEBIRD (Vocal: Carmen Lombardo) / THE NEARNESS OF YOU (Vocal: Mert Curtis)... *Decca 3214* 2-4 40

BLUES IN THE NIGHT / FRANKIE AND JOHNNY.................. *Decca 4177* 2-4 42
(Vocals: Unknown)

BLUES SERENADE, A / CONCERT IN THE PARK (Vocals: by trio)... *Decca 2521* 2-4 39

BOO-HOO (Vocals: by trio) / I CAN'T LOSE THAT LONGING FOR YOU (Vocal: Carmen Lombardo).... *Victor 25522* 2-4 37

BROKEN RECORD, THE (Vocals: by trio) / ALONE AT A TABLE FOR TWO (Vocal: Carmen Lombardo)............... *Victor 25210* 3-5 36

BY THE LIGHT OF THE SILVERY MOON / CUDDLE UP A LITTLE CLOSER, LOVEY MINE...... *Decca 3985* 3-5 41
(Vocals: Kenny Gardner & trio)

CHEEK TO CHEEK (Vocals: by trio) / BROADWAY RHYTHM..................... *Decca 549* 3-5 35

CONFESSIN' GOOD EVENIN'....... *Columbia 2259-D* 3-5 30
(Vocals: Unknown)

COQUETTE / BELOVED........... *Columbia 1345-D* 3-5 28
(Vocals: Carmen Lombardo)

COTTAGE FOR SALE, A (Vocal: Carmen Lombardo) / WITHOUT YOU, EMALINE (Vocals: Unknown)................... *Columbia 2156-D* 3-5 30

COTTON PICKER'S BALL / MAMA'S GONE, GOODBYE................... *Gennett 5417* 15-20 24

DEEP IN THE HEART OF TEXAS / SWEETHEARTS OR STRANGERS...................... *Decca 4264* 2-4 42
(Vocals: Unknown)

DID YOU EVER SEE A DREAM WALKING? (Vocal: Carmen Lombardo) / I RAISED MY HAT (Vocals: by trio)................. *Brunswick 6713* 3-5 34

DON'T BLAME ME / NOTHING BUT THE BEST..................... *Banner 33157* 3-5 34
(Vocals: Carmen Lombardo)

DON'T BLAME ME / NOTHING BUT THE BEST.................. *Conqueror 8380* 3-5 34
(Vocals: Carmen Lombardo)

DON'T BLAME ME / NOTHING BUT THE BEST................. *Melotone M-13124* 3-5 34
(Vocals: Carmen Lombardo)

DON'T BLAME ME / NOTHING BUT THE BEST......................... *Oriole 2959* 3-5 34
(Vocals: Carmen Lombardo)

DON'T BLAME ME / NOTHING BUT THE BEST...................... *Perfect 15985* 3-5 34
(Vocals: Carmen Lombardo)

DON'T BLAME ME / NOTHING BUT THE BEST....................... *Romeo 2333* 3-5 34
(Vocals: Carmen Lombardo)
(Simultaneously released on six labels)

DOWN BY THE OLD MILL STREAM / LOVE IN BLOOM (Vocal: Carmen Lombardo)........ *Decca 102* 4-6 34

DOWN BY THE RIVER / WHAT'S THE REASON (I'M NOT PLEASIN' YOU).................... *Decca 393* 2-4 35
(Vocals: Carmen Lombardo)

FARE THEE WELL (Vocal: Liebert Lombardo) / THE SWEETEST MUSIC THIS SIDE OF HEAVEN (Vocal: Carmen Lombardo)............. *Brunswick 6874* 3-5 34

FARE THEE WELL / LOVE, CAN'T YOU HEAR ME CALLING?........... *Banner 33205* 3-5 34
(Vocals: Liebert Lombardo)

FARE THEE WELL / LOVE, CAN'T YOU HEAR ME CALLING?....... *Melotone M-13172* 3-5 34
(Vocals: Liebert Lombardo)

FARE THEE WELL / LOVE, CAN'T YOU HEAR ME CALLING?............. *Oriole 3000* 3-5 34
(Vocals: Liebert Lombardo)

FARE THEE WELL / LOVE, CAN'T YOU HEAR ME CALLING?........... *Perfect 16012* 3-5 34
(Vocals: Liebert Lombardo)

FARE THEE WELL / LOVE, CAN'T YOU HEAR ME CALLING?............ *Romeo 2374* 3-5 34
(Vocals: Liebert Lombardo)
(Simultaneously released on five labels)

FINE ROMANCE, A / THE WAY YOU LOOK TONIGHT................. *Victor 25372* 3-5 36
(Vocals: Carmen Lombardo)

GO HOME AND TELL YOUR MOTHER / I'M DOIN' THAT THING.................... *Columbia 2276-D* 4-6 30
(Vocals: Unknown)

GOODNIGHT, SWEETHEART / I WOULDN'T CHANGE YOU FOR THE WORLD.......... *Columbia 2547-D* 3-5 31
(Vocals: Unknown)

GOOFUS / VILIA..................... *Brunswick 6466* 3-5 33

HAVE A LITTLE FAITH IN ME / CRYING FOR THE CAROLINES... *Columbia 2062-D* 4-6 30
(Vocals: Unknown)

HERE IT IS MONDAY AND I'VE STILL GOT A DOLLAR / JUST A LITTLE HOME FOR THE OLD FOLKS................. *Brunswick 6440* 3-5 33
(Vocals: Carmen Lombardo)

HI-DIDDLE-DIDDLE / THREE LITTLE FISHIES.............. *Decca 2446* 2-4 39
(Vocals: Carmen Lombardo, Larry Owen, & Fred Henry)

HIGH UP ON A HILL TOP / THE SPELL OF THE BLUES.................. *Columbia 1653-D* 5-8 29

HOT TIME IN THE OLD TOWN TONIGHT / THE MUSIC GOES 'ROUND AND AROUND......... *Decca 24792* 2-4 49
(Vocals: Kenny Gardner)

HOW DEEP IS THE OCEAN? (Vocal: Carmen Lombardo) / PINK ELEPHANTS (Vocals: by trio)... *Brunswick 6399* 4-6 32

HOW DO I KNOW IT'S REAL? / THERE WON'T BE A SHORTAGE OF LOVE................ *Decca 4199* 3-5 42
(Vocals: Unknown)

HUMMING BIRD, THE (Vocals: Bobby Gibson & trio) / PUT-PUT-PUT (YOUR ARMS AROUND ME) (Vocals: Rose Marie Lombardo & trio)................ *Decca 4344* 2-4 42

I CAN'T FIND ANYTHING TO SUIT MY MOOD (Vocal: Carmen Lombardo) / PENNY SERENADE... *Decca 2291* 2-4 39

I DON'T WANT TO SET THE WORLD ON FIRE (Vocal: Kenny Gardner) / CONCERTO (TCHAIKOVSKY)........... *Decca 3999* 3-5 41

I GET THE BLUES WHEN IT RAINS / KIDS AGAIN.......... *Columbia 1888-D* 3-5 29
(Vocals: Unknown)

I GUESS I'LL HAVE TO CHANGE MY PLAN / AS LONG AS LOVE LIVES ON............... *Brunswick 6363* 3-5 32
(Vocals: Carmen Lombardo)

I HAVEN'T TOLD HER, SHE HASN'T TOLD ME / SOMEBODY AND ME........ *Columbia 1093-D* 3-5 27
(Vocals: Unknown)

I'LL NEVER BE THE SAME / WE JUST COULDN'T SAY GOODBYE.................. *Brunswick 6350* 3-5 32
(Vocals: Carmen Lombardo)

I'LL SEE YOU IN MY DREAMS / GOODNIGHT, SWEETHEART.......... *Decca 3713* 2-4 41
(Vocals: Kenny Gardner)

I LOVE TO BUMPITY BUMP (ON A BUMPY ROAD WITH YOU (Vocals: by trio) / WITHERED ROSES (Vocals: Unknown)........... *Columbia 1757-D* 3-5 29

I LOVE YOU TRULY / STARLIGHT AND TULIPS (by Thelma Terry & Her Play Boys)..... *Columbia 1532-D* 3-5 28

I'M ALWAYS CHASING RAINBOWS / MAKE BELIEVE...................... *Decca 18789* 2-4 46
(Vocals: Mert Curtis)

I'M MORE THAN SATISFIED (Vocals: by trio) / THE CANNON BALL............. *Columbia 1451-D* 4-6 28

I'M PUTTING ALL MY EGGS IN ONE BASKET / BUT WHERE ARE YOU?.................. *Victor 25242* 3-5 36
(Vocals: Carmen Lombardo)

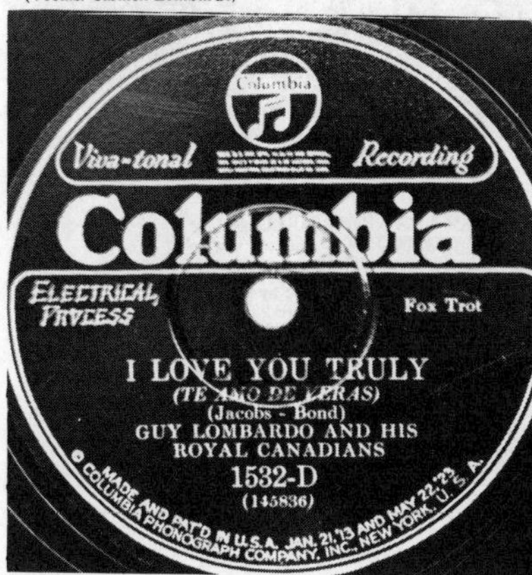

INTERMEZZO / STAR DUST (Vocal: Kenny Gardner) .... *Decca 3674* 2-4 41

IT AIN'T NECESSARILY SO / I GOT PLENTY O' NUTTIN' .... *Victor 25204* 3-5 36
(Vocals: Carmen Lombardo)

IT MUST BE TRUE (Vocal: Carmen Lombardo) / HEARTACHES (Vocals: by trio)...... *Columbia 2390-D* 3-5 31

IT'S EASIER SAID THAN DONE (Vocal: Carmen Lombardo) / BEI MIR BIST DU SCHOEN (Vocals: by trio)........................ *Victor 25739* 2-4 38

IT WAS WONDERFUL THEN / I COULD WRITE A BOOK .... *Decca 3658* 2-4 41
(Vocals: Kenny Gardner)

I WANT TO BE IN WINCHELL'S COLUMN (Vocals: by trio) / SWEET SOMEONE (Vocal: Carmen Lombardo) .... *Victor 25709* 2-4 37

JINGLE JANGLE JINGLE (Vocals: Kenny Gardner & trio) / IDAHO (Vocal: Rose Marie Lombardo) ...... *Decca 18399* 2-4 42

JUNE IN JANUARY / WITH EVERY BREATH I TAKE .... *Decca 307* 3-5 34
(Vocals: Carmen Lombardo)

JUNGLE DRUMS / INKA DINKA DOO (Vocals: by trio) .... *Banner 33152* 3-5 34

JUNGLE DRUMS / INKA DINKA DOO (Vocals: by trio).......... *Conqueror 8375* 3-5 34

JUNGLE DRUMS / INKA DINKA DOO (Vocals: by trio)........ *Melotone M-13119* 3-5 34

JUNGLE DRUMS / INKA DINKA DOO (Vocals: by trio) .... *Oriole 2954* 3-5 34

JUNGLE DRUMS / INKA DINKA DOO (Vocals: by trio)........... *Perfect 15980* 3-5 34

JUNGLE DRUMS / INKA DINKA DOO (Vocals: by trio)............ *Romeo 2328* 3-5 34
(Simultaneously released on six labels)

JUST A LITTLE DANCE, MAM'SELLE / I STILL GET A THRILL.......... *Columbia 2286-D* 3-5 30
(Vocals: Unknown)

LAST ROUND-UP / ANNIE DOESN'T LIVE HERE ANYMORE........... *Brunswick 6662* 3-5 33
(Vocals: Carmen Lombardo & trio)

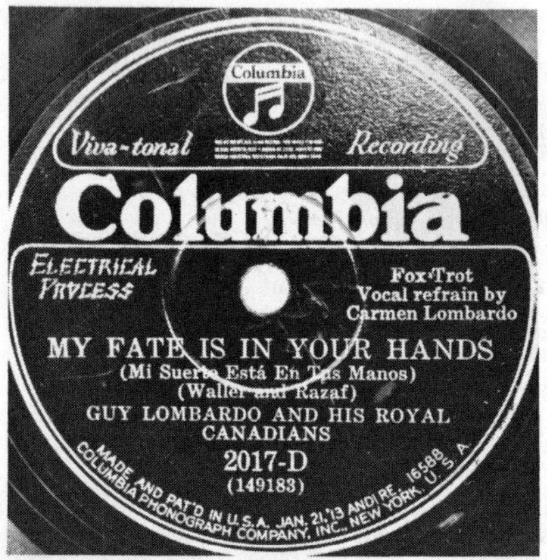

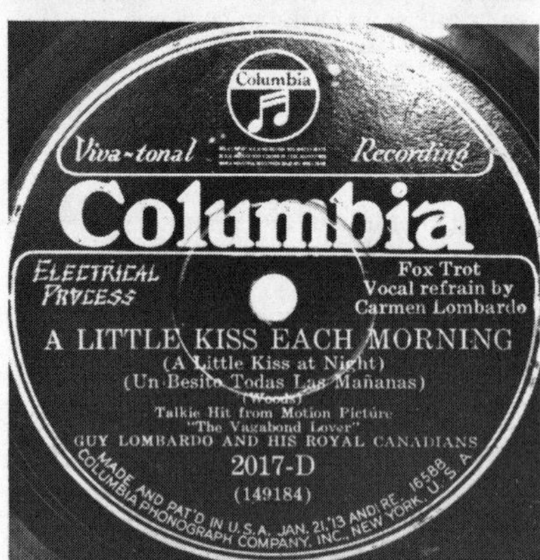

LAWD, YOU MAKE THE NIGHT TOO LONG / A MOMENT IN THE DARK .... *Brunswick 6300* 4-6 32
(Vocals: Carmen Lombardo)

LET'S ALL SING TOGETHER (Vocals: by trio) / THE SINGING HILLS (Vocal: Mert Curtis).... *Decca 3007* 2-4 40

LIEBESTRAUM / SWEETHEARTS ON PARADE (Vocal: Carmen Lombardo)....... *Victor 25493* 3-5 37

LIGHT A CANDLE IN THE CHAPEL / LOVE IS A SONG .... *Decca 18445* 2-4 42
(Vocals: Bobby Gibson)

LITTLE DUTCH MILL / YOU OUGHTA BE IN PICTURES................. *Brunswick 6781* 3-5 34
(Vocals: by trio)

LITTLE SIR ECHO / I CAN'T GET YOU OUT OF MY MIND .... *Decca 2306* 2-4 39
(Vocals: Carmen Lombardo)

LOST / THERE IS NO GREATER LOVE.... *Victor 25271* 3-5 36
(Vocals: Carmen Lombardo)

LOVE BUG WILL BITE YOU, THE / DREAMY EYES.......... *Victor 25548* 3-5 37
(Vocals: by trio)

LOVELY ONE / THAT OLD FEELING ... *Victor 25629* 2-4 37
(Vocals: Carmen Lombardo)

LOVE ME OR LEAVE ME (Vocal: Carmen Lombardo) / I'M STILL CARING (Vocals: Unknown) ... *Columbia 1782-D* 3-5 29

MANAGUA – NICARAGUA / WHAT MORE CAN I ASK FOR? .... *Decca 23782* 2-4 46
(Vocals: Don Rodney)

MARCH FOR THE NEW INFANTRY / EV'RYBODY EV'RY PAYDAY .... *Decca 4408* 3-5 42
(Vocals: Unknown)

MEMPHIS BLUES / S-H-I-N-E............ *Decca 4077* 3-5 41
(Vocals: Kenny Gardner)

MOON GLOW / BLUE IN LOVE........... *Decca 103* 4-6 34
(Vocals: Carmen Lombardo)

MOON IS LOW, THE (Vocals: Unknown) / LAZY LOU'SIANA MOON (Vocal: Carmen Lombardo)................. *Columbia 2135-D* 3-5 30

MOONLIGHT AND ROSES / THE LAST ROUND-UP (Vocal: Kenny Gardner) .... *Decca 3722* 2-4 41

MOONLIGHT-SAVING TIME (Vocal: Carmen Lombardo) / WHEN THE SHEPHERD LEADS THE SHEEP BACK HOME (Vocals: Unknown) .... *Columbia 2457-D* 3-5 31

MY BEST GIRL (Vocals: Carmen Lombardo, Larry Owen, & Fred Henry) / EASTER PARADE (Vocal: Carmen Lombardo) .... *Decca 2345* 2-4 39

MY FATE IS IN YOUR HANDS / A LITTLE KISS EACH MORNING .... *Columbia 2017-D* 4-6 29
(Vocals: Carmen Lombardo)

MY OLD FLAME / GIVE ME A HEART TO SING TO................ *Banner 33204* 3-5 34
(Vocals: Carmen Lombardo)

MY OLD FLAME / GIVE ME A HEART TO SING TO .... *Melotone M-13171* 3-5 34
(Vocals: Carmen Lombardo)

MY OLD FLAME / GIVE ME A HEART TO SING TO.................. *Oriole 2999* 3-5 34
(Vocals: Carmen Lombardo)

MY OLD FLAME / GIVE ME A HEART TO SING TO .... *Perfect 16011* 3-5 34
(Vocals: Carmen Lombardo)

MY OLD FLAME / GIVE ME A HEART TO SING TO................. *Romeo 2373* 3-5 34
(Vocals: Carmen Lombardo)
(Simultaneously released on five labels)

MY OLD FLAME / THE LIGHTS ARE LOW – THE MUSIC IS SWEET .... *Brunswick 6909* 3-5 34
(Vocals: Carmen Lombardo)

NIGHTINGALE SANG IN BERKELEY SQUARE, A / DID ANYONE CALL? .... *Decca 3453* 2-4 40
(Vocals: Carmen Lombardo)

NIGHT ON THE WATER / INKA DINKA DOO .... *Brunswick 6714* 3-5 34
(Vocals: by trio)

NO MORE LOVE (Vocal: Carmen Lombardo) / JUST BECAUSE YOU'RE YOU (Vocals: by trio)...................... *Brunswick 6417* 3-5 32

ON THE SENTIMENTAL SIDE / THIS IS MY NIGHT TO DREAM....... *Victor 25764* 2-4 38
(Vocals: Carmen Lombardo)

PERFECT SONG, THE / DOWN BY THE OLD MILL STREAM .... *Victor 25807* 2-4 38

RAINBOW ON THE RIVER (Vocal: Carmen Lombardo) / WHEN MY DREAMBOAT COMES HOME (Vocal: Liebert Lombardo) .... *Victor 25435* 2-4 36

RED SAILS IN THE SUNSET / MADONNA MINE...................... *Decca 585* 3-5 35
(Vocals: Carmen Lombardo)

RUNNING BETWEEN THE RAINDROPS / BY THE RIVER SAINTE MARIE.......... *Columbia 2401-D* 3-5 31
(Vocals: Carmen Lombardo)

SAILBOAT IN THE MOONLIGHT, A / GONE WITH THE WIND.......................... *Victor 25594* 3-5 37
(Vocals: Carmen Lombardo)

SEPTEMBER IN THE RAIN / WHAT WILL I TELL MY HEART?.................. *Victor 25526* 3-5 37
(Vocals: Carmen Lombardo)

SHANGHAI LIL / ANNIE DOESN'T LIVE HERE ANYMORE.............. *Banner 33158* 4-6 33
(Vocals: Carmen Lombardo)

SHANGHAI LIL / ANNIE DOESN'T LIVE HERE ANYMORE........... *Conqueror 8381* 4-6 33
(Vocals: Carmen Lombardo)

SHANGHAI LIL / ANNIE DOESN'T LIVE HERE ANYMORE.......... *Melotone M-13125* 4-6 33
(Vocals: Carmen Lombardo)

SHANGHAI LIL / ANNIE DOESN'T LIVE HERE ANYMORE................ *Oriole 2960* 4-6 33
(Vocals: Carmen Lombardo)

SHANGHAI LIL / ANNIE DOESN'T LIVE HERE ANYMORE.............. *Perfect 15986* 4-6 33
(Vocals: Carmen Lombardo)

SHANGHAI LIL / ANNIE DOESN'T LIVE HERE ANYMORE............... *Romeo 2334* 4-6 33
(Vocals: Carmen Lombardo)
(Simultaneously released on six labels)

SHANGHAI LIL / BY A WATERFALL... *Brunswick 6653* 3-5 33
(Vocals: Carmen Lombardo)

SINGIN' IN THE BATHTUB (Vocals: by trio) / LITTLE BY LITTLE (Vocal: Carmen Lombardo).... *Columbia 2045-D* 4-6 30

SING SONG SERENADE / BLUE AFTERGLOW .... *Decca 3665* 2-4 41
(Vocals: Kenny Gardner)

SMILES / ROSE ROOM................... *Decca 3841* 2-4 41
(Vocals: Kenny Gardner)

SO LITTLE TIME / LITTLE LADY MAKE-BELIEVE............... *Victor 25823* 2-4 38
(Vocals: Carmen Lombardo)

SONG OF INDIA / I WON'T DANCE (Vocals: by trio).......... *Decca 404* 4-6 35

SO RARE (Vocal: Carmen Lombardo) / LITTLE HEAVEN OF THE SEVEN SEAS (Vocals: by trio) ... *Victor 25626* 2-4 37

SO THIS IS VENICE / CRY............. *Gennett 5416* 12-15 24

SOUTH OF THE BORDER / OLD MILL WHEEL .... *Decca 2768* 2-4 39
(Vocals: Carmen Lombardo)

STARS FELL ON ALABAMA / GIVE ME A HEART TO SING TO .... *Decca 104* 4-6 34
(Vocals: Carmen Lombardo)

STAY OUT OF MY DREAMS / STORMY WEATHER .... *Brunswick 6550* 3-5 33
(Vocals: Carmen Lombardo)

STEPHEN FOSTER MEDLEY / ST. LOUIS BLUES............... *Columbia 50256-D* 4-6 30
(Vocals: Unknown)
(This is an oversize 12-inch 78 rpm)

ST. LOUIS BLUES (Vocals: by chorus) / AULD LANG SYNE (theme song) .... *Decca 2478* 2-4 39

STREET OF DREAMS / I CALLED TO SAY GOODNIGHT............. *Brunswick 6455* 3-5 33
(Vocals: Carmen Lombardo)

SUMMERTIME / I'LL SEE YOU IN MY DREAMS.................... *Victor 25716* 2-4 38

SUN VALLEY ROSE / A BOY IN KHAKI – A GIRL IN LACE .... *Decca 4349* 3-5 42
(Vocals: Bobby Gibson)

SWEET AND LOVELY / BEGGING FOR LOVE...................... *Columbia 2500-D* 3-5 31
(Vocals: Unknown)

SWEETHEARTS ON PARADE (Vocal: Carmen Lombardo) / AFTER THE BALL (Vocal: Kenny Gardner) .... *Decca 3890* 2-4 41

SWEETHEARTS ON PARADE / THAT'S HOW I FEEL ABOUT YOU.............. *Columbia 1628-D* 3-5 28
(Vocals: Carmen Lombardo)

SWEETHEART WALTZ / STAY AS SWEET AS YOU ARE.......................... *Decca 274* 3-5 34
(Vocals: Carmen Lombardo)

TAKING A CHANCE ON LOVE (Vocals: Carmen Lombardo, Mert Curtis, and Fred Henry) / WE'LL MEET AGAIN (Vocal: Carmen Lombardo) .... *Decca 3575* 2-4 41

TEA FOR TWO (Vocal: Kenny Gardner) / I'M ALWAYS CHASING RAINBOWS (Vocal: Mert Curtis)... *Decca 3586* 2-4 41

THANKS FOR EV'RYTHING (Vocal: Carmen Lombardo) / DEEP PURPLE........................ *Decca 2215* 2-4 39

THAT NAUGHTY WALTZ / MISSOURI WALTZ .... *Decca 2843* 2-4 40

THERE'S DANGER IN YOUR EYES, CHERIE / WITH YOU............ *Columbia 2107-D* 4-6 30
(Vocals: Carmen Lombardo)

THERE'S YES! YES! IN YOUR EYES (Vocals: Carmen Lombardo, Mert Curtis, & Fred Henry) / ALL THE THINGS YOU ARE (Vocal: Mert Curtis) .... *Decca 2949* 2-4 40

TOO LATE / RIVER, STAY 'WAY FROM MY DOOR .... *Columbia 2578-D* 5-8 32
(Vocals: Kate Smith)

TO YOU, SWEETHEART, ALOHA (Vocal: Liebert Lombardo) / MY KINGDOM FOR A KISS (Vocal: Carmen Lombardo) .... *Victor 15414* 2-4 36

TURN ON THE OLD MUSIC BOX (Vocals: Carmen Lombardo, Mert Curtis, & Fred Henry) / WHEN YOU WISH UPON A STAR (Vocal: Carmen Lombardo)... *Decca 2969* 4-6 40

UMBRELLA MAN, THE (Vocals: by trio) / WE SPEAK OF YOU OFTEN (Vocal: Carmen Lombardo) ..... *Decca 2221* 2-4 39

UNDER A TEXAS MOON / CAN'T YOU UNDERSTAND? .... *Columbia 2089-D* 4-6 30
(Vocals: Unknown)

THE MOON / CHARMAINE .... *Columbia 1048-D* 3-5 27
(Vocals: Unknown)

UNTIL WE MEET AGAIN, SWEETHEART / SWINGIN' IN A HAMMOCK .... *Columbia 2237-D* 3-5 30
(Vocals: Unknown)

WAITIN' FOR KATY (Vocals: by trio) / I CAN'T DO WITHOUT YOU (Vocal: Carmen Lombardo).... *Columbia 1395-D* 4-6 28

WAITING FOR THE ROBERT E. LEE (Vocals: by trio) / HOW ABOUT YOU? (Vocals: Unknown)..... *Decca 4133* 2-4 42

WHEN DID YOU LEAVE HEAVEN? / SWEET MISERY OF LOVE............................ *Victor 25357* 2-4 36
(Vocals: Carmen Lombardo)

WHEN THE ORGAN PLAYED AT TWILIGHT (Vocal: Mert Curtis) / DRIFTING AND DREAMING (Vocal: Kenny Gardner)........ *Decca 3878* 2-4 41

WHERE DO I GO FROM YOU? / WHEN THE SWALLOWS COME BACK TO CAPISTRANO... *Decca 3213* 2-4 40
(Vocals: Carmen Lombardo)

WHERE THE SHY LITTLE VIOLETS GROW (Vocals: by trio) / ME AND THE MAN IN THE MOON (Vocals: Unknown).... *Columbia 1679-D* 3-5 29

WHISTLING IN THE DARK / BUILDING A HOME FOR YOU .... *Columbia 2444-D* 3-5 31
(Vocals: Unknown)

WINTER WONDERLAND (Vocals: by trio) / WATER UNDER THE BRIDGE (Vocal: Carmen Lombardo) .... *Decca 294* 3-5 34

WITH A SMILE AND A SONG (Vocal: Carmen Lombardo) / WHISTLE WHILE YOU WORK (Vocals: by trio)............................ *Victor 25748* 4-6 38

YOU DO THE DARNDEST THINGS, BABY (Vocals: by trio) / IT'S LOVE I'M AFTER (Vocal: Carmen Lombardo)................ *Victor 25421* 2-4 36

YOU HAVE EVERYTHING (Vocals: by trio) / I SEE YOUR FACE BEFORE ME (Vocal: Carmen Lombardo)................ *Victor 25684* 2-4 37

YOU MADE ME LOVE YOU / MANDY IS TWO (Vocals: Unknown)........ *Decca 4155* 4 42

YOU'RE DRIVING ME CRAZY! / MY LOVE FOR YOU.................. *Columbia 2335-D* 3-5 30
(Vocals: Carmen Lombardo)

YOU'RE THE SWEETEST GIRL THIS SIDE OF HEAVEN (Vocals: Unknown) / ROLLIN' DOWN THE RIVER (Vocal: Carmen Lombardo)..... *Columbia 2188-D* 3-5 30

LONG, Johnny, & His Orchestra
(Johnny Long: circa 1916 – 10/31/72)

BACK THE RED, WHITE AND BLUE WITH GOLD / FOR THE FLAG, FOR THE HOME, FOR THE FAMILY.............. *Decca 4231* 3-5 42
(Vocals: Unknown)

BLUE SHADOWS AND WHITE GARDENIAS / SING ME A SONG OF THE ISLANDS......... *Decca 4190* 2-4 42
(Vocals: Unknown)

BLUE SKIES (Vocal: Bob Houston) / BEAU NIGHT IN HOTCHKISS CORNERS (Vocal: Helen Young)...................... *Decca 3823* 2-4 41

BOOGIE MAN (Vocal: Paul Harman) / THE MOON WON'T TALK (Vocal: Bob Houston)................ *Decca 3670* 3-5 41

CAN'T GET OUT OF THIS MOOD (Vocals: The Four Teens) / SOFT-HEARTED (Vocal: Bob Houston)..... *Decca 4369* 2-4 42

CHATTANOOGA CHOO CHOO (Vocal: Paul Harman) / THE BOOGLIE WOOGLIE PIGGY (Vocal: Helen Young)...................... *Decca 3905* 3-5 41

CONSTANTLY (Vocal: Helen Young) / MOONLIGHT BECOMES YOU (Vocals: Bob Houston & The Four Teens)............. *Decca 4389* 2-4 42

DEAR ARABELLA (Vocals: Unknown) / HE'S 1-A IN THE ARMY AND HE'S A-1 IN MY HEART (Vocal: Helen Young).......... *Decca 4115* 3-5 42

DON'T TAKE YOUR LOVE FROM ME (Vocal: Bob Houston) / KISS THE BOYS GOODBYE (Vocal: Helen Young)..... *Decca 3907* 2-4 41

DO YOU MISS YOUR SWEETHEART? / AFTER TAPS......................... *Decca 4209* 3-5 42
(Vocals: Unknown)

GIRL OF MY DREAMS (Vocal: Rod Kinder) / WITCHCRAFT (Vocals: Barbara Hammond & Rod Kinder)........................ *Mercury 70374* 2-4

I HEARD IT ON THE HIT PARADE / CONCHITA, MARQUITA, LOLITA, PEPITA, ROSITA, JUANITA LOPEZ.............. *Decca 4341* 2-4 42
(Vocals: Bob Houston & The Four Teens)

I'M BREATHLESS (Vocals: Helen Young & Bob Houston) / HOE DOWN (Vocals: Helen Young & "Swede" Nielsen)...................... *Decca 4191* 2-4 42

IN A SHANTY IN OLD SHANTY TOWN (Vocals: chorus) / SWING ME BACH (Vocal: Helen Young).... *Decca 3409* 2-4 40

(BACK HOME AGAIN) IN INDIANA / THAT'S WHAT I LIKE ABOUT THE SOUTH............. *Decca 3786* 2-4 41
(Vocals: Bob Houston)

JUST A KID NAMED JOE (Vocal: Jack Edmondson) / JOHN BROWN'S TEN LITTLE INDIANS (Vocal: Paul Harman).................. *Vocalion 4463* 3-5 38

JUST LIKE THAT (Vocals: chorus) / THE WHITE STAR OF SIGMA NU (theme song) (Vocals: Glee Club & chorus)................ *Decca 4350* 2-4 42

LOUISE (Vocal: Jack Edmondson) / MOONLIGHT ON THE GANGES...................... *Decca 3239* 2-4 40

MISS JOHNSON 'PHONED AGAIN TODAY (Vocal: Helen Young) / TAKE IT JACKSON............ *Decca 3785* 3-5 41

NOBODY'S SWEETHEART (Vocals: The Longshots & Glee Club) / THE NIGHT WAS MADE FOR LOVE............................ *King 15109* 2-4

PAPA NICCOLINI / AS WE WALK INTO THE SUNSET.................. *Decca 4179* 2-4 42
(Vocals: Unknown)

PRETTY LITTLE BUSYBODY / CHANCES ARE........................ *Decca 4139* 2-4 42
(Vocals: Unknown)

SHEPHERD SERENADE / I WISH I HAD A SWEETHEART................ *Decca 4017* 2-4 41
(Vocals: Bob Houston)

SOMEDAY I'LL MEET YOU AGAIN / SAN FERNANDO VALLEY............. *Decca 4437* 2-4 42
(Vocals: Gene Williams)

TEN PRETTY GIRLS (Vocal: Paul Harman) / I'LL TAKE ROMANCE (Vocal: Jack Edmondson)..... *Vocalion 3888* 2-4 38

THIS NEVER HAPPENED BEFORE / LET'S GIVE LOVE ANOTHER CHANCE.......... *Vocalion 3897* 2-4 38
(Vocals: Jack Edmondson)

TIME TO SING, THE (Vocal: Helen Young) / THE ANNIVERSARY WALTZ (Vocal: Bob Houston).................... *Decca 4078* 2-4 41

WALKIN' BY THE RIVER (Vocal: Bob Houston) / ACCIDENT'LY ON PURPOSE (Vocal: Helen Young)...................... *Decca 3660* 2-4 41

WHEN I GROW TOO OLD TO DREAM / SHADOWS ON THE SAND........................... *Decca 3574* 2-4 41
(Vocals: Bob Houston)

WHEN I TAKE MY SUGAR TO TEA (Vocal: Paul Harman) / LOOKING AT THE WORLD THROUGH ROSE-COLORED GLASSES (Vocals: by trio)................ *Decca 3341* 2-4 40

YES, MY DARLING DAUGHTER (Vocal: Helen Young) / JOHNNY PEDDLER (Vocals: Helen Young & Paul Harman)......................... *Decca 3560* 2-4 41

LOPEZ, Vincent, & His Casa Lopez Orchestra
(Vincent Lopez: 12/30/98 – 9/75)
(The Vincent Lopez Orchestra continues to play engagements in the Philadelphia area. On weekends the band is joined by Jan Eberle Gordon, daughter of the late Ray Eberle, famed Glenn Miller vocalist. Jan sings Glenn Miller/Ray Eberle tunes accompanied by the Lopez Orchestra, and she hosts a weekly radio program, "Glen Miller," on WWFM, New Jersey.)

ARE YOU HAPPY? (Vocal: Franklyn Baur) / KISS AND MAKE-UP (Vocal: Irving Kaufman)..... *Brunswick 3643* 5-8 27

BABY MINE / JUST LIKE A BUTTERFLY.................. *Brunswick 3573* 4-6 27
(Vocals: Franklyn Baur)

BIRTH OF THE BLUES (Vocal: Irving Kaufman) / ST. LOUIS BLUES................ *Brunswick 20065* 5-8 28
(This is an oversize 12-inch 78 rpm)

BLUE SHADOWS (Vocal: Jack Parker) / ONCE IN A LIFETIME (Vocals: Ed Smalle & Dick Robertson).................. *Brunswick 4059* 3-5 28

BLUE SKIES / SINCE I FOUND YOU... *Brunswick 3426* 3-5 27
(Vocals: Frank Munn)

CUP OF COFFEE, A SANDWICH AND YOU, A / WHO?.................. *Okeh 40542* 3-5 26

DARKTOWN STRUTTERS' BALL, THE (Vocals: The Ritz Quartette) / ALEXANDER'S RAGTIME BAND (Vocals: Ed Smalle & Dick Robertson).......... *Brunswick 20066* 5-8 28
(This is an oversize 12-inch 78 rpm)

DON'T WAKE ME UP (LET ME DREAM) / I NEVER KNEW...................... *Okeh 40535* 3-5 26

JUST A MEMORY (Vocal: Frank Munn) / SOMEDAY YOU'LL SAY "O.K." (Vocal: Irving Kaufman).............. *Brunswick 3633* 4-6 27

LITTLE LOG CABIN OF DREAMS (Vocal: Frank Luther) / SAY "YES" TODAY (Vocals: Ed Smalle & Dick Robertson).................. *Brunswick 3907* 4-6 28

LONELY LITTLE BLUEBIRD (Vocal: Frank Munn) / BLUE GRASS (Vocals: Phil Dewey, Frank Luther, & Jack Parker)...................... *Brunswick 4002* 3-5 28

SCATTER YOUR SMILES / LAY ME DOWN TO SLEEP IN CAROLINA................... *Brunswick 3339* 3-5 26
(Vocals: Irving Kaufman)

SO BLUE / WHAT DOES IT MATTER?................ *Brunswick 3473* 3-5 27
(Vocals: Frank Munn)

SONG OF THE FLAME / RHYTHM OF THE DAY................ *Okeh 40586* 5-8 26

SONG OF THE VAGABONDS / FOND OF YOU....................... *Okeh 40540* 2-4 26

THAT CERTAIN FEELING / DOROTHY... *Okeh 40574* 2-4 26
(Vocals: Bruce Wallace)

T-N-T / BLACK HORSE STOMP.......... *Okeh 40552* 5-8 26

YOU TOOK ADVANTAGE OF ME (Vocal: Dick Robertson) / DO I HEAR YOU SAYING "I LOVE YOU"? (Vocal: Laurence Wolfe).................. *Brunswick 3936* 4-6 28

LOPEZ, Vincent, & His Hotel Pennsylvania Orchestra

ADORING YOU / LONELY LITTLE MELODY..................... *Okeh 40165* 2-4 24

AFTER THE STORM/FOR-GET-ME-NOT... *Okeh 40123* 2-4 24

AWAY DOWN EAST IN MAINE (Vocal: Aileen Stanley) / SWANEE SMILES..................... *Okeh 4736* 2-4 22

BURNING SANDS / AGGRAVATIN' PAPA... *Okeh 4783* 3-5 23

CRINOLINE DAYS / PACK UP YOUR SINS AND GO TO THE DEVIL................ *Okeh 4762* 3-5 23

DANCING FOOL / DIXIE HIGHWAY...... *Okeh 4662* 2-4 22

DEEDLE-DEEDLE-DUM / I'M JUST WILD ABOUT HARRY....................... *Okeh 4647* 3-5 22

DOWN IN MARYLAND / RUNNIN' WILD.... *Okeh 4772* 3-5 23

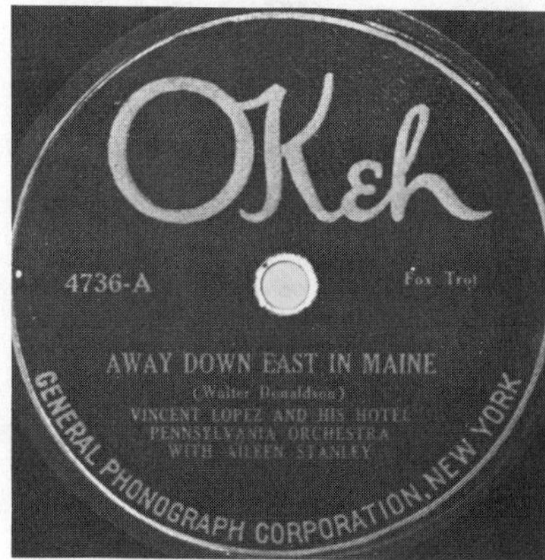

ELIZA / COLD, COLD MAMAS (BURN ME UP) (Vocal: Billy Jones)........ *Okeh 40221* 3-5 24

HOMESICK / TOOT, TOOT, TOOTSIE....... *Okeh 4706* 3-5 22

I CAN'T GET THE ONE I WANT / ALL ALONE WITH YOU IN A LITTLE RENDEZVOUS...... *Okeh 40151* 2-4 24

LAZY / WHAT'LL I DO?.................. *Okeh 40097* 2-4 24

LITTLE OLD NEW YORK / RAGGEDY ANN....................... *Okeh 40009* 2-4 24

LOVEY COME BACK / THERE'S NOBODY ELSE BUT YOU...................... *Okeh 40035* 2-4 24

MADELINE / O KATHARINA!........... *Okeh 40307* 2-4 25

MAYTIME / JUNE NIGHT.............. *Okeh 40149* 2-4 24

ME AND THE BOY FRIEND / DREAMER OF DREAMS............... *Okeh 40199* 2-4 24
(Vocals: Billy Jones)

NEGRO SPIRITUALS / I WANT TO BE HAPPY............................. *Okeh 40175* 3-5 24

NOLA (theme song) / ROSY POSY.......... *Okeh 4579* 2-4 22

ON THE RADIO / TAKE ME............. *Okeh 40234* 2-4 25

RAGGING THE SCALE / GLORIA......... *Okeh 4921* 2-4 23

RUBETOWN FROLICS / SALLY LOU..... *Okeh 40132* 2-4 24

SHOW ME THE WAY TO GO HOME / PADDLIN' MADELIN' HOME (Vocal: Bruce Wallace)... *Okeh 40516* 3-5 26

SITTIN' IN A CORNER / COVERED WAGON DAYS................... *Okeh 4946* 2-4 23

SOME LITTLE SOMEONE / YOU KNOW YOU BELONG TO SOMEBODY ELSE.................. *Okeh 4788* 2-4 23

SOMEONE LOVES YOU AFTER ALL / STEPPIN' OUT........................ *Okeh 40024* 2-4 24

STOMP OFF, LET'S GO / THE MEANEST KIND O' BLUES..................... *Okeh 40478* 5-8 25

SWEET INDIANA HOME / THE YANKEE DOODLE BLUES...................... *Okeh 4654* 2-4 22

SWEET LOVIN' MAMA / YOU'VE GOT TO SEE MAMA EV'RY NIGHT.......................... *Okeh 4819* 4-6 23

TEASIN' / KISS ME BY WIRELESS........ *Okeh 4591* 2-4 22

TODDLE ALONG / LITTLE PEACH....... *Okeh 40355* 2-4 25

TRICKS / COAL BLACK MAMMY........ *Okeh 4673* 2-4 22

WILL YOU REMEMBER ME?/DEAR ONE.... *Okeh 40266* 2-4 25

WONDERFUL ONE / ON A MOONLIGHT NIGHT.............................. *Okeh 4878* 2-4 23

YES! WE HAVE NO BANANAS / LONG-LOST MAMA.................... *Okeh 4901* 3-5 23

LOPEZ, Vincent, & His Hotel St. Regis Orchestra

I NEVER SLEPT A WINK LAST NIGHT / SLEEPY HEAD..... *Bluebird B-5524* 3-5 34
(Vocals: Frances Hunt)

MARIA, MY OWN (Vocal: Paul Small) / THE VOODOO..................... *Brunswick 6112* 3-5 31

MUCHACHA / MAMA INEZ.......... *Brunswick 6084* 3-5 31
(Vocals: Paul Small)

RIDIN' AROUND IN THE RAIN (Vocal: Frances Hunt) / STAIRWAYS..................... *Bluebird B-5442* 3-5 34

RIPTIDE / AN OLD WATER MILL... *Bluebird B-5441* 3-5 34
(Vocals: Jack Campbell)

SPELLBOUND (Vocal: Johnny Morris) / SO HELP ME (Vocal: Frances Hunt)... *Bluebird B-5523* 3-5 34

LOPEZ, Vincent, & His Orchestra

CHANT OF THE JUNGLE / MY SWEETER THAN SWEET...................... *Domino 4448* 4-6 30
(Vocals: Irving Kaufman)

CHANT OF THE JUNGLE / MY SWEETER THAN SWEET................ *Pathe Actuelle 37069* 5-8 30
(Vocals: Irving Kaufman)

CHANT OF THE JUNGLE / MY SWEETER THAN SWEET....................... *Perfect 15250* 4-6 30
(Vocals: Irving Kaufman)

CHANT OF THE JUNGLE / MY SWEETER THAN SWEET........................ *Regal 8896* 4-6 30
(Vocals: Irving Kaufman)
(Simultaneously released on four labels)

CHARMING / SHOULD I?........ *Pathe Actuelle 37078* 4-6 30
(Vocals: Jack Parker)

CHARMING / SHOULD I?.............. *Perfect 15259* 3-5 30
(Vocals: Jack Parker)
(Simultaneously released on two labels)

CHEERFUL LITTLE EARFUL (Vocal: Smith Ballew)............ *Hit Of The Week 1120* 4-6 31
(Hit Of The Week records are one-sided paper discs)

GLOOMY SUNDAY (FAMOUS HUNGARIAN SUICIDE SONG) / I DON'T WANT TO MAKE HISTORY................ *Conqueror 8640* 4-6 36
(Vocals: Unknown)

GLOOMY SUNDAY (FAMOUS HUNGARIAN SUICIDE SONG) / I DON'T WANT TO MAKE HISTORY............... *Melotone 6-05-07* 4-6 36
(Vocals: Unknown)
(Simultaneously released on two labels)

HAPPY DAYS ARE HERE AGAIN / 'TAIN'T NO SIN (TO DANCE AROUND IN YOUR BONES)................ *Domino 4483* 4-6 30
(Vocals: Jack Parker)

HAPPY DAYS ARE HERE AGAIN / 'TAIN'T NO SIN (TO DANCE AROUND IN YOUR BONES)..................... *Oriole 1826* 4-6 30
(Vocals: Jack Parker)

HAPPY DAYS ARE HERE AGAIN / 'TAIN'T NO SIN (TO DANCE AROUND IN YOUR BONES)............. *Pathe Actuelle 37085* 5-8 30
(Vocals: Jack Parker)

HAPPY DAYS ARE HERE AGAIN / 'TAIN'T NO SIN (TO DANCE AROUND IN YOUR BONES).................. *Perfect 15266* 4-6 30
(Vocals: Jack Parker)

HAPPY DAYS ARE HERE AGAIN / 'TAIN'T NO SIN (TO DANCE AROUND IN YOUR BONES).................. *Regal 8928* 4-6 30
(Vocals: Jack Parker)
(Simultaneously released on five labels)

HARMONICA HARRY / LOOK FOR THE SILVER LINING................. *Domino 4478* 4-6 30
(Vocals: Jack Parker)

HARMONICA HARRY / LOOK FOR THE SILVER LINING.......... *Pathe Actuelle 37081* 5-8 30
(Vocals: Jack Parker)

HARMONICA HARRY / LOOK FOR THE SILVER LINING .... *Perfect 15262* 4-6 30
(Vocals: Jack Parker)

HARMONICA HARRY / LOOK FOR THE SILVER LINING .... *Regal 8925* 4-6 30
(Vocals: Jack Parker)
(Simultaneously released on four labels)

HERE COMES THE SUN (Vocal: Jack Parker) .... *Hit Of The Week 1089* 4-6 30
(Hit Of The Week records are one-sided paper discs)

I'D RATHER LEAD A BAND (Vocal: Johnny Morris) / DREAM SHADOWS (Vocal: Stanley Worth) .... *Bluebird B-6265* 3-5 36

JUST A GIGOLO (Vocal: Jack Parker) .... *Hit Of The Week 1128* 4-6 31
(Hit Of The Week records are one-sided paper discs)

LET YOURSELF GO (Vocal: Maxine Tappan) / LET'S FACE THE MUSIC AND DANCE (Vocal: Stanley Worth) .... *Bluebird B-6264* 3-5 36

LITTLE WHITE LIES (Vocal: Jack Parker) .... *Hit Of The Week 1088* 5-8 30
(Hit Of The Week records are one-sided paper discs)

LONESOME LOVER (Vocal: Jack Parker) .... *Hit Of The Week 1127* 4-6 31
(Hit Of The Week records are one-sided paper discs)

LOVELY LADY (Vocal: Stanley Worth with whistling by Fred Lowery) / A LITTLE RENDEVOUS IN HONOLULU (Vocal: Maxine Tappan) .... *Bluebird B-6263* 3-5 36

LOVE (YOUR SPELL IS EVERYWHERE) / WHY? .... *Domino 4451* 3-5 30
(Vocals: Irving Kaufman)

LOVE (YOUR SPELL IS EVERYWHERE) / WHY? .... *Pathe Actuelle 37068* 4-6 30
(Vocals: Irving Kaufman)

LOVE (YOUR SPELL IS EVERYWHERE) / WHY? .... *Perfect 15249* 3-5 30
(Vocals: Irving Kaufman)

LOVE (YOUR SPELL IS EVERYWHERE) / WHY? .... *Regal 8895* 3-5 30
(Vocals: Irving Kaufman)
(Simultaneously released on four labels)

MY FATE IS IN YOUR HANDS..... *Hit Of The Week 1022* 4-6 30
(Hit Of The Week records are one-sided paper discs)

MY SWEETER THAN SWEET... *Hit Of The Week 1023* 4-6 30
(Hit Of The Week records are one-sided paper discs)

OLD FASHIONED GIRL / BY THE SAPPHIRE SEA .... *Paramount 20114* 3-5 22

OLD FASHIONED GIRL / BY THE SAPPHIRE SEA .... *Puritan 11114* 2-4 22
(Simultaneously released on two labels)

PALESTEENA / CARESSES .... *Columbia A-3349* 2-4 21

SHEIK OF ARABY / TY-TEE .... *Puritan 11086* 3-5 22

SHEPHERD'S SERENADE / I'M A DREAMER – AREN'T WE ALL? .... *Pathe Actuelle 37072* 3-5 30
(Vocals: Jack Parker)

SHEPHERD'S SERENADE / I'M A DREAMER – AREN'T WE ALL? .... *Perfect 15253* 2-4 30
(Vocals: Jack Parker)
(Simultaneously released on two labels)

SPRINGTIME IN THE ROCKIES (Vocal: Scrappy Lambert as Rodman Lewis) .... *Hit Of The Week 1050* 3-5 30
(Hit Of The Week records are one-sided paper discs)

THERE'S DANGER IN YOUR EYES, CHERIE .... *Hit Of The Week 1029* 4-6 30
(Hit Of The Week records are one-sided paper discs)

THERE'S DANGER IN YOUR EYES, CHERIE / SINGING A VAGABOND SONG........ *Perfect 15279* 3-5 30
(Vocals: Jack Parker)

THERE'S HONEY ON THE MOON TONIGHT / THE SPELLING BEE .... *Vocalion 4141* 4-6 38
(Vocals: Johnny Russell)

WHEN I'M LOOKING AT YOU / THE ROGUE SONG .... *Perfect 15275* 3-5 30
(Vocals: Jack Parker)

LOPEZ, Vincent, & His Suave Swing Orchestra

BLUE MOON / HOW AM I TO KNOW? .... *Bluebird B-10268* 2-4 39

CREAKING OLD MILL ON THE CREEK, THE (Vocal: Sonny Schuyler) / DON'T KISS AND TELL (Vocal: Penny Parker) .... *Bluebird B-10588* 2-4 40

DARK EYES / SWINGING WITH THE GOONS .... *Bluebird B-10283* 3-5 39

DAUGHTER OF SWEET GEORGIA BROWN, THE / WHISTLING IN THE WILDWOOD... *Bluebird B-10225* 3-5 39
(Vocals: Sonny Schuyler)

HOW MANY TIMES? (Vocal: Penny Parker) / NOLA (theme song) .... *Bluebird B-10601* 2-4 40

IGLOO (Vocal: Betty Hutton) / CONCERT IN THE PARK (Vocals: Betty Hutton & Sonny Schuyler) .... *Bluebird B-10300* 3-5 39
(Betty Hutton later became famous as an actress on stage & screen, and starred in her own television series)

JITTERBUG, THE (Vocal: Betty Hutton) / IF I ONLY HAD A BRAIN (Vocal: Sonny Schuyler)..... *Bluebird B-10367* 4-6 39

MY LOVE FOR YOU / ESPECIALLY FOR YOU .... *Bluebird B-10312* 2-4 39
(Vocals: Sonny Schuyler)

PUT YOUR LITTLE FOOT THERE / BOOMPS-A-DAISY .... *Bluebird B-10579* 2-4 40
(Vocals: Penny Parker)

ROSE O'DAY (Vocal: Sonny Schuyler) / SOMEBODY NOBODY LOVES (Vocals: Unknown) ... *Philharmonic 54* 3-5 42

SOMETIMES / ROSE O'DAY.............. *Elite 5013* 2-4 42
(Vocals: Sonny Schuyler)

THERE'S A SMALL HOTEL / I'M FOREVER BLOWING BUBBLES .... *Bluebird B-10318* 2-4 39

THIS HEART OF MINE / EACH TIME YOU SAY GOOD-BYE............ *Bluebird B-10354* 2-4 39
(Vocals: Sonny Schuyler)

TUMBLING TUMBLEWEEDS (Vocal: Sonny Schuyler) / DIANE......................... *Bluebird B-10534* 2-4 39

WHEN THE ROSES BLOOM AGAIN / SOMEBODY NOBODY LOVES .... *Elite 5014* 2-4 42
(Vocals: Unknown)

YOU'RE DRIVING ME CRAZY / ALL ALONE.................... *Bluebird B-10397* 2-4 39

LORCH, Carl, & His Orchestra

ANGRY (Vocal: Shirley Dean) / LET'S SAY GOODNIGHT TO THE LADIES (AND WE'LL COME RIGHT BACK AGAIN) (Vocals: by orchestra)........ *Bluebird B-10411* 3-5 39

DON'T PUT THE BEE ON ME / DOES YOUR HEART BEAT FOR ME?................. *Bluebird B-10418* 4-6 39
(Vocals: Shirley Dean)

YOU'RE GONNA FALL AND BREAK YOUR HEART / SWING, LITTLE INDIANS, SWING (Vocal: Shirley Dean) .... *Bluebird B-10428* 5-8 39

LOUISVILLE RHYTHM KINGS, The:
see POLLACK, Ben, & His Park Central Orchestra

LOWN, Bert, & His Hotel Biltmore Orchestra

BYE BYE BLUES (theme song) (Vocals: Scrappy Lambert)......... *Hit Of The Week 1090* 5-8 30
(Hit Of The Week records are one-sided paper discs)

CONGRATULATIONS (Vocals: Unknown) .... *Hit Of The Week 1032* 3-5 30
(Hit Of The Week records are one-sided paper discs)

HEARTACHES (Vocals: The Biltmore Trio) / SAY "HELLO" TO THE FOLKS BACK HOME (Vocal: Elmer Feldkamp)........... *Victor 22612* 3-5 31

I LOVE YOU, BELIEVE ME, I LOVE YOU / THE PERFECT SONG.......... *Pathe Actuelle 37089* 4-6 30
(Vocals: Scrappy Lambert)

I LOVE YOU, BELIEVE ME, I LOVE YOU / THE PERFECT SONG................ *Perfect 15270* 3-5 30
(Vocals: Scrappy Lambert)

I LOVE YOU, BELIEVE ME, I LOVE YOU / THE PERFECT SONG...................... *Regal 8939* 3-5 30
(Vocals: Scrappy Lambert)
(Simultaneously released on three labels)

I'M SO AFRAID OF YOU / BY MY SIDE..... *Victor 22623* 4-6 31
(Vocals: Elmer Feldkamp)

I'VE FOUND WHAT I WANTED IN YOU (Vocals: The Biltmore Trio) / WERE YOU SINCERE? (Vocal: Elmer Feldkamp).................. *Victor 26653* 4-6 31

LOVING YOU THE WAY I DO (Vocals: The Biltmore Rhythm Boys) / THE PENALTY OF LOVE (Vocal: Elmer Feldkamp) .... *Victor 22568* 4-6 30

MAYBE IT'S LOVE / I'LL BE BLUE, JUST THINKING OF YOU .... *Columbia 2292-D* 5-8 30
(Vocals: Elmer Feldkamp)

MY SUCCESS / ALONE IN A CORNER... *Victor 22787* 5-8 31
(Vocals: Elmer Feldkamp)

NEVER (Vocals: The Biltmore Trio) / I'M PAINTING PICTURES (Vocal: Elmer Feldkamp) .... *Victor 22725* 4-6 31

NOW YOU'RE IN MY ARMS (Vocal: Elmer Feldkamp) / I WANNA SING ABOUT YOU (Vocals: The Biltmore Trio)............... *Victor 22689* 4-6 31

PLEASE DON'T TALK ABOUT ME WHEN I'M GONE (Vocal: Elmer Feldkamp) / WHEN YOUR LOVER HAS GONE (Vocals: The Biltmore Trio).......... *Victor 22652* 4-6 31

SWEET SUMMER BREEZE / YOU CALL IT MADNESS, BUT I CALL IT LOVE................ *Victor 22804* 3-5 31
(Vocals: Elmer Feldkamp)

THAT LITTLE BOY OF MINE / THE HOUR OF PARTING........................ *Victor 22738* 4-6 31
(Vocals: Elmer Feldkamp)

UNDER THE MOON IT'S YOU / BYE BYE BLUES (theme song)...... *Columbia 2258-D* 5-8 30
(Vocals: The Biltmore Rhythm Boys)

WHEN I TAKE MY SUGAR TO TEA (Vocals: The Biltmore Trio) / RUNNING BETWEEN THE RAINDROPS (Vocal: Elmer Feldkamp)..... *Victor 22654* 4-6 31

YOU'RE SIMPLY DELISH (Vocals: The Biltmore Rhythm Boys) / AND THEN YOUR LIPS MET MINE (Vocal: Elmer Feldkamp)...................... *Victor 22582* 4-6 31

YOU'RE THE ONE I CARE FOR (Vocal: Elmer Feldkamp) / CRYING MYSELF TO SLEEP (Vocals: The Biltmore Rhythm Boys) .... *Victor 22583* 4-6 31

LOWN, Bert, & His Orchestra

CHARLIE'S HOME (Vocal: Elmer Feldkamp) / BLACK PANTHER................ *Bluebird B-5100* 5-8 33

CHARLIE'S HOME (Vocal: Elmer Feldkamp) / BLACK PANTHER............... *Electradisk 2015* 15-20 33

CHARLIE'S HOME (Vocal: Elmer Feldkamp) / BLACK PANTHER................ *Sunrise S-31810* 15-20 33
(Simultaneously released on three labels)

I CAN'T BELIEVE IT'S TRUE / GOODBYE TO LOVE................. *Victor 24086* 3-5 32

I COVER THE WATERFRONT (Vocal: Mac Ceppos) / MISSISSIPPI BASIN (Vocal: Eddie Farley) .... *Bluebird B-5068* 5-8 33

I COVER THE WATERFRONT (Vocal: Mac Ceppos) / MISSISSIPPI BASIN (Vocal: Eddie Farley)...................... *Electradisk 1991* 15-20 33

I COVER THE WATERFRONT (Vocal: Mac Ceppos) / MISSISSIPPI BASIN (Vocal: Eddie Farley) .... *Sunrise S-3150* 15-20 33
(Simultaneously released on three labels)

I'll BUILD A NEST / MY HEART'S DESIRE............ *Bluebird B-5087* 4-6 33
(Vocals: Ted Holt)

I'll BUILD A NEST / MY HEART'S DESIRE............ *Electradisk 2003* 12-15 33
(Vocals: Ted Holt)

I'll BUILD A NEST / MY HEART'S DESIRE.............. *Sunrise S-3162* 12-15 33
(Vocals: Ted Holt)
(Simultaneously released on three labels)

IT WAS A NIGHT IN JUNE / ISN'T IT HEAVENLY?............. *Bluebird B-5067* 3-5 33
(Vocals: Ted Holt)

IT WAS A NIGHT IN JUNE / ISN'T IT HEAVENLY?............ *Electradisk 1990* 10-12 33
(Vocals: Ted Holt)
(Simultaneously released on two labels)

MOONSTRUCK (Vocal: Ted Holt) / HERE YOU COME WITH LOVE (Vocal: Elmer Feldkamp) ... *Bluebird B-5099* 3-5 33

MOONSTRUCK (Vocal: Ted Holt) / HERE YOU COME WITH LOVE (Vocal: Elmer Feldkamp)... *Electradisk 2014* 10-12 33

MOONSTRUCK (Vocal: Ted Holt) / HERE YOU COME WITH LOVE (Vocal: Elmer Feldkamp) ... *Sunrise S-3180* 10-12 33
(Simultaneously released on three labels)

MORE YOU HURT ME, THE / WAS THAT THE HUMAN THING TO DO?.......................... *Victor 22908* 3-5 32
(Vocals: Elmer Feldkamp)

OVER THE WEEK-END / I'M YOURS FOR TONIGHT...................... *Victor 24087* 3-5 32
(Vocals: Elmer Feldkamp)

LOWN, Bert, & His Orchestra as The Park Central Orchestra

I'VE GOT TO PASS YOUR HOUSE TO GET TO MY HOUSE / CAN'T WE MEET AGAIN?......... *Bluebird B-5090* 3-5 33
(Vocals: Ted Holt)

I'VE GOT TO PASS YOUR HOUSE TO GET TO MY HOUSE / CAN'T WE MEET AGAIN?......... *Electradisk 2006* 10-12 33
(Vocals: Ted Holt)

I'VE GOT TO PASS YOUR HOUSE TO GET TO MY HOUSE / CAN'T WE MEET AGAIN?.......... *Sunrise S-3165* 10-12 33
(Vocals: Ted Holt)
(Simultaneously released on three labels)

LEARN TO CROON / A FOOL IN LOVE .... *Bluebird B-5091* 3-5 33
(Vocals: Ted Holt)

LEARN TO CROON / A FOOL IN LOVE.................. *Electradisk 2007* 10-12 33
(Vocals: Ted Holt)

LEARN TO CROON / A FOOL IN LOVE .... *Sunrise S-3166* 10-12 33
(Vocals: Ted Holt)
(Simultaneously released on three labels)

LOYD, Ed, & His Band:
see MARTIN, Freddy, & His Orchestra

LOYD, Ed, & His Orchestra:
see CALIFORNIA RAMBLERS, The, as Ted Wallace & His Orchestra
see KARDOS, Gene, & His Orchestra

LUCAS, Clyde, & His Orchestra

I SAID NO / BLUES IN THE NIGHT........ *Elite 5010* 3-5 42
(Vocals: Eadie Lang)

LUCAS, Clyde, & His California Dons
(Clyde Lucas: circa 1901 –)

BIG APPLE, THE / SONG OF THE SAMOVAR...................... *Vocalion 3782* 4-6 37

MOONLIGHT ON THE CAMPUS / LITTLE FRATERNITY PIN.................... *Vocalion 3785* 3-5 37

SHE'S WAY UP THAR (I'M WAY DOWN YAR) (Vocals: Clyde Lucas & The Four Men Only) / CHINESE RHUMBA (Vocal: Lynn Lucas)................... *Columbia 35935* 3-5 41

SO MANY MEMORIES / GARDENIAS AND KISSES .... *Vocalion 3783* 3-5 37

STOP! YOU'RE BREAKIN' MY HEART / WHISPERS IN THE DARK .... *Vocalion 3774* 4-6 37

SWINGIN' IN A JUG / CHINESE RHUMBA .... *Variety 667* 4-6 37

WHEN BUDDHA SMILES (Vocals: The Four Men Only) / INTERMEZZO .... *Columbia 36017* 3-5 41

WHY TALK ABOUT LOVE? / I'D LIKE TO SEE SAMOA OF SAMOA .... *Vocalion 3786* 3-5 37

LUCKY STRIKE DANCE ORCHESTRA, The:

see SELVIN, Ben, & His Orchestra

LUNCEFORD, Jimmie, & His Chickasaw Syncopators

(Jimmie Lunceford: 6/6/02 – 7/13/47)

IN DAT MORNIN' (preaching by Moses Allen) / SWEET RHYTHM .... *Victor V-38141* 20-25 30

LUNCEFORD, Jimmie, & His Orchestra

ANNIE LAURIE / FRISCO FOG .... *Decca 1569* 5-8 37

BABY, WON'T YOU PLEASE COME HOME? (Vocal: Joe Thomas) / BLUE BLAZES .... *Vocalion 4667* 4-6 39

BACK DOOR STUFF / BACK DOOR STUFF, PART II .... *Decca 18594* 3-5 42

BATTLE AXE / CHOCOLATE .... *Decca 3807* 3-5 41

BECAUSE YOU'RE YOU (Vocal: Henry Wells) / RAIN (Vocals: by trio) .... *Decca 415* 5-8 35

BIRD OF PARADISE / RHAPSODY JUNIOR .... *Decca 639* 5-8 35

BLACK AND TAN FANTASY / SINCE MY BEST GAL TURNED ME DOWN (Vocals: by trio) .... *Decca 453* 5-8 35

BLUE PRELUDE / PEACE AND LOVE FOR ALL .... *Decca 3892mm2-4*

BLUE PRELUDE / PEACE AND LOVE FOR ALL .... *Decca 3892* 2-4 41
(Vocals: Dan Grissom)

BREAKFAST BALL (Vocal: Sy Oliver) / HERE GOES (Vocal: Henry Wells) .... *Victor 24601* 8-10 34

BUGS PARADE / CHOPIN'S PRELUDE NO. 7 .... *Columbia 35547* 3-5 40

CALL IT ANYTHING (IT WASN'T LOVE) (Vocal: Henry Wells) / RHYTHM IN MY NURSERY RHYMES (Vocal: Willie Smith) .... *Decca 572* 5-8 35

COQUETTE (Vocal: Dan Grissom) / FOR DANCERS ONLY .... *Decca 1340* 5-8 37

COUNT ME OUT / LINGER AWHILE .... *Decca 1229* 4-6 37
(Vocals: Dan Grissom)

DREAM OF YOU / HITTIN' THE BOTTLE .... *Decca 765* 5-8 35
(Vocals: Sy Oliver)

EASTER PARADE (Vocal: Trummy Young) / I'M ALONE WITH YOU .... *Columbia 35484* 2-4 40

FLAMINGO (Vocal: Dan Grissom) / SIETA AT THE FIESTA .... *Decca 3931* 3-5 41

FOR DANCERS ONLY / WHITE HEAT .... *V-Disc 135* 5-8 -
(A World War II release)

GONE (Vocal: Dan Grissom) / IMPROMPTU .... *Decca 4083* 3-5 41

HE AIN'T GOT RHYTHM (Vocal: Joe Thomas) / SLUMMING ON PARK AVENUE (Vocals: by trio) .... *Decca 1128* 5-8 37

HELL'S BELLS / PUT ON YOUR OLD GREY BONNET (Vocal: Eddie Tompkins) .... *Decca 1506* 4-6 37

HI SPOOK / YARD DOG MAZURKA .... *Decca 4032* 3-5 41

HONEYDIPPER, THE / BABY, ARE YOU KIDDIN'? .... *Decca 23451* 3-5 46
(Vocals: The Delta Rhythm Boys)

I CAN'T ESCAPE FROM YOU (Vocal: Dan Grissom) / HARLEM SHOUT .... *Decca 980* 5-8 36

I HAD A PREMONITION (Vocal: Dan Grissom) / TWENTY-FOUR ROBBERS (Vocals: Trummy Young & orchestra) .... *Decca 3718* 2-4 41

I'LL SEE YOU IN MY DREAMS (Vocal: Dan Grissom) / THE MERRY-GO-ROUND BROKE DOWN (Vocal: Sy Oliver) .... *Decca 1318* 5-8 37

I'LL TAKE THE SOUTH / THE MELODY MAN .... *Decca 805* 5-8 36
(Vocals: Sy Oliver)

I'M GONNA MOVE TO THE OUTSKIRTS OF TOWN / I'M GONNA MOVE TO THE OUTSKIRTS OF TOWN, PART II .... *Decca 18324* 3-5 42
(Vocals: Dan Grissom)

I'M IN AN AWFUL MOOD (Vocal: Trummy Young) / BLUES IN THE GROOVE .... *Conqueror 9498* 3-5 40

I'M IN AN AWFUL MOOD (Vocal: Trummy Young) / BLUES IN THE GROOVE .... *Vocalion 5395* 3-5 40
(Simultaneously released on two labels)

I'M LOSING MY MIND (BECAUSE OF YOU) (Vocal: Dan Grissom) / LIFE IS FINE (Vocal: Trummy Young) .... *Decca 4289* 2-4 42

I'M WALKING THROUGH HEAVEN WITH YOU (Vocal: Henry Wells) / I'M NUTS ABOUT SCREWY MUSIC (Vocal: Willie Smith) .... *Decca 682* 5-8 36

IT HAD TO BE YOU (Vocals: by quartet) / KEEP SMILIN', KEEP LAUGHIN', BE HAPPY (Vocal: Joe Thomas) .... *Decca 18504* 3-5 42

I USED TO LOVE YOU (BUT IT'S ALL OVER NOW) (Vocal: Joe Thomas) / LIZA .... *Conqueror 9500* 3-5 39

I USED TO LOVE YOU (BUT IT'S ALL OVER NOW) (Vocal: Joe Thomas) / LIZA .... *Vocalion 5276* 3-5 39
(Simultaneously released on two labels)

I WANNA HEAR SWING SONGS (Vocal: Trummy Young) / SONATA (BEETHOVEN) .... *Columbia 35453* 3-5 40

JAZZNOCRACY (early theme song) / CHILLUN, GET UP (Vocals: Henry Wells & trio) .... *Victor 24522* 5-8 34

JEALOUS (Vocal: Henry Wells) / THE BEST THINGS IN LIFE ARE FREE (Vocal: Dan Grissom) .... *Decca 78* 5-8 36

JIMMIES, THE / I NEED A LIFT (Vocals: by ensemble) .... *Majestic 1060* 2-4 46

LIKE A SHIP AT SEA (Vocal: Dan Grissom) / MARGIE (Vocal: Trummy Young) .... *Decca 1617* 3-5 38

LIVING FROM DAY TO DAY (Vocal: Dan Grissom) / 'TAIN'T GOOD (LIKE A NICKEL MADE OF WOOD) (Vocals: by trio) .... *Decca 960* 5-8 36

LONESOME ROAD (Vocal: Trummy Young) / MANDY .... *Vocalion 4831* 4-6 39

MINNIE THE MOOCHER IS DEAD (Vocal: The Dandridge Sisters) / PAVANNE .... *Columbia 35700* 3-5 40

MIXUP / BLUE AFTERGLOW (Vocal: Dan Grissom) .... *Columbia 35919* 3-5 41

MONOTONY IN FOUR FLATS / I AIN'T GONNA STUDY WAR NO MORE (Vocals: Dandridge Sisters) .... *Columbia 35567* 3-5 40

MOOD INDIGO / ROSE ROOM .... *Decca 131* 5-8 34

MUDDY WATER (A MISSISSIPPI MOAN) (Vocals: by trio) / HONEST AND TRULY (Vocal: Dan Grissom) .... *Decca 1219* 5-8 37

(THIS IS) MY LAST AFFAIR (Vocal: Dan Grissom) / RUNNING A TEMPERATURE (Vocal: Sy Oliver) .... *Decca 1035* 5-8 37

MY MELANCHOLY BABY / BY THE RIVER SAINTE MARIE .... *Decca 1808* 3-5 38
(Vocals: Dan Grissom)

NANA (Vocal: Henry Wells) / MISS OTIS REGRETS (Vocal: Sy Oliver) .... *Decca 130* 5-8 34

OH BOY / CHARMAINE (Vocal: Dan Grissom) .... *Decca 628* 4-6 35

OH WHY, OH WHY / I LOVE YOU .... *Vocalion 4979* 3-5 39

OKAY FOR BABY / FLIGHT OF THE JITTERBUG .... *Columbia 35967* 3-5 41

ON THE BEACH AT BALI-BALI / ME AND THE MOON .... *Decca 915* 5-8 36
(Vocals: Sy Oliver)

PIGEON WALK / I'M LAUGHING UP MY SLEEVE (Vocal: Sy Oliver) .... *Decca 1659* 4-6 38

POSIN' (Vocal: Willie Smith) / HONEY, KEEP YOUR EYE ON ME (Vocal: Dan Grissom) .... *Decca 1355* 5-8 37

PRETTY EYES (Vocal: Dan Grissom) / IT'S TIME TO JUMP AND SHOUT .... *Conqueror 9499* 3-5 40

PRETTY EYES (Vocal: Dan Grissom) / IT'S TIME TO JUMP AND SHOUT .... *Okeh 5430* 3-5 40

PRETTY EYES (Vocal: Dan Grissom) / IT'S TIME TO JUMP AND SHOUT .... *Vocalion 5430* 3-5 40
(Simultaneously released on three labels)

PRETTY EYES (Vocal: Dan Grissom) / LUNCEFORD SPECIAL .... *V-Disc 69* 5-8 -
(A World War II release)

PUT IT AWAY (Vocal: Willie Smith) / I'M IN AN AWFUL MOOD (Vocal: Trummy Young) .... *V-Disc 97* 5-8 -
(A World War II release)

PUT IT AWAY (Vocal: Willie Smith) / UPTOWN BLUES (later theme song) .... *Conqueror 9502* 3-5 40

PUT IT AWAY (Vocal: Willie Smith) / UPTOWN BLUES (later theme song) .... *Vocalion 5362* 3-5 40
(Simultaneously released on two labels)

RAGGING THE SCALE / THE FIRST TIME I SAW YOU (Vocal: Dan Grissom) .... *Decca 1364* 5-8 37

RAININ' (Vocal: Dan Grissom) / LE JAZZ HOT .... *Vocalion 4595* 4-6 39

RED WAGON / YOU AIN'T NOWHERE .... *Columbia 35782* 3-5 40
(Vocals: The Dandridge Sisters)

ROCK IT FOR ME (Vocal: Joe Thomas) / BAREFOOT BLUES (Vocal: Willie Smith) .... *Columbia 35860* 3-5 40

ROCK IT FOR ME (Vocal: Joe Thomas) / WHAM (RE-BOP-BOOM-BAM) (Vocal: Willie Smith) .... *V-Disc 39* 8-10 -
(A World War II release)

RUNNIN' WILD (Vocals: by orchestra) / FOUR OR FIVE TIMES (Vocal: Sy Oliver) .... *Decca 503* 5-8 35

SASSIN' THE BOSS (Vocal: Willie Smith) / I WANT THE WAITER (WITH THE WATER) (Vocals: Trummy Young & orchestra) .... *Conqueror 9316* 4-6 39

SLEEPY-TIME GAL / ORGAN GRINDER'S SWING .... *Decca 908* 5-8 36

SOPHISTICATED LADY / UNSOPHISTICATED SUE (Vocals: by trio) .... *Decca 129* 5-8 34

STAR DUST (Vocal: Henry Wells) / RHYTHM IS OUR BUSINESS (2nd theme song) (Vocal: Willie Smith) .... *Decca 369* 5-8 35

STOMP IT OFF / MY BLUE HEAVEN (Vocals: by trio) .... *Decca 712* 5-8 36

STRATOSPHERE / SOLITUDE (Vocal: Henry Wells) .... *Decca 299* 5-8 35

STRICTLY INSTRUMENTAL / KNOCK ME A KISS (Vocal: Willie Smith) .... *Decca 18463* 3-5 42

SWANEE RIVER / AVALON .... *Decca 668* 5-8 35

SWINGIN' ON C / LET'S TRY AGAIN (Vocal: Dan Grissom) .... *Columbia 35725* 3-5 40

SWINGIN' UPTOWN / REMEBER WHEN (Vocal: Henry Wells) .... *Victor 24669* 8-10 34

'TAIN'T WHAT YOU DO (IT'S THE WAY THAT YOU DO IT) / CHEATIN' ON ME .... *Vocalion 4582* 4-6 39
(Vocals: Trummy Young & chorus)

TEASIN' TESSIE BROWN (Vocal: Eddie Tompkins) / THE LOVE NEST (Vocal: Dan Grissom) .... *Decca 1734* 5-8 38

THEM WHO HAS – GETS (Vocal: Joe Thomas) / SHUT-OUT .... *Majestic 1077* 3-5 46

TIME'S A-WASTIN' (Vocal: Sy Oliver) / WELL, ALL RIGHT THEN (Vocals: by orchestra) .... *Vocalion 4887* 4-6 39

WHAM (RE-BOP-BOOM-BAM) (Vocal: Willie Smith) / LUNCEFORD SPECIAL .... *Vocalion 5326* 3-5 40

WHATCHA KNOW, JOE? (Vocal: Trummy Young) / PLEASE SAY THE WORD (Vocal: Dan Grissom) .... *Columbia 35625* 3-5 40

WHAT IS THIS THING CALLED SWING? (Vocal: Joe Thomas) / AIN'T SHE SWEET? (Vocals: Trummy Young and trio) .... *Vocalion 4875* 4-6 39

WHAT'S YOUR STORY, MORNIN' GLORY? / I GOT IT (Vocal: Trummy Young) .... *Columbia 35510* 3-5 40

WHITE HEAT / LEAVING ME (Vocal: Henry Wells) .... *Victor 24586* 8-10 34

WHITE HEAT / YOU CAN FOOL SOME OF THE PEOPLE (SOME OF THE TIME) (Vocal: Trummy Young) .... *Vocalion 5156* 4-6 39

WHO DID YOU MEET LAST NIGHT? (Vocal: Dan Grissom) / SASSIN' THE BOSS (Vocal: Willie Smith) .... *Vocalion 5116* 4-6 39

YOU LET ME DOWN (Vocal: Dan Grissom) / I WANT THE WAITER (WITH THE WATER) (Vocals: Trummy Young & orchestra) .... *Vocalion 5033* 3-5 39

YOU'RE ALWAYS IN MY DREAMS (Vocal: Dan Grissom) / EASY STREET (Vocal: Trummy Young) .... *Decca 18534* 3-5 42

YOU'RE JUST A DREAM / I'VE ONLY MYSELF TO BLAME .... *Vocalion 4754* 3-5 39
(Vocals: Dan Grissom)

YOU SET ME ON FIRE (Vocal: Dan Grissom) / SHOEMAKER'S HOLIDAY .... *Vocalion 4712* 4-6 39

LUSTIG, Billy:

see SCRANTON SIRENS Orchestra, The

LYMAN, Abe, & His Californians

(Abe Lyman: 8/4/97 – 10/23/57)

AFTER I SAY I'M SORRY (Vocal: Ed Holly) / YOU DON'T HOW MUCH YOU CAN SUFFER (Vocal: Rose Blane) .... *Bluebird B-10325* 2-4 39

AT THE BALALAIKA (Vocal: Ed Holly) / YODELIN' JIVE (Vocal: Rose Blane) .... *Bluebird B-10533* 3-5 40

DEBUTANTE WALTZ / THAT NAUGHTY WALTZ .... *Bluebird B-10544* 2-4 40
(Vocals: Ed Holly)

FEED BOX FREDDY (Vocal: Rose Blane) / DAWN (Vocal: Eddie Holly) .... *Bluebird B-11158* 2-4 41

FOR ME AND MY GAL / LA GOLONDRINA .... *Bluebird B-11549* 2-4 42
(Vocals: Bill Sherman)

GOLDEN GATE / SAN FRANCISCO .... *Decca 2435* 2-4 39
(Vocals: The Century Quartet)

HE WEARS A PAIR OF SILVER WINGS (Vocal: Billy Sherman) / AMEN (Vocals: Rose Blane & orchestra) .... *Bluebird B-11542* 3-5 42

HONEST JOHN (Vocal: Ed Holly) / GOOD MORNING (Vocal: Rose Blane) .... *Bluebird B-10424* 2-4 39

HOW DID HE LOOK? (Vocal: Ed Holly) / YOU'RE IN THE ARMY NOW (Vocals: chorus) .... *Bluebird B-10971* 3-5 41

I'LL ALWAYS REMEMBER (Vocals: Rose Blane & Billy Sherman) / MANDY IS TWO (Vocal: Billy Sherman) .... *Bluebird B-11434* 3-5 42

INDIANS THREW ROCKS AT COLUMBUS, THE (Vocal: Rose Blane) / A BEAUTIFUL LADY IN BLUE (Vocal: Larry Stewart) .... *Bluebird B-11261* 2-4 41

I WISH I HAD A DIME (Vocal: Rose Blane) / HORSE 'N' BOOGIE .... *Bluebird B-11360* 2-4 41

LET'S PUT THE AXE TO THE AXIS (Vocals: The Four Eton Boys) / BABY BOOGIE (Vocal: Rose Blane) .... *Bluebird B-11410* 3-5 42

MARIA ELENA (Vocal: Bob Hannon) / THE PRISONER'S SONG (Vocal: Rose Blane) .... *Bluebird B-11005* 2-4 41

MISSOURI SCRAMBLER / OH! HOW I HATE TO GET UP IN THE MORNING (Vocal: Frank Parrish) .... *Bluebird B-10992* 3-5 41

MOON OVER AMERICA / LONELY BREEZE .... *Bluebird B-11026* 2-4 41
(Vocals: Ed Holly)

SHE'LL BE COMIN' ROUND THE MOUNTAIN / HAND ME DOWN MY WALKIN' CANE .... *Bluebird B-10869* 2-4 40
(Vocals: The Escorts)

SHOEMAKER'S HOLIDAY / DANGER! MEN BLASTING .... *Bluebird B-10337* 2-4 39
(Vocals: Rose Blane)

STOP KICKING MY HEART AROUND (Vocal: Ed Holly) / THE MONKEYS HAVE NO TAILS IN PAGO PAGO (Vocal: Rose Blane) .... *Bluebird B-10407* 3-5 39

(I WANNA GO WHERE YOU GO) THEN I'LL BE HAPPY (Vocal: Rose Blane) / LET THERE BE LOVE (Vocal: Ed Holly) .... *Bluebird B-10685* 2-4 40

TO YOU, SWEETHEART, ALOHA (Vocal: Frank Parrish) / SWEET LITTLE YOU (Vocal: Rose Blane) .... *Bluebird B-10496* 2-4 39

VIOLETS FOR YOUR FURS (Vocal: Billy Sherman) / SUNSET NEAR VINE .... *Bluebird B-11378* 2-4 41

WHEN THE LILACS BLOOM AGAIN (Vocal: Frank Parrish) / LOVE, YOU ARE MINE TONIGHT (Vocal: Eddie Holly) .... *Bluebird B-11177* 2-4 41

WRAP YOUR DREAMS IN THE RED, WHITE AND BLUE / HE'S MY UNCLE .... *Bluebird B-10924* 3-5 40
(Vocals: Rose Blane)

YOURS (Vocals: Rose Blane & Frank Parrish) / JOHNSON SPECIAL............. *Bluebird B-11241* 3-5 41

LYMAN, Abe, & His Orchestra / California Ambassador Hotel Orchestra / California Orchestra

ACE IN THE HOLE / MANDY (Vocal: Frank Sylvano)........ *Brunswick 3241* 4-6 26

AFTER I SAY I'M SORRY (Vocal: Charles Kaley) / SHAKE THAT THING .... *Brunswick 3069* 4-6 26

AIN'T MISBEHAVIN' / BASHFUL BABY.................. *Brunswick 4443* 3-5 29
(Vocals: Unknown)

AMONG MY SOUVENIRS / KEEP SWEEPING THE COBWEBS OFF THE MOON........ *Brunswick 3753* 3-5 28
(Vocals: Phil Neely)

AS LONG AS WE'RE TOGETHER (Vocal: Olga Sardi) / THE GRASS IS JUST AS GREEN
(Vocal: Rose Blane).................. *Bluebird B-7580* 3-5 38

BABY / I CAN'T GIVE YOU ANYTHING BUT LOVE............ *Brunswick 4136* 3-5 29
(Vocals: Phil Neely)

BESIDE A GARDEN WALL / WISTFUL AND BLUE .... *Brunswick 3317* 3-5 26
(Vocals: Unknown)

BREEZIN' ALONG WITH THE BREEZE / WHERE'D YOU GET THOSE EYES?........... *Brunswick 3240* 3-5 26
(Vocals: Frank Sylvano)

BUGLE CALL RAG / QUEEN OF EGYPT................ *Brunswick 2481* 4-6 23

BYE-BYE, PRETTY BABY / JUST ANOTHER DAY WASTED AWAY .... *Brunswick 3615* 2-4 27
(Vocals: Unknown)

CALIFORNIA BLUES / I DON'T WANT YOU TO CRY OVER ME.............. *Brunswick 2530* 3-5 23

COCOANUT TROT / I WANT YOU BACK, OLD PAL (Vocal: Billy Jones).......... *Brunswick 2749* 3-5 24

CUT YOURSELF A PIECE OF CAKE / NO, NO, NORA (Vocal: Charles Kaley) .... *Brunswick 2476* 2-4 23

DID YOU MEAN IT? / CHARMAINE.... *Brunswick 3648* 2-4 27
(Vocals: Phil Neely)

DREAM HOUSE / DARLING......... *Brunswick 3970* 2-4 28
(Vocals: Unknown)

DREAM TRAIN / DON'T BE LIKE THAT...................... *Brunswick 4137* 2-4 28
(Vocals: Phil Neely)

EVERYBODY STOMP / PRETENDING (Vocal: Charles Kaley)... *Brunswick 2980* 3-5 25

GIRL ON THE POLICE GAZETTE / THIS YEAR'S KISSES................. *Decca 1127* 4-6 37
(Vocals: Sonny Schuyler)

GIVE ME YOUR AFFECTION (HONEY) / WHY DANCE? .... *Brunswick 6154* 3-5 31
(Vocals: Phil Neely)

GOLDEN SANDS / HULLABALOO ... *Brunswick 4912* 3-5 30
(Vocals: Unknown)

GONE / LOVE, WHAT ARE YOU DOING TO MY HEART? .... *Decca 1098* 4-6 36
(Vocals: Sonny Schuyler)

GOOD NEWS (Vocals: by trio) / THE VARSITY DRAG (Vocal: Phil Neely)............. *Brunswick 3901* 3-5 28

I COVER THE WATERFRONT (Vocal: Gracie Barrie) / LYING IN THE HAY (Vocal: Frank Sylvano)............... *Brunswick 6572* 3-5 33

I'M ONLY MAKING BELIEVE / ANOTHER NIGHT................ *Brunswick 4555* 3-5 29
(Vocals: Unknown)

I'M WAITING FOR SHIPS THAT NEVER COME IN / I THINK OF WHAT YOU USED TO THINK OF ME............... *Brunswick 3904* 2-4 28
(Vocals: Phil Neely)

JEALOUS (Vocal: Charles Kaley) / IF YOU DO WHAT YOU DO........ *Brunswick 2639* 2-4 24

JIMMY HAD A NICKEL / MUSIC MAKES ME................ *Brunswick 6756* 3-5 34
(Vocals: by trio)

LET'S TALK ABOUT MY SWEETIE / TENDERLY...................... *Brunswick 3070* 3-5 26
(Vocals: Charles Kaley)

LOVE AND LEARN (Vocal: Tony Wolfe) / WANTED (Vocal: Sonny Schuyler) .... *Decca 1105* 4-6 37

LOVE IS HERE TO STAY (Vocal: Frank Parrish) / I WAS DOING ALL RIGHT
(Vocal: Olga Sardi).................... *Bluebird B-7369* 2-4 38

MIGHTY BLUE / THAT'S ALL THERE IS .... *Brunswick 2934* 2-4 25
(Vocals: Charles Kaley)

MILENBERG JOYS / HIGH SOCIETY... *Brunswick 6325* 5-8 32

MY SUPPRESSED DESIRE / SWEETHEARTS ON PARADE..................... *Brunswick 4117* 2-4 29
(Vocals: Unknown)

NEW KIND OF MAN, A / ROMANY DAYS.................. *Brunswick 2679* 2-4 24

NOTHING ELSE TO DO / TOO BAD... *Brunswick 3084* 3-5 26

ON THE SENTIMENTAL SIDE (Vocal: Frank Parrish) / THIS IS MY NIGHT TO DREAM
(Vocal: Olga Sardi) .... *Bluebird B-7366* 3-5 38

OOH! THAT KISS / YOU'RE MY EVERYTHING................ *Brunswick 6208* 3-5 31
(Vocals: Dick Robertson)

PAGAN MOON / I WONDER WHO'S UNDER THE MOON WITH YOU TONIGHT?... *Brunswick 6232* 3-5 32
(Vocals: Smith Ballew)

POP! GOES YOUR HEART (Vocal: Phil Neely) / I'M IN LOVE (Vocal: Louis Rapp)...... *Brunswick 6968* 3-5 34

RHYTHM OF THE RAIN (Vocal: Phil Neely) / I WAS LUCKY (Vocal: Louis Rapp) .... *Brunswick 7371* 3-5 35

RISE 'N' SHINE (Vocal: Paul Small) / TURN OUT THE LIGHT........... *Brunswick 6444* 3-5 33

ROGUE SONG, THE (Vocals: by chorus) / WHEN I'M LOOKING AT YOU (Vocals: Unknown)... *Brunswick 4696* 3-5 30

SHEPHERD'S SERENADE, THE / IF HE CARED .... *Brunswick 4633* 3-5 30
(Vocals: Unknown)

SOME RAINY DAY (Vocals: Unknown) / A JAZZ HOLIDAY................ *Brunswick 4155* 5-8 29

STORMY WEATHER (Vocal: Frank Sylvano) / GOLD DIGGERS OF 1933 (Vocals: Frank Sylvano & Phil Neely) .... *Brunswick 20122* 5-8 33
(This is an oversize 12-inch 78 rpm)

SUMMER NIGHT / THE LITTLE HOUSE THAT LOVE BUILT.......................... *Decca 1104* 3-5 37
(Vocals: Sonny Schuyler)

SUNDAY / HAVIN' LOTS OF FUN..... *Brunswick 3286* 3-5 26
(Vocals: Unknown)

THAT'S MY WEAKNESS NOW / JUST IMAGINE.................... *Brunswick 3971* 3-5 28
(Vocals: Unknown)

THERE'S A BLUE RIDGE IN MY HEART, VIRGINIA / BURGUNDY....................... *Brunswick 3139* 2-4 26

THERE'S SOMETHING ABOUT AN OLD-FASHIONED GIRL / NEVER SWAT A FLY .... *Brunswick 4924* 4-6 30
(Vocals: Unknown)

TWELFTH STREET RAG / FAREWELL BLUES................ *Brunswick 6314* 5-8 32

TWELFTH STREET RAG / THE NEW ST. LOUIS BLUES................. *Brunswick 3316* 5-8 26

UKELELE BABY / IF YOU KNEW SUSIE (Vocal: Charles Kaley).... *Brunswick 2903* 3-5 25

WEARY BLUES / THE NEW ST. LOUIS BLUES................. *Brunswick 6637* 5-8 33

WEARY WEASEL / BEFORE YOU GO... *Brunswick 2504* 5-8 23

WHEN THE REST OF THE CROWD GOES HOME (I ALWAYS GO HOME ALONE) / WHERE THE BLUE OF THE NIGHT (MEETS THE GOLD OF THE DAY)..................... *Brunswick 6224* 3-5 32
(Vocals: Les Reis)

WHEN THE STARS GO TO SLEEP / IT'S THE DREAMER IN ME .... *Bluebird B-7578* 2-4 38
(Vocals: Ed Holly)

WHEN YOU WERE THE GIRL ON THE SCOOTER (AND I WAS THE BOY ON THE BIKE)
(Vocals: The Revere Sisters) / DOIN' THE UPTOWN LOWDOWN (Vocal: Ella Logan)........ *Brunswick 6674* 4-6 33

WITHOUT THAT GAL! / AT YOUR COMMAND .... *Brunswick 6142* 3-5 31
(Vocals: Unknown)

WITH YOU, DEAR, IN BOMBAY / SING A SONG (Vocal: Charles Kaley) ... *Brunswick 2912* 10-12 25
(The orchestra is directed by Charlie Chaplin, who plays the violin solos, as Chaplin's compositions are recorded.)

WON'T YOU TELL ME, HON' (WHEN WE'RE GONNA BE ONE) (Vocal: Phil Neely) / GIVE YOUR LITTLE BABY LOTS OF LOVIN' (Vocals: Unknown) ... *Brunswick 4175* 3-5 29

WRAP YOUR TROUBLES IN DREAMS / JUST ONE MORE CHANCE .... *Brunswick 6125* 3-5 31
(Vocals: Phil Neely)

YOU AND THE MOON AND ME (Vocals: Gracie Barrie & Phil Neely) / MY! OH MY!
(Vocal: Frank Sylvano)................. *Brunswick 6578* 2-4 33

YOU CAN'T STOP ME FROM LOVIN' YOU (Vocal: Marvin Warner) / I CAN'T GET MISSISSIPPI OFF MY MIND
(Vocal: Harry Podal)................... *Brunswick 6158* 3-5 31

YOU'RE A REAL SWEETHEART / DOWN WHERE THE SUN GOES DOWN............ *Brunswick 3994* 2-4 28
(Vocals: Unknown)

YOU'RE SO EASY TO REMEMBER / LOVE BABY......... *Brunswick 3632* 2-4 27
(Vocals: Unknown)

YOU'RE THAT CERTAIN SOMEONE / SALLY'S GOT THE BLUES...................... *Brunswick 2780* 3-5 24

YOU WILL COME BACK TO ME / WORRYIN' OVER YOU .... *Brunswick 4774* 3-5 30
(Vocals: Unknown)

LYNCH, Al, & His Orchestra:

see RICH, Fred, as Fred Rich's Dance Orchestra

LYNN, Al, as Al Lynn's Music Masters

AT SUNDOWN / ME AND MY SHADOW... *Edison 52086* 5-8 27
(Vocals: J. Donald Parker)

HOOSIER SWEETHEART (Vocal: Jack Kaufman) / SOMETIMES I'M HAPPY
(Vocal: Vaughn de Leath)................. *Edison 52041* 4-6 27

INDIAN BUTTERFLY / WHAT MAKES MY BABY CRY? .... *Edison 51952* 4-6 27

THERE AIN'T NO MAYBE IN MY BABY'S EYES / IT'S A HAPPY OLD WORLD AFTER ALL.... *Edison 52004* 5-8 27
(Vocals: John Ryan)

WHISPER SWEET AND LOW / LAURETTA.......................... *Edison 52270* 8-10 28
(Vocals: Unknown)

LYTE, Glen, as Glen Lyte's Orchestra

BEGGING FOR LOVE / PARDON ME, PRETTY BABY.................... *Broadway 1475* 5-8 31
(Vocals: Unknown)

WHEN I TAKE MY SUGAR TO TEA (Vocals: by duet) / OUT OF NOWHERE
(Vocals: Unknown).................... *Braodway 1459* 5-8 31

MACK, Ted, & His Orchestra

CARELESSLY / WORDS FAIL ME.... *Bluebird B-6920* 5-8 37
(Vocals: Ted Mack)

I HUM A WALTZ / A LOVE SONG OF LONG AGO.................. *Bluebird B-6934* 4-6 37
(Vocals: Ted Mack)

SPRING CLEANING / ON A LITTLE DREAM RANCH.................. *Bluebird B-6922* 5-8 37
(Vocals: Ted Mack)

MAD HATTERS, The:

see ROBERTSON, Dick, & His Orchestra

MADRIGUERA, Enric, & His Hotel Biltmore Orchestra

(Enric Madriguera: 2/17/04 – 9/7/73)

LET'S HAVE ANOTHER CUP O'COFFEE / LOVABLE....... *Columbia 2651-D* 3-5 32
(Vocals: Unknown)

MADRIGUERA, Enric, & His Hotel Weylin Orchestra

BLOW, GABRIEL, BLOW / WHERE THERE'S SMOKE, THERE'S FIRE....................... *Victor 24818* 2-4 35
(Vocals: Tony Sacco)

SHE'S A LATIN FROM MANHATTAN / THE LITTLE THINGS YOU USED TO DO........... *Victor 25000* 2-4 35
(Vocals: Tony Sacco)

YOU AND THE NIGHT AND THE MUSIC / IF THERE'S SOMEONE LOVELIER THAN YOU..... *Victor 24768* 2-4 34
(Vocals: Tony Sacco)

MADRIGUERA, Enric, & His Orchestra

CARIOCA / HEAT WAVE
(Vocal: Patricia Gilmore).................. *Victor 27592* 2-4 41

CHASING SHADOWS (Vocal: Bob Bunch) / WHEN A GYPSY MAKES HIS VIOLIN CRY
(Vocals: Enric Madriguera & Tony Sacco)..... *Victor 25047* 2-4 35

FULL MOON / IF YOU ARE BUT A DREAM....................... *Victor 27858* 2-4 42
(Vocals: Patricia Gilmore)

LIVING IN DREAMS / THE SONG THAT BROKE MY HEART............... *Brunswick 6316* 2-4 32
(Vocals: Richard Barry)

LULLABY OF THE LEAVES / GOODBYE BLUES................. *Brunswick 6310* 3-5 32
(Vocals: Richard Barry)

MILLION TIMES A DAY, A / VOODOO MOON (Vocal: Tito Rodriguez) .... *Victor 27759* 2-4 41

ORCHIDS IN THE MOONLIGHT (Vocals: Unknown) / CARIOCA........................ *Columbia 2885-D* 5-8 34
(This record was pressed in blue shellac.)

ORCHIDS IN THE MOONLIGHT / TABOO............. *Brunswick 8407* 2-4 39
(Vocals: The Skylarks)

STAR GAZING (Vocal: Tony Sacco) / EV'RY SINGLE LITTLE TINGLE OF MY HEART
(Vocal: Helen Dell) .... *Victor 25064* 2-4 35

TENDER IS THE NIGHT / I FOUND A DREAM.................. *Victor 25162* 2-4 35
(Vocals: Tony Sacco)

TAKE IT AWAY (Vocal: Patricia Gilmore) / BABALU (Vocal: Eddie Gomez)............. *Cosmo 462* 3-5 46

WE'LL MAKE HAY WHILE THE SUN SHINES / AFTER SUNDOWN..... *Columbia 2849-D* 5-8 34
(Vocals: Unknown)

MADRIGUERA, Enric, as Enric Madriguera's Havana Casino Orchestra

SIBONEY / ADIOS................. *Columbia 2434-D* 3-5 31

MAJESTIC DANCE ORCHESTRA, The:

see GLANTZ, Nathan, & His Orchestra
see HARING, Bob, & His Orchestra
see LANIN, Sam, & His Orchestra
see SAMUELS, Joseph, & His Orchestra
see SAMUELS, Joseph, as Joseph Samuel's Master Players, and
see SCHUBERT, Adrian, & His Salon Orchestra

MALNECK, Matty, & His Orchestra

(Matty Malneck: 12/10/04 – 3/81)

BY THE WATERS OF MINNETONKA / LAZY RHAPSODY (Vocal: Martha Mears)... *Decca 2616* 2-4 39

CARNIVAL OF VENICE / WILLIAM TELL OVERTURE....... *Columbia 35299* 3-5 39

HEARTS AND FLOWERS / SING, YOU SINNERS................. *Decca 2060* 2-4 38

HURRY BACK TO SORRENTO (Vocal: Helen Ward) / LITTLE GIRL IN BLUE............ *Columbia 36184* 3-5 41

LONDONDERRY AIR / LISTEN TO THE MOCKING BIRD.............. *Brunswick 8413* 2-4 39

PARK AVENUE FANTASY / THEN I WROTE THE MINUET IN G..................... *Columbia 35212* 3-5 39

SHANGRI-LA / SHANGRI-LA, PART II .... *Columbia 37877* 2-4 48

SOUVENIR / FLIGHT OF THE BUMBLE-BEE .... *Brunswick 8396* 3-5 39

ST. LOUIS BLUES / HUMORESQUE....... *Decca 2182* 4-6 38

MANHATTAN DANCE MAKERS, The:

see SELVIN, Ben

MANHATTAN IMPERIAL ORCHESTRA, The:

see STRAIGHT, Charley, & His Orchestra

MANHATTAN MADCAPS, The:

see FENTON, Carl, & His Orchestra

MANNERS, Zeke, & His Band

FAT MAN BLUES (Vocal: Zeke Manners) / EENY MEENY DIXIE DEENY
(Vocals: Singing Lariateers)................ *Victor 20-2139* 3-5 46

MANONE, Joe, "Wingy", & His Club Royale Orchestra

(Joe "Wingy" Manone: 2/13/04 – 7/9/82)
(On some labels the name Manone is spelled Mannone)

DOWNRIGHT DISGUSTED / FARE THEE WELL .... *Vocalion 15728* 20-25 28
(Vocals: Wingy Manone)

TRYING TO STOP MY CRYING / ISN'T THERE A LITTLE LOVE? .... *Vocalion 15797* 20-25 29
(Vocals: Wingy Manone)

MANONE, Wingy, & His Orchestra

ABOUT A QUARTER TO NINE / LET'S SPILL THE BEANS........................ *Vocalion 2934* 8-10 35

BASIN STREET BLUES (Vocal: Wingy Manone) / PANAMA........................ *Bluebird B-6411* 5-8 36

BEALE STREET BLUES (Vocal: Wingy Manone) / FAREWELL BLUES............. *Bluebird B-10401* 3-5 39

BLUES HAVE GOT ME, THE / BREEZE........................... *Banner 33356* 5-8 35
(Vocals: Wingy Manone)

BLUES HAVE GOT ME, THE / BREEZE .... *Melotone M-13323* 5-8 35
(Vocals: Wingy Manone)

BLUES HAVE GOT ME, THE / BREEZE............................. *Oriole 3098* 5-8 35
(Vocals: Wingy Manone)

BLUES HAVE GOT ME, THE / BREEZE .... *Perfect 16081* 5-8 35
(Vocals: Wingy Manone)

BLUES HAVE GOT ME, THE / BREEZE .... *Romeo 2472* 5-8 35
(Vocals: Wingy Manone)
(Simultaneously released on five labels)

BOO-HOO / OH, SAY, CAN YOU SWING? .... *Bluebird B-6806* 5-8 37
(Vocals: Wingy Manone)

DALLAS BLUES (Vocal: Wingy Manone) / SWINGIN' AT THE HICKORY HOUSE (Vocals: Wingy Manone & Nappy Lamare).................... *Bluebird B-6375* 5-8 36

DON'T EVER CHANGE / YOU'RE PRECIOUS TO ME.......................... *Bluebird B-7002* 4-6 37
(Vocals: Wingy Manone)

DOWNRIGHT DISGUSTED BLUES / BOOGIE WOOGIE .... *Bluebird B-10296* 4-6 39
(Vocals: Wingy Manone)

DOWN STREAM / WHERE'S THE WAITER?.................... *Bluebird B-7391* 4-6 38
(Vocals: Wingy Manone)

EVERY LITTLE MOMENT / BLACK COFFEE .... *Vocalion 2963* 5-8 35
(Vocals: Wingy Manone)

EVERY NOW AND THEN (Vocal: Wingy Manone) / I'VE GOT A NOTE (Vocals: Wingy Manone, Jack Teagarden, & Johnny Mercer)................... *Vocalion 3071* 8-10 35

FANCY MEETING YOU (Vocal: Wingy Manone) / A GOOD MAN IS HARD TO FIND (Vocals: Wingy Manone & Sally Sharon)...................... *Bluebird B-6537* 5-8 36

FARE THEE WELL, ANNABELLE / ON THE GOOD SHIP LOLLIPOP .... *Vocalion 2914* 8-10 35
(Vocals: Wingy Manone & Nappy Lamare)

FROM THE TOP OF YOUR HEAD / TAKES TWO TO MAKE A BARGAIN............... *Vocalion 3023* 5-8 35
(Vocals: Wingy Manone)

HEART OF MINE / LITTLE JOE FROM CHICAGO .... *Bluebird B-7622* 4-6 38
(Vocals: Wingy Manone)

HESITATION BLUES / SING ME A SWING SONG.................. *Bluebird B-6394* 5-8 36
(Vocals: Wingy Manone)

I AIN'T GOT NOBODY / JAZZ ME BLUES.................. *Bluebird B-7198* 5-8 37
(Vocals: Wingy Manone)

MONONE, Wingy, & His Orchestra

IF I COULD BE WITH YOU ONE HOUR TONIGHT (Vocal: Kay Starr) / TIN ROOF BLUES........ *Ara 145* 3-5 46

I'M SHOOTING HIGH / THE MUSIC GOES 'ROUND AND AROUND .... *Vocalion 3134* 5-8 36
(Vocals: Wingy Manone)

IN THE GROOVE (Vocal: Wingy Manone) / HONEY, PLEASE DON'T TURN YOUR BACK ON ME (by Amanda Randolph & Her Orchestra; Vocal: Amanda Randolph).................. *Bluebird B-6616* 5-8 36

IT'S NO FUN / RHYTHM SAVED THE WORLD .... *Bluebird B-6360* 5-8 36
(Vocals: Wingy Manone)

JUMPY NERVES / CASEY JONES
(Vocal: Wingy Manone)............... *Bluebird B-10289* 4-6 39

JUMPY NERVES / CASEY JONES
(Vocal: Wingy Manone)....... *Montgomery Ward M-8354* 4-6 39
(Simultaneously released on two labels)

JUST ONE GIRL / SHE'S CRYING FOR ME... *Okeh 41569* 10-12 34

LET ME CALL YOU SWEETHEART / EASY LIKE....................... *Bluebird B-6618* 5-8 36
(Vocals: Wingy Manone)

LET'S BREAK THE GOOD NEWS / MANNONE BLUES............... *Bluebird B-7633* 4-6 38
(Vocals: Wingy Manone)

LET'S SWING IT / RHYTHM IS OUR BUSINESS..................... *Vocalion 2990* 8-10 35
(Vocals: Wingy Manone)

MARTHA / THE FLAT FOOT FLOOGIE.................. *Bluebird B-7621* 4-6 38
(Vocals: Wingy Manone)

NICKEL IN THE SLOT (with dialog between Wingy Manone & Nappy Lamare) / SWING, BROTHER, SWING (Vocals: Wingy Manone)........... *Okeh 41573* 8-10 35

NO CALLING CARD / STRANGE BLUES................ *Brunswick 6911* 8-10 34
(Vocals: Wingy Manone & Nappy Lamare)

OCHI CHORNYA / THE BOOGIE BEAT'LL GETCHA............... *Bluebird B-11298* 3-5 41
(Vocals: Wingy Manone)

OLD MAN MOSE / PLEASE BELIEVE ME....................... *Vocalion 3159* 5-8 36
(Vocals: Wingy Manone)

RIVER MAN / AFTERGLOW......... *Bluebird B-6483* 4-6 36
(Vocals: Wingy Manone)

ROYAL GARDEN BLUES / ZERO......... *Okeh 41570* 10-12 34

SEND ME / WALKIN' THE STREET ... *Brunswick 6940* 8-10 34
(Vocals: Wingy Manone)

SWEET AND LOW / LULU'S BACK IN TOWN.......................... *Vocalion 2972* 5-8 35
(Vocals: Wingy Manone)

YOU LET ME DOWN / I'VE GOT MY FINGERS CROSSED.......................... *Vocalion 3135* 5-8 36
(Vocals: Wingy Manone)

YOU'RE AN ANGEL / I'M IN LOVE ALL OVER AGAIN .... *Vocalion 2933* 5-8 35

YOU STARTED ME DREAMING / TORMENTED...................... *Bluebird B-6359* 5-8 36
(Vocals: Wingy Manone)

MARIGOLD ENTERTAINERS, The

JEALOUS / WHEN MY SUGAR WALKS DOWN THE STREET............... *Vocalion 15800* 5-8 29
(Vocals: Art White)

MARIGOLD SERENADERS, The

BREEZIN' ALONG (TO GEORGIA) / (YOU FORGOT TO) REMEMBER .... *Champion 15019* 3-5 25

BREEZIN' ALONG (TO GEORGIA) / (YOU FORGOT TO) REMEMBER........................ *Gennett 3133* 4-6 25
(Simultaneously released on two labels)

DANGER / CUDDLES AND KISSES..... *Gennett 5689* 3-5 25

MARKEL & HIS DANCE ORCHESTRA:

see MARKEL, Mike

MARKEL, Mike, & His Orchestra / Markel's Orchestra / Mike Markel's Orchestra

AFRICA / DICTY BLUES (by William Finzel as Finzel's Arcadia Orchestra of Detroit)............ *Okeh 40161* 4-6 24

ALABAMA BLUES / BLUE-EYED BLUES.... *Okeh 4656* 3-5 22

CROSS YOUR HEART / THAT'S WHY I LOVE YOU......................... *Edison 51794* 4-6 26

DAWN / WE TWO........................ *Okeh 40959* 2-4 28
(Vocals: Unknown)

DEEP HENDERSON / WHO'D BE BLUE?... *Okeh 40625* 5-8 26

DIRTY HANDS! DIRTY FACE! / WHEN JUNE COMES ALONG WITH A SONG................. *Okeh 4897* 2-4 23

DOLL DANCE / RED LIPS, KISS MY BLUES AWAY (Vocal: Russell Douglas)................... *Okeh 40805* 4-6 27

DON'T BE TOO SURE / IF ANYONE CAN STEAL YOU (THEN YOU'RE NOT THE MAN FOR ME).................... *Okeh 4827* 2-4 23

EARLY IN THE MORNING BLUES / BLUE......................... *Okeh 4691* 3-5 22

FLAMIN' MAMIE (Vocal: Al Bernard) / CHINKY BUTTERFLY............. *Brunswick 3091* 5-8 26

FOOLING ME / SOUTH SEA ISLES........ *Okeh 4417* 2-4 21

FOOLISH CHILD / YOU ARE EASY TO REMEMBER (BUT NOT SO EASY TO FORGET)........ *Okeh 4939* 2-4 23

GEORGIA CABIN DOOR / BLUE EYES (YOU MAKE ME BLUE)..................... *Okeh 4821* 2-4 23

I CRIED FOR YOU (NOW IT'S YOUR TURN TO CRY OVER ME) / ROSETIME AND YOU....... *Okeh 4884* 2-4 23

IDOLA / HIGH BROWN BLUES........... *Okeh 4593* 3-5 22

I'LL BUILD A STAIRWAY TO PARADISE / TWO LITTLE RUBY RINGS.................. *Okeh 4715* 2-4 22

I LOST MY HEART TO YOU / ORANGE BLOSSOMS..................... *Okeh 4328* 2-4 21

IN THE LITTLE RED SCHOOL HOUSE / SWANEE RIVER MOON.......................... *Okeh 4624* 2-4 22

ISLE OF TANGERINE / YOU AND I (ATTA BABY)............... *Okeh 4586* 2-4 22

KITTY'S KISSES (Vocal: Arthur Hall) / HER BEAUS ARE ONLY RAINBOWS................... *Edison 51764* 3-5 26

LITTLE PEACH / BESIDE A SILV'RY STREAM................. *Columbia 372-D* 2-4 25

LO LA LO / DOO DAH BLUES............. *Okeh 4549* 2-4 22

LULU BELLE / JUST A LITTLE DANCE.................. *Brunswick 3189* 3-5 26

MY HONEY'S LOVIN' ARMS / WHENEVER YOU'RE LONESOME (JUST TELEPHONE ME).... *Okeh 4641* 3-5 22

NOBODY BUT FANNY / SUGAR PLUM..................... *Columbia 475-D* 3-5 25

POOR PAPA / TONIGHT'S MY NIGHT WITH BABY................. *Edison 51752* 5-8 26

PRECIOUS (Vocal: Johnny Marvin) / DOWN ON THE BANKS OF THE OLD YAZOO........... *Okeh 40668* 2-4 26

SAN / IT'S ABOUT TIME................ *Okeh 40098* 3-5 24

SAW MILL RIVER ROAD / PEGGY DEAR.... *Okeh 4802* 2-4 23

SNEAK, THE / NOBODY LIED............ *Okeh 4648* 2-4 22

SOUTHERN MOONLIGHT / YOU'VE HAD YOUR DAY........................ *Okeh 4628* 2-4 22

STAVIN' CHANGE (THE MEANEST MAN IN NEW ORLEANS) / I'VE GOT A SONG FOR SALE (THAT MY SWEETIE TURNED DOWN)................ *Okeh 4967* 2-4 23

31ST STREET BLUES / TWO BLUE EYES... *Okeh 40045* 5-8 24

WHEN FRANCIS DANCES WITH ME / MONASTERY BELLS (by The Green Brothers' Novelty Band)... *Okeh 4467* 2-4 22

WORLD IS WAITING FOR THE SUNRISE, THE / WHEN THE LEAVES COME TUMBLING DOWN...... *Okeh 4675* 3-5 22

MARKEL, Mike, as Markel & His Dance Orchestra

BLACK HORSE STOMP / BIRDIE .... *Columbia 617-D* 5-8 26

MARKEL, Mike, as Markel's Society Orchestra

ONCE IN A LIFETIME / TO KNOW YOU IS TO LOVE YOU...................... *Okeh 41161* 2-4 29
(Vocals: Unknown)

TEACH ME TO SMILE / CROSS ROADS ... *Domino 4249* 2-4 29
(Vocals: Irving Kaufman)

TEACH ME TO SMILE / CROSS ROADS ... *Regal 8689* 2-4 29
(Vocals: Irving Kaufman)
(Simultaneously released on two labels)

MARKEL, Mike, as Mike Markel's Orchestra:
see MARKEL, Mike, & His Orchestra

MARKEL'S ORCHESTRA:
see MARKEL, Mike, & His Orchestra

MARKEL'S SOCIETY ORCHESTRA:
see MARKEL, Mike

MARLOW, Earl, as Earl Marlow's Orchestra:
see RICH, Fred, & His Orchestra

MARLOW, Rudy, & His Orchestra:
see SELVIN, Ben, & His Orchestra

MARSALA, Joe, & His Delta Six:
see FEATHER, Leonard, as Leonard Feather's All-Star Jam Band

MARSHALL, Ted, & His Orchestra:
see ROYAL TROUBADOURS, The

MARSHARD, Jack, & His Orchestra

ASLEEP OR AWAKE / MY LAST GOODBYE........................ *Brunswick 8383* 3-5 39
(Vocals: Gil Phelan)

HOW LONG HAS THIS BEEN GOING ON? / I JUST GOT A LETTER....................... *Columbia 35306* 2-4 39
(Vocals: Gil Phelan)

IF I DIDN'T CARE / BLUE EVENING... *Brunswick 8374* 3-5 39
(Vocals: Gil Phelan)

I'M IN LOVE WITH THE HONORABLE MR. SO-AND-SO / YOURS FOR A SONG... *Brunswick 8369* 3-5 39
(Vocals: Gil Phelan)

IN THE MIDDLE OF A DREAM / OUT OF THIS WORLD............. *Brunswick 8402* 3-5 39
(Vocals: Gil Phelan)

IT'S ALL YOURS / THIS IS IT........ *Brunswick 8342* 3-5 39
(Vocals: Gil Phelan)

IT'S A WHOLE NEW THING / SWEET DREAMS, SWEETHEART.......... *Columbia 35292* 2-4 39
(Vocals: Gil Phelan)

MY LOVE FOR YOU (Vocal: Vaughn Monroe) / DON'T LOOK NOW (Vocal: Gil Phelan)........ *Brunswick 8398* 3-5 39

READING, WRITING AND RHYTHM / WE CAN LIVE ON LOVE (WE HAVEN'T GOT A POT TO COOK IN).............. *Brunswick 8408* 3-5 39
(Vocals: Gil Phelan)

SNUG AS A BUG IN A RUG / I NEVER KNEW HEAVEN COULD SPEAK.................... *Brunswick 8349* 3-5 39
(Vocals: Gil Phelan)

'S WONDERFUL / IN THE STILL OF THE NIGHT.................. *Brunswick 8417* 3-5 39
(Vocals: Vaughn Monroe)

MARTIN, Freddy, & His Orchestra
(Freddy Martin: 12/9/06 – 9/30/83)

Martin's Orchestra was among those having the greatest longevity of all the big bands. In a 1976 interview at Disneyland in Anaheim, California, where his orchestra was fulfilling one of its many engagements, Freddy Martin told the author that he had first formed his orchestra in 1932, had never disbanded, and that he had played in and directed the band since that time. When questioned about the lean years for the big bands, from the mid-1940s to the early 1970s when most orchestras disbanded entirely or re-formed into small groups, and many musicians were forced into other types of employment, Martin said that his band had always worked quite steadily, playing concerts and for dances, and making records. Freddy Martin and His Orchestra continued playing engagements nationwide until shortly before his death from a series of strokes.)

ALL OR NOTHING AT ALL (Vocal: Clyde Rogers) / I SHOULD HAVE KNOWN YOU YEARS AGO (Vocal: Eddie Stone)..... *Bluebird B-10928* 2-4 40

APPLE BLOSSOMS AND CHAPEL BELLS / SAND .... *Bluebird B-10567* 2-4 40
(Vocals: Bill Stoker)

APRIL IN PARIS / COUNT YOUR BLESSINGS............... *Brunswick 6717* 3-5 34
(Vocals: Elmer Feldkamp)

ARAB DANCE / CHINESE DANCE...... *Victor 27901* 2-4 42

AS FAR AS I'M CONCERNED / DANCING ON A ROOFTOP.................. *Brunswick 6918* 3-5 34
(Vocals: Elmer Feldkamp)

BEAUTIFUL GIRL (Vocal: Terry Shand) / I'M DANCIN' ON A RAINBOW (Vocals: by trio)......... *Brunswick 6659* 3-5 33

BE CAREFUL (Vocal: Elmer Feldkamp) / GATHER LIP ROUGE WHILE YOU MAY (Vocal: Terry Shand).................. *Brunswick 6658* 3-5 33

BLAME IT ON MY YOUTH (Vocal: Elmer Feldkamp) / WINTER WONDERLAND (Vocal: Terry Shand).................. *Brunswick 7316* 3-5 34

BLUE CHAMPAGNE / BE HONEST WITH ME (Vocals: Clyde Rogers, Eddie Stone & orchestra) ... *Bluebird B-11256* 2-4 41

BREAKFAST FOR TWO / SHADOWS IN THE NIGHT.................. *Bluebird B-11086* 2-4 41
(Vocals: Clyde Rogers)

CALL OF LOVE / ALL I DO IS DREAM OF YOU................ *Brunswick 6888* 3-5 34
(Vocals: Elmer Feldkamp)

CAN'T GET OUT OF THIS MOOD (Vocals: Bob Haymes & The Martin Men) / I GET THE NECK OF THE CHICKEN (Vocal: Eddie Stone)................ *Victor 20-1515* 2-4 42
(Bob Haymes is the younger brother of singer Dick Haymes)

CARELESS RHAPSODY (Vocal: Clyde Rogers) / EVERYTHING I'VE GOT (Vocal: Eddie Stone).......................... *Victor 27919* 2-4 42

CARMEN CARMELA / TONIGHT WE LOVE (theme song)............. *Bluebird B-11320* 2-4 41
(Vocals: Clyde Rogers)

CLOSE TO ME (Vocal: Elmer Feldkamp) / ODDS AND ENDS................ *Brunswick 6739* 3-5 34

CLOSE YOUR EYES / LET'S MAKE UP................. *Brunswick 6620* 3-5 33
(Vocals: Elmer Feldkamp)

CORN SILK / TOO BEAUTIFUL TO LAST........................ *Bluebird B-11050* 2-4 41
(Vocals: Eddie Stone)

DANCE OF SUGAR PLUM FAIRIES / RUSSIAN DANCE.................... *Victor 27900* 2-4 42

DANCE OF THE REED FLUTES / WALTZ OF THE FLOWERS................ *Victor 27902* 2-4 42

DAY DREAMS / STARS FELL ON ALABAMA (Vocal: Buddy Clarke).... *Brunswick 6976* 3-5 34

DON'T WAKE UP MY HEART (Vocal: Elmer Feldkamp) / I'VE BEEN SAVING MYSELF FOR YOU (Vocal: Gene Walsh)................ *Bluebird B-7634* 3-5 38

DOWN WHERE THE TRADE WINDS BLOW (Vocal: Terry Shand) / I SEE YOUR FACE BEFORE ME (Vocal: Elmer Feldkamp) .... *Brunswick 8045* 3-5 38

FORBIDDEN LOVE / SOMEDAY WE'LL MEET AGAIN..................... *Brunswick 6408* 5-8 32
(Vocals: Elmer Feldkamp)

FROM TWILIGHT TILL DAWN (Vocals: Bob Haymes & The Martin Men) / WARSAW CONCERTO... *Victor 20-1535* 2-4 42
(Bob Haymes is the younger brother of singer Dick Haymes)

GOODBYE TO LOVE / WE JUST COULDN'T SAY GOODBYE .... *Columbia 2703-D* 4-6 32
(Vocals: Elmer Feldkamp)

GOOD USED HEART, A / SINNER OR SAINT............ *RCA Victor 20-4946* 2-4 56
(Vocals: Stuart Wade)

GRIEG PIANO CONCERTO / SERENADE FOR STRINGS.................. *Bluebird B-11430* 2-4 42

HOME TOWN BAND / LET'S PUT OUT THE LIGHTS AND GO TO SLEEP .... *RCA Victor 20-3614* 2-4 50
(Vocals: Merv Griffin. Now star and host of his own TV series.)

HOW'S CHANCES? (Vocal: Elmer Feldkamp) / EASTER PARADE (Vocals: by trio) .... *Brunswick 6678* 3-5 33

I LOOK AT HEAVEN (WHEN I LOOK AT YOU) / I CAN'T GIVE YOU ANYTHING BUT LOVE...................... *Bluebird B-11487* 2-4 42
(Vocals: Dinah Shore)

I MET HER ON MONDAY (Vocal: Eddie Stone) / JINGLE, JANGLE, JINGLE (Vocals: Clyde Rogers, & Stuart Wade)................ *Victor 27909* 2-4 42

IN A SHELTER FROM A SHOWER (Vocals: by trio) / THERE GOES MY HEART (Vocal: Elmer Feldkamp) .... *Brunswick 6766* 3-5 34

INTERMEZZO (Vocal: Clyde Rogers) / NICE DREAMIN', BABY (Vocal: Eddie Stone)............ *Bluebird B-11123* 2-4 41

ISN'T IT A SHAME? / IN THE QUIET OF AN AUTUMN NIGHT........... *Brunswick 6982* 3-5 34
(Vocals: Buddy Clark)

IT'S YOU I ADORE (Vocal: Elmer Feldkamp) / NIGHT WIND (Vocals: Terry Shand & trio) ..... *Brunswick 7387* 3-5 35

I'VE GOTTA GET UP AND GO TO WORK / AH! BUT IS IT LOVE? .... *Brunswick 6621* 3-5 33
(Vocals: Elmer Feldkamp)

JAYWALK / BYE-LO-BYE LULLABY (early theme song) (Vocal: Bill Stoker)................ *Bluebird B-10104* 2-4 39

JOHNNY DOUGHBOY FOUND A ROSE IN IRELAND (Vocal: Clyde Rogers) / I'LL KEEP THE LOVELIGHT BURNING (Vocal: Stuart Wade)...... *Bluebird B-11503* 3-5 42

KARLSTAD BALL (SWEDISH SCOTTISCHE) / THE HUT-SUT SONG (A SWEDISH SERENADE) (Vocal: Eddie Stone)................ *Bluebird B-11147* 2-4 41

LADY FROM TWENTY-NINE PALMS, THE (Vocals: The Martin Men) / CUMANA.......... *RCA Victor 20-2347* 2-4 47

LIGHTS OUT (Vocal: Elmer Feldkamp) / JUST ONE OF THOSE THINGS (Vocal: Terry Shand) ... *Brunswick 7579* 3-5 36

LOUISIANA HAYRIDE (Vocal: Terry Shand) / A RAINY DAY (Vocal: Elmer Feldkamp).......... *Brunswick 6407* 5-8 32

MAKE-BELIEVE BALLROOM / WHEN MY DREAM BOAT COMES HOME.............. *Brunswick 7754* 3-5 36
(Vocals: Unknown)

MAMA'S GONE, GOODBYE (Vocals: Glenn Hughes & trio) / EARLY IN THE MORNING (Vocal: Bill Stoker)................... *Bluebird B-10447* 3-5 39

MELODY FARM (Vocal: Terry Shand) / THE ONE I LOVE (Vocal: Elmer Feldkamp)........ *Brunswick 8056* 3-5 38

MY DANCING LADY / EVERYTHING I HAVE IS YOURS... *Brunswick 6677* 3-5 33
(Vocals: Elmer Feldkamp)

NEIGHBORS / OVER SOMEBODY ELSE'S SHOULDER (Vocal: Elmer Feldkamp)... *Brunswick 6777* 3-5 34

NOW AND FOREVER (Vocal: Artie Wayne) / BUMBLE BOOGIE... *RCA Victor 20-1829* 2-4 46

ONE-ZY, TWO-ZY (Vocals: The Martin Men) / SLEEPY BABY (Vocals: Artie Wayne & The Martin Men)... *RCA Victor 20-1826* 2-4 46

OVERTURE MINIATURE / MARCH... *Victor 27899* 2-4 42

PENNY ARCADE, THE / JUST PLAIN LONESOME... *Bluebird B-11524* 2-4 42
(Vocals: Stuart Wade & quartet)

PENNY WHISTLE BLUES / APRIL IN PORTUGAL... *RCA Victor 20-5052* 2-4 56

PENTHOUSE FOR RENT (Vocal: Bill Stokes) / SCATTER-BRAIN (Vocal: Glenn Hughes)... *Bluebird B-10436* 2-4 39

RACHMANINOFF CONCERTO NO. 2 / I'M GLAD I WAITED FOR YOU (Vocal: Clyde Rogers)... *RCA Victor 20-1749* 2-4 46

ROOF TOP SERENADE / YOU ALONE... *Brunswick 6720* 3-5 34
(Vocals: Elmer Feldkamp)

ROSEANNA / SUNDAY OUT IN THE COUNTRY... *RCA Victor 20-3484* 2-4 49
(Vocals: Merv Griffin, now star and host of his own TV series.)

SATURDAY'S CHILDREN (Vocal: Clyde Rogers) / I'D LOVE TO (Vocal: Eddie Stone)... *Bluebird B-10643* 2-4 40

SHAME ON YOU (Vocal: Terry Shand) / BLESS YOUR HEART (Vocal: Elmer Feldkamp)... *Brunswick 6631* 3-5 33

SITTIN' ON A BACKYARD FENCE / HONEYMOON HOTEL... *Brunswick 6654* 3-5 33
(Vocals: Terry Shand)

SPEAK EASY / EASY TO LOVE (Vocal: Clyde Rogers)... *Brunswick B-10678* 2-4 40

SPIN A LITTLE WEB OF DREAMS (Vocal: Elmer Feldkamp) / WHEN TOMORROW COMES... *Brunswick 6760* 3-5 34

THERE'S A STRANGE LITTLE CHANGE IN ME / A SERENADE TO THE STARS... *Bluebird B-7380* 3-5 38
(Vocals: Elmer Feldkamp)

THERE'S ONLY ONE LOVE / AN OLD-FASHIONED TUNE IS ALWAYS NEW... *Bluebird B-10326* 2-4 39
(Vocals: Bill Stoker)

THREE ON A MATCH/NIGHTFALL... *Columbia 2708-D* 4-6 32
(Vocals: Elmer Feldkamp)

THREE WISHES / A MOONLIGHT MEMORY... *Brunswick 6645* 3-5 33
(Vocals: Elmer Feldkamp)

'TILL REVEILLE (Vocal: Clyde Rogers) / FLAMINGO... *Bluebird B-11167* 2-4 41

TO EACH HIS OWN / YOU PUT A SONG IN MY HEART... *RCA Victor 20-1921* 2-4 46
(Vocals: Stuart Wade)

TUMBLEDOWN RANCH IN ARIZONA / THE SAME OLD STORY... *Bluebird B-10830* 2-4 40
(Vocals: Clyde Rogers)

WABASH BLUES / SLEEPY-TIME GAL (Vocal: Freddy Martin)... *Bluebird B-7378* 3-5 38

WHAT A DIFFERENCE A DAY MADE / BE STILL MY HEART... *Brunswick 6998* 3-5 34
(Vocals: Elmer Feldkamp)

WHEN LOVE COMES SWINGIN' ALONG (Vocals: by trio) / SAY WHEN (Vocal: Elmer Feldkamp)... *Brunswick 7313* 3-5 35

WHERE THERE'S SMOKE – THERE'S FIRE / ISLE OF CAPRI... *Brunswick 7344* 4-6 35
(Vocals: Elmer Feldkamp)

WHEREVER YOU ARE / WHAT DOES A SOLDIER DREAM OF?... *Bluebird B-11475* 3-5 42
(Vocals: by chorus)

WHY DO I DREAM THOSE DREAMS? (Vocal: Terry Shand) / WONDER BAR... *Brunswick 6770* 3-5 34

WHY DON'T WE DO THIS MORE OFTEN? (Vocal: Eddie Stone) / PIANO CONCERTO IN B FLAT... *Bluebird B-11211* 2-4 41

WOLVERINE BLUES / MILENBERG JOYS... *Bluebird B-7712* 4-6 38

YOU COULDN'T BE CUTER / JUST LET ME LOOK AT YOU... *Bluebird B-7396* 3-5 38
(Vocals: Elmer Feldkamp)

MARTIN, Freddy, & His Orchestra as Allan Burns & His Orchestra

NIGHT AND DAY / A TREE WAS A TREE... *Conqueror 8105* 4-6 33
(Vocals: Elmer Feldkamp)

NIGHT AND DAY / WHEN THE MORNING ROLLS AROUND... *Banner 32663* 4-6 33
(Vocals: Elmer Feldkamp)

NIGHT AND DAY / WHEN THE MORNING ROLLS AROUND... *Melotone M-12592* 4-6 33
(Vocals: Elmer Feldkamp)

NIGHT AND DAY / WHEN THE MORNING ROLLS AROUND... *Oriole 2635* 4-6 33
(Vocals: Elmer Feldkamp)

NIGHT AND DAY / WHEN THE MORNING ROLLS AROUND... *Perfect 15724* 4-6 33
(Vocals: Elmer Feldkamp)

NIGHT AND DAY / WHEN THE MORNING ROLLS AROUND... *Romeo 2008* 4-6 33
(Vocals: Elmer Feldkamp)
(Simultaneously released on five labels)

TREE WAS A TREE, A / WHY CAN'T THIS NIGHT GO ON FOREVER?... *Banner 32678* 4-6 33
(Vocals: Elmer Feldkamp)

TREE WAS A TREE, A / WHY CAN'T THIS NIGHT GO ON FOREVER?... *Melotone M-12611* 4-6 33
(Vocals: Elmer Feldkamp)

TREE WAS A TREE, A / WHY CAN'T THIS NIGHT GO ON FOREVER?... *Oriole 2645* 4-6 33
(Vocals: Elmer Feldkamp)

TREE WAS A TREE, A / WHY CAN'T THIS NIGHT GO ON FOREVER?... *Perfect 15732* 4-6 33
(Vocals: Elmer Feldkamp)

TREE WAS A TREE, A / WHY CAN'T THIS NIGHT GO ON FOREVER?... *Romeo 2018* 4-6 33
(Vocals: Elmer Feldkamp)
(Simultaneously released on five labels)

MARTIN, Freddy, & His Orchestra as Bob Causer & His Cornellians

DINNER AT EIGHT / GIVE ME LIBERTY OR GIVE ME LOVE... *Banner 32865* 3-5 33
(Vocals: Elmer Feldkamp)

DINNER AT EIGHT / GIVE ME LIBERTY OR GIVE ME LOVE... *Melotone M-12791* 3-5 33
(Vocals: Elmer Feldkamp)

DINNER AT EIGHT / GIVE ME LIBERTY OR GIVE ME LOVE... *Oriole 2761* 3-5 33
(Vocals: Elmer Feldkamp)

DINNER AT EIGHT / GIVE ME LIBERTY OR GIVE ME LOVE... *Perfect 15820* 3-5 33
(Vocals: Elmer Feldkamp)

DINNER AT EIGHT / GIVE ME LIBERTY OR GIVE ME LOVE... *Romeo 2134* 3-5 33
(Vocals: Elmer Feldkamp)
(Simultaneously released on five labels)

IT MIGHT HAVE BEEN A DIFF'RENT STORY / DON'T BLAME ME... *Banner 32815* 3-5 33
(Vocals: Elmer Feldkamp)

IT MIGHT HAVE BEEN A DIFF'RENT STORY / DON'T BLAME ME... *Melotone M-12751* 3-5 33
(Vocals: Elmer Feldkamp)

IT MIGHT HAVE BEEN A DIFF'RENT STORY / DON'T BLAME ME... *Oriole 2730* 3-5 33
(Vocals: Elmer Feldkamp)

IT MIGHT HAVE BEEN A DIFF'RENT STORY / DON'T BLAME ME... *Perfect 15794* 3-5 33
(Vocals: Elmer Feldkamp)

IT MIGHT HAVE BEEN A DIFF'RENT STORY / DON'T BLAME ME... *Romeo 2103* 3-5 33
(Vocals: Elmer Feldkamp)
(Simultaneously released on five labels)

LEARN TO CROON / MOONSTRUCK... *Banner 32790* 3-5 33
(Vocals: Elmer Feldkamp)

LEARN TO CROON / MOONSTRUCK... *Melotone M-12723* 3-5 33
(Vocals: Elmer Feldkamp)

LEARN TO CROON / MOONSTRUCK... *Oriole 2715* 3-5 33
(Vocals: Elmer Feldkamp)

LEARN TO CROON / MOONSTRUCK... *Perfect 15782* 3-5 33
(Vocals: Elmer Feldkamp)

LEARN TO CROON / MOONSTRUCK... *Romeo 2088* 3-5 33
(Vocals: Elmer Feldkamp)
(Simultaneously released on five labels)

LET'S CALL IT A DAY / STORMY WEATHER... *Banner 32742* 4-6 33
(Vocals: Elmer Feldkamp)

LET'S CALL IT A DAY / STORMY WEATHER... *Melotone M-12671* 4-6 33
(Vocals: Elmer Feldkamp)

LET'S CALL IT A DAY / STORMY WEATHER... *Oriole 2682* 4-6 33
(Vocals: Elmer Feldkamp)

LET'S CALL IT A DAY / STORMY WEATHER... *Perfect 15757* 4-6 33
(Vocals: Elmer Feldkamp)

LET'S CALL IT A DAY / STORMY WEATHER... *Romeo 2055* 4-6 33
(Vocals: Elmer Feldkamp)
(Simultaneously released on five labels)

LOVE TALES / FAREWELL TO ARMS... *Banner 32700* 4-6 33
(Vocals: Elmer Feldkamp)

LOVE TALES / FAREWELL TO ARMS... *Melotone M-12631* 4-6 33
(Vocals: Elmer Feldkamp)

LOVE TALES / FAREWELL TO ARMS... *Oriole 2653* 4-6 33
(Vocals: Elmer Feldkamp)

LOVE TALES / FAREWELL TO ARMS... *Perfect 15737* 4-6 33
(Vocals: Elmer Feldkamp)

LOVE TALES / FAREWELL TO ARMS... *Romeo 2026* 4-6 33
(Vocals: Elmer Feldkamp)
(Simultaneously released on five labels)

MAYBE I LOVE YOU TOO MUCH / WHAT HAVE WE GOT TO LOSE?... *Banner 32719* 3-5 33
(Vocals: Elmer Feldkamp)

MAYBE I LOVE YOU TOO MUCH / WHAT HAVE WE GOT TO LOSE?... *Melotone M-12648* 3-5 33
(Vocals: Elmer Feldkamp)

MAYBE I LOVE YOU TOO MUCH / WHAT HAVE WE GOT TO LOSE?... *Oriole 2668* 3-5 33
(Vocals: Elmer Feldkamp)

MAYBE I LOVE YOU TOO MUCH / WHAT HAVE WE GOT TO LOSE?... *Perfect 15746* 3-5 33
(Vocals: Elmer Feldkamp)

MAYBE I LOVE YOU TOO MUCH / WHAT HAVE WE GOT TO LOSE?... *Romeo 2041* 3-5 33
(Vocals: Elmer Feldkamp)
(Simultaneously released on five labels)

STORMY WEATHER (Vocal: Elmer Feldkamp) / SWEETHEART DARLIN' (Vocal: George Beuchler)... *Conqueror 8150* 4-6 33

MARTIN, Freddy, & His Orchestra as Owen Fallon & His Californians

STAY OUT OF MY DREAMS / I LAY ME DOWN TO SLEEP... *Banner 32745* 4-6 33
(Vocals: Elmer Feldkamp)

STAY OUT OF MY DREAMS / I LAY ME DOWN TO SLEEP... *Melotone M-12673* 4-6 33
(Vocals: Elmer Feldkamp)

STAY OUT OF MY DREAMS / I LAY ME DOWN TO SLEEP... *Oriole 2685* 4-6 33
(Vocals: Elmer Feldkamp)

STAY OUT OF MY DREAMS / I LAY ME DOWN TO SLEEP... *Perfect 15760* 4-6 33
(Vocals: Elmer Feldkamp)

STAY OUT OF MY DREAMS / I LAY ME DOWN TO SLEEP... *Romeo 2058* 4-6 33
(Vocals: Elmer Feldkamp)
(Simultaneously released on five labels)

MARTIN, Freddy, & His Orchestra as The Hotel Bossert Orchestra

IN THE PARK IN PAREE / LOOK WHAT I'VE GOT... *Columbia 2769-D* 4-6 33
(Vocals: Elmer Feldkamp)

MARTIN, Freddy, & His Orchestra as Eddie Jackson & His Orchestra

THROW ANOTHER LOG ON THE FIRE / ALICE IN WONDERLAND... *Vocalion 2618* 3-5 34
(Vocals: Dick Robertson)

MARTIN, Freddy, & His Orchestra as Ed Loyd & His Band

I'VE GOT TO SING A TORCH SONG / REMEMBER MY FORGOTTEN MAN... *Banner 32767* 4-6 33
(Vocals: Helen Rowland)

I'VE GOT TO SING A TORCH SONG / REMEMBER MY FORGOTTEN MAN... *Melotone M-12696* 4-6 33
(Vocals: Helen Rowland)

I'VE GOT TO SING A TORCH SONG / REMEMBER MY FORGOTTEN MAN... *Oriole 2700* 4-6 33
(Vocals: Helen Rowland)

I'VE GOT TO SING A TORCH SONG / REMEMBER MY FORGOTTEN MAN... *Perfect 15771* 4-6 33
(Vocals: Helen Rowland)

I'VE GOT TO SING A TORCH SONG / REMEMBER MY FORGOTTEN MAN... *Romeo 2073* 4-6 33
(Vocals: Helen Rowland)
(Simultaneously released on five labels)

MORNING, NOON AND NIGHT (Vocal: Elmer Feldkamp) / LYING IN THE HAY (Vocal: Terry Shand)... *Banner 32805* 4-6 33

MORNING, NOON AND NIGHT (Vocal: Elmer Feldkamp) / LYING IN THE HAY (Vocal: Terry Shand)... *Melotone M-12738* 4-6 33

MORNING, NOON AND NIGHT (Vocal: Elmer Feldkamp) / LYING IN THE HAY (Vocal: Terry Shand)... *Oriole 2723* 4-6 33

MORNING, NOON AND NIGHT (Vocal: Elmer Feldkamp) / LYING IN THE HAY (Vocal: Terry Shand)... *Perfect 15788* 4-6 33

MORNING, NOON AND NIGHT (Vocal: Elmer Feldkamp) / LYING IN THE HAY (Vocal: Terry Shand)... *Romeo 2096* 4-6 33
(Simultaneously released on five labels)

MARTIN, Freddy, & His Orchestra as Will Osborne & His Orchestra

HOLD YOUR MAN / IMAGINARY SWEETHEART... *Banner 32789* 3-5 33
(Vocals: Will Osborne)

HOLD YOUR MAN / IMAGINARY SWEETHEART... *Melotone M-12722* 3-5 33
(Vocals: Will Osborne)

HOLD YOUR MAN / IMAGINARY SWEETHEART... *Oriole 2714* 3-5 33
(Vocals: Will Osborne)

HOLD YOUR MAN / IMAGINARY SWEETHEART... *Perfect 15781* 3-5 33
(Vocals: Will Osborne)

HOLD YOUR MAN / IMAGINARY SWEETHEART... *Romeo 2087* 3-5 33
(Vocals: Will Osborne)
(Simultaneously released on five labels)

I COVER THE WATERFRONT / ISN'T IT HEAVENLY?... *Banner 32769* 4-6 33
(Vocals: Will Osborne)

I COVER THE WATERFRONT / ISN'T IT HEAVENLY?... *Melotone M-12698* 4-6 33
(Vocals: Will Osborne)

I COVER THE WATERFRONT / ISN'T IT HEAVENLY?... *Oriole 2702* 4-6 33
(Vocals: Will Osborne)

I COVER THE WATERFRONT / ISN'T IT HEAVENLY? .... *Perfect 15773* 4-6 33
(Vocals: Will Osborne)

I COVER THE WATERFRONT / ISN'T IT HEAVENLY? .... *Romeo 2075* 4-6 33
(Vocals: Will Osborne)
(Simultaneously released on five labels)

IN THE VALLEY OF THE MOON / I CAN'T REMEMBER .... *Banner 32741* 3-5 33
(Vocals: Will Osborne)

IN THE VALLEY OF THE MOON / I CAN'T REMEMBER .... *Melotone M-12670* 3-5 33
(Vocals: Will Osborne)

IN THE VALLEY OF THE MOON / I CAN'T REMEMBER .... *Oriole 2681* 3-5 33
(Vocals: Will Osborne)

IN THE VALLEY OF THE MOON / I CAN'T REMEMBER .... *Perfect 15756* 3-5 33
(Vocals: Will Osborne)

IN THE VALLEY OF THE MOON / I CAN'T REMEMBER .... *Romeo 2054* 3-5 33
(Vocals: Will Osborne)
(Simultaneously released on five labels)

LOVE IS A DREAM / MEET ME IN THE GLOAMING .... *Banner 32718* 3-5 33
(Vocals: Will Osborne)

LOVE IS A DREAM / MEET ME IN THE GLOAMING .... *Melotnoe M-12647* 3-5 33
(Vocals: Will Osborne)

LOVE IS A DREAM / MEET ME IN THE GLOAMING .... *Oriole 2667* 3-5 33
(Vocals: Will Osborne)

LOVE IS A DREAM / MEET ME IN THE GLOAMING .... *Perfect 15745* 3-5 33
(Vocals: Will Osborne)

LOVE IS A DREAM / MEET ME IN THE GLOAMING .... *Romeo 2040* 3-5 33
(Vocals: Will Osborne)
(Simultaneously released on five labels)

UNDER A BLANKET OF BLUE / I COULDN'T TELL THEM WHAT TO DO .... *Banner 32803* 3-5 33
(Vocals: Will Osborne)

UNDER A BLANKET OF BLUE / I COULDN'T TELL THEM WHAT TO DO .... *Melotone M-12736* 3-5 33
(Vocals: Will Osborne)

UNDER A BLANKET OF BLUE / I COULDN'T TELL THEM WHAT TO DO .... *Oriole 2721* 3-5 33
(Vocals: Will Osborne)

UNDER A BLANKET OF BLUE / I COULDN'T TELL THEM WHAT TO DO .... *Perfect 15786* 3-5 33
(Vocals: Will Osborne)

UNDER A BLANKET OF BLUE / I COULDN'T TELL THEM WHAT TO DO .... *Romeo 2094* 3-5 33
(Vocals: Will Osborne)
(Simultaneously released on five labels)

YOU'RE BEAUTIFUL TONIGHT, MY DEAR / HERE IS MY HEART .... *Banner 32730* 3-5 33
(Vocals: Will Osborne)

YOU'RE BEAUTIFUL TONIGHT, MY DEAR / HERE IS MY HEART .... *Melotone M-12659* 3-5 33
(Vocals: Will Osborne)

YOU'RE BEAUTIFUL TONIGHT, MY DEAR / HERE IS MY HEART .... *Oriole 2674* 3-5 33
(Vocals: Will Osborne)

YOU'RE BEAUTIFUL TONIGHT, MY DEAR / HERE IS MY HEART .... *Perfect 15750* 3-5 33
(Vocals: Will Osborne)

YOU'RE BEAUTIFUL TONIGHT, MY DEAR / HERE IS MY HEART .... *Romeo 2047* 3-5 33
(Vocals: Will Osborne)
(Simultaneously released on five labels)

MARTIN, Freddy, & His Orchestra as Frank Parker & His Orchestra

OLD SPINNING WHEEL, THE / CLOSE TO ME .... *Vocalion 2606* 4-6 34
(Vocals: Frank Parker)

MARTIN, Freddy, & His Orchestra as Albert Taylor & His Orchestra

THROW ANOTHER LOG ON THE FIRE / IN THE VALLEY OF YESTERDAY .... *Banner 32926* 3-5 34
(Vocals: Russ Morgan)

THROW ANOTHER LOG ON THE FIRE / IN THE VALLEY OF YESTERDAY .... *Melotone M-12869* 3-5 34
(Vocals: Russ Morgan)

THROW ANOTHER LOG ON THE FIRE / IN THE VALLEY OF YESTERDAY .... *Oriole 2814* 3-5 34
(Vocals: Russ Morgan)

THROW ANOTHER LOG ON THE FIRE / IN THE VALLEY OF YESTERDAY .... *Perfect 15864* 3-5 34
(Vocals: Russ Morgan)

THROW ANOTHER LOG ON THE FIRE / IN THE VALLEY OF YESTERDAY .... *Romeo 2187* 3-5 34
(Vocals: Russ Morgan)
(Simultaneously released on five labels)

TRY A LITTLE TENDERNESS / IF YOU DON'T WANT TO BE SWEETHEARTS .... *Banner 32664* 4-6 33
(Vocals: Elmer Feldkamp)

TRY A LITTLE TENDERNESS / IF YOU DON'T WANT TO BE SWEETHEARTS .... *Melotone M-12594* 4-6 33
(Vocals: Elmer Feldkamp)

TRY A LITTLE TENDERNESS / IF YOU DON'T WANT TO BE SWEETHEARTS .... *Oriole 2636* 4-6 33
(Vocals: Elmer Feldkamp)

TRY A LITTLE TENDERNESS / IF YOU DON'T WANT TO BE SWEETHEARTS .... *Perfect 15725* 4-6 33
(Vocals: Elmer Feldkamp)

TRY A LITTLE TENDERNESS / IF YOU DON'T WANT TO BE SWEETHEARTS .... *Romeo 2009* 4-6 33
(Vocals: Elmer Feldkamp)
(Simultaneously released on five labels)

WE'RE OUT OF THE RED / STAND UP AND CHEER! .... *Banner 32931* 3-5 34
(Vocals: by trio)

WE'RE OUT OF THE RED / STAND UP AND CHEER! .... *Melotone M-12990* 3-5 34
(Vocals: by trio)

WE'RE OUT OF THE RED / STAND UP AND CHEER! .... *Oriole 2882* 3-5 34
(Vocals: by trio)

WE'RE OUT OF THE RED / STAND UP AND CHEER! .... *Perfect 15921* 3-5 34
(Vocals: by trio)

WE'RE OUT OF THE RED / STAND UP AND CHEER! .... *Romeo 2256* 3-5 34
(Vocals: by trio)
(Simultaneously released on five labels)

YOU AND THE MOON AND ME (Vocal: Elmer Feldkamp) / DON'T DO ANYTHING I WOULDN'T DO (Vocal: Terry Shand) .... *Banner 32781* 3-5 33

YOU AND THE MOON AND ME (Vocal: Elmer Feldkamp) / DON'T DO ANYTHING I WOULDN'T DO (Vocal: Terry Shand) .... *Melotone M-12716* 3-5 33

YOU AND THE MOON AND ME (Vocal: Elmer Feldkamp) / DON'T DO ANYTHING I WOULDN'T DO (Vocal: Terry Shand) .... *Oriole 2709* 3-5 33

YOU AND THE MOON AND ME (Vocal: Elmer Feldkamp) / DON'T DO ANYTHING I WOULDN'T DO (Vocal: Terry Shand) .... *Perfect 15779* 3-5 33

YOU AND THE MOON AND ME (Vocal: Elmer Feldkamp) / DON'T DO ANYTHING I WOULDN'T DO (Vocal: Terry Shand) .... *Romeo 2082* 3-5 33
(Simultaneously released on five labels)

MARTIN, Nat, & His Orchestra

DOWN IN WAH WAH TOWN / TELL ME, DREAMY EYES .... *Edison 51431* 5-8 24

IF I HAD A GIRL LIKE YOU / SO THAT'S THE KIND OF GIRL YOU ARE .... *Edison 51615* 5-8 25

MARTIN, Paul, & His Orchestra

DOWN AMONG THE SHELTERING PALMS (Vocals: by quartet) / ALONG MIAMI SHORE...... *Exclusive 76X* 3-5 49

MARTIN, Paul, & His Soothing Music

HOW CAN WE BE WRONG? / SIMPLE AND SWEET .... *Bluebird B-7798* 4-6 38
(Vocals: The Three Cheers)

HOW LITTLE I KNEW (Vocals: The Three Cheers) / SUMMER SOUVENIRS (Vocal: Phil Hanna) .... *Bluebird B-7811* 4-6 38

SOMEDAY SWEETHEART (Vocals: The Three Cheers) / A KISS FOR CINDERELLA (Vocal: Phil Hanna) .... *Bluebird B-7827* 5-8 38

MARTIN, Skip, & His Orchestra

(Skip Martin: 5/14/16 –)

I CONCENTRATE ON YOU / VILIA ...... *MGM 11248* 2-4

I'M BEWILDERED / TO SAY YOU'RE MINE .... *Abbott 3002* 2-4
(Vocals: The DeCastro Sisters)

ROSE ROOM / THERE'S DANGER IN YOUR EYES, CHERIE............. *MGM 11342* 2-4

MARX, Chico, & His Orchestra

(Chico Marx: 3/22/91 – 1961)

SWEET ELOISE / HERE YOU ARE......... *Hit 7004* 5-8 42
(Vocals: Skip Nelson)

WE MUST BE VIGILANT / JOHNNY DOUGHBOY FOUND A ROSE IN IRELAND .... *Hit 7003* 5-8 42
(Vocals: Siggy Lane)

MASON, Albert, as Albert Mason's Orchestra:

see LANIN, Sam, & His Famous Players & Singers

MASTERS, Frankie, & His Orchestra

(Frankie Masters: 4/12/04 –)

ALL BY MYSELF (Vocals: Phyllis Miles & quartet) / SNIFFLE SONG (Vocals: Frankie Masters & quartet) .... *Vogue 772* 8-10 46
(Vogue records are picture discs)

ALL THE THINGS YOU ARE (Vocal: Harlan Rogers) / THAT LUCKY FELLOW (Vocal: Frankie Masters)...................... *Vocalion 5265* 2-4 40

ARISE, MY LOVE (Vocal: Marion Francis) / A LITTLE TOO LATE.................. *Okeh 5885* 2-4 40

BACK TO BACK (Vocal: Frankie Masters) / WHEN WINTER COMES (Vocals: Marion Francis & Frankie Masters)..................... *Vocalion 4892* 2-4 39

BLUE CHAMPAGNE (Vocal: Phyllis Miles) / HARBOR OF DREAMS (Vocals: Phyllis Miles & The Masters Voices).......................... *Okeh 6279* 2-4 41

BLUE CHAMPAGNE (Vocal: Phyllis Miles) / HUMPTY DUMPTY HEART (Vocal: Lou Hurst)... *Conqueror 9833* 2-4 41

BUTCH, THE BEACH BOY (Vocals: Frankie Masters & The Masters Voices) / BABY ME (Vocal: Marion Francis)..................... *Vocalion 5024* 2-4 39

CABIN IN THE SKY (Vocals: Marion Francis & The Masters Voices) / BIRDS OF A FEATHER (Vocal: Frankie Masters) .... *Conqueror 9792* 2-4 41

CABIN IN THE SKY (Vocals: Marion Francis & The Masters Voices) / TAKING A CHANCE ON LOVE (Vocals: Frankie Masters & Marion Francis) .... *Okeh 5910* 2-4 41

CLEAR OUT OF THIS WORLD / BLUE LOVEBIRD .... *Vocalion 5565* 2-4 40
(Vocals: Marion Francis)

CONFUCIUS SAY / DOWN THE ALLEY AND OVER THE FENCE........................ *Vocalion 5300* 2-4 40
(Vocals: Frankie Masters & The Masters Voices)

CREAKING OLD MILL ON THE CREEK, THE (Vocals: Frankie Masters& Marion Francis) / GAUCHO SERENADE (Vocal: Gordon Goodman)................ *Vocalion 5328* 2-4 40

DON'T CRY, BABY / IS IT GONNA BE LONG (TILL YOU BELONG TO ME?) .... *Victor 21602* 3-5 28
(Vocals: Frankie Masters)

FALLING LEAVES / THROW YOUR HEART IN THE RING (Vocal: Frankie Masters) .... *Okeh 5803* 2-4 40

FIRST ONE TO SAY GOOD MORNING, THE (Vocal: Lou Hurst) / YOURS (Vocal: Marion Francis) ...... *Okeh 6190* 2-4 41

FOR WANT OF A STAR (Vocal: Marion Francis) / MY HEART AT THY SWEET VOICE .... *Conqueror 9747* 2-4 41

FOR WANT OF A STAR (Vocal: Marion Francis) / MY HEART AT THY SWEET VOICE ..... *Okeh 6132* 2-4 41
(Simultaneously released on two labels)

FRIENDLY TAVERN POLKA (Vocals: Frankie Masters & The Masters Voices) / DOLORES (Vocal: Frankie Masters).......... *Okeh 6142* 2-4 41

GAUCHO SERENADE (Vocal: Gordon Goodman) / I'VE GOT MY EYES ON YOU (Vocal: Marion Francis) .... *Conqueror 9483* 2-4 40

GOODBYE MAMA (I'M OFF TO YOKOHAMA) / THE SUN WILL SOON BE SETTING (FOR THE LAND OF THE RISING SUN) .... *Okeh 6545* 3-5 42
(Vocals: Frankie Masters)

HEAR MY SONG, VIOLETTA (Vocal: Frankie Masters) / THE BREEZE AND I (Vocal: Marión Francis) .... *Conqueror 9491* 2-4 40

HERE'S TO YOU, MAC ARTHUR / THE YANKS ARE COMIN' AGAIN........................ *Okeh 6608* 3-5 42
(Vocals: Frankie Masters & The Masters Voices)

HUT-SUT SONG (Vocals: The Swingmasters) / I WENT OUT OF MY WAY (Vocal: Phyllis Miles) .... *Okeh 6223* 2-4 41

I DO / NOW AND FOREVER .... *Okeh 6625* 2-4 42
(Vocals: Phyllis Miles)

I LIKE TO RECOGNIZE THE TUNE (Vocals: Frankie Masters & The Masters Voices) / I DIDN'T KNOW WHAT TIME IT WAS (Vocal: Marion Francis) .... *Vocalion 5158* 2-4 40

I'LL WAIT FOR YOU (Vocal: Phyllis Miles) / GOT SOMETHING IN MY EYE (Vocal: Frankie Masters).................... *Okeh 6467* 3-5 41

I'M WALKING ON AIR / OUR BUNGALOW OF DREAMS .... *Victor 21102* 3-5 28
(Vocals: Frankie Masters)

IN APPLE BLOSSOM TIME (Vocal: Frankie Masters) / IN THE HUSH OF THE NIGHT (Vocal: Marion Francis) .... *Conqueror 9789* 2-4 41

IN APPLE BLOSSOM TIME (Vocal: Frankie Masters) / IN THE HUSH OF THE NIGHT (Vocal: Marion Francis)..................... *Okeh 6176* 2-4 41
(Simultaneously released on two labels)

IRENE (Vocal: Frankie Masters) / ALICE BLUE GOWN (Vocal: Marion Francis) ... *Conqueror 9481* 2-4 40

IRENE (Vocal: Frankie Masters) / ALICE BLUE GOWN (Vocal: Marion Francis)........ *Okeh 5455* 2-4 40

IRENE (Vocal: Frankie Masters) / ALICE BLUE GOWN (Vocal: Marion Francis) .... *Vocalion 5455* 2-4 40
(Simultaneously released on three labels)

IT'S ALWAYS YOU (Vocal: Lou Hurst) / BIRDS OF A FEATHER (Vocal: Frankie Masters) .... *Okeh 6059* 2-4 41

I WALK WITH MUSIC (Vocal: Harlan Rogers) / CHARMING LITTLE FAKER (Vocal: Frankie Masters) .... *Conqueror 9482* 2-4 40

I WALK WITH MUSIC (Vocal: Harlan Rogers) / CHARMING LITTLE FAKER (Vocal: Frankie Masters)................. *Vocalion 5394* 2-4 40
(Simultaneously released on two labels)

LOVER'S LULLABY / THE WOODPECKER SONG (Vocals: Marion Francis & The Masters Voices) .... *Conqueror 9480* 2-4 40

LOVER'S LULLABY / THE WOODPECKER SONG (Vocals: Marion Francis & The Masters Voices) .... *Vocalion 5443* 2-4 40
(Simultaneously released on two labels)

MERRY OLD LAND OF OZ, THE (Vocals: Frankie Masters & The Masters Voices) / IF I ONLY HAD A BRAIN (Vocals: Frankie Masters, Jack Allison, & Buddy Seger) .... *Vocalion 5034* 4-6 39

OH! LOOK AT ME NOW (Vocals: Frankie Masters & The Swingmasters) / FRIENDLY TAVERN POLKA (Vocals: Frankie Masters & The Masters Voices).... *Conqueror 9617* 2-4 41

POLKA DOTS AND MOONBEAMS (Vocal: Frankie Masters) / WATCHING THE CLOCK (Vocal: Marion Francis) .... *Conqueror 9479* 2-4 40

POLKA DOTS AND MOONBEAMS (Vocal: Frankie Masters) / WATCHING THE CLOCK (Vocal: Marion Francis).................... *Vocalion 5480* 2-4 40
(Simultaneously released on two labels)

SAME OLD STORY, THE (Vocals: Frankie Masters & The Masters Voices) / FERRY BOAT SERENADE (Vocals: Marion Francis & The Masters Voices) .... *Okeh 5716* 2-4 40

SAY WHEN (Vocals: Frankie Masters & The Masters Voices) / ORCHIDS FOR REMEMBRANCE (Vocal: Marion Francis).... *Okeh 5630* 2-4 40

SOMEBODY'S THINKING OF YOU TONIGHT (Vocal: Phyllis Miles) / THE FERRIS WHEEL (Vocals: Frankie Masters & The Swingmasters)........... *Columbia 36612* 3-5 42

SUNSET AT SEA / WALKIN' BY THE RIVER .... *Okeh 5986* 2-4 41
(Vocals: Marion Francis)

TAKE ME OUT TO THE BALL GAME (Vocals: The Masters Voices) / SCATTER-BRAIN (theme song) (Vocal: Frankie Masters)................ *Vocalion 4915* 2-4 39

TAKING A CHANCE ON LOVE (Vocals: Frankie Masters & Marion Francis) / IT'S ALWAYS YOU (Vocal: Lou Hurst)..................... *Conqueror 9619* 2-4 41

THAT'S FOR ME (Vocal: Frankie Masters) / SHADES OF TWILIGHT (Vocal: Marion Francis).......... *Okeh 5702* 2-4 40

THUMBS UP! (official song of the British War Relief Society) (Vocals: Frankie Masters & The Masters Voices) / LET'S PUT TWO AND TWO TOGETHER (Vocal: Frankie Masters) .... *Conqueror 9848* 3-5 41

TUMBLEDOWN RANCH IN ARIZONA (Vocals: Frankie Masters & The Swingmasters) / EXACTLY LIKE YOU (Vocals: The Swingmasters) .... *Okeh 5603* 2-4 40

TUMBLEDOWN RANCH IN ARIZONA (Vocals: Frankie Masters & The Swingmasters) / EXACTLY LIKE YOU (Vocals: The Swingmasters) .... *Vocalion 5603* 2-4 40
(Simultaneously released on two labels)

UNDER BLUE CANADIAN SKIES / BELOW THE EQUATOR................. *Conqueror 9849* 2-4 41
(Vocals: Frankie Masters & The Masters Voices)

UNTIL TOMORROW (Vocal: Lou Hurst) / AURORA (Vocals: Frankie Masters & The Swingmasters) .... *Okeh 6201* 2-4 41

WE'RE IN THE ARMY NOW (Vocals: chorus) / G'BYE NOW (Vocal: Frankie Masters) ... *Conqueror 9620* 3-5 41

WE'RE IN THE ARMY NOW (Vocals: chorus) / G'BYE NOW (Vocal: Frankie Masters)........ *Okeh 6155* 3-5 41
(Simultaneously released on two labels)

WILL YOU STILL BE MINE? (Vocals: Frankie Masters & Phyllis Miles) / DADDY (Vocals: The Swingmasters) .... *Okeh 6232* 2-4 41

WIND BLOWS FREE, THE (Vocal: Phyllis Miles) / UNDER BLUE CANADIAN SKIES (Vocals: Frankie Masters & The Masters Voices) ... *Okeh 6322* 2-4 41

YOU'VE GOT ME THIS WAY (Vocal: Frankie Masters) / DON'T THINK IT AIN'T BEEN CHARMING (Vocals: Marion Francis & The Masters Voices) .... *Okeh 5837* 2-4 40

MATLOCK, Matty, & His All Stars
(Matty Matlock: 4/27/09 – 6/14/78)

PLAY A SIMPLE MELODY / SAM'S SONG... *Decca 27112* 3-5 51
(Vocals: Bing Crosby & Gary Crosby as Gary Crosby and Friends)

MAXWELL HOUSE ORCHESTRA, The:
see VOORHEES, Don

MAYERS, Duncan:
see SAVOY BEARCATS, The

MAYHEW, Nye, & His Orchestra

BLUE ROSES / IT ISN'T FAIR......... *Banner 32827* 3-5 33
(Vocals: Douglas Newman)

BLUE ROSES / IT ISN'T FAIR...... *Melotone M-12757* 3-5 33
(Vocals: Douglas Newman)

BLUE ROSES / IT ISN'T FAIR........... *Oriole 2737* 3-5 33
(Vocals: Douglas Newman)

BLUE ROSES / IT ISN'T FAIR.......... *Perfect 15800* 3-5 33
(Vocals: Douglas Newman)

BLUE ROSES / IT ISN'T FAIR........... *Romeo 2110* 3-5 33
(Vocals: Douglas Newman)
(Simultaneously released on five labels)

COCKTAILS FOR TWO / I'LL STRING ALONG WITH YOU................. *Vocalion 2692* 3-5 34
(Vocals: Douglas Newman)

I CAN'T FORGET (Vocal: Dick Robertson) / THIS TIME IT'S LOVE (Vocals: Unknown) .... *Banner 32839* 2-4 33

I CAN'T FORGET (Vocal: Dick Robertson) / THIS TIME IT'S LOVE (Vocals: Unknown)........... *Melotone M-12767* 2-4 33

I CAN'T FORGET (Vocal: Dick Robertson) / THIS TIME IT'S LOVE (Vocals: Unknown) .... *Oriole 2744* 2-4 33

I CAN'T FORGET (Vocal: Dick Robertson) / THIS TIME IT'S LOVE (Vocals: Unknown)................ *Perfect 15806* 2-4 33

I CAN'T FORGET (Vocal: Dick Robertson) / THIS TIME IT'S LOVE (Vocals: Unknown)................. *Romeo 2117* 2-4 33
(Simultaneously released on five labels)

I LOVED YOU WEDNESDAY (Vocal: Douglas Newman) / THERE'S NO HARM IN HOPING...... *Banner 32851* 2-4 33

I LOVED YOU WEDNESDAY (Vocal: Douglas Newman) / THERE'S NO HARM IN HOPING... *Melotone M-12778* 2-4 33

I LOVED YOU WEDNESDAY (Vocal: Douglas Newman) / THERE'S NO HARM IN HOPING....... *Oriole 2752* 2-4 33

I LOVED YOU WEDNESDAY (Vocal: Douglas Newman) / THERE'S NO HARM IN HOPING...... *Perfect 15812* 2-4 33

I LOVED YOU WEDNESDAY (Vocal: Douglas Newman) / THERE'S NO HARM IN HOPING....... *Romeo 2125* 2-4 33
(Simultaneously released on five labels)

LIFE'S SO COMPLETE / THIS IS ROMANCE................. *Banner 32865* 2-4 33
(Vocals: Douglas Newman)

LIFE'S SO COMPLETE / THIS IS ROMANCE............. *Melotone M-12792* 2-4 33
(Vocals: Douglas Newman)

LIFE'S SO COMPLETE / THIS IS ROMANCE.................... *Oriole 2761* 2-4 33
(Vocals: Douglas Newman)

LIFE'S SO COMPLETE / THIS IS ROMANCE .... *Perfect 15821* 2-4 33
(Vocals: Douglas Newman)

LIFE'S SO COMPLETE / THIS IS ROMANCE.................... *Romeo 2134* 2-4 33
(Vocals: Douglas Newman)
(Simultaneously released on five labels)

MADEMOISELLE / RIPTIDE.......... *Vocalion 2709* 3-5 34
(Vocals: Douglas Newman)

MOON GOT IN MY EYES, THE (Vocal: Douglas Newman) / IT'S THE NATURAL THING TO DO (Vocal: Helen Reynolds) .... *Vocalion 3617* 3-5 37

ORCHIDS IN THE MOONLIGHT (Vocal: Douglas Newman) / CARIOCA..... *Vocalion 2627* 2-4 34

TEMPTATION / WE'LL MAKE HAY WHILE THE SUN SHINES........... *Vocalion 2626* 2-4 34
(Vocals: Douglas Newman)

THIS IS OUR LAST NIGHT TOGETHER (Vocal: Douglas Newman) / BABY, TAKE A BOW! (Vocal: Russ Morgan) .... *Vocalion 2691* 3-5 34

WHEN (WILL YOU BELONG TO ME?) / DANCING UNDER THE STARS .... *Vocalion 3606* 3-5 37
(Vocals: Douglas Newman)

MAYHEW, Nye, & His Orchestra as Art Kahn's Orchestra

IN THE VINE-COVERED CHURCH 'WAY BACK HOME / LITTLE LOCKET OF LONG AGO ..... *Banner 32828* 2-4 33
(Vocals: Douglas Newman)

IN THE VINE-COVERED CHURCH 'WAY BACK HOME / LITTLE LOCKET OF LONG AGO ... *Melotone M-12758* 2-4 33
(Vocals: Douglas Newman)

IN THE VINE-COVERED CHURCH 'WAY BACK HOME / LITTLE LOCKET OF LONG AGO........ *Oriole 2738* 2-4 33
(Vocals: Douglas Newman)

IN THE VINE-COVERED CHURCH 'WAY BACK HOME / LITTLE LOCKET OF LONG AGO...... *Perfect 15801* 2-4 33
(Vocals: Douglas Newman)

IN THE VINE-COVERED CHURCH 'WAY BACK HOME / LITTLE LOCKET OF LONG AGO .... *Romeo 2111* 2-4 33
(Vocals: Douglas Newman)
(Simultaneously released on five labels)

MAYHEW, Nye, & His Orchestra as Will Osborne & His Orchestra

THANKS / THE DAY YOU CAME ALONG .... *Banner 32850* 2-4 33
(Vocals: Will Osborne)

THANKS / THE DAY YOU CAME ALONG.................. *Melotone M-12777* 2-4 33
(Vocals: Will Osborne)

THANKS / THE DAY YOU CAME ALONG .... *Oriole 2751* 2-4 33
(Vocals: Will Osborne)

THANKS / THE DAY YOU CAME ALONG....................... *Perfect 15811* 2-4 33
(Vocals: Will Osborne)

THANKS / THE DAY YOU CAME ALONG....................... *Romeo 2124* 2-4 33
(Vocals: Will Osborne)
(Simultaneously released on five labels)

MAYHEW, Nye, & His Orchestra as Dan Ritchie & His Orchestra

ORCHIDS IN THE MOONLIGHT / SPIN A LITTLE WEB OF DREAMS.................... *Banner 32958* 2-4 34
(Vocals: Russ Morgan)

ORCHIDS IN THE MOONLIGHT / SPIN A LITTLE WEB OF DREAMS...................... *Conqueror 8282* 2-4 34
(Vocals: Russ Morgan)

ORCHIDS IN THE MOONLIGHT / SPIN A LITTLE WEB OF DREAMS.................. *Melotone M-12908* 2-4 34
(Vocals: Russ Morgan)

ORCHIDS IN THE MOONLIGHT / SPIN A LITTLE WEB OF DREAMS......................... *Oriole 2837* 2-4 34
(Vocals: Russ Morgan)

ORCHIDS IN THE MOONLIGHT / SPIN A LITTLE WEB OF DREAMS........................ *Perfect 15879* 2-4 34
(Vocals: Russ Morgan)

ORCHIDS IN THE MOONLIGHT / SPIN A LITTLE WEB OF DREAMS.......................... *Romeo 2207* 2-4 34
(Vocals: Russ Morgan)
(Simultaneously released on six labels)

MAYHEW, Nye, & His Orchestra as Bob Snyder & His Orchestra

ON THE WRONG SIDE OF THE FENCE (Vocal: Douglas Newman) / THERE GOES MY HEART (Vocal: Russ Morgan)........ *Vocalion 2628* 3-5 34

McALPINEERS, The:
see CALIFORNIA RAMBLERS, The

McCOMBER, Ken:
see HIGH HATTERS, The

McCONNELL, Ray:
see FOLEY, Bill, as Bill Foley's Keystone Serenaders

McCOY, Clyde, & His Drake Hotel Orchestra
(Clyde McCoy: 12/29/03 –)
(The following four records were pressed in blue shellac.)

NOBODY'S SWEETHEART / WAH WAH LAMENT............. *Columbia 2808-D* 5-8 33

SMOKE RINGS / NEW BASIN STREET BLUES .... *Columbia 2794-D* 5-8 33

SOME OF THESE DAYS / IN THE COOL OF THE NIGHT.................. *Columbia 2801-D* 5-8 33

'WAY DOWN YONDER IN NEW ORLEANS / TEAR IT DOWN.................. *Columbia 2909-D* 4-6 33

McCOY, Clyde, & His Orchestra

BLACK AND TAN FANTASY / MOOD INDIGO.......................... *Decca 1152* 4-6 37

BLACK AND TAN FANTASY / THE NIGHTMARE .... *Columbia 2466-D* 4-6 31

BLUE FANTASY / BLUE PRELUDE...... *Decca 1917* 3-5 38

BLUE SUGAR / ROSELAND STOMP .... *Decca 833* 4-6 36

BUGLES IN THE SKY (Vocals: Dick Lee & the Bennett Sisters) / LOVE CAN DO THE DARNDEST THINGS (Vocals: The Bennett Sisters)................ *Decca 3581* 2-4 41

DON'T LOOK NOW (Vocals: The Bennett Sisters) / YOU ARE MY DREAM (Vocal: Wayne Gregg) .... *Decca 2630* 2-4 39

DOODLE DOO DOO / I CAN'T GIVE YOU ANYTHING BUT LOVE (BABY) (Vocal: Wayne Gregg) ... *Decca 1230* 3-5 37

DRY ICE / WAH! WAH! LAMENT.......... *Decca 566* 4-6 35

GOONA GOO, THE / WHEN YOU'RE SMILING........................ *Decca 1109* 3-5 37

GYPSY IN MY SOUL, THE / ONE MORE DREAM .... *Decca 1766* 2-4 38

JAPANESE SANDMAN / TEA FOR TWO ... *Decca 382* 3-5 35

I FOUND YOU, LOVED YOU, LOST YOU (Vocal: Wayne Gregg) / YOU'RE THE ONE (YOU BEAUTIFUL SON-OF-A-GUN) (Vocals: The Bennett Sisters & chorus) .... *Decca 3074* 2-4 40

I'M GONNA PLAY IN THE VARSITY BAND (Vocals: chorus) / BASIN STREET BLUES .... *Decca 620* 3-5 35

IT LOOKS LIKE LOVE / A LONELY GONDOLIER (theme song) .... *Columbia 2453-D* 3-5 31

I'VE FOUND A NEW BABY / CHINA BOY .... *Decca 422* 4-6 35

I WANT MY MAMA (Vocals: by chorus) / I WAS WATCHING A MAN PAINT A FENCE (Vocal: Wayne Gregg)............ *Decca 2995* 2-4 40

MAPLE LEAF RAG / THE NIGHTMARE ... *Decca 681* 4-6 35

OLD-FASHIONED LOVE / TWELFTH STREET RAG................ *Decca 509* 4-6 35

PALOOKA / LIKE ME A LITTLE BIT LESS.............. *Columbia 2865-D* 5-8 34
(Vocals: Unknown)
(This record was pressed in blue shellac)

RIDIN' TO GLORY ON A TRUMPET / YOU GAVE ME THE RUN-A-ROUND......................... *Decca 758* 4-6 36
(Vocals: Unknown)

SHADES OF GREY / A LONELY GONDOLIER (theme song)................. *Decca 2737* 2-4 39
(Vocals: Wayne Gregg)

SUGAR BLUES (theme song) / BASIN STREET BLUES.................. *Vogue 707* 8-10 46
(Vogue records are picture discs)

SUGAR BLUES (theme song) / READIN', RITIN', RHYTHM....... *Columbia 2389-D* 3-5 31

TEAR IT DOWN / SUGAR BLUES (theme song)................ *Decca 381* 2-4 35

TELL ME YOU'LL FORGIVE ME (Vocals: by quartet) / SURRENDER TO THE BLUES .... *Decca 3633* 2-4 41

TEN LITTLE MILES FROM NOWHERE / MY PILLOW AND ME .... *Decca 1788* 2-4 38

THERE'LL BE SOME CHANGES MADE (Vocal: Rosalind Marquis) / WHISPERING .... *Decca 461* 3-5 35

TOM, TOM, THE PIPER'S SON (Vocals: Wayne Gregg & The Bennett Sisters) / OL' MAN RIVER .... *Decca 2217* 2-4 38

TOOT, TOOT, TOOSIE (GOO'BYE) / DOO WACKA DOO .... *Decca 1297* 3-5 37

YA GOT ME (Vocals: The Bennett Sisters) / TEN PINS IN THE SKY (Vocal: Wayne Gregg) .... *Decca 2149* 2-4 38

McCOY, Clyde, & His Orchestra as Billy Clyde & His Orchestra

AFTER YOU'VE GONE / SOME OF THESE DAYS .... *Champion 40108* 4-6 35

ROSE ROOM / OH BABY .... *Champion 40102* 4-6 35

McDONOUGH, Dick, & His Orchestra

(Dick McDonough: 1904 – 5/25/38)

DARDANELLA / BETWEEN THE DEVIL AND THE DEEP BLUE SEA .... *Melotone 7-02-04* 5-8 37

DON'T EVER CHANGE / TWO HEARTS ARE DANCING .... *Melotone 7-07-16* 3-5 37
(Vocals: Barry McKinley)

HE AIN'T GOT RHYTHM / THE GIRL ON THE POLICE GAZETTE .... *Melotone 7-03-11* 5-8 37
(Vocals: Chick Bullock)

I CAN'T LOSE THAT LONGING FOR YOU / THE GOONA GOO .... *Melotone 7-03-12* 5-8 37
(Vocals: Art Gentry)

I'M NEVER BLUE WHERE THE GRASS IS GREEN / SPRING CLEANING (GETTING READY FOR LOVE) .... *Melotone 7-06-03* 4-6 37
(Vocals: Barry McKinley)

I'M ONE STEP AHEAD OF MY SHADOW / NOW OR NEVER .... *Melotone 6-12-02* 5-8 36
(Vocals: Chick Bullock)

IT AIN'T RIGHT (Vocal: Buddy Clark) / IN A SENTIMENTAL MOOD .... *Melotone 6-11-02* 5-8 36

I'VE GOT BEGINNER'S LUCK / SHALL WE DANCE? .... *Melotone 7-05-18* 4-6 37
(Vocals: Barry McKinley)

LOVE IS ON THE AIR TONIGHT / HAVE YOU GOT ANY CASTLES, BABY? .... *Conqueror 8907* 5-8 37

LOVE, WHAT ARE YOU DOING TO MY HEART? / YOU'RE GIVING ME A SONG AND A DANCE .... *Melotone 6-12-03* 5-8 36
(Vocals: Larry Stewart)

SCENE CHANGES, THE / ON THE BEACH AT BALI-BALI .... *Conqueror 8678* 5-8 36
(Vocals: Chick Bullock)

SCENE CHANGES, THE / ON THE BEACH AT BALI-BALI .... *Melotone 6-08-08* 5-8 36
(Vocals: Chick Bullock)
(Simultaneously released on two labels)

SOUTH SEA ISLAND MAGIC / AFTERGLOW .... *Conqueror 8750* 5-8 36
(Vocals: Buddy Clark)

SOUTH SEA ISLAND MAGIC / AFTERGLOW .... *Melotone 6-11-01* 5-8 36
(Vocals: Buddy Clark)
(Simultaneously released on two labels)

SUMMER HOLIDAY / I'M GRATEFUL TO YOU .... *Melotone 6-09-07* 4-6 37
(Vocals: Buddy Clark)

TAKE MY HEART (Vocal: Chick Bullock) / STARS IN MY EYES (Vocal: Dorothy Dreslin) .... *Melotone 6-08-07* 4-6 37

TEA ON THE TERRACE / THERE'S FROST ON THE MOON .... *Melotone 7-01-11* 4-6 37
(Vocals: Chick Bullock)

WHEN THE MOON HANGS HIGH / MIDNIGHT BLUE .... *Melotone 6-11-04* 5-8 36
(Vocals: Buddy Clark)

WITH THEE I SWING / I'M IN A DANCING MOOD .... *Conqueror 8761* 5-8 37
(Vocals: Chick Bullock)

WITH THEE I SWING / I'M IN A DANCING MOOD .... *Melotone 7-01-07* 5-8 37
(Vocals: Chick Bullock)
(Simultaneously released on two labels)

YOU AND I KNOW / THAT OLD FEELING .... *Conqueror 8903* 5-8 37
(Vocals: Howard Phillips)

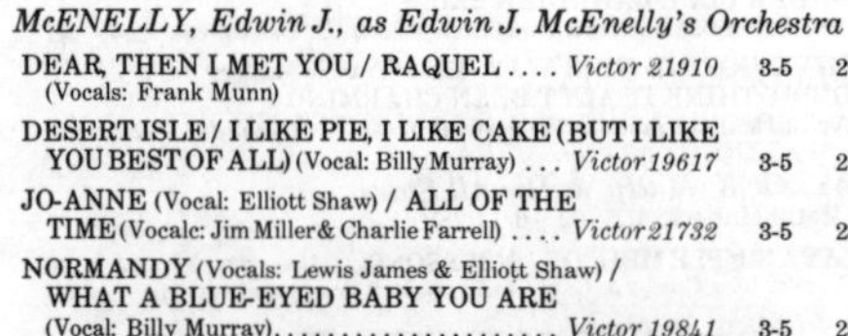

McENELLY, Edwin J., as Edwin J. McEnelly's Orchestra

DEAR, THEN I MET YOU / RAQUEL .... *Victor 21910* 3-5 29
(Vocals: Frank Munn)

DESERT ISLE / I LIKE PIE, I LIKE CAKE (BUT I LIKE YOU BEST OF ALL) (Vocal: Billy Murray) ... *Victor 19617* 3-5 25

JO-ANNE (Vocal: Elliott Shaw) / ALL OF THE TIME (Vocals: Jim Miller & Charlie Farrell) .... *Victor 21732* 3-5 28

NORMANDY (Vocals: Lewis James & Elliott Shaw) / WHAT A BLUE-EYED BABY YOU ARE (Vocal: Billy Murray) .... *Victor 19841* 3-5 25

McFARLAND TWINS & THEIR ORCHESTRA, The

directed by Artie and George McFarland

HEY, ZEKE (YOUR COUNTRY'S CALLIN') (Vocals: Don Cornell, Betty Norton & orchestra) / WHEN DAY IS DONE (Vocals: Don Cornell, The Norton Sisters, & The Twin Choir) .... *Bluebird B-11449* 5-8 42

ROW THAT ROWBOAT (Vocals: The Norton Sisters) / IF I COULD ONLY PLAY A CONCERTINA (Vocals: The Twinsters Three) .... *Bluebird B-11484* 5-8 42

McGHEE, Howard, & His Orchestra

(Howard McGhee: 2/16/18 –)

DIALATED PUPILS / MIDNIGHT AT MINTON'S .... *Dial 1011* 5-8 47

DOROTHY / NIGHT MIST .... *Dial 1027* 5-8 48

MAN WITH A HORN / TWELFTH STREET BOP .... *Hi-Lo 1414* 5-8 -

McGHEE JUMPS / McGHEE SPECIAL .... *Modern Music MM136* 5-8 46

UP IN DODO'S ROOM / HIGH WIND IN HOLLYWOOD .... *Dial 1010* 5-8 47

McHUGH, Jimmy, as Jimmy McHugh's Bostonians

(Jimmy McHugh: 7/10/94 –)

GIRL OF MY DREAMS / WHEN LOVE COMES STEALING .... *Harmony 743-H* 5-8 28
(Vocals: Tommy Weir)

LET'S SIT AND TALK ABOUT YOU / IN A GREAT BIG WAY .... *Harmony 823-H* 8-10 29
(Vocals: Irving Kaufman as Jim Andrews)

WHOOPEE STOMP, THE / FUTURISTIC RHYTHM (Vocal: Irving Kaufman as Marvin Young) .... *Harmony 836-H* 10-12 29

McINTIRE, Dick, as Dick McIntire's Harmony Hawaiians

ONE ROSE, THE / KUKUNA OKA LA ...... *Decca 558* 3-5 35

McINTIRE, Lani, & His Aloha Islanders

MAI POINA OE IA'U (Vocals: Lani McIntire, Leilani Iaea, & Samson Akaka) / PARADISE ISLE (Vocal: Lani McIntire) .... *Sonora 1094* 3-5 45

McINTYRE, Hal, & His Orchestra

(Hal McIntyre: 11/29/14 – 5/5/59)

BIM BAM BOOGIE (Vocals: Betty Norton & Johnny Turnbull) / SPRING IN DECEMBER (Vocal: Frankie Lester) .... *MGM 10167* 2-4 48

DAISY MAE / I THREW A KISS IN THE OCEAN (Vocal: Penny Parker) .... *Victor 27878* 4-6 42

FOOLED / I'LL NEVER FORGET .... *Victor 27777* 3-5 42
(Vocals: Carl Denny)

FRIDAY AFTERNOON / YOU'RE IN LOVE WITH SOMEONE ELSE (Vocal: Frances Gaynor) ... *Victor 27924* 3-5 42

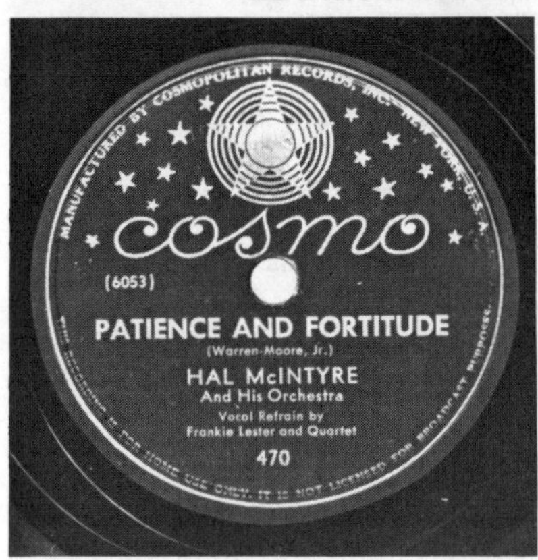

HOW DO I KNOW IT'S REAL? (Vocals: Carl Denny) / THE COMMANDO SERENADE .... *Victor 27796* 3-5 42

I'LL PRAY FOR YOU / DO YOU MISS YOUR SWEETHEART (LIKE YOUR SWEETHEART MISSES YOU?) .... *Victor 27821* 3-5 42
(Vocals: Carl Denny)

I'M GETTING TIRED SO I CAN SLEEP / THIS IS THE ARMY, MR. JONES .... *Victor 27951* 3-5 42
(Vocals: Jerry Stuart)

KILLE KILLE (INDIAN LOVE TALK (Vocals: Four Lytle Sisters) / WHY DON'T YOU FALL IN LOVE WITH ME? (Vocal: Jerry Stuart) .... *Victor 27964* 2-4 42

LORETTA / SHE'LL ALWAYS REMEMBER .... *Victor 27805* 3-5 42
(Vocals: Carl Denny)

MEM'RY OF THIS DANCE / THERE ARE RIVERS TO CROSS .... *Victor 27840* 3-5 42
(Vocals: Carl Denny)

PATIENCE AND FORTITUDE / THERE'S NO ONE BUT YOU .... *Cosmo 470* 4-6 46
(Vocals: Frankie Lester & quartet)

PUT 'EM IN A BOX TIE 'EM WITH A RIBBON (Vocal: Johnny Turnbull) / ON AN ISLAND WITH YOU (Vocal: Frankie Lester) .... *MGM 10193* 2-4 48

SOUTH BAYOU SHUFFLE / I'LL KEEP THE LOVE-LIGHT BURNING (Vocal: Carl Denny) ..... *Victor 27855* 3-5 42

STORY OF A STARRY NIGHT, THE (Vocal: Carl Denny) / WE'LL MEET AGAIN (Vocal: Penny Parker) .... *Victor 27859* 3-5 42

TANGERINE / WHEN THE ROSES BLOOM AGAIN .... *Victor 27803* 2-4 42
(Vocals: Carl Denny)

WHEN YOU'RE A LONG, LONG WAY FROM HOME (Vocal: Jerry Stuart) / PLAY NUMBER FORTY-NINE .... *Victor 27942* 3-5 42

McKAY, Marion, & His Orchestra

AT THE END OF THE ROAD / SWANEE BUTTERFLY.............. *Gennett 5673* 4-6 25

HONEST AND TRULY / DOO WACKA DOO .... *Gennett 5615* 5-8 25

I'M ON MY WAY TO DREAMLAND / SUGAR PLUM .... *Gennett 3217* 4-6 26

LITTLE BUTTERFLY/HOOTENANNY... *Gennett 20025* 4-6 24

TELL ME, LITTLE DAISY (Vocal: Roger Beals) / MY BLUE HEAVEN (Vocal: Fred Stuart)..... *Gennett 6294* 5-8 28

McKAY, Marion, & His Orchestra as The Dreamland Harmonists

HONEST AND TRULY / DOO WACKA DOO............... *Claxtonola 40408* 10-12 25

McKAY, Marion, & His Orchestra as Harold Ross & His Southerners

BEGGAR, THE / MY BLUE HEAVEN (Vocal: Fred Stuart) .... *Champion 15385* 4-6 28

McKAY, Marion, & His Orchestra as Bill Williams & His Gang

HONEST AND TRULY / DOO WACKA DOO............... *Champion 15011* 5-8 28

McKENZIE, Red, & His Orchestra
(Red McKenzie: 10/14/99 – 2/7/48)

FAREWELL, MY LOVE / SAIL ALONG, SILVERY MOON .... *Vocalion 3875* 5-8 38
(Vocals: Red McKenzie)

YOU'RE OUT OF THIS WORLD / GEORGIANNA..................... *Vocalion 3898* 5-8 38
(Vocals: Red McKenzie)

McKENZIE, Red, & His Rhythm Kings

DON'T COUNT YOUR KISSES (BEFORE YOU'RE KISSED) / I DON'T KNOW YOUR NAME (BUT YOU'RE BEAUTIFUL)................... *Decca 721* 5-8 36
(Vocals: Red McKenzie)

DOUBLE TROUBLE / THAT'S WHAT YOU THINK.......................... *Decca 521* 5-8 35
(Vocals: Red McKenzie)

I CAN'T GET STARTED WITH YOU / I CAN PULL A RABBIT OUT OF MY HAT.............. *Decca 790* 5-8 36
(Vocals: Red McKenzie)

MURDER IN THE MOONLIGHT (IT'S LOVE IN THE FIRST DEGREE) / LET'S SWING IT...... *Decca 507* 5-8 35
(Vocals: Red McKenzie)

SING AN OLD FASHIONED SONG (TO A YOUNG SOPHISTICATED LADY) / I'M BUILDING UP TO AN AWFUL LETDOWN...................... *Decca 667* 5-8 36
(Vocals: Red McKenzie)

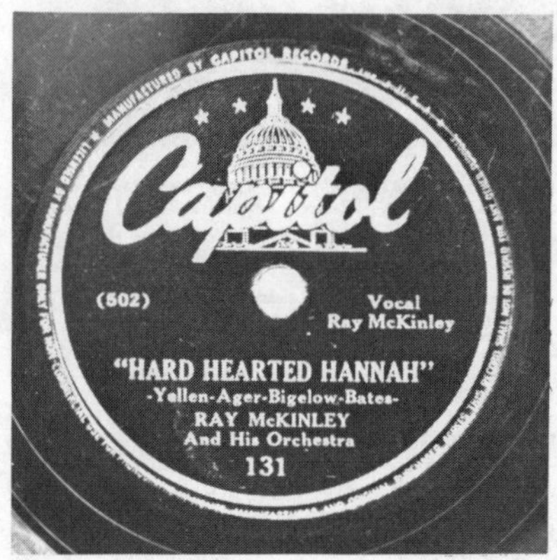

McKINLEY, Ray, & His Orchestra
(Ray McKinley: 6/18/10 –)

DOWN THE ROAD A PIECE (Vocal: Ray McKinley) / ONE LOVE (Vocal: Teddy Norman)....... *Majestic 7189* 3-5 46

HARD HEARTED HANNAH (Vocal: Ray McKinley) / BIG BOY (Vocal: Imogene Lynn) .... *Capitol 131* 4-6 43

IN THE LAND OF THE BUFFALO NICKEL (Vocal: Ray McKinley) / SANDSTORM .... *Majestic 7184* 2-4 46

RED SILK STOCKINGS AND GREEN PERFUME (Vocals: Ray McKinley & band) / JIMINY CRICKETS .... *Majestic 7216* 2-4 47

SARONG / WHERE DID THE WILD WEST GO?............... *RCA Victor 20-3546* 2-4 49
(Vocals: Ray McKinley)

YOUR RED WAGON / A MAN'S BEST FRIEND IS A BED................... *Majestic 7275* 3-5 47
(Vocals: Ray McKinley)

McKINLEY, Ray, as Ray McKinley's Jazz Band

LOVE IN THE FIRST DEGREE / NEW ORLEANS PARADE............. *Decca 1019* 5-8 36

SHACK IN THE BACK / FINGERWAVE... *Decca 1020* 5-8 36

MELODY DANCE PLAYERS, The:
see KATZMAN, Louis, as Katzman's Orchestra

MELODY MEN, The

AFTER I'VE CALLED YOU SWEETHEART / BY THE WATERS OF MINNETONKA............. *Bell 568* 3-5 27

BABY FACE / WHERE'D YOU GET THOSE EYES? .... *Bell 424* 3-5 26

OOH! MAYBE IT'S YOU / NEVER .... *Bell 545* 3-5 27

MELODY SHEIKS, The:
see LANIN, Sam

MELODY WALTZ ORCHESTRA, The:
see BARTH, Harry

MEMPHIS HOT SHOTS, The:
see ELLINGTON, Duke, & His Orchestra as The Harlem Footwarmers

MEMPHIS MELODY BOYS, The:
see CALIFORNIA RAMBLERS, The, as The Vagabonds

MEROFF, Benny, & His Orchestra
also see LANIN, Sam, & His Famous Players
see LANIN, Sam, & His Famous Players and Singers and
see TRUMBAUER, Frankie, as Frankie Trumbauer's Augmented Orchestra
(Benny Meroff: 4/19/01 – 1973)

ARISTOCRAT OF HARLEM / THE PLEASURE WAS ALL MINE!................. *Columbia 3065-D* 5-8 35
(This record was pressed in blue shellac)

COWBOY IN MANHATTAN / YANKEE IN HAVANA .... *Columbia 3072-D* 5-8 35
(This record was pressed in blue shellac)

HAPPY DAYS ARE HERE AGAIN (Vocal: Dusty Rhodes) / THE TALK OF THE TOWN......... *Brunswick 4709* 5-8 30

SMILING SKIES / ME AND THE MAN IN THE MOON.................. *Okeh 41171* 12-15 29
(Vocals: Benny Meroff)

THERE'S A TRICK IN PICKIN' A CHICK-CHICK-CHICKEN / THAT'S DOLLY..... *Okeh 40847* 5-8 27
(Vocals: Unknown)

MERRY MELODY MEN, The

FANCIES / TUCK ME TO SLEEP IN MY OLD 'TUCKY HOME .... *Pathe Actuelle 020650* 2-4 21

HOME AGAIN BLUES / LOOK FOR THE SILVER LINING.................. *Arto 9046* 2-4 20

HONOLULU EYES / CARESSES.... *Paramount 20038* 3-5 21

I CALL YOU SUNSHINE / IN THE DEVIL'S GARDEN........... *Vocalion 14178* 2-4 21

I WONDER IF YOU STILL CARE? / WHO'LL BE THE NEXT ONE TO CRY OVER YOU?..... *Cardinal 2064* 2-4 21

JUST LIKE A RAINBOW / ROSY CHEEKS.... *Arto 9098* 2-4 21

MY SUNNY TENNESSEE / SUNNYSIDE SAL............ *Pathe Actuelle 020594* 2-4 21

PUCKER UP AND WHISTLE (whistling by Margaret McKee) / SNUGGLES.......... *Gennett 4720* 2-4 21

REMEMBER THE ROSE / ALL BY MYSELF .... *Gennett 4770* 2-4 21

SCANDINAVIA / I FOUND A ROSE IN THE DEVIL'S GARDEN.......... *Olympic 15102* 2-4 21

WABASH BLUES / BLUE MOON...... *Emerson 10468* 3-5 21

MERRY SPARKLERS, The

DANCIN' DAN / BLUE ROSE .... *Edison 51288* 3-5 24

I WANT YOU BACK, OLD PAL (Vocal: Arthur Hall) / HONEST AND TRULY (Vocal: Charles Hart) .... *Edison 51507* 3-5 25

OUT OF A MILLION YOU'RE THE ONLY ONE (Vocal: Charles Hart) / HAVE A LITTLE FUN (Vocal: Arthur Hall)................ *Edison 51434* 4-6 25

THAT'S GEORGIA / THE SUNSHINE ALWAYS SHINES FOR ME .... *Edison 51408* 5-8 24
(Vocals: Vernon Dalhart)

THERE'S YES! YES! IN YOUR EYES / LAZY (by the Atlantic Dance Orchestra)............. *Edison 51325* 3-5 24

WHERE'S MY SWEETIE HIDING? / MY ROAD......................... *Edison 51427* 3-5 24

MESSNER, Johnny, & His Music Box Band
(Johnny Messner: 10/13/09 –)

BABY MINE (Vocal: Jack Ryan) / WHEN I SEE AN ELEPHANT FLY (Vocals: Johnny Messner & Jeanne D'Arcy)................. *Decca 4061* 2-4 41

CHEW-CHEW-CHEW (CHEW YOUR BUBBLE GUM) (Vocal: Jeanne D'Arcy) / BOOM! (Vocals: The Three Jacks)................ *Bluebird B-10275* 2-4 39

CONCERTO FOR TWO (Vocals: Unknown) / CLARINET IN A HAUNTED HOUSE .... *Decca 4040* 3-5 41

DADDY (Vocals: Unknown) / MOBILE FLAG STOP................... *Decca 3816* 3-5 41

DEVIL WITH THE DEVIL, THE (Vocal: Johnny Messner) / COULD BE (Vocal: Jeanne D'Arcy).... *Bluebird B-10107* 2-4 39

DO YOU REMEMBER LAST NIGHT? (Vocal: Jeanne D'Arcy) / MIDNIGHT ON THE TRAIL (Vocal: Johnny Messner)....... *Bluebird B-10065* 2-4 39

DUST BE MY DESTINY (Vocal: Johnny Messner) / MEXICONGA (Vocals: Johnny Messner & The Three Jacks)............... *Bluebird B-10400* 2-4 39

HAVE A HEART / DAWN OF A NEW DAY............... *Bluebird B-10101* 2-4 39
(Vocals: Bobby King)

HAWAII SANG ME TO SLEEP (Vocal: Shorty Skipper) / HEY! GOOD LOOKING (Vocals: Johnny Messner, Jeanne D'Arcy, & The Three Jacks) .... *Bluebird B-10449* 2-4 39

HOW MUCH DO YOU MEAN TO ME? (Vocal: Johnny Messner) / DON'T CROSS YOUR FINGERS, CROSS YOUR HEART (Vocals: The Three Jacks).............. *Bluebird B-7750* 2-4 38

HUT-SUT SONG (Vocals: by trio) / AT A GEORGIA CAMP MEETING (Vocals: Johnny Messner & chorus)... *Decca 3817* 2-4 41

LINGERING ON YOUR DOORSTEP (Vocals: Johnny Messner & Jeanne D'Arcy) / IT'S A HUNDRED TO ONE (I'M IN LOVE) (Vocals: Jeanne D'Arcy & The Three Jacks).................. *Bluebird B-10387* 2-4 39

MA-MA-MARIA (Vocals: by trio) / MAMA (Vocals: Johnny Messner, Jeanne D'Arcy, & chorus) .... *Decca 4039* 2-4 41

MAN ON THE FLYING TRAPEZE / THERE IS A TAVERN IN THE TOWN .... *Decca 3776* 2-4 41
(Vocals: Johnny Messner & chorus)

MAN WITH THE LOLLYPOP SONG (Vocal: Johnny Messner) / SAYS WHO? SAYS YOU, SAYS I! (Vocals: Johnny Messner & Jeanne D'Arcy)..... *Decca 4085* 2-4 42

MODERN DESIGN (Vocal: Johnny Messner) / THE SKUNK SONG (Vocals: by quartet) .... *Decca 4086* 3-5 42

MOON WAS DREAMING, THE (Vocals: Unknown) / IF I COULD ONLY PLAY A CONCERTINA... *Decca 4192* 2-4 42

PENNY POLKA (Vocals: Johnny Messner & Jack Ryan) / THE BIGGEST ASPIDASTRA IN THE WORLD (Vocals: Jeanne D'Arcy & Johnny Messner)..... *Decca 4148* 3-5 41

PLEASE COME OUT OF YOUR DREAM (Vocal: Johnny Messner) / AMONG THOSE SAILING (Vocal: Jeanne D'Arcy)...... *Bluebird B-10058* 2-4 39

SHABBY OLD CABBY / YOU TOOK ME OUT OF THIS WORLD................ *Bluebird B-10343* 2-4 39
(Vocals: Johnny Messner)

SHE HAD TO GO AND LOSE IT AT THE ASTOR (Vocals: by ensemble) / JOHNNY'S MESSIN' 'ROUND........................... *Varsity 8083* 3-5 39

SINGIN' IN THE SADDLE (Vocal: Johnny Messner) / LET'S STOP THE CLOCK (Vocal: Jeanne D'Arcy).............. *Bluebird B-10110* 2-4 39

START THE DAY RIGHT (Vocals: Johnny Messner & orchestra) / I MUST HAVE ONE MORE KISS KISS KISS (Vocals: Johnny Messner, Jeanne D'Arcy, & The Three Jacks)................ *Bluebird B-10348* 2-4 39

THAT WEEK IN PARIS / SPANITA.... *Bluebird B-7747* 2-4 38
(Vocals: Jeanne D'Arcy)

TOY PIANO MINUET / ALEXANDER THE SWOOSE (Vocals: by trio)........... *Decca 3777* 2-4 41

UMBRELLA MAN, THE / POLLY PUT YOUR SLIPPERS ON .... *Bluebird B-10048* 2-4 39
(Vocals: The Three Jacks)

MESSNER, Johnny, & His Orchestra

STOP! AND RECONSIDER (Vocal: Jeanne D'Arcy) / A GARDEN IN GRANADA (Vocal: Shorty Skipper) .... *Conqueror 9023* 2-4 38

STOP! AND RECONSIDER (Vocal: Jeanne D'Arcy) / A GARDEN IN GRANADA (Vocal: Shorty Skipper)................ *Vocalion 4088* 2-4 38
(Simultaneously released on two labels)

YOU DIDN'T HAVE TO TELL ME (Vocal: Johnny Messner) / COWBOY FROM BROOKLYN (Vocals: The Three Rangers)............. *Vocalion 4112* 2-4 38

METZGER'S NIGHT OWLS:
see METZGER, Ted, & His Campus Owls

METZGER, Ted, & His Campus Owls

I KEEP REMEMBERING / I'M HAPPY WHEN YOU'RE HAPPY .... *Champion 16741* 8-10 31
(Vocals: Wendell Merthe)

METZGER, Ted, & His Campus Owls as Metzger's Night Owls

I KEEP REMEMBERING (Vocal: Wendell Merthe) / IT'S THAT RHYTHM..................... *Superior 2646* 10-12 31

WHEN DREAMS COME TRUE / I'M HAPPY WHEN YOU'RE HAPPY..................... *Superior 2629* 8-10 31
(Vocals: Wendell Merthe)

MEYERS, Vic, & His Hotel Butler Orchestra

ESTRELLITA / BLOW THE SMOKE AWAY................... *Columbia 1516-D* 3-5 28

NOBODY'S SWEETHEART / JA-DA... *Columbia 1530-D* 3-5 28

WHETHER IT RAINS, WHEATHER IT SHINES / NOW THAT YOU'RE GONE............ *Columbia 1168-D* 3-5 27

MEYERS, Vic, & His Orchestra

BURMALONE / HEARTBROKEN .... *Brunswick 2685* 3-5 24

MEAN, MEAN MAMA / SHAKE IT AND BREAK IT......... *Brunswick 2501* 5-8 23

NAY, DEARIE, NAY / THREE O'CLOCK BLUES................... *Vocalion 15056* 5-8 25

NO WONDER (I LOVE YOU) / THE ONLY, ONLY ONE FOR ME (Vocal: Frank Bessinger)...... *Brunswick 2774* 3-5 24

SHIMMY / SAD (Vocal: Frank Bessinger) ... *Brunswick 2800* 3-5 25

SPRINGTIME RAG / HELEN GONE.... *Brunswick 2630* 5-8 24

WEARY BLUES / BEETS AND TURNIPS......................... *Brunswick 2664* 5-8 24

MEYERS, Vic, as Vic Meyers' Music

BESIDE AN OPEN FIREPLACE / IF I'M DREAMING .... *Columbia 2049-D* 4-6 30
(Vocals: Unknown)

CONGRATULATIONS / MELANCHOLY .... *Columbia 2026-D* 4-6 29
(Vocals: Unknown)

MIAMI BEACH ORCHESTRA, The

ALWAYS / SYMPATHY................. *Gennett 3252* 2-4 26
(Vocals: Arthur Fields)

OLD-FASHIONED LOVE / I'VE GOT A SONG FOR SALE.................. *Federal 5343* 3-5 23

REMEMB'RING / SWEET BUTTER...... *Federal 5350* 3-5 24

MIAMI DANCE ORCHESTRA, The

WHILE YOU WERE MAKING BELIEVE / YOU SAID SOMETHING WHEN YOU SAID "DIXIE"........... *Pathe Actuelle 020936* 3-5 23

WHILE YOU WERE MAKING BELIEVE / YOU SAID SOMETHING WHEN YOU SAID "DIXIE".................. *Perfect 14118* 2-4 23
(Simultaneously released on two labels)

MIAMI MELODISTS, The:
see GOLD, Lou, & His Orchestra

MIDNIGHT RAMBLERS, The:
see RESER, Harry, as The Rounders

MIDNIGHT SERENADERS, The:
see RICH, Fred, as Fred Rich's Dance Orchestra

MILES, Eddie, & His Florentine Club Orchestra

GIVE ME A NIGHT IN JUNE / IS IT POSSIBLE?..................... *Gennett 6247* 5-8 27
(Vocals: Sol Bearman)

ONE O'CLOCK BABY (Vocal: Wallace Chambers) / AT SUNDOWN (Vocal: Sol Bearman)...... *Gennett 6200* 5-8 27

MILLER, Glenn, & His Orchestra
(Glenn Miller: 3/1/04 – missing since 12/15/44)

(Glenn Miller was lost in a plane flight which left England December 15, 1944 and never arrived at Paris, France. Glenn Miller's career as bandleader spanned about five years, yet in that length of time he created and directed apparently the most popular, most memorable big dance band of all time.

In 1942, his recording "Chattanooga Choo Choo" was the first Gold Record ever awarded, and interestingly, was the first million-seller since 1927. The motion picture version of his life, *"The Glenn Miller Story"* was one of the top ten of 1954.

Today, forty years after his death, the Miller estate continues to receive substantial royalties from his original recordings, and astonishingly, fan letters are still written to Glenn Miller as if he were alive!

The present-day Glenn Miller Orchestra, directed by Dick Gerhart and utilizing largely original Miller arrangements, appears worldwide for concerts and dancing, fifty weeks annually.

ALICE BLUE GOWN / WONDERFUL ONE .... *Bluebird B-10701* 3-5 40

ALONG THE SANTA FE TRAIL (Vocal: Ray Eberle) / YES, MY DARLING DAUGHTER (Vocal: Marion Hutton)............... *Bluebird B-10970* 3-5 40

AMERICAN PATROL / SOLDIER, LET ME READ YOU LETTER (Vocals: Ray Eberle & The Modernaires)...................... *Victor 27873* 3-5 42

AND THE ANGELS SING (Vocal: Ray Eberle) / THE CHESTNUT TREE (Vocals: Marion Hutton & the band)......................... *Bluebird B-10201* 3-5 39

ANGEL CHILD (Vocal: Ray Eberle) / BE HAPPY (Vocal: Marion Hutton).... *Bluebird B-10796* 3-5 40

ANGEL IN A FURNISHED ROOM, AN (Vocal: Ray Eberle) / LOVE WITH A CAPITAL "YOU" (Vocal: Kay Starr).... *Bluebird B-10383* 3-5 39

ANVIL CHORUS / ANVIL CHORUS, PART II........ *Bluebird B-10982* 2-4 40

APRIL PLAYED THE FIDDLE (Vocal: Ray Eberle) / I HAVEN'T TIME TO BE A MILLIONAIRE (Vocal: Tex Beneke)... *Bluebird B-10694* 3-5 40

AT THE PRESIDENT'S BALL (Vocals: Marion Hutton & The Modernaires) / ANGELS OF MERCY (Vocals: Ray Eberle & chorus)................ *Bluebird B-11429* 5-8 42
("Angels of Mercy" was dedicated to the American Red Cross)

BASKET WEAVER / ON A LITTLE STREET IN SINGAPORE............ *Victor 20-1585* 2-4 44
(Vocals: Ray Eberle)
(The first side is a 1939 recording first released in 1944; the second side is a reissue from Bluebird B-10526.)

BEAT ME DADDY, EIGHT TO THE BAR (Vocals: Jack Lathrop & band) / FALLING LEAVES............... *Bluebird B-10876* 4-6 40

BLESS YOU / SPEAKING OF HEAVEN .... *Bluebird B-10455* 4-6 39
(Vocals: Ray Eberle)

BLUEBERRY HILL / A MILLION DREAMS AGO.................... *Bluebird B-10768* 3-5 40
(Vocals: Ray Eberle)

BLUE MOONLIGHT / MY PRAYER ... *Bluebird B-10404* 3-5 39
(Vocals: Ray Eberle)

BLUE ORCHIDS (Vocal: Ray Eberle) / BABY ME (Vocal: Kay Starr)......... *Bluebird B-10372* 3-5 39

BLUE RAIN / WHO'S SORRY NOW? ... *Bluebird B-10486* 3-5 39
(Vocals: Ray Eberle)

BLUES SERENADE, A / MOONLIGHT ON THE GANGES............... *Columbia 3051-D* 20-25 35
(Vocals: Smith Ballew)
(This record was pressed in blue shellac)

BOULDER BUFF / THE BOOGLIE WOOGLIE PIGGY (Vocals: Tex Beneke, The Modernaires, & Paula Kelly) .... *Bluebird B-11163* 3-6 41

BUT IT DIDN'T MEAN A THING (Vocal: Marion Hutton) / RUNNIN' WILD.................... *Bluebird B-10269* 3-5 39

BY THE WATERS OF MINNETONKA (Vocals: by orchestra) / BY THE WATERS OF MINNETONKA, PART II........... *Bluebird B-7870* 3-5 38

CALL OF THE CANYON / OUR LOVE AFFAIR.............. *Bluebird B-10845* 3-5 40
(Vocals: Ray Eberle)

CAN I HELP IT? (Vocal: Ray Eberle) / I JUST GOT A LETTER (Vocal: Marion Hutton)...... *Bluebird B-10448* 4-6 39

CARELESS / VAGABOND DREAMS... *Bluebird B-10520* 3-5 39
(Vocals: Ray Eberle)

CINDERELLA (STAY IN MY ARMS) / MOON LOVE.................... *Bluebird B-10303* 3-5 39
(Vocals: Ray Eberle)

CONCHITA, MARGUITA, LOLITA, PEPITA, ROSITA, JUANITA LOPEZ (Vocals: Marion Hutton, Tex Beneke, & The Modernaires) / LONG TALL MAMA... *Victor 27943* 4-6 42

COWBOY SERENADE, THE (Vocal: Ray Eberle) / BELOW THE EQUATOR (Vocals: Ray Eberle & The Modernaires)................ *Bluebird B-11235* 4-6 41

CROSSTOWN (Vocal: Jack Lathrop) / WHAT'S YOUR STORY, MORNING GLORY (Vocal: Tex Beneke) .... *Bluebird B-10832* 4-6 40

CUCKOO IN THE CLOCK / ROMANCE RUNS IN THE FAMILY......................... *Bluebird B-10145* 5-8 39
(Vocals: Marion Hutton)

DAY DREAMING (Vocals: Ray Eberle & The Modernaires) / A STRING OF PEARLS........... *Bluebird B-11382* 2-4 41

DEAR ANABELLA (Vocals: Marion Hutton, Tex Beneke, & The Modernaires) / ORANGE BLOSSOM LANE (Vocal: Ray Eberle).................. *Bluebird B-11326* 5-8 41

DEARLY BELOVED / I'M OLD-FASHIONED .... *Victor 27953* 3-5 42
(Vocals: Skip Nelson)

DEAR MOM (Vocals: Ray Eberle & The Modernaires) / KEEP 'EM FLYING.................. *Bluebird B-11443* 5-8 42

DEVIL MAY CARE / I'M STEPPING OUT WITH A MEMORY TONIGHT............ *Bluebird B-10717* 3-5 40
(Vocals: Ray Eberle)

DON'T CRY, CHERIE (Vocal: Ray Eberle) / SWEETER THAN THE SWEETEST (Vocals: Paula Kelly & The Modernaires) .... *Bluebird B-11183* 3-5 41

DON'T WAKE UP MY HEART (Vocal: Ray Eberle) / WHY'D YA MAKE ME FALL IN LOVE? (Vocal: Gail Reese) .... *Brunswick 8152* 12-15 38

DO YOU KNOW WHY (Vocal: Ray Eberle) / ISN'T THAT JUST LIKE LOVE (Vocal: Jack Lathrop)................ *Bluebird B-10936* 5-8 40

DREAMSVILLE, OHIO (Vocals: Ray Eberle & The Modernaires) / PAPA NICCOLINI (Vocals: Ray Eberle, Tex Beneke, & The Modernaires) .... *Bluebird B-11342* 4-6 41

ELMER'S TUNE (Vocals: Ray Eberle, & The Modernaires) / DELILAH (Vocals: Tex Beneke & The Modernaires)..................... *Bluebird B-11274* 3-5 41

EVERY DAY'S A HOLIDAY / SWEET STRANGER............... *Brunswick 8041* 12-15 37
(Vocals: Kathleen Lane)

EV'RYTHING I LOVE / BABY MINE... *Bluebird B-11365* 3-5 41
(Vocals: Ray Eberle)

FAITHFUL FOREVER (Vocal: Ray Eberle) / BLUEBIRDS IN THE MOONLIGHT (Vocal: Marion Hutton).............. *Bluebird B-10465* 3-5 39

FAITHFUL TO YOU / IT'S A BLUE WORLD..................... *Bluebird B-10536* 3-5 40
(Vocals: Ray Eberle)

FOOLED (Vocal: Ray Eberle) / IT HAPPENED IN HAWAII (Vocals: Ray Eberle & The Modernaires)... *Bluebird B-11416* 4-6 42

FOOLS RUSH IN (Vocal: Ray Eberle) / YOURS IS MY HEART ALONE.... *Bluebird B-10728* 3-5 40

FRENESI / MY BLUE HEAVEN.... *Bluebird B-10994* 3-5 41

FROM ONE LOVE TO ANOTHER / I'M THRILLED.................. *Bluebird B-11287* 4-6 41
(Vocals: Ray Eberle)

GIVE A LITTLE WHISTLE (Vocal: Marion Hutton) / THE SKY FELL DOWN.......... *Bluebird B-10580* 3-5 40

GLENN MILLER AND HIS ORCHESTRA Limited Edition, Volume One (45 rpm)........... *RCA Victor (M) SPD-18* 40-45 55
(a 10-record boxed set)

GUESS I'LL GO BACK HOME (Vocal: Tex Beneke) / SLIP HORN JIVE................ *Bluebird B-10317* 3-5 39

HANDFUL OF STARS, A / YESTERTHOUGHTS .... *Bluebird B-10893* 3-5 40
(Vocals: Ray Eberle)

HEAR MY SONG, VIOLETTA / STARLIGHT AND MUSIC......... *Bluebird B-10684* 3-5 40
(Vocals: Ray Eberle)

HELPLESS (Vocal: Ray Eberle) / WHEN JOHNNY COMES MARCHING HOME (Vocals: Tex Beneke, Marion Hutton, & The Modernaires) .... *Victor 20-1600* 3-5 44
(The first side is a 1940 recording first released in 1944, and the second side is a reissue from Bluebird B-11480.)

HOW AM I TO KNOW? (Vocal: Doris Kerr) / MOONLIGHT BAY (Vocals: by orchestra).... *Decca 1239* 15-20 37

HUMORESQUE / DOIN' THE JIVE (Vocals: Kathleen Lane & band with dialog between Glenn Miller & Chummy MacGregor)............... *Brunswick 8062* 15-20 38

HUMPTY DUMPTY HEART / THIS IS NO LAUGHING MATTER............ *Bluebird B-11369* 3-5 41
(Vocals: Ray Eberle)

I'D KNOW YOU ANYWHERE (Vocal: Ray Eberle) / YOU'VE GOT ME THIS WAY (Vocal: Marion Hutton).............. *Bluebird B-10906* 3-5 40

I DO, DO YOU? / YOU ARE THE ONE....................... *Bluebird B-11020* 4-6 41
(Vocals: Ray Eberle)

I DREAMT I DWELT IN HARLEM / A STONE'S THROW FROM HEAVEN (Vocal: Ray Eberle)................. *Bluebird B-11063* 4-6 41

I GOT RHYTHM / TIME ON MY HANDS....................... *Brunswick 7915* 15-20 37

I GUESS I'LL HAVE TO DREAM THE REST (Vocal: Ray Eberle) / TAKE THE "A" TRAIN ... *Bluebird B-11187* 3-5 41

I KNOW WHY (Vocals: Paula Kelly and The Modernaires) / CHATTANOOGA CHOO CHOO (Vocals: Tex Beneke, The Modernaires, & Paula Kelly)........... *Bluebird B-11230* 2-4 41
(This was the first "Gold Record" ever awarded. In commemoration of the first million-selling record since 1927, officials from RCA Victor presented a gold-plated recording of "Chattanooga Choo Choo" to Glenn Miller on Feb. 10, 1942. This was the beginning of the Gold Record concept, the practice of awarding a Gold Record to an artist whose recording had sold a million or more copies.)

IMAGINATION (Vocal: Ray Eberle) / SAY "SI SI" (Vocal: Marion Hutton) ... *Bluebird B-10622* 3-5 40

I'M SORRY FOR MYSELF (Vocals: Marion Hutton & Tex Beneke, with dialog between Glenn Miller & Tex Beneke) / BACK TO BACK (Vocal: Marion Hutton).............. *Bluebird B-10299* 4-6 39

IN A LITTLE SPANISH TOWN / SOLO HOP....................... *Columbia 3058-D* 20-25 35

IN AN OLD DUTCH GARDEN (BY AN OLD DUTCH MILL) / STARLIT HOUR.......... *Bluebird B-10553* 3-5 40
(Vocals: Ray Eberle)

INDIAN SUMMER (Vocal: Ray Eberle) / FAREWELL BLUES.............. *Bluebird B-10495* 3-5 39

IN THE MOOD / I WANT TO BE HAPPY .... *Bluebird B-10416* 2-4 39

IT HAPPENED IN SUN VALLEY (Vocals: Paula Kelly, Ray Eberle, Tex Beneke, & The Modernaires) / THE KISS POLKA (Vocals: Paula Kelly, Ernie Caceres, & The Modernaires) .... *Bluebird B-11263* 3-5 41

IT MUST BE JELLY ('CAUSE JAM DON'T SHAKE LIKE THAT) (Vocals: The Modernaires) / RAINBOW RHAPSODY.............. *Victor 20-1546* 3-5 44

IT'S ALWAYS YOU (Vocal: Ray Eberle) / IDA! SWEET AS APPLE CIDER (Vocal: Tex Beneke)... *Bluebird B-11079* 2-4 41

IT WAS WRITTEN IN THE STARS (Vocal: Ray Eberle) / JOHNSON RAG.................. *Bluebird B-10498* 2-4 40

I WOULDN'T TAKE A MILLION (Vocal: Ray Eberle) / FIFTH AVENUE (Vocals: Marion Hutton & Tex Beneke) .... *Bluebird B-10860* 4-6 40

JINGLE BELLS (Vocals: Tex Beneke, Ernie Caseras, & The Modernaires) / SANTA CLAUS IS COMIN' TO TOWN (by Alvino Rey & His Orchestra; Vocals: The Four King Sisters)......... *Bluebird B-11353* 4-6 41

JUKE BOX SATURDAY NIGHT (Vocals: Marion Hutton, Tex Beneke, & The Modernaires) / SLEEPY TOWN TRAIN............. *Victor 20-1509* 2-4 42

(I'VE GOT A GAL IN) KALAMAZOO (Vocals: Tex Beneke, Marion Hutton, & The Modernaires) / AT LAST (Vocal: Ray Eberle) ...... Victor 27934 2-4 42

KNIT ONE, PURL TWO (Vocals: Marion Hutton & The Modernaires) / LULLABY OF THE RAIN (Vocals: Ray Eberle & The Modernaires) ...... Victor 27894 5-8 42

LAMP IS LOW, THE / BLUE EVENING ...... Bluebird B-10290 3-5 39 (Vocals: Ray Eberle)

LAMPLIGHTER'S SERENADE, THE (Vocals: Ray Eberle & The Modernaires) / DON'T SIT UNDER THE APPLE TREE (Vocals: Marion Hutton, Tex Beneke, & The Modernaires) ...... Bluebird B-11474 2-4 42

LET'S HAVE ANOTHER CUP O' COFFEE (Vocals: Marion Hutton, Ernie Caseras, & The Modernaires) / CHIP OFF THE OLD BLOCK ...... Bluebird B-11450 3-5 42

LITTLE BROWN JUG / PAVANNE ...... Bluebird B-10286 2-4 39

LITTLE OLD CHURCH IN ENGLAND, A (Vocals: Ray Eberle, Dorothy Claire, & The Modernaires) / WHEN THAT MAN IS DEAD AND GONE (Vocals: Tex Beneke, & The Modernaires) ...... Bluebird B-11069 5-8 41

MAKE BELIEVE BALLROOM TIME (Vocals: The Modernaires) / OLD BLACK JOE ...... Bluebird B-10913 3-5 40

MAN IN THE MOON, THE (Vocal: Ray Eberle) / MA-MA-MARIA (Vocals: Ray Eberle & The Modernaires) ...... Bluebird B-11299 3-5 41

MAN WITH THE MANDOLIN, THE (Vocal: Marion Hutton) / THE LITTLE MAN WHO WASN'T THERE (Vocal: Tex Beneke with dialog between Glenn Miller & Tex Beneke) ...... Bluebird B-10358 4-6 39

MELANCHOLY LULLABY / (WHY COULDN'T IT LAST) LAST NIGHT ...... Bluebird B-10423 3-5 39 (Vocals: Ray Eberle)

MEM'RY OF A ROSE / PRAIRIELAND LULLABY ...... Bluebird B-11011 3-5 41 (Vocals: Ray Eberle)

MISSOURI WALTZ / BEAUTIFUL OHIO ...... Bluebird B-10587 3-5 40

MOONLIGHT BECOMES YOU / MOONLIGHT MOOD ...... Victor 20-1520 3-5 44 (Vocals: Skip Nelson & The Modernaires)

MOONLIGHT COCKTAIL (Vocals: Ray Eberle & The Modernaires) / HAPPY IN LOVE (Vocal: Marion Hutton) ...... Bluebird B-11401 2-4 42

MOONLIGHT SONATA / SLUMBER SONG ...... Bluebird B-11386 2-4 42

MY FINE FEATHERED FRIEND / SILHOUETTED IN THE MOONLIGHT ...... Brunswick 8034 12-15 38 (Vocals: Kathleen Lane)

MY ISLE OF GOLDEN DREAMS / WHAM (RE-BOP-BOOM-BAM) (Vocals: Marion Hutton & band) ...... Bluebird B-10399 3-5 39

MY LAST GOODBYE (Vocal: Ray Eberle) / THE LADY'S IN LOVE WITH YOU (Vocal: Tex Beneke with dialog between Glenn Miller & Tex Beneke) ...... Bluebird B-10229 4-6 39

MY! MY! (Vocal: Marion Hutton) / SAY IT (Vocal: Ray Eberle) ...... Bluebird B-10631 3-5 40

MY REVERIE (Vocal: Ray Eberle) / KING PORTER STOMP ...... Bluebird B-7853 3-5 38

NEARNESS OF YOU, THE (Vocal: Ray Eberle) / MISTER MEADOWLARK (Vocal: Jack Lathrop) ...... Bluebird B-10745 3-5 40

OH JOHNNY, OH JOHNNY, OH! (Vocal: Marion Hutton) / CIRI-BIRI-BIN (Vocal: Ray Eberle) ...... Bluebird B-10507 2-4 40

OH, YOU CRAZY MOON (Vocal: Ray Eberle) / AIN'T CHA COMIN' OUT? (Vocals: Marion Hutton & Tex Beneke) ...... Bluebird B-10329 3-5 39

ON A LITTLE STREET IN SINGAPORE / THIS CHANGING WORLD ...... Bluebird B-10526 3-5 40 (Vocals: Ray Eberle)

ONE I LOVE (BELONGS TO SOMEBODY ELSE), THE (Vocals: Ray Eberle & The Modernaires) / SUN VALLEY JUMP ...... Bluebird B-11110 3-5 41

ON THE OLD ASSEMBLY LINE / WHEN JOHNNY COMES MARCHING HOME ...... Bluebird B-11480 4-6 42 (Vocals: Tex Beneke, Marion Hutton, & The Modernaires)

OOH! WHAT YOU SAID (Vocal: Marion Hutton) / I BEG YOUR PARDON (Vocal: Ray Eberle) ...... Bluebird B-10561 4-6 40

OUT OF SPACE / SO MANY TIMES ...... Bluebird B-10438 3-5 39 (Vocals: Ray Eberle)

OVER THE RAINBOW (Vocal: Ray Eberle) / DING-DONG! THE WITCH IS DEAD (Vocal: Marion Hutton) ...... Bluebird B-10366 4-6 39

PEEKABOO TO YOU (Vocals: The Modernaires & Paula Kelly) / CRADLE SONG (Vocals: Ray Eberle & chorus) ...... Bluebird B-11203 4-6 41

PEG O' MY HEART / I'M SITTIN' ON TOP OF THE WORLD ...... Decca 1342 15-20 37

PENNSYLVANIA SIX-FIVE THOUSAND / RUG CUTTER'S SWING ...... Bluebird B-10754 2-4 40

PERFIDIA (Vocals: Dorothy Claire & The Modernaires) / SPRING WILL BE SO SAD (Vocals: Ray Eberle & The Modernaires) ...... Bluebird B-11095 2-4 41

POLKA DOTS AND MOONBEAMS (Vocal: Ray Eberle) / WHAT'S THE MATTER WITH ME (Vocal: Marion Hutton) ...... Bluebird B-10657 3-5 40

RENDEZVOUS TIME IN PAREE (Vocal: Ray Eberle) / WE CAN LIVE ON LOVE (WE HAVEN'T GOT A POT TO COOK IN) (Vocal: Marion Hutton) ...... Bluebird B-10309 5-8 39

RHAPSODY IN BLUE / ALONG THE SANTA FE TRAIL (Vocal: Ray Eberle) ...... Victor 20-1529 3-5 42
(The first side is a 1940 recording first released in 1942, and the second side is a reissue from Bluebird B-10970.)

RHUMBA JUMPS, THE (Vocals: Marion Hutton & Tex Beneke) / I'LL NEVER SMILE AGAIN (Vocal: Ray Eberle) ...... Bluebird B-10673 5-8 40

SERENADE IN BLUE (Vocals: Ray Eberle & The Modernaires) / THAT'S SABOTAGE (Vocal: Marion Hutton) ...... Victor 27935 4-6 42

SHADOWS ON THE SAND (Vocal: Ray Eberle) / FIVE O'CLOCK WHISTLE (Vocals: Marion Hutton & band) ...... Bluebird B-10900 4-6 40

SHAKE DOWN THE STARS (Vocal: Ray Eberle) / BOOG-IT (Vocal: Marion Hutton) ...... Bluebird B-10689 3-5 40

SHE'LL ALWAYS REMEMBER (Vocals: Ray Eberle & The Modernaires) / SHHH, IT'S A MILITARY SECRET (Vocals: Marion Hutton, Tex Beneke, & The Modernaires) ...... Bluebird B-11493 5-8 42

(GOTTA GET SOME) SHUT-EYE (Vocal: Marion Hutton) / HOW I'D LIKE TO BE WITH YOU IN BERMUDA (Vocal: Ray Eberle) ...... Bluebird B-10139 4-6 39

SIERRA SUE / MOMENTS IN THE MOONLIGHT ...... Bluebird B-10638 3-5 40 (Vocals: Ray Eberle)

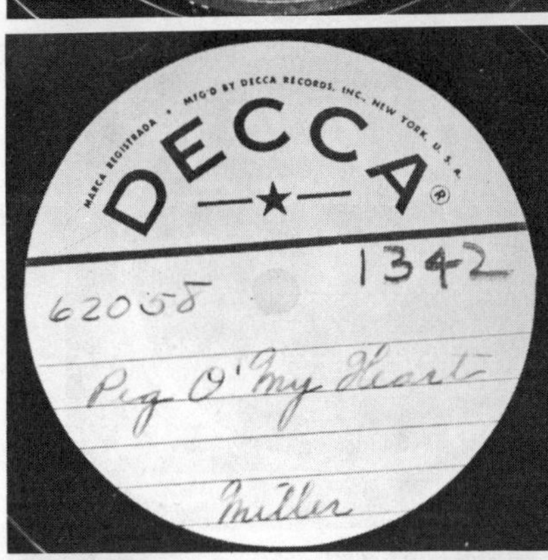

RARE TEST CUTS OF DECCA 1342

SLEEPY-TIME GAL / COMMUNITY SWING ...... Brunswick 7923 15-20 37

SLOW FREIGHT / BUGLE CALL RAG ...... Bluebird B-10740 3-5 40

SOLD AMERICAN / DIPPER MOUTH BLUES ...... Brunswick 8173 15-20 38 (Vocals: by orchestra)

SOLD AMERICAN (Vocals: by orchestra) / PAGAN LOVE SONG ...... Bluebird B-10352 3-5 39

SOMEWHERE (Vocal: Ray Eberle) / FRESH AS A DAISY (Vocals: Marion Hutton, Jack Lathrop, & Tex Beneke) ...... Bluebird B-10959 3-5 40

SONG OF THE VOLGA BOATMAN / CHAPEL IN THE VALLEY (Vocal: Ray Eberle) ...... Bluebird B-10029 3-5 40

SPIRIT IS WILLING, THE / THE AIR MINDED EXECUTIVE (Vocals: Tex Beneke, Dorothy Claire, & the band) ...... Bluebird B-11135 3-5 41

STAIRWAY TO THE STARS / TO YOU ...... Bluebird B-10276 3-5 39 (Vocals: Ray Eberle)

STARDUST / MY MELANCHOLY BABY (Vocal: Tex Beneke) ...... Bluebird B-10665 3-5 40

STORY OF A STARRY NIGHT, THE / SKYLARK ...... Bluebird B-11462 3-5 42 (Vocals: Ray Eberle)

SUNRISE SERENADE / MOONLIGHT SERENADE (theme song) ...... Bluebird B-10214 2-4 39
(Glenn Miller was co-composer of Moonlight Serenade, his theme song)

SWEET ELOISE / SLEEP SONG ...... Victor 27879 2-4 42 (Vocals: Ray Eberle & The Modernaires)

THAT OLD BLACK MAGIC (Vocals: Skip Nelson & The Modernaires) / A PINK COCKTAIL FOR A BLUE LADY (Vocal: Skip Nelson) ...... Victor 20-1523 2-4 44

THREE LITTLE FISHIES (Vocals: Marion Hutton, Tex Beneke, & band) / WISHING (WILL MAKE IT SO) (Vocal: Ray Eberle) ...... Bluebird B-10219 3-5 39

THIS TIME THE DREAM'S ON ME (Vocal: Ray Eberle) / SAYS WHO? SAYS YOU, SAYS I! (Vocals: Marion Hutton, Tex Beneke, & The Modernaires) ...... Bluebird B-11315 2-4 41

TOO ROMANTIC (Vocal: Ray Eberle) / SWEET POTATO PIPER (Vocals: Marion Hutton & Tex Beneke) ...... Bluebird B-10605 3-5 40

TUXEDO JUNCTION / DANNY BOY (LONDONDERRY AIR) ...... Bluebird B-10612 2-4 40

TWILIGHT INTERLUDE (Vocal: Ray Eberle) / GLEN ISLAND SPECIAL ...... Bluebird B-10388 3-5 39

UNDER BLUE CANADIAN SKIES (Vocal: Ray Eberle) / ADIOS ...... Bluebird B-11219 2-4 41

WANNA HAT WITH CHERRIES (Vocal: Marion Hutton) / THE DAY WE MEET AGAIN (Vocal: Ray Eberle) ...... Bluebird B-10344 4-6 39

WHEN THE SWALLOWS COME BACK TO CAPISTRANO (Vocal: Ray Eberle) / A CABANA IN HAVANA (Vocal: Marion Hutton) ...... Bluebird B-10776 3-5 40

WHEN YOU WISH UPON A STAR / GAUCHO SERENADE ...... Bluebird B-10570 4-6 40 (Vocals: Ray Eberle)

(THERE'LL BE BLUE BIRDS OVER) WHITE CLIFFS OF DOVER, THE / WE'RE THE COUPLE IN THE CASTLE ...... Bluebird B-11397 4-6 41 (Vocals: Ray Eberle)

WISTFUL AND BLUE (Vocal: Doris Kerr) / ANYTIME, ANYDAY, ANYWHERE (Vocals: Sterling Bose & The Tune Twisters) ...... Decca 1284 15-20 37

WOODPECKER SONG, THE / LET'S ALL SING TOGETHER ...... Bluebird B-10598 3-5 40 (Vocals: Marion Hutton)

YESTERDAY'S GARDENIAS (Vocals: Ray Eberle & The Modernaires) / THE HUMMING-BIRD (Vocals: Marion Hutton, Tex Beneke, & The Modernaires) ...... Victor 27933 5-8 42

YOU AND I / THE ANGELS CAME THRU ...... Bluebird B-11215 2-4 41 (Vocals: Ray Eberle)

YOU STEPPED OUT OF A DREAM (Vocals: Ray Eberle & The Modernaires) / RING, TELEPHONE, RING (Vocal: Ray Eberle) ...... Bluebird B-11042 4-6 41

GLENN MILLER ORCHESTRA, The
directed by Tex Beneke

BLUES OF THE RECORD MAN, THE (Vocal: Tex Beneke) / WHY DON'T WE SAY WE'RE SORRY? (Vocals: Garry Stevens, Tex Beneke, & The Mello Larks) ...... RCA Victor 20-2190 2-4 47

GIRL THAT I REMEMBER, A (Vocal: Garry Stevens) / SURPRISE SYMPHONY ...... RCA Victor 20-2497 2-4 47

HOODLE ADDLE (Vocal: Tex Beneke) / ANNIVERSARY SONG (Vocal: Garry Stevens) ...... RCA Victor 20-2126 2-4 47

OH, BUT I DO (Vocal: Artie Malvin) / A GAL IN CALICO (Vocal: Tex Beneke) ...... RCA Victor 20-1991 2-4 47

SPEAKING OF ANGELS / IT MIGHT HAVE BEEN A DIFFERENT STORY ...... RCA Victor 20-2123 2-4 47 (Vocals: Garry Stevens)

WOODCHUCK SONG, THE (Vocal: Tex Beneke) / PASSE (Vocal: Lillian Lane) ...... RCA Victor 20-1951 2-4 47

MILLER, Ray, & His Hotel Gibson Orchestra

BLUE BABY / YEP! 'LONG ABOUT JUNE ...... Brunswick 3676 5-8 27 (Vocals: Ray Miller, Mort Clavner & Cookie Trantham)

I AIN'T GOT NOBODY (Vocal: Ray Miller) / WEARY BLUES ...... Brunswick 3677 5-8 27

IS SHE MY GIRL FRIEND? / I WISH I COULD SHIMMY LIKE MY SISTER KATE ...... Brunswick 3829 5-8 28

SORRY / MY HONEY'S LOVIN' ARMS ...... Brunswick 3828 5-8 27

MILLER, Ray, & His Orchestra

ANYTHING YOU SAY / IF I HAD YOU.................... *Brunswick 4077* 3-5 28
(Vocals: Harry Maxfield)

BAGDAD / RED HOT MAMA......... *Brunswick 2681* 5-8 24

BECAUSE OF YOU / BREEZIN' ALONG (TO GEORGIA) .... *Brunswick 2947* 3-5 25

BENEATH MONTANA SKIES / MONTANA .... *Brunswick 4857* 2-4 30
(Vocals: Unknown)

BLUE HOOSIER BLUES / MARCH OF THE MANNIKINS.............. *Columbia A-3926* 2-4 23

BY THE LAKE / NOBODY KNOWS WHAT A RED-HEAD MAMA CAN DO............ *Brunswick 2778* 5-8 25

DEEDLE DEEDLE DUM / I'M JUST WILD ABOUT HARRY............ *Columbia A-3640* 2-4 22

DOODLE-DOO-DOO / ADORING YOU... *Brunswick 2724* 4-6 24

HARLEM MADNESS / AIN'T YOU, BABY?................ *Brunswick 4692* 4-6 30
(Vocals: Dusty Rhodes)

HOOSIER HOP / NOBODY'S USING IT NOW.......................... *Brunswick 4687* 4-6 30

I CAN'T GET THE ONE I WANT (THOSE I GET I DON'T WANT) / SALLY LOU............ *Brunswick 2643* 5-8 24

INDIAN LOVE CALL / YOU AND I ... *Brunswick 2789* 3-5 25

IN MY GARDEN OF MEMORY / DREAMING THE WALTZ AWAY................ *Brunswick 3313* 2-4 26

I WANT YOU TO WANT ME TO WANT YOU / OH! OH! WHAT A NIGHT .... *Brunswick 3133* 4-6 26

JUST A LITTLE DRINK / MOONLIGHT AND ROSES......... *Brunswick 2866* 3-5 25
(Vocals: Frank Wright & Frank Bessinger)

KISS ME WITH YOUR EYES / WHEN IT'S SPRINGTIME IN THE ROCKIES.... *Brunswick 4735* 3-5 30
(Vocals: Unknown)

LONELY LITTLE MELODY / SOMEBODY LOVES ME........... *Brunswick 2669* 4-6 24

LOTS O' MAMA / FROM ONE TILL TWO (I ALWAYS DREAM OF YOU)................ *Brunswick 2613* 5-8 24

MAMA'S GONE, GOODBYE / WHERE IS THAT OLD GIRL OF MINE? (Vocal: Billy Jones) ... *Brunswick 2632* 5-8 24

MINDIN' MY BUS'NESS / IF YOU'LL COME BACK...................... *Brunswick 2564* 3-5 24

NINE O'CLOCK SAL / TWO BLUE EYES .... *Brunswick 2573* 3-5 24

ON THE WAY TO MONTEREY / THAT'S MY GIRL................ *Brunswick 2823* 3-5 25

PLEASE / CHARLESTON CABIN .... *Brunswick 2666* 3-5 24

RED HOT HENRY BROWN / LET IT RAIN – LET IT POUR .... *Brunswick 2855* 5-8 25

ROSE OF MANDALAY (Vocal: Bob Nolan) / WHO WOULDN'T BE JEALOUS OF YOU? (Vocal: Dick Teela) .... *Brunswick 4131* 4-6 29

STOMP YOUR STUFF / THE SIGN OF THE ROSE .... *Brunswick 3132* 5-8 26

TESSIE (STOP TEASING ME) / WILL YOU REMEMBER ME?................. *Brunswick 2830* 4-6 25

THAT'S A PLENTY / ANGRY (Vocal: Bob Nolan) .... *Brunswick 4224* 5-8 29

WE'RE BACK TOGETHER AGAIN / I'LL TAKE HER BACK IF SHE WANTS TO COME BACK (Vocal: Irving Kaufman).... *Brunswick 2847* 3-5 25

MILLER, Ray, as Ray Miller's Black And White Melody Boys

BEALE STREET BLUES / MAKE BELIEVE .... *Okeh 4274* 4-6 21

BRIGHT EYES / MOLLY.................. *Okeh 4251* 2-4 20

CAN YOU TELL? / ROSE OF SPAIN ... *Vocalion 14106* 3-5 20

DOO DAH BLUES / LOLA LO .... *Columbia A-3563* 3-5 22

HUMMING / WITHOUT YOU .... *Cardinal 2035* 3-5 21

LOOK FOR THE SILVER LINING / NIGHTINGALE......... *Grey Gull L-1050* 2-4 21

LOVEY DOVE / DO IT AGAIN ...... *Columbia A-3595* 2-4 22

MOLLY / TWO SWEET LIPS........... *Cardinal 2034* 3-5 21

ROSE OF SPAIN / JUNE............... *Gennett 9075* 3-5 20

SWEET LAVENDER / CONGO NIGHTS.... *Okeh 4277* 2-4 21

'TWAS IN THE MERRY MONTH OF MAY / PARADE OF THE WOODEN SOLDIERS .... *Columbia A-3628* 2-4 22

WEEP NO MORE (MY MAMMY) / THE SHEIK..................... *Columbia A-3519* 3-5 21

WITHOUT YOU / SANDMAN BLUES ...... *Okeh 4304* 3-5 21

MILLINDER, Lucky, & His Orchestra
(Lucky Millinder: 8/8/00 – 9/28/66)

APOLLO JUMP / ARE YOU READY? (Vocals: Trevor Bacon & chorus)............................ *Decca 18529* 3-5 42

FIGHTIN' DOUG MAC ARTHUR / WE'RE GONNA HAVE TO SLAP THE DIRTY LITTLE JAP.................... *Decca 4261* 4-6 42
(Vocals: Trevor Bacon & orchestra)

LET ME OFF UPTOWN (Vocal: Trevor Bacon) / HOW ABOUT THAT MESS?............. *Decca 4099* 3-5 41

MASON FLYER / LITTLE JOHN SPECIAL................. *Brunswick 03406* 5-8 42
(British release)

RIDE, RED, RIDE (theme song) (Vocal: Lucky Millinder) / HEY HUSS (Vocals: Trevor Bacon & orchestra)........... *Decca 4146* 3-5 42

ROCK ME (Vocal: Sister Rosetta Tharpe) / SAVOY (Vocals: Trevor Bacon & orchestra)... *Decca 18353* 3-5 42

SHOUT, SISTER, SHOUT / I WANT A TALL SKINNY PAPA .... *Decca 18386* 3-5 42
(Vocals: Sister Rosetta Tharpe)

SLIDE, MR. TROMBONE (Vocal: Trevor Bacon) / ROCK, DANIEL (Vocal: Sister Rosetta Tharpe) ...... *Decca 3956* 3-5 41

THAT'S ALL (Vocal: Sister Rosetta Tharpe) / WHEN THE LIGHTS GO ON AGAIN (Vocal: Trevor Bacon) .... *Decca 18496* 4-6 42

TROUBLE IN MIND (Vocal: Sister Rosetta Tharpe) / BIG FAT MAMA (Vocal: Trevor Bacon).......... *Decca 4041* 3-5 41

TROUBLE IN MIND / THAT'S ALL .... *V-Disc 129* 8-10
(Vocals: Sister Rosetta Tharpe)
(A World War II release)

MILLS CAVALCADE ORCHESTRA: The,
see BRUNIS, George

MILLS, Floyd, & His Marylanders

HARD LUCK / CHICAGO RHYTHM..... *Gennett 6909* 12-15 29

ON DONNA CLARA / NINETY-NINE OUT OF A HUNDRED (WANNA BE LOVED) (Vocal: Clem Garity) .... *Superior 2664* 5-8 31

OUT OF NOWHERE (Vocal: David Gotwals, Jr.) / OH DONNA CLARA.............. *Champion 16265* 5-8 31

MILLS, Floyd, & His Marylanders as Geroge Drew & His Orchestra

HARD LUCK / CHICAGO RHYTHM..... *Superior 2829* 10-12 29

MILLS, Floyd, & His Marylanders as The Hottentots

HARD LUCK / CHICAGO RHYTHM.... *Supertone 9447* 10-12 29

MILLS, Floyd, & His Marylanders as Red Owens & His Band

HARD LUCK / CHICAGO RHYTHM.... *Champion 16423* 10-12 29

MILLS, Irving, & His Hotsy Totsy Gang / The Hotsy Totsy Gang
(Irving Mills: 1/16/94 – 4/85)

AIN'T MISBEHAVIN' / DOIN' THE NEW LOW DOWN..................... *Brunswick 4535* 10-12 29
(Both sides feature tap dancing by Bill "Bojangles" Robinson)

CAN'T WE GET TOGETHER? / SWEET SAVANNAH SUE................. *Brunswick 4482* 10-12 29
(Vocals: Lillian Morton)

CRAZY 'BOUT MY GAL / RAILROAD MAN................. *Brunswick 4838* 10-12 30

DEEP HARLEM / STRUT, MISS LIZZIE (Vocal: Dick Robertson) .... *Brunswick 4983* 20-25 30

DOIN' THE NEW LOW DOWN / DIGA DIGA DOO .... *Brunswick 4014* 10-12 28
(Vocals: Elizabeth Welch)

FUTURISTIC RHYTHM / OUT WHERE THE BLUES BEGIN .... *Brunswick 4200* 10-12 29
(Vocals: Smith Ballew)

HARVEY (Vocal: Hoagy Carmichael) / MARCH OF THE HOODLUMS...... *Brunswick 4559* 10-12 29

HIGH AND DRY (Vocal: Hoagy Carmichael) / BARBARIC .... *Brunswick 4920* 10-12 30

MANHATTAN RAG / WHAT KIND OF MAN IS YOU?................ *Brunswick 4641* 8-10 30

WHAT A NIGHT! (Vocals: Unknown) / I WONDER WHAT MY GAL IS DOIN?................ *Brunswick 4998* 8-10 30

MILLS, Irving, & His Hotsy Totsy Gang as Jimmy Bracken's Toe Ticklers

FOUR OR FIVE TIMES / ICKY BLUES (by Irving Mills & His Hotsy Totsy Gang as The Kentucky Grasshoppers; Vocal: Dick Morgan) .... *Conqueror 7303* 10-12 29

ICKY BLUES (Vocals: Dick Morgan as Icky Morgan) / FOUR OR FIVE TIMES .... *Domino 4278* 10-12 29

SHIRT TAIL STOMP / IT'S TIGHT LIKE THAT (Vocal: Jack Teagarden)...... *Domino 4274* 10-12 29

MILLS, Irving, & His Hotsy Totsy Gang as Lou Connor's Collegians

IT'S TIGHT LIKE THAT (Vocal: Jack Teagarden) / FOUR OR FIVE TIMES .... *Jewel 5520* 10-12 29

IT'S TIGHT LIKE THAT (Vocal: Jack Teagarden) / FOUR OR FIVE TIMES................ *Oriole 1483* 10-12 29
(Simultaneously released on two labels)

MILLS, Irving, & His Hotsy Totsy Gang as The Kentucky Grasshoppers

ICKY BLUES (Vocal: Dick Morgan) / FOUR OR FIVE TIMES (by Irving Mills & His Hotsy Totsy Gang as Jimmy Bracken's Toe Ticklers)........... *Conqueror 7303* 10-12 29

IT'S TIGHT LIKE THAT (Vocal: Jack Teagarden) / FOUR OR FIVE TIMES................ *Banner 6295* 10-12 29

MILLS, Irving, & His Orchestra as Mills' Merry Makers

MOANIN' LOW (Vocal: Al Shayne as Roy Stewart) / MILWAUKEE WALK................. *Cameo 9203* 8-10 29

MOANIN' LOW (Vocal: Al Shayne as Roy Stewart) / MILWAUKEE WALK................ *Lincoln 3230* 8-10 29

MOANIN' LOW (Vocal: Al Shayne as Roy Stewart) / MILWAUKEE WALK................. *Romeo 1005* 8-10 29
(Simultaneously released on three labels)

MILLS, Irving, as Goody's Good Timers recorded under the name The Dixie Daisies

DIGA DIGA DOO / 'CAUSE I'M IN LOVE .... *Cameo 9004* 8-10 29
(Vocals: Irving Mills)

DIGA DIGA DOO / 'CAUSE I'M IN LOVE .... *Lincoln 3033* 8-10 29
(Vocals: Irving Mills)

DIGA DIGA DOO / 'CAUSE I'M IN LOVE .... *Romeo 808* 8-10 29
(Vocals: Irving Mills)
(Simultaneously released on three labels)

MILLS, Irving, as Mills' Merry Makers recorded under the name Jimmy Bracken's Toe Ticklers

AFTER YOU'VE GONE (Vocal: Jack Kaufman) / TWELFTH STREET RAG (Vocal: Dick Morgan) .... *Banner 6441* 10-12 29

MILLS, Irving, as Mills' Merry Makers recorded under the name The Dixie Jazz Band

AFTER YOU'VE GONE (Vocal: Jack Kaufman) / TWELFTH STREET RAG (Vocal: Dick Morgan) .... *Jewel 5648* 10-12 29

AFTER YOU'VE GONE (Vocal: Jack Kaufman) / TWELFTH STREET RAG (Vocal: Dick Morgan)....................... *Oriole 1624* 10-12 29
(Simultaneously released on two labels)

MILLS, Irving, as Mills' Merry Makers recorded under the name The Whoopee Makers

TWELFTH STREET RAG (Vocal: Dick Morgan) / IT'S SO GOOD (Vocal: Jack Teagarden) ..... *Pathe Actuelle 37036* 10-12 29

TWELFTH STREET RAG (Vocal: Dick Morgan) / IT'S SO GOOD (Vocal: Jack Teagarden)............ *Perfect 15217* 8-10 29
(Simultaneously released on two labels)

MILLS, Irving, as Mills' Musical Clowns

FUTURISTIC RHYTHM / OUT WHERE THE BLUES BEGIN........................ *Pathe Actuelle 36944* 10-12 29
(Vocals: Mildred Roselle)

FUTURISTIC RHYTHM / OUT WHERE THE BLUES BEGIN .... *Perfect 15125* 8-10 29
(Vocals: Mildred Roselle)
(Simultaneously released on two labels)

I USED TO LOVE HER IN THE MOONLIGHT (Vocals: Billy Murray & Walter Scanlan) / WIPIN' THE PAN (Vocal: Irving Kaufman) .... *Pathe Actuelle 36974* 5-8 29

I USED TO LOVE HER IN THE MOONLIGHT (Vocals: Billy Murray & Walter Scanlan) / WIPIN' THE PAN (Vocal: Irving Kaufman).................. *Perfect 15155* 4-6 29
(Simultaneously released on two labels)

MILLS, Irving, as Mills' Swingphonic Orchestra

LULLABY TO A LAMP POST / AT A CUBAN CABARET .... *Master 119* 5-8 37

MERRY WIDOW ON A SPREE / DEAR, DEAR, WHAT CAN THE MATTER BE? .... *Master 126* 5-8 37

MILLS' MERRY MAKERS:
see LANIN, Sam, & His Orchestra
see MILLS, Irving, and
see MILLS, Irving, & His Orchestra

MILLS' MUSICAL CLOWNS:
see MILLS, Irving

MILLS' SWINGPHONIC ORCHESTRA:
see MILLS, Irving

MILLS' TEN BLACK BERRIES:
see ELLINGTON, Duke, & His Cotton Club Orchestra

MISSOURI JAZZ BAND, The:
see SAMUELS, Joseph, & His Orchestra
see SCHUBERT, Adrian, & His Salon Orchestra
see SELVIN, Ben, & His Orchestra, and
see SISSLE, Noble, & His Orchestra

MISSOURI JAZZ HOUNDS, The:
see SAMUELS, Joseph, as Joseph Samuels' Melody Masters

MITCHELL, Al, & His Orchestra

HOME TIES / DANCING WITH MY SHADOW .... *Bluebird B-5732* 3-5 35
(Vocals: Dick Robertson)

ISLE OF CAPRI / HANDS ACROSS THE TABLE .... *Bluebird B-5729* 4-6 35
(Vocals: Dick Robertson)

LULLABY IN BLUE / IN A SHELTER FROM A SHOWER .... *Bluebird B-5372* 3-5 34
(Vocals: Dick Robertson)

LULLABY IN BLUE / IN A SHELTER FROM A SHOWER .... *Sunrise S-3453* 10-12 34
(Vocals: Dick Robertson)
(Simultaneously released on two labels)

MITCHELL, Al, & His Orchestra as Sid Peltyn & Orchestra

LITTLE DUTCH MILL / DELTA BOUND .... *Bluebird B-5417* 4-6 34
(Vocals: Dick Robertson)

MITCHELL, Al, & His Orchestra as Leo Zollo & His Orchestra

OLD COVERED BRIDGE / ARMFUL O' SWEETNESS .... *Bluebird B-5415* 4-6 34
(Vocals: Dick Robertson)

MOBILE TRIO, The

STRUTTIN' JIM / LAST NIGHT ON THE BACK PORCH (Vocals: Unknown) ... *Gennett 5246* 3-5 23

MODERNISTS, The:
see GOODMAN, Benny, & His Music Hall Orchestra

MONARCH ORCHESTRA, The:
see RESER, Harry, as Harry Reser's Syncopators

MONDELLO, Toots, & His Orchestra
(Toots Mondello: circa 1910 –)

AT SUNDOWN / I'LL SEE YOU IN MY DREAMS .... *Brunswick 8105* 5-8 38

LET ME DAY DREAM / I LOVE YOU JUST BECAUSE .... *Brunswick 8094* 5-8 38
(Vocals: Barry McKinley)

LET THAT BE A LESSON TO YOU / THANKS FOR THE MEMORY .... *Brunswick 8031* 4-6 38
(Vocals: Barry McKinley)

ST. LOUIS GAL / LOUISIANA .... *Varsity 8118* 8-10 39

SWEET LORRAINE / BEYOND THE MOON .... *Varsity 8110* 8-10 39

YOU'RE IN LOVE WITH LOVE / NAUGHTY, NAUGHTY .... *Brunswick 8061* 5-8 38
(Vocals: Barry McKinley)

MONROE, Vaughn, & His Orchestra
(Vaughn Monroe: 10/7/11 – 5/21/73)

ACCIDENT'LY ON PURPOSE (Vocal: Johnny Turnbull) / THE LAST ROUND-UP
(Vocal: Vaughn Monroe) .... *Bluebird B-10997* 2-4 41

AREN'T YOU KIND OF GLAD WE DID? / CHANGING MY TUNE .... *Victor 20-1946* 2-4 46
(Vocals: Betty Norton & Vaughn Monroe)

CABIN IN THE SKY / YOU DANCED WITH DYNAMITE .... *Bluebird B-10966* 2-4 41
(Vocals: Vaughn Monroe)

COMING OUT PARTY / ALL I NEED IS YOU (Vocal: Marilyn Duke) .... *Victor 27910* 3-5 42

DADDY (Vocal: Marilyn Duke) / DON'T BE BLUE, LITTLE PAL, DON'T BE BLUE
(Vocal: Vaughn Monroe) .... *Bluebird B-11189* 2-4 41

DARDANELLA / THERE'LL BE SOME CHANGES MADE
(Vocal: Marilyn Duke) .... *Bluebird B-11025* 2-4 41

GENTLEMAN NEEDS A SHAVE, THE / IF YOU SEE MARGIE .... *Bluebird B-10798* 2-4 40
(Vocals: Vaughn Monroe)

HARVARD SQUARE / I GOT IT BAD AND THAT AIN'T GOOD (Vocal: Marilyn Duke) ... *Bluebird B-11310* 3-5 41

HIP HIP HOORAY (Vocals: The Four V's) / WHEN THE LIGHTS GO ON AGAIN (ALL OVER THE WORLD)
(Vocal: Vaughn Monroe) .... *Victor 27945* 3-5 42

HOW SOON? / TRUE .... *Victor 20-2523* 2-4 47
(Vocals: Vaughn Monroe & The Moon Maids)

IF I COULD BE THE SWEETHEART OF A GIRL LIKE YOU / IT'S MY LAZY DAY ...... *RCA Victor 20-3000* 2-4 47
(Vocals: Vaughn Monroe & The Moon Maids)

I GUESS I'LL BE ON MY WAY (Vocals: Vaughn Monroe) / I DON'T WANT TO WALK WITHOUT YOU (Vocal: Marilyn Duke) .... *Bluebird B-11399* 3-5 41

LAST TIME I SAW PARIS / HIGH ON A WINDY HILL .... *Bluebird B-10976* 2-4 41
(Vocals: Vaughn Monroe)

LET IT SNOW! LET IT SNOW! LET IT SNOW! / WHEN THE SANDMAN RIDES THE TRAIL .... *Victor 20-1759* 2-4 46
(Vocals: Vaughn Monroe & The Norton Sisters)

MAKE BELIEVE (Vocals: Vaughn Monroe) / THAT LUCKY OLD SUN (Vocal: Vaughn Monroe & The Moon Men) .... *RCA Victor 20-3531* 2-4 49

MUSIC MAKERS / G'BYE NOW ..... *Bluebird B-11114* 2-4 41
(Vocals: Marilyn Duke)

MY DEVOTION (Vocal: Vaughn Monroe) / WHEN I GROW UP (Vocal: Ziggy Talent) .... *Victor 27925* 2-4 42

MY LITTLE COUSIN (Vocal: Marilyn Duke) / COMMODORE CLIPPER .... *Bluebird B-11488* 3-5 42

MY ONE ROMANCE (Vocal: Marilyn Duke) / TAKE IT, JACKSON .... *Bluebird B-11045* 3-5 41

NIGHTINGALE / A SOLDIER DREAMS (OF YOU TONIGHT) .... *Victor 27877* 3-5 42
(Vocals: Vaughn Monroe)

REQUESTFULLY YOURS (Vocals: Marilyn Duke & Vaughn Monroe) / RACING WITH THE MOON (theme song)
(Vocals: Vaughn Monroe) .... *Bluebird B-11070* 2-4 41

SALUD, DINERO Y AMOR (HEALTH, WEALTH AND LOVE) / THE DONKEY SERENADE .... *Bluebird B-10866* 2-4 40
(Vocals: Vaughn Monroe)

SEEING YOU AGAIN DID ME NO GOOD (Vocal: Vaughn Monroe) / ARTHUR MURRAY TAUGHT ME DANCING IN A HURRY (Vocal: Ziggy Talent) ... *Bluebird B-11441* 2-4 42

SINNER KISSED AN ANGEL, A / AND SO IT ENDED .... *Bluebird B-11361* 2-4 41
(Vocals: Vaughn Monroe)

SOMEBODY ELSE IS TAKING MY PLACE (Vocal: Vaughn Monroe) / HONEY DEAR
(Vocal: Marilyn Duke) .... *Bluebird B-11454* 2-4 42

TALLAHASSEE / I WISH I DIDN'T LOVE YOU SO .... *Victor 20-2294* 2-4 47
(Vocals: Vaughn Monroe & The Moon Maids)

THERE I GO / WHATEVER HAPPENED TO YOU? .... *Bluebird B-10848* 2-4 40
(Vocals: Vaughn Monroe)

THINGS WE DID LAST SUMMER, THE / MORE NOW THAN EVER (Vocals: Vaughn Monroe & The Moon Maids) .... *Victor 20-1972* 2-4 46

THIS IS WORTH FIGHTING FOR (Vocal: Vaughn Monroe) / THE CORPORAL TOLD THE PRIVATE
(Vocals: The Four V's) .... *Victor 27921* 3-5 42

THREE LITTLE SISTERS (Vocals: The Four V's) / BE BRAVE, BELOVED
(Vocal: Vaughn Monroe) .... *Bluebird B-11508* 3-5 42

TICA-TI — TICA-TA (Vocal: Marilyn Duke) / TANGERINE
(Vocal: Vaughn Monroe) .... *Bluebird B-11433* 2-4 42

TUNE TOWN SHUFFLE / ONE FOOT IN HEAVEN
(Vocal: Vaughn Monroe) .... *Bluebird B-11354* 3-5 41

TWO PAIR OF SHOES (Vocal: Mildred Law) / SAM, YOU MADE THE PANTS TOO LONG
(Vocal: Ziggy Talent) .... *Bluebird B-11260* 2-4 41

YOU WERE NEVER LOVELIER (Vocal: Marilyn Duke) / AFTER IT'S OVER (Vocal: Vaughn Monroe) ... *Victor 27958* 3-5 42

MOONEY, Art, & His Orchestra

AGAIN / FIVE FOOT TWO .... *MGM 10398* 2-4 48

BABY FACE / ENCORE, CHERIE .... *MGM 10156* 2-4 48

I'LL NEVER BE FREE (Vocals: The Skylarks) / TO THINK YOU'VE CHOSEN ME! (Vocals: Bob Manning & The Skylarks) .... *MGM 10839* 2-4 51

I'M LOOKING OVER A FOUR-LEAF CLOVER / BIG BRASS BAND FROM BRAZIL .... *MGM 10119* 2-4 48

KENTUCKY (Vocals: Cathy Ryan & The Cloverleafs) / 720 IN THE BOOKS (Vocal: Cathy Ryan) .... *MGM 11514* 2-4 57

LAZY RIVER / HONESTLY .... *MGM 11347* 2-4 55

MOGAMBO / OFF SHORE .... *MGM 11610* 2-4 57

SERENADE IN BLUE (Vocals: Matt DeLila & The Cloverleafs) / (I'M A DREAMER) AREN'T WE ALL?
(Vocals: The Cloverleafs) .... *MGM 10822* 2-4 51

SUNSET TO SUNRISE (theme song) / BLUEBIRD OF HAPPINESS .... *MGM 10207* 2-4 48

TOOT TOOT TOOTSIE / I NEVER SEE MAGGIE ALONE .... *MGM 10548* 2-4 49

MOONEY, Joe, as the Joe Mooney Quartet
(Joe Mooney: 1911 –)

LAZY COUNTRYSIDE (Vocal: Joe Mooney) / STARS IN MY EYES .... *Decca 24174* 2-4 47

MEET ME AT NO SPECIAL PLACE / I CAN'T GET UP THE NERVE TO KISS YOU .... *Decca 23909* 2-4 47
(Vocals: Joe Mooney)

SEPTEMBER SONG / JUST A GIGOLO ... *Decca 23790* 2-4 47
(Vocals: Joe Mooney)

TEA FOR TWO / WARM KISS AND A COLD HEART .... *Decca 23842* 2-4 47

MOORE, Phil, as Phil Moore's Orchestra
(Philip Moore: 2/20/18 –)

AND HER TEARS FLOWED LIKE WINE / MY BABY SAID YES .... *Victor 20-1624* 2-4 45

CONCERTO FOR TROMBONE / CONCERTO FOR TROMBONE, PART II .... *Discovery 1200* 3-5 49
(An oversize 12-inch 78 rpm)

CORNUCOPIA / 125TH STREET PROPHET .... *Discovery 100* 2-4 48

I HADN'T ANYONE TILL YOU / YOU'RE MINE, YOU .... *Discovery 135* 2-4 49
(Vocals: Mary Ann McCall)

I LOVES YOU, PORGY / SYMPHONY ... *Musicraft 15048* 2-4 45

MISTY MOON BLUES / BARROOM PIANO .... *Discovery 101* 3-5 49

OL' MAN RIVER / I'VE GOT SIXPENCE .... *Musicraft 15055* 2-4 46

ROMANCE WITHOUT FINANCE IS A NUISANCE / SHE'S A RANK CHICK .... *Musicraft 15076* 2-4 46

MORAND, Jose, & His Orchestra

GAY RANCHERO / SPANISH CAPRICE ... *Decca 4026* 2-4 41

MARIA ELENA / LA PALOMA .... *Decca 3847* 2-4 41

SAND IN MY SHOES / MISIRLOU .... *Decca 3974* 2-4 41

SOUTH AMERICAN WAY / MEXICONGA ... *Decca 2787* 2-4 39
(Vocals: Larry Burke)

MOREHOUSE, Chauncey, & His Orchestra
(Chauncey Morehouse: 3/11/02 –)

KU-LI-A / ORIENTAL NOCTURNE ... *Brunswick 8142* 5-8 38

PLASTERED IN PARIS / MAZI-PANI (NO WORK, NO PAY) ... *Brunswick 8122* 8-10 38

MOREHOUSE, Chauncey, & His Swing Six

BLUES IN B FLAT / ON THE ALAMO .... *Variety 608* 8-10 37

MORGAN, Joe, & His Palais D'Or Orchestra

I HAD TO LOSE YOU (TO LEARN YOU WERE MEANT FOR ME) (Vocal: Dick Robertson) / JUST A GIGOLO (Vocal: Charles Lawman) .... *Banner 32072* 4-6 31

SAY A LITTLE PRAYER FOR ME / I LOST MY GAL AGAIN .... *Conqueror 7777* 4-6 31

SAY A LITTLE PRAYER FOR ME / I LOST MY GAL AGAIN .... *Perfect 15449* 4-6 31
(Simultaneously released on two labels)

MORGAN, Russ, & His Orchestra
(Russ Morgan: 4/29/04 – 8/8/69)
(The Russ Morgan Orchestra under the leadership of son Jack continues to play engagements coast-to-coast. Fifty years of "Music in the Morgan Manner" was celebrated aboard the steamer Mississippi Queen, in September, 1985)

ABSENCE MAKES THE HEART GROW FONDER / I REMEMBER YOU FROM SOMEWHERE .... *Odeon ONY-36097* 5-8 30
(Vocals: Unknown)

ALABAMY BOUND (Vocals: The Morganaires) / THE POPCORN SONG
(Vocals: Russ Morgan & quartet) .... *Decca 29606* 2-4

ALL THOSE WONDERFUL YEARS / SWEET ELOISE .... *Decca 4300* 2-4 42

AT THE PERFUME COUNTER (Vocal: Russ Morgan) / OOOOOH BOOM! .... *Brunswick 8080* 2-4 38

BASIN STREET BLUES / BASIN STREET BLUES, PART II .... *Brunswick 7941* 4-6 37
(Vocals: Jimmy Lewis)

BEI MIR BIST DU SCHOEN (Vocal: Russ Morgan) / I DOUBLE-DARE YOU
(Vocal: Bernice Parks) .... *Brunswick 8037* 3-5 38

BLUEBERRY HILL (Vocal: Carol Kay) / I'M HOME AGAIN (Vocal: Russ Morgan) .... *Decca 3290* 2-4 40

BLUE HAWAII (Vocals: Russ Morgan & The Muller Sisters) / WHEN THE POPPIES BLOOM AGAIN
(Vocal: Mert Curtis) .... *Brunswick 7845* 2-4 37

BOO-HOO (Vocal: Judy Richards) / IF MY HEART COULD ONLY TALK (Vocal: Russ Morgan) ..... *Brunswick 7814* 2-4 37

CHINA DOLL PARADE / JOHNSON RAG ... *Decca 2778* 3-5 39

CROSS-EYED COWBOY ON THE CROSS-EYED HORSE, THE (Vocal: Russ Morgan) / THE GREATEST MISTAKE OF MY LIFE
(Vocal: Lewis Julian) .... *Brunswick 8032* 3-5 38

CRUISING DOWN THE RIVER / SUNFLOWER .... *Decca 24568* 2-4 49
(Vocals: The Skylarks)

DOES YOUR HEART BEAT FOR ME? (theme song) / I FOUND A ROSE .... *Brunswick 7672* 2-4 36
(Vocals: Unknown)

DON'T SAY A WORD – JUST DANCE / YOU STARTED ME DREAMING .... *Brunswick 7641* 3-5 36
(Vocals: Unknown)

DROP A NICKEL IN THE SLOT
(Vocal: Russ Morgan) / JOSEPH! JOSEPH!
(Vocal: Carolyn Clarke) .... *Brunswick 8097* 3-5 38

ELI GREEN'S CAKE WALK / GOODBYE MY LADY LOVE .... *Decca 2266* 2-4 39

EV'RY SINGLE LITTLE TINGLE OF MY HEART / IN A LITTLE GYPSY TEA ROOM .... *Columbia 3064-D* 5-8 35
(Vocals: Unknown)
(This record was pressed in blue shellac)

EV'RY TIME (Vocal: Phyllis Lynne) / BUCKLE DOWN, WINSOCKI (Vocal: Russ Morgan) .... *Decca 4069* 2-4 41

FAREWELL BLUES / MOONLIGHT ON THE GANGES (Vocal: Russ Morgan) .... *Brunswick 7918* 3-5 37

FERRIS WHEEL, THE / GOODNIGHT, LITTLE ANGEL .... *Decca 18317* 2-4 42

FLOWER OF DAWN / VAGABOND DREAMS .... *Decca 2822* 2-4 39
(Vocals: Russ Morgan)

GETTING SOME FUN OUT OF LIFE
(Vocal: Russ Morgan) / SO MANY MEMORIES
(Vocal: Mert Curtis) .... *Brunswick 7959* 3-5 37

GIRL ON THE POLICE GAZETTE, THE
(Vocal: Russ Morgan) / THE CALL TO ARMS
(Vocal: Mert Curtis) .... *Brunswick 7822* 2-4 37

GOODBYE, JONAH (Vocal: Lewis Julian) / IF YOU WERE SOMEONE ELSE
(Vocal: Bernice Parks) .... *Brunswick 7955* 2-4 37

HAVE YOU WRITTEN HOME TO MOTHER?
(Vocal: Jack Fulton) / 'WAY BACK HOME
(Vocal: Russ Morgan) .... *Banner 33423* 4-6 35

HAVE YOU WRITTEN HOME TO MOTHER?
(Vocal: Jack Fulton) / 'WAY BACK HOME
(Vocal: Russ Morgan) .... *Conqueror 8520* 4-6 35

HAVE YOU WRITTEN HOME TO MOTHER?
(Vocal: Jack Fulton) / 'WAY BACK HOME
(Vocal: Russ Morgan) .... *Melotone M-13390* 4-6 35

HAVE YOU WRITTEN HOME TO MOTHER?
(Vocal: Jack Fulton) / 'WAY BACK HOME
(Vocal: Russ Morgan) .... *Oriole 3136* 4-6 35

HAVE YOU WRITTEN HOME TO MOTHER?
(Vocal: Jack Fulton) / 'WAY BACK HOME
080(Vocal: Russ Morgan) .... *Perfect 16112* 4-6 35

HAVE YOU WRITTEN HOME TO MOTHER?
(Vocal: Jack Fulton) / 'WAY BACK HOME
(Vocal: Russ Morgan) .... *Romeo 2510* 4-6 35
(Simultaneously released on six labels)

HEART OF STONE / DON'T CRY, SWEETHEART .... *Decca 18348* 2-4 42

HILLS OF OLD WYOMIN', THE / IT'S A SIN TO TELL A LIE .... *Brunswick 7637* 3-5 36
(Vocals: Unknown)

HOW HIGH THE MOON / YOU GORGEOUS DANCING DOLL .... *Decca 3030* 2-4 40
(Vocals: Russ Morgan)

I CAN'T ESCAPE FROM YOU / EMPTY SADDLES .... *Brunswick 7697* 3-5 36
(Vocals: Unknown)

I LOVE A LASSIE / CASEY JONES ... *Brunswick 8127* 3-5 38
(Vocals: The Swing Fourteen)

I'M GOING SHOPPIN' WITH YOU / THE WORDS ARE IN MY HEART .... *Banner 33347* 4-6 35
(Vocals: Chick Bullock)

I'M GOING SHOPPIN' WITH YOU / THE WORDS ARE IN MY HEART .... *Melotone M-13314* 4-6 35
(Vocals: Chick Bullock)

I'M GOING SHOPPIN' WITH YOU / THE WORDS ARE IN MY HEART .... *Oriole 3081* 4-6 35
(Vocals: Chick Bullock)

I'M GOING SHOPPIN' WITH YOU / THE WORDS ARE IN MY HEART .... *Perfect 16075* 4-6 35
(Vocals: Chick Bullock)

I'M GOING SHOPPIN' WITH YOU / THE WORDS ARE IN MY HEART .... *Romeo 2465* 4-6 35
(Vocals: Chick Bullock)
(Simultaneously released on five labels)

ISLE OF CAPRI / WANG-WANG BLUES .... *Brunswick 7758* 4-6 36

I THREW A BEAN BAG AT THE MOON / IT'S YOU I ADORE .... *Banner 33354* 4-6 35
(Vocals: Chick Bullock)

I THREW A BEAN BAG AT THE MOON / IT'S YOU I ADORE .... *Melotone M-13321* 4-6 35
(Vocals: Chick Bullock)

I THREW A BEAN BAG AT THE MOON / IT'S YOU I ADORE .... *Oriole 3096* 4-6 35
(Vocals: Chick Bullock)

I THREW A BEAN BAG AT THE MOON / IT'S YOU I ADORE .... *Perfect 16079* 4-6 35
(Vocals: Chick Bullock)

I THREW A BEAN BAG AT THE MOON / IT'S YOU I ADORE .... *Romeo 2470* 4-6 35
(Vocals: Chick Bullock)
(Simultaneously released on five labels)

I'VE GOT A POCKETFUL OF DREAMS / DON'T LET THAT MOON GET AWAY .... *Decca 1936* 2-4 38
(Vocals: Russ Morgan)

I WANNA BE IN WINCHELL'S COLUMN / BROADWAY'S GONE HAWAII ..... *Brunswick 8014* 3-5 37
(Vocals: Russ Morgan)

I WANT YOU FOR CHRISTMAS (Vocal: Russ Morgan) / THE DIPSY DOODLE .... *Brunswick 8005* 3-5 37

JEZEBEL (Vocal: Mert Curtis) / IT'S EASIER SAID THAN DONE (Vocal: Carolyn Clarke) .... *Brunswick 8101* 2-4 38

LIGHTS OUT (Vocal: Mert Curtis) / RAGGING THE SCALE .... *Brunswick 7925* 3-5 37

LIMEHOUSE BLUES / BUZZ MIRANDY .... *Brunswick 7878* 3-5 37

LITTLE SUNSHINE / WHEN THE ORGAN PLAYED AT TWILIGHT .... *Odeon ONY-36140* 5-8 30
(Vocals: Unknown)

LITTLE WHITE LIGHTHOUSE, A (Vocal: Russ Morgan) / TWO DREAMS GOT TOGETHER
(Vocal: Mert Curtis) .... *Brunswick 8047* 3-5 38

LOVELINESS OF YOU, THE (Vocal: Mert Curtis) / TILL THE CLOCK STRIKES THREE
(Vocal: Russ Morgan) .... *Brunswick 7931* 3-5 37

LOVE ME FOREVER / THE ROSE IN HER HAIR .... *Columbia 3063-D* 4-6 35
(Vocals: Unknown)

MIDSUMMER MATINEE (Vocals: The Morganaires) / THEN YOU'RE A LONG, LONG WAY FROM HOME
(Vocal: Russ Morgan) .... *Decca 18443* 2-4 42

MUST WE SAY GOODNIGHT / BE STILL, MY HEART! .... *Banner 33238* 5-8 34
(Vocals: Chick Bullock)

MUST WE SAY GOODNIGHT / BE STILL, MY HEART! .... *Melotone M-13205* 5-8 34
(Vocals: Chick Bullock)

MUST WE SAY GOODNIGHT / BE STILL, MY HEART! .... *Oriole 3026* 5-8 34
(Vocals: Chick Bullock)

MUST WE SAY GOODNIGHT / BE STILL, MY HEART! .... *Perfect 16023* 5-8 34
(Vocals: Chick Bullock)

MUST WE SAY GOODNIGHT / BE STILL, MY HEART! .... *Romeo 2400* 5-8 34
(Vocals: Chick Bullock)
(Simultaneously released on five labels)

MY LITTLE BUCKAROO (Vocal: Mert Curtis) / SWING HIGH, SWING LOW
(Vocal: Judy Richards) .... *Brunswick 7833* 3-5 37

NIGHTINGALE (Vocal: Elizabeth Rogers) / I'M GETTIN' MIGHTY LONESOME FOR YOU
(Vocal: Russ Morgan) .... *Decca 18393* 2-4 42

PAVANNE / YESTERDAY .... *Decca 2555* 2-4 39

PHANTOM FANTASIE / SLIPHORN SAM .... *Columbia 3067-D* 8-10 35

SHEIK OF ARABY (Vocal: Gloria Whitney) / 'WAY DOWN YONDER IN NEW ORLEANS ...... *Brunswick 8157* 3-5 38

SHINE ON, HARVEST MOON (Vocal: Bernice Parks) / CANADIAN CAPERS .... *Brunswick 7902* 3-5 37

SMALL FRY (Vocal: Russ Morgan) / LAUGH AND CALL IT LOVE (Vocal: Mert Curtis) .... *Decca 1935* 2-4 38

SOPHISTICATED SWING / DIGA DIGA DOO .... *Brunswick 8128* 3-5 38

TEN LITTLE MILES FROM TOWN
(Vocals: Russ Morgan & The Swing Fourteen) / WILL YOU REMEMBER TONIGHT, TOMORROW?
(Vocal: Russ Morgan) .... *Brunswick 8119* 3-5 38

(DID YOU EVER GET) THAT FEELING IN THE MOONLIGHT / YOU'RE NOBODY 'TIL SOMEBODY LOVES YOU .... *Decca 18724* 2-4 45
(Vocals: Russ Morgan)

THAT RUSSIAN WINTER / I LEFT MY HEART AT THE STAGE DOOR CANTEEN .... *Decca 18444* 3-5 42
(Vocals: Russ Morgan)

TIDAL WAVE / MIDNIGHT OIL ..... *Columbia 3050-D* 8-10 35

TOODLE-OO (Vocal: Bernice Parks) / THE MERRY-GO-ROUND BROKE DOWN
(Vocal: Jimmy Lewis) .... *Brunswick 7888* 3-5 37

VALSE TRISTE / IF YOU EVER CHANGE YOUR MIND (Vocal: Jimmy Lewis) .... *Decca 2455* 2-4 39

WABASH BLUES/LINGER AWHILE ... *Brunswick 7704* 3-5 36

WEDDING OF THE WOODEN SOLDIER (AND THE PAINTED DOLL) (Vocal: Carolyn Clarke) / THE GIRL WITH THE PIGTAILS IN HER HAIR (Vocals: Russ Morgan & Carolyn Clarke) .... *Decca 2823* 2-4 39

WHISPERS IN THE DARK (Vocal: Bernice Parks) / STOP! YOU'RE BREAKING MY HEART
(Vocals: Russ Morgan & Dave Franklin) ... *Brunswick 7910* 2-4 37

WHY DOESN'T SOMEBODY TELL ME THESE THINGS? (Vocals: Carolyn Clarke & Russ Morgan) / LAMBETH WALK (Vocal: Jimmy Lewis) .... *Decca 2009* 2-4 38

WINDMILL UNDER THE STARS / JUST AS THOUGH YOU WERE HERE .... *Decca 18374* 2-4 42
(Vocals: Russ Morgan)

WOODPECKER SONG / IN AN OLD DUTCH GARDEN (Vocal: Russ Morgan) .... *Decca 2954* 2-4 40

YOU'RE AN EDUCATION (Vocal: Bernice Parks) / TWO BOUQUETS (Vocal: Mert Curtis) .... *Brunswick 8084* 2-4 38

MORGAN, Russ, & His Orchestra as Bob Causer & His Cornellians

IRRESISTIBLE / WERE YOU FOOLIN'? .... *Banner 33239* 5-8 34
(Vocals: Chick Bullock)

IRRESISTIBLE / WERE YOU FOOLIN'? .... *Melotone M-13206* 5-8 34
(Vocals: Chick Bullock)

IRRESISTIBLE / WERE YOU FOOLIN'? .... *Oriole 3027* 5-8 34
(Vocals: Chick Bullock)

IRRESISTIBLE / WERE YOU FOOLIN'? .... *Perfect 16024* 5-8 34
(Vocals: Chick Bullock)

IRRESISTIBLE / WERE YOU FOOLIN'? .... *Romeo 2401* 5-8 34
(Vocals: Chick Bullock)
(Simultaneously released on five labels)

MORRIS, Al, & His Playmates:
see LANIN, Sam, as The University Orchestra

MORRIS, Joe, & His Orchestra:
see LANIN, Sam, as The University Orchestra

MORRIS, Mel:
see PICCADILLY PLAYERS, The

MORTON, Benny, & His Orchestra
(Benny Morton: 1/31/07 –)

GET GOIN' / FARE THEE WELL TO HARLEM .... *Columbia 2902-D* 15-20 34
(Vocals: Jerry Blake)

TAYLOR MADE / THE GOLD DIGGERS' SONG (Vocal: Henry Allen) .... *Columbia 2924-D* 15-20 34

MOULIN ROUGE ORCHESTRA, The
also see SELVIN, Ben

NA-JO / DO YOU EVER THINK OF ME (Vocal: Arthur Hall) .... *Blue Bird 20048* 30-35 21
(Possibly one of Ben Selvin's orchestras)
(An exceptionally rare release produced by the Blue Bird Talking Machine Company in Los Angeles, California.)

MUNDY, Jimmy, & His Orchestra
(Jimmy Mundy: 6/28/07 –)

LITTLE OLD LADY FROM BALTIMORE / A LOVER IS BLUE............................ *Varsity 8136* 4-6 40
(Vocals: Madeleine Greene)

SUNDAY SPECIAL / ALL ABOARD ..... *Varsity 8148* 5-8 40

MUNDY, Jimmy, & His Swing Club Seven

I SURRENDER, DEAR / AIN'T MISBEHAVIN'.................. *Varsity 598* 8-10 37
(Vocals: Walter Fuller)

MURPHY, Lyle "Spud", & His Orchestra
(Lyle Murphy: 8/19/08 –)

BLAME IT ON MY LAST AFFAIR (Vocal: Lucy Ann Matthews) / IT'S EASY TO BLAME THE WEATHER (Vocal: Clyde Rogers)................ *Bluebird B-10151* 3-5 39

DANCE OF THE DOINKS / BOOLY JA-JA (JUNGLE DANCE) .... *Bluebird B-10539* 4-6 40

HOLD OUT FOR LOVE / JUST A PHRASE................. *Bluebird B-10157* 3-5 39

PINETOP BREAKAWAY / SAND DUNE .... *Bluebird B-10875* 4-6 40

QUAKER CITY JAZZ / CHEROKEE .... *Decca 2040* 3-5 38

TRANS-CONTINENTAL / MY LITTLE GIRL...................... *Decca 1853* 3-5 38

MURRAY, Billy, & His Merry Melody Men

SHE'S GOT GREAT IDEAS! / KANSAS CITY KITTY................ *Edison 52559* 5-8 29
(Vocals: Billy Murray)

MURRAY, Billy, as Billy Murray's Melody Men

SOMEBODY / I LIKE TO DO IT........ *Vocalion 14046* 3-5 20

WIGWAM / POLLY................... *Vocalion 14078* 3-5 20

MURRAY, Kel, & His Orchestra

ANDANTE CANTABILE / SOUVENIR ... *Sonora 1075* 2-4 46

CLOUDS (Vocal: Harold van Emburgh) / THINGS MIGHT HAVE BEEN SO DIFF'RENT (Vocal: Mary Welsh).................... *Banner 33352* 4-6 35

CLOUDS (Vocal: Harold van Emburgh) / THINGS MIGHT HAVE BEEN SO DIFF'RENT (Vocal: Mary Welsh)................ *Melotone M-13319* 4-6 35

CLOUDS (Vocal: Harold van Emburgh) / THINGS MIGHT HAVE BEEN SO DIFF'RENT (Vocal: Mary Welsh) .... *Oriole 3094* 4-6 35

CLOUDS (Vocal: Harold van Emburgh) / THINGS MIGHT HAVE BEEN SO DIFF'RENT (Vocal: Mary Welsh)..................... *Perfect 16077* 4-6 35

CLOUDS (Vocal: Harold van Emburgh) / THINGS MIGHT HAVE BEEN SO DIFF'RENT (Vocal: Mary Welsh)...................... *Romeo 2468* 4-6 35
(Simultaneously released on five labels)

MY HEART IS AN OPEN BOOK (Vocal: Mary Welsh) / LET ME SING YOU TO SLEEP WITH A LOVE SONG (Vocal: Harold van Emburgh)............. *Banner 33351* 3-5 35

MY HEART IS AN OPEN BOOK (Vocal: Mary Welsh) / LET ME SING YOU TO SLEEP WITH A LOVE SONG (Vocal: Harold van Emburgh) .... *Melotone M-13318* 3-5 35

MY HEART IS AN OPEN BOOK (Vocal: Mary Welsh) / LET ME SING YOU TO SLEEP WITH A LOVE SONG (Vocal: Harold van Emburgh)............... *Oriole 3093* 3-5 35

MY HEART IS AN OPEN BOOK (Vocal: Mary Welsh) / LET ME SING YOU TO SLEEP WITH A LOVE SONG (Vocal: Harold van Emburgh).............. *Perfect 16076* 3-5 35

MY HEART IS AN OPEN BOOK (Vocal: Mary Welsh) / LET ME SING YOU TO SLEEP WITH A LOVE SONG (Vocal: Harold van Emburgh)............... *Romeo 2467* 3-5 35
(Simultaneously released on five labels)

MUSICAL COMEDY ORCHESTRA, The:
see SELVIN, Ben, & His Orchestra

MUSICAL MANIACS, The:
see FAZOLA, Irving

MUSICAL MUSKETEERS, The:
see RAY, Jimmy, & His Orchestra

MUSICAL STEVEDORES, The

HAPPY RHYTHM / HONEYCOMB HARMONY..................... *Columbia 14406-D* 15-20 29

MUSICAL VOYAGERS, The:
see DORSEY BROTHERS' ORCHESTRA, The

MYERS, Vic, & His Orchestra

AUTUMN MOON / WHEN THE DREAMS OF A DREAMER COME TRUE........ *Columbia 1040-D* 3-5 27

MYERS, Vick, as Vick Myers' Atlantic Melody Artists

BLUE-EYED SALLY / IF YOU DON'T WANT ME, STOP DOGGIN' ME AROUND .... *Okeh 40281* 5-8 25

MAMIE / FLAG THAT TRAIN (TO ALABAM')................. *Okeh 40364* 5-8 25

OH! THAT SWEET IN SUITE 16 (Vocal: Billy Meyers) / SWEET MAN BLUES.................. *Okeh 40386* 5-8 25

SAVE YOUR SORROW / NANTUCKET NAN.................... *Okeh 40434* 5-8 25

NAPOLEON, Phil, & His Emperors Of Rhythm
(Phil Napoleon: 9/2/01 –)

THAT'S A PLENTY / SWING PATROL.... *Variety 669* 5-8 37

NAPOLEON, Phil, & His Orchestra

GO JOE, GO / TIGER RAG.............. *Edison 51908* 15-20 27

MARY, DEAR, I MISS YOU MOST OF ALL (Vocal: J. Donald Parker) / UNDERNEATH THE WEEPING WILLOW .... *Edison 51996* 5-8 27

RUBBER HEELS / CLARINET MARMALADE....................... *Edison 52021* 12-15 27

TAKE YOUR FINGER OUT OF YOUR MOUTH (Vocal: Billy Murray) / GO, JOE, GO .... *Victor 20605* 5-8 27

NAPOLEON, Phil, & His Whispering Rhythm

LOVE ME (Vocal: Ruth Denning) / BLUE BAYOU (Vocal: Ford Leary)......... *Variety 656* 4-6 37

NAPOLEON, Phil, as Napoleon's Emperors

ANYTHING / YOU CAN'T CHEAT A CHEATER....................... *Victor V-38069* 15-20 29

MEAN TO ME / MY KINDA LOVE..... *Victor V-38057* 15-20 29

NAPOLEON, Phil, as Napoleon's Emperors recorded under the name Joe Venuti & His Orchestra

GETTIN' HOT (WATERLOO) / SOME OF THESE DAYS (by Dave Nelson and The Kings Men; Vocal: Dave Nelson) .... *Victor 23039* 20-25 31
(Dave Nelson was the nephew of Joe "King" Oliver)

NAPOLEON'S EMPERORS:
see NAPOLEON, Phil

NASH, Sam, & His Orchestra:
see SELVIN, Ben, & His Orchestra

NATZY, Hazay, & His Biltmore Orchestra

CUTIE / ANGEL CHILD................ *Gennett 4830* 4-6 22

JUST KEEP A THOUGHT FOR ME / EVERY NIGHT......................... *Okeh 4349* 3-5 21

LOUISIAN' / COAL BLACK MAMMY .... *Gennett 4939* 4-6 22

MOONLIGHT / SUNSHINE .... *Gennett 4714* 3-5 21

NATZY, Hazay, & His Orchestra

ANGEL CHILD / CUTIE............. *Connorized 3063* 5-8 22

LOVELIGHT IN YOUR EYES, THE / FALLING.................... *Pathe Actuelle 020898* 3-5 23

LOVELIGHT IN YOUR EYES, THE / FALLING........................... *Perfect 14088* 2-4 23
(Simultaneously released on two labels)

TALE OF A FAN, THE / TEMPTING.................. *Pathe Actuelle 020845* 3-5 22

TALE OF A FAN, THE / TEMPTING.......................... *Perfect 14064* 2-4 22
(Simultaneously released on two labels)

NAYLOR, Oliver, as Oliver Naylor's Orchestra

EVANGELINE / I'M JUST A VAGABOND LOVER................ *Okeh 41247* 5-8 29
(Vocals: Unknown)

SWEET GEORGIA BROWN / RIVERBOAT SHUFFLE (by the Benson Orchestra of Chicago)........ *Victor 19688* 5-8 25

NAYLOR, Oliver, as Naylor's Seven Aces

DRIFTWOOD / SAY, SAY, SADIE (Vocal: Jack Kaufman)........... *Gennett 5470* 12-15 24

HIGH SOCIETY / 31 ST STREET BLUES... *Gennett 5392* 15-20 24

HUGO (I GO WHERE YOU GO) / YOU.... *Gennett 5375* 12-15 24

OH, JOHNNY! PLEASE DON'T — MOM-MA! / SO I TOOK FIFTY THOUSAND DOLLARS ... *Gennett 5386* 15-20 24

RINGLEBERG BLUES / AIN'T THAT HATEFUL?......................... *Gennett 5393* 15-20 24

SHE WOULDN'T DO WHAT I ASKED HER TO / I'VE GOT A CROSS-EYED PAPA (BUT HE LOOKS STRAIGHT AT ME).................. *Gennett 5376* 15-20 24

SUSQUEHANNA HOME / TAKE ME .... *Gennett 5638* 12-15 25

NEIBAUR, Eddie:
see Seattle Harmony Kings, The

NELSON, Dave, & The King's Men
(Dave Nelson: 1905 – 4/7/46)
(Dave Nelson was the nephew of Joe "King" Oliver)

I AIN'T GOT NOBODY / WHEN DAY IS DONE............................ *Victor 22639* 15-20 31
(Vocals: Dave Nelson)

SOME OF THESE DAYS (Vocal: Dave Nelson) / GETTIN' HOT (WATERLOO) (by Phil Napoleon as Napoleon's Emperors recorded under the name Joe Venuti & His Orchestra)......................... *Victor 23039* 20-25 31

NELSON, Ozzie, & His Orchestra
(Ozzie Nelson: 3/20/06 – 6/3/75)
(Ozzie Nelson married his vocalist, Harriet Hilliard, and in later years, the two starred in the long-running radio, then television series "Adventures of Ozzie and Harriet". Parents of Ricky Nelson, a teenage rock star of the 1960s.)

ABOUT A QUARTER TO NINE / SHE'S A LATIN FROM MANHATTAN .... *Brunswick 7325* 3-5 35
(Vocals: Ozzie Nelson)

ALMA MATER (CORNELL) (Vocals: The Uptowners) / THE EYES OF TEXAS .... *Victor 27426* 2-4 41

ANGEL IN DISGUISE (Vocal: Ozzie Nelson) / ALICE BLUE GOWN (Vocal: Rose Ann Stevens) .... *Bluebird B-10659* 2-4 40

AT LEAST YOU COULD SAY HELLO / HOW LONG HAS THIS BEEN GOING ON? (Vocal: Ozzie Nelson) .... *Bluebird B-10497* 2-4 39

AT LONG LAST LOVE (Vocal: Ozzie Nelson) / FORGET IF YOU CAN (Vocal: Harriet Hilliard) ..... *Bluebird B-7825* 3-5 39

BLACK CAT, THE / DON'T BE THAT WAY...................... *Bluebird B-7502* 5-8 38

BODY AND SOUL / SOMETHING TO REMEMBER YOU BY......................... *Brunswick 4922* 5-8 30
(Vocals: Unknown)

CENTRAL AVENUE SHUFFLE / SIR WALTER'S SERENADE...... *Bluebird B-11543* 3-5 42

CHANGE PARTNERS / THE NIGHT IS FILLED WITH MUSIC.................... *Bluebird B-7734* 3-5 38
(Vocals: Ozzie Nelson)

CHRISTMAS NIGHT IN HARLEM / DR. HECKLE AND MR. JIBE......................... *Brunswick 6861* 5-8 34
(Vocals: Ozzie Nelson)

DOIN' THE PROM / STOMPIN' AT THE SAVOY.................. *Brunswick 7659* 5-8 36

DO I REALLY DESERVE IT FROM YOU? / DREAM A LITTLE DREAM OF ME .... *Brunswick 6060* 8-10 31
(Vocals: Ozzie Nelson)

EVER SO QUIET / WAVE-A-STICK BLUES......................... *Bluebird B-10233* 3-5 39
(Vocals: Ozzie Nelson)

FLOWER OF DAWN (Vocal: Ozzie Nelson) / LITTLE SHEPHERD OF MY DREAMS (Vocal: Harriet Hilliard)............. *Bluebird B-10516* 2-4 40

GOIN' TO HEAVEN ON A MULE / 'LONG ABOUT MIDNIGHT........... *Vocalion 2636* 3-5 34
(Vocals: Ozzie Nelson)

HAPPY ENDING / JOSEPH, JOSEPH! .... *Bluebird B-7465* 2-4 38
(Vocals: Ozzie Nelson)

HAVE YOU EVER BEEN LONELY? (Vocal: Ozzie Nelson) / HEADIN' FOR A WEDDIN' (Vocals: Ozzie Nelson & Harriet Hilliard) .... *Brunswick 6547* 4-6 33

HEAVEN ONLY KNOWS / PUDDIN' HEAD JONES............. *Vocalion 2582* 3-5 33
(Vocals: Ozzie Nelson)

I'M GONNA CLAP MY HANDS (Vocal: Ozzie Nelson) / DON'T COUNT YOUR KISSES (BEFORE YOU'RE KISSED) (Vocals: Ozzie Nelson & Harriet Hilliard) .... *Brunswick 7326* 3-5 35

I'M JUST AN ORDINARY HUMAN / I'LL NEVER SAY "NEVER AGAIN" AGAIN.......... *Brunswick 7326* 3-5 35
(Vocals: Ozzie Nelson)

IN THE VALLEY OF THE MOON / BABY BOY....................... *Brunswick 6551* 3-5 33
(Vocals: Ozzie Nelson)

I STILL GET A THRILL (THINKING OF YOU) / I DON'T MIND WALKING IN THE RAIN.... *Brunswick 4897* 4-6 30
(Vocals: Ozzie Nelson)

IT'S ME AGAIN (Vocal: Harriet Hilliard) / I WANT THE WAITER (WITH THE WATER) (Vocal: Ozzie Nelson) .... *Bluebird B-10365* 2-4 39

I WANT TO BE IN WINCHELL'S COLUMN / SWEET SOMEONE............... *Bluebird B-7267* 2-4 38
(Vocals: Ozzie Nelson)

I WANT YOU – I NEED YOU (Vocal: Ozzie Nelson) / NOBODY LOVES ME LIKE THAT DALLAS MAN (Vocal: Harriet Hilliard) .... *Vocalion 2581* 5-8 33

JOSEPHINE / GEE, BUT IT'S GREAT TO MEET A FRIEND (FROM YOUR HOME TOWN)....... *Bluebird B-7157* 2-4 37
(Vocals: Ozzie Nelson)

LET'S HAVE ANOTHER CIGARETTE / ROSES IN DECEMBER............ *Bluebird B-7034* 2-4 37
(Vocals: Harriet Hilliard)

MAKE-BELIEVE DANCELAND / I'M LOOKING FOR A GUY WHO PLAYS ALSO AND CLARINET AND DOUBLES ON BARITONE AND WEARS A SIZE 37 SUIT .... *Bluebird B-10666* 3-5 40
(Vocals: Ozzie Nelson & Rose Ann Stevens)

MAPLE LEAF RAG / YES SUH! (Vocal: Ozzie Nelson) .... *Bluebird B-7726* 5-8 38

MARY (I'M IN LOVE WITH YOU) / I PROMISE YOU.................. *Brunswick 6228* 3-5 32
(Vocals: Ozzie Nelson)

MISS JOHNSON 'PHONED AGAIN TODAY / I'M NOBODY'S BABY............ *Bluebird B-10722* 2-4 40
(Vocals: Rose Ann Stevens)

MISTER MAGICIAN (WON'T YOU BRING MY BABY BACK TO ME?) / WHAT'S FOOD FOR THE GOOSE (IS GOOD FOR THE GANDER) .... *Vocalion 2642* 4-6 34
(Vocals: Ozzie Nelson & Harriet Hilliard)

MOUNTAIN MUSIC (Vocal: Ozzie Nelson) / SATAN TAKES A HOLIDAY....... *Bluebird B-6965* 5-8 37

MRS. ASTOR'S HORSE / MAMA DON'T ALLOW IT....................... *Brunswick 7580* 4-6 36
(Vocals: Ozzie Nelson)

NEVER IN A MILLION YEARS / IT'S SWELL OF YOU .... *Bluebird B-6896* 2-4 37
(Vocals: Ozzie Nelson)

NO! NO! A THOUSAND TIMES NO! (Vocals: Ozzie Nelson & Harriet Hilliard) / DOWN'T UNCLE BILL'S (Vocal: Ozzie Nelson) .... *Brunswick 7340* 4-6 35

OH! SUSANNA, DUST OFF THAT OLD PIANNA (Vocals: Ozzie Nelson & Harriet Hilliard) / RIGMAROLE........................... *Brunswick 7375* 3-5 35

OLD PLAYMATE / GUILTY.......... *Brunswick 6186* 3-5 31
(Vocals: Ozzie Nelson)

ON, WISCONSIN! / RAMBLING WRECK FROM GEORGIA TECH .... *Bluebird B-7723* 2-4 38
(Vocals: Ozzie Nelson)

OUR PENTHOUSE ON 3RD AVENUE (Vocal: Harriet Hilliard) / LOVE IS NEVER OUT OF SEASON (Vocal: Ozzie Nelson) .... *Bluebird B-6987* 2-4 37

PECKIN' / THE JELLY-FISH .... *Bluebird B-6974* 5-8 37

PERFIDIA / THE MAN WHO COMES AROUND (Vocal: Rose Ann Stevens)... *Bluebird B-10626* 3-5 40

PUT ON YOUR OLD GRAY BONNET (Vocal: Ozzie Nelson) / COME ON, GET UP (Vocals: Ozzie Nelson & Harriet Hilliard).... *Vocalion 2574* 2-4 33

QUEEN ISABELLA / ONCE IN AWHILE (Vocal: Harriet Hilliard)... *Bluebird B-7256* 4-6 38

RED SKIES IN THE NIGHT / LITTLE SKIPPER................ *Bluebird B-10187* 2-4 39
(Vocals: Ozzie Nelson)

RIFF INTERLUDE / OUT TO LUNCH................. *Bluebird B-10802* 3-5 40

SAY IT ISN'T SO (Vocal: Ozzie Nelson) / GOT YOU WHERE I WANT YOU (RIGHT IN MY ARMS) (Vocals: Ozzie Nelson & Harriet Hilliard)......... *Brunswick 6372* 3-5 32

SAY "SI SI" (Vocal: Ozzie Nelson) / I LOVE YOU..................... *Bluebird B-10293* 2-4 39

SAYS MY HEART (Vocal: Harriet Hilliard) / YOU LEAVE ME BREATHLESS (Vocal: Ozzie Nelson) .... *Bluebird B-7528* 2-4 38

SHACK IN THE BACK OF THE HILLS, A / THE OLD APPLE TREE.......... *Bluebird B-7430* 2-4 38
(Vocals: Ozzie Nelson)

SHEIK OF ARABY, THE / YOU'LL BE REMINDED OF ME (Vocal: Ozzie Nelson) .... *Bluebird B-7517* 5-8 38

SHOUTIN' IN THAT AMEN CORNER (Vocal: Ozzie Nelson) / YOU'RE IN MY POWER......................... *Vocalion 2637* 4-6 34

SOUTH AMERICAN WAY (Vocal: Harriet Hilliard) / IS IT POSSIBLE? (Vocal: Ozzie Nelson)..... *Bluebird B-10298* 2-4 39

STOMPIN' AT THE STADIUM / WHO BLEW OUT THE FLAME? (Vocal: Ozzie Nelson) .... *Bluebird B-7814* 5-8 38

STRANGERS IN THE DARK (Vocal: Shirley Lloyd) / HAPPY BIRTHDAY TO LOVE (Vocal: Ozzie Nelson) .... *Bluebird B-7037* 2-4 37

STREAMLINE STRUT / IS IT TRUE WHAT THEY SAY ABOUT DIXIE? (Vocal: Ozzie Nelson).... *Brunswick 7651* 4-6 36

SUBWAY / GOBLIN BAND .... *Bluebird B-7268* 3-5 38

SWAMP FIRE / SOLILOQUY.......... *Brunswick 7414* 3-5 35

SWEETHEART OF SIGMA CHI (Vocals: The Uptowners) / WASHINGTON AND LEE SWING...... *Victor 27425* 2-4 41

SWINGIN' ON THE GOLDEN GATE / JERSEY JIVE............... *Bluebird B-11180* 3-5 41

'TAIN'T GOOD (LIKE A NICKEL MADE OF WOOD) (Vocal: Ozzie Nelson) / SOPHISTICATED SWING.......... *Brunswick 7770* 3-5 37

THERE'S SOMETHING ABOUT A SOLDIER (Vocals: Ozzie Nelson & Harriet Hilliard) / GOODNIGHT, MY DARLING (Vocal: Ozzie Nelson) .... *Vocalion 2601* 3-5 34

THEY CAN'T TAKE THAT AWAY FROM ME / THEY ALL LAUGHED............. *Bluebird B-6873* 3-5 37
(Vocals: Ozzie Nelson)

THREE FOOT SKIPPER JONES / LEANIN' ON THE OLD TOP RAIL.................. *Bluebird B-10499* 2-4 40
(Vocals: Rose Ann Stevens)

TWENTY-FOUR HOURS IN GEORGIA / IF I HAD A MILLION DOLLARS............... *Brunswick 6991* 3-5 34
(Vocals: Ozzie Nelson)

WHISPER SONG, THE / TIGER RAG... *Brunswick 7523* 4-6 35

WHOA BABE / POOR ROBINSON CRUSOE (Vocal: Ozzie Nelson) .... *Bluebird B-6875* 4-6 37

YOU AND I KNOW / EBB TIDE...... *Bluebird B-7169* 3-5 37
(Vocals: Ozzie Nelson)

YOU CAN'T RUN AWAY FROM LOVE TONIGHT / 'CAUSE MY BABY SAYS IT'S SO ... *Bluebird B-6909* 3-5 37
(Vocals: Ozzie Nelson)

YOU CAN'T STOP ME FROM DREAMING / THE BIG APPLE.................. *Bluebird B-7159* 3-5 37
(Vocals: Ozzie Nelson)

YOU HAVE EVERYTHING / I SEE YOUR FACE BEFORE ME................ *Bluebird B-7216* 2-4 37
(Vocals: Ozzie Nelson)

YOU'RE NOT THE ONLY OYSTER IN THE STEW / IT'S DARK ON OBSERVATORY HILL.... *Brunswick 6999* 3-5 34
(Vocals: Ozzie Nelson)

YOU'RE SUCH A COMFORT TO ME (Vocals: Ozzie Nelson & Harriet Hilliard) / YOU'RE GONNA LOSE YOUR GAL (Vocal: Ozzie Nelson) .... *Vocalion 2600* 3-5 34

NEWMAN, Ruby, & His Orchestra
(Ruby Newman: circa 1902 –)

ABOUT A QUARTER TO NINE / (THERE'S A) LITTLE PICTURE PLAYHOUSE IN MY HEART... *Victor 24894* 2-4 35
(Vocals: Ray Morton)

APPLE A DAY, AN / ONE NEVER KNOWS – DOES ONE?................ *Victor 25468* 2-4 37
(Vocals: Barry McKinley)

DARKTOWN STRUTTERS BALL / I'M JUST WILD ABOUT HARRY.................Decca 23621 2-4 46

FROM NOW ON / GET OUT OF TOWN.....Decca 2192 2-4 38
(Vocals: Ray Morton)

I GET A KICK OUT OF YOU / SMOKE GETS IN YOUR EYES.......................Decca 23617 2-4 46

I'LL SEE YOU AGAIN / WHO? ....Decca 23620 2-4 46

I'M JUST BEGINING TO CARE / WE'LL REST AT THE END OF THE TRAIL..................Victor 25344 2-4 36
(Vocals: Barry McKinley)

I SEND MY LOVE WITH THESE ROSES / THREE GUESSES....................Victor 24043 3-5 32
(Vocals: The Funnybones)

JOHNNY ONE NOTE (Vocal: Wynn Murray) / WHERE OR WHEN (Vocal: Ray Heatherton)..............Victor 25546 2-4 37
(Ray Heatherton is father of Joey Heatherton, motion picture and television actress and dancer.)

JUST ONE OF THOSE THINGS / NIGHT AND DAY...........................Decca 23618 2-4 46

LET'S ADD UP THE SCORE / IMAGINATION.........................Victor 25005 2-4 35
(Vocals: Ray Morton)

LOVE FOR SALE / BY MYSELF..........Decca 23619 3-5 46

MY SILENT LOVE (Vocal: Gordon Graham) / AM I WASTING MY TIME?
(Vocals: The Funnybones)..................Victor 24042 3-5 32

NEVER GONNA DANCE / MAGNOLIAS IN THE MOONLIGHT.....................Victor 25402 3-5 36
(Vocals: Barry McKinley)

PORQUE? (WHY?); CHITARRA ROMANA / BASIN STREET BLUES; MEMPHIS BLUES....Decca 15052 3-5 41
(An oversize 12-inch 78 rpm)

SAY IT WITH A KISS (Vocal: Ray Morton) / PLEASE COME OUT OF YOUR DREAM
(Vocal: Ruby Newman)......................Decca 2191 2-4 39

SEMPER FIDELIS; NATIONAL EMBLEM MARCH / OUR DIRECTOR; WASHINGTON POST MARCH...............................Decca 15051 3-5 40
(An oversize 12-inch 78 rpm)

SHORTEST DAY OF THE YEAR, THE / THIS CAN'T BE LOVE.................Decca 2211 2-4 39
(Vocals: Ray Morton)

SING, BABY, SING / MAKE-BELIEVE BALLROOM..........................Victor 25401 4-6 36
(Vocals: Barry McKinley)

SWEET LEILANI / SWING HIGH, SWING LOW.........................Victor 25543 2-4 37
(Vocals: Ray Heatherton)

TONIGHT (PERFIDIA) / ONE-TWO-THREE-KICK................Decca 2846 2-4 40
(Vocals: Larry Taylor)

NEWMAN, Ruby, & His Rainbow Room Orchestra

IT'S A SIN TO TELL A LIE / SMALL TOWN GIRL..................Victor 25327 2-4 36
(Vocals: Barry McKinley)

IT'S HIGH TIME I GOT THE LOW-DOWN ON YOU / TONIGHT'S THE NIGHT...............Victor 25328 2-4 36
(Vocals: Barry McKinley)

NEWMAN, Ruby, & His Ritz-Carlton Hotel Orchestra

WINNIE THE WAILER / LAFFIN' AT THE FUNNIES.......................Victor 22934 3-5 32

NEW MUSIC OF REGINALD FORESYTHE, The:

see FORESYTHE, Reginald

NEW ORLEANS BLACKBIRDS, The:

see PETTIS, Jack, & His Pets

NEWPORT SOCIETY ORCHESTRA, The:

see SAMUELS, Joseph, & His Orchestra

NEWTON, Frank, & His Cafe Society Orchestra

(Frank Newton: 1/4/06 – 3/11/54)

JITTERS / JAM FEVER................Vocalion 4851 5-8 39

TAB'S BLUES / FRANKIE'S JUMP......Vocalion 4821 5-8 39

VAMP / PARALLEL FIFTHS............Vocalion 5410 5-8 39

NEWTON, Frank, & His Uptown Serenaders

EASY LIVING / WHERE OR WHEN.......Variety 616 8-10 37
(Vocals: Leon LaFell)

I FOUND A NEW BABY / THE BRITTWOOD STOMP (I'M A DING DONG DADDY)............Variety 571 10-12 37

THERE'S NO TWO WAYS ABOUT IT / 'CAUSE MY BABY SAYS IT'S SO...................Variety 550 10-12 37
(Vocals: Slim Gaillard)

WHO'S SORRY NOW? / THE ONYX HOP (Vocals: Frank Newton & Pete Brown)....Variety 647 10-12 37

YOU SHOWED ME THE WAY (Vocal: Clarence Palmer) / PLEASE DON'T TALK ABOUT ME WHEN I'M GONE............................Variety 518 8-10 37

NEWTON, Frankie, & Orchestra

MINOR JIVE / ROMPIN'.............Bluebird B-10186 5-8 39

ROSETTA / THE WORLD IS WAITING FOR THE SUNRISE...............Bluebird B-10176 5-8 39

WHO? / THE BLUES MY BABY GAVE ME.................Bluebird B-10216 5-8 39

NEWTOWN PIPPINS, The

HIGHWAYS ARE HAPPY WAYS (Vocal: Eddie Russell) / AT SUNDOWN (Vocal: Jerry White).......Herwin 8045 15-20 28

HIGHWAYS ARE HAPPY WAYS (Vocal: Eddie Russell) / AT SUNDOWN (Vocal: Jerry White).....Supertone 9007 5-8 28
(Simultaneously released on two labels)

OUR BUNGALOW OF DREAMS (Vocals: Eddie & Elmer Russell) / BEAUTIFUL
(Vocal: Jerry White)..........................Herwin 8042 12-15 28

OUR BUNGALOW OF DREAMS (Vocals: Eddie & Elmer Russell) / BEAUTIFUL
(Vocal: Jerry White)....................Supertone 9017 4-6 28
(Simultaneously released on two labels)

RAIN (Vocal: Jerry White) / TOGETHER, WE TWO (Vocal: Elmer Russell)..........Herwin 8043 15-20 28

NEW YORKERS, The:

see FENTON, Carl, & His Orchestra, and
see KARDOS, Gene, & His Orchestra

NEW YORK SYNCOPATORS, The:

see CALIFORNIA RAMBLERS, The, as Ted Wallace & His Orchestra
see LANIN, Sam, & His Famous Players & Singers
see RESER, Harry, & His Orchestra
see RICH, Fred, & His (La Palina) Orchestra, and
see RICH, Fred, & His Orchestra

NICHOLS, Ray, & His Four Towers Orchestra

AND THEN SOME (Vocal: Billie Hibbard) / (DO YOU INTEND TO PUT AN END TO) A SWEET BEGINNING LIKE THIS? (Vocal: Al Graf)..........Bluebird B-6012 3-5 35

IN THE SWEET LONG AGO / TO CALL YOU MY OWN...........Bluebird B-5903 3-5 35
(Vocals: Jeanne LaRue)

MOONLIGHT AND MAGNOLIAS / A LITTLE DOOR, A LITTLE LOCK, A LITTLE KEY.........Bluebird B-6010 3-5 35
(Vocals: Al Graf)

WHAT A LITTLE MOONLIGHT CAN DO (Vocal: Al Graf) / MURDER IN THE MOONLIGHT (Vocal: Billie Hibbard).......................Bluebird B-6011 4-6 35

WHO'S SORRY NOW? / ROSETTA (Vocal: Al Graf)............Bluebird B-5902 5-8 35

NICHOLS, Ray, & His Palace Royal Orchestra

I'LL ALWAYS BE IN LOVE WITH YOU / LOUISE.................................Harmony 902-H 3-5 29
(Vocals: Irving Kaufman)

NICHOLS, Red, & His Orchestra

(Red Nichols: 5/8/05 – 6/28/65)

CREAM PUFF / TWILIGHT IN TURKEY...Variety 655 5-8 37

DAVENPORT BLUES / WAIL OF THE WINDS (theme song)...........Bluebird B-10408 3-5 39

EVERYBODY LOVES MY BABY (Vocal: Red Nichols) / I'M SORRY I MADE YOU CRY
(Vocal: Tony Sacco)..................Brunswick 6461 5-8 33

HOT LIPS / THE PARADE OF THE PENNIES...................Bluebird B-10360 3-5 39

HOUR OF PARTING, THE / THE KING KONG...................Bluebird B-10190 3-5 39

HUMORESQUE / O SOLE MIO...........Variety 595 4-6 37

I LIVE AGAIN / YOU'RE THE GREATEST DISCOVERY (SINCE 1492)......................Bluebird B-10451 2-4 39
(Vocals: Bill Darnell)

I NEVER KNEW HEAVEN COULD SPEAK / TEARS FROM MY INKWELL.......Bluebird B-10200 2-4 39
(Vocals: Bill Darnell)

LOVE, NUTS AND NOODLES (BRING 'EM BACK ALIVE) (Vocal: Ernie Mathias) / HEAT WAVES.....................Brunswick 6451 5-8 32

LOWLAND BLUES / BEAT ME, DADDY (EIGHT TO A BAR).............Okeh 5676 4-6 40
(Vocals: Harry Jaeger)

OUR LOVE / YOU'RE SO DESIRABLE.....................Bluebird B-10179 2-4 39
(Vocals: Bill Darnell)

OVERNIGHT HOP / MEET MISS EIGHT BEAT..........................Okeh 5648 4-6 40

POOR BUTTERFLY (Vocals: orchestra) / A PRETTY GIRL IS LIKE A MELODY...............Bluebird B-10522 3-5 39

SASSIN' THE BOSS / POOR LOULIE JEAN (Vocal: Bill Darnell)............Bluebird B-10328 3-5 39

SUGAR / DINAH LOU................Brunswick 6534 5-8 33
(Vocals: Ernie Mathias)

THEY ALL LAUGHED / LET'S CALL THE WHOLE THING OFF.......................Variety 502 5-8 37
(Vocals: The Three Songies)

THREE LITTLE WORDS (Vocals: The Songcopators) / HARLEM (Vocals: King Harvey & The Songcopators).................Brunswick 7460 5-8 34

TROUBLESOME TRUMPET (Vocals: The Three Songies) / LOVE'S OLD SWEET SONG.............Variety 545 5-8 37

WHEN YOU AND I WERE YOUNG, MAGGIE / DARDANELLA......................Brunswick 7358 5-8 34

NICHOLS, Red, & His World-Famous Pennies

I'M HUMMIN', I'M WHISTLIN', I'M SINGIN' (Vocals: The Songcopators) / STRAIGHT FROM THE SHOULDER (Vocal: King Harvey)......Bluebird B-5552 4-6 34

JUNGLE FEVER (Vocals: The Songcopators) / ROCKIN' IN RHYTHM ....Bluebird B-5547 5-8 34

PRIZE WALTZ, THE (Vocal: King Harvey) / LET ME CALL YOU MINE (Vocals: The Songcopators)....Bluebird B-5549 3-5 34

ROLLIN' HOME (Vocals: King Harvey & The Songcopators) / THE VERY THOUGHT OF YOU
(Vocal: King Harvey)...................Bluebird B-5548 5-8 34

SHINE / RUNNIN' WILD.............Bluebird B-5553 5-8 34
(Vocals: The Songcopators)

SILVER THREADS AMONG THE GOLD / OLD WHITE'S WHISKERS (Vocals: The Songcopators)...Bluebird B-5583 5-8 34

NIGHT CLUB ORCHESTRA, The:

see RESER, Harry

NOBLE, Leighton, & His Orchestra

MY HEART IS UNEMPLOYED (Vocal: Edith Caldwell) / HOW LONG CAN LOVE KEEP LAUGHING?
(Vocal: Leighton Noble)..................Vocalion 4410 4-6 38

WHITE STAR OF SIGNA NU / SWEETHEART OF SIGMA CHI.........................Coral 60579 2-4 51

WHY DOESN'T SOMEBODY TELL ME THESE THINGS (Vocals: by trio) / I'VE GOT A HEART FULL OF RHYTHM (Vocal: Johnny McAfee)........Vocalion 4385 4-6 38

NOBLE, Ray, & His Orchestra

(Ray Noble: 12/17/03 – 1977)

ALONG THE SANTA FE TRAIL / A HANDFUL OF STARS.........................Columbia 35775 2-4 40
(Vocals: Larry Stewart)

APRIL SHOWERS / I WONDER WHO'S KISSING HER NOW.............................Columbia 37544 2-4 47
(Vocals: Snooky Lanson & The Sportsmen)

BUGLE CALL RAG / DINAH.............Victor 25223 5-8 35

BUT DEFINITELY / WHEN I'M WITH YOU...........................Victor 25336 4-6 36
(Vocals: Al Bowlly)

BY THE WATERS OF MINNETONKA / CHEROKEE.......................Brunswick 8247 4-6 38

CAPTAIN CUSTARD (Vocal: Ray Noble) / SWEET POTATO PIPER
(Vocal: Elizabeth Tilton)...............Columbia 35392 2-4 40

CAROLINA IN THE MORNING (Vocals: by trio) / IF I HAD MY WAY (Vocal: Larry Stewart)........Columbia 35577 2-4 40

COMANCHE WAR DANCE / IROQUOIS.......................Columbia 35258 3-5 39

DOUBLE TROUBLE (Vocals: The Freshmen) / WHY STARS COME OUT AT NIGHT (Vocal: Al Bowlly)....Victor 25105 4-6 35

EASY TO LOVE / I'VE GOT YOU UNDER MY SKIN...............Victor 25422 4-6 36
(Vocals: Al Bowlly)

EMPTY SADDLES (Vocal: Al Bowlly) / BIG CHIEF DE SOTO (Vocals: Al Bowlly & Sterling Bose)....Victor 25346 5-8 36

FRIDAY NIGHT AT THE HARTYS / SATURDAY NIGHT AT THE NOBLES...........Brunswick 8351 3-5 39

FROM OAKLAND TO BURBANK / HARLEM NOCTURNE..............Columbia 35708 2-4 40

FULL MOON AND EMPTY ARMS / IT MIGHT AS WELL BE SPRING.......................Columbia 36893 2-4 45
(Vocals: Roy Lanson)

I'LL DANCE AT YOUR WEDDING / THOSE THINGS MONEY CAN'T BUY................ *Columbia 37967* 2-4 48
(Vocals: Buddy Clark)

I'LL NEVER SMILE AGAIN (Vocal: Larry Stewart) / MAYBE (Vocal: Don Bonnee)........... *Columbia 35596* 2-4 40

IS IT POSSIBLE? / RENDEZVOUS TIME IN PAREE.................. *Brunswick 8399* 3-5 39
(Vocals: Larry Stewart)

JUST LET ME LOOK AT YOU / YOU COULDN'T BE CUTER........................ *Brunswick 8076* 3-5 38
(Vocals: Tony Martin)

KISS THE BOYS GOODBYE / IS THAT GOOD?.................. *Columbia 36256* 2-4 41
(Vocals: Unknown)

LET'S CALL A HEART A HEART / ONE, TWO, BUTTON YOUR SHOE......................... *Victor 25428* 4-6 36
(Vocals: Al Bowlly)

LET'S SWING IT (Vocals: The Freshmen) / CHINATOWN, MY CHINATOWN....... *Victor 25070* 5-8 35

LET YOURSELF GO (Vocals: Al Bowlly & The Freshmen) / LET'S FACE THE MUSIC AND DANCE (Vocal: Al Bowlly)........................ *Victor 25241* 5-8 36

LIFE BEGINS AT SWEET SIXTEEN (Vocals: The Freshmen) / I'M THE FELLOW WHO LOVES YOU (Vocals: Al Bowlly & The Freshmen)......... *Victor 25190* 4-6 35

LITTLE BIT OF BLARNEY, A / MY WILD IRISH ROSE............ *Columbia 36162* 2-4 41
(Vocals: Larry Stewart)

LOUISIANA PURCHASE (Vocal: Don Bonnee) / OUTSIDE OF THAT I LOVE YOU (Vocals: Mary Ann Warren & Larry Stewart)........... *Columbia 35507* 2-4 40

LOVE IS A RANDOM THING / LINDA... *Columbia 37215* 2-4 46
(Vocals: Buddy Clark)

MARCHING ALONG WITH TIME (Vocal: Tony Martin) / ALEXANDER'S RAGTIME BAND... *Brunswick 8180* 3-5 38

MOONLIGHT IN HILO / BLAZIN' THE TRAIL.................. *Victor 25282* 4-6 36
(Vocals: Al Bowlly)

MOON OF MANAKOORA / I HADN'T ANYONE TILL YOU................ *Brunswick 8079* 3-5 38
(Vocals: Tony Martin)

MOON OVER BURMA / ARISE MY LOVE.................. *Columbia 35804* 2-4 40
(Vocals: Larry Stewart)

MY WALKING STICK / NOW IT CAN BE TOLD..................... *Brunswick 8153* 3-5 38
(Vocals: Tony Martin)

NIGHTINGALE SANG IN BERKELEY SQUARE, A (Vocal: Larry Stewart) / WE THREE (MY ECHO, MY SHADOW AND ME (Vocals: We Three)... *Columbia 35733* 2-4 40

NOW / LITTLE OLD LADY............. *Victor 25448* 3-5 36
(Vocals: Al Bowlly)

PRAIRIE FAIRY TALE / THE MOON OVER MADISON SQUARE......... *Columbia 35646* 2-4 40
(Vocals: Larry Stewart)

RED ROOF COTTAGE/ISOLA BELLA... *Columbia 35814* 2-4 40
(Vocals: Larry Stewart)

SEMINOLE / SLEEPY-TIME GAL (Vocals: Larry Stewart)........... *Columbia 35557* 2-4 40

SIOUX SUE / FAR AWAY............ *Columbia 35850* 2-4 40

SLUMMING ON PARK AVENUE (Vocal: The Merry Macs) / I'VE GOT MY LOVE TO KEEP ME WARM (Vocal: Howard Phillips)................. *Victor 25507* 3-5 37

SOUTH AMERICAN WAY (Vocal: Larry Stewart) / PEER GYNT SUITE............... *Brunswick 8390* 2-4 39

SWING LOW, SWEET CHARIOT (Vocals: Unknown) / ON THE ALAMO (Vocal: Larry Stewart)... *Columbia 36212* 2-4 41

THAT'S FOR ME (Vocal: Larry Stewart) / RHYTHM ON THE RIVER (Vocal: Don Bonnee)...... *Columbia 35630* 2-4 40

THERE'S SOMETHING IN THE AIR / WHERE THE LAZY RIVER GOES BY................ *Victor 25459* 4-6 36
(Vocals: Al Bowlly)

TILL I KISSED YOU GOODBYE (Vocal: Larry Stewart) / WHEN IRISH EYES ARE SMILING... *Columbia 35311* 2-4 39

TOO ROMANTIC / THE MOON AND THE WILLOW TREE......... *Columbia 35385* 2-4 40
(Vocals: Larry Stewart)

TOP HAT (Vocals: Al Bowlly & The Freshmen) / PICCOLINO (Vocal: Al Bowlly)........... *Victor 25094* 5-8 35

VERY THOUGHT OF YOU, THE (opening theme) / GOODNIGHT SWEETHEART (closing theme)...................... *Columbia 36546* 2-4 41
(Vocals: Snooky Lanson)

VILIA / CRAZY RHYTHM........... *Brunswick 8098* 4-6 38

'WAY DOWN YONDER IN NEW ORLEANS / ST. LOUIS BLUES (Vocal: Al Bowlly)............. *Victor 25082* 5-8 35

WE SAW THE SEA (Vocals: The Freshmen) / IF YOU LOVE ME (Vocal: Al Bowlly)............. *Victor 25240* 4-6 36

WHERE AM I? (AM I IN HEAVEN?) / DINNER FOR ONE, PLEASE JAMES................ *Victor 25187* 5-8 35
(Vocals: Al Bowlly)

WHILE MY LADY SLEEPS / BY THE LIGHT OF THE SILV'RY MOON............ *Columbia 36479* 2-4 42
(Vocals: Snooky Lanson)

WHY DREAM / I WISHED ON THE MOON...................... *Victor 25104* 4-6 35
(Vocals: Al Bowlly)

YOURS TRULY IS TRULY YOURS / THE TOUCH OF YOUR LIPS...................... *Victor 25277* 4-6 36
(Vocals: Al Bowlly)

NORVO, Red, & His Orchestra
(Red Norvo: 3/31/08 –)

ALWAYS AND ALWAYS / IT'S WONDERFUL................ *Brunswick 8069* 5-8 38
(Vocals: Mildred Bailey)

CLAP HANDS, HERE COMES CHARLIE / RUSSIAN LULLABY............... *Brunswick 7975* 5-8 37

CUCKOO IN THE CLOCK (Vocal: Mildred Bailey) / WE'LL NEVER KNOW (Vocal: Terry Allen)...... *Vocalion 4698* 4-6 39

DAY DREAMIN' / SAVIN' MYSELF FOR YOU......................... *Brunswick 8145* 5-8 38
(Vocals: Mildred Bailey)

EVERYONE'S WRONG BUT ME / POSIN'............................ *Brunswick 7928* 5-8 37
(Vocals: Mildred Bailey)

GARDEN OF THE MOON / JUMP JUMP'S HERE............. *Brunswick 8202* 5-8 38
(Vocals: Mildred Bailey)

GRAMERCY SQUARE / DECCA STOMP.... *Decca 691* 5-8 36

HOW CAN YOU FORGET? (Vocal: Terry Allen) / THERE'S A BOY IN HARLEM (Vocal: Mildred Bailey)................. *Brunswick 8089* 5-8 38

I CAN READ BETWEEN THE LINES / YOURS FOR A SONG................ *Vocalion 4818* 4-6 39
(Vocals: Terry Allen)

I GET ALONG WITHOUT YOU VERY WELL / KISS ME WITH YOUR EYES.................. *Vocalion 4648* 4-6 39
(Vocals: Terry Allen)

IN THE MIDDLE OF A DREAM / MY LOVE FOR YOU........................... *Vocalion 4953* 3-5 39
(Vocals: Terry Allen)

IT ALL BEGINS AND ENDS WITH YOU / PICTURE ME WITHOUT YOU.................. *Brunswick 7732* 5-8 36
(Vocals: Mildred Bailey)

IT CAN HAPPEN TO YOU (Vocal: Mildred Bailey) / WHEN IS A KISS NOT A KISS? (Vocal: Lou Hirst)................. *Brunswick 7761* 5-8 36

I WAS DOING ALL RIGHT / LOVE IS HERE TO STAY.................. *Brunswick 8068* 5-8 38
(Vocals: Mildred Bailey)

JEANNINE / TEA TIME............ *Brunswick 8103* 4-6 38

JERSEY BOUNCE / ARTHUR MURRAY TAUGHT ME DANCING IN A HURRY (Vocals: Mildred Bailey)............... *Columbia 36557* 2-4 42

LIZA / I WOULD DO ANYTHING FOR YOU............ *Brunswick 7868* 8-10 37

MORNING AFTER, THE / DO YOU EVER THINK OF ME?.................. *Brunswick 7932* 5-8 37
(Vocals: Mildred Bailey)

POLLY WOLLY DOODLE / THE WEDDING OF JACK AND JILL..................... *Decca 670* 5-8 36
(Vocals: by trio)

PORTER'S LOVE SONG TO A CHAMBERMAID, A (Vocal: Mildred Bailey) / I KNOW THAT YOU KNOW....................... *Brunswick 7744* 5-8 36

PUT YOUR HEART IN A SONG / THE SUNNY SIDE OF THINGS..... *Brunswick 8182* 5-8 38
(Vocals: Mildred Bailey)

REHEARSIN' FOR A NERVOUS BREAKDOWN / BLUE EVENING (Vocal: Terry Allen).... *Vocalion 4833* 5-8 39

REMEMBER / JIVING THE JEEP.... *Brunswick 7896* 5-8 37

SAYS MY HEART / YOU LEAVE ME BREATHLESS................ *Brunswick 8135* 5-8 38
(Vocals: Mildred Bailey)

SERENADE IN THE STARS, A (Vocal: Terry Allen) / MORE THAN EVER (Vocal: Mildred Bailey)......... *Brunswick 8085* 5-8 38

SLUMMIN' ON PARK AVENUE / I'VE GOT MY LOVE TO KEEP ME WARM.............. *Brunswick 7813* 5-8 37
(Vocals: Mildred Bailey)

SOME LIKE IT HOT / HAVE MERCY... *Vocalion 5009* 5-8 39

TEARS IN MY HEART / WORRIED OVER YOU............ *Brunswick 7970* 5-8 37
(Vocals: Mildred Bailey)

THEY SAY / I GO FOR THAT.......... *Vocalion 4548* 4-6 39
(Vocals: Mildred Bailey)

THIS IS MADNESS / WHO BLEW OUT THE FLAME?................. *Brunswick 8230* 5-8 38
(Vocals: Mildred Bailey)

THOUSAND DREAMS OF YOU, A / SWEET DREAMS.................. *Brunswick 7815* 5-8 37
(Vocals: Mildred Bailey)

TOADIE TODDLE / THERE'LL NEVER BE ANOTHER YOU (Vocal: Mildred Bailey)............. *Vocalion 4738* 5-8 39

UNDECIDED / THANKS FOR EVERYTHING (Vocal: Mildred Bailey)... *Brunswick 8288* 5-8 39

WEEK-END OF A PRIVATE SECRETARY, THE / PLEASE BE KIND................. *Brunswick 8088* 5-8 38
(Vocals: Mildred Bailey)

WIGWAMMIN' / HOW CAN I THINK YOU?................... *Brunswick 8194* 5-8 38
(Vocals: Mildred Bailey)

YOU'RE A SWEET LITTLE HEADACHE / I HAVE EYES..................... *Brunswick 8227* 4-6 38
(Vocals: Terry Allen)

NORVO, Red, & His Swing Octet / Septet

BUGHOUSE / BLUES IN E FLAT.... *Columbia 3079-D* 12-15 35

I SURRENDER, DEAR / TOMBOY... *Columbia 2977-D* 8-10 34

NIGHT IS BLUE, THE / WITH ALL MY HEART AND SOUL.............. *Columbia 3026-D* 10-12 35
(This record was pressed in blue shellac)

OLD FASHIONED LOVE / HONEYSUCKLE ROSE........... *Columbia 3059-D* 10-12 35
(This record was pressed in blue shellac)

NORVO, Red, & His Swing Sextette

I GOT RHYTHM / OH! LADY BE GOOD..... *Decca 779* 5-8 36

NORVO, Red, xylophone or marimba solos accompanied by a recording group

IN A MIST / DANCE OF THE OCTUPUS................... *Brunswick 6906* 10-12 34

KNOCKIN' ON WOOD / HOLE IN THE WALL.............. *Brunswick 6562* 10-12 33

NOVAK, Frank, & His Orchestra

AT YOUR COMMAND (Vocals: Unknown) / I'M ALL DRESSED UP WITH A BROKEN HEART.................. *Crown 3168* 3-5 31

I'VE TOLD EVERY LITTLE STAR / MORE BEAUTIFUL THAN EVER......................... *Crown 3409* 4-6 33
(Vocals: Unknown)

LOVE ME TONIGHT / MUSIC, MUSIC EVERYWHERE. ...... *Crown 3368* 3-5 32
(Vocals: Unknown)

YOU'RE SO DESIRABLE (Vocal: Terry Allen) / THREE LITTLE FISHES (ITTY BITTY POO) (Vocal: Mildred Bailey).................. *Vocalion 4785* 4-6 39

NORVO, Red, & His Orchestra as Len Herman & His Orchestra

IF YOU LOVE ME / LET YOURSELF GO (by Red Norvo & His Orchestra as Ken Kenny & His Orchestra)........... *Champion 40100* 5-8 36
(Vocals: Unknown)

LIFE BEGINS WHEN YOU'RE IN LOVE / MISTY ISLANDS OF THE HIGHLANDS (by Red Norvo & His Orchestra as Ken Kenny and His Orchestra)......... *Champion 40101* 5-8 36
(Vocals: Unknown)

NORVO, Red, & His Orchestra as Ken Kenny & His Orchestra

LET YOURSELF GO / IF YOU LOVE ME (by Red Norvo & His Orchestra as Len Herman & His Orchestra).......... *Champion 40100* 5-8 36
(Vocals: Unknown)

MISTY ISLANDS OF THE HIGHLANDS / LIFE BEGINS WHEN YOU'RE IN LOVE (by Red Norvo & His Orchestra as Len Herman & His Orchestra)... *Champion 40101* 5-8 36
(Vocals: Unknown)

YOU STARTED ME DREAMING / WHAT'S THE NAME OF THAT SONG?................. *Champion 40107* 5-8 36
(Vocals: Unknown)

O'HARE, Husk, as Husk O'Hare's Super Orchestra of Chicago
(Husk O'Hare: circa 1890 – 4/29/70)

ALL MUDDLED UP / SWANEE SMILES... *Starr 9312* 5-8 22
(Canadian release)

BOO HOO HOO / TIGER RAG........... *Gennett 4850* 10-12 22

BOO HOO HOO / TIGER RAG............. *Starr 9237* 12-15 22
(Simultaneously released on 2 labels, one Canadian [Starr])

CLOVER BLOSSOM BLUES / NIGHT.... *Gennett 4921* 8-10 22

CLOVER BLOSSOM BLUES / NIGHT...... *Starr 9276* 10-12 22
(Simultaneously released on 2 labels, one Canadian [Starr])

YOU GAVE ME YOUR HEART / SWANEE SMILES.................... *Gennett 4983* 5-8 22

O'HARE, Husk, as Husk O'Hare's Wolverines

MILENBERG JOYS / MY DADDY ROCKS ME........................ *Vocalion 15646* 15-30 28
(Vocals: Turk Savage)

OHMAN, Phil, & His Orchestra
(Phil Ohman: 10/7/96 – 8/8/54)

CHEEK TO CHEEK / TOP HAT, WHITE TIE AND TAILS.................. *Columbia 3077-D* 3-5 35
(Vocals: Unknown)

NO STRINGS / ISN'T THIS A LOVELY DAY?................ *Columbia 3076-D* 3-5 35
(Vocals: Unknown)

OHMAN, Phil, as Phil Ohman's Trio

WILDFLOWER / EVERYTHING IS K.O. IN KENTUCKY................ *Emerson 10602* 2-4 23

OKEH DANCE BAND / ORCHESTRA, The

MARY / BEAUTIFUL OHIO............... *Okeh 1165* 2-4 19

PETER GINK / RUSSIAN RAG.............. *Okeh 4002* 2-4 19

STARLIGHT LOVE / DREAMY AMAZON... *Okeh 4034* 2-4 19

THAT'S WORTH WAITING FOR / THAT NAUGHTY WALTZ............... *Okeh 4033* 2-4 19

TILL WE MEET AGAIN / RAINY DAY BLUES........................... *Okeh 1166* 2-4 19

OKEH MARIMBA BAND, The

BLUE JEANS / JUST ANOTHER KISS..... *Okeh 4644* 2-4 22

DREAMY PARADISE / JUST WE TWO..... *Okeh 4263* 2-4 21

DROWSY HEAD / SLEEPY HEAD......... *Okeh 4444* 2-4 21

SLEEPY HOLLOW / THE HULA BLUES... *Okeh 4227* 2-4 20

OKEH MELODIANS, The:
see LANIN, Sam

OKEH SALON ORCHESTRA, The:
see RING, Justin

OKEH SYNCOPATORS, The:
see RADERMAN, Harry, as the Red Hotters and see RESER, Harry

OLIVER, Earl, as Earl Oliver's Jazz Babies:
see RESER, Harry

OLIVER, Sy, & His Orchestra
(Sy Oliver: 12/17/10 –)

BIBBIDI-BOBBIDI-BOO (Vocals: The Aristokats) / A DREAM IS A WISH YOUR HEART MAKES (Vocals: Jack Haskell & The Aristokats)........ *Decca 24807* 4-6 50

CASTLE ROCK (Vocal: Sy Oliver) / ABOARD THE SENTIMENTAL TRAIN (Vocals: The Tune Timers)............. *Decca 27707* 3-5 50

NASHVILLE BLUES (Vocal: Truly Richards) / WE'LL BUILD A BUNGALOW (Vocal: Sy Oliver)........................ *Decca 24840* 3-5 50

NEVER HAVE I FELT LIKE THIS BEFORE / I DIDN'T KNOW WHAT TIME IT WAS........... *Decca 24978* 3-5 50
(Vocals: Eileen Wilson)

"O" (OH!) (Vocal: Sy Oliver) / I'M WALKING BEHIND YOU (Vocal: Tony Russo)........... *Bell 1010* 5-8
(This is a 7-inch 78 rpm record with microgrooves, containing the same amount of music as the usual 10-inch records.)

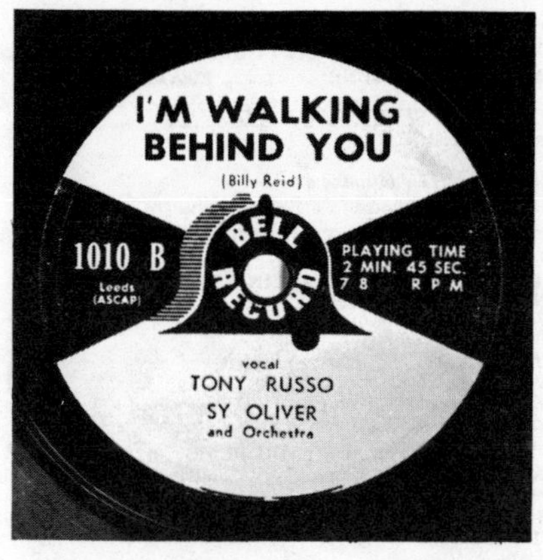

OLSEN, George, & His Music
(George Olsen: 3/18/93 – 3/18/71)
(Fred McMurray, of later motion picture and television fame, played tenor saxophone with this orchestra in 1929-30.)

ALL-AMERICAN GIRL (Vocal: Fran Frey) / AND SO TO BED (Vocals: Paul Small & Ethel Shutta).... *Victor 24125* 4-6 32

ALWAYS IN ALL WAYS / BEYOND THE BLUE HORIZON (theme song)................ *Victor 22530* 2-4 30
(Vocals: Bob Borger)

BECAUSE MY BABY DON'T MEAN "MAYBE" NOW (Vocal: Bob Borger) / JUST LIKE A MELODY OUT OF THE SKY (Vocal: Fran Frey)............ *Victor 21452* 3-5 28

BLUE SKIES / WHERE'S THAT RAINBOW?.................... *Victor 20455* 2-4 27
(Vocals: Fran Frey, Bob Borger, & Bob Rice)

BREAKAWAY / BIG CITY BLUES....... *Victor 21961* 3-5 29
(Vocals: Fran Frey)

DO-DO-DO (Vocals: Fran Frey, Bob Borger, & Bob Rice) / CLAP YO' HANDS (by Roger Wolfe Kahn & His Orchestra)........................ *Victor 20327* 4-6 27

DRIFTWOOD (Vocal: Bob Borger) / TEN LITTLE MILES FROM TOWN (Vocals: Fran Frey, Bob Borger, & Bob Rice)................. *Victor 21589* 2-4 28

FOND OF YOU / JOURNEY'S END....... *Victor 19896* 2-4 26

GOOD NEWS (Vocals: Fran Frey, Bob Borger, & Bob Rice) / THE VARSITY DRAG (Vocal: Fran Frey).... *Victor 20875* 3-5 27

GOSH DARN! (Vocals: Ethel Shutta & Fran Frey) / I'M SO ALONE WITH THE CROWD (Vocal: Ethel Shutta).................... *Victor 22994* 3-5 32

HE'S THE HOTTEST MAN IN TOWN / A NEW KIND OF MAN............... *Victor 19375* 5-8 24

I FEEL AT HOME WITH YOU / MY HEART STOOD STILL (Vocals: Fran Frey, Bob Borger, & Bob Rice)............... *Victor 21034* 2-4 27

IF YOU BELIEVED IN ME / SONG OF THE MOONBEAMS.................. *Victor 22065* 2-4 29
(Vocals: Fran Frey)

I'M IN SEVENTH HEAVEN / LITTLE PAL........................ *Victor 21954* 2-4 29
(Vocals: Fran Frey)

I'M KNEE-DEEP IN DAISIES (Vocals: Fran Frey & Bob Rice) / HOT AIRE....................... *Victor 19761* 3-5 25

IT'S ONLY A PAPER MOON (Vocal: Bob Borger) / NIGHT OWL (Vocal: Ethel Shutta).... *Columbia 2811-D* 5-8 33

I'VE GOT THE GIRL (Vocal: Fran Frey) / TONIGHT YOU BELONG TO ME (by Roger Wolfe Kahn & His Orchestra; Vocal: Franklyn Baur).................. *Victor 20359* 4-6 27

LET'S MAKE UP (Vocals: Bob Borger & Fran Frey) / HELLO, ALOHA! (Vocal: Fran Frey)...... *Victor 20060* 2-4 26

LOU'SIANA LULLABY / LET'S MAKE UP...................... *Columbia 2790-D* 5-8 33
(Vocals: Unknown)
(This record was pressed in blue shellac.)

LOVE, YOU FUNNY THING (Vocal: Fran Frey) / BY THE FIRESIDE (Vocals: Bob Borger & Ethel Shutta).............. *Victor 22947* 3-5 32

LUCKY IN LOVE (Vocals: Fran Frey, Bob Borger & Bob Rice) / THE BEST THINGS IN LIFE ARE FREE (Vocal: Bob Borger)..................... *Victor 20872* 2-4 27

MAKIN' WHOOPEE! / UNTIL YOU GET SOMEBODY ELSE.............. *Victor 21816* 3-5 29
(Vocals: Fran Frey)

MONTANA CALL (Vocals: by sextet) / THE MOON IS LOW (Vocal: Fran Frey).............. *Victor 22392* 3-5 30

MY BEST GIRL / PUT AWAY A LITTLE RAY OF SUNSHINE FOR A RAINY DAY....... *Victor 19518* 3-5 25

OUT OF THE DARKNESS (Vocal: Dave Marshall) / AH, BUT I'VE LEARNED (Vocal: Ethel Shutta).................... *Victor 24166* 3-5 32

OUT OF THE TEMPEST (Vocal: Fran Frey) / THE FIRST KISS (Vocal: Bob Borger)..... *Victor 21652* 2-4 28

ROCK-A-BYE MOON (Vocal: Ethel Shutta) / PLAY, FIDDLE, PLAY (Vocal: Dave Marshall).... *Victor 24165* 3-5 32

ROLLIN' ON OUR ROLLER SKATES / THE LAST ROUND-UP..................... *Columbia 2791-D* 5-8 33
(Vocals: Unknown)
(This record was pressed in blue shellac.)

SAY ARABELLA (WHAT'S A FELLA TO DO?) (Vocal: Billy Murray) / ROW! ROW! ROW! (Vocals: Billy Murray & Ed Smalle).......... *Victor 19710* 3-5 25

SAY IT ISN'T SO / LOVE ME TONIGHT.... *Victor 24124* 2-4 32
(Vocals: Paul Small)

SHE'S A CORNFED INDIANA GIRL (BUT SHE'S MAMA TO ME (Vocals: Fran Frey & Bob Rice) / TOO BAD........................... *Victor 20024* 4-6 26

SIXTY SECONDS GOT TOGETHER / LITTLE LADY MAKE-BELIEVE...................... *Decca 1786* 2-4 38
(Vocals: Unknown)

SLAVE OF LOVE, THE / BECAUSE THEY ALL LOVE YOU (Barney Rapp & His Orchestra)........ *Victor 19497* 3-5 24

SUNNY / WHO? (Vocals: Fran Frey, Bob Rice, & Jack Fulton).................. *Victor 19840* 2-4 26

THERE I GO DREAMING AGAIN (Vocals: Ethel Shutta) / YOU CAN MAKE MY LIFE A BED OF ROSES (Vocals: Fran Frey).................. *Victor 22937* 3-5 32

THIS LITTLE PIGGIE WENT TO MARKET / IN OTHER WORDS – WE'RE THROUGH...... *Columbia 2878-D* 5-8 34
(Vocals: Unknown)

UNDERNEATH THE ARCHES (Vocal: Ethel Shutta) / VAS VILLST DU HABEN? (Vocal: George Olsen)................... *Victor 24229* 4-6 33

WALKING WITH SUSIE (Vocal: Fran Frey) / THAT'S YOU BABY (Vocal: Erwin McGee).............. *Victor 21927* 3-5 29

WHAT'S THE USE OF TALKING? (Vocals: Bob Borger & Bob Rice) / BYE-BYE BLACKBIRD (Vocals: Fran Frey, Bob Borger, & Bob Rice)................... *Victor 20089* 2-4 26

WHY DO YOU WANT TO KNOW WHY? (Vocals: Fran Frey, Bob Borger, & Bob Rice) / TING-A-LING, THE BELLS'LL RING (by Roger Wolfe Kahn & His Orchestra)... *Victor 20116* 3-5 26

YOU ARE TOO BEAUTIFUL (Vocal: Bob Borger) / HALLELUJAH, I'M A BUM (Vocal: Fran Frey).................. *Victor 24221* 4-6 33

YOU NEED SOMEONE TO LOVE (Vocals: Fran Frey, Bob Borger, & Bob Rice) / ADORABLE (by Roger Wolfe Kahn & His Orchestra; Vocal: Gladys Rice & Carl Mathieu).................... *Victor 20106* 3-5 26

OLSEN, Ole, & His Orchestra

SADIE GREEN (THE VAMP OF NEW ORLEANS) (Vocal: John Ryan) / SNAG IT..... *Pathe Actuelle 36488* 5-8 26

SADIE GREEN (THE VAMP OF NEW ORLEANS) (Vocal: John Ryan) / SNAG IT........... *Perfect 14669* 3-5 26
(Simultaneously released on two labels)

OLYMPIC DANCE ORCHESTRA, The

AUNT HAGAR'S CHILDREN BLUES / AGGRAVATIN' PAPA................ *Olympic 1421* 5-8 23

O'NEILL, Walker:
see SPECHT, Paul, as The Georgians

OPERAPHONE DANCE ORCHESTRA, The:
see SAMUELS, Joseph, & His Orchestra

OPPENHEIM'S Benjamin Franklin Hotel Orchestra:
see HARING, Bob, & His Orchestra

ORCHESTRE CHEZ FYSHER, The:
see SELVIN, Ben

ORESTE & His Queensland Orchestra

EYEFUL OF YOU (Vocal: Arthur Fields) / SIDE BY SIDE (Vocal: Jack Kaufman) .... *Edison 52087* 4-6 27

HIGH HAT HARRY (Vocal: Jack Kaufman) / ROSY CHEEKS (Vocal: J. Donald Parker) ... *Edison 52017* 8-10 27

I NEVER KNEW WHAT THE MOONLIGHT COULD DO (Vocal: Charles Hart) / EV'RYTHING'S PEACHES .... *Edison 51857* 8-10 26

I WANT TO BE MILES AWAY FROM EVERYONE (AND JUST A LITTLE CLOSER TO YOU) / I'M LOOKING OVER A FOUR-LEAF CLOVER .... *Edison 51983* 5-8 27
(Vocals: Jack Davis)

LOVELY LADY / DANGER! (LOOK OUT FOR THAT GAL)..................... *Edison 52214* 8-10 28
(Vocals: The Songsters)

TEAR DROPS / ME AND THE CLOCK .... *Edison 52592* 8-10 29
(Vocals: The Rollickers)

TEN LITTLE MILES FROM TOWN / ANYTHING YOU SAY! .... *Edison 52383* 8-10 28

ORIGINAL SIX, The:
see KELLY, George

ORIGINAL ST. LOUIS CRACKERJACKS, The
directed by Chick Finney

CHASING THE BLUES AWAY / LONESOME MOMENTS (Vocal: Austin Wright).......... *Decca 7265* 4-6 36

CRACKERJACK STOMP / BLUE THINKING OF YOU (Vocal: Austin Wright)................ *Decca 7236* 4-6 36

ECHO IN THE DARK / FUSSIN' .... *Decca 7248* 5-8 36

GOOD OLD BOSOM BREAD / SWING JACKSON...................... *Decca 7235* 5-8 36

ORIGINAL WOLVERINES, The
(also see WOLVERINE ORCHESTRA, The)
directed by Dick Voynow

IF I HAD YOU / I FAW DOWN AND GO 'BOOM'!.................... *Vocalion 15766* 8-10 29
(Vocals: Frank Sylvano)

LIMEHOUSE BLUES / DEAR OLD SOUTHLAND (Vocals: Unknown)....... *Vocalion 15708* 12-15 28

ROYAL GARDEN BLUES / A GOOD MAN IS HARD TO FIND............................ *Brunswick 4000* 12-15 27

SHIM-ME-SHA-WABBLE / THE NEW TWISTER .... *Brunswick 3707* 12-15 27

SWEETHEARTS ON PARADE / I'LL GET BY....................... *Vocalion 15751* 8-10 29
(Vocals: Frank Sylvano)

THERE'S A RAINBOW 'ROUND MY SHOULDER / SONNY BOY........................ *Vocalion 15732* 8-10 29
(Vocals: Harry Maxfield)

ORIGINAL YELLOW JACKETS, The

BUSINESS AFTER MIDNIGHT / THE HOUR OF PARTING (Vocal: Aubrey Yancey) ... *Vocalion 03504* 10-12 37

CROSS STREET SWING / BLUE DRAG (Vocal: Aubrey Yancey).... *Vocalion 03591* 12-15 37

SWINGIN' AT THE CHAT 'N' CHEW / YELLOW-JACKETS GET TOGETHER .... *Vocalion 03549* 12-15 37

ORIOLE ORCHESTRA, The:
see RUSSO & FIO RITO'S ORIOLE Orchestra

ORIOLE TERRACE ORCHESTRA, The:
see RUSSO & FIO RITO'S ORIOLE Orchestra

ORLANDO, Nicholas, as Nicholas Orlando's Orchestra

APRIL SHOWERS (Vocal: Ernest Hare) / SAL-O-MAY (SALOME) .... *Pathe Actuelle 020664* 2-4 21

HINDU ROSE / YOU DON'T NEED THE WINE TO HAVE A WONDERFUL TIME (Vocal: Arthur Fields) .... *Pathe 22165* 3-5 19

HONEYMOON (Vocal: Henry Burr as Harry McClaskey) / WILL O' THE WISP .... *Pathe 22166* 2-4 19
(Henry Burr's pseudonym, Harry McClaskey, is his real name)

I KNOW WHY / SO THIS IS PARIS....... *Pathe 22342* 2-4 20

I'M SO SYMPATHETIC / MY ISLE OF GOLDEN DREAMS .... *Pathe 22269* 2-4 20

MAKE BELIEVE / TWO SWEET LIPS............ *Pathe Actuelle 022501* 2-4 21

MARY ANN / JUST A LITTLE GOLD BAND................. *Pathe Actuelle 36754* 2-4 21
(Vocals: Frank Bessinger)

MON HOMME (MY MAN) / IDOL MINE ... *Edison 50781* 3-5 21

OH, WHAT A PAL WAS MARY / PATCHES........................... *Pathe 22210* 2-4 19

SIDEWALK, THE / MOLLY ON A TROLLEY.............. *Pathe Actuelle 020593* 2-4 21

ORLANDO, Nicholas, as Nicholas Orlando's Orchestra
recorded under the name The EMPIRE DANCE ORCHESTRA

YOU DON'T NEED THE WINE TO HAVE A WONDERFUL TIME (Vocal: Arthur Fields) / WILL O' THE WISP.................. *Empire 31113* 4-6 19

ORLANDO, Nicholas as Nicholas Orlando's Orchestra
recorded under the name The Hot Springs Novelty Orchestra

EARLY IN THE MORNING BLUES / TWO LITTLE RUBY RINGS................ *Pathe Actuelle 020847* 3-5 22

EARLY IN THE MORNING BLUES / TWO LITTLE RUBY RINGS........................ *Perfect 14066* 2-4 22
(Simultaneously released on two labels)

SNEAK, THE / JUST BECAUSE YOU'RE MINE – THAT'S WHY I LOVE YOU .... *Pathe Actuelle 020800* 3-5 22

SNEAK, THE / JUST BECAUSE YOU'RE MINE – THAT'S WHY I LOVE YOU............ *Perfect 14033* 2-4 22
(Simultaneously released on two labels)

ORLANDO, Nicholas, as Orlando's Society Orchestra

I NEVER KNEW / HONOLULU EYES... *Emerson 10330* 2-4 21

SOMEONE CARES / JUNE .... *Emerson 10293* 2-4 20

ORLANDO'S SOCIETY ORCHESTRA:
see ORLANDO, Nicholas

ORMANDY, Dr. Eugene as
Dr. Eugene Ormandy's Salon Orchestra

GO TO BED / DANCE AWAY THE NIGHT... *Okeh 41300* 5-8 29
(Vocals: Unknown)

I NEVER DREAMT (YOU'D FALL IN LOVE WITH ME) / ONLY A ROSE .... *Okeh 41401* 8-10 30
(Vocals: Scrappy Lambert)

OSBORNE, Will, & His Orchestra
(Will Osborne: 11/25/06 – 10/22/81)
also see MARTIN, Freddy, & His Orchestra, and see MAYHEW, Nye, & His Orchestra

BLUE MOMENTS (WITHOUT YOU, DEAR) / TILL TOMORROW.................. *Banner 32645* 3-5 33
(Vocals: Will Osborne)

BLUE MOMENTS (WITHOUT YOU, DEAR) / TILL TOMORROW .... *Melotone M-12585* 3-5 33
(Vocals: Will Osborne)

BLUE MOMENTS (WITHOUT YOU, DEAR) / TILL TOMORROW..................... *Oriole 2625* 3-5 33
(Vocals: Will Osborne)

BLUE MOMENTS (WITHOUT YOU, DEAR) / TILL TOMORROW .... *Perfect 15714* 3-5 33
(Vocals: Will Osborne)

BLUE MOMENTS (WITHOUT YOU, DEAR) / TILL TOMORROW..................... *Romeo 1994* 3-5 33
(Vocals: Will Osborne)
(Simultaneously released on five labels)

BY THE RIVER SAINTE MARIE / BY MY SIDE..................... *Melotone M-12102* 3-5 31
(Vocals: Will Osborne)

COCKTAILS FOR TWO / LIVE AND LOVE TONIGHT..................... *Banner 33037* 3-5 34
(Vocals: Will Osborne)

COCKTAILS FOR TWO / LIVE AND LOVE TONIGHT................. *Melotone M-12996* 3-5 34
(Vocals: Will Osborne)

COCKTAILS FOR TWO / LIVE AND LOVE TONIGHT....................... *Oriole 2886* 3-5 34
(Vocals: Will Osborne)

COCKTAILS FOR TWO / LIVE AND LOVE TONIGHT..................... *Perfect 15925* 3-5 34
(Vocals: Will Osborne)

COCKTAILS FOR TWO / LIVE AND LOVE TONIGHT .... *Romeo 2260* 3-5 34
(Vocals: Will Osborne)
(Simultaneously released on five labels)

DANNY BOY (Vocals: Unknown) / YOU'RE GONNA SEE A LOT OF ME (Vocal: Lynn Davis) .... *Decca 2232* 2-4 39

DO I LOVE YOU? / WITH MY EYES WIDE OPEN I'M DREAMING............... *Banner 33075* 3-5 34
(Vocals: Will Osborne)

DO I LOVE YOU? / WITH MY EYES WIDE OPEN I'M DREAMING .... *Melotone M-13039* 3-5 34
(Vocals: Will Osborne)

DO I LOVE YOU? / WITH MY EYES WIDE OPEN I'M DREAMING................. *Oriole 2909* 3-5 34
(Vocals: Will Osborne)

DO I LOVE YOU? / WITH MY EYES WIDE OPEN I'M DREAMING .... *Perfect 15942* 3-5 34
(Vocals: Will Osborne)

DO I LOVE YOU? / WITH MY EYES WIDE OPEN I'M DREAMING................ *Romeo 2283* 3-5 34
(Vocals: Will Osborne)
(Simultaneously released on five labels)

DOWN BY THE RIVER / IT'S EASY TO REMEMBER..................... *Banner 33362* 3-5 35
(Vocals: Will Osborne)

DOWN BY THE RIVER / IT'S EASY TO REMEMBER................. *Melotone M-13329* 3-5 35
(Vocals: Will Osborne)

DOWN BY THE RIVER / IT'S EASY TO REMEMBER..................... *Oriole 3099* 3-5 35
(Vocals: Will Osborne)

DOWN BY THE RIVER / IT'S EASY TO REMEMBER .... *Perfect 16082* 3-5 35
(Vocals: Will Osborne)

DOWN BY THE RIVER / IT'S EASY TO REMEMBER .... *Romeo 2473* 3-5 35
(Vocals: Will Osborne)
(Simultaneously released on five labels)

DOWN HOME RAG / WHERE HAS MY LITTLE DOG GONE? (Vocals: by chorus) .... *Decca 2262* 2-4 39

DOWN THE RIVER OF GOLDEN DREAMS / THE SONG WITHOUT A NAME... *Columbia 2212-D* 3-5 30
(Vocals: Will Osborne)

FOR ALL WE KNOW / LET ME CALL YOU MINE......................... *Banner 33109* 2-4 34
(Vocals: Will Osborne)

FOR ALL WE KNOW / LET ME CALL YOU MINE..................... *Melotone M-13076* 2-4 34
(Vocals: Will Osborne)

FOR ALL WE KNOW / LET ME CALL YOU MINE.......................... *Oriole 2930* 2-4 34
(Vocals: Will Osborne)

FOR ALL WE KNOW / LET ME CALL YOU MINE .... *Perfect 15960* 2-4 34
(Vocals: Will Osborne)

FOR ALL WE KNOW / LET ME CALL YOU MINE .... *Romeo 2304* 2-4 34
(Vocals: Will Osborne)
(Simultaneously released on five labels)

FOR YOUR CARESSES / WITHOUT THAT GAL! .... *Melotone M-12206* 3-5 31
(Vocals: Will Osborne)

GENTLEMAN AWAITS, THE (theme song) / TELL ME, PRETTY MAIDEN (Vocals: Will Osborne & Lynn Davis).......... *Decca 2442* 2-4 39

GET RHYTHM IN YOUR FEET (AND MUSIC IN YOUR SOUL) / IF YOU WANT MY HEART (IT BELONGS TO YOU)........... *Melotone M-13419* 5-8 35
(Vocals: Will Osborne)

GET RHYTHM IN YOUR FEET (AND MUSIC IN YOUR SOUL) / IF YOU WANT MY HEART (IT BELONGS TO YOU)............... *Perfect 16125* 5-8 35
(Vocals: Will Osborne)
(Simultaneously released on two labels)

GOODNIGHT MOON / CAROLINA'S CALLING ME.................... *Melotone M-12301* 3-5 32
(Vocals: Will Osborne)

HAVE YOU FORGOTTEN? / TO WHISPER, DEAR, I LOVE YOU.................... *Melotone M-12130* 2-4 31
(Vocals: Will Osborne)

HEARTACHES / WHEN YOUR HAIR HAS TURNED TO SILVER .... *Meltone M-12078* 3-5 31
(Vocals: Will Osborne)

HELLO! BEAUTIFUL / ONE LITTLE RAINDROP......... *Melotone M-12099* 4-6 31
(Vocals: Will Osborne)

HOT CHOC'LATE SOLDIERS / I'VE HAD MY MOMENTS............ *Banner 33051* 3-5 34
(Vocals: Will Osborne)

HOT CHOC'LATE SOLDIERS / I'VE HAD MY MOMENTS......... *Melotone M-13013* 3-5 34
(Vocals: Will Osborne)

HOT CHOC'LATE SOLDIERS / I'VE HAD MY MOMENTS .... *Oriole 2895* 3-5 34
(Vocals: Will Osborne)

HOT CHOC'LATE SOLDIERS / I'VE HAD MY MOMENTS............. *Perfect 15930* 3-5 34
(Vocals: Will Osborne)

HOT CHOC'LATE SOLDIERS / I'VE HAD MY MOMENTS.............. *Romeo 2269* 3-5 34
(Vocals: Will Osborne)
(Simultaneously released on five labels)

I CAN'T BELIEVE IT'S TRUE / MUSIC, MUSIC EVERYWHERE (BUT NOT A SONG IN MY HEART).................. *Melotone M-12461* 3-5 32
(Vocals: Will Osborne)

IF I CAN COUNT ON YOU (Vocal: John Whitney) / THERE'S A GOLD MINE IN THE SKY (Vocal: Will Osborne)...................... *Decca 1455* 4-6 37

IF YOU WERE AS LOVELY (AS YOU ARE LOVELY) / THAT'S WHAT YOU THINK......... *Columbia 3080-D* 5-8 35
(Vocals: Will Osborne)

I KNEW WE TWO WERE ONE / THEY ALL FALL IN LOVE .... *Columbia 2044-D* 4-6 30
(Vocals: Will Osborne)

I'LL NEVER SAY "NEVER AGAIN" AGAIN / HOW CAN I HOLD YOU CLOSE ENOUGH? .... *Melotone M-13445* 4-6 35
(Vocals: Will Osborne)

I'LL NEVER SAY "NEVER AGAIN" AGAIN / HOW CAN I HOLD YOU CLOSE ENOUGH?.... *Perfect 16137* 4-6 35
(Vocals: Will Osborne)
(Simultaneously released on two labels)

ILL WIND / AS LONG AS I LIVE....... *Banner 32997* 3-5 34
(Vocals: Will Osborne)

ILL WIND / AS LONG AS I LIVE.... *Melotone M-12949* 3-5 34
(Vocals: Will Osborne)

ILL WIND / AS LONG AS I LIVE .... *Oriole 2861* 3-5 34
(Vocals: Will Osborne)

ILL WIND / AS LONG AS I LIVE........ *Perfect 15992* 3-5 34
(Vocals: Will Osborne)

ILL WIND / AS LONG AS I LIVE......... *Romeo 2236* 3-5 34
(Vocals: Will Osborne)
(Simultaneously released on five labels)

IN A BOAT OUT TO SEA / THE HOUR OF PARTING......... *Melotone M-12237* 3-5 31
(Vocals: Will Osborne)

INKA DINKA DOO (Vocals: by trio) / LIKE ME A LITTLE BIT LESS (LOVE ME A LITTLE BIT MORE) (Vocal: Nedra Gordinier)................. *Banner 32927* 3-5 34

INKA DINKA DOO (Vocals: by trio) / LIKE ME A LITTLE BIT LESS (LOVE ME A LITTLE BIT MORE) (Vocal: Nedra Gordinier) .... *Melotone M-12880* 3-5 34

INKA DINKA DOO (Vocals: by trio) / LIKE ME A LITTLE BIT LESS (LOVE ME A LITTLE BIT MORE) (Vocal: Nedra Gordinier)......................... *Oriole 2818* 3-5 34

INKA DINKA DOO (Vocals: by trio) / LIKE ME A LITTLE BIT LESS (LOVE ME A LITTLE BIT MORE) (Vocal: Nedra Gordinier) .... *Perfect 15867* 3-5 34

INKA DINKA DOO (Vocals: by trio) / LIKE ME A LITTLE BIT LESS (LOVE ME A LITTLE BIT MORE) (Vocal: Nedra Gordinier) .... *Romeo 2191* 3-5 34
(Simultaneously released on five labels)

IN THE STILL OF THE NIGHT (Vocal: John Whitney) / ROSALIE (Vocal: Will Osborne) .... *Decca 1467* 4-6 37

IT'S DE-LOVELY (Vocal: Dick Rogers & Dorothy Rogers) / TEA ON THE TERRACE (Vocal: Dorothy Rogers).................... *Decca 1058* 4-6 37

I WISH I COULD LEAVE YOU ALONE / TELL ME WHILE WE'RE DANCING........ *Melotone M-12341* 2-4 32
(Vocals: Will Osborne)

JUST A KID NAMED JOE / ANYWHERE I HANG MY HAT .... *Decca 2225* 2-4 39
(Vocals: Will Osborne)

JUST AN ECHO IN THE VALLEY / IT'S WITHIN YOUR POWER............................ *Banner 32660* 3-5 33
(Vocals: Will Osborne)

JUST AN ECHO IN THE VALLEY / IT'S WITHIN YOUR POWER......................... *Melotone M-12589* 3-5 33
(Vocals: Will Osborne)

JUST AN ECHO IN THE VALLEY / IT'S WITHIN YOUR POWER.............................. *Oriole 2632* 3-5 33
(Vocals: Will Osborne)

JUST AN ECHO IN THE VALLEY / IT'S WITHIN YOUR POWER .... *Perfect 15721* 3-5 33
(Vocals: Will Osborne)

JUST AN ECHO IN THE VALLEY / IT'S WITHIN YOUR POWER .... *Romeo 2005* 3-5 33
(Vocals: Will Osborne)
(Simultaneously released on five labels)

JUST A YEAR AGO TONIGHT / GOODNIGHT, LITTLE GIRL OF MY DREAMS .... *Conqueror 8219* 2-4 33
(Vocals: Will Osborne)

JUST A YEAR AGO TONIGHT / GOODNIGHT, LITTLE GIRL OF MY DREAMS........... *Melotone M-12805* 2-4 33
(Vocals: Will Osborne)

JUST A YEAR AGO TONIGHT / GOODNIGHT, LITTLE GIRL OF MY DREAMS................ *Oriole 2769* 2-4 33
(Vocals: Will Osborne)

JUST A YEAR AGO TONIGHT / GOODNIGHT, LITTLE GIRL OF MY DREAMS............... *Perfect 15828* 2-4 33
(Vocals: Will Osborne)

JUST A YEAR AGO TONIGHT / GOODNIGHT, LITTLE GIRL OF MY DREAMS................ *Romeo 2142* 2-4 33
(Vocals: Will Osborne)
(Simultaneously released on five labels)

JUST FRIENDS / ONE MORE KISS, THEN GOODNIGHT............. *Melotone M-12298* 3-5 32
(Vocals: Will Osborne)

JUST THINK OF ME SOMETIME / WITH YOU WHERE YOU ARE....................... *Columbia 2064-D* 4-6 30
(Vocals: Will Osborne)

JUST YOU ALONE / LET ME CALL YOU SWEETHEART........ *Columbia 2369-D* 3-5 30
(Vocals: Will Osborne)

LADY, PLAY YOUR MANDOLIN / A TEAR WAS BORN .... *Meltone M-12087* 3-5 31
(Vocals: Will Osborne)

LAST ROUND-UP, THE / HOME ON THE RANGE .... *Banner 32849* 3-5 33
(Vocals: Will Osborne)

LAST ROUND-UP, THE / HOME ON THE RANGE........... *Conqueror 8214* 3-5 33
(Vocals: Will Osborne)

LAST ROUND-UP, THE / HOME ON THE RANGE.......... *Melotone M-12776* 3-5 33
(Vocals: Will Osborne)

LAST ROUND-UP, THE / HOME ON THE RANGE............... *Oriole 2750* 3-5 33
(Vocals: Will Osborne)

LAST ROUND-UP, THE / HOME ON THE RANGE.............. *Perfect 15810* 3-5 33
(Vocals: Will Osborne)

LAST ROUND-UP, THE / HOME ON THE RANGE............... *Romeo 2123* 3-5 33
(Vocals: Will Osborne)
(Simultaneously released on six labels)

LET ME BORROW AN HOUR OF TOMORROW / SO LITTLE TIME .... *Decca 1769* 2-4 38
(Vocals: Will Osborne)

LET'S CALL IT ALL A DREAM / WHAT A DIFFERENCE A DAY MADE......... *Banner 33256* 3-5 34
(Vocals: Will Osborne)

LET'S CALL IT ALL A DREAM / WHAT A DIFFERENCE A DAY MADE ..... *Melotone M-13223* 3-5 34
(Vocals: Will Osborne)

LET'S CALL IT ALL A DREAM / WHAT A DIFFERENCE A DAY MADE........... *Oriole 3036* 3-5 34
(Vocals: Will Osborne)

LET'S CALL IT ALL A DREAM / WHAT A DIFFERENCE A DAY MADE .... *Perfect 16027* 3-5 34
(Vocals: Will Osborne)

LET'S CALL IT ALL A DREAM / WHAT A DIFFERENCE A DAY MADE.......... *Romeo 2410* 3-5 34
(Vocals: Will Osborne)
(Simultaneously released on five labels)

LITTLE DRUMMER BOY / I'LL STILL BE LOVING YOU .... *Decca 1926* 2-4 38
(Vocals: Will Osborne)

LOVE IN BLOOM / STRAIGHT FROM THE SHOULDER (RIGHT FROM THE HEART) .... *Banner 33110* 2-4 34
(Vocals: Will Osborne)

LOVE IN BLOOM / STRAIGHT FROM THE SHOULDER (RIGHT FROM THE HEART)........ *Conqueror 8408* 2-4 34
(Vocals: Will Osborne)

LOVE IN BLOOM / STRAIGHT FROM THE SHOULDER (RIGHT FROM THE HEART)...... *Melotone M-13077* 2-4 34
(Vocals: Will Osborne)

LOVE IN BLOOM / STRAIGHT FROM THE SHOULDER (RIGHT FROM THE HEART) .... *Oriole 2931* 2-4 34
(Vocals: Will Osborne)

LOVE IN BLOOM / STRAIGHT FROM THE SHOULDER (RIGHT FROM THE HEART).......... *Perfect 15961* 2-4 34
(Vocals: Will Osborne)

LOVE IN BLOOM / STRAIGHT FROM THE SHOULDER (RIGHT FROM THE HEART)........... *Romeo 2305* 2-4 34
(Vocals: Will Osborne)
(Simultaneously released on six labels)

LOVER / (I DON'T STAND) A GHOST OF A CHANCE WITH YOU.......................... *Banner 32710* 3-5 33
(Vocals: Will Osborne)

LOVER / (I DON'T STAND) A GHOST OF A CHANCE WITH YOU...................... *Melotone M-12637* 3-5 33
(Vocals: Will Osborne)

LOVER / (I DON'T STAND) A GHOST OF A CHANCE WITH YOU............................ *Oriole 2661* 3-5 33
(Vocals: Will Osborne)

LOVER / (I DON'T STAND) A GHOST OF A CHANCE WITH YOU .... *Perfect 15741* 3-5 33
(Vocals: Will Osborne)

LOVER / (I DON'T STAND) A GHOST OF A CHANCE WITH YOU .... *Romeo 2034* 3-5 33
(Vocals: Will Osborne)
(Simultaneously released on five labels)

LOVE THY NEIGHBOR / ONCE IN A BLUE MOON...................... *Banner 33036* 2-4 34
(Vocals: Will Osborne)

LOVE THY NEIGHBOR / ONCE IN A BLUE MOON................. *Melotone M-12995* 2-4 34
(Vocals: Will Osborne)

LOVE THY NEIGHBOR / ONCE IN A BLUE MOON........................ *Oriole 2885* 2-4 34
(Vocals: Will Osborne)

LOVE THY NEIGHBOR / ONCE IN A BLUE MOON .... *Perfect 15924* 2-4 34
(Vocals: Will Osborne)

LOVE THY NEIGHBOR / ONCE IN A BLUE MOON .... *Romeo 2259* 2-4 34
(Vocals: Will Osborne)
(Simultaneously released on five labels)

LUCILLE! / CHANCES ARE........ *Melotone M-12275* 3-5 31
(Vocals: Will Osborne)

MUSIC, MUSIC EVERYWHERE (BUT NOT A SONG IN MY HEART) / MOON.............. *Conqueror 8036* 3-5 32
(Vocals: Will Osborne)

MUSIC, MUSIC EVERYWHERE (BUT NOT A SONG IN MY HEART) / MOON .... *Perfect 15666* 3-5 32
(Vocals: Will Osborne)
(Simultaneously released on two labels)

NEEDLE IN A HAYSTACK, A / THE CONTINENTAL............... *Banner 33187* 3-5 34
(Vocals: Will Osborne)

NEEDLE IN A HAYSTACK, A / THE CONTINENTAL........... *Melotone M-13154* 3-5 34
(Vocals: Will Osborne)

NEEDLE IN A HAYSTACK, A / THE CONTINENTAL................. *Oriole 2985* 3-5 34
(Vocals: Will Osborne)

NEEDLE IN A HAYSTACK, A / THE CONTINENTAL............... *Perfect 15997* 3-5 34
(Vocals: Will Osborne)

NEEDLE IN A HAYSTACK, A / THE CONTINENTAL............... *Romeo 2359* 3-5 34
(Vocals: Will Osborne)
(Simultaneously released on five labels)

NOW THAT YOU'RE GONE / LINDA.......................... *Melotone M-12234* 3-5 31
(Vocals: Will Osborne)

OLD SPINNING WHEEL, THE / COUNT YOUR BLESSINGS.......... *Banner 32919* 3-5 34
(Vocals: Will Osborne)

OLD SPINNING WHEEL, THE / COUNT YOUR BLESSINGS........ *Conqueror 8266* 3-5 34
(Vocals: Will Osborne)

OLD SPINNING WHEEL, THE / COUNT YOUR BLESSINGS....... *Melotone M-12863* 3-5 34
(Vocals: Will Osborne)

OLD SPINNING WHEEL, THE / COUNT YOUR BLESSINGS............ *Oriole 2809* 3-5 34
(Vocals: Will Osborne)

OLD SPINNING WHEEL, THE / COUNT YOUR BLESSINGS .... *Perfect 15859* 3-5 34
(Vocals: Will Osborne)

OLD SPINNING WHEEL, THE / COUNT YOUR BLESSINGS .... *Romeo 2180* 3-5 34
(Vocals: Will Osborne)
(Simultaneously released on six labels)

ON A BLUE AND MOONLESS NIGHT / IMAGINE...................... *Columbia 2128-D* 4-6 30
(Vocals: Will Osborne)

ONE I LOVE (BELONGS TO SOMEBODY ELSE), THE / MELODY FARM .... *Decca 1637* 3-5 38

PERHAPS / SAME OLD MOON...... *Columbia 1988-D* 4-6 29
(Vocals: Will Osborne)

PLEASE / HERE LIES LOVE .... *Banner 32599* 2-4 32
(Vocals: Will Osborne)

PLEASE / HERE LIES LOVE......... *Conqueror 8074* 2-4 32
(Vocals: Will Osborne)

PLEASE / HERE LIES LOVE....... *Melotone M-12499* 2-4 32
(Vocals: Will Osborne)

PLEASE / HERE LIES LOVE............ *Oriole 2587* 2-4 32
(Vocals: Will Osborne)

PLEASE / HERE LIES LOVE........... *Perfect 15686* 2-4 32
(Vocals: Will Osborne)

PLEASE / HERE LIES LOVE .... *Romeo 1959* 2-4 32
(Vocals: Will Osborne)
(Simultaneously released on six labels)

PLEASE / JUST AN ECHO IN THE VALLEY.................. *Vocalion 15880* 3-5 33
(Vocals: Will Osborne)

PLEASE PARDON US, WE'RE IN LOVE (Vocals: Will Osborne & Dorothy Rogers) / AFRAID TO DREAM (Vocal: Dorothy Rogers)................. *Decca 1371* 4-6 37

REMEMBER ME? / AM I IN LOVE? (Vocal: Will Osborne).............. *Decca 1383* 4-6 37

RIDIN' AROUND IN THE RAIN / A LAZY DAY IN THE SUN....................... *Banner 33076* 3-5 34
(Vocals: Will Osborne)

RIDIN' AROUND IN THE RAIN / A LAZY DAY IN THE SUN .... *Melotone M-13040* 3-5 34
(Vocals: Will Osborne)

RIDIN' AROUND IN THE RAIN / A LAZY DAY IN THE SUN........................ *Oriole 2910* 3-5 34
(Vocals: Will Osborne)

RIDIN' AROUND IN THE RAIN / A LAZY DAY IN THE SUN........................ *Perfect 15943* 3-5 34
(Vocals: Will Osborne)

RIDIN' AROUND IN THE RAIN / A LAZY DAY IN THE SUN......................... *Romeo 2284* 3-5 34
(Vocals: Will Osborne)
(Simultaneously released on five labels)

SAY IT ISN'T SO / AFTER TONIGHT................. *Conqueror 8021* 3-5 32
(Vocals: Will Osborne)

SAY IT ISN'T SO / AFTER TONIGHT................. *Perfect 15670* 3-5 32
(Vocals: Will Osborne)
(Simultaneously released on two labels)

SILVER ON THE SAGE / WHEN TWILIGHT COMES .... *Decca 1951* 2-4 38
(Vocals: Will Osborne)

SINGIN' THE BLUES / BUZZ MIRANDY.... *Decca 1717* 3-5 38

SING, MY HEART (Vocal: Lynn Davis) / THE MOON IS A SILVER DOLLAR (Vocal: Will Osborne)..... *Decca 2335* 2-4 39

SNUGGLED ON YOUR SHOULDER / SHADOWS ON THE WINDOW.................. *Melotone M-12312* 3-5 32
(Vocals: Will Osborne)

STREET OF DREAMS / I CALLED TO SAY GOODNIGHT............... *Banner 32637* 3-5 33
(Vocals: Will Osborne)

STREET OF DREAMS / I CALLED TO SAY GOODNIGHT .... *Melotone M-12564* 3-5 33
(Vocals: Will Osborne)

STREET OF DREAMS / I CALLED TO SAY GOODNIGHT................. *Oriole 2609* 3-5 33
(Vocals: Will Osborne)

STREET OF DREAMS / I CALLED TO SAY GOODNIGHT................ *Perfect 15711* 3-5 33
(Vocals: Will Osborne)

STREET OF DREAMS / I CALLED TO SAY GOODNIGHT................. *Romeo 1991* 3-5 33
(Vocals: Will Osborne)
(Simultaneously released on five labels)

THAT LITTLE BOY OF MINE / SAY A LITTLE PRAYER FOR ME............... *Melotone M-12118* 3-5 31
(Vocals: Will Osborne)

THERE GOES MY HEART / IT'S AN OLD-FASHIONED WORLD AFTER ALL............... *Banner 32960* 2-4 34
(Vocals: Will Osborne)

THERE GOES MY HEART / IT'S AN OLD-FASHIONED WORLD AFTER ALL............ *Melotone M-12910* 2-4 34
(Vocals: Will Osborne)

THERE GOES MY HEART / IT'S AN OLD-FASHIONED WORLD AFTER ALL.................... *Oriole 2836* 2-4 34
(Vocals: Will Osborne)

THERE GOES MY HEART / IT'S AN OLD-FASHIONED WORLD AFTER ALL.................. *Perfect 15880* 2-4 34
(Vocals: Will Osborne)

THERE GOES MY HEART / IT'S AN OLD-FASHIONED WORLD AFTER ALL................... *Romeo 2209* 2-4 34
(Vocals: Will Osborne)
(Simultaneously released on five labels)

THERE WILL NEVER BE ANOTHER MARY / THE LANGUAGE OF LOVE....... *Columbia 2093-D* 4-6 30
(Vocals: Will Osborne)

THREE ON A MATCH / 'TWAS ONLY A SUMMER NIGHT'S DREAM .... *Conqueror 8022* 3-5 32
(Vocals: Will Osborne)

THREE ON A MATCH / 'TWAS ONLY A SUMMER NIGHT'S DREAM .... *Perfect 15674* 3-5 32
(Vocals: Will Osborne)
(Simultaneously released on two labels)

TILL THE CLOCK STRIKES THREE / DON'T EVER CHANGE................. *Decca 1361* 4-6 37
(Vocals: Will Osborne)

(LET'S DRINK A DRINK) TO THE FUTURE! / I'M ALL DRESSED UP WITH A BROKEN HEART........... *Melotone M-12201* 3-5 31
(Vocals: Will Osborne)

WAGON WHEELS / LULLABY IN BLUE .... *Banner 32969* 2-4 34
(Vocals: Will Osborne)

WAGON WHEELS / LULLABY IN BLUE........................ *Conqueror 8266* 2-4 34
(Vocals: Will Osborne)

WAGON WHEELS / LULLABY IN BLUE....................... *Melotone M-12919* 2-4 34
(Vocals: Will Osborne)

WAGON WHEELS / LULLABY IN BLUE............................. *Oriole 2841* 2-4 34
(Vocals: Will Osborne)

WAGON WHEELS / LULLABY IN BLUE.......................... *Perfect 15885* 2-4 34
(Vocals: Will Osborne)

WAGON WHEELS / LULLABY IN BLUE.............................. *Romeo 2214* 2-4 34
(Vocals: Will Osborne)
(Simultaneously released on six labels)

WATER UNDER THE BRIDGE / P.S. – I LOVE YOU.................... *Banner 33232* 2-4 34
(Vocals: Will Osborne)

WATER UNDER THE BRIDGE / P.S. – I LOVE YOU .... *Melotone M-13199* 2-4 34
(Vocals: Will Osborne)

WATER UNDER THE BRIDGE / P.S. – I LOVE YOU...................... *Oriole 3020* 2-4 34
(Vocals: Will Osborne)

WATER UNDER THE BRIDGE / P.S. – I LOVE YOU .... *Perfect 16017* 2-4 34
(Vocals: Will Osborne)

WATER UNDER THE BRIDGE / P.S. – I LOVE YOU.................... *Romeo 2394* 2-4 34
(Vocals: Will Osborne)
(Simultaneously released on five labels)

WHEN I CLOSE MY EYES AND DREAM / SO BEATS MY HEART FOR YOU .... *Columbia 2269-D* 3-5 30
(Vocals: Will Osborne)

WHERE THE BLUE OF THE NIGHT (MEETS THE GOLD OF THE DAY) / SHOULD I BE SORRY? .... *Melotone M-12287* 2-4 32
(Vocals: Will Osborne)

WHISPER WALTZ / A KISS IN THE MOONLIGHT .... *Banner 32709* 2-4 33
(Vocals: Will Osborne)

WHISPER WALTZ / A KISS IN THE MOONLIGHT .... *Melotone M-12636* 2-4 33
(Vocals: Will Osborne)

WHISPER WALTZ / A KISS IN THE MOONLIGHT .... *Oriole 2660* 2-4 33
(Vocals: Will Osborne)

WHISPER WALTZ / A KISS IN THE MOONLIGHT .... *Perfect 15740* 2-4 33
(Vocals: Will Osborne)

WHISPER WALTZ / A KISS IN THE MOONLIGHT .... *Romeo 2033* 2-4 33
(Vocals: Will Osborne)
(Simultaneously released on five labels)

WHISTLE AND BLOW YOUR BLUES AWAY / WHERE ARE YOU .... *Melotone M-12351* 3-5 32
(Vocals: Will Osborne)

WHO'LL BUY MY VIOLETS? / I SURRENDER, DEAR .... *Melotone M-12112* 3-5 31
(Vocals: Will Osborne)

WITH EVERY BREATH I TAKE / JUNE IN JANUARY .... *Banner 33285* 2-4 34
(Vocals: Will Osborne)

WITH EVERY BREATH I TAKE / JUNE IN JANUARY .... *Conqueror 8425* 2-4 34
(Vocals: Will Osborne)

WITH EVERY BREATH I TAKE / JUNE IN JANUARY .... *Melotone M-13252* 2-4 34
(Vocals: Will Osborne)

WITH EVERY BREATH I TAKE / JUNE IN JANUARY .... *Oriole 3053* 2-4 34
(Vocals: Will Osborne)

WITH EVERY BREATH I TAKE / JUNE IN JANUARY .... *Perfect 16042* 2-4 34
(Vocals: Will Osborne)

WITH EVERY BREATH I TAKE / JUNE IN JANUARY .... *Romeo 2426* 2-4 34
(Vocals: Will Osborne)
(Simultaneously released on six labels)

WITHOUT A WORD OF WARNING / I WISH I WERE ALADDIN .... *Columbia 3081-D* 5-8 35
(Vocals: Will Osborne)

WOULD'ST COULD I BUT KISS THY HAND, OH BABE (Vocal: "Doghouse" Dale Jones) / THE MAN WHO COMES AROUND (Vocals: Dale, Barbara, Stinky, Will & orchestra) .... *Varsity 8143* 4-6 39

YAAKA HULA HICKEY DULA (Vocals: by trio) / TWELFTH STREET RAG .... *Decca 1534* 5-8 37

YOU'LL ALWAYS BE THE SAME SWEETHEART / MOON .... *Melotone M-12473* 2-4 32
(Vocals: Will Osborne)

OSBORNE, Will, & His Orchestra as Dan Ritchie & His Orchestra

WHISTLE AND BLOW YOUR BLUES AWAY / TELL ME WHILE WE'RE DANCING .... *Perfect 15589* 3-5 32
(Vocals: Dick Robertson)

OSSMAN, Vess L., as Vess Ossman's Banjo Orchestra

BENEATH A BALCONY / HILDA .... *Edison 50427* 8-10 16

GO TO IT / RAG-A-MINOR .... *Gennett 7630* 8-10 17

KANGAROO HOP / MERRY WHIRL ..... *Victor 35536* 5-8 16
(an oversize 12-inch 78 rpm)

MY HAWAIAN SUNSHINE / YOU'LL ALWAYS BE THE SAME SWEET BABY ..... *Columbia A-5928* 5-8 17

POOR BUTTERFLY / HELLO, I'VE BEEN LOOKING FOR YOU .... *Operaphone 1631* 8-10 17
(7 inch)

TOPSY / HAVANOLA .... *Operaphone 1632* 8-10 17
(7 inch)

OSWALD, Glen, as Glen Oswald's Serenaders

BUCKTOWN BLUES / BURMALONE (AN ECHO FROM THE SOUTH SEAS) .... *Victor 19733* 5-8 25

GO YOUR WAY AND I'LL GO MINE / OH PETER .... *Victor 19410* 4-6 24

I AIN'T GOT NOBODY TO LOVE / (IF IT WASN'T FOR YOU) I WOULDN'T BE CRYING NOW .... *Victor 19611* 4-6 25

OWENS, Harry, & His Arizona Biltmore Hotel Orchestra
(Harry Owens: 4/18/02 –)

TUNE IN ON MY HEART / WHAT DO I CARE? .... *Brunswick 4599* 5-8 29
(Vocals: by trio)

OWENS, Harry, & His Royal Hawaiian Hotel Orchestra

DOWN WHERE THE TRADE WINDS BLOW (Vocal: Raymond Andrade) / SYNCOPATED HULA LOVE SONG (Vocals: by quartet) .... *Decca 1243* 4-6 37

FAREWELL MALIHINI (Vocal: Bob Hamlin) / DOWN ON AMI AMI ONI ONI ISLE (Vocals: by trio) .... *Capitol 20003* 2-4 45

LITTLE BUTCH (Vocal: Bob Hamlin) / SWEET LEILANI (theme song) (Vocals: by trio) .... *Capitol 20004* 2-4 45

SING A HULA SONG (Vocals: by trio) / O MA KA LA PUA (Vocals: Raymond Andrade & Alvin Kaleolani) .... *Decca 2039* 2-4 38

OWENS, Red, & His Band:
see MILLS, Floyd, & His Marylanders

OXLEY, Harold, & His Post Lodge Orchestra

STEP, HENRIETTA / BURNING KISSES ... *Okeh 40134* 5-8 24

PAGE, Hot Lips, & His Band
(Hot Lips Page: 1/27/08 – 11/5/54)

(A SKY OF BLUE, WITH YOU) AND SO FORTH (Vocal: Dolores Payne) / WILL YOU REMEMBER TONIGHT TOMORROW? (Vocal: Ben Bowers) .... *Bluebird B-7680* 4-6 38
DOWN ON THE LEVEE (LEVEE LULLABY) / OLD MAN BEN .... *Decca 7433* 5-8 38
(Vocals: Hot Lips Page)
FEELIN' HIGH AND HAPPY / AT YOUR BECK AND CALL .... *Bluebird B-7569* 5-8 38
(Vocals: Hot Lips Page)
GOOD OLD BOSOM BREAD (Vocal: Hot Lips Page) / HE'S PULLING HIS WHISKERS .... *Decca 7451* 5-8 38
HARLEM RHUMBAIN' THE BLUES / NO MATTER WHERE YOU ARE (WHEN EVENING DRAWS HER CURTAIN) (Vocal: Bea Morton) .... *Decca 8531* 5-8 41
I AIN'T GOT NOBODY (Vocals: The Harlem Highlanders) / GONE WITH THE GIN .... *Decca 7714* 5-8 40
IF I WERE YOU (Vocal: Delores Payne) / SMALL FRY (Vocal: Hot Lips Page) .... *Bluebird B-7684* 4-6 38
I WOULD DO ANYTHING FOR YOU / I WON'T BE HERE LONG .... *Decca 7699* 4-6 40
(Vocals: Hot Lips Page)
JUMPIN' / SKULLDUGGERY .... *Bluebird B-7583* 5-8 38
LAFAYETTE / SOUTH .... *Decca 18124* 4-6 41
PIED PIPER, THE / I'M GONNA LOCK MY HEART AND THROW AWAY THE KEY .... *Bluebird B-7682* 5-8 38
(Vocals: Hot Lips Page)
PORTER'S LOVE SONG TO A CHAMBERMAID (Vocal: Romayne Jackson) / WALK IT TO ME ...... *Decca 7757* 5-8 40
ROCK IT FOR ME (Vocal: Hot Lips Page) / I LET A SONG GO OUT OF MY HEART .... *Bluebird B-7567* 5-8 38

PAGE, Hot Lips, as Hot Lips Page Trio

EVIL MAN'S BLUES (Vocal: Teddy Bunn) / DO IT IF YOU WANNA .... *Bluebird B-8634* 5-8 41
JUST ANOTHER WOMAN / MY FIGHTIN' GAL .... *Bluebird B-8660* 5-8 41
(Vocals: Hot Lips Page)
THIRSTY MAMA BLUES / — .... *Bluebird B-8981* 5-8 41

PAGE, Walter, as Walter Page's Blue Devils
(Walter Page: 2/9/00 – 12/20/57)

BLUE DEVIL BLUES (Vocal: Jimmy Rushing) / SQUABBLIN' .... *Vocalion 1463* 40-50 29

PAIGE, Raymond, & His Orchestra
(Raymond Paige: — –8/7/65)

GOT ME DOIN' THINGS (Vocals: The Rhythmettes) / MY HEART IS AN OPEN BOOK (Vocal: Hugh Grant) .... *Victor 24866* 3-5 35
LOVE THY NEIGHBOR (Vocals: The Three Rhythm Kings) / ONCE IN A BLUE MOON (Vocals: Unknown) .... *Victor 24604* 3-5 34
POP! GOES YOUR HEART (Vocals: The Rhythm Kings) / BEAUTY MUST BE LOVED (Vocals: Unknown) .... *Victor 24706* 3-5 34
WHEN MY PRINCE CHARMING COMES ALONG / A LITTLE WHITE GARDENIA .... *Victor 24857* 2-4 35
(Vocals: Marion Manfield)
YOU'RE NOTHIN' BUT A NOTHIN' (Vocals: by orchestra) / TALKIN' TO MYSELF (Vocals: The Rhythm Kings) .... *Victor 24703* 3-5 34

PALACE DANCE ORCHESTRA, The:
see SCHUBERT, Adrian, & His Salon Orchestra

PALACE TRIO, The:
see WIEDOFT, Rudy

PALACE TRIO & ORCHESTRA, The:
see WIEDOFT, Rudy

PALAIS D'OR ORCHESTRA, The

BLACK-EYED SUSAN BROWN / I'M NUTS ABOUT MUTTS .... *Crown 3450* 4-6 33
(Vocals: Unknown)
UNDERNEATH THE ARCHES / YOU MUST BELIEVE ME .... *Crown 3443* 3-5 33
(Vocals: Unknown)

PALAIS ROYAL ORCHESTRA, The

MAMMY'S LULLABY (Vocal: Arthur Fields) / HEAD OVER HEELS .... *Pathe 40154* 2-4 19
MY DESERT FANTASY / SWEET SIAMESE (Vocal: Arthur Fields) .... *Pathe 22101* 2-4 19
OH, SUSIE, BEHAVE / LOVE IS LOVE ... *Pathe 40162* 2-4 19

PALLEDO ORCHESTRA OF ST. LOUIS, The

CLOSE YOUR EYES / WHAT-CHA-CALL-'EM BLUES .... *Okeh 40521* 5-8 25

PALLOY, Charlie, & His Orchestra

BROTHER, CAN YOU SPARE A DIME? / IT DON'T MEAN A THING(IF IT AIN'T GOT THAT SWING) .... *Crown 3392* 5-8 32
(Vocals: Charlie Palloy)
PETTIN' IN THE PARK / WE'RE IN THE MONEY (THE GOLD DIGGERS' SONG) .... *Crown 3512* 5-8 33
(Vocals: Charlie Palloy)
WHAT A PERFECT COMBINATION / AND SO I MARRIED THE GIRL .... *Crown 3410* 5-8 32
(Vocals: Charlie Palloy)
YOU'RE TELLING ME / ONE LITTLE WORD LED TO ANOTHER .... *Crown 3389* 5-8 32
(Vocals: Charlie Palloy)

PALM BEACH SOCIETY ORCHESTRA, The

APPLE SAUCE / DOWN IN MARYLAND .... *Olympic 1425* 4-6 23

PALMER, Skeeter, & His Orchestra

I'M BUBBLING OVER / NEVER IN A MILLION YEARS .... *Vocalion 3512* 5-8 37
(Vocals: Skeeter Palmer)
WHEN LOVE IS YOUNG / DID ANYONE EVER TELL YOU?..... .... *Vocalion 3502* 5-8 37
(Vocals: Skeeter Palmer)

PALMQUIST, Ernie, & His Carolina Collegians

FADED SUMMER LOVE (Vocal: Maurice Cross) / YOU RASCAL, YOU (Vocal: Harry Jaeger).... *Champion 16352* 4-6 32
MARTY / OLD PLAYMATE.......... *Champion 16359* 3-5 32
(Vocals: Unknown)
MARTY / OLD PLAYMATE............ *Superior 2767* 3-5 32
(Vocals: Unknown)
(Simultaneously released on two labels)

PALMQUIST, Ernie, & His Carolina Collegians as Harlan Hasty & His Orchestra

GEE, BUT I'D LIKE TO MAKE YOU HAPPY (Vocal: Art Lombardi) / HOW CAN I SMILE? (Vocal: Ernie Palmquist)................. *Superior 2553* 3-5 30
GOODNIGHT, SWEETHEART (Vocal: Ernie Palmquist) / YOU RASCAL, YOU (Vocal: Harry Jaeger).................... *Superior 2759* 4-6 32

PALMQUIST, Ernie, & His Carolina Collegians as Bud Reynolds & His Orchestra

GOODNIGHT, SWEETHEART (Vocal: Ernie Palmquist) / YOU CALL IT MADNESS (Vocal: Maurice Cross)............... *Champion 16353* 4-6 32

PALMQUIST, Ernie, & His Carolina Collegians as Chuck Winters & His Boys

FADED SUMMER LOVE / YOU CALL IT MADNESS......................... *Superior 2758* 4-6 32
(Vocals: Maurice Cross)

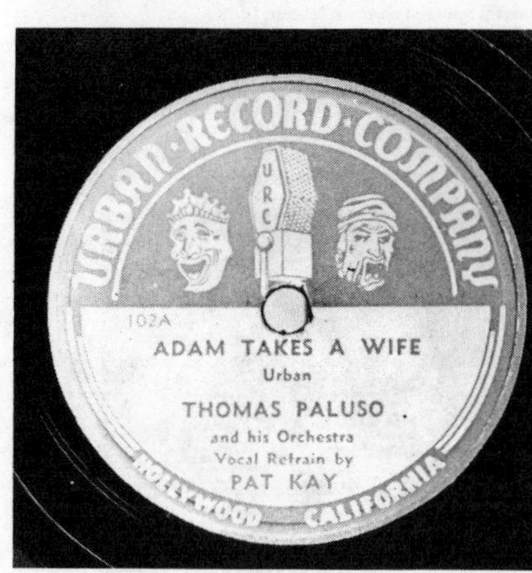

PALUSO, Thomas, & His Orchestra

ADAM TAKES A WIFE / ON THE SPUR OF THE MOMENT.................... *Urban 102* 5-8 46
(Vocals: Pat Kay)

PAN-AMERICAN MARIMBA BAND, The
directed by Antonio Cibelli

FAROLITO (Vocal: Luis Alvarez) / LA MARIMBA (Vocal: Ducal) .... *Victor 25203* 3-5 35

PANCHO, & His Orchestra

ADIOS, MUCHACHOS / TANGO DELLE ROSE................. *Decca 1982* 2-4 38
ALLA EN EL RANCHO GRANDE / DOWN ARGENTINE WAY.............. *Decca 3474* 2-4 40
AURORA / I CAME, I SAW, I CONGA'D.... *Decca 3742* 2-4 41
FRENESI / DARDANELLA.............. *Decca 3589* 2-4 41
HEY AI YEA / IMPROVISANDO.......... *Apollo 1036* 3-5 47
HINDUSTAN / TIGER RAG.............. *Decca 3620* 2-4 41
LA VEEDA / MINNIE FROM TRINIDAD.... *Decca 3957* 2-4 41
RHUMBOOGIE / DARK EYES .... *Decca 3480* 2-4 40

PANICO, Louis, & His Orchestra

DON'T LET YOUR LOVE GO WRONG / WHY DON'T YOU PRACTICE WHAT YOU PREACH?... *Decca 230* 5-8 34
WABASH BLUES (theme song) / OH DOCTOR (Vocals: Unknown)....... *Brunswick 4736* 8-10 30
WABASH BLUES (theme song) / SOMEDAY, SWEETHEART............. *Decca 159* 5-8 34

PAPALIA, Russ, as Papalia & His Orchestra

CROSS-WORD MAMA YOU'RE PUZZLING ME / SOMETIME WHEN YOU'RE ALONE.... *Okeh 40347* 15-20 25

PARAMOUNT DANCE ORCHESTRA, The

JUNE NIGHTS / MANDALAY ...... *Paramount 20338* 3-5 24
NONA / ROSES AT TWILIGHT ...... *Paramount 30089* 3-5 19
OH! HOW I LOVE MY DARLING (Vocals: Unknown) / I WANT TO SEE MY TENNESSEE... *Paramount 20366* 3-5 24
PLEASE / THERE'S YES! YES! IN YOUR EYES (Vocals: Unknown)... *Paramount 20335* 3-5 24
ROSE-MARIE / I WONDER WHAT'S BECOME OF SALLY? .... *Paramount 20355* 3-5 24

PARAMOUNT–PUBLIX RECORDING ORCHESTRA, The,
directed by Irvin Talbot

I'M CRAZY 'BOUT MY BABY (AND MY BABY'S CRAZY 'BOUT ME) / THE SAME AS WE USED TO BE .... *Perfect 15447* 3-5 31
(Vocals: Frank Parker)

PARAMOUNTEERS, The
see CALIFORNIA RAMBLERS, The

PARISIAN RED HEADS, The

I'LL THINK OF YOU / I STILL LOVE YOU................ *Brunswick 3795* 4-6 28
(Vocals: Bobby Grice)
(This was an all-girl band including Bobby Grice, the vocalist.)

PARK CENTRAL ORCHESTRA, The:
see LOWN, Bert, & His Orchestra

PARKER, Charlie
(Charlie Parker: 8/29/20 – 3/12/55)

CHARLIE PARKER WITH STRINGS (a 3-record album set) .... *Mercury C-509* 15-25 48
Individual records in the set, listed numerically (with value of each)
YOU CAME ALONG FROM OUT OF NOWHERE / EAST OF THE SUN.............. *Mercury 11070* 5-8 -
THEY CAN'T TAKE THAT AWAY FROM ME / I'M IN THE MOOD FOR LOVE .... *Mercury 11071* 5-8 -
EASY TO LOVE / I'LL REMEMBER APRIL............................ *Mercury 11072* 5-8 -

PARKER, Don, & His Strand Roof Orchestra

FOOLISH CHILD / COVERED WAGON DAYS (Vocal: Arthur Grant)...... *Pathe Actuelle 021068* 3-5 23
FOOLISH CHILD / COVERED WAGON DAYS (Vocal: Arthur Grant).............. *Perfect 14171* 2-4 23
(Simultaneously released on two labels)

PARKER, Don, as Don Parker's Entertainers

SOMEONE LOVES YOU AFTER ALL / TWELVE O'CLOCK AT NIGHT.......... *Pathe Actuelle 036040* 3-5 24
SOMEONE LOVES YOU AFTER ALL / TWELVE O'CLOCK AT NIGHT .... *Perfect 14221* 2-4 24
(Simultaneously released on two labels)

PARKER, Don, as Don Parker's Western Melody Boys
(A Dance Band)

DEAREST (YOU'RE THE NEAREST TO MY HEART) / LITTLE ROVER (Vocals: Unknown)... *Pathe Actuelle 020914* 3-5 23
DEAREST (YOU'RE THE NEAREST TO MY HEART) / LITTLE ROVER (Vocals: Unknown) ...... *Perfect 14098* 2-4 23
(Simultaneously released on two labels)
EVERYTHING IS K.O. IN K.Y. / ROSE OF BRAZIL............... *Pathe Actuelle 020937* 3-5 23
EVERYTHING IS K.O. IN K.Y. / ROSE OF BRAZIL.......................... *Perfect 14119* 2-4 23
(Simultaneously released on two labels)
I'M ALWAYS STUTTERING / YANKEE DOODLE BLUES.... *Pathe Actuelle 020824* 4-6 22
I'M ALWAYS STUTTERING / YANKEE DOODLE BLUES........... *Perfect 14050* 3-5 22
(Simultaneously released on two labels)

PARKER, Don, as The Don Parker Trio

I LOVE HER – SHE LOVES ME / NOLA .... *Pathe Actuelle 020769* 3-5 22
IT'S GETTING DARK ON OLD BROADWAY / VAMP ME (AND I'LL VAMP YOU)......... *Pathe Actuelle 020844* 3-5 22
SILVER STARS / WHO'LL TAKE MY PLACE?................. *Pathe Actuelle 020809* 3-5 22
SILVER STARS / WHO'LL TAKE MY PLACE? .... *Perfect 14040* 2-4 22
SILVER STARS / WHO'LL TAKE MY PLACE?............. .... *Davega 5035* 10-12 22
(Simultaneously released on three labels)

PARKER, Frank, & His Orchestra:
see MARTIN, Freddy, & His Orchestra

PARK LANE ORCHESTRA, The:
see RESER, Harry

PAR-O-KET (DANCE) ORCHESTRA, The
(Par-O-Ket records are rare.)

I'M A-LONGIN' FO' YOU / WILD FLOWERS .... *Par-O-Ket 94* 15-20 17
JOHNNY, GET A GIRL / RED FOX TROT .... *Par-O-Ket 53* 20-25 16
MISSOURI WALTZ / I'M GOING TO HIT THE TRAIL .... *Par-O-Ket 55* 15-20 16
OH, JOHNNY! OH, JOHNNY! OH / IF YOU CAN'T MAKE A HIT IN A BALL GAME ..... *Par-O-Ket 124* 20-25 17

PASTOR, Tony, & His Orchestra
(Tony Pastor: 10/26/07 – 10/31/69)

ABSENT-MINDED MOON / THE LAMP OF MEMORY .... *Bluebird B-11435* 2-4 42
(Vocals: John McAfee)
AIN'T MISBEHAVIN' / BROTHER BILL .... *Bluebird B-11550* 3-5 42
(Vocals: Tony Pastor)
BELLS OF SAN RAQUEL, THE (Vocal: Eugenie Baird) / A PRETTY CO-ED HAS GONE TO MY HEAD .... *Bluebird B-11307* 2-4 41
(Vocals: John McAfee)
BLUES (MY NAUGHTY SWEETIE GIVES TO ME) (Vocal: Eugenie Baird) / GREEN EYES (Vocal: Dorsey Anderson) .... *Bluebird B-11168* 2-4 41
CONFESSIN' (Vocal: Tony Pastor) / I CLOSE MY EYES (Vocal: Dorsey Anderson) .... *Bluebird B-11105* 2-4 41
COPLEY SQUARE / BRAGGIN' (Vocal: Tony Pastor) ...... *Bluebird B-11119* 3-5 41
DANCE WITH A DOLLY (WITH A HOLE IN HER STOCKING) (Vocal: Tony Pastor) / WATCHING THE CLOCK (Vocal: Elisse Cooper) ... *Bluebird B-10582* 2-4 40
DEAREST, DAREST I? (Vocals: Kay Little & Tony Pastor) / I'VE GOT YOU UNDER MY SKIN (Vocal: Tony Pastor) .... *Bluebird B-10915* 2-4 40
DINAH (Vocal: Tony Pastor) / ALL ALONE AND LONELY (Vocal: John McAfee) .... *Bluebird B-11185* 2-4 41
FLAGWAVER / DOIN' THE RATAMACUE (Vocal: Tony Pastor) ... *Bluebird B-11421* 3-5 41
FULL MOON (Vocal: Eugenie Baird) / OBEY YOUR AIR RAID WARDEN (Vocal: Tony Pastor) ... *Bluebird B-11525* 3-5 42
GET HAPPY / BLOSSOMS (theme song) .... *Bluebird B-11376* 3-5 41
GOOD MORNING, MR. ZIP-ZIP-ZIP! (Vocals: Eugenie Baird, Tony Pastor, & John McAfee) / THE MARINES' HYMN (Vocal: John McAfee) .... *Bluebird B-11452* 3-5 42
HELEN OF TROY / HURRY BACK TO SORRENTO (Vocal: John McAfee) ... *Bluebird B-11139* 3-5 41
I'LL PRAY FOR YOU / NOT MINE ... *Bluebird B-11467* 3-5 42
(Vocals: Eugenie Baird)
I'M GETTING TIRED SO I CAN SLEEP (Vocal: Eugenie Baird) / MASSACHUSETTS (Vocal: Tony Pastor) .... *Bluebird B-11585* 2-4 42
I'M NEW AT THIS (Vocal: Dorsey Anderson) / DON'T LET JULIA FOOL YA (Vocal: Tony Pastor) .... *Bluebird B-11247* 2-4 41
I'M SORRY I DIDN'T SAY I'M SORRY (Vocals: Tony Pastor, Rose Mary Clooney) / THE LADY FROM TWENTY-NINE PALMS (Vocal: Tony Pastor) .... *Columbia 37562* 2-4 47
LET'S DO IT (LET'S FALL IN LOVE) (Vocal: Tony Pastor) / READY, GET SET, JUMP .... *Bluebird B-10902* 3-5 40
LET'S GIVE LOVE A CHANCE (Vocal: John McAfee) / THE MEMORY OF THIS DANCE (Vocals: Eugenie Baird & John McAfee) .... *Bluebird B-11481* 2-4 42
LOUISIANA PURCHASE (Vocal: Kay Foster) / THE LORD DONE FIXED UP MY SOUL (Vocal: Tony Pastor) .... *Bluebird B-10725* 3-5 40
LOVE OF MY LIFE (Vocal: Kay Little) / LET'S DREAM THIS ONE OUT (Vocal: Dorsey Anderson) .... *Bluebird B-10938* 2-4 40
MARIA ELENA (Vocal: Dorsey Anderson) / MADE UP MY MIND (Vocal: John McAfee) .... *Bluebird B-11127* 2-4 41
NOTHING BUT YOU (Vocal: Bob Carroll) / IT NEVER ENTERED MY MIND (Vocal: Kay Foster) .... *Bluebird B-10634* 2-4 40
ON A SIMMERY SUMMERY DAY (Vocal: Kay Foster) / I BOUGHT A WOODEN WHISTLE (Vocal: Tony Pastor) .... *Bluebird B-10747* 2-4 40
PALE MOON / HEP-TEE-HOOTIE (JUKE BOX JIVE) .... *Bluebird B-11040* 3-5 40
(Vocals: Tony Pastor)
PARADIDDLE JOE (Vocal: Tony Pastor) / ADIOS .... *Bluebird B-11008* 3-5 41
SHEPHERD SERENADE (Vocal: John McAfee) / YOO-HOO (Vocal: Tony Pastor) .... *Bluebird B-11264* 2-4 41
SOFT-HEARTED (Vocal: Eugenie Baird) / HEY, MABEL! (Vocal: Tony Pastor) ... *Bluebird 30-0802* 2-4 42
SO NEAR AND YET SO FAR (Vocal: Eugenia Baird) / DREAM DANCING (Vocal: John McAfee) .... *Bluebird B-11267* 2-4 41
SUNDAY IN SAVANNAH (Vocal: Tony Pastor) / JOHNNIE'S IN THE PANTRY (Vocal: Eugenie Baird) .... *Bluebird B-11340* 2-4 41
TELL IT TO A STAR / DEAR LITTLE BOY OF MINE .... *Bluebird B-11533* 2-4 42
(Vocals: Eugenie Baird)
THAT AIN'T THE WAY I DREAMED IT (Vocal: John McAfee) / FIGHTIN' DOUG MacARTHUR (Vocal: Tony Pastor) ... *Bluebird B-11502* 3-5 42
THERE'S A MAN AT THE DOOR (Vocals: Tony Pastor & The Clooney Sisters) / I WANNA SLEEP (Vocal: Tony Pastor) .... *Columbia 38178* 2-4 48
TWENTY-ONE DOLLARS A DAY – ONCE A MONTH (Vocal: Tony Pastor) / I FOUND YOU IN THE RAIN (Vocal: Eugenie Baird) .... *Bluebird B-11231* 3-5 41
WHO'S GOT A TENT FOR RENT? (Vocals: Tony Pastor & Virginia Maxey) / ALL THAT GLITTERS IS NOT GOLD (Vocals: Tony Pastor, Virginia Maxey, & The Tunetimers) .... *Cosmo 474* 5-8 46
WIGWAM STOMP / MARIA, MARIA (Vocal: Tony Pastor) .... *Bluebird B-11087* 3-5 41
YOU CAN DEPEND ON ME / EL CHOCLO .... *Bluebird B-11359* 2-4 41
(Vocals: Tony Pastor)
YOUR RED WAGON (Vocal: Tony Pastor) / GONNA GET A GIRL (Vocals: Tony Pastor & The Clooney Sisters) .... *Columbia 37973* 2-4 47

PAYNE, Art, & His Orchestra

BLUE NIGHT / JO-ANNE .... *Gennett 6694* 10-12 29
(Vocals: Doug Williamson)
IGLOO STOMP / TAKE YOUR TOMORROW .... *Gennett 6644* 10-12 28
JINGLE BELLS / YOU'VE GOT TO SEE YOUR MAMA EVERY NIGHT .... *Gennett 5064* 5-8 23
LET ME CALL YOU SWEETHEART / SOME WINTER NIGHT .... *Gennett 5063* 4-6 23
OH MAUD / YOU CAN'T MAKE A WOMAN CHANGE HER MIND .... *Gennett 5631* 5-8 25

PAYNE, Art, & His Orchestra, as Art Kahn & His Orchestra

BLUE NIGHT / JO-ANNE .... *Supertone 9334* 8-10 29
(Vocals: Doug Williamson)

PEABODY, Eddie, & His Band
(Eddie Peabody: circa 1901 – 11/7/70)

HELLO SANDY (Vocals: Unknown) / FRESHIE .... *Banner 1640* 4-6 26
HELLO SANDY (Vocals: Unknown) / FRESHIE .... *Domino 3611* 4-6 26
(Simultaneously released on two labels)
TILL THE END OF THE WORLD WITH YOU / WHEN I DREAM OF THE LAST WALTZ WITH YOU .... *Banner 1645* 3-5 25
TILL THE END OF THE WORLD WITH YOU / WHEN I DREAM OF THE LAST WALTZ WITH YOU .... *Domino 3616* 3-5 25
TILL THE END OF THE WORLD WITH YOU / WHEN I DREAM OF THE LAST WALTZ WITH YOU .... *Regal 9950* 3-5 25
(Simultaneously released on three labels)
WHOOPEE! / CLAP HANDS! (HERE COMES CHARLEY!) (Vocals: Unknown) .... *Banner 1643* 5-8 26
WHOOPEE! / CLAP HANDS! (HERE COMES CHARLEY!) (Vocals: Unknown) .... *Domino 3615* 5-8 26
WHOOPEE! / CLAP HANDS! (HERE COMES CHARLEY!) (Vocals: Unknown) .... *Regal 9944* 5-8 26
(Simultaneously released on three labels)

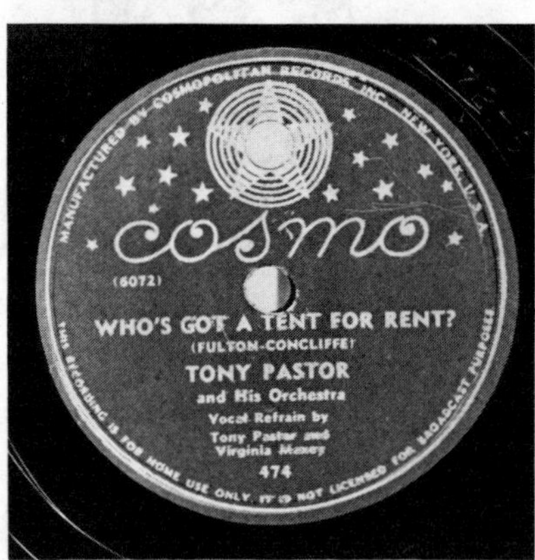

PEARL, Ray, & His Orchestra

CHOIR BOY (Vocal: Fran Schneider) / THE MOON IS IN THE SKY (Vocal: Bud Madison) .... *Vocalion 3536* 4-6 37
I LOVE YOU FROM COAST TO COAST (Vocal: Walt Link) / GONE (Vocal: Bub Madison) .... *Vocalion 3408* 5-8 37
I'M HATIN' THIS WAITIN' AROUND (Vocal: Art Link) / WANTED (Vocal: Bud Madison) .... *Vocalion 3522* 5-8 37
TIMBER (Vocal: Bud Madison) / SMOKE DREAMS (Vocal: Fran Schneider) .... *Vocalion 3420* 5-8 37

PEERLESS SERENADERS of Al Tearney's Town Club
directed by Al Hall & Howard Israel
(Al Hall: 3/18/15 –)

YOU BROKE MY HEART / I'VE LOST MY DOG .... *Okeh 40729* 5-8 27

PELHAM HEATH INN SOCIETY Orchestra, The:
see RADERMAN, Lou

PELHAM INN SOCIETY Orchestra, The:
see RADERMAN, Lou

PELTYN, Sid, & His Orchestra
also see MITCHELL, Al, & His Orchestra

SAME OLD MOON / ROAMIN' FOR ROMANCE .... *Victor 24082* 3-5 32
(Vocals: James Harkins)

PELTYN, Sid, & His Orchestra, as Eliot Everett & His Orchestra

MOON (Vocal: James Harkins) / I FOUND A BRAND NEW SWEETHEART (Vocals: James Harkins & George Stone) .... *Victor 24120* 3-5 32
THREE KISSES (Vocal: James Harkins) / LOUISIANA HAYRIDE (Vocals: James Harkins & George Stone) .... *Victor 24130* 4-6 32

PELTYN, Sid, & His Orchestra as Jim Harkins & His Orchestra
(These releases are early 8-inch Electradisks, exceptionally rare)

CLOUDS WILL SOON ROLL BY, THE / GEE, BUT I HATE TO SAY GOODNIGHT .... *Electradisk 1809* 20-25 32
(Vocals: James Harkins)
NIGHT SHALL BE FILLED WITH MUSIC, THE / IN THE DREAMY HILLS OF HOME, SWEET HOME .... *Electradisk 1805* 20-25 32
(Vocals: James Harkins)

PELTYN, Sid, & His Orchestra as Charles Prince & His Ochestra

GREAT BIG BUNCH OF YOU, A / NOW YOU'VE GOT ME WORRYIN' FOR YOU .... *Electradisk 1806* 20-25 32
(Vocals: James Harkins)
(An exceptionally rare early 8-inch Electradisk)

PELTYN, Sid, & His Orchestra as Les Sims & His Orchestra

YOU'VE GOT ME IN THE PALM OF YOUR HAND / MY DREAM HOUSE ON AIR CASTLE ROAD .... *Electradisk 1804* 20-25 32
(Vocals: James Harkins)
(An exceptionally rare early 8-inch Electradisk)

PENDARVIS, Paul, & His Orchestra
(Paul Pendarvis: 1907 –)

I'M IN LOVE ALL OVER AGAIN (Vocal: Patricia Norman) / WOULD THERE BE LOVE? (Vocals: Unknown) .... *Columbia 3032-D* 4-6 35
LITTLE ANGEL TOLD ME SO, A (Vocal: Eddie Stone) / I'VE GOT AN INVITATION TO A DANCE (Vocal: Patricia Norman) .... *Columbia 2974-D* 4-6 34
MISSISSIPPI HONEYMOON (Vocal: Eddie Stone) / THE OBJECT OF MY AFFECTION (Vocal: Patricia Norman) .... *Columbia 2973-D* 5-8 34
(This record was pressed in blue shellac)
PAGE MISS GLORY (Vocals: The Pendarvis Boys) / ACCENT ON YOUTH (Vocal: Jimmy Stewart) ... *Columbia 3082-D* 4-6 35
SOON / IT'S EASY TO REMEMBER ... *Columbia 3025-D* 4-6 35
(Vocals: Jimmy Stewart)
THANKS A MILLION (Vocal: Marjorie Beatty) / I'M SITTIN' HIGH ON A HILL TOP (Vocal: Eddie Stone) .... *Columbia 3091-D* 3-5 35

PENNINGTON ORCHESTRA, The

ADORING YOU / DREAM GIRL .... *Triangle 11424* 3-5 24
BROKEN DREAMS / MOONLIGHT MEMORIES .... *Lyraphone 11416* 5-8 24
BROKEN DREAMS / MOONLIGHT MEMORIES .... *Triangle 11416* 3-5 24
(Simultaneously released on two labels)

PENNSYLVANIA COLLEGIANS, The
see KARDOS, Gene, & His Orchestra

PENNSYLVANIA DANCE ORCHESTRA, The

TWO LIPS TO KISS MY CARES AWAY / IT'S THE LAST TIME (7-inch) .... *Marathon 228* 15-20 28
(Vocals: Unknown)
(Marathon records are rare.)

PENNSYLVANIA PLAYERS, The

ARE YOU HAPPY? / A NICE HONEYMOON .... *Bell 543* 3-5 27
(Vocals: Unknown)
BYE-BYE, PRETTY BABY / STOP YOUR CRYIN' .... *Bell 532* 3-5 27
(Vocals: Unknown)

PERKINS, Doc, & His Orchestra

I'M SORRY, DEAR / TOO LATE .... *Champion 16376* 5-8 32
(Vocals: Unknown)

PERRINE, Cliff, & His Orchestra

MYSTERIOUS MOSE / I LOST MY GAL FROM MEMPHIS .... *Gennett 7214* 5-8 30
(Vocals: Cliff Perrine)
MYSTERIOUS MOSE / I LOST MY GAL FROM MEMPHIS .... *Champion 15999* 4-6 30
(Vocals: Cliff Perrine)
(Simultaneously released on two labels)

PERRY, Bill, as Bill Perry's Entertainers

CRAZY WORDS – CRAZY TUNE / COCK-A-DOODLE, I'M OFF MY NOODLE (MY BABY'S BACK) .... *Banner 1922* 3-5 27
(Vocals: The Radio Imps)

PERRY'S HOT DOGS

HAS BEEN BLUES / I'M GONNA HANG AROUND MY SUGAR (Vocal: Arthur Fields) .... *Banner 1641* 5-8 26
HAS BEEN BLUES / I'M GONNA HANG AROUND MY SUGAR (Vocal: Arthur Fields) .... *Domino 3614* 5-8 26
HAS BEEN BLUES / I'M GONNA HANG AROUND MY SUGAR (Vocal: Arthur Fields) .... *Regal 9945* 5-8 26
(Simultaneously released on three labels)
SHOW ME THE WAY TO GO HOME / THERE AIN'T NO FLIES ON AUNTIE .... *Banner 1615* 5-8 25
(Vocals: Arthur Fields)
SHOW ME THE WAY TO GO HOME / THERE AIN'T NO FLIES ON AUNTIE .... *Domino 3589* 5-8 25
(Vocals: Arthur Fields)
SHOW ME THE WAY TO GO HOME / THERE AIN'T NO FLIES ON AUNTIE .... *Regal 9917* 5-8 25
(Vocals: Arthur Fields)
(Simultaneously released on three labels)

PERRY'S ORCHESTRA

THAT CERTAIN PARTY (Vocal: Arthur Hall) / HEADIN' FOR LOUISVILLE .... *Paramount 20431* 5-8 26
THAT CERTAIN PARTY (Vocal: Arthur Hall) / HEADIN' FOR LOUISVILLE .... *Puritan 11431* 4-6 26
(Simultaneously released on two labels)

PETTIS, Jack, & His Band
(Jack Pettis: 1902 –)

IT ALL DEPENDS ON YOU (Vocals: Scrappy Lambert & Billy Hillpot) / MUDDY WATER (Vocal: Scrappy Lambert) .... *Banner 1927* 5-8 27
IT ALL DEPENDS ON YOU (Vocals: Scrappy Lambert & Billy Hillpot) / MUDDY WATER (Vocal: Scrappy Lambert) .... *Domino 3897* 5-8 27
(Simultaneously released on two labels)
ONCE OVER LIGHTLY / STEPPIN' IT OFF .... *Domino 4094* 5-8 28
ONCE OVER LIGHTLY / STEPPIN' IT OFF .... *Regal 8483* 5-8 28
(Simultaneously released on two labels)

PETTIS, Jack, & His Band, as The Dixie Jazz Band

HE'S THE LAST WORD / ST. LOUIS SHUFFLE .... *Oriole 799* 5-8 27

PETTIS, Jack, & His Orchestra

FRESHMAN HOP / SWEETEST MELODY .... *Okeh 41411* 15-20 29
HAWAIIAN HEAT WAVE / SWING SESSION IN SIBERIA .... *Variety 558* 5-8 37

PETTIS, Jack, & His Orchestra as Jack Binney & His Orchestra

FRESHMAN HOP / BAG O' BLUES .... *Parlophone PNY-34076* 15-20 29

PETTIS, Jack, & His Pets

BAG O' BLUES, A / FRESHMAN HOP (Vocals: Erwin McGee) ... *Victor 21793* 10-12 28
DRY MARTINI / HOT HEELS .... *Vocalion 15703* 12-15 28
SPANISH DREAM / DOIN' THE NEW LOW DOWN .... *Victor 21559* 10-12 28

PETTIS, Jack, & His Pets as The New Orleans Blackbirds

HONOLULU BLUES (Vocal: Erwin McGee) / BABY (Vocal: Irving Mills) .... *Victor V-38026* 15-20 28

PHILLIPS, Flip, as The Flip Phillips Quartet
(Flip Phillips: 2/26/15 –)

FLIP PHILLIPS (a 3-record album set) .... *Mercury C-105* 12-15 49
Individual records in the set, listed numerically (with value of each)
LOVER / BLUE ROOM .... *Mercury 8918* 3-5 -
DON'T TAKE YOUR LOVE FROM ME / LOVER COME BACK TO ME .... *Mercury 8919* 3-5 -
FEELIN' THE BLUES / FLIP'S BOOGIE .... *Mercury 8920* 4-6 -

PICCADILLY PLAYERS, The
directed by Mel Morris

FEELIN' GOOD / RAIN OR SHINE .... *Edison 52232* 10-12 28
IN THE HUSH OF THE NIGHT / TIP-TOE THROUGH THE TULIPS WITH ME .... *Edison 14056* 15-20 29
(Vocals: Unknown)
(A rare lateral-cut thin Edison disc)
MY ONE AND ONLY / I'M RIDING TO GLORY .... *Edison 52280* 10-12 28
(Vocals: Unknown)
ROSE ROOM / I FELL HEAD OVER HEELS IN LOVE .... *Edison 52215* 8-10 28
(Vocals: Unknown)
SONNY BOY / TAKE YOUR TOMORROW .... *Edison 52391* 8-10 28
(Vocals: Unknown)
THINK OF ME THINKING OF YOU / I'M SORRY, SALLY .... *Edison 52442* 8-10 29
WALKING WITH SUSIE / BREAKAWAY .... *Edison 52613* 12-15 29
WANTING YOU / DEEP IN THE ARMS OF LOVE .... *Edison 14088* - -
(This record session was the final one for commercial issue in the Edison Studios. The record was never released.)
WEARY RIVER / SUSIANNA .... *Edison 52527* 12-15 29
WHAT'LL YOU DO? / I JUST ROLL ALONG .... *Edison 52198* 10-12 29
(Vocals: Vaughn de Leath)
YOU OUGHT TO SEE MY NEW BABY / EV'RY DAY AWAY FROM YOU .... *Edison 52635* 10-12 29
(Vocals: Elliott Stewart)
YOU'RE JUST A GREAT BIG BABY DOLL / JUST A LITTLE BIT O' DRIFTWOOD .... *Edison 52327* 8-10 28
YOU WERE MEANT FOR ME / A NIGHT OF MEMORIES .... *Edison 52545* 8-10 29

PIERCE, Charles, & His Orchestra

BULL FROG BLUES / CHINA BOY .... *Paramount 12619* 40-50 28
JAZZ ME BLUES / SISTER KATE .... *Paramount 12640* 40-50 28

PIETRO & HIS BLUE HORSE TAVERN ORCHESTRA:
see DEIRO, Pietro

PINKIE'S BIRMINGHAM FIVE:
see GERBRECHT, Edward "Pinkie"

PITT, Merle, & His Make Believe Ballroom Orchestra

MAKE BELIEVE BALLROOM (Vocal: Mildred Craig) / WITH A SMILE AND A SONG (Vocal: Don Richards) .... *Vocalion 3959* 5-8 38
START THE DAY WITH A SMILE (Vocal: Alan Courtney) / PAGLIACCI .... *Vocalion 3945* 5-8 38

PLANTATION DANCE / JAZZ ORCHESTRA, The:
see RADERMAN, Harry

PLETCHER, Stew, & His Orchestra
(Stew Pletcher: 2/21/07 –)

TOUCH OF YOUR LIPS, THE / I HOPE GABRIEL LIKES MY MUSIC .... *Bluebird B-6345* 8-10 36
(Vocals: Stew Pletcher)
WILL I EVER KNOW? / I DON'T WANT TO MAKE HISTORY .... *Bluebird B-6344* 8-10 36
(Vocals: Stew Pletcher)
YOU / YOU NEVER LOOKED SO BEAUTIFUL .... *Bluebird B-6343* 8-10 36
(Vocals: Stew Pletcher)

PLETCHER, Stew, as Pletcher's Eli Prom Trotters

I LIKE TO DO THINGS FOR YOU (Vocal: Stew Pletcher) / THAT'S WHERE YOU'RE WRONG .... *QRS Q-1055* 25-30 30

PLUMB, Neely, & His Orchestra

TAKES TWO TO TANGO (Vocal: Dottie O'Brien) / OH HAPPY DAY (Vocal: Ralph Brackett) ... *Ace-Hi 1012* 2-4 51

PLUMB, Neely, as Neely Plumb's Four Star Rhythm Section

RHYTHM BLUES (slow tempo) / RHYTHM BLUES (jump tempo) .... *Rhythm Records R-110* 4-6 46

POLLACK, Ben, & His Californians
(Ben Pollack: 6/22/03 – 6/7/71)

SINGAPORE SORROWS (Vocal: Ben Pollack) / SWEET SUE – JUST YOU (Vocal: Franklyn Baur) ... *Victor 21437* 10-12 28
YOU'RE THE ONE FOR ME (Vocal: Ilomay Bailey) / HIGH FEVER (by the Coon-Sanders Orchestra) ... *Victor 20461* 15-20 27

POLLACK, Ben, & His Orchestra

AFTER YOU'VE GONE / LOOKING AT THE WORLD THROUGH ROSE-COLORED GLASSES ... *Decca 2057* 3-5 38
CRYIN' FOR THE CAROLINES (Vocal: Ben Pollack) .... *Hit Of The Week 1027* 10-12 30
(Hit Of The Week records are one-sided paper discs.)
DANCING IN THE MOONLIGHT (Vocal: Ben Pollack) / OLE MAMMY AIN'T GONNA SING NO MORE (Vocal: Joe Harris) .... *Columbia 2901-D* 8-10 34
'DEED I DO / I NEED LOVIN' (by The Coon-Sanders Orchestra; Vocal: Joe Sanders) .... *Victor 20408* 5-8 27
DEEP ELM / THE MOON IS GRINNING AT ME (Vocal: Ben Pollack) .... *Variety 504* 5-8 37
DEEP JUNGLE / SWING OUT .... *Columbia 2879-D* 10-12 34
EVERYBODY'S DOIN' IT / THIS IS THE LIFE; THE INTERNATIONAL RAG .... *Decca 1891* 3-5 38
(Vocals: Paula Gayle)
FRECKLE FACE, YOU'RE BEAUTIFUL (Vocal: Joe Harris) / I'VE GOT A WARM SPOT FOR YOU (Vocal: Doris Robbins) .... *Columbia 2931-D* 8-10 34
GOT THE JITTERS (Vocal: Nappy Lamare) / I'M FULL OF THE DEVIL (Vocal: Ben Pollack) .... *Columbia 2870-D* 10-12 34
HAVE YOU EVER BEEN IN HEAVEN? / MAMMA, I WANNA MAKE RHYTHM .... *Decca 1476* 5-8 37
(Vocals: Frances Hunt)
HERE GOES (Vocal: Joe Harris) / THE BEAT O' MY HEART (Vocals: Unknown) .... *Columbia 2905-D* 8-10 34
(This record was pressed in blue shellac)
IF I COULD BE WITH YOU ONE HOUR TONIGHT (Vocal: Jack Teagarden as Roland Lance) / THERE'S A WAH-WAH GIRL IN AGUA CALIENTE (Vocals: by trio) .... *Conqueror 7576* 10-12 30
IF I COULD BE WITH YOU ONE HOUR TONIGHT (Vocal: Jack Teagarden as Roland Lance) / THERE'S A WAH-WAH GIRL IN AGUA CALIENTE (Vocals: by trio) .... *Domino 4588* 10-12 30
IF I COULD BE WITH YOU ONE HOUR TONIGHT (Vocal: Jack Teagarden as Roland Lance) / THERE'S A WAH-WAH GIRL IN AGUA CALIENTE (Vocals: by trio) .... *Perfect 15325* 10-12 30
(Simultaneously released on three labels)
IF YOU SHOULD EVER LEAVE / I'M DEPENDABLE .... *Decca 1435* 5-8 37
(Vocals: Frances Hunt)
I'M FOLLOWING YOU (Vocal: Ben Pollack) .... *Hit Of The Week 1026* 10-12 30
(Hit Of The Week records are one-sided paper discs)
I'M ONE STEP AHEAD OF MY SHADOW (Vocal: Lois Still) / I COULDN'T BE MAD AT YOU (Vocals: Carol McKay) .... *Brunswick 7751* 5-8 36
IN A SENTIMENTAL MOOD / PECKIN' (Vocals: Ben Pollack & trio) .... *Variety 556* 5-8 37
I'VE GOT FIVE DOLLARS (Vocal: Ben Pollack as Ted Bancroft) / SWEET AND HOT (Vocals: by Ben Pollack as Ted Bancroft, Jack Teagarden & Nappy Lamare) .... *Banner 32104* 10-12 31
I'VE GOT FIVE DOLLARS (Vocal: Ben Pollack as Ted Bancroft) / SWEET AND HOT (Vocals: by Ben Pollack as Ted Bancroft, Jack Teagarden & Nappy Lamare) .... *Conqueror 7684* 10-12 31
I'VE GOT FIVE DOLLARS (Vocal: Ben Pollack as Ted Bancroft) / SWEET AND HOT (Vocals: by Ben Pollack as Ted Bancroft, Jack Teagarden & Nappy Lamare) .... *Jewel 6213* 10-12 31
I'VE GOT FIVE DOLLARS (Vocal: Ben Pollack as Ted Bancroft) / SWEET AND HOT (Vocals: by Ben Pollack as Ted Bancroft, Jack Teagarden & Nappy Lamare) .... *Oriole 2213* 10-12 31
I'VE GOT FIVE DOLLARS (Vocal: Ben Pollack as Ted Bancroft) / SWEET AND HOT (Vocals: by Ben Pollack as Ted Bancroft, Jack Teagarden & Nappy Lamare) .... *Perfect 15431* 10-12 31
I'VE GOT FIVE DOLLARS (Vocal: Ben Pollack as Ted Bancroft) / SWEET AND HOT (Vocals: by Ben Pollack as Ted Bancroft, Jack Teagarden & Nappy Lamare) .... *Regal 10273* 10-12 31
I'VE GOT FIVE DOLLARS (Vocal: Ben Pollack as Ted Bancroft) / SWEET AND HOT (Vocals: by Ben Pollack as Ted Bancroft, Jack Teagarden & Nappy Lamare) .... *Romeo 1576* 10-12 31
(Simultaneously released on seven labels)
LINGER A LITTLE LONGER IN THE TWILIGHT (Vocal: Doris Robbins) / TWO TICKETS TO GEORGIA (Vocal: Nappy Lamare) .... *Victor 24284* 8-10 33
MEET THE BEAT OF MY HEART / WHAT ARE YOU DOING TONIGHT? .... *Decca 2005* 3-5 38
(Vocals: Paula Gayle)
MY LITTLE GRASS SHACK IN KEALAKEKUA, HAWAII (Vocals: Doris Robbins, Nappy Lamare, & Joe Harris) / GOIN' TO HEAVEN ON A MULE (Vocal: Joe Harris) .... *Columbia 2886-D* 5-8 34
NATURALLY / SO UNEXPECTEDLY .... *Decca 2012* 2-4 38
(Vocals: Paula Gayle)
NIGHT ON THE DESERT / SLEEPY HEAD .... *Columbia 2929-D* 5-8 34
(Vocals: Joe Harris)
SHOULD I / DON'T MEDDLE IN MY MOOD .... *Jewel J-1001* 4-6 45
(Vocals: Kay Starr)
SING A SONG OF SIXPENCE / AS LONG AS I LIVE .... *Decca 2006* 3-5 38
(Vocals: Paula Gayle)

SING-SONG GIRL (LITTLE YELLA CINDERELLA) (Vocal: Ben Pollack as Ted Bancroft) / (WHEN YOU FALL IN LOVE) FALL IN LOVE WITH ME (Vocal: Eddie Gale as Ted Bancroft) .... *Banner 32074* 8-10 31

SING-SONG GIRL (LITTLE YELLA CINDERELLA) (Vocal: Ben Pollack as Ted Bancroft) / (WHEN YOU FALL IN LOVE) FALL IN LOVE WITH ME (Vocal: Eddie Gale as Ted Bancroft) ...... *Conqueror 7772* 8-10 31

SING-SONG GIRL (LITTLE YELLA CINDERELLA) (Vocal: Ben Pollack as Ted Bancroft) / (WHEN YOU FALL IN LOVE) FALL IN LOVE WITH ME (Vocal: Eddie Gale as Ted Bancroft) .... *Jewel 6193* 8-10 31

SING-SONG GIRL (LITTLE YELLA CINDERELLA) (Vocal: Ben Pollack as Ted Bancroft) / (WHEN YOU FALL IN LOVE) FALL IN LOVE WITH ME (Vocal: Eddie Gale as Ted Bancroft) .... *Oriole 2193* 8-10 31

SING-SONG GIRL (LITTLE YELLA CINDERELLA) (Vocal: Ben Pollack as Ted Bancroft) / (WHEN YOU FALL IN LOVE) FALL IN LOVE WITH ME (Vocal: Eddie Gale as Ted Bancroft) .... *Perfect 15424* 8-10 31

SING-SONG GIRL (LITTLE YELLA CINDERELLA) (Vocal: Ben Pollack as Ted Bancroft) / (WHEN YOU FALL IN LOVE) FALL IN LOVE WITH ME (Vocal: Eddie Gale as Ted Bancroft) .... *Regal 10250* 8-10 31

SING-SONG GIRL (LITTLE YELLA CINDERELLA) (Vocal: Ben Pollack as Ted Bancroft) / (WHEN YOU FALL IN LOVE) FALL IN LOVE WITH ME (Vocal: Eddie Gale as Ted Bancroft) .... *Romeo 1561* 8-10 31
(Simultaneously released on seven labels)

SONG OF THE ISLANDS (theme song) / I'M YOURS FOR THE ASKING (Vocal: Frances Hunt) .... *Decca 1424* 4-6 37

SONG OF THE ISLANDS (theme song) / JIMTOWN BLUES (by Ben Pollack as The Dean & His Kids) .... *Brunswick 7764* 5-8 36

THRU' THE COURTESY OF LOVE (Vocal: Ben Pollack) / NOW OR NEVER (by Ben Pollack as The Dean & His Kids; Vocal: Joe Harris) .... *Brunswick 7747* 5-8 36

WAITIN' FOR KATIE (Vocals: by trio) / MEMPHIS BLUES .... *Victor 21184* 10-12 27

YOU'LL BE REMINDED OF ME / THERE'S RAIN IN MY EYES .... *Decca 1815* 2-4 38
(Vocals: Paula Gayle)

POLLACK, Ben, & His Park Central Orchestra

BUY, BUY FOR BABY (OR BABY WILL BYE-BYE YOU) / SHE'S ONE SWEET SHOW GIRL .... *Victor 21743* 8-10 28
(Vocals: Belle Mann)

IN THE HUSH OF THE NIGHT / WON'TCHA .... *Victor 22071* 5-8 29
(Vocals: Scrappy Lambert as Burt Lorin.)

LOUISE / WAIT 'TIL YOU SEE "MA CHERIE" .... *Victor 21941* 8-10 29
(Vocals: Smith Ballew as Charles Roberts.)

MY KINDA LOVE (Vocal: Smith Ballew as Charles Roberts) / ON WITH THE DANCE! (Vocal: Ben Pollack) .... *Victor 21944* 8-10 29

THEN CAME THE DAWN (Vocal: Dick Robertson) / SENTIMENTAL BABY (Vocal: Gene Austin) .... *Victor 21827* 5-8 29

YOU'VE MADE ME HAPPY TODAY / FROM NOW ON .... *Victor 22158* 5-8 29
(Vocals: Smith Ballew as Charles Roberts)

POLLACK, Ben, & His Park Central Orchestra as Ben's Bad Boys

WANG-WANG BLUES / YELLOW DOG BLUES (Vocal: Ben Pollack) .... *Victor 21971* 10-12 29

POLLACK, Ben, & His Park Central Orchestra as The Louisville Rhythm Kings

LET'S SIT AND TALK ABOUT YOU (Vocal: Smith Ballew) / IN A GREAT BIG WAY (Vocals: by trio) .... *Okeh 41189* 15-20 29

POLLACK, Ben, & His Pick-A-Rib Boys

ALICE BLUE GOWN / CUDDLE UP A LITTLE CLOSER (Vocal: Peggy Mann) .... *Decca 1546* 5-8 37

AT THE JAZZ BAND BALL / DIXIELAND ONE STEP .... *Modern 214* 4-6 48

BOOGIE WOOGIE / CALIFORNIA, HERE I COME .... *Decca 1517* 5-8 37

FIDGETY FEET / STOMPIN' AT THE SAVOY .... *Two-Beat T. B. 8551* 5-8 46

IF IT'S THE LAST THING I DO / YOU MADE ME LOVE YOU .... *Decca 1465* 4-6 37
(Vocals: Peggy Mann)

I'M IN MY GLORY (Vocal: Peggy Mann) / THE SNAKE CHARMER .... *Decca 1488* 5-8 37

MOROCCO / NOBODY'S GONNA TAKE YOU AWAY FROM ME (Vocal: Paula Gayle) .... *Decca 1851* 3-5 38

MY WILD IRISH ROSE / DON'T YOU HEAR ME CALLING, CAROLINE? (Vocal: Peggy Mann) .... *Decca 1458* 5-8 37

SONG OF INDIA / SENTIMENTAL JOURNEY .... *Modern 211* 3-5 48

THAT DA-DA STRAIN / STOMPIN' AT THE SAVOY .... *Savoy 791* 4-6 47

TIN ROOF BLUES / SAN ANTONIO SHOUT .... *Discovery 132* 3-5 50

POLLACK, Ben, as The Dean & His Kids

JIMTOWN BLUES / SONG OF THE ISLANDS (theme song) (by Ben Pollack & His Orchestra) ... *Brunswick 7764* 5-8 36

NOW OR NEVER (Vocal: Joe Harris) / THRU' THE COURTESY OF LOVE (by Ben Pollack & His Orchestra; Vocal: Ben Pollack) .... *Brunswick 7747* 5-8 36

SPREADIN' KNOWLEDGE AROUND / ZOOM ZOOM ZOOM (Vocal: Harry James) .... *Vocalion 3342* 8-10 36

POLLA, W. C., & His Orchestra

LUCKY BOY / SUGAR PLUM .... *Columbia 525-D* 2-4 25

POLLA, W. C., as Polla's Clover Garden Orchestra / The Clover Garden Orchestra, W. C. Polla, director

BESIDE A SILV'RY STREAM / ONE SMILE .... *Edison 51585* 3-5 25

I DON'T WANT TO GET MARRIED (I'M HAVING TOO MUCH FUN) / CHINA GIRL .... *Columbia 321-D* 3-5 25

I'LL SEE YOU IN MY DREAMS / THE ONLY, ONLY ONE .... *Columbia 269-D* 3-5 25

IT'LL GET YOU / TOO TIRED .... *Edison 51440* 3-5 25

I WANT A LOVABLE BABY / GIVE UP THE CHARLESTON .... *Columbia 412-D* 4-6 25

I WANT YOU ALL FOR ME / I LEFT HER BY THE SHORES OF MINNETONKA .... *Columbia 441-D* 3-5 25

KICKIN' THE CLOUDS AWAY / WHY DO I LOVE YOU? .... *Columbia 362-D* 3-5 25

MADEIRA / SAVE YOUR SORROW (FOR TOMORROW) .... *Edison 51586* 3-5 25

MOONLIGHT AND ROSES / WHEN YOU AND I WERE SEVENTEEN .... *Edison 51540* 3-5 25
(Vocals: Helen Clark & Joseph Phillips)

TRAVELING BLUES / ALL ALONE WITH YOU (IN A LITTLE RENDEZVOUS) .... *Edison 51456* 4-6 25

POLLOCK, Harry, & His Diamonds

DO-DO-DO / WOULDN'T YOU? .... *Gennett 6016* 5-8 27
(Vocals: Helen Spring & Elliott Stewart)

POLLOCK, Harry, & His Orchestra

HONEY / LOUISE .... *Gennett 6834* 5-8 29
(Vocals: Roy Strom)

HONEY / LOUISE .... *Supertone 9419* 4-6 29
(Vocals: Roy Strom)
(Simultaneously released on two labels)

POLLOCK, Harry, as Harry Pollack's Blue Diamonds

I'M GONNA MEET MY SWEETIE NOW / YOU CAN'T CRY OVER MY SHOULDER .... *Gennett 6067* 5-8 27
(Vocals: Al Shayne)

SHEPHERD OF THE HILLS / THERE AIN'T NO SWEET MAN THAT'S WORTH THE SALT OF MY TEARS .... *Gennett 6383* 5-8 28
(Vocals: Gloria Gray)

POLLOCK, Harry, as Harry Pollack's Maurice Club Diamonds

HALF A MOON (Vocal: Charles Forsythe) / WHEN DAY IS DONE (Vocal: Arthur Hall) .... *Gennett 3401* 4-6 26

POMAR, Harry, & His Hotel Ansley Orchestra

I STILL HAVE YOU IN MY DREAMS / RAINY DAYS .... *Okeh 41111* 2-4 28

NOTHIN' TO DO / WOND'RING WHAT YOU'LL DO .... *Okeh 41150* 2-4 28

YOU'VE MADE MY DREAMS COME TRUE / WEDNESDAY NIGHT WALTZ .... *Okeh 41236* 2-4 29

POPE, Bob, & His Hotel Charlotte Orchestra

BIG CHIEF DE SOTA (Vocal: Bob Pope) / THESE FOOLISH THINGS REMIND ME OF YOU (Vocal: Nolan Canova) .... *Bluebird B-6452* 5-8 36

BREAKIN' IN A PAIR OF SHOES (Vocal: Dixie Lee Sothern) / WAH-HOO! (Vocals: Dixie Lee Sothern, Bob Pope, & Nolan Canova) .... *Bluebird B-6285* 5-8 36

BUG, THE / STOP THAT DOG (HE'S GOIN' MAD) (Vocal: Dixie Lee Sothern) .... *Bluebird B-6300* 5-8 36

GREEN FIELDS AND BLUEBIRDS (Vocal: Nolan Canova) / SHOE-SHINE BOY (Vocal: Dixie Lee Sothern) .... *Bluebird B-6286* 5-8 36

LET'S GET HOT AND TRUCK (Vocal: Nolan Canova) / SWAMP FIRE .... *Bluebird B-6471* 5-8 36

MADHOUSE / SLAT'S SHUFFLE (by Jimmie Gunn & His Orchestra) .... *Bluebird B-6508* 5-8 36

ON THE ALAMO / WHEN MY BABY SMILES AT ME .... *Bluebird B-6502* 4-6 36
(Vocals: Nolan Canova)

SADDLE YOUR BLUES TO A WILD MUSTANG (Vocal: Nolan Canova) / MOON ROSE (Vocal: Bob Pope) .... *Bluebird B-6284* 5-8 36

TAKE MY HEART / LET'S SING AGAIN .... *Bluebird B-6454* 4-6 36
(Vocals: Nolan Canova)

THAT LOVELY NIGHT IN BUDAPEST / THAT NEVER-TO-BE-FORGOTTEN NIGHT .... *Bluebird B-6299* 4-6 36
(Vocals: Nolan Canova)

THERE'S A SMALL HOTEL (Vocal: Nolan Canova) / ON YOUR TOES .... *Bluebird B-6453* 4-6 36

WEST WIND (Vocal: Nolan Canova) / EARLY BIRD (Vocal: Bob Pope) ...... *Bluebird B-6283* 4-6 36

POPE, Bob, & His Orchestra

BLUE SKIES / THE FIRST TIME I SAW YOU .... *Melotone 7-06-16* 4-6 37

I'LL ALWAYS BE IN LOVE WITH YOU / WHOA BABE! (Vocal: Bob Pope) ...... *Melotone 7-07-05* 5-8 37

WHEN YOU GOT TO GO YOU GOT TO GO (Vocal: Bob Pope) / STOP TEASING ME (Vocals: Bob Pope & The Creole Sisters) .... *Decca 8509* 5-8 40

POPPER, Herman, & His S.S. George Washington Orchestra

MY RAMBLER ROSE / LIST'NING ON SOME RADIO .... *Okeh 4668* 4-6 22

PORTER, Dick, & His Orchestra

MAY I HAVE THE NEXT ROMANCE WITH YOU? / THERE'S NO TWO WAYS ABOUT IT ... *Vocalion 3469* 5-8 37
(Vocals: Dick Porter)

SWEET THING / (I'D LIKE TO SEE GRANDPA) SWINGIN' TO A SWING TUNE .... *Vocalion 3355* 8-10 36
(Vocals: Dick Porter)

SWING, BOY, SWING / POOR ROBINSON CRUSOE .... *Vocalion 3478* 8-10 37
(Vocals: Dick Porter)

PORTER'S BLUE DEVILS

"E FLAT" BLUES / ORIGINAL CHARLESTON STRUT .... *Gennett 5210* 5-8 23

MAMA GOES WHERE PAPA GOES (Vocal: Ernest Hare) / SOMEBODY'S WRONG .... *Gennett 5251* 5-8 23

WALK, JENNY, WALK / HOT DAWG! ... *Gennett 5282* 5-8 23

WHEN IT'S NIGHT TIME IN ITALY (Vocal: Jack Kaufman) / I'M SITTIN' PRETTY IN A PRETTY LITTLE CITY .... *Gennett 5305* 4-6 23

PORT OF HARLEM JAZZMEN, The

MIGHTY BLUES / ROCKING THE BLUES ... *Blue Note 3* 8-10 39

POWELL, Jimmie, as Powell's Jazz Monarchs

(Jimmie Powell: 10/24/14 –)

CHAUFFEUR'S SHUFFLE / LAUGHING BLUES (Vocal: William Calloway) .... *Okeh 8333* 15-20 26

POWELL, Mel, & His Orchestra

(Mel Powell: 2/12/23 –)

WHEN DID YOU LEAVE HEAVEN? / BLUE SKIES .... *Commodore 543* 5-8 42

WORLD IS WAITING FOR THE SUNRISE, THE / MOOD AT TWILIGHT .... *Commodore 544* 5-8 42

POWELL'S JAZZ MONARCHS:

see POWELL, Jimmie

POWELL, Teddy, & His Orchestra

(Teddy Powell: 3/1/05 –)

ALL I NEED (Vocal: Ruth Gaylor) / SANS CULOTTES (theme song) ...... *Bluebird B-11201* 3-5 41

ALL THOSE WONDERFUL YEARS / THERE WON'T BE A SHORTAGE OF LOVE ...... *Bluebird B-11499* 3-5 42
(Vocals: Peggy Mann)

AM I BLUE? (Vocal: Ruth Gaylor) / RIDIN' THE SUBWAYS .... *Decca 3094* 2-4 40

BE CAREFUL, IT'S MY HEART (Vocal: Tommy Taylor) / MIDSUMMER MATINEE (Vocal: Peggy Mann) .... *Bluebird B-11554* 2-4 42

BLUEBIRD BOOGIE WOOGIE / THAT OLD GANG OF MINE (Vocal: Ruth Gaylor) .... *Bluebird B-11082* 3-5 41

BLUE DANUBE / A RENDEZVOUS IN RIO (Vocal: Ruth Gaylor) .... *Bluebird B-11132* 2-4 41

BOOGIN' ON THE DOWNBEAT / TIME ON MY HANDS (Vocal: Ruth Gaylor) ..... *Bluebird B-11176* 3-5 41

FEATHER MERCHANT'S BALL / TEDDY BEAR BOOGIE .... *Decca 3234* 3-5 40

FLEA ON A SPREE / THE SPHINX .... *Decca 2985* 3-5 40

FRIENDLY TAVERN / THE THINGS I LOVE .... *Bluebird B-11113* 2-4 41
(Vocals: Ruth Gaylor)

HELPLESS / (AS LONG AS YOU'RE NOT IN LOVE WITH ANYONE ELSE) WHY DON'T YOU FALL IN LOVE WITH ME? .... *Bluebird B-11575* 2-4 42
(Vocals: Peggy Mann)

HEREAFTER / YOU'RE NOT THE KIND (Vocal: Ruth Gaylor) ...... *Bluebird B-11358* 2-4 41

HOE DOWN / HOW ABOUT YOU? ... *Bluebird B-11380* 2-4 41
(Vocals: Peggy Mann)

HOW DO YOU DO WITHOUT ME? (Vocals: Peggy Mann & Dick Judge) / ALL THROUGH THE NIGHT (Vocal: Peggy Mann) .... *Bluebird B-11427* 2-4 41

I'D LOVE YOU AGAIN (Vocal: Dick Judge) / YES INDEED! (Vocals: Ruth Gaylor & chorus) .... *Bluebird B-11248* 2-4 41

I LOVE YOU BEST OF ALL (Vocal: Ruth Gaylor) / SERENADE TO A MAID (A BRONX SERENADE) (Vocals: by orchestra) .... *Bluebird B-11373* 2-4 41

IN A PERSIAN MARKET / MARCH OF THE TOYS .... *Decca 2906* 3-5 39

IN PINETOP'S FOOTSTEPS / MICKEY (Vocal: Ruth Gaylor) .... *Bluebird B-11276* 3-5 41

I SEE A MILLION PEOPLE (BUT ALL I CAN SEE IS YOU) (Vocal: Ruth Gaylor) / JUNGLE BOOGIE .... *Bluebird B-11232* 3-5 41

IT ALL COMES BACK TO ME NOW (Vocal: Ruth Gaylor) / SUNSET AT SEA (Vocal: Jimmy Blair) .... *Bluebird B-11000* 2-4 40

IT'S SAD BUT TRUE (Vocal: Jimmy Blair) / I CAN'T RUB YOU OUT OF MY EYES (Vocals: Ruth Gaylor & quartet) .... *Bluebird B-10974* 2-4 40

I USED TO LOVE YOU (BUT IT'S ALL OVER NOW) / HONEY ... *Bluebird B-11270* 2-4 41
(Vocals: Ruth Gaylor)

I WENT OUT OF MY WAY (Vocal: Ruth Gaylor) / ODE TO SPRING ... *Bluebird B-11152* 2-4 41

JIM (Vocal: Ruth Gaylor) / STEADY TEDDY ... *Bluebird B-11213* 3-5 41

KICKIN' THE CONGA AROUND (Vocal: Peggy Mann) / GOODBYE MAMA (I'M OFF TO YOKOHAMA) (Vocals: Dick Judge, Peggy Mann, & chorus) ... *Bluebird B-11412* 3-5 41

LET'S GET LOST / "MURDER," HE SAYS ... *Bluebird 30-0809* 2-4 42
(Vocals: Peggy Mann)

LOVE IS A SONG / TAPESTRY IN BLUE ... *Bluebird B-11556* 2-4 42
(Vocals: Peggy Mann)

MAKE LOVE TO ME / THE BIRTH OF THE BLUES ... *Bluebird B-11300* 3-5 41
(Vocals: Ruth Gaylor)

ONE I LOVE, THE (Vocal: Ruth Gaylor) / I GET THE BLUES WHEN IT RAINS (Vocal: Jimmy Blair) ... *Decca 3034* 2-4 40

PLEASE TAKE A LETTER, MISS BROWN (Vocal: Jimmy Blair) / OUTSIDE OF THAT, I LOVE YOU (Vocal: Ruth Gaylor) ... *Decca 3218* 2-4 40

PUSSY IN THE CORNER / SOME DAY ... *Decca 2941* 3-5 39

SLAP-HAPPY LASSIE / ALL NIGHT LONG ... *Bluebird B-11039* 2-4 41
(Vocals: Ruth Gaylor)

SOMEBODY'S THINKING OF YOU TONIGHT (Vocal: Peggy Mann) / GOT THE MOON IN MY POCKET (Vocal: Tommy Taylor) ... *Bluebird B-11520* 2-4 42

'TAIN'T NO GOOD (LIKE A NICKEL MADE OF WOOD) (Vocals: Peggy Mann & Tommy Taylor) / IF YOU ARE BUT A DREAM ... *Bluebird B-11516* 3-5 42

TAKING A CHANCE ON LOVE / HERE'S MY HEART ... *Bluebird B-11016* 2-4 41
(Vocals: Ruth Gaylor)

TALKING TO THE WIND (Vocal: Ruth Gaylor) / STRAIGHT EIGHT BOOGIE ... *Bluebird B-11092* 3-5 41

TEDDY'S BOOGIE-WOOGIE / JAMAICA JAM ... *Decca 2806* 3-5 39

THERE WILL NEVER BE ANOTHER YOU (Vocal: Peggy Mann) / A BOY IN KHAKI – A GIRL IN LACE (Vocal: Tommy Taylor) ... *Bluebird B-11568* 3-5 42

WHEN YOUR WEDDING RING WAS NEW (Vocals: by quartet) / SWEETHEARTS OR STRANGERS (Vocal: Dick Judge) ... *Bluebird B-11338* 2-4 41

WISE OLD OWL, THE / TWO HEARTS THAT PASS IN THE NIGHT ... *Bluebird B-11089* 2-4 41
(Vocals: Ruth Gaylor)

POWELL, Tommy, & His Hi-De-Ho Boys

HI-DE-HO SWING / THAT CAT IS HIGH ... *Decca 7231* 10-12 36

JUST ABOUT THE TIME / GOT THE BLUES FOR HARLEM ... *Decca 7255* 10-12 37

POWELL, Walter, & His Orchestra

DEVIL'S HOLIDAY / DEFINITION OF SWING ... *Vocalion 4612* 10-12 39

PRICE, Sam, & His Texas Blusicians

(Sam Price: 10/6/08 –)

COW COW BLUES / SWING OUT IN THE GROOVE (Vocal: Sam Price) ... *Decca 7732* 8-10 40

DO YOU DIG MY JIVE? (Vocals: by chorus) / BOOGIE WOOGIE MOAN ... *Decca 8575* 8-10 41

FETCH IT TO ME / SWEEPIN' THE BLUES AWAY ... *Decca 7781* 8-10 40

GOON DRAG, THE / I LOST LOVE (WHEN I LOST YOU) (Vocal: Sam Price) ... *Decca 8547* 5-8 41

I KNOW HOW TO DO IT / VALETTA ... *Decca 8566* 5-8 41
(Vocals: Sam Price)

MATCH BOX BLUES (Vocal: Jack Meredith) / BLOW, KATY, BLOW ... *Decca 8624* 8-10 42

ME AND MY CHAUFFEUR / I'VE GOT TOO MANY BLUES ... *Decca 8601* 10-12 42
(Vocals: Mabel Robinson)

TEED UP / FRANTIC ... *Decca 8642* 5-8 42

THINGS 'BOUT COMING MY WAY (Vocal: Yack Taylor) / JUST JIVIN' AROUND ... *Decca 8557* 5-8 41

THINKING (Vocal: Sam Price) / JUMPIN' THE BOOGIE ... *Decca 8515* 5-8 41

WHY DON'T YOU LOVE ME ANY MORE? / HARLEM GIN BLUES ... *Decca 8609* 8-10 42
(Vocals: Ruby Smith. Ruby is the niece of Bessie Smith, the legendary "Empress of the Blues.")

PRICE, Sam, & His Texas Blusicians as Lem Johnson & His Washboard Band

QUEEN STREET BLUES / LOUISE LOUISE ... *Decca 7820* 8-10 41
(Vocals: Lem Johnson)

PRIMA, Louis, & His Band

(Louis Prima: 12/7/11 – 8/24/78)

EXACTLY LIKE YOU / NOW AND THEN ... *Decca 2279* 4-6 39
(Vocals: Louis Prima)

SHOW ME THE WAY TO GO HOME (Vocal: Louis Prima) / JITTERBUGS ON PARADE ... *Decca 2242* 4-6 39

WHERE HAVE WE MET BEFORE / NOW THEY CALL IT SWING ... *Decca 1674* 4-6 38
(Vocals: Louis Prima)

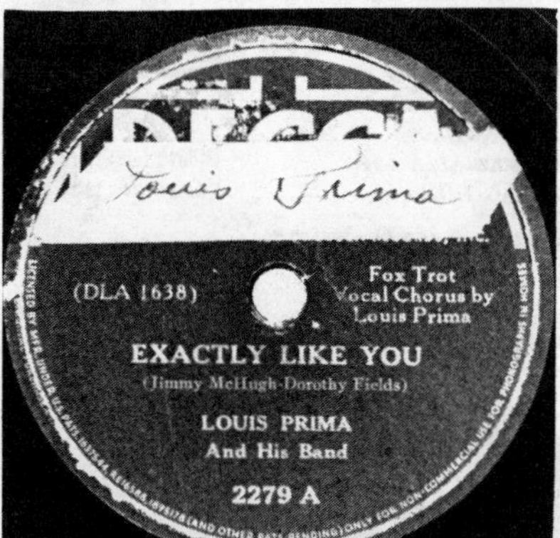

PRIMA, Louis, & His Gleeby Rhythm Orchestra

DANCE WITH A DOLLY (WITH A HOLE IN HER STOCKING) (Vocals: Louise Prima, Lily Ann Carol, & Frank Frederico) / LOOK OUT ... *Varsity 8245* 3-5 40

DAYDREAMS COME TRUE AT NIGHT (Vocal: Lily Ann Carol) / PERCY, HAVE MERCY (Vocals: Louis Prima, Lily Ann Carol & chorus) ... *Varsity 8247* 3-5 40

SING-A-SPELL (MUSICAL SPELLING BEE) (Vocals: by orchestra) / GLEEBY RHYTHM IS BORN (Vocal: Louis Prima) ... *Varsity 8166* 2-4 40

TO YOU, SWEETHEART, ALOHA / SAY "SI SI" (Vocal: Louis Prima) ... *Varsity 8170* 2-4 40

PRIMA, Louis, & His New Orleans Gang

AT THE DARKTOWN STRUTTERS' BALL / ALICE BLUE GOWN ... *Brunswick 7657* 5-8 36
(Vocals: Louis Prima)

CHINATOWN, MY CHINATOWN / BASIN STREET BLUES ... *Brunswick 7456* 8-10 35
(Vocals: Louis Prima)

CONFESSIN' / LET'S HAVE FUN ... *Brunswick 7709* 5-8 36
(Vocals: Louis Prima)

CROSS PATCH / SWING ME A LULLABY ... *Brunswick 7680* 5-8 36
(Vocals: Louis Prima)

DANGER, LOVE AT WORK / AFRAID TO DREAM ... *Vocalion 3628* 5-8 37
(Vocals: Louis Prima)

DINAH / LAZY RIVER ... *Brunswick 7666* 5-8 36
(Vocals: Louis Prima)

FIFTY-SECOND STREET / THE LOVE BUG WILL BITE ... *Vocalion 3509* 5-8 37
(Vocals: Louis Prima)

GOOD MAN IS HARD TO FIND, A / IF I COULD BE WITH YOU ONE HOUR TONIGHT ... *Decca 2660* 3-5 39
(Vocals: Louis Prima)

HOUSE RENT PARTY DAY / BRIGHT EYES ... *Brunswick 7376* 8-10 35
(Vocals: Louis Prima)

HOW'M I DOIN' (HEY-HEY) / SOLITUDE ... *Brunswick 7531* 5-8 35
(Vocals: Louis Prima)

I JUST CAN'T BELIEVE YOU'RE GONE / RHYTHM ON THE RADIO ... *Vocalion 3921* 5-8 37
(Vocals: Louis Prima)

I'M SHOOTING HIGH / I'VE GOT MY FINGERS CROSSED ... *Brunswick 7586* 5-8 36
(Vocals: Louis Prima)

IT'S BEEN SO LONG / SING, SING, SING ... *Brunswick 7628* 8-10 36
(Vocals: Louis Prima)

IT'S THE RHYTHM IN ME / WORRY BLUES ... *Brunswick 7471* 8-10 35
(Vocals: Louis Prima)

LADY IN RED, THE / CHASING SHADOWS ... *Brunswick 7448* 8-10 35
(Vocals: Louis Prima)

LET'S GET TOGETHER AND SWING / THE STARS KNOW (I'M FALLING IN LOVE WITH YOU) ... *Brunswick 7740* 8-10 36
(Vocals: Louis Prima)

LONG ABOUT MIDNIGHT / STAR DUST ... *Brunswick 7335* 8-10 34
(Vocals: Louis Prima)

MR. GHOST GOES TO TOWN / THE GOOSE HANGS HIGH ... *Vocalion 3388* 8-10 37

OF THEE I SING / SWEET AND LOW DOWN ... *Decca 2749* 4-6 39
(Vocals: Louis Prima)

PENNIES FROM HEAVEN / WHAT WILL SANTA CLAUS SAY? ... *Vocalion 3376* 5-8 36
(Vocals: Louis Prima)

PLAIN OLD ME / WEATHER MAN ... *Brunswick 7499* 5-8 35
(Vocals: Louis Prima)

PUT ON AN OLD PAIR OF SHOES / I'M LIVIN' IN A GREAT BIG WAY ... *Brunswick 7419* 5-8 35
(Vocals: Louis Prima)

SING IT 'WAY LOW DOWN / LET'S HAVE A JUBILEE ... *Brunswick 7394* 8-10 35
(Vocals: Louis Prima)

SUGAR IS SWEET AND SO ARE YOU / SWING ME WITH RHYTHM ... *Brunswick 7431* 5-8 35
(Vocals: Louis Prima)

SWEET SUE / I LOVE YOU TRULY ... *Brunswick 7596* 5-8 36
(Vocals: Louis Prima)

THAT'S WHERE THE SOUTH BEGINS (Vocal: Louis Prima) / JAMAICA SHOUT ... *Brunswick 7524* 8-10 34

WHY SHOULD I PRETEND? / DOIN' THE SERPENTINE ... *Decca 1953* 4-6 38
(Vocals: Louis Prima)

YES, THERE AIN'T NO MOONLIGHT (SO WHAT) / ROSALIE ... *Decca 1618* 3-5 38
(Vocals: Louis Prima)

YOU CALL IT MADNESS (BUT I CALL IT LOVE) / NOTHING'S TOO GOOD FOR YOU ... *Decca 1871* 2-4 38
(Vocals: Louis Prima)

YOU CAN'T HAVE EVERYTHING (Vocal: Louis Prima) / TIN ROOF BLUES ... *Vocalion 3657* 5-8 37

PRIMA, Louis, & His Orchestra

BIGGER THE FIGURE, THE (Vocal: Louis Prima) / BONEY BONES ... *Columbia 39735* 2-4 50

FLEA AND A FLY IN A FLUE, A (Vocals: Louis Prima & The Tune-Timers) / NOSY-BODY (Vocals: Louis Prima & Judy Lynn) ... *Majestic 1076* 2-4 46

I AIN'T GONNA TAKE IT SETTIN' DOWN (Vocals: Louis Prima & Keely Smith) / ENJOY YOURSELF (IT'S LATER THAN YOU THINK) (Vocal: Louis Prima) ... *Mercury 5361* 2-4 51

ROBIN HOOD / I'LL WALK ALONE (Vocal: Lily Ann Carol) ... *Hit 7083* 3-5 44

SENTIMENTAL JOURNEY / THERE! I'VE SAID IT AGAIN ... *Majestic 7140* 3-5 45
(Vocals: Lily Ann Carol)

TICA-TEE, TICA-TA (Vocals: Lily Ann Carol & Louis Prima) / FORGIVE ME (Vocal: Louis Prima) ... *Okeh 6520* 2-4 41

PRINCE, Charles, & His Orchestra:

see PELTYN, Sid, & His Orchestra

PRINCE, Charles A.:

see COLUMBIA DANCE ORCHESTRA, The, and see PRINCE'S BAND / ORCHESTRA

PRINCE, Graham, & His Palais D'Or Orchestra

LAWD, YOU MADE THE NIGHT TOO LONG (Vocal: Leo Kelsen) / THE CLOUDS WILL SOON ROLL BY (Vocal: Walter Darrach) ... *Electradisk 2505* 15-20 32

LET'S TRY AGAIN / WHERE ARE YOU? ... *Victor 24058* 4-6 32
(Vocals: Walter Darrach)

MY SILENT LOVE (Vocal: Walter Darrach) / RAIN, RAIN, GO AWAY (Vocal: Graham Prince) ... *Electradisk 2500* 12-15 32

WHISTLE AND BLOW YOUR BLOWS AWAY / A GREAT BIG BUNCH OF YOU ... *Electradisk 2501* 15-20 32
(Vocals: Phil Dooley)

PRINCE'S BAND / ORCHESTRA,

also see COLUMBIA DANCE ORCHESTRA, The
directed by Charles A. Prince

A LA HABANA / YANKEE ... *Columbia A-2500* 2-4 18

BEALE STREET / LILY OF THE VALLEY ... *Columbia A-2327* 3-5 17

BEN HUR CHARIOT RACE MARCH ... *Little Wonder 329* 25-30 -
(A one-sided record.)
("Little Wonders" are 5½ inch records produced from 1911 to 1919 without performer credits. However, the label on this release does list Prince's Band as the recording artists, and is one of only five known "Little Wonder" issues released with performer identification on the label.)

CENTURY GIRL / FOR ME AND MY GAL ... *Columbia A-5957* 2-4 17

DREAMY MELODY / GOODNIGHT ... *Paramount 20225* 4-6 23

FOR THE FREEDOM OF THE WORLD / EVERYBODY'S JAZZIN' IT ... *Columbia A-2347* 3-5 17

GIRLS, IF YOU EVER GET MARRIED / ALLAH'S HOLIDAY ... *Columbia A-5945* 2-4 18

GOING UP / EVERYBODY OUGHT TO KNOW HOW TO DO THE TICKLE TOE ... *Columbia A-2524* 2-4 18

HESITATING BLUES / ST. LOUIS BLUES ... *Columbia A-5772* 4-6 16

HY-SINE / THE MAN BEHIND THE HAMMER AND THE PLOUGH ... *Columbia A-5973* 2-4 17

IF THEY EVER PUT A TAX ON LOVE / JUST LIKE WASHINGTON CROSSED THE DELAWARE, GENERAL PERSHING WILL CROSS THE RHINE ... *Columbia A-6049* 3-5 18

I'LL BE WITH YOU IN APPLE BLOSSOM TIME / BABY DREAMS ... *Columbia A-6177* 2-4 21

I'M ALABAMA BOUND / PORCUPINE RAG ... *Columbia A-901* 3-5 10

I'M ALWAYS CHASING RAINBOWS / OH! FRENCHY! ... *Columbia A-6064* 2-4 18

I'M CRAZY OVER EVERY GIRL IN FRANCE / OVER THERE ... *Columbia A-2387* 3-5 17

I'M FOREVER BLOWING BUBBLES / TUMBLEDOWN SHACK IN ATHLONE ... *Columbia A-6104* 2-4 19

I'M GOING TO FOLLOW THE BOYS / CLEOPATRA HAD A JAZZ BAND ... *Columbia A-6017* 3-5 18

IT'S A LONG WAY TO BERLIN, BUT WE'LL GET THERE! / THERE'S ALWAYS SOMETHING DOING DOWN IN DIXIE ... *Columbia A-2414* 3-5 17

IT'S A LONG WAY TO DEAR OLD BROADWAY / MUSLIN RAG .... *Columbia A-6084* 2-4 18

IT'S TIME FOR EVERY BOY TO BE A SOLDIER / COTTON PICKIN' TIME IN ALABAM' .... *Columbia A-2267* 3-5 17

I WONDER WHY / YOU'RE IN LOVE .... *Columbia A-5962* 2-4 17

LASSUS TROMBONE (DE CULUD VALET TO MISS TROMBONE) / MISS TROMBONE (A SLIPPERY RAG) .... *Columbia A-2825* 3-5 18

LIBERTY BELL, IT'S TIME TO RING AGAIN / JUST A BABY'S PRAYER AT TWILIGHT .... *Columbia A-6029* 3-5 18

LOVE BOAT, THE / LET THE REST OF THE WORLD GO BY .... *Columbia A-6165* 2-4 20

MY BELGIAN ROSE / BEAUTIFUL OHIO .... *Columbia A-6081* 2-4 18

MY HAWAIIAN SUNSHINE / I'VE GOT THE ARMY BLUES .... *Columbia A-5951* 3-5 17

MY MIND'S MADE UP TO MARRY CAROLINA / KEEP THE TRENCH FIRES GOING ...... *Columbia A-6043* 3-5 18

OH, WHAT A PAL WAS MARY / CAROLINA SUNSHINE .... *Columbia A-6137* 2-4 20

OLD-FASHIONED GARDEN / APPLE BLOSSOMS .... *Columbia A-2874* 2-4 20

ON THE LEVEL YOU'RE A LITTLE DEVIL / WHAT YANKEE DOODLE SAYS HE'LL DO, HE'LL DO .... *Columbia A-6079* 3-5 18

PACK UP YOUR TROUBLES IN YOUR OLD KIT BAG AND SMILE, SMILE, SMILE / WHAT KIND OF AN AMERICAN ARE YOU? .... *Columbia A-2317* 3-5 17

PEGGY O'NEILL / THE LAST WALTZ .... *Columbia A-6188* 2-4 21

PEG O' THE RING / SEND ME AWAY WITH A SMILE .... *Columbia A-5990* 3-5 17

PETER GINK / ARABIAN NIGHTS ... *Columbia A-6099* 2-4 18

PRETTY LITTLE CINDERELLA / PICKANINNY BLUES .... *Columbia A-6162* 2-4 20

RAG-A-MINOR / RIGOLETTO RAG ... *Columbia A-2499* 2-4 18

SINCE I FIRST KNEW YOU / OVER THE TOP .... *Columbia A-6009* 2-4 18

SO LONG MOTHER / THE BRAVEST HEART OF ALL .... *Columbia A-6003* 3-5 17

SOMEWHERE IN FRANCE / WAIT TILL THE COWS COME HOME .... *Columbia A-2448* 3-5 17

SOUTH SEAS SWEETHEART / SWANEE RIVER MOON .... *Columbia A-6213* 2-4 22

TACKIN' 'EM DOWN / IF HE CAN FIGHT LIKE HE LOVE, GOODNIGHT, GERMANY! ... *Columbia A-6058* 3-5 18

THAT NAUGHTY WALTZ / MY ISLE OF GOLDEN DREAMS .... *Columbia A-6139* 2-4 19

THREE O'CLOCK IN THE MORNING / LA GOLONDRINA .... *Columbia A-3724* 2-4 22

TRIPOLI / ROMANCE .... *Columbia A-6157* 2-4 20

WHEN YOU COME BACK / SMILES ... *Columbia A-6077* 3-5 18

WHERE DO WE GO FROM HERE? / HELP! HELP! I'M SINKING .... *Columbia A-5985* 2-4 17

WHERE THOSE COTTON BLOSSOMS GROW / ROSE ROOM .... *Columbia A-6047* 2-4 18

YAH-DE-DAH / NEW ORLEANS JAZZ .... *Columbia A-5983* 3-5 17

YOU'RE A GRAND OLD FLAG / SOMEWHERE ON BROADWAY ... *Columbia A-5978* 3-5 17

YOU SAID SOMETHING / HOME AGAIN .... *Columbia A-5968* 2-4 17

PRINCETON TRIANGLE CLUB JAZZ BAND, The
(The following are Columbia Personal Records)

I'LL BUILD AN IGLOO FOR YOU / MY WHITE ROSE .... *Columbia 59-P* 12-15 25

INDIAN MOON / BROKE AGAIN ...... *Columbia 63-P* 15-20 25

PRETTY PLEASE / GONDOLA MAID ... *Columbia 85-P* 12-15 26

RHYTHMIC REFRAIN / MELODY MOON .... *Columbia 100-P* 15-20 27

SEA OF DREAMS / PIRATE GOLD .. *Columbia 31-P* 15-20 24

SHIPS THAT PASS IN THE NIGHT / JOIN THE NAVY .... *Columbia 30-P* 15-20 24

WHERE LOVE IS KING / TWILIGHT .... *Columbia 84-P* 12-15 26

YOU KNOW WHO / EVERYBODY AND YOU .... *Columbia 114-P* 15-20 28

PRINCETON TRIANGLE CLUB JAZZ BAND, The as The Equinox Orchestra Of Princeton, New Jersey

CHINA BOY / THAT'S A PLENTY .... *Columbia 115-P* 15-20 28

PROFIT, Clarence, as The Clarence Profit Trio
(Clarence Profit: 6/26/12 – 10/22/44)

BODY AND SOUL / I DIDN'T KNOW WHAT TIME IT WAS .... *Columbia 35378* 4-6 40

DARK EYES / AZURE .... *Decca 8527* 5-8 40

THERE'LL BE SOME CHANGES MADE / TEA FOR TWO .... *Brunswick 8341* 5-8 39

TIMES SQUARE BLUES / HOT AND BOTHERED .... *Decca 8503* 8-10 40

PRYOR, Arthur, as Arthur Pryor's Band
(Victor records from this period are one-sided)

COON BAND CONTEST (7-inch) .... *Victor 4069* 12-15 04

DARKIES' SPRING SONG .... *Victor 5395* 3-5 07

KING OF RAGS (A TWO-STEP ODDITY) ... *Victor 5301* 3-5 07

MR. BLACK MAN (7-inch) .... *Victor 2557* 12-15 04

RAZZAZZA MAZZAZZA (8-inch) .... *Victor 4525* 12-15 06

ST. LOUIS RAG, THE (8-inch) .... *Victor 2783* 12-15 06

PRYOR, Roger, & His Orchestra
(Roger Pryor: circa 1901 – 1/31/74)

NOW IT CAN BE TOLD / MY WALKING STICK .... *Vocalion 4164* 4-6 38

WHISTLER AND HIS DOG, THE (theme song) / MARCHE SLAV .... *Vocalion 4256* 4-6 38

PURPLE PIRATES ORCHESTRA, The

TIGER RAG / CHINA BOY .... *W* 12-15 26
(The performers were the collegiate orchestra at Williams College. Recorded by Paramount, but not for general release, thus, there is no catalog number.)

PURVIS, Jack, & His Orchestra
(Jack Purvis: 12/11/06 – 3/30/62)

DISMAL DAN / BE BO BO (Vocal: J. C. Higginbotham) .... *Okeh 8808* 15-20 30

POOR RICHARD (Vocals: Jack Purvis, J.C. Higginbotham & Will Johnson) / DOWN GEORGIA WAY ..... *Okeh 8782* 15-20 30

WHAT'S THE USE OF CRYIN', BABY? / WHEN YOU'RE FEELIN' BLUE ... *Odeon ONY-36093* 15-20 30

QUADLING, Lew, as Lew Quadling's Orchestra

TIMELESS / YOU KISSED ME, REMEMBER? .... *Kem 2708* 2-4 -
(Vocals: The Country Gentlemen.)

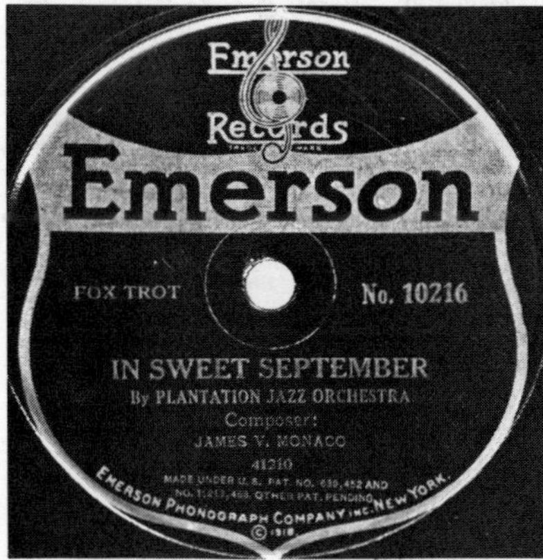

RADERMAN, Harry, as
The Plantation Dance / Jazz Orchestra

IN SWEET SEPTEMBER / RED FOX TROT (by Rudy Wiedoeft's Palace Trio) .... *Emerson 10216* 2-4 20

RADERMAN, Harry, as Raderman's Dance Orchestra

BRIGHT EYES / BROADWAY ROSE ... *Cardinal 2020* 3-5 21
DEENAH (MY ARGENTINE ROSE) / MAZIE .... *Cardinal 2025* 3-5 21
FORGIVE ME / HOOSIER SWEETHEART... *Okeh 40773* 2-4 27
(Vocals: Unknown)
HALLELUJAH! / SWEET MARIE .... *Okeh 40829* 2-4 27
(Vocals: Unknown)
JAPANESE SANDMAN / WHISPERING .... *Cardinal 2007* 3-5 20
JEALOUS / AFTER THE STORM.... *Paramount 20325* 5-8 24
JEALOUS / AFTER THE STORM ...... *Triangle 11371* 3-5 24
(Simultaneously released on two labels)
MANDALAY / IT HAD TO BE YOU ..... *Edison 51390* 4-6 24
MANDY, MAKE UP YOUR MIND / MY BABY'S BABY BLUE EYES .... *Edison 51450* 4-6 25
ON THE BLUE LAGOON / WHAT'LL I DO? .... *Broadway 11360* 4-6 24
ON THE BLUE LAGOON / WHAT'LL I DO? .... *Lyraphone 11360* 4-6 24
ON THE BLUE LAGOON / WHAT'LL I DO? .... *Paramount 20321* 5-8 24
(Simultaneously released on three labels)
SAY IT AGAIN / AFTER THE STORM... *Edison 51331* 3-5 24

RADERMAN, Harry, as The Bal Taberin Jazz Orchestra

DARDANELLA / BLUES MY NAUGHTY SWEETIE GIVES .... *Lyric 4211* 5-8 20
LAUGH SONG, THE / YELLOW DOG BLUES .... *Lyric 4212* 5-8 20
VAMP / YOU'D BE SURPRISED .... *Lyric 4210* 4-6 20

RADERMAN, Harry, as The Bal Taberin Jazz Orchestra recorded under the name The Concert Taberin Jazz Orchestra

BLUES MY NAUGHTY SWEETIE GIVES TO ME / YELLOW DOG BLUES .... *Concert 1007* 30-40 20
(Concert records are very rare.)

RADERMAN, Harry, as Harry Raderman's
Biltmore Cascade Roof Orchestra

KOSHER KITTY KELLY / SEMINOLA .... *Everybody's 1067* 10-12 25
ONE SMILE / OH SAY, CAN I SEE YOU TONIGHT? .... *Everybody's 1068* 10-12 25

RADERMAN, Harry, as Harry Raderman's Jazz Orchestra

ALL FOR YOU / MAKE BELIEVE...... *Cardinal 2032* 4-6 21
APACHE LOVE / MA! .... *Edison 50846* 4-6 21
CUTIE / DON'T LEAVE ME, MAMMY... *Edison 50930* 3-5 22
DREAM OF YOUR SMILE / WEEP NO MORE, MY MAMMY .... *Edison 50889* 3-5 21
I CALL YOU SUNSHINE / TODDLE..... *Edison 50757* 3-5 21
I FOUND A ROSE IN THE DEVIL'S GARDEN / CHERIE .... *Edison 50783* 3-5 21
JUST LIKE A RAINBOW / YOU'RE THE SWEETEST GIRL IN ALL THE WORLD........ *Edison 50798* 3-5 21
LEARN TO SMILE / STOLEN KISSES... *Edison 50822* 3-5 21
MAKE THAT TROMBONE LAUGH / ALEXANDRIA .... *Okeh 4089* 3-5 20
MAKE THAT TROMBONE LAUGH / DARDANELLA .... *Edison 50637* 4-6 20
NEAR ME / JUST BECAUSE .... *Okeh 4378* 2-4 21
NOW AND THEN / DOLLY, I LOVE YOU... *Okeh 4237* 2-4 21
OH JOY! / ANGEL EYES .... *Edison 50834* 3-5 21
OH JOY! / ILO .... *Okeh 4404* 2-4 21
PAY DAY BLUES / WET YO' THUMB...... *Okeh 4923* 3-5 23
SHUFFLE ALONG MEDLEY / BIRDS OF A FEATHER .... *Edison 50866* 3-5 21
SONG OF OMAR / BLUES MY NAUGHTY SWEETIE GIVES TO ME .... *Gennett 9035* 3-5 20
TIN ROOF BLUES / WOLVERINE BLUES ... *Okeh 4885* 3-5 23
TWO LITTLE GIRLS IN BLUE / CANADIAN CAPERS .... *Edison 50802* 3-5 21

RADERMAN, Harry, as Harry Raderman's Orchestra

HULA BLUES, THE / ANNIE, MY OWN ... *Gennett 4648* 3-5 20
LOVABLE EYES / ROAMING .... *Gennett 4902* 3-5 22
LOVE'S SYMPHONY / BURNING SANDS .... *Edison 51047* 3-5 22
MOXIE (instrumental) / MOXIE (Vocals: Unknown) .... *Moxie (un-numbered)* 50-60 21
(A promotional record for the Moxie soft drink, extremely rare.)
MY SOUTHERN HOME / COW BELLS .... *Edison 51032* 3-5 22
OH, ME! OH, MY! / DAISY DAYS........ *Gennett 4750* 3-5 21
(Vocals: Arthur Fields)
OH! MIN / HOT ROASTED PEANUTS... *Broadway 11294* 5-8 23
OH! MIN / HOT ROASTED PEANUTS... *Claxtonola 40262* 10-12 23
(Simultaneously released on two labels)

SOMEWHERE IN NAPOLI (Vocal: Vernon Dalhart) / IN DREAMS WITH YOU (Vocal: Charles Hart) .... *Edison 51356* 4-6 24

RADERMAN, Harry, as Raderman's Novelty Orchestra

ROSIE CHEEKS / YOU TAUGHT ME TO CARE .... *Clarion 1110* 3-5 21

RADERMAN, Harry, as Raderman's Radio Orchestra

WHY DO YOU WANT TO KNOW WHY? / BYE BYE BLACKBIRD .... *Okeh 40663* 3-5 26

RADERMAN, Harry, as
Raderman's Red Hotters / The Red Hotters

CROSS YOUR HEART / THAT NIGHT IN ARABY .... *Okeh 40712* 2-4 26
HORSES / SOMEBODY'S LONELY........ *Okeh 40610* 2-4 26
JUST A LITTLE DANCE / I'D CLIMB THE HIGHEST MOUNTAIN .... *Okeh 40642* 3-5 26
LOVE BOUND / LOOKING FOR A BOY.... *Okeh 40570* 3-5 26
LUCKY DAY / THE BIRTH OF THE BLUES .... *Okeh 40652* 3-5 26
MARIE, MARIE, MARIE / LET IT RAIN, LET IT POUR........ *Okeh 40324* 2-4 25
OH! HEINRICH! (YOU'RE SO NICE) / EV'RYTHING IS HOTSY TOTSY NOW... *Okeh 40380* 3-5 25
(Vocals: Henry Cogert)
PANGO PANGO MAID / WHAT DO I CARE – WHAT DO I CARE, MY SWEETIE TURNED ME DOWN .... *Okeh 40443* 2-4 25
ROLL 'EM, GIRLS / YOU TOLD ME TO GO... *Okeh 40523* 3-5 26
SONYA (YUP, ALAY YUP!) / I MISS MY SWISS (MY SWISS MISS MISSES ME) (by Harry Raderman as The Red Hotters recorded under the name The Okeh Syncopators) .... *Okeh 40425* 2-4 25
(Vocals: Billy Jones)
TOO MANY MAMAS / OH, SAY! CAN I SEE YOU TONIGHT? .... *Okeh 40449* 3-5 25
WHAT DID I TELL YA? / SMILE A LITTLE BIT .... *Okeh 40543* 3-5 26
WHAT IS THE USE? / I FOUND A WAY TO LOVE YOU (BUT I CAN'T FIND A WAY TO FORGET) .... *Okeh 40360* 2-4 25

RADERMAN, Harry, as The Red Hotters recorded under the name The Okeh Syncopators

I MISS MY SWISS (MY SWISS MISS MISSES ME) / SONYA (YUP, ALAY YUP!) (by Harry Raderman as The Red Hotters) .... *Okeh 40425* 2-4 25
(Vocals: Billy Jones)
I'M TIRED OF EVERYTHING BUT YOU / IF YOU HADN'T GONE AWAY .... *Okeh 40450* 2-4 25

RADERMAN, Harry, as Raderman's Roysterers

I'M KNEE-DEEP IN DAISIES (Vocal: Billy West) / I AIN'T GOT NOBODY .... *Harmony 48-H* 3-5 25
WHO WOULDN'T LOVE YOU? / SWEET MAN .... *Harmony 22-H* 3-5 25

RADERMAN, Lou, & His Orchestra as
Ray Beagle & His Hounds of Music

IT GOES TO YOUR FEET / PECKIN'.... *Vocalion 3573* 3-5 37

RADERMAN, Lou, & His Pelham Heath Inn Orchestra

IN A LITTLE TWO BY FOUR FOR TWO / I'M RIDING TO GLORY .... *Domino 4134* 5-8 28
(Vocals: Unknown)
WHY DO I LOVE YOU? (Vocal: Irving Kaufman) / OL' MAN RIVER (Vocal: Harry Donahey) .... *Harmony 607-H* 10-12 28

RADIO DANCE ORCHESTRA, The

I'M ALONE BECAUSE I LOVE YOU (Vocals: Unknown) / —........ *Empire 52* 40-50 31
(This is the only known release by this group, an extremely rare British flexible record.)

RADIOLITES, The:
see GOODMAN, Benny, & His Orchestra and see SELVIN, Ben

RADLACH, Karl, & His Orchestra

AROUND THE CORNER (Vocals: Unknown) / HAND ME DOWN MY WALKIN' CANE (Vocals: by orchestra) .... *Perfect 15316* 4-6 30
BE CAREFUL WITH THOSE EYES (Vocals: Unknown) / YOU BROUGHT A NEW KIND OF LOVE TO ME (by Harry Reser as The Clevelanders).... *Perfect 15311* 4-6 30

RAEBURN, Boyd, & His Orchestra
(Boyd Raeburn: 10/27/13 – 8/2/66)

BLUE ECHOES / LITTLE BOYD BLUE.... *Jewel D1-4-6* 4-6 45
BLUE PRELUDE / YOU'VE GOT ME CRYING AGAIN .... *Guild 134* 4-6 45
BOYD MEETS STAVINSKY / I ONLY HAVE EYES FOR YOU .... *Jewel 10002* 4-6 46
BOYD'S NEST / OUT OF NOWHERE .... *Guild 133* 4-6 45
HIP BOYD'S / THE MAN WITH THE HORN .... *Jewel GN-10,003* 4-6 46
I PROMISED YOU / THIS HEART OF MINE .... *Guild 108* 2-4 45
OVER THE RAINBOW / BODY AND SOUL .... *Jewel D1-2-3* 3-5 45
PRELUDE TO THE DAWN / DUCK WADDLE .... *Jewel 10004* 3-5 46
SUMMERTIME / MARCH OF THE BOYDS.... *Guild 111* 4-6 45
TONSILECTOMY / FORGETFUL .... *Jewel 10000* 3-5 46
YERXA / RIP VAN WINKLE .... *Jewel 10001* 3-5 46

RAGON, Ike, & His Orchestra

SLAP THAT BASS (Vocal: Ike Ragon) / MAPLE LEAF RAG .... *Vocalion 03513* 10-12 37
TRUCKIN' ON THE OLD CAMP GROUND / HARLEM BLUES .... *Vocalion 03547* 12-15 37
(Vocals: Ike Ragon)

RAMBLERS, The

HONEY IN THE BEE BALL / LONESOME RAILROAD .... *Decca 2499* 5-8 39
(Vocals: O'Neil Spencer)
'TAIN'T WHAT YOU DO (IT'S THE WAY THAT CHA DO IT) (Vocals: Teddy Bunn & O'Neil Spencer) / MONEY IS HONEY (Vocal: O'Neil Spencer) .... *Decca 2470* 5-8 39

RAMOS, Jose, as The Jose Ramos Tango Orchestra

EL CHOCLO / ADIOS, MUCHACHOS .... *Decca 818* 3-5 35
MEDIA LUZ (DIM LIGHT) / DONDE ESTAS CORAZON? (WHERE ARE YOU, MY HEART?)........ *Decca 563* 3-5 35
QUEJA PAMPERA / MADELEINE .... *Decca 636* 3-5 35

RANDALL, Bobby, as Bobby Randall's Band-Its

SOMEBODY'S LONELY / JUST A COTTAGE SMALL (BY A WATERFALL) .... *Gennett 3263* 5-8 26
(Vocals: Bobby Randall)

RANDALL, Slatz, & His Orchestra

BESSIE COULDN'T HELP IT (Vocal: Joe Roberts) / I GET THE BLUES WHEN IT RAINS (Vocals: Unknown) .... *Brunswick 4331* 5-8 29
BLAME IT ON THE MOON / I'D DO ANYTHING FOR YOU (Vocals: Unknown)........ *Brunswick 4562* 4-6 29
GOT A GREAT BIG DATE WITH A LITTLE BITTA GIRL / LET'S DON'T 'N' SAY WE DID ..... *Brunswick 4568* 5-8 29
(Vocals: Unknown)
HELLO! GORGEOUS / MY MOM...... *Brunswick 6304* 5-8 32
(Vocals: Unknown)
SKIRTS (Vocal: Slatz Randall) / I'M A DING-DONG DADDY (FROM DUMAS) (Vocals: Unknown) .... *Brunswick 4779* 5-8 30
WHAT A PERFECT NIGHT FOR LOVE / SWEETHEART TRAIL .... *Brunswick 4719* 4-6 30
(Vocals: Unknown)

RANDELL, Jay, & His Orchestra

I'M IN LOVE / TAKE THIS LITTLE ROSE .... *Columbia 3112-D* 4-6 36
(Vocals: Unknown)
THIS IS THE KISS OF ROMANCE / WHEN APRIL COMES AGAIN..... *Columbia 3113-D* 4-6 36
(Vocals: Unknown)

RANDOLPH, Amanda, & Her Orchestra

DOIN' THE SUZIE-Q / PLEASE DON'T TALK ABOUT MY MAN .... *Bluebird B-6615* 5-8 36
(Vocals: Amanda Randolph)

FOR SENTIMENTAL REASONS / HE MAY BE YOUR MAN (BUT HE COMES TO SEE ME SOMETIMES) .... *Bluebird B-6617* 5-8 36
(Vocals: Amanda Randolph)

HONEY, PLEASE DON'T TURN YOUR BACK ON ME (Vocal: Amanda Randolph) / IN THE GROOVE (by Wingy Manone & His Orchestra; Vocal: Wingy Manone) .... *Bluebird B-6616* 5-8 36

I'VE GOT SOMETHING IN MY EYE (Vocal: Amanda Randolph) / RAINBOW ON THE RIVER (by Charlie Barnet & His Orchestra; Vocal: Charlie Barnet)... *Bluebird B-6619* 4-6 36

RANDOLPH, Earl, as Earl Randolph's Orchestra:
see RICH, Fred, as Fred Rich's Dance Orchestra
see SAMUELS, Joseph as Joseph Samuels' Master Players, and
see SAMUELS, Joseph as Joseph Samuels' Music Masters

RAPEE, Erno, as Erno Rapee's Orchestra
(Erno Rapee: 6/4/91 – 6/26/45)
(Hit Of The Week records are one-sided paper discs; some, including the following, have two titles on the one side.)

RIVER, STAY 'WAY FROM MY DOOR; SOME OF THESE DAYS .... *Hit Of The Week 1185* 5-8 32
(Vocals: Helen Rowland)

SAVE THE LAST DANCE FOR ME (Vocal: Paul Small) ; IDA .... *Hit Of The Week B-2-3* 5-8 32

THIS IS THE MISSUS (Vocal: Paul Small) ; THE MERRY WIDOW WALTZ .... *Hit Of The Week B-4-C-1* 5-8 32

RAPH, Ted, & His Orchestra
see BALLEW, Smith, & His Orchestra

RAPP, Barney, & His New Englanders
(Barney Rapp: – circa 1970)

BUILD A LITTLE HOME / NO MORE LOVE .... *Bluebird B-5250* 4-6 33
(Vocals: Bunny Welcome)

BUILD A LITTLE HOME / NO MORE LOVE .... *Electradisk 2130* 12-15 33
(Vocals: Bunny Welcome)

BUILD A LITTLE HOME / NO MORE LOVE .... *Sunrise S-3333* 12-15 33
(Vocals: Bunny Welcome)
(Simultaneously released on three labels)

HEAVEN ONLY KNOWS / CHIMES IN THE CHAPEL .... *Bluebird B-5238* 4-6 33
(Vocals: Eddie Ryan)

HEAVEN ONLY KNOWS / CHIMES IN THE CHAPEL .... *Electradisk 2121* 12-15 33
(Vocals: Eddie Ryan)

HEAVEN ONLY KNOWS / CHIMES IN THE CHAPEL .... *Sunrise S-3321* 12-15 33
(Vocals: Eddie Ryan)
(Simultaneously released on three labels)

WHEN SHALL WE MEET AGAIN? / AND SO GOODBYE .... *Bluebird B-5237* 4-6 33
(Vocals: Eddie Ryan)

WHEN SHALL WE MEET AGAIN? / AND SO GOODBYE .... *Electradisk 2120* 12-15 33
(Vocals: Eddie Ryan)

WHEN SHALL WE MEET AGAIN? / AND SO GOODBYE .... *Sunrise S-3320* 12-15 33
(Vocals: Eddie Ryan)
(Simultaneously released on three labels)

RAPP, Barney, & His Orchestra

BECAUSE THEY ALL LOVE YOU / THE SLAVE OF LOVE (by George Olsen & His Music) .... *Victor 19497* 3-5 24

WALK, JENNIE, WALK / SOMEBODY ELSE TOOK YOU OUT OF MY ARMS .... *Victor 19182* 5-8 23

WHEN DIXIE STARS ARE PLAYING PEEK-A-BOO (yodeling by Frank Kamplain) / I NEED SOME PETTIN' .... *Victor 19341* 4-6 24

RAVAZZA, Carl, & His Orchestra
also see RAVELL, Carl, & His Orchestra)
(Carl Ravazza: circa 1915 – 7/29/68. Also known as Carl Ravell.)

LOVE TALES / SOUTH OF PAGO PAGO .... *Bluebird B-10833* 3-5 40
(Vocals: Carl Ravazza)

NIGHT HAS A THOUSAND EYES, THE / TESSIE, STOP TEASING ME .... *Bluebird B-10882* 4-6 40
(Vocals: Carl Ravazza)

SOMEBODY TOLD ME THEY LOVED ME (Vocals: Carl Ravazza, Paul Durand, Lester Randolph, & George Porter) / I LOVED YOU BEFORE I MEET YOU (FOR I SAW YOU IN MY DREAMS) (Vocal: Carl Ravazza) .... *Bluebird B-10629* 3-5 40

VIENI SU (theme song) / CRAZY LITTLE DREAM .... *Bluebird B-10583* 3-5 40
(Vocals: Carl Ravazza)

RAVELL, Carl, & His Orchestra
also see RAVAZZA, Carl, & His Orchestra
(Carl Ravell was also known as Carl Ravazza)

HARBOR LIGHTS / LOVE IS A MERRY-GO-ROUND .... *Melotone 7-08-04* 4-6 37
(Vocals: Carl Ravell)

SO RARE / GONE WITH THE WIND .... *Conqueror 8910* 4-6 37
(Vocals: Carl Ravell)

SO RARE / GONE WITH THE WIND ... *Melotone 7-08-07* 4-6 37
(Vocals: Carl Ravell)
(Simultaneously released on two labels)

YOU'LL NEVER GO TO HEAVEN (IF YOU BREAK MY HEART) / WHEN TWO LOVE EACH OTHER (JUST AS YOU AND I) .... *Melotone 7-07-18* 3-5 37
(Vocals: Carl Ravell)

RAY, Floyd, & His Orchestra

JAMMIN' THE BLUES (Vocal: Ivy Ann Glascoe) / SIDE BY SIDE (Vocals: Ivy, Verne, & Von) ... *Decca 2618* 5-8 39

LOVE IS SIMPLY GRAND (Vocals: Ivy, Verne, & Von) / FIREFLY STOMP .... *Decca 2500* 5-8 39

MY LITTLE DREAM GIRL (Vocal: Joe Alexander) / BLUES AT NOON (Vocals: Ivy, Verne, & Von) .... *Decca 2923* 5-8 39

THREE O'CLOCK IN THE MORNING (Vocals: chorus) / COMIN' ON WITH THE BLUES (Vocal: Ivy Ann Glascoe) .... *Decca 2337* 5-8 39

RAY, Jimmy, & His Orchestra
(Jimmy Ray: circa 1915 –)

I WANT YOU FOR CHRISTMAS / I TOLD SANTA CLAUS TO BRING ME YOU .... *Bluebird B-7282* 3-5 38
(Vocals: Jimmy Ray)

ON TREASURE ISLAND / TAKE ME BACK TO MY BOOTS AND SADDLES .... *Bluebird B-6128* 4-6 35
(Vocals: Jimmy Ray)

ROLLIN' PLAINS / BE A GOOD SPORT .... *Bluebird B-7285* 3-5 38
(Vocals: Jimmy Ray)

SHAME ON YOU / STICKS AND STONES WILL BREAK MY BONES .... *Bluebird B-7084* 3-5 37
(Vocals: Jimmy Ray)

SO RARE / YOU'RE MY DESIRE..... *Bluebird B-7077* 4-6 37
(Vocals: Jimmy Ray)

RAY, Jimmy, & His Orchestra as The Musical Musketeers

SO MANY MEMORIES / MY CABIN OF DREAMS .... *Bluebird B-7082* 3-5 37
(Vocals: Jimmy Ray)

SONG OF THE MARINES (WE'RE SHOVIN' RIGHT OFF AGAIN) / THE DREAM IN MY HEART .... *Bluebird B-7080* 3-5 37
(Vocals: Jimmy Ray)

RAY, Jimmy, & His Orchestra as The Southern Rhythm Kings

CARAVAN / JOSEPHINE .... *Bluebird B-7079* 3-5 37

RAY, Jimmy, & His Orchestra as The Southern Serenaders Orchestra

LITTLE BOY THAT SANTA CLAUS FORGOT, THE / TWO LITTLE WOODEN PONIES ON THE MERRY-GO-ROUND ...... *Bluebird B-7284* 2-4 38
(Vocals: Jimmy Ray)

PELL STREET BLUES / THE DANCE OF THE BLUE DANUBE .... *Bluebird B-7321* 3-5 38

WHEN THE BAND PLAYS "HOME SWEET HOME" / ON THE SUNNY SIDE OF THE ROCKIES .... *Bluebird B-7307* 2-4 38
(Vocals: Jimmy Ray)

RAYMOND, Frank, as Frank Raymond's Dance Orchestra:
see RICH, Fred, & His Orchestra

RAYMOND, Joe, & His Orchestra

MY SWEETIE WENT AWAY (SHE DIDN'T SAY WHERE, WHEN OR WHY) / DIRTY HANDS! DIRTY FACE! .... *Victor 19110* 2-4 23

REMEMB'RING / SALT YOUR SUGAR... *Victor 19178* 2-4 23

REARDON, Casper, & His Group
(Casper Reardon: 4/15/07 – 3/9/41)

WASHBOARD BLUES / WHAT IS THIS THING CALLED LOVE? .... *Liberty Music Shop L-218* 5-8 37

REARDON, Casper, & His Orchestra

AIN'T MISBEHAVIN' / IN A SENTIMENTAL MOOD .... *Master 133* 5-8 37

WASHBOARD BLUES / A BLUES SERENADE .... *Master 139* 5-8 37

REARDON, Casper, harp solos accompanied by a recording group

I CAN'T GIVE YOU ANYTHING BUT LOVE / EASY TO LOVE .... *Schirmer 511* 5-8 40
(Vocals: Loulie Jean)

I GOT RHYTHM / THEY DIDN'T BELIEVE ME .... *Schirmer 512* 5-8 40
(Vocals: Loulie Jean)

REARDON, Casper, His Harp & His Orchestra

IN A SENTIMENTAL MOOD / TORMENTED .... *Liberty Music Shop L-193* 4-6 36

SUMMERTIME / (IF YOU CAN'T SING IT) YOU'LL HAVE TO SWING IT (Vocal: Bea Giersdorf) .... *Liberty Music Shop L-199* 5-8 36

RECTOR'S ORCHESTRA

TILL WE MEET AGAIN / BEAUTIFUL OHIO .... *Arto 9001* 4-6 19

RED HOTTERS, The:
see RADERMAN, Harry, as Raderman's Red Hotters

REDMAN, Don, & His Orchestra
(Don Redman: 7/29/00 – 11/30/64)

BABY, WON'T YOU PLEASE COME HOME? (Vocal: Quentin Jackson) / AIN'T I GOOD TO YOU? (Vocal: Don Redman) .... *Victor 26266* 5-8 39

CHANT OF THE WEED (theme song) / SHAKIN' THE AFRICAN (Vocal: Don Redman) .... *Brunswick 6211* 10-12 31

CHEW-CHEW-CHEW (YOUR BUBBLE GUM) (Vocals: Don Redman & Laurel Watson) / IGLOO (Vocal: Laurel Watson) .... *Victor 26258* 5-8 39

DOIN' THE NEW LOW-DOWN (Vocal & tap dancing by Bill "Bojangles" Robinson) / SHUFFLE YOUR FEET; BANDANNA BABIES (Vocals: Harry & Donald Mills) .... *Brunswick 6520* 8-10 33

DOIN' WHAT I PLEASE / NAGASAKI .. *Brunswick 6429* 8-10 32
(Vocals: Don Redman)

DOWN HOME RAG / MARGIE (Vocals: chorus) .... *Bluebird B-10061* 5-8 39

EXACTLY LIKE YOU / ON THE SUNNY SIDE OF THE STREET .... *Variety 580* 5-8 37
(Vocals: The Swing Choir)

HOW'M I DOIN'? / TRY GETTING A GOOD NIGHT'S SLEEP .... *Brunswick 6273* 8-10 32
(Vocals: Ron Redman)

IF IT'S TRUE (Vocal: Harlan Lattimore) / HOT AND ANXIOUS (Vocal: Ron Redman) .... *Brunswick 6368* 10-12 32

I FOUND A NEW WAY TO GO TO TOWN (Vocal: Harlan Lattimore) / NO ONE LOVES ME LIKE THAT DALLAS MAN (Vocal: Ron Redman) .... *Brunswick 6684* 8-10 33

I GOT YA (Vocal: Ron Redman) / AULD LANG SYNE (Vocals: chorus) .... *Bluebird B-10095* 5-8 39

I'M PLAYING SOLITAIRE (Vocal: Quentin Jackson) / MILENBERG JOYS .... *Bluebird B-10071* 5-8 39

IT'S A GREAT WORLD AFTER ALL (Vocal: Ron Redman) / YOU GAVE ME EVERYTHING BUT LOVE (Vocal: Harlan Lattimore) .... *Brunswick 6344* 5-8 32

I WANNA BE LOVED (Vocal: Harlan Lattimore) / GOT THE JITTERS (Vocal: Ron Redman) .... *Brunswick 6745* 5-8 34

I WON'T TELL (Vocal: Ron Redman) / IT'S ALL YOUR FAULT (Vocal: Harlan Lattimore) ...... *Brunswick 6585* 5-8 33

LAZY BONES (Vocal: Harlan Lattimore) / WATCHING THE KNIFE AND FORK SPOON (Vocal: Ron Redman) .... *Brunswick 6622* 5-8 33

LAZY WEATHER / MOONRISE
ON THE LOWLANDS ... *Melotone 6-07-09* 5-8 36
(Vocals: Harold Lattimore)

MAN ON THE FLYING TRAPESE, THE (Vocal: Ron
Redman) / THAT NAUGHTY WALTZ ... *Variety 635* 5-8 37

PAGAN PARADISE (Vocal: Harlan Lattimore) /
TWO-TIME MAN (Vocal: Ron Redman) ... *Brunswick 6412* 8-10 32

SHIM-ME-SHA-WABBLE /
CHANT OF THE WEED ... *Bluebird B-10765* 5-8 40

SOPHISTICATED LADY / THAT BLUE-EYED
BABY FROM MEMPHIS
(Vocal: Harlan Lattimore) ... *Brunswick 6560* 5-8 33

STORMY WEATHER (Vocals: The Swing Choir) /
SWEET SUE ... *Variety 605* 8-10 37

SWEET LEILANI (Vocals: chorus) / 'DEED I DO
(Vocals: Laurel Watson & chorus) ... *Bluebird B-10081* 5-8 39

TEA FOR TWO (Vocal: Harlan Lattimore) /
I GOT RHYTHM ... *Brunswick 6354* 5-8 32

TOO BAD (Vocal: Ron Redman) /
BUGLE CALL RAG ... *Melotone 6-12-18* 5-8 36

TOO BAD (Vocal: Ron Redman) /
BUGLE CALL RAG ... *Vocalion 3354* 5-8 36
(Simultaneously released on two labels)

TROUBLE, WHY PICK ON ME? (Vocal: Lois Deppe) /
I HEARD (Vocal: Ron Redman) ... *Brunswick 6233* 10-12 31

UNDERNEATH THE HARLEM MOON / AIN'T I THE
LUCKY ONE? ... *Brunswick 6401* 5-8 32
(Vocals: Harlan Lattimore)

WHO WANTS TO SING MY LOVE SONG
(Vocal: Harlan Lattimore) / WE DON'T KNOW FROM
NOTHIN' (Vocal: Ron Redman) ... *Melotone 7-03-03* 5-8 37

WHO WANTS TO SING MY LOVE SONG
(Vocal: Harlan Lattimore) / WE DON'T KNOW FROM
NOTHIN' (Vocal: Ron Redman) ... *Vocalion 3359* 5-8 37
(Simultaneously released on two labels)

YOU AIN'T NOWHERE (Vocals: Ron Redman & chorus) /
ABOUT RIP VAN WINKLE (Vocals: Ron Redman,
Bootsie Garrison & chorus) ... *Bluebird B-10615* 5-8 40

YOU TOLD ME BUT HALF THE STORY /
LONELY CABIN ... *Brunswick 6935* 8-10 33
(Vocals: Harlan Lattimore)

REDMAN, Don, & His Orchestra as Billy Bunch & His Smoky Rhythm

THREE LITTLE MAIDS (Vocals: The Three Little Maids) /
THE FLOWERS THAT BLOOM IN THE SPRING
(Vocals: Ron Redman & Eddie Williams) ... *Bluebird B-10305* 5-8 39

REDMAN, Don, & His Orchestra as Bob Causer & His Cornellians

PUDDIN' HEAD JONES /
MY OLD MAN ... *Melotone M-12848* 8-10 34
(Vocals: Chick Bullock)

PUDDIN' HEAD JONES /
MY OLD MAN ... *Perfect 15852* 8-10 34
(Vocals: Chick Bullock)
(Simultaneously released on two labels)

REDMAN, Don, & His Orchestra as Earl Harlan & His Orchestra

GOT THE SOUTH IN MY SOUL (Vocal: Harlan Lattimore) /
WEST BOUND FREIGHT (by Dick Robertson & His
Orchestra; Vocal: Dick Robertson) ... *Melotone M-12417* 5-8 32

OUR BIG LOVE SCENE /
AFTER SUNDOWN ... *Melotone M-12840* 5-8 34
(Vocals: Chick Bullock)

OUR BIG LOVE SCENE /
AFTER SUNDOWN ... *Perfect 15847* 5-8 34
(Vocals: Chick Bullock)
(Simultaneously released on two labels)

TIRED OF IT ALL / KEEP ON DOIN' WHAT
YOU'RE DOIN' ... *Melotone M-12867* 8-10 34
(Vocals: Chick Bullock)

TIRED OF IT ALL / KEEP ON DOIN' WHAT
YOU'RE DOIN' ... *Perfect 15862* 8-10 34
(Vocals: Chick Bullock)
(Simultaneously released on two labels)

RED, WHITE AND BLUE MARIMBA BAND, The

(AT THE) COTTON PICKERS' BALL / THERE'S A LUMP
OF SUGAR DOWN IN DIXIE ... *Columbia A-2550* 2-4 18

REGAL DANCE ORCHESTRA, The:

see SELVIN, Ben, as The Moulin Rouge Orchestra

REGA, Milo, as The Rega Dance Orchestra

BAMBOO ISLE / JA DA BLUES ... *Okeh 4695* 2-4 22

DON'T WE CARRY ON? / I LOVE ME
(I'M WILD ABOUT MYSELF) ... *Okeh 4843* 2-4 23
(Vocals: Billy Jones)

FLOWER OF ARABY /
IVY (CLING TO ME) ... *Okeh 4763* 2-4 23

I WISH THERE WAS A WIRELESS TO HEAVEN /
RADIO EYES ... *Okeh 4674* 2-4 22

JOKES (OKEH LAUGHING DANCE RECORD) /
JOKES (OKEH LAUGHING DANCE
RECORD), PART II ... *Okeh 4731* 5-8 23

LEARN TO SMILE / BRING BACK
MY BLUSHING ROSE ... *Okeh 4396* 2-4 21

MARY-ELLEN (SINCE I FELL IN LOVE WITH YOU) /
GEORGETTE ... *Okeh 4661* 2-4 22

MOON RIVER / THREE O'CLOCK IN THE MORNING
(whistling by Sibyl Sanderson Fagan) ... *Okeh 4514* 2-4 22

'N' THAT'S BETTER / STELLA ... *Okeh 4877* 2-4 23
(Vocals: Billy Jones)

OH! OH! (Vocal: Jack Kaufman) /
DARDANELLA ... *Okeh 4057* 2-4 20

OLD FAVORITES / IRISH MEDLEY ... *Okeh 4335* 2-4 21

PEGGY / PATCHES ... *Okeh 4001* 2-4 19

PICKLES (Vocals: Billy Jones & Ernest Hare) /
NUTSEY FAGAN (Vocal: Billy Jones) ... *Okeh 4909* 3-5 23

RED MOON / WALTZ OF LOVE ... *Okeh 4787* 2-4 23

SALLY / LOVE BIRD ... *Okeh 4258* 2-4 21
(whistling by Sibyl Sanderson Fagan)

STOP IT! / KARZAN ... *Okeh 4099* 2-4 20

THAT CAT STEP / I'M A JAZZ VAMPIRE ... *Okeh 4178* 2-4 20

TUCK ME TO SLEEP IN MY OLD 'TUCKY HOME /
EVERYBODY STEP ... *Okeh 4452* 2-4 21

VENETIAN MOON / OH! BY JINGO ... *Okeh 4090* 2-4 20

WATERMELON WHISPERS / SOUTH AMERICAN
FOX TROT ... *Okeh 1041* 3-5 18

WHEN THE SUN GOES DOWN IN CAIRO TOWN /
ORIENTAL STARS ... *Okeh 4101* 2-4 20

WHISTLE THE BLUES AWAY (whistling by Sibyl
Sanderson Fagan) / THRILLS ... *Okeh 4496* 2-4 22

REICHMAN, Joe, & His Orchestra

(Joe Reichman: circa 1898 – 4/14/70)

ANDANTE CANTABILE / MY MELANCHOLY BABY
(Vocal: Chester LeRoy) ... *Victor 27882* 2-4 42

BE FAIR (Vocal: Gene Schill) /
I'M THRILLED (Vocal: Larry Neill) ... *Victor 27668* 2-4 41

BONJOUR, MAM'SELLE /
PARIS IN SPRING ... *Melotone M-13420* 2-4 35
(Vocals: Unknown)

DANCE OF THE BAYOU / IF THIS
BE LOVE (Vocal: Marion Shaw) ... *Victor 27408* 2-4 41

DANCING WITH MY SHADOW / WHERE THERE'S
SMOKE – THERE'S FIRE ... *Banner 33290* 3-5 35
(Vocals: Paul Small)

DANCING WITH MY SHADOW / WHERE THERE'S
SMOKE – THERE'S FIRE ... *Melotone M-13257* 3-5 35
(Vocals: Paul Small)

DANCING WITH MY SHADOW / WHERE THERE'S
SMOKE – THERE'S FIRE ... *Oriole 3057* 3-5 35
(Vocals: Paul Small)

DANCING WITH MY SHADOW / WHERE THERE'S
SMOKE – THERE'S FIRE ... *Perfect 16045* 3-5 35
(Vocals: Paul Small)

DANCING WITH MY SHADOW / WHERE THERE'S
SMOKE – THERE'S FIRE ... *Romeo 2431* 3-5 35
(Vocals: Paul Small)
(Simultaneously released on five labels)

DON'T BE BLUE, LITTLE PAL, DON'T BE BLUE /
FOOLED ... *Victor 27463* 2-4 41
(Vocals: Larry Neill)

FIRESIDE CHAT, A / WHEREVER
YOU ARE ... *Victor 27800* 2-4 42
(Vocals: Siggy Lane)

GAUCHO, THE / LOVE ME
FOREVER (Vocals: Unknown) ... *Melotone M-13449* 2-4 35

HANDS ACROSS THE TABLE / THE OBJECT
OF MY AFFECTION ... *Banner 33270* 3-5 35
(Vocals: Paul Small)

HANDS ACROSS THE TABLE / THE OBJECT
OF MY AFFECTION ... *Conqueror 8461* 3-5 35
(Vocals: Paul Small)

HANDS ACROSS THE TABLE / THE OBJECT
OF MY AFFECTION ... *Melotone M-13237* 3-5 35
(Vocals: Paul Small)

HANDS ACROSS THE TABLE / THE OBJECT
OF MY AFFECTION ... *Oriole 3044* 3-5 35
(Vocals: Paul Small)

HANDS ACROSS THE TABLE / THE OBJECT
OF MY AFFECTION ... *Perfect 16034* 3-5 35
(Vocals: Paul Small)

HANDS ACROSS THE TABLE / THE OBJECT
OF MY AFFECTION ... *Romeo 2418* 3-5 35
(Vocals: Paul Small)
(Simultaneously released on six labels)

HEY! STOP KISSIN' MY SISTER / IT WAS
WONDERFUL THEN ... *Victor 27378* 2-4 41
(Vocals: Marion Shaw)

I HEAR A RHAPSODY / I COULD
WRITE A BOOK ... *Victor 27325* 2-4 41
(Vocals: Marion Shaw)

I'LL CLOSE MY EYES TO EVERYONE ELSE /
BUTTERFLY ... *Banner 33126* 3-5 34
(Vocals: Mildred Monson)

I'LL CLOSE MY EYES TO EVERYONE ELSE /
BUTTERFLY ... *Melotone M-13093* 3-5 34
(Vocals: Mildred Monson)

I'LL CLOSE MY EYES TO EVERYONE ELSE /
BUTTERFLY ... *Oriole 2939* 3-5 34
(Vocals: Mildred Monson)

I'LL CLOSE MY EYES TO EVERYONE ELSE /
BUTTERFLY ... *Perfect 15967* 3-5 34
(Vocals: Mildred Monson)

I'LL CLOSE MY EYES TO EVERYONE ELSE /
BUTTERFLY ... *Romeo 2313* 3-5 34
(Vocals: Mildred Monson)
(Simultaneously released on five labels)

I ONLY HAVE EYES FOR YOU / TRY TO SEE
IT MY WAY ... *Banner 33087* 3-5 34
(Vocals: Joseph Sudy)

I ONLY HAVE EYES FOR YOU / TRY TO SEE
IT MY WAY ... *Melotone M-13051* 3-5 34
(Vocals: Joseph Sudy)

I ONLY HAVE EYES FOR YOU / TRY TO SEE
IT MY WAY ... *Oriole 2917* 3-5 34
(Vocals: Joseph Sudy)

I ONLY HAVE EYES FOR YOU / TRY TO SEE
IT MY WAY ... *Perfect 15950* 3-5 34
(Vocals: Joseph Sudy)

I ONLY HAVE EYES FOR YOU / TRY TO SEE
IT MY WAY ... *Romeo 2291* 3-5 34
(Vocals: Joseph Sudy)
(Simultaneously released on five labels)

ISN'T IT A SHAME? (Vocal: Mildred Monson) /
SOMEWHERE IN YOUR HEART
(Vocal: Chick Bullock) ... *Banner 33197* 3-5 34

ISN'T IT A SHAME? (Vocal: Mildred Monson) /
SOMEWHERE IN YOUR HEART
(Vocal: Chick Bullock) ... *Melotone M-13164* 3-5 34

ISN'T IT A SHAME? (Vocal: Mildred Monson) /
SOMEWHERE IN YOUR HEART
(Vocal: Chick Bullock) ... *Oriole 2992* 3-5 34

ISN'T IT A SHAME? (Vocal: Mildred Monson) /
SOMEWHERE IN YOUR HEART
(Vocal: Chick Bullock) ... *Perfect 16004* 3-5 34

ISN'T IT A SHAME? (Vocal: Mildred Monson) /
SOMEWHERE IN YOUR HEART
(Vocal: Chick Bullock) ... *Romeo 2366* 3-5 34
(Simultaneously released on five labels)

I WOKE UP TOO SOON / I THRILL WHEN
THEY MENTION YOUR NAME ... *Banner 33300* 2-4 35
(Vocals: Paul Small)

I WOKE UP TOO SOON / I THRILL WHEN
THEY MENTION YOUR NAME ... *Melotone M-13267* 2-4 35
(Vocals: Paul Small)

I WOKE UP TOO SOON / I THRILL WHEN
THEY MENTION YOUR NAME ... *Oriole 3064* 2-4 35
(Vocals: Paul Small)

I WOKE UP TOO SOON / I THRILL WHEN
THEY MENTION YOUR NAME ... *Perfect 16050* 2-4 35
(Vocals: Paul Small)

I WOKE UP TOO SOON / I THRILL WHEN
THEY MENTION YOUR NAME ... *Romeo 2438* 2-4 35
(Vocals: Paul Small)
(Simultaneously released on five labels)

KASHMIRI SONG / LITTLE
THOUGHTS (Vocal: Chester LeRoy) ... *Victor 27975* 2-4 42

KEEP AN EYE ON YOUR HEART / I'M ALWAYS
CHASING RAINBOWS ... *Victor 27333* 2-4 41
(Vocals: Marion Shaw)

KISS ME GOODNIGHT / LOVE SONG
OF TAHITI ... *Melotone M-13421* 2-4 35
(Vocals: Unknown)

LULLABY TO A SWEET PAPOOSE /
MOONLIGHT COCKTAIL ... *Victor 27810* 2-4 42

ME WITHOUT YOU / A LITTLE ANGEL
TOLD ME SO ... *Banner 33289* 2-4 35
(Vocals: Paul Small)

ME WITHOUT YOU / A LITTLE ANGEL
TOLD ME SO ... *Melotone M-13256* 2-4 35
(Vocals: Paul Small)

ME WITHOUT YOU / A LITTLE ANGEL
TOLD ME SO ... *Oriole 3056* 2-4 35
(Vocals: Paul Small)

ME WITHOUT YOU / A LITTLE ANGEL
TOLD ME SO ... *Perfect 16044* 2-4 35
(Vocals: Paul Small)

ME WITHOUT YOU / A LITTLE ANGEL
TOLD ME SO ... *Romeo 2430* 2-4 35
(Vocals: Paul Small)
(Simultaneously released on five labels)

MRS. AUSTIN FROM BOSTON (Vocals: Margie Stuart &
Larry Neill) / MOONLIGHT SONATA ... *Victor 27484* 2-4 41

NEW MOON IS OVER MY SHOULDER, A /
FROM NOW ON ... *Banner 33127* 3-5 34
(Vocals: Chris Fletcher)

NEW MOON IS OVER MY SHOULDER, A /
FROM NOW ON ... *Melotone M-13094* 3-5 34
(Vocals: Chris Fletcher)

NEW MOON IS OVER MY SHOULDER, A /
FROM NOW ON ... *Oriole 2940* 3-5 34
(Vocals: Chris Fletcher)

NEW MOON IS OVER MY SHOULDER, A /
FROM NOW ON ... *Perfect 15968* 3-5 34
(Vocals: Chris Fletcher)

NEW MOON IS OVER MY SHOULDER, A /
FROM NOW ON ... *Romeo 2314* 3-5 34
(Vocals: Chris Fletcher)
(Simultaneously released on five labels)

NIGHTY NIGHT / THE MONKEY
ON A STRING ... *Victor 27448* 3-5 41
(Vocals: Janette)

PARIS IN SPRING /
LOVE ME FOREVER ... *Conqueror 8538* 2-4 35
(Vocals: Unknown)

STAR GAZING / AND THEN SOME ... *Melotone M-13446* 2-4 35
(Vocals: Joe Martin)

STAR GAZING / AND THEN SOME ... *Perfect 16138* 2-4 35
(Vocals: Joe Martin)
(Simultaneously released on two labels)

THANK YOU FOR A LOVELY EVENING /
BECAUSE IT'S LOVE ... *Banner 33079* 3-5 34
(Vocals: Joseph Sudy)

THANK YOU FOR A LOVELY EVENING /
BECAUSE IT'S LOVE ... *Melotone M-13043* 3-5 34
(Vocals: Joseph Sudy)

THANK YOU FOR A LOVELY EVENING /
BECAUSE IT'S LOVE ... *Oriole 2913* 3-5 34
(Vocals: Joseph Sudy)

THANK YOU FOR A LOVELY EVENING /
BECAUSE IT'S LOVE ... *Perfect 15946* 3-5 34
(Vocals: Joseph Sudy)

THANK YOU FOR A LOVELY EVENING /
BECAUSE IT'S LOVE ... *Romeo 2287* 3-5 34
(Vocals: Joseph Sudy)
(Simultaneously released on five labels)

TONIGHT WE LOVE (Vocal: Larry Neill) / I WISH I HAD A
SWEETHEART (Vocal: Gene Schill) ... *Victor 27618* 2-4 41

WINE SONG (Vocal: Paul Small) /
HA-CHA-CHA (Vocal: Chick Bullock) ... *Banner 33221* 3-5 34

WINE SONG (Vocal: Paul Small) /
HA-CHA-CHA (Vocal: Chick Bullock) ... *Melotone M-13188* 3-5 34

WINE SONG (Vocal: Paul Small) /
HA-CHA-CHA (Vocal: Chick Bullock) ... *Oriole 3015* 3-5 34

WINE SONG (Vocal: Paul Small) /
HA-CHA-CHA (Vocal: Chick Bullock) ... *Perfect 16007* 3-5 34

WINE SONG (Vocal: Paul Small) /
HA-CHA-CHA (Vocal: Chick Bullock) ... *Romeo 2389* 3-5 34
(Simultaneously released on five labels)

WISE OLD OWL (Vocal: Marion Shaw) /
TOY PIANO MINUET ... *Victor 27360* 2-4 41

YOU'LL NEVER KNOW /
THE HUT-SUT SONG ... *Victor 27420* 3-5 41
(Vocals: Janette)

YOU'RE A BUILDER-UPPER (Vocal: Chick Bullock) / WHY AM I BLUE? (Vocal: Mildred Monson) .... *Banner 33186* 3-5 34

YOU'RE A BUILDER-UPPER (Vocal: Chick Bullock) / WHY AM I BLUE? (Vocal: Mildred Monson) .... *Melotone M-13153* 3-5 34

YOU'RE A BUILDER-UPPER (Vocal: Chick Bullock) / WHY AM I BLUE? (Vocal: Mildred Monson) .... *Oriole 2984* 3-5 34

YOU'RE A BUILDER-UPPER (Vocal: Chick Bullock) / WHY AM I BLUE? (Vocal: Mildred Monson) .... *Perfect 15996* 3-5 34

YOU'RE A BUILDER-UPPER (Vocal: Chick Bullock) / WHY AM I BLUE? (Vocal: Mildred Monson) .... *Romeo 2358* 3-5 34
(Simultaneously released on five labels)

REICHMAN, Joe, & His Orchestra as Carl Shaw & His Orchestra

DON'T LET IT BOTHER YOU / OUT IN THE COLD AGAIN .... *Vocalion 2786* 3-5 34
(Vocals: Mildred Monson)

I SAW STARS / HAVE A LITTLE DREAM ON ME .... *Vocalion 2785* 3-5 34
(Vocals: Chick Bullock)

REILLY-FARLEY & THEIR ONYX CLUB BOYS:
see RILEY, Mike – Eddie Farley & Their Onyx Club Boys

REISMAN, Leo, & His Orchestra
(Leo Reisman: 1897 – 12/18/61)

ALONE TOGETHER / A SHINE ON YOUR SHOES .... *Victor 24131* 3-5 32
(Vocals: Frank Luther)

AT DAWNING / DREAMING OF TOMORROW .... *Columbia 464-D* 3-5 25

BEFORE YOU GO / TELL ME, RADIO .... *Columbia 152-D* 3-5 24

BEGIN THE BEGUINE / CAN'T WE DREAM A MIDSUMMER NIGHT'S DREAM? ... *Brunswick 7575* 3-5 36
(Vocals: Unknown)

BESS, YOU IS MY WOMAN NOW (Vocals: Helen Dowdy & Avon Long) / I GOT PLENTY OF NUTTIN' (Vocal: Avon Long) .... *Decca 18323* 2-4 42

BIRTH OF THE BLUES / HERE I AM ... *Columbia 701-D* 4-6 26

BROTHER, CAN YOU SPARE A DIME? (Vocal: Milton Douglas) / WHISTLING FOR A KISS (Vocal: George Wheeler) .... *Victor 24156* 3-5 32

BROWN EYES – WHY ARE YOU BLUE? / CLOSE YOUR EYES .... *Columbia 456-D* 3-5 25

BYE BYE BLUES (Vocal: Don Howard) / AROUND THE CORNER (Vocal: Philip Steele) .... *Victor 22459* 3-5 30

BYGONES / LONESOME HOURS ...... *Vocalion 14314* 2-4 22

CALL ME DARLING / BEND DOWN, SISTER .... *Victor 22849* 3-5 31
(Vocals: Leo Reisman)

CAN'T WE BE FRIENDS? / EVANGELINE .... *Victor 22070* 3-5 29
(Vocals: Lew Conrad)

CHEEK TO CHEEK / NO STRINGS ... *Brunswick 7486* 5-8 35
(Vocals: Fred Astaire)

CLOSE / ROSALIE .... *Victor 25698* 2-4 37
(Vocals: Lee Sullivan)

COLLETTE / RED LIPS – KISS MY BLUES AWAY .... *Columbia 973-D* 2-4 27
(Vocals: Unknown)

DAWN / WE TWO .... *Columbia 1205-D* 2-4 28
(Vocals: Unknown)

DINNER AT EIGHT (Vocal: Frank Luther) / SAVAGE SERENADE (Vocal: Sally Schermerhorn) ... *Victor 24419* 3-5 33

DON'T BLAME ME (Vocal: Howard Phillips) / HERE YOU COME WITH LOVE (Vocal: Leo Reisman) .... *Victor 24359* 3-5 33

DOWN ARGENTINA WAY (Vocal: Sara Horn) / YOU'RE NEARER (Vocal: Jack Kilty) ..... *Victor 26765* 2-4 40

EASTER PARADE / HOW'S CHANCES (Vocal: Clifton Webb) ... *Victor 24418* 3-5 33
(Clifton Webb starred in Broadway Productions and was in silent films in the early 1920's. His motion picture career extended into the 1960s, probably best remembered as Mr. Belvedere in several comedy films.)

FERRY BOAT SERENADE / NOW I LAY ME DOWN TO DREAM .... *Victor 26718* 2-4 40
(Vocals: Anita Boyer)

FLAMINGOS AND MOONLIGHT / BEWITCHED (Vocal: Anita Boyer) .... *Victor 27344* 2-4 41

FUN TO BE FOOLED / SHOEIN' THE MARE .... *Brunswick 6942* 5-8 34
(Vocals: Harold Arlen)

GIGOLETTE / THE WORLD IS MINE ... *Brunswick 7305* 3-5 34
(Vocals: Lew Conrad)

HAPPY AS THE DAY IS LONG (Vocal: Harold Arlen) / THE GOLD DIGGERS' SONG (Vocal: Fred Astaire) .... *Victor 24315* 5-8 33

HEARTACHES / MAYBE .... *Columbia 75-D* 3-5 24

HELLO MA! I DONE IT AGAIN (Vocal: Sara Horn) / WISHFUL THINKING (Vocal: Hal Lieber) ... *Victor 27275* 2-4 41

HE'S NOT WORTH YOUR TEARS / HURT ... *Victor 22605* 3-5 31
(Vocals: Ben Gordon)

I FEEL A SONG COMIN' ON (Vocal: Frank Luther) / SPEAKING CONFIDENTIALLY (Vocal: Sally Singer) .... *Brunswick 7483* 3-5 35

IF IT AIN'T LOVE / NIGHT SHALL BE FILLED WITH MUSIC .... *Victor 24011* 3-5 32
(Vocals: Frank Luther)

I GET A KICK OUT OF YOU / ANYTHING GOES .... *Brunswick 7332* 3-5 35
(Vocals: Sally Singer)

I GOT PLENTY O' NUTTIN' (Vocals: Unknown) / IT AIN'T NECESSARILY SO (Vocal: Edward Matthews) .... *Brunswick 7562* 2-4 35

I LIKE TO DO THINGS FOR YOU / HAPPY FEET .... *Victor 22398* 4-6 30
(Vocals: Lew Conrad)

ILL WIND (Vocal: Thelma Nevins) / AS LONG AS I LIVE (Vocal: Sally Singer) .... *Brunswick 6789* 4-6 34

I LOOK AT HEAVEN / THE LAMPLIGHTER'S SERENADE .... *Decca 18299* 2-4 42
(Vocals: Unknown)

I LOVE LOUISA / NEW SUN IN THE SKY .... *Victor 22755* 5-8 31
(Vocals: Fred Astaire)

I MAY BE DANCING WITH SOMEBODY ELSE / BYE-BYE BLACKBIRD .... *Columbia 653-D* 3-5 26

I'M IN THE MOOD FOR LOVE (Vocal: Frank Luther) / TAKE IT EASY (Vocal: Sally Singer) ... *Brunswick 7482* 3-5 35

IN A BAMBOO GARDEN / 'CAUSE I FEEL LOW-DOWN ...... *Columbia 1467-D* 3-5 28
(Vocals: Unknown)

INDIAN LOVE CALL / BECAUSE THEY ALL LOVE YOU .... *Columbia 242-D* 3-5 24

IN THE SHADE OF THE NEW APPLE TREE / GOD'S COUNTRY .... *Victor 25714* 3-5 38
(Vocals: Harold Arlen)

IT AIN'T NECESSARILY SO / A WOMAN IS A SOMETIME THING .... *Decca 18281* 2-4 42
(Vocals: Avon Long)

IT'S THE GIRL (Vocal: Leo Reisman) / TAKE IT FROM ME (I'M TAKING TO YOU) (Vocal: Lee Wiley) .... *Victor 22757* 4-6 31

I WANT TO LIVE (AS LONG AS YOU LOVE ME) (Vocal: Joan Whitney) / SUCH STUFF AS DREAMS ARE MADE OF (Vocal: Jack Kilty) .... *Victor 26758* 2-4 40

I WON'T DANCE / LOVELY TO LOOK AT .... *Brunswick 7393* 3-5 35
(Vocals: Phil Dewey)

I, YI, YI, YI, YI (I LIKE YOU VERY MUCH) (Vocal: Sara Horn) / BOA NOITE (GOODNIGHT) (Vocal: Anita Boyer) .... *Victor 27351* 2-4 41

JUST A GIGOLO / I'M ALONE BECAUSE I LOVE YOU .... *Victor 22606* 3-5 31
(Vocals: Ben Gordon)

KENTUCKY'S WAY OF SAYIN' "GOOD MORNING!" / HERE IN MY ARMS .... *Columbia 573-D* 2-4 26

LA PETITE AMIE / BLACK MAN'S LULLABY .... *Victor 25746* 3-5 38
(Vocals: Eve Symington)

LAST TIME I SAW PARIS, THE (Vocal: Phil Dewey) / WHAT MAKES A SONG? (Vocal: Mary Alcott) .... *Victor 27223* 2-4 40

LIZA (Vocal: Lew Conrad) / DO WHAT YOU DO! (Vocal: Smith Ballew) .... *Victor 22069* 3-5 29

LOOK WHAT YOU'VE DONE TO ME / DOIN' THE BOOM-BOOM .... *Victor 22115* 4-6 29
(Vocals: L. Levin)

LOVE BIRD / BRIGHT EYES .... *Columbia A-3366* 2-4 21

LOVE SONGS OF THE NILE (Vocal: Howard Phillips) / MY TEMPTATION (Vocal: Fred Astaire) .... *Victor 24312* 5-8 33

LUCKY ME – LOVABLE YOU / HAPPY DAYS ARE HERE AGAIN .... *Victor 22221* 4-6 30
(Vocals: L. Levin)

LUCKY SEVEN / SING SOMETHING SIMPLE .... *Victor 22538* 3-5 30
(Vocals: Frank Luther)

MA BELLE / MARCH OF THE MUSKETEERS .... *Columbia 1351-D* 2-4 28
(Vocals: Unknown)

MEAN TO ME / THAT'S WHAT I CALL HEAVEN .... *Victor 21921* 3-5 29
(Vocals: Ran Weeks)

MOANIN' LOW / AIN'T MISBEHAVIN' ... *Victor 22047* 4-6 29
(Vocals: Lew Conrad)

MOON OF MANAKOORA / LOVE WALKED IN .... *Victor 25790* 3-5 38
(Vocals: Felix Knight)

MY ELECTRIC GIRL / IN A TENT ... *Columbia A-3960* 2-4 23

MY LITTLE BUNCH OF HAPPINESS / ANGEL EYES .... *Columbia 855-D* 2-4 27

MY WOMAN / TOO MANY TEARS .... *Victor 22961* 3-5 32
(Vocals: Fran Frey)

NEEDLE IN A HAYSTACK (Vocal: Lew Conrad) / THE CONTINENTAL .... *Brunswick 6973* 3-5 34

NIGHT AND DAY / I'VE GOT YOU ON MY MIND .... *Victor 24193* 5-8 33
(Vocals: Fred Astaire)

NOT FOR ALL THE RICE IN CHINA (Vocal: Clifton Webb) / SUPPER TIME (Vocal: Thelma Nevins) ... *Victor 24428* 3-5 33
(Clifton Webb starred in Broadway Productions and was in silent films in the early 1920's. His motion picture career extended into the 1960s, probably best remembered as Mr. Belvedere in several comedy films.)

NOTHING BUT YOU / EV'RY SUNDAY AFTERNOON .... *Victor 26533* 3-5 40
(Vocals: The Deep River Boys)

ON THE ALAMO / MY CASTLE IN SPAIN IS A SHACK IN THE LANE (Vocals: Unknown) .... *Columbia 1767-D* 3-5 29

ON THE BEACH AT BALI BALI / AFTERGLOW .... *Brunswick 7696* 3-5 36
(Vocals: Larry Stewart)

PETRUSHKA / ALABAMA STOMP ... *Columbia 776-D* 4-6 26

PICCOLINO, THE (Vocal: Fred Astaire) / TODDLIN' ALONG WITH YOU (Vocal: Frank Luther) .... *Brunswick 7488* 5-8 35

POOR BUTTERFLY / LIMEHOUSE BLUES .... *Victor 27435* 3-5 41

RAINY DAY, A (Vocal: George Wheeler) / LOUISIANA HAYRIDE (Vocals: Arthur Schwartz & The Eva Jessye Choir) .... *Victor 24157* 3-5 32

RIDDLE ME THIS / HOW DO YOU DO IT .... *Victor 24132* 3-5 32
(Vocals: Frank Luther)

ROSE OF THE MOONLIGHT / LADY OF THE NILE .... *Columbia 355-D* 2-4 25

ROSES BROUGHT ME YOU, THE / I NEVER KNEW HOW WONDERFUL YOU WERE ... *Columbia 575-D* 2-4 26

SMILE WILL GO A LONG, LONG WAY, A / THE ONLY GIRL .... *Columbia 71-D* 2-4 24

SMOKE GETS IN YOUR EYES (Vocal: Tamara) / THE TOUCH OF YOUR HAND (Vocal: Bernice Claire) .... *Brunswick 6715* 3-5 34

SMOKE RINGS (Vocal: Harold Arlen) / HEART OF STONE (Vocal: Fred Astaire) .... *Victor 24358* 5-8 33

SOMETHING TO REMEMBER YOU BY / BODY AND SOUL .... *Victor 22537* 4-6 30
(Vocals: Frank Luther)

SONG OF THE VAGABONDS / CUP OF COFFEE, A SANDWICH AND YOU .... *Columbia 517-D* 3-5 26

SPAIN / DRIFTWOOD .... *Columbia 134-D* 2-4 24

STORMY WEATHER (Vocal: Harold Arlen) / MAYBE I LOVE YOU TOO MUCH (Vocal: Fred Astaire) .... *Victor 24262* 5-8 33

SWEET MADNESS / ME FOR YOU FOREVER .... *Victor 24398* 3-5 33
(Vocals: Vivian Ruth)

SWINGIN' IN A HAMMOCK / CHEER UP (GOOD TIMES ARE COMIN') .... *Victor 22453* 4-6 30
(Vocals: Lew Conrad)

TALES FROM THE VIENNA WOODS / ST. LOUIS BLUES .... *Victor 25745* 3-5 38

TELL ME, DREAMY EYES / PUT AWAY A LITTLE RAY OF GOLDEN SUNSHINE ...... *Columbia 230-D* 2-4 24

THERE'S A BOAT DAT'S LEAVING SOON FOR NEW YORK (Vocal: Avon Long) / SUMMERTIME (Vocal: Helen Dowdy) .... *Decca 18282* 2-4 42

THEY MET IN RIO (Vocal: Sara Horn) / CHICA CHICA BOOM CHIC (Vocal: Anita Boyer) .... *Victor 27383* 2-4 41

TOO MARVELOUS FOR WORDS / JUST A QUIET EVENING .... *Brunswick 7831* 2-4 37
(Vocals: Jimmy Brierley)

TWILIGHT (THE STARS AND YOU) / IN THE PURPLE TWILIGHT .... *Columbia 384-D* 2-4 25

UNTIL THE REAL THING COMES ALONG / DREAM AWHILE .... *Brunswick 7713* 3-5 36
(Vocals: Unknown)

WATERS OF THE PERKIOMEN / CHEERIE-BEERIE-BE .... *Columbia 1112-D* 2-4 27

WEARY (Vocals: Unknown) / LET IT BE ME (Vocal: Sally Singer) .... *Brunswick 7585* 3-5 36

WHAT IS THIS THING CALLED LOVE? (theme song) (Vocal: Anita Boyer) / PENTHOUSE SERENADE .... *Victor 27629* 2-4 41

WHAT IS THIS THING CALLED LOVE? (theme song) / SHE'S SUCH A COMFORT TO ME ...... *Victor 22282* 4-6 30
(Vocals: Lew Conrad)

WHEN LOVE BECKONED (Vocal: Gertrude Niesen) / IT WAS WRITTEN IN THE STARS (Vocal: Dick Smart) .... *Victor 26434* 2-4 40

WHEN THE MOON COMES OVER THE MOUNTAIN (Vocal: Ben Gordon) / WITHOUT THAT GAL! (Vocal: Leo Reisman) .... *Victor 22746* 4-6 31

WHEN YOU'RE COUNTING THE STARS ALONE / NEEDIN' YOU LIKE I DO .... *Victor 22181* 4-6 31
(Vocals: L. Levin)

WHITE HEAT (Vocal: Fred Astaire) / HOOPS (Vocals: Fred & Adele Astaire) ...... *Victor 22836* 5-8 31

WHY WAS I BORN? / HERE AM I .... *Victor 22187* 3-5 29
(Vocals: L. Levin)

WITH A SONG IN MY HEART / YOURS SINCERELY.................. *Victor 21923* 2-4 29
(Vocals: Ran Weeks)

WITH MY EYES WIDE OPEN I'M DREAMING / DO I LOVE YOU?...................... *Brunswick 6896* 4-6 34
(Vocals: George Beuler)

YEAR FROM TODAY, A / MY SWEETER THAN SWEET...................... *Victor 22194* 3-5 29
(Vocals: L. Levin)

YOU AND THE NIGHT AND THE MUSIC / WHEN YOU LOVE ONLY ONE..................... *Brunswick 7331* 3-5 35
(Vocals: Phil Dewey)

YOU DIDN'T KNOW THE MUSIC (Vocal: Ben Gordon) / TIME ON MY HANDS (Vocal: Lee Wiley).... *Victor 22839* 4-6 31

YOU DO SOMETHING TO ME / YOU'VE GOT THAT THING........... *Victor 22244* 4-6 30
(Vocals: Frank Luther)

YOU GAVE ME EV'RYTHING BUT LOVE / IN THE STILL OF THE NIGHT............... *Victor 24029* 3-5 32
(Vocals: Frank Luther)

YOU'LL BE MINE IN APPLE BLOSSOM TIME / FOR YOU........................... *Victor 22670* 3-5 31
(Vocals: Frank Munn)

YOU'RE A BUILDER-UPPER / WHAT CAN YOU SAY IN A LOVE SONG?............... *Brunswick 6941* 4-6 34
(Vocals: Harold Arlen)

YOURS IS MY HEART ALONE / OUT OF NOWHERE................. *Victor 22668* 3-5 31
(Vocals: Frank Munn)

RENARD, Jacques, & His Cocoanut Grove Orchestra

LONELY IN A CROWD (Vocal: Elliott Shaw) / BENEATH VENETIAN SKIES (Vocal: Lewis James).... *Victor 21093* 2-4 28

MARY ANN / AUF WEIDERSEH'N...... *Victor 21234* 2-4 28
(Vocals: Scrappy Lambert & Billy Hillpot)

THERE'LL NEVER BE ANOTHER YOU (Vocals: Phil Dewey, Frank Luther & Jack Parker) / SWEET ELLA MAY (Vocal: Frank Marvin).................... *Victor 21601* 2-4 28

WHEN MORNING GLORIES WAKE UP IN THE MORNING (Vocal: Johnny Marvin) / BLUE RIVER (by Jean Goldkette & His Orchestra; Vocal: Lewis James)................ *Victor 20981* 5-8 27

RENARD, Jacques, & His Orchestra

AS TIME GOES BY / I'M SORRY, DEAR................ *Brunswick 6205* 3-5 31
(Vocals: Unknown)

CLOSE TO YOUR HEART / JUST CALL ON ME (Vocal: Lewis James)............ *Victor 20728* 2-4 27

DINNER AT EIGHT / GIVE ME LIBERTY OR GIVE ME LOVE................ *Vocalion 2549* 3-5 33
(Vocals: Howard Phillips)

HEARTACHES / REACHING FOR THE MOON........................ *Brunswick 6033* 3-5 31
(Vocals: Chester Gaylord)

HIGH AND LOW (I'VE LOOKING FOR YOU) / DANCING IN THE DARK.......... *Brunswick 6136* 3-5 31
(Vocals: Frank Munn)

I'D RATHER LISTEN TO YOUR EYES (Vocal: Smith Ballew) / I'D LOVE TO TAKE ORDERS FROM YOU (Vocal: Chick Bullock)............... *Columbia 3086-D* 3-5 35

IF I KNEW YOU BETTER / READIN', RITIN', RHYTHM........ *Brunswick 4940* 3-5 30
(Vocals: Unknown)

IF YOU HAVEN'T GOT LOVE / COME TO ME..................... *Brunswick 6106* 3-5 31
(Vocals: Paul Small)

I'M ALL DRESSED UP WITH A BROKEN HEART / AS LONG AS YOU'RE THERE...... *Brunswick 6144* 3-5 31
(Vocals: Paul Small)

IT'S THE TALK OF THE TOWN / TIME TO GO................. *Vocalion 2525* 3-5 33
(Vocals: Paul Small)

JUST ANOTHER DREAM OF YOU / MASQUERADE.................. *Brunswick 6326* 3-5 32

LONELY / YOU WENT AWAY TOO FAR AND STAYED AWAY TOO LONG (Vocal: Johnny Marvin)... *Victor 20487* 2-4 27

LOVE ME TONIGHT / ISN'T IT ROMANTIC?............. *Brunswick 6378* 4-6 32
(Vocals: Smith Ballew)

LOVING YOU THE WAY I DO / CAN THIS BE LOVE?........... *Brunswick 4919* 3-5 30
(Vocals: Unknown)

LUCKY SEVEN / SING SOMETHING SIMPLE............ *Brunswick 4918* 3-5 30
(Vocals: Unknown)

NIGHT WHEN LOVE WAS BORN, THE / NIGHT SHALL BE FILLED WITH MUSIC.... *Brunswick 6327* 3-5 32
(Vocals: Paul Small)

NIGHT / WHEN THE LIGHTS ARE SOFT AND LOW............. *Brunswick 6299* 4-6 32
(Vocals: Smith Ballew)

NOT THAT I CARE (Vocal: Frank Munn) / WHEN YOUR BOY BECOMES A MAN (Vocal: Grace Johnston)............... *Brunswick 6180* 4-6 31

'R' YOU LIST'NIN'? (Vocal: Smith Ballew with dialog by Tony Wons) / TELL ME WITH A LOVE SONG (Vocal: Smith Ballew)............... *Brunswick 6238* 4-6 32

SINCE AN ANGEL LIKE MARY LOVES A DEVIL LIKE ME / HAPPY LITTLE TUNE.... *Brunswick 6113* 3-5 31
(Vocals: Paul Small)

SOMETHING IN THE NIGHT / NIGHTFALL...................... *Brunswick 6383* 4-6 32
(Vocals: Smith Ballew)

THIS IS ROMANCE / BLESS YOUR HEART.............. *Vocalion 2557* 3-5 33
(Vocals: Howard Phillips)

THIS TIME IT'S LOVE / CLOSE YOUR EYES............ *Vocalion 2524* 3-5 33
(Vocals: Paul Small)

THREE LITTLE WORDS / A GIRL FRIEND OF A BOY FRIEND OF MINE.................. *Brunswick 4939* 3-5 30
(Vocals: Unknown)

UNDER THE SPELL OF YOUR KISS / LITTLE SPANISH DANCER....... *Brunswick 4995* 3-5 31
(Vocals: Chester Gaylord)

WE'RE FRIENDS AGAIN (Vocal: Chester Gaylord) / HE'S MY SECRET PASSION (Vocals: Unknown)................. *Brunswick 4994* 3-5 31

WHO AM I? / WHAT IS IT?........... *Brunswick 6183* 4-6 31

RESER, Harry, & His Eskimos
(Harry Reser: – 9/27/65)

I'M DANCIN' ON A RAINBOW (Vocals: by trio) / BEAUTIFUL GIRL (Vocals: Jimmy Brierley)................... *Melotone M-12803* 2-4 33

I'M DANCIN' ON A RAINBOW (Vocals: by trio) / BEAUTIFUL GIRL (Vocal: Jimmy Brierley)......................... *Oriole 2707* 2-4 33

I'M DANCIN' ON A RAINBOW (Vocals: by trio) / BEAUTIFUL GIRL (Vocal: Jimmy Brierley)....................... *Perfect 15826* 2-4 33

I'M DANCIN' ON A RAINBOW (Vocals: by trio) / BEAUTIFUL GIRL (Vocal: Jimmy Brierley)........................ *Romeo 2140* 2-4 33
(Simultaneously released on four labels)

WHO'S AFRAID OF THE BIG BAD WOLF? (Vocal: Loretta Clemens) / YOU GOTTA BE A FOOTBALL HERO (Vocal: Jimmy Brierley).......... *Conqueror 8218* 4-6 33

WHO'S AFRAID OF THE BIG BAD WOLF? (Vocal: Loretta Clemens) / YOU GOTTA BE A FOOTBALL HERO (Vocal: Jimmy Brierley)........ *Melotone M-12804* 4-6 33

WHO'S AFRAID OF THE BIG BAD WOLF? (Vocal: Loretta Clemens) / YOU GOTTA BE A FOOTBALL HERO (Vocal: Jimmy Brierley)............ *Oriole 2768* 4-6 33

WHO'S AFRAID OF THE BIG BAD WOLF? (Vocal: Loretta Clemens) / YOU GOTTA BE A FOOTBALL HERO (Vocal: Jimmy Brierley)............ *Perfect 15827* 4-6 33
(Simultaneously released on four labels)

RESER, Harry, & His Orchestra / Harry Reser's Orchestra

HA-CHA-CHA / CROSS-EYED SALLY (FROM PENN-SYL-VAN-EYE-AY)........ *Decca 263* 4-6 34
(Vocals: Tom Stack)

HIGHWAYS ARE HAPPY WAYS / KISS AND MAKE UP................ *Domino 4049* 3-5 27
(Vocals: Tom Stacks)

HIGHWAYS ARE HAPPY WAYS / KISS AND MAKE UP................ *Regal 8416* 3-5 27
(Vocals: Tom Stacks)
(Simultaneously released on two labels)

HOOK AND LADDER 31 / THE WEST-BOUND FREIGHT......... *Variety 588* 4-6 37

I AIN'T THAT KIND OF A BABY / ROAM ON, MY LITTLE GYPSY SWEETHEART.... *Domino 4008* 3-5 27
(Vocals: Tom Stacks)

I AIN'T THAT KIND OF A BABY / ROAM ON, MY LITTLE GYPSY SWEETHEART..... *Regal 8379* 3-5 27
(Vocals: Tom Stacks)
(Simultaneously released on two labels)

I WALKED BACK FROM THE BUGGY RIDE / WHO WAS THE LADY?.............. *Okeh 40856* 3-5 27
(Vocals: Tom Stacks)

I WONDER WHO'S DANCING WITH YOU TONIGHT / MONA VANA..................... *Paramount 20311* 3-5 24

I WONDER WHO'S DANCING WITH YOU TONIGHT / MONA VANA...................... *Puritan 11311* 3-5 24
(Simultaneously released on two labels)

JIMINY GEE / HE LOOKS AT HER AND THEN HE GOES HA-HA-HA-HA-HA!........ *Broadway 11380* 4-6 24
(Vocals: Arthur Hall)

JIMINY GEE / HE LOOKS AT HER AND THEN HE GOES HA-HA-HA-HA-HA!......... *Pennington 1380* 25-30 24
(Vocals: Arthur Hall)
(Pennington records are rare)

JIMINY GEE / HE LOOKS AT HER AND THEN HE GOES HA-HA-HA-HA-HA!.......... *Triangle 11380* 4-6 24
(Vocals: Arthur Hall)
(Simultaneously released on three labels)

NO! NO! A THOUSAND TIMES NO! / YOU'RE NOT THE ONLY OYSTER IN THE STEW........... *Decca 284* 4-6 34
(Vocals: Tom Stacks)

OUR BUNGALOW OF DREAMS / WHEN THE ROBERT E. LEE COMES TO TOWN...... *Pathe Actuelle 36740* 3-5 28
(Vocals: Harold Miller)

OUR BUNGALOW OF DREAMS / WHEN THE ROBERT E. LEE COMES TO TOWN............ *Perfect 14921* 3-5 28
(Vocals: Harold Miller)
(Simultaneously released on two labels)

ROCK AND ROLL (Vocal: Tom Stacks) / ONE LITTLE KISS (Vocal: Paul Small)...... *Decca 285* 4-6 34
(One of the first occasions in which the term "Rock And Roll" was used in, or as, a song title.)

SMILE WILL GO A LONG, LONG WAY, A / BEFORE YOU GO................ *Paramount 20318* 3-5 24

TOP OF THE TOWN / THAT FOOLISH FEELING............. *Variety 510* 4-6 37
(Vocals: Unknown)

WHAT DO YOU DO SUNDAY, MARY? / MAMA GOES WHERE PAPA GOES (Vocal: Arthur Hall)................. *Harmograph 875* 8-10 23

WHAT DO YOU DO SUNDAY, MARY? / MAMA GOES WHERE PAPA GOES (Vocal: Arthur Hall)................. *Paramount 20282* 5-8 23
(Simultaneously released on two labels)

WHEN YOU DO WHAT YOU DO / TITINA.................. *Gennett 5705* 3-5 25

WHY DID I KISS THAT GIRL? / SINCE MA IS PLAYING MAH JONGG........... *Paramount 20320* 4-6 24
(Vocals: Arthur Fields as Charles Dale)

YOU'RE GONNA LOSE YOUR GAL / MY GALVESTON GAL........... *Columbia 2840-D* 4-6 33
(Vocals: Unknown)

RESER, Harry, & His Orchestra as Frank Harrison's Banjo Orchestra

THERE ARE SOME THINGS YOU NEVER FORGET / DANCING HONEYMOON..... *Pathe Actuelle 036026* 3-5 24

THERE ARE SOME THINGS YOU NEVER FORGET / DANCING HONEYMOON............. *Perfect 14207* 2-4 24
(Simultaneously released on two labels)

RESER, Harry, & His Orchestra as Tom Rock & His Orchestra

LITTLE JOE / TWO HEARTS...... *Odeon ONY-36201* 3-5 31

RESER, Harry, & His Orchestra as The New York Syncopators

SIBONEY / MAMA INEZ........... *Odeon ONY-36200* 3-5 31

RESER, Harry, & His Orchestra as Tom Stacks & His Minute Men

I LOVE THE COLLEGE GIRLS / COCK-A-DOODLE, I'M OFF MY NOODLE (MY BABY'S BACK).... *Okeh 40756* 3-5 27
(Vocals: Tom Stacks)

LITTLE WHITE HOUSE / JERSEY WALK... *Okeh 40742* 3-5 27
(Vocals: Tom Stacks)

RESER, Harry, & His Orchestra as Tom Stacks & His Orchestra

'S WONDERFUL / MAYBE I'LL BABY YOU............................ *Okeh 40954* 2-4 28
(Vocals: Tom Stacks)

RESER, Harry, as The Bostonians

NO MAN'S MAMA / I'VE FOUND A NEW BABY...................... *Vocalion 15298* 3-5 26
(Vocals: Tom Stacks)

SO DOES YOUR OLD MANDARIN / LET'S TALK ABOUT MY SWEETIE.............. *Vocalion 15275* 3-5 26
(Vocals: Tom Stacks)

RESER, Harry, as The Clevelanders

ALL FOR YOU / RHYTHM OF THE DAY........................ *Brunswick 3047* 3-5 26

DUSTY STEVEDORE / GUESS WHO'S IN TOWN.................... *Brunswick 4109* 3-5 28
(Vocals: Dick Robertson)

LOOK AT THE WORLD AND SMILE / SOMEBODY ELSE.................. *Brunswick 3456* 3-5 27
(Vocals: Vaughn de Leath)

MY CUTEY'S DUE AT TWO-TO-TWO TODAY / SHE BELONGS TO ME............ *Brunswick 3279* 3-5 26
(Vocals: Tom Stacks)

PRETTY LIPS / WHEN I FIRST ME MARY............... *Brunswick 3440* 3-5 27
(Vocals: Frank Munn)

THINKING OF YOU / TAKE IN THE SUN, HANG OUT THE MOON.................... *Brunswick 3375* 3-5 27

YA GOTTA KNOW HOW TO LOVE (Vocals: Lester O'Keefe, Frank Wright & Frank Bessinger) / THAT NIGHT IN ARABY (Vocals: Tom Stacks)....... *Brunswick 3304* 3-5 26

YOU BROUGHT A NEW KIND OF LOVE TO ME / BE CAREFUL WITH THOSE EYES (by Karl Radlach & His Orchestra; Vocal: Unknown)............ *Perfect 15311* 4-6 30

RESER, Harry, as The Clicquot Club Eskimos

AT SUNDOWN / MY SUNDAY GIRL... *Columbia 921-D* 3-5 27

CLICQUOT / ADORABLE............ *Columbia 687-D* 2-4 26

COME ON, BABY / AVALON TOWN.............. *Columbia 687-D* 3-5 28
(Vocals: Tom Stacks)

CRYIN' FOR THE CAROLINES / HAVE A LITTLE FAITH IN ME (by The Dorsey Brothers' Orchestra)........ *Perfect 15265* 5-8 30
(Vocals: Scrappy Lambert as Rodman Lewis)

HELLO BLUEBIRD! (Vocals: Tom Stacks) / SOMEDAY............................ *Columbia 795-D* 2-4 26

HENRY'S MADE A LADY OUT OF LIZZIE / GEE! BUT I'M GLAD I'M HOME... *Columbia 1281-D* 3-5 28
(Vocals: Tom Stacks)

LITTLE WHITE LIES (Vocals: Speed Young) / MY LITTLE BUTTERFLY (by Ernie Golden & His Orchestra; Vocal: Tom & Roy)............... *Banner 0755* 3-5 30

SOMEBODY'S LONELY / LONESOME AND SORRY........... *Columbia 637-D* 3-5 26

WINGS (Vocals: Unknown) / HUMORESKIMO.................. *Columbia 1322-D* 2-4 28

YOU DO SOMETHING TO ME / YOU'VE GOT THAT THING.......... *Domino 4464* 3-5 29
(Vocals: Scrappy Lambert as Rodman Lewis)

YOU DO SOMETHING TO ME / YOU'VE GOT THAT THING..... *Pathe Actuelle 37079* 3-5 29
(Vocals: Scrappy Lambert as Rodman Lewis)

YOU DO SOMETHING TO ME / YOU'VE GOT THAT THING.......... *Perfect 15260* 3-5 29
(Vocals: Scrappy Lambert as Rodman Lewis)

YOU DO SOMETHING TO ME / YOU'VE GOT THAT THING.......... *Regal 8916* 3-5 29
(Vocals: Scrappy Lambert as Rodman Lewis)
(Simultaneously released on four labels)

RESER, Harry, as The Jazz Pilots / Harry Reser's Jazz Pilots

DANCING THE CHARLESTON / PASSION FLOWER.......... *Okeh 40702* 3-5 25

GIGOLO / MEADOW LARK.......... *Okeh 40701* 2-4 26
(Vocals: Tom Stacks)

GIMME A LI'L KISS, WILL YA, HUH? / LULU LOU.......... *Okeh 40611* 3-5 26
(Vocals: Tom Stacks)

HOW COULD RE RIDING HOOD? / I'M TELLIN' THE BIRDS – TELLIN' THE BEES HOW I LOVE YOU.......... *Okeh 40719* 3-5 27
(Vocals: Tom Stacks)

JUDGE CLIFF DAVIS BLUES, THE (Vocals: Ernest Hare) / CHICK, CHICK, CHICK, CHICKEN (Vocals: Tom Stacks).......... *Okeh 40665* 4-6 26

MONKEY DOODLE-DOO / I WISH'T I WAS IN PEORIA.......... *Okeh 40548* 3-5 26
(Vocals: Tom Stacks)

RAMBLING WRECK FROM GEORGIA TECH (Vocals: Johnny Marvin) / SLEEPY-TIME GAL (Vocals: Tom Stacks).......... *Okeh 40502* 3-5 26

SHE DON'T WANNA / PASTAFAZOOLA... *Okeh 40918* 3-5 27
(Vocals: Tom Stacks)

SHE KNOWS HER ONIONS / THAT'S MY GIRL.......... *Okeh 40688* 3-5 26
(Vocals: Tom Stacks)

THANKS FOR THE BUGGY RIDE (Vocals: Tom Stacks) / YOU OUGHT TO SEE WHAT'S WAITING FOR ME.......... *Okeh 40569* 3-5 28

THAT'S MY WEAKNESS NOW / HAPPY-GO-LUCKY LANE.......... *Okeh 41066* 3-5 28
(Vocals: Tom Stacks)

RESER, Harry, as Jimmy Johnston's Rebels

HORSES / POOR PAPA.......... *Paramount 20449* 5-8 26
(Vocals: Tom Stacks)

HORSES / POOR PAPA.......... *Puritan 11449* 3-5 26
(Vocals: Tom Stacks)
(Simultaneously released on two labels)

LULU LOU / TONIGHT'S MY NIGHT WITH BABY.......... *Broadway 1014* 3-5 26
(Vocals: Tom Stacks)

LULU LOU / TONIGHT'S MY NIGHT WITH BABY.......... *Silvertown 3531* 3-5 26
(Vocals: Tom Stacks)
(Simultaneously released on two labels)

SHOW THAT FELLO THE DOOR / WHAT A MAN!.......... *Paramount 20452* 5-8 26
(Vocals: Tom Stacks)

SHOW THAT FELLO THE DOOR / WHAT A MAN!.......... *Puritan 11452* 3-5 26
(Vocals: Tom Stacks)
(Simultaneously released on two labels)

RESER, Harry, as The Night Club Orchestra

BECAUSE I LOVE YOU / TONIGHT YOU BELONG TO ME.......... *Vocalion 15471* 2-4 26

FLAMIN' MAMIE (Vocals: Tom de Arman) / BEHIND THE CLOUDS.......... *Harmony 102-H* 3-5 26

FLAPPER WIFE, THE / AH-HA!..... *Vocalion 15031* 2-4 25

I DO NOT CHOOSE TO RUN / HEY! HEY! HAZEL.......... *Harmony 624-H* 2-4 28
(Vocals: Tom Stacks)

I'M GONNA DANCE WIT DE GUY WOT BRUNG ME / WHO-OO? YOU-OO, THAT'S WHO!... *Harmony 473-H* 2-4 27
(Vocals: Unknown)

I WANT YOU ALL FOR ME / WHO WOULDN'T LOVE YOU? (Vocals: Irving Kaufman).......... *Vocalion 15097* 2-4 25

MANHATTAN / I WANT A LOVABLE BABY.......... *Vocalion 15074* 2-4 25

MY SUGAR / SOME DAY WE'LL MEET AGAIN.......... *Vocalion 15107* 2-4 25

THANKS FOR THE BUGGY RIDE (Vocals: Al Bernard) / BLINKY MOON BAY (Vocals: Tom Stacks).......... *Vocalion 15278* 3-5 26

RESER, Harry, as The Night Club Orchestra recorded under the name The Seven Wild Men

I'M JUST WILD ABOUT ANIMAL CRACKERS / THE LUNATIC'S LULLABY.......... *Harmony 193-H* 5-8 26

RESER, Harry, as The Okeh Syncopators

BIRMINGHAM PAPA (YOUR MEMPHIS MAMA'S COMIN' TO TOWN) / IT'S ALL THE SAME TO ME.......... *Okeh 40316* 3-5 25
(Vocals: Earl Rickard)

BLACK SHEEP BLUES / OH, YOU LITTLE SUN-UV-ER-GUN (Vocals: Unknown).......... *Okeh 4978* 3-5 23

DON'T BRING LULU / ARABELLA.......... *Okeh 41413* 3-5 25

EVERYBODY'S DOIN' THE CHARLESTON / FOOTLOOSE.......... *Okeh 40493* 3-5 25

GOTTA GETTA GIRL / ROSE MARIE..... *Okeh 40231* 3-5 24

I'M WALKING AROUND IN CIRCLES / BLACK BOTTOM.......... *Okeh 40641* 3-5 26

JUST A LITTLE DANCE / I'D CLIMB THE HIGHEST MOUNTAIN IF I KNEW I'D FIND YOU.... *Okeh 40642* 2-4 26

NOBODY KNOWS WHAT A RED HEAD MAMA CAN DO / MY GAL DON'T LOVE ME ANY MORE.......... *Okeh 40282* 3-5 25

PLEASE / CHARLEY, MY BOY.......... *Okeh 40166* 3-5 24

SHINE / SAVANNAH (THE GEORGIANNA BLUES).......... *Okeh 40100* 3-5 24

SWEET LITTLE YOU / TOO TIRED.......... *Okeh 40207* 2-4 24

WHY DID I KISS THAT GIRL? / NOBODY'S SWEETHEART.......... *Okeh 40072* 3-5 24

RESER, Harry, as Earl Oliver's Jazz Babies

CHICK, CHICK, CHICK, CHICKEN / SHOW THAT FELLOW THE DOOR.......... *Edison 51745* 5-8 26
(Vocals: Tom Stacks as Tom Howard)

FIRE! (AN ALARMING NOVELTY) / COWS.......... *Edison 51977* 5-8 27
(Vocals: Tom Stacks as Tom Howard)

JIG WALK (Vocals: Tom Stacks as Tom Howard) / HORSES.......... *Edison 51724* 5-8 26

SAM, THE OLD ACCORDION MAN (Vocals: Tom Stacks as Tom Howard) / I LOVE THE COLLEGE GIRLS (Vocals: Harry Reser, Larry Abbott & Tom Stacks as Tom Howard)...... *Edison 51929* 5-8 27

SHE'S A CORNFED INDIANA GIRL (BUT SHE'S MAMA TO ME) / LET'S TAKE A FERRYBOAT.......... *Edison 51776* 5-8 26
(Vocals: Tom Stacks as Tom Howard)

THANKS FOR THE BUGGY RIDE / THE VILLAGE BLACKSMITH OWNS THE VILLAGE NOW.......... *Edison 51698* 5-8 26
(Vocals: Tom Stacks as Tom Howard)

WHERE DO YOU WORK-A, JOHN? / PRETTY LIPS.......... *Edison 51900* 5-8 27
(Vocals: Tom Stacks as Tom Howard)

RESER, Harry, as The Park Lane Orchestra

COVER ME UP WITH SUNSHINE (Vocals: Irving Kaufman) / SWEET THING.......... *Brunswick 3343* 3-5 26

'DEED I DO / I LOVE YOU BUT I DON'T KNOW WHY.......... *Brunswick 3454* 3-5 27
(Vocals: The Bonnie Laddies)

DOROTHY / NO FOOLIN'.......... *Brunswick 3167* 3-5 26

FRESHIE / SHOW ME THE WAY TO GO HOME.......... *Vocalion 15158* 3-5 26
(Vocals: Billy Jones, Frank Muny, & Lester O'Keefe)

I DON'T WANT NOBODY BUT YOU / CAMILLE.......... *Brunswick 3276* 3-5 26
(Vocals: Frank Munn)

LITTLE MUSIC IN THE MOONLIGHT, A / I'D LOVE TO CALL YOU MY SWEETHEART.......... *Brunswick 3356* 2-4 26
(Vocals: Herman Horn)

SWEET SOMEONE / DO YOU LOVE ME?.......... *Brunswick 3578* 2-4 27
(Vocals: Al Lynch)

RESER, Harry, as Harry Reser's Banjo Boys

WHEN THE ROBERT E. LEE COMES TO TOWN / DOWN SOUTH.......... *Victor 21321* 3-5 28
(Vocals: Tom Stacks)

RESER, Harry, as Harry Reser's Jazz Pilots:
see RESER, Harry, as The Jazz Pilots

RESER, Harry, as Harry Reser's Orchestra:
see RESER, Harry, & His Orchestra

RESER, Harry, as Harry Reser's Rounders:
see RESER, Harry, as The Rounders

RESER, Harry, as Harry Reser's String Orchestra

WHAT DOES IT MATTER? / JUST WOND'RING.......... *Okeh 40759* 2-4 27
(Vocals: Unknown)

RESER, Harry, as Harry Reser's Syncopators

BLUE-EYES SALLY / UNDERNEATH A SUNNY SKY.... *Columbia 276-D* 3-5 25

CRAVING / THE FLAPPER WIFE.... *Columbia 393-D* 3-5 25

CRAZY RHYTHM / IMAGINATION.... *Columbia 1378-D* 3-5 28
(Vocals: Tom Stacks)

DON'T BE LIKE THAT / MY TROUBLES ARE OVER.......... *Columbia 1696-D* 2-4 29
(Vocals: Tom Stacks)

FLIPPITY FLOP, THE / THE WHOOPEE HAT BRIGADE.......... *Columbia 1884-D* 3-5 29
(Vocals: Tom Stacks)

FOND OF YOU / IT MUST BE LOVE.... *Columbia 510-D* 2-4 25

HERE COMES THE SHOW BOAT / WHERE DID YOU GET THAT NAME?.......... *Columbia 1835-D* 3-5 29
(Vocals: Tom Stacks)

I GOT A "CODE" IN MY "DOZE" / IT AIN'T NO FAULT OF MINE.......... *Columbia 1806-D* 3-5 29
(Vocals: Tom Stacks)

KANSAS CITY KITTY / I'M WILD ABOUT HORNS ON AUTOMOBILES THAT GO "TA-TA-TA-TA".......... *Columbia 1761-D* 3-5 29
(Vocals: Tom Stacks)

LOVE BOUND / I'M AS BLUE AS THE BLUE GRASS OF KENTUCKY...... *Columbia 604-D* 2-4 26

LULU LOU / JUST A LITTLE DANCE... *Columbia 678-D* 2-4 26

NOBODY'S GONNA KEEP ME AWAY FROM MY GAL / GONE AGAIN GAL.......... *Vocalion 15436* 3-5 26
(Vocals: Tom Stacks)

OH! HOW I LOVE BULGARIANS / SUSIE'S "FELLER".......... *Columbia 774-D* 3-5 26
(Vocals: Tom Stacks)

PICCOLO PETE / COLLEGIATE SAM... *Columbia 1973-D* 3-5 29
(Vocals: Tom Stacks)

SHAKING THE BLUES AWAY / OOH! MAYBE IT'S YOU.......... *Columbia 1109-D* 3-5 27
(Vocals: Tom Stacks)

SING-LOO / BY THE LIGHT OF THE STARS.......... *Columbia 366-D* 2-4 25

(WHAT DO I CARE WHAT) SOMEBODY SAID / I'M IN LOVE AGAIN.......... *Columbia 981-D* 2-4 27
(Vocals: Tom Stacks)

SPEECH! (Vocals: Billy Jones) / SWEET MAN.......... *Columbia 454-D* 3-5 25

SWANEE SHORE / MEET ME IN THE MOONLIGHT.......... *Columbia 1087-D* 2-4 27

TURKISH TOWEL / WASN'T IT NICE?... *Columbia 725-D* 2-4 26

UKULELE LADY / ON A NIGHT LIKE THIS.......... *Columbia 413-D* 3-5 25

WE'LL HAVE A KINGDOM / FIRE! (Vocals: Tom Stacks).......... *Columbia 803-D* 3-5 26

WHEN THE ROBERT E. LEE COMES TO TOWN / I SCREAM – YOU SCREAM – WE ALL SCREAM FOR ICE CREAM.......... *Columbia 1244-D* 4-6 28
(Vocals: Tom Stacks)

WHO WOULDN'T? / SOMEONE IS LOSIN' SUSAN.......... *Columbia 708-D* 3-5 26

YEARNING (JUST FOR YOU) / WHEN YOU DO WHAT YOU DO.......... *Columbia 319-D* 3-5 25

RESER, Harry, as Harry Reser's Syncopators recorded under the name The Monarch Orchestra

YOU CAN'T HANG OUT WITH ANNIE ('CAUSE ANNIE HANGS OUT WITH ME) / ME TOO.......... *Vocalion 15414* 3-5 26
(Vocals: Tom Stacks)

RESER, Harry, as The Rio Trio

SOUTHLAND MEDLEY / SEND BACK MY HONEYMAN.......... *Gennett 4923* 3-5 22

RESER, Harry, as The Rounders / Harry Reser's Rounders

DOWN AMONG THE SUGAR CANE / THAT'S WHAT I CALL HEAVEN.......... *Domino 4279* 2-4 29
(Vocals: Irving Kaufman)

DOWN AMONG THE SUGAR CANE / THAT'S WHAT I CALL HEAVEN.......... *Regal 8727* 2-4 29
(Vocals: Irving Kaufman)
(Simultaneously released on two labels)

HELLO CUTIE (Vocals: Tom Stacks) / MARIONETTE.......... *Edison 52034* 5-8 27

HELLO, MONTREAL! / YOU CAN'T BLAME ME FOR THAT.......... *Domino 4118* 2-4 28
(Vocals: Tom Stacks)

HELLO, MONTREAL! / YOU CAN'T BLAME ME FOR THAT.......... *Regal 8518* 2-4 28
(Vocals: Tom Stacks)
(Simultaneously released on two labels)

HIGHWAYS ARE HAPPY WAYS / OUR BUNGALOW OF DREAMS.......... *Edison 52184* 4-6 28
(Vocals: Tom Stacks)

I DON'T KNOW WHAT TO DO / HEY! HEY! HAZEL.......... *Edison 52282* 5-8 28
(Vocals: Tom Stacks as Tom Howard)

I'M WILD ABOUT HORNS ON AUTOMOBILES THAT GO "TA-TA-TA-TA" / I FAW DOWN AN' GO "BOOM".......... *Domino 4257* 4-6 29
(Vocals: Billy Murray)

I'M WILD ABOUT HORNS ON AUTOMOBILES THAT GO "TA-TA-TA-TA" / I FAW DOWN AN' GO "BOOM".......... *Regal 8703* 4-6 29
(Vocals: Billy Murray)
(Simultaneously released on two labels)

MARY (WHAT ARE YOU WAITING FOR?) / WITHOUT YOU, SWEETHEART .... *Broadway 1132* 3-5 28
(Vocals: Tom Stacks)

STEPPIN' ALONG / TOO WONDERFUL FOR WORDS........................ *Domino 4403* 3-5 29
(Vocals: Scrappy Lambert)

STEPPIN' ALONG / TOO WONDERFUL FOR WORDS.......................... *Regal 8851* 3-5 29
(Vocals: Scrappy Lambert)
(Simultaneously released on two labels)

TOO BUSY / JUST LIKE A MELODY OUT OF THE SKY..................... *Regal 8573* 2-4 28
(Vocals: Irving Kaufman)

WHEN YOU'RE WITH SOMEBODY ELSE / CHANGES .... *Domino 4015* 3-5 28
(Vocals: Tom Stacks)

WHEN YOU'RE WITH SOMEBODY ELSE / CHANGES .... *Regal 8499* 3-5 28
(Vocals: Tom Stacks)
(Simultaneously released on two labels)

RESER, Harry, as The Rounders recorded under the name The Midnight Ramblers

DEEP NIGHT / DOWN AMONG THE SUGAR CANE................. *Broadway 1257* 3-5 29

WHERE THE SWEET FORGET-ME-NOTS REMEMBER/AIN'T MISBEHAVIN'... *Broadway 1302* 3-5 29

RESER, Harry, as The Rounders recorded under the name The Ten Freshmen

STEPPIN' ALONG / TOO WONDERFUL FOR WORDS................. *Pathe Actuelle 37039* 4-6 29
(Vocals: Scrappy Lambert)

STEPPIN' ALONG / TOO WONDERFUL FOR WORDS........................ *Perfect 15220* 3-5 29
(Vocals: Scrappy Lambert)
(Simultaneously released on two labels)

RESER, Harry, as The Rounders recorded under the name The University Boys

HELLO MONTREAL! / WHEN THE ROBERT E. LEE COMES TO TOWN........................ *Jewel 5234* 3-5 28
(Vocals: Tom Stacks as Sid Clayton)

RESER, Harry, as The Seven Little Polar Bears

HI-DIDDLE-DIDDLE / I WONDER WHAT'S BECOME OF JOE?................ *Lincoln 2536* 2-4 26
(Vocals: Tom Stacks)

HI-HO! THE MERRIO / I LOVE HER!.... *Lincoln 2527* 2-4 26
(Vocals: Tom Stacks)

I'M JUST WILD ABOUT ANIMAL CRACKERS / I LOVE HER! .... *Cameo 952* 3-5 26
(Vocals: Tom Stacks)

LULU LOU / HORRAY FOR THE IRISH ... *Cameo 935* 3-5 26
(Vocals: Tom Stacks)

SINCE SHE LEARNED TO RIDE A HORSE (Vocals: Tom Stacks) / CLICQUOT .... *Cameo 8243* 2-4 28

SINCE SHE LEARNED TO RIDE A HORSE (Vocals: Tom Stacks) / CLICQUOT .... *Lincoln 2891* 2-4 28

SINCE SHE LEARNED TO RIDE A HORSE (Vocals: Tom Stacks) / CLICQUOT .... *Romeo 666* 2-4 28
(Simultaneously released on three labels)

SOMEONE IS LOSIN' SUSAN / HORSES... *Cameo 915* 3-5 26
(Vocals: Tom Stacks)

YOU NEVER GET NOWHERE HOLDING HANDS / I WALKED BACK FROM THE BUGGY RIDE.......................... *Cameo 1182* 3-5 27
(Vocals: Tom Stacks)

YOU NEVER GET NOWHERE HOLDING HANDS / I WALKED BACK FROM THE BUGGY RIDE...................... *Lincoln 2644* 3-5 27
(Vocals: Tom Stacks)
(Simultaneously released on two labels)

RESER, Harry, as The Seven Little Polar Bears recorded under the name Phil Hughes & His High Hatters

HEY! HEY! HAZEL! / HELLO MONTREAL! .... *Pathe Actuelle 36777* 3-5 28
(Vocals: Tom Stacks)

HEY! HEY! HAZEL! / HELLO MONTREAL!.................... *Perfect 14958* 2-4 28
(Vocals: Tom Stacks)
(Simultaneously released on two labels)

SINCE SHE LEARNED TO RIDE A HORSE / OH! YOU HAVE NO IDEA...... *Pathe Actuelle 36807* 3-5 28
(Vocals: Tom Stacks)

SINCE SHE LEARNED TO RIDE A HORSE / OH! YOU HAVE NO IDEA .... *Perfect 14988* 2-4 28
(Vocals: Tom Stacks)
(Simultaneously released on two labels)

RESER, Harry, as The Six Jumping Jacks

CHARLESTON BALL / THE VILLAGE BLACKSMITH OWNS THE VILLAGE NOW
(Vocals: Tom Stacks)................. *Brunswick 3064* 3-5 26

COCK-A-DOODLE, I'M OFF MY NOODLE / THE COAT AND PANTS DO ALL THE WORK AND THE VEST GETS ALL THE GRAVY .... *Brunswick 3412* 3-5 27
(Vocals: Tom Stacks)

COLLEGIATE SAM / MY WIFE IS ON A DIET................... *Brunswick 4589* 3-5 29
(Vocals: Tom Stacks)

DAN THE ELEVATOR MAN / SEND FOR OUR FREE BOOKLET .... *Brunswick 4759* 4-6 30
(Vocals: Tom Stacks)

ETIQUETTE BLUES (Vocals: Larry Abbott, Harry Reser & Tom Stacks) / C-O-N-S-T-A-N-T-I-N-O-P-L-E
(Vocals: Tom Stacks)................. *Brunswick 3940* 3-5 28

HENRY'S MADE A LADY OUT OF LIZZIE / (I SCREAM – YOU SCREAM – WE ALL SCREAM FOR) ICE CREAM...................... *Brunswick 3782* 4-6 28
(Vocals: Tom Stacks)

I'M GONNA DANCE WIT DE GUY WOT BRUNG ME / SHE'S JUST WHAT THE DOCTOR ORDERED....................... *Brunswick 3623* 3-5 27
(Vocals: Tom Stacks)

I'M JUST WILD ABOUT ANIMAL CRACKERS / THE PUMP SONG................ *Brunswick 3216* 3-5 26
(Vocals: Tom Stacks)

IT'S A GREAT LIFE (IF YOU DON'T WEAKEN) (Vocals: Tom Stacks) / YOU'RE SIMPLY DELISH (Vocals: Unknown)............ *Brunswick 4948* 4-6 30

MORE WE ARE TOGETHER, THE / YOU NEVER GET NOWHERE HOLDING HANDS..... *Brunswick 3524* 3-5 27
(Vocals: orchestra)

OH! LOOK AT THAT BABY / GET 'EM IN A RUMBLE SEAT................ *Brunswick 3856* 3-5 28
(Vocals: Tom Stacks)

PRUNE SONG / I NEVER KISSED A BABY LIKE YOU............... *Brunswick 4073* 3-5 28
(Vocals: Tom Stacks)

SAY, MISTER! HAVE YOU MET ROSIE'S SISTER? / SITTIN' AROUND................ *Brunswick 3131* 3-5 26
(Vocals: Tom Stacks)

SHE'S GOT "IT" / GONNA GET A GIRL............. *Brunswick 3603* 3-5 27
(Vocals: Tom Stacks)

THANKS FOR THE BUGGY RIDE / SHE WAS JUST A SAILOR'S SWEETHEART.......... *Brunswick 3094* 3-5 26
(Vocals: Tom Stacks)

TWENTY SWEDES RAN THROUGH THE WEEDS (CHASING ONE NORWEGIAN) / THE WEDDING IN THE ARK....................... *Brunswick 6007* 3-5 31
(Vocals: Unknown)

WHEN SWEET SUSIE GOES STEPPIN' BY / NAGASAKI...................... *Brunswick 4011* 3-5 28
(Vocals: Tom Stacks)

WHEN YOU DUNK A DOUGHNUT, DON'T IT MAKE IT NICE? / HOW COULD RED RIDING HOOD (HAVE BEEN SO GOOD AND STILL KEEP THE WOLF FROM THE DOOR?) .... *Brunswick 3254* 3-5 26
(Vocals: Tom Stacks)

WHERE DO YOU WORK-A, JOHN? / IF YOU CAN'T LAND 'ER ON THE OLD VERANDAH (THEN YOU CAN'T LAND 'ER AT ALL)......... *Brunswick 3374* 3-5 27
(Vocals: Tom Stacks)

WHOOPEE HAT BRIGADE / PICCOLO PETE.................. *Brunswick 4459* 3-5 29
(Vocals: Tom Stacks)

WIND BLEW THROUGH HIS WHISKERS / WIMMIN, AAH! .... *Brunswick 3031* 3-5 26
(Vocals: Tom Stacks)

RESER, Harry, as The Six Jumping Jacks recorded under the name The Six Hayseeds

CHARLESTON BALL / THE VILLAGE BLACKSMITH OWNS THE VILLAGE NOW
(Vocals: Tom Stacks)................. *Vocalion 15244* 3-5 26

RESER, Harry, as The Volunteer Firemen

BLINKY MOON BAY / WAIT TILL TOMORROW NIGHT............. *Brunswick 3077* 3-5 26
(Vocals: Al Bernard & Frank Kamplain)

SHOW ME THE WAY TO GO HOME / WHY AREN'T YEZ EATIN' MORE ORANGES? .... *Brunswick 3025* 3-5 25
(Vocals: Unknown)

REY, Alvino, & His Orchestra
(Alvino Rey: 7/1/11 –)

AMONG MY SOUVENIRS (Vocals: JoAnne Ryan, The Blue Reys, & The Glee Club) / SAVE YOUR SORROW
(Vocals: JoAnne Ryan) .... *Capitol 338* 2-4 44

ARMY AIR CORPS, THE (Vocals: The Four King Sisters, Bill Schallen, & orchestra) / LITTLE HAWK .... *Bluebird B-11476* 3-5 42

AS I REMEMBER YOU (Vocals: Bill Schallen) / A ROMANTIC GUY, I (Vocals: Skeets Herfurt)................ *Bluebird B-11186* 2-4 41

BLUE SHADOWS AND WHITE GARDENIAS (Vocals: Alyce King) / SING ME A SONG OF THE ISLANDS (Vocals: Bill Schallen) ...... *Bluebird B-11448* 2-4 42

DEARLY BELOVED (Vocals: Bill Schallen) / I'M OLD-FASHIONED
(Vocals: Alyce King)............... *Bluebird B-11579* 2-4 42

DON'T TAKE YOUR LOVE FROM ME / JEALOUS............. *Bluebird B-11272* 2-4 41
(Vocals: Yvonne King)

DROWSY OLD RIFF / HOW GREEN WAS MY VALLEY (Vocals: Alyce King) .... *Bluebird B-11238* 2-4 41

FEED THAT EAGLE (Vocals: Yvonne King) / (THE BELLE OF THE VILLAGE BALL) AROUND AND AROUND SHE GOES (Vocals: Alyce King & quartet)............. *Bluebird B-11381* 3-5 41

FERRIS WHEEL, THE (Vocals: Skeets Herfurt) / HE WEARS A PAIR OF SILVER WINGS
(Vocals: Alyce King) .... *Victor 27920* 3-5 42

HARBOR OF CREAMS (Vocals: Bill Schallen) / IN THE HALL OF THE MOUNTAIN KING... *Bluebird B-11216* 2-4 41

HERE COMES THE BRIDE / DANCING WITH A DREAM
(Vocals: Bill Schallen).............. *Bluebird B-11254* 2-4 41

HINDUSTAN / EVERYTHING HAPPENS TO ME (Vocals: Alyce King).......... *Bluebird B-11136* 2-4 41

IDAHO (Vocals: Yvonne King) / IT ISN'T A DREAM ANY MORE (Vocals: Alyce King) .... *Bluebird B-11331* 2-4 41

IF IT'S TRUE (Vocals: Yvonne King) / SATURDAY NITE............. *Bluebird B-11170* 2-4 41

I'M GLAD THERE IS YOU (Vocals: Alyce King) / PICNIC IN PURGATORY (Vocals: Charles Brosen)............. *Bluebird B-11501* 2-4 42

I SAID NO (Vocals: Yvonne King) / DEEP IN THE HEART OF TEXAS (Vocals: Bill Schallen & Skeets Herfurt)............. *Bluebird B-11391* 3-5 42

KEEP SMILIN', KEEP LAUGHIN', BE HAPPY (Vocals: The Four King Sisters) / THE SINGING SANDS OF ALAMOSA (Vocals: Bill Schallen) .... *Victor 27936* 2-4 42

KISS THE BOYS GOODBYE (Vocals: Yvonne King) / IT'S YOURS (Vocals: The Four King Sisters).... *Bluebird B-11196* 2-4 41

LIEBESTRAUM / NOT A STAR IN SIGHT (Vocals: Alyce King) .... *Bluebird B-11404* 2-4 42

LIGHT CALVARY / AMAPOLA...... *Bluebird B-11108* 2-4 41

MAJOR AND THE MINOR, THE / STRIP-POLKA (Vocals: The King Sisters)..... *Bluebird B-11573* 2-4 42

MUSIC 'TIL DAWN (Vocals: The Four King Sisters) / MY BUDDY............... *Bluebird B-11517* 3-5 42

NIGHTY-NIGHT (theme song) (Vocals: Yvonne King) / MY PRODIGAL (Vocals: Alyce King)...... *Bluebird B-11041* 2-4 41

OH, FOR HEAVEN'S SAKE (Vocals: Yvonne King & Skeets Herfurt) / WOODLAND SYMPHONY............ *Bluebird B-11143* 2-4 41

SANTA CLAUS IS COMIN' TO TOWN (Vocals: The Four King Sisters) / JINGLE BELLS (by Glenn Miller & His Orchestra; Vocals: Tex Beneke, Ernie Caceras, & The Modernaires)..................... *Bluebird B-11353* 4-6 41

SMILE FOR ME (Vocals: Four King Sisters) / DO YOU MISS YOUR SWEETHEART (LIKE YOUR SWEETHEART MISSES YOU?) (Vocal: Yvonne King) ... *Bluebird B-11461* 3-5 42

ST. LOUIS BLUES / ROW, ROW, ROW YOUR BOAT............... *Bluebird B-10948* 3-5 41
(Vocals: The Four King Sisters)

TIGER RAG (Vocals: Four King Sisters) / ROSE ROOM.................. *Bluebird B-11002* 3-5 41

WE'LL GATHER LILACS (Vocals: JoAnne Ryan) / CEMENT MIXER (PUT-TI PUT-TI)
(Vocals: Rocky Coluccio)................ *Capitol 248* 2-4 43

WHEN IT'S MOONLIGHT ON THE BLUE PACIFIC (Vocals: Bill Schallen & The Four King Sisters) / I NEVER KNEW (I COULD LOVE ANYBODY LIKE I'M LOVING YOU) (Vocals: Alyce King)............... *Victor 27948* 2-4 42

WHERE ARE YOU (Vocals: Alyce King) / I TAKE TO YOU
(Vocals: Yvonne King) .... *Bluebird B-11151* 2-4 41

WHO CALLS? (Vocals: Bill Schallen) / ON THE ALAMO............... *Bluebird B-11319* 2-4 41

WILLIAM TELL / WILLIAM TELL, PART II.......... *Bluebird B-1072* 3-5 41

YOU ARE THE LYRIC (TO THE LOVE SONG IN MY HEART) (Vocals: Bill Schallen) / THE SKUNK SONG
(Vocals: Dick Morgan) .... *Bluebird B-11363* 3-5 41

REYNOLDS, Bob, & His Band

OVERNIGHT / MY IDEAL.............. *Crown 3053* 4-6 31
(Vocals: Unknown)

REYNOLDS, Bud, & His Orchestra:
see PALMQUIST, Ernie, & His Carolina Collegians

REYNOLDS, Frankie, & His Orchestra

CHICKEN ON THE APPLE / PARADISE...................... *Bluebird B-7137* 5-8 37

LADY, BE GOOD (Vocals: Barbara Lane) / AIN'T MISBEHAVIN' (by Boots Douglas as Boots & His Buddies; Vocal: Cora Woods) .... *Bluebird B-7241* 5-8 37

REYNOLDS, Ross, & His Palais Gardens Orchestra

CREOLE / PIPPIN .... *Gennett 5611* 8-10 25

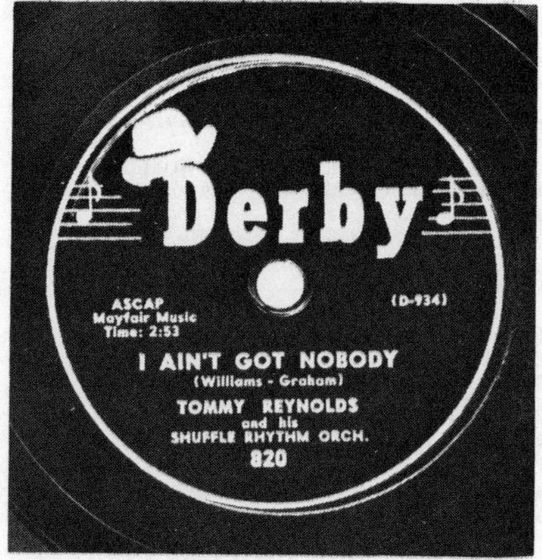

REYNOLDS, Tommy, & His Orchestra
(Tommy Reynolds: 1/17/17 –)

DOLLY DOOLITTLE (Vocals: Sally Richards) / TWO GUITARS.... Vocalion 5554 2-4 40
I AIN'T GOT NOBODY / IT'S A WONDERFUL WORLD (Vocals: Bon Bon).... Derby 820 3-5 50
I DON'T WANT TO CRY ANY MORE / STOP PRETENDING (Vocals: Sally Richards).... Okeh 5718 2-4 40
IF IT WEREN'T FOR YOU / MOMENTS IN THE MOONLIGHT.... Vocalion 5431 2-4 40
(Vocals: Sally Richards)
IF YOU SEE MARGIE (Vocals: Ralph Young) / HALFWAY DOWN THE STREET
(Vocals: Mary Ann McCall).... Okeh 5807 2-4 40
JAZZ FOR HAPPY FEET, VOL. 1 (EP).... King (M) KEP 379 3-5 57
(With picture cover)
JAZZ FOR HAPPY FEET, VOL. 2 (EP).... King (M) KEP 380 3-5 57
(With picture cover)
JUNGLE JIVE / I'LL TELL IT TO THE BREEZE (Vocals: Sally Richards).... Okeh 5791 3-5 40
MAKE LOVE WITH A GUITAR (Vocals: Penny Porter) / MOMENTS IN THE MOONLIGHT
(Vocals: Sally Richards).... Conqueror 9518 2-4 40
MARCHETA / DEEP NIGHT.... Conqueror 9517 2-4 40
MARCHETA / DEEP NIGHT.... Vocalion 5339 2-4 40
(Simultaneously released on two labels)
MISSOURI SCRAMBLER / I'LL WAIT FOR YOU FOREVER (Vocals: Sally Richards).... Vocalion 5594 3-5 40
NIGHT AFTER NIGHT WITH YOU / IT'S A BLUE WORLD.... Vocalion 5317 2-4 40
(Vocals: Marion Page)
NOW YOU KNOW (Vocals: Penny Porter) / PIP DREAMS (theme song).... Conqueror 9515 2-4 40
NOW YOU KNOW (Vocals: Penny Porter) / PIP DREAMS (theme song).... Vocalion 5418 2-4 40
(Simultaneously released on two labels)
ON A SIMMERY SUMMERY DAY / I LOVE TO WATCH THE MOONLIGHT.... Vocalion 5569 2-4 40
(Vocals: Sally Richards)
PLEASE TAKE A LETTER, MISS BROWN (Vocals: Gene Sanders) / ONCE OVER LIGHTLY.... Vocalion 5645 2-4 40
SAILOR WITH THE NAVY BLUE EYES (Vocals: Sally Richards & Gene Sanders) / I BOUGHT A WOODEN WHISTLE (Vocals: Sally Richards).... Vocalion 5604 2-4 40
SIERRA SUE / I CAN'T LOVE YOU ANY MORE (ANY MORE THAN I DO).... Vocalion 5521 2-4 40
(Vocals: Sally Richards)
SOMETHING TO LIVE FOR (Vocals: Ralph Young) / NICKEL'S WORTH OF RHYTHM
(Vocals: Mary Ann McCall).... Okeh 5902 2-4 40
WHISPERING GRASS (Vocals: Sally Richards) / JUST A MEMORY.... Conqueror 9516 2-4 40
WHISPERING GRASS (Vocals: Sally Richards) / JUST A MEMORY.... Vocalion 5468 2-4 40
(Simultaneously released on two labels)
WOULDST COULD I BUT KISS THY HAND, OH BABE / MAKE LOVE WITH A GUITAR.... Vocalion 5373 2-4 40
(Vocals: Penny Porter)

RHYTHMODIC ORCHESTRA, The:
see FENTON, Carl

RICHARDS, Jay, & His Orchestra

LITTLE PAL / I'M IN SEVENTH HEAVEN.... Vocalion 15813 3-5 29
(Vocals: Unknown)
MY SONG OF THE NILE (Vocals: by duet) / OUT WHERE THE MOONBEAMS ARE BORN
(Vocals: Unknown).... Vocalion 15827 3-5 29
SWEETNESS / I DON'T WANT YOUR KISSES (IF I CAN'T HAVE YOUR LOVE).... Vocalion 15835 5-8 29
(Vocals: Elmo Tanner)
WHY CAN'T YOU? / USED TO YOU.... Vocalion 15812 3-5 29
(Vocals: Unknown)

RICHARDSON, Florence, & Her Orchestra

BLUE MOON / I WOKE UP TOO SOON.... Bluebird B-5764 5-8 35
(Vocals: Jerry Lee)
JUST A FAIR-WEATHER FRIEND / I THRILL WHEN THEY MENTION YOUR NAME.... Bluebird B-5766 5-8 35
(Vocals: Jerry Lee)
OLE FAITHFUL (Vocals: Jerry Lee) / WALTZ TIME IN VIENNA.... Bluebird B-5763 4-6 35

RICH, Fred, & His Hotel Astor Orchestra
(Fred Rich: 1/3/98 – 9/8/56)

ALL ALONE MONDAY / WHEN DAY IS DONE.... Columbia 777-D 3-5 26
(Vocals: Irving Kaufman as Frank Harris)
AND THEN I FORGET / LOOKING AT THE WORLD THRU ROSE-COLORED GLASSES.... Cameo 1001 3-5 26
BLUE ROOM / KATINKA (Vocals: Ray Stillwell).... Columbia 660-D 3-5 26
CLAP YO' HANDS (Vocals: The Crooners) / DO-DO-DO.... Columbia 802-D 3-5 26
COULD I? – I CERTAINLY COULD / GIMME ME A LITTLE KISS, WILL YA, HUH?
(Vocals: Bob Nelson).... Harmony 136-H 3-5 26
DO I HEAR YOU SAYING "I LOVE YOU?" / YOU TOOK ADVANTAGE OF ME.... Columbia 1389-D 3-5 28
(Vocals: James Melton)
DON'T WAKE ME UP / SOMEONE'S STOLEN MY SWEET BABY.... Harmony 90-H 3-5 26
FAR AWAY BELLS / WEAR YOUR SUNDAY SMILE.... Columbia 945-D 2-4 27
(Vocals: Lewis James)
FEELIN' KIND O' BLUE / MIAMI.... Harmony 38-H 3-5 25
FLAMIN' MAMIE / SHAKE THAT THING.... Cameo 872 4-6 26
HELLO, ALOHA! HOW ARE YOU? / I LOVE A UKELELE.... Harmony 171-H 2-4 26
(Vocals: Ray Stilwell)
HIGH-HIGH-HIGH UP IN THE HILLS / CRAZY WORDS – CRAZY TUNE.... Columbia 871-D 2-4 27
(Vocals: Johnny Marvin)
HOW MANY TIMES? / WHO WOULDN'T.... Okeh 40664 3-5 26
(Vocals: Ray Stilwell)
I LOVE THE MOONLIGHT / I STILL BELIEVE IN YOU.... Columbia 843-D 3-5 27
JUST A LITTLE LONGER / I STILL BELIEVE IN YOU.... Okeh 40718 3-5 27
(Vocals: The Crooners)
LUCKY IN LOVE / GOOD NEWS.... Columbia 1108-D 2-4 27
(Vocals: Franklyn Baur, Frank Luther, & Elliott Shaw)
ON THE RIVIERA / BARCELONA.... Columbia 706-D 2-4 26
(Vocals: Lewis James)
PLAY, GYPSIES – DANCE GYPSIES / MOONLIGHT ON THE GANGES.... Columbia 734-D 2-4 26
POOR PAPA / BELL HOPPIN' BLUES.... Harmony 119-H 4-6 26
POOR PAPA / BELL HOPPIN' BLUES.... Silvertone 3269 4-6 26
(Simultaneously released on two labels)
SOMEBODY ELSE / IT ALL DEPENDS ON YOU.... Columbia 900-D 2-4 27
(Vocals: Irving Kaufman as Vincent Van Tuyl)
TING-A-LING, THE BELLS'LL RING / TRUDY.... Columbia 720-D 3-5 26
(Vocals: Ray Stilwell)

RICH, Fred, & His Hotel Astor Orchestra as The Astorites

AND THEN I FORGOT / UP AND DOWN THE EIGHT MILE ROAD.... Harmony 228-H 3-5 26
BLACK BOTTOM / HUGS AND KISSES (Vocals: Paul Hagan).... Harmony 251-H 3-5 26
HOW MANY TIMES? / WHO WOULDN'T.... Harmony 201-H 3-5 26
(Vocals: Irving Kaufman)
I STILL BELIEVE IN YOU / TUCK IN KENTUCKY AND SMILE.... Harmony 285-H 2-4 26
IT MADE YOU HAPPY WHEN YOU MADE ME CRY / THINKING OF YOU.... Harmony 303-H 2-47
ME AND MY SHADOW / HALLELUJAH!.... Harmony 412-H 3-5 27
(Vocals: Unknown)
MOONLIT WATERS / DREAM KISSES.... Harmony 497-H 2-4 27
(Vocals: Unknown)
THERE MUST BE SOMEBODY ELSE / DID YOU MEAN IT?.... Harmony 527-H 2-4 27
(Vocals: Unknown)
TREE IN THE PARK, A / WHO DO YOU LOVE?.... Harmony 376-H 2-4 27
(Vocals: Irving Kaufman)

RICH, Fred, & His Hotel Astor Orchestra as The Happy Hour Orchestra

AND THEN I FORGOT / BLUE HAWAIIAN MOONLIGHT.... Pathe Actuelle 36506 3-5 26
(Vocals: Ray Stilwell)
AND THEN I FORGOT / BLUE HAWAIIAN MOONLIGHT.... Perfect 14687 2-4 26
(Vocals: Ray Stilwell)
(Simultaneously released on two labels)
MOUNTAIN GREENERY / PEGGY'S DU.... Pathe Actuelle 36504 3-5 26
MOUNTAIN GREENERY / PEGGY'S DU.... Perfect 14685 2-4 26
(Simultaneously released on two labels)
WHO DO YOU LOVE? / I'VE GROWN SO LONESOME, THINKING OF YOU.... Okeh 40735 3-5 27
(Vocals: Sammy Fain & Artie Dunn)

RICH, Fred, & His (La Palina) Orchestra

EMBRACEABLE YOU / I GOT RHYTHM.... Columbia 2328-D 8-10 30
(Vocals: Paul Small)

RICH, Fred, & His (La Palina) Orchestra as Bud Blue & His Orchestra

I'LL BE BLUE, JUST THINKING OF YOU / SOMEONE SANG A SWEETER SONG TO MARY.... Okeh 41466 8-10 30
(Vocals: Smith Ballew)

RICH, Fred, & His (La Palina) Orchestra as The Deauville Syncopators

BABY'S BIRTHDAY PARTY / WEDDING OF THE BIRDS (by Fred Rich & His (La Palina) Orchestra as George Wells & His Orchestra).... Parlophone PNY-34158 4-6 31
(Vocals: Smith Ballew)
CHEERFUL LITTLE EARFUL / THE LITTLE THINGS IN LIFE (by Fred Rich & His (La Palina) Orchestra as George Wells & His Orchestra).... Parlophone PNY-3415& 8-10 31
SWEETHEART OF MY STUDENT DAYS / YOU'RE LUCKY TO ME.... Parlophone PNY-34138 5-8 30
(Vocals: Dick Robertson as Chester Leighton)

RICH, Fred, & His (La Palina) Orchestra as Lloyd Keating & His Music / Lloyd Keating's Music

BABY'S BIRTHDAY PARTY / WEDDING OF THE BIRDS.... Harmony 1239-H 3-6 31
(Vocals: Smith Ballew)
I'LL BE BLUE, JUST THINKING OF YOU / A PEACH OF A PAIR (by Fred Rich & His (La Palina) Orchestra as Chester Leighton & His Sophomores).... Harmony 1233-H 5-8 30
(Vocals: Smith Ballew)

RICH, Fred, & His (La Palina) Orchestra as Chester Leighton & His Sophomores

PEACH OF A PAIR, A / I'LL BE BLUE, JUST THINKING OF YOU (by Fred Rich & His (La Palina) Orchestra as Lloyd Keating & His Music).... Harmony 1233-H 5-8 30
(Vocals: Smith Ballew)
YOU'RE LUCKY TO ME / MEMORIES OF YOU.... Harmony 1215-H 4-6 30
(Vocals: Dick Robertson as Chester Leighton)

RICH, Fred, & His (La Palina) Orchestra as Harold Lem & His Orchestra

I GOT RHYTHM / MY LOVE FOR YOU.... Okeh 41465 8-10 30
(Vocals: Smith Ballew)

RICH, Fred, & His (La Palina) Orchestra as The New York Syncopators

CHEERFUL LITTLE EARFUL / I'M TICKLED WITH A BLUE-EYED BABY.... Odeon ONY-36165 8-10 31
(Vocals: Smaith Ballew)
WASTING MY LOVE ON YOU / SWEETHEART OF MY STUDENT DAYS.... Odeon ONY-36145 5-8 30
(Vocals: Dick Robertson as Chester Leighton)
YOU'RE LUCKY TO ME / MEMORIES OF YOU.... Odeon ONY-36146 5-8 30
(Vocals: Dick Robertson as Chester Leighton)

RICH, Fred, & His (La Palina) Orchestra as George Wells & His Orchestra

LITTLE THINGS IN LIFE, THE / CHEERFUL LITTLE EARFUL (by Fred Rich & His (La Palina) Orchestra as The Deauville Syncopators).... Parlophone PNY-34157 8-10 31
(Vocals: Smith Ballew)
WEDDING OF THE BIRDS / BABY'S BIRTHDAY PARTY (by Fred Rich & His (La Palina) Orchestra as The Deauville Syncopators).... Parlophone PNY-34158 4-6 31
(Vocals: Smith Ballew)

RICH, Fred, & His Orchestra

ALL THAT I'M ASKING IS SYMPATHY / PAL OF MY SWEETHEART DAYS.... Banner 6517 3-5 29
(Vocals: Smith Ballew as Buddy Blue)
AS LONG AS WE'RE IN LOVE / LET'S SIT AND TALK ABOUT YOU.... Columbia 1713-D 3-5 29
(Vocals: Billy Murray)
AT YOUR COMMAND (Vocals: Bunny Berigan) / PARDON ME, PRETTY BABY
(Vocals: Scrappy Lambert).... Columbia 2484-D 8-10 31
BABY'S BIRTHDAY PARTY / WEDDING OF THE BIRDS.... Okeh 41472 4-6 31
(Vocals: Smith Ballew)
DON'T HANG YOUR DREAMS ON A RAINBOW / SONG OF THE MOONBEAMS.... Columbia 1893-D 4-6 29
(Vocals: Smith Ballew)
DREAM AVENUE / FOR YOU.... Columbia 2195-D 3-5 30
(Vocals: Unknown)
GOOD EVENIN' / WHEN THE ORGAN PLAYED AT TWILIGHT.... Perfect 15346 2-4 30
(Vocals: Scrappy Lambert as Rogman Lewis)
GOT THE BENCH – GOT THE PARK / I'M THE LAST ONE LEFT ON THE CORNER.... Columbia 2427-D 4-6 31
(Vocals: Elmer Feldkamp)
HE'S SO UNUSUAL / DIXIE JAMBOREE.... Columbia 2043-D 8-10 30
(Vocals: The Rollickers)
HOUR OF PARTING, THE / AS LONG AS YOUR'RE THERE.... Columbia 2494-D 3-5 31
(Vocals: Unknown)
HOUSE WITH A LITTLE RED BARN, A / HOW HIGH THE MOON.... Vocalion 5420 3-5 40
(Vocals: Rosemary Calvin)
I'D WRITE A SONG / YOU ARE THE SONG.... Columbia 2751-D 3-5 33
(Vocals: Paul Small)
IF I DIDN'T HAVE YOU / AS TIME GOES BY.... Columbia 2536-D 4-6 31
(Vocals: Smith Ballew)
IF LOVE WERE ALL (Vocals: The Rollickers) / I'LL SEE YOU AGAIN (Vocals: Smith Ballew).... Columbia 2090-D 3-5 30
I'M JUST A DANCING SWEETHEART / KISS ME GOODNIGHT, NOT GOODBYE.... Columbia 2534-D 3-5 31
(Vocals: Smith Ballew)
I SURRENDER, DEAR (Vocals: Bill Coty) / WERE YOU SINCERE? (Vocals: Larry Murphy).... Okeh 41488 3-5 31
KINGS' HORSES, THEvvThe Roundtown Quartet) / THE ONE-MAN BAND (Vocals: Larry Murphy).... Okeh 41480 4-6 31
LET'S FALL IN LOVE (Vocals: Phil Regan) / LOVE IS LOVE ANYWHERE
(Vocals: Vera Van).... Columbia 2868-D 3-5 34
MY FIRST LOVE / TWO LIPS.... Columbia 2868-D 3-5 34
(Vocals: by trio)
REVOLUTIONARY RHYTHM / WHEN THE REAL THING COMES ALONG.... Columbia 1965-D 5-8 29
(Vocals: The Rollickers)
SEND FOR ME / STRIKE UP THE BAND!.... Columbia 2132-D 5-8 30
(Vocals: Unknown)
SINGIN' IN THE RAIN / NOBODY BUT YOU.... Columbia 1838-D 5-8 29
(Vocals: The Rollickers)
SING SOMETHING SIMPLE / IF I'D ONLY LISTENED TO YOU.... Columbia 2299-D 5-8 30
(Vocals: Small Paul)
SOME SWEET DAY / I GET THE BLUES WHEN IT RAINS.... Regal 8761 5-8 29
(Vocals: Irving Kaufman)
SOME SWEET DAY / I GET THE BLUES WHEN IT RAINS.... Conqueror 7333 5-8 29
(Vocals: Irving Kaufman)
SOME SWEET DAY / I GET THE BLUES WHEN IT RAINS.... Regal 8761 5-8 29
(Vocals: Irving Kaufman)
(Simultaneously released on two labels)
TILL WE MEET AGAIN / I'M FOREVER BLOWING BUBBLES.... Vocalion 5507 3-5 40

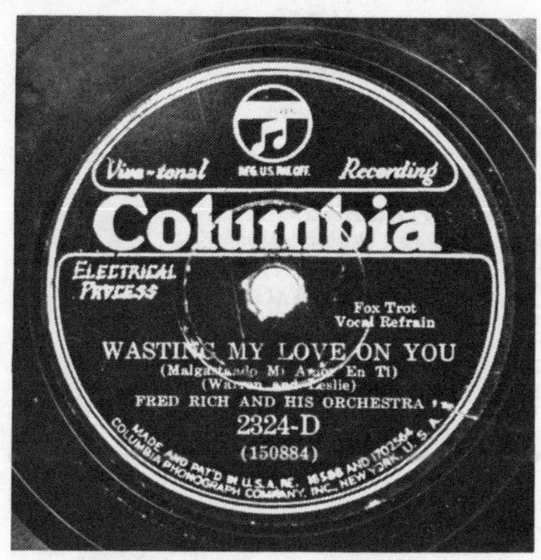

WASTING MY LOVE ON YOU (Vocal: Paul Small) / WEDDING BELLS ARE RINGING FOR SALLY (by Ben Selvin & His Orchestra as The Cavaliers; Vocals: Unknown) .... *Columbia 2324-D* 5-8 30

WHAT IS THIS THING CALLED LOVE? / WHAT WOULD I CARE? .... *Columbia 2099-D* 3-5 30
(Vocals: Unknown)

WHEN YOU WERE THE BLOSSOM OF BUTTERCUP LANE / TIE A LITTLE STRING AROUND YOUR FINGER .... *Columbia 2387-D* 5-8 31
(Vocals: Unknown)

WHY CAN'T YOU? / USED TO YOU .... *Columbia 1878-D* 3-5 29
(Vocals: Unknown)

YOU ARE TOO BEAUTIFUL / THERE'S A HOUSE ON A HILL .... *Columbia 2752-D* 3-5 33
(Vocals: Paul Small)

YOURS SINCERELY / I KISS YOUR HAND, MADAME .... *Columbia 1778-D* 3-5 29
(Vocals: The Rollickers)

RICH, Fred, & His Orchestra as Frank Auburn & His Orchestra

I'M SO AFRAID OF YOU / WOULD YOU LIKE TO TAKE A WALK? .... *Harmony 1269-H* 8-10 31
(Vocals: Elmer Feldkamp)

RICH, Fred, & His Orchestra as The Deauville Syncopators

I'M SO AFRAID OF YOU / TRULY (by Fred Rich & His Orchestra as George Wells & His Orchestra) .... *Parlophone PNY-34171* 4-6 31
(Vocals: Elmer Feldkamp)

I'M THE LAST ONE LEFT ON THE CORNER (Vocals: The RounTowners Quartet) / SWEET AND HOT (by Fred Rich & His Orchestra as Richard Hampton & His Orchestra; Vocal: Larry Murphy) ... *Parlophone PNY-34186* 8-10 31

LOVE FOR SALE / BY THE RIVER SAINTE MARIE .... *Parlophone PNY-34180* 4-6 31
(Vocals: Bill Coty)

RICH, Fred, & His Orchestra as Richard Hampton & His Orchestra

SWEET AND HOT (Vocal: Larry Murphy) / I'M THE LAST ONE LEFT ON THE CORNER (by Fred Rich & His Orchestra as The Deauville Syncopators; Vocal: RounTowners Quartet) ..... *Parlophone PNY-34186* 8-10 31

RICH, Fred, & His Orchestra as Lloyd Keating's Music

LONESOME LOVER / TRULY .... *Harmony 1268-H* 4-6 31
(Vocals: Elmer Feldkamp)

RICH, Fred, & His Orchestra as The La Palina Orchestra

ALL THAT I'M ASKING IS SYMPATHY / PAL OF MY SWEETHEART DAYS .... *Domino 4409* 3-5 29
(Vocals: Smith Ballew)

RAINBOW MAN, THE / CHRISTINA .... *Pathe Actuelle 36980* 4-6 29
(Vocals: Irving Kaufman)

RAINBOW MAN, THE / CHRISTINA .... *Perfect 15161* 3-4 29
(Vocals: Irving Kaufman)
(Simultaneously released on two labels)

RICH, Fred, & His Orchestra as Chester Leighton & His Sophomores

WHEN I TAKE MY SUGAR TO TEA / DREAM A LITTLE DREAM OF ME .... *Harmony 1307-H* 5-8 31
(Vocals: Dick Robertson as Chester Leighton)

RICH, Fred, & His Orchestra as Earl Marlow's Orchestra

PLEASE DON'T TALK ABOUT ME WHEN I'M GONE / WHEN YOUR HAIR HAS TURNED TO SILVER .... *Parlophone PNY-34181* 4-6 31
(Vocals: Bill Coty)

Rich, Fred, & His Orchestra as The New York Syncopators

IT SEEMS TO BE SPRING / BEWARE OF LOVE .... *Okeh 41434* 4-6 30
(Vocals: Scrappy Lambert)

LONESOME LOVER / FALLING IN LOVE AGAIN .... *Odeon ONY-36178* 4-6 31
(Vocals: Elmer Feldkamp)

RICH, Fred, & His Orchestra as Frank Raymond's Dance Orchestra

LITTLE BY LITTLE / HOW AM I TO KNOW? .... *Paramount 20757* 5-8 29
(Vocals: Irving Kaufman)

PICOLLO PETE (Vocal: Irving Kaufman) / PAL OF MY SWEETHEART DAYS (Vocal: Smith Ballew as Sturgis Anderson) .... *Broadway 1327* 4-6 30

SOME SWEET DAY / THE THINGS THAT WERE MADE FOR LOVE .... *Broadway 1269* 4-6 29
(Vocals: Irving Kaufman as Ray Minh)

RICH, Fred, & His Orchestra as Tom Rock & His Orchestra

TRULY / WOULD YOU LIKE TO TAKE A WALK? .... *Odeon ONY-36179* 5-8 31
(Vocals: Elmer Feldkamp)

RICH, Fred, & His Orchestra as George Wells & His Orchestra

TRULY / I'M SO AFRAID OF YOU (by Fred Rich & His Orchestra as The Deauville Syncopators) .... *Parlophone PNY-34171* 4-6 31
(Vocals: Elmer Feldkamp)

RICH, Fred, as Freddie Rich's Radio Orchestra

(Hit Of The Week records are one-sided paper discs; some have two titles on the one side.)

I'M JUST A DANCING SWEETHEART (Vocal: Ben Alley); AS THE BACKS GO TEARING BY (Vocals: by trio) .... *Hit Of The Week L-1* 5-8 31

IT'S THE GIRL (Vocal: Elmer Feldkamp) .... *Hit Of The Week K-1* 5-8 31

LITTLE GIRL (Vocal: Elmer Feldkamp) .... *Hit Of The Week J-4* 5-8 31

RICH, Fred, as Fred Rich's Dance Orchestra

I NEVER THOUGHT / THAT'S MY MAMMY .... *Domino 4147* 2-4 28
(Vocals: Scrappy Lambert)

I NEVER THOUGHT / THAT'S MY MAMMY .... *Regal 8558* 2-4 28
(Vocals: Scrappy Lambert)
(Simultaneously released on two labels)

THREE IN THE PARK, A / I WONDER HOW I LOOK WHEN I'M ASLEEP? .... *Banner 1930* 2-4 27
(Vocals: Sammy Fain & Artie Dunn)

WHEREVER YOU ARE / PLAYGROUND IN THE SKY .... *Conqueror 7023* 2-4 27
(Vocals: Sammy Fain & Artie Dunn)

WHEREVER YOU ARE / PLAYGROUND IN THE SKY .... *Domino 4044* 2-4 27
(Vocals: Sammy Fain & Artie Dunn)
(Simultaneously released on two labels)

RICH, Fred, as Fred Rich's Orchestra recorded under the name Al Lynch & His Orchestra

SO TIRED / DREAM KISSES .... *Broadway 1133* 2-4 28
(Vocals: Scrappy Lambert)

SO TIRED / DREAM KISSES .... *Paramount 20575* 3-5 28
(Vocals: Scrappy Lambert)
(Simultaneously released on two labels)

WHEREVER YOU ARE / PLAYGROUND IN THE SKY .... *Regal 8424* 3-5 27
(Vocals: Sammy Fain & Artie Dunn)

RICH, Fred, as Fred Rich's Dance Orchestra recorded under the name The Midnight Serenaders

CAN'T YOU HEAR ME SAY "I LOVE YOU"? / SWWETHEART MEMORIES .... *Broadway 1129* 3-5 27
(Vocals: Irving Kaufman as Frank Harris)

CAN'T YOU HEAR ME SAY "I LOVE YOU"? / SWWETHEART MEMORIES ...... *Paramount 20557* 5-8 27
(Vocals: Irving Kaufman as Frank Harris)
(Simultaneously released on two labels)

RICKETTS, Bob, as Bob Ricketts' Band

MEAN, MEAN MAMA / IF YOU WANT TO KEEP YOUR DADDY HOME .... *Gennett 5156* 5-8 23

MEAN, MEAN MAMA / IF YOU WANT TO KEEP YOUR DADDY HOME .... *Starr 9403* 8-10 23
(Simultaneously released on two labels, one Canadian [Starr])

RILEY, Mike, & His Orchestra

also see RILEY, Mike – Eddie Farley & Their Onyx Club Boys
(Mike Riley: 1/15/04 –)

I'M HATIN' THIS WAITIN' AROUND / SPENDIN' ALL MY TIME WITH THE BLUES .... *Decca 1263* 5-8 37
(Vocals: Mike Riley)

THAT'S SOUTHERN HOSPITALITY / JAMMIN' .... *Decca 1271* 5-8 37
(Vocals: Mike Riley)

RILEY, Mike, & His Round And Round Boys

CACHITA / OH, DEAR, WHAT CAN THE MATTER BE? .... *Decca 1662* 4-6 38
(Vocals: Mike Riley)

OOOH BOOM! / YOU'RE GIVING ME THE RUN-AROUND .... *Decca 1655* 4-6 38
(Vocals: Mike Riley)

RILEY, Mike – Eddie Farley, & Their Onyx Club Boys

also see FARLEY, Eddie, & His Orchestra
see RILEY, Mike, & His Orchestra, and
see RILEY, Mike, & His Round And Round Boys
(Eddie Farley: 7/16/05 –
(The name Riley is spelled "Reilly" on some labels.)

HEY - HEY / WITH THEE I SWING .... *Decca 1041* 5-8 36
(Vocals: Mike Riley)

I'M GONNA CLAP MY HANDS / NOT ENOUGH .... *Decca 683* 8-10 36
(Vocals: Mike Riley)

I WISH I WERE ALADDIN (Vocal: Mike Riley) / YOU'RE WICKY, YOU'RE WACKY, YOU'RE WONDERFUL (Vocals: Unknown) .... *Decca 684* 8-10 36

MUSIC GOES 'ROUND AND AROUND (theme song) (Vocal: Mike Riley & Eddie Farley) / LOOKING FOR LOVE .... *Decca 578* 5-8 35

SANTA CLAUS IS COMIN' TO TOWN / JINGLE BELLS .... *Decca 1031* 5-8 35
(Vocals: Unknown)

SOUTH / I NEVER KNEW .... *Decca 619* 8-10 35

TROUBLE DON'T LIKE MUSIC / A HIGH HAT, A PICCOLO, AND A CANE .... *Decca 994* 5-8 36
(Vocals: Mike Riley)

WABASH BLUES / BLUE CLARINET STOMP .... *Decca 641* 8-10 35

RILEY, Mike – Eddie Farley & Their Onyx Club Boys as Ted Russell & His Orchestra

DINNER FOR ONE, PLEASE JAMES / A BEAUTIFUL LADY IN BLUE .... *Champion 40089* 5-8 36
(Vocals: Unknown)

DOUBLE TROUBLE / RHYTHM IS OUR BUSINESS .... *Champion 40042* 8-10 35
(Vocals: Unknown)

HERE'S TO ROMANCE / AT YOUR SERVICE, MADAME .... *Champion 40066* 5-8 35
(Vocals: Wayne Gregg)

I FOUND A DREAM / NO OTHER ONE.................. *Champion 40071* 5-8 36
(Vocals: Unknown)

IN THE MIDDLE OF A KISS / WHEN I GROW TOO OLD TO DREAM....................... *Champion 40041* 4-6 35
(Vocals: Unknown)

LOVE IS LIKE A CIGARETTE / KNICK-KNACKS ON THE MANTEL.......................... *Champion 40110* 5-8 36
(Vocals: Hal Burke)

MELODY FROM THE SKY / TWILIGHT ON THE TRAIL................... *Champion 40109* 5-8 36
(Vocals: Hal Burke)

QUICKER THAT YOU CAN SAY "JACK ROBINSON" / I FEEL LIKE A FEATHER IN THE BREEZE .... *Champion 40079* 5-8 36
(Vocals: Unknown)

SANTA CLAUS IS COMIN' TO TOWN / JINGLE BELLS................... *Champion 40056* 5-8 35
(Vocals: Unknown)

TWENTY-FOUR HOURS A DAY / DON'T GIVE UP THE SHIP .... *Champion 40065* 5-8 36
(Vocals: Unknown)

YOU ARE MY LUCKY STAR / I'M IN THE MOOD FOR LOVE............ *Champion 40057* 5-8 35
(Vocals: Unknown)

YOU'RE ALL I NEED / I WISHED ON THE MOON.................. *Champion 40040* 5-8 35
(Vocals: Unknown)

YOU TOOK MY BREATH AWAY / WHEN A GREAT LOVE COMES ALONG............ *Champion 40072* 5-8 36
(Vocals: Unknown)

RINES, Joe, & His Hotel St. Regis Orchestra

FROM ALPHA TO OMEGA / FOR NO RHYME OR REASON.................... *Victor 26022* 2-4 38
(Vocals: Joe Rines)

LAMBETH WALK (Vocal: Joe Rines) / JE NE SAIS PAPA (Vocals: Fifi D'Orsay & Joe Rines).......... *Victor 26015* 2-4 38

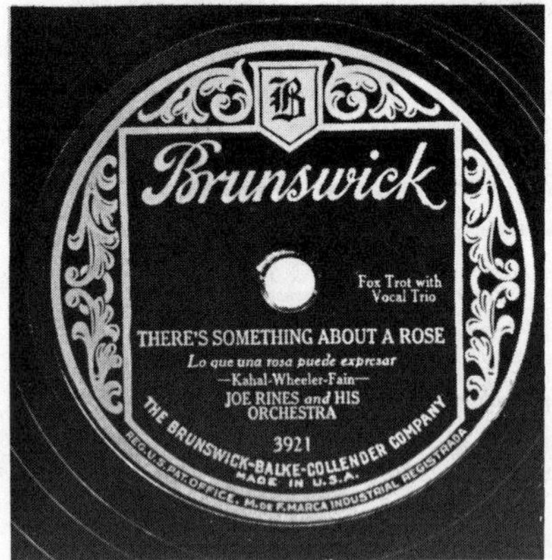

RINES, Joe, & His Orchestra

ANYTHING TO MAKE YOU HAPPY / ONE MORE NIGHT................ *Brunswick 3753* 2-4 28
(Vocals: Joe Rines)

HAVE YOU EVER BEEN IN HEAVEN? (Vocal: Frank Parrish) / MAMA, I WANNA MAKE RHYTHM (Vocal: Joe Rines).... *Brunswick 7962* 3-5 37

I STILL LOVE TO KISS YOU GOODNIGHT / I'D LIKE TO SEE SAMOA OF SAMOA........... *Brunswick 7944* 2-4 37
(Vocals: Frank Parrish)

LADY IS A TRAMP, THE (Vocal: Bebe Best) / WHY TALK ABOUT LOVE? (Vocal: Frank Parrish) ... *Brunswick 7967* 2-4 37

LANGUAGE OF RHYTHM (Vocals: Joe Rines & Carlotta Ryan) / THEY CUT DOWN THE OLD PINE TREE (Vocals: Joe Rines & Jerry Lipson) .... *Victor 24230* 3-5 32

PUT ON YOUR OLD GREY BONNET / BAMBALINA .... *Brunswick 7948* 2-4 37
(Vocals: Frank Parrish)

SONG I LOVE, THE / CAROLINA MOON................ *Brunswick 4146* 2-4 29
(Vocals: Scrappy Lambert)

SWEETHEART OF ALL MY DREAMS (Vocal: Joe Rines) / FASHIONETTE ... *Brunswick 4199* 2-4 29

TABOO TABOO (Vocals: Joe Rines & orchestra) / MY LOVE'S A COUNTRY GAL (I GUESS I'LL HAVE TO MARRY HER) (Vocals: Joe Rines & Carlotta Ryan) ... *Victor 24155* 3-5 32

THERE'S SOMETHING ABOUT A ROSE (Vocals: Dave Bernie, Ray Covert & Maxwell Covert) / JUST A LITTLE WAY AWAY FROM HOME (Vocals: Ed Smalle & Dick Robertson).................... *Brunswick 3921* 2-4 28

THIS NEVER HAPPENED BEFORE (Vocal: Lee Sullivan) / LET'S GIVE LOVE ANOTHER CHANCE (Vocal: Fred Steele).................. *Brunswick 8024* 2-4 37

UNDERNEATH THE HARLEM MOON (Vocal: Joe Rines) / SAVE A RAINY DAY FOR ME (Vocal: Carlotta Ryan)...................... *Victor 24151* 4-6 32

YOU'RE A SWEETHEART / HAVE YOU MET MISS JONES? .... *Brunswick 8012* 2-4 37
(Vocals: Lee Sullivan)

RINES, Joe, & His Triadors

THO' YOU'VE FORGOTTEN / HELLO MARGOT!................. *Brunswick 4527* 3-5 29
(Vocals: Unknown)

RINGER, Johnny, as Johnny Ringer's Rosemont Orchestra

RUBBER HEELS / SWAMP BLUES ..... *Gennett 6199* 12-15 27

VARSITY DRAG, THE (Vocals: Arthur Fields) / GOLD DIGGER....................... *Gennett 6280* 10-12 27

WHO'S THAT KNOCKIN' AT MY DOOR? / MOONLIT WATERS................. *Gennett 6264* 10-12 27
(Vocals: Arthur Fields)

RING, Harry, as Harry Ring's Southern Melody Artists

YOU CAN'T TAKE MY MEM'RIES FROM ME / TENNESSEE........................ *Okeh 45285* 4-6 29

RING, Justin, & His Dance Orchestra as as Dick Cherwin & His Orchestra

CHIMES OF SPRING / WABASH MOON... *Perfect 15430* 2-4 31
(Vocals: Joe White)

I'M KEEPIN' COMPANY / AS LONG AS YOU'RE THERE.................. *Perfect 15493* 3-5 31
(Vocals: Chick Bullock)

LITTLE JOE / FOOL ME SOME MORE... *Perfect 15450* 3-5 31
(Vocals: Mildred Hunt)

RING, Justin, & His Okeh Orchestra

HERE I AM, BROKEN HEARTED / MEET ME IN THE MOONLIGHT................. *Okeh 40849* 2-4 27
(Vocals: Unknown)

ONE MORE WALTZ / MOONLIGHT ON THE COLORADO .... *Okeh 41459* 3-5 30
(Vocals: Smith Ballew)

REVENGE / DOLORES...................... *Okeh 41120* 2-4 28
(Vocals: Seger Ellis)

RING, Justin, & His Orchestra

AH, SWEET MYSTERY OF LIFE (Vocal: Jack Parker) / GYPSY LOVE SONG (Vocal: Walter Preston) ... *Decca 231* 3-5 34

BEAUTIFUL GARDEN OF ROSES / SMILES.................................. *Decca 149* 3-5 34
(Vocals: Jack Parker)

MY ISLE OF GOLDEN DREAMS / YOUR EYES HAVE TOLD ME SO.......................... *Decca 354* 3-5 34
(Vocals: Walter Preston)

MY WILD IRISH ROSE / WHEN IRISH EYES ARE SMILING.......................... *Decca 148* 3-5 34
(Vocals: Jack Parker)

SUNRISE AND YOU / DEAR LITTLE BOY OF MINE........................ *Decca 1027* 3-5 34
(Vocals: Jack Parker)

WALTZ CLOG MEDLEY / WALTZ CLOG MEDLEY, PART II...................... *Decca 150* 3-5 34

RING, Justin, as The Okeh Salon Orchestra

ONLY A BROKEN STRING OF PEARLS / WHISPERING TREES (MEMORIES AND YOU) .... *Okeh 40676* 2-4 26
(Vocals: Henry Moeller)

RIO TRIO, The;

see RESER, Harry

RISKIN, Irving, as Rex Irving & The Boys

ACROBAT, THE / BABUSHKA HOP .... *Elite 5035* 3-5 40

ELEGY TO A JITTERBUG / THE ACROBAT....................... *Royale 1845* 4-6 40

GOSSIP / 2ND AVENUE CLAMBAKE .... *Royale 1842* 4-6 40

OVERTURE BEGINS AT FORTE / BABUSHKA HOP .... *Varsity 8262* 2-4 40

PICKANINNY DOLLS / YE OLDE TIME MOVIES...................... *Varsity 8279* 2-4 40

SWING MARCH / TOY DEPARTMENT ... *Royale 1787* 3-5 39

THEY'RE OFF / DANCE HENRY .... *Royale 1797* 3-5 39

RITCHIE, Dan, & His Orchestra:

see MAYHEW, Nye, & His Orchestra
see OSBORNE, Will, & His Orchestra, and
see ROSE, Vincent, & His Orchestra

RIZZO, Vincent, & His Hotel Sylvania Orchestra Of Philadelphia

DO-DO-DO / CLAP YO' HANDS........... *Okeh 40725* 4-6 27

JUST LEAVE ME ALONE (THAT'S ALL I ASK OF YOU) / SPAIN.............................. *Okeh 40130* 2-4 24

NIGHTINGALE (whistling by Sibyl Sanderson Fagan) / BELIEVE ME .... *Okeh 40135* 2-4 24

THAT SOOTHING MELODY / GIGOLETTE .... *Okeh 40356* 2-4 25
(whistling by Sibyl Sanderson Fagan.)

VALENCIA / MY CASTLE IN SPAIN...... *Okeh 40609* 2-4 26

ROANE, Kenneth:

see HAITIAN ORCHESTRA, The

ROANE'S PENNSYLVANIANS

Directed by Carl Gross. Roane's Pennsylvanians was a fine, swinging band, years before the word "swing" was coined in regard to dance music. Little information has been available about this orchestra or its members, but these pictures and the following have been furnished by William Picher, whose father was with the band. Frank Picher played trumpet, was an arranger and sang the melody lines in some of the ensemble vocals with Roane's Pennsylvanians. Picher also played with other bands, including Leo Hannon and His Musical Bell Hops, and served as copyist/arranger for AFM Local 9 in Boston. Frank Picher also began playing piano and organ, which he played with various bands, in addition to trumpet. In the late 1930's Picher began playing organ in roller-skating rinks in Massachusetts, which provided a steady income and eliminated the necessity of traveling with a band, so that he could be at home with his family. In the late 1940s he recorded for the Dance-Tone label. In later years, though still occasionally playing on weekends, Picher retired in his home state of Maine, and died there 4/24/83.

IS I IN LOVE? I IS / GOODBYE BLUES... *Victor 24036* 5-8 32
(Vocals: Snowball & Cliff Nazarro)

(WE'VE GOT TO) PUT THAT SUN BACK IN THE SKY (Vocals: chorus) / BETWEEN THE DEVIL AND THE DEEP BLUE SEA (Vocals: Bobby Roberts, Snowball, & chorus)..................... *Victor 22922* 5-8 32

WHEN YOU AND I WERE YOUNG, MAGGIE (Vocals: chorus) / CHINATOWN, MY CHINATOWN (Vocal: Bobby Roberts) .... *Victor 22919* 5-8 32

ROBBINS, Sam, & His Hotel McAlpin Orchestra

DON'T LET IT BOTHER YOU / A NEEDLE IN A HAYSTACK................. *Bluebird B-5630* 3-5 34
(Vocals: Sam Robbins)

I'M LONESOME FOR YOU, CAROLINE (Vocals: orchestra) / THE DRUNKARD SONG (Vocal: Sam Robbins) .... *Bluebird B-5644* 5-8 34

INKA DINKA DOO / CINDERELLA'S FELLA........... *Bluebird B-5276* 4-6 34
(Vocals: Sam Robbins)

INKA DINKA DOO / CINDERELLA'S FELLA........... *Electradisk 2150* 12-15 34
(Vocals: Sam Robbins)

INKA DINKA DOO / CINDERELLA'S FELLA............ *Sunrise S-3357* 12-15 34
(Vocals: Sam Robbins)
(Simultaneously released on three labels)

I RAISED MY HAT / MY OLD MAN... *Bluebird B-5267* 3-5 34
(Vocals: Sam Robbins)

I RAISED MY HAT / MY OLD MAN .... *Electradisk 2142* 10-12 34
(Vocals: Sam Robbins)

I RAISED MY HAT / MY OLD MAN... *Sunrise S-3348* 10-12 34
(Vocals: Sam Robbins)
(Simultaneously released on three labels)

IS I GOTTA GO TO SCHOOL, MA? (Vocals: June Joy & Sam Robbins) / A BOWL OF CHOP SUEY AND YOU-EY (Vocal: Sam Robbins).................. *Bluebird B-5480* 4-6 34

I'VE GOT A WARM SPOT IN MY HEART FOR YOU / HAVING YOU IS HEAVEN......... *Bluebird B-5479* 3-5 34
(Vocals: Sydney Schiff)

MISTER MAGICIAN (WON'T YOU BRING MY BABY BACK TO ME?) / IN OTHER WORDS, WE'RE THROUGH .... *Bluebird B-5353* 3-5 34
(Vocals: Sam Robbins)

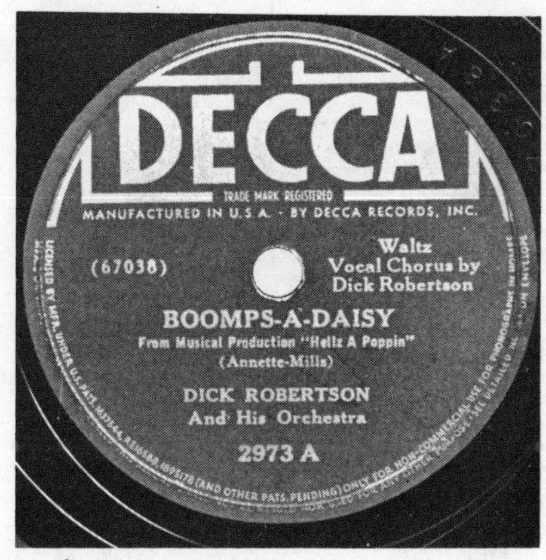

OLD SPINNING WHEEL, THE (Vocal: Sydney Schiff) / SITTIN' ON A LOG (PETTIN' MY DOG)
(Vocal: Sam Robbins)........ *Bluebird B-5268* 3-5 34

OLD SPINNING WHEEL, THE (Vocal: Sydney Schiff) / SITTIN' ON A LOG (PETTIN' MY DOG)
(Vocal: Sam Robbins)........ *Electradisk 2143* 10-12 34

OLD SPINNING WHEEL, THE (Vocal: Sydney Schiff) / SITTIN' ON A LOG (PETTIN' MY DOG)
(Vocal: Sam Robbins)........ *Sunrise S-3349* 10-12 34
(Simultaneously released on three labels)

OUT IN THE COLD AGAIN (Vocal: Roland Jessop) / IT'S ALL FORGOTTEN NOW
(Vocal: Sydney Schiff)........ *Bluebird B-5641* 4-6 34

THIS LITTLE PIGGIE WENT TO MARKET / A DAY WITHOUT YOU........ *Bluebird B-5351* 4-6 34
(Vocals: Sam Robbins)

WONDER BAR / WAGON WHEELS.... *Bluebird B-5352* 3-5 34
(Vocals: Sydney Schiff)

YOU OUGHT TO BE ARRESTED (Vocal: June Joy) / THE LIGHTS ARE LOW
(Vocal: Sydney Schiff)........ *Bluebird B-5638* 4-6 34

ROBERTSON, Dick, & His Orchestra

(Dick Robertson: 7/3/03 – 1979)

AIN'T YOU ASHAMED? / LITTLE GIRL... *Decca 3124* 2-4 40
(Vocals: Dick Robertson)

ALL ALONE / ROW, ROW, ROW........ *Decca 3031* 2-4 40
(Vocals: Dick Robertson)

ALONE / IF I SHOULD LOSE YOU... *Champion 40088* 5-8 36
(Vocals: Dick Robertson)

ARE YOU HAVIN' ANY FUN? / COMES LOVE........ *Decca 2827* 2-4 39
(Vocals: Dick Robertson)

BE HONEST WITH ME / GOODBYE, DEAR, I'LL BE BACK IN A YEAR........ *Decca 3791* 2-4 41
(Vocals: Dick Robertson)

BOB WHITE (WHATCHA GONNA SWING TONIGHT?) / YOU STARTED SOMETHING........ *Decca 1620* 3-5 38
(Vocals: Dick Robertson)

BOOMPS-A-DAISY / PLAYMATES........ *Decca 2973* 2-4 40
(Vocals: Dick Robertson)

BUT WHERE ARE YOU? / I'M PUTTING ALL MY EGGS IN ONE BASKET........ *Champion 40092* 5-8 36
(Vocals: Dick Robertson)

BUY AMERICAN! / IF I EVER GET A JOB AGAIN........ *Crown 3438* 5-8 33
(Vocals: Dick Robertson)

CHINESE LAUNDRY BLUES (MR. WU) / FERDINAND THE BULL........ *Decca 1847* 4-6 38
(Vocals: Dick Robertson)

CHING / ISABELLA KISSED A FELLA.... *Decca 4365* 2-4 42
(Vocals: Dick Robertson & The Three Larks)

CRY, BABY, CRY / OH! MA-MA!........ *Decca 1726* 2-4 38
(Vocals: Dick Robertson)

DROP A NICKEL IN THE SLOT / YOU WENT TO MY HEAD........ *Decca 1706* 2-4 38
(Vocals: Dick Robertson)

EADIE WAS A LADY / I PLAYED THE FIDDLE FOR THE CZAR........ *Crown 3427* 4-6 33
(Vocals: Dick Robertson)

EXTRA! / WHAT'S GOOD FOR THE GOOSE........ *Bluebird B-5369* 3-5 34
(Vocals: Dick Robertson)

EXTRA! / WHAT'S GOOD FOR THE GOOSE........ *Sunrise S-3450* 10-12 34
(Vocals: Dick Robertson)
(Simultaneously released on two labels)

FERRYBOAT SERENADE / ON A SIMMERY SUMMERY DAY........ *Decca 3305* 2-4 40
(Vocals: Dick Robertson)

GLORY OF LOVE, THE / BLAZIN' THE TRAIL........ *Champion 40116* 4-6 36
(Vocals: Dick Robertson)

GOODBYE, LITTLE DARLIN', GOODBYE / I'LL NEVER SMILE AGAIN........ *Decca 3304* 2-4 40
(Vocals: Dick Robertson)

GOOD MORNIN' / THE MERRY-GO-ROUND BROKE DOWN........ *Decca 1334* 4-6 37
(Vocals: Dick Robertson)

GOODNIGHT, ANGEL / LET'S SAIL TO DREAMLAND........ *Decca 1707* 3-5 38
(Vocals: Dick Robertson)

GOODNIGHT, MY LOVE / WHEN MY DREAM BOAT COMES HOME........ *Decca 1131* 3-5 37
(Vocals: Dick Robertson)

GUY NEEDS A GAL, THE / THE GANG THAT SANG "HEART OF MY HEART"........ *Decca 3189* 2-4 40
(Vocals: Dick Robertson)

HAPPY DAYS ARE HERE AGAIN / WHILE WE DANCED AT THE MARDI GRAS........ *Decca 1125* 3-5 37
(Vocals: Dick Robertson0)

HELLO! LITTLE GIRL OF MY DREAMS / IT'S A MIGHTY PRETTY NIGHT FOR LOVE.... *Decca 3410* 2-4 40
(Vocals: Dick Robertson)

HILLS OF OLD WYOMIN' / IS IT TRUE WHAT THEY SAY ABOUT DIXIE?........ *Champion 40105* 5-8 36
(Vocals: Dick Robertson)

HI YO, SILVER! (Vocals: Dick Robertson & The Men About Town) / WHEN MOTHER NATURE SINGS HER LULLABY (Vocal: Dick Robertson).... *Decca 1914* 3-5 38

HO HUM! / MOONLIGHT SAVING TIME........ *Melotone M-12162* 5-8 31
(Vocals: Dick Robertson)

HOLDING MY HONEY'S HAND / THERE'S OCEANS OF LOVE BY THE BEAUTIFUL SEA........ *Melotone M-12408* 5-8 32
(Vocals: Dick Robertson)

HOUSE ON THE HILL, THE / SAIL ALONG, SILV'RY MOON........ *Decca 1599* 3-5 38
(Vocals: Dick Robertson)

I CRIED FOR YOU / GARDENIAS........ *Decca 2260* 2-4 38
(Vocals: Dick Robertson)

IF I COULD BE WITH YOU ONE HOUR TONIGHT / I WANT A GIRL JUST LIKE THE GIRL THAT MARRIED DEAR OLD DAD........ *Decca 3141* 2-4 40
(Vocals: Dick Robertson)

IF I HAVE TO GO ON WITHOUT YOU / CAN'T YOU SEE?........ *Melotone M-12266* 3-5 31
(Vocals: Dick Robertson)

I'LL BET YOU TELL THAT TO ALL THE GIRLS / ON THE BEACH AT BALI BALI... *Champion 40118* 5-8 36
(Vocals: Dick Robertson)

I'M ALONE BECAUSE I LOVE YOU / I DON'T WANT TO SET THE WORLD ON FIRE........ *Decca 3981* 2-4 41
(Vocals: Dick Robertson)

I'M A LUCKY DEVIL (TO FIND AN ANGEL LIKE YOU) / I'M BUILDING A SAILBOAT OF DREAMS........ *Decca 2364* 2-4 39
(Vocals: Dick Robertson)

I MAY STAY AWAY A LITTLE LONGER / GOODBYE MAMA (I'M OFF TO YOKOHAMA)........ *Decca 4116* 3-5 42
(Vocals: Dick Robertson & The American Four)

I'M IN LOVE WITH THE GIRL I LEFT BEHIND ME / KEEP 'EM FLYING........ *Decca 4283* 3-5 42
(Vocals: Dick Robertson)

I'M JUST A DANCING SWEETHEART / THE KISS THAT YOU'VE FORGOTTEN...... *Melotone M-12226* 3-5 31
(Vocals: Dick Robertson)

IN A SHANTY IN OLD SHANTY TOWN / I WONDER WHO'S KISSING HER NOW?........ *Decca 1512* 3-5 37
(Vocals: Dick Robertson)

IN MY MERRY OLDSMOBILE / DAISY BELL; LITTLE ANNIE ROONEY........ *Decca 1511* 3-5 37
(Vocals: Dick Robertson)

IT'S A SIN TO TELL A LIE / THE TOUCH OF YOUR LIPS....... *Champion 40106* 5-8 36
(Vocals: Dick Robertson)

JUST A LITTLE BIT SOUTH OF NORTH CAROLINA / G'BYE NOW........ *Decca 3792* 2-4 41
(Vocals: Dick Robertson)

KISSABLE BABY / I'M HAPPY WHEN YOU'RE JEALOUS........ *Melotone M-12267* 3-5 31
(Vocals: Dick Robertson)

LET'S FACE THE MUSIC AND DANCE / I'D RATHER LEAD A BAND........ *Champion 40093* 5-8 36
(Vocals: Dick Robertson)

LIGHTS OUT / A LITTLE RENDEZVOUS IN HONOLULU.... *Champion 40087* 5-8 36
(Vocals: Dick Robertson)

LILACS IN THE RAIN / OH! JOHNNY, OH! JOHNNY, OH!........ *Decca 2845* 2-4 39
(Vocals: Dick Robertson)

LITTLE LESS MOONLIGHT, A / WHAT IS IT?........ *Melotone M-12229* 3-5 31
(Vocals: Dick Robertson)

LITTLE OLD LADY / TOO MARVELOUS FOR WORDS........ *Decca 1209* 3-5 37
(Vocals: Dick Robertson)

LITTLE SKIPPER / IT MAKES NO DIFFERENCE NOW........ *Decca 2419* 2-4 39
(Vocals: Dick Robertson)

LOST / WELCOME STRANGER...... *Champion 40104* 5-8 36
(Vocals: Dick Robertson)

LOVELY LADY / WITH ALL MY HEART........ *Champion 40078* 5-8 35
(Vocals: Dick Robertson)

MAYBE / AIN'T CHA COMIN' OUT?....... *Decca 2541* 2-4 39
(Vocals: Dick Robertson)

MAY I HAVE THE NEXT ROMANCE WITH YOU? / MARIE........ *Decca 1169* 4-6 37
(Vocals: Dick Robertson)

MEMORIES / YOU'RE THE VERY LAST WORD IN LOVE........ *Decca 2146* 2-4 38
(Vocals: Dick Robertson)

MICKEY / CONNIE'S GOT CONNECTIONS IN CONNECTICUT..... *Decca 3462* 2-4 40
(Vocals: Dick Robertson)

MILLER'S DAUGHTER MARIANNE, THE / GONE WITH THE WIND........ *Decca 1335* 4-6 37
(Vocals: Dick Robertson)

MINNIE THE MOOCHER / KICKIN' THE GONG AROUND........ *Crown 3306* 5-8 32
(Vocals: Dick Robertson)

MOON OVER MIAMI / CLING TO ME... *Champion 40077* 5-8 36
(Vocals: Dick Robertson)

MY CABIN OF DREAMS / HEAVEN HELP THIS HEART OF MINE........ *Decca 1374* 4-6 37
(Vocals: Dick Robertson)

MY GAL SAL / TAKE ME OUT TO THE BALL GAME........ *Decca 1735* 2-4 38
(Vocals: Dick Robertson)

MY LITTLE BUCKEROO / SEPTEMBER IN THE RAIN........ *Decca 1215* 5-8 37
(Vocals: Dick Robertson)

MY MELANCHOLY BABY / KERMIT THE HERMIT........ *Decca 2276* 2-4 39
(Vocals: Dick Robertson)

NO WONDER / INDIANA MOONLIGHT... *Decca 2022* 2-4 38
(Vocals: Dick Robertson)

OH! HOW I HATE TO GET UP IN THE MORNING / OH, THEY'RE MAKING ME ALL OVER IN THE ARMY........ *Decca 3558* 3-5 41
(Vocals: Dick Robertson)

ONE FOR ALL – ALL FOR ONE / I PAID MY INCOME TAX TODAY........ *Decca 4151* 3-5 42
(Vocals: Dick Robertson & The American Four)

PUT YOUR LITTLE FOOT RIGHT OUT / AS 'ROUND AND 'ROUND WE GO........ *Decca 2926* 2-4 40
(Vocals: Dick Robertson)

REMEMBER PEARL HARBOR / YOU'RE A SAP, MISTER JAP........ *Decca 4144* 3-5 42
(Vocals: Dick Robertson & The American Four)

ROLLIN' PLAINS / I WANT YOU FOR CHRISTMAS........ *Decca 1498* 3-5 37
(Vocals: Dick Robertson)

ROSES IN DECEMBER / GETTING SOME FUN OUT OF LIFE........ *Decca 1487* 3-5 37
(Vocals: Dick Robertson)

SAN ANTONIO ROSE / I USED TO LOVE YOU (BUT IT'S ALL OVER NOW)........ *Decca 3559* 2-4 41
(Vocals: Dick Robertson)

SHE DON'T WANNA / ONE DOZEN ROSES........ *Decca 4294* 2-4 42
(Vocals: Dick Robertson)

SHE HAD TO GO AND LOSE IT AT THE ASTOR / MA (HE'S MAKING EYES AT ME)........ *Decca 2920* 3-5 40
(Vocals: Dick Robertson)

SHE SHALL HAVE MUSIC / A WALTZ WAS BORN IN VIENNA........ *Champion 40117* 4-6 36
(Vocals: Dick Robertson)

SIDEWALKS OF NEW YORK / COME, JOSEPHINE, IN MY FLYING MACHINE........ *Decca 1436* 4-6 37
(Vocals: Dick Robertson)

SOMEBODY STOLE MY GAL / BLUES MY NAUGHTY SWEETIE GIVES TO ME........ *Decca 3669* 2-4 41
(Vocals: Dick Robertson)

SOMEBODY TOLD ME THEY LOVED ME / HELLO, MISTER KRINGLE........ *Decca 2828* 2-4 39
(Vocals: Dick Robertson)

SWEET ROSIE O'GRADY / IN THE GOOD OLD SUMMER TIME........ *Decca 1758* 2-4 38
(Vocals: Dick Robertson)

SWINGY LITTLE THINGY / IT'S THE TALK OF THE TOWN........ *Bluebird B-5153* 3-5 33
(Vocals: Dick Robertson)

SWINGY LITTLE THINGY / IT'S THE TALK OF THE TOWN........ *Electradisk 2052* 10-12 33
(Vocals: Dick Robertson)

SWINGY LITTLE THINGY / IT'S THE TALK OF THE TOWN........ *Sunrise S-3234* 10-12 33
(Vocals: Dick Robertson)
(Simultaneously released on three labels)

TEACHER'S PET / DUST........ *Decca 1823* 2-4 38
(Vocals: Dick Robertson)

TEN PRETTY GIRLS / IN A LITTLE WHITE LIGHTHOUSE........ *Decca 1585* 4-6 38
(Vocals: Dick Robertson)

THAT OLD GANG OF MINE / WON'T YOU COME OVER TO MY HOUSE?........ *Decca 1536* 3-5 37
(Vocals: Dick Robertson)

THAT'S HOW I NEED YOU / OH! HOW I MISS YOU TONIGHT........ *Decca 1952* 2-4 38
(Vocals: Dick Robertson)

THIS TIME / HATS OFF TO MacARTHUR (AND OUR BOYS DOWN THERE)........ *Decca 4318* 3-5 42
(Vocals: Dick Robertson)

THREE O'CLOCK IN THE MORNING / THE WALTZ YOU SAVED FOR ME........ *Decca 1099* 3-5 37
(Vocals: Dick Robertson)

TIE A LITTLE STRING AROUND YOUR FINGER / WOULD YOU LIKE TO TAKE A WALK?........ *Melotone M-12082* 5-8 31
(Vocals: Dick Robertson)

TWENTY-ONE DOLLARS A DAY – ONCE A MONTH (Vocals: Dick Robertson & The Norsemen) / ANSWER TO YOU ARE MY SUNSHINE
(Vocal: Dick Robertson)........ *Decca 3908* 3-5 41

TWENTY-ONE YEARS / I HATE TO LOSE YOU........ *Decca 4233* 2-4 42
(Vocals: Dick Robertson)

TWO LITTLE GIRLS IN BLUE / I WONDER WHAT'S BECOME OF SALLY?........ *Decca 1675* 2-4 38
(Vocals: Dick Robertson)

WALKING THE FLOOR OVER YOU / ON THE STREET OF REGRET .... *Decca 4189* 2-4 42
(Vocals: Dick Robertson)

WEDDING BELLS (ARE BREAKING UP THAT OLD GANG OF MINE) / TILL WE MEET AGAIN .... *Decca 4031* 2-4 41
(Vocals: Dick Robertson)

WE DID IT BEFORE (AND WE CAN DO IT AGAIN) / EVERYONE'S A FIGHTING SON OF THAT OLD GANG OF MINE .... *Decca 4117* 3-5 41
(Vocals: Dick Robertson & The American Four)

WEST BOUND FREIGHT (Vocal: Dick Robertson) / GOT THE SOUTH IN MY SOUL
(by Don Redman & His Orchestra as Earl Harlan & His Orchestra; Vocal: Harlan Lattimore) .... *Melotone M-12417* 5-8 32

WHAT'S THE GOOD OF MOONLIGHT (WHEN YOU HAVEN'T GOT A GIRL TO LOVE?) / GOT A LETTER FROM MY KID TODAY .... *Decca 3961* 2-4 41
(Vocals: Dick Robertson)

WHEN I GET YOU ALONE TONIGHT / BREAKING MY HEART TO KEEP AWAY FROM YOU.... *Decca 3349* 2-4 40
(Vocals: Dick Robertson)

WHEN THE POPPIES BLOOM AGAIN / WANTED .... *Decca 1181* 4-6 37
(Vocals: Dick Robertson)

WHEN YOUR OLD WEDDING RING WAS NEW / I HAD SOMEONE ELSE BEFORE I HAD YOU (AND I'LL HAVE SOMEONE AFTER YOU'VE GONE) .... *Decca 4129* 2-4 42
(Vocals: Dick Roberts)

WHERE DO YOU WORK-A, JOHN? / PIPPINELLA .... *Decca 2497* 2-4 39
(Vocals: Dick Robertson)

WHO DID YOU MEET LAST NIGHT? / I ONLY WANT A BUDDY – NOT A SWEETHEART .... *Decca 2807* 2-4 39
(Vocals: Dick Robertson)

WINGS OVER THE NAVY / EYES OF THE FLEET .... *Decca 4308* 3-5 42
(Vocals: Dick Robertson & The American Four)

WISE OLD OWL, THE / SIDEWALK SERENADE .... *Decca 3659* 2-4 41
(Vocals: Dick Robertson)

WRECK OF THE OLD 97 / I WISH I HAD DIED IN MY CRADLE (BEFORE I GREW UP TO LOVE YOU) .... *Decca 3125* 2-4 40
(Vocals: Dick Robertson)

YOU CAN'T STOP ME FROM DREAMING / BLOSSOMS ON BROADWAY .... *Decca 1415* 3-5 37
(Vocals: Dick Robertson)

YOU GOTTA BE A FOOTBALL HERO (TO GET ALONG WITH THE BEAUTIFUL GIRLS) / ALL-AMERICAN GIRL .... *Decca 2023* 2-4 38
(Vocals: Dick Robertson)

YOU GOTTA QUIT CHEATIN' ON ME / UNCLE EPH'S GOT THE COON .... *Decca 4330* 3-5 41
(Vocals: Dick Robertson)

YOU'RE A GRAND OLD FLAG / I AM AN AMERICAN .... *Decca 3323* 3-5 40
(Vocals: Dick Robertson & The Century Quartet)

YOU'RE A SWEETHEART / SOMEBODY'S THINKING OF YOU TONIGHT .... *Decca 1619* 2-4 38
(Vocals: Dick Robertson)

YOU'RE THE ONLY STAR (IN MY BLUE HEAVEN) / TUTTI-FRUTTI .... *Decca 2059* 2-4 38
(Vocals: Dick Robertson)

ROBERTSON, Dick, & His Orchestra as The Mad Hatters

IT ISN'T FAIR / LET'S MAKE UP .... *Bluebird B-5151* 3-5 33
(Vocals: Dick Robertson)

IT ISN'T FAIR / LET'S MAKE UP.... *Electradisk 2050* 10-12 33
(Vocals: Dick Robertson)

IT ISN'T FAIR / LET'S MAKE UP ..... *Sunrise S-3232* 10-12 33
(Vocals: Dick Robertson)
(Simultaneously released on three labels)

ROBERTSON, Dick, & His Orchestra as Sonny South & His Collegians

MY OWN / I COULDN'T TELL THEM WHAT TO DO .... *Bluebird B-5152* 3-5 33
(Vocals: Dick Robertson)

MY OWN / I COULDN'T TELL THEM WHAT TO DO .... *Electradisk 2051* 10-12 33
(Vocals: Dick Robertson)

MY OWN / I COULDN'T TELL THEM WHAT TO DO .... *Sunrise S-3233* 10-12 33
(Vocals: Dick Robertson)
(Simultaneously released on three labels)

ROBISON, Carson, as The Carson Robison Orchestra

(Carson Robison: 8/4/90 – 3/24/57)
(While Carson Robison was best known for his performances and compositions in the early country and western field of music, the following releases come within the dance band/jazz category.)

NOTHIN' / LESS THAN THAT .... *Okeh 41389* 8-10 29

ROBISON, Carson, as Carson Robison's Kansas City Jack-Rabbits

STUFF / NONSENSE .... *Victor V-38074* 10-12 29

ROBISON, Carson, as Carson Robison's Madcaps

STUFF / NONSENSE .... *Edison 14085* 10-12 29
(A rare lateral-cut thin Edison disc)

ROBISON, Willard, & His Orchestra

(Willard Robison: 9/18/94 – 6/24/68)

BELOVED / THO' YOU THREW ME DOWN .... *Pathe Actuelle 36789* 3-5 28
(Vocals: Jason Hawkes)

BELOVED / THO' YOU THREW ME DOWN .... *Perfect 14970* 2-4 28
(Vocals: Jason Hawkes)
(Simultaneously released on two labels)

BROADWAY / MANHATTAN MARY .... *Pathe Actuelle 36692* 3-5 27
(Vocals: The Deep River Quartet)

BROADWAY / MANHATTAN MARY .... *Perfect 14873* 2-4 27
(Vocals: The Deep River Quartet)
(Simultaneously released on two labels)

CALLING / TAKE IN THE SUN, HANG OUT THE MOON .... *Pathe Actuelle 36566* 3-5 27
(Vocals: Jack Kaufman as Walter Neff)

CALLING / TAKE IN THE SUN, HANG OUT THE MOON .... *Perfect 14747* 2-4 27
(Vocals: Jack Kaufman as Walter Neff)
(Simultaneously released on two labels)

I FELL HEAD OVER HEELS IN LOVE (Vocal: Vic Hall) / WHEN THE MORNING GLORIES WAKE UP IN THE MORNING (Vocal: Paul Hagen) .... *Pathe Actuelle 36727* 3-5 27

I FELL HEAD OVER HEELS IN LOVE (Vocal: Vic Hall) / WHEN THE MORNING GLORIES WAKE UP IN THE MORNING (Vocal: Paul Hagen) .... *Perfect 14908* 2-4 27
(Simultaneously released on two labels)

IT WON'T BE LONG NOW / FIVE STEP .... *Pathe Actuelle 36706* 3-5 27
(Vocals: The Deep River Quintet)

IT WON'T BE LONG NOW / FIVE STEP .... *Perfect 14887* 2-4 27
(Vocals: The Deep River Quintet)
(Simultaneously released on two labels)

JAPANESE SANDMAN / SMILES... *Pathe Actuelle 36796* 5-8 28
(Vocals: Annette Hanshaw)

JAPANESE SANDMAN / SMILES .... *Perfect 14977* 4-6 28
(Vocals: Annette Hanshaw)
(Simultaneously released on two labels)

LAZY WEATHER (Vocal: Murray John) / LA DOODLE LA DA DA (Vocals: Murray John & trio) ... *Pathe Actuelle 36638* 5-8 27

LAZY WEATHER (Vocal: Murray John) / LA DOODLE LA DA DA (Vocals: Murray John & trio) .... *Perfect 14819* 4-6 27
(Simultaneously released on two labels)

LOTUS LOVE / FLAPPERETTE.... *Pathe Actuelle 36655* 3-5 27

LOTUS LOVE / FLAPPERETTE .... *Perfect 14836* 2-4 27
(Simultaneously released on two labels)

MAN I LOVE, THE (Vocal: Frank Bessinger) / THOU SWELL .... *Pathe Actuelle 36744* 5-8 28

MAN I LOVE, THE (Vocal: Frank Bessinger) / THOU SWELL .... *Perfect 14925* 4-6 28
(Simultaneously released on two labels)

THERE AIN'T NO SWEET MAN THAT'S WORTH THE SALT OF MY TEARS / I LOVE MY OLD-FASHIONED MAN .... *Pathe Actuelle 36782* 5-8 28
(Vocals: Annette Hanshaw)

THERE AIN'T NO SWEET MAN THAT'S WORTH THE SALT OF MY TEARS / I LOVE MY OLD-FASHIONED MAN .... *Perfect 14963* 4-6 28
(Vocals: Annette Hanshaw)
(Simultaneously released on two labels)

WHY DO I LOVE YOU? / I CAN'T HELP LOVIN' DAT MAN .... *Pathe Actuelle 36765* 3-5 28
(Vocals: Joe Wilbur)

WHY DO I LOVE YOU? / I CAN'T HELP LOVIN' DAT MAN .... *Perfect 14946* 2-4 28
(Vocals: Joe Wilbur)
(Simultaneously released on two labels)

ROBISON, Willard, & His Orchestra as The Deep River Orchestra

BLUE RIVER / NEW HAMPSHIRE HIGHWAY .... *Pathe Actuelle 36668* 3-5 27
(Vocals: The Deep River Quintet)

BOARDWALK NIGHTS (Vocal: Bob Christie) / SOLILOQUY .... *Pathe Actuelle 36647* 3-5 27

BOARDWALK NIGHTS (Vocal: Bob Christie) / SOLILOQUY .... *Perfect 14828* 2-4 27
(Simultaneously released on two labels)

EV'RYTHING WE LIKE WE LIKE ALIKE / BLUE SHADOWS .... *Pathe Actuelle 36860* 4-6 28
(Vocals: The Willis – Knight Hawks)

EV'RYTHING WE LIKE WE LIKE ALIKE / BLUE SHADOWS .... *Perfect 15041* 3-5 28
(Vocals: The Willis – Knight Hawks)
(Simultaneously released on two labels)

IN SWEETHEART TIME (Vocal: Arthur Hall) / PALS, JUST PALS (Vocals: The Willis – Knight Hawks) .... *Pathe Actuelle 36882* 3-5 28

IN SWEETHEART TIME (Vocal: Arthur Hall) / PALS, JUST PALS (Vocals: The Willis – Knight Hawks) .... *Perfect 15063* 2-4 28
(Simultaneously released on two labels)

JUST A NIGHT FOR MEDITATION / JUST A LITTLE BIT O' DRIFTWOOD .... *Pathe Actuelle 36799* 3-5 28
(Vocals: John Ryan)

JUST A NIGHT FOR MEDITATION / JUST A LITTLE BIT O' DRIFTWOOD .... *Perfect 14980* 2-4 28
(Vocals: John Ryan)
(Simultaneously released on two labels)

MUSIC OF A MOUNTAIN STREAM / TAMPICO .... *Pathe Actuelle 36574* 4-6 27

MUSIC OF A MOUNTAIN STREAM / TAMPICO .... *Perfect 14755* 3-5 27
(Simultaneously released on two labels)

MY BLUE HEAVEN / DIANE .... *Pathe Actuelle 36694* 3-5 27
(Vocals: The Deep River Quartet)

MY BLUE HEAVEN / DIANE .... *Perfect 14875* 2-4 27
(Vocals: The Deep River Quartet)
(Simultaneously released on two labels)

OH! SWEET MYSTERY OF LIFE / MOTHER MACHREE .... *Pathe Actuelle 36773* 2-4 28
(Vocals: Billy Jones)

RHAPSODY IN BLUE / RHAPSODY IN BLUE, PART II .... *Pathe Actuelle 36644* 5-8 27

RHAPSODY IN BLUE / RHAPSODY IN BLUE, PART II .... *Perfect 14825* 4-6 27
(Simultaneously released on two labels)

12TH STREET RAG / PECK HORN BLUES .... *Pathe Actuelle 36635* 5-8 27

12TH STREET RAG / PECK HORN BLUES .... *Perfect 14816* 4-6 27
(Simultaneously released on two labels)

WHEREVER YOU ARE / PLAYGROUND IN THE SKY .... *Pathe Actuelle 36704* 3-5 27

WHEREVER YOU ARE / PLAYGROUND IN THE SKY .... *Perfect 14885* 2-4 27
(Simultaneously released on two labels)

WHERE IN THE WORLD (IS THERE SOMEONE FOR ME?) (Vocal: Paul Hagen) / OLD NAMES OF OLD FLAMES (Vocals: Vic Hall & Ken Christie) .... *Pathe Actuelle 36730* 3-5 27

WHERE IN THE WORLD (IS THERE SOMEONE FOR ME?) (Vocal: Paul Hagen) / OLD NAMES OF OLD FLAMES (Vocals: Vic Hall & Ken Christie) .... *Perfect 14911* 2-4 27
(Simultaneously released on two labels)

ROCKAWAY RAMBLERS, The:

see CALIFORNIA RAMBLERS, The

ROCK, Tom, & His Orchestra:

see RESER, Harry, & His Orchestra, and see RICH, Fred, & His Orchestra

RODEMICH, Gene, & His Orchestra

ARKANSAS MULE, THE / SOMEHOW (I'M ALWAYS TO BLAME) .... *Brunswick 2550* 3-5 24

BAMBOO BAY / BROKEN-HEARTED BLUES .... *Brunswick 2290* 3-5 22

BLUE GRASS BLUES / YOU DARLING YOU .... *Brunswick 2527* 3-5 24

BY THE PYRAMIDS / RIGHT OR WRONG .... *Brunswick 2183* 3-5 21

CHOO-CHOO (GOTTA HURRY HOME) / LONELY AND BLUE .... *Brunswick 2775* 3-5 25

DREARY WEATHER / DEAR ONE... *Brunswick 2756* 3-5 24
(Vocals: Frank Sylvano)

EVERYBODY LOVES MY BABY / WHEN I THINK OF YOU .... *Brunswick 2843* 3-5 25

FANCIES / GYPSY BLUES .... *Brunswick 2152* 3-5 21

HOT NOTES / I'M LONELY WITHOUT YOU .... *Brunswick 3073* 3-5 26

HOW COME YOU DO ME LIKE YOU DO? / ONE STOLEN KISS .... *Brunswick 2824* 3-5 25

ISN'T SHE THE SWEETEST THING? / GOT NO TIME .... *Brunswick 2892* 2-4 25

JUST LIKE A RAINBOW / CRY BABY BLUES .... *Brunswick 2159* 3-5 21

JUST SNAP YOUR FINGERS AT CARE / CASTLE OF DREAMS .... *Brunswick 2059* 2-4 21

MARGIE / HOME AGAIN BLUES ..... *Brunswick 2060* 3-5 21

MOBILE BLUES / TENTH INTERVAL RAG .... *Brunswick 2599* 4-6 24

ON THE ISLE OF WICKI-WACKI-WOO / OH SISTER AIN'T THAT HOT? .... *Brunswick 2474* 3-5 23

PATCHES / SWANEE .... *Brunswick 2026* 2-4 19

ROSE OF SUNNY ITALY / ST. LOUIS TICKLE .... *Brunswick 2480* 3-5 23

SCISSOR GRINDER JOE / WOND'RING BLUES (MILLER BLUES) .... *Brunswick 2663* 3-5 24

SHANGHAI SHUFFLE / HONOLULU (Vocal: Frank Sylvano) .... *Brunswick 2760* 2-4 24

SHE WOULDN'T DO WHAT I ASKED HER TO / WHO WILL IT BE? .... *Brunswick 2556* 2-4 24

SNOWFLAKE / APRIL SHOWERS.... *Brunswick 2169* 2-4 21

ST. LOUIS GAL / JUST ONE MORE KISS .... *Brunswick 2558* 2-4 24

TEDDY BEAR BLUES / FATE .... *Brunswick 2379* 2-4 23

THAT'S GEORGIA / WORRYIN' BLUES .... *Brunswick 2731* 3-5 24

THREE LITTLE WORDS / FLOWER OF ARABY .... *Brunswick 2381* 2-4 23

TIA JUANA / JUST A FUNNY LITTLE TUNE .... *Brunswick 2680* 2-4 24

TREASURE ISLAND / JUNE .... *Brunswick 2064* 2-4 21

WOLVERINE BLUES / WHEN JUNE COMES ALONG WITH A SONG .... *Brunswick 2455* 3-5 23

YOU'RE SO NEAR AND YET SO FAR / I HAD SOMEONE ELSE BEFORE I HAD YOU .... *Brunswick 2867* 2-4 25

ROGERS, Richard, & His Orchestra
(Richard Rodgers: 6/28/02 – 12/30/79)

FALLING IN LOVE WITH LOVE; LOVER (Vocal: Lee Sullivan) / THERE'S A SMALL HOTEL; IT'S GOT TO BE LOVE (Vocals: Deane Janis & Lee Sullivan) ... *Columbia 35382* 3-5 40

MY HEART STOOD STILL; THOU SWELL (Vocal: Lee Sullivan) / DO I HEAR YOU SAYING "I LOVE YOU?"; YOU TOOK ADVANTAGE OF ME (Vocal: Deane Janis) ... *Columbia 35379* 3-5 40

THIS CAN'T BE LOVE; SING FOR YOUR SUPPER (Vocal: Deane Janis) / WITH A SONG IN MY HEART; YOURS SINCERELY (Vocal: Lee Sullivan) ... *Columbia 35381* 3-5 40

WHERE OR WHEN; JOHNNY ONE NOTE (Vocal: Lee Sullivan) / THE GIRL FRIEND; THE BLUE ROOM ... *Columbia 35380* 3-5 40

ROEHR, Alvin, as Alvin Roehr's Hotel Alma Orchestra

DON'T BE LIKE THAT / MY OLD GIRL'S MY NEW GIRL NOW ... *Gennett 6696* 4-6 29
(Vocals: Tony Salamack)

JUMPING JACK / HIGH UP ON A HILL TOP (Vocal: Tony Salamack) ... *Gennett 6678* 5-8 28

ROGERS, Buddy, & His California Cavaliers

I BEG YOUR PARDON, MADEMOISELLE / WITH MY SWEETIE IN THE MOONLIGHT ... *Victor 24031* 5-8 32
(Vocals: Buddy Rogers)

IN MY HIDEAWAY (Vocal: Frank Parrish) / HAPPY-GO-LUCKY YOU (AND BROKEN-HEARTED ME) (Vocal: Buddy Rogers) ... *Victor 24015* 5-8 32

PLEASE HANDLE WITH CARE (Vocal: Buddy Rogers) / ASK YOURSELF WHO LOVES YOU (Vocal: Louis Rapp) ... *Victor 24049* 5-8 32

YOU FASCINATE ME / HELLO, GORGEOUS ... *Victor 24001* 5-8 32
(Vocals: Buddy Rogers)

ROGERS, Buddy, & His Famous Swing Band

FIGARO / MEET THE BEAT OF MY HEART ... *Vocalion 4227* 4-6 38
(Vocals: Bob Hannon)

HAPPY AS A LARK (Vocal: Buddy Rogers) / THE SUNNY SIDE OF THINGS (Vocal: Joe Mooney) ... *Vocalion 4240* 5-8 38

LOVELIGHT IN THE STARLIGHT / THIS TIME IT'S REAL ... *Vocalion 4058* 4-6 38
(Vocals: Bob Hannon)

MOONSHINE OVER KENTUCKY (Vocal: Buddy Rogers) / LITTLE LADY MAKE-BELIEVE (Vocal: Bob Hannon) ... *Vocalion 4071* 5-8 38

THIS IS MADNESS (Vocal: Bob Hannon) / RAINBOW 'ROUND THE MOON ... *Vocalion 4422* 5-8 38

YOU CAN'T BE MINE (AND SOMEONE ELSE'S TOO) / WHILE A CIGARETTE WAS BURNING ... *Vocalion 4408* 5-8 38
(Vocals: Elizabeth Tilton)

ROGERS, Buddy, vocals, accompanied by recording groups

ANY TIME'S THE TIME TO FALL IN LOVE / SWEEPIN' THE CLOUDS AWAY ... *Columbia 2143-D* 8-10 30
(Vocals: Buddy Rogers)

I'D LIKE TO BE A BEE IN YOUR BOUDOIR / MY FUTURE JUST PASSED ... *Columbia 2183-D* 8-10 30
(Vocals: Buddy Rogers)

ROGERS, Dick, & His Orchestra

DIXIE GIRL / TWENTY-ONE DOLLARS A DAY – ONCE A MONTH (Vocals: Dick Rogers, Dale Jones & chorus) ... *Okeh 6393* 4-6 41

IF I COULD ONLY PLAY A CONCERTINA (Vocals: chorus) / MY FOOLISH HEART AND I (Vocal: Bobbi Engel) ... *Okeh 6441* 3-5 41

ROGERS, Mack, & His Gunter Hotel Orchestra

AFTER ALL / SPANISH BUTTERFLY ... *Bluebird B-5830* 4-6 35
(Vocals: Paul White)

BABY, WON'T YOU PLEASE COME HOME? (Vocal: Sibyl Hopkins) / HERE COMES THE SHOW BOAT ... *Bluebird B-5835* 5-8 35

BETTER FOR BOTH OF US / SAY IT ... *Bluebird B-5601* 4-6 34
(Vocals: Paul White)

IN THE SHADE OF THE OLD APPLE TREE / CASA LOMA STOMP ... *Bluebird B-5603* 5-8 34

WORDS ARE IN MY HEART, THE / I'M GOIN' SHOPPIN' WITH YOU ... *Bluebird B-5829* 4-6 35
(Vocals: Paul White)

ROGERS, Walter B. as Walter B. Rogers Band
also see VICTOR MILITARY BAND, The,
directed by Walter B. Rogers
(Paroquette records are rare)

ALABAMA SLIDE / BEAUTIFUL EYES ... *Paroquette 43* 20-25 16

BANANA PEEL RAG / HONEYSUCKLE ... *Paroquette 95* 20-25 17

BLUE GOOSE RAG / TAR BABIES RAG ... *Paroquette 72* 20-25 17

HAWAIIAN BLUES / LOG CABIN RAG ... *Paroquette 71* 20-25 17

IN THE SWEET LONG AGO / BLUSH ROSES ... *Paroquette 41* 15-20 16

JOE TURNER BLUES / SOUTHERN LAND ... *Paroquette 105* 25-30 17

JUST ONE DAY / UNISON BLUES ... *Paroquette 37* 20-25 16

MIGHTY LAK' A ROSE / MY HAWAIIAN SUNSHINE ... *Paroquette 39* 15-20 16

MISS SPRINGTIME / BACK TO TEXAS ... *Paroquette 86* 20-25 17

ON THE SOUTH SEA ISLE / THE BOAT TO DIXIE ... *Paroquette 36* 20-25 16

PLAY BALL / CABARET SPORTS ... *Paroquette 87* 20-25 17

SHADES OF NIGHT / HOP SING (A LAUNDRY RAG) ... *Paroquette 44* 20-25 16

TEASING THE CAT / UNDER EGYPTIAN SKIES ... *Paroquette 38* 20-25 16

ROLFE, B. A., & His Concert Orchestra
(B. A. Rolfe: 10/24/78 – 4/23/56)

MY LADY'S BOUDOIR – SUITE / THE MERRY WIDOW SELECTIONS: OH! PROMISE ME – ROBIN HOOD; THE CHOCOLATE SOLDIER SELECTIONS (by B. A. Rolfe & His Palais D'Or Orchestra) ... *Edison 10008* 50-60 27
(This is a long-play disc released in 1927 which required a special attachment on the Edison phonograph. These records played at 80 rpm, as do the standard Edison discs, but with the use of microgrooves, the 10-inch records contained 24 minutes of music. There were also 12-inch long-play discs which played for 40 minutes. The microgrooves, 450 to the inch, are so fine that they are barely visible to the naked eye. In comparison, the standard Edison discs have 150 grooves per inch, and modern LPs contain an average of 250 grooves to the inch. The records were not commercially successful and were withdrawn after a few months, which accounts for their extreme rarity.)

ROLFE, B. A., & His Lucky Strike Dance Orchestra

BIRMINGHAM BERTHA / AM I BLUE? ... *Edison 52604* 5-8 29
(Vocals: Vaughn de Leath)

FLIPPITY FLOP, THE / TRUE BLUE LOU ... *Edison 14033* 10-12 29
(A rare lateral-cut thin Edison disc.)

HELLO MARGOT! / WON'T YOU GIVE IN? ... *Edison 14068* 10-12 29
(Vocals: by trio)
(A rare lateral-cut thin Edison disc.)

HELLO SWEETIE / DANCE OF THE PAPER DOLLS ... *Edison 52548* 4-6 29

IF I HAD YOU / FIORETTA ... *Edison 52531* 4-6 29

LIZA (ALL THE CLOUDS'LL ROLL AWAY) / DO WHAT YOU DO! ... *Edison 14049* 12-15 29
(Vocals: J. Donald Parker)
(A rare lateral-cut thin Edison disc.)

POLLY PRIMROSE / WOULDN'T IT BE WONDERFUL? ... *Edison 14059* 10-12 29
(A rare lateral-cut thin Edison disc.)

SINGIN' IN THE RAIN (Vocal: Walter Scanlan) / YOUR MOTHER AND MINE (Vocal: Phil Dewey) ... *Edison 52626* 4-6 29

SORROWS (Vocal: Phil Dewey) / SPANISH DOLL ... *Edison 52597* 4-6 29

WHY CAN'T YOU? / LITTLE PAL ... *Edison 52645* 4-6 29
(Vocals: J. Donald Parker)

ROLFE, B. A., & His Palais D'Or Orchestra

BEAUTIFUL (Vocals: Unknown) / ST. LOUIS BLUES ... *Edison 52295* 12-15 28

BLUE BONNET – YOU MAKE ME FEEL BLUE / GIVE ME TODAY ... *Edison 51761* 4-6 26

BLUE HAWAII / MEAN TO ME ... *Edison 52584* 5-8 29
(Vocals: Unknown)

BLUE NIGHT (Vocals: Theo Alban) / GYPSY ... *Edison 52455* 4-6 29

BUFFALO RHYTHM / ROCKY MOUNTAIN BLUES ... *Edison 52037* 12-15 27

BYE BYE BLACKBIRD / TALKING TO THE MOON ... *Edison 51757* 5-8 26

CAN'T YOU HEAR ME SAY "I LOVE YOU"? / PLAYGROUND IN THE SKY ... *Edison 52130* 5-8 27

CAROLINA MOON / MY ANGELINA ... *Edison 52536* 4-6 29
(Vocals: Theo Alban)

CHOCOLATE SOLDIER / THE MERRY WIDOW ... *Edison 51991* 4-6 27

CRAZY QUILT / I'D RATHER BE THE GIRL IN YOUR ARMS ... *Edison 51790* 4-6 26

DANCE, LITTLE LADY / A ROOM WITH A VIEW ... *Edison 52462* 5-8 29
(Vocals: Theo Alban)

FOR OLD TIMES' SAKE / CHIQUITA (Vocals: The Rollikers) ... *Edison 52346* 4-6 28

I WON'T GO HOME TONIGHT / ONLY YOU AND LONELY ME ... *Edison 51782* 4-6 26

MAKIN' WHOOPEE / I'M BRINGING A RED, RED ROSE ... *Edison 52474* 10-12 29
(Vocals: J. Donald Parker)

ROLFE, B. A. & His Palais D'Or Orchestra

MERRY WIDOW SELECTIONS, THE; OH! PROMISE ME – ROBIN HOOD; THE CHOCOLATE SOLDIER SELECTIONS / MY LADY'S BOUDIOR – SUITE (by B. A. Rolfe & His Concert Orchestra) ... *Edison 10008* 50-60 27
(This is a long-play disc released in 1927 which required a special attachment on the Edison phonograph. These records played at 80 rpm, as do the standard Edison discs, but with the use of microgrooves, the 10-inch records contained 24 minutes of music. There were also 12-inch long-play discs which played for 40 minutes. The microgrooves, 450 to the inch, are so fine that they are barely visible to the naked eye. In comparison, the standard Edison discs have 150 grooves per inch, and modern LPs contain an average of 250 grooves to the inch. The records were not commercially successful and were withdrawn after a few months, which accounts for their extreme rarity.)

MIA BELLA ROSA / LET'S DO IT ... *Edison 52505* 5-8 29
(Vocals: Theo Alban)

MY HEART STOOD STILL / MY RAINBOW (Vocal: Charles Hart) ... *Edison 52210* 5-8 28

ONE SUMMER NIGHT / THERE'S EVERYTHING NICE ABOUT YOU ... *Edison 52002* 5-8 27
(Vocals: J. Donald Parker)

PLAY, GYPSIES – DANCE GYPSIES / THE ONE I'M LOOKING FOR ... *Edison 51817* 4-6 26

RAG DOLL / HIDING IN THE CORNER OF YOUR SMILE (Vocals: The Rollickers) ... *Edison 52268* 4-6 28

SHE DIDN'T SAY "YES", SHE DIDN'T SAY "NO", SHE ONLY SAID "MAYBE" / TWO BLUE EYES ... *Edison 52300* 10-12 28
(Vocals: The Rollickers)

SINGAPORE SORROWS (Vocals: The Rollickers) / AMONG MY SOUVENIRS ... *Edison 52156* 5-8 29

SOME OTHER DAY (Vocal: J. Donald Parker) / THE DOLL DANCE ... *Edison 52013* 5-8 27

THAT'S MY WEAKNESS NOW (Vocal: Jack Kaufman) / JUST LIKE A MELODY OUT OF THE SKY ... *Edison 52343* 10-12 28

TOGETHER / WHAT'LL I DO IF THE MISSISSIPPI GOES DRY? ... *Edison 52261* 10-12 28
(Vocals: Theo Alban)

TOMORROW'S TOMORROW (Vocals: Unknown) / DEEP HOLLOW ... *Edison 52319* 10-12 28

WHAT DOES IT MATTER? (Vocal: Walter Scanlan) / IT'S O.K., KATY, WITH ME (Vocal: Van Buren Clark) ... *Edison 51954* 5-8 27

WHAT GOOD IS GOOD MORNING? / REACHING FOR THE MOON ... *Edison 51750* 4-6 26

WHO WOULDN'T BE BLUE? (Vocals: Unknown) / WHEN SWEET SUSIE GOES STEPPIN' BY ... *Edison 52326* 10-12 28

WHY DO I LOVE YOU? / CAN'T HELP LOVIN' DAT MAN ... *Edison 52223* 10-12 28

ROLLINI, Adrian, & His Orchestra
(Adrian Rollini: 6/28/04 – 5/15/56)

AH, BUT IS IT LOVE? (Vocal: Howard Phillips) / I GOTTA GET UP AND GO TO WORK (Vocal: Red McKenzie) ... *Banner 32826* 5-8 33

AH, BUT IS IT LOVE? (Vocal: Howard Phillips) / I GOTTA GET UP AND GO TO WORK (Vocal: Red McKenzie) ... *Melotone M-12756* 5-8 33

AH, BUT IS IT LOVE? (Vocal: Howard Phillips) / I GOTTA GET UP AND GO TO WORK (Vocal: Red McKenzie) ... *Oriole 2736* 5-8 33

AH, BUT IS IT LOVE? (Vocal: Howard Phillips) / I GOTTA GET UP AND GO TO WORK (Vocal: Red McKenzie) ... *Perfect 15799* 5-8 33

AH, BUT IS IT LOVE? (Vocal: Howard Phillips) / I GOTTA GET UP AND GO TO WORK (Vocal: Red McKenzie) ... *Romeo 2109* 5-8 33
(Simultaneously released on five labels)

BILL / BEI MIR BIST DU SCHOEN (by The Adrian Rollini Quintet; Vocal: Sonny Schuyler) ... *Decca 1638* 3-5 38

BY A WATERFALL / SITTIN' ON A BACK YARD FENCE ... *Banner 32867* 8-10 33
(Vocals: Herb Weil)

BY A WATERFALL / SITTIN' ON A BACK YARD FENCE ... *Domino 139* 8-10 33
(Vocals: Herb Weil)

BY A WATERFALL / SITTIN' ON A BACK YARD FENCE ... *Melotone M-12788* 8-10 33
(Vocals: Herb Weil)

BY A WATERFALL / SITTIN' ON A BACK YARD FENCE ... *Oriole 2757* 8-10 33
(Vocals: Herb Weil)

BY A WATERFALL / SITTIN' ON A BACK YARD FENCE ... *Perfect 15817* 8-10 33
(Vocals: Herb Weil)

BY A WATERFALL / SITTIN' ON A BACK YARD FENCE ... *Romeo 2130* 8-10 33
(Vocals: Herb Weil)
(Simultaneously released on six labels)

DAVENPORT BLUES / SOMEBODY LOVES ME ... *Decca 359* 10-12 34

HAVE YOU EVER BEEN LONELY? / YOU MUST BELIEVE ME ... *Banner 32698* 10-12 33
(Vocals: Dick Robertson)

HAVE YOU EVER BEEN LONELY? / YOU MUST BELIEVE ME ... *Oriole 2651* 10-12 33
(Vocals: Dick Robertson)

HAVE YOU EVER BEEN LONELY? / YOU MUST BELIEVE ME ... *Romeo 2024* 10-12 33
(Vocals: Dick Robertson)
(Simultaneously released on three labels)

HUNDRED YEARS FROM TODAY, A (Vocal: Chick Bullock) / HOW CAN IT BE A BEAUTIFUL DAY? (Vocal: Joey Nash) ... *Vocalion 2675* 8-10 34

IF I HAD SOMEBODY TO LOVE (Vocal: Howard Phillips) / DREAM ON (Vocal: Red McKenzie) ... *Banner 32837* 5-8 33

IF I HAD SOMEBODY TO LOVE (Vocal: Howard Phillips) / DREAM ON (Vocal: Red McKenzie) ... *Melotone M-12766* 5-8 33

IF I HAD SOMEBODY TO LOVE (Vocal: Howard Phillips) / DREAM ON (Vocal: Red McKenzie) ... *Oriole 2743* 5-8 33

IF I HAD SOMEBODY TO LOVE (Vocal: Howard Phillips) / DREAM ON (Vocal: Red McKenzie) ... *Perfect 15805* 5-8 33

IF I HAD SOMEBODY TO LOVE (Vocal: Howard Phillips) / DREAM ON (Vocal: Red McKenzie) ... *Romeo 2116* 5-8 33
(Simultaneously released on five labels)

I'LL BE FAITHFUL / BELOVED ... *Banner 32863* 5-8 33
(Vocals: Herb Weil)

I'LL BE FAITHFUL / BELOVED ... *Domino 141* 5-8 33
(Vocals: Herb Weil)

I'LL BE FAITHFUL / BELOVED ... *Melotone M-12790* 5-8 33
(Vocals: Herb Weil)

I'LL BE FAITHFUL / BELOVED ... *Oriole 2759* 5-8 33
(Vocals: Herb Weil)

I'LL BE FAITHFUL / BELOVED ... *Perfect 15819* 5-8 33
(Vocals: Herb Weil)

I'LL BE FAITHFUL / BELOVED ... *Romeo 2132* 5-8 33
(Vocals: Herb Weil)
(Simultaneously released on six labels)

ON THE WRONG SIDE OF THE FENCE / OL' PAPPY ... *Banner 32949* 8-10 34
(Vocals: Herb Weil)

ON THE WRONG SIDE OF THE FENCE / OL' PAPPY ... *Melotone M-12892* 8-10 34
(Vocals: Herb Weil)

ON THE WRONG SIDE OF THE FENCE / OL' PAPPY ... *Oriole 2828* 8-10 34
(Vocals: Herb Weil)

ON THE WRONG SIDE OF THE FENCE / OL' PAPPY ... *Perfect 15876* 8-10 34
(Vocals: Herb Weil)

ON THE WRONG SIDE OF THE FENCE / OL' PAPPY ... *Romeo 2201* 8-10 34
(Vocals: Herb Weil)
(Simultaneously released on five labels)

SITTIN' ON A LOG (Vocal: June Vance) / I RAISED MY HAT (Vocal: Herb Weil)................ *Banner 32912* 5-8 34

SITTIN' ON A LOG (Vocal: June Vance) / I RAISED MY HAT (Vocal: Herb Weil)............... *Conqueror 8262* 5-8 34

SITTIN' ON A LOG (Vocal: June Vance) / I RAISED MY HAT (Vocal: Herb Weil)............ *Melotone M-12855* 5-8 34

SITTIN' ON A LOG (Vocal: June Vance) / I RAISED MY HAT (Vocal: Herb Weil)................... *Oriole 2803* 5-8 34

SITTIN' ON A LOG (Vocal: June Vance) / I RAISED MY HAT (Vocal: Herb Weil)................. *Perfect 15855* 5-8 34

SITTIN' ON A LOG (Vocal: June Vance) / I RAISED MY HAT (Vocal: Herb Weil)................... *Romeo 2176* 5-8 34
(Simultaneously released on six labels)

SLAP THAT BASS / LET'S CALL THE WHOLE THING OFF.................. *Master 114* 5-8 37

SONG OF SURRENDER / COFFEE IN THE MORNING AND KISSES IN THE NIGHT......... *Banner 32923* 5-8 34
(Vocals: Howard Phillips)

SONG OF SURRENDER / COFFEE IN THE MORNING AND KISSES IN THE NIGHT..... *Melotone M-12866* 5-8 34
(Vocals: Howard Phillips)

SONG OF SURRENDER / COFFEE IN THE MORNING AND KISSES IN THE NIGHT........... *Oriole 2811* 5-8 34
(Vocals: Howard Phillips)

SONG OF SURRENDER / COFFEE IN THE MORNING AND KISSES IN THE NIGHT......... *Perfect 15861* 5-8 34
(Vocals: Howard Phillips)

SONG OF SURRENDER / COFFEE IN THE MORNING AND KISSES IN THE NIGHT.......... *Romeo 2184* 5-8 34
(Vocals: Howard Phillips)
(Simultaneously released on five labels)

SUGAR / RIVERBOAT SHUFFLE.......... *Decca 265* 8-10 34

SWING LOW / STUFF, ETC............... *Decca 807* 5-8 36

TAP ROOM SWING / LESSONS IN LOVE... *Decca 787* 5-8 36

THOUSAND GOODNIGHTS, A / BUTTERFINGERS.................. *Vocalion 2672* 8-10 34
(Vocals: Joey Nash)

WAITIN' AT THE GATE FOR KATY / LITTLE DID I DREAM.............. *Vocalion 2673* 8-10 34
(Vocals: Joey Nash)

WHO WALKS IN WHEN I WALK OUT? (Vocal: Howard Weil) / GOT THE JITTERS (Vocal: Chick Bullock).................. *Banner 32950* 8-10 34

WHO WALKS IN WHEN I WALK OUT? (Vocal: Howard Weil) / GOT THE JITTERS (Vocal: Chick Bullock)............... *Melotone M-12893* 8-10 34

WHO WALKS IN WHEN I WALK OUT? (Vocal: Howard Weil) / GOT THE JITTERS (Vocal: Chick Bullock)..................... *Oriole 2829* 8-10 34

WHO WALKS IN WHEN I WALK OUT? (Vocal: Howard Weil) / GOT THE JITTERS (Vocal: Chick Bullock)................... *Perfect 15877* 8-10 34

WHO WALKS IN WHEN I WALK OUT? (Vocal: Howard Weil) / GOT THE JITTERS (Vocal: Chick Bullock)..................... *Romeo 2202* 8-10 34
(Simultaneously released on five labels)

YOU'VE GOT EVERYTHING / AND SO, GOODBYE................. *Banner 32873* 5-8 33
(Vocals: Herb Weil)

YOU'VE GOT EVERYTHING / AND SO, GOODBYE................ *Conqueror 8249* 5-8 33
(Vocals: Herb Weil)

YOU'VE GOT EVERYTHING / AND SO, GOODBYE............. *Melotone M-12815* 5-8 33
(Vocals: Herb Weil)

YOU'VE GOT EVERYTHING / AND SO, GOODBYE.................... *Oriole 2775* 5-8 33
(Vocals: Herb Weil)

YOU'VE GOT EVERYTHING / AND SO, GOODBYE.................. *Perfect 15831* 5-8 33
(Vocals: Herb Weil)

YOU'VE GOT EVERYTHING / AND SO, GOODBYE.................... *Romeo 2148* 5-8 33
(Vocals: Herb Weil)
(Simultaneously released on six labels)

YOU'VE GOT ME CRYIN' AGAIN / HUSTLIN' AND BUSTLIN' FOR BABY................ *Banner 32699* 10-12 33
(Vocals: Dick Robertson)

YOU'VE GOT ME CRYIN' AGAIN / HUSTLIN' AND BUSTLIN' FOR BABY............ *Melotone M-12630* 10-12 33
(Vocals: Dick Robertson)

YOU'VE GOT ME CRYIN' AGAIN / HUSTLIN' AND BUSTLIN' FOR BABY................. *Oriole 2652* 10-12 33
(Vocals: Dick Robertson)

YOU'VE GOT ME CRYIN' AGAIN / HUSTLIN' AND BUSTLIN' FOR BABY................ *Perfect 15736* 10-12 33
(Vocals: Dick Robertson)

YOU'VE GOT ME CRYIN' AGAIN / HUSTLIN' AND BUSTLIN' FOR BABY................. *Romeo 2025* 10-12 33
(Vocals: Dick Robertson)
(Simultaneously released on five labels)

ROLLINI, Adrian, & his Orchestra as Owen Fallon & His Californians

HAVE YOU EVER BEEN LONELY? / YOU MUST BELIEVE ME........ *Melotone M-12629* 10-12 33
(Vocals: Dick Robertson)

HAVE YOU EVER BEEN LONELY? / YOU MUST BELIEVE ME............. *Perfect 15735* 10-12 33
(Vocals: Dick Robertson)
(Simultaneously released on two labels)

ROLLINI, Adrian, as Adrian & His Orchestra

BLUE PRELUDE / HAPPY AS THE DAY IS LONG............... *Columbia 2785-D* 15-20 33
(Vocals: Howard Phillips)

ROLLINI, Adrian, as Adrian & His Tap Room Gang

BOUNCIN' IN RHYTHM / HONEYSUCKLE ROSE (Vocal: Putney Dandridge).......... *Victor 25208* 5-8 35

GOT A NEED FOR YOU (Vocal: Jeanne Burns) / WEATHER MAN (Vocals: Wingy Manone & Putney Dandridge)..................... *Victor 25072* 5-8 35

NAGASAKI (Vocal: Putney Dandridge) / JAZZ O' JAZZ (Vocal: Jeanne Burns)............... *Victor 25085* 5-8 35

ROLLINI, Adrian, as Adrian's Ramblers

BETTER TO LOVE YOU, MY DEAR, THE (Vocal: Chick Bullock) / I WISH I WERE TWINS (Vocal: Ella Logan)........................ *Brunswick 6889* 8-10 34

I'VE GOT A WARM SPOT IN MY HEART FOR YOU / WHY DON'T YOU PRACTICE WHAT YOU PREACH?................... *Brunswick 6877* 8-10 34
(Vocals: Chick Bullock)

KEEP ON DOIN' WHAT YOU'RE DOIN' / GET GOIN'....................... *Brunswick 6786* 8-10 34
(Vocals: Chick Bullock)

ROLLINI, Adrian, as The Adrian Rollini Quintet

BEI MIR BIST DU SCHOEN (Vocal: Sonny Schuyler) / BILL (by Adrian Rollini & His Orchestra)..... *Decca 1638* 3-5 38

I WISH I HAD YOU / ON THE BUMPY ROAD TO LOVE.................... *Vocalion 4257* 3-5 38
(Vocals: The Tune Twisters)

JOSEPHINE / YOU'RE A SWEETHEART... *Decca 1639* 3-5 38
(Vocals: Sonny Schuyler)

(HOW TO MAKE LOVE IN) TEN EASY LESSONS / SMALL FRY........................ *Vocalion 4212* 3-5 38
(Vocals: The Tune Twisters)

TRUE CONFESSION / I'VE HITCHED MY WAGON TO A STAR.................. *Decca 1654* 3-5 38
(Vocals: Sonny Schuyler)

ROLLINI, Adrian, as The Adrian Rollini Trio

DRIFTIN' / REBOUND.................. *Decca 1157* 3-5 37

ESTRELLITA / DARK EYES........... *Vocalion 5435* 2-4 39

HONKY TONK TRAIN BLUES / MARTHA... *Okeh 5582* 3-5 40

I CAN'T BELIEVE THAT YOU'RE IN LOVE WITH ME; I CAN'T GIVE YOU ANYTHING BUT LOVE / DARDANELLA..................... *Vocalion 5621* 2-4 39

ISLE OF CAPRI / THE GIRL WITH THE LIGHT BLUE HAIR............... *Okeh 5979* 2-4 40

MOONGLOW / PAVANNE............ *Vocalion 5200* 2-4 39

STAR DUST; SOLITUDE / DIGA DIGA DOO.................... *Vocalion 5376* 3-5 39

VIBROLLINI / JITTERS................... *Decca 1132* 3-5 37

ROLLINS, Todd, & His Orchestra

AM I TO BLAME? / DID SHE ASK FOR ME?...................... *Banner 33293* 3-5 35
(Vocals: Chick Bullock)

AM I TO BLAME? / DID SHE ASK FOR ME?.................. *Melotone M-13260* 3-5 35
(Vocals: Chick Bullock)

AM I TO BLAME? / DID SHE ASK FOR ME?......................... *Oriole 3060* 3-5 35
(Vocals: Chick Bullock)

AM I TO BLAME? / DID SHE ASK FOR ME?....................... *Perfect 16048* 3-5 35
(Vocals: Chick Bullock)

AM I TO BLAME? / DID SHE ASK FOR ME?....................... *Romeo 2434* 3-5 35
(Vocals: Chick Bullock)
(Simultaneously released on five labels)

BLUE SKY AVENUE / TALKIN' TO MYSELF.......................... *Banner 33189* 3-5 34
(Vocals: Chick Bullock)

BLUE SKY AVENUE / TALKIN' TO MYSELF....................... *Melotone M-13156* 3-5 34
(Vocals: Chick Bullock)

BLUE SKY AVENUE / TALKIN' TO MYSELF............................. *Oriole 2987* 3-5 34
(Vocals: Chick Bullock)

BLUE SKY AVENUE / TALKIN' TO MYSELF........................... *Perfect 15999* 3-5 34
(Vocals: Chick Bullock)

BLUE SKY AVENUE / TALKIN' TO MYSELF............................ *Romeo 2361* 3-5 34
(Vocals: Chick Bullock)
(Simultaneously released on five labels)

BOOGIE MAN, THE / TAKE A LESSON FROM THE LARK.................. *Banner 33080* 5-8 34
(Vocals: Chick Bullock)

BOOGIE MAN, THE / TAKE A LESSON FROM THE LARK............... *Melotone M-13044* 5-8 34
(Vocals: Chick Bullock)

BOOGIE MAN, THE / TAKE A LESSON FROM THE LARK..................... *Oriole 2914* 5-8 34
(Vocals: Chick Bullock)

BOOGIE MAN, THE / TAKE A LESSON FROM THE LARK.................. *Perfect 15947* 5-8 34
(Vocals: Chick Bullock)

BOOGIE MAN, THE / TAKE A LESSON FROM THE LARK.................... *Romeo 2288* 5-8 34
(Vocals: Chick Bullock)
(Simultaneously released on five labels)

CHRISTMAS NIGHT IN HARLEM / MOON COUNTRY.................. *Banner 33043* 5-8 34
(Vocals: Dick Robertson)

CHRISTMAS NIGHT IN HARLEM / MOON COUNTRY................ *Melotone M-13005* 5-8 34
(Vocals: Dick Robertson)

CHRISTMAS NIGHT IN HARLEM / MOON COUNTRY...................... *Oriole 2891* 5-8 34
(Vocals: Dick Robertson)

CHRISTMAS NIGHT IN HARLEM / MOON COUNTRY.................... *Perfect 15927* 5-8 34
(Vocals: Dick Robertson)

CHRISTMAS NIGHT IN HARLEM / MOON COUNTRY..................... *Romeo 2265* 5-8 34
(Vocals: Dick Robertson)
(Simultaneously released on five labels)

DOWN'T UNCLE BILL'S / THE MAN FROM SCOTLAND YARD.................. *Banner 33303* 4-6 35
(Vocals: Chick Bullock)

DOWN'T UNCLE BILL'S / THE MAN FROM SCOTLAND YARD............... *Melotone M-13270* 4-6 35
(Vocals: Chick Bullock)

DOWN'T UNCLE BILL'S / THE MAN FROM SCOTLAND YARD..................... *Oriole 3067* 4-6 35
(Vocals: Chick Bullock)

DOWN'T UNCLE BILL'S / THE MAN FROM SCOTLAND YARD................... *Perfect 16053* 4-6 35
(Vocals: Chick Bullock)

DOWN'T UNCLE BILL'S / THE MAN FROM SCOTLAND YARD.................... *Romeo 2441* 4-6 35
(Vocals: Chick Bullock)
(Simultaneously released on five labels)

FARE-THEE-WELL TO HARLEM / GET GOIN'......................... *Banner 32989* 5-8 34
(Vocals: Dick Robertson)

FARE-THEE-WELL TO HARLEM / GET GOIN'...................... *Melotone M-12938* 5-8 34
(Vocals: Dick Robertson)

FARE-THEE-WELL TO HARLEM / GET GOIN'........................... *Oriole 2857* 5-8 34
(Vocals: Dick Robertson)

FARE-THEE-WELL TO HARLEM / GET GOIN'......................... *Perfect 15899* 5-8 34
(Vocals: Dick Robertson)

FARE-THEE-WELL TO HARLEM / GET GOIN'.......................... *Romeo 2231* 5-8 34
(Vocals: Dick Robertson)
(Simultaneously released on five labels)

I BELIEVE IN MIRACLES / DON'T BE AFRAID TO TELL YOUR MOTHER.............. *Banner 33335* 2-4 35
(Vocals: Chick Bullock)

I BELIEVE IN MIRACLES / DON'T BE AFRAID TO TELL YOUR MOTHER........... *Melotone M-13302* 2-4 35
(Vocals: Chick Bullock)

I BELIEVE IN MIRACLES / DON'T BE AFRAID TO TELL YOUR MOTHER................ *Oriole 3085* 2-4 35
(Vocals: Chick Bullock)

I BELIEVE IN MIRACLES / DON'T BE AFRAID TO TELL YOUR MOTHER................. *Perfect 16069* 2-4 35
(Vocals: Chick Bullock)

I BELIEVE IN MIRACLES / DON'T BE AFRAID TO TELL YOUR MOTHER................ *Romeo 2459* 2-4 35
(Vocals: Chick Bullock)
(Simultaneously released on five labels)

I HATE MYSELF (FOR BEING SO MEAN TO YOU) / I KNEW YOU WHEN............... *Banner 33016* 3-5 34
(Vocals: Chick Bullock)

I HATE MYSELF (FOR BEING SO MEAN TO YOU) / I KNEW YOU WHEN............ *Melotone M-12975* 3-5 34
(Vocals: Chick Bullock)

I HATE MYSELF (FOR BEING SO MEAN TO YOU) / I KNEW YOU WHEN .... *Oriole 2873* 3-5 34
(Vocals: Chick Bullock)

I HATE MYSELF (FOR BEING SO MEAN TO YOU) / I KNEW YOU WHEN................. *Perfect 15913* 3-5 34
(Vocals: Chick Bullock)

I HATE MYSELF (FOR BEING SO MEAN TO YOU) / I KNEW YOU WHEN.................. *Romeo 2247* 3-5 34
(Vocals: Chick Bullock)
(Simultaneously released on five labels)

I'LL SEE YOU IN CHURCH / JUNK MAN......................... *Banner 32963* 4-6 34
(Vocals: Chick Bullock)

I'LL SEE YOU IN CHURCH / JUNK MAN..................... *Melotone M-12913* 4-6 34
(Vocals: Chick Bullock)

I'LL SEE YOU IN CHURCH / JUNK MAN........................... *Oriole 2839* 4-6 34
(Vocals: Chick Bullock)

I'LL SEE YOU IN CHURCH / JUNK MAN.......................... *Perfect 15883* 4-6 34
(Vocals: Chick Bullock)

I'LL SEE YOU IN CHURCH / JUNK MAN........................... *Romeo 2212* 4-6 34
(Vocals: Chick Bullock)
(Simultaneously released on five labels)

I'M SATISFIED / I'M COUNTING ON YOU........................... *Banner 33122* 2-4 34
(Vocals: Chick Bullock)

I'M SATISFIED / I'M COUNTING ON YOU........................ *Melotone M-13089* 2-4 34
(Vocals: Chick Bullock)

I'M SATISFIED / I'M COUNTING ON YOU.............................. *Oriole 2936* 2-4 34
(Vocals: Chick Bullock)

I'M SATISFIED / I'M COUNTING ON YOU............................ *Perfect 15966* 2-4 34
(Vocals: Chick Bullock)

I'M SATISFIED / I'M COUNTING ON YOU............................ *Romeo 2310* 2-4 34
(Vocals: Chick Bullock)
(Simultaneously released on five labels)

JUNGLE FEVER / SLEEPY HEAD ..... *Banner 33067* 4-6 34
(Vocals: Chick Bullock)

JUNGLE FEVER / SLEEPY HEAD ... *Melotone M-13031* 4-6 34
(Vocals: Chick Bullock)

JUNGLE FEVER / SLEEPY HEAD........ *Oriole 2906* 4-6 34
(Vocals: Chick Bullock)

JUNGLE FEVER / SLEEPY HEAD...... *Perfect 15939* 4-6 34
(Vocals: Chick Bullock)

JUNGLE FEVER / SLEEPY HEAD....... *Romeo 2280* 4-6 34
(Vocals: Chick Bullock)
(Simultaneously released on five labels)

KISSING GAMES / BORN TO BE KISSED......................... *Banner 33113* 3-5 34
(Vocals: Chick Bullock)

KISSING GAMES / BORN TO BE KISSED...................... *Melotone M-13080* 3-5 34
(Vocals: Chick Bullock)

KISSING GAMES / BORN TO BE KISSED........................... *Oriole 2934* 3-5 34
(Vocals: Chick Bullock)

KISSING GAMES / BORN TO BE KISSED......................... *Perfect 15964* 3-5 34
(Vocals: Chick Bullock)

KISSING GAMES / BORN TO BE KISSED.......................... *Romeo 2308* 3-5 34
(Vocals: Chick Bullock)
(Simultaneously released on five labels)

MOONLIGHT PARADE / MY HAT'S ON THE SIDE OF MY HEAD...................... *Banner 33091* 2-4 34
(Vocals: Chick Bullock)

MOONLIGHT PARADE / MY HAT'S ON THE SIDE OF MY HEAD.................. *Melotone M-13055* 2-4 34
(Vocals: Chick Bullock)

MOONLIGHT PARADE / MY HAT'S ON THE SIDE OF MY HEAD........................ *Oriole 2921* 2-4 34
(Vocals: Chick Bullock)

MOONLIGHT PARADE / MY HAT'S ON THE SIDE OF MY HEAD........................ *Perfect 15954* 2-4 34
(Vocals: Chick Bullock)

MOONLIGHT PARADE / MY HAT'S ON THE SIDE OF MY HEAD........................ *Romeo 2295* 2-4 34
(Vocals: Chick Bullock)
(Simultaneously released on five labels)

ONE MORNING IN MAY (Vocal: Dick Robertson) / IN A SHELTER FROM A SHOWER
(Vocal: Chick Bullock)........................ *Banner 32988* 3-5 34

ONE MORNING IN MAY (Vocal: Dick Robertson) / IN A SHELTER FROM A SHOWER
(Vocal: Chick Bullock) .... *Melotone M-12937* 3-5 34

ONE MORNING IN MAY (Vocal: Dick Robertson) / IN A SHELTER FROM A SHOWER
(Vocal: Chick Bullock)................... *Oriole 2856* 3-5 34

ONE MORNING IN MAY (Vocal: Dick Robertson) / IN A SHELTER FROM A SHOWER
(Vocal: Chick Bullock).................... *Perfect 15898* 3-5 34

ONE MORNING IN MAY (Vocal: Dick Robertson) / IN A SHELTER FROM A SHOWER
(Vocal: Chick Bullock)..................... *Romeo 2230* 3-5 34
(Simultaneously released on five labels)

POOR GIRL / THE HOUSE IS HAUNTED (BY THE ECHO OF YOUR LAST GOODBYE).... *Banner 33032* 3-5 34
(Vocals: Chick Bullock)

POOR GIRL / THE HOUSE IS HAUNTED (BY THE ECHO OF YOUR LAST GOODBYE)... *Melotone M-12991* 3-5 34
(Vocals: Chick Bullock)

POOR GIRL / THE HOUSE IS HAUNTED (BY THE ECHO OF YOUR LAST GOODBYE)....... *Oriole 2883* 3-5 34
(Vocals: Chick Bullock)

POOR GIRL / THE HOUSE IS HAUNTED (BY THE ECHO OF YOUR LAST GOODBYE) .... *Perfect 15922* 3-5 34
(Vocals: Chick Bullock)

POOR GIRL / THE HOUSE IS HAUNTED (BY THE ECHO OF YOUR LAST GOODBYE)...... *Romeo 2257* 3-5 34
(Vocals: Chick Bullock)
(Simultaneously released on five labels)

ROLL OUT OF BED WITH A SMILE / JIMMY HAD A NICKEL............. *Banner 32946* 4-6 34
(Vocals: Chick Bullock)

ROLL OUT OF BED WITH A SMILE / JIMMY HAD A NICKEL.......... *Melotone M-12889* 4-6 34
(Vocals: Chick Bullock)

ROLL OUT OF BED WITH A SMILE / JIMMY HAD A NICKEL............... *Oriole 2825* 4-6 34
(Vocals: Chick Bullock)

ROLL OUT OF BED WITH A SMILE / JIMMY HAD A NICKEL .... *Perfect 15874* 4-6 34
(Vocals: Chick Bullock)

ROLL OUT OF BED WITH A SMILE / JIMMY HAD A NICKEL .... *Romeo 2198* 4-6 34
(Vocals: Chick Bullock)
(Simultaneously released on five labels)

(IF LOVE MAKES YOU GIVE UP) STEAK AND POTATOES / HOT DOGS AND SASPARELLA................. *Banner 33092* 3-5 34
(Vocals: Chick Bullock)

(IF LOVE MAKES YOU GIVE UP) STEAK AND POTATOES / HOT DOGS AND SASPARELLA............. *Melotone M-13056* 3-5 34
(Vocals: Chick Bullock)

(IF LOVE MAKES YOU GIVE UP) STEAK AND POTATOES / HOT DOGS AND SASPARELLA .... *Oriole 2922* 3-5 34
(Vocals: Chick Bullock)

(IF LOVE MAKES YOU GIVE UP) STEAK AND POTATOES / HOT DOGS AND SASPARELLA................. *Perfect 15955* 3-5 34
(Vocals: Chick Bullock)

(IF LOVE MAKES YOU GIVE UP) STEAK AND POTATOES / HOT DOGS AND SASPARELLA.................. *Romeo 2296* 3-5 34
(Vocals: Chick Bullock)
(Simultaneously released on five labels)

SURPRISE / YOU'RE IN MY POWER (HA-HA-HA-HA-HA!)........ *Banner 32964* 3-5 34
(Vocals: Chick Bullock)

SURPRISE / YOU'RE IN MY POWER (HA-HA-HA-HA-HA!) .... *Melotone M-12914* 3-5 34
(Vocals: Chick Bullock)

SURPRISE / YOU'RE IN MY POWER (HA-HA-HA-HA-HA!).......... *Oriole 2840* 3-5 34
(Vocals: Chick Bullock)

SURPRISE / YOU'RE IN MY POWER (HA-HA-HA-HA-HA!) .... *Perfect 15884* 3-5 34
(Vocals: Chick Bullock)

SURPRISE / YOU'RE IN MY POWER (HA-HA-HA-HA-HA!).......... *Romeo 2213* 3-5 34
(Vocals: Chick Bullock)
(Simultaneously released on five labels)

SWEETIE PIE / YOU CAN PUT IT IN THE PAPERS .... *Banner 33176* 3-5 34
(Vocals: Chick Bullock)

SWEETIE PIE / YOU CAN PUT IT IN THE PAPERS............. *Melotone M-13143* 3-5 34
(Vocals: Chick Bullock)

SWEETIE PIE / YOU CAN PUT IT IN THE PAPERS.................. *Oriole 2978* 3-5 34
(Vocals: Chick Bullock)

SWEETIE PIE / YOU CAN PUT IT IN THE PAPERS................. *Perfect 15992* 3-5 34
(Vocals: Chick Bullock)

SWEETIE PIE / YOU CAN PUT IT IN THE PAPERS.................. *Romeo 2352* 3-5 34
(Vocals: Chick Bullock)
(Simultaneously released on five labels)

ROLLINS, Todd, & His Orchestra as Chick Bullock & His Levee Loungers

FRANKIE AND JOHNNIE / I CAN'T DANCE (I GOT ANTS IN MY PANTS)............... *Banner 33050* 5-8 34
(Vocals: Chick Bullock)

FRANKIE AND JOHNNIE / I CAN'T DANCE (I GOT ANTS IN MY PANTS) .... *Melotone M-13012* 5-8 34
(Vocals: Chick Bullock)

FRANKIE AND JOHNNIE / I CAN'T DANCE (I GOT ANTS IN MY PANTS)................. *Oriole 2894* 5-8 34
(Vocals: Chick Bullock)

FRANKIE AND JOHNNIE / I CAN'T DANCE (I GOT ANTS IN MY PANTS) .... *Perfect 15929* 5-8 34
(Vocals: Chick Bullock)

FRANKIE AND JOHNNIE / I CAN'T DANCE (I GOT ANTS IN MY PANTS)................. *Romeo 2268* 5-8 34
(Vocals: Chick Bullock)
(Simultaneously released on five labels)

ROMANCE OF HARMONY ORCHESTRA, The

DOODLE DOO DOO / BLUE EVENING BLUES.................. *Gennett 20068* 5-8 24

ROMANCERS, The:

see SPECHT, Paul, & His Hotel Alamac Orchestra

ROMANELLI, Luigi, & His King Edward Hotel Orchestra

PERHAPS / PRETENDING............ *Edison 14077* 12-15 29
(A rare lateral-cut thin Edison disc)

ROMANO, Phil, & His Orchestra

I'M GOIN' OUT IF LIZZIE COMES IN (Vocal: Billy Murray) / KEEP ON CROONIN' A TUNE......... *Victor 19803* 5-8 25

ROSE, Dave, & His Orchestra

SHADOWS / JIG-SAW RHTYTHM .... *Bluebird B-5708* 5-8 33

ROSE, Dave, as The Hotcha Trio

CHINATOWN, MY CHINATOWN / DINAH.......................... *Bluebird B-5296* 5-8 33
(Vocals: Louis Prima)

CHINATOWN, MY CHINATOWN / DINAH.......................... *Electradisk 2167* 15-20 33
(Vocals: Louis Prima)

CHINATOWN, MY CHINATOWN / DINAH.......................... *Sunrise S-3377* 15-20 33
(Vocals: Louis Prima)
(Simultaneously released on three labels)

ROSE, David, & His Orchestra

(David Rose: 6/15/10 –)

AMERICAN IN PARIS, AN / LIZA .... *MGM 30409* 2-4 51

MOON OF MANAKOORA / BEWITCHED... *MGM 30120* 2-4 50

POINCIANA / DANCE OF THE SPANISH ONION................ *Victor 27888* 2-4 42

ROSEMONT MELODY BOYS, The:

see SMALL, Abe

ROSEMONT ORCHESTRA, The:

see SMALL, Abe

ROSE, Vincent, & His Montmarte Orchestra

also see GOODMAN, Benny, & His Music Hall Orchestra, and see ROSE, Vincent – Jackie Taylor & Their Hollywood Orchestra

SINCE YOU'VE BEEN GONE / I DON'T KNOW WHY I LOVE YOU(I ONLY KNOW IT DO) ..... *Victor 19515* 2-4 24
(Vocals: Buddy Burns)

ROSE, Vincent, & His Orchestra

(Vincent Rose: 6/13/80 – 5/20/44)

also see GOODMAN, Benny, & His Music Hall Orchestra, and see ROSE, Vincent – Jackie Taylor & Their Hollywood Orchestra

SINCE YOU'VE BEEN GONE / I DON'T KNOW WHY I LOVE YOU............ *Victor 19515* 2-4 24
(Vocals: Buddy Burns)

ROSE, Vincent, & His Orchestra

AFTER THINKING IT OVER / AM I A PASSING FANCY? .... *Supertone 9414* 3-5 29
(Vocals: Joe Prince)

AFTER THINKING IT OVER / YOU'RE MY SILVER LINING OF LOVE................... *Gennett 6848* 4-6 29
(Vocals: Joe Prince)

HOUSE WHERE I WAS BORN, THE (Vocal: Dick Robertson) / ON THE GOOD SHIP LOLLIPOP
(Vocal: Dorothy Brent) .... *Banner 33301* 4-6 35

HOUSE WHERE I WAS BORN, THE (Vocal: Dick Robertson) / ON THE GOOD SHIP LOLLIPOP
(Vocal: Dorothy Brent).............. *Melotone M-13268* 4-6 35

HOUSE WHERE I WAS BORN, THE (Vocal: Dick Robertson) / ON THE GOOD SHIP LOLLIPOP
(Vocal: Dorothy Brent) .... *Oriole 3063* 4-6 35

HOUSE WHERE I WAS BORN, THE (Vocal: Dick Robertson) / ON THE GOOD SHIP LOLLIPOP
(Vocal: Dorothy Brent)................. *Perfect 16051* 4-6 35

HOUSE WHERE I WAS BORN, THE (Vocal: Dick Robertson) / ON THE GOOD SHIP LOLLIPOP
(Vocal: Dorothy Brent)................... *Romeo 2439* 4-6 35
(Simultaneously released on five labels)

LOVE PASSES BY / TWO HEADS AGAINST THE MOON......................... *Banner 33383* 3-5 35
(Vocals: Chick Bullock)

LOVE PASSES BY / TWO HEADS AGAINST THE MOON..................... *Melotone M-13350* 3-5 35
(Vocals: Chick Bullock)

LOVE PASSES BY / TWO HEADS AGAINST THE MOON .... *Oriole 3113* 3-5 35
(Vocals: Chick Bullock)

LOVE PASSES BY / TWO HEADS AGAINST THE MOON......................... *Perfect 16092* 3-5 35
(Vocals: Chick Bullock)

LOVE PASSES BY / TWO HEADS AGAINST THE MOON......................... *Romeo 2487* 3-5 35
(Vocals: Chick Bullock)
(Simultaneously released on five labels)

MY DOG LOVES YOUR DOG / NASTY MAN...................... *Banner 33001* 3-5 34
(Vocals: Lynn Dori)

MY DOG LOVES YOUR DOG / NASTY MAN .... *Melotone M-12952* 3-5 34
(Vocals: Lynn Dori)

MY DOG LOVES YOUR DOG / NASTY MAN. .... *Oriole 2864* 3-5 34
(Vocals: Lynn Dori)

MY DOG LOVES YOUR DOG / NASTY MAN .... *Perfect 15905* 3-5 34
(Vocals: Lynn Dori)

MY DOG LOVES YOUR DOG / NASTY MAN .... *Romeo 2238* 3-5 34
(Vocals: Lynn Dori)
(Simultaneously released on five labels)

POP! GOES YOUR HEART / HAPPINESS AHEAD .... Banner 33236 3-5 34
(Vocals: Chick Bullock)

POP! GOES YOUR HEART / HAPPINESS AHEAD .... Conqueror 8420 3-5 34
(Vocals: Chick Bullock)

POP! GOES YOUR HEART / HAPPINESS AHEAD .... Melotone M-13203 3-5 34
(Vocals: Chick Bullock)

POP! GOES YOUR HEART / HAPPINESS AHEAD .... Oriole 3024 3-5 34
(Vocals: Chick Bullock)

POP! GOES YOUR HEART / HAPPINESS AHEAD .... Perfect 16021 3-5 34
(Vocals: Chick Bullock)

POP! GOES YOUR HEART / HAPPINESS AHEAD .... Romeo 2398 3-5 34
(Vocals: Chick Bullock)
(Simultaneously released on six labels)

RHYTHM OF THE RAIN / EV'RYTHING'S BEEN DONE BEFORE .... Banner 33382 3-5 35
(Vocals: Chick Bullock)

RHYTHM OF THE RAIN / EV'RYTHING'S BEEN DONE BEFORE .... Melotone M-13349 3-5 35
(Vocals: Chick Bullock)

RHYTHM OF THE RAIN / EV'RYTHING'S BEEN DONE BEFORE .... Oriole 3112 3-5 35
(Vocals: Chick Bullock)

RHYTHM OF THE RAIN / EV'RYTHING'S BEEN DONE BEFORE .... Perfect 16091 3-5 35
(Vocals: Chick Bullock)

RHYTHM OF THE RAIN / EV'RYTHING'S BEEN DONE BEFORE .... Romeo 2486 3-5 35
(Vocals: Chick Bullock)
(Simultaneously released on five labels)

STAY AS SWEET AT YOU ARE / LET'S GIVE THREE CHEERS FOR LOVE .... Banner 33251 3-5 34
(Vocals: Smith Ballew)

STAY AS SWEET AT YOU ARE / LET'S GIVE THREE CHEERS FOR LOVE .... Conqueror 8447 3-5 34
(Vocals: Smith Ballew)

STAY AS SWEET AT YOU ARE / LET'S GIVE THREE CHEERS FOR LOVE .... Melotone M-13218 3-5 34
(Vocals: Smith Ballew)

STAY AS SWEET AT YOU ARE / LET'S GIVE THREE CHEERS FOR LOVE .... Oriole 3032 3-5 34
(Vocals: Smith Ballew)

STAY AS SWEET AT YOU ARE / LET'S GIVE THREE CHEERS FOR LOVE .... Perfect 16026 3-5 34
(Vocals: Smith Ballew)

STAY AS SWEET AT YOU ARE / LET'S GIVE THREE CHEERS FOR LOVE .... Romeo 2406 3-5 34
(Vocals: Smith Ballew)
(Simultaneously released on six labels)

SWEET AND SIMPLE / HOLD MY HAND .... Banner 33000 2-4 34
(Vocals: Slim Fortier)

SWEET AND SIMPLE / HOLD MY HAND .... Melotone M-12951 2-4 34
(Vocals: Slim Fortier)

SWEET AND SIMPLE / HOLD MY HAND .... Oriole 2868 2-4 34
(Vocals: Slim Fortier)

SWEET AND SIMPLE / HOLD MY HAND .... Perfect 15904 2-4 34
(Vocals: Slim Fortier)

SWEET AND SIMPLE / HOLD MY HAND .... Romeo 2237 2-4 34
(Vocals: Slim Fortier)
(Simultaneously released on five labels)

TONIGHT OR NEVER / I IDOLIZE MY BABY'S EYES .... Perfect 15523 3-5 31
(Vocals: Chick Bullock)

WHEN YOU WERE THE BLOSSOM OF BUTTERCUP LANE (AND I WAS YOUR LITTLE BOY BLUE) / WHY MUST I ALWAYS BE WITHOUT YOU?... Perfect 15441 3-5 31
(Vocals: Scrappy Lambert as Rodman Lewis)

ROSE, Vincent, & His Orchestra as Dan Ritchie & His Orchestra

IF I HAVE TO GO ON WITHOUT YOU / KISSABLE BABY .... Perfect 15525 3-5 31
(Vocals: Scrappy Lambert)

ROSE, Vincent–Jackie Taylor & Their Hollywood Orchestra
also see ROSE, Vincent, & His Montmarte Orchestra
see ROSE, Vincent, & His Orchestra, and
see TAYLOR, Jackie, & His Orchestra

DID YOU MEAN IT? / BLUE RIVER .... Columbia 1177-D 4-6 27
(Vocals: Unknown)

I'M TELLING YOU / I WANT YOU... Columbia 1461-D 3-5 28
(Vocals: Unknown)

IN MY LITTLE DREAM HOUSE ON THE HILL / LOVELY LITTLE SILHOUETTE... Columbia 1309-D 3-5 27
(Vocals: Unknown)

ROSS, Alonzo, as The Ross Deluxe Syncopators

DON'T YOU WANNA KNOW? (Vocal: Margaret Miller) / BELIEVE ME, DEAR .... Victor 21537 15-20 27

MARY BELL (Vocal: Casper Tower) / LADY MINE .... Victor 20952 15-20 27

MONIA (Vocal: Robert "Cookie" Mason) / BABY, STOP TEASIN' ME
(Vocals: Earl Evans & Alonzo Ross) .... Victor 21077 15-20 27

SKAD-O-LEE (Vocal: Margaret Miller) / FLORIDA RHYTHM (Vocal: Frank Houston) .... Victor 20961 15-20 27

ROSS DE LUXE SYNCOPATORS, The:
see ROSS, Alonzo

ROSS, Harold, & His Southerners:
see McKAY, Marion, & His Orchestra

ROSS, Roy, & His Orchestra

SONG HITS OF 1937 (a 4-record album set) .... Decca A-1937 8-10 42
(Individual records in the set, listed numerically (with value of each))

HARBOR LIGHTS; WHEN MY DREAM BOAT COMES HOME; CAN I FORGET YOU? / BOO HOO; THAT OLD FEELING; ORGAN GRINDER'S SWING .... Decca 24080 2-4 -
(Vocals: Don Rodney)

WHISPERS IN THE DARK; TOO MARVELOUS FOR WORDS; SEPTEMBER IN THE RAIN / THE ONE ROSE; IN A WHILE; BLUE HAWAII ... Decca 24081 2-4 -
(Vocals: Don Rodney)

REMEMBER ME?; SERENADE IN THE NIGHT; SWEET LEILANI/WHAT WILL I TELL MY HEART?; MOONLIGHT AND SHADOWS; NEVER IN A MILLION YEARS .... Decca 24082 2-4 -
(Vocals: Don Rodney)

IT LOOKS LIKE RAIN IN CHERRY BLOSSOM LANE; LITTLE OLD LADY; ROSALIE / A SAILBOAT IN THE MOONLIGHT; I'VE GOT MY LOVE TO KEEP ME WARM; VIENI VIENI .... Decca 24083 2-4 -
(Vocals: Don Rodney)

ROSS, Sam, & His Orchestra

I'VE GOT THE WORLD ON A STRING / THERE'S A NEW DAY COMIN' .... Crown 3455 5-8 33
(Vocals: Unknown)

STRIKE ME PINK / GOING! GOING!! GONE!!! .... Crown 3458 5-8 33
(Vocals: Unknown)

ROUNDERS, The:
see RESER, Harry

ROYAL DANCE ORCHESTRA, The

TOODLE-OO, SO LONG / JUST A BLUE-EYED BLONDE .... Broadway 1467 3-5 31
(Vocals: Unknown)

ROYALE TRIO, The

CRAZY JO / PICKIN'S.......... Pathe Actuelle 020896 3-5 23

CRAZY JO / PICKIN'S .... Perfect 11095 2-4 23
(Simultaneously released on two labels)

ROYAL RHYTHM BOYS, The

BLUE SKIES / PEACE, BROTHER, PEACE .... Decca 7759 10-12 39
(Vocals: Slam Stewart)

IN A SHANTY IN OLD SHANTY TOWN / BEAT IT OUT, BUMPIN' BOY .... Decca 2830 10-12 39
(Vocals: Slam Stewart)

ROYAL SOCIETY ORCHESTRA, The:
see SAMUELS, Joseph, as Joseph Samuel's Dance Orchestra

ROYAL TROUBADOURS, The

ADORABLE (Vocal: Arthur Hall) / UNEXPECTED PAPA .... Gennett 3341 3-5 26

BEEDLE-UM-BO / POSITIVELY – ABSOLUTELY .... Silvertone 5047 2-4 27
(Vocals: Jack Kaufman)

GEORGIANNA / MOONLIGHT AND ROSES BLUES (Vocals: The Two Jounards) .... Gennett 3287 3-5 26

I LOVE A UKULELE / I'D RATHER BE THE GIRL IN YOUR ARMS .... Gennett 3346 3-5 26
(Vocals: Vaughn de Leath)

IN YOUR GREEN HAT (Vocals: Unknown) / THANKS FOR THE BUGGY RIDE ..... Gennett 3232 4-6 26

MUDDY WATER (A MISSISSIPPI MOAN) / ORIENTAL MOONLIGHT .... Harmony 346-H 4-6 27

WATERS OF PERKIOMEN / LO NAH (Vocals: Unknown) .... Gennett 3257 3-5 26

ROYAL TROUBADOURS, The, as The Arabian Knights

PETRUSHKA / THAT NIGHT IN ARABY (Vocal: Bert Lewis) .... Gennett 3372 3-5 26

ROYAL TROUBADOURS, The, as The Hill Top Inn Orchestra

GIVE ME A UKULELE (AND A UKULELE BABY) (Vocal: Artie Mehlinger) / MEADOW LARK (Vocal: Arthur Fields) .... Champion 15167 3-5 26

ROYAL TROUBADOURS, The, as Ted Marshall & His Orchestra

IN YOUR GREEN HAT (Vocals: Unknown) / THANKS FOR THE BUGGY RIDE .... Champion 15063 3-5 26

RUGOLO, Pete, & His Orchestra
(Pete Rugolo: 12/25/15 –)

CALIFORNIA MELODIES / 360 SPECIAL .... Columbia 40222 2-4 -

EARLY STAN / LAURA .... Columbia 40195 3-5 -

JINGLE BELLS MAMBO / THEME FROM LOMBARDO ENDING .... Columbia 40369 2-4 -

KING PORTER STOMP / QUIET VILLAGE .... Columbia 40519 3-5 -

MANANA / IN THE SHADE OF THE OLD APPLE TREE .... Columbia 40262 3-5 -

THAT OLD BLACK MAGIC / COME BACK LITTLE ROCKET ..... Columbia 40194 3-5 -

YOU STEPPED OUT OF A DREAM / BAZAAR .... Columbia 40223 3-5 -

RUMSEY, Howard, as Howard Rumsey's Lighthouse All-Stars
(Howard Rumsey: 11/7/17 –)

LUAU / THE DUKE YOU SAY! ... Contemporary C 355 5-8 55

WITCH DOCTOR / MAMBO LOS FELIZ .... Contemporary C 359 5-8 55

RUSSELL, Luis, & His Orchestra
(Luis Russell: 8/6/02 – 12/11/63)

AFTER THE HOUR / GARBAGE MAN BLUES (Vocals: Unknown) .... Manor 1022 8-10 46

AT THE DARKTOWN STRUTTERS' BALL / OL' MAN RIVER .... Banner 33179 15-20 34
(Vocals: Sonny Woods)

AT THE DARKTOWN STRUTTERS' BALL / OL' MAN RIVER .... Melotone M-13146 15-20 34
(Vocals: Sonny Woods)

AT THE DARKTOWN STRUTTERS' BALL / OL' MAN RIVER .... Oriole 2981 15-20 34
(Vocals: Sonny Woods)

AT THE DARKTOWN STRUTTERS' BALL / OL' MAN RIVER .... Perfect 15995 15-20 34
(Vocals: Sonny Woods)

AT THE DARKTOWN STRUTTERS' BALL / OL' MAN RIVER .... Romeo 2355 15-20 34
(Vocals: Sonny Woods)
(Simultaneously released on five labels)

FEELIN' THE SPIRIT (Vocal: J. C. Higginbotham) / DOCTOR BLUES .... Okeh 8766 20-25 30

GHOST OF THE FREAKS (Vocals: The Palmer Brothers) / HOKUS POKUS .... Banner 33367 15-20 34

GHOST OF THE FREAKS (Vocals: The Palmer Brothers) / HOKUS POKUS .... Melotone M-13334 15-20 34

GHOST OF THE FREAKS (Vocals: The Palmer Brothers) / HOKUS POKUS .... Oriole 3104 15-20 34

GHOST OF THE FREAKS (Vocals: The Palmer Brothers) / HOKUS POKUS .... Perfect 16086 15-20 34

GHOST OF THE FREAKS (Vocals: The Palmer Brothers) / HOKUS POKUS .... Romeo 2478 15-20 34
(Simultaneously released on five labels)

GOIN' TO TOWN / SAY THE WORD...... Victor 22789 20-25 31
(Vocals: Chick Bullock)

LOUSIANA SWING / ON REVIVAL DAY (Vocal: Andy Razaf) .... Okeh 8811 20-25 30

NEW CALL OF THE FREAKS, THE (theme song) (Vocals: by trio) / JERSEY LIGHTNING .... Okeh 8734 20-25 29

PANAMA / HIGH TENSION............... Okeh 8849 25-30 30

POOR LI'L ME (Vocal: Jesse Cryor) / MUGGIN' LIGHTLY .... Okeh 8830 20-25 30

SARATOGA SHOUT / SONG OF THE SWANEE .... Okeh 8780 25-30 30

SWEET MEMORY / DON'T TAKE YOUR LOVE FROM ME .... Apollo 1020 5-8 46
(Vocals: Unknown)

RUSSELL, Ted, & His Orchestra:
see RILEY, Mike – Eddie Farley & Their Onyx Club Boys

RUSSO & Fio Rito's Oriole Orchestra / Oriole Terrace Orchestra
directed by Dan Russo & Ted Fio Rito (12/20/00 – 7/22/71)
also see FIO RITO, Ted, & His Orchestra
see RUSSO, Dan, & His Oriole Orchestra, and
see RUSSO, Dan, & His Orioles

BACK WHERE THE DAFFODILS GROW / OH! MABEL (Vocal: Nick Lucas) ...... Brunswick 2769 3-5 25

CAROLITA / FOOLISH CHILD .... Brunswick 2509 3-5 23

CHANSONETTE / BONNIE .... *Brunswick 2505* 2-4 23

CHICAGO / CAROLINA IN THE MORNING .... *Brunswick 2324* 3-5 22

CLOVER BLOSSOM BLUES / TOOT, TOOT, TOOTSIE! .... *Brunswick 2337* 3-5 22

COPENHAGEN / MY ROSE MARIE .... *Brunswick 2752* 4-6 24

DREAMY MELODY / A KISS IN THE DARK (by Carl Fenton & His Orchestra) ... *Brunswick 2428* 2-4 23

ELIZA / MANDY, MAKE UP YOUR MIND .... *Brunswick 2741* 4-6 24

GEORGETTE / KEEP ON BUILDING CASTLES IN THE AIR .... *Brunswick 2294* 2-4 22

I DON'T BELIEVE IT, BUT SAY IT AGAIN / LET'S TALK ABOUT MY SWEETIE
(Vocal: Mark Fisher) .... *Victor 19989* 3-5 26

I'M SO ASHAMED / UKULELE LADY .... *Brunswick 2875* 2-4 25
(Vocals: Mark Fisher)

IN A COZY TEA ROOM / THAT'S EVERYTHING .... *Brunswick 2533* 2-4 23

I WISH'T I WAS IN PEORIA (Vocals: by chorus) / SOMEBODY'S EYES .... *Victor 19924* 3-5 26

LITTLE OLD CLOCK ON THE MANTEL / I NEED SOME PETTIN' .... *Brunswick 2637* 3-5 24

LOST MELODY / BIT BY BIT YOU'RE BREAKING MY HEART .... *Brunswick 2489* 2-4 23

LUCKY KENTUCKY / FLAG THAT TRAIN (TO ALABAM') .... *Brunswick 2856* 3-5 25

MAGIC EYES / BESIDE A BABBLING BROOK .... *Brunswick 2437* 2-4 23

OH, HOW I MISS YOU TONIGHT / AH-HA .... *Brunswick 2874* 2-4 25
(Vocals: Mark Fisher)

ORIOLE BLUES / SERENADE BLUES .... *Brunswick 2300* 3-5 22

PORCELAIN MAID / JOURNEY'S END .... *Brunswick 2378* 2-4 23

RITZI-MITZI / SHIM-ME-SHA-WABBLE .... *Brunswick 2466* 4-6 23

ROSE OF THE RIO GRANDE / ALL MUDDLED UP .... *Brunswick 2356* 2-4 23

SLOW POKE / SOUTH SEA ISLES .... *Brunswick 2473* 3-5 23

SOBBIN' BLUES / A SMILE WILL GO A LONG, LONG WAY .... *Brunswick 2560* 3-5 24

STEP, HENRIETTA! / YOU'LL NEVER GET TO HEAVEN WITH THOSE EYES .... *Brunswick 2633* 3-5 24

THAT CERTAIN PARTY (Vocal: Mark Fisher) / I WANNA GO WHERE YOU GO – DO WHAT YOU DO – THEN I'LL BE HAPPY .... *Victor 19917* 3-5 26

THERE'S YES! YES! IN YOUR EYES / THAT LULLABY STRAIN .... *Brunswick 2587* 3-5 24

'WAY DOWN HOME / OFF AND GONE .... *Brunswick 2832* 3-5 25

RUSSO, Dan, & His Oriole Orchestra

also see RUSSO & Fio Rito's Oriole Orchestra / Oriole Terrace Orchestra

HOLLYWOOD / MY LITTLE HONEY AND ME .... *Brunswick 4622* 4-6 29
(Vocals: Unknown)

ILLINOIS LOYALTY SONG, THE / WAVE THE FLAG OF OLD CHICAGO; MARCH OF THE MAROONS .... *Brunswick 4563* 3-5 29
(Vocals: Unknown)

I'M THE MEDICINE MAN FOR THE BLUES / WOULDN'T IT BE WONDERFUL? ... *Brunswick 4490* 4-6 29
(Vocals: Unknown)

SWEETHEART / TAIN'T NO SIN (TO DANCE AROUND IN YOUR BONES) .... *Brunswick 4708* 4-6 30
(Vocals: Unknown)

(YOU MADE ME LOVE YOU) WHY DID YOU (Vocals: Unknown) / AN OLD ITALIAN LOVE SONG .... *Brunswick 4439* 2-4 29

RUSSO, Dan, & His Orioles

GOOFUS/I'M A DING DONG DADDY ... *Columbia 2641-D* 8-10 32
(Vocals: Unknown)
(This record was pressed in blue shellac)

NOAH'S ARK / OLD MacDONALD HAD A FARM .... *Columbia 2642-D* 5-8 32
(Vocals: Unknown)
(This record was pressed in blue shellac)

RYAN, Joe, & His Orchestra

LOVE MADE A GYPSY OUT OF ME / A LITTLE KISS EACH MORNING .... *Pathe Actuelle 37071* 5-8 30
(Vocals: Smith Ballew as Buddy Blue)

LOVE MADE A GYPSY OUT OF ME / A LITTLE KISS EACH MORNING .... *Perfect 15252* 4-6 30
(Vocals: Smith Ballew as Buddy Blue)
(Simultaneously released on two labels)

LOVE ME / DANCE AWAY THE NIGHT .... *Pathe Actuelle 37058* 4-6 29
(Vocals: Scrappy Lambert as Harold Lang)

LOVE ME / DANCE AWAY THE NIGHT .... *Perfect 15239* 3-5 29
(Vocals: Scrappy Lambert as Harold Lang)
(Simultaneously released on two labels)

RYAN, Joe, & His Orchestra as The Bostonians

LOVE MADE A GYPSY OUT OF ME / A LITTLE KISS EACH MORNING .... *Domino 4452* 4-6 30
(Vocals: Smith Ballew as Buddy Blue)

LOVE MADE A GYPSY OUT OF ME / A LITTLE KISS EACH MORNING .... *Regal 8898* 4-6 30
(Vocals: Smith Ballew as Buddy Blue)
(Simultaneously released on two labels)

LOVE ME / DANCE AWAY THE NIGHT ... *Domino 4425* 3-5 29
(Vocals: Scrappy Lambert as Harold Lang)

LOVE ME / DANCE AWAY THE NIGHT ... *Regal 8872* 3-5 29
(Vocals: Scrappy Lambert as Harold Lang)
(Simultaneously released on two labels)

SACK, Albert, & His Orchestra

FELLOW ON A FURLOUGH (Vocal: Bob Matthews) / DANCE OF THE TROPICAL MOONBEAMS (Vocal: Eileen Wilson) .... *Premier AS 101* 3-5 44

SALON DANCE SEXTET, The

I'LL BE YOUR BABY VAMPIRE (Vocal: Esther Walker) / I WANT A DADDY WHO WILL ROCK ME TO SLEEP .... *Aeolian Vocalion 12200* 3-5 19

I MIGHT BE YOUR ONCE-IN-A-WHILE / IRENE O'DARE .... *Vocalion 14025* 2-4 19

PRETTY GIRL IS LIKE A MELODY, A / WILD FLOWERS .... *Aeolian Vocalion 12193* 3-5 19

SALTER, Harry, & His Willys-Knighters

OLD PALS ARE THE BEST PALS AFTER ALL / DREAM RIVER .... *Cameo 8249* 3-5 28
(Vocals: Jack Kaufman)

OLD PALS ARE THE BEST PALS AFTER ALL / DREAM RIVER .... *Lincoln 2897* 3-5 28
(Vocals: Jack Kaufman)

OLD PALS ARE THE BEST PALS AFTER ALL / DREAM RIVER .... *Romeo 672* 3-5 28
(Vocals: Jack Kaufman)
(Simultaneously released on three labels)

SAMPSON, Edgar, & His Orchestra
(Edgar Sampson: 8/31/07 – 1/17/73)

DON'T TRY YOUR JIVE ON ME / PICK YOUR OWN LICK .... *Vocalion 4942* 10-12 39
(Vocals: The Three Swingsters)

SAMUELS, Joseph, & His Orchestra / Joseph Samuels' Dance Orchestra / Joseph Samuels' Orchestra

ALEXANDER'S BAND IS BACK IN DIXIELAND / DREAMY ALABAMA .... *Lyric 4209* 5-8 19

SAMUELS, Joseph, & His Orchestra / Joseph Samuels' Dance Orchestra / Joseph Samuels' Orchestra

ALEXANDER'S BAND IS BACK IN DIXIELAND / DREAMY ALABAMA .... *Lyric 4209* 5-8 19

ARCADY / LOVEY CAME BACK .... *Federal 5348* 3-5 23

BY THE CAMP FIRE / HOW YA GONNA KEEP 'EM DOWN ON THE FARM? .... *Pathe 40157* 3-5 19

BY THE SHALIMAR / WONDERFUL ONE .... *Gennett 5077* 3-5 23

CAT STEP, THE / WHEN I FOUND YOU... *Lyric 4231* 5-8 20

DUMBELL / I'M THROUGH SHEDDING TEARS OVER YOU .... *Triangle 11186* 2-4 23

FULL O' PEP / ROUND THE TOWN...... *Pathe 22098* 3-5 19

HINDUSTAN / KISSES .... *Pathe 40155* 3-5 19

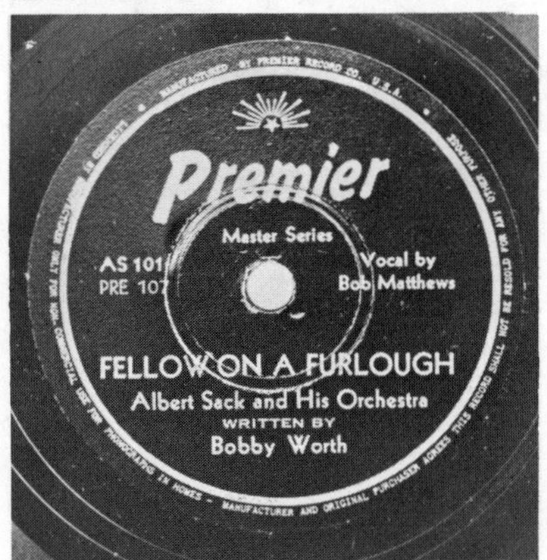

LAZY / WHAT'LL I DO? .... *Emerson 10739* 2-4 24

MANYANA / POLLY .... *Pathe 22368* 3-5 20

MORNING (WON'T YOU EVER COME 'ROUND) / LONELY LITTLE MELODY ... *Pathe Actuelle 036132* 3-5 24

MORNING (WON'T YOU EVER COME 'ROUND) / LONELY LITTLE MELODY .... *Perfect 14313* 3-5 24
(Simultaneously released on two labels)

MY CAIRO LOVE / LIMBO LAND .... *Pathe 40171* 2-4 19

NIJIGO NOVGO / MY SWEETIE WENT AWAY (by Joseph Samuels & His Orchestra as The Six Black Diamonds; Vocal: Earnest Hare as Bob Thomas) .... *Banner 1227* 3-5 23

NO-ONE LOVES YOU BETTER THAN YOUR M-A-DOUBLE-M-Y / MAXIE JONES (THE KING OF THE SAXOPHONES) .... *Pathe Actuelle 020932* 3-5 23

NO-ONE LOVES YOU BETTER THAN YOUR M-A-DOUBLE-M-Y / MAXIE JONES (THE KING OF THE SAXOPHONES) .... *Perfect 14144* 2-4 23
(Simultaneously released on two labels)

PAGE MR. PADEREWSKI / DUSTING THE KEYS .... *Pathe Actuelle 021045* 3-5 23

PAGE MR. PADEREWSKI / DUSTING THE KEYS .... *Perfect 14163* 2-4 23
(Simultaneously released on two labels)

SALLY GREEN, THE VILLAGE VAMP / I WANT TO GO WHERE THE SWEET DADDIES GROW... *Lyric 4230* 4-6 20

SLOW POKE / THAT BIG BLONDE MAMA (Vocal: Vernon Dalhart as Bob White).... *Regal 9525* 3-5 23

SOMEWHERE IN NAPLES / COLORADO AND YOU .... *Emerson 10522* 2-4 22

SOMEWHERE IN NAPLES / COLORADO AND YOU .... *Regal 9208* 2-4 22
(Simultaneously released on two labels)

TAXI / CHU-CHU-SAN .... *Pathe 22179* 3-5 19

TENTS OF ARABS / PEGGY .... *Pathe 22267* 3-5 20

THAT NAUGHTY WALTZ / IRENE O'DARE .... *Pathe 22309* 3-5 20

THAT'S ALL THERE IS, THERE AIN'T NO MORE (Vocal: Arthur Hall) / LADY OF MY CIGARETTE .... *Perfect 14410* 2-4 25

'WAY OUT IN KENTUCKY / THAT BIG BLONDE MAMA (Vocal: Vernon Dalhart as Bob White) .... *Banner 1240* 3-5 23

WHEN MY SWEETIE COMES BACK TO ME / SWEET HAWAIIAN MOONLIGHT...... *Pathe 40170* 2-4 19

WHY DID I KISS THAT GIRL? (Vocal: Vernon Dalhart) / I'VE GOT A CROSS-EYED PAPA .... *Federal 5368* 3-5 24

YOU'D BE SURPRISED / MY BABY'S ARMS .... *Lyric 4210* 4-6 19

YOU'RE THE ONE (THAT I WANT) (Vocal: Henry Burr as Harry McClaskey, his real name) / WHEN THE RAINBOW OF LOVE APPEARS .... *Pathe 22178* 2-4 19

SAMUELS, Joseph, & His Orchestra as The Banner Dance Orchestra

BUGLE CALL RAG / EVERY STEP BRINGS ME CLOSER TO YOU .... *Banner 1229* 3-5 23

WONDER IF SHE'S LONELY TOO / JUST A GIRL THAT MEN FORGET .... *Banner 1251* 2-4 23

SAMUELS, Joseph, & His Orchestra as The Castle-By-The-Sea Orchestra

ANNABELLE / BEBE (by Joseph Samuels & His Orchestra as The Hollywood Dance Orchestra) .... *Regal 9511* 2-4 23

SAMUELS, Joseph, & His Orchestra as Roy Collins' Orchestra

CAROLINA MAMMY / I LOVE ME (by Joseph Samuels & His Orchestra as The Newport Society Orchestra; Vocal: Billy Jones as Billy West) .... *Banner 1213* 2-4 23

MAMA GOES WHERE PAPA GOES / SITTIN' IN A CORNER .... *Banner 1270* 3-5 23

MIDNIGHT ROSE / SOMEBODY'S WRONG... *Regal 9528* 2-4 23

'NEATH EGYPTIAN SKIES / STEAMBOAT SAL (Vocal: Arthur Hall) ... *Banner 1239* 2-4 23

OH! GEE, OH! GOSH, OH! GOLLY, I'M IN LOVE / WALK, JENNY, WALK! (by Joseph Samuels & His Orchestra as The Six Black Diamonds) .... *Banner 1278* 3-5 23
(Vocals: Billy Jones as Billy West)

SUN-KIST ROSE / THAT OLD GANG OF MINE .... *Banner 1255* 2-4 23

SAMUELS, Joseph, & His Orchestra as The Empire Dance Orchestra

IN YOUR ARMS (Vocal: Lewis James) / DREAMY AMAZON .... *Empire 31125* 4-6 19

SAMUELS, Joseph, & His Orchestra as Joseph Franklin's Orchestra

LIFE OF A ROSE, THE / SOMEDAY YOU'LL CRY OVER SOMEONE (by Joseph Samuels & His Orchestra as The Hollywood Dance Orchestra) .... *Banner 1231* 2-4 23

LOVE TALES / INDIANA MOON .... *Banner 1241* 2-4 23

SITTIN' IN A CORNER / LAST NIGHT ON THE BACK PORCH .... *Regal 9557* 3-5 23

'WAY OUT IN KENTUCKY / HOT ROASTED PEANUTS (by Joseph Samuels & His Orchestra as aThe Six Black Diamonds; Vocal: Arthur Hall) .... *Regal 9524* 2-4 23

SAMUELS, Joseph, & His Orchestra as Sam Franklin's Orchestra

I CRIED FOR YOU / BEALE STREET MAMA (by Joseph Samuels & His Orchestra as The Six Black Diamonds) .... *Regal 9503* 3-5 23

SAMUELS, Joseph, & His Orchestra as The Great Western Serenaders

THAT'S ALL THERE IS, THERE AIN'T NO MORE (Vocal: Arthur Hall) / LADY OF MY CIGARETTE .... *Pathe Actuelle 036229* 3-5 25

SAMUELS, Joseph, & His Orchestra as Eph Hannaford's Broadway Orchestra

I'M GOIN' SOUTH / SOMEBODY STOLE MY GAL (by Joseph Samuels & His Orchestra as The Hollywood Dance Orchestra; Vocal: Arthur Hall) .... *Regal 9585* 3-5 24

SLEEP / CIELITO LINDO (by Joseph Samuels & His Orchestra as The Imperial Dance Orchestra) .... *Banner 1298* 2-4 24

TWELVE O'CLOCK AT NIGHT / CHILI-BOM-BOM .... *Regal 9597* 2-4 24

SAMUELS, Joseph, & His Orchestra as The Hollywood Dance Orchestra

ANNABELLE / FIRST, LAST AND ALWAYS .... *Banner 1226* 2-4 23

BEBE / ANNABELLE (by Joseph Samuels & His Orchestra as The Castle-By-The-Sea Orchestra) .... *Regal 9511* 2-4 23

CAROLINA MAMMY / I AIN'T NEVER HAD NOBODY CRAZY OVER ME (by Joseph Samuels & His Orchestra as The Six Black Diamonds) .... *Regal 9501* 2-4 23

DOWN AMONG THE SLEEPY HILLS OF TEN-TEN-TENNESSEE / WHILE YOU WERE MAKING BELIEVE (by Joseph Samuels & His Orchestra as The Majestic Dance Orchestra) .... *Regal 9471* 2-4 23

FOOLISH CHILD (Vocal: Billy Jones as Billy West) / LAST NIGHT ON THE BACK PROCH .... *Banner 1263* 2-4 23

SOMEBODY STOLE MY GAL (Vocal: Arthur Hall) / I'M GOIN' SOUTH (by Joseph Samuels & His Orchestra as Eph Hannaford's Broadway Orchestra) .... *Regal 9585* 3-5 24

SOMEDAY YOU'LL CRY OVER SOMEONE / THE LIFE OF A ROSE (by Joseph Samuels & His Orchestra as Joseph Franklin's Orchestra) .... *Banner 1231* 2-4 23

SOMEWHERE IN THE WORLD / NIGHTS IN THE WOODS .... *Regal 9647* 2-4 24

WHEN JUNE COMES ALONG WITH A SONG / BORN AND BRED IN BROOKLYN .... *Banner 1253* 2-4 23

SAMUELS, Joseph, & His Orchestra as The Imperial Dance Orchestra

CIELITO LINDO / SLEEP (by Joseph Samuels & His Orchestra as Eph Hannaford's Broadway Orchestra) .... *Banner 1298* 2-4 24

RAGGEDY ANN / IN LOVE WITH LOVE .... *Regal 9584* 2-4 24

SAMUELS, Joseph, & His Orchestra as The Majestic Dance Orchestra

WHEN JUNE COMES ALONG WITH A SONG / BORN AND BRED IN BROOKLYN ...... *Regal 9540* 2-4 23

WHILE YOU WERE MAKING BELIEVE / DOWN AMONG THE SLEEPY HILLS OF TEN-TEN-TENNESSEE (by Joseph Samuels & His Orchestra as The Hollywood Dance Orchestra) .... *Regal 9471* 2-4 23

SAMUELS, Joseph, & His Orchestra as The Missouri Jazz Band

EVERY NIGHT I CRY MYSELF TO SLEEP OVER YOU / SOBBIN' BLUES .... *Banner 1265* 3-5 23

I'M SITTING PRETTY IN A PRETTY LITTLE CITY / MAMA GOES WHERE PAPA GOES...... *Regal 9552* 3-5 23

MAMA LOVES PAPA, PAPA LOVES MAMA (Vocal: Arthur Hall) / WALK, JENNY, WALK (Vocal: Billy Jones as Billy West) .... *Regal 9568* 3-5 23

SAMUELS, Joseph, & His Orchestra as The Newport Society Orchestra

I LOVE ME (Vocal: Billy Jones as Billy West) / CAROLINA MAMMY (by Joseph Samuels & His Orchestra as Roy Collins' Orchestra) .... *Banner 1213* 2-4 23

SAMUELS, Joseph & His Orchestra as The Operaphone Dance Orchestra

IN YOUR ARMS (Vocal: Lewis James) / DREAMY AMAZON .... *Operaphone 31125* 4-6 19

MISSISSIPPI SHORE / POLLY (by Joseph Samuels & His Orchestra as The Society Dance Orchestra) .... *Operaphone 31145* 4-6 20

SAMUELS, Joseph, & His Orchestra as The Six Black Diamonds

APPLE SAUCE / FAREWELL BLUES..... *Regal 9458* 3-5 23

BEALE STREET MAMA / I CRIED FOR YOU (by Joseph Samuels & His Orchestra as Sam Franklin's Orchestra) .... *Regal 9503* 3-5 23

HOT ROASTED PEANUTS (Vocal: Arthur Hall) / 'WAY OUT IN KENTUCKY (by Joseph Samuels & His Orchestra as Joseph Franklin's Orchestra)...... *Regal 9524* 2-4 23

I AIN'T NEVER HAD NOBODY CRAZY OVER ME / CAROLINA MAMMY (by Joseph Samuels & His Orchestra as The Hollywood Dance Orchestra) .... *Regal 9501* 2-4 23

MY SWEETIE WENT AWAY (Vocal: Ernest Hare as Bob Thomas) / NIJIGO NOVGO (by Joseph Samuels & His Orchestra) .... *Banner 1227* 3-5 23

WALK, JENNY, WALK / OH! GEE, OH! GOSH, OH! GOLLY, I'M IN LOVE (by Joseph Samuels & His Orchestra as Roy Collins' Orchestra) .... *Banner 1278* 3-5 23
(Vocals: Billy Jones as Billy West)

SAMUELS, Joseph, & His Orchestra as The Society Dance Orchestra

POLLY / MISSISSIPPI SHORE (by Joseph Samuels & His Orchestra as The Operaphone Dance Orchestra) .... *Operaphone 31145* 4-6 20

SAMUELS, Joseph, as Joseph Samuels' Dance Orchestra:
see SAMUELS, Joseph, & His Orchestra

SAMUELS, Joseph, as Joseph Samuels' Jazz Band

HOME AGAIN BLUES / CRAZY BLUES.... *Okeh 4250* 3-5 21

NUTHIN' BUT / YOU'VE GOT TO SEE MAMA EV'RY NIGHT .... *Paramount 20206* 4-6 23

OH BOY! / PULLMAN PORTER BLUES.... *Okeh 4370* 3-5 21

RUNNIN' WILD / LOOSE FEET....... *Grey Gull 1143* 3-5 23

RUNNIN' WILD / LOOSE FEET..... *Harmograph 772* 10-12 23

RUNNIN' WILD / LOOSE FEET....... *National 12190* 5-8 23

RUNNIN' WILD / LOOSE FEET..... *Paramount 20190* 5-8 23

RUNNIN' WILD / LOOSE FEET....... *Puretone 11198* 10-12 23

RUNNIN' WILD / LOOSE FEET........ *Puritan 11190* 3-5 23

RUNNIN' WILD / LOOSE FEET......... *Radiex 7012* 3-5 23

RUNNIN' WILD / LOOSE FEET....... *Triangle 11198* 3-5 23
(Simultaneously released on eight labels)

SCANDINAVIA / I'M NOBODY'S BABY.... *Okeh 4302* 3-5 21

TROPICAL BLUES / JABBERWOCKY...... *Okeh 4282* 3-5 21

SAMUELS, Joseph, as Joseph Samuels' Master Players

DUMBELL / SUNNY JIM............. *Puritan 11180* 2-4 23

JAPANESE MOON / I'M THROUGH SHEDDING TEARS OVER YOU.................. *Gennett 4998* 3-5 22

SAY IT WHILE DANCING / WHEN THE LEAVES COME TUMBLING DOWN .... *Gennett 4942* 3-5 22

SAMUELS, Joseph, as Joseph Samuels' Master Players recorded under the name The Majestic Dance Orchestra

ONE NIGHT IN JUNE / BABY BLUE EYES............... *Broadway 11184* 3-5 23

SAMUELS, Joseph, as Joseph Samuels' Master Players recorded under the name Earl Randolph's Orchestra

TRICKS / COOL BLACK MAMMY (by Ben Selvin as The Moulin Rouge Orchestra recorded under the name the Frisco Syncopators)............... *Claxtonola 40152* 5-8 22

SAMUELS, Joseph, as Joseph Samuels' Melody Masters recorded under the name The Missouri Jazz Hounds

OH! HAROLD / YES! WE HAVE NO BANANAS...................... *Banner 1200* 3-5 23
(Vocals: Arthur Hall)

OH! HAROLD / YES! WE HAVE NO BANANAS......................... *Regal 9488* 3-5 23
(Vocals: Arthur Hall)
(Simultaneously released on two labels)

SAMUELS, Joseph, as Joseph Samuels' Music Masters

AIN'T WE GOT FUN? / WHERE?.................... *Pathe Actuelle 020598* 3-5 21

APACHE LOVE / WHEN THE HONEYMOON WAS OVER .... *Pathe Actuelle 020630* 3-5 21

LADY OF MY CIGARETTE / LITTLE PEACH................... *Emerson 10857* 2-4 25

LIPS / MON HOMME (MY MAN)... *Pathe Actuelle 020540* 2-4 21

MOONBEAMS / SOME LITTLE BIRD ... *Emerson 10346* 2-4 21

OH JOSEPH! / GET YOURSELF A BROOM AND SWEEP YOUR TROUBLES AWAY (Vocal: Billy Jones)............ *Emerson 10839* 2-4 25

ROSIE (MAKE IT ROSY FOR ME) / NO WONDER I'M BLUE............... *Pathe 40215* 3-5 20

SOMEONE ELSE / SKIES OF NORMANDY................ *Pathe Actuelle 020517* 3-5 21

SWEETHEART / MADELINE......... *Emerson 10369* 2-4 21

WHEN THE HONEYMOON WAS OVER / TENDERLY .... *Emerson 10453* 2-4 21

SAMUELS, Joseph, as Joseph Samuels' Music Masters recorded under the name Earl Randolph's Orchestra

STUMBLING / SOME SUNNY DAY.... *Claxtonola 40128* 5-8 22

STUMBLING / SOME SUNNY DAY..... *Puritan 11120* 3-5 22
(Simultaneously released on two labels)

SAMUELS, Joseph, as Joseph Samuels' Orchestra:

see SAMUELS, Joseph, & His Orchestra

SAMUELS, Joseph, as The Synco Jazz Band

ALCOHOLIC BLUES / AT THE JAZZ BAND BALL....................... *Empire 31110* 5-8 19

ALCOHOLIC BLUES / AT THE JAZZ BAND BALL.................... *Operaphone 31110* 5-8 19
(Simultaneously released on two labels)

BIG BAD BILL IS SWEET WILLIAM NOW / NOBODY KNOWS WHAT A RED HEAD MAMA CAN DO .... *Pathe Actuelle 036190* 3-5 25

BLACKSMITH RAG / THE MOAN.................. *Pathe Actuelle 020461* 4-6 20

BLUES HAVE GOT ME / OH! MABEL.................. *Pathe Actuelle 036200* 4-6 25

CAROLINA BLUES / ON THE 'GIN 'GIN 'GINNY SHORE .... *Pathe Actuelle 020699* 3-5 22

CAROLINA BLUES / ON THE 'GIN 'GIN 'GINNY SHORE.......................... *Perfect 14013* 2-4 22
(Simultaneously released on two labels)

CHICAGO / CLOVER BLOSSOM BLUES............ *Pathe Actuelle 020812* 3-5 22

CHICAGO / CLOVER BLOSSOM BLUES.................... *Perfect 14043* 2-4 22
(Simultaneously released on two labels)

DANGEROUS BLUES / MYSTERIOUS BLUES....................... *Pathe Actuelle 020665* 3-5 21

HOT LIPS / STATE STREET BLUES............... *Pathe Actuelle 020770* 4-6 22

HOT LIPS / STATE STREET BLUES...................... *Perfect 14022* 3-5 22
(Simultaneously released on two labels)

I'VE GOT THE WONDER WHERE HE WENT AND WHEN HE'S COMING BACK BLUES / NO USE CRYING.............. *Pathe Actuelle 020721* 3-5 22

JAZZOLA / BLUIN' THE BLUES........... *Arto 9003* 4-6 20

LAND OF COTTON BLUES / DO-DOODLE-OOM............... *Pathe Actuelle 036016* 3-5 23

LASSUS TROMBONE / ALCOHOLIC BLUES............................... *Pathe 22117* 4-6 19

LASSUS TROMBONE / MISSOURI BLUES.................. *Empire 31115* 4-6 19

LASSUS TROMBONE / MISSOURI BLUES............... *Operaphone 31115* 4-6 19
(Simultaneously released on two labels)

LUCKY DOG BLUES / SATANIC BLUES............ *Pathe Actuelle 020558* 4-6 21

OLD JOE BLUES / HUNKATIN.......... *Pathe 22207* 3-5 19

RAILROAD BLUES / SWEET MAMA (PAPA'S GETTING MAD) .... *Pathe Actuelle 020499* 4-6 21

SLIM TROMBONE / EVERYONE SHIMMIES NOW...................... *Pathe 22099* 3-5 19

SOMEBODY'S WRONG / HOUSE OF DAVID BLUES .... *Pathe Actuelle 021075* 3-5 23

TOREADOR HUMORESQUE / AT THE JAZZ BAND BALL......................... *Pathe 22122* 3-5 19

SANDERS, Joe, & His Orchestra

also see COON-SANDERS ORCHESTRA, The, and see COON-SANDERS ORIGINAL NIGHTHAWK Orchestra, The
(Joe Sanders: 10/15/96 – 5/15/65)

ANYTHING YOUR LITTLE HEART DESIRES (Vocal: Jack Swift) / I COULD BE IN HEAVEN (IF YOU'D COME DOWN TO EARTH) (Vocal: Joe Sanders)..... *Decca 956* 4-6 36

I FOUND A ROSE IN THE SNOW / I'LL NEVER FORGET I LOVE YOU (opening theme song).... *Decca 659* 4-6 36
(Vocals: Joe Sanders)

I GOT LOVE / HOLLYWOOD AT VINE (Vocal: Joe Sanders).................. *Decca 676* 5-8 36

I'LL NEVER LET YOU GO / I'M ONE STEP AHEAD OF MY SHADOW........................... *Decca 850* 4-6 36
(Vocals: Joe Sanders)

LET IT BE ME / WEARY................. *Decca 658* 5-8 36
(Vocals: Barbara Parks)

NIGHTY-NIGHT DEAR (closing theme song) / HERE COMES MY BALL AND CHAIN.... *Decca 692* 4-6 36
(Vocals: Joe Sanders)

THERE GOES MY ATTRACTION / AND THEY SAID IT WOULDN'T LAST!...................... *Decca 955* 4-6 36
(Vocals: Joe Sanders)

THESE FOOLISH THINGS / MY FIRST THRILL..................... *Decca 843* 4-6 36
(Vocals: Joe Sanders)

YOU'RE SLIGHTLY TERRIFIC (Vocal: Jack Swift) / YOU DO THE DARNDEST THINGS, BABY (Vocal: Joe Sanders)....................... *Decca 952* 5-8 36

SANDERS, Red, & His Orchestra

CLOSE YOUR EYES / PEACEFUL VALLEY................. *Gennett 3157* 5-8 25

WHAT COULD BE SWEETER THAN YOU? / WHAT DO WE CARE IF IT'S ONE O'CLOCK? ..... *Gennett 3147* 5-8 25
(Vocals: James Teele)

WHEN I DREAM OF THE LAST WALTZ WITH YOU (Vocals: Unknown) / I NEVER KNEW HOW WONDERFUL YOU WERE............ *Gennett 3177* 4-6 25

SANFORD'S FAMOUS DANCE ORCHESTRA

DESERT DREAMS / THERE SHE GOES (Vocals: Unknown) .... *Emerson 10170* 2-4 20

MYSTERY / FAR EAST.............. *Emerson 10155* 2-4 20

ON MIAMI SHORE / SWANEE........ *Emerson 10185* 2-4 20

SANNELLA, Andy, & His All Star Orchestra

(Andy Sannella: 3/11/00 – 1961)

LET'S GET FRIENDLY / I'M MAD ABOUT YOU .... *Victor 22675* 3-5 31
(Vocals: Chick Bullock)

SANNELLA, Andy, & His All Star Trio

AUF WIEDERSEH'N / I STILL LOVE YOU .... *Harmony 599-H* 2-4 28
(Vocals: Unknown)

BEAUTIFUL / I CAN'T DO WITHOUT YOU.................... *Harmony 613-H* 2-4 28
(Vocals: Unknown)

DREAM MOTHER / EVANGELINE... *Columbia 1846-D* 2-4 29
(Vocals: Unknown)

I'LL SEE YOU THRU' (Vocal: Smith Ballew) / SERENADING THE MOON (Vocals: Unknown)................. *Columbia 2060-D* 3-5 29

I'M IN HEAVEN WHEN I SEE YOU SMILE, DIANE / YESTERDAY .... *Harmony 519-H* 2-4 27
(Vocals: Unknown)

JACK AND JILL / RAG DOLL........ *Harmony 656-H* 3-5 28

JAPANSY / LOU'SIANA LULLABY... *Harmony 642-H* 2-4 28
(Vocals: Unknown)

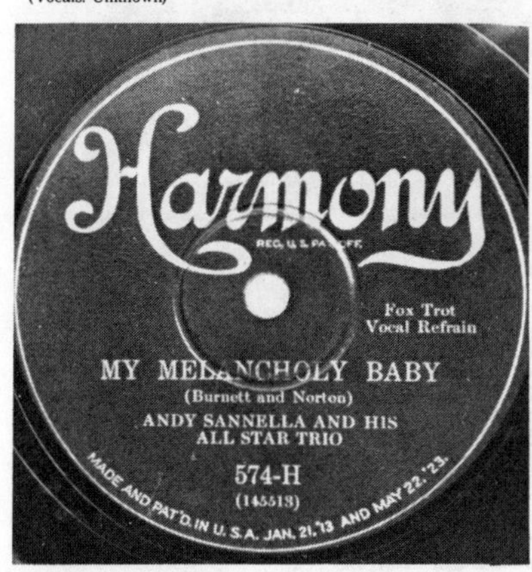

LADY OF THE MORNING / PERFUME OF ROSES .... *Columbia 1804-D* 3-5 29
(Vocals: Smith Ballew)

LITTLE LOG CABIN OF DREAMS / THE DANCE OF THE BLUE DANUBE.............. *Harmony 623-H* 2-4 28
(Vocals: Unknown)

MY MELANCHOLY BABY / AFTER MY LAUGHTER CAME TEARS .... *Harmony 574-H* 3-5 28
(Vocals: Unknown)

ROSETTE / FOR OLD TIMES' SAKE ... *Harmony 663-H* 2-4 28
(Vocals: Unknown)

WHEREVER YOU ARE / MY LADY.... *Harmony 538-H* 2-4 27
(Vocals: Unknown)

SANNELLA, Andy, & His Orchestra

(Hit Of The Week records are one-sided paper discs. Some, including the following, have two titles on the one side.)

LAWD, YOU MADE THE NIGHT TOO LONG; SHARING.................. *Hit Of The Week F-2-3* 5-8 32
(Vocals: Ralph Kirberry)

ONE HOUR WITH YOU; I BEG YOUR PARDON, MADEMOISELLE............ *Hit Of The Week F-1-2* 4-6 32
(Vocals: Ralph Kirberry)

TEA FOR TWO / YAAKA HULA HICKEY DOOLA................ *Variety 561* 4-6 37

SANNELLA, Andy, & His Pennzoil Orchestra

RUNNING BETWEEN THE RAINDROPS / PLEASE DON'T TALK ABOUT ME WHEN I'M GONE .... *Perfect 15438* 3-5 31
(Vocals: Chick Bullock)

SANNELLA, Andy, as Andy Sannella's Novelty Salon Orchestra

ICH LIEBE DICH (I LOVE YOU) / AT THE CLOSE OF DAY............................. *Okeh 41278* 2-4 29
(Vocals: Unknown)

SAN REMO DANCE ORCHESTRA, The

ADIOS / LADY OF SPAIN .... *Crown 3286* 3-5 32

AMAPOLA / THE MASKED ONE......... *Crown 3320* 5-8 32
(Vocals: Elmer Feldkamp)

I'M SURE OF EVERYTHING BUT YOU / SWEET MUCHACHA.................. *Crown 3407* 3-5 33
(Vocals: Unknown)

JEALOUSY / TANGO OF THE ROSES .... *Crown 3495* 3-5 33

WHEN YOUR HAIR HAS TURNED TO SILVER / I'M ALONE BECAUSE I LOVE YOU .... *Crown 3030* 3-5 31
(Vocals: Unknown)

SANTELMANN, Lt. William H.:

see UNITED STATES MARINE BAND, The

SANTREY, Henry, & His Cameo Record Orchestra

BABY – WHAT IS YOUR NAME? / —...... *Cameo 598* 3-5 24

BABY – WHAT IS YOUR NAME? / —.... *Lincoln 2275* 3-5 24
(Simultaneously released on two labels)

DREAM DADDY / —...................... *Cameo 475* 3-5 24

LONESOME AND BLUE / SAY IT AGAIN (by Bob Haring & His Velvetone Orchestra) .... *Cameo 501* 2-4 24

SAUSAGE, Doctor, & His Five Pork Chops:

see TYSON, "Dr. Sausage"

SAUTER – FINEGAN ORCHESTRA, The
directed by Eddie Sauter and Bill Finegan
(Eddie Sauter: 12/2/14 – 4/21/81. Bill Finegan: 4/3/17 –)

DOODLETOWN FIFERS (theme song) / AZURE-TE .... *RCA Victor 20-4866* 3-5 52
JOEY'S THEME / DOODLETOWN RACES......... *RCA Victor 20-5506* 3-5 55
MIDNIGHT SLEIGH RIDE / WHEN HEARTS ARE YOUNG.................. *RCA Victor 20-4995* 4-6 52
MOONLIGHT ON THE GANGES / APRIL IN PARIS............... *RCA Victor 20-4927* 3-5 52
NINA NEVER KNEW / LOVE IS A SIMPLE THING............. *RCA Victor 20-5065* 3-5 53
"O" / THE MOON IS BLUE (45 rpm)................ *RCA Victor 47-5359* 2-4 54
YANKEE DOODLETOWN / NOW THAT I'M IN LOVE.................. *RCA Victor 20-5248* 3-5 54

SAVANNAH NIGHT HAWKS, The:
see TRENT, Alphonse, & His Orchestra

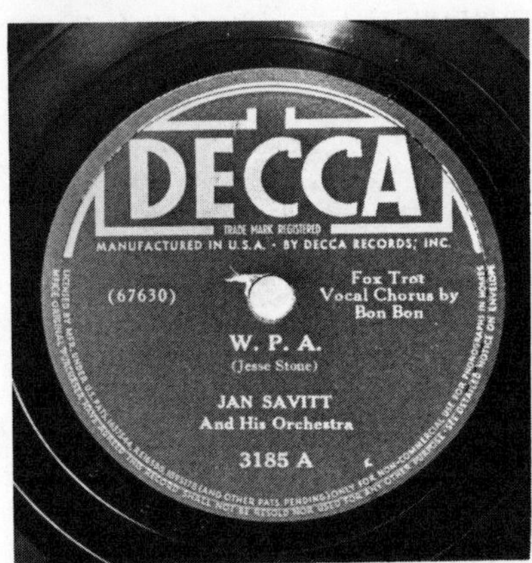

SAVITT, Jan, & His Orchestra
(Jan Savitt: 9/4/13 – 10/4/48)

APRIL SHOWERS (Vocal: Allan DeWitt) / BIG BEAVER......................... *Decca 3695* 2-4 41
BLUES IN THE GROOVE / ROSE OF THE RIO GRANDE (Vocal: Bon Bon)............ *Decca 3019* 3-5 40
HER NAME WAS ROSITA / I'M STEPPING OUT WITH A MEMORY TONIGHT .... *Decca 3196* 2-4 40
(Vocals: Allan DeWitt)
IF I CARED A LITTLE BIT LESS (Vocal: Joe Martin) / ROMANCE A LA MODE
(Vocal: Gloria DeHaven) .... *Bluebird 30-0800* 3-5 42
(Gloria DeHaven later became a motion picture star and was active on the stage and in television)
IT'S A WONDERFUL WORLD / HONESTLY.......................... *Decca 2836* 2-4 39
(Vocals: Bon Bon)
JOLLY PETER / BY HECK .... *Decca 3724* 3-5 41
LEIBESTRAUM / MEADOWBROOK SHUFFLE............................ *Decca 3876* 3-5 41
LES PRELUDES / GREEN GOON JIVE.... *Decca 3671* 3-5 41
MAID OF THE MIST / AFTER ALL (Vocal: Bon Bon) .... *Decca 2847* 2-4 39
MAKE-BELIEVE ISLAND / ASK YOUR HEART .... *Decca 3188* 2-4 40
(Vocals: Bon Bon)
MAKE LOVE WITH A GUITAR / IMAGINATION......................... *Decca 2990* 2-4 40
(Vocals: Bon Bon)
MANHATTAN SERENADE (Vocal: Joe Martin) / IF YOU EVER, EVER LOVED ME (LOVE ME TONIGHT)
(Vocal: Gloria DeHaven)............. *Bluebird B-11584* 3-5 42
MEDITATION / BELOVED FRIEND (Vocal: Allan DeWitt)............ *Decca 4124* 2-4 41
NOCTURNE IN E FLAT MAJOR / TELL ME (Vocal: Allan DeWitt)............ *Decca 3937* 2-4 41
SECRETS IN THE MOONLIGHT (Vocal: Bon Bon) / WHERE WAS I? (Vocal: Allan DeWitt)...... *Decca 3153* 2-4 40
TURKEY IN THE STRAW / PARADE OF THE WOODEN SOLDIERS.................. *Decca 3041* 2-4 40
TUXEDO JUNCTION / KANSAS CITY MOODS............................ *Decca 2989* 3-5 40
W.P.A. (Vocal: Bon Bon) / IT'S TIME TO JUMP AND SHOUT.................... *Decca 3185* 4-6 40
YOU CAN'T BRUSH ME OFF / IT'S A LOVELY DAY TOMORROW............. *Decca 3178* 2-4 40
(Vocals: Allan DeWitt)
YOUNG PRINCE AND THE YOUNG PRINCESS, THE / MY HEART AT THY SWEET VOICE..... *Decca 3640* 2-4 41
YOU'RE LONELY AND I'M LONELY / THE LORD DONE FIXED UP MY SOUL............ *Decca 3177* 2-4 40
(Vocals: Allan Dewitt)

SAVITT, Jan, & His Top Hatters

AFTERNOON OF A FAUN / AFTERNOON OF A FAUN, PART II...................... *Victor 27594* 2-4 41
ALWAYS IN MY HEART (Vocal: Joe Martin) / JERSEY BOUNCE...................... *Victor 27809* 2-4 42
AND THE ANGELS SING / SNUG AS A BUG IN A RUG............................ *Decca 2390* 2-4 39
(Vocals: Bon Bon)
AS WE WALK INTO THE SUNSET (Vocal: Allan DeWitt) / CHATTANOOGA CHOO CHOO......... *Victor 27573* 3-5 41
BEWILDERED (Vocal: Carlotta Dale) / SOMETHING TELLS ME (Vocal: Bon Bon).......... *Bluebird B-7490* 4-6 38
COULD BE; KINDA LONESOME; THE MASQUERADE IS OVER; ROMANCE RUNS IN THE FAMILY / ON THE ROAD TO MANDALAY; LOVE, YOUR MAGIC SPELL IS EVERYWHERE; BEGIN THE BEGUINE; HAVE IT YOUR WAY.............. *Thesaurus 621* 12-15 39
(An electrical transcription produced for radio broadcast, not for commercial release)
DROP IN THE BUCKET, A / WHY DON'T WE DO THIS MORE OFTEN?.......................... *Victor 27584* 2-4 41
(Vocals: Allan DeWitt)
DUST / IT'S THE LITTLE THINGS THAT COUNT........... *Bluebird B-7607* 5-8 38
(Vocals: Bon Bon)
EV'RY TIME / THERE'S A BOAT DAT'S LEAVIN' SOON FOR NEW YORK.............. *Victor 27706* 3-5 41
(Vocals: Bon Bon)
FOL DA ROL DOL (Vocal: Bon Bon) / WHEN TWILIGHT COMES (Vocal: Carlotta Dale) .... *Bluebird B-7670* 3-5 38
GOOD MORNING / MANY DREAMS AGO ... *Decca 2805* 3-5 39
(Vocals: Bon Bon)
GYPSY IN MY SOUL / I LIVE THE LIFE I LOVE..................... *Bluebird B-7295* 4-6 38
(Vocals: Bon Bon)
HOW COULD YOU? / I'LL NEVER TELL YOU I LOVE YOU (Vocal: Carlotta Dale) .... *Variety 506* 5-8 37
IF WHAT YOU SAY IS TRUE / STRANGER THINGS HAVE HAPPENED .... *Decca 2792* 2-4 39
(Vocals: Bon Bon)
I'LL ALWAYS BE IN LOVE WITH YOU / GET HAPPY........................... *Decca 2583* 2-4 39
IN A MOMENT OF WEAKNESS / I'M HAPPY ABOUT THE WHOLE THING.................. *Decca 2330* 2-4 39
(Vocals: Bon Bon)
INDIAN SUMMER / SWEET DREAMS, SWEETHEART ...... *Decca 2821* 2-4 39
(Vocals: Bon Bon)
IN THE HALL OF THE MOUNTAIN KING / LITTLE FUGUE (FUGUE IN G MINOR)......... *Victor 27670* 3-5 41
I REMEMBER YOU / TICA-TI — TICA-TA .... *Victor 27775* 2-4 42
(Vocals: Bon Bon)
IT'S A HUNDRED TO ONE (I'M IN LOVE) / THE PAPER PICKER ...... *Decca 2738* 2-4 39
(Vocals: Bon Bon)
IT'S SO PEACEFUL IN THE COUNTRY (Vocal: Allan DeWitt) / SUGAR FOOT STRUT......... *Victor 27464* 3-5 41
I WENT OUT OF MY WAY (Vocal: Allan DeWitt) / THROWING PEBBLES IN THE MILLSTREAM
(Vocal: Jane Ward)...................... *Victor 27423* 2-4 41
JO-JO, THE HOBO (Vocals: The Toppers) / TOPPER................................ *Victor 27477* 3-5 41
JUST A KID NAMED JOE (Vocal: Bon Bon) / HURRY HOME (Vocal: Carlotta Dale)......... *Bluebird B-10013* 2-4 38
LA CINQUANTAINE / I SEE A MILLION PEOPLE (BUT ALL I CAN SEE IS YOU)
(Vocal: Allan DeWitt)...................... *Victor 27577* 2-4 41
LA DE DOODY DOO (Vocal: Harry Roberts) / WHAT ARE YOU DOIN' TONIGHT?
(Vocal: Bon Bon)..................... *Bluebird B-7737* 3-5 38
LET'S PLAY GEOGRAPHY / SUPPOSING.... *Variety 542* 5-8 37
LITTLE SIR ECHO (Vocal: Bon Bon) / I WANT MY SHARE OF LOVE (Vocal: Carlotta Dale) .... *Decca 2391* 2-4 39
LOVE OF MY LIFE (Vocal: Carlotta Dale) / I HAVEN'T CHANGED A THING
(Vocal: Bon Bon)..................... *Bluebird B-7748* 3-5 38
LOVE'S GOT NOTHIN' ON ME (Vocal: Jack Palmer) / WHEN THE SUN COMES OUT
(Vocal: Allan DeWitt)..................... *Victor 27515* 2-4 41
MOONSHINE OVER KENTUCKY (Vocal: Bon Bon) / LOVELIGHT IN THE STARLIGHT
(Vocal: Carlotta Dale)................. *Bluebird B-7504* 5-8 38
M-O-T-H-E-R / MOONLIGHT MASQUERADE....................... *Victor 27699* 2-4 41
(Vocals: Bon Bon)
MY HEAVEN ON EARTH / AM I IN ANOTHER WORLD?.............. *Bluebird B-7281* 4-6 38
(Vocals: Bon Bon)
MY MARGARITA / SWEET AND TENDER.................. *Bluebird B-7593* 3-5 38
(Vocals: Bon Bon)
NOT A CARE IN THE WORLD / A NICKEL TO MY NAME........................ *Victor 27720* 2-4 42
(Vocals: Bon Bon)
PRELUDE TO CARMEN / THE SORCERER'S APPRENTICE...... *Victor 27570* 3-5 41
720 IN THE BOOKS / ALLA EN RANCHO GRANDE (Vocal: Bon Bon)................ *Decca 2771* 2-4 39
'S GOOD ENOUGH FOR ME / SO LOVELY........................ *Bluebird B-7679* 3-5 38
(Vocals: Bon Bon)
SHABBY OLD CABBY (Vocal: Phil Brito) / MOONLIGHT SERENADE (Vocal: Carlotta Dale) .... *Decca 2600* 3-5 39
SING ME A SONG OF THE ISLANDS / BLUE SHADOWS AND WHITE GARDENIAS... *Victor 27778* 2-4 42
STOP! AND RECONSIDER (Vocals: The Three Toppers) / WEEK-END OF A PRIVATE SECRETARY
(Vocal: Carlotta Dale)................. *Bluebird B-7493* 4-6 38
STOP! IT'S WONDERFUL / THE LAST TWO WEEKS IN JULY .... *Decca 2770* 2-4 39
(Vocals: Bon Bon)
SUGAR FOOT STOMP / QUAKER CITY JAZZ (theme song) .... *Bluebird B-10005* 3-5 38
SWEETHEART OF SIGMA CHI / WHEN I GO A-DREAMIN'.................. *Bluebird B-7786* 3-5 38
(Vocals: Bon Bon)
THAT'S A PLENTY / FUTURISTIC SHUFFLE .... *Bluebird B-7733* 5-8 38
THERE'S NO PLACE LIKE YOUR ARMS / YA GOT ME........................ *Bluebird B-7797* 4-6 38
(Vocals: Bon Bon)

THINGS I LOVE, THE (Vocal: Allan DeWitt) / MANHATTAN SUNRISE.............. *Victor 27403* 3-5 41
TOMORROW'S SUNRISE / ME AND MY MELINDA........................ *Victor 27822* 2-4 42
(Vocals: Joe Martin)
TROPICAL MAGIC / A WEEK-END IN HAVANA......................... *Victor 27615* 2-4 41
(Vocals: Allan DeWitt)
TWILIGHT INTERLUDE (Vocal: Carlotta Dale) / VOL VISTU GAILY STAR (Vocal: Bon Bon)...... *Decca 2739* 2-4 39
WAIT UNTIL MY HEART FINDS OUT / GARDENIAS.................... *Bluebird B-10018* 3-5 38
(Vocals: Bon Bon)
WE GO WELL TOGETHER (Vocals: Jack Palmer & The Toppers) / HORIZON.............. *Victor 27382* 3-5 41
WE, THE PEOPLE (Vocals: The Three Toppers) / HI-YO SILVER (Vocal: Bon Bon) ...... *Bluebird B-7666* 5-8 38
WHEN BUDDHA SMILES / THAT'S A PLENTY .... *Decca 2540* 3-5 39
WHERE YOU ARE (Vocal: Allan DeWitt) / I TAKE TO YOU
(Vocals: Jack Palmer & The Toppers)........ *Victor 27414* 2-4 41
WHO CALLS? / 'TIS AUTUMN.......... *Victor 27643* 2-4 41
(Vocals: Allan DeWitt)
WHY'D YA MAKE ME FALL IN LOVE?
(Vocals: The Three Toppers) / I'VE GOT A GUY
(Vocal: Carlotta Dale)................ *Bluebird B-7595* 4-6 38
YONKEL DOODLE GOES STEPPIN' / CROSS COUNTRY HOP................ *Variety 585* 5-8 37
YOU DON'T KNOW WHAT LOVE IS / NOW AND FOREVER................ *Victor 27724* 2-4 42
(Vocals: Bon Bon)
YOU GO TO MY HEAD (Vocal: Carlotta Dale) / TUTTIE FRUTTI (Vocals: Bon Bon & Harry Roberts)...................... *Bluebird B-7783* 5-8 38
YOU STARTED SOMETHING / A KISS FOR CONSOLATION .... *Bluebird B-7283* 5-8 37
YOU TAUGHT ME TO LOVE AGAIN
(Vocal: Carlotta Dale) / RUNNING THROUGH MY MIND (Vocal: Phil Brito)............... *Decca 2614* 3-5 39

SAVOY BEARCATS, The, directed by Duncan Mayers

HOW COULD I BE BLUE? / BEARCAT STOMP.................... *Victor 20307* 10-12 26
SENEGALESE STOMP / NIGHTMARE... *Victor 20182* 10-12 26
STAMPEDE / HOT NOTES.............. *Victor 20460* 10-12 26

SAWYER, Chuck, & His Syncopators:
see HOWARD, Gordon, & His Multnomah Chieftains

SAWYER, Duane, & His Novelty Orchestra

KARZAN / MY SAHARA ROSE .... *Pathe 22364* 3-5 20

SAWYER, Duane, & His Society Orchestra

BEAUTIFUL HAWAII / KISS ME AGAIN..................... *Gennett 9046* 3-5 20

SAXOJAZZ ORCHESTRA, The

LIVERY STABLE BLUES / THE DARKTOWN STRUTTERS' BALL.............. *Paramount 30033* 5-8 18

SAXOPHONE SEXTET, The

HINDUSTAN/SWEET 'N' PRETTY... *Paramount 30088* 5-8 18

SAXO SEXTETTE, The

ALLAH'S HOLIDAY / POOR BUTTERFLY............... *Columbia A-2203* 3-5 17
ALL BLUES MEDLEY / — .... *Columbia A-2196* 2-4 17
MY CASTLE IN THE AIR / WHAT DO YOU WANT TO MAKE THOSE EYES AT ME FOR?...................... *Columbia A-2205* 2-4 17

SCHOEN, Vic, & His Orchestra
(Vic Schoen: circa 1917 –)

HIT THE ROAD (Vocal: Don Raye) / ARABIAN NIGHTS .... *Decca 3227* 2-4 40
SERENADE TO THE STARS (MORNING GLORY) / OF MAESTRO AND MEN.................. *Decca 3237* 2-4 40

SCHUBERT, Adrian, & His Orchestra

ADORABLE / MY HEART'S DESIRE .... *Crown 3496* 3-5 33
(Vocals: Unknown)

BEAUTIFUL LOVE / WHEN THE MOON COMES OVER THE MOUNTAIN .... *Crown 3162* 4-6 31
(Vocals: Unknown)

BOY AND GIRL WERE DANCING, A / THE CLOCK STRIKES THE HOUR OF LOVE .... *Crown 3411* 3-5 32
(Vocals: Unknown)

BUTTERFLIES IN THE RAIN / YOU'LL NEVER GET TO HEAVEN THAT WAY .... *Crown 3483* 4-6 33
(Vocals: Unknown)

CAN'T WE TALK IT OVER? / I'LL MISS YOU IN THE EVENING .... *Crown 3269* 4-6 32
(Vocals: Unknown)

DANCING IN THE DARK / YOURS IS MY HEART ALONE .... *Crown 3164* 4-6 31
(Vocals: Unknown)

FALLING IN LOVE AGAIN / TWO HEARTS IN WALTZ TIME .... *Crown 3066* 4-6 31
(Vocals: Smith Ballew)

HOLD MY HAND / IT WAS SO BEAUTIFUL .... *Crown 3348* 3-5 32
(Vocals: Unknown)

HOLD YOUR MAN / DREAMING .... *Crown 3508* 4-6 33
(Vocals: Unknown)

HOUR OF PARTING, THE / WHY DANCE? .... *Crown 3178* 3-5 31
(Vocals: Unknown)

HOW-DEEP-IS-THE-OCEAN? / SAME OLD MOON .... *Crown 3388* 4-6 32
(Vocals: Unknown)

I'M PLAYING WITH FIRE / WHY CAN'T THIS NIGHT GO ON FOREVER? .... *Crown 3439* 4-6 33
(Vocals: Unknown)

I'M SORRY, DEAR / WHY DID IT HAVE TO BE ME? .... *Crown 3225* 3-5 31
(Vocals: Unknown)

I'M WITH YOU / GOODNIGHT, SWEETHEART .... *Crown 3206* 4-6 31
(Vocals: Smith Ballew)

I'M YOURS FOR TONIGHT / MOONLIGHT ON THE RIVER .... *Crown 3364* 3-5 32
(Vocals: Unknown)

JUST FRIENDS / I PROMISE YOU .... *Crown 3245* 3-5 31
(Vocals: Unknown)

KISS ME GOODNIGHT / THE CUTE LITTLE THINGS YOU DO .... *Crown 3207* 4-6 31
(Vocals: Smith Ballew)

LADY I LOVE, THE / WHILE WE DANCED AT THE MARDI GRAS .... *Crown 3359* 3-5 32
(Vocals: Unknown)

LADY, PLAY YOUR MANDOLIN / JUST A GIGOLO .... *Crown 3052* 4-6 31
(Vocals: Unknown)

LOVE SONGS OF THE NILE / SWEETHEART DARLIN' .... *Crown 3493* 3-5 33
(Vocals: Unknown)

MANY HAPPY RETURNS OF THE DAY / COME TO ME .... *Crown 3151* 3-5 31
(Vocals: Unknown)

MY SILENT LOVE / LAZY DAY .... *Crown 3317* 4-6 32
(Vocals: Unknown)

NIGHT WHEN LOVE WAS BORN, THE / MASQUERADE .... *Crown 3335* 3-5 32
(Vocals: Unknown)

NOW YOU'RE IN MY ARMS / THERE OUGHT TO BE A MOONLIGHT SAVING TIME .... *Crown 3129* 4-6 31
(Vocals: Unknown)

NOW YOU'VE GOT ME WORRYIN' FOR YOU / AS YOU DESIRE ME .... *Crown 3350* 4-6 32
(Vocals: Unknown)

OLD TIME WALTZES MEDLEY / OLD TIME WALTZES MEDLEY, PART II .... *Crown 3393* 3-5 32

ONE HOUR WITH YOU / WE WILL ALWAYS BE SWEETHEARTS .... *Crown 3282* 3-5 32
(Vocals: Unknown)

ONE LITTLE RAINDROP / THAT LITTLE BOY OF MINE .... *Crown 3088* 4-6 31
(Vocals: Unknown)

PARADISE / BY THE FIRESIDE .... *Crown 3274* 3-5 32
(Vocals: Unknown)

PETTIN' IN THE PARK / I'VE GOT TO SING A TORCH SONG .... *Crown 3484* 4-6 33
(Vocals: Unknown)

PLAY, FIDDLE, PLAY / A LITTLE STREET WHERE OLD FRIENDS MEET .... *Crown 3408* 3-5 32
(Vocals: Unknown)

SAME AS WE USED TO DO / AFTER THE DANCE .... *Crown 3110* 3-5 31
(Vocals: Unknown)

STARLIGHT / OH! WHAT A THRILL .... *Crown 3257* 3-5 32
(Vocals: Unknown)

SWEETHEART OF MY STUDENT DAYS / ALWAYS IN ALL WAYS .... *Crown 3004* 3-5 30
(Vocals: Frank Luther)

TO WHOM IT MAY CONCERN / STOLEN MOMENTS .... *Crown 3034* 3-5 31
(Vocals: Unknown)

TRULY (I LOVE YOU) / IT'S A LONESOME OLD TOWN (WHEN YOU'RE NOT AROUND) .... *Crown 3062* 4-6 31
(Vocals: Smith Ballew)

WAS THAT THE HUMAN THING TO DO? / HOW LONG WILL IT LAST? .... *Crown 3258* 4-6 32
(Vocals: Unknown)

WHEN THE LIGHTS ARE SOFT AND LOW / GOSH DARN! .... *Crown 3303* 3-5 32
(Vocals: Unknown)

SCHUBERT, Adrian, & His Salon Orchestra / Adrian Schubert's Salon Orchestra

BLAME IT ON THE WALTZ / WHEN YOU'RE DANCING 'NEATH THE DIXIE MOON .... *Regal 8156* 2-4 26

C'EST VOUS / THAT SAXOPHONE WALTZ .... *Regal 8403* 2-4 27
(Vocals: Charles Harrison)

CHEERIE-BEERIE-BE / LONESOME FOR YOU .... *Domino 4025* 2-4 27
(Vocals: Scrappy Lambert)

CHEERIE-BEERIE-BE / LONESOME FOR YOU .... *Regal 8395* 2-4 27
(Vocals: Scrappy Lambert)
(Simultaneously released on two labels)

FALLING IN LOVE WITH YOU / STARLIGHT .... *Banner 1865* 2-4 26

FALLING IN LOVE WITH YOU / STARLIGHT .... *Domino 3837* 2-4 26

FALLING IN LOVE WITH YOU / STARLIGHT .... *Regal 8180* 2-4 26
(Simultaneously released on three labels)

IF MY DREAMS OF YOU COULD ONLY COME TRUE / WORRYIN' .... *Domino 4015* 2-4 27

IF MY DREAMS OF YOU COULD ONLY COME TRUE / WORRYIN' .... *Regal 8378* 2-4 27
(Simultaneously released on two labels)

JUST ANOTHER KISS / MY DEAR .... *Domino 4354* 2-4 29
(Vocals: Scrappy Lambert)

JUST ANOTHER KISS / MY DEAR .... *Regal 8799* 2-4 29
(Vocals: Scrappy Lambert)
(Simultaneously released on two labels)

LIVING A LIFE OF DREAMS (Vocal: Ray O'Hara) / IN MEMORY OF YOU (by Adrian Schubert & His Salon Orchestra as The Hollywood Dance Orchestra; Vocals: Scrappy Lambert) .... *Perfect 15336* 3-5 30

MERRY WIDOW, THE / VICTOR HERBERT WALTZ MEDLEY .... *Banner 1751* 2-4 26

MERRY WIDOW, THE / VICTOR HERBERT WALTZ MEDLEY .... *Domino 3717* 2-4 26
(Simultaneously released on two labels)

MY OHIO LULLABY / THE HOURS I SPENT WITH YOU .... *Domino 4077* 2-4 28
(Vocals: Scrappy Lambert)

MY OHIO LULLABY / THE HOURS I SPENT WITH YOU .... *Regal 8458* 2-4 28
(Vocals: Scrappy Lambert)
(Simultaneously released on two labels)

MY SWEETHEART (Vocal: Arthur Hall) / IN A LITTLE SPANISH TOWN (Vocal: Irving Kaufman) .... *Banner 1885* 2-4 27

MY SWEETHEART (Vocal: Arthur Hall) / IN A LITTLE SPANISH TOWN (Vocal: Irving Kaufman) .... *Domino 3858* 2-4 27
(Simultaneously released on two labels)

MY WINDOW OF DREAMS / CHIQUITA .... *Domino 4172* 2-4 28
(Vocals: Frank Luther)

MY WINDOW OF DREAMS / CHIQUITA .... *Regal 8601* 2-4 28
(Vocals: Frank Luther)
(Simultaneously released on two labels)

PARADISE / MARIE .... *Domino 4230* 2-4 28
(Vocals: Scrappy Lambert)

PARADISE / MARIE .... *Regal 8666* 2-4 28
(Vocals: Scrappy Lambert)
(Simultaneously released on two labels)

PLAY ME AN OLD-FASHIONED WALTZ / CHERIE, I LOVE YOU (Vocal: Irving Kaufman) .... *Banner 1768* 2-4 26

PLAY ME AN OLD-FASHIONED WALTZ / CHERIE, I LOVE YOU (Vocal: Irving Kaufman) .... *Domino 3740* 2-4 26

PLAY ME AN OLD-FASHIONED WALTZ / CHERIE, I LOVE YOU (Vocal: Irving Kaufman) .... *Regal 8073* 2-4 26
(Simultaneously released on three labels)

SLEEPY HEAD / I WISH YOU WERE JEALOUS OF ME (Vocal: Charles Harrison) .... *Broadway 1031* 2-4 26

SLEEPY HEAD / I WISH YOU WERE JEALOUS OF ME (Vocal: Charles Harrison) .... *Paramount 20473* 4-6 26

SLEEPY HEAD / I WISH YOU WERE JEALOUS OF ME (Vocal: Charles Harrison) .... *Regal 8108* 2-4 26
(Simultaneously released on three labels)

THAT CERTAIN ONE / TONIGHT YOU BELONG TO ME (Vocal: Irving Kaufman) .... *Banner 1909* 2-4 27

THAT CERTAIN ONE / TONIGHT YOU BELONG TO ME (Vocal: Irving Kaufman) .... *Domino 3879* 2-4 27

THAT CERTAIN ONE / TONIGHT YOU BELONG TO ME (Vocal: Irving Kaufman) .... *Regal 8224* 2-4 27
(Simultaneously released on three labels)

WHAT A MAN! / WHAT GOOD IS GOOD MORNING? (by Adrian Schubert & His Salon Orchestra as The Hollywood Dance Orchestra) .... *Banner 1727* 2-4 26

WHAT A MAN! / WHAT GOOD IS GOOD MORNING? (by Adrian Schubert & His Salon Orchestra as The Hollywood Dance Orchestra) .... *Domino 3699* 2-4 26
(Simultaneously released on two labels)

WHERE IN THE WORLD / GIRL OF MY DREAMS .... *Domino 4072* 2-4 28
(Vocals: Leroy Montesanto)

WHERE IN THE WORLD / GIRL OF MY DREAMS .... *Regal 8461* 2-4 28
(Vocals: Leroy Montesanto)
(Simultaneously released on two labels)

WHISP'RING TREES / I WISH YOU WERE JEALOUS OF ME (Vocal: Charles Harrison) .... *Banner 1801* 2-4 26

WHISP'RING TREES / I WISH YOU WERE JEALOUS OF ME (Vocal: Charles Harrison) .... *Domino 3771* 2-4 26
(Simultaneously released on two labels)

SCHUBERT, Adrian, & His Salon Orchestra as Roy Carlson's Dance Orchestra

WHENEVER I THINK OF YOU (Vocals: The Strollers Quartet) / I'VE GOT TO HAVE YOU (by Adrian Schubert & His Salon Orchestra as The Hollywood Dance Orchestra) .... *Banner 0573* 3-5 30

SCHUBERT, Adrian, & His Salon Orchestra as The Hollywood Dance Orchestra

CHEERIE-BEERIE-BE / LET'S BE THE SAME AGAIN .... *Banner 6081* 2-4 27
(Vocals: Scrappy Lambert)

CLIMBING UP THE LADDER OF LOVE / PLAY, GYPSIES – DANCE, GYPSIES .... *Banner 1843* 2-4 26

CLIMBING UP THE LADDER OF LOVE / PLAY, GYPSIES – DANCE, GYPSIES .... *Domino 3815* 2-4 26
(Simultaneously released on two labels)

HUGS AND KISSES (Vocals: Unknown) / ALL ALONE MONDAY .... *Banner 1871* 2-4 26

HUGS AND KISSES (Vocals: Unknown) / ALL ALONE MONDAY .... *Domino 3838* 2-4 26
(Simultaneously released on two labels)

IDOLIZING / THERE AIN'T NO MAYBE IN MY BABY'S EYES .... *Domino 3843* 3-5 26
(Vocals: Arthur Fields)

IDOLIZING / THERE AIN'T NO MAYBE IN MY BABY'S EYES (by Adrian Schubert & His Salon Orchestra as The Missouri Jazz Band) .... *Banner 1870* 3-5 26
(Vocals: Arthur Fields)

IF I LOST YOU / WAS IT LOVE? .... *Domino 4208* 2-4 28

IF I LOST YOU / WAS IT LOVE? .... *Regal 8683* 2-4 28
(Simultaneously released on two labels)

IN MEMORY OF YOU (Vocal: Scrappy Lambert) / LIVING A LIFE OF DREAMS (by Adrian Schubert & His Salon Orchestra; Vocal: Ray O'Hara) .... *Perfect 15336* 3-5 30

I'VE GOT TO HAVE YOU / WHENEVER I THINK OF YOU (by Adrian Schubert & His Salon Orchestra as Roy Carlson's Dance Orchestra; Vocals: The Stollers Quartet) .... *Banner 0573* 3-5 30

MEADOW LARK (Vocal: Irving Kaufman) / I CAN'T GET OVER A GIRL LIKE YOU (Vocal: Arthur Hall) .... *Regal 8148* 2-4 26

MY LITTLE NEST (OF HEAVENLY BLUE) / THAT NIGHT IN ARABY (Vocal: Irving Kaufman) .... *Regal 8124* 2-4 26

ROSES REMIND ME OF YOU / WHERE DOES SHE LIVE? (by Adrian Schubert & His Salon Orchestra as The Missouri Jazz Band) .... *Banner 1766* 2-4 26

ROSES REMIND ME OF YOU / WHERE DOES SHE LIVE? (by Adrian Schubert & His Salon Orchestra as The Missouri Jazz Band) .... *Domino 3734* 2-4 26
(Simultaneously released on two labels)

SHE'LL BE COMIN' 'ROUND THE MOUNTAIN / OH! DEM GOLDEN SLIPPERS .... *Perfect 15329* 3-5 30
(Vocals: Irving Kaufman)

SOMEBODY ELSE / DIXIE VAGABOND .... *Regal 8269* 2-4 27
(Vocals: Irving Kaufman)

SOMEBODY'S LONELY / HONEY BUNCH (Vocal: Irving Kaufman) .... *Domino 3700* 2-4 26

TRAIL OF DREAMS / BECAUSE I LOVE YOU .... *Domino 3818* 2-4 26
(Vocals: Arthur Hall)

TRAIL OF DREAMS / BECAUSE I LOVE YOU .... *Regal 8147* 2-4 26
(Vocals: Arthur Hall)
(Simultaneously released on two labels)

WHAT GOOD IS GOOD MORNING? / SHOW THAT FELLOW THE DOOR (by Adrian Schubert & His Salon Orchestra as The Imperial Dance Orchestra; Vocal: Billy Jones) .... *Regal 8041* 2-4 26

WHAT GOOD IS GOOD MORNING / WHAT A MAN! (by Adrian Schubert & His Salon Orchestra) .... *Banner 1727* 2-4 26

WHAT GOOD IS GOOD MORNING / WHAT A MAN! (by Adrian Schubert & His Salon Orchestra) .... *Domino 3699* 2-4 26
(Simultaneously released on two labels)

SCHUBERT, Adrian, & His Salon Orchestra as The Imperial Dance Orchestra

CLAP YO' HANDS / DO-DO-DO .... *Regal 8201* 3-5 27

CLIMBING UP THE LADDER OF LOVE / PLAY, GYPSIES – DANCE GYPSIES .... *Regal 8157* 2-4 26

DREAM LOVER / YOU'RE ALWAYS IN MY ARMS .... *Domino 4468* 3-5 30
(Vocals: Smith Ballew as Buddy Blue)

DREAM LOVER / YOU'RE ALWAYS IN MY ARMS .... *Regal 8911* 3-5 30
(Vocals: Smith Ballew as Buddy Blue)
(Simultaneously released on two labels)

HELLO BABY (Vocals: The Strollers Quartet) / I'VE GOT TO HAVE YOU .... *Domino 4479* 3-5 30

HELLO BABY (Vocals: The Strollers Quartet) / I'VE GOT TO HAVE YOU .... *Pathe Actuelle 37083* 4-6 30

HELLO BABY (Vocals: The Strollers Quartet) / I'VE GOT TO HAVE YOU .... *Perfect 15264* 3-5 30

HELLO BABY (Vocals: The Strollers Quartet) / I'VE GOT TO HAVE YOU .... *Regal 8924* 3-5 30
(Simultaneously released on four labels)

HUGS AND KISSES (Vocals: Unknown) / ALL ALONE MONDAY .... *Regal 8182* 2-4 26

JUST THE SAME / SWEET MARIE .... *Regal 8313* 2-4 27
(Vocals: Scrappy Lambert as Harold Miller)

LOOKING AT THE WORLD THRU' ROSE-COLORED GLASSES / THAT'S ANNABELLE .... *Banner 1798* 2-4 26
(Vocals: Irving Kaufman)

MY LITTLE NEST (OF HEAVENLY BLUE) / THAT NIGHT IN ARABY (Vocal: Irving Kaufman) .... *Banner 1816* 2-4 26

MY LITTLE NEST (OF HEAVENLY BLUE) / THAT NIGHT IN ARABY (Vocal: Irving Kaufman) .... *Domino 3790* 2-4 26
(Simultaneously released on two labels)

ORIENTAL MOONLIGHT / CORONADO NIGHTS .... *Banner 1923* 2-4 27

ORIENTAL MOONLIGHT / CORONADO NIGHTS .... *Domino 3896* 2-4 27
(Simultaneously released on two labels)

SHOW THAT FELLOW THE DOOR (Vocal: Billy Jones) / WHAT GOOD IS GOOD MORNING? (by Adrian Schubert & His Salon Orchestra as The Hollywood Dance Orchestra) .... *Regal 8041* 2-4 26

WHY SHOULD YOU CRY OVER ME / BLUE SKIES (Vocal: Arthur Fields) .... *Banner 1905* 2-4 27

WHY SHOULD YOU CRY OVER ME / BLUE SKIES (Vocal: Arthur Fields)....... *Domino 3878* 2-4 27
(Simultaneously released on two labels)

SCHUBERT, Adrian, & His Salon Orchestra as The Majestic Dance Orchestra

NEVER / C'EST VOUS (Vocal: Charles Harrison) .... *Banner 6077* 2-4 27

WAS IT LOVE? / JUST A KISS IN THE MOONLIGHT................. *Banner 7245* 2-4 28

WILL WE EVER MEET AGAIN? (Vocal: Leroy Montesanto) / EVERYWHERE YOU GO (Vocal: Frank Luther)................... *Banner 7011* 2-4 28

SCHUBERT, Adrian, & His Salon Orchestra as The Missouri Jazz Band

CLAP YO' HANDS / DO-DO-DO.......... *Banner 1888* 3-5 27

CLAP YO' HANDS / DO-DO-DO......... *Domino 3857* 3-5 27
(Simultaneously released on two labels)

EVERYBODY'S GOT A GIRL BUT ME / OUT IN THE NEW-MOWN HAY.................... *Banner 1797* 2-4 26
(Vocals: Irving Kaufman)

EVERYBODY'S GOT A GIRL BUT ME / OUT IN THE NEW-MOWN HAY................... *Domino 3765* 2-4 26
(Vocals: Irving Kaufman)
(Simultaneously released on two labels)

HERE COMES FATIMA (Vocal: Irving Kaufman) / SUSIE, OH SUSIE, WHY WON'T YOU MARRY ME? (by Adrian Schubert & His Salon Orchestra as The Six Black Diamonds; Vocal: Billy Jones) .... *Domino 3807* 3-5 26

NOBODY'S SWEETHEART / THE MAN FROM THE SOUTH .... *Perfect 15273* 3-5 30
(Vocals: Scrappy Lambert as Ralph Haines)

NOBODY'S SWEETHEART / THE MAN FROM THE SOUTH .... *Regal 8942* 3-5 30
(Vocals: Scrappy Lambert as Ralph Haines)
(Simultaneously released on two labels)

SHE BELONGS TO ME / OUT IN THE NEW-MOWN HAY...................... *Regal 8110* 2-4 26
(Vocals: Irving Kaufman)

SUSIE, OH SUSIE, WHY WON'T YOU MARRY ME? (Vocal: Billy Jones) / HERE COMES FATIMA (Vocal: Irving Kaufman).................. *Banner 1842* 3-5 26

THAT CAPTIVATING RHYTHM / HI-DIDDLE-DIDDLE (Vocal: Arthur Fields) .... *Banner 1819* 2-4 26

THAT CAPTIVATING RHYTHM / HI-DIDDLE-DIDDLE (Vocal: Arthur Fields)........... *Domino 3785* 2-4 26
(Simultaneously released on two labels)

THERE AIN'T NO MAYBE IN MY BABY'S EYES / IDOLIZING (by Adrian Schubert & His Salon Orchestra as The Hollywood Dance Orchestra) .... *Banner 1870* 3-5 26
(Vocals: Arthur Fields)

WHERE DOES SHE LIVE? / ROSES REMIND ME OF YOU (by Adrian Schubert & His Salon Orchestra as The Hollywood Dance Orchestra)................ *Banner 1766* 2-4 26

WHERE DOES SHE LIVE? / ROSES REMIND ME OF YOU (by Adrian Schubert & His Salon Orchestra as The Hollywood Dance Orchestra) .... *Domino 3734* 2-4 26
(Simultaneously released on two labels)

WHO ARE YOU FOOLING TONIGHT? / HOW COULD RED RIDING HOOD? .... *Banner 1904* 3-5 27

SCHUBERT, Adrian, & His Salon Orchestra as The Palace Dance Orchestra

I'M FOLLOWING YOU (Vocal: Smith Ballew as Jimmy Green) / CRYING FOR THE CAROLINAS (by the Collegians, a pseudonym for an unidentified band)...... *Broadway 1349* 3-5 30

SCHUBERT, Adrian, & His Salon Orchestra as The Six Black Diamonds

SUSIE, OH SUSIE, WHY WON'T YOU MARRY ME (Vocal: Billy Jones) / HERE COMES FATIMA (by Adrian Schubert & His Salon Orchestra as The Missouri Jazz Band; Vocal: Irving Kaufman).................. *Domino 3807* 3-5 26

SCHUBERT, Adrian, & His Salon Orchestra as The Southampton Society Orchestra

PUT YOUR ARMS WHERE THEY BELONG / SILVER MOON................ *Pathe Actuelle 36629* 3-5 27
(Vocals: Scrappy Lambert as Harold Clarke)

PUT YOUR ARMS WHERE THEY BELONG / SILVER MOON........................ *Perfect 14810* 2-4 27
(Vocals: Scrappy Lambert as Harold Clarke)
(Simultaneously released on two labels)

SCHUBERT, Adrian, as Adrian Schubert's Salon Orchestra: *see SCHUBERT, Adrian, & His Salon Orchestra*

SCHULTZ, Bernie, & His Crescent Orchestra

HOLD EVERYTHING / SOMEBODY AND ME .... *Gennett 6234* 10-12 27

SHOW ME THAT KIND OF A GIRL (Vocals: Unknown) / — .... *Gennett 6235* 10-12 27

SHOW ME THAT KIND OF A GIRL (Vocals: Unknown) / — .... *Silvertone 25107* 8-10 27
(Simultaneously released on two labels)

SWEET VIOLETS / SWEETHEART OF SIGMA CHI...................... *Gennett 6216* 8-10 27
(Vocals: by Chorus)

SCHUTT, Arthur, & His Orchestra
(Arthur Schutt: 11/21/02 – 1/28/65)

HAVE A LITTLE FAITH IN ME / CRYIN' FOR THE CAROLINES............... *Odeon ONY-36028* 5-8 30
(Vocals: Smith Ballew)

HAVE A LITTLE FAITH IN ME / CRYIN' FOR THE CAROLINES..................... *Okeh 41359* 5-8 30
(Vocals: Smith Ballew)
(Simultaneously released on two labels)

'LEVEN THIRTY SATURDAY NIGHT (Vocal: Smith Ballew) / —.... *Odeon ONY-36056* 10-12 30

'LEVEN THIRTY SATURDAY NIGHT (Vocal: Smith Ballew) / — .... *Okeh 41400* 10-12 30
(Simultaneously released on two labels)

MONTANA CALL / THE MOON IS LOW .... *Odeon ONY-36055* 5-8 30
(Vocals: Smith Ballew)

MONTANA CALL / THE MOON IS LOW .... *Okeh 41391* 5-8 30
(Vocals: Smith Ballew)
(Simultaneously released on two labels)

MY FATE IS IN YOUR HANDS / IF I'M DREAMING..................... *Okeh 41346* 5-8 30
(Vocals: Smith Ballew)

SHARING / THE SONG WITHOUT A NAME .... *Odeon ONY-36096* 5-8 30
(Vocals: Smith Ballew)

SCHWARZ, Dickinson, as Dickinson Schwarz' Four-Leaf Clovers

HELLO CUTIE! / I WANT TO BE MILES AWAY FROM EVERYONE............ *Gennett 6119* 4-6 27
(Vocals: Tom Low)

SCOGGIN, Chic, & His Pla-Mor Orchestra

IF I COULD WRITE A SONG / SHE CHILLS ME.................. *Brunswick 4654* 5-8 30
(Vocals: Unknown)

SCOTT, Blue, & His Blue Boys: *see SCOTT, Leonard*

SCOTT, Cecil, & His Bright Boys
(Cecil Scott: 11/22/05 – 1/5/64)

LAWD, LAWD (Vocals: Frank Newton & chorus) / IN A CORNER..................... *Victor V-38098* 30-35 30

SCOTT, Cecil, & His Orchestra

BRIGHT BOY BLUES / SPRINGFIELD STOMP.............. *Victor V-38117* 30-35 30

SCOTT, Leonard, as Blue Scott & His Blue Boys

I CAN DISH IT – CAN YOU TAKE IT? / RUBBIN', RUBBIN'................ *Bluebird B-6520* 12-15 36
(Vocals: Leonard Scott)

YOU CAN'T LOSE / AT THE BOTTOM................. *Bluebird B-6557* 10-12 36
(Vocals: Leonard Scott)

SCOTT, Lloyd, & His Orchestra

SYMPHONIC SCRONCH / HAPPY HOUR BLUES......................... *Victor 20495* 20-25 27

SCOTT, Raymond, & His New Orchestra
(Raymond Scott: 9/10/10 –)

BEAU NIGHT IN HOTCHKISS CORNERS (Vocal: Gloria Hart) / THE MERRY CARROUSEL (Vocal: Clyde Burke)..... *Columbia 36288* 2-4 41

BLUES MY GIRL FRIEND TAUGHT ME / EVENING STAR.................. *Columbia 35980* 3-5 41

CRAZY RHYTHM / MOUNTAIN HIGH, VALLEY LOW .... *Audivox 107* 3-5 -
(Vocals: Dorothy Collins)

EAGLE BEAK / COPYRIGHT 1950.... *Columbia 35911* 2-4 41

FOUR BEAT SHUFFLE / BIRDSEED SPECIAL.................. *Columbia 35565* 3-5 40

GET HAPPY / GIRL AT THE TYPEWRITER (by The Raymond Scott Quintette)............. *Columbia 37359* 3-5 39

I DON'T WANT TO CRY ANY MORE / HALF WAY DOWN THE STREET.................. *Columbia 35773* 2-4 40
(Vocals: Clyde Burke)

IN A MOONBOAT / A MILLION DREAMS AGO.......................... *Columbia 35698* 2-4 40
(Vocals: Nan Wynn)

I TOUCHED A STAR / DO YOU CARE?.................. *Columbia 36161* 2-4 41
(Vocals: Clyde Burke)

I UNDERSTAND / THE THINGS I LOVE .... *Columbia 36083* 2-4 41
(Vocals: Clyde Burke)

JUST A GIGOLO / HUCKLEBERRY DUCK........... *Columbia 35363* 3-5 40

JUST A LITTLE BIT SOUTH OF NORTH CAROLINA / IN THE HUSH OF THE NIGHT..... *Columbia 36103* 2-4 41
(Vocals: Clyde Burke)

KEEP COOL, FOOL (Vocal: Gloria Hart) / WHERE ARE YOU (Vocal: Clyde Burke) .... *Columbia 36149* 2-4 41

MEXICAN JUMPING BEAN / IN A SUBWAY FAR FROM IRELAND.................. *Columbia 36211* 3-5 40

MOTHER TALK / TICO TICO........... *Audivox 102* 2-4 -
(Vocals: Dorothy Collins)

MR BASIE GOES TO WASHINGTON / MAGIC GARDEN..................... *Sonora 3008* 4-6 46

NOW I LAY ME DOWN TO DREAM / AND SO DO I................ *Columbia 35623* 2-4 40
(Vocals: Nan Wynn)

PEANUT VENDOR / BUSINESS MEN'S BOUNCE.................. *Columbia 35364* 3-5 40

PRETTY LITTLE PETTICOAT (theme song) / A NICE DAY IN THE COUNTRY.... *Columbia 35803* 2-4 40

SHADOW DANCE / MYSTERY WALTZ... *Audivox 101* 3-5 -

SINGIN' IN THE RAIN / TIGER RAG .... *Audivox 104* 4-6 -
(Vocals: Dorothy Collins)

TOONERVILLE TROLLEY / ENCHANTED FOREST .... *Sonora 3003* 4-6 46

WHEN COOTIE LEFT THE DUKE / PETITE.......................... *Columbia 35940* 3-5 41

YESTERTHOUGHTS (Vocal: Nan Wynn) / STRANGER (Vocal: Clyde Burke) .... *Columbia 35745* 2-4 40

SCOTT, Raymond, & His Orchestra

CARRIER PIGEON / CAREFUL CONVERSATION AT A DIPLOMATIC FUNCTION........... *Decca 18422* 2-4 42

CATEPILLAR CREEP / SYMPHONY UNDER THE STARS................. *Decca 18264* 2-4 42

EIGHT LETTERS IN THE MAILBOX / KODACHROME....................... *Decca 18276* 2-4 42

SECRET AGENT / PAN-AMERICAN HOT-SPOT........... *Decca 18377* 3-5 42

SCOTT, Raymond, as The Raymond Scott Quintette

BUMPY WEATHER OVER NEWARK / PETER TAMBOURINE................ *Columbia 35585* 2-4 39

GIRL AT THE TYPEWRITER / GET HAPPY (by Raymond Scott & his New Orchestra)............. *Columbia 37359* 3-5 39

HAPPY FARMER / EGYPTIAN BARN DANCE..................... *Brunswick 8144* 3-5 38

IN AN 18TH-CENTURY DRAWING-ROOM / BOY SCOUT IN SWITZERLAND.... *Brunswick 8404* 3-5 39

LITTLE BIT OF RIGOLETTO / THE QUINTETTE PLAYS CARMEN................. *Columbia 37360* 2-4 39

MINUET IN JAZZ / TWILIGHT IN TURKEY................ *Master 108* 4-6 37

MOMENT MUSICAL / MANHATTAN MINUET.................. *Columbia 37361* 2-4 39

NEW YEAR'S EVE IN A HAUNTED HOUSE / THE GIRL WITH THE LIGHT BLUE HAIR............... *Columbia 35247* 3-5 39

RECKLESS NIGHT ON BOARD AN OCEAN LINER / DINNER MUSIC FOR A PACK OF HUNGRY CANNIBALS............. *Master 136* 4-6 37

SIBERIAN SLEIGH-RIDE / THE TOBACCO AUCTIONEER ..... *Brunswick 8452* 3-5 39

TOY TRUMPET (theme song) / POWERHOUSE....................... *Master 111* 4-6 37

WAR DANCE FOR WOODEN INDIANS / THE PENGUIN................. *Brunswick 8058* 3-5 38

SCOTTI, Bill, & His Orchestra

ALICE IN WONDERLAND / KEEP YOUNG AND BEAUTIFUL................ *Bluebird B-5310* 3-5 34
(Vocals: Lee Sullivan)

ALICE IN WONDERLAND / KEEP YOUNG AND BEAUTIFUL............... *Electradisk 2177* 10-12 34
(Vocals: Lee Sullivan)

ALICE IN WONDERLAND / KEEP YOUNG AND BEAUTIFUL................ *Sunrise S-3391* 10-12 34
(Vocals: Lee Sullivan)
(Simultaneously released on three labels)

GATHER LIP ROUGE WHILE YOU MAY (Vocal: Harold van Emburgh) / BE CAREFUL (Vocal: Tom Low)................. *Bluebird B-5196* 3-5 33

GATHER LIP ROUGE WHILE YOU MAY (Vocal: Harold van Emburgh) / BE CAREFUL (Vocal: Tom Low)................. *Electradisk 2086* 10-12 33

GATHER LIP ROUGE WHILE YOU MAY (Vocal: Harold van Emburgh) / BE CAREFUL (Vocal: Tom Low)................. *Sunrise S-3277* 10-12 33
(Simultaneously released on three labels)

I JUST COULDN'T TAKE IT, BABY / YOUR MOTHER'S SON-IN-LAW .... *Bluebird B-5308* 4-6 34
(Vocals: Lee Sullivan)

I JUST COULDN'T TAKE IT, BABY / YOUR MOTHER'S SON-IN-LAW.................... *Electradisk 2175* 12-15 34
(Vocals: Lee Sullivan)

I JUST COULDN'T TAKE IT, BABY / YOUR MOTHER'S SON-IN-LAW .... *Sunrise S-3389* 12-15 34
(Vocals: Lee Sullivan)
(Simultaneously released on three labels)

IT'S ONLY A PAPER MOON (Vocal: Larry Murphy) / THE ROAD IS OPEN AGAIN (Vocals: Larry Murphy & Tom Low)...... *Bluebird B-5181* 4-6 33

IT'S ONLY A PAPER MOON (Vocal: Larry Murphy) / THE ROAD IS OPEN AGAIN (Vocals: Larry Murphy & Tom Low) ..... *Electradisk 2074* 12-15 33

IT'S ONLY A PAPER MOON (Vocal: Larry Murphy) / THE ROAD IS OPEN AGAIN (Vocals: Larry Murphy & Tom Low)....... *Sunrise S-3261* 12-15 33
(Simultaneously released on three labels)

TEMPTATION / ORCHIDS IN THE MOONLIGHT .... *Bluebird B-5309* 4-6 34
(Vocals: Lee Sullivan)

TEMPTATION / ORCHIDS IN THE MOONLIGHT...................... *Electradisk 2176* 12-15 34
(Vocals: Lee Sullivan)

TEMPTATION / ORCHIDS IN THE MOONLIGHT .... *Sunrise S-3390* 12-15 34
(Vocals: Lee Sullivan)
(Simultaneously released on three labels)

THANKS (Vocal: Larry Murphy) / THE DAY YOU CAME ALONG (Vocal: Tom Low) .... *Bluebird B-5180* 3-5 33

THANKS (Vocal: Larry Murphy) / THE DAY YOU CAME ALONG (Vocal: Tom Low)........... *Electradisk 2073* 10-12 33

THANKS (Vocal: Larry Murphy) / THE DAY YOU CAME ALONG (Vocal: Tom Low)............. *Sunrise S-3260* 10-12 33
(Simultaneously released on three labels)

SCRANTON SIRENS ORCHESTRA, The directed by Billy Lustig

COMMON STREET BLUES / CLARINET MARMALADE BLUES (by Jimmy Joy's St. Anthony Hotel Orchestra).............. *Okeh 40329* 10-12 25

WHY SHOULD I BELIEVE IN YOU? / AFRAID TO CARE (by Tobin's Midnight Serenaders)...... *Okeh 40297* 8-10 25

SEARS, Al, & His Orchestra
(Al Sears: 2/22/10 –)

BALTIMORE BOUNCE / NOW RIDE "D" TRAIN.................... *King 4489* 3-5

MARSHALL PLAN / BERRY WELL....... *King 4520* 3-5

SEARS, Jerry, as The Jerry Sears Session with Peg La Centra

ALEXANDER'S BACK IN TOWN / NOODLIN'...................... *Bluebird B-10021* 5-8 38
(Vocals: Peg La Centra)

BLUE GRASS / A BLIND MAN COULD SEE THAT I LOVE YOU.............. *Bluebird B-10097* 4-6 38
(Vocals: Peg La Centra)

WHO THREW THE MUSH IN GRANDPA'S WHISKERS / BIG MOUTH MINNIE........... *Bluebird B-10050* 5-8 38
(Vocals: Peg La Centra)

SEATTLE HARMONY KINGS, The directed by Eddie Neibaur

BREEZIN' ALONG WITH THE BREEZE / TELL ME YOU LOVE ME (by Art Landry & His Orchestra)........... *Victor 20142* 3-5 26

HOW MANY TIMES? / OH, IF I ONLY HAD YOU (by Ted Weems & His Orchestra; Vocals: Parker Gibbs, Bill Comfort, & Dusty Rhodes)...................... *Victor 20133* 3-5 26

IF I HAD A GIRL LIKE YOU / DARKTOWN SHUFFLE.............. *Victor 19772* 5-8 25

SEDRIC, Gene, & His Honey Bears
(Gene Sedric: 6/17/07 – 4/3/63)

CHOO CHOO / WAIL OF THE SCROMPH.................... *Vocalion 4552* 10-12 39

JOINT IS JUMPIN', THE / OFF TIME... *Vocalion 4576* 10-12 39
(Vocals: Myra Johnson)

SEELEY, Ray, & His Orchestra
also see SELVIN, Ben, & His Orchestra

DOWN THE RIVER OF GOLDEN DREAMS / THE RANGER'S SONG........... *Odeon ONY-36085* 2-4 30
(Vocals: Unknown)

GAZING AT THE STARS / YOU'RE THE ONE I CARE FOR............... *Odeon ONY-36174* 3-5 31
(Vocals: Unknown)

HURT / UNDER THE SPELL OF YOUR KISS.................. *Odeon ONY-36168* 3-5 31
(Vocals: Unknown)

TO WHOM IT MAY CONCERN / THERE'S SOMETHING MISSING IN YOUR EYES........ *Odeon ONY-36175* 3-5 31
(Vocals: Unknown)

YOU'RE DRIVING ME CRAZY / HURT.... *Okeh 41475* 3-5 31
(Vocals: Unknown)

YOU'RE DRIVING ME CRAZY / I HATE MYSELF (FOR FALLING IN LOVE WITH YOU).... *Odeon ONY-36167* 3-5 31
(Vocals: Unknown)

SEIDEL, Emil, & His Orchestra

BEST THINGS IN LIFE ARE FREE, THE (Vocal: Cliff Williams) / DOWN SOUTH (Vocals: chorus)...................... *Silvertone 5500* 10-12 28

COUNTING THE DAYS / MOONLIGHT LANE.................. *Gennett 6355* 5-8 28
(Vocals: Jimmy Fisher)

DEAR, ON A NIGHT LIKE THIS / ONE MORE NIGHT.................. *Gennett 6340* 8-10 28
(Vocals: Cliff Williams)

DID YOU MEAN IT? (Vocal: Jimmy Fisher) / FOR MY BABY (Vocals: chorus).......... *Superior 303* 8-10 28

DOWN SOUTH (Vocals: chorus) / THE HOURS I SPENT WITH YOU (Vocal: Cliff Williams)......... *Gennett 6309* 12-15 28

FOR MY BABY (Vocals: chorus) / THE SONG IS ENDED (Vocal: Cliff Williams)......... *Gennett 6327* 8-10 28

SHE WEARS THE PIN OF A XI PSI PHI (Vocal: Cliff Williams) / BEAUTIFUL (Vocal: Benny Benson)....... *Gennett 6367* 5-8 28

TOGETHER, WE TWO (Vocal: Cliff Williams) / DID YOU MEAN IT? (Vocal: Jimmy Fisher)......... *Gennett 6324* 12-15 28

TOGETHER, WE TWO / THE SONG IS ENDED............... *Superior 300* 5-8 28
(Vocals: Cliff Williams)

SEIDEL, Emil, & His Orchestra as Jack Crawford & His Boys

COUNTING THE DAYS (Vocal: Jimmy Fisher) / ONE MORE NIGHT (Vocal: Cliff Williams)... *Champion 15418* 5-8 28

DEAR, ON A NIGHT LIKE THIS / SHE WEARS THE PIN OF A XI PSI PHI............. *Champion 15439* 5-8 28

DID YOU MEAN IT? (Vocal: Jimmy Fisher) / FOR MY BABY (Vocals: chorus)...... *Champion 15404* 8-10 28

TOGETHER, WE TWO / THE SONG IS ENDED....................... *Champion 15400* 5-8 28
(Vocals: Cliff Williams)

SELVIN, Ben

Ben Selvin (1898 – 7/15/80) was the most prolific of all the recording bandleaders. He led many orchestras of varying sizes, beginning in 1919. His contribution of dance records reportedly exceeded nine thousand different titles, on virtually every label in existence during his career, which extended into 1934.

SELVIN, Ben, & His Orchestra

ALABAMY BOUND / I CAN'T REALIZE (YOU LOVE ME).................... *Vocalion 14964* 3-5 25

ALL OF ME (Vocals: Unknown) / I FOUND YOU (Vocal: "Le Dandy")......................... *Columbia 2585-D* 5-8 32

AM I BLUE? / MY SONG OF THE NILE....................... *Columbia 1900-D* 3-5 29
(Vocals: Smith Ballew)

AMONG MY SOUVENIRS (Vocal: Cyril Pitts) / DREAM KISSES (by Sam Lanin as The Ipana Troubadours; Vocal: Harold Lambert).... *Columbia 1188-D* 3-5 27

ANY ICE TODAY, LADY? (Vocal: Irving Kaufman) / SHE KNOWS HER ONIONS (Vocal: Ben Selvin)......................... *Brunswick 3301* 3-5 26

BABY FACE / WHO WOULDN'T!..... *Brunswick 3253* 3-5 26
(Vocals: Ben Selvin)

BARCELONA / ON THE RIVIERA.... *Brunswick 3284* 2-4 26
(Vocals: Irving Kaufman)

BEND DOWN, SISTER / POTATOES ARE CHEAPER, TOMATOES ARE CHEAPER, NOW'S THE TIME TO FALL IN LOVE............ *Columbia 2575-D* 8-10 32
(Vocals: Dick Robertson as Roy Carroll)

BETTY (Vocal: Ben Selvin) / VALENCIA (Vocal: Irving Kaufman).... *Brunswick 3172* 3-5 26

BREEZIN' ALONG (TO GEORGIA) / LET'S WANDER AWAY........... *Vocalion 15083* 2-4 25

BROADWAY MELODY / YOU WERE MEANT FOR ME (by Ben Selvin & His Orchestra as The Broadway Nitelites)............ *Columbia 1738-D* 3-5 29
(Vocals: Unknown)

BROWN EYES, WHY ARE YOU BLUE? / YA! YA! ALMA (Vocal: Ben Selvin)..... *Vocalion 15110* 2-4 25

CABIN IN THE COTTON (Vocal: Helen Rowland) / HUMMIN' TO MYSELF (Vocals: Unknown)................. *Columbia 2669-D* 8-10 32

CHARLEY, MY BOY (Vocal: Irving Kaufman) / RED HOT MAMA.................. *Vocalion 14853* 3-5 24

CHARLIE CADET / LITTLE MARY BROWN.......... *Columbia 2554-D* 8-10 31
(Vocals: The Rondoliers)

CHEERIE-BEERIE-BE / I COULD WALTZ ON FOREVER.............. *Brunswick 3634* 2-4 27
(Vocals: Frank Munn)

CHEER UP (GOOD TIMES ARE COMIN') (Vocals: Unknown) / I REMEMBER YOU FROM SOMEWHERE (Vocal: Ruth Etting)... *Columbia 2207-D* 4-6 30

CRAZY PEOPLE / IS I IN LOVE? I IS... *Columbia 2661-D* 8-10 32
(Vocals: by trio)

DANCING ON THE CEILING / JUST FRIENDS................. *Columbia 2618-D* 4-6 32
(Vocals: Unknown)

DAY DREAMING / HONEST AND TRULY............. *Vocalion 14932* 2-4 24

DINNER AT EIGHT / EMPEROR JONES............... *Columbia 2813-D* 4-6 33
(Vocals: Unknown)

DON'T BRING LULU / LET IT RAIN, LET IT POUR........ *Vocalion 15003* 3-5 25
(Vocals: Irving Kaufman)

DO THE NEW YORK (Vocals: The Pickens Sisters & The Rondoliers) / HIKIN' DOWN THE HIGHWAY (Vocals: The Rondoliers)............. *Columbia 2499-D* 8-10 31

DREAM HOUSE / JUST IMAGINE... *Columbia 1490-D* 3-5 28
(Vocals: Unknown)

FUNNY, DEAR, WHAT LOVE CAN DO / 'TAIN'T NO SIN (TO DANCE AROUND IN YOUR BONES)............... *Columbia 2096-D* 4-6 30
(Vocals: Unknown)

GOOD NEWS / LUCKY IN LOVE..... *Brunswick 3641* 3-5 27
(Vocals: Franklyn Baur)

GREY MORN / ON THE ALAMO......... *Banner 1065* 2-4 22

HAPPY DAYS ARE HERE AGAIN / THE ONE GIRL................. *Columbia 2116-D* 4-6 30
(Vocals: Unknown)

HERE I AM (Vocal: Ben Selvin) / ONLY YOU AND LONELY ME (Vocals: The Keller Sisters and Lynch)..... *Vocalion 15365* 2-4 26

HE'S NOT WORTH YOUR TEARS / WOULD YOU LIKE TO TAKE A WALK?............. *Columbia 2381-D* 8-10 31
(Vocals: Helen Rowland)

HIGH AND LOW (Vocals: by trio) / DANCING IN THE DARK (Vocals: Unknown)........... *Columbia 2473-D* 5-8 31

HOLDING MY HONEY'S HAND / SLEEP (COME ON AND TAKE ME)... *Columbia 2676-D* 5-8 32

HOODLE-DEE-DOO-DEE-DOO (Vocal: Ben Selvin) / WHEN THE RED, RED ROBIN COMES BOB, BOB, BOBBIN' ALONG (Vocals: The Keller Sisters & Lynch).......................... *Brunswick 3213* 3-5 26

HOOSIER SWEETHEART (Vocal: Ben Selvin) / CLOSE TO YOUR HEART (Vocal: Frank Munn)..................... *Brunswick 3504* 3-5 27

I AM THE WORDS – YOU ARE THE MELODY / OLD-FASHIONED GIRL.......... *Columbia 2298-D* 4-6 30
(Vocals: Unknown)

IF I HAD YOU / CAROLINA MOON.... *Columbia 1719-D* 3-5 29
(Vocals: Unknown)

I MISS A LITTLE MISS (Vocals: by quartet) / CHEERFUL LITTLE EARFUL (Vocal: Helen Rowland)................. *Columbia 2356-D* 8-10 31

I'M JUST A VAGABOND LOVER / THE ONE IN THE WORLD............... *Columbia 1831-D* 3-5 29
(Vocals: Unknown)

I'M SORRY, SALLY (Vocal: Jack Palmer) / IF YOU WANT THE RAINBOW (YOU MUST HAVE THE RAIN) (Vocal: Larry Murphy)................. *Columbia 1617-D* 3-5 28

I'M TIRED OF EVERYTHING BUT YOU / DESERT ISLE.................. *Vocalion 15049* 2-4 25

I'M YOURS / DIXIANA............... *Columbia 2287-D* 5-8 30
(Vocals: Irving Kaufman)

IN A LITTLE LOVE BOAT / SUITE 16.... *Vocalion 15029* 2-4 25

INDIAN CRADLE SONG (Vocal: Lewis James) / I'M AFRAID OF YOU (Vocals: Unknown)... *Columbia 1399-D* 3-5 28

I ONLY HAVE EYES FOR YOU / BORN TO BE KISSED............. *Columbia 2966-D* 4-6 34
(Vocals: Unknown)

I WANT A LITTLE LOVIN' / JUST A LITTLE DRINK (Vocal: Arthur Hall)...... *Banner 1599* 3-5 25

I WANT A LITTLE LOVIN' / JUST A LITTLE DRINK (Vocal: Arthur Hall)..... *Domino 3572* 3-5 25
(Simultaneously released on two labels)

I WISH'T I WAS IN PEORIA / SWEET CHILD...................... *Vocalion 15220* 3-5 26
(Vocals: Ben Selvin)

JEANNINE, I DREAM OF LILAC TIME / GRIEVING........................ *Columbia 1512-D* 2-4 28
(Vocals: Unknown)

JUST A LITTLE CUTER (THAN THE REST) / MARIANETTE.................. *Brunswick 3545* 2-4 27
(Vocals: Franklyn Baur)

KEEP ON CROONIN' A TUNE / SOMEBODY'S STOLEN MY SWEET, SWEET BABY.......... *Vocalion 15168* 3-5 26

KENTUCKY LULLABY / TRAIL OF DREAMS................... *Brunswick 3272* 2-4 26
(Vocals: Franklyn Baur)

KINKY KIDS' PARADE (Vocal: Ben Selvin) / CHARLESTONETTE............... *Vocalion 15105* 3-5 25

LADY WHIPPORWILL / RIGHT OUT OF HEAVEN........... *Columbia 1538-D* 2-4 28
(Vocals: Unknown)

LET'S DRINK A DRINK TO THE FUTURE (Vocals: by quartet) / JUST ONE MORE CHANCE (Vocals: The Rondoliers)............. *Columbia 2487-D* 8-10 31

LONELY / LO LO................... *Columbia 2234-D* 4-6 30

LOOKING AT YOU ACROSS THE BREAKFAST TABLE / LET ME SING AND I'M HAPPY ... *Columbia 2150-D* 5-8 30
(Vocals: Smith Ballew)

LOVING YOU / JUST A LITTLE WHILE ... *Columbia 2312-D* 4-6 30
(Vocals: Smith Ballew)

LULLABY OF THE LEAVES / WHISTLE AND BLOW YOUR BLUES AWAY ... *Columbia 2654-D* 4-6 32
(Vocals: Unknown)

MISS YOU / JUNIOR ... *Columbia 1875-D* 4-6 29
(Vocals: Smith Ballew)

MOONLIGHT MEMORIES / LAND OF MY SUNSET DREAMS (Vocal: Irving Kaufman) ... *Vocalion 14834* 2-4 24

MY HEART STOOD STILL / THOU SWELL ... *Columbia 1187-D* 2-4 27
(Vocals: Unknown)

MY LOVE PARADE / DREAM LOVER ... *Harmony 1027-H* 3-5 29

MY MAN FROM CAROLINE (Vocal: Eva Taylor) / STILL I LOVE HER (Vocal: Lew Conrad) ... *Columbia 2323-D* 8-10 30

MY SIN / HONEY ... *Columbia 1800-D* 3-5 29
(Vocals: Unknown)

MY SONG / THIS IS THE MISSUS ... *Columbia 2515-D* 5-8 31
(Vocals: Paul Small)

MY SWEET TOOTH SAYS "I WANNA" (BUT MY WISDOM TOOTH SAYS "NO") / NOBODY LOVES NO BABY LIKE MY BABY LOVES ME! ... *Columbia 2501-D* 8-10 31
(Vocals: The Pickens Sisters)

NANCY / ON THE WAY TO MONTEREY ... *Vocalion 14909* 2-4 24
(Vocals: Irving Kaufman)

NEVER WITHOUT YOU / EV'RY LITTLE WHILE ... *Brunswick 3455* 3-5 27
(Vocals: Ben Selvin)

99 OUT OF A HUNDRED WANNA BE LOVED (Vocal: Helen Rowland) / LOVE FOR SALE ... *Columbia 2400-D* 8-10 31

OH GEE! OH JOY! / SAY SO! ... *Columbia 1285-D* 2-4 28
(Vocals: Unknown)

OH! IF I ONLY HAD YOU / THAT'S ANNABELLE ... *Brunswick 3277* 3-5 26
(Vocals: Ben Selvin)

OH! WHAT A THRILL / GOODNIGHT, MOON ... *Columbia 2592-D* 4-6 32
(Vocals: Unknown)

ON A LITTLE BALCONY IN SPAIN / LADY, PLAY YOUR MANDOLIN ... *Columbia 2367-D* 5-8 31
(Vocals: Smith Ballew)

ONLY LOVE IS REAL / THE WOMAN IN THE SHOE ... *Columbia 2014-D* 5-8 29
(Vocals: Smith Ballew)

OOH! MAYBE IT'S YOU / SHAKING THE BLUES AWAY ... *Brunswick 3639* 3-5 27
(Vocals: Franklyn Baur)

OUT OF THE TEMPEST / SOMEDAY, SOMEWHERE ... *Columbia 1575-D* 4-6 28
(Vocals: Larry Murphy)

PETER PAN, I LOVE YOU / DOES MY SWEETIE DO – AND HOW! ... *Vocalion 14982* 3-5 25

POOR KID (Vocal: Sid Garry) / NOW YOU'RE IN MY ARMS (Vocal: Helen Rowland) ... *Columbia 2463-D* 5-8 31

POOR LITTLE RICH GIRL / A CUP OF COFFEE, A SANDWICH, AND YOU (Vocal: Ben Selvin) ... *Vocalion 15208* 2-4 26

RAIN ON THE ROOF / AUF WIEDERSEHEN, MY DEAR ... *Columbia 2614-D* 3-5 32
(Vocals: "Le Dandy")

RAMONA / IN MY BOUQUET OF MEMORIES ... *Columbia 1337-D* 2-4 28
(Vocals: Unknown)

REDSKIN / "YO TE AMO" MEANS "I LOVE YOU" (by Ben Selvin & His Orchestra as The Columbians) ... *Columbia 1739-D* 3-5 29
(Vocals: Unknown)

REFLECTIONS IN THE WATER / MORNING, NOON AND NIGHT (Vocal: Jack Miller) ... *Columbia 2789-D* 5-8 33

REMINISCING / I LOVE YOU SO ... *Columbia 2159-D* 5-8 30
(Vocals: Smith Ballew)

ROGUE SONG / WHEN I'M LOOKING AT YOU ... *Columbia 2080-D* 3-5 29
(Vocals: Unknown)

ROLLIN' HOME / THE PRIZE WALTZ ... *Columbia 2965-D* 3-5 34
(Vocals: Unknown)

ROOM WITH A VIEW / DANCE, LITTLE LADY ... *Columbia 1693-D* 4-6 29
(Vocals: Unknown)

SHEPHERD'S SERENADE / CHARMING ... *Columbia 2066-D* 5-8 30
(Vocals: Smith Ballew)

SLEEPY-TIME GAL / WHOOPEE! ... *Vocalion 15154* 3-5 26
(Vocals: Ben Selvin)

SMILE, DARN YA, SMILE / THE ONE MAN BAND ... *Columbia 2421-D* 5-8 31
(Vocals: Joe & Dan Mooney, The Sunshine Boys)

SO DOES YOUR OLD MANDARIN / WHAT GOOD IS GOOD MORNING ... *Brunswick 3151* 3-5 26
(Vocals: Ben Selvin)

SONG OF THE FOOL (Vocals: Unknown) / WHO'S CALLING YOU SWEETHEART TONIGHT? ... *Columbia 2345-D* 3-5 31

SONYA (YUP, ALAY YUP!) (Vocal: Irving Kaufman) / MAMIE ... *Vocalion 15081* 3-5 25

SO THAT'S THE KIND OF GIRL YOU ARE (Vocal: Arthur Fields) / LOUD-SPEAKIN' PAPA ... *Banner 1586* 3-5 25

SO THAT'S THE KIND OF GIRL YOU ARE (Vocal: Arthur Fields) / LOUD-SPEAKIN' PAPA ... *Domino 3557* 3-5 25

SO THAT'S THE KIND OF GIRL YOU ARE (Vocal: Arthur Fields) / LOUD-SPEAKIN' PAPA ... *Regal 9888* 3-5 25
(Simultaneously released on three labels)

STARS ARE THE WINDOWS OF HEAVEN / WHEN YOU WALTZ WITH THE ONE YOU LOVE ... *Brunswick 3353* 2-4 26
(Vocals: Frank Munn)

STEPPIN' IN SOCIETY / CHARLESTON ... *Vocalion 15038* 3-5 25

SUNNY SIDE UP / LOVE, YOUR SPELL IS EVERYWHERE ... *Columbia 1994-D* 5-8 29
(Vocals: Smith Ballew)

SWANEE BUTTERFLY / WILL YOU REMEMBER ME? ... *Vocalion 14981* 2-4 25

TAMIAMI TRAIL / POOR PAPA ... *Vocalion 15277* 3-5 26
(Vocals: Unknown)

TENTIN' DOWN IN TENNESSEE (Vocal: Ben Selvin) / AFTER I SAY I'M SORRY ... *Vocalion 15258* 3-5 26

THAT HAUNTING MELODY / NIGHTINGALE (whistling by Sibyl Sanderson Fagan) ... *Vocalion 14925* 2-4 24

THAT'S A GOOD GIRL / PRETTY CINDERELLA ... *Brunswick 3340* 2-4 26
(Vocals: Ben Selvin)

THAT'S THE GOOD OLD SUNNY SOUTH / WHO WOULDN'T BE JEALOUS OF YOU? ... *Columbia 1748-D* 3-5 29
(Vocals: Unknown)

THEN I'LL BE HAPPY (Vocals: Frank Bessinger & Frank Wright) / I WONDER WHERE MY BABY IS TONIGHT (Vocal: Ben Selvin) ... *Vocalion 15199* 2-4 26

THERE'S A RAINBOW 'ROUND MY SHOULDER (Vocal: Jack Palmer) / WHEN SUMMER IS GONE (by Ben Selvin & His Orchestra as The Columbians; Vocal: Jack Parker) ... *Columbia 1605-D* 4-6 28

TREES / YOURS IS MY HEART ALONE ... *Columbia 2524-D* 4-6 31
(Vocals: Unknown)

UNDER THE UKULELE TREE (Vocal: Ben Selvin) / (I'D CLIMB THE HIGHEST MOUNTAIN) IF I KNEW I'D FIND YOU (Vocal: Frank Munn) ... *Brunswick 3130* 2-4 26

WAS IT WRONG? / WHEN IT'S SLEEPY TIME DOWN SOUTH ... *Clarion 5387-C* 4-6 31
(Vocals: Dick Robertson as Phil Hughes)

WAS IT WRONG? / WHEN IT'S SLEEPY TIME DOWN SOUTH ... *Harmony 1373-H* 4-6 31
(Vocals: Dick Robertson as Phil Hughes)

WAS IT WRONG? / WHEN IT'S SLEEPY TIME DOWN SOUTH ... *Velvet Tone 2451-V* 4-6 31
(Vocals: Dick Robertson as Phil Hughes)
(Simultaneously released on three labels)

WAS THAT THE HUMAN THING TO DO? / DELISHIOUS ... *Columbia 2604-D* 4-6 32
(Vocals: Unknown)

WEB OF LOVE, THE / I'M IN LOVE WITH YOU ... *Columbia 1964-D* 4-6 29
(Vocals: Smith Ballew)

WHAT COULD BE SWEETER? / SHE WAS JUST A SAILOR'S SWEETHEART ... *Bell 370* 3-5 25

WHEN IT'S SPRINGTIME IN THE ROCKIES (Vocals: Unknown) / DANCING WITH TEARS IN MY EYES (Vocal: Ruth Etting) ... *Columbia 2206-D* 4-6 30

WHEN / TELL ME YOU'RE SORRY ... *Columbia 1321-D* 2-4 28
(Vocals: Irving Kaufman as Frank Harris)

WHEN WE'RE ALONE (PENTHOUSE SERENADE) / YOU'RE MY EVERYTHING ... *Columbia 2596-D* 4-6 32
(Vocals: Unknown)

WHEN YOU'RE WITH SOMEBODY ELSE / WE'LL HAVE A NEW HOME (IN THE MORNIN') ... *Columbia 1274-D* 2-4 28

WHEREVER YOU ARE / PLAYGROUND IN THE SKY ... *Columbia 1133-D* 2-4 27
(Vocals: Unknown)

WHITE HOUSE OF OUR OWN, A / STREET OF DREAMS ... *Columbia 2734-D* 4-6 33
(Vocals: Unknown)

WHY? / CROSS YOUR FINGERS ... *Columbia 2077-D* 4-6 30
(Vocals: Unknown)

WHY HAVE YOU FORGOTTEN WAIKIKI? / IT'S EASY TO FALL IN LOVE ... *Columbia 2255-D* 5-8 30
(Vocals: Eddie Walters)

YES SHE DO (NO SHE DON'T) (Vocals: Ben Selvin & Bill Percy) / I CALL YOU SUGAR (Vocal: Ben Selvin) ... *Brunswick 3636* 3-5 27

YOU'RE GETTING TO BE A HABIT WITH ME (Vocals: Unknown) / YOUNG AND HEALTHY (Vocals: Muriel Sherman & Elmer Feldkamp) ... *Columbia 2731-D* 5-8 33

YOURS AND MINE (Vocal: Smith Ballew) / LITTLE SPANISH DANCER (Vocals: Unknown) ... *Columbia 2366-D* 8-10 31

YOU SAID IT / LEARN TO CROON ... *Columbia 2426-D* 5-8 31
(Vocals: Helen Rowland & Paul Small)

YOU TOLD ME TO GO / OH, LOVEY, BE MINE (Vocal: Ben Selvin) ... *Vocalion 15129* 2-4 25

SELVIN, Ben, & His Orchestra as Mickie Alpert & His Orchestra

SING SONG GIRL (LITTLE YELLA CINDERELLA) (Vocals: by trio) / I SURRENDER, DEAR (Vocal: Helen Rowland) ... *Columbia 2403-D* 5-8 31

WE'RE FRIENDS AGAIN / HURT ... *Columbia 2344-D* 5-8 31
(Vocals: Unknown)

YOU CAN MAKE MY LIFE A BED OF ROSES / SAY ... *Columbia 2629-D* 4-6 32
(Vocals: Unknown)

SELVIN, Ben, & His Orchestra as Frank Auburn & His Orchestra

BETWEEN THE DEVIL AND THE DEEP BLUE SEA (Vocal: Dick Robertson) / KISS BY KISS (by Ben Selvin & His Orchestra as Roy Carroll & His Sands Point Orchestra; Vocal: Paul Small) ... *Clarion 5455-C* 5-8 32

BETWEEN THE DEVIL AND THE DEEP BLUE SEA (Vocal: Dick Robertson) / KISS BY KISS (by Ben Selvin & His Orchestra as Roy Carroll & His Sands Point Orchestra; Vocal: Paul Small) ... *Harmony 1412-H* 5-8 32

BETWEEN THE DEVIL AND THE DEEP BLUE SEA (Vocal: Dick Robertson) / KISS BY KISS (by Ben Selvin & His Orchestra as Roy Carroll & His Sands Point Orchestra; Vocal: Paul Small) ... *Velvet Tone 2515-V* 5-8 32
(Simultaneously released on three labels)

MY CRADLE SWEETHEART / FAITHFULLY YOURS ... *Clarion 5335-C* 4-6 31
(Vocals: Scrappy Lambert as Tom Frawley)

MY CRADLE SWEETHEART / FAITHFULLY YOURS ... *Harmony 1327-H* 4-6 31
(Vocals: Scrappy Lambert as Tom Frawley)

MY CRADLE SWEETHEART / FAITHFULLY YOURS ... *Velvet Tone 2399-V* 4-6 31
(Vocals: Scrappy Lambert as Tom Frawley)
(Simultaneously released on three labels)

ONE LITTLE QUARREL (Vocal: Dick Robertson) / WHEN WE'RE ALONE (PENTHOUSE SERENADE) (by Ben Selvin & His Orchestra as the D'Orsay Dance Orchestra; Vocals: Unknown) ... *Clarion 5451-C* 4-6 32

ONE LITTLE QUARREL (Vocal: Dick Robertson) / WHEN WE'RE ALONE (PENTHOUSE SERENADE) (by Ben Selvin & His Orchestra as the D'Orsay Dance Orchestra; Vocals: Unknown) ... *Harmony 1410-H* 4-6 32

ONE LITTLE QUARREL (Vocal: Dick Robertson) / WHEN WE'RE ALONE (PENTHOUSE SERENADE) (by Ben Selvin & His Orchestra as the D'Orsay Dance Orchestra; Vocals: Unknown) ... *Velvet Tone 2511-V* 4-6 32
(Simultaneously released on three labels)

ROCKY MOUNTAIN LULLABY (Vocal: Smith Ballew as Robert Wood) / WHEN THE MOON COMES OVER THE MOUNTAIN (Vocal: Smith Ballew as Chester Leighton) ... *Clarion 5320-C* 4-6 31

ROCKY MOUNTAIN LULLABY (Vocal: Smith Ballew as Robert Wood) / WHEN THE MOON COMES OVER THE MOUNTAIN (Vocal: Smith Ballew as Chester Leighton) ... *Harmony 1321-H* 4-6 31

ROCKY MOUNTAIN LULLABY (Vocal: Smith Ballew as Robert Wood) / WHEN THE MOON COMES OVER THE MOUNTAIN (Vocal: Smith Ballew as Chester Leighton) ... *Velvet Tone 2386-V* 4-6 31
(Simultaneously released on three labels)

SELVIN, Ben, & His Orchestra as The Broadway Nitelites

BYE, BYE, PRETTY BABY / JUST ANOTHER DAY WASTED AWAY ... *Columbia 1085-D* 2-4 27
(Vocals: Bob Carroll)

I WANNA BE LOVED BY YOU (Vocal: Vaughn de Leath) / YOU'RE THE CREAM IN MY COFFEE (Vocal: Jack Parker) ... *Columbia 1604-D* 4-6 28

MY HEART STOOD STILL / THOU SWELL ... *Columbia 1187-D* 2-4 27
(Vocals: Unknown)

YOU WERE MEANT FOR ME / BROADWAY MELODY (by Ben Selvin & His Orchestra) ... *Columbia 1738-D* 3-5 29
(Vocals: Unknown)

SELVIN, Ben, & His Orchestra as Buddy Campbell & His Orchestra

MOONLIGHT SAVING TIME / ROLL ON, MISSISSIPPI, ROLL ON ... *Okeh 41499* 5-8 31
(Vocals: Paul Small)

ROCKY MOUNTAIN LULLABY (Vocal: Smith Ballew as Robert Wood) / WHEN THE MOON COMES OVER THE MOUNTAIN (Vocal: Smith Ballew as Chester Leighton) ... *Okeh 41495* 4-6 31

SELVIN, Ben, & His Orchestra as Roy Carroll & His Sands Point Orchestra

BEND DOWN SISTER (Vocal: Dick Robertson as Roy Carroll) / BY THE SYCAMORE TREE (by Ben Selvin & His Orchestra as Jerry Fenwyck & His Orchestra; Vocal: Smith Ballew as Jerry Fenwyck) ... *Clarion 5420-C* 5-8 32

BEND DOWN SISTER (Vocal: Dick Robertson as Roy Carroll) / BY THE SYCAMORE TREE (by Ben Selvin & His Orchestra as Jerry Fenwyck & His Orchestra; Vocal: Smith Ballew as Jerry Fenwyck) ... *Harmony 1397-H* 5-8 32

BEND DOWN SISTER (Vocal: Dick Robertson as Roy Carroll) / BY THE SYCAMORE TREE (by Ben Selvin & His Orchestra as Jerry Fenwyck & His Orchestra; Vocal: Smith Ballew as Jerry Fenwyck) ... *Velvet Tone 2480-V* 5-8 32
(Simultaneously released on three labels)

DANCING IN THE DARK / HIGH AND LOW ... *Clarion 5343-C* 5-8 31
(Vocals: Scrappy Lambert as Roy Carroll)

DANCING IN THE DARK / HIGH AND LOW ... *Harmony 1334-H* 5-8 31
(Vocals: Scrappy Lambert as Roy Carroll)

DANCING IN THE DARK / HIGH AND LOW ... *Velvet Tone 2407-V* 5-8 31
(Vocals: Scrappy Lambert as Roy Carroll)
(Simultaneously released on three labels)

KISS BY KISS (Vocal: Paul Small) / BETWEEN THE DEVIL AND THE DEEP BLUE SEA (by Ben Selvin & His Orchestra as Frank Auburn & His Orchestra; Vocal: Dick Robertson) ... *Clarion 5455-C* 5-8 32

KISS BY KISS (Vocal: Paul Small) / BETWEEN THE DEVIL AND THE DEEP BLUE SEA (by Ben Selvin & His Orchestra as Frank Auburn & His Orchestra; Vocal: Dick Robertson) ... *Harmony 1412-H* 5-8 32

KISS BY KISS (Vocal: Paul Small) / BETWEEN THE DEVIL AND THE DEEP BLUE SEA (by Ben Selvin & His Orchestra as Frank Auburn & His Orchestra; Vocal: Dick Robertson) ... *Velvet Tone 2515-V* 5-8 32
(Simultaneously released on three labels)

LET'S GET FRIENDLY / ONE MORE TIME ... *Clarion 5338-C* 5-8 31
(Vocals: Dick Robertson as Roy Carroll)

LET'S GET FRIENDLY / ONE MORE TIME ... *Harmony 1329-H* 5-8 31
(Vocals: Dick Robertson as Roy Carroll)

LET'S GET FRIENDLY / ONE MORE TIME ... *Velvet Tone 2402-V* 5-8 31
(Vocals: Dick Robertson as Roy Carroll)
(Simultaneously released on three labels)

MOONLIGHT SAVING TIME / ROLL ON, MISSISSIPPI, ROLL ON............ *Clarion 5321-C* 5-8 31
(Vocals: Paul Small)

MOONLIGHT SAVING TIME / ROLL ON, MISSISSIPPI, ROLL ON........... *Harmony 1322-H* 5-8 31
(Vocals: Paul Small)

MOONLIGHT SAVING TIME / ROLL ON, MISSISSIPPI, ROLL ON......... *Velvet Tone 2387-V* 5-8 31
(Vocals: Paul Small)
(Simultaneously released on three labels)

SELVIN, Ben, & His Orchestra as The Cavaliers

ALL THROUGH THE NIGHT / THE KISS WALTZ................ *Columbia 2267-D* 3-5 30
(Vocals: Unknown)

AUF WIEDERSEH'N / MY STORMY WEATHER PAL................. *Columbia 1331-D* 2-4 28
(Vocals: Unknown)

DAY-DREAMING / FUNNY.......... *Columbia 428-D* 2-4 25

DON'T FORGET ME IN YOUR DREAMS / LITTLE SWEETHEART OF THE PRAIRIE... *Columbia 2382-D* 3-5 31
(Vocals: Unknown)

DREAMY CAROLINA MOON (Vocal: Vernon Dalhart) / TAKE ME BACK, MARGUERITE... *Columbia 390-D* 3-5 25

FADED SUMMER LOVE (Vocals: by trio) / CALL ME DARLING (Vocals: Unknown)........ *Columbia 2555-D* 3-5 31

I COULD WALTZ ON FOREVER WITH YOU, SWEETHEART (Vocal: Billy Jones) / THE LOVE WALTZ (Vocal: Irving Kaufman as Frank Harris)..................... *Columbia 919-D* 2-4 27

IF WE SHOULD NEVER MEET AGAIN / WHEN YOU COME TO THE END OF THE DAY.................... *Columbia 1904-D* 3-5 29
(Vocals: Unknown)

I'M SOMEONE WHO'S NO-ONE TO YOU / HONEST AND TRULY............ *Columbia 224-D* 2-4 24

IN A LITTLE SPANISH TOWN / TRAIL OF DREAMS............... *Columbia 805-D* 2-4 27

I'VE FOUND MY SWEETHEART SALLY / OH, HOW I MISS YOU TONIGHT............ *Columbia 359-D* 2-4 25

I WISH I HAD MY OLD GAL BACK AGAIN (Vocal: Franklyn Baur) / WALTZING THE BLUES AWAY.................... *Columbia 616-D* 2-4 26

JUST BROUGHT THE ROSES / THE MIDNIGHT WALTZ.......... *Columbia 331-D* 2-4 25

LAY MY HEAD BENEATH A ROSE / KENTUCKY LULLABY........... *Columbia 684-D* 2-4 26

LAZY RIVER (FLOWING TO THE SOUTHLAND) (Vocals: Lewis James & Elliott Shaw) / THAT SAXOPHONE WALTZ (Vocal: Lewis James)......... *Columbia 889-D* 2-4 27

MASQUERADE / SYLVIA.......... *Columbia 2670-D* 2-4 32
(Vocals: Unknown)

MOLLY MALONE / LIKE THE WANDERING MINSTREL........ *Columbia 1137-D* 2-4 27
(Vocals: Unknown)

MOONLIGHT LANE / AFTER WE KISS................. *Columbia 1311-D* 2-4 28
(Vocals: Unknown)

NIGHT OF LOVE / SYMPATHY WALTZ.............. *Columbia 597-D* 2-4 26

PUT YOUR ARMS WHERE THEY BELONG / AM I WASTING MY TIME ON YOU?... *Columbia 703-D* 2-4 26
(Vocals: Franklyn Baur)

SLEEPY HEAD / FALLING IN LOVE WITH YOU................ *Columbia 753-D* 2-4 26

SWEET SUZANNE / LADY DIVINE... *Columbia 1765-D* 3-5 29
(Vocals: Unknown)

THAT SOOTHING MELODY / LOVER'S WALTZ................ *Columbia 270-D* 2-4 25

TOO MANY PARTIES AND TOO MANY PALS (Vocal: Arthur Fields) / SOMEONE TO LOVE... *Columbia 584-D* 2-4 26

WABASH MOON / WHEN YOUR HAIR HAS TURNED TO SILVER..................... *Columbia 2399-D* 4-6 31
(Vocals: Unknown)

WAITING BY THE SILV'RY RIO GRANDE / I'M ALONE BECAUSE I LOVE YOU........... *Columbia 2339-D* 4-6 31
(Vocals: Unknown)

WEDDING BELLS ARE RINGING FOR SALLY (Vocals: Unknown) / WASTING MY LOVE ON YOU (by Fred Rich & His Orchestra; Vocal: Paul Small).................. *Columbia 2324-D* 5-8 30

WHEN I DREAM OF THE LAST WALTZ WITH YOU / GOLDEN MEMORIES.......... *Columbia 481-D* 2-4 25
(Vocals: Lewis James)

WHEN I LOOK TO THE WEST / WHEN THE ORGAN PLAYED AT TWILIGHT.......... *Columbia 2279-D* 3-5 30
(Vocals: Unknown)

SELVIN, Ben, & His Orchestra as The Cloverdale Country Club Orchestra

ALL OF ME (Vocal: Unknown) / I FOUND YOU (Vocal: "Le Dandy")........ *Okeh 41542* 5-8 32

SELVIN, Ben, & His Orchestra as The Columbians

BLAME IT ON THE WALTZ / CHERITZA (PRETTY LITTLE VIENNESE).............. *Columbia 778-D* 2-4 26

BUY, BUY, FOR BABY (OR BABY WILL BYE-BYE YOU) / I'M WALKING BETWEEN THE RAINDROPS (by Ben Selvin & His Orchestra as The Knickerbockers).............. *Columbia 1661-D* 4-6 29
(Vocals: Unknown)

WHEN SUMMER IS GONE (Vocal: Jack Parker) / THERE'S A RAINBOW 'ROUND MY SHOULDER (by Ben Selvin & His Orchestra; Vocal: Jack Palmer)............................ *Columbia 1605-D* 4-6 28

"YO TE AMO" MEANS "I LOVE YOU" / REDSKIN (by Ben Selvin & His Orchestra)............ *Columbia 1739-D* 3-5 29
(Vocals: Unknown)

SELVIN, Ben, & His Orchestra as The Columbia Photo Players

DARK NIGHT / DUST.............. *Columbia 2196-D* 5-8 30
(Vocals: The Rondoliers)

"FREE AND EASY", THE (Vocal: Eddie Walters) / IT MUST BE YOU (Vocal: Smith Ballew)......................... *Columbia 2149-D* 5-8 30

I'M LEARNING A LOT FROM YOU / ONE MORE WALTZ............. *Columbia 2285-D* 3-5 30
(Vocals: Unknown)

KISS ME WITH YOUR EYES / YOU DARLIN'.................... *Columbia 2197-D* 4-6 30
(Vocals: Smith Ballew)

LEAVE IT THAT WAY (Vocal: Lew Conrad) / THE WHOLE DARN THING'S FOR YOU (Vocal: Don Howard)................ *Columbia 2177-D* 5-8 30

LIVE AND LOVE TODAY / JUST A LITTLE CLOSER......... *Columbia 2256-D* 4-6 30
(Vocals: Unknown)

MY LOVE PARADE / DREAM LOVER................. *Columbia 2000-D* 4-6 29
(Vocals: Smith Ballew)

SITTING BY THE WINDOW / MONA... *Columbia 2105-D* 4-6 30
(Vocals: Unknown)

SWEEPIN' THE CLOUDS AWAY (Vocal: Smith Ballew) / IN MY LITTLE HOPE CHEST (Vocals: Unknown)..................... *Columbia 2131-D* 5-8 30

WHAT IS LIFE WITHOUT LOVE? / TO BE FORGOTTEN.............. *Columbia 2030-D* 4-6 29
(Vocals: Smith Ballew)

SELVIN, Ben, & His Orchestra as The D'Orsay Dance Orchestra

I FOUND YOU (Vocal: "Le Dandy") / YOU'RE MY EVERYTHING (Vocals: Unknown)...................... *Clarion 5440-C* 5-8 32

I FOUND YOU (Vocal: "Le Dandy") / YOU'RE MY EVERYTHING (Vocals: Unknown).................. *Harmony 1401-H* 5-8 32

I FOUND YOU (Vocal: "Le Dandy") / YOU'RE MY EVERYTHING (Vocals: Unknown)................. *Velvet Tone 2500-V* 5-8 32
(Simultaneously released on three labels)

IT'S THE DARNDEST THING (Vocals: Unknown) / LITTLE MARY BROWN (Vocals: The Nitecaps).......................... *Clarion 5394-C* 5-8 31

IT'S THE DARNDEST THING (Vocals: Unknown) / LITTLE MARY BROWN (Vocals: The Nitecaps)....................... *Harmony 1380-H* 5-8 31

IT'S THE DARNDEST THING (Vocals: Unknown) / LITTLE MARY BROWN (Vocals: The Nitecaps)..................... *Velvet Tone 2458-V* 5-8 31
(Simultaneously released on three labels)

KISS ME GOODNIGHT / (YOU ONLY WANT ME) WHEN NOBODY ELSE IS AROUND (by Ben Selvin as The Bar Harbor Society Orchestra)....... *Clarion 5466-C* 5-8 32
(Vocals: Unknown)

KISS ME GOODNIGHT / (YOU ONLY WANT ME) WHEN NOBODY ELSE IS AROUND (by Ben Selvin as The Bar Harbor Society Orchestra)..... *Harmony 1419-H* 5-8 32
(Vocals: Unknown)

KISS ME GOODNIGHT / (YOU ONLY WANT ME) WHEN NOBODY ELSE IS AROUND (by Ben Selvin as The Bar Harbor Society Orchestra).... *Velvet Tone 2526-V* 5-8 32
(Vocals: Unknown)
(Simultaneously released on three labels)

WHEN WE'RE ALONE (PENTHOUSE SERENADE) (Vocals: Unknown) / ONE LITTLE QUARREL (by Ben Selvin & His Orchestra as Frank Auburn & His Orchestra; Vocal: Dick Robertson)................ *Clarion 5451-C* 4-6 32

WHEN WE'RE ALONE (PENTHOUSE SERENADE) (Vocals: Unknown) / ONE LITTLE QUARREL (by Ben Selvin & His Orchestra as Frank Auburn & His Orchestra; Vocal: Dick Robertson)................ *Harmony 1410-H* 4-6 32

WHEN WE'RE ALONE (PENTHOUSE SERENADE) (Vocals: Unknown) / ONE LITTLE QUARREL (by Ben Selvin & His Orchestra as Frank Auburn & His Orchestra; Vocal: Dick Robertson)............. *Velvet Tone 2511-V* 4-6 32
(Simultaneously released on three labels)

SELVIN, Ben, & His Orchestra as Wally Edwards & His Orchestra

IF YOU SHOULD EVER NEED ME / OH, DONNA CLARA............ *Odeon ONY-36202* 5-8 31
(Vocals: Lou Brady)

SELVIN, Ben, & His Orchestra as Jerry Fenwyck & His Orchestra

BY THE SYCAMORE TREE (Vocal: Smith Ballew as Jerry Fenwyck) / BEND DOWN, SISTER (by Ben Selvin & His Orchestra as Roy Carroll & His Sands Point Orchestra; Vocal: Dick Robertson as Roy Carroll).......... *Clarion 5420-C* 8-10 32

BY THE SYCAMORE TREE (Vocal: Smith Ballew as Jerry Fenwyck) / BEND DOWN, SISTER (by Ben Selvin & His Orchestra as Roy Carroll & His Sands Point Orchestra; Vocal: Dick Robertson as Roy Carroll)........ *Harmony 1397-H* 8-10 32

BY THE SYCAMORE TREE (Vocal: Smith Ballew as Jerry Fenwyck) / BEND DOWN, SISTER (by Ben Selvin & His Orchestra as Roy Carroll & His Sands Point Orchestra; Vocal: Dick Robertson as Roy Carroll)....... *Velvet Tone 2480-V* 8-10 32
(Simultaneously released on three labels)

I WOULDN'T CHANGE YOU FOR THE WORLD / SAVE THE LAST DANCE FOR ME........ *Clarion 5421-C* 5-8 32
(Vocals: Smith Ballew as Jerry Fenwyck)

I WOULDN'T CHANGE YOU FOR THE WORLD / SAVE THE LAST DANCE FOR ME...... *Harmony 1398-H* 5-8 32
(Vocals: Smith Ballew as Jerry Fenwyck)

I WOULDN'T CHANGE YOU FOR THE WORLD / SAVE THE LAST DANCE FOR ME..... *Velvet Tone 2481-V* 5-8 32
(Vocals: Smith Ballew as Jerry Fenwyck)
(Simultaneously released on three labels)

NOBODY LOVES NO BABY LIKE MY BABY LOVES ME / DO THE NEW YORK... *Clarion 5364-C* 8-10 31
(Vocals: Dick Robertson as Jerry Fenwyck)

NOBODY LOVES NO BABY LIKE MY BABY LOVES ME / DO THE NEW YORK........ *Harmony 1352-H* 8-10 31
(Vocals: Dick Robertson as Jerry Fenwyck)

NOBODY LOVES NO BABY LIKE MY BABY LOVES ME / DO THE NEW YORK....... *Velvet Tone 2428-V* 8-10 31
(Vocals: Dick Robertson as Jerry Fenwyck)
(Simultaneously released on three labels)

SLOW BUT SURE / SWEET SUMMER BREEZE......... *Clarion 5371-C* 5-8 31
(Vocals: Dick Robertson as Jerry Fenwyck)

SLOW BUT SURE / SWEET SUMMER BREEZE....... *Harmony 1359-H* 5-8 31
(Vocals: Dick Robertson as Jerry Fenwyck)

SLOW BUT SURE / SWEET SUMMER BREEZE...... *Velvet Tone 2435-V* 5-8 31
(Vocals: Dick Robertson as Jerry Fenwyck)
(Simultaneously released on three labels)

SELVIN, Ben, & His Orchestra as Fran Frey & His Orchestra

PUDDIN' HEAD JONES / SITTIN' ON A LOG............... *Columbia 2841-D* 5-8 33
(Vocals: Unknown)

SELVIN, Ben, & His Orchestra as The Globe Music Masters

SNEAK, THE / SAY IT WHILE DANCING.......... *Emerson 10540* 2-4 22

SELVIN, Ben, & His Orchestra as The Golden Terrace Orchestra

FAITHFULLY YOURS (Vocal: Scrappy Lambert as Tom Frawley) / UNDER YOUR WINDOW TONIGHT (Vocal: Scrappy Lambert as Robert Wood)..... *Okeh 41505* 5-8 31

SWEET AND LOVELY / I CAN'T GET MISSISSIPPI OFF MY MIND............ *Okeh 41514* 5-8 31
(Vocals: Phil Hughes)

WRAP YOUR TROUBLES IN DREAMS / I WANNA SING ABOUT YOU........... *Okeh 41500* 5-8 31
(Vocals: Paul Small)

SELVIN, Ben, & His Orchestra as The Harmonians

IF YOU SHOULD EVER NEED ME / OH, DONNA CLARA .... *Harmony 1308-H* 5-8 31
(Vocals: Lew Conrad as Lou Brady)

SELVIN, Ben, & His Orchestra as The Harmony Dance Orchestra

CECILIA / YES, SIR, THAT'S MY BABY (Vocal: Billy Jones).......... *Harmony 10-H* 3-5 25

DINAH / TWEEDLE-DEE, TWEEDLE-DOO.................... *Harmony 60-H* 3-5 25

SELVIN, Ben, & His Orchestra as Phil Hughes & His High Hatters

TREAT ME LIKE A BABY (Vocal: Scrappy Lambert as Phil Hughes) / LOOK IN THE LOOKING GLASS (Vocals: The Rondoliers, a quartet, but the label credits Phil Hughes).............. *Clarion 5342-C* 5-8 31

TREAT ME LIKE A BABY (Vocal: Scrappy Lambert as Phil Hughes) / LOOK IN THE LOOKING GLASS (Vocals: The Rondoliers, a quartet, but the label credits Phil Hughes)............. *Harmony 1333-H* 5-8 31

TREAT ME LIKE A BABY (Vocal: Scrappy Lambert as Phil Hughes) / LOOK IN THE LOOKING GLASS (Vocals: The Rondoliers, a quartet, but the label credits Phil Hughes) .... *Velvet Tone 2406-V* 5-8 31
(Simultaneously released on three labels)

SELVIN, Ben, & His Orchestra as Lloyd Keating & His Music

HAVE YOU FORGOTTEN? / UNDER YOUR WINDOW TONIGHT................ *Clarion 5334-C* 5-8 31
(Vocals: Scrappy Lambert as Robert Wood)

HAVE YOU FORGOTTEN? / UNDER YOUR WINDOW TONIGHT............. *Harmony 1326-H* 5-8 31
(Vocals: Scrappy Lambert as Robert Wood)

HAVE YOU FORGOTTEN? / UNDER YOUR WINDOW TONIGHT............ *Velvet Tone 2398-V* 5-8 31
(Vocals: Scrappy Lambert as Robert Wood)
(Simultaneously released on three labels)

LOOKING AT YOU ACROSS THE BREAKFAST TABLE / MY FUTURE JUST PASSED....... *Harmony 1145-H* 5-8 30

TOM BOY / THE BIRTHDAY OF A KISS...................... *Clarion 11000-C* 15-20 31
(Vocals: Jack Miller)

TOM BOY / THE BIRTHDAY OF A KISS...................... *Harmony 6000-H* 15-20 31
(Vocals: Jack Miller)

TOM BOY / THE BIRTHDAY OF A KISS.................... *Velvet Tone 10000-V* 15-20 31
(Vocals: Jack Miller)
(Simultaneously released on three labels.)
(These issues are dual-track records with one track containing the vocal version, and the instrumental arrangement on the other.)

WRAP YOUR TROUBLES IN DREAMS / I WANNA SING ABOUT YOU .... *Clarion 5322-C* 5-8 31
(Vocals: Paul Small)

WRAP YOUR TROUBLES IN DREAMS / I WANNA SING ABOUT YOU .... *Harmony 1323-H* 5-8 31
(Vocals: Paul Small)

WRAP YOUR TROUBLES IN DREAMS / I WANNA SING ABOUT YOU............. *Velvet Tone 2388-V* 5-8 31
(Vocals: Paul Small)
(Simultaneously released on three labels)

SELVIN, Ben, & His Orchestra as The Kensington Serenaders

I FOUND A ROUND-ABOUT WAY TO HEAVEN / TELL ME YOU LOVE ME .... *Vocalion 15351* 2-4 26
(Vocals: Irving Kaufman)

LEAVE ME SOMETHING TO REMEMBER / MY LITTLE NEST................ *Vocalion 15383* 2-4 26
(Vocals: Irving Kaufman)

MEET ME IN THE MOONLIGHT / LAY ME DOWN TO SLEEP IN CAROLINA............ *Vocalion 15432* 2-4 26
(Vocals: The Keller Sisters and Lynch as The Vaudeville Trio)

OOH! MAYBE IT'S YOU / GOOD NEWS...................... *Vocalion 15628* 2-4 27
(Vocals: Franklyn Baur)

SHAKING THE BLUES AWAY / LUCKY IN LOVE.................. *Vocalion 15629* 3-5 27
(Vocals: Franklyn Baur)

SHOW THAT FELLOW THE DOOR / TONIGHT'S MY NIGHT WITH BABY................ *Vocalion 15340* 3-5 26
(Vocals: Ben Selvin)

SELVIN, Ben, & His Orchestra as The Knickerbockers

ALL ABOARD FOR HEAVEN / THE ORIGINAL CHARLESTON .... *Columbia 355-D* 3-5 25

AWAY FROM YOU / DON'T KEEP ME IN THE DARK, BRIGHT EYES.................. *Columbia 1462-D* 3-5 28
(Vocals: Unknown)

DELILAH / I FOUND A MILLION-DOLLAR BABY .... *Columbia 870-D* 2-4 27
(Vocals: Unknown)

FROM NOW ON / YOU'VE MADE ME HAPPY TODAY .... *Columbia 2003-D* 5-8 29
(Vocals: Smith Ballew)

GOOD FOR YOU – BAD FOR ME / THANK YOUR FATHER.......... *Columbia 2129-D* 5-8 30
(Vocals: Smith Ballew)

HAPPY DAYS AND LONELY NIGHTS / DOIN' THE RACCOON........... *Columbia 1596-D* 3-5 28
(Vocals: Unknown)

HONG KONG DREAM GIRL / TEA FOR TWO.................... *Columbia 358-D* 2-4 25

I CAN'T GIVE YOU ANYTHING BUT LOVE / I MUST HAVE THAT MAN........ *Columbia 1424-D* 5-8 28
(Vocals: Vaughn de Leath)

I'M WALKING BETWEEN THE RAINDROPS / BUY, BUY FOR BABY (OR BABY WILL BYE-BYE YOU) (by Ben Selvin & His Orchestra as The Columbians).................... *Columbia 1661-D* 4-6 29
(Vocals: Unknown)

I WONDER WHERE MY BABY IS TONIGHT? (Vocal: Ben Selvin as Robert Benjamin) / WHAT A BLUE-EYED BABY YOU ARE .... *Columbia 494-D* 2-4 25

LADY I LOVE, THE / ALL OF A SUDDEN .... *Columbia 2679-D* 5-8 32
(Vocals: Unknown)
(This record was pressed in blue shellac)

LOOKING FOR A BOY / SWEET AND LOW DOWN .... *Columbia 549-D* 3-5 26

MANHATTAN / SENTIMENTAL ME............... *Columbia 422-D* 2-4 25

MISS ANNABELLE LEE / ROAM ON, MY LITTLE GYPSY SWEETHEART ... *Columbia 1088-D* 2-4 27
(Vocals: Irving Kaufman)

MY MAN IS ON THE MAKE (Vocal: Eva Taylor) / WHY DO YOU SUPPOSE? (Vocal: Smith Ballew) ... *Columbia 2067-D* 8-10 30

REALLY AND TRULY (Vocal: Irving Kaufman as Frank Harris) / WHAT'S THE REASON? (Vocals: The Three Melodians) .... *Columbia 1398-D* 2-4 28

RIO RITA (Vocal: Charles Kaley) / THE KINKAJOU (Vocal: Johnny Marvin)................ *Columbia 893-D* 2-4 27

ROSY CHEEKS / ONE SUMMER NIGHT........... *Columbia 1012-D* 2-4 27
(Vocals: Unknown)

SLOW BUT SURE / ME! .... *Columbia 2502-D* 5-8 31
(Vocals: Dick Robertson)

SOMEONE / HALF A MOON .... *Columbia 832-D* 2-4 27

SONG OF SIBERIA / SONG OF THE BLUES (Vocal: Smith Ballew).... *Columbia 1940-D* 5-8 29

STEPPIN' IN SOCIETY / COLLEGIATE..................... *Columbia 391-D* 2-4 25

TONIGHT'S MY NIGHT WITH BABY (Vocal: Ben Selvin as Robert Benjamin) / HI-HO! THE MERRIO (Vocal: Arthur Fields)................... *Columbia 650-D* 2-4 26

WHEN YUBA PLAYS THE RHUMBA ON THE TUBA / SING A LITTLE JINGLE.......... *Columbia 2483-D* 4-6 31
(Vocals: Unknown)

WHERE ARE YOU, DREAM GIRL? / IF I WERE YOU, I'D FALL IN LOVE WITH ME ..... *Columbia 1901-D* 4-6 29
(Vocals: Unknown)

WHERE THE BLUE OF THE NIGHT MEETS THE GOLD OF THE DAY / YOU WERE MY SALVATION...... *Columbia 2576-D* 5-8 32
(Vocals: Unknown)

WHO CARES? / OF THEE I SING.... *Columbia 2598-D* 5-8 32
(Vocals: Unknown)

WHO'S YOUR LITTLE WHO-ZIS? / WITH LOVE IN MY HEART....... *Columbia 2591-D* 5-8 31
(Vocals: Unknown)

WONDER / WHERE CAN YOU BE?.... *Columbia 2241-D* 4-6 30

SELVIN, Ben, & His Orchestra as The Kolster Dance Orchestra

WHEN I AM HOUSEKEEPING FOR YOU (Vocal: Eva Taylor) / DO YA LOVE ME? (Vocal: Smith Ballew)................ *Columbia 2072-D* 8-10 30

SELVIN, Ben, & His Orchestra as Chester Leighton & His Sophomores

LOVE IS LIKE THAT / TWO LITTLE, BLUE LITTLE EYES............... *Clarion 5337-C* 5-8 31
(Vocals: Dick Robertson as Bobby Dix)

LOVE IS LIKE THAT / TWO LITTLE, BLUE LITTLE EYES............. *Harmony 1328-H* 5-8 31
(Vocals: Dick Robertson as Bobby Dix)

LOVE IS LIKE THAT / TWO LITTLE, BLUE LITTLE EYES............ *Velvet Tone 2401-V* 5-8 31
(Vocals: Dick Robertson as Bobby Dix)
(Simultaneously released on three labels)

NOW THAT YOU'RE GONE / GUILTY.......................... *Clarion 5383-C* 5-8 31
(Vocals: Dick Robertson as Chester Leighton)

NOW THAT YOU'RE GONE / GUILTY......................... *Harmony 1370-H* 5-8 31
(Vocals: Dick Robertson as Chester Leighton)

NOW THAT YOU'RE GONE / GUILTY........................ *Velvet Tone 2447-V* 5-8 31
(Vocals: Dick Robertson as Chester Leighton)
(Simultaneously released on three labels)

NOW YOU'RE IN MY ARMS (Vocal: Smith Ballew as Chester Leighton) / STAR DUST (Vocal: Smith Ballew as Robert Wood)................ *Clarion 5319-C* 5-8 31

NOW YOU'RE IN MY ARMS (Vocal: Smith Ballew as Chester Leighton) / STAR DUST (Vocal: Smith Ballew as Robert Wood).............. *Harmony 1320-H* 5-8 31

NOW YOU'RE IN MY ARMS (Vocal: Smith Ballew as Chester Leighton) / STAR DUST (Vocal: Smith Ballew as Robert Wood)............. *Velvet Tone 2385-V* 5-8 31
(Simultaneously released on three labels)

ON THE BEACH WITH YOU (Vocal: Eddie Walters as Chester Leighton) / WITHOUT THAT GAL! (Vocal: Dick Robertson as Chester Leighton).......... *Clarion 5351-C* 5-8 31

ON THE BEACH WITH YOU (Vocal: Eddie Walters as Chester Leighton) / WITHOUT THAT GAL! (Vocal: Dick Robertson as Chester Leighton)........ *Harmony 1340-H* 5-8 31

ON THE BEACH WITH YOU (Vocal: Eddie Walters as Chester Leighton) / WITHOUT THAT GAL! (Vocal: Dick Robertson as Chester Leighton)....... *Velvet Tone 2415-V* 5-8 31
(Simultaneously released on three labels)

SELVIN, Ben, & His Orchestra as The Lucky Strike Dance Orchestra

MY DREAM GIRL / DRIFTING DOWN ON HONOLULU BAY................. *Domino 391* 2-4 24

SELVIN, Ben, & His Orchestra as Rudy Marlow & His Orchestra

I'VE WAITED A LIFETIME FOR YOU / HOW AM I TO KNOW?............ *Harmony 988-H* 2-4 29

SHEPHERD'S SERENADE / CHARMING .... *Harmony 1082-H* 4-6 30

SUNNY SIDE UP / DANCE AWAY THE NIGHT .... *Harmony 1020-H* 3-5 29

WEB OF LOVE, THE / I'M IN LOVE WITH YOU .... *Harmony 1007-H* 3-5 29

SELVIN, Ben, & His Orchestra as The Missouri Jazz Band

WHO? / NOBODY'S BUSINESS (Vocal: Arthur Fields)......... *Banner 1657* 3-5 26

WHO? / NOBODY'S BUSINESS (Vocal: Arthur Fields)......... *Domino 3629* 3-5 26
(Simultaneously released on two labels)

SELVIN, Ben, & His Orchestra as The Musical Comedy Orchestra

MOON OF MY DELIGHT / I MUST HAVE YOU .... *Harmony 751-H* 2-4 28
(Vocals: Irving Kaufman as Robert Wood)

SELVIN, Ben, & His Orchestra as Sam Nash & His Orchestra

I LOVE YOU SO MUCH (Vocals: Scrappy Lambert) / YOU'RE THE SWEETEST GIRL (THIS SIDE OF HEAVEN) ... *Parlophone PNY-34099* 3-5 30

SELVIN, Ben, & His Orchestra as Ray Seeley & His Orchestra

CAN I HELP IT? (Vocal: Scrappy Lambert) / YOU'RE THE SWEETEST GIRL (THIS SIDE OF HEAVEN)........ *Odeon ONY-36107* 4-6 30

SWINGIN' IN A HAMMOCK / I LOVE YOU SO MUCH.......... *Odeon ONY-36106* 5-8 30
(Vocals: Scrappy Lambert)

YOU'LL BE MINE IN APPLE BLOSSOM TIME / I'M CRAZY 'BOUT MY BABY..... *Odeon ONY-36203* 5-8 31
(Vocals: Lew Conrad as Lou Brady)

YOU / MY LOVE .... *Odeon ONY-36103* 5-8 30

SELVIN, Ben, & His Orchestra as Perley Stevens & His Orchestra

I KISS YOUR HAND, MADAME / OLD-FASHIONED LADY .... *Harmony 889-H* 2-4 29
(Vocals: Irving Kaufman as Jim Andrews)

SELVIN, Ben, & His Orchestra as Barney Trimble & His Olkahomans

NOBODY'S FAULT BUT YOUR OWN / I'LL SEE YOU THRU' .... *Harmony 885-H* 4-6 29
(Vocals: Irving Kaufman as Jim Andrews)

SELVIN, Ben, & His Orchestra as Jack Whitney & His Orchestra

YOU FORGOT YOUR GLOVES / FALLING IN LOVE................ *Clarion 5344-C* 5-8 31
(Vocals: Scrappy Lambert as Jerry Fenwyck)

YOU FORGOT YOUR GLOVES / FALLING IN LOVE.............. *Harmony 1335-H* 5-8 31
(Vocals: Scrappy Lambert as Jerry Fenwyck)

YOU FORGOT YOUR GLOVES / FALLING IN LOVE .... *Velvet Tone 2408-V* 5-8 31
(Vocals: Scrappy Lambert as Jerry Fenwyck)
(Simultaneously released on three labels)

SELVIN, Ben, as The Bar Harbor Orchestra / Bar Harbor Society Orchestra

AFTER EVERY PARTY / RED MOON ... *Vocalion 14530* 2-4 23

CAROLINA IN THE MORNING / VAMP ME .... *Vocalion 14448* 2-4 22

CUT YOURSELF A PIECE OF CAKE (Vocal: Irving Kaufman) / THAT BIG BLONDE MAMA ... *Vocalion 14639* 2-4 23

DO IT AGAIN / I'M JUST WILD ABOUT HARRY.............. *Vocalion 14346* 3-5 22

DON'T BE AFRAID TO COME HOME / TOO MANY PARTIES AND TOO MANY PALS (by Sam Lanin & His Orchestra)..... *Pathe Actuelle 36376* 5-8 26
(Vocals: Arthur Hall)

DON'T BE AFRAID TO COME HOME / TOO MANY PARTIES AND TOO MANY PALS (by Sam Lanin & His Orchestra) .... *Perfect 14557* 4-6 26
(Vocals: Arthur Hall)
This record was pressed in brown shellac)
(Simultaneously released on two labels.)

HIGH BROWN BLUES (Vocals: Unknown) / GEORGIA............................ *Vocalion 14330* 3-5 22

ONE ALONE / THE DESERT SONG.... *Harmony 654-H* 3-5 28

ONE ALONE / THE DESERT SONG......... *Special Record 1001-P* 5-8 28
(Simultaneously released on two labels)

SHINE / IT AIN'T GONNA RAIN NO MO' (Vocal: Irving Kaufman).... *Vocalion 14816* 3-5 24

SOFT LIGHT AND SWEET MUSIC / BY THE FIRESIDE................ *Clarion 5465-C* 4-6 32
(Vocals: Unknown)

SOFT LIGHT AND SWEET MUSIC / BY THE FIRESIDE............... *Harmony 1418-H* 4-6 32
(Vocals: Unknown)

SOFT LIGHT AND SWEET MUSIC / BY THE FIRESIDE .... *Velvet Tone 2525-V* 4-6 32
(Vocals: Unknown)
(Simultaneously released on three labels)

SOMEWHERE IN OLD WYOMING (Vocal: Irving Kaufman as Robert Wood) / LOVE VOWS (by Lou Gold & His Orchestra as Rex King & His Sovereigns; Vocal: Chick Bullock as Rex King) .... *Clarion 5089-C* 4-6 30

STARLIGHT / DELISHIOUS...... *Velvet Tone 10505-V* 8-10 31
(Vocals: Chet Watson)
(This is a rare double-track record with one track containing an instrumental arrangement, while the other has a vocal version of the same tune. Each side of this 10-inch 78 rpm record plays for five minutes, and Velvet Tone's sister labels, Clarion, Diva and Harmony, had similar releases. This was another unsuccessful early attempt at long-play, but these records suffered the same fate as the 1926-27 Edison 10-inch and 12-inch discs which contained 24 minutes and 40 minutes of music respectively, as well as the early 1930s 10-inch 33⅓ rpm Victor records which featured approximately 10 minutes playing time on each side. For a description of the Edison long-playing discs, see ROLFE, B. A. & His Concert Orchestra, and SOMAN, Herbert, as Herbert Soman's Salon Orchestra, and see SHILKRET, Nat as The Victor Salon Group for further details of the Victor 33⅓ rpm issues.
The first successful long-play commercial records were introduced by Columbia in 1948.)

(YOU ONLY WANT ME) WHEN NOBODY ELSE IS AROUND / KISS ME GOODNIGHT (by Ben Selvin & His Orchestra as The D'Orsay Dance Orchestra)...................... *Clarion 5466-C* 5-8 32
(Vocals: Unknown)

(YOU ONLY WANT ME) WHEN NOBODY ELSE IS AROUND / KISS ME GOODNIGHT (by Ben Selvin & His Orchestra as The D'Orsay Dance Orchestra).................... *Harmony 1419-H* 5-8 32
(Vocals: Unknown)

(YOU ONLY WANT ME) WHEN NOBODY ELSE IS AROUND / KISS ME GOODNIGHT (by Ben Selvin & His Orchestra as The D'Orsay Dance Orchestra).................. *Velvet Tone 2526-V* 5-8 32
(Vocals: Unknown)
(Simultaneously released on three labels)

SELVIN, Ben, as The Broadway Syncopators

BURNING SANDS / WITHOUT YOU... *Vocalion 14475* 2-4 23
HOUSE OF DAVID BLUES / BONNIE... *Vocalion 14670* 2-4 23
I AIN'T NEVER HAD NOBODY CRAZY OVER ME / TWO-TIME DAN.................. *Vocalion 14598* 3-5 23
LOUISVILLE LOU / BLUE HOOSIER BLUES........... *Vocalion 14586* 3-5 23
SITTIN' IN A CORNER / BIT BY BIT YOU'RE BREAKIN' MY HEART............ *Vocalion 14675* 2-4 23

SELVIN, Ben, as The Manhattan Dance Makers

ANGEL EYES / I NEED LOVIN'..... *Harmony 313-H* 3-5 27
DAWNING / JUST A MEMORY (Vocal: Unknown).......... *Harmony 486-H* 2-4 27
DOLORES / SIREN OF THE NILE.... *Harmony 641-H* 2-4 28
I CAN'T SEE THE BEAUTIFUL SEA (Vocals: Billy Jones) / SHE'S DRIVIN' ME WILD........... *Columbia 440-D* 3-5 25
I WONDER WHERE MY BABY IS TONIGHT? / WHAT A BLUE-EYED BABY YOU ARE..... *Harmony 49-H* 2-4 25
JUST AROUND THE CORNER / SLEEPY-TIME GAL............... *Harmony 63-H* 2-4 26
KINKY KIDS' PARADE, THE / THERE AIN'T NO FLIES ON AUNTIE................ *Harmony 24-H* 3-5 25
(Vocals: Ernest Hare)
LET ME LINGER LONGER IN YOUR ARMS (Vocal: Lewis James) / HOLD ME IN YOUR ARMS............ *Columbia 392-D* 2-4 25
LOVE ME ALL THE TIME / TONIGHT YOU BELONG TO ME (Vocal: Jimmy Flynn).......... *Harmony 280-H* 2-4 26
MOONLIGHT AND ROSES / GOLDEN MEMORIES............ *Columbia 344-D* 2-4 25
ONE MORE NIGHT / DOWN SOUTH... *Harmony 604-H* 2-4 28
ROW, ROW ROSIE (Vocal: Arthur Fields) / STEPPIN' IN SOCIETY.............. *Harmony 7-H* 3-5 25
SOMEBODY'S EYES / THE LONESOMEST GIRL IN TOWN................. *Harmony 83-H* 2-4 26

YEP! 'LONG ABOUT JUNE / SWEET STRANGER.............. *Harmony 552-H* 2-4 28
YOU GOTTA BE GOOD TO ME / MARY ANN..................... *Harmony 586-H* 2-4 28

SELVIN, Ben, as The Moulin Rouge Orchestra

BLUE-EYED BLUES / LIST'NING ON SOME RADIO......................... *Banner 1085* 2-4 22
DANCING FOOL / THE SNEAK........... *Arto 9161* 3-5 22
GRIEVING FOR YOU / BRING BACK MY LOVE DREAMS (by Ben Selvin as Selvin's Novelty Orchestra)...................... *Arto 9024* 3-5 20
HALF-PAST TEN / WHEN CLOUDS HAVE VANISHED AND SKIES ARE BLUE (Vocal: Irving Kaufman)................ *Vocalion 14724* 2-4 24
I WONDER WHO'S DANCING WITH YOU TONIGHT? / TURN ON YOUR RADIO (AND LISTEN IN ON YOUR HOME TOWN)..................... *Vocalion 14754* 2-4 24
(Vocals: Irving Kaufman)

JUST KEEP A THOUGHT FOR ME / ALL BY MYSELF (by Ben Selvin as Selvin's Novelty Orchestra).... *Arto 9067* 3-5 21
(Vocals: Earnest Hare)
MAKE BELIEVE (Vocal: Arthur Hall) / I LOST MY HEART TO YOU............. *Arto 9048* 3-5 21
MAYBE / IF YOU DO – WHAT YOU DO... *Vocalion 14771* 2-4 24
MOONLIGHT / I FOUND A ROSE IN THE DEVIL'S GARDEN (by Ben Selvin as Selvin's Novelty Orchestra; Vocal: Arthur Hall)......................... *Arto 9061* 3-5 21
OLD TIMER'S FOX TROT / OH, SING-A-LOO.................... *Banner 1067* 2-4 22
ON THE OLD LAKE TRAIL / SOMEONE LOVES YOU AFTER ALL............... *Vocalion 14737* 2-4 24
SOME SUNNY DAY / ON THE ALAMO..... *Arto 9145* 3-5 22
TAKE, OH TAKE THOSE LIPS AWAY / RAGGEDY ANN................... *Vocalion 14723* 3-5 24
THREE O'CLOCK IN THE MORNING / CUTIE.............................. *Radiex 1099* 2-4 22
TRULY / COAL BLACK MAMMY........ *Banner 1099* 3-5 22
TWO BLUE EYES / NOBODY'S SWEETHEART......... *Vocalion 14779* 2-4 24
WOULD YOU? I'LL SAY YOU WOULD (Vocal: Arthur Hall) / UNDERNEATH HAWAIIAN SKIES (by Ben Selvin as Selvin's Novelty Orchestra)........... *Arto 9059* 3-5 21

SELVIN, Ben, as The Moulin Rouge Orchestra recorded under the name The Frisco Syncopators

BLUE-EYED BLUES / LIST'NING ON SOME RADIO................ *Broadway 11146* 3-5 22
BLUE-EYED BLUES / LIST'NING ON SOME RADIO.................. *Puritan 11146* 3-5 22
(Simultaneously released on two labels)
COAL BLACK MAMMY / TRICKS (by Joseph Samuels' Master Players as Earl Randolph's Orchestra)......... *Claxtonola 40152* 5-8 22
OLD TIMER'S FOX TROT / OH, SING-A-LOO................... *Puritan 11133* 2-4 22

SELVIN, Ben, as The Moulin Rouge Orchestra recorded under the name the Regal Dance Orchestra

DO IT AGAIN / OPERA TROT NO. 3....... *Regal 9324* 3-5 22

SELVIN, Ben, as The Orchestra Chez Fysher

EV'RYTHING'S GONNA BE ALL RIGHT (Vocal: Ben Selvin) / ALWAYS (Vocal: Frank Bessinger).............. *Brunswick 3089* 2-4 22
I WISH'T I WAS IN PEORIA / SWEET CHILD.................... *Brunswick 3030* 2-4 26
(Vocals: Ben Selvin)
POOR LITTLE RICH GIRL / A CUP OF COFFEE, A SANDWICH, AND YOU (Vocal: Ben Selvin).................. *Brunswick 3023* 2-4 26

SELVIN, Ben, as The Radiolites

BECAUSE I LOVE YOU (Vocal: Charles Hart) / I'M ON MY WAY HOME (Vocal: Charles Kaley).... *Columbia 759-D* 2-4 26
CORONADO NIGHTS / 'DEED I DO (Vocals: Unknown)............. *Columbia 885-D* 2-4 27
DANCING TAMBOURINE / THE VARSITY DRAG (by Cass Hagan & His Park Central Hotel Orchestra; Vocals: Franklyn Baur, Lewis James, & Elliot Shaw)..................... *Columbia 1114-D* 5-8 27
HOW MANY TIMES? / I'M WALKING AROUND IN CIRCLES............. *Columbia 676-D* 2-4 26
(Vocals: Irving Kaufman as Frank Harris)
I'D LOVE TO MEET THAT OLD SWEETHEART OF MINE / LAY ME DOWN TO SLEEP IN CAROLINA... *Columbia 714-D* 2-4 26
I'M HAPPY WHEN YOU'RE HAPPY / WERE YOU SINCERE?........... *Columbia 2405-D* 2-4 31
(Vocals: Unknown)
I STILL LOVE YOU (Vocals: Unknown) / MY OHIO HOME (by Cass Hagan & His Park Central Hotel Orchestra; Vocals: Irving Kaufman as Frank Harris)....... *Columbia 1301-D* 3-5 28
NEVERTHELESS (I'M IN LOVE WITH YOU) / WHEN THE MOON COMES OVER THE MOUNTAIN............ *Columbia 2485-D* 2-4 31
(Vocals: Unknown)
RAIN OR SHINE / FOREVER AND EVER........... *Columbia 1326-D* 2-4 28
(Vocals: Unknown)
SONG OF SHANGHAI / AIN'T SHE SWEET? (Vocal: Charles Kaley)........ *Columbia 903-D* 3-5 27
SUNDAY / IF I'D ONLY BELIEVED IN YOU.............. *Columbia 793-D* 2-4 26
(Vocals: Charles Kaley)

THERE'S A CRADLE IN CAROLINE / EVERYBODY LOVES MY GIRL.... *Columbia 1150-D* 2-4 27
(Vocals: Unknown)
THERE'S A LITTLE WHITE HOUSE / I'D LOVE TO CALL YOU MY SWEETHEART..... *Columbia 811-D* 2-4 27
(Vocals: Charles Kaley)

SELVIN, Ben, as Selvin's Dance Orchestra

CHERIE / MOONLIGHT.............. *Vocalion 14182* 2-4 21
DARLING / GRIEVING FOR YOU...... *Vocalion 14127* 2-4 20
DO YOU EVER THINK OF ME? / LOVE BIRD........................ *Vocalion 14155* 2-4 21
GOODBYE, PRETTY BUTTERFLIES / SMILIN'............................ *Brunswick 2182* 2-4 22
GRIEVING FOR YOU / FEATHER YOUR NEST............. *Cardinal 2008* 3-5 21
IN A BOAT / SUNSHINE.............. *Vocalion 14196* 2-4 21
IRISH SONG MEDLEY / IRISH SONG MEDLEY, PART II................. *Vocalion 14288* 2-4 22
I'VE GOT MY HABITS ON / JUST A LITTLE LOVE SONG........ *Vocalion 14277* 2-4 22
REMEMBER THE ROSE / LEAVE ME WITH A SMILE......... *Vocalion 14233* 2-4 21
SAL-O-MAY (SALOME) / CANADIAN CAPERS.............. *Brunswick 2164* 2-4 21
SAY IT WITH MUSIC / TENDERLY.... *Vocalion 14239* 2-4 21

SELVIN, Ben, as Selvin's Novelty Orchestra

AFGHANISTAN / VENETIAN MOON.............. *Paramount 20007* 3-5 20
ALL BY MYSELF / JUST KEEP A THOUGHT FOR ME (by Ben Selvin as The Moulin Rouge Orchestra)... *Arto 9067* 3-5 21
(Vocals: Ernest Hare)
APRIL SHOWERS / SONG OF LOVE... *Cardinal 2071* 3-5 21
AVALON / CUBAN MOON................ *Lyric 4224* 3-5 20
BRING BACK MY LOVE DREAMS / GRIEVING FOR YOU (by Ben Selvin as The Moulin Rouge Orchestra)................ *Arto 9024* 3-5 20
DAISY DAYS / PAPER DOLL......... *Vocalion 14180* 3-5 21
DARDANELLA / MY ISLE OF GOLDEN DREAMS................ *Victor 18633* 2-4 20
DO YOU EVER THINK OF ME? (Vocal: Arthur Hall) / KISS-A-MISS (by the Arto Dance Orchestra, a pseudonym for an unidentified band)......................... *Arto 9052* 3-5 21
GOODBYE, PRETTY BUTTERFLIES / SONG OF LOVE............. *Pathe Actuelle 020654* 3-5 21
GOODBYE, PRETTY BUTTERFLIES / SONG OF LOVE.......................... *Perfect 14106* 2-4 21
(Simultaneously released on two labels)
I FOUND A ROSE IN THE DEVIL'S GARDEN (Vocal: Arthur Hall) / MOONLIGHT (by Ben Selvin as The Moulin Rouge Orchestra)....................... *Arto 9061* 3-5 21
I NEVER KNEW / NOW AND THEN................ *Cardinal 2017* 4-6 21
I NEVER KNEW / NOW AND THEN...................... *Lyric 4238* 4-6 21
(Simultaneously released on two labels)

IN OLD MANILA / JAPANESE SANDMAN . . . *Arto 9019* 3-5 20

IRENE / DESERT DREAMS . . . *Paramount 20008* 3-5 20

MAKE BELIEVE / LOVE IN LILAC TIME . . . *Emerson 10341* 2-4 21

MANDY / NOVELTY ONE-STEP . . . *Victor 18614* 2-4 19

MAYBE / SWEET LOVE . . . *Emerson 10371* 2-4 21

MELLO 'CELLO / EMALINE . . . *Pathe Actuelle 020577* 2-4 21

MY ISLE OF GOLDEN DREAMS / PEGGY . . . *Paramount 20002* 3-5 20

MY MAMMY / HUMMING . . . *Vocalion 35000* 3-5 21
(This is an oversize 12-inch 78 rpm)

MY MAMMY (Vocals: Unknown) / WHY DON'T YOU? . . . *Cardinal 2016* 3-5 21

MY SUNNY TENNESSEE / FIGARO . . . *Cardinal 2063* 3-5 21

OLD TIMERS WALTZ MEDLEY / OLD TIMERS WALTZ MEDLEY, PART II . . . *Paramount 20034* 3-5 20

ONE KISS / LOVE WILL FIND A WAY . . . *Brunswick 2144* 2-4 21

ON THE 'GIN 'GIN 'GINNY SHORE / I'M CUCKOO OVER YOU . . . *Paramount 20104* 4-6 22

ON THE 'GIN 'GIN 'GINNY SHORE / I'M CUCKOO OVER YOU . . . *Puritan 11104* 2-4 22
(Simultaneously released on two labels)

PEACHES / SWEETHEARTS ALL THE TIME . . . *Pathe Actuelle 020578* 2-4 21

SCANDAL WALK / TELL ME LITTLE GYPSY . . . *Lyric 4225* 3-5 20

SNUGGLE / SUNSHINE . . . *Pathe Actuelle 020536* 2-4 21

TEA LEAVES / MOONLIGHT . . . *Okeh 4331* 2-4 21

THAT NAUGHTY WALTZ / DARDANELLA . . . *Paramount 20001* 4-6 20

THAT NAUGHTY WALTZ / DARDANELLA . . . *Puritan 11001* 2-4 20
(Simultaneously released on two labels)

UNDERNEATH HAWAIIAN SKIES / WOULD YOU? I'LL SAY YOU WOULD (by Ben Selvin as The Moulin Rouge Orchestra; Vocal: Arthur Hall) . . . *Arto 9059* 3-5 21

VENETIA / IN SWEET SEPTEMBER . . . *Paramount 20016* 3-5 20

WILD ROSE / MAKE BELIEVE . . . *Vocalion 14169* 2-4 21

WILL-O'-THE-WISP / NOBODY KNOWS (AND NOBODY SEEMS TO CARE) . . . *Paramount 33049* 3-5 19

WITHOUT YOU / JUST LIKE A RAINBOW . . . *Pathe Actuelle 020537* 2-4 21

YELLOW DOG BLUES / IN SHADOWLAND . . . *Emerson 10133* 3-5 20

SELVIN, Ben, as Selvin's Orchestra

AM I TO BLAME? / THINK OF ME . . . *Vocalion 14531* 2-4 23

ANGEL CHILD / LOLA LO . . . *Brunswick 2249* 2-4 22

ARGENTINE / BAMBALINA . . . *Vocalion 14532* 2-4 23

DIRTY HANDS! DIRTY FACE! / OTHER LIPS . . . *Vocalion 14660* 2-4 23

DON'T THINK YOU'LL BE MISSED / SEVEN OR ELEVEN (MY DIXIE PAIR O' DICE) . . . *Vocalion 14545* 2-4 23

DOWN AMONG THE SLEEPY HILLS OF TENNESSEE / DON'T BE TOO SURE . . . *Vocalion 14544* 2-4 23

DREAMY MELODY / INDIANA MOON . . . *Vocalion 14621* 2-4 23

HOOT MON / JUST A GIRL THAT MEN FORGET . . . *Vocalion 14664* 2-4 23

I FOUND A FOUR-LEAF CLOVER / I'LL BUILD A STAIRWAY TO PARADISE . . . *Vocalion 14434* 3-5 22

I'M THROUGH (SHEDDING TEARS OVER YOU) / WHO CARES? . . . *Vocalion 14477* 2-4 22

KISS IN THE DARK / BROKEN-HEARTED MELODY . . . *Vocalion 14583* 3-5 23

LOVE IS JUST A FLOWER / HAVANA . . . *Vocalion 14604* 2-4 23

LOVELIGHT IN YOUR EYES, THE / DOWN IN MARYLAND (Vocal: Irving Kaufman) . . . *Vocalion 14493* 2-4 23

LOVIN' SAM (THE SHEIK OF ALABAM') / TIME WILL TELL . . . *Vocalion 14447* 3-5 22

OH! HAROLD (Vocal: Irving Kaufman) / ANNABELLE . . . *Vocalion 14637* 2-4 23

ONE KISS / LOVE WILL FIND A WAY . . . *Brunswick 2144* 2-4 21

OPEN YOUR ARMS, MY ALABAMY / THE FUZZY WUZZY BIRD . . . *Vocalion 14472* 3-5 22

RITZI-MITZI / YES! WE HAVE NO BANANAS . . . *Vocalion 14590* 3-5 23
(Vocals: Irving Kaufman)

ROMANY LOVE / NO USE CRYING . . . *Brunswick 2273* 2-4 22

ROSY POSY / EVERY DAY . . . *Brunswick 2262* 2-4 22

SAW MILL RIVER ROAD / FALLING . . . *Vocalion 14509* 3-5 23

SO THIS IS LOVE / THE WALTZ OF LONG AGO . . . *Vocalion 14690* 2-4 23

THREE O'CLOCK IN THE MORNING (Vocals: Unknown) / ISLE OF SWEETHEARTS . . . *Vocalion 14488* 2-4 23

TRULY / CHANSON . . . *Vocalion 14395* 2-4 22

WEST, A NEST AND YOU, THE / SLEEP . . . *Vocalion 14695* 2-4 23

WILL YOU ALWAYS LOVE ME? / I CRIED FOR YOU . . . *Vocalion 14568* 2-4 23

WONDEFUL ONE / MELLOW MOON . . . *Vocalion 14508* 2-4 23

SENATORS, The:
see LANIN, Sam, as The Broadway Broadcasters

SENTER, Boyd, & His Senterpedes
(Boyd Senter: 11/30/99 – 6/10/82)

BEALE STREET BLUES / COPENHAGEN . . . *Victor 22303* 10-12 30

DOIN' YOU GOOD / SHINE . . . *Victor 21912* 8-10 29
(Vocals: Paul Small)

GIVE IT TO ME RIGHT AWAY / SMILES . . . *Victor 23032* 10-12 30
(Vocals: Ray Stilwell)

RICH MAN, POOR MAN, BEGGAR MAN, THIEF / I'M IN THE JAILHOUSE NOW . . . *Victor 22010* 5-8 29

SWEETHEART BLUES / NO-ONE (Vocal: Dan Calker) . . . *Victor 22464* 8-10 29

WABASH BLUES / GOIN' BACK TO TENNESSEE (Vocals: Unknown) . . . *Victor 21864* 8-10 29

WATERLOO (Vocal: Ray Stilwell) / A GOOD MAN IS HARD TO FIND (by Snooks Friedman as Snooks & His Memphis Ramblers with Julia Gerity recorded under the name Julia Gerity & Her Playboys; Vocals: Ken Herlin, Walter Ashby, Elly Bellare, & Julia Gerity) . . . *Victor 22812* 8-10 31

SEVEN ACES, The:
see BENNETT, Ralph

SEVEN BLACK DOTS, The

LOVE WILL FIND A WAY / BANDANA DAYS . . . *Pathe Actuelle 020655* 4-6 21

SHAKE IT AND BREAK IT / WANG-WANG BLUES . . . *Pathe Actuelle 020634* 5-8 21

SEVEN BLUE BABIES, The:
see CALIFORNIA RAMBLERS, The

SEVEN LITTLE CLOUDS OF JOY, The:
see KIRK, Andy

SEVEN LITTLE POLAR BEARS, The:
see RESER, Harry

SEVEN WILD MEN, The:
see RESER, Harry, as The Night Club Orchestra

SHAND, Terry, & His Orchestra
(Terry Shand: 10/1/04 –)

BACK HOME / WHEN THE CIRCUS CAME TO TOWN . . . *Vocalion 4113* 3-5 38
(Vocals: Terry Shand)

CINDY / FOR SEV'N LONG YEARS . . . *Decca 3835* 2-4 41
(Vocals: Terry Shand)

DANCE WITH A DOLLY (WITH A HOLE IN HER STOCKING) (Vocals: Terry Shand & chorus) / DON'T MAKE ME LAUGH (WITH TEARS IN MY EYES) (Vocal: Louanne) . . . *Decca 2927* 2-4 40

HOLD MY HAND / ON THE BUMPY ROAD OF LOVE . . . *Decca 1928* 2-4 38
(Vocals: Terry Shand)

I CAN'T LOVE YOU ANY MORE / PRETTY BABY . . . *Decca 3127* 2-4 40
(Vocals: Terry Shand)

I'LL BE BACK / SH-H, IT'S A MILITARY SECRET . . . *Decca 4284* 3-5 42
(Vocals: Terry Shand)

I LOVE ME / MY EXTRAORDINARY GAL . . . *Decca 3190* 2-4 40
(Vocals: Terry Shand)

I'M SORRY THAT WE SAID GOODBYE / JUST ONE GIRL . . . *Decca 4242* 2-4 42
(Vocals: Terry Shand)

I NEED LOVIN' (Vocal: Louanne) / AIN'T WE GOT FUN? (Vocals: Terry Shand & Louanne) . . . *Decca 3136* 2-4 40

I'VE BEEN WORKING ON THE RAILROAD / CASEY JONES . . . *Decca 3714* 2-4 41
(Vocals: Terry Shand)

I WISH I WAS THE WILLOW / LET'S BREAK THE GOOD NEWS . . . *Decca 1918* 2-4 38
(Vocals: Terry Shand)

K-K-K-KATY / WABASH CANNON-BALL . . . *Decca 3783* 2-4 41
(Vocals: Terry Shand)

KNICK KNACK POLLY WAH JINGASOL / SWEET POTATO PIPER . . . *Decca 3010* 2-4 40
(Vocals: Terry Shand)

LET'S DO IT / SLAP-HAPPY LASSIE . . . *Decca 3587* 2-4 41
(Vocals: Terry Shand)

LI'L BOY LOVE (Vocal: Louanne) / MY PIGGY BANK IS JING-A-LING AGAIN (Vocal: Terry Shand) . . . *Decca 3421* 2-4 40

NEW RIVER TRAIN / FILIPINO HOMBRE . . . *Decca 3836* 2-4 41
(Vocals: Terry Shand)

PAY ME NO MIND / IT'S BEEN A LONG, LONG TIME . . . *Decca 4256* 3-5 42
(Vocals: Terry Shand)

PRACTICE MAKES PERFECT (Vocal: Terry Shand) / WILLIE, WILLIE, WILLIE (WHY YOU CRY?) (Vocal: Louanne) . . . *Decca 3399* 2-4 40

SCARED / GIVE ME THE MOONLIGHT, GIVE ME THE GIRL . . . *Decca 3250* 2-4 40
(Vocals: Terry Shand)

SOUTHERN FRIED / MISSOURI SCRAMBLER . . . *Decca 3472* 3-5 40

TALKIN' OUT OF TURN (Vocal: Louanne) / PIERRE OF SASKATCHEWAN (Vocal: Terry Shand) . . . *Decca 3641* 2-4 41

TALL, TALL CORN / FERDINAND THE BULL . . . *Vocalion 4131* 4-6 38
(Vocals: Terry Shand)

WAIT TILL THE GIRLS GET INTO THE ARMY, BOYS / DON'T FORGET TO SAY "NO", BABY . . . *Decca 4320* 3-5 42
(Vocals: Terry Shand)

YOU'RE LETTIN' THE GRASS GROW (RIGHT UNDER YOUR FEET) / BLAME THE IMP . . . *Decca 2940* 2-4 39
(Vocals: Terry Shand)

SHARKEY & HIS SHARKS OF RHYTHM:
see BONANO, Sharkey

SHARP, Bee, & Orchestra

NOT FOR ALL THE RICE IN CHINA / EASTER PARADE . . . *Bluebird B-5219* 3-5 33
(Vocals: Dick Robertson)

NOT FOR ALL THE RICE IN CHINA / EASTER PARADE . . . *Electradisk 2105* 10-12 33
(Vocals: Dick Robertson)

NOT FOR ALL THE RICE IN CHINA / EASTER PARADE . . . *Sunrise S-3302* 10-12 33
(Vocals: Dick Robertson)
(Simultaneously released on three labels)

SUPPER TIME (Vocal: Bee Sharp) / HEAT WAVE (Vocal: Dick Robertson) . . . *Bluebird B-5218* 4-6 33

SUPPER TIME (Vocal: Bee Sharp) / HEAT WAVE (Vocal: Dick Robertson) . . . *Electradisk 2104* 12-15 33

SUPPER TIME (Vocal: Bee Sharp) / HEAT WAVE (Vocal: Dick Robertson) . . . *Sunrise S-3301* 12-15 33
(Simultaneously released on three labels)

SHAW, Artie, & His Gramercy Five
(Artie Shaw: 5/23/10 –)
(After 30 years' retirement, Artie Shaw has a new orchestra which is again touring the country. The new band's first engagement was the re-opening of the legendary Glen Island Casino on Long Island, which launched numerous bands to stardom in the big band era.)

DR. LIVINGSTONE, I PRESUME? / WHEN THE QUAIL COME BACK TO SAN QUENTIN . . . *Victor 27289* 3-5 41

GRABTOWN GRAPPLE, THE / THE SAD SACK . . . *Victor 20-1647* 2-4 45

MY BLUE HEAVEN / MOONGLOW (by Artie Shaw & His Orchestra) . . . *Victor 27405* 2-4 41

SMOKE GETS IN YOUR EYES / DANCING IN THE DARK (by Artie Shaw & His Orchestra) . . . *Victor 27335* 2-4 41

SPECIAL DELIVERY STOMP / KEEPIN' MYSELF FOR YOU . . . *Victor 26762* 3-5 40

SUMMIT RIDGE DRIVE / CROSS YOUR HEART . . . *Victor 26763* 3-5 40

SHAW, Artie, & His New Music

AFRAID TO DREAM / IF YOU SHOULD EVER LEAVE . . . *Brunswick 7934* 5-8 37
(Vocals: Peg La Centra)

ALL ALONE / BECAUSE I LOVE YOU . . . *Brunswick 7899* 4-6 37

ALL GOD'S CHILLUN GOT RHYTHM / IT GOES TO YOUR FEET . . . *Brunswick 7895* 5-8 37
(Vocals: Tony Pastor)

BLUES, THE / THE BLUES, PART II . . . *Brunswick 7947* 8-10 37

BLUES, THE / THE BLUES, PART II . . . *Vocalion 4401* 3-5 39
(The Vocalion release is a reissue)

FEE FI FO FUM (Vocal: Leo Watson) / THE CHANT . . . *Brunswick 7952* 8-10 37

I'M YOURS / JUST YOU, JUST ME . . . *Brunswick 8010* 5-8 37

I SURRENDER, DEAR / BLUE SKIES . . . *Brunswick 7907* 5-8 37

IT'S A LONG, LONG WAY TO TIPPERARY / NIGHTMARE (theme song) . . . *Brunswick 7965* 4-6 37

I'VE A STRANGE NEW RHYTHM IN MY HEART (Vocal: Leo Watson) / IF IT'S THE LAST THING I DO (Vocal: Beatrice Wayne) . . . *Brunswick 7971* 5-8 37

JOHNNIE ONE NOTE: NEVER IN A MILLION YEARS (Vocal: Dorothy Howe); WAKE UP AND LIVE; I'VE GOT BEGINNER'S LUCK (Vocal: Dorothy Howe) / BORN TO SWING; SOMEDAY SWEETHEART; NIGHT AND DAY; UBANGI; BUS BLUES......... *Thesaurus 389* 15-20 37
(An electrical transcription produced for radio broadcast, not for commercial release)

LET 'ER GO / STRANGE LONELINESS (Vocal: Dolores O'Neil) ... *Brunswick 7986* 5-8 37

MONSOON / FREE FOR ALL......... *Brunswick 8019* 8-10 37

NIGHT AND DAY / SOMEDAY, SWEETHEART .... *Brunswick 7914* 5-8 37

OLD APPLE TREE; LOST IN THE SHUFFLE; IF DREAMS COME TRUE; MOONLIGHT ON THE SUNSET TRAIL (Vocal: Nita Bradley) / MORE THAN EVER; I'LL NEVER LET YOU CRY; IN THE SHADE OF THE NEW APPLE TREE; IT'S WONDERFUL (Vocal: Nita Bradley)................... *Theasaurus 500* 15-20 38
(An electrical transcription produced for radio broadcast, not for commercial release.)

SHOOT THE LIKKER TO ME, JOHN BOY / FREE WHEELING .... *Brunswick 7976* 8-10 37
(Vocals: Leo Watson)

SWEET ADELINE (Vocal: Tony Pastor) / HOW DRY I AM.................. *Brunswick 7936* 5-8 37

SWEET VARSITY SUE; I WANT A NEW ROMANCE; SHOOT THE LIKKER TO ME, JOHN BOY (Vocal: Leo Watson); FREE WHEELIN' (Vocal: Leo Watson) / S.O.S.; HOW DRY I AM; BLACK AND BLUE; FEE FI FO FUM (Vocal: Leo Watson)..................... *Theasurus 496* 15-20 37
(An electrical transcription produced for radio broadcast, not for commercial release.)

TWILIGHT IN TURKEY; ALIBI BABY (Vocal: Tony Pastor); NIGHT OVER SHANGHAI; STUDY IN BROWN / I'LL NEVER TELL YOU I LOVE YOU (Vocal: Dorothy Howe); WITHOUT YOUR LOVE (Vocal: Dorothy Howe); THE LOVE BUG WILL BITE YOU (Vocal: Tony Pastor) .... *Theasurus 388* 15-20 37
(An electronic transcription produced for radio broadcast, not for commercial release.)

WHISTLE WHILE YOU WORK (Vocal: Tony Pastor) / ONE SONG (Vocal: Nita Bradley) ...... *Brunswick 8050* 5-8 38

SHAW, Artie, & His Orchestra

ALL IN FUN / ALL THE THINGS YOU ARE........................ *Bluebird B-10492* 2-4 39
(Vocals: Helen Forrest)

ALONE TOGETHER / ROSE ROOM ... *Bluebird B-10148* 3-5 39

ANY OLD TIME (Vocal: Billy Holiday) / ZIGEUNER............................ *V-Disc 399* 8-10 -
(A World War II release)

APRIL IN PARIS / KING FOR A DAY.... *Victor 26654* 2-4 40

BACK BAY SHUFFLE / ANY OLD TIME (Vocal: Billie Holiday)........... *Bluebird B-7759* 5-8 38

BEGIN THE BEGUINE / INDIAN LOVE CALL (Vocal: Tony Pastor)............ *Bluebird B-7746* 3-5 38

BETWEEN A KISS AND A SIGH / THANKS FOR EVERYTHING..... *Bluebird B-10055* 2-4 39
(Vocals: Helen Forrest)

BLUES / BLUES, PART II............... *Victor 27411* 4-6 41

CALYPSO, THE / BEAU NIGHT IN HOTCHKISS CORNERS............... *Victor 27315* 3-5 41
(Vocals: Anita Boyer)

CARIOCA / BILL (Vocal: Helen Forrest).......... *Bluebird B-10124* 3-5 39

CARNIVAL / NEEDLENOSE............ *Victor 27860* 3-5 42

CHANTEZ-LES BAS (SING 'EM LOW) / DANZA LUCUMI .... *Victor 27354* 4-6 40

COMIN' ON / I CAN'T BELIEVE THAT YOU'RE IN LOVE WITH ME.................. *Bluebird B-7772* 4-6 38

CONCERTO FOR CLARINET / CONCERTO FOR CLARINET, PART II.................. *Victor 36383* 5-8 41
(This is an oversize 12-inch 78 rpm)

COPENHAGEN / MY BLUE HEAVEN ... *Brunswick 7827* 5-8 37

DANCING IN THE DARK / SMOKE GETS IN YOUR EYES (by Artie Shaw & His Gramercy Five).... *Victor 27335* 2-4 41

DAY IN – DAY OUT (Vocal: Helen Forrest) / PUT THAT DOWN IN WRITING (Vocal: Tony Pastor)................ *Bluebird B-10406* 3-5 39

DEEP IN A DREAM / DAY AFTER DAY............... *Bluebird B-10046* 2-4 39
(Vocals: Helen Forrest)

DEEP PURPLE (Vocal: Helen Forrest) / PASTEL BLUE.................. *Bluebird B-10178* 3-5 39

DON'T FALL ASLEEP / GLOOMY SUNDAY............... *Bluebird B-26563* 3-5 40
(Vocals: Pauline Byrne)

DREAMING OUT LOUD / NOW WE KNOW .... *Victor 26642* 2-4 40
(Vocals: Pauline Byrne)

FRENESI / ADIOS, MARIQUITA LINDA.... *Victor 26542* 2-4 40

GEORGIA ON MY MIND / WHY SHOULDN'T I?.................. *Victor 27499* 2-4 41

GO FLY A KITE (Vocal: Tony Pastor) / A MAN AND HIS DREAM (Vocal: Helen Forrest) ... *Bluebird B-10347* 2-4 39

GUILTY (Vocals: Mel Torme & The Mel-Tones) / ANNIVERSARY SONG.................. *Musicraft 428* 2-4 47

HOW DEEP IS THE OCEAN (Vocal: Hal Stevens) / THE HORNET .... *Musicraft 409* 2-4 47

I ASK THE STARS / TAKE YOUR SHOES OFF, BABY (Vocal: Hot Lips Page) .... *Victor 27719* 3-5 41

I CAN'T AFFORD TO DREAM (Vocal: Tony Pastor) / COMES LOVE (Vocal: Helen Forrest) ... *Bluebird B-10324* 2-4 39

IF I HAD YOU / IT HAD TO BE YOU.................... *Victor 27536* 3-5 41

IF IT'S YOU / OLD CASTLE IN SCOTLAND.................... *Victor 26760* 2-4 40
(Vocals: Anita Boyer)

I'LL NEVER BE THE SAME / 'S WONDERFUL........................ *Victor 20-1638* 2-4 45

I'LL REMEMBER / EASY TO SAY... *Bluebird B-10345* 3-5 39
(Vocals: Helen Forrest)

I'M COMING, VIRGINIA / OUT OF NOWHERE................ *Bluebird B-10320* 4-6 39

I POURED MY HEART INTO A SONG (Vocal: Helen Forrest) / WHEN WINTER COMES (Vocal: Tony Pastor)................ *Bluebird B-10307* 3-5 39

IS IT TABOO? / BEYOND THE BLUE HORIZON...................... *Victor 27641* 2-4 41

IT'S ALL YOURS / THIS IS IT....... *Bluebird B-10141* 3-5 39
(Vocals: Helen Forrest)

I USED TO BE ABOVE LOVE / NO REGRETS..................... *Brunswick 7698* 5-8 36
(Vocals: Wes Vaughn)

I WANT MY SHARE OF LOVE (Vocal: Helen Forrest) / DELIGHTFUL DELIRIUM (Vocal: Tony Pastor)................ *Bluebird B-10134* 3-5 39

JAPANESE SANDMAN / A PRETTY GIRL IS LIKE A MELODY.................. *Brunswick 7688* 5-8 36

JUNGLE DRUMS / IT HAD TO BE YOU..................... *Bluebird B-10091* 2-4 39

JUST KIDDIN' AROUND / SOMETIMES I FEEL LIKE A MOTHERLESS CHILD (Vocal: Hot Lips Page) .... *Victor 27806* 3-5 42

LOVE AND LEARN / MOON FACE... *Brunswick 7787* 5-8 37
(Vocals: Peg La Centra)

LOVE IS GOOD FOR ANYTHING THAT AILS YOU; NO MORE TEARS (Vocal: Peg La Centra); SEPTEMBER IN THE RAIN (Vocal: Peg La Centra); THE MOOD THAT I'M IN / TRUST IN ME (Vocal: Peg La Centra); A MESSAGE FROM THE MAN IN THE MOON; WAS IT RAIN? (Vocal: Peg La Centra); SWING HIGH, SWING LOW .... *Thesaurus 366* 15-20 37
(An electrical transcription produced for radio broadcast, not for commercial release.)

LOVE IS GOOD FOR ANYTHING THAT AILS YOU / WAS IT RAIN?.................... *Brunswick 7841* 5-8 37
(Vocals: Peg La Centra)

LOVE ME A LITTLE LITTLE / DON'T TAKE YOUR LOVE FROM ME .... *Victor 27509* 5-8 41
(Vocals: Lena Horne)

LOVE OF MY LIFE / A HANDFUL OF STARS .... *Victor 26790* 3-5 40
(Vocals: Anita Boyer)

LOVE OF MY LIFE / THE GLIDER ..... *Musicraft 378* 2-4 46

LOVER COME BACK TO ME / ROSALIE (Vocal: Tony Pastor) .... *Bluebird B-10126* 2-4 39

MAKE LOVE TO ME (Vocal: Paula Kelly) / SOLID SAM........................ *Victor 27705* 3-5 41

MANY DREAMS AGO (Vocal: Helen Forrest) / IF WHAT YOU SAY IS TRUE (Vocal: Tony Pastor)................ *Bluebird B-10446* 2-4 39

MARINELA / I COVER THE WATERFRONT................. *Victor 27362* 2-4 41

MOON GLOW / MY BLUE HEAVEN (by Artie Shaw & His Gramercy Five) .... *Victor 27405* 2-4 41

MOONRAY / MELANCHOLY MOOD... *Bluebird B-10334* 3-5 39
(Vocals: Helen Forrest)

MY FANTASY (Vocal: Pauline Byrne) / MISTER MEADOWLARK (Vocal: Jack Pearle)...... *Victor 26614* 2-4 40

MY HEART STOOD STILL / THE DONKEY SERENADE....... *Bluebird B-10125* 3-5 39

NIGHTMARE (theme song) / NON-STOP FLIGHT .... *Bluebird B-7875* 3-5 38

NOCTURNE / THROUGH THE YEARS... *Victor 27703* 3-5 41

NO MORE TEARS / MOONLIGHT AND SHADOWS...... *Brunswick 7835* 5-8 37
(Vocals: Peg La Centra)

NOT MINE / ABSENT-MINDED MOON.... *Victor 27779* 3-5 42
(Vocals: Fredda Gibson, later known as Georgia Gibbs)

OCTOROON / ALL I REMEMBER IS YOU (Vocal: Helen Forrest)........... *Bluebird B-10319* 3-5 39

OH! LADY BE GOOD / I SURRENDER, DEAR .... *Bluebird B-10430* 2-4 39

ONE NIGHT STAND / ONE FOOT IN THE GROOVE............. *Bluebird B-10202* 3-5 39

ONE, TWO, BUTTON YOUR SHOE (Vocal: Tony Pastor) / LET'S CALL A HEART A HEART (Vocal: Peg La Centra) .... *Brunswick 7750* 5-8 36

PRELUDE IN C MAJOR / WHAT IS THERE TO SAY?.................... *Victor 27432* 3-5 41

ROCKIN' CHAIR / IF I LOVE AGAIN..... *Victor 27664* 3-5 41

SAME OLD LINE / YOU CAN TELL SHE COMES FROM DIXIE (Vocal: Peg La Centra).......... *Brunswick 7794* 5-8 37

SAY IT WITH A KISS / IT TOOK A MILLION YEARS .... *Bluebird B-10079* 3-5 39
(Vocals: Helen Forrest)

SEPTEMBER SONG / LITTLE JAZZ.... *Victor 20-1668* 3-5 45

SHADOWS / I DIDN'T KNOW WHAT TIME IT WAS (Vocal: Helen Forrest) .... *Bluebird B-10502* 2-4 39

SKELETON IN THE CLOSET / THERE'S FROST ON THE MOON (Vocal: Peg La Centra)..... *Brunswick 7771* 5-8 36

SOBBIN' BLUES / CREAM PUFF..... *Brunswick 7806* 8-10 37

SOBBIN' BLUES / CREAM PUFF....... *Vocalion 4686* 3-5 39
(The Vocalion release is a reissue)

SOFTLY AS IN A MORNING SUNRISE / COPENHAGEN .... *Bluebird B-10054* 3-5 39

SOMEBODY NOBODY LOVES (Vocal: Fredda Gibson) / HINDUSTAN......................... *Victor 27798* 3-5 42
(Fredda Gibson was later known as Georgia Gibbs)

SOMEONE'S ROCKING MY DREAMBOAT / I DON'T WANT TO WALK WITHOUT YOU...... *Victor 27746* 3-5 42
(Vocals: Paula Kelly)

SOUTH SEA ISLAND MAGIC / IT AIN'T RIGHT................... *Brunswick 7721* 5-8 36
(Vocals: Peg La Centra)

ST. JAMES'S INFIRMARY / ST. JAMES'S INFIRMARY, PART II................ *Victor 27895* 3-5 42
(Vocals: Hot Lips Page)

SUGAR FOOT STOMP / THOU SWELL........................ *Brunswick 7735* 8-10 36

SUPPER TIME (Vocal: Helen Forrest) / ZIGEUNER.................. *Bluebird B-10127* 2-4 39

TABLE IN A CORNER, A / WITHOUT A DREAM TO MY NAME.................... *Bluebird B-10468* 3-5 39
(Vocals: Helen Forrest)

TEMPTATION / STAR DUST............ *Victor 27230* 2-4 40

THERE'S SOMETHING IN THE AIR / TAKE ANOTHER GUESS.......... *Brunswick 7778* 5-8 36
(Vocals: Peg La Centra)

THEY SAY / A ROOM WITH A VIEW .... *Bluebird B-10075* 2-4 39
(Vocals: Helen Forrest)

THIS IS ROMANCE / PYRAMID......... *Victor 27343* 3-5 41

THIS TIME THE DREAM'S ON ME (Vocal: Bonnie Lake) / BLUES IN THE NIGHT (Vocal: Hot Lips Page) .... *Victor 27609* 4-6 41

TO A BROADWAY ROSE / DEUCES WILD.................... *Victor 27838* 3-5 42

TRAFFIC JAM / SERENADE TO A SAVAGE .... *Bluebird B-10385* 3-5 39

TWO BLIND LOVES / THE LAST TWO WEEKS IN JULY................. *Bluebird B-10412* 2-4 39
(Vocals: Helen Forrest)

VILIA / THE MAN I LOVE............... *Bluebird B-10128* 3-5 39

WHO'S EXCITED? / ALONE TOGETHER... *Victor 27385* 3-5 41

YOU GROW SWEETER AS THE YEARS GO BY / IF YOU EVER CHANGE YOUR MIND ..... *Bluebird B-10195* 2-4 39
(Vocals: Helen Forrest)

YOU'RE A LUCKY GUY (Vocal: Tony Pastor) / LOVE IS HERE (Vocal: Helen Forrest)......... *Bluebird B-10482* 2-4 39

YOU'RE GIVING ME A SONG AND A DANCE / DARLING, NOT WITHOUT YOU.... *Brunswick 7741* 4-6 36
(Vocals: Peg La Centra)

YOU'RE SO INDIFF'RENT (Vocal: Helen Forrest) / SNUG AS A BUG IN A RUG (Vocal: Tony Pastor)................ *Bluebird B-10215* 2-4 39

SHAW, Artie, & His Strings

COUNT EVERY STAR / IF YOU WERE ONLY MINE........................... *Decca 27042* 3-5 50
(Vocals: Dick Haymes)
(A Canadian release)

STREAMLINE / SWEET LORRAINE... *Brunswick 7852* 5-8 37

SHAW, Carl, & His Orchestra:

see REICHMAN, Joe, & His Orchestra

SHAW, Joel, & His Orchestra

AVALON / MARGIE.................... *Crown 3382* 4-6 32
(Vocals: Dick Robertson as Bob Dixon)

BARNACLE BILL (THE SAILOR) / STOP THE SUN, STOP THE MOON.................. *Crown 3273* 5-8 32
(Vocals: Dick Robertson as Bob Dixon)

BUSINESS IN F / SWEET VIOLETS...... *Crown 3271* 5-8 32
(Vocals: Dick Robertson as Bob Dixon)

DINAH / THE DARKTOWN STRUTTERS' BALL.................. *Crown 3319* 5-8 32
(Vocals: Dick Robertson as Bob Dixon)

GET CANNIBAL (Vocal: Dick Robertson as Bob Dixon) / BASIN STREET BLUES.............. *Crown 3362* 5-8 32

HOW'M I DOIN' / THE SCAT SONG ...... *Crown 3333* 5-8 32
(Vocals: Dick Robertson as Bob Dixon)

IDA (Vocal: Dick Robertson as Bob Dixon) / ORIGINAL DIXIELAND ONE-STEP.... *Crown 3444* 5-8 33

IF IT AIN'T LOVE / LAWD, YOU MADE THE NIGHT TOO LONG.......................... *Crown 3298* 5-8 32
(Vocals: Dick Robertson as Bob Dixon)

KICKIN' THE GONG AROUND / MINNIE THE MOOCHER.............. *Crown 3306* 5-8 32
(Vocals: Dick Robertson as Bob Dixon)

REEFER MAN / GOIN' TO TOWN........ *Crown 3423* 8-10 32
(Vocals: Dick Robertson as Bob Dixon)

SOME OF THESE DAYS / ALEXANDER'S RAGTIME BAND................................ *Crown 3285* 5-8 32
(Vocals: Dick Robertson as Bob Dixon)

THAT'S A PLENTY / LET'S HAVE A PARTY (Vocal: Dick Robertson as Bob Dixon)........ *Crown 3352* 5-8 32

TIGER RAG / CLARINET MARMALADE.... *Crown 3383* 8-10 32

WHO'S YOUR LITTLE WHO-ZIS? / ONE MORE KISS, THEN GOODNIGHT.................. *Crown 3244* 4-6 32
(Vocals: Dick Robertson as Bob Dixon)

YEAH MAN / JAZZ PIE .... *Crown 3414* 8-10 32
(Vocals: Dick Robertson as Bob Dixon)

SHAW, Milt, & His Detroiters

COLLEGIANA / BORNEO............ *Vocalion 15666* 5-8 28
(Vocals: Al Shayne)

DAUGHTER OF THE LATIN QUARTER / MY LOVE FOR YOU....................... *Melotone M-12021* 4-6 30
(Vocals: Unknown)

I'M MAD ABOUT YOU (Vocal: Ronnie Perry) / I'M BIDDING MY BUDDY GOODBYE
(Vocals: Unknown)................. *Melotone M-12165* 4-6 31

I'M SO AFRAID OF YOU / THE RIVER AND ME....................... *Melotone M-12060* 5-8 31
(Vocals: Ronnie Perry)

IT'S AN OLD SPANISH CUSTOM IN THE MOONLIGHT / BABY'S BIRTHDAY PARTY..... *Melotone M-12020* 3-5 30
(Vocals: Unknown)

POOR PEOPLE (Vocal: Scrappy Lambert) / THAT'S MY WEAKNESS NOW (Vocal: Al Shayne)... *Vocalion 15697* 5-8 28

PRECIOUS LITTLE THING CALLED LOVE, A / MIA BELLA ROSA.................... *Okeh 41196* 5-8 29
(Vocals: Smith Ballew)

SLEEPY TOWN EXPRESS, THE / THE KING'S HORSES (AND THE KING'S MEN)......... *Melotone M-12061* 3-5 31
(Vocals: Ronnie Perry)

SUNSHINE (Vocal: Eddy Thomas) / GOLDEN GATE (Vocal: Al Shayne)..... *Vocalion 15665* 5-8 28

WALKING WITH SUSIE / BREAKAWAY.................. *Columbia 1811-D* 5-8 29
(Vocals: Unknown)

WALKIN' MY BABY BACK HOME / RUNNIN' BETWEEN THE RAINDROPS.... *Melotone M-12098* 5-8 31
(Vocals: Scrappy Lambert)

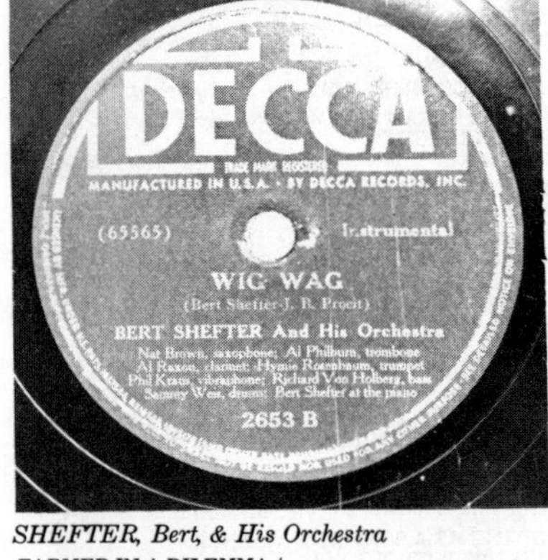

SHEFTER, Bert, & His Orchestra

FARMER IN A DILEMMA / DESERTED DESERT................. *Decca 2584* 3-5 39

MONKEY ON A STRING / TRAMMIN' AT THE FAIR............. *Decca 2525* 4-6 39

WIG WAG / TOAST TO PAGANINI'S GHOST.................. *Decca 2653* 4-6 39

SHEFTER, Bert, & His Rhythm Octet

CHOPIN'S GHOST / MAHOGANY HALL STOMP
(by Bunny Berigan & His Orchestra)......... *Victor 25622* 5-8 37

S.O.S. / LOCOMOTIVE.................... *Victor 25614* 5-8 37

SHIELD, Leroy, & The Victor Hollywood Orchestra

SING-SONG GIRL (Vocal: James Blackstone) / SONG OF THE BIG TRAIL (Vocal: Bud Jamieson).... *Victor 22548* 3-5 30

SHILKRET, Jack, & His Orchestra
(Jack Shilkret: 10/13/96 – 6/16/64)

ABOUT A QUARTER TO NINE / THE LITTLE THINGS YOU USED TO DO................ *Bluebird B-5884* 3-5 35
(Vocals: Unknown)

MELODY FROM THE SKY / I'M A FOOL FOR LOVING YOU (Vocal: Chick Bullock)............. *Oriole 6-06-07* 4-6 36

MISTY ISLANDS OF THE HIGHLANDS / A LITTLE RENDEZ-VOUS IN HONOLULU.... *Brunswick 7602* 4-6 36
(Vocals: Chick Bullock)

SING AN OLD-FASHIONED SONG / THE DAY I LET YOU GET AWAY................. *Brunswick 7603* 4-6 36
(Vocals: Chick Bullock)

SHILKRET, Nat, & The Victor Orchestra
(Nat Shilkret: 12/15/95 –)

AIN'T SHE SWEET? (Vocal: Franklyn Baur) / MUDDY WATER (by Paul Whiteman and His Orchestra; Vocal: Bing Crosby)..................... *Victor 20508* 5-8 27

BABY'S BLUE (Vocal: Johnny Marvin) / THE CALINDA (by Paul Whiteman & His Orchestra; Vocals: Bing Crosby, Jack Fulton, Charles Gaylord, & Austin Young).... *Victor 20882* 3-5 27

BOTTOMS UP / BIGGER AND BETTER THAN EVER......................... *Victor 22109* 2-4 29
(Vocals: Don Howard)

BROADWAY BABY DOLLS / WISHING AND WAITING FOR LOVE (Vocal: Belle Mann).......... *Victor 22019* 2-4 29

DIXIANA / MR. AND MRS. SIPPI........ *Victor 22472* 2-4 30
(Vocals: Frank Luther)

DUSKY STEVEDORE (Vocals: Wilfred Glenn & Elliott Shaw) / WHEN SWEET SUSIE GOES STEPPIN' BY........................ *Victor 21515* 3-5 28

HALF A MOON (Vocal: Johnny Marvin) / JERSEY WALK (by Roger Wolfe Kahn & His Orchestra)...... *Victor 20231* 4-6 26

HITTIN' THE CEILING (Vocal: Scrappy Lambert as Burt Lorin) / SING A LITTLE LOVE SONG (Vocal: Don Howard).................... *Victor 21969* 2-4 29

I CAN DO WONDERS WITH YOU (Vocal: Scrappy Lambert) / MY MAN IS ON THE MAKE (Vocal: Belle Mann)...................... *Victor 22185* 3-5 29

I'M THE MEDICINE MAN FOR THE BLUES / WOULDN'T IT BE WONDERFUL?..... *Victor 22055* 3-5 29
(Vocals: Johnny Marvin)

IN THE GOOD OLD SUMMER TIME / THE SIDEWALKS OF NEW YORK..... *Victor 21493* 2-4 28
(Vocals: Lewis James)

I WANT A DADDY TO CUDDLE ME / BECAUSE I KNOW YOU'RE MINE..... *Victor 21818* 3-5 29
(Vocals: Belle Mann)

PULL YOURSELF TOGETHER / WHERE HAVE YOU BEEN ALL MY LIFE?................ *Victor 20902* 2-4 27
(Vocals: Johnny Marvin)

UNTIL THE REAL THING COMES ALONG (Vocal: Scrappy Lambert as Burt Lorin) / HELLO BABY (by Fred Waring & His Pennsylvanians; Vocal: Will Morgan)...................... *Victor 22266* 4-6 30

WHAT DOES IT MATTER? (Vocal: Elliott Shaw) / HOOSIER SWEETHEART (by Jean Goldkette and His Orchestra; Vocal: Ray Muerer)............ *Victor 20471* 5-8 27

WHEREVER YOU GO (Vocal: Lewis James) / I'M IN LOVE AGAIN (by Paul Whiteman & His Orchestra; Vocals: Jack Fulton, Charles Gaylord, Austin Young, Bing Crosby & Al Rinker)............... *Victor 20646* 3-5 27

YOU WOULDN'T FOOL ME, WOULD YOU? (Vocal: Johnny Marvin) / I WANT TO BE BAD (Vocal: Belle Mann)................ *Victor 21859* 3-5 29

SHILKRET, Nat, as The Havana Novelty Orchestra

ADIOS / BONITA....................... *Victor 22963* 2-4 32

LADY, PLAY YOUR MANDOLIN (Vocal: Paul Small) / MAMA INEZ......................... *Victor 22597* 3-5 31

SHILKRET, Nat, as The Hilo Hawaiian Orchestra

COLORADO SUNSET / THAT NIGHT IN AVALON...................... *Bluebird B-7749* 2-4 38
(Vocals: Jimmy Ray)

DOWN THE RIVER OF GOLDEN DREAMS (Vocal: Johnny Marvin) / WHEN IT'S SPRINGTIME IN THE ROCKIES (Vocals: Frank Luther & Carson Robison)...................... *Victor 22339* 2-4 30

HEARTS ARE NEVER BLUE IN BLUE KALUA / SAILING AWAY FROM THE ISLANDS............. *Bluebird B-7760* 2-4 38
(Vocals: Jimmy Ray)

SHILKRET, Nat, as The International Novelty Orchestra

LET IT RAIN (Vocal: Vernon Dalhart) / MY KID............................ *Victor 19624* 3-5 25

PRISONER'S SONG, THE (Vocal: Vernon Dalhart) / AFTER THE BALL (Vocal: Henry Burr)... *Victor 19714* 2-4 25

ROSITA / ABANDONADO.............. *Victor 19218* 2-4 24

SHILKRET, Nat, as Shilkret's Rhythm-Melodists

CHLOE / WHEN YOU'RE WITH SOMEBODY ELSE............ *Victor 21298* 5-8 28

I CAN'T GIVE YOU ANYTHING BUT LOVE (BABY) / I'M SORRY, SALLY...................... *Victor 21688* 3-5 28

SHILKRET, Nathaniel, as The Victor Salon Group

VICTOR HERBET MELODIES – PAN AMERICANA; I'VE BEEN DECORATED; TWILIGHT BARAKECSH; ROSE OF THE WORLD; YESTERTHOUGHTS / VICTOR HERBET MELODIES, PART II – PUNCHINELLO; JIG ERIN'S ISLE; EILEEN ALANNA ASTHORE; THE IRISH HAVE A GREAT DAY TONIGHT; YOU'RE THE ONLY GIRL FOR ME; WHEN YOU'RE AWAY... *Victor Program Transcription L-4506* 10-12 32
(This is one record, an early 33 1/3 rpm disc containing about ten minutes of music on each side. Although these long-play records were produced from 1931 until 1934, sales were always small due to the economic condition of the time, which accounts for their rarity today.)

SHORT, Arthur E., & His Tivoli Syncopators

BY THE SHALIMAR / LONG AGO..... *Vocalion 14553* 2-4 23

DREAMS OF INDIA / DOWN IN SWEETHEART TOWN............. *Vocalion 14552* 2-4 23

LIZA / WOLVERINE BLUES.......... *Vocalion 14554* 3-5 23

MIDNIGHT ROSE / BEBE .... *Vocalion 14641* 2-4 23

MY OLD RAMSHACKLE SHACK / IN A TENT........................ *Vocalion 14613* 2-4 23

NO, NO, NORA / TWEET TWEET (whistling by Sibyl Sanderson Fagan).................. *Vocalion 14640* 2-4 23

SLOW POKE / BUGLE CALL RAG..... *Vocalion 14658* 3-5 23

SOBBIN' BLUES / LONG-LOST MAMA (DADDY MISSES YOU)............ *Vocalion 14600* 3-5 23

SIGNORELLI, Frank, & His Orchestra
(Frank Signorelli: 5/24/01 –)

SHE'S STILL MY BABY / —...... *Pathe Actuelle 36518* 5-8 26

ST. LOUIS HOP / A BLUES SERENADE......... *Pathe Actuelle 36535* 5-8 26

ST. LOUIS HOP / A BLUES SERENADE............... *Perfect 14716* 4-6 26
(Simultaneously released on two labels)

SILVERMAN, David H., & His Orchestra

MEAN BLUES / MAMA GOES WHERE PAPA GOES (OR PAPA DON'T GO OUT TONIGHT).... *Victor 19195* 4-6 23

ONE HOUR OF LOVE / NIGHT IN THE WOODS......................... *Victor 19200* 2-4 23

SIMS, Les, & His Orchestra:
see PELTYN, Sid, & His Orchestra

SISSLE, Noble, & His Orchestra
(Noble Sissle: 7/10/89 –)

GOT THE BENCH, GOT THE PARK / LOVELESS LOVE .... *Brunswick 6073* 15-20 31
(Vocals: Noble Sissle)

I TAKE TO YOU (Vocal: Lena Horne) / RHYTHM OF THE BROADWAY MOON (Vocal: Noble Sissle).... *Decca 847* 8-10 36

I WONDER WHO MADE RHYTHM (Vocal: Billy Banks) / 'TAIN'T A FIT NIGHT OUT FOR MAN OR BEAST (Vocal: Noble Sissle)...................... *Decca 766* 8-10 36

THAT'S WHAT LOVE DID TO ME (Vocal: Lena Horne) / YOU CAN'T LIVE IN HARLEM (Vocal: Billy Banks)........................ *Decca 778* 8-10 36

WHA'D YA DO TO ME? / ROLL ON, MISSISSIPPI, ROLL ON........... *Brunswick 6111* 15-20 31
(Vocals: Noble Sissle)

SISSLE, Noble & His Orchestra as The Missouri Jazz Band

GOT THE BENCH, GOT THE PARK / LOVELESS LOVE .... *Supertone S-2173* 12-15 31
(Vocals: Noble Sissle)

SISSON, Ken, & His Orchestra

BAMBOOLA / BLUE HEAVEN....... *Brunswick 3595* 2-4 27
(Vocals: Vaughn de Leath)

DON'T KEEP ME IN THE DARK, BRIGHT EYES (Vocal: Jack Parker) / IF YOU DON'T LOVE ME (Vocal: Frank Luther)............. *Brunswick 4018* 2-4 28

LA LO LA / HELLO, CUTIE.......... *Brunswick 3502* 2-4 27
(Vocals: Vaughn de Leath)

OL' MAN RIVER (Vocal: Irving Kaufman) / WHY DO I LOVE YOU? (Vocal: Franklyn Baur).......... *Brunswick 3766* 3-5 28

WHOLE WORLD KNOWS I LOVE YOU, THE (Vocal: Frank Luther) / 'ROUND EVENING (Vocal: Eddy Thomas)................. *Brunswick 4120* 3-5 28

SIX BLACK DIAMONDS, The:
see CALIFORNIA RAMBLERS, The
see SAMUELS, Joseph, & His Orchestra, and
see SCHUBERT, Adrian, & His Salon Orchestra

SIX BROWN BROTHERS, The, directed by Tom Brown

FATIMA / 12TH STREET RAG........ *Emerson 10205* 2-4 20

I'LL SAY SHE DOES / MISSOURI BLUES.................. *Emerson 1056* 2-4 19

PUSSYFOOT MARCH / BULL FROG BLUES .... *Victor 18097* 2-4 16

RAINBOW OF MY DREAMS / JAZZ BAND BLUES................. *Emerson 10195* 2-4 20

SAXOPHONE SAM / THE GHOST OF THE SAXOPHONE.................. *Victor 18309* 2-4 17

WHEN AUNT DINAH'S DAUGHTER HANNAH BANGS ON THAT PIANO / CHASING THE CHICKENS............ *Victor 18476* 2-4 18

SIX HAYSEEDS, The:
see RESER, Harry, as The Six Jumping Jacks

SIX JOLLY JESTERS, The:
see ELLINGTON, Duke

SIX JUMPING JACKS, The:
see RESER, Harry

SIZZLERS, The

DIGA DIGA DOO / SOMEBODY STOLE MY GAL..................... *Edison 52463* 8-10 29

SLACK, Freddy, & His Eight Beats
(Freddy Slack: 8/7/10 – 8/10/65)

BOOGIE WOOGIE ON KITTEN ON THE KEYS / THAT PLACE DOWN THE ROAD A-PIECE (Vocals: Don Raye & Jo Jo Hoffman) .... *Decca 4043* 2-4 41

STRANGE CARGO (theme song)) / PIG FOOT PETE (Vocal: Don Raye) .... *Decca 4130* 2-4 41

SLACK, Freddie, & His Orchestra

AIN'T THAT JUST LIKE A MAN (Vocal: Margaret Whiting) / SWINGING ON A STAR (Vocals: The Brian Sisters) .... *Capitol 160* 2-4 44

COW-COW BOOGIE (Vocal: Ella Mae Morse) / HERE YOU ARE (Vocal: David Street) .... *Capitol 102* 2-4 42

FREDDIE SLACK'S BOOGIE WOOGIE (a 4-record album set) .... *Capitol Set BD 12* 8-10 44
(Individual records in the set, listed numerically with value of each)

BEHIND THE EIGHT BEAT / RIB JOINT .... *Capitol 20029* 2-4 -

SOUTHPAW SERENADE / STRANGE CARGO (theme song) .... *Capitol 20030* 2-4 -

BLACKOUT BOOGIE / A CAT'S NINTH LIFE .... *Capitol 20031* 2-4 -

KITTEN ON THE KEYS / BASHFUL BABY BLUES .... *Capitol 20032* 2-4 -

GEE CHI SONG / A KISS GOODNIGHT (Vocal: Liza Morrow) .... *Capitol 203* 2-4 45

HE'S MY GUY (Vocal: Ella Mae Morse) / DOLL DANCE .... *Capitol 113* 2-4 42

HOUSE OF BLUE LIGHTS / HEY MR. POSTMAN .... *Capitol 251* 3-5 46
(Vocals: Ella Mae Morse)

SILVER WINGS IN THE MOONLIGHT (Vocal: Margaret Whiting) / FURLOUGH FLING .... *Capitol 146* 3-5 43

STEAL AWAY EASY, BABY (Vocal: Charlotte Blackburn) / KITTEN ON THE KEYS .... *Capitol 15155* 2-4 46

THAT OLD BLACK MAGIC (Vocal: Margaret Whiting) / HIT THE ROAD TO DREAMLAND (Vocals: The Mellowaires) .... *Capitol 126* 2-4 42

WAITIN' FOR THE EVENIN' MAIL (Vocals: Johnny Mercer) / THE OLD MUSIC MASTER (by Paul Whiteman & His Orchestra: Vocals: Johny Mercer & Jack Teagarden) .... *Capitol 137* 3-5 42

SLIM & HIS HOT BOYS:
see LAMAR, Slim

SMALL, Abe, & His Melody Boys

AUNT HAGAR'S BLUES / I WISH I COULD SHIMMY LIKE MY SISTER KATE .... *Strong 10002* 50-60 23

GEORGIA CABIN DOOR / LOVE'S LAMENT .... *Strong 10003* 45-50 23
(Strong records are exceedingly rare)

TOMORROW (I'LL BE IN MY DIXIE HOME) / SISTER KATE .... *Federal 5228* 5-8 23

SMALL, Abe, as Abe Small's Rosemont Melody Boys

GEORGIA CABIN DOOR / AGGRAVATIN' PAPA .... *Silvertone 5246* 5-8 23

TOMORROW (I'LL BE IN MY DIXIE HOME) / SISTER KATE .... *Silvertone 5228* 5-8 23

WABASH BLUES / VIRGINIA BLUES .... *Silvertone 2277* 5-8 23

SMALL, Abe, as Abe Small's Rosemont Orchestra

GEORGIA CABIN DOOR / AGGRAVATIN' PAPA .... *Federal 5246* 5-8 23

WABASH BLUES / VIRGINIA BLUES .... *Federal 5277* 5-8 23

SMALL, Abe, as The Carolina Cotton Pickers

GEORGIA CABIN DOOR / DUMBELL .... *Gennett 5016* 5-8 23

SMALL, Abe, as Small's Melodian Men recorded under the name The Famous Rosemont Dance Orchestra

LAST NIGHT I SAW MARIE HOME / COME, MY SWEETHEART, WE'LL DRINK A GLASS OF LIQUEUR .... *Strong 10001* 40-45 23
(Strong records are exceedingly rare)

SMALL, Allan, & His Orchestra

LEARN TO CROON / MOONSTRUCK .... *Crown 3505* 4-6 33
(Vocals: Unknown)

MOON / I ONLY FOUND YOU FOR SOMEBODY ELSE .... *Crown 3380* 4-6 32
(Vocals: Unknown)

PINK ELEPHANTS / 'TWAS ONLY A SUMMER NIGHT'S DREAM .... *Crown 3378* 5-8 32
(Vocals: Unknown)

SMALL, Paul, as Paul Small's Collegians

GUILTY / WHO AM I? .... *Crown 3196* 4-6 31
(Vocals: Paul Small)

OF THEE I SING / AUF WIEDERSEHEN, MY DEAR .... *Crown 3256* 4-6 32
(Vocals: Paul Small)

SMALL'S MELODIAN MEN:
see SMALL, Abe

SMELSER, Cornell, as Cornell & His Orchestra

COLLEGIATE LOVE / ACCORDION JOE (Vocal: Artie Dunn) .... *Odeon ONY-36069* 8-10 30
(There's no vocal on side 1, although some labels credit one.)

COLLEGIATE LOVE / ACCORDION JOE (Vocal: Artie Dunn) .... *Okeh 41386* 8-10 30
(There's no vocal on side 1, although some labels credit one.)
(Simultaneously released on two labels)

SMITH, Cal, as Cal Smith's American Orchestra

LOVELIGHT IN YOUR EYES, THE / DOWN IN MARYLAND .... *Gennett 5020* 3-5 23

PACK UP YOUR SINS AND GO TO THE DEVIL / WHO DID YOU FOOL AFTER ALL? .... *Gennett 5011* 4-6 23

SMITH, Harl, & His Orchestra

BRING BACK THOSE ROCK-A-BYE BABY DAYS / ROSE MARIE .... *Pathe Actuelle 036158* 5-8 24

SMITH, Harl, as The Lido Venice Dance Orchestra

WHEN THINGS GO WRONG / SAN .... *Pathe Actuelle 036110* 5-8 24

WHEN THINGS GO WRONG / SAN .... *Perfect 14291* 4-6 24
(Simultaneously released on two labels)

SMITH, Joe, as Joe Smith's Martha Lee Club Orchestra
(Joe Smith: 1902 – 12/2/37)

JOANNA / THE MIDNIGHT WALTZ .... *Okeh 40351* 4-6 25
(Vocals: Unknown)

NORA LEE / DON'T BOTHER ME .... *Okeh 40322* 5-8 25

SMITH, Joseph C., as Joseph C. Smith's Orchestra

CALICOCO / MY DOUGH BOY .... *Victor 18478* 3-5 18

CHING-A-LING'S JAZZ BAZAAR / IRENE .... *Victor 35695* 2-4 20
(This is an oversize 12-inch 78 rpm)

EVENSONG / GET OFF MY FOOT .... *Victor 18247* 2-4 17

FASCINATION / FOR ME AND MY GAL .... *Victor 35640* 2-4 17
(This is an oversize 12-inch 78 rpm)

HINDUSTAN / 'N' EVERYTHING .... *Victor 18507* 2-4 18

LOVE AND THE MOON / WONDERFUL YOU .... *Brunswick 2402* 2-4 23

MELLO 'CELLO / LEGEND .... *Victor 18761* 2-4 21

MONEY BLUES / I'VE A SHOOTING BOX IN SCOTLAND .... *Victor 18165* 2-4 16

NOW THAT I NEED YOU, YOU'RE GONE / STELLA .... *Brunswick 2447* 2-4 23

OH! JOHNNY! OH, JOHNNY! OH! / DANCE AND GROW THIN .... *Victor 18313* 2-4 17

ON MIAMI SHORE / PEGGY (Vocal: Harry MacDonough) .... *Victor 18632* 2-4 19

POOR BUTTERFLY / ALLAH'S HOLIDAY .... *Victor 18246* 2-4 17

RAINY DAY BLUES / OUT OF THE EAST .... *Victor 18561* 2-4 19

SMILES (Vocal: Harry MacDonough) / ROSE ROOM .... *Victor 18473* 2-4 18

STEALING / I WANT MY MAMMY .... *Victor 18845* 2-4 22

SWEETHEART OF SIGMA CHI / MARIANNA .... *Brunswick 2440* 2-4 23

TELL ME (Vocal: Arthur Fields) / THE VAMP (Vocals: Harry MacDonough & Billy Murray) .... *Victor 18594* 3-5 19

TULIP TIME / YELLOW DOG BLUES .... *Victor 18618* 3-5 19

WHOSE BABY ARE YOU? / LEFT ALL ALONE AGAIN BLUES .... *Victor 18661* 2-4 20

YOU'RE IN LOVE / THIS WAY OUT .... *Victor 18275* 2-4 17

SMITH, Leroy, & His Orchestra

INDIAN LOVE CALL / DIXIE DREAMS .... *Everybody's 1027* 15-20 24

MORNING (WON'T YOU EVER COME ROUND?) / STOP AND LISTEN .... *Blue-Disc 1001* 50-60 24
(Blue Disc is an extrememly rare record)

RHAPSODY IN BLUE / ST. LOUIS BLUES .... *Victor 21328* 8-10 28

SATURDAY / LOVE WILL FIND A WAY .... *Vocalion 14218* 5-8 21

SMITH, Willie "The Lion":
see HAITIAN ORCHESTRA, The

SNOOKS & HIS MEMPHIS RAMBLERS / STOMPERS:
see FRIEDMAN, Snooks

SNYDER, Bob, & His Orchestra:
see, DORSEY BROTHERS' Orchestra, The and see MAYHEW, Nye, & His Orchestra

SNYDER, Carl, & His Orchestra:
see HAYMES, Joe, & His Orchestra

SOCIETY DANCE ORCHESTRA, The;
see SAMUELS, Joseph, & His Orchestra

SOCIETY NIGHT CLUB ORCHESTRA, The:
see HARING, Bob, & His Orchestra

SOCIETY SYNCOPATORS, The:
see SPECHT, Paul as Specht's Jazz Outfit

SOMAN, Herbert as Herbert Soman's Salon Orchestra

RECOLLECTIONS OF GILBERT AND SULLIVAN (including selections from "H.M.S. Pinafore", "The Pirates of Penzance" and "The Mikado") / MEMORIES OF VICTOR HERBERT (including "Naughty Marietta", "The Red Mill", "Mlle. Modeste", "Babes in Toyland" and "The Fortune Teller") .... *Edison 10002* 50-60 27
(This is one record, a long-play disc released in 1927 which required a special attachment on the Edison phonograph. These records played at 80 rpm, as do the standard Edison discs, but with the use of microgrooves, the 10-inch records contained 24 minutes of music. There were also 12-inch long-play discs which played for 40 minutes. The microgrooves, 450 to the inch, are so fine that they are barely visible to the naked eye. In comparison, the standard Edison discs have 150 grooves per inch, and modern LPs contain an average of 250 grooves to the inch. The records were not commercially successful and were discontinued after a few months, which accounts for their extreme rarity.)

SOPHISTICATS, The:
see LEASH, Paul

SOSNIK, Harry, & His Edgewater Beach Hotel Orchestra
(Harry Sosnik 7/13/06 –)

COUNT YOUR BLESSINGS (Vocal: Bob Hannon) / CARIOCA .... *Victor 24488* 2-4 34

HOW DO I KNOW IT'S SUNDAY? (Vocal: Bob Hannon) / HOT CHOC'LATE SOLDIERS (Vocals: The Campus Trio) .... *Victor 24623* 2-4 34

NO MORE HEARTACHES, NO MORE TEARS / FOOL THAT I AM .... *Victor 24626* 2-4 34
(Vocals: Bob Hannon)

THAT'S LOVE / LET'S PUT TWO AND TWO TOGETHER .... *Victor 24570* 2-4 34
(Vocals: Bob Hannon)

WINTER INTERLUDE / LAZY RHAPSODY (theme song) .... *Victor 24572* 2-4 34
(Vocals: Bob Hannon)

SOSNIK, Harry, & His Orchestra

MISS YOU / MINKA .... *Decca 4088* 2-4 42
(Vocals: Bob Hannon)

MOON AT SEA / HERE COMES THE SANDMAN .... *Decca 1466* 3-5 37
(Vocals: Dave Marshall)

SOTHERN, Larry, & His Orchestra

DAY IN – DAY OUT / LITTLE OLD BAND OF GOLD .... *Vocalion 5050* 2-4 39
(Vocals: Larry Sothern)

MAN AND HIS DREAM, A / OLD MILL WHEEL .... *Vocalion 4996* 2-4 39
(Vocals: Larry Sothern)

(YOU TOOK ME) OUT OF THIS WORLD / IT MUST HAVE BEEN TWO OTHER PEOPLE ... *Vocalion 4944* 2-4 39
(Vocals: Larry Sothern)

WHISPER WHILE WE DANCE / WHO'S SORRY NOW? .... *Vocalion 5075* 2-4 39
(Vocals: Larry Sothern)

SOUDERS, Jackie, & His Orchestra

BY THE ALAMO / EVERY LITTLE THING .... *Columbia 837-D* 3-5 26
(Vocals: Walton McKinney)

KISS ME AND THEN SAY GOODNIGHT / I NEVER KNEW WHAT THE MOONLIGHT COULD DO .... *Columbia 785-D* 2-4 26
(Vocals: Unknown)

MEDITATION / PALE MOON .... *Columbia 1216-D* 2-4 27

WHEN YOU DREAM, DREAM OF ME / PROMISE .... *Columbia 958-D* 2-4 27
(Vocals: Unknown)

SOUSA'S BAND, directed by John Philip Sousa
(John Philip Sousa: 11/6/1854 – 3/6/32)
("Berliners" are the original disc records, highly prized as collector's items, and have become extremely rare. Both Berliner and Victor records of this period are one-sided.)

AT A GEORGIA CAMP MEETING .... *Berliner 136* 50-60 98
COON BAND CONTEST, A .... *Berliner 01170* 50-60 00
COTTON BLOSSOMS .... *Berliner 104* 45-50 98
HOT TIME IN THE OLD TOWN TONIGHT, A .... *Victor 316* 5-8 00
HULA HULA CAKE WALK .... *Berliner 01201* 40-45 00
LEVEE REVELS – AN AFRO-AMERICAN CAN-HOP .... *Berliner 38* 50-60 97
ORANGE BLOSSOMS .... *Berliner 65* 45-50 97
SILENCE AND FUN – A RAG TIME ODDITY .... *Victor 4538* 3-5 05
SOUTHERN HOSPITALITY CAKE-WALK .... *Berliner 081* 40-45 99
TROMBONE SNEEZE – A HUMORESQUE CAKE-WALK .... *Victor 1223* 5-8 02
WHISTLING RUFUS .... *Berliner 0181* 40-45 99

SOUTHAMPTON SOCIETY ORCHESTRA, The:
see SCHUBERT, Adrian, & His Salon Orchestra

SOUTH, Eddie, & His Alabamians
(Eddie South: 11/27/04 – 4/25/62)

BY THE WATERS OF MINNETONKA / LA ROSITA .... *Victor 21151* 5-8 28

VOICE OF THE SOUTHLAND / MY OHIO HOME .... *Victor 21155* 5-8 28
(Vocals: Eddie South & Jerome Burke)

SOUTH, Eddie, & His Orchestra

MY! OH MY! (Vocal: Eddie South) / GOTTA GO! (Vocals: Eddie South & Everett Barksdale) .... *Victor 24343* 8-10 33

NAGASAKI (Vocal: Everett Barksdale) / MAMA MOCKINGBIRD .... *Victor 24383* 8-10 33

OH, LADY BE GOOD / STOMPIN' AT THE SAVOY .... *Columbia 36193* 3-5 41

OLD MAN HARLEM (Vocal: Milt Hinton) / NO MORE BLUES (Vocal: Eddie South) .... *Victor 24324* 10-12 33

PRETTY GIRL IS LIKE A MELODY, A / PARDON, MADAME .... *Columbia 35633* 2-4 40

ZIGEUNER / MELODIE IN A .... *Columbia 35634* 2-4 40

SOUTHERN MELODY ARTISTS, The:
see RING, Harry

SOUTHERN RHYTHM KINGS, The:
see RAY, Jimmy, & His Orchestra

SOUTHERN SERENADERS ORCHESTRA, The:
see RAY, Jimmy, & His Orchestra

SOUTH, Sonny, & His Collegians:
see ROBERTSON, Dick, & His Orchestra

SPANIER, Muggsy, & His Orchestra
(Muggsy Spanier: 11/09/06 – 2/12/67)

AMERICAN PATROL / MORE THAN YOU KNOW (Vocal: Dottie Reid) .... *Decca 4328* 3-5 42

CAN'T WE BE FRIENDS? / CHICAGO ..... *Decca 4168* 3-5 42

LITTLE DAVID, PLAY ON YOUR HARP / HESITATING BLUES (by Muggsy Spanier & His Ragtimers) ... *Decca 4271* 3-5 42

WRECK OF THE OLD 97, THE (Vocal: Ford Leary) / TWO O'CLOCK JUMP .... *Decca 4336* 3-5 42

SPANIER, Muggsy, & His Ragtime Band

AT SUNDOWN / BLUIN' THE BLUES .... *Bluebird B-10719* 4-6 40

AT THE JAZZ BAND BALL / LIVERY STABLE BLUES (BARNYARD BLUES) .... *Bluebird B-10518* 3-5 40

BIG BUTTER AND EGG MAN (Vocal: George Brunies) / ECCENTRIC .... *Bluebird B-10417* 4-6 39

DINAH (Vocal: George Brunies) / (WHAT DID I DO TO BE SO) BLACK AND BLUE .... *Bluebird B-10682* 4-6 40

I WISH I COULD SHIMMY LIKE MY SISTER KATE (Vocal: George Brunies) / DIPPERMOUTH BLUES .... *Bluebird B-10506* 4-6 40

LONESOME ROAD / MANDY, MAKE UP YOUR MIND .... *Bluebird B-10766* 4-6 40

RIVERBOAT SHUFFLE / RELAXIN' AT THE TOURO (theme song) .... *Bluebird B-10532* 4-6 40

SPANIER, Muggsy, & His Ragtimers

HESITATING BLUES / LITTLE DAVID, PLAY ON YOUR HARP (by Muggsy Spanier & His Orchestra) .... *Decca 4271* 3-5 42

SPARTON SYNCOPATORS, The:
see SPECHT, Paul, & His Orchestra

SPECHT, Paul, & His Hotel Alamac Orchestra
(Paul Specht: circa 1895 – 1954)

ALL BROKEN UP OVER YOU / BLUE EVENING BLUES (by Art Kahn & His Orchestra) .... *Columbia 104-D* 3-5 24

DREARY WEATHER / DEAR ONE ... *Columbia 232-D* 2-4 24

FORGET-ME-NOT / FROM ONE TILL TWO .... *Columbia 135-D* 2-4 24

I CAN'T GET THE ONE I WANT / MANDALAY .... *Columbia 160-D* 2-4 24

PATSY / MORNING (by Art Kahn & His Orchestra) .... *Columbia 215-D* 3-5 24

TAKE, OH TAKE THOSE LIPS AWAY / DEAR OLD LADY .... *Columbia 27-D* 3-5 24

WORRIED / WHAT'LL I DO? .... *Columbia 118-D* 3-5 24

SPECHT, Paul, & His Hotel Alamac Orchestra as The Romancers

ARIZONA STARS / ON THE BLUE LAGOON .... *Columbia 97-D* 2-4 24

BRING BACK THAT OLD-FASHIONED WALTZ / WHEN LIGHTS ARE LOW .... *Columbia 41-D* 2-4 24

DREAMER OF DREAMS / COME BACK TO ME (WHEN THEY THROW YOU DOWN) ... *Columbia 187-D* 2-4 24

HALF-PAST TEN / HULA HULA DREAM GIRL .... *Columbia 59-D* 2-4 24

SPECHT, Paul, & His Orchestra

ALL ALONE / NO WONDER (I LOVE YOU) .... *Columbia 284-D* 2-4 25

BAMBOOLA / WHOOPEE! .... *Columbia 497-D* 2-4 25

CHANSONETTE / EASY MELODY .... *Columbia A-3992* 2-4 23

CHANT OF THE JUNGLE / THAT WONDERFUL SOMETHING IS LOVE .... *Columbia 2002-D* 3-5 29
(Vocals: Unknown)

HITTIN' THE CEILING (Vocal: Johnny Morris) / SING A LITTLE LOVE SONG (Vocals: Unknown) .... *Columbia 1836-D* 4-6 29

I FOUND A MILLION-DOLLAR BABY / WRAP YOUR TROUBLES IN DREAMS .... *Columbia 2482-D* 3-5 31
(Vocals: Unknown)

I'VE GROWN SO LONESOME, THINKING OF YOU / IT MADE YOU HAPPY WHEN YOU MADE ME CRY .... *Columbia 819-D* 3-5 27
(Vocals: Johnny Morris)

KEEPIN' MYSELF FOR YOU / THE HARBOR OF MY HEART .... *Columbia 2106-D* 5-8 30
(Vocals: Johnny Morris)

OH PETER (YOU'RE SO NICE) / BYE-BYE, BABY (Vocals: Unknown) .... *Columbia 258-D* 3-5 25

ORIENTAL MOONLIGHT / I'M LOOKING OVER A FOUR-LEAF CLOVER .... *Columbia 902-D* 2-4 27
(Vocals: Johnny Morris)

ROLL UP THE CARPETS / HOT FEET (Vocal: Johnny Morris) .... *Columbia 1186-D* 4-6 27

SING A NEW SONG / KEEPIN' OUT OF MISCHIEF NOW .... *Clarion 5470-C* 3-5 32
(Vocals: Unknown)

SING A NEW SONG / KEEPIN' OUT OF MISCHIEF NOW .... *Harmony 1423-H* 3-5 32
(Vocals: Unknown)

SING A NEW SONG / KEEPIN' OUT OF MISCHIEF NOW .... *Velvet Tone 2530-V* 3-5 32
(Vocals: Unknown)
(Simultaneously released on three labels)

SO THIS IS LOVE / THE WALTZ OF LONG AGO .... *Columbia 13-D* 2-4 23

STATIC STRUT / SHOW THAT FELLOW THE DOOR (Vocal: Johnny Morris) .... *Columbia 627-D* 5-8 26

ST. LOUIS SHUFFLE / CORNFED ... *Columbia 1307-D* 5-8 27

WHEN WILL THE SUN SHINE FOR ME? / NIGHT AFTER NIGHT .... *Columbia A-3903* 2-4 23

WHEN YOU AND I WERE YOUNG MAGGIE BLUES / MY BUDDY .... *Columbia A-3817* 4-6 23

WORLD IS WAITING FOR THE SUNRISE, THE / ROSES OF PICARDY .... *Columbia A-3870* 2-4 23

YOU FORGOT YOUR GLOVES / FALLING IN LOVE .... *Columbia 2472-D* 4-6 31
(Vocals: Johnny Morris)

SPECHT, Paul, & His Orchestra as The Carolina Club Orchestra

SUNSHINE / AFRAID OF YOU ... *Pathe Actuelle 36764* 3-5 28
(Vocals: Johnny Morris)

SUNSHINE / AFRAID OF YOU .... *Perfect 14945* 2-4 28
(Vocals: Johnny Morris)
(Simultaneously released on two labels)

SPECHT, Paul, & His Orchestra as The Consolidated Club Orchestra

SWEET LORRAINE / I'D RATHER CRY OVER YOU .... *Pathe Actuelle 36806* 3-5 28
(Vocals: Johnny Morris)

SWEET LORRAINE / I'D RATHER CRY OVER YOU .... *Perfect 14987* 2-4 28
(Vocals: Johnny Morris)
(Simultaneously released on two labels)

SPECHT, Paul, & His Orchestra as The Spartan Syncopators

MIA CARA / IF I HAD A GIRL LIKE YOU .... *Odeon ONY-36082* 3-5 30
(Vocals: Unknown)

SWEETHEART, WE NEED EACH OTHER / YOU'RE ALWAYS IN MY ARMS (BUT ONLY IN MY DREAMS) .... *Okeh 41331* 3-5 30
(Vocals: Unknown)

SPECHT, Paul, as The Georgians
(The Georgians were a small "hot dance" unit with members from Paul Specht's Orchestra, directed by Frank Guarente, who played trumpet, or by Walker O'Neill, pianist.

ARE THEY PICKIN' ON YOUR BABY? / CHARLESTON BABY O'MINE .... *Columbia 407-D* 5-8 25

BIG BOY / SOMEDAY, SWEETHEART .... *Columbia 117-D* 4-6 24
(Vocals: Dolly Kay)

BRINGIN' HOME THE BACON / A NEW KIND OF MAN WITH A NEW KIND OF LOVE FOR ME .... *Columbia 136-D* 4-6 24
(Vocals: Blossom Seeley)

FAREWELL BLUES / SNAKES HIPS .... *Columbia A-3864* 4-6 23

GEORGIA PINES / I WON'T BELIEVE IT'S RAINING .... *Harmony 1023-H* 4-6 29
(Vocals: Irving Kaufman as Jim Andrews)

HENPECKED BLUES / LONG LOST MAMA .... *Columbia A-3907* 3-5 23

HOME TOWN BLUES / YOU MAY BE FAST, BUT MAMA'S GONNA SLOW YOU DOWN ... *Columbia 23-D* 4-6 23

I'M SITTING PRETTY IN A PRETTY LITTLE CITY / LEARN TO DO THE STRUT .... *Columbia 11-D* 3-5 23

I WISH I COULD SHIMMY LIKE MY SISTER KATE / CHICAGO .... *Columbia A-3775* 3-5 23

LAND OF COTTON BLUES / MAMA LOVES PAPA .... *Columbia A-3987* 3-5 23

LET'S DO IT / GLORIANNA .... *Harmony 776-H* 2-4 28
(Vocals: Johnny Morris)

LOOSE FEET / AGGRAVATIN' PAPA .... *Columbia A-3825* 3-5 23

LOVEY COME BACK / DANCIN' DAN ... *Columbia 62-D* 2-4 24

MAMA GOES WHERE PAPA GOES / SOMEBODY'S WRONG .... *Columbia A-3996* 2-4 23

ME QUERES? / S'POSIN' .... *Harmony 929-H* 2-4 29
(Vocals: Johnny Morris)

MINDIN' MY BUS'NESS / IF YOU'LL COME BACK .... *Columbia 102-D* 4-6 24

MY BEST GIRL / EVERYBODY LOVES MY BABY .... *Columbia 252-D* 4-6 25

O, GEE, GEORGIE! / IF YOU DO–WHAT YOU DO .... *Columbia 56-D* 5-8 24
(Vocals: Eddie Cantor)

OLD KING TUT / BARNEY GOOGLE .... *Columbia A-3902* 4-6 23

SAVANNAH / DOODLE-DOO-DOO ... *Columbia 142-D* 4-6 24

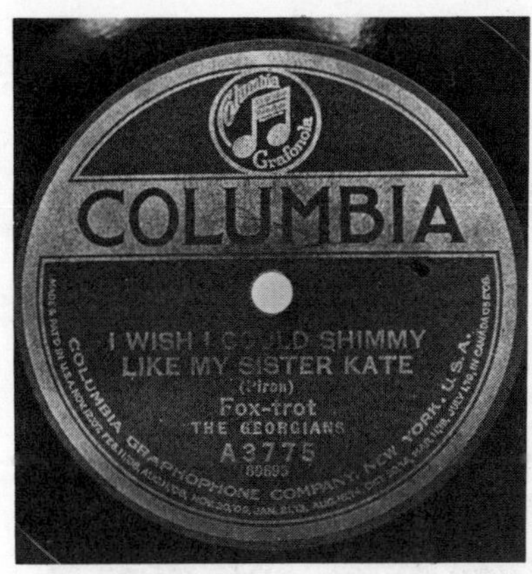

SHAKE YOUR FEET / OLD-FASHIONED
LOVE .... *Columbia 30-D* 4-6 24

SPANISH SHAWL / CLAP HANDS! HERE COMES CHARLEY! (Vocal: Johnny Morris)..... *Columbia 523-D* 3-5 26

'WAY DOWN YONDER IN NEW ORLEANS / NOTHIN' BUT.................. *Columbia A-3804* 3-5 23

YOU'D BETTER KEEP BABYING BABY / I'VE GOT A CROSS-EYED PAPA................ *Columbia 40-D* 3-5 24
(Vocals: Billy Jones)

YOU TELL HER – I STUTTER / YOU'VE GOT TO SEE MAMA EV'RY NIGHT............ *Columbia A-3857* 3-5 23

SPECHT, Paul, as Specht's Jazz Outfit

YOU CAN HAVE HIM, I DON'T WANT HIM BLUES / HOT LIPS..................... *Broadway 11148* 4-6 22

SPECHT, Paul, as Specht's Jazz Outfit recorded under the name The Society Syncopators

YOU CAN HAVE HIM, I DON'T WANT HIM BLUES / HOT LIPS............................ *Regal 9341* 4-6 22

SPECHT, Paul, as Specht's Jazz Outfit recorded under the name Specht's Society Serenaders

YOU CAN HAVE HIM, I DON'T WANT HIM BLUES / HOT LIPS............................ *Banner 1090* 4-6 22

SPECHT'S JAZZ OUTFIT:
see Specht, Paul

SPECHT'S SOCIETY SERENADERS:
see SPECHT, Paul, as Specht's Jazz Outfit

SPECIALE, Mike, & His Bamboo Gardens Orchesi

I WISH I HAD MY OLD GAL BACK AGAIN / A NIGHT OF LOVE..................... *Pathe Actuelle 36406* 3-5
(Vocals: Arthur Hall)

I WISH I HAD MY OLD GAL BACK AGAIN / A NIGHT OF LOVE............................ *Perfect 14587* 2-4 26
(Vocals: Arthur Hall)
(Simultaneously released on two labels)

SPECIALE, Mike, & His Carlton Terrace Hotel Orchestra

ALONE AT LAST / OH BOY! WHAT A GIRL (Vocal: Arthur Hall)............ *Edison 51614* 4-6 25

KINKY KIDS' PARADE / WHEN THE DEAR OLD SUMMER GOES (Vocal: Arthur Hall)..... *Edison 51612* 5-8 25

OH! HOW I LOVE MY DARLING / TAKE ME................... *Pathe Actuelle 036173* 2-4 25

PRETTY LITTLE BABY / KENTUCKY'S WAY OF SAYIN' "GOOD MORNIN' "......... *Harmony 78-H* 2-4 26

SPECIALE, Mike, & His Flippen Club Orchestra

I'VE LOST ALL MY LOVE FOR YOU / EMBERS..................... *Pathe Actuelle 36715* 3-5 27
(Vocals: Scrappy Lambert)

I'VE LOST ALL MY LOVE FOR YOU / EMBERS.......................... *Perfect 14896* 2-4 27
(Vocals: Scrappy Lambert)

SPECIALE, Mike, & His Orchestra

I'M LONELY WITHOUT YOU (Vocal: Arthur Hall) / THE BLUE ROOM.................. *Edison 51751* 4-6 26

JUST A COTTAGE SMALL / DINAH..... *Perfect 14569* 3-5 26
(Vocals: Arthur Hall)

MAMMY CHASING BLUES / I WANNA GO WHERE YOU DO, DO WHAT YOU DO (Vocal: Jimmy Flynn)............ *Perfect 14526* 3-5 26
(This record was pressed in brown shellac)

MY INSPIRATION IS YOU / CARESSING YOU.................... *Edison 52498* 4-6 29

SPENCER, Herbert, & His Orchestra / Spencer's Dance Orchestra

SHE'S A GREAT, GREAT GIRL / LILA................................ *Domino 4119* 3-5 28
(Vocals: Unknown)

SHE'S A GREAT, GREAT GIRL / LILA .... *Regal 8516* 3-5 28
(Vocals: Unknown)
(Simultaneously released on two labels)

SPENCER'S DANCE ORCHESTRA:
see SPENCER, Herbert, & His Orchestra

SPITALNY, Phil, & His Music / Phil Spitalny's Music
(Phil Spitalny: 11/7/90 – 10/11/70)

BLUE SKIES / SEVILLE.................. *Vogue 733* 5-8 46
(Vogue records are picture discs.)

BOTTOMS UP / BIGGER AND BETTER THAN EVER......................... *Edison 14076* 12-15 29
(A rare lateral-cut thin Edison disc)

BY THE WAY / JUST YOU, JUST ME.... *Edison 14062* 10-12 29
(A rare lateral-cut thin Edison disc)

"Hit Of The Week" records are one-sided paper discs. Some, including most of the following, have two titles on the one side.

GOODNIGHT, SWEETHEART (Vocals: The Paull Sisters); IN THE SHADE OF THE OLD APPLE TREE (Vocals: by trio)................ *Hit Of The Week M-1* 4-6 31

GUILTY (Vocals: The Paull Sisters); SHE'LL BE COMIN' 'ROUND THE MOUNTAIN (Vocals: by trio)................. *Hit Of The Week L-2* 4-6 31

HERE WE ARE / S'POSIN'............. *Edison 52589* 4-6 29

LET'S HAVE ANOTHER CUP O' COFFEE (Vocals: Helen Rowland & trio); STRANGERS (Vocals: Unknown)............. *Hit Of The Week D-3-4* 4-6 32

LULLABY OF THE LEAVES (Vocal: Ben Alley); BETTY BOOP (Vocals: by trio).......... *Hit Of The Week F-3-4* 5-8 32

MY SILENT LOVE (Vocal: Ben Alley); HUMMIN' TO MYSELF (Vocals: by trio)....... *Hit Of The Week F-4-5* 3-5 32

NOW'S THE TIME TO FALL IN LOVE; AFTER THE BALL................. *Hit Of The Week A-2-3* 4-6 32
(Vocals: Paul Small)
(A picture of Phil Spitalny is featured on the reverse of this record.)

SHINE ON, HARVEST MOON (Vocal: Helen Rowland); OH SUSANNA (Vocals: Bill Coty & trio)......................... *Hit Of The Week L-4* 3-5 31

SOMEBODY LOVES YOU; ONE MORE KISS, THEN GOODNIGHT............... *Hit Of The Week D-1-2* 5-8 32
(Vocals: Paul Small)

SWINGIN' IN A HAMMOCK (Vocal: Bill Coty)................ *Hit Of The Week 1083* 4-6 30

TIME ON MY HANDS; JINGLE BELLS .... *Hit Of The Week M-3-4* 3-5 31
(Vocals: Bill Coty)

WHEN IT'S SLEEPY-TIME DOWN SOUTH (Vocal: Helen Rowland); SAILING (Vocals: by trio)...................... *Hit Of The Week A-1-2* 5-8 31

WHEN MY DREAMS COME TRUE / BABY, OH! WHERE CAN YOU BE? .... *Edison 52605* 4-6 29
(Vocals: The Paull Sisters)

SPITALNY, Phil, & His Orchestra

BALLYHOO (Vocals: Eddie Cantor).... *Hit Of The Week K-6* 10-12 31
(Hit Of The Week records are one-sided paper discs)

BEYOND THE BLUE HORIZON / MAYBE IT'S LOVE .... *Brunswick 4917* 3-5 30
(Vocals: Unknown)

CAN'T YOU SEE? / TO BE WORTHY OF YOU........................ *Perfect 15532* 3-5 31
(Vocals: Helen Rowland)

CHINESE MOON / KISS ME WITH YOUR EYES (Vocal: Billy Murray)........ *Victor 20287* 2-4 26

I APOLOGIZE (Vocal: Paul Small); FIGHT FOR CALIFORNIA .... *Hit Of The Week K-4* 5-8 31
(Hit Of The Week records are one-sided paper discs)

I MUST HAVE COMPANY / WORRIED... *Victor 19307* 2-4 24

JACKASS BLUES / UP AND AT 'EM..... *Victor 20108* 4-6 26

MY SWEETIE AND ME / HOW I LOVE THAT GIRL................... *Victor 19562* 2-4 25

NO MEANS YES / FEELING THE WAY I DO........................... *Victor 19306* 2-4 24

ONLY YOU AND LONELY ME / HELLO BABY (Vocal: Dennie Looney)..... *Victor 20115* 3-5 26

SOMEONE IS LOSIN' SUSAN / THAT'S MY GIRL (by Ted Weems & His Orchstra; Vocals: Parker Gibbs, Bill Comfort, & Dusty Rhodes)................... *Victor 20196* 3-5 26

SWEET AND LOVELY (Vocal: Paul Small); NOTRE DAME VICTORY MARCH ...... *Hit Of The Week K-5* 5-8 31
(Hit Of The Week records are one-sided paper discs)

YOU CALL IT MADNESS (BUT I CALL IT LOVE) / MY SONG......................... *Perfect 15522* 3-5 31
(Vocals: Chick Bullock)

SPITALNY, Phil, & His Hour Of Charm All-Girl Orchestra
(Phil Spitalny: 11/7/90 – 10-11/70)

SILENT NIGHT / CAROL OF THE BELLS; GOD REST YE MERRY, GENTLEMEN .... *Charm 1000* 3-5 48

SPITALNY, Phil, as Phil Spitalny's Music:
see LANIN, Sam, as Sam Lanin's Dance Ensemble and see SPITALNY, Phil, & His Music

SPIVAK, Charlie, & His Orchestra
(Charlie Spivak: 2/17/06 – 3/1/82)

ALONG WITH ME / SPRING MAGIC................ *RCA Victor 20-1876* 2-4 46
(Vocals: Jimmy Saunders & The Stardreamers)

ANGELS OF MERCY (DEDICATED TO THE AMERICAN RED CROSS) (Vocals: Gary Stevens & The Stardusters) / THE PRESIDENT'S BIRTHDAY BALL (Vocals: The Stardusters) .... *Okeh 6572* 3-5 42

ARTHUR MURRAY TAUGHT ME DANCING IN A HURRAY (Vocal: June Hutton) / I REMEMBER YOU (Vocals: Gary Stevens, June Hutton & The Stardusters)............. *Okeh 6593* 2-4 42

AUTUMN NOCTURNE / THE CLOCK SONG (Vocals: The Stardusters)......... *Conqueror 9956* 2-4 41

AUTUMN NOCTURNE / THE CLOCK SONG (Vocals: The Stardusters) .... *Okeh 6476* 2-4 41
(Simultaneously released on two labels)

BELLS OF ST. MARY'S, THE / YOU CAN CRY ON SOMEBODY ELSE'S SHOULDER............ *RCA Victor 20-1791* 2-4 46
(Vocals: Jimmy Saunders)

DEAR MOM (Vocal: Gary Stevens) / REMEMBER PEARL HARBOR (Vocals: Gary Stevens & The Stardusters).................. *Okeh 6555* 3-5 42

DON'T CRY / EVERYTHING HAPPENS TO ME .... *Okeh 6096* 2-4 41
(Vocals: Gary Stevens)

DON'T TAKE YOUR LOVE FROM ME (Vocal: Gary Stevens) / IF IT'S TRUE (Vocals: Gary Stevens & The Debs) .... *Okeh 6321* 2-4 41

EVERYTHING HAPPENS TO ME (Vocal: Gary Stevens) / INTERMEZZO..................... *Conqueror 9649* 2-4 41

FLAT FEET / YOU ARE TOO BEAUTIFUL (Vocal: Jimmy Saunders) .... *RCA Victor 20-1913* 2-4 46

GOLDEN EARRINGS (Vocal: Irene Daye) / TENDERLY .... *RCA Victor 20-2585* 2-4 47

HOW LUCKY YOU ARE (Vocal: Tommy Mercer) / AT DAWNING................. *RCA Victor 20-2500* 2-4 47

IF IT'S TRUE (Vocals: Gary Stevens & The Debs) / IN THE DARK OF THE MOON...... *Conqueror 9904* 2-4 41

I'LL NEVER LET A DAY PASS BY / TIME WAS............................ *Okeh 6257* 2-4 41
(Vocals: Gary Stevens)

I'LL REMEMBER APRIL / WHAT DOES A SOLDIER DREAM OF? .... *Okeh 6646* 3-5 42
(Vocals: Gary Stevens)

IN THE DARK OF THE MOON / UNDER YOUR WINDOW................ *Okeh 6431* 2-4 41
(Vocals: Gary Stevens)

IT'S ALL OVER NOW / FOR SENTIMENTAL REASONS.................... *RCA Victor 20-1981* 2-4 46
(Vocals: Jimmy Saunders)

IT'S SO PEACEFUL IN THE COUNTRY (Vocal: Gary Stevens) / WHAT WORD IS SWEETER THAN SWEETHEART? (Vocals: Gary Stevens & The Debs) .... *Okeh 6291* 2-4 41

I UNDERSTAND / TWO HEARTS THAT PASS IN THE NIGHT..................... *Okeh 6110* 2-4 41
(Vocals: Gary Stevens)

LET'S PUT OUR DREAMS TOGETHER (Vocal: Jimmy Saunders) / LEAVE SOME........ *RCA Victor 20-2144* 2-4 47

MINKA (Vocal: Gary Stevens) / A WEEK-END IN HAVANA (Vocals: The Stardusters).......... *Okeh 6415* 2-4 41

MY DEVOTION / I LEFT MY HEART AT THE STAGE DOOR CANTEEN................. *Columbia 36620* 3-5 42
(Vocals: Gary Stevens)

NO GREATER LOVE / BORN TO BE BLUE..................... *RCA Victor 20-2202* 2-4 47
(Vocals: Tommy Mercer)

OLD DEVIL MOON (Vocals: Unknown) / IF THIS ISN'T LOVE (Vocals: The Stardreamers) ... *RCA Victor 20-2065* 2-4 47

PAPA NICCOLINI (Vocals: Gary Stevens & The Stardusters) / DREAMSVILLE, OHIO (Vocal: June Hutton) ... *Okeh 6518* 2-4 42

PEOPLE LIKE YOU AND ME (Vocals: The Stardusters) / AT LAST (Vocals: Gary Stevens & The Stardusters)......................... *Columbia 36642* 2-4 42

PRAIRELAND LULLABY / THE MEM'RY OF A ROSE .... *Okeh 6036* 2-4 41
(Vocals: Frank Howard)

RED LILACS (Vocal: Joe Tucker) / SENTIMENTAL TRUMPET .... *King 15225* 2-4 53

ROSE AND A PRAYER, A / THE ANGELS CAME THRU' .... *Okeh 6280* 2-4 41
(Vocals: Gary Stevens)

SIMPATICA (Vocal: Gary Stevens) / INTERMEZZO.......................... *Okeh 6120* 2-4 41

SPRING WILL BE SO SAD (WHEN SHE COMES THIS YEAR) (Vocal: Gary Stevens) / SLAP-SLAP (THAT'S THE WAY TO SAY HELLO) (Vocal: Ginger Maylon) .... *Okeh 6191* 2-4 41

STAR DREAMS (theme song) / I SURRENDER, DEAR (Vocals: The Stardusters) .... *Okeh 6546* 2-4 42

SWEETHEART OF ALL MY DREAMS / MY BABY SAID YES .... *Victor 20-1646* 2-4 45
(Vocals: Irene Daye)

TALE OF TWO CITIES (Vocal: Gary Stevens) / MOVE OVER (Vocal: Ginger Maylon) .... *Okeh 6146* 2-4 41

THIS IS NO LAUGHING MATTER (Vocal: Gary Stevens) / WHEN I SEE AN ELEPHANT FLY (Vocals: The Stardusters) .... *Okeh 6458* 2-4 41

THIS TIME (Vocals: The Stardusters) / THE STORY OF A STARRY NIGHT (Vocals: Gary Stevens, June Hutton, & The Stardusters) .... *Okeh 6637* 2-4 42

TIME WAS / IT'S SO PEACEFUL IN THE COUNTRY .... *Conqueror 9902* 2-4 41
(Vocals: Gary Stevens)

TO YOUR HEART'S CONTENT / LET'S GO HOME .... *Okeh 6366* 3-5 41

WHAT'S COOKIN'? / HEY, SIT DOWN, BUD .... *Okeh 6061* 3-5 41

WHEN THE SUN COMES OUT (Vocal: Gary Stevens) / CHARLIE HORSE .... *Okeh 6246* 2-4 41

WHITE CHRISTMAS / YESTERDAY'S GARDENIAS .... *Columbia 36649* 2-4 42
(Vocals: Gary Stevens)

STABILE, Dick, & His Orchestra
(Dick Stabile: 5/29/09 – 1980)

BE CAREFUL, IT'S MY HEART / YOU'RE EASY TO DANCE WITH .... *Decca 4351* 2-4 42
(Vocals: Paul Warner)

CUBAN CABBY / GONE .... *Bluebird B-6720* 4-6 37
(Vocals: Bert Shaw)

HE'S MY GUY / AT LAST .... *Decca 4352* 3-5 42
(Vocals: Gracie Barrie)
(During Dick Stabile's military service in WW II, the band was fronted by his wife, singer Gracie Barrie.)

IF I COULD BE WITH YOU ONE HOUR TONIGHT (Vocal: Billy Wilson) / JA DA .... *Decca 977* 5-8 36

I HEAR BLUEBIRDS / SIX LESSONS FROM MADAME LA ZONGA .... *Vocalion 5593* 2-4 40
(Vocals: Shirley Gay)

I LOVE YOU FROM COAST TO COAST (Vocal: Billie Trask) / SUMMER NIGHT (Vocal: Bert Shaw) .... *Bluebird B-6726* 3-5 37

I'M STILL CRAZY FOR YOU (Vocals: Gracie Barrie & Paul Warner) / BY THE LIGHT OF THE SILVERY MOON (Vocal: Paul Warner) .... *Decca 4364* 2-4 42
(During Dick Stabile's military service in WW II, the band was fronted by his wife, singer Gracie Barrie)

IN OLD CHICAGO (Vocal: Bert Shaw) / MY FIRST IMPRESSION OF YOU (Vocal: Paula Kelly) .... *Bluebird B-7390* 3-5 38

IN THE SHADE OF THE NEW APPLE TREE / LOST IN THE SHUFFLE .... *Bluebird B-7388* 4-6 38
(Vocals: Paula Kelly)

JOHN PEEL (Vocal: Paula Kelly) / YOU CALL IT MADNESS (BUT I CALL IT LOVE) ... *Bluebird B-7480* 3-5 38

JUST BECAUSE / DEEP ELM BLUES .... *Decca 716* 5-8 36
(Vocals: Billy Wilson)

MOMENTS LIKE THIS / I SIMPLY ADORE YOU .... *Bluebird B-7394* 2-4 38
(Vocals: Bert Shaw)

MY HEART IS TAKING LESSONS / LOST AND FOUND .... *Bluebird B-7476* 2-4 38
(Vocals: Paula Kelly)

SOMEBODY ELSE IS TAKING MY PLACE / WHAT DOES A SOLDIER DREAM OF? .... *Decca 4297* 3-5 42
(Vocals: Unknown)

TEA ON THE TERRACE / I WAS SAYING TO THE MOON .... *Vocalion 3358* 3-5 36
(Vocals: Unknown)

THOUSAND DREAMS OF YOU, A (Vocal: Frank Fleming) / GOODNIGHT MEDLEY .... *Bluebird B-6722* 3-5 37

WHAT A DUMMY LOVE HAS MADE OF ME (Vocal: Bert Shaw) / RIFFIN' AT THE RITZ .... *Vocalion 3368* 4-6 36

WHERE HAVE WE MET BEFORE? (Vocal: Paula Kelly) / AIN'T YOU COMIN' BACK FROM CALIFORNIA? .... *Bluebird B-7492* 3-5 38

YOU KNOW / JEALOUS .... *Decca 4301* 2-4 42

STACKS, Tom, & His Minute Men:
see RESER, Harry, & His Orchestra

STACKS, Tom, & His Orchestra:
see RESER, Harry, & His Orchestra

STACY, Jess, & His Orchestra
(Jess Stacy: 8/4/04 –)

BREEZE (fox trot tempo) / BREEZE (blues) ... *Varsity 8121* 4-6 40

CAN'T WE BE FRIENDS? / IMAGINATION .... *Capitol 1136* 3-5 50

DAYBREAK SERENADE / IT'S ONLY A PAPER MOON .... *RCA Victor 20-1708* 2-4 45

I CAN'T BELIEVE THAT YOU'RE IN LOVE WITH ME / CLARINET BLUES .... *Varsity 8132* 5-8 40

JESS STAY BLUES / NONI ... *Montgomery Ward 10088* 5-8 39

JESS STAY BLUES / NONI .... *Varsity 8076* 5-8 39
(Simultaneously released on two labels)

WHAT'S NEW? / MELANCHOLY MOOD ..... *Montgomery Ward 10089* 5-8 39
(Vocals: Carlotta Dale)

WHAT'S NEW? / MELANCHOLY MOOD ... *Varsity 8064* 5-8 39
(Vocals: Carlotta Dale)
(Simultaneously released on two labels)

STAFFON, Bill, & His Orchestra

AM I BLUE? (Vocal: Bill Staffon) / BABY, WON'T YOU PLEASE COME HOME? .... *Bluebird B-6175* 5-8 35

HEARTSTRINGS (Vocal: Joe Dixon) / SITTIN' AROUND ON SUNDAY (Vocal: Bill Staffon) ...... *Bluebird B-6048* 4-6 35

WHY STARS COME OUT AT NIGHT (Vocal: Bill Staffon) / LOST MY RHYTHM, LOST MY MUSIC, LOST MY MAN (Vocals: The Bennett Sisters) .... *Bluebird B-6049* 5-8 35

STAFFORD, Jesse, & His Orchestra

ALL A-TWITTER (Vocal: Craig Leitch) / I WANNA GO PLACES AND DO THINGS (Vocal: Clyde Lucas) .... *Bluebird B-4250* 3-5 29

BENCH IN THE PARK, A / RAGAMUFFIN ROMEO .... *Brunswick 4824* 3-5 30
(Vocals: by chorus)

CAMPUS CAPERS (Vocal: Edna O'Keefe) / SOPHOMORE PROM (Vocal: Charlie Blane) .... *Brunswick 4549* 2-4 29

DOIN' THE RACCOON (Vocal: Clyde Lucas) / GLORIANNA (Vocals: Clyde Lucas & Leon Lucas) ...... *Brunswick 4129* 3-5 29

FEELIN' THE WAY I DO / LAST NIGHT, HONEY .... *Brunswick 4527* 3-5 29
(Vocals: Charlie Blane)

HOW'S YOUR UNCLE? / BEGGING FOR LOVE .... *Brunswick 6171* 3-5 31
(Vocals: Paul Small)

I DON'T WANT YOUR KISSES (IF I CAN'T HAVE YOUR LOVE) / UNTIL THE END .... *Brunswick 4548* 4-6 29
(Vocals: Charlie Blane)

I LIKE TO DO THINGS FOR YOU / CHINNIN' AND CHATTIN' WITH MAY .... *Brunswick 4822* 3-5 30
(Vocals: by trio)

I LOVE YOU TRULY / RYE .... *Brunswick 4032* 2-4 28

I'M FOLLOWING YOU! / I'M SAILING ON A SUNBEAM .... *Brunswick 4630* 4-6 30
(Vocals: Laurence Grey)

MY SWEETER THAN SWEET / THE PREP STEP .... *Brunswick 4629* 3-5 30
(Vocals: by trio)

RIGHT KIND OF MAN, THE (Vocal: Jane Davies) / LITTLE BY LITTLE (Vocal: Charlie Blane) ...... *Brunswick 4526* 3-5 29

SHINE / CINDERELLA BLUES ...... *Brunswick 4048* 4-6 28

SHOULD I? / ONLY LOVE IS REAL .... *Brunswick 4660* 3-5 30
(Vocals: by chorus)

SPELL OF THE BLUES (Vocals: Clyde & Leon Lucas) / YOU'LL NEVER KNOW (Vocal: Leon Lucas) .... *Brunswick 4198* 4-6 29

STEPPIN' ALONG (Vocal: Charlie Blane) / TOO WONDERFUL FOR WORDS (Vocal: Ray Kinney) .... *Brunswick 4525* 3-5 29

TONIGHT (Vocals: by chorus) / ANCHORS AWEIGH (Vocals: by quintet) .... *Brunswick 4818* 3-5 30

WHOLE DARN THING'S FOR YOU, THE (Vocals: chorus) / DUST (Vocals: by trio) .... *Brunswick 4823* 3-5 30

STARITA, Al, & His Society Orchestra

TWO SWEET LIPS / LOVE BIRD .... *Grey Gull L-1059* 2-4 21

STARITA, Al, as The Starita Saxophone Quartette

COMEDY TOM / WHEN IT'S MOONLIGHT ON THE SWANEE SHORE .... *Grey Gull L-1012* 2-4 20

LUCILLE / MY ISLE OF GOLDEN DREAMS .... *Grey Gull L-1011* 2-4 20

STECK, Gus, as Gus Steck's Chanticleer Orchestra

MY! OH MY! / THERE'S A CABIN IN THE PINES .... *Crown 3507* 4-6 33
(Vocals: Unknown)

STEELE, Blue, & His Orchestra

ALL MUGGLED UP (Vocal: Frank Myers) / SHOOIN' FLIES (Vocal: Kay Austin) ...... *Victor 23014* 12-15 30

ANOTHER NIGHT OF HAPPINESS (Vocal: George Marks) / ARE YOU LONESOME? (Vocal: Clyde Davis) .... *Victor V-40182* 4-6 29

BEYOND THE SUNSET (Vocals: Kenny Sargent, Ted Delmarter & Bob Noland) / I KNEW I'D MISS YOU (Vocal: Kenny Sargent) .... *Victor 21530* 2-4 28

CORONADO (Vocal: George Marks) / YOU'RE SO DIFFERENT (Vocal: Clyde Davis) ...... *Victor V-40140* 4-6 29

GIRL OF MY DREAMS, I LOVE YOU (Vocal: Kenny Sargent) / SUGAR BABE, I'M LEAVIN'! (Vocals: Blue Steele, Kenny Sargent, & Pete Schmidt) ...... *Victor 20971* 4-6 27

LET'S FORGIVE AND FORGET / I'M DRIFTING BACK TO DREAMLAND .... *Victor 21068* 2-4 27
(Vocals: Bob Noland)

MISSOURI MOON (Vocal: George Marks) / WORRIES ON MY MIND (Vocal: Clyde Davis) .... *Victor 23501* 10-12 30

MISTAKES (Vocal: George Marks) / ROCK ME TO SLEEP IN YOUR ARMS (Vocal: Clyde Davis) ...... *Victor 22142* 3-5 29

SEARCHING / SWEETHEART, I LOVE YOU .... *Victor 23002* 10-12 30
(Vocals: Clyde Davis)

SHADOWS OF LOVE / TENNESSEE MEMORIES .... *Victor V-40161* 3-5 29
(Vocals: George Marks)

THOUGH YOU WENT AWAY (Vocal: Blue Steele) / BE MY BABY (Vocal: Kenny Sargent) .... *Victor 21355* 5-8 28

'TIL THE END OF THE WORLD (Vocal: George Marks) / HOW CAN YOU FORGET? (Vocal: Clyde Davis) .... *Victor V-40288* 4-6 30

VIRGINIA LEE (Vocal: Blue Steele) / BECAUSE YOU ARE MY DREAM GIRL (Vocal: Bob Noland) .... *Victor 21400* 4-6 28

WASHINGTON AND LEE SWING (Vocals: chorus) / WHERE HAS MY OLD GANG GONE? (Vocals: Kenny Sargent, Ted Delmarter, & Bob Nolan) ...... *Victor 21262* 5-8 28

YOU DARLIN' (Vocal: Ernie Wimburn) / THERE'S A TEAR FOR EVERY SMILE IN HOLLYWOOD (Vocal: Mabel Batson) .... *Victor 22436* 4-6 30

STENNETT, Billy, as Billy Stennett's Carolina Stompers

BUFFALO RHYTHM / "RED NICHOLS" FIVE PENNIES .... *Broadway 1194* 8-10 28

SOMEBODY SWEET IS SWEET ON ME / DOWN WHERE THE SUN GOES DOWN .... *Broadway 1193* 5-8 28
(Vocals: Earl Riggs)

STERN, Harold, & The Biltmore Orchestra

FAREWELL TO ARMS / JUST A LITTLE FLOWER SHOP AROUND THE CORNER ..... *Bluebird B-5018* 5-8 33

FAREWELL TO ARMS / JUST A LITTLE FLOWER SHOP AROUND THE CORNER .... *Electradisk 1955* 15-20 33
(Simultaneously released on two labels)

MAYBE I LOVE YOU TOO MUCH (Vocals: by trio) / THE SIDEWALK WALTZ (Vocal: Bill Smith) .... *Bluebird B-5020* 4-6 33

MAYBE I LOVE YOU TOO MUCH (Vocals: by trio) / THE SIDEWALK WALTZ (Vocal: Bill Smith) .... *Electradisk 1957* 12-15 33
(Simultaneously released on two labels)

REMEMBER ME / I WAKE UP SMILING .... *Bluebird B-5019* 4-6 33
(Vocals: Bill Smith)

REMEMBER ME / I WAKE UP SMILING .... *Electradisk 1956* 12-15 33
(Vocals: Bill Smith)
(Simultaneously released on two labels)

STERN, Harold, & His Hotel Belleclaire Orchestra

ALONG THE GYPSY TRAIL / MY SWEETIE'S EYES .... *Edison 51805* 4-6 26

SHE BELONGS TO ME / BLACK BOTTOM .... *Edison 51815* 5-8 26

STERN, Harold, & His Orchestra

ISN'T IT ROMANTIC? / LOVE ME TONIGHT .... *Columbia 2718-D* 4-6 32
(Vocals: Unknown)

'TWAS ONLY A SUMMER NIGHT DREAM (Vocals: The Park Avenue Promenaders) / YOU'LL ALWAYS BE THE SAME SWEETHEART (Vocal: Bill Smith) .... *Columbia 2717-D* 3-5 32

STEVENS, Leith, & His Saturday Night Swing Club Orchestra

LOVE'S OLD SWEET SONG / TWELFTH STREET RAG .... *Vocalion 4350* 4-6 38

MEMPHIS BLUES / LA-DE-DOODY-DOO .... *Vocalion 4210* 5-8 38

STEVENS, Les, & His Orchestra

CANNIBOLA / STEAMBOAT SAL .... *Pathe Actuelle 021072* 4-6 23

CANNIBOLA / STEAMBOAT SAL .... *Perfect 14175* 3-5 23
(Simultaneously released on two labels)

STEVENS, Les, as Les Stevens' Clover Gardens Orchestra

DON'T CRY, SWANEE / BARNEY GOOGLE .... *Pathe Actuelle 020982* 5-8 23

DON'T CRY, SWANEE / BARNEY GOOGLE .... *Perfect 14133* 3-5 23
(Simultaneously released on two labels)

WHO'S SORRY NOW? / SOUTH SEA EYES .... *Pathe Actuelle 020972* 4-6 23

WHO'S SORRY NOW? / SOUTH SEA EYES .... *Perfect 14124* 3-5 23
(Simultaneously released on two labels)

STEVENSON, Carlyle, as Carlyle Stevenson's Bon Ton Orchestra

CHARLESTON / I MISS MY SWISS....... *Sunset 1114* 15-20 25
(Sunset records are rare)

STEVENSON, Carlyle, as Carlyle Stevenson's El Patio Orchestra

(Sunset records are rare)

CECILIA / SUMMER NIGHTS........... *Sunset 1119* 12-15 25
(Vocals: Carl Edwards)

COLLEGIATE (Vocals: by trio) / YOU TOLD ME TO GO (Vocal: Walter Dupre)............. *Sunset 1120* 12-15 25

I'M TIRED OF EVERYTHING BUT YOU / MEXICALI ROSE .... *Sunset 1121* 15-20 25

MILENBERG JOYS / YES, SIR! THAT'S MY BABY (Vocal: Carl Edwards) .... *Sunset 1117* 15-20 25

STEVENS, Perley, & His Orchestra:

see SELVIN, Ben, & His Orchestra

STILLMAN CLUB ORCHESTRA, The:

see STILLMAN, Jack

STILLMAN, Jack, as Jack Stillman's Orchestra

ALL THAT I'M ASKING IS SYMPATHY / DANCE AWAY THE NIGHT............... *Champion 15864* 3-5 30
(Vocals: Joe Wilbur)

ALL THAT I'M ASKING IS SYMPATHY / DREAM LOVER...................... *Gennett 7057* 4-6 30
(Vocals: Joe Wilbur)

AT PEACE WITH THE WORLD (Vocal: James Doherty) / IN THE MIDDLE OF THE NIGHT........ *Edison 51756* 4-6 26

BURGUNDY / FOR HEAVEN'S SAKE... *Edison 51726* 5-8 26

DREAMING OF A CASTLE IN THE AIR / LOVE BOUND......................... *Edison 51679* 4-6 26

DREAM LOVER / DANCE AWAY THE NIGHT....................... *Supertone 9581* 3-5 30

EVANGELINE / JUST BEYOND THE BLUE........................... *Edison 14054* 8-10 29
(A rare lateral-cut thin Edison disc.)

FUNNY / DAY DREAMING .... *Edison 51581* 4-6 25

GO TO BED / ROCK ME TO SLEEP IN YOUR ARMS.............. *Edison 14065* 8-10 29
(A rare lateral-cut thin Edison disc.)

I CAN'T FORGET YOU / BLUE WATERS .... *Edison 52552* 4-6 29

IF I'M DREAMING DON'T WAKE ME UP / THE SHEPARD'S SERENADE...... *Supertone 9607* 3-5 30
(Vocals: Joe Wilbur)

I WANT ANOTHER CHANCE WITH YOU / THE WORLD IS SUCH A LONESOME PLACE .... *Edison 51600* 4-6 25

JAPANSY / WHEN LOVE COMES STEALING.................. *Edison 52211* 4-6 28
(Vocals: The Rollickers)

JUST BEYOND THE BLUE / SILVERY MOON......................... *Edison 52631* 4-6 29

LAUGH, CLOWN, LAUGH! (Vocal: Happy Jack) / THERE'LL NEVER BE ANOTHER YOU....................... *Edison 52372* 4-6 28

LET IT RAIN (Vocal: Vernon Dalhart) / TODDLE ALONG....................... *Edison 51537* 5-8 25

LET US WALTZ AS WE SAY GOODBYE (Vocals: Helen Clark & Charles Hart) / CLOSE YOUR EYES .... *Edison 51659* 4-6 26

LITTLE GIRL – A LITTLE BOY – A LITTLE MOON / I'M WALTZING IN LOVE WITH YOU ... *Edison 52048* 4-6 27

MIDNIGHT WALTZ / THE VALE OF GOLDEN DREAMS .... *Edison 51553* 4-6 25

MOLLY MALONE / MOONLIGHT LANE .... *Edison 52154* 4-6 28
(Vocals: The Rollickers)

'N' YOU! (Vocals: The Songsters) / AH! SWEET MYSTERY OF LIFE (Vocal: Victor Hall)............ *Edison 52175* 4-6 28

ONLY A BROKEN STRING OF PEARLS / WAIT TILL TOMORROW NIGHT...... *Edison 51710* 4-6 26

PAGAN LOVE SONG / WITMARK THEME WALTZETTE..... *Edison 52639* 4-6 29
(Vocals: Walter Scanlon)

RAINBOW OF LOVE / YOU ONLY WANT ME WHEN YOU'RE LONESOME (Vocals: Helen Clark & John Ryan).......... *Edison 51984* 5-8 27

SILVER MOON / YESTERDAY .... *Edison 52011* 4-6 27

SOMEBODY'S LONELY / ROSES (Vocal: Arthur Fields)............ *Edison 51734* 5-8 26

SONG IS ENDED, THE / THE SWEETHEART OF SIGMA CHI .... *Edison 52140* 4-6 27

STILL WATERS / LET'S FORGIVE AND FORGET .... *Edison 51906* 3-5 27

THAT SAXOPHONE WALTZ / LOVE ME ALL THE TIME .... *Edison 51940* 4-6 27
(Vocals: Unknown)

TOMORROW'S ANOTHER DAY / THAT'S MY GIRL....................... *Edison 51451* 5-8 25
(Vocals: Unknown)

WHAT DO WE CARE IF IT'S ONE O'CLOCK? / CAROLINA SWEETHEART (Vocals: Arthur Hall & John Ryan)........................ *Edison 51638* 4-6 25

STILLMAN, Jack, as Jack Stillman's Oriole Orchestra

COOLER HOT / ANY BLUES........... *Gennett 3183* 5-8 25

ROLL 'EM, GIRLS / CLAP HANDS, HERE COMES CHARLEY!........ *Paramount 20427* 5-8 26
(Vocals: Arthur Hall)

ROLL 'EM, GIRLS / CLAP HANDS, HERE COMES CHARLEY!........... *Puritan 11427* 4-6 26
(Vocals: Arthur Hall)

ROLL 'EM, GIRLS / CLAP HANDS, HERE COMES CHARLEY!.......... *Silvertone 3501* 4-6 26
(Vocals: Arthur Hall)
(Simultaneously released on three labels)

SAY IT AGAIN / LINGERING LIPS ... *Broadway 1001* 3-5 26
(Vocals: Harry Jockin)

SAY IT AGAIN / LINGERING LIPS ... *Paramount 20443* 4-6 26
(Vocals: Harry Jockin)

SAY IT AGAIN / LINGERING LIPS .... *Puritan 11443* 3-5 26
(Vocals: Harry Jockin)
(Simultaneously released on three labels)

SWEET GEORGIA BROWN / YOU'RE MY BABY .... *Bell 368* 5-8 25

STILLMAN, Jack, as Jack Stillman's Orioles / Stillman's Orioles

CORONADO NIGHTS / THERE NEVER WAS A PAL LIKE MY DADDY'S GAL....... *Pathe Actuelle 36695* 4-6 27
(Vocals: Joe Sherman)

CORONADO NIGHTS / THERE NEVER WAS A PAL LIKE MY DADDY'S GAL .... *Perfect 14776* 3-5 27
(Vocals: Joe Sherman)
(Simultaneously released on two labels)

IF TEARS COULD BRING YOU BACK TO ME / GONE AGAIN GAL....................... *Bell 457* 4-6 26
(Vocals: Unknown)

I WISH'T I WAS IN PEORIA / I WANNA GO WHERE YOU GO – DO WHAT YOU DO, THEN I'LL BE HAPPY............................. *Bell 382* 4-6 25
(Vocals: Unknown)

I WONDER WHERE MY BABY IS TONIGHT? / I'M GONNA CHARLESTON BACK TO CHARLESTON .... *Paramount 20423* 5-8 25
(Vocals: Irving Post)

STILLMAN, Jack, as The Stillman Club Orchestra

LANTERN OF LOVE (Vocal: Frank Bessinger) / MYSTERIOUS EYES.......................... [illegible] 5-8 26

STILLMAN'S ORIOLES:

see STILLMAN, Jack, as Jack Stillman's Orioles

STOCK, Bert, & His Orchestra

GET HAPPY (Vocal: Paul Dillon) / YOU CAN'T GET TO HEAVEN THAT WAY (Vocal: Doc Mayers)................. *Champion 16018* 4-6 30

GET HAPPY (Vocal: Paul Dillon) / YOU CAN'T GET TO HEAVEN THAT WAY (Vocal: Doc Mayers)..................... *Gennett 7213* 5-8 30

GET HAPPY (Vocal: Paul Dillon) / YOU CAN'T GET TO HEAVEN THAT WAY (Vocal: Doc Mayers).................. *Supertone 9751* 4-6 30
(Simultaneously released on three labels)

TURN ON THE HEAT (Vocal: Doc Mayers) / HONEYSUCKLE ROSE (Vocal: Paul Dillon)...................... *Gennett 7059* 8-10 29

TURN ON THE HEAT (Vocal: Doc Mayers) / HONEYSUCKLE ROSE (Vocal: Paul Dillon)...................... *Supertone 9585* 5-8 29
(Simultaneously released on two labels)

STODDARD, Harry, as The Harry Stoddard Orchestra

I AIN'T NEVER HAD NOBODY CRAZY OVER ME / LONG-LOST MAMA (DADDY MISSES YOU) .... *Emerson 10626* 4-6 23

STOLL, Georgie, & His Orchestra

BLUE MOON / YOU WERE MEANT FOR ME........................ *MGM 30049* 2-4 49

GIRL FRIEND, THE / SWANEE .... *Decca 976* 5-8 36

LOUISE / I'M IN THE MOOD FOR LOVE.... *MGM 30051* 2-4 49

OVER THE RAINBOW / PAGAN LOVE SONG.................. *MGM 30052* 2-4 49

SEPTEMBER IN THE RAIN / TEMPTATION.......................... *MGM 30050* 2-4 49

STONE, Eddie, & His Orchestra

(Eddie Stone: circa 1908 – 6/26/83)

CAMPBELLS ARE SWINGING, THE / MR. SWEENEY'S LEARNED TO SWING.... *Vocalion 3996* 5-8 38

CASEY JONES (Vocal: Eddie Stone) / CARAVAN.................................. *Vocalion 3576* 5-8 37

MOROCCO / BURPING BASSOON ...... *Vocalion 3984* 4-6 38

RHYTHM ON THE LOOSE / UP POPPED THE DEVIL (Vocal: Eddie Stone)........ *Vocalion 3585* 5-8 37

SATAN TAKES A HOLIDAY / A STUDY IN BROWN................ *Vocalion 3555* 5-8 37

SMUGGLER'S NIGHTMARE / THE GOBLIN BAND................. *Vocalion 4101* 5-8 38

STANSHAW STOMP / LISTEN, MY CHILDREN, AND YOU SHALL HEAR (Vocal: Eddie Stone)... *Vocalion 3703* 5-8 37

STRAETER, Ted, & His Orchestra

(Ted Straeter: circa 1914 – deceased)

BETWEEN FRIENDS (Vocals: The Ted Straeter Singers) / PEOPLE LIKE YOU (Vocal: Ted Straeter)........................ *Columbia 35873* 2-4 41

DANCING IN THE DARK (Vocal: Dorothy Rochelle) / TEA FOR TWO......................... *Columbia 35588* 2-4 40

HERE IN THE VELVET NIGHT (Vocal: Dorothy Rochelle) / DON'T LET IT GET YOU DOWN (Vocal: Ted Straeter).................... *Columbia 35641* 2-4 40

IMAGINATION / A HOUSE WITH A LITTLE RED BARN............ *Columbia 35406* 2-4 40
(Vocals: Dorothy Rochelle)

JUST ONE OF THOSE THINGS / THEY DIDN'T BELIEVE ME .... *Columbia 35430* 2-4 40
(Vocals: Dorothy Rochelle)

STRAIGHT, Charley, & His Orchestra

(Charlie Straight: 1/16/91 – 9/21/40)

ARKANSAS MULE / BATHING BEAUTY BLUES................ *Paramount 20264* 5-8 23

BUDDY'S HABITS / HENPECKED BLUES .... *National 12244* 4-6 23

BUDDY'S HABITS / HENPECKED BLUES............ *Paramount 20244* 5-8 23
(Simultaneously released on two labels)

DEEP HENDERSON / HOBO'S PRAYER................. *Brunswick 3224* 5-8 26

HER BEAUS ARE ONLY RAINBOWS (Vocal: Frank Sylvano) / THAT'S WHY I LOVE YOU .... *Brunswick 3203* 2-4 26

LAST NIGHT I DREAMED YOU KISSED ME / FROM MIDNIGHT TO DAWN.......... *Brunswick 3944* 3-5 28
(Vocals: Frank Sylvano)

MY OHIO HOME / EVERYWHERE YOU GO .... *Brunswick 3797* 3-5 28
(Vocals: Frank Sylvano)

MY SUNFLOWER MAID / FORGETFUL BLUES............. *Paramount 20291* 4-6 24

ROSE OF SUNNY ITALY / LOVE, MY HEART IS CALLING YOU................ *Paramount 20265* 3-5 23

SIDE BY SIDE / NESTING TIME..... *Brunswick 3516* 2-4 27
(Vocals: The Keller Sisters and Lynch)

STEALING TO VIRGINIA / THAT OLD GANG OF MINE .... *Paramount 20266* 5-8 23

SWEET HENRY / EASY MELODY... *Harmograph 862* 8-10 23

SWEET HENRY / EASY MELODY.... *Paramount 20271* 5-8 23
(Simultaneously released on two labels)

SWEET SOUTHERN BREEZE / TALKING TO THE MOON.......... *Brunswick 3076* 3-5 26

SWEET SUE – JUST YOU / SENTIMENTAL BABY............ *Brunswick 3900* 3-5 28
(Vocals: Frank Sylvano)

TELL ME TONIGHT / WHAT'S THE USE OF CRYING? .... *Brunswick 3324* 2-4 26
(Vocals: Frank Sylvano)

THAT'S WHAT I CALL KEEN / PERSIAN RUG.................. *Brunswick 3899* 3-5 28
(Vocals: Frank Sylvano)

TOO BUSY / JUST A NIGHT FOR MEDITATION................ *Brunswick 3945* 4-6 28
(Vocals: Frank Sylvano)

TWEET TWEET / SITTIN' IN THE CORNER.................. *Paramount 20270* 5-8 23

WAITING AND DREAMING (Vocals: The Vagabonds) / DO YOU, DON'T YOU?............ *Brunswick 4026* 2-4 28

WHAT A MAN! / HI-DIDDLE-DIDDLE .... *Brunswick 3136* 3-5 26
(Vocals: Hannah & Dorothea Williams)

STRAIGHT, Charley, & His Orchestra as The Frisco Syncopators

ARKANSAS MULE / BATHING BEAUTY BLUES................ *Claxtonola 40264* 5-8 23

BUDDY'S HABITS / HENPECKED BLUES............ *Claxtonola 40244* 5-8 23

BUDDY'S HABITS / HENPECKED BLUES............... *Puritan 11244* 4-6 23
(Simultaneously released on two labels)

MY SUNFLOWER MAID / FORGETFUL BLUES................ *Puritan 11291* 3-5 23

SWEET HENRY / EASY MELODY ..... *Puritan 11271* 4-6 23

STRAIGHT, Charley, & His Orchestra as The Harmograph Dance Orchestra

MY SUNFLOWER MAID / FORGETFUL BLUES............. *Harmograph 889* 5-8 23

STRAIGHT, Charley, & His Orchestra as The Manhattan Imperial Orchestra

ARKANSAS MULE / BATHING BEAUTY BLUES.................. *Puritan 11264* 4-6 23

STRATAKOS, Ellis, & His Hotel Jung Orchestra

PRECIOUS LITTLE THING CALLED LOVE, A / WEARY RIVER .... *Vocalion 15792* 20-25 29
(Vocals: Fred Loyacano)

STRAUN'S PULLMAN PORTERS:

see GLANTZ, Nathan, & His Orchestra

STRONG, Benny, & His Orchestra

(Benny Strong: 3/17/11 –)

BABY FACE / SWEET GEORGIA BROWN.............................. *Tower 1255* 3-5 47

FIVE FOOT TWO, EYES OF BLUE / DREAM BABY .... *Tower 1456* 2-4 49
(Vocals: Benny Strong)

I NEVER SEE MAGGIE ALONE / WHEN MY SUGAR WALKS DOWN THE STREET........ *Capitol 57-750* 2-4 49
(Vocals: Benny Strong)

TESSIE / LAST NIGHT ON THE BACK PORCH.................. *Capitol 1003* 2-4 50
(Vocals: Benny Strong)

THAT CERTAIN PARTY / MY BEST GIRL....................... *Tower 1271* 3-5 47
(Vocals: Benny Strong)

THAT OLD GANG OF MINE / THAT GANG THAT SANG OF MY HEART................ *Capitol 1179* 2-4 50
(Vocals: Benny Strong)

THREE-HANDED WOMAN / I DON'T CARE...................... *Capitol 1326* 2-4 50
(Vocals: Benny Strong)

SUDY, Joe, & His Orchestra

IT'S A HAP-HAP-HAPPY DAY / I HEAR A DREAM............... *Bluebird B-10491* 3-5 39
(Vocals: Joe Sudy)

IT'S NEVER TOO LATE / RAINBOW VALLEY.............. *Bluebird B-10165* 3-5 39
(Vocals: Joe Sudy)

MY HANDS ARE TIED / I LONG TO BELONG TO YOU................ *Bluebird B-10173* 3-5 39
(Vocals: Joe Sudy)

NOTHING IS TOO PERFECT FOR YOU / DIARY OF DREAMS............. *Bluebird B-10155* 3-5 39
(Vocals: Joe Sudy)

WIND AT MY WINDOW, THE / I SHOULDA STOOD IN BED.................. *Bluebird B-10483* 4-6 39
(Vocals: Joe Sudy)

SULLIVAN, Joe, & His Cafe Society Orchestra

(Joe Sullivan: 11/5/06 - 10/13/71)

I'VE GOT A CRUSH ON YOU (Vocal: Helen Ward) / COQUETTE............................ *Okeh 5647* 4-6 40

OH, LADY BE GOOD / I CAN'T GIVE YOU ANYTHING BUT LOVE (Vocal: Joe Turner).......... *Vocalion 5496* 5-8 40

POM POM / I COVER THE WATERFRONT (Vocal: Helen Ward).... *Vocalion 5556* 5-8 40

SOLITUDE / LOW DOWN DIRTY SHAME (Vocal: Joe Turner)...... *Vocalion 5531* 5-8 40

SWANEE SWINGERS, THE:

see JONES, Isham, as Isham Jones' Juniors

SWIFT, Sammy, as Sammy Swift's Jazz Band:

see HENDERSON, Fletcher, as Henderson's Dance Players

SYLVANO, Frank, & His Orchestra

AFTER SUNDAY AFTERNOON / SO SWEET......................... *Brunswick 4835* 4-6 30
(Vocals: Frank Sylvano)

SYLVESTER, Bob, & His Orchestra

COULD I WRITE A BOOK? / I NEED YOU........................ *Vocalion 3852* 3-5 37

DOWN WHERE THE TRADE WINDS BLOW / I SEE YOUR FACE BEFORE ME........... *Vocalion 3946* 3-5 38

SOPHISTICATED SWING / HUGGIN' AND MUGGIN'.............. *Variety 661* 5-8 37

SUNDAY IN THE PARK / DO YOU KNOW YOUR A.B.C.?........................ *Vocalion 3971* 4-6 38

SYLVESTER, Johnny, & His Orchestra

HOT-HOT-HOTTENTOT / KING PORTER STOMP.............. *Pathe Actuelle 036211* 5-8 25

I'M GOIN' OUT IF LIZZIE COMES IN / EVERYBODY'S DOIN' THE CHARLESTON NOW........... *Pathe Actuelle 36331* 5-8 25

I'M GOIN' OUT IF LIZZIE COMES IN / EVERYBODY'S DOIN' THE CHARLESTON NOW...... *Perfect 14512* 4-6 25
(Simultaneously released on two labels)

RIO RITA / THE KINKAJOU............... *Pathe Actuelle 36597* 4-6 27
(Vocals: Frank Gould)

RIO RITA / THE KINKAJOU............ *Perfect 14778* 3-5 27
(Vocals: Frank Gould)
(Simultaneously released on two labels)

ROSIE O'RYAN (Vocal: Frank Gould) / WHAT'S THE USE? (Vocal: Bob Blake).......... *Pathe Actuelle 36599* 4-6 27
(A rare marbled shellac disc, forerunner of the multi-colored vinyl records which would become so popular fifty years later.)

ROSIE O'RYAN (Vocal: Frank Gould) / WHAT'S THE USE? (Vocal: Bob Blake)................. *Perfect 14780* 3-5 27
(Simultaneously released on two labels)

SWEET MAN JOE / CLEARING HOUSE BLUES............... *Pathe Actuelle 036086* 5-8 24

SWEET MAN JOE / CLEARING HOUSE BLUES........................ *Perfect 14267* 4-6 24
(Simultaneously released on two labels)

SYLVESTER, Johnny, & His Playmates

MINE (Vocals: The Four Bachelors) / WHEREVER YOU GO-WHATEVER YOU DO (Vocal: Al Shayne)... *Gennett 6095* 8-10 27

SONG OF THE WANDERER (Vocal: Lou de Fabbia) / —............... *Gennett 6027* 8-10 27

SYLVESTER, Johnny, & His Playmates as Bobby Jones & His Orchestra

SONG OF THE WANDERER (Vocal: Lou de Fabbia) / —............ *Champion 15202* 5-8 27

WHEREVER YOU GO - WHATEVER YOU DO (Vocal: Al Shayne) / ST. LOUIS BLUES........ *Champion 15294* 5-8 27

SYMPHONIA DANCE ORCHESTRA, The

BEAUTIFUL CALIFORNIA / POINSETTA ... *Arto 9158* 2-4 22

BEAUTIFUL CALIFORNIA / POINSETTA... *Bell P-158* 2-4 22
(Simultaneously released on two labels)

I'M JUST A LITTLE BLUE FOR YOU / NOVEMBER ROSE, GOODBYE...................... *Globe 7197* 2-4 23

LOVELY LUCERNE / UNDERNEATH THE MELLOW MOON............. *Globe 7171* 2-4 22

LOVE'S LAMENT / WISTFUL WALTZ...... *Arto 9166* 2-4 22

LOVE'S LAMENT / WISTFUL WALTZ..... *Bell P-166* 2-4 22
(Simultaneously released on two labels)

OUT OF THE SHADOWS / RED MOON .... *Globe 7188* 2-4 22

STEAL A LITTLE KISS WHILE DANCING / HONEYMOON TIME..................... *Globe 7213* 2-4 23

SWANEE RIVER MOON / TAKE ME HOME......................... *Arto 9152* 2-4 22

SWANEE RIVER MOON / TAKE ME HOME...................... *Globe 7152* 2-4 22
(Simultaneously released on two labels)

THRU' THE NIGHT / LET US SAY GOODBYE WITH A WALTZ............ *Globe 7187* 2-4 22

WALTZ OF LOVE / HONEY, DAT'S ALL... *Globe 7209* 2-4 23

WONDERFUL ONE / A KISS IN THE DARK......................... *Globe 7203* 2-4 23

SYNCO JAZZ BAND, The:

see SAMUELS, Joseph

TAGGART, Milt, as Milt Taggart's Eleven Vagabonds Of The Air

STARLIGHT AND YOU (Vocal: Milt Taggart) / WHEN I LOOK TO THE WEST (Vocal: Glen Horsley) ... *Victor 22427* 4-6 30

WHEN IT'S SPRINGTIME IN THE ROCKIES (Vocal: Jerry Wilford) / THE UTAH TRAIL .... *Victor 22431* 4-6 30
(The label on the second side also credits Jerry Wilford as vocalist, but it is an instrumental arrangement.)

TALBOT, Irvin:
see PARAMOUNT-PUBLIX Recording Orchestra, The

TAMMS, Bob, & His Orchestra

BLUE IS THE NIGHT (Vocals: Unknown) / WHEN IT'S SPRINGTIME IN THE ROCKIES (Vocals: by quartet) .... *Broadway 1372* 3-5 30

STRIKE UP THE BAND / THE WOMAN IN THE SHOE .... *Broadway 1373* 3-5 30
(Vocals: Unknown)

TATUM, Art, & His Band
(Art Tatum: 10/13/10 – 11/5/56)

CORRINE CORRINA / LONESOME GRAVEYARD .... *Decca 8563* 20-25 41
(Vocals: Joe Turner)

LUCILLE / ROCK ME, MAMA .... *Decca 8577* 20-25 41
(Vocals: Joe Turner)

STOMPIN' AT THE SAVOY / LAST GOOD BYE BLUES (Vocal: Joe Turner) .... *Decca 8536* 15-20 41

WEE BABY BLUES (Vocal: Joe Turner) / BATTERY BOUNCE .... *Decca 8526* 15-20 41

TATUM, Art, & His Swingsters

BODY AND SOUL / WHAT WILL I TELL MY HEART? .... *Decca 1197* 8-10 37

WITH PLENTY OF MONEY AND YOU / I'VE GOT MY LOVE TO KEEP ME WARM .... *Decca 1198* 8-10 37

TAYLOR, Albert, & His Orchestra:
see MARTIN, Freddy, & His Orchestra

TAYLOR, Dick, & His "Taylor Made" Music

LAST WALTZ, THE (Vocal: Bob Braman) / SHUFFLIN' BOOGIE .... *Skylark SK 528* 3-5 –

WHO'S GONNA BE SWEET TO YOU? / SAY YOU'LL BE MINE .... *Master 377* 3-5 –
(Vocals: June Bruner)

TAYLOR, Jackie, & His Orchestra
also see ROSE, Vincent – Jackie Taylor & Their Hollywood Orchestra

NIGHT OF HAPPINESS / SITTING BY THE WINDOW .... *Victor 22217* 4-6 29
(Vocals: Buster Dees)

WE'RE ON THE HIGHWAY TO HEAVEN (Vocals: The Boswell Sisters) / WHEN LOVE COMES IN THE MOONLIGHT (Vocal: Leigh Harline) .... *Victor 22500* 5-8 30

TEAGARDEN, Jack, & His Orchestra
(Jack Teagarden: 8/20/05 – 1/15/64)

ACCIDENTALLY ON PURPOSE (Vocal: Lynne Clark) / IT ALL COMES BACK TO ME NOW (Vocal: David Allen) .... *Viking 104* 5-8 41

AT LEAST YOU COULD SAY HELLO / STOP KICKING MY HEART AROUND .... *Columbia 35245* 5-8 39
(Vocals: Kitty Kallen)

BEALE STREET BLUES (Vocal: Jack Teagarden) / SWINGIN' ON THE TEAGARDEN GATE .... *Columbia 35323* 5-8 39

BLUE RIVER (Vocal: Jack Teagarden) / RHYTHM HYMN (Vocals: chorus) .... *Decca 4071* 4-6 41

CAN'T WE TALK IT OVER? (Vocal: Jack Teagarden) / THE BLUES .... *Montgomery Ward 10012* 5-8 40

CAN'T WE TALK IT OVER? (Vocal: Jack Teagarden) / THE BLUES .... *Varsity 8218* 5-8 40
(Simultaneously released on two labels)

CINDERELLA, STAY IN MY ARMS (Vocal: Jack Teagarden) / THAT'S RIGHT – I'M WRONG (Vocal: Jean Arnold) ...... *Brunswick 8378* 5-8 39

CLASS WILL TELL / IF IT'S GOOD (THEN I WANT IT) .... *Brunswick 8373* 5-8 39
(Vocals: Jack Teagarden)

DARK EYES / CHICKS IS WONDERFUL .... *Decca 3701* 3-5 41

DEVIL MAY CARE / NIGHT ON THE SHALIMAR .... *Varsity 8278* 3-5 40
(Vocals: Marianne Dunne)

ESPECIALLY FOR YOU / YOU'RE THE MOMENT IN MY LIFE .... *Brunswick 8431* 4-6 39
(Vocals: Linda Keene)

FRENESI / HERE'S MY HEART (Vocal: David Allen) .... *Viking 103* 5-8 41

HUNDRED YEARS FROM TODAY, A / NOBODY KNOWS THE TROUBLE I'VE SEEN ..... *Decca 4317* 3-5 41
(Vocals: Jack Teagarden)

IF I COULD BE WITH YOU / MY MELANCHOLY BABY .... *Varsity 8209* 4-6 40
(Vocals: Jack Teagarden)

IF I COULD BE WITH YOU (Vocal: Jack Teagarden) / THE BLUES .... *Philmarmonic 83* 5-8 40

I GOTTA RIGHT TO SING THE BLUES (theme song) (Vocal: Jack Teagarden) / YANKEE DOODLE (Vocal: Jean Arnold) .... *Brunswick 8397* 4-6 39

I HEAR BLUEBIRDS (Vocal: Marianne Dunne) / FATIMA'S DRUMMER BOY (Vocal: Jack Teagarden) .... *Varsity 8273* 3-5 40

I'M TAKIN' MY TIME WITH YOU / I WANNA HAT WITH CHERRIES .... *Columbia 35224* 4-6 39
(Vocals: Kitty Kallen)

I SWUNG THE ELECTION (Vocals: Jack Teagarden & chorus) / AUNT HAGAR'S BLUES (Vocal: Jack Teagarden) .... *Columbia 35206* 5-8 39

IT'S A HUNDRED TO ONE (Vocal: Jack Teagarden) / I'LL REMEMBER (Vocal: Kitty Kallen) ..... *Columbia 35215* 4-6 39

I'VE GOT "IT" / PLANTATION MOODS .... *Columbia 2913-D* 15-20 33

JUNKMAN / CASA LOMA STOMP (by Glen Gray & The Casa Loma Orchestra) .... *Brunswick 7652* 8-10 33

LOVE FOR SALE / WHAM (RE-BOP-BOOM-BAM) .... *Varsity 8202* 4-6 40
(Vocals: Kitty Kallen)

MUDDY RIVER BLUES (Vocal: Jack Teagarden) / WOLVERINE BLUES .... *Columbia 35297* 5-8 39

NOW I LAY ME DOWN TO DREAM (Vocal: David Allen) / RIVER HOME (Vocal: Jack Teagarden) .... *Varsity 8374* 4-6 40

ON REVIVAL DAY (Vocal: Jack Teagarden) / WOLVERINE BLUES .... *V-Disc 724* 10-12 –
(This is an oversize 12-inch 78 rpm, a World War II release.)

PERSIAN RUG / THE SHEIK OF ARABY (Vocals: Jack Teagarden & Meredith Blake) .... *Brunswick 8370* 4-6 39

PICKIN' FOR PATSY / UNDERTOW .... *Brunswick 8401* 4-6 39

PRELUDE IN C SHARP MINOR / BLUES TO THE LONELY (Vocal: Jack Teagarden) ...... *Decca 3642* 3-5 41

PRELUDE TO THE BLUES / THE BLUES HAVE GOT ME (Vocal: Jack Teagarden) .... *Decca 4409* 3-5 41

PUTTIN' AND TAKIN' (Vocal: Jack Teagarden) / BLUES TO THE DOLE .... *Brunswick 8454* 4-6 39

RED WING / SOMEWHERE A VOICE IS CALLING .... *Columbia 35450* 3-5 39

RIPPLING WATERS / PEG O' MY HEART .... *Columbia 35727* 3-5 39

ROCKIN' CHAIR (Vocals: Eddie Miller & Nappy Lamare) / LOVELESS LOVE (Vocal: Jack Teagarden) ... *Crown 3051* 15-20 31

SHAKE YOUR HIPS / SOMEBODY STOLE GABRIEL'S HORN (Vocal: Jack Teagarden) .... *Columbia 2802-D* 15-20 33
(This record was pressed in blue shellac)

STARS FELL ON ALABAMA / YOUR GUESS IS JUST AS GOOD AS MINE .... *Brunswick 6993* 5-8 34
(Vocals: Jack Teagarden)

ST. JAMES' INFIRMARY / WHAT DID I DO TO BE SO BLACK AND BLUE .... *Decca 3844* 3-5 41
(Vocals: Jack Teagarden)

TABLE IN A CORNER, A / SO MANY TIMES .... *Columbia 35252* 5-8 39
(Vocals: Kitty Kallen)

TWO BLIND LOVES / HAWAII SANG ME TO SLEEP .... *Columbia 35233* 4-6 39
(Vocals: Kitty Kallen)

WAIT 'TILL I CATCH YOU IN MY DREAMS (Vocal: David Allen) / AND SO DO I (Vocal: Marianne Dunne) .... *Varsity 8388* 2-4 40

WHITE SAILS (Vocal: Linda Keene) / OCTOROON (Vocal: Jack Teagarden) ... *Brunswick 8388* 4-6 39

YOU KNOW JUST AS WELL AS I KNOW / THE LITTLE MAN WHO WASN'T THERE .... *Brunswick 8435* 4-6 39
(Vocals: Jack Teagarden)

YOU RASCAL, YOU / THAT'S WHAT I LIKE ABOUT YOU .... *Columbia 2588-D* 10-12 31
(Vocals: Jack Teagarden & Fats Waller)

TEAGARDEN, Jack, as Jack Teagarden's Big Eight

ST. JAMES INFIRMARY (Vocal: Jack Teagarden) / SHINE .... *Hot Record Society 2006* 5-8 41
(This is an oversize 12-inch 78 rpm)

WORLD IS WAITING FOR THE SUNRISE, THE / THE BIG EIGHT BLUES .... *Hot Record Society 2007* 5-8 41
(This is an oversize 12-inch 78 rpm)

TEAGARDEN, Jack, with Orchestral Accompaniment

HUNDRED YEARS FROM TODAY, A / I JUST COULDN'T TAKE IT, BABY .... *Brunswick 6716* 5-8 33
(Vocals: Jack Teagarden)

LOVE ME / BLUE RIVER .... *Brunswick 6741* 8-10 33
(Vocals: Jack Teagarden)

TEN BLACK BERRIES, The:
see ELLINGTON, Duke, & His Cotton Club Orchestra

TEN FRESHMEN, The:
see RESER, Harry, as The Rounders

TERR, Max, & His Orchestra

ARGENTINE / THE MAN IN THE MOON .... *Pathe Actuelle 020931* 2-4 23

DREAM DADDY / RAGGEDY ANN .... *Pathe Actuelle 036030* 3-5 24

DREAM DADDY / RAGGEDY ANN ...... *Perfect 14211* 2-4 24
(Simultaneously released on two labels)

GOO-GOO-GOODNIGHT / WHO DO YOU LOVE? .... *Pathe Actuelle 036159* 2-4 24

HAWAIIAN MOON / WHEN THE SUN GOES DOWN ON THE LONESOME PINE .... *Pathe Actuelle 036162* 3-5 25

HAWAIIAN MOON / WHEN THE SUN GOES DOWN ON THE LONESOME PINE .... *Perfect 14343* 2-4 25
(Simultaneously released on two labels)

I FOUND A FOUR-LEAF CLOVER / I'LL BUILD A STAIRWAY TO PARADISE .... *Pathe Actuelle 020828* 3-5 22

I FOUND A FOUR-LEAF CLOVER / I'LL BUILD A STAIRWAY TO PARADISE .... *Perfect 14054* 2-4 22
(Simultaneously released on two labels)

IN LOVE WITH LOVE / STEPPIN' OUT .... *Pathe Actuelle 036047* 3-5 24

IN LOVE WITH LOVE / STEPPIN' OUT .... *Perfect 14228* 2-4 24
(Simultaneously released on two labels)

LOOK-A WHAT I GOT NOW! / MANDA (Vocal: Billy Jones) ...... *Pathe Actuelle 036144* 3-5 24

LOOK-A WHAT I GOT NOW! / MANDA (Vocal: Billy Jones) .... *Perfect 14325* 2-4 24
(Simultaneously released on two labels)

MOONLIGHT AND ROSES / BESIDE A SILVERY STREAM .... *Perfect 14438* 2-4 25

MURMURING / TRULY .... *Pathe Actuelle 020810* 2-4 22

NO, NO NORA! (Vocals: Unknown) / BONNIE .... *Pathe Actuelle 021050* 3-5 23

NO, NO NORA! (Vocals: Unknown) / BONNIE .... *Perfect 14168* 2-4 23
(Simultaneously released on two labels)

SERENADE / NOCTURNE IN E FLAT .... *Pathe Actuelle 036087* 3-5 24

SERENADE / NOCTURNE IN E FLAT .... *Perfect 14268* 2-4 24
(Simultaneously released on two labels)

SUSIE / SOUTHERN MOON ..... *Pathe Actuelle 020811* 2-4 22

TERRY, Bob, & His Orchestra

IT'S BEEN SO LONG / SING AN OLD-FASHIONED SONG .... *Champion 40094* 10-12 36
(Vocals: Wayne Gregg)

MOONBURN / MY HEART AND I .... *Champion 40093* 10-12 36
(Vocals: Wayne Gregg)

TERRY, Thelma, & Her Play Boys

LADY OF HAVANA / VOICE OF THE SOUTHLAND .... *Columbia 1390-D* 4-6 28

MAMA'S GONE, GOODBYE / HEY! HEY! (by Charles Fulcher & His Orchestra; Vocal: Charles Fulcher) ...... *Columbia 1706-D* 5-8 28

STARLIGHT AND TULIPS / I LOVE YOU TRULY (by Guy Lombardo & His Royal Canadians) ...... *Columbia 1532-D* 3-5 28

WHEN SWEET SUSIE GOES STEPPIN' BY (Vocal: Wayne Smith) / DUSKY STEVEDORE (Vocal: Joe Davis) .... *Columbia 1588-D* 5-8 28

TEXAS TEN, The:
see GLANTZ, Nathan, & His Orchestra

THIES, Henry, & His Castle Farm Orchestra
(Henry Thies: 11/1/93 – 6/12/35)

DREAM GARDEN / ANGRY .... *Gennett 3118* 5-8 25

SPANISH MELODY / SOME OTHER BIRD WHISTLED A TUNE (by Bob Deikman & His Orchestra) ... *Gennett 3142* 5-8 25

THIES, Henry, & His Hotel Sinton Orchestra

ROSE OF MANDALAY / SWEET LIZA ... *Victor 21890* 4-6 29
(Vocals: Don Dewey)

WHEN YOU'RE SMILING / THAT'S MY MAMMY .... *Victor 21462* 3-5 28
(Vocals: Don Dewey)

THIES, Henry, & His Orchestra

HAVIN' YOU AROUND IS HEAVEN (Vocal: Charles Dameron) / HERE COMES EMILY BROWN (Vocals: The Howard Trio) .... *Victor 22476* 4-6 30

JUNE KISSES (Vocal: Jane Froman) / UNDER VESUVIAN SKIES (Vocal: Charles Dameron)........... *Victor 22460* 4-6 30

MY SWEETHEART SERENADE (Vocal: Charles Dameron) / SHARING (Vocal: Jane Froman) .... *Victor 22461* 4-6 30

THIES' DETROIT RITZ ORCHESTRA:
see THIES, Henry

THIES, Henry, as Thies' Detroit Ritz Orchestra

CAN YOU FORGET? / BLUE MOON ... *Vocalion 14274* 3-5 22

DAPPER DAN / I WANT MY MAMMY ... *Vocalion 14273* 3-5 22

NOW I LAY ME DOWN TO SLEEP / LITTLE GIRL...................... *Vocalion 14207* 2-4 21

THOMAS, Howard, & His Orchestra

BUSINESS IN F / AN EVENING IN CAROLINE (Vocals: Unknown) .... *Champion 16380* 10-12 32

HOME / TEMPORARILY BLUE .... *Superior 2785* 4-6 32
(Vocals: Unknown)

I PROMISE YOU / TEMPORARILY BLUE............ *Champion 16377* 4-6 32
(Vocals: Unknown)

SINCE YOU'VE GONE AWAY / THAT'S ALL I WANT IN LIFE............................ *Gennett 7195* 5-8 30
(Vocals: Howard Thomas)

SINCE YOU'VE GONE AWAY / YOU OUGHTA KNOW............. *Champion 15998* 4-6 30
(Vocals: Howard Thomas)

THOMPSON, Kay, & Her Orchestra
(Kay Thompson: 11/9/13 –)

CARELESSLY (Vocals: Kay Thompson & chorus) / THERE'S A LULL IN MY LIFE (Vocal: Kay Thompson).................... *Victor 25564* 5-8 37

IT HAD TO BE YOU / EXACTLY LIKE YOU................ *Victor 25582* 5-8 37
(Vocals: Kay Thompson & chorus)

THOMPSON, Kay, & The Boys

OUT OF SIGHT, OUT OF MIND / DON'T MENTION LOVE TO ME..................... *Brunswick 7564* 5-8 36
(Vocals: Kay Thompson)

YOU LET ME DOWN / YOU HIT THE SPOT............... *Brunswick 7560* 5-8 36
(Vocals: Kay Thompson)

THORNHILL, Claude, & His Orchestra
(Claude Thornhill: 8/10/09 – 7/1/65)

ALT WIEN (OLD VIENNA) / LOVE TALES... *Okeh 5988* 2-4 40

AMERICA, I LOVE YOU / SOMETHING TO REMEMBER YOU BY.............. *Columbia 36578* 3-5 42
(Vocals: The Pair Of Pairs)

ANTHROPOLOGY / FOR HEAVEN'S SAKE .... *Columbia 38224* 2-4 48

AUTUMN NOCTURNE / WHERE HAS MY LITTLE DOG GONE?........... *Columbia 36435* 3-5 41

BAD HUMOR MAN (Vocal: Bob Jenney) / I'VE GOT A ONE-TRACK MIND (Vocal: Jane Essex).......... *Okeh 5838* 2-4 40

BE CAREFUL, IT'S MY HEART (Vocal: Lillian Lane) / LULLABY OF THE RAIN .... *Columbia 36616* 3-5 42

BELLS OF SAN RAQUEL / I FOUND YOU IN THE RAIN............................. *Columbia 36431* 2-4 41
(Vocals: Dick Harding)

BUSTER'S LAST STAND / I DON'T KNOW WHY (Vocals: The Snowflakes) .... *Columbia 36858* 2-4 42

DO I WORRY? (Vocal: Dick Harding) / SLEEPY SERENADE...................... *Okeh 6178* 2-4 41

EBB TIDE (Vocal: Barry McKinley) / DON'T SAVE YOUR LOVE (Vocal: Maxine Sullivan)... *Brunswick 7957* 5-8 37

EV'RYTHING I LOVE (Vocal: Lillian Lane) / I HATE YOU, DARLING (Vocal: Dick Harding)....... *Columbia 36456* 2-4 42

GRIEG'S PIANO CONCERTO / I'LL PRAY FOR YOU (Vocal: Dick Harding) .... *Columbia 36535* 3-5 42

HARBOR LIGHTS (Vocal: Jimmy Farrell) / GONE WITH THE WIND (Vocal: Maxine Sullivan)...... *Vocalion 3595* 5-8 37

I'M GETTING TIRED SO I CAN SLEEP (Vocal: Terry Allen) / ROCK-A-BYE BABY (Vocals: Lillian Lane & The Snowflakes)... *Columbia 36658* 2-4 42

JIM (Vocal: Kay Doyle) / CONCERTO FOR TWO (Vocal: Dick Harding)................. *Columbia 36371* 2-4 41

LOVE OF MY LIFE / THE LEGEND OF OLD CALIFORNIA.................. *Okeh 5901* 2-4 40
(Vocals: Dick Harding)

LOVERS IN GLASS HOUSES / MANDY IS TWO................... *Columbia 36361* 2-4 41
(Vocals: Dick Harding)

MEMORY LANE / THE LAMP OF MEMORY...................... *Columbia 36527* 2-4 42
(Vocals: Dick Harding)

MISS YOU (Vocal: Dick Harding) / BABY MINE (Vocal: Lillian Lane)...... *Columbia 36413* 3-5 41

MOONLIGHT MASQUERADE / ORANGE BLOSSOM LANE................. *Columbia 36391* 2-4 41
(Vocals: Dick Harding)

NIGHT AND DAY / STEALIN' APPLES ... *V-Disc 612* 5-8 –
(This is an oversize 12-inch 78 rpm, a World War II release.)

PORTRAIT OF A GUINEA FARM / ALL I NEED IS YOU (Vocal: Dick Harding).............. *Okeh 6234* 2-4 41

ROBBINS NEST / JUST ABOUT THIS TIME LAST NIGHT............... *Columbia 38136* 2-4 48

ROSE O' DAY (Vocals: Lillian Lane, Martha Wayne, Dick Harding & Buddy Stewart) / SOMEBODY NOBODY LOVES (Vocal: Lillian Lane).......... *Columbia 36458* 2-4 42

SHE'LL ALWAYS REMEMBER (Vocal: Dick Harding) / COUNT ME IN (Vocals: Martha Wayne & Buddy Stewart)................... *Columbia 36560* 3-5 42

SING A LOVE SONG / I'M THRILLED... *Columbia 36287* 3-5 41
(Vocals: Dick Harding)

SMILES (Vocals: The Pair Of Pairs) / NIGHT AND DAY................. *Columbia 37055* 2-4 46

SNOWFALL (theme song) / WHERE OR WHEN................ *Columbia 36268* 2-4 41

SOMEBODY ELSE IS TAKING MY PLACE (Vocals: The Pair of Pairs) / YA LU-BLU (Vocal: Dick Harding) ..... *Columbia 36513* 2-4 42

STACK OF BARLEY / HUNGARIAN DANCE NO. 5......................... *Okeh 6168* 3-5 41

SUNDAY KIND OF LOVE, A (Vocal: Fran Warren) / SONATA (Vocal: Buddy Hughes)....... *Columbia 37219* 3-5 47

THERE'S A SMALL HOTEL / MOONLIGHT BAY................. *Columbia 36725* 2-4 42
(Vocals: The Snowflakes)

THIS LOVE OF MINE (Vocal: Lillian Lane) / CHATTANOOGA CHOO CHOO (Vocals: Lillian Lane & Bob Jenney) .... *Columbia 36472* 2-4 42

WE'RE THE COUPLE IN THE CASTLE (Vocal: Dick Harding) / I SAID NO (Vocal: Lillian Lane)......................... *Columbia 36477* 4-6 42

WHEN THE LILACS BLOOM AGAIN / OVERNIGHT.......................... *Okeh 6202* 2-4 41
(Vocals: Dick Harding)

WHISPERS IN THE DARK (Vocal: Jimmy Farrell) / STOP! YOU'RE BREAKING MY HEART (Vocal: Maxine Sullivan)................. *Vocalion 3616* 5-8 37

YOU AND I KNOW / AN OLD FLAME NEVER DIES .... *Brunswick 7951* 5-8 37
(Vocals: Barry McKinley)

YOURS IS MY HEART ALONE / GOTTA GET ME SOMEBODY TO LOVE (Vocal: Buddy Hughes)................ *Columbia 37098* 2-4 46

YOU WERE MEANT FOR ME (Vocal: Dick Harding) / PARADISE (Vocal: Kay Doyle) .... *Columbia 36298* 2-4 41

TICKLE TOE TEN, The

BY THE LIGHT OF THE STARS (Vocal: Bruce Wallace) / JUST A LITTLE DRINK (Vocal: Billy Jones)......................... *Okeh 40414* 3-5 25

I'LL TAKE HER BACK / YEARNING..... *Okeh 40325* 3-5 25

PROMENADE WALK / WHAT A WORLD THIS WOULD BE (Vocal: Bruce Wallace)... *Okeh 40428* 3-5 25

TIMOTHY, Tom, & His Frivolity Club Orchestra

MY PET / TELL ME YOU'RE SORRY.... *Edison 52311* 5-8 28
(Vocals: Unknown)

TIN PAN PARADERS, The:
see HALL, Fred

TOBIN, John, as John Tobin's Midnight Serenaders

I'M AFRAID TO CARE FOR YOU / WHY SHOULD I BELIEVE IN YOU? (by The Scranton Sirens Orchestra)....................... *Okeh 40297* 8-10 25

TOBIN'S MIDNIGHT SERENADERS:
see TOBIN, John

TOLBERT, Skeets, & His Gentlemen of Swing

BOUNCING IN RHYTHM / THE STUFF'S OUT (IT JUMPED JUST A MINUTE AGO) (Vocal: Lem Johnson).................. *Decca 7630* 5-8 39

C. O. D. / HEY MAN, HEY MAN........... *Decca 8641* 5-8 42
(Vocals: by chorus)

DELTA LAND BLUES (Vocal: Herbert Goodwin) / RIDE ON (Vocal: Jean Eldridge)............ *Decca 8608* 5-8 42

FILL UP / BECAUSE I LOVE MY DADDY SO (Vocal: Nora Lee King) .... *Decca 8617* 4-6 42

FINE PIECE OF MEAT (Vocal: Babe Wallace) / SWING OUT.......................... *Decca 7669* 5-8 39

GIMME SOMETHING LIKE THAT (Vocal: Clarence Easter) / PAPA'S IN BED WITH HIS BRITCHES ON (Vocals: by chorus)............................ *Decca 7751* 5-8 40

HOLE HOLY ROLY-POLY (Vocals: by chorus) / HARLEM AIN'T WHAT IT USTA BE (Vocal: Clarence Easter).................. *Decca 7717* 5-8 40

I'VE LOST MY HEAD OVER YOU / THIS IS THE END.................... *Decca 7591* 4-6 39
(Vocals: Babe Hines)

JUMPIN' LIKE MAD / HIT THAT JIVE, JACK .... *Decca 8528* 5-8 41
(Vocals: by chorus)

LAZY GAL BLUES (Vocal: Charles Richards) / GIT IT ('CAUSE I LOVE TO SEE YOU WID IT) (Vocal: Babe Wallace) .... *Decca 8589* 5-8 41

RAILROAD BLUES (Vocal: Lem Johnson) / I'M BLOWIN' MY TOP (Vocal: Babe Wallace)............. *Decca 7653* 5-8 39

RHUMBA BLUES (Vocals: by chorus) / JUMPIN' IN THE NUMBERS (Vocal: Wingy Carpenter)........ *Decca 8565* 5-8 41

SAMMY'S CHOPPIN' BLOCK (Vocals: by chorus) / FOUR O'CLOCK BLUES (Vocal: Babe Wallace)..... *Decca 8534* 5-8 41

SKIN 'EM BACK (Vocals: Unknown) / GET UP................................ *Decca 7570* 5-8 39

SUGAR BOOGIE / I'LL MAKE IT WORTH YOUR WHILE................. *Decca 8506* 5-8 40
(Vocals: Yack Taylor)

THAT'S THAT MESSY BOOGIE / WHAT IS THE MATTER NOW? (Vocal: Jean Eldridge) ..... *Decca 8631* 5-8 41

THOSE DRAFTIN' BLUES (Vocal: Yack Taylor) / BUGLE BLUES......................... *Decca 8516* 5-8 41

UNCLE EPH'S DREAM / BIG FAT BUTTERFLY (Vocals: by chorus)........... *Decca 8579* 4-6 41

W. P. A. (Vocals: by chorus) / I CAN'T GO FOR YOU (Vocal: Charles Richards)......... *Decca 7722* 5-8 40

TOMPKINS, Tommy "Red", & His Orchestra

DEEP SHADOWS (Vocal: Billy Pritchard) / MONOPOLY SWING.................... *Variety 543* 5-8 37

OH BABE – MAYBE SOMEDAY / I NEVER HAD A DREAM........................ *Variety 610* 4-6 37
(Vocals: Billy Pritchard)

VIPER'S DREAM / SUMPIN' 'BOUT RHYTHM........... *Vocalion 3293* 5-8 36

WHAT THE HEART BELIEVES / JES' NATCH'ULLY LAZY............ *Vocalion 3271* 5-8 36
(Vocals: Sally Ann Harris)

TOP NOTCHERS, The

ALONG THE OLD LAKE TRAIL / SOMEONE LOVES YOU AFTER ALL............... *Edison 51404* 4-6 24

FORGET-ME-NOT / WHEN THE ONE YOU LOVE LOVES YOU.............. *Edison 51453* 4-6 25
(Vocals: Charles Hart)

HONEY BABE / MY BEAUTIFUL MEXICAN ROSE...................... *Edison 51342* 5-8 24

JUST LIKE A BABY / DON'T MIND THE RAIN.......................... *Edison 51318* 4-6 24
(Vocals: Unknown)

OKLAHOMA INDIAN JAZZ / — .... *Edison 51297* 5-8 24

TAKE ME BACK TO YOUR HEART (Vocal: Charles Hart) / MY MOTHER'S HUMMING LULLABY... *Edison 51499* 3-5 24

TRACE, Al, & His Orchestra
(Al Trace: 12/25/00 –)

CHERRY LIPS / HONKY TONK MELODY............. *Mercury 5828* 2-4 52

I HAD MY HEART SET ON YOU / I'M THROUGH CALLING EVERYBODY DARLING...... *Columbia 38431* 2-4 48

LINGER AWHILE / YOU CALL EVERYBODY DARLING........... *Regent 117* 2-4 48
(Vocals: Bob Vincent)

MAIRZY DOATS / WHERE DID YOU GET THAT GIRL?........................ *Hit 8079* 2-4 43

TRAVELERS, The:
see DORSEY BROTHERS' Orchestra, The

TRAVERS, Vincent, & His Hotel Walton Orchestra

FRASQUITA SERENADE / SONG OF THE ISLANDS................... *Bluebird B-5176* 3-5 33

FRASQUITA SERENADE / SONG OF THE ISLANDS.................. *Electradisk 2070* 10-12 33

FRASQUITA SERENADE / SONG OF THE ISLANDS..................... *Sunrise S-3257* 10-12 33
(Simultaneously released on three labels)

THREE OF US (Vocal: Pat Harrington) / JUNGLE DRUMS.................. *Bluebird B-5174* 4-6 33

THREE OF US (Vocal: Pat Harrington) / JUNGLE DRUMS .... *Electradisk 2068* 12-15 33

THREE OF US (Vocal: Pat Harrington) / JUNGLE DRUMS.................. *Sunrise S-3255* 12-15 33
(Simultaneously released on three labels)

TRAVERS, Vincent, & His Orchestra

LOVE IS GOOD FOR ANYTHING THAT AILS YOU (Vocal: Tiny Wolfe) / WAS IT RAIN? (Vocal: Buddy Blaisdell).......... *Vocalion 3476* 3-5 37

LOVE IS GOOD FOR ANYTHING THAT AILS YOU (Vocal: Tiny Wolfe) / WAS IT RAIN? (Vocal: Buddy Blaisdell)........ *Melotone 7-04-21* 3-5 37

LOVE IS GOOD FOR ANYTHING THAT AILS YOU (Vocal: Tiny Wolfe) / WAS IT RAIN? (Vocal: Buddy Blaisdell) .... *Perfect 7-04-21* 3-5 37
(Simultaneously released on three labels)

MESSAGE FROM THE MAN IN THE MOON / TOMORROW IS ANOTHER DAY ...... *Vocalion 3546* 3-5 37
(Vocals: Buddy Blaisdell)

TRAYMORE ORCHESTRA, The:
see ELLINGTON, Duke, & His Orchestra as The Washingtonians

TREMAINE, Paul, & His Orchestra

ARISTOCRATIC STOMP / FOUR-FOUR RHYTHM (Vocal: Paul Tremaine) .... *Victor V-40176* 5-8 29

GIVE YOUR AFFECTION, HONEY / I CAN'T GET MISSISSIPPI OFF MY MIND ...... *Columbia 2510-D* 3-5 31
(Vocals: Unknown)

GOSPEL TRAIN (Vocals: by chorus) / IS THERE A PLACE UP THERE FOR ME?
(Vocals: Unknown) .... *Columbia 2302-D* 5-8 31

HAND ME DOWN MY WALKIN' CANE / SHE'LL BE COMIN' AROUND THE MOUNTAIN .... *Columbia 2130-D* 5-8 30
(Vocals: Paul Tremaine)

IT'S SUNDAY DOWN IN CAROLINE / IN THE PARK IN PAREE .... *Bluebird B-5050* 4-6 33
(Vocals: Paul Tremaine)

IT'S SUNDAY DOWN IN CAROLINE / IN THE PARK IN PAREE .... *Electradisk 1976* 12-15 33
(Vocals: Paul Tremaine)

IT'S SUNDAY DOWN IN CAROLINE / IN THE PARK IN PAREE .... *Sunrise S-3124* 12-15 33
(Vocals: Paul Tremaine)
(Simultaneously released on three labels)

ROCKIN' CHAIR (Vocals: Unknown) / ANCHORS AWEIGH (Vocals: by chorus) .... *Columbia 2200-D* 4-6 30

SIGHING FOR THE MOON / SARAH LEE .... *Victor V-40230* 5-8 29
(Vocals: Paul Tremaine)

STORMY WEATHER (Vocal: Paul Tremaine) / HAND ME DOWN MY WALKIN' CANE
(Vocals: Paul Tremaine & Orchestra) ..... *Bluebird B-5049* 4-6 33

STORMY WEATHER (Vocal: Paul Tremaine) / HAND ME DOWN MY WALKIN' CANE
(Vocals: Paul Tremaine & Orchestra) ..... *Electradisk 1975* 12-15 33

STORMY WEATHER (Vocal: Paul Tremaine) / HAND ME DOWN MY WALKIN' CANE
(Vocals: Paul Tremaine & Orchestra) ...... *Sunrise S-3123* 12-15 33
(Simultaneously released on three labels)

WHEN GABRIEL BLOWS DAT HORN / I WANNA SING ABOUT YOU .... *Columbia 2462-D* 5-8 30
(Vocals: Unknown)

WHEN THE DAY'S WORK'S ALL BEEN DONE (Vocals: Unknown) / STEAMBOAT BILL
(Vocals: Paul Tremaine & chorus) .... *Columbia 2229-D* 4-6 30

TRENT, Alphonse & His Orchestra
(Alphonse Trent: 8/24/05 – 10/14/59)

AFTER YOU'VE GONE (Vocal: Stuff Smith) / ST. JAMES INFIRMARY (Vocals: by chorus) .... *Champion 15956* 15-20 30

AFTER YOU'VE GONE (Vocal: Stuff Smith) / ST. JAMES INFIRMARY (Vocals: by chorus) .... *Gennett 7161* 20-25 30
(Simultaneously released on two labels)

BLACK AND BLUE RHAPSODY / NIGHTMARE .... *Gennett 6710* 20-25 29

CLEMENTINE / I'VE FOUND A NEW BABY .... *Champion 16587* 20-25 33
(Vocals: Peanuts Holland)

LOUDER AND FUNNIER (Vocals: Snub Mosley, Stuff Smith & John Fielsing) / GILDED KISSES
(Vocal: John Fielsing) .... *Gennett 6664* 20-25 28

TRENT, Alfonse, & His Orchestra as Duke Diggs & His Orcehstra

AFTER YOU'VE GONE (Vocal: Stuff Smith) / ST. JAMES INFIRMARY (Vocals: by chorus) .... *Supertone 9653* 15-20 30

BLACK AND BLUE RHAPSODY / NIGHTMARE .... *Supertone 9487* 15-20 29

TRENT, Alfonse, & His Orchestra as Deacon Foster & His Boys

GILDED KISSES (Vocal: John Fielsing) / BLACK AND BLUE RHAPSODY .... *Champion 15656* 15-20 29

TRENT, Alphonse, & His Orchestra as The Savannah Night Hawks

LOUDER AND FUNNIER (Vocals: Snub Mosley, Stuff Smith, & John Fielsing) / NIGHTMARE
(Vocal: John Fielsing) .... *Champion 15641* 20-25 28

TRIMBLE, Barney, & His Oklahomans:
see GOLD, Lou, & His Orchestra, and see SELVIN, Ben, & His Orchestra

TRINI, Anthony, & His Orchestra

I'M SORRY, DEAR / CUBAN LOVE SONG .... *Melotone M-12286* 3-5 32
(Vocals: Anthony Trini)

WHEN THE REST OF THE CROWD GOES HOME (I ALWAYS GO HOME ALONE) / SAVE THE LAST DANCE FOR ME .... *Meltone M-12285* 3-5 32
(Vocals: Anthony Trini)

WHY SHOULDN'T I? / WHEN THE SHEPHERD LEADS THE SHEEP BACK HOME ... *Melotone M-12197* 3-5 31
(Vocals: Anthony Trini)

YOU CALL IT MADNESS / LOVE LETTERS IN THE SAND .... *Melotone M-12243* 4-6 31
(Vocals: Anthony Trini)

TRINI, Anthony, & The Village Barn Orchestra

BREEZE (THAT'S BRINGIN' MY BABY BACK TO ME) / BORN TO BE KISSED .... *Bluebird B-5555* 4-6 34
(Vocals: Anthony Trini)

DILLY DALLY / AND THE BIG BAD WOLF WAS DEAD .... *Bluebird B-5551* 5-8 34
(Vocals: Beth Challis)

I NEVER HAD A CHANCE / THE MOONLIGHT PARADE .... *Bluebird B-5554* 4-6 34
(Vocals: Anthony Trini)

TROUBADOURS, The:
see LANIN, Sam, & His Orchestra

TRUESDALE, William:
see FOOR-ROBINSON Carolina Club Orchestra, The

TRUMBAUER, Frankie, & His Orchestra
(Frankie Trumbauer: 5/30/01 – 6/11/56)

BABY, WON'T YOU PLEASE COME HOME?
(Vocal: Frank Trumbauer) / I LIKE THAT ... *Okeh 41286* 25-30 29

BLESS YOU! SISTER / DUSKY STEVEDORE .... *Okeh 41100* 25-30 28
(Vocals: Frank Trumbauer & Dee Orr)

BLUE MOON / DOWN'T UNCLE BILL'S ... *Victor 24812* 8-10 35
(Vocals: Dick Robertson)

BLUE RIVER / THERE'S A CRADLE IN CAROLINE .... *Okeh 40879* 20-25 27
(Vocals: Seger Ellis)

BORNEO / MY PET .... *Okeh 41039* 25-30 28
(Vocals: Scrappy Lambert)

BREAKIN' IN A PAIR OF SHOES / I HOPE GABRIEL LIKES MY MUSIC (Vocals: Jack Teagarden & Frank Trumbauer) ..... *Brunswick 7613* 8-10 36

BREAK IT DOWN / JUBA DANCE .... *Brunswick 6763* 8-10 34

BYE BYE BLUES (Vocal: Smith Ballew) / CHOO CHOO .... *Okeh 41450* 10-12 30

CINDERELLA'S WEDDING DAY / BASS DRUM DAN .... *Columbia 2879-D* 10-12 32
(Vocals: Leroy Buck)

CLARINET MARMALADE / SINGIN' THE BLUES (theme song) .... *Okeh 40772* 15-20 27
(Some issues add the credit "with Bix" or "with Bix and Lang")

CRYING ALL DAY / A GOOD MAN IS HARD TO FIND .... *Okeh 40966* 15-20 27

EMALINE / 'LONG ABOUT MIDNIGHT .... *Brunswick 6788* 8-10 34
(Vocals: Jack Teagarden)

FLIGHT OF A HAYBAG / ANNOUNCER'S BLUES .... *Brunswick 7629* 8-10 36

FUTURISTIC RHYTHM (Vocal: Frank Trumbauer) / RAISIN' THE ROOF .... *Okeh 41209* 25-30 29

GEORGIA ON MY MIND (Vocals: Art Jarrett & trio) / HONEYSUCKLE ROSE
(Vocal: Art Jarrett) .... *Brunswick 6159* 8-10 31

GET HAPPY / DEEP HARLEM .... *Okeh 41431* 10-12 30
(Vocals: Frank Trumbauer)

HAPPY FEET (Vocal: Smith Ballew) / I LIKE TO DO THINGS FOR YOU (Vocal: Jeannie Lang) ... *Okeh 41421* 10-12 30

HIGH UP ON A HILL TOP / SENTIMENTAL BABY .... *Okeh 41128* 25-30 28
(Vocals: Charles Gaylord)

HONKY TONK TRAIN BLUES / LITTLE ROCK GETAWAY .... *Varsity 8236* 4-6 40

HUMPTY DUMPTY / BALTIMORE .... *Okeh 40926* 20-25 27

I DON'T STAND A GHOST OF A CHANCE (Vocal: Fredda Gibson) / SUGAR FOOT STOMP .... *Varsity 8256* 4-6 40
(Fredda Gibson was later known as Georgia Gibbs)

I'M AN OLD COWHAND (Vocal: Jack Teagarden) / DIGA DIGA DOO .... *Brunswick 7687* 5-8 36

I'M COMING, VIRGINIA / 'WAY DOWN YONDER IN NEW ORLEANS .... *Okeh 40843* 15-20 27

IN A MIST / WILD HONEY (by Anson Weeks & His California Orchestra; Vocal: Ben Gage) .... *Brunswick 6997* 5-8 34

IN THE MERRY MONTH OF MAYBE / CRAZY QUILT .... *Brunswick 6146* 8-10 31
(Vocals: Art Jarrett & trio)

I THINK YOU'RE A HONEY (Vocals: The Nitecaps) / BUSINESS IN Q .... *Columbia 2710-D* 10-12 32

JIMTOWN BLUES / THE LAZIEST GAL IN TOWN (Vocal: Fredda Gibson) .... *Varsity 8223* 5-8 40
(Fredda Gibson as later known as Georgia Gibbs)

JUBILEE / I'M MORE THAN SATISFIED (by Larry Abbott & His orchestra; Vocals: by duet) .... *Okeh 41044* 25-30 28

LADY BE GOOD / WRAP YOUR TROUBLES IN DREAMS .... *Varsity 8269* 4-6 40

LOUISE / WAIT TILL YOU SEE "MA CHERIE" .... *Okeh 41231* 20-25 29
(Vocals: Smith Ballew)

LOVE AIN'T NOTHIN' BUT THE BLUES / HOW AM I TO KNOW? .... *Okeh 41301* 10-12 29
(Vocals: Smith Ballew)

MANHATTAN RAG / WHAT WOULDN'T I DO FOR THAT MAN? (Vocal: Smith Ballew) .... *Okeh 41330* 10-12 29

MAYOR OF ALABAM' (Vocals: Jack Teagarden & chorus) / 'S WONDERFUL .... *Brunswick 7663* 5-8 36

NEVER-NEVER LAND FANTASY / NATIONAL EMBLEM MARCH .... *Varsity 8243* 3-5 40

NEWEST ST. LOUIS BLUES, THE (Vocal: Leroy Buck) / BETWEEN THE DEVIL AND THE DEEP BLUE SEA
(Vocals: Frank Trumbauer & Leroy Buck) ... *Columbia 2729-D* 15-20 32
(This record was pressed in blue shellac)

NOBODY BUT YOU / GOT A FEELIN' FOR YOU .... *Okeh 41252* 10-12 29
(Vocals: Smith Ballew)

NOT ON THE FIRST NIGHT, BABY (Vocals: Wayne Williams, Frank Trumbauer, & Fredda Gibson) / WALKIN' THE DOG (Vocals: chorus) ..... *Varsity 8225* 4-6 40
(Fredda Gibson was later known as Georgia Gibbs)

OSTRICH WALK / RIVERBOAT SHUFFLE .... *Okeh 40822* 12-15 27

OUR BUNGALOW OF DREAMS / LILA .... *Okeh 41019* 12-15 28
(Vocals: Noel Taylor)

PLANTATION MOODS / TROUBLED .... *Victor 24834* 5-8 35

SEMPER FIDELIS / STARS AND STRIPES FOREVER .... *Varsity 8253* 3-5 40

SHIVERY STOMP / REACHING FOR SOMEONE (Vocal: Smith Ballew) .... *Okeh 41268* 10-12 29

SOMEBODY LOVES ME / AIN'T MISBEHAVIN' .... *Brunswick 7665* 5-8 36
(Vocals: Jack Teagarden)

TAKE YOUR TOMORROW (Vocal: Frank Trumbauer) / LOVE AFFAIRS (Vocal: Scrappy Lambert) .... *Okeh 41145* 25-30 28

THERE'LL COME A TIME / MISSISSIPPI MUD (Vocals: Bing Crosby & Frank Trumbauer) .... *Okeh 40979* 20-25 28

THREE BLIND MICE / KRAZY KAT ...... *Okeh 40903* 15-20 27

TURN ON THE HEAT / SUNNY SIDE UP ... *Okeh 41313* 10-12 29
(Vocals: Smith Ballew)

WEARING OF THE GREEN; IRISH WASHER-WOMAN / NO RETARD (CHINA BOY) ... *Varsity 8215* 4-6 40

WHAT'S THE USE? (Vocal: Smith Ballew) / HITTIN' THE BOTTLE (Vocal: Frank Trumbauer) .... *Okeh 41437* 8-10 30

TRUMBAUER, Frankie, as Frankie Trumbauer's Augmented Orchestra recorded under the name Benny Meroff & His Orchestra

JUST AN HOUR OF LOVE / I'M WONDERIN' WHO .... *Okeh 40912* 15-20 27
(Vocals: Irving kaufman)

TUCKER, Orrin, & His Orchestra
(Orrin Tucker: 2/17/11 –)
(Orrin Tucker is retired from the band business, and currently is in real estate in Palm Springs, California)

ABSENCE MAKES THE HEART GROW FONDER (FOR SOMEBODY ELSE) (Vocal: Bonnie Baker) / GEORGIA ON MY MIND (Vocals: Orrin Tucker & The Bodyguards) .... *Columbia 36049* 2-4 41

ALL ALONE AND LONELY (Vocals: Orrin Tucker & The Bodyguards) / YOU TALK TOO MUCH (Vocals: Bonnie Baker & Orrin Tucker) .... *Columbia 36172* 2-4 41

AREN'T YOU GONNA KISS ME GOODNIGHT? (Vocal: Bonnie Baker) / THE LAST TIME I SAW PARIS (Vocal: Orrin Tucker) ...... *Columbia 35948* 2-4 41

ARE YOU KIDDIN' / UNDER BLUE CANADIAN SKIES (Vocals: Unknown) ... *Columbia 36382* 2-4 41

AT THE BLALAIKA (Vocal: Gil Mershon) / DRIFTING AND DREAMING (theme song)
(Vocals: The Bodyguards) .... *Columbia 35332* 2-4 40

BILLY (Vocals: Bonnie Baker) / EVERYBODY LOVES MY BABY (Vocal: Orrin Tucker) .... *Vocalion 4914* 2-4 39

CALLING ALL HEARTS (Vocal: Orrin Tucker) / YOU CAN DEPEND ON ME
(Vocal: Bonnie Baker) .... *Columbia 36093* 2-4 41

DO I WORRY? (Vocals: Bonnie Baker & Orrin Tucker) / I WENT OUT OF MY WAY
(Vocal: Orrin Tucker) .... *Columbia 36102* 2-4 41

DO SOMETHING / SHE DON'T WANNA (Vocals: Unknown) .... *Columbia 36490* 2-4 42

DRINK THE BARREL DRY (Vocals: The Bodyguards) / YOU BETCHA MY LIFE
(Vocal: Bonnie Baker) .... *Columbia 36192* 2-4 41

EACH TIME YOU SAY GOODBYE (I DIE A LITTLE)
(Vocal: Gil Mershon) /
LOVELINESS (Vocal: Orrin Tucker) .... *Columbia 35229* 2-4 39

ESPECIALLY FOR YOU (Vocal: Bonnie Baker) / I NEED LOVIN' (Vocal: Orrin Tucker) .... *Conqueror 9313* 3-5 38

ESPECIALLY FOR YOU (Vocal: Bonnie Baker) / I NEED LOVIN' (Vocal: Orrin Tucker) .... *Vocalion 4241* 3-5 38
(Simultaneously released on two labels)

FOR TONIGHT (Vocal: Sim Sims) / BLUE ORCHIDS (Vocal: Orrin Tucker) ... *Vocalion 5076* 2-4 39

GO AWAY – CAN'T YOU SEE I'M DREAMING? (Vocal: Bonnie Baker) / GET THE MOON OUT OF YOUR EYES (Vocal: Orrin Tucker) .... *Columbia 35546* 2-4 40

GOODBYE, MAMA (I'M OFF TO YOKOHAMA) (Vocal: Eddie Rice) / YOU'RE A SAP, MR. JAP
(Vocals: Orrin Tucker & chorus) .... *Columbia 36502* 3-5 42

HAVIN' MYSELF A TIME (Vocal: Bonnie Baker) / CATHEDRAL IN THE PINES
(Vocal: Orrin Tucker) .... *Vocalion 4099* 2-4 38

HI NEIGHBOR! / WHISTLER'S MOTHER-IN-LAW (Vocals: Bonnie Baker & Orrin Tucker) .... *Columbia 36362* 2-4 41

HOW STRANGE (Vocal: Gil Mershon) / WISHING (WILL MAKE IT SO) (Vocal: Orrin Tucker) ...... *Vocalion 4762* 2-4 39

IF I COULD BE THE DUMMY ON YOUR KNEE (Vocal: Bonnie Baker) / IF IT WASN'T FOR THE MOON
(Vocal: Orrin Tucker) .... *Columbia 35390* 2-4 40

IF I COULD ONLY PLAY A CORCERTINA (Vocals: Lorraine Benson & Orrin Tucker) / WHEREVER YOU ARE (Vocal: Bob Haymes) .... *Columbia 36539* 2-4 42
(Bob Haymes is the younger brother of singer Dick Haymes)

IF I KNEW THEN (Vocal: Bonnie Baker) / ALL IN FAVOR SAY AYE! (Vocals: Orrin Tucker & The Bodyguards) . . . Columbia 35256 2-4 39

IF YOU LOVE ME (Vocals: Bonnie Baker & The Bodyguards) / YOU THINK OF EV'RYTHING (Vocal: Orrin Tucker) . . . Columbia 35489 2-4 40

I KNOW SOMEBODY WHO LOVES YOU (Vocal: Bonnie Baker) / TAKE CARE (Vocal: Orrin Tucker) . . . Columbia 35699 2-4 40

KEEP YOUR EYE ON YOUR HEART (Vocals: Bonnie aker & The Bodyguards) / BREAKFAST FOR TWO (Vocal: Orrin Tucker) . . . Columbia 36016 2-4 41

LA ROSITA / I LOVE YA, I BETCHA (Vocal: Bonnie Baker) . . . Columbia 35722 2-4 40

LITTLE GIRL (Vocal: Orrin Tucker) / YOU'D BE SURPRISED (Vocal: Bonnie Baker) . . . Columbia 35344 2-4 40

LYDIA, THE TATTOED LADY (Vocals: orchestra) / STOP! IT'S WONDERFUL (Vocal: Bonnie Baker) . . . Columbia 35249 2-4 39

MAKE BELIEVE (Vocal: Gil Mershon) / WHERE'D YOU GET THOSE EYES? (Vocals: Bonnie Baker & The Bodyguards) . . . Columbia 36307 2-4 40

MARY, MARY, QUITE CONTRARY (Vocal: Bonnie Baker) / A STONE'S THROW FROM HEAVEN (Vocal: Jack Bartell) . . . Columbia 36175 2-4 41

MIDNIGHT (Vocal: Gil Mershon) / WHAT ARE LITTLE GIRLS MADE OF? (Vocals: Bonnie Baker & The Bodyguards) . . . Vocalion 4805 2-4 39

MOON AND I, THE (Vocal: Unknown) / THE YOGI WHO LOST HIS WILL POWER (Vocal: Jerry Colonna) . . . Columbia 35866 3-5 41

MY GREATEST MISTAKE (Vocal: Orrin Tucker) / YOUR FLAG AND MINE (Vocals: The Bodyguards) . . . Columbia 35622 2-4 40

MY RESISTANCE IS LOW (Vocal: Bonnie Baker) / BEEN LOOKIN' FOR LOVE (Vocal: Orrin Tucker) . . . Columbia 35468 2-4 40

NO FOOLIN' (Vocal: Orrin Tucker) / IT WAS WONDERFUL THEN (Vocal: Bonnie Baker) . . . Columbia 35997 2-4 41

NOT YET (Vocal: Bonnie Baker) / WHERE DO I GO FROM YOU? (Vocal: Orrin Tucker) . . . Columbia 35452 2-4 40

OH JOHNNY, OH JOHNNY, OH! (Vocal: Bonnie Baker) / HOW MANY TIMES? (Vocal: Orrin Tucker) . . . Columbia 35228 2-4 39

ON THE OUTSIDE LOOKING IN (Vocal: Bonnie Baker) / RENDEZVOUS IN RIO (Vocal: Jack Bartell) . . . Columbia 36151 2-4 41

PINCH ME / WOULDJA MIND? . . . Columbia 35328 2-4 39 (Vocals: Bonnie Baker)

RIDE, TENDERFOOT, RIDE / I'LL DREAM TONIGHT . . . Vocalion 4111 2-4 38 (Vocals: Orrin Tucker)

SH! BABY'S ASLEEP (Vocals: Bonnie Baker & The Bodyguards) / APPLE BLOSSOMS AND CHAPEL BELLS (Vocal: Orrin Tucker) . . . Columbia 35405 2-4 40

SOME MUST WIN (Vocals: The Bodyguards) / WILL YOU MARRY ME, MR. LARAMIE? (Vocal: Bonnie Baker) . . . Columbia 36223 2-4 41

SOMEONE'S ROCKIN' MY DREAMBOAT / DEAR MOM . . . Columbia 36515 3-5 42 (Vocals: Orrin Tucker)

SUCH STUFF AS DREAMS ARE MADE OF / I WANT TO LIVE (AS LONG AS YOU LOVE ME) . . . Columbia 35813 2-4 40 (Vocals: Unknown)

TANGERINE / ALWAYS IN MY HEART . . . Columbia 36565 2-4 42 (Vocals: Bob Haymes) (Bob Haymes is the younger brother of singer Dick Haymes)

THEM THERE EYES (Vocal: Orrin Tucker) / OH, LADY! BE GOOD (Vocals: Bonnie Baker & The Bodyguards) . . . Columbia 35576 2-4 40

TOO BUSY (Vocal: Orrin Tucker) / I'LL COME TO YOU (Vocals: Bonnie Baker & The Bodyguards) . . . Columbia 35528 2-4 40

TWILIGHT INTERLUDE / MANY DREAMS AGO . . . Columbia 35303 2-4 39 (Vocals: Orrin Tucker)

WHAT ARE LITTLE GIRLS MADE OF? (Vocals: Bonnie Baker & the Bodyguards) / EVERYBODY LOVES MY BABY (Vocal: Orrin Tucker) . . . Conqueror 9312 2-4 39

WHO CALLS? / AS WE WALK INTO THE SUNSET (Vocals: Unknown) . . . Columbia 36459 2-4 42

YOU'RE NEARER (Vocals: Unknown) / LI'L ABNER . . . Columbia 35792 4-6 40

YOU'RE THE ONE (Vocals: Orrin Tucker & The bodyguards) / GEE! I WISH I'D LISTENED TO MY MOTHER (Vocals: Bonnie Baker & The Bodyguards) . . . Columbia 35848 2-4 40

YOU'VE GOT WHAT IT TAKES (Vocals: Bonnie Baker & The Bodyguards) / DANCING ON A DIME (Vocal: Orrin Tucker) . . . Columbia 35744 2-4 40

TUCKER, Tommy, & His Californians

(Tommy Tucker: 5/18/08 –)

BLUE PRELUDE / GOOD EVENIN', MR. NIGHTINGALE . . . Crown 3497 5-8 33 (Vocals: Unknown)

HIAWATHA'S LULLABY / MY GYPSY RHAPSODY . . . Crown 3478 4-6 33 (Vocals: Unknown)

I CAN'T REMEMBER / STAY OUT OF MY DREAMS . . . Crown 3477 5-8 33 (Vocals: Unknown)

SPRING IN MY HEART / TIME TO SING . . . Crown 3471 4-6 33 (Vocals: Unknown)

TWO-BUCK TIM FROM TIMBUCTOO / TONY'S WIFE . . . Crown 3479 5-8 33 (Vocals: Unknown)

YOU AND THE NIGHT AND THE MUSIC / A FOOL IN LOVE . . . Crown 3499 4-6 33 (Vocals: Unknown)

TUCKER, Tommy, & His Orchestra

I LOVE YOU (OH HOW I LOVE YOU) (theme song) / LOVE IN JUNE . . . Brunswick Special un-numbered 15-20 36

REMEMBER ME (Vocals: The Voices Four) / AM I IN LOVE? (Vocal: Ray Hoskins) . . . Vocalion 3667 2-4 37

TUCKER, Tommy, as Tommy Tucker Time

AIN'T IT A SHAME ABOUT MAME? (Vocal: Amy Arnell) / RHYTHM ON THE RIVER (Vocal: Al Knapp) . . . Okeh 5688 3-5 40

ALL ALONE AND LONELY (Vocal: Don Brown) / WHERE THE MOUNTAINS MEET THE MOON (Vocals: The Voices Three & chorus) . . . Okeh 6236 2-4 41

AS TIME GOES BY (Vocal: Peter Hanley) / TWO SWEETHEARTS (Vocals: The Voices Four) . . . MGM 11619 2-4 52

BABY DOLL (Vocal: Karen Rich) / WITH NO ONE TO LOVE TONIGHT (Vocal: Peter Hanley . . . MGM 11162 2-4 51

BARTENDER POLKA (Vocals: The Voices Three) / THE MAN DON'T COME TO OUR HOUSE ANYMORE (Vocal: Kerwin Somerville) . . . Okeh 5717 3-5 40

BROWN SKIN (Vocals: The Voices Five) / SHE'LL BE COMIN' 'ROUND THE MOUNTAIN (Vocal: Amy Arnell) . . . Vocalion 4739 3-5 39

CALLING ALL HEARTS (Vocal: Amy Arnell) / ON THE OUTSIDE LOOKING IN (Vocal: Al Knapp) . . . Okeh 6048 2-4 41

CANCEL THE FLOWERS (Vocals: Don Brown & The Voices Four) / THE SKUNK SONG (Vocals: Kerwin Somerville & The Voices Four) . . . Conqueror 9955 3-5 41

CANCEL THE FLOWERS (Vocals: Don Brown & The Voices Four) / THE SKUNK SONG (Vocals: Kerwin Somerville & The Voices Four) . . . Okeh 6466 3-5 41 (Simultaneously released on two labels)

DEAR OLD PAL OF MINE (Vocals: Amy Arnell, Don Brown, & The Voices Five) / WHISPER THAT YOU LOVE ME (Vocals: Amy Arnell, Don Brown, & The Voices Four) . . . Columbia 36728 2-4 42

EBB TIDE / I STILL LOVE TO KISS YOU GOODNIGHT . . . Conqueror 8958 3-5 37 (Vocals: Unknown)

EBB TIDE / I STILL LOVE TO KISS YOU GOODNIGHT . . . Vocalion 3680 3-5 37 (Vocals: Unknown) (Simultaneously released on two labels)

EV'RYBODY EV'RY PAYDAY (Vocals: Amy Arnell & The Voices Three) / MARCH FOR THE NEW INFANTRY (Vocals: Don Brown & The Voices Four) . . . Okeh 6701 3-5 44

EV'RY SUNDAY AFTERNOON (Vocals: The Voices Three) / WHERE DO I GO FROM YOU? (Vocals: The Voices Four) . . . Conqueror 9526 2-4 40

EV'RY SUNDAY AFTERNOON (Vocals: The Voices Three) / WHERE DO I GO FROM YOU? (Vocals: The Voices Four) . . . Vocalion 5505 2-4 40 (Simultaneously released on two labels)

HAVING A LONELY TIME (Vocal: Don Brown) / SUGAR DADDY (Vocals: Amy Arnell & chorus) . . . Conqueror 9901 3-5 41

HAVING A LONELY TIME (Vocal: Don Brown) / WHEN THIS CRAZY WORLD IS SANE AGAIN (Vocals: Amy Arnell, Don Brown, & chorus) . . . Okeh 6412 3-5 41

HOW COME, BABY, HOW COME? (Vocal: Amy Arnell) / SEVEN BEERS WITH THE WRONG WOMAN (Vocal: Kerwin Somerville) . . . Okeh 5815 3-5 40

HOW DO I KNOW IT'S REAL? (Vocals: Amy Arnell & chorus) / LORETTA (Vocals: Don Brown & The Voices Five) . . . Okeh 6592 2-4 42

I DON'T WANT TO SET THE WORLD ON FIRE (Vocals: Amy Arnell & The Voices Three) / CONCERTO FOR TWO (Vocal: Don Brown) . . . Conqueror 9898 2-4 41

I FOUND A MILLION-DOLLAR BABY (Vocal: Don Brown) / BLUES (MY NAUGHTY SWEETIE GIVES TO ME) (Vocal: Amy Arnell) . . . Okeh 6188 2-4 41

I HADN'T ANYONE TILL YOU (Vocal: Amy Arnell) / YES, THERE AIN'T NO MOONLIGHT (SO WHAT) (Vocal: Archie Berdahl) . . . Vocalion 4031 2-4 38

I'LL PRAY FOR YOU (Vocals: Amy Arnell, Don Brown & The Voices Four) / JOHNNY DOUGHBOY FOUND A ROSE IN IRELAND (Vocal: Don Brown) . . . Okeh 6620 3-5 42

I'M GONNA LASSO A DREAM (Vocals: Don Brown & The Three Two Timers) / ANYBODY'S LOVE SONG (Vocal: Don Brown) . . . Columbia 37233 2-4 47

I'M NOBODY'S BABY (Vocal: Amy Arnell) / BUDS WON'T BUD (Vocal: Al Knapp) . . . Okeh 5634 2-4 40

IN A LITTLE HULA HEAVEN / SWEET LEILANI . . . Melotone 7-05-17 2-4 37 (Vocals: Unknown)

IN A LITTLE HULA HEAVEN / SWEET LEILANI . . . Vocalion 3489 2-4 37 (Vocals: Unknown) (Simultaneously released on two labels)

IS THAT THE WAY TO TREAT A SWEETHEART? / THE CUTE LITTLE HAT CHECK GIRL (Vocal: Ray Hawkins) . . . Vocalion 4399 2-4 38

IT HAPPENED IN KALOHA (Vocals: The Voices Three) / SHAKE DOWN THE STARS (Vocal: Kelly Rand) . . . Vocalion 5457 2-4 40

I THREW A KISS IN THE OCEAN (Vocals: Amy Arnell & The Voices Five) / OH, HOW I MISS YOU TONIGHT (Vocals: Don Brown & The Voices Five) . . . Okeh 6645 3-5 42

JACK AND JILL (Vocals: Amy Arnell) / CONCERTO FOR TWO (Vocals: Don Brown) . . . Okeh 6402 2-4 41

KISS THE BOYS GOODBYE / JIM . . . Conqueror 9899 3-5 41 (Vocals: Amy Arnell)

KISS THE BOYS GOODBYE (Vocal: Amy Arnell) / TATTLETALE (Vocal: Don Brown) . . . Okeh 6268 3-5 41

LAST CALL FOR LOVE (Vocals: Don Brown & The Voices Five) / HEAVENLY, ISN'T IT? (Vocal: Amy Arnell) . . . Columbia 36592 3-5 42

LAZY RIVER (Vocals: Don Brown & The Voices Four) / I LOVE YOU (theme song) (Vocals: The Voices Three) . . . Conqueror 9629 2-4 41

LAZY RIVER (Vocals: Don Brown & The Voices Four) / I LOVE YOU (theme song) (Vocals: The Voices Three) . . . Okeh 6145 2-4 41 (Simultaneously released on two labels)

LET HIM LIVE (Vocal: Kerwin Somerville) / LAST NIGHT A MIRACLE HAPPENED (Vocal: Amy Arnell) . . . Vocalion 4650 2-4 39

LET'S SAY GOODNIGHT WITH A DANCE (Vocal: Don Brown) / I DON'T WANT TO WALK WITHOUT YOU (Vocal: Amy Arnell) . . . Okeh 6554 3-5 42

LI'L ABNER (Vocals: Amy Arnell & Tommy Tucker) / BIG AND FAT AND FORTY-FOUR (Vocal: Kerwin Somerville) . . . Okeh 5949 4-6 41

LOVE OF MY LIFE (Vocal: Amy Arnell) / FOR THE FIRST TIME (Vocals: The Voices Four) . . . Vocalion 4367 2-4 38

MAN COMES AROUND, THE (Vocal: Kerwin Somerville) / HONESTLY (Vocal: Ernest MacLean) . . . Conqueror 9524 3-5 39

MAN COMES AROUND, THE (Vocal: Kerwin Somerville) / HONESTLY (Vocal: Ernest MacLean) . . . Vocalion 5199 3-5 39 (Simultaneously released on two labels)

MAYBE YOU'LL BE THERE / ANOTHER NIGHT LIKE THIS . . . Columbia 37339 2-4 47 (Vocals: Don Brown & The Three Two Timers)

MIRRORS DON'T TELL LIES (Vocals: The Voices Three) / THERE'S A BRAND NEW PICTURE IN MY PICTURE FRAME (Vocal: Ray Hawkins) . . . Vocalion 4228 2-4 38

MOONLIGHT COCKTAIL (Vocals: Don Brown & The Voices Three) / I SAID NO (Vocal: Amy Arnell) . . . Okeh 6526 2-4 42

MY SHIP (Vocal: Amy Arnell) / JENNY (Vocals: Amy Arnell & The Voices Three) . . . Conqueror 9630 2-4 41

MY SHIP (Vocal: Amy Arnell) / JENNY (Vocals: Amy Arnell & The Voices Three) . . . Okeh 6131 2-4 41 (Simultaneously released on two labels)

NICE DREAMIN', BABY (Vocal: Don Brown) / NUMBER TEN, LULLABY LANE (Vocals: Amy Arnell & Don Brown) .... *Conqueror 9628* 2-4 41

NICE DREAMIN', BABY (Vocal: Don Brown) / NUMBER TEN, LULLABY LANE (Vocals: Amy Arnell & Don Brown)........... *Okeh 6156* 2-4 41 (Simultaneously released on two labels)

NIGHT MUST FALL (Vocal: Amy Arnell) / WELL, ALL RIGHT (TONIGHT'S THE NIGHT) (Vocal: Kerwin Somerville) .... *Vocalion 4931* 2-4 39

OCEANA ROLL (Vocals: Amy Arnell & The Voices Three) / PAPA'S IN BED WITH HIS BRITCHES ON (Vocal: Amy Arnell)......................... *Okeh 5861* 2-4 40

PRETTY LITTLE BUSY-BODY (Vocals: Don Brown & Amy Arnell) / SOMETIMES (Vocals: Don Brown & The Voices Three) .... *Okeh 6571* 2-4 42

RELUCTANT DRAGON, THE (Vocals: Don Brown & The Voices Four) / YES INDEED! (Vocals: Amy Arnell, Kerwin Somerville, & chorus)...................... *Okeh 6290* 2-4 41

ROSE O'DAY (Vocals: Don Brown & The Glee Club) / WHEN YOUR OLD WEDDING RING WAS NEW (Vocals: The Voices Three) .... *Okeh 6448* 2-4 41

ROSE OF THE ROCKIES (Vocals: by chorus) / THE TWO LITTLE SQUIRRELS (NUTS TO YOU) (Vocals: Amy Arnell, Don Brown, & Tommy Tucker) .... *Okeh 6082* 2-4 41

SHEPHERD SERENADE (Vocals: Don Brown & The Voices Three) / JIM (Vocal: Amy Arnell) .... *Okeh 6353* 2-4 41

SING ME A SONG OF THE ISLANDS (Vocals: Amy Arnell & The Voices Five) / SLEEPY LAGOON (Vocal: Don Brown)........................ *Okeh 6638* 2-4 42

SNOOTIE LITTLE CUTIE (Vocals: Amy Arnell & Don Brown) / A SOLDIER DREAMS (OF YOU TONIGHT) (Vocals: Don Brown & The Voices Five) ... *Columbia 36607* 3-5 43

SO MANY TIMES / HOW LONG HAS THIS BEEN GOING ON? .... *Vocalion 5254* 2-4 39 (Vocals: Amy Arnell)

SOMEDAY, SOMEWHERE (Vocals: The Three Two Timers) / BAIA (Vocals: Don Brown & The Three Two Timers)................ *Columbia 36799* 2-4 45

STARS OVER THE CAMPUS (Vocals: Amy Arnell, Don Brown, & chorus) / BECAUSE OF YOU (Vocal: Don Brown)........................ *Okeh 5899* 2-4 40

SUGAR DADDY / SOME SUNNY DAY ..... *Okeh 6429* 2-4 41 (Vocals: Amy Arnell)

TANGERINE (Vocal: Amy Arnell) / DEEP IN THE HEART OF TEXAS (Vocals: Amy Arnell, Kerwin Somerville, & chorus) .... *Okeh 6583* 2-4 42

THAT OLD SWEETHEART OF MINE (Vocals: Don Brown, Tommy Tucker, & chorus) / YOU'RE A LUCKY FELLOW, MR. SMITH (Vocals: Don Brown, Tommy Tucker, & The Voices Three)......................... *Okeh 6023* 3-5 41

THERE'S A LULL IN MY LIFE / WAKE UP AND LIVE............... *Vocalion 3500* 2-4 37 (Vocals: Unknown)

THERE WILL NEVER BE ANOTHER YOU / JUST AS THOUGH YOU WERE HERE........... *Okeh 6702* 3-5 42 (Vocals: Unknown)

THIS LOVE OF MINE (Vocals: by chorus) / I DON'T WANT TO SET THE WORLD ON FIRE (Vocals: Amy Arnell & The Voices Three)......................... *Okeh 6320* 3-5 41

THIS LOVE OF MINE (Vocals: by chorus) / SHEPHERD SERENADE (Vocals: Don Brown & The Voices Three).................. *Conqueror 9900* 3-5 41

TIME AND TIME AGAIN / MINNIE FROM TRINIDAD............. *Okeh 6177* 2-4 41 (Vocals: Amy Arnell)

TOO TIRED (Vocals: Amy Arnell & Tommy Tucker) / LITTLE NELL'S A BIG GIRL NOW (Vocal: Amy Arnell)................... *Conqueror 9525* 2-4 40

TOO TIRED (Vocals: Amy Arnell & Tommy Tucker) / LITTLE NELL'S A BIG GIRL NOW (Vocal: Amy Arnell) .... *Vocalion 5491* 2-4 40 (Simultaneously released on two labels)

WALKIN' THROUGH MOCKIN' BIRD LANE (Vocals: Don Brown & The Voices Three) / YOU WALK BY (Vocals: Amy Arnell & Don Brown)........... *Okeh 5973* 2-4 41

WHEN I SAW YOU (Vocal: Amy Arnell) / ALL THINGS COME TO THOSE WHO WAIT (Vocals: by chorus) .... *Okeh 5923* 2-4 40

WHITE CLIFFS OF DOVER, THE (Vocals: Amy Arnell, Don Brown, & The Voices Five) / THE TRAIN SONG (Vocals: Amy Arnell & The Voices Three) .... *Okeh 6487* 3-5 41

WILLIE, WILLIE, WILL YA? (Vocals: Amy Arnell & Tommy Tucker) / YOU TAUGHT ME TO LOVE AGAIN (Vocal: Amy Arnell) .... *Vocalion 4972* 2-4 39

(GIMME A LITTLE KISS) WILL YA, HUH? (Vocal: Amy Arnell) / WHO COULDN'T (Vocal: Al Knapp)................... *Vocalion 5578* 2-4 40

YAM, THE (Vocals: The Voices Four) / THE NIGHT IS FILLED WITH MUSIC (Vocal: Amy Arnell) .... *Vocalion 4269* 3-5 38

YOU ARE MY SUNSHINE (Vocals: Don Brown & The Voices Three) / NEW WORRIED MIND (Vocal: Amy Arnell)................... *Conqueror 9897* 2-4 41

YOU ARE MY SUNSHINE (Vocals: Don Brown & The Voices Three) / NEW WORRIED MIND (Vocal: Amy Arnell)......................... *Okeh 6211* 2-4 41 (Simultaneously released on two labels)

YOU DARLIN' (Vocals: The Voices Three) / AIN'T YOU ASHAMED? (Vocals: Amy Arnell & Tommy Tucker)...... *Vocalion 5543* 2-4 40

YOU STARTED SOMETHING (Vocal: Don Brown) / LOVELINESS AND LOVE (Vocals: Amy Arnell & Don Brown)........... *Okeh 6245* 2-4 41

YOU WALK BY (Vocals: Amy Arnell & Don Brown) / YOU'RE DANGEROUS (Vocal: Amy Arnell)................... *Conqueror 9752* 2-4 41

TULLER, Eddie, & His Redondo Pavilion Orchestra

CHARLESTON CHARLEY / I'LL SEE YOU IN MY DREAMS.................. *Hollywood 1067* 20-25 25 (Hollywood is a very rare label)

TUNNELL, Bon Bon, as Bon Bon & His Buddies

(Bon Bon Tunnell: 1903 –)

BLOW, GABRIEL, BLOW / ALL THAT MEAT AND NO POTATOES.................. *Decca 8567* 5-8 41 (Vocals: Bon Bon Tunnell)

I DON'T WANT TO SET THE WORLD ON FIRE / SWEET MAMA, PAPA'S GETTING MAD ... *Decca 3980* 5-8 41 (Vocals: Bon Bon Tunnell)

I'M NOT MUCH ON LOOKS / RICKETY ROCKING CHAIR .... *Decca 8628* 4-6 42 (Vocals: Bon Bon Tunnell)

SEEING YOU AGAIN DID ME NO GOOD / SLEEPY OLD TOWN.................. *Decca 8603* 4-6 42 (Vocals: Bon Bon Tunnell)

TURNER, Lloyd, & His Villa Venice Orchestra

MY MAMA'S IN TOWN / TING-A-LING, THE BELLS'LL RING (by Sam Lanin as The Arkansaw Travelers) .... *Okeh 40674* 4-6 26

ROSES / LET'S FORGET................. *Okeh 40658* 3-5 26

TYSON, "Dr. Sausage", as Doctor Sausage & His Five Pork Chops

CUCKOO CUCKOO CHICKEN RHYTHM / BIRTHDAY PARTY.................. *Decca 7776* 5-8 40 (Vocals: by chorus)

WHAM (RE-BOP-BOOM-BAM) (Vocals: by chorus) / DOCTOR SAUSAGE BLUES (Vocal: Doctor Sausage Tyson)............... *Decca 7736* 5-8 40

UNDERWOOD, Jimmy, & His Orchestra:
see HAYMES, Joe, & His Orchestra

UNITED STATES HOTEL ORCHESTRA, The

CREOLE BLUES / IN OLD MANILA...... *Pathe 22424* 4-6 20

MARION / SOME PRETTY DAY.......... *Pathe 40202* 3-5 20

UNITED STATES MARINE BAND, The
Directed by Lt. William H. Santelmann

(Following are some excellent examples of early ragtime recording, despite the fact that the United States Marine Band is generally not noted for playing dance music.
Berliners are the original disc records, highly prized as collector's items, and have become extremely rare. Both Berliner and Victor records of this period are one-sided.)

HOT STUFF – A NEGRO ODDITY...... *Berliner 0506* 40-50 99

MAPLE LEAF RAG...................... *Victor 4911* 3-5 06

YOU GOT TO PLAY RAGTIME.......... *Berliner 0520* 40-50 99

UNIVERSITY BOYS, The:
see RESER, Harry, as The Rounders

UNIVERSITY ORCHESTRA, The:
see LANIN, Sam

UNIVERSITY SIX, The:
see CALIFORNIA RAMBLERS, The

VAGABONDS, The:
see CALIFORNIA RAMBLERS, The

VALLE, Rudy, & His Connecticut Yankees
(Rudy Vallee: 7/28/01 –)

AS TIME GOES BY/
BEGGING FOR LOVE................. *Victor 22773* 2-4 31
(Vocals: Rudy Vallee)

BESIDE AN OPEN FIREPLACE / LOVE MADE
A GYPSY OUT OF ME................. *Victor 22284* 3-5 30
(Vocals: Rudy Vallee)

BETTY CO-ED (Vocal: Rudy Vallee) /
VIOLET; FRIENDS.................. *Victor 22473* 3-5 30

BROTHER, CAN YOU SPARE A DIME? / I'LL NEVER
HAVE TO DREAM AGAIN........ *Columbia 2725-D* 3-5 32
(Vocals: Rudy Vallee)

BY A WATERFALL (Vocal: Rudy Vallee) / HONEYMOON
HOTEL (Vocal: Alice Faye)........... *Bluebird B-5171* 5-8 33

BY A WATERFALL (Vocal: Rudy Vallee) / HONEYMOON
HOTEL (Vocal: Alice Faye)........... *Electradisc 2065* 15-20 33

BY A WATERFALL (Vocal: Rudy Vallee) / HONEYMOON
HOTEL (Vocal: Alice Faye)............ *Sunrise S-3252* 15-20 33
(Simultaneously released on three labels)

BYE AND BYE, SWEETHEART / MY TIME IS YOUR
TIME (theme song)..................... *Victor 21924* 2-4 29
(Vocals: Rudy Vallee)

BY THE FIRESIDE;
LOVABLE.................. *Hit Of The Week D-2-3* 3-5 32
(Hit Of The Week records are one-sided paper discs; this release has two titles on the one side.)

BY THE SYCAMORE TREE
(Vocal: Rudy Vallee)............ *Hit Of The Week B-1-2* 4-6 32
(Hit Of The Week records are one-sided paper discs. A picture of Rudy Vallee is featured on the reverse.)

CONFESSIN' / MY BLUEBIRD WAS
CAUGHT IN THE RAIN.............. *Victor 22506* 3-5 30
(Vocals: Rudy Vallee)

DANCING IN THE MOONLIGHT /
CAROLINA.......................... *Victor 24558* 2-4 34
(Vocals: Rudy Vallee)

DEEP NIGHT (Vocal: Rudy Vallee) /
KITTY FROM KANSAS CITY (Vocals: Rudy Vallee & The Gentlemen Songsters)...... *Bluebird B-7140* 3-5 37

DEEP NIGHT / WEARY RIVER......... *Victor 21868* 3-5 29
(Vocals: Rudy Vallee)

DOIN' THE RACCOON /
BYE AND BYE, SWEETHEART.... *Harmony 759-H* 3-5 28
(Vocals: Rudy Vallee)

DON'T BLAME ME / STRINGIN' ALONG
ON A SHOESTRING............... *Bluebird B-5115* 4-6 33
(Vocals: Rudy Vallee)

DON'T BLAME ME / STRINGIN' ALONG
ON A SHOESTRING............... *Electradisk 2025* 12-15 33
(Vocals: Rudy Vallee)

DON'T BLAME ME / STRINGIN' ALONG
ON A SHOESTRING................ *Sunrise S-3196* 12-15 33
(Vocals: Rudy Vallee)
(Simultaneously released on three labels)

DON'T SAY GOODNIGHT / GOIN' TO
HEAVEN ON A MULE............... *Victor 24554* 3-5 34
(Vocals: Rudy Vallee)

DREAM DUST / A TWINKLE
IN YOUR EYE.................... *Bluebird B-7649* 2-4 38
(Vocals: Rudy Vallee)

DREAM SWEETHEART (Vocal: Sleep Ward) /
SALAAMING THE RAJAH
(Vocal: George Morrow)............... *Harmony 728-H* 2-4 28

DRUNKARD SONG, THE (THERE IS A TAVERN IN
THE TOWN) / LOST IN A FOG......... *Victor 24721* 2-4 34
(Vocals: Rudy Vallee)

EMPTY SADDLES /
RHYTHM ON THE RANGE........ *Melotone 6-08-09* 2-4 36
(Vocals: Rudy Vallee)

EVERYTHING'S IN RHYTHM WITH MY HEART /
SAY THE WORD AND IT'S YOURS..... *Victor 25233* 2-4 36
(Vocals: Rudy Vallee)

FADED SUMMER LOVE
(Vocal: Rudy Vallee)............ *Hit Of The Week M-4-5* 4-6 31
(Hit Of The Week records are one-sided paper discs. This release features a picture of Rudy Vallee on the reverse side.)

(WHEN YOU FALL IN LOVE) FALL IN LOVE WITH
ME / THE WIND IN THE WILLOWS... *Victor 22615* 2-4 31
(Vocals: Rudy Vallee)

FINE ROMANCE, A / THE WALTZ
IN SWING TIME.................. *Melotone 6-10-10* 2-4 36
(Vocals: Rudy Vallee)

HA-CHA-CHA (Vocals: Rudy Vallee & The Debutantes) /
OUT IN THE COLD AGAIN
(Vocal: Rudy Vallee)..................... *Victor 24722* 2-4 34

HAPPY BOY – HAPPY GIRL (Vocals: Rudy Vallee & Alice Faye) / EMPTY DAYS
(Vocal: Rudy Vallee).................. *Bluebird B-5182* 5-8 33

HAPPY BOY – HAPPY GIRL (Vocals: Rudy Vallee & Alice Faye) / EMPTY DAYS
(Vocal: Rudy Vallee).................. *Electradisk 2075* 15-20 33

HAPPY BOY – HAPPY GIRL (Vocals: Rudy Vallee & Alice Faye) / EMPTY DAYS
(Vocal: Rudy Vallee)................... *Sunrise S-3262* 15-20 33
(Simultaneously released on three labels)

HAVE YOU MET MISS JONES? /
I'D RATHER BE RIGHT........... *Bluebird B-7238* 2-4 37
(Vocals: Rudy Vallee)

HAWAIIAN WAR CHANT (Vocals: The Gentlemen Songsters) / PHIL THE FLUTER'S BALL
(Vocal: Rudy Vallee)................. *Bluebird B-7667* 2-4 38

HEART OF STONE /
LAZY BONES..................... *Bluebird B-5114* 4-6 33
(Vocals: Rudy Vallee)

HEART OF STONE /
LAZY BONES.................... *Electradisk 2024* 12-15 33
(Vocals: Rudy Vallee)

HEART OF STONE /
LAZY BONES...................... *Sunrise S-3195* 12-15 33
(Vocals: Rudy Vallee)
(Simultaneously released on three labels)

HEAVEN HELP THIS HEART OF MINE /
HARBOR LIGHTS................. *Bluebird B-7067* 3-5 37
(Vocals: Rudy Vallee)

HEIGH-HO! EVERYBODY, HEIGH-HO! /
MISS YOU........................... *Victor 22029* 2-4 29
(Vocals: Rudy Vallee)

HIS MAJESTY THE BABY / I COULDN'T
BELIEVE MY EYES.................. *Victor 25089* 2-4 35
(Vocals: Rudy Vallee)

HOME (Vocal: Rudy Vallee)........ *Hit Of The Week A-3-4* 3-5 32
(Hit Of The Week records are one-sided paper discs.)

HOW COME YOU DO ME LIKE YOU DO? /
OLD NEW ENGLAND MOON.......... *Victor 22445* 3-5 30
(Vocals: Rudy Vallee)

HOW-DEEP-IS-THE-OCEAN? /
PLEASE......................... *Columbia 2724-D* 4-6 32
(Vocals: Rudy Vallee)

HYPNOTIZED (Vocal: Rudy Vallee) /
MOONBURN (by Eddy Duchin & His Orchestra; Vocal: Lew Sherwood).......... *Victor 25231* 3-5 36

I CAN WIGGLE MY EARS / HE WOOED HER (AND
WOOED HER AND WOOED HER)..... *Victor 25234* 2-4 36
(Vocals: Rudy Vallee)

I DON'T WANT TO MAKE HISTORY / THERE ISN'T
ANY LIMIT TO MY LOVE............. *Victor 25267* 2-4 36
(Vocals: Rudy Vallee)

IF I HAD YOU / MAKIN' WHOOPEE.... *Harmony 825-H* 3-5 29
(Vocals: Rudy Vallee)

I'LL TAKE ROMANCE (Vocals: Rudy Vallee & The Gentlemen Songsters) / A LITTLE WHITE LIGHTHOUSE
(Vocal: Rudy Vallee).................. *Bluebird B-7331* 2-4 38

I LOVE YOU, BELIEVE ME, I LOVE YOU /
IF YOU WERE THE ONLY GIRL
IN THE WORLD...................... *Victor 22227* 3-5 30
(Vocals: Rudy Vallee)

I'M HUMMIN' – I'M WHISTLIN' – I'M SINGIN' /
PANAMA........................... *Victor 24697* 2-4 34
(Vocals: Rudy Vallee)

I'M KEEPIN' COMPANY / WHEN YUBA PLAYS THE
RHUMBA ON THE TUBA............. *Victor 22742* 2-4 31
(Vocals: Rudy Vallee)

I'M PLAYING WITH FIRE /
A BEDTIME STORY.............. *Columbia 2737-D* 4-6 33
(Vocals: Rudy Vallee)

I'M STILL CARING / I'M JUST
A VAGABOND LOVER................ *Victor 21967* 2-4 29
(Vocals: Rudy Vallee)

I NEVER DREAMT /
I STILL REMEMBER................. *Victor 22361* 3-5 30
(Vocals: Rudy Vallee)

I RAISED MY HAT /
PUDDIN' HEAD JONES............... *Victor 24475* 2-4 34
(Vocals: Rudy Vallee)

I WANNA GO BACK TO BALI /
DAY DREAMING.................... *Victor 25836* 2-4 38
(Vocals: Rudy Vallee)

I WAS SAYING TO THE MOON /
YOU LOVES YOU?................ *Melotone 7-01-01* 2-4 37

JUST A LITTLE CLOSER /
GOOD EVENIN'...................... *Victor 22489* 3-5 30
(Vocals: Rudy Vallee)

KITTY FROM KANSAS CITY /
IF I HAD A GIRL LIKE YOU.......... *Victor 22419* 3-5 30
(Vocals: Rudy Vallee)

LANGUAGE OF LOVE / JUST AN ECHO
IN THE VALLEY................. *Columbia 2733-D* 4-6 33
(Vocals: Rudy Vallee)
(This record was pressed in blue shellac)

LAST ROUND-UP /
SHANGHAI LIL.................. *Bluebird B-5172* 4-6 33
(Vocals: Rudy Vallee)

LAST ROUND-UP /
SHANGHAI LIL.................. *Electradisk 2066* 12-15 33
(Vocals: Rudy Vallee)

LAST ROUND-UP /
SHANGHAI LIL.................. *Sunrise S-3253* 12-15 33
(Vocals: Rudy Vallee)
(Simultaneously released on three labels)

LATIN QUARTER /
A STRANGER IN PAREE............. *Victor 25835* 2-4 38
(Vocals: Rudy Vallee)

LET'S DO IT (LET'S FALL IN LOVE) / COME WEST,
LITTLE GIRL, COME WEST........ *Harmony 808-H* 3-5 29
(Vocals: Rudy Vallee)

LETTER FROM LONDON / I JUST
COULDN'T SAY IT BEFORE.......... *Victor 27823* 4-6 42
(Vocals: Rudy Vallee)

LIFE IS A SONG /
YOU OPENED MY EYES.............. *Victor 24895* 3-5 35
(Vocals: Rudy Vallee)

LIFE IS JUST A BOWL OF CHERRIES /
THIS IS THE MISSUS................ *Victor 22783* 4-6 31
(Vocals: Rudy Vallee)

LIFE IS JUST A BOWL OF CHERRIES (Vocals: Rudy Vallee, Sy Baker, & Frank Friselle) / OUTSIDE
(Vocal: Rudy Vallee).................. *Bluebird B-7368* 2-4 38

LINGER A LITTLE LONGER IN THE
TWILIGHT WITH ME / A JUG OF WINE, A LOAF
OF BREAD...................... *Columbia 2738-D* 4-6 33
(Vocals: Rudy Vallee)

LITTLE KISS EACH MORNING, A /
I'LL BE REMINDED OF YOU.......... *Victor 22193* 3-5 29
(Vocals: Rudy Vallee)

LOVER, COME BACK TO ME / COQUETTE .... *Victor 21880* 2-4 29
(Vocals: Rudy Vallee)

MAD DOGS AND ENGLISHMEN / THE WHIFFENPOOF SONG........ *Bluebird B-7135* 2-4 37
(Vocals: Rudy Vallee & The Gentlemen Songsters)

MAKIN' FACES AT THE MOON / HIKIN' DOWN THE HIGHWAY........ *Victor 22751* 2-4 31
(Vocals: Rudy Vallee)

MAORI / I GUESS I'LL HAVE TO CHANGE MY PLAN (THE BLUE PAJAMAS SONG)..... *Columbia 2700-D* 3-5 32
(Vocals: Rudy Vallee)

MARIE / CARESSING YOU.......... *Harmony 834-H* 3-5 29
(Vocals: Rudy Vallee)

MEET ME IN THE GLOAMING / MAYBE I LOVE YOU TOO MUCH .... *Columbia 2756-D* 4-6 33
(Vocals: Rudy Vallee)

MELODY FARM / THE ONE I LOVE.......................... *Bluebird B-7342* 2-4 38
(Vocals: Rudy Vallee)

ME MINUS YOU / LET'S PUT OUT THE LIGHTS (AND GO TO BED) .... *Columbia 2715-D* 4-6 32
(Vocals: Rudy Vallee)

MOONLIGHT DOWN LOVERS' LANE / TO BE OR NOT TO BE IN LOVE.... *Bluebird B-5118* 4-6 33
(Vocals: Rudy Vallee)

MOONLIGHT DOWN LOVERS' LANE / TO BE OR NOT TO BE IN LOVE.... *Electradisk 2028* 12-15 33
(Vocals: Rudy Vallee)

MOONLIGHT DOWN LOVERS' LANE / TO BE OR NOT TO BE IN LOVE..... *Sunrise S-3199* 12-15 33
(Vocals: Rudy Vallee)
(Simultaneously released on three labels)

MY BEST WISHES / NATURALLY ... *Bluebird B-7645* 2-4 38
(Vocals: Rudy Vallee)

MY DANCING LADY / EVERYTHING I HAVE IS YOURS .... *Victor 24458* 2-4 33
(Vocals: Rudy Vallee)

MY SONG / THE THRILL IS GONE ...... *Victor 22784* 2-4 31
(Vocals: Rudy Vallee)

MY TEMPTATION / WHEN YOUR HAIR HAS TURNED TO SILVER .... *Victor 22595* 3-5 31
(Vocals: Rudy Vallee)

NASTY MAN (Vocals: Rudy Vallee & The Do-Re-Mi Trio) / HOLD MY HAND (Vocals: Rudy Vallee, The Cavaliers, & The Do-Re-Mi Trio) .... *Victor 24581* 3-5 34

NINETY-NINE OUT OF A HUNDRED / WOULD YOU LIKE TO TAKE A WALK?............. *Victor 22611* 3-5 31
(Vocals: Rudy Vallee)

OH! MA-MA (Vocals: Red Stanley & The Gentlemen Songsters) / LONESOME, THAT'S ALL
(Vocal: Rudy Vallee).................. *Bluebird B-7543* 3-5 38

OLD MAN HARLEM / HERE IS MY HEART............. *Columbia 2764-D* 5-8 33
(Vocals: Rudy Vallee)

OLD SOW SONG / WITH HER HEAD TUCKED UNDERNEATH HER ARM......... *Bluebird B-7078* 3-5 37
(Vocals: Cyril Smith)

ONE IN THE WORLD, THE / S'POSIN'... *Victor 21998* 2-4 29
(Vocals: Rudy Vallee)

ON THE AIR / MY MOONLIGHT MADONNA....................... *Bluebird B-5097* 10-12 33
(Vocals: Rudy Vallee)

ON THE AIR / MY MOONLIGHT MADONNA....................... *Electradisk 2012* 10-12 33
(Vocals: Rudy Vallee)

ON THE AIR / MY MOONLIGHT MADONNA........................ *Sunrise S-3178* 8-10 33
(Vocals: Rudy Vallee)
(Simultaneously released on three labels)

ON THE ALAMO / ME QUERES? (DO YOU LOVE ME) .... *Victor 22084* 2-4 29
(Vocals: Rudy Vallee)

ORCHIDS IN THE MOONLIGHT / FLYING DOWN TO RIO .... *Victor 24459* 2-4 33
(Vocals: Rudy Vallee)

PAGE MISS GLORY (Vocal: Rudy Vallee) / PLAIN OLD ME (Vocals: Rudy Vallee & The Stewart Sisters) .... *Victor 25109* 2-4 35

PARDON ME, PRETTY BABY / MANY HAPPY RETURNS OF THE DAY .... *Victor 22752* 2-4 31
(Vocals: Rudy Vallee)

PERHAPS / THE ALBUM OF MY DREAMS......................... *Victor 22118* 2-4 29
(Vocals: Rudy Vallee)

PIG GOT UP AND SLOWLY WALKED AWAY, THE / THE GENTLEMAN OBVIOUSLY DOESN'T BELIEVE (IN LOVE)................. *Victor 25092* 3-5 35
(Vocals: Rudy Vallee)

PRETENDING YOU CARE / WHISPER WALTZ................ *Columbia 2746-D* 4-6 33
(Vocals: Rudy Vallee)

PRETTY GIRL IS LIKE A MELODY, A
(Vocal: Rudy Vallee) / ON THE GOOD SHIP LOLLIPOP
(Vocals: The Stewart Sisters) .... *Victor 24838* 4-6 35

REMINISCING / THE VERDICT IS LIFE (WITH YOU).................... *Victor 22412* 3-5 30
(Vocals: Rudy Vallee)

RIGHT OUT OF HEAVEN (Vocal: Sleepy Ward) / LADY WHIPPOORWILL
(Vocal: George Morrow) .... *Harmony 724-H* 2-4 28

SAVAGE SERENADE (Vocal: Rudy Vallee) / NAGASAKI....................... *Bluebird B-5177* 4-6 33

SAVAGE SERENADE (Vocal: Rudy Vallee) / NAGASAKI...................... *Electradisk 2071* 12-15 33

SAVAGE SERENADE (Vocal: Rudy Vallee) / NAGASAKI......................... *Sunrise S-3258* 12-15 33
(Simultaneously released on three labels)

SAY IT ISN'T SO / THREE'S A CROWD.............. *Columbia 2714-D* 4-6 32
(Vocals: Rudy Vallee)

SEEIN' IS BELIEVIN' / LOVE DROPPED IN FOR TEA .... *Victor 24899* 2-4 35
(Vocals: Rudy Vallee)

SEVENTH HEAVEN / THE CORONATION WALTZ........ *Meltone 7-05-26* 2-4 37
(Vocals: Rudy Vallee)

SHADOW WALTZ / I'VE GOT TO SING A TORCH SONG.................. *Columbia 2773-D* 5-8 33
(Vocals: Rudy Vallee)

SHAME ON YOU (Vocal: Alice Faye) / LOVE IS THE SWEETEST THING
(Vocal: Rudy Vallee).................. *Bluebird B-5175* 5-8 33

SHAME ON YOU (Vocal: Alice Faye) / LOVE IS THE SWEETEST THING
(Vocal: Rudy Vallee)................. *Electradisk 2069* 15-20 33

SHAME ON YOU (Vocal: Alice Faye) / LOVE IS THE SWEETEST THING
(Vocal: Rudy Vallee).................. *Sunrise S-3256* 15-20 33
(Simultaneously released on three labels)

SHE LOVES ME JUST THE SAME / WASHINGTON AND LEE SWING .... *Victor 22574* 4-6 30
(Vocals: Rudy Vallee)

SHE SHALL HAVE MUSIC / THE GLORY OF LOVE .... *Conqueror 8649* 2-4 36
(Vocals: Rudy Vallee)

SHE SHALL HAVE MUSIC / THE GLORY OF LOVE .... *Melotone 6-06-09* 2-4 36
(Vocals: Rudy Vallee)
(Simultaneously released on two labels)

SLEEPY HEAD / THE SWEETEST MUSIC THIS SIDE OF HEAVEN......................... *Victor 24642* 2-4 34
(Vocals: Rudy Vallee)

SOMEWHERE IN YOUR HEART / JUST AN OLD BANJO .... *Victor 24702* 2-4 34
(Vocals: Rudy Vallee)

SONG WITHOUT A NAME / MY HEART BELONGS TO THE GIRL WHO BELONGS TO SOMEBODY ELSE.................... *Victor 22435* 3-5 30
(Vocals: Rudy Vallee)

SPEAKING OF THE WEATHER / ALL'S FAIR IN LOVE AND WAR .... *Meltone 7-01-04* 2-4 37
(Vocals: Rudy Vallee)

SPELLBOUND / SO HELP ME........... *Victor 24646* 2-4 34
(Vocals: Rudy Vallee)

STEIN SONG (Vocals: Rudy Vallee, Joe Miller, Jules de Vorzon & Ray Toland) / ST. LOUIS BLUES
(Vocal: Rudy Vallee) .... *Victor 22321* 4-6 30

STOLEN MOMENTS / SWEETHEART OF MY STUDENT DAYS .... *Victor 22560* 3-5 30
(Vocals: Rudy Vallee)

STRANGE INTERLUDE / SAME OLD MOON (Vocal: Rudy Vallee) ..... *Columbia 2702-D* 3-5 32

STRANGE / P.S. – I LOVE YOU.......... *Victor 24723* 2-4 34
(Vocals: Rudy Vallee)

SUDDENLY / WHAT IS THERE TO SAY?.............................. *Victor 24476* 2-4 34
(Vocals: Rudy Vallee)

SWEETHEART OF ALL MY DREAMS / THE SONG I LOVE.............. *Harmony 811-H* 2-4 29
(Vocals: Rudy Vallee)

SWEET MUSIC / EV'RY DAY............ *Victor 24827* 2-4 35
(Vocals: Rudy Vallee)

SWEET SUZANNE / HONEY............ *Victor 21869* 2-4 29
(Vocals: Rudy Vallee)

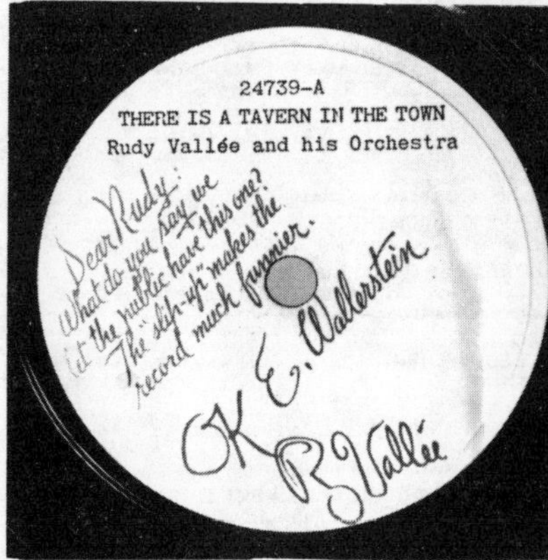

TATTOOED LADY (Vocals: Rudy Vallee & orchestra) / THE DRUNKARD SONG (THERE IS A TAVERN IN THE TOWN) (Vocal: Rudy Vallee)......... *Victor 24739* 5-8 34
(Certain copies of Victor 24739 have a white label with the following printed in red handwriting: "Dear Rudy, What do you say we let the public have this one? The slip-up makes the record much funnier. – E. Wallerstein. – O.K. – R. Vallee." The value listed is for issues with such label; the common copies of the same record are worth $2. to $4.)

TEARS / DON'T FORGET ME IN YOUR DREAMS.................... *Victor 22585* 2-4 31
(Vocals: Rudy Vallee)

THAT'S WHEN I LEARNED TO LOVE YOU / A KISS TO REMEMBER.............. *Victor 22090* 2-4 29
(Vocals: Rudy Vallee)

THESE FOOLISH THINGS (REMIND ME OF YOU) / DREAM TIME.................... *Melotone 6-08-04* 3-5 36
(Vocals: Rudy Vallee)

THINKING OF YOU, DEAR / YOU'RE DRIVING ME CRAZY! .... *Victor 22572* 3-5 31
(Vocals: Rudy Vallee)

THREE WISHES / FREE .... *Bluebird B-5132* 4-6 33
(Vocals: Rudy Vallee)

THREE WISHES / FREE............ *Electradisk 2038* 12-15 33
(Vocals: Rudy Vallee)

THREE WISHES / FREE .... *Sunrise S-3213* 12-15 33
(Vocals: Rudy Vallee)
(Simultaneously released on three labels)

TILL TOMMOROW / HERE IT IS MONDAY AND I'VE STILL GOT A DOLLAR .... *Columbia 2730-D* 4-6 33
(Vocals: Rudy Vallee)

TO THE LEGION / SONG OF THE NAVY ... *Victor 24075* 2-4 31
(Vocals: Rudy Vallee, Lambert Murphy, Charles Harrison, Walter J. Preston & Frank Croxton)

TURN OFF THE MOON / THAT'S SOUTHERN HOSPITALITY......... *Melotone 7-06-11* 2-4 37
(Vocals: Rudy Vallee)

TWO LITTLE BLUE LITTLE EYES / YOU'RE JUST A LOVER.............. *Victor 22679* 2-4 31
(Vocals: Rudy Vallee)

VALLEE SURPRISES: RUDY VALLEE INTRODUCES –SWEET SUE; DINAH (parodies sung by Red Stanley) / VALLEE SURPRISES: RUDY VALLEE INTRODUCES – HOW FIGHTS BEGAN IN SALOONS
(dialog by Cyril Smith) .... *Bluebird B-10069* 3-5 37

VIENI, VIENI (Vocals: Rudy Vallee & The Gentlemen Songsters) / DON'T PLAY WITH FIRE
(Vocal: Rudy Vallee).................. *Bluebird B-7069* 2-4 37

WAS THAT THE HUMAN THING TO DO?
(Vocals: Rudy Vallee)............ *Hit Of The Week C-1-2* 5-8 32
(Hit Of The Week records are one-sided paper discs. A picture of Rudy Vallee is featured on the reverse.)

WAY YOU LOOK TONIGHT, THE / BOJANGLES OF HARLEM......... *Melotone 6-10-11* 3-5 36
(Vocals: Rudy Vallee)

WHEN THE ORGAN PLAYED "O PROMISE ME" / IN THE MISSION BY THE SEA .... *Bluebird B-7226* 2-4 37
(Vocals: Rudy Vallee)

WHEN THE SWEET MAGNOLIAS BLOOM AGAIN / THANK HEAVEN FOR YOU .... *Bluebird B-5098* 4-6 33
(Vocals: Rudy Vallee)

WHEN THE SWEET MAGNOLIAS BLOOM AGAIN / THANK HEAVEN FOR YOU....... *Electradisk 2013* 12-15 33
(Vocals: Rudy Vallee)

WHEN THE SWEET MAGNOLIAS BLOOM AGAIN / THANK HEAVEN FOR YOU .... *Sunrise S-3179* 12-15 33
(Vocals: Rudy Vallee)
(Simultaneously released on three labels)

WHERE ARE YOU, DREAM GIRL? / PRETENDING .... *Victor 22062* 2-4 29
(Vocals: Rudy Vallee)

WHIFFENPOOF SONG, THE (Vocals: Rudy Vallee & The King's Men) / THIS CHRISTMAS
(Vocal: Rudy Vallee)..... *private recording, un-numbered* 10-12 –
(A release of undetermined date. This is a private recording, without label name or number, featuring a picture of Rudy Vallee on the label, originally for complimentary distribution by record/phonograph dealers.)

WHISTLING IN THE DARK / MY CIGARETTE LADY .... *Victor 22672* 2-4 31
(Vocals: Rudy Vallee)

WITHOUT THAT CERTAIN THING (Vocal: Rudy Vallee) / YOU OUGHTA BE IN PICTURES (Vocals: Rudy Vallee & The Do-Re-Mi Trio)................. *Victor 24580* 3-5 34

WOODEN SOLDIER AND THE CHINA DOLL, THE
(Vocal: Rudy Vallee)............. *Hit Of The Week C-5-4* 3-5 32
(Hit Of The Week records are one-sided paper discs)

WOULD YOU? / US ON A BUS........ *Conqueror 8650* 2-4 36
(Vocals: Rudy Vallee)

WOULD YOU? / US ON A BUS .... *Melotone 6-06-08* 2-4 36
(Vocals: Rudy Vallee)
(Simultaneously released on two labels)

YOU'RE JUST ANOTHER MEMORY / BABY, OH! WHERE CAN YOU BE? .... *Victor 22034* 2-4 29
(Vocals: Rudy Vallee)

YOU TRY SOMEBODY ELSE
(Vocal: Rudy Vallee) .... *Hit Of The Week MM-4-5* 5-8 31
(Hit Of The Week records are one-sided paper discs. This release features a picture of Rudy Vallee on the reverse side.)

YOU WANT LOVIN' BUT I WANT LOVE / LONELY TROUBADOUR.............. *Victor 22136* 3-5 29
(Vocals: Rudy Vallee)

VAN & HIS HOTEL HALF MOON ORCHESTRA:
see VAN STEEDEN, Peter

VAN & HIS ORCHESTRA:
see VAN STEEDEN, Peter

VAN EMBURGH, Harold, & His Orchestra

ALL-AMERICAN GIRL / SHE WENT TO OLD ST. MARY'S .... *Crown 3390* 4-6 32
(Vocals: Harold Van Emburgh)

DON'T TELL A SOUL / SO ASHAMED.... *Crown 3361* 4-6 32
(Vocals: Harold Van Emburgh)

Title	Label	Price	Year
HAPPY-GO-LUCKY YOU (AND BROKEN-HEARTED ME) / CABIN IN THE COTTON (Vocals: Harold Van Emburgh)	Crown 3336	5-8	32
IF YOU WERE ONLY MINE / JUST ANOTHER DREAM OF YOU (Vocals: Harold Van Emburgh)	Crown 3346	4-6	32
LOVABLE / BENEATH THE SILVERY MOON (Vocals: Harold Van Emburgh)	Crown 3284	4-6	32
MY MOM / BY A RIPPLING STREAM (Vocals: Harold Van Emburgh)	Crown 3299	4-6	32
STRANGE INTERLUDE / YOU ALWAYS BE THE SAME SWEETHEART (Vocals: Harold Van Emburgh)	Crown 3366	4-6	32

VAN EPS, Fred, as The Van Eps Banjo Orchestra

Title	Label	Price	Year
I WANT TO BACK TO MICHIGAN / SOUP TO NUTS	Columbia A-1629	5-8	14
MY HINDOO MAN / THANKS FOR THE LOBSTER	Columbia A-1593	5-8	14
POOR LITTLE BUTTERFLY / THE SMILER (Paroquette records are rare.)	Paroquette 42	20-25	16
SANS SOUCI / SOME BABY	Columbia A-1594	5-8	14

VAN EPS, Fred, as the Van Eps Dance Orchestra

Title	Label	Price	Year
DREAM OF ME, DARLING, TONIGHT / THE OLD COVERED BRIDGE (Vocals: Dick Robertson)	Banner 33026	3-5	34
DREAM OF ME, DARLING, TONIGHT / THE OLD COVERED BRIDGE (Vocals: Dick Robertson)	Melotone M-12985	3-5	34
DREAM OF ME, DARLING, TONIGHT / THE OLD COVERED BRIDGE (Vocals: Dick Robertson)	Oriole 2877	3-5	34
DREAM OF ME, DARLING, TONIGHT / THE OLD COVERED BRIDGE (Vocals: Dick Robertson)	Perfect 15917	3-5	34
DREAM OF ME, DARLING, TONIGHT / THE OLD COVERED BRIDGE (Vocals: Dick Robertson) (Simultaneously released on five labels)	Romeo 2251	3-5	34
OLD ROSES / NEIGHBORS (Vocals: Unknown)	Banner 33017	4-6	34
OLD ROSES / NEIGHBORS (Vocals: Unknown)	Melotone M-12976	4-6	34
OLD ROSES / NEIGHBORS (Vocals: Unknown)	Oriole 2874	4-6	34
OLD ROSES / NEIGHBORS (Vocals: Unknown)	Perfect 15914	4-6	34
OLD ROSES / NEIGHBORS (Vocals: Unknown) (Simultaneously released on five labels)	Romeo 2248	4-6	34

VAN EPS, Fred, as The Van Eps Quartette

Title	Label	Price	Year
MOONBEAMS / SNUGGLE (CLOSE TO MY HEART)	Vocalion 14177	3-5	21
'ROUND THE CORNER / TURKO (by The Green Brothers Xylophone Orchestra) (This release has the "Indian Head" label.)	Okeh 4048	5-8	20

VAN'S COLLEGIANS:

see VAN STEEDEN, Peter

VAN STEEDEN, Peter, & His Orchestra

(Peter Van Steeden: 4/13/04 –)

Title	Label	Price	Year
EVERYTHING MUST HAVE AN ENDING (Vocal: Chick Bullock) / LAWD, YOU MADE THE NIGHT TOO LONG (by Paul Whiteman & His Orchestra; Vocal: Red McKenzie)	Victor 22984	4-6	32
HOME / I PROMISE YOU (Vocals: Dick Robertson)	Victor 22868	3-5	32
I'LL ALWAYS REMEMBER SEPTEMBER / I CAN SYMPATHIZE WTIH YOU (Vocals: Smith Ballew)	Victor 22858	4-6	31
I WILL SHARE / WITH LOVE IN MY HEART (Vocals: Dick Robertson)	Victor 22884	3-5	32
SOMEBODY LOVES YOU / YOU'RE DANCING ON MY HEART (Vocals: Chick Bullock)	Victor 22948	3-5	32

VAN STEEDEN, Peter, as Van & His Hotel Half Moon Orchestra

Title	Label	Price	Year
IF YOU WANT THE RAINBOW / TEN LITTLE MILES FROM TOWN (Vocals: Roy Strom)	Gennett 6556	3-5	28
IN MY BOUQUET OF MEMORIES / JUST A LITTLE AWAY FROM HOME (Vocals: Jerry White)	Gennett 6455	3-5	28
JUST A LITTLE AWAY FROM HOME / MY BLUE RIDGE MOUNTAIN HOME (Vocals: Jerry White)	Supertone 9014	5-8	28
JUST ANOTHER DAY WASTED AWAY / I'M LOOKING OVER A FOUR-LEAF CLOVER (Vocals: Carl Mathieu)	Silvertone 8055	3-5	28
JUST ANOTHER DAY WASTED AWAY / I'M LOOKING OVER A FOUR-LEAF CLOVER (Vocals: Carl Mathieu) (Simultaneously released on two labels)	Supertone 9008	3-5	28
LET A SMILE BE YOUR UMBRELLA (Vocal: Billy Ross) / DREAM KISSES (Vocal: Carl Mathieu)	Silvertone 8039	3-5	28
LET A SMILE BE YOUR UMBRELLA (Vocal: Billy Ross) / DREAM KISSES (Vocal: Carl Mathieu) (Simultaneously released on two labels)	Supertone 9005	3-5	28
SHADY TREE, A / AMONG MY SOUVENIRS (Vocals: Jerry White)	Silvertone 8038	3-5	28
SHADY TREE, A / AMONG MY SOUVENIRS (Vocals: Jerry White) (Simultaneously released on two labels)	Supertone 9001	3-5	28
WITHOUT YOU, SWEETHEART / LET A SMILE BE YOUR UMBRELLA (Vocals: Scrappy Lambert)	Pathe Actuelle 36737	4-6	28
WITHOUT YOU, SWEETHEART / LET A SMILE BE YOUR UMBRELLA (Vocals: Scrappy Lambert) (Simultaneously released on two labels)	Perfect 14918	3-5	28

VAN STEEDEN, Peter, as Van & His Orchestra

Title	Label	Price	Year
WHO ARE YOU VAMPING TONIGHT? / SWEET THING (Vocals: Arthur Fields)	Pathe Actuelle 36559	3-5	26
WHO ARE YOU VAMPING TONIGHT? / SWEET THING (Vocals: Arthur Fields) (Simultaneously released on two labels)	Perfect 14740	2-4	26

VAN STEEDEN, Peter, as Van's Collegians

Title	Label	Price	Year
JIG WALK / —	Pathe Actuelle 36422	8-10	26
JIG WALK / — (Simultaneously released on two labels)	Perfect 14603	5-8	26
WHOSE WHO ARE YOU? / —	Pathe Actuelle 36432	8-10	26
WHOSE WHO ARE YOU? / — (Simultaneously released on two labels)	Perfect 14613	5-8	26

VARSITY EIGHT, The:

see CALIFORNIA RAMBLERS, The

VENUTI, Joe, & His Blue Five

(Joe Venuti: 9/1/04 – 8/15/78)

Title	Label	Price	Year
VIBRAPHONIA / JIG SAW PUZZLE BLUES (by The Joe Venuti – Eddie Lang Blue Five) (This record was pressed in blue shellac)	Columbia 2782-D	12-15	33

VENUTI, Joe, & His New Yorkers

Title	Label	Price	Year
BECAUSE MY BABY DON'T MEAN "MAYBE" NOW / JUST LIKE A MELODY OUT OF THE SKY (Vocals: Scrappy Lambert & Billy Hillpot)	Okeh 41056	10-12	28
CHANT OF THE JUNGLE / THAT WONDERFUL SOMETHING (IS LOVE) (Vocals: Smith Ballew)	Okeh 41320	12-15	29
DOIN' THINGS / I MUST HAVE THAT MAN (Vocal: Chauncey Morehouse)	Okeh 41133	12-15	28
I AM ONLY HUMAN AFTER ALL / OUT OF BREATH (Vocals: Scrappy Lambert)	Odeon ONY-36138	8-10	30
I AM ONLY HUMAN AFTER ALL / OUT OF BREATH (Vocals: Scrappy Lambert) (Simultaneously released on two labels)	Okeh 41451	8-10	30
I'M IN SEVENTH HEAVEN / LITTLE PAL (Vocals: Smith Ballew)	Okeh 41263	8-10	29
I MUST BE DREAMING / 'TAIN'T SO, HONEY, 'TAIN'T SO (Vocals: Scrappy Lambert)	Okeh 41051	10-12	28
PICKIN' COTTON / I'M ON THE CREST OF A WAVE (Vocals: Scrappy Lambert)	Okeh 41087	8-10	28
PROMISES / DANCING WITH TEARS IN MY EYES (Vocals: Smith Ballew)	Odeon ONY-36098	10-12	30
PROMISES / DANCING WITH TEARS IN MY EYES (Vocals: Smith Ballew) (Simultaneously released on two labels)	Okeh 41427	10-12	30
THAT'S THE GOOD OLD SUNNY SOUTH / WEARY RIVER (Vocals: Smith Ballew)	Okeh 41192	12-15	29

VENUTI, Joe, & His Orchestra

(also see NAPOLEON, Phil, as Napoleon's Emperors)

Title	Label	Price	Year
BUILD A LITTLE HOME / NO MORE LOVE (Vocals: Howard Phillips)	Banner 32896	4-6	33
BUILD A LITTLE HOME / NO MORE LOVE (Vocals: Howard Phillips)	Melotone M-12839	4-6	33
BUILD A LITTLE HOME / NO MORE LOVE (Vocals: Howard Phillips)	Oriole 2792	4-6	33
BUILD A LITTLE HOME / NO MORE LOVE (Vocals: Howard Phillips)	Perfect 15846	4-6	33
BUILD A LITTLE HOME / NO MORE LOVE (Vocals: Howard Phillips) (Simultaneously released on five labels)	Romeo 2165	4-6	33
CINDERELLA'S FELLA / ALICE IN WONDERLAND (Vocals: Slim Fortier)	Banner 32943	4-6	34
CINDERELLA'S FELLA / ALICE IN WONDERLAND (Vocals: Slim Fortier)	Melotone M-12886	4-6	34
CINDERELLA'S FELLA / ALICE IN WONDERLAND (Vocals: Slim Fortier)	Oriole 2822	4-6	34
CINDERELLA'S FELLA / ALICE IN WONDERLAND (Vocals: Slim Fortier)	Perfect 15871	4-6	34
CINDERELLA'S FELLA / ALICE IN WONDERLAND (Vocals: Slim Fortier) (Simultaneously released on five labels)	Romeo 2195	4-6	34
EENY MEENY MINEY MO (Vocal: Ruth Lee) / TWENTY-FOUR HOURS A DAY (Vocal: Tony Pasteur)	Columbia 3103-D	5-8	35
EVERYBODY SHUFFLE / MOON GLOW	Bluebird B-5520	5-8	33
FIDDLESTICKS / GOBLIN MARKET	Okeh 41586	8-10	34
FIDDLESTICKS / PHANTOM RHAPSODY	Bluebird B-5293	5-8	33
FLIP / FLOP	Decca 2313	4-6	39
HEAT WAVE / EASTER PARADE (Vocals: Dolores Read)	Banner 32879	5-8	33
HEAT WAVE / EASTER PARADE (Vocals: Dolores Read)	Melotone M-12828	5-8	33
HEAT WAVE / EASTER PARADE (Vocals: Dolores Read)	Oriole 2783	5-8	33
HEAT WAVE / EASTER PARADE (Vocals: Dolores Read)	Perfect 15838	5-8	33
HEAT WAVE / EASTER PARADE (Vocals: Dolores Read) (Simultaneously released on five labels)	Romeo 2156	5-8	33
I WANT TO RING BELLS / GATHER LIP-ROUGE WHILE YOU MAY (Vocals: Don Elton)	Domino 152	5-8	33
I WANT TO RING BELLS / GATHER LIP-ROUGE WHILE YOU MAY (Vocals: Don Elton)	Melotone M-12807	5-8	33
I WANT TO RING BELLS / GATHER LIP-ROUGE WHILE YOU MAY (Vocals: Don Elton)	Oriole 2771	5-8	33
I WANT TO RING BELLS / GATHER LIP-ROUGE WHILE YOU MAY (Vocals: Don Elton)	Perfect 15830	5-8	33
I WANT TO RING BELLS / GATHER LIP-ROUGE WHILE YOU MAY (Vocals: Don Elton) (Simultaneously released on five labels)	Romeo 2144	5-8	33
MOON GLOW / CHEESE AND CRACKERS	Banner 32883	5-8	33
MOON GLOW / CHEESE AND CRACKERS	Melotone M-12831	5-8	33
MOON GLOW / CHEESE AND CRACKERS	Oriole 2787	5-8	33

MOON GLOW / CHEESE
AND CRACKERS .... *Perfect 15842* 5-8 33

MOON GLOW / CHEESE
AND CRACKERS.................... *Romeo 2160* 5-8 33
(Simultaneously released on five labels)

MY DANCING LADY / EVERYTHING I HAVE
IS YOURS.......................... *Banner 32895* 4-6 33
(Vocals: Howard Phillips)

MY DANCING LADY / EVERYTHING I HAVE
IS YOURS .... *Melotone M-12838* 4-6 33
(Vocals: Howard Phillips)

MY DANCING LADY / EVERYTHING I HAVE
IS YOURS............................. *Oriole 2791* 4-6 33
(Vocals: Howard Phillips)

MY DANCING LADY / EVERYTHING I HAVE
IS YOURS .... *Perfect 15845* 4-6 33
(Vocals: Howard Phillips)

MY DANCING LADY / EVERYTHING I HAVE
IS YOURS .... *Romeo 2164* 4-6 33
(Vocals: Howard Phillips)
(Simultaneously released on five labels)

MY MAN FROM CAROLINE (Vocal: Irene Beasley) /
I LIKE A LITTLE GIRL LIKE THAT
(Vocal: Frank Luther)...................... *Victor 23015* 12-15 30

ONE MINUTE TO ONE / YOU HAVE
TAKEN MY HEART................. *Banner 32939* 4-6 34
(Vocals: Slim Fortier)

ONE MINUTE TO ONE / YOU HAVE
TAKEN MY HEART.............. *Melotone M-12882* 4-6 34
(Vocals: Slim Fortier)

ONE MINUTE TO ONE / YOU HAVE
TAKEN MY HEART.................. *Oriole 2820* 4-6 34
(Vocals: Slim Fortier)

ONE MINUTE TO ONE / YOU HAVE
TAKEN MY HEART................. *Perfect 15869* 4-6 34
(Vocals: Slim Fortier)

ONE MINUTE TO ONE / YOU HAVE
TAKEN MY HEART.................. *Romeo 2193* 4-6 34
(Vocals: Slim Fortier)
(Simultaneously released on five labels)

SOMETHING / NOTHING .... *Decca 2312* 4-6 39

STOP, LOOK AND LISTEN / YANKEE DOODLE
NEVER WENT TO TOWN......... *Columbia 3104-D* 5-8 35
(Vocals: Ruth Lee)

YOU'RE MY PAST, PRESENT AND FUTURE /
DOIN' THE UPTOWN LOWDOWN... *Conqueror 8250* 5-8 33
(Vocals: Don Elton)

YOU'RE MY PAST, PRESENT AND FUTURE /
DOIN' THE UPTOWN LOWDOWN...... *Domino 154* 5-8 33
(Vocals: Don Elton)

YOU'RE MY PAST, PRESENT AND FUTURE /
DOIN' THE UPTOWN LOWDOWN... *Melotone M-12816* 5-8 33
(Vocals: Don Elton)

YOU'RE MY PAST, PRESENT AND FUTURE /
DOIN' THE UPTOWN LOWDOWN ...... *Oriole 2776* 5-8 33
(Vocals: Don Elton)

YOU'RE MY PAST, PRESENT AND FUTURE /
DOIN' THE UPTOWN LOWDOWN..... *Perfect 15832* 5-8 33
(Vocals: Don Elton)

YOU'RE MY PAST, PRESENT AND FUTURE /
DOIN' THE UPTOWN LOWDOWN...... *Romeo 2149* 5-8 33
(Vocals: Don Elton)
(Simultaneously released on six labels)

VENUTI, Joe, as Joe Venuti's Blue Four

BLUE ROOM / SENSATION.............. *Okeh 41144* 10-12 28
(Vocals: Rube Bloom)

CHEESE AND CRACKERS /
A MUG OF ALE .... *Okeh 40897* 10-12 27

DINAH / THE WILD DOG................ *Okeh 41025* 12-15 28

KICKIN' THE CAT /
BEATIN' THE DOG......................... *Okeh 40853* 10-12 27

LITTLE GIRL (Vocal: Harold Arlen) /
TEMPO DI MODERNAGE......... *Columbia 2488-D* 10-12 31

MAN FROM THE SOUTH (Vocal: Rube Bloom) /
PRETTY TRIX........................... *Okeh 41076* 10-12 28

MY HONEY'S LOVIN' ARMS /
GOIN' HOME.......................... *Okeh 41251* 12-15 29
(Vocals: Rube Bloom)

PARDON ME, PRETTY BABY (Vocal: Harold Arlen) /
LITTLE BUTTERCUP.................. *Okeh 41506* 10-12 31

PENN BEACH BLUES /
FOUR STRING JOE........................ *Okeh 40947* 12-15 28

WILD DOG, THE / REALLY BLUE....... *Victor 23021* 12-15 30

VENUTI, Joe, as Joe Venuti's Rhythm Boys

THERE'S NO OTHER GIRL / NOW THAT I NEED YOU,
YOU'RE GONE.................. *Columbia 2535-D* 8-10 31
(Vocals: Harold Arlen)

WOLF WOBBLE / WHY DID IT HAVE TO
BE ME? (by The Dorsey Brothers' Orchestra;
Vocal: Wes Vaughn) .... *Columbia 2589-D* 10-12 32

VENUTI, Joe – Eddie Lang, & Their All-Star Orchestra
(Eddie Lang: 10/25/02 – 3/26/33)

BEALE STREET BLUES /
AFTER YOU'VE GONE........... *Melotone M-12294* 20-25 31
(Vocals: Jack Teagarden)

BEALE STREET BLUES /
AFTER YOU'VE GONE .... *Vocalion 15864* 20-25 31
(Vocals: Jack Teagarden)
(Simultaneously released on two labels)

FAREWELL BLUES /
SOMEDAY, SWEETHEART....... *Melotone M-12277* 20-25 31

FAREWELL BLUES /
SOMEDAY, SWEETHEART .... *Vocalion 15858* 20-25 31
(Simultaneously released on two labels)

VENUTI, Joe – Eddie Lang Blue Five, The

JIG SAW PUZZLE BLUES / VIBRAPHONIA (by Joe Venuti
& His Blue Five).................... *Columbia 2782-D* 12-15 33
(This record was pressed in blue shellac)

RAGGIN' THE SCALE / CHANT OF THE SWAMP (by Art
Kassel & His Kassels-In-The-Air)....... *Columbia 2765-D* 10-12 33
(This record was pressed in blue shellac)

VENUTI, Joe, His Violin & His All Star Orchestra

YOU CALL IT MADNESS, BUT I CALL IT LOVE /
I SURRENDER, DEAR...... *Pan-American PAN 064* 4-6 45
(Vocals: John Laurenz)

VEO, Harold, & His Arrowhead Inn Orchestra

RHAPSODIE RUSSE / PALE MOON .... *Edison 51923* 4-6 27

VEO, Harold, as Harold Veo's Orchestra

DON'T LEAVE ME, DADDY /
THE ZOO STEP.......................... *Victor 18372* 3-5 17

VEO, Harold, as Veo's Hotel McAlpin Orchestra

AS LONG AS WE ARE IN LOVE / LET'S SIT
AND TALK ABOUT YOU....... *Pathe Actuelle 36928* 3-5 29
(Vocals: Harold Van Emburgh)

AS LONG AS WE ARE IN LOVE / LET'S SIT
AND TALK ABOUT YOU .... *Perfect 15109* 2-4 29
(Vocals: Harold Van Emburgh)
(Simultaneously released on two labels)

DO YOU THINK OF ME? /
IN OLD VIENNA.............. *Pathe Actuelle 36921* 2-4 29
(Vocals: Harold Van Emburgh)

MY ANGELINE /
DADDY O' MINE .... *Pathe Actuelle 36951* 2-4 29
(Vocals: Harold Van Emburgh)

SWEETHEART OF ALL MY DREAMS /
I'M NOT SORRY............... *Pathe Actuelle 36936* 3-5 29
(Vocals: Harold Van Emburgh)

SWEETHEART OF ALL MY DREAMS /
I'M NOT SORRY .... *Perfect 15117* 2-4 29
(Vocals: Harold Van Emburgh)

VEO'S HOTEL McALPIN ORCHESTRA:
see VEO, Harold

VERNON – OWENS HOTEL WINTON ORCHESTRA OF CLEVELAND, OHIO, The

DREAMING ALONE / WHEN WILL
I KNOW?........................... *Gennett 5044* 3-5 23

SONG OF SONGS / THE WORLD IS WAITING
FOR THE SUNRISE.................. *Gennett 5046* 4-6 23

WHEN HEARTS ARE YOUNG /
CRINOLINE DAYS.................... *Gennett 5045* 3-5 23

VERNON TRIO, The

FEATHER YOUR NEST / MY MIDNIGHT
FROLIC GIRL....................... *Vocalion 14118* 2-4 20

FEATHER YOUR NEST /
MY WONDER GIRL................. *Emerson 10282* 2-4 20

GRIEVING FOR YOU / ANYTIME,
ANYDAY, ANYWHERE .... *Paramount 20036* 4-6 20

NIGHTINGALE / MARGIE............. *Gennett 4658* 3-5 21

WHISPERING / MY MIDNIGHT
FROLIC GIRL.................... *Brunswick 2049* 3-5 20

VERTMONTE ORCHESTRA, The

I'D RATHER BE ALONE /
WESTWARD........................ *Vocalion 15302* 2-4 26

THERE'S NOTHIN' ON MY MIND /
NEVER MIND...................... *Vocalion 15299* 2-4 26
(Vocals: Elliott Shaw)

VICTOR MILITARY BAND, The Directed by Walter B. Rogers
(also see ROGERS, Walter B., as Walter B. Rogers' Band)
(Despite the name of this band, its output was mainly dance music, and following are examples of their ragtime and early blues recordings.)

BALLIN' THE JACK / —................ *Victor 35405* 3-5 14
(This is an oversize 12-inch 78 rpm)

BLAME IT ON THE BLUES / — .... *Victor 17764* 2-4 15

BUGLE CALL RAG / — .... *Victor 35533* 3-5 16
(This is an oversize 12-inch 78 rpm)

HESITATION BLUES /
KANSAS CITY BLUES................ *Victor 18163* 2-4 16

RAG-A-MUFFIN RAG /
MEMPHIS BLUES.................... *Victor 17619* 2-4 14

VICTOR SALON GROUP, The:
see SHILKRET, Nathaniel

VIRGINIA CREEPERS, The:
see GOLD, Lou, & His Orchestra

VIRGINIANS, The:
see WHITEMAN, Paul, & His Orchestra

VOLTAIRE, Harry, as Harry Voltaire's Voice of Central Park Orchestra

BIMINY / BAGDAD .... *Triangle 11414* 3-5 24

I WONDER WHAT'S BECOME OF SALLY? /
LONELY LITTLE MELODY....... *Pennington 11415* 20-25 24
(Pennington records are rare.)

I WONDER WHAT'S BECOME OF SALLY? /
LONELY LITTLE MELODY......... *Triangle 11415* 3-5 24
(Simultaneously released on two labels)

VOLUNTEER FIREMEN, The:
see RESER, Harry

VOORHEES, Don, & His Earl Carroll Vanities Orchestra

CLIMBING UP THE LADDER OF LOVE /
HUGS AND KISSES .... *Columbia 765-D* 4-6 26

DANCING THE DEVIL AWAY (Vocal: Vaughn de Leath) /
THE SAME OLD MOON
(Vocal: J. Donald Parker)................ *Edison 51999* 10-12 27

FANTASY ON ST. LOUIS BLUES / FANTASY ON ST.
LOUIS BLUES, PART II........... *Columbia 1078-D* 5-8 27

JUST ONE MORE KISS / I'D LOVE
TO CALL YOU MY SWEETHEART.... *Edison 51855* 5-8 26
(Vocals: Scrappy Lambert)

NEVER WITHOUT YOU / I STILL BELIEVE
IN YOU............................. *Edison 51963* 8-10 27
(Vocals: Hal Yates)

ONE ALONE (Vocal: Charles Kaley) / THE RIFF SONG
(Vocals: The Shannon Quartet).......... *Columbia 835-D* 5-8 27

ROOM FOR TWO (Vocal: Hal Yates) /
WITH SOMEONE LIKE YOU.......... *Edison 52024* 5-8 27

SHOW ME THAT KIND OF A GIRL /
TWO LITTLE PRETTY BIRDS........ *Edison 52070* 5-8 27

WHO DO YOU LOVE? (Vocal: Hal Yates) /
BLUE SKIES (Vocals: Cooper Lawley
& Hal Yates).......................... *Edison 51919* 8-10 27

WHO DO YOU LOVE? /
MUDDY WATER................. *Columbia 881-D* 8-10 27
(Vocals: Charles Kaley)

VOORHEES, Don, & His Orchestra

CAN'T HELP LOVIN' DAT MAN
(Vocal: Vaughn de Leath) / OL' MAN RIVER
(Vocal: Wilfred Glenn)............ *Columbia 1284-D* 5-8 28

GO HOME AND TELL YOUR MOTHER
(Vocal: Scrappy Lambert)......... *Hit Of The Week 1091* 4-6 30
(Hit Of The Week records are one-sided paper discs.)

HIGHWAYS ARE HAPPY WAYS /
WHEN THE MORNING GLORIES WAKE UP
IN THE MORNING............... *Columbia 1124-D* 5-8 27
(Vocals: Irving Kaufman as Vincent Van Tuyl)

I FOUND A MILLION-DOLLAR BABY
(Vocals: by trio).................. *Hit Of The Week J-2* 4-6 31
(Hit Of The Week records are one-sided paper discs.)

I'M THROUGH WITH LOVE
(Vocal: Scrappy Lambert)......... *Hit Of The Week 1154* 4-6 31
(Hit Of The Week records are one-sided paper discs.)

RAIN (Vocal: Billy Day) / THAT'S WHAT I THINK OF YOU
(by Al Handler & His Hotel Davis Orchestra;
Vocal: Frank Sylvano)................ *Columbia 1126-D* 5-8 27

SOLILOQUY / MY BLUE
HEAVEN (Vocal: Lewis James)....... *Columbia 1129-D* 5-8 27

SOME DAY / THE SPHINX....... *Pathe Actuelle 36567* 5-8 27

SOME DAY / THE SPHINX............. *Perfect 14748* 4-6 27
(Simultaneously released on two labels)

TIP-TOE THROUGH THE TULIPS WITH ME
(Vocals: Unknown) .... *Hit Of The Week 2-D* 4-6 30
(Hit Of The Week records are one-sided paper discs.)

WHO DO YOU LOVE? /
SOMEBODY'S EYES........... *Pathe Actuelle 36594* 5-8 27
(Vocals: Herb Hobbs)

WHO DO YOU LOVE? /
SOMEBODY'S EYES................. *Perfect 14775* 4-6 27
(Vocals: Herb Hobbs)
(Simultaneously released on two labels)

VOORHEES, Don, as The Maxwell House Orchestra

MANY HAPPY RETURNS OF THE DAY
(Vocals: Unknown)................ *Hit Of The Week J-3* 4-6 31
(Hit Of The Week records are one-sided paper discs.)

ROLL ON, MISSISSIPPI, ROLL ON
(Vocal: Scrappy Lambert)......... *Hit Of The Week 1155* 5-8 31
(Hit Of The Week records are one-sided paper discs.)

VOYNOW, Dick:
see ORIGINAL WOLVERINES, The, and
see WOLVERINE ORCHESTRA, The

WADE, Jimmy, & His Dixielanders
(Jimmy Wade: circa 1895 – 2/57)

MISSISSIPPI WOBBLE /
GATES BLUES (Vocal: Punch Miller)..... *Vocalion 1236* 50-60 28

WADE, Jimmy, as Jimmy Wade's Club Alabam Orchestra

ALL THAT I HAD IS GONE / ORIGINAL
BLACK BOTTOM DANCE.............. *Gennett 6105* 70-80 27
(Vocals: Perry Bradford)

ALL THAT I HAD IS GONE / ORIGINAL
BLACK BOTTOM DANCE.......... *Black Patti 8019* 100-125 27
(Vocals: Perry Bradford)
(Black Patti is an extremely rare label.)
(Simultaneously released on two labels)

WADE, Jimmy, as Wade's Moulin Rouge Orchestra

SOMEDAY SWEETHEART /
MOBILE BLUES.................. *Harmograph 893* 50-60 24

SOMEDAY SWEETHEART /
MOBILE BLUES................. *Paramount 20295* 40-50 24

SOMEDAY SWEETHEART /
MOBILE BLUES................... *Puritan 11295* 30-40 24
(Simultaneously released on three labels)

WADE'S MOULIN ROUGE ORCHESTRA:
see WADE, Jimmy

WADSWORTH, F. Wheeler, as Wadsworth's Novelty Dance Orchestra

BEALE STREET BLUES /
THE WEARY BLUES................. *Pathe 20441* 3-5 18

BEALE STREET BLUES /
THE WEARY BLUES......... *Pathe Actuelle 020925* 3-5 18

BEALE STREET BLUES /
THE WEARY BLUES................ *Perfect 14107* 2-4 18
(Simultaneously released on three labels)

HINDUSTAN / FRIVOLITY............. *Pathe 20443* 2-4 19

"PEE GEE'S" BLUES /
OLE MISS BLUES.................... *Pathe 22206* 3-5 19

SENSATION / RINGTAIL BLUES........ *Pathe 22050* 3-5 19

SENSATION /
RINGTAIL BLUES............ *Pathe Actuelle 020927* 3-5 19

SENSATION / RINGTAIL BLUES....... *Perfect 14109* 2-4 19
(Simultaneously released on three labels)

ST. LOUIS BLUES /
YELLOW DOG RAG................... *Pathe 22038* 3-5 19

ST. LOUIS BLUES /
YELLOW DOG RAG........... *Pathe Actuelle 020926* 3-5 19

ST. LOUIS BLUES /
YELLOW DOG RAG.................. *Perfect 14108* 2-4 19
(Simultaneously released on three labels)

WADSWORTH'S NOVELTY DANCE ORCHESTRA:
see WADSWORTH, F. Wheeler

WAGER, Roy, & His Orchestra:
see HAYMES, Joe, & His Orchestra

WAGNER, Sol S., & His Orchestra

COUNTIN' THE DAYS /
EVERYWHERE YOU GO.............. *Okeh 40973* 4-6 28
(Vocals: Paul Small)

I'M IN LOVE AGAIN / SOUTH WIND..... *Okeh 40827* 4-6 27
(Vocals: Russell Douglas)

MY SWEET GAL / TEACH ME.......... *Gennett 5311* 5-8 24

OKLAHOMA INDIAN JAZZ / HAVANA.... *Gennett 5313* 5-8 24

WALD, Jerry, & His Orchestra
(Jerry Wald: 1/15/19 – 1973)

POINCIANA / MISSISSIPPI DREAM BOAT... *Decca 4433* 2-4 44

SOMEONE TO WATCH OVER ME /
THE CONTINENTAL................ *Majestic 7150* 2-4 46

STRICTLY INSTRUMENTAL / HE WEARS A
PAIR OF SILVER WINGS
(Vocal: Anita Boyer)................... *Decca 4340* 3-5 42

TRAINS IN THE NIGHT / MAD ABOUT HIM, SAD
WITHOUT HIM, HOW CAN I BE GLAD WITHOUT
HIM BLUES (Vocal: Anita Boyer).......... *Decca 4345* 3-5 42

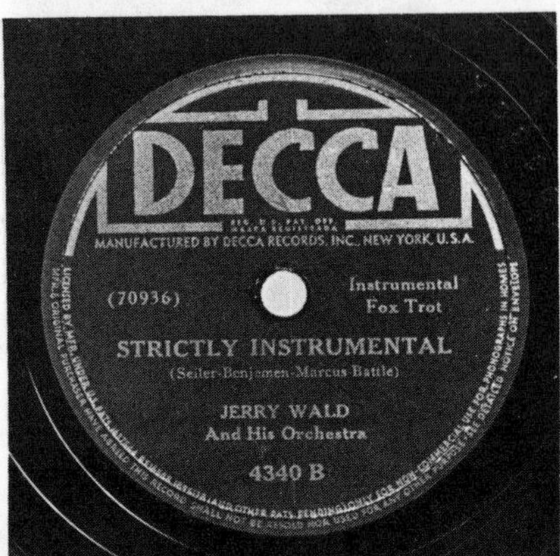

WALDMAN, Herman, & His Orchestra

LAZY RIVER (Vocals: Ken Switzer & Vernon Mills) /
GOT NO HONEY (Vocal: Ken Switzer)... *Brunswick 6181* 4-6 31

MARBLES / WAITING............... *Brunswick 4649* 5-8 29

OUT FOR NO GOOD (Vocal: Meri Bell) / FAIR AND
WARMER (Vocal: Rex Preis)............. *Bluebird B-5439* 5-8 34

WALKER, Don, & His Orchestra:
see KING, Henry, & His Orchestra

WALKUP, Johnny, as Jack/Johnny Walkup's Orchestra

I LIKE A LITTLE GIRL LIKE THAT /
ALONG THE HIGHWAY OF LOVE... *Champion 16108* 3-5 30
(Vocals: Russ Ebker)

I LIKE A LITTLE GIRL LIKE THAT /
ALONG THE HIGHWAY OF LOVE..... *Gennett 7300* 4-6 30
(Vocals: Russ Ebker)
(Simultaneously released on two labels)

I'M TICKLED PINK WITH A BLUE-EYED BABY /
THREE LITTLE WORDS.......... *Champion 16133* 4-6 31
(Vocals: Russ Ebker)
(The following two records are the last Champions by the Starr Piano Company.)

OUT IN THE COLD AGAIN / THE MOON
WAS YELLOW.................... *Champion 16832* 4-6 34
(Vocals: Juanita Sigritz)

P.S. – I LOVE YOU (Vocal: Juanita Sigritz) / BIGGER THAN
THE MOON (Vocal: Eddie James)..... *Champion 16831* 4-6 34

WALLACE, Ted, & His Campus Boys:
see CALIFORNIA RAMBLERS, The

WALLACE, Ted, & His Orchestra:
see CALIFORNIA RAMBLERS, The

WALLER, Thomas "Fats", & His Buddies
(Thomas Waller: 5/21/04 – 12/15/43)

LOOKIN' FOR ANOTHER SWEETIE /
WHEN I'M ALONE................ *Victor V-38110* 25-30 30
(Vocals: Orlando Roberson)

LOOKIN' GOOD BUT FEELIN' BAD /
I NEED SOMEONE LIKE YOU....... *Victor V-38086* 25-30 29
(Vocals: The Four Wanderers)

MINOR DRAG / HARLEM FUSS....... *Victor V-38050* 20-25 29

RIDIN' BUT WALKIN' / WON'T YOU GET
OFF IT, PLEASE?.................. *Victor V-38119* 25-30 30

WALLER, Thomas "Fats", & His Rhythm

ABDULLAH / WHO'LL TAKE
MY PLACE?..................... *Bluebird B-10419* 3-5 39
(Vocals: Fats Waller)

ALL MY LIFE / IT'S NO FUN........... *Victor 25296* 5-8 36
(Vocals: Fats Waller)

AM I IN ANOTHER WORLD? / MY FIRST
IMPRESSION OF YOU............... *Victor 25753* 3-5 38
(Vocals: Fats Waller)

AT TWILIGHT / FAT AND GREASY... *Bluebird B-10803* 4-6 40
(Vocals: Fats Waller)

BABY BROWN / BECAUSE OF
ONCE UPON A TIME................. *Victor 24846* 10-12 35
(Vocals: Fats Waller)

BACH UP TO ME (dialog by Fats Waller) / THE MEANEST
THING YOU EVER DID WAS KISS ME
(Vocal: Fats Waller)..................... *Victor 25536* 4-6 37

BELIEVE IT, BELOVED /
IF IT ISN'T LOVE.................... *Victor 24808* 5-8 34
(Vocals: Fats Waller)

BLACK MARIA (Vocal: Fats Waller) /
THE MOON IS LOW............. *Bluebird B-10624* 4-6 40

BLACK RASPBERRY JAM / PASWONKY... *Victor 25359* 8-10 36
(dialog by Fats Waller.)

BLESS YOU / IT'S THE TUNE
THAT COUNTS................ *Bluebird B-10393* 3-5 39
(Vocals: Fats Waller)

BOO-HOO / THE LOVE BUG
WILL BITE YOU..................... *Victor 25563* 4-6 37

BUCKIN' THE DICE / ALL THAT MEAT
AND NO POTATOES............ *Bluebird B-11102* 4-6 41
(Vocals: Fats Waller)

BUCK JUMPIN' / THE BELLS OF
SAN RAQUEL (Vocal: Fats Waller)... *Bluebird B-11324* 4-6 41

BY THE LIGHT OF THE SILVERY MOON (Vocals: Fats Waller & The Deep River Boys) / SWING OUT TO VICTORY
(Vocal: Fats Waller)............... *Bluebird B-11569* 4-6 42

CHRISTOPHER COLUMBUS /
US ON A BUS....................... *Victor 25295* 5-8 36
(Vocals: Fats Waller)

CLARINET MARMALADE / WINTER
WEATHER (Vocal: Fats Waller)...... *Bluebird B-11469* 4-6 42

COPPER COLORED GAL (Vocal: Fats Waller) /
I'M AT THE MERCY OF LOVE......... *Victor 25409* 5-8 36

CROSS PATCH / CABIN IN THE SKY.... *Victor 25315* 5-8 36
(Vocals: Fats Waller)

CRYIN' MOOD / TO A SWEET
PRETTY THING...................... *Victor 25551* 4-6 37
(Vocals: Fats Waller)

DARKTOWN STRUTTERS' BALL (Vocal: Fats Waller) /
I CAN'T GIVE YOU ANYTHING BUT LOVE
(Vocals: Fats Waller & Una Mae Carlisle)... *Bluebird B-10573* 3-5 39

DID ANYONE EVER TELL YOU? /
WHEN LOVE IS YOUNG............. *Victor 25537* 4-6 37
(Vocals: Fats Waller)

DINAH (Vocals: Fats Waller) /
LATCH ON (dialog by Fats Waller)........ *Victor 25471* 5-8 37

DON'T GIVE ME THAT JIVE / YOU MUST
BE LOSING YOUR MIND (by Fats Waller, His
Rhythm, & His Orchestra)........... *Bluebird B-11539* 5-8 42
(Vocals: Fats Waller)

DON'T YOU KNOW OR DON'T YOU CARE? /
LOST LOVE......................... *Victor 25604* 4-6 37
(Vocals: Fats Waller)

DO YOU HAVE TO GO? /
TWENTY-FOUR ROBBERS....... *Bluebird B-11222* 4-6 41
(Vocals: Fats Waller)

DREAM MAN / I'M GROWING
FONDER OF YOU.................... *Victor 24801* 5-8 34
(Vocals: Fats Waller)

EVERYBODY LOVES MY BABY (Vocal: Fats Waller) /
SCRAM!......................... *Bluebird B-10989* 4-6 40

EVERY DAY'S A HOLIDAY /
NEGLECTED......................... *Victor 25749* 4-6 38
(Vocals: Fats Waller)

GEORGIA MAY (Vocal: Fats Waller) / DON'T LET IT
BOTHER YOU (Vocal: Fats Waller with
dialog by Harry Dial)................... *Victor 24714* 5-8 34

GEORGIA ROCKIN' CHAIR / BROTHER, SEEK AND
YOU SHALL FIND.................. *Victor 25175* 4-6 35
(Vocals: Fats Waller)

GOT A BRAN' NEW SUIT /
THIEF IN THE NIGHT................ *Victor 25123* 4-6 35
(Vocals: Fats Waller)

HALLELUJAH! THINGS LOOK ROSY NOW /
TAIN'T GOOD (LIKE A NICKEL
MADE OF WOOD)................... *Victor 25478* 4-6 37
(Vocals: Fats Waller)

HAVIN' A BALL / I'M SORRY
I MADE YOU CRY................... *Victor 25515* 4-6 37
(Vocals: Fats Waller)

HONEY HUSH / YOU MEET THE NICEST PEOPLE IN
YOUR DREAMS................. *Bluebird B-10346* 4-6 39
(Vocals: Fats Waller)

HOW CAN YOU FACE ME? /
SWEETIE PIE....................... *Victor 24737* 5-8 34
(Vocals: Fats Waller)

I AIN'T GOT NOBODY / (OH SUSANNAH) DUST OFF
THAT OLD PIANNA................. *Victor 24888* 5-8 35
(Vocals: Fats Waller)

I JUST MADE UP WITH THAT OLD GIRL OF MINE /
THE CURSE OF AN ACHING HEART.... *Victor 25394* 4-6 36
(Vocals: Fats Waller)

I'LL NEVER SMILE AGAIN /
STAYIN' AT HOME.............. *Bluebird B-10841* 3-5 40
(Vocals: Fats Waller)

I LOVE TO WHISTLE / FLORIDA FLO... *Victor 25806* 4-6 38
(Vocals: Fats Waller)

I'M A HUNDRED PER CENT FOR YOU /
YOU FIT INTO THE PICTURE......... *Victor 24863* 5-8 35
(Vocals: Fats Waller)

I'M ALWAYS IN THE MOOD FOR YOU / SHE'S TALL,
SHE'S TAN, SHE'S TERRIFIC.......... *Victor 25671* 4-6 37
(Vocals: Fats Waller)

I'M CRAZY 'BOUT MY BABY / UNTIL THE REAL
THING COMES ALONG............... *Victor 25374* 4-6 36
(Vocals: Fats Waller)

I'M GONNA SALT AWAY SOME SUGAR /
BLUE EYES..................... *Bluebird B-10943* 4-6 40
(Vocals: Fats Waller)

I REPENT / HEADLINES
IN THE NEWS................... *Bluebird B-11188* 3-5 41
(Vocals: Fats Waller)

IT'S A SIN TO TELL A LIE /
BIG CHIEF DE SOTA................. *Victor 25342* 4-6 36
(Vocals: Fats Waller)

IT'S YOU WHO TAUGHT IT TO ME /
YOU'RE LETTIN' THE GRASS GROW
UNDER YOUR FEET............ *Bluebird B-10527* 4-6 39
(Vocals: Fats Waller)

I USED TO LOVE YOU (BUT IT'S ALL OVER NOW) /
ANITA.......................... *Bluebird B-10369* 3-5 39
(Vocals: Fats Waller)

I'VE GOT A NEW LEASE ON LOVE /
SWEET HEARTACHE................ *Victor 25580* 4-6 37
(Vocals: Fats Waller)

I'VE GOT MY FINGERS CROSSED /
SPREADIN' RHYTHM AROUND....... *Victor 25211* 5-8 35
(Vocals: Fats Waller)

I WANNA HEAR SWING SONGS / LET'S GET AWAY
FROM IT ALL (by Fats Waller at the electric organ,
accompanied by guitar & drums)....... *Bluebird B-11115* 4-6 41
(Vocals: Fats Waller)

I WISH I WERE TWINS /
ARMFUL O' SWEETNESS............ *Victor 24641* 5-8 34
(Vocals: Fats Waller)

JOINT IS JUMPIN', THE /
A HOPELESS LOVE AFFAIR.......... *Victor 25689* 4-6 38
(Vocals: Fats Waller)

LAST NIGHT A MIRACLE HAPPENED /
KISS ME WITH YOUR EYES...... *Bluebird B-10136* 4-6 39
(Vocals: Fats Waller)

LITTLE BIT INDEPENDENT, A /
SWEET THING...................... *Victor 25196* 4-6 36
(Vocals: Fats Waller)

LIVER LIP JONES / COME DOWN
TO EARTH, MY ANGEL.......... *Bluebird B-11010* 4-6 41
(Vocals: Fats Waller)

LOUSIANA FAIRY TALE / CINDERS.... *Victor 24898* 5-8 35
(Vocals: Fats Waller)

LOUNGING AT THE WALDORF (dialog by Fats Waller) /
LA-DE-DE, LA-DE-DA
(Vocal: Fats Waller)..................... *Victor 25430* 4-6 36

LOVE, I'D GIVE MY LIFE FOR YOU / I'LL DANCE AT
YOUR WEDDING............... *Bluebird B-10070* 4-6 38
(Vocals: Fats Waller)

LULU'S BACK IN TOWN /
SWEET AND SLOW................. *Victor 25063* 5-8 35
(Vocals: Fats Waller)

MAMACITA / SHORTNIN' BREAD
(Vocals: Fats Waller & chorus)....... *Bluebird B-11078* 4-6 41

MANDY / YOU'RE NOT THE ONLY
OYSTER IN THE STEW.............. *Victor 24738* 5-8 34
(Vocals: Fats Waller)

MIGHTY FINE / EEP, IPE,
WANNA PIECE OF PIE.......... *Bluebird B-10744* 4-6 40
(Vocals: Fats Waller)

MOON ROSE / GARBO GREEN.......... *Victor 25281* 5-8 36
(Vocals: Fats Waller)

MORE I KNOW YOU, THE /
LET'S SING AGAIN................ *Victor 25348* 4-6 36
(Vocals: Fats Waller)

MY MOMMIE SENT ME TO THE STORE / DRY BONES ... *Bluebird B-10892* 4-6 40
(Vocals: Fats Waller)

MY WINDOW FACES THE SOUTH / WHY DO HAWAIIANS SING ALOHA? ... *Victor 25762* 3-5 38
(Vocals: Fats Waller)

NIGHT WIND / I BELIEVE IN MIRACLES ... *Victor 24853* 5-8 35
(Vocals: Fats Waller)

OH! FRENCHY / CHEATIN' ON ME ... *Bluebird B-10658* 3-5 40
(Vocals: Fats Waller)

OLD GRAND DAD / LITTLE CURLY HAIR IN A HIGH CHAIR ... *Bluebird B-10698* 3-5 40
(Vocals: Fats Waller)

ON THE BUMPY ROAD TO LOVE / WE, THE PEOPLE ... *Victor 25898* 4-6 38
(Vocals: Fats Waller)

OOOH! LOOK-A THERE, AIN'T SHE PRETTY? / THAT NEVER-TO-BE-FORGOTTEN NIGHT ... *Victor 25255* 5-8 36
(Vocals: Fats Waller)

OUR LOVE WAS MEANT TO BE / I'D RATHER CALL YOU BABY ... *Victor 25681* 3-5 37
(Vocals: Fats Waller)

PANIC IS ON, THE / SUGAR ROSE ... *Victor 25266* 5-8 36
(Vocals: Fats Waller)

PAN-PAN / OH BABY, SWEET BABY (WHAT ARE YOU DOING TO ME?) ... *Bluebird B-11383* 4-6 41
(Vocals: Fats Waller)

PANTIN' IN THE PANTHER ROOM / I UNDERSTAND ... *Bluebird B-11175* 4-6 41
(Vocals: Fats Waller)

PLEASE KEEP ME IN YOUR DREAMS / NERO ... *Victor 25498* 3-5 37
(Vocals: Fats Waller)

PORTER'S LOVE SONG TO A CHAMBERMAID / DO ME A FAVOR ... *Victor 24648* 5-8 34
(Vocals: Fats Waller)

RHYME FOR LOVE / I ADORE YOU ... *Victor 25491* 4-6 37
(Vocals: Fats Waller)

RHYTHM AND ROMANCE / A SWEET BEGINNING LIKE THIS ... *Victor 25131* 5-8 35
(Vocals: Fats Waller)

SAD SAP SUCKER AM I / RUMP STEAK SERENADE (by Fats Waller, His Rhythm, & His Orchestra) ... *Bluebird B-11296* 4-6 41
(Vocals: Fats Waller)

SERENADE FOR A WEALTHY WIDOW (dialog by Fats Waller) / LET'S PRETEND THERE'S A MOON (Vocal: Fats Waller) ... *Victor 24742* 5-8 34

SHAME! SHAME! / TELL ME WITH YOUR KISSES ... *Bluebird B-7885* 5-8 38
(Vocals: Fats Waller)

SMARTY / I'M GONNA PUT YOU IN YOUR PLACE ... *Victor 25608* 5-8 37
(Vocals: Fats Waller)

SOMEBODY STOLE MY GAL / SUGAR BLUES ... *Victor 25194* 5-8 35
(Vocals: Fats Waller)

SOME RAINY DAY / 'TAIN'T WHAT YOU DO (IT'S THE WAY THAT CHA DO IT) ... *Bluebird B-10192* 4-6 39
(Vocals: Fats Waller)

SOMETHING TELLS ME / DON'T TRY TO CRY YOUR WAY BACK TO ME ... *Victor 25817* 4-6 38
(Vocals: Fats Waller)

S'POSIN' / FLOATIN' DOWN TO COTTON TOWN ... *Victor 25415* 5-8 36
(Vocals: Fats Waller)

(YOU'RE A) SQUARE FROM DELAWARE / "SEND ME" JACKSON ... *Bluebird B-10730* 4-6 40
(Vocals: Fats Waller)

STEP UP AND SHAKE MY HAND / UNDECIDED ... *Bluebird B-10184* 4-6 39
(Vocals: Fats Waller)

STOP PRETENDING / HEY! STOP KISSIN' MY SISTER ... *Bluebird B-10829* 4-6 40
(Vocals: Fats Waller)

SUITCASE SUSIE / YOUR FEET'S TOO BIG ... *Bluebird B-10500* 3-5 39
(Vocals: Fats Waller)

SWINGA-DILLA STREET / "FATS" WALLER'S ORIGINAL E FLAT BLUES (Vocal: Fats Waller) ... *Bluebird B-10858* 4-6 40

SWINGIN' THEM JINGLE BELLS / A THOUSAND DREAMS OF YOU ... *Victor 25483* 4-6 37
(Vocals: Fats Waller)

'TAIN'T NOBODY'S BIZNESS IF I DO / ABERCROMBIE HAD A ZOMBIE ... *Bluebird B-10967* 4-6 40
(Vocals: Fats Waller)

TAKE IT EASY / THERE'S GOING TO BE THE DEVIL TO PAY ... *Victor 25078* 5-8 35
(Vocals: Fats Waller)

THAT GETS IT, MR. JOE / CASH FOR YOUR TRASH ... *Bluebird B-11425* 5-8 42
(Vocals: Fats Waller)

THEN I'LL BE TIRED OF YOU / HAVE A LITTLE DREAM OF ME ... *Victor 24708* 5-8 34
(Vocals: Fats Waller)

THERE GOES MY ATTRACTION / BYE-BYE, BABY ... *Victor 25388* 5-8 36
(Vocals: Fats Waller)

THERE'S HONEY ON THE MOON TONIGHT / FAIR AND SQUARE ... *Victor 25891* 4-6 38
(Vocals: Fats Waller)

TRUCKIN' / THE GIRL I LEFT BEHIND ME ... *Victor 25116* 5-8 35
(Vocals: Fats Waller)

TWELFTH STREET RAG / SWEET SUE ... *Victor 25087* 5-8 35
(Vocals: Fats Waller)

TWO SLEEPY PEOPLE / I'LL NEVER FORGIVE MYSELF ... *Bluebird B-10000* 4-6 38
(Vocals: Fats Waller)

WAIT AND SEE / SQUEEZE ME ... *Bluebird B-10405* 4-6 39
(Vocals: Fats Waller)

WEST WIND / SING AN OLD FASHIONED SONG ... *Victor 25253* 4-6 36
(Vocals: Fats Waller)

WHAT A PRETTY MISS (Vocal: Fats Waller) / BOND STREET ... *Bluebird B-10437* 4-6 39

WHEN SOMEBODY THINKS YOU'RE WONDERFUL / YOU STAYED AWAY TOO LONG ... *Victor 25222* 4-6 36
(Vocals: Fats Waller)

WHERE IS THE SUN? / OLD PLANTATION ... *Victor 25550* 4-6 37
(Vocals: Fats Waller)

WHO'S AFRAID OF LOVE? / ONE IN A MILLION ... *Victor 25499* 4-6 37
(Vocals: Fats Waller)

WHOSE HONEY ARE YOU? / ROSETTA ... *Victor 24892* 5-8 35
(Vocals: Fats Waller)

WOE! IS ME (Vocal: Fats Waller) / LOAFIN' TIME (Vocals: Fats Waller & Herman Autrey) ... *Victor 25140* 4-6 35

YOU ASKED FOR IT – YOU GOT IT / GOT NO TIME ... *Bluebird B-10170* 4-6 39
(Vocals: Fats Waller)

YOU OUT-SMARTED YOURSELF / HOLD TIGHT ... *Bluebird B-10116* 3-5 39
(Vocals: Fats Waller)

YOU'RE LAUGHING AT ME / I CAN'T BREAK THE HABIT OF YOU ... *Victor 25530* 4-6 37
(Vocals: Fats Waller)

YOU'RE MY DISH / MORE POWER TO YOU ... *Victor 25679* 4-6 37
(Vocals: Fats Waller)

YOU'RE NOT THE KIND / WHY DO I LIE TO MYSELF ABOUT YOU? ... *Victor 25353* 4-6 36
(Vocals: Fats Waller)

YOU'RE SO DARN CHARMIN' / I'M ON A SEE-SAW ... *Victor 25120* 5-8 35
(Vocals: Fats Waller)

YOU'RE THE CUTEST ONE / I HATE TO TALK TO MYSELF ... *Victor 25039* 5-8 35
(Vocals: Fats Waller)

YOU'RE THE PICTURE / MY VERY GOOD FRIEND THE MILKMAN ... *Victor 25075* 4-6 35
(Vocals: Fats Waller)

YOUR SOCKS DON'T MATCH / UP JUMPED YOU WITH LOVE ... *Bluebird 30-0814* 3-5 42
(Vocals: Fats Waller)

YOU RUN YOUR MOUTH, I'LL RUN MY BUSINESS / TOO TIRED ... *Bluebird B-10779* 4-6 40
(Vocals: Fats Waller)

YOU SHOWED ME THE WAY / SAN ANTON' ... *Victor 25579* 4-6 37
(Vocals: Fats Waller)

YOU'VE BEEN READING MY MAIL / SPRING CLEANING ... *Victor 25554* 4-6 37
(Vocals: Fats Waller)

YOU'VE BEEN TAKING LESSONS IN LOVE / I'M GONNA SIT RIGHT DOWN AND WRITE MYSELF A LETTER ... *Victor 25044* 3-5 35
(Vocals: Fats Waller)

YOU'VE GOT ME UNDER YOUR THUMB / BEAT IT OUT ... *Victor 25672* 4-6 37
(Vocals: Fats Waller)

YOU WENT TO MY HEAD / LOST AND FOUND ... *Victor 25812* 4-6 38
(Vocals: Fats Waller)

WALLER, Thomas "Fats", His Rhythm & His Orchestra

CHANT OF THE GROOVE / COME AND GET IT (Vocal: Fats Waller) ... *Bluebird B-11262* 4-6 41

HOLD MY HAND / INSIDE ... *Victor 26045* 3-5 39
(Vocals: Fats Waller)

IN THE GLOAMING / THE SHEIK OF ARABY (Vocal: Fats Waller) ... *Victor 25847* 4-6 38

LET'S BREAK THE GOOD NEWS / I SIMPLY ADORE YOU ... *Victor 25830* 3-5 38
(Vocals: Fats Waller)

RUMP STEAK SERENADE / SAD SAP SUCKER AM I (by Fats Waller & His Rhythm) ... *Bluebird B-11296* 4-6 41
(Vocals: Fats Waller)

WE NEED A LITTLE LOVE (Vocal: Fats Waller) / JITTERBUG WALTZ ... *Bluebird B-11518* 3-5 42

YOU HAD AN EVENING TO SPARE / SKRONTCH ... *Victor 25834* 4-6 38
(Vocals: Fats Waller)

YOU MUST BE LOSING YOUR MIND / DON'T GIVE ME THAT JIVE (by Fats Waller & His Rhythm) ... *Bluebird B-11539* 5-8 42
(Vocals: Fats Waller)

WANDERERS, The

FOOTWARMER / NEALSKI ... *Bluebird B-5994* 5-8 35

GOOD MAN IS HARD TO FIND, A / IT'S YOU I ADORE ... *Bluebird B-5834* 5-8 35
(Vocals: Bert Dodson)

TIGER RAG (Vocals: by chorus) / NO-ONE TO SAY GOODBYE (Vocal: Dick Reinhart) ... *Bluebird B-5887* 5-8 35

WANDERERS' STOMP / I AIN'T GOT NOBODY (Vocals: by trio) ... *Bluebird B-5869* 5-8 35

WARD, Joe, as Joe Ward's Swanee Club Orchestra

TRAFFIC JAM / SCORCHIN' (Vocals: by trio) ... *Cameo 9026* 5-8 29

TRAFFIC JAM / SCORCHIN' (Vocals: by trio) ... *Lincoln 3055* 5-8 29

TRAFFIC JAM / SCORCHIN' (Vocals: by trio) ... *Romeo 830* 5-8 29
(Simultaneously released on three labels)

WARING, Fred, & His Pennsylvanians

(Fred Waring: 6/9/00 – 7/29/84)

(Waring remained active all his life, having conducted a concert less than 48 hours before his death, and a tour was planned for Fall 1984 to celebrate his 69th year in show business. Waring's Pennsylvanians recorded more than 2,000 titles, and in the 1940s he was the first band leader to adopt television with his own prime time show, a part of the General Electric program. Prior to that, the *Fred Waring Show* was the most popular radio show from 1940 to 1945. Waring and his band also starred in *Syncopation*, one of the first of the lavish Hollywood musicals.

ANCHORS AWEIGH / BUCKLE DOWN, WINSOCKI ... *Decca 23717* 2-4 46
(Vocals: orchestra and glee club)

ANY ICE TODAY, LADY? (Vocal: Poley McClintock) / THE PUMP SONG (by Irving Aaronson & His Commanders; Vocal: Phil Saxe) ... *Victor 20083* 3-5 26

BUTTON UP YOUR OVERCOAT (Vocals: by trio) / MY LUCKY STAR (Vocal: Roy Cropper) ... *Victor 21861* 2-4 29

COLLEGE MEDLEY / COLLEGE MEDLEY, PART II ... *Victor 24169* 2-4 32

DANCE OF THE BLUE DANUBE (Vocal: Tom Waring) / LAUGH, CLOWN, LAUGH! (Vocal: Fred Waring) ... *Victor 21308* 2-4 28

DANCING IN THE DARK / HIGH AND LOW ... *Victor 22708* 3-5 31
(Vocals: The Three Waring Girls & orchestra)

DREARY WEATHER (Vocal: Tom Waring) / ANY WAY THE WIND BLOWS ... *Victor 19422* 2-4 24

FAREWELL BLUES (Vocals: Fred Waring & orchestra) / STACK O' LEE BLUES ... *Victor 21508* 5-8 28

GLORIANNA (Vocal: Clare Hanlon) / LOVE TALE OF ALSACE LORRAINE (Vocals: Clare Hanlon, Fred Waring, & Nelson Keller) ... *Victor 21836* 3-5 29

GOOD FOR YOU, BAD FOR ME (Vocals: The Three Girl Friends) / THANK YOUR FATHER (Vocals: Will Morgan & The Three Girl Friends) ... *Victor 22326* 3-5 30

GOODNIGHT, SLEEP TIGHT (Vocal: Tom Waring) / THAT SWANEE RIVER SONG ... *Victor 19362* 2-4 24

HAVE A LITTLE FAITH IN ME (Vocal: Stuart Churchill) / CRYING FOR THE CAROLINES (Vocals: Will Morgan & orchestra) ... *Victor 22272* 3-5 30

HAY FOOT, STRAW FOOT / LET'S WANDER AWAY ... *Victor 19814* 2-4 25

HELLO BABY (Vocal: Will Morgan) / UNTIL THE REAL THING COMES ALONG (by Nat Shilkret & The Victor Orchestra; Vocal: Scrappy Lambert as Burt Lorin) ... *Victor 22266* 4-6 30

HERE IT IS MONDAY, AND I'VE STILL GOT A DOLLAR (Vocals: Fred Waring, Tom Waring, & Clare Hanlon) / ANYBODY'S COLLEGE SONG (Vocals: by orchestra) ... *Victor 24181* 3-5 33

HONEST! REALLY! TRULY! (Vocal: Clare Hanlon) / I'M ONLY GUESSIN' (Vocals: The Three Waring Girls) ... *Victor 22900* 2-4 32

HOW'M I DOIN'? (HEY-HEY) / RHYMES ... *Victor 22978* 3-5 32
(Vocals: Johnny "Scat" Davis, Poley McClintock, & orchestra)

I CAN'T MAKE HER HAPPY (Vocal: Clare Hanlon) / THE SONG I LOVE (Vocal: Fred Waring) ... *Victor 21810* 2-4 29

I FOUND A MILLION-DOLLAR BABY (Vocals: Clare Hanlon & The Three Waring Girls) / SING A LITTLE JINGLE (Vocals: The Three Waring Girls & orchestra) ... *Victor 22707* 3-5 31

IN A LITTLE GARDEN / TONIGHT'S MY NIGHT WITH BABY ... *Victor 20078* 2-4 26
(Vocals: Tom Waring)

I SAY IT'S SPINACH / ON A ROOF IN MANHATTAN ... *Victor 22939* 3-5 32
(Vocals: Nelson Keller, Stuart Churchill, & Clare Hanlon)

I'VE NEVER SEEN A STRAIGHT BANANA (Vocals: by orchestra) / I WONDER HOW I LOOK WHEN I'M ASLEEP (Vocals: Tom Waring & orchestra) ... *Victor 20562* 2-4 27

I WANT THE WORLD TO KNOW / SAY THAT YOU LOVE ME ... *Victor 21783* 2-4 28
(Vocals: Fred Waring)

I WANT TO BE HAPPY (Vocals: Clare Hanlon, Will Morgan, & Poley McClintock) / TEA FOR TWO (Vocals: The Three Girl Friends) ... *Victor 22292* 3-5 30

JERICHO (Vocals: Fred Waring & orchestra) / I'LL ALWAYS BE IN LOVE WITH YOU (Vocals: Clare Hanlon & chorus) ... *Victor 21870* 2-4 29

JUST A COTTAGE SMALL / IN MY GONDOLA (Vocals: by orchestra) ... *Victor 20010* 2-4 26

JUST ANOTHER DAY WASTED AWAY / SING ME A BABY SONG ... *Victor 20724* 2-4 27
(Vocals: Tom Waring)

JUST HOT! / — ... *Victor 19377* 3-5 24

KEEP SMILING AT TROUBLE / OH! MABEL ... *Victor 19533* 4-6 25

LET'S HAVE ANOTHER CUP O' COFFEE (Vocals: Chick Bullock & The Three Waring Girls) / SOFT LIGHTS AND SWEET MUSIC (Vocals: The Three Waring Girls) ... *Victor 22936* 3-5 32

LITTLE PEACH (Vocal: Tom Waring) / SWANEE BUTTERFLY ... *Victor 19636* 2-4 25

LITTLE WHITE LIES / GEE, BUT I'D LIKE TO MAKE YOU HAPPY ... *Victor 22492* 3-5 30
(Vocals: Clare Hanlon)

LOOK AT THOSE EYES (Vocal: Tom Waring) / COLLEGIATE (Vocals: by orchestra) ... *Victor 19648* 2-4 25

LOVE FOR SALE / WHERE HAVE YOU BEEN? ... *Victor 22598* 3-5 31
(Vocals: The Three Waring Girls)

MAYBE I'LL BABY YOU / IF I CAN'T HAVE YOU ... *Victor 21206* 2-4 28
(Vocals: Tom Waring)

MAYBE THIS IS LOVE / POMPANOLA ... *Victor 21788* 2-4 29
(Vocals: Fred Waring)

MEMORY LANE (Vocal: Tom Waring) / DOWN HOME BLUES ... *Victor 19303* 3-5 24

MIGHTY BLUE (Vocal: Tom Waring) / FRESHIE (Vocals: by orchestra) ... *Victor 19784* 2-4 25

MY CASTLE IN SPAIN IS A SHACK IN THE LANE / I USED TO LOVE HER IN THE MOONLIGHT ... *Victor 21900* 2-4 29
(Vocals: Clare Hanlon)

MY SIN (Vocal: Clare Hanlon) / WHEN MY DREAMS COME TRUE (Vocals: by trio) ... *Victor 21977* 2-4 29

NAVY BLUES / ALMA MAMMY ... *Victor 22254* 3-5 30
(Vocals: Clare Hanlon)

OH DONNA CLARA! (Vocal: Clare Hanlon) / ELIZABETH (Vocals: The Three Waring Girls) ... *Victor 22655* 3-5 31

OLD YAZOO (Vocals: Frank Zullo & orchestra) / THE OLD MAN OF THE MOUNTAIN (Vocals: Poley McClintock & Chick Bullock) ... *Victor 24062* 3-5 32

OUT OF A MILLION (YOU'RE THE ONLY ONE) (Vocal: Tom Waring) / HAVE A LITTLE FUN ... *Victor 19471* 2-4 24

PICNIC FOR TWO (Vocals: Nelson Keller, Clare Hanlon, & Tom Waring) / I HEARD (Vocals: Johnny "Scat" Davis, Frank Zullo & Poley McClintock) ... *Victor 24030* 2-4 32

RED-HOT CHICAGO (Vocal: Fred Waring) / WASN'T IT BEAUTIFUL WHILE IT LASTED? (Vocals: Stuart Churchill & The Three Girl Friends) ... *Victor 22325* 3-5 30

ROSES OF YESTERDAY / MY WINDOW OF DREAMS (Vocal: Tom Waring) ... *Victor 21676* 2-4 28

SINCE I FOUND YOU / HELLO, SWANEE, HELLO! ... *Victor 20467* 2-4 27
(Vocals: Tom Waring)

STACK O' LEE BLUES / STAVIN' CHANGE (by Paul Whiteman & His Orchestra as The Virginians; Vocal: Vernon Dalhart) ... *Victor 19189* 4-6 23

TELL ME WHY YOU SMILE, MONA LISA (Vocal: Tom Waring) / WITH SUMMER COMING ON (Vocals: Fred Waring, Nelson Keller, Clare Hanlon, & Tom Waring) ... *Victor 24016* 2-4 32

THAT MELODY OF LOVE (Vocals: Fred & Tom Waring) / WAS IT A DREAM? (Vocal: Tom Waring) ... *Victor 21297* 2-4 28

THEN YOU'VE NEVER BEEN BLUE (Vocal: Clare Hanlon) / MY ANNAPOLIS AND YOU (Vocals: Unknown) ... *Victor 21974* 2-4 29

WEST, A NEST AND YOU, THE / SLEEP (theme song) (Vocals: Fred & Tom Waring) ... *Victor 19172* 2-4 23

WHAT A NIGHT FOR SPOONING / HIGH UP ON A HILL TOP ... *Victor 21715* 2-4 28
(Vocals: Clare Hanlon)

WHERE DO YOU WORK-A, JOHN? / I LOVE THE COLLEGE GIRLS ... *Victor 20378* 2-4 27
(Vocals: by orchestra)

WHO'S BLUE NOW? (Vocals: by orchestra) / STAY OUT OF THE SOUTH (by The Coon-Sanders Orchestra; Vocals: Carleton Coon & Joe Sanders) ... *Victor 21258* 4-6 28

WITHOUT LOVE (Vocal: Tom Waring) / SO BEATS MY HEART FOR YOU (Vocals: Stuart Churchill & The Three Girl Friends) ... *Victor 22486* 3-5 30

WITH YOU (Vocals: Nelson Keller, Clare Hanlon & Will Morgan) / THERE'S DANGER IN YOUR EYES, CHERIE (Vocal: Clare Hanlon) ... *Victor 22293* 3-5 30

WOB-A-LY WALK (Vocal: Fred Waring) / I SCREAM – YOU SCREAM – WE ALL SCREAM FOR ICE CREAM (Vocals: Fred Waring, Poley McClintock, & orchestra) ... *Victor 21099* 3-5 28

YALE BLUES (Vocals: Fred Waring, Francis Foster & Fred Culley) / COLLEGIANA (Vocals: Fred & Tom Waring) ... *Victor 21307* 3-5 28

YOU'LL GET BY (WITH A TWINKLE IN YOUR EYE) (Vocals: Fred Waring, Nelson Keller, & Clare Hanlon) / FIT AS A FIDDLE (Vocal: Frank Zullo) ... *Victor 24168* 3-5 32

WARNER, Byron H., as Warner's Seven Aces

also see BENNETT, Ralph, as Warner's Seven Aces

ACE OF SPADES / I'D LIKE TO BE YOUR SHEIK FOR AWHILE ... *Okeh 40080* 3-5 24

BESSIE COULDN'T HELP IT (Vocal: J. L. Richmond) / LONGING FOR YOU ... *Okeh 40198* 4-6 24

BLUES HAVE GOT ME, THE / WHO TOLD YOU? ... *Columbia 336-D* 3-5 25

IN A TENT / EDDIE STEADY ... *Okeh 4888* 3-5 23

LONESOME LOVESICK GOT-TO-HAVE-MY-DADDY BLUES / MEAN EYES ... *Okeh 4924* 3-5 23

LOVE TIME / ROCK-A-BYE MY BABY BLUES ... *Okeh 40201* 3-5 24

WHEN MY SUGAR WALKS DOWN THE STREET / CHEATIN' ON ME ... *Columbia 305-D* 4-6 25

WONDER IF SHE'S LONELY TOO? / DREAM GIRL OF PI K. A. ... *Okeh 4911* 3-5 23

WARNER'S SEVEN ACES:

see BENNETT, Ralph, and see WARNER, Byron H.

WARNOW, Mark, & His Orchestra

(Mark Warnow: 4/10/02 – 10/49)

COCKTAILS FOR TWO (Vocal: Barry Wood) / THE MUSIC GOES 'ROUND AND AROUND (Vocals: The Hit Paraders) ... *Victor 27868* 2-4 42

I DON'T WANT TO SET THE WORLD ON FIRE (Vocals: Barry Wood & The Hit Paraders) / ALL THE THINGS YOU ARE (Vocal: Joan Edwards) ... *Victor 27866* 2-4 42

WHERE OR WHEN (Vocals: The Hit Paraders) / TI-PI-TIN (Vocals: Joan Edwards, Barry Wood, & The Hit Paraders) ... *Victor 27865* 2-4 42

WOODPECKER SONG (Vocals: Joan Edwards & The Hit Paraders) / THESE FOOLISH THINGS REMIND ME OF YOU (Vocal: Barry Wood) ... *Victor 27867* 2-4 42

WASHINGTONIANS, The:

see ELLINGTON, Duke, & His Orchestra

WASHINGTON, Steve, & His Orchestra

(Steve Washington: circa 1900 – circa 1/36)

BLUE RIVER / LOVE ME ... *Vocalion 2609* 10-12 34
(Vocals: Steve Washington)

WE WERE THE BEST OF FRIENDS / SING A LITTLE LOW-DOWN TUNE ... *Vocalion 2598* 12-15 34
(Vocals: Steve Washington)

WATSON, Leo, & His Orchestra

(Leo Watson: 2/27/98 – 5/2/50)

JA DA / IT'S THE TUNE THAT COUNTS ... *Decca 2959* 5-8 39
(Vocals: Leo Watson)

MAN WITH THE MANDOLIN, THE / UTT DA ZAY (THE TAILOR SONG) ... *Decca 2750* 5-8 39
(Vocals: Leo Watson)

WEBB, Chick, & His Little Chicks

(Chick Webb: 2/10 circa 1909 – 6/16/39)

I GOT RHYTHM / SWEET SUE, JUST YOU ... *Decca 1759* 5-8 37

IN A LITTLE SPANISH TOWN / I AIN'T GOT NOBODY ... *Decca 1513* 5-8 37

WEBB, Chick, & His Orchestra

ARE YOU HERE TO STAY? (Vocal: Charles Linton) / LOVE AND KISSES (Vocal: Ella Fitzgerald) ... *Decca 494* 5-8 35

A-TISKET, A-TASKET (Vocals: Ella Fitzgerald & chorus) / LIZA ... *Decca 1840* 2-4 38

BLUE LOU / SWINGING ON THE RESERVATION (Vocal: Ella Fitzgerald) ... *Decca 1065* 5-8 36

DIPSY DOODLE (Vocal: Ella Fitzgerald) / MIDNITE IN A MADHOUSE ... *Decca 1587* 4-6 38

DOWN HOME RAG / CRYING MY HEART OUT FOR YOU (Vocal: Ella Fitzgerald) ... *Decca 785* 5-8 36

ELLA (Vocals: Ella Fitzgerald & Taft Jordan) / I FOUND MY YELLOW BASKET (Vocal: Ella Fitzgerald) ... *Decca 2148* 2-4 36

FACTS AND FIGURES / SING ME A SWING SONG (Vocal: Ella Fitzgerald) ... *Decca 830* 5-8 36

GO HARLEM / DEVOTING MY TIME TO YOU (Vocal: Ella Fitzgerald) ... *Decca 995* 5-8 36

GOTTA PEBBLE IN MY SHOW (Vocal: Ella Fitzgerald) / WHO YA HUNCHIN'? ... *Decca 2231* 4-6 38

HEEBIE JEEBIES / SOFT AND SWEET ... *Vocalion 1607* 20-25 31

I CAN'T STOP LOVING YOU / 'TAIN'T WHAT YOU DO (IT'S THE WAY THAT CHA DO IT) ... *Decca 2310* 3-5 39
(Vocals: Ella Fitzgerald)

I GOT A GUY (Vocal: Ella Fitzgerald) / HARLEM CONGO ... *Decca 1681* 4-6 37

I'LL CHASE THE BLUES AWAY (Vocal: Ella Fitzgerald) / I MAY BE WRONG BUT I THINK YOU'RE WONDERFUL (Vocal: Taft Jordan) ... *Decca 640* 5-8 35

I'M JUST A JITTERBUG (Vocal: Ella Fitzgerald) / AZURE ... *Decca 1899* 3-5 38

I'M UP A TREE / HAVE MERCY ... *Decca 2468* 3-5 39
(Vocals: Ella Fitzgerald)

IT'S FOXY / MY HEART BELONGS TO DADDY ... *Decca 2309* 3-5 39
(Vocals: Ella Fitzgerald)

IT'S OVER BECAUSE WE'RE THROUGH (Vocal: Taft Jordan) / DON'T BE THAT WAY ... *Decca 483* 5-8 35

IT'S SLUMBERTIME ALONG THE SWANEE / CHEW-CHEW-CHEW (YOUR BUBBLE GUM) ... *Decca 2389* 3-5 39
(Vocals: Ella Fitzgerald)

I WANT TO BE HAPPY / HALLELUJAH! ... *Decca 15039* 5-8 38
(Vocals: Ella Fitzgerald.)
(This is an oversize 12-inch 78 rpm)

JUST A SIMPLE MELODY / HOLIDAY IN HARLEM ... *Decca 1521* 5-8 37
(Vocals: Ella Fitzgerald)

LOVE IS THE THING, SO THEY SAY (Vocals: Ella Fitzgerald) / THAT NAUGHTY WALTZ ... *Decca 1356* 5-8 37

LOVE MARCHES ON (Vocal: by trio) / GEE, BUT YOU'RE SWELL (Vocal: Louis Jordan) ... *Decca 1115* 4-6 37

LOVE, YOU'RE JUST A LAUGH (Vocal: Ella Fitzgerald) / THERE'S FROST ON THE MOON (Vocals: by trio) ... *Decca 1114* 5-8 37

MacPHERSON IS REHEARSIN' (TO SWING) / I LET A TEAR FALL IN THE RIVER ... *Decca 2080* 3-5 38
(Vocals: Ella Fitzgerald)

ONE SIDE OF ME / LITTLE WHITE LIES ... *Decca 2556* 3-5 39
(Vocals: Ella Fitzgerald)

ON THE SUNNY SIDE OF THE STREET (Vocal: Taft Jordan) / BLUE MINOR ... *Decca 172* 8-10 34

PACK UP YOUR SINS AND GO TO THE DEVIL / EVERYBODY STEP ... *Decca 1894* 3-5 38
(Vocals: Ella Fitzgerald)

RHYTHM AND ROMANCE (Vocal: Ella Fitzgerald) / MOONLIGHT AND MAGNOLIAS (Vocal: Charles Linton) ... *Decca 588* 5-8 35

RUSTY HINGE (Vocal: Louis Jordan) / CRYIN' MOOD (Vocal: Ella Fitzgerald) ... *Decca 1273* 4-6 37

SPINNIN' THE WEBB / WACKY DUST (Vocal: Ella Fitzgerald) ... *Decca 2021* 3-5 38

SQUEEZE ME / IF DREAMS COME TRUE (Vocal: Ella Fitzgerald) ... *Decca 1716* 3-5 38

STRICTLY JIVE / ROCK IT FOR ME (Vocal: Ella Fitzgerald) ... *Decca 1586* 5-8 37

SUGAR PIE / THAT WAS MY HEART ... *Decca 2665* 3-5 39
(Vocals: Ella Fitzgerald)

THAT RHYTHM MAN (Vocal: Taft Jordan) / LONA ... *Decca 173* 8-10 34

UNDECIDED (Vocal: Ella Fitzgerald) / IN THE GROOVE AT THE GROVE ... *Decca 2323* 3-5 39

UNDER THE SPELL OF THE BLUES / A LITTLE BIT LATER ON ... *Decca 831* 5-8 36
(Vocals: Ella Fitzgerald)

WAKE UP AND LIVE (Vocals: Ella Fitzgerald & trio) / IT'S SWELL OF YOU (Vocal: Louis Jordan) ... *Decca 1213* 4-6 37

WHAT A SHUFFLE / I'VE GOT THE SPRING FEVER BLUES (Vocal: Ella Fitzgerald) ... *Decca 1087* 5-8 36

WHEN I GET LOW I GET HIGH / TAKE ANOTHER GUESS ... *Decca 1123* 5-8 37
(Vocals: Ella Fitzgerald)

(IF YOU CAN'T SING IT) YOU'LL HAVE TO SWING IT / VOTE FOR MR. RHYTHM ... *Decca 1032* 5-8 36
(Vocals: Ella Fitzgerald)

YOU SHOWED ME THE WAY (Vocal: Ella Fitzgerald) / CLAP HANDS! HERE COMES CHARLEY ... *Decca 1220* 5-8 37

WEBB, Chick, as Chick Webb's Savoy Orchestra

BLUE MINOR / LONESOME MOMENTS ... *Okeh 41572* 15-20 34

I CAN'T DANCE (I GOT ANTS IN MY PANTS) (Vocal: Taft Jordan) / IMAGINATION (Vocal: Chuck Richards) ... *Columbia 2920-D* 12-15 34

IF DREAMS COME TRUE / LET'S GET TOGETHER (theme song) ... *Columbia 2883-D* 12-15 34

TRUE / IF IT AIN'T LOVE ... *Okeh 41571* 12-15 34
(Vocals: Charles Linton)

WHY SHOULD I BEG FOR LOVE? (Vocal: Taft Jordan) / STOMPING AT THE SAVOY ... *Columbia 2926-D* 12-15 34

WEBB'S NOVELTY ENTERTAINERS

JADE LADY / GEMS ... *Pathe 22383* 2-4 20

OLD MAN JAZZ / WHOSE BABY ARE YOU? ... *Pathe 22367* 3-5 20

WEBSTER, Carl, as Carl Webster's Yale Collegians

IF I'M WITHOUT YOU (Vocals: Stew Pletcher, Bob Bruce, Al Thompson & Neil Waterman) / DREAM CHILD ... *Columbia 139-P* 10-12 30
(This is a personal recording)

PUTTIN' ON THE RITZ (Vocal: Stew Pletcher) / WITH YOU (Vocal: Dick Webster) ... *Odeon ONY-36054* 5-8 30

PUTTIN' ON THE RITZ (Vocal: Stew Pletcher) / WITH YOU (Vocal: Dick Webster) ... *Okeh 41393* 5-8 30
(Simultaneously released on two labels)

WEEKS, Anson, & His California Orchestra

(Anson Weeks: 2/14/96 – 2/7/69)

EARFUL OF MUSIC, AN / YOUR HEAD ON MY SHOULDER ... *Brunswick 6989* 2-4 34
(Vocals: Kay St. Germaine)

IN MY COUNTRY THAT MEANS LOVE / IF IT ISN'T LOVE ... *Brunswick 7350* 2-4 35
(Vocals: Ben Gage)

LONELY FEET / WE WERE SO YOUNG........................ *Brunswick 7349* 2-4 34
(Vocals: Kay St. Germaine)

SWEETIE PIE / MY WHOLE DAY IS SPOILED.................. *Brunswick 6965* 2-4 34
(Vocals: Kay St. Germaine)

WHAT ABOUT ME? (Vocal: Ben Gage) / HAVE A LITTLE DREAM ON ME
(Vocals: Kay St. Germaine & Ben Gage)... *Brunswick 6969* 2-4 34

WHEN MY SHIP COMES IN (Vocal: Ben Gage) / OKAY, TOOTS (Vocal: Frank Saputo)... *Brunswick 6990* 3-5 34

WEEKS, Anson, & His Hotel Mark Hopkins Orchestra

IF I HAD A GIRL LIKE YOU (Vocal: Warren Luce) / RO-RO-ROLLIN' ALONG
(Vocal: Irving Kaufman).............. *Columbia 2211-D* 3-5 30

I'M SORRY, DEAR / WAS IT WRONG?................ *Columbia 2552-D* 3-5 31
(Vocals: Don Raymond)

SENORITA / PLODDIN' ALONG.... *Columbia 1742-D* 2-4 29

SOME DAY SOON / ONLY FOR YOU (Vocal: Warren Luce)....... *Columbia 1915-D* 2-4 29

SUSIANNA / GIVE YOUR LITTLE BABY LOTS OF LOVIN'.......... *Columbia 40004-D* 3-5 29
(Vocals: Unknown)

WEEKS, Anson, & His Orchestra

BREEZE, THE (Vocal: Kay St. Germaine) / AND I STILL DO
(Vocal: Pete Fylling).................. *Brunswick 6946* 2-4 34

BUCKIN' THE WIND (Vocal: Carl Ravazza) / GIVE ME LIBERTY OR GIVE ME LOVE
(Vocal: Bob Crosby).................. *Brunswick 6665* 3-5 33

DREAM HOUSE / WOB-A-LY WALK... *Columbia 1409-D* 3-5 28

FAREWELL TO ARMS / MEET ME IN THE GLOAMING..... *Brunswick 6524* 3-5 33
(Vocals: Donald Novis)

GIRL WITH THE DREAMY EYES / I'M ON A SEE-SAW................ *Brunswick 7510* 2-4 35
(Vocals: Unknown)

I ONLY HAVE EYES FOR YOU (Vocal: Kay St. Germaine) / A NEW MOON IS OVER MY SHOULDER
(Vocal: Fred Williams).................. *Brunswick 6944* 3-5 34

IT'S NOT A SECRET ANY MORE (Vocal: Bob Crosby) / LOUISVILLE LADY
(Vocal: Carl Ravazza).................. *Brunswick 6604* 3-5 33

IT WAS A NIGHT IN JUNE (Vocal: Harriet Lee) / IT'S SUNDAY DOWN IN CAROLINE
(Vocals: Anson Weeks)................ *Brunswick 6569* 3-5 33

I'VE GOT A FEELIN' YOU'RE FOOLIN' (Vocal: Unknown) / BROADWAY RHYTHM........... *Brunswick 7515* 2-4 35

MAN ON THE FLYING TRAPEZE / MAN ON THE FLYING TRAPEZE, PART II.. *Brunswick 6639* 3-5 33
(Vocals: Frank Saputo)

MARCHING ALONG TOGETHER (Vocal: Bob Crosby) / BLUE ROSES (Vocal: Carl Ravazza).. *Brunswick 6619* 3-5 33

MELODY IN A / SONG OF INDIA..... *Brunswick 6772* 3-5 34

MOONLIGHT AND SHADOWS (Vocal: Frank Saputo) / HOW COULD YOU? (Vocal: Margie Dee).... *Decca 1134* 4-6 37

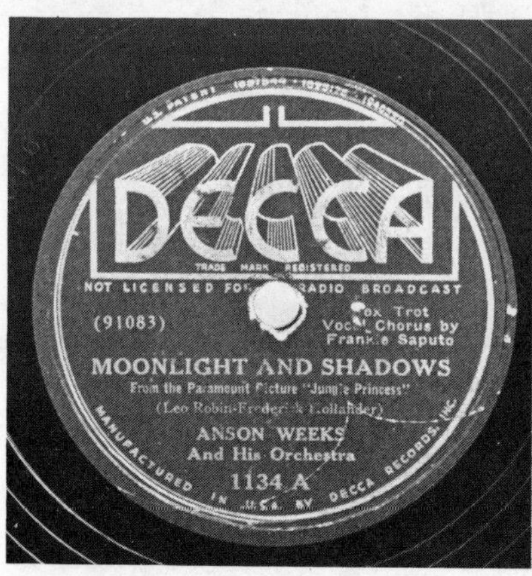

MY BLUEBIRD'S SINGING THE BLUES / THANK HEAVEN FOR YOU....... *Brunswick 6575* 3-5 33
(Vocals: Anson Weeks)

MY VERY GOOD FRIEND THE MILKMAN / THE TRAFFIC WAS TERRIFIC..... *Brunswick 7477* 2-4 35
(Vocals: Unknown)

SITTIN' ON A LOG / SITTIN' UP WAITIN' FOR YOU................ *Brunswick 6727* 2-4 34
(Vocals: Bob Crosby)

THROW ANOTHER LOG ON THE FIRE (Vocal: Frank Saputo) / MEMPHIS BY MORNIN'
(Vocal: Pete Fylling).................. *Brunswick 6730* 3-5 34

WAITIN' AT THE GATE FOR KATY / OH ME! OH MY! OH YOU!.......................... *Brunswick 6795* 3-5 34
(Vocals: Bob Crosby)

WILD HONEY (Vocal: Ben Gage) / IN A MIST (by Frankie Trumbauer & His Orchestra)... *Brunswick 6997* 5-8 34

YOU CAN TELL SHE COMES FROM DIXIE (Vocal: Frank Saputo) / TWINKLE, TWINKLE, LITTLE STAR
(Vocal: Margie Dee)..................... *Decca 1140* 4-6 37

YOU'VE GOT EVERYTHING (Vocal: Bob Crosby) / I'LL BE FAITHFUL
(Vocal: Pete Fylling).................. *Brunswick 6661* 2-4 33

WEEMS, Ted, & His Orchestra

(Ted Weems: 9/26/01 – 5/6/63)

BABY DOLL (Vocal: Parker Gibbs) / IF YOU WANT THE RAINBOW (YOU MUST HAVE THE RAIN)
(Vocal: Art Jarrett)...................... *Victor 21670* 3-5 28

BIG BOY! / SAVANNAH (THE GEORGIANNA BLUES)......... *Victor 19344* 4-6 24

BLUE ROSE / DON'T FORGET TO REMEMBER..................... *Victor 19274* 2-4 24

BLUE SKY AVENUE / TALKIN' TO MYSELF........... *Columbia 2957-D* 5-8 34
(Vocals: Red Ingle)

BUT LOVE / LITTLE JOE.............. *Victor 22624* 5-8 31
(Vocals: Art Jarrett)

CELEBRATIN' (Vocal: Red Ingle) / LAZY WEATHER (Vocal: Perry Como with whistling by Elmo Tanner)............... *Decca 822* 4-6 36

COVERED WAGON DAYS / SOMEBODY STOLE MY GAL.......... *Victor 19212* 3-5 24

DOIN' THE UPTOWN LOWDOWN / BUCKIN' THE WIND............. *Bluebird B-5236* 5-8 33
(Vocals: Parker Gibbs)

DOIN' THE UPTOWN LOWDOWN / BUCKIN' THE WIND.............. *Electradisk 2119* 15-20 33
(Vocals: Parker Gibbs)

DOIN' THE UPTOWN LOWDOWN / BUCKIN' THE WIND............... *Sunrise S-3319* 15-20 33
(Vocals: Parker Gibbs)
(Simultaneously released on three labels)

FIVE-PIECE BAND (Vocal: Parker Gibbs) / FOOLED BY THE MOON (Vocal: Perry Como with whistling by Elmo Tanner)............... *Decca 921* 4-6 36

GIRL FRIEND OF A BOY FRIEND OF MINE, A (Vocal: Parker Gibbs) / MY BABY JUST CARES FOR ME
(Vocal: Art Jarrett)...................... *Victor 22499* 4-6 30

HARMONICA HARRY (Vocal: Parker Gibbs) / THE MAN FROM THE SOUTH (Vocals: Art Jarrett, Parker Gibbs, & chorus).................. *Victor 22238* 5-8 30

HEARTACHES (whistling by Elmo Tanner) / MARCHING ALONG TOGETHER (Vocals: Dudley Fosdick, Wes Vaughn, & Elmo Tanner)... *Bluebird B-5131* 3-5 33

HEARTACHES (whistling by Elmo Tanner) / MARCHING ALONG TOGETHER (Vocals: Dudley Fosdick, Wes Vaughn, & Elmo Tanner)... *Electradisk 2037* 10-12 33

HEARTACHES (whistling by Elmo Tanner) / MARCHING ALONG TOGETHER (Vocals: Dudley Fosdick, Wes Vaughn, & Elmo Tanner).... *Sunrise S-3212* 10-12 33
(Simultaneously released on three labels)

HIGHWAYS ARE HAPPY WAYS (Vocal: Parker Gibbs & Dusty Rhodes) / IT WAS ONLY A SUN SHOWER
(Vocal: Dusty Rhodes).................... *Victor 20910* 4-6 27

HE'S TALL, DARK AND HANDSOME / NOTHIN' ON MY MIND................ *Victor 21364* 4-6 28
(Vocals: Parker Gibbs)

HOLD YOUR MAN (Vocal: Andrea Marsh) / TROUBLE IN PARADISE (Vocal: Andrea Marsh with whistling by Elmo Tanner)......... *Bluebird B-5130* 5-8 33

HOLD YOUR MAN (Vocal: Andrea Marsh) / TROUBLE IN PARADISE (Vocal: Andrea Marsh with whistling by Elmo Tanner)......... *Electradisk 2036* 15-20 33

HOLD YOUR MAN (Vocal: Andrea Marsh) / TROUBLE IN PARADISE (Vocal: Andrea Marsh with whistling by Elmo Tanner)......... *Sunrise S-3211* 15-20 33
(Simultaneously released on three labels)

HY'A DUCHESS (Vocals: Andrea Marsh, Parker Gibbs, & chorus) / JUGGLING A JIGSAW
(Vocal: Red Ingle)..................... *Victor 24265* 5-8 33

IF I EVER CRY (YOU'LL NEVER KNOW) / SIBERIA............................ *Victor 19722* 4-6 25

IF I HAD SOMEBODY TO LOVE / LET ME GIVE MY HAPPINESS TO YOU............. *Bluebird B-5148* 5-8 33
(Vocals: Elmo Tanner)

IF I HAD SOMEBODY TO LOVE / LET ME GIVE MY HAPPINESS TO YOU............. *Electradisk 2047* 15-20 33
(Vocals: Elmo Tanner)

IF I HAD SOMEBODY TO LOVE / LET ME GIVE MY HAPPINESS TO YOU.............. *Sunrise S-3229* 15-20 33
(Vocals: Elmo Tanner)
(Simultaneously released on three labels)

I LIKE MOUNTAIN MUSIC (Vocal: Elmo Tanner) / SHE CHANGED HER HI-DE-HI-DE
(Vocals: Red Ingle & trio)................. *Victor 24266* 5-8 33

I'LL KEEP WARM ALL WINTER (WITH MY SUNNY SUMMER LOVE) (Vocal: Red Ingle) / WINTER WONDERLAND (Vocal: Parker Gibbs)........................ *Columbia 2976-D* 5-8 35

I'M FOR YOU A HUNDRED PER CENT / THAT'S WHAT I LIKE ABOUT YOU.... *Victor 22838* 5-8 31
(Vocals: Parker Gibbs)

I'M GROWING FONDER OF YOU (Vocal: Fred Waldmar) / ONE LITTLE KISS
(Vocal: Gene Glennan)............... *Columbia 2975-D* 5-8 35

IN A ONE-ROOM FLAT / I'M A LOVER OF PAREE.......... *Bluebird B-5235* 4-6 33
(Vocals: Elmo Tanner)

IN A ONE-ROOM FLAT / I'M A LOVER OF PAREE.......... *Electradisk 2118* 12-15 33
(Vocals: Elmo Tanner)

IN A ONE-ROOM FLAT / I'M A LOVER OF PAREE........... *Sunrise S-3318* 12-15 33
(Vocals: Elmo Tanner)
(Simultaneously released on three labels)

I WONDER WHO'S KISSING HER NOW / ON THE ISLAND OF CATALINA........ *Decca 2919* 2-4 39
(Vocals: Perry Como)

JELLY BEAN (Vocal: Red Ingle) / THE MARTINS AND THE COYS (Vocal: Elmo Tanner)........... *Decca 810* 5-8 36

JIMINY CRICKET (Vocals: Elmo Tanner & Mary Lee) / MONSTRO THE WHALE (Vocals: Red Ingle & Marvell Maxwell)......................... *Decca 2793* 4-6 39
(Marvel Maxwell was later known as Marilyn Maxwell, motion picture star.)

LONELY PARK (Vocal: Andrea Marsh) / WHEN THE MORNING ROLLS AROUND
(Vocal: Parker Gibbs).................... *Victor 24227* 5-8 33

LOOK WHO'S HERE! / HATS OFF, HERE COMES A LADY............... *Victor 24308* 5-8 33
(Vocals: Parker Gibbs)

ME AND THE MAN IN THE MOON (Vocal: Art Jarret) / MY TROUBLES ARE OVER
(Vocal: Parker Gibbs)..................... *Victor 21809* 3-5 29

MISS ANNABELLE LEE (Vocals: Parker Gibbs & Dusty Rhodes) / BARBARA (Vocal: Dusty Rhodes)... *Victor 20846* 4-6 27

MY CUTEY'S DUE AT TWO-TO-TWO TODAY / I'M GONNA PARK MYSELF IN YOUR ARMS........................ *Victor 20120* 3-5 26
(Vocals: Parker Gibbs)

MYSTERIOUS MOSE / SLAPPIN' THE BASS................. *Victor 22411* 5-8 30
(Vocals: Parker Gibbs)

NOBODY'S BABY IS SOMEBODY'S BABY NOW (Vocal: Red Ingle) / ANY CORNER IS A COZY CORNER
(Vocal: Wes Vaughn)..................... *Victor 22829* 4-6 31

NOLA / ROBINS AND ROSES (Vocal: Perry Como)................ *Decca 2041* 2-4 38

OH, IF I ONLY HAD YOU (Vocals: Parker Gibbs, Bill Comfort, & Dusty Rhodes) / HOW MANY TIMES? (by The Seattle Harmony Kings)..................... *Victor 20133* 3-5 26

OH! MONAH (Vocal: Country Washburn) / I LOVE TO HEAR A MILITARY BAND
(Vocal: Parker Gibbs).................. *Victor 22822* 4-6 31

OH MONAH! (Vocal: Country Washburn) / OUT OF THE NIGHT (theme song)
(whistling by Elmo Tanner)................. *Decca 3697* 2-4 41

OLLIE OLLIE OUTS IN FREE / DEEP IN THE HEART OF TEXAS............................ *Decca 4138* 2-4 42
(Vocals: Perry Como)

ONE OF US WAS WRONG (Vocal: Elmo Tanner) / CAROLINA'S CALLING ME
(Vocal: Wes Vaughn)..................... *Victor 22877* 3-5 31

OUT WHERE THE BLUE BEGINS / DARLING, NOT WITHOUT YOU......... *Decca 959* 4-6 36
(Vocals: Perry Como)

PICTURE ME WITHOUT YOU (Vocal: Perry Como with whistling by Elmo Tanner) / COTTAGE BY THE MOON
(Vocal: Elmo Tanner)....................... *Decca 958* 4-6 36

PLAY THAT HOT GUITAR (Vocal: Parker Gibbs) / DEEP SEA LOW DOWN (by Bernie Cummins & His Hotel New Yorker Orchestra; Vocal: Bernie Cummins)... *Victor 24053* 5-8 31

POOR PINOCCHIO'S NOSE (Vocal: Elmo Tanner) / GAMBLER'S BLUES................ *Decca 2408* 4-6 39

RAINBOW ON THE RIVER (Vocal: Perry Como with whistling by Elmo Tanner) / HEY, BABE, HEY! (Vocals: Red Ingle, Elmo Tanner & Parker Gibbs)........... *Decca 969* 4-6 36

SHE'LL NEVER FIND A FELLOW LIKE ME / FROM SATURDAY NIGHT TILL MONDAY MORNING................. *Victor 21009* 3-5 27
(Vocals: Parker Gibbs)

SHE'S SO NICE (Vocal: Parker Gibbs) / THIS IS MY LOVE SONG (Vocal: Wes Vaughn)............... *Victor 22881* 4-6 32

SITTIN' UP WAITIN' FOR YOU (Vocal: Red Ingle) / THE ROOFTOP SERENADE (Vocals: Dudley Fosdick, Wes Vaughn & Elmo Tanner)........... *Bluebird B-5290* 5-8 34

SITTIN' UP WAITIN' FOR YOU (Vocal: Red Ingle) / THE ROOFTOP SERENADE (Vocals: Dudley Fosdick, Wes Vaughn & Elmo Tanner).......... *Electrodisk 2161* 15-20 34

SITTIN' UP WAITIN' FOR YOU (Vocal: Red Ingle) / THE ROOFTOP SERENADE (Vocals: Dudley Fosdick, Wes Vaughn & Elmo Tanner)............ *Sunrise S-3371* 15-20 34
(Simultaneously released on three labels)

SMILE WILL GO A LONG, LONG, WAY, A / NINE O'CLOCK SAL.................. *Victor 19258* 3-5 24

SONG OF SURRENDER (Vocal: Wes Vaughn) / BOULEVARD OF BROKEN DREAMS
(Vocal: Elmo Tanner)................. *Bluebird B-5288* 4-6 34

SONG OF SURRENDER (Vocal: Wes Vaughn) / BOULEVARD OF BROKEN DREAMS
(Vocal: Elmo Tanner)................. *Electradisk 2159* 12-15 34

SONG OF SURRENDER (Vocal: Wes Vaughn) / BOULEVARD OF BROKEN DREAMS
(Vocal: Elmo Tanner)................. *Sunrise S-3369* 12-15 34
(Simultaneously released on three labels)

SWINGIN' IN THE CORN / A SHACK IN THE BACK OF THE HILLS (Vocals: Unknown)............ *Decca 1705* 2-4 38

'TAIN'T SO (Vocals: Red Ingle, Country Washburn, & Elmo Tanner) / THE MUSIC MAN
(Vocals: by chorus)................. *Bluebird B-5289* 5-8 34

'TAIN'T SO (Vocals: Red Ingle, Country Washburn, & Elmo Tanner) / THE MUSIC MAN
(Vocals: by chorus).................... *Electradisk 2168* 15-20 34

'TAIN'T SO (Vocals: Red Ingle, Country Washburn, & Elmo Tanner) / THE MUSIC MAN
(Vocals: by chorus)..................... *Sunrise S-3370* 15-20 34
(Simultaneously released on three labels)

TEN YARDS TO GO (Vocal: Parker Gibbs) / OUT OF THE NIGHT (theme song)
(Vocals & whistling by Elmo Tanner).... *Columbia 2956-D* 5-8 34

THAT'S MY GIRL (Vocals: Parker Gibbs, Bill Comfort, & Dusty Rhodes) / SOMEONE IS LOSIN' SUSAN (by Phil Spitalny & His Orchestra)....................... *Victor 20196* 3-5 26

THERE'LL BE SOME CHANGES MADE (Vocal: Mary Lee) / MOONLIGHT (Vocal: Elmo Tanner)....... *Decca 3044* 2-4 39

THERE'S TOO MANY EYES THAT WANNA MAKE EYES AT TWO PRETTY EYES I LOVE (Vocal: Art Jarrett) / REMARKABLE GIRL
(Vocal: Country Washburn)................ *Victor 22157* 4-6 29

THREE SHIF'LESS SKUNKS (Vocals: unknown) / BUFFOON............................ *Decca 1884* 3-5 38

UNTIL TODAY (Vocal: Perry Como) / BYE BYE BABY (Vocal: Parker Gibbs)....... *Decca 895* 4-6 36

WALKIN' MY BABY BACK HOME / I LOST MY GAL AGAIN............. *Victor 22637* 4-6 31
(Vocals: Parker Gibbs)

WHAT A DAY! (Vocal: Parker Gibbs) / AM I A PASSING FANCY? (Vocal: Art Jarrett)............. *Victor 22038* 3-5 29

YOU'RE THE CREAM IN MY COFFEE (Vocal: Parker Gibbs) / ANYTHING YOUR HEART DESIRES
(Vocal: Art Jarrett)...................... *Victor 21767* 3-5 28

WELK, Lawrence, & His Champagne Music
(Lawrence Welk: 3/11/03 –)

CHANGE PARTNERS (Vocal: Lois Best) / I USED TO BE COLOR BLIND (Vocal: Walter Bloom) .... *Vocalion 4270* 2-4 38

COLORADO SUNSET (Vocal: Walter Bloom) / THERE'S A FARAWAY LOOK IN YOUR EYE (Vocal: Lois Best) .... *Vocalion 4284* 2-4 38

COMIN' THRO' THE RYE / THE HOIRIGER SCHOTTISCHE (Vocal: Bob Page) .... *Vocalion 5064* 2-4 39

EIGHT LITTLE NOTES (Vocal: Lois Best) / WHEN TWILIGHT COMES (Vocal: Walter Bloom) .... *Vocalion 4323* 2-4 38

FROM NOW ON (Vocal: Lois Best) / GET OUT OF TOWN (Vocal: Walter Bloom) .... *Vocalion 4512* 2-4 39

GIRL BEHIND THE VENETIAN BLIND, THE (Vocal: Parnell Grina) / BUT IT DIDN'T MEAN A THING (Vocal: Walter Bloom)... *Vocalion 4817* 2-4 39

GIRL WITH THE PIGTAILS IN HER HAIR / ANGEL .... *Vocalion 5365* 2-4 40
(Vocals: Jayne Walton)

HAVE YOU FORGOTTEN SO SOON? (Vocal: Walter Bloom) / IT'S A LONELY TRAIL (WHEN YOU'RE TRAVELIN' ALL ALONE) (Vocal: Lois Best) .... *Vocalion 4458* 2-4 38

HELLO, MY DARLING (Vocal: Jules Herman) / A LOVE LIKE OURS (Vocals: Lois Best & Walter Bloom) .... *Vocalion 4585* 2-4 38

HOW CAN I EVER BE ALONE? (Vocal: Jayne Walton) / TENNESEE FISH FRY (Vocal: Parnell Grina) .... *Okeh 5581* 3-5 40

HOW CAN I EVER BE ALONE? (Vocal: Jayne Walton) / TENNESEE FISH FRY (Vocal: Parnell Grina) .... *Vocalion 5581* 3-5 40
(Simultaneously released on two labels)

I PAID FOR THE LIE I TOLD YOU (Vocal: Tommy Allen) / IF I HADN'T MET YOU (Vocal: Joe Bohner) .... *Vocalion 4929* 2-4 39

KENTUCKY'S WAY OF SAYIN' "GOOD MORNIN'" / IF YOU TALK IN YOUR SLEEP, DON'T MENTION MY NAME (Vocal: Parnell Grina) .... *Okeh 5677* 2-4 40

LET'S TIE THE OLD FORGET-ME-NOT (Vocal: Jules Herman) / HARD-TO-GET GERTIE (Vocal: Parnell Grina) .... *Vocalion 5022* 2-4 39

LINGER AWHILE (Vocal: Walter Bloom) / TOYTOWN JAMBOREE (Vocal: Parnell Grina) .... *Vocalion 4478* 2-4 38

LITTLE DRUMMER BOY / I'LL STILL BE LOVING YOU .... *Vocalion 4194* 2-4 38
(Vocals: Walter Bloom)

LOVELAND IN THE WINTER TIME (Vocal: Walter Bloom) / THE PIED PIPER OF HAMLIN TOWN (Vocal: Parnell Grina) .... *Vocalion 4525* 2-4 38

LOVIN' SAM (THE SHEIK OF ALABAM') (Vocal: Lois Best) / LOUISVILLE LOU (THE VAMPIN' LADY) (Vocal: Parnell Grina) .... *Vocalion 4633* 3-5 39

MASQUERADE IS OVER, THE (Vocal: Walter Bloom) / IT'S EASY TO BLAME THE WEATHER (Vocal: Lois Best) .... *Vocalion 4679* 2-4 39

MEET MR. CALLAGHAN / FLIRTATION WALTZ .... *Coral 60828* 2-4 –

MISTER MEADOWLARK (Vocal: Jayne Walton) / ON THE OLD PARK BENCH (Vocal: Parnell Grina) .... *Vocalion 5555* 2-4 40

MOON IS A SILVER DOLLAR, THE (Vocal: Walter Bloom) / I'M A LUCKY DEVIL (Vocal: Parnell Grina) .... *Vocalion 4681* 2-4 39

OLD CURIOSITY SHOP, AN (Vocal: Walter Bloom) / SHE'S MY GIRL (Vocal: Parnell Grina) .... *Vocalion 4597* 2-4 39

ONE-TWO-THREE-KICK (Vocal: Jayne Walton) / THE MAN ON THE FERRY (Vocals: Jayne Walton & Parnell Grina) .... *Vocalion 5222* 2-4 39

ON SWEETHEART BAY (Vocal: Walter Bloom) / BUBBLES IN THE WINE (theme song) .... *Conqueror 9082* 2-4 38

ON SWEETHEART BAY (Vocal: Walter Bloom) / BUBBLES IN THE WINE (theme song) .... *Vocalion 4368* 2-4 38
(Simultaneously released on two labels)

OR HAVE I? / MARIA ELENA .... *Conqueror 9650* 2-4 41
(Vocals: Jayne Walton)

SING FOR YOUR SUPPER (Vocal: Lois Best) / THIS CAN'T BE LOVE (Vocal: Walter Bloom) .... *Vocalion 4535* 2-4 38

SO HELP ME / LAUGH AND CALL IT LOVE .... *Vocalion 4298* 2-4 38
(Vocals: Lois Best)

START THE DAY RIGHT (Vocal: Joe Bohner) / IT SEEMS LIKE OLD TIMES (Vocal: Mildred Stanley) .... *Vocalion 4918* 2-4 39

STUMBLING / MY MAN .... *Vocalion 4848* 2-4 39

SWEET AND LOW (Vocals: Jayne Walton & Parnell Grina) / LITTLE SLEEPY HEAD (Vocal: Jayne Walton) .... *Okeh 5976* 2-4 41

SWEET DREAMS, SWEETHEART (Vocal: Bob Page) / YOU TELL ME YOUR DREAM (Vocal: Walter Bloom) .... *Vocalion 5103* 2-4 39

SWEET POTATO PIPER / ANGEL .... *Conqueror 9507* 2-4 40
(Vocals: Jayne Walton)

SWEET POTATO PIPER (Vocal: Jayne Walton) / CAPTAIN CUSTARD (Vocal: Parnell Grina) .... *Vocalion 5374* 2-4 40

SWINGIN' DOWN THE LANE (Vocal: Roberta Linn) / YOU'RE SOMEBODY ELSE'S SWEETHEART (Vocals: Roberta Linn & The Sparklers) .... *Coral 60630* 2-4 –

TEACH ME TO FORGET YOU (Vocal: Walter Bloom) / HOLD ON TO YOUR HEART (Vocal: Lois Best) .... *Vocalion 4572* 2-4 39

THAT'S A PLENTY / EMALINE .... *Vocalion 4497* 3-5 38

TIGER RAG / MILITARY POLKA .... *Mercury 5529* 2-4 51

TWO HEARTS ARE BETTER THAN ONE / ONE LOOK AT YOU .... *Vocalion 5184* 2-4 39
(Vocals: Bob Page)

TWO SLEEPY PEOPLE / I WON'T TELL A SOUL (I LOVE YOU) .... *Vocalion 4435* 2-4 38
(Vocals: Walter Bloom)

UMBRELLA MAN, THE (Vocals: Lois Best & Walter Bloom) / I FELL UP TO HEAVEN (Vocal: Lois Best) .... *Vocalion 4561* 2-4 39

UNFORTUNATE BLUES / THE STARLIT HOUR (Vocal: Bob Page) .... *Vocalion 5303* 3-5 39

VILLAGE TAVERN POLKA / BEER BARREL POLKA .... *Vocalion 4788* 2-4 39

YOU GROW SWEETER AS THE YEARS GO BY (Vocal: Walter Bloom) / THE CHESTNUT TREE (Vocal: Parnell Grina) .... *Vocalion 4765* 2-4 39

WELK, Lawrence, & His Orchestra

DOIN' THE NEW LOWDOWN / — .... *Gennett 6697* 20-25 29

FRIENDLY TAVERN POLKA / YOU ARE MY SUNSHINE .... *Decca 3725* 2-4 41
(Vocals: Shirley Grundy & Parnell Grina)

RAISE THE WINDOW DOWN (Vocal: Jo Ann Hubbard) / NICKEL POLKA (Vocals: Jo Ann Hubbard & Parnell Grina) .... *Decca 4018* 2-4 41

SPIKED BEER / SHANGHAI HONEYMOON (Vocal: Gordon Malie) ..... *Gennett 20341* 20-25 29

THRILL ME / SMILE, DARN YA, SMILE .... *Broadway 1462* 15-20 31
(Vocals: Frankie Sanders)

WELLS, George, & His Orchestra:
see RICH, Fred, & His (La Palina) Orchestra and see RICH, Fred, & His Orchestra

WHEELER, "Doc", & His Sunset Orchestra

FOO-GEE (Vocal: Julius Watson) / HOW 'BOUT THAT MESS? .... *Bluebird B-11314* 5-8 41

GABBY / BIG AND FAT AND FORTY-FOUR (Vocals: "Doc" Wheeler & The Hardway Four) .... *Bluebird B-11389* 5-8 42

ME AND MY MELINDA (Vocal: James Otis Lewis) / SARGHUM SWITCH .... *Bluebird B-11529* 5-8 42

WHO THREW THE WHISKEY IN THE WELL (Vocals: "Doc" Wheeler & The Hardway Four) / KEEP JUMPIN' .... *Bluebird B-11559* 5-8 42

WHITEMAN, Paul, & His Ambassador Orchestra
(Paul Whiteman: 3/28/90 – 12/29/67)
(Paul Whiteman, called the "King of Jazz", was the most widely known orchestra leader throughout the world in the 1920s' "jazz age")

WANG WANG BLUES / ANYTIME, ANYDAY, ANYWHERE .... *Victor 18694* 2-4 20

WHITEMAN, Paul, & His Concert Orchestra
(The following releases by The Paul Whiteman Concert Orchestra are oversize 12-inch 78 rpm records)

JUBILEE MEDLEY / JUBILEE MEDLEY, PART II .... *Victor 36175* 4-6 35

MISSISSIPPI SUITE / MISSISSIPPI SUITE, PART II .... *Victor 35859* 8-10 27

PARK AVENUE FANTASY / DEEP PURPLE .... *Victor 36131* 4-6 34

PETER, PETER, PUMPKIN EATER / PETER, PETER, PUMPKIN EATER, PART II .... *Victor 36143* 4-6 34

RHAPSODY IN BLUE (theme song) / RHAPSODY IN BLUE, PART II .... *Victor 55225* 8-10 24
(The composer George Gershwin is featured as solo pianist on this release)

TOP HAT MEDLEY / TOP HAT MEDLEY, PART II .... *Victor 36174* 4-6 35

WHITEMAN, Paul, & His Orchestra
(Certain Columbia releases have picture labels featuring the head of Paul Whiteman in caricature form, commonly called the "potato head" label. Those known issues are noted and priced accordingly, and any other releases with the picture labels would have similar values.)

ALL ASHORE (Vocals: The Four Modernaires) / MY REVERIE .... *Decca 2075* 3-5 38

ALL THE THINGS YOU ARE / ALL IN FUN .... *Decca 2912* 2-4 40

ALL THROUGH THE NIGHT (Vocal: Bob Lawrence) / ANYTHING GOES (Vocal: Ramona Davies) ... *Victor 24770* 3-5 34

AT TWILIGHT / WHEN YOU'RE COUNTING THE STARS ALONE .... *Columbia 1993-D* 8-10 29
(Vocals: Bing Crosby, Jack Fulton & Al Rinker)
(This release has a picture label featuring the head of Paul Whiteman in caricature form, commonly called the "potato head" label.)

BACK IN YOUR OWN BACK YARD / SUNSHINE (Vocals: Bing Crosby, Al Rinker, Jack Fulton, Charles Gaylord & Austin Young) ..... *Victor 21240* 5-8 28

BEAUTIFUL OHIO (Vocal: Jack Fulton) / MISSOURI WALTZ (Vocals: Bing Crosby, Al Rinker, Jack Fulton, Charles Gaylord & Austin Young) ... *Victor 20973* 3-5 27

BELL HOPPIN' BLUES / ST. LOUIS BLUES .... *Victor 20092* 5-8 26

BIRTH OF THE BLUES (Vocals: Jack Fulton, Charles Gaylord, & Austin Young) / COUNTESS MARITZA .... *Victor 20138* 3-5 26

BLUE HAWAII (Vocals: Jack Fulton & Charles Gaylord) / LOUISE (Vocal: Bing Crosby) .... *Columbia 1771-D* 4-6 29
(This release has a picture label featuring the head of Paul Whiteman in caricature form, commonly called the "potato head" label.)

BODY AND SOUL (Vocal: Jack Fulton) / SOMETHING TO REMEMBER YOU BY (Vocals: The King's Jesters) .... *Columbia 2297-D* 5-8 30
(This release has a picture label featuring the head of Paul Whiteman in caricature form, commonly called the "potato head" label.)

BORN TO BE KISSED (Vocal: Ramona Davies) / I SAW YOU IN MY DREAMS (Vocal: Jack Fulton) .... *Victor 24670* 3-5 34

BUTTON UP YOUR OVERCOAT (Vocal: Vaughn de Leath) / MY LUCKY STAR (Vocal: Norman Clark) .... *Columbia 1736-D* 5-8 29
(This release has a picture label featuring the head of Paul Whiteman in caricature form, commonly called the "potato head" label.)

CALINDA, THE (Vocals: Bing Crosby, Al Rinker, Jack Fulton, Charles Gaylord & Austin Young) / BABY'S BLUE (by Nat Shilkret & The Victor Orchestra; Vocal: Johnny Marvin) .... *Victor 20882* 3-5 27

CALL OF THE SOUTH / ALABAMY BOUND .... *Victor 19557* 2-4 25

CAROLINA IN THE MORNING / HOMESICK .... *Victor 18963* 2-4 22

CHANGES (Vocals: Bing Crosby, Al Rinker, Harry Barris, Jack Fulton, Charles Gaylord & Austin Young) / MARY (WHAT ARE YOU WAITING FOR?) (Vocal: Bing Crosby) .... *Victor 21103* 5-8 28

CHINA BOY / OH! MISS HANNAH (Vocal: Bing Crosby) .... *Columbia 1945-D* 12-15 29
(This release has a picture label featuring the head of Paul Whiteman in caricature form, commonly called the "potato head" label.)

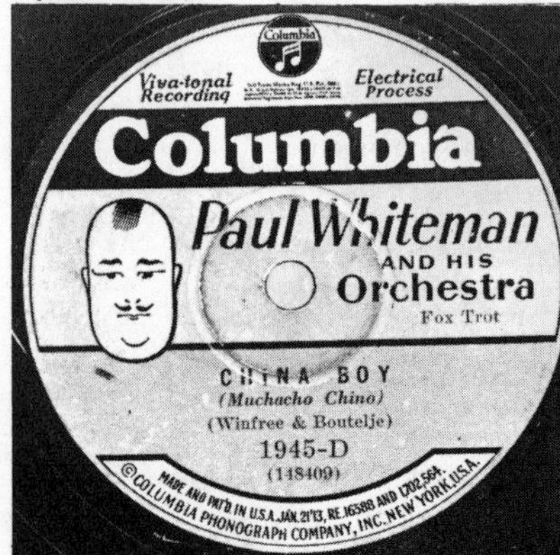

CHIQUITA (Vocal: Jack Fulton) / LONESOME IN THE MOONLIGHT (Vocals: Bing Crosby, Al Rinker & Harry Barris) .... *Columbia 1448-D* 5-8 28
(This release has a picture label featuring the head of Paul Whiteman in caricature form, commonly called the "potato head" label.)

COLLETTE / BROKEN-HEARTED....... *Victor 20757* 4-6 27
(Vocals: Jack Fulton, Charles Gaylord & Austin Young)

C-O-N-S-T-A-N-T-I-N-O-P-L-E (Vocals: Al Rinker, Harry Barris & trio) / GET OUT AND GET UNDER THE MOON (Vocals: Bing Crosby & trio)........... *Columbia 1402-D* 5-8 28
(This release has a picture label featuring the head of Paul Whiteman in caricature form, commonly called the "potato head" label.)

COQUETTE / MY ANGELINE....... *Columbia 1755-D* 5-8 29
(Vocals: Bing Crosby)
(This release has a picture label featuring the head of Paul Whiteman in caricature form, commonly called the "potato head" label.)

CREAKING OLD MILL ON THE CREEK, THE / THE GAUCHO SERENADE............. *Decca 2938* 2-4 39

CUTIE / LONESOME HOURS........... *Victor 18865* 2-4 22

DARKTOWN STRUTTERS' BALL (Vocal: Jack Teagarden) / FAREWELL BLUES .... *Victor 25192* 5-8 35

DARN THAT DREAM / MY FANTASY .... *Decca 2937* 2-4 39

DAYBREAK (Vocal: Red McKenzie) / TOSELLI'S SERENADE.............. *Victor 24017* 4-6 32

DEAREST / 'WAY DOWN YONDER IN NEW ORLEANS.................. *Victor 19030* 2-4 23

DEAR OLD SOUTHLAND / THEY CALL IT DANCING............ *Victor 18856* 2-4 22

DIXIE DAWN (Vocal: Austin Young) / LOUISIANA (Vocals: Bing Crosby, Jack Fulton, Charles Gaylord & Austin Young).......... *Victor 21438* 8-10 28

DODGING A DIVORCEE / AIN'T MISBEHAVIN' (Vocal: Jack Teagarden).... *Victor 25086* 5-8 35

DO I HEAR YOU SAYING (Vocals: Bing Crosby, Al Rinker, & Charles Gaylord) / YOU TOOK ADVANTAGE OF ME (Vocals: Bing Crosby, Jack Fulton, Charles Gaylord & Austin Young)....................... *Victor 21398* 5-8 28

DUKE INSISTS, THE / GARDEN OF WEED .... *Victor 25113* 5-8 35

EADIE WAS A LADY (Vocals: Ramona Davies & The Rhythm Boys) / YOU'RE AN OLD SMOOTHIE (Vocal: Ramona Davies) .... *Victor 24202* 3-5 33

EASTER PARADE / SAY IT ISN'T SO..... *Decca 2692* 2-4 39
(Vocals: Joan Edwards & Clarke Dennis)

FAREWELL TO ARMS / A WHITE HOUSE OF OUR OWN....................... *Victor 24236* 3-5 33
(Vocals: Jack Fulton)

FASCINATING RHYTHM / OH! LADY BE GOOD.......................... *Victor 19551* 3-5 25

FIVE STEP / IT WON'T BE LONG NOW .... *Victor 20883* 5-8 27
(Vocals: Bing Crosby, Al Rinker, & Harry Barris)

G BLUES / TAIL SPIN.................. *Victor 24668* 5-8 34

GETTIN' SENTIMENTAL (Vocals: The Romancers) / MY GOODBYE TO YOU (Vocal: Mildred Bailey)................. *Victor 22876* 4-6 31

GREAT DAY (Vocals: Bing Crosby, Jack Fulton, Al Rinker & Harry Barris) / WITHOUT A SONG (Vocal: Bing Crosby)................. *Columbia 2023-D* 5-8 29
(This release has a picture label featuring the head of Paul Whiteman in caricature form, commonly called the "potato head" label.)

GYPSY BLUES / WHEN BUDDHA SMILES............ *Victor 18839* 2-4 21

HAPPY FEET (Vocals: Bing Crosby, Al Rinker & Harry Barris) / A BENCH IN THE PARK (Vocals: Bing Crosby, Al Rinker, Harry Barris, & The Brox Sisters) ...... *Columbia 2164-D* 8-10 30
(This release has a picture label featuring the head of Paul Whiteman in caricature form, commonly called the "potato head" label.)

HARD-HEARTED HANNAH / BAGDAD... *Victor 19447* 2-4 24

HEAVEN IN MY ARMS / THAT LUCKY FELLOW................ *Decca 2913* 2-4 40

HERE'S HOPING (Vocal: Jack Fulton) / THREE ON A MATCH (Vocal: Red McKenzie) .... *Victor 24089* 4-6 32

HONEY, I'M IN LOVE WITH YOU / CHARLESTON .... *Victor 19671* 2-4 25

IDA – I DO / CHARLESTONETTE .... *Victor 19785* 2-4 25

I FEEL A SONG COMIN' ON (Vocals: Ramona Davies & The King's Men) / I'M IN THE MOOD FOR LOVE (Vocal: Ramona Davies) .... *Victor 25091* 3-5 35

IF I LOVE AGAIN / WAGON WHEELS.................... *Victor 24517* 3-5 34
(Vocals: Bob Lawrence)

I FOUND A NEW BABY / THE GENERAL JUMPED AT DAWN.................. *Capitol 101* 3-5 42
(This was the first Capitol release.)

I GET A KICK OUT OF YOU (Vocal: Ramona Davies) / YOU'RE THE TOP (Vocals: Peggy Healey & John Hauser)........................ *Victor 24769* 3-5 34

I GUESS I'LL HAVE TO CHANGE MY PLAN (Vocal: Ramona Davies) / YOU'LL ALWAYS BE THE SAME SWEETHEART TO ME (Vocal: Jack Fulton)............. *Victor 24097* 3-5 32

I'LL FOLLOW YOU (Vocal: Ramona Davies) / HOW DEEP IS THE OCEAN? (Vocal: Jack Fulton) ..... *Victor 24141* 3-5 32

I'LL NEVER BE THE SAME / WE JUST COULDN'T SAY GOODBYE..................... *Victor 24088* 4-6 32
(Vocals: Mildred Bailey)

I'M A DREAMER – AREN'T WE ALL? (Vocals: Bing Crosby, Jack Fulton, Al Rinker, & Harry Barris) / IF I HAD A TALKING PICTURE OF YOU (Vocals: Bing Crosby)........ *Columbia 2010-D* 5-8 29
(This release has a picture label featuring the head of Paul Whiteman in caricature form, commonly called the "potato head" label.)

I'M BRINGING A RED, RED ROSE (Vocal: Jack Fulton) / MAKIN' WHOOPEE (Vocals: Bing Crosby & trio)................................ *Columbia 1683-D* 5-8 29
(This release has a picture label featuring the head of Paul Whiteman in caricature form, commonly called the "potato head" label.)

I'M COMING, VIRGINIA (Vocals: Bing Crosby, Al Rinker, & Harry Barris) / JUST ONCE AGAIN (Vocal: Austin Young) .... *Victor 20751* 5-8 27

I'M COUNTING ON YOU (Vocal: Ramona Davies) / I SAW STARS (Vocal: Peggy Healey) ...... *Victor 24705* 3-5 34

I'M IN LOVE AGAIN (Vocals: Jack Fulton, Charles Gaylord, Austin Young, Bing Crosby & Al Rinker) / WHEREVER YOU GO (by Nat Shilkret & The Victor Orchestra; Vocal: Lewis James) .... *Victor 20646* 3-5 27

I MISS MY SWISS (Vocal: John Sperzel with yodeling by Fritz Zimmerman) / THE KINKY KIDS' PARADE (Vocal: John Sperzel)....................... *Victor 19753* 2-4 25

I NEVER KNEW / DO YOU EVER THINK OF ME?.......................... *Victor 18734* 2-4 21

IS IT GONNA BE LONG? / I'D RATHER CRY OVER YOU (Vocals: Bing Crosby & trio)...... *Columbia 1496-D* 8-10 28
(This release has a picture label featuring the head of Paul Whiteman in caricature form, commonly called the "potato head" label.)

IT HAD TO BE YOU / THE HOODOO MAN .... *Victor 19339* 2-4 24

IT HAPPENED IN MONTEREY (Vocal: Jack Fulton) / SONG OF THE DAWN (Vocals: Bing Crosby & chorus) .... *Columbia 2163-D* 5-8 30
(This release has a picture label featuring the head of Paul Whiteman in caricature form, commonly called the "potato head" label.)

IT'S GOT TO BE LOVE (Vocal: John Hauser) / THERE'S A SMALL HOTEL (Vocal: Durrelle Alexander)................ *Victor 25270* 3-5 36

IT'S ONLY A PAPER MOON (Vocal: Peggy Healey) / NIGHT OWL (Vocals: The Rhythm Boys) ... *Victor 24400* 4-6 33

IVY (CLING TO ME) / I GAVE YOU UP JUST BEFORE YOU THREW ME DOWN........... *Victor 19003* 2-4 23

JUNE BUGS' DANCE / SHOEMAKER'S HOLIDAY (Vocals: The Four Modernaries).... *Decca 2505* 2-4 39

JUST A LITTLE BIT OF DRIFTWOOD (Vocal: Austin Young) / OUT O' TOWN GAL (Vocals: Bing Crosby, Al Rinker, & Harry Barris)............ *Columbia 1505-D* 10-12 28
(This release has a picture label featuring the head of Paul Whiteman in caricature form, commonly called the "potato head" label.)

JUST LIKE A MELODY OUT OF THE SKY (Vocals: Jack Fulton, Charles Gaylord, & Austin Young) / BECAUSE MY BABY DON'T MEAN "MAYBE" NOW (Vocals: Bing Crosby & trio)........... *Columbia 1441-D* 8-10 28
(This release has a picture label featuring the head of Paul Whiteman in caricature form, commonly called the "potato head" label.)

LAST NIGHT I DREAMED YOU KISSED ME (Vocal: Jack Fulton) / EVENING STAR (Vocals: Bing Crosby & trio)........... *Columbia 1401-D* 5-8 28
(This release has a picture label featuring the head of Paul Whiteman in caricature form, commonly called the "potato head" label.)

LAST NIGHT ON THE BACK PORCH / IF I CAN'T HAVE THE SWEETIE I WANT .... *Victor 19139* 2-4 23

LAWD, YOU MADE THE NIGHT TOO LONG (Vocal: Red McKenzie) / EVERYTHING MUST HAVE AN ENDING (by Peter Van Steeden & His Orchestra; Vocal: Chick Bullock).................... *Victor 22984* 4-6 32

LET'S PUT OUT THE LIGHTS (AND GO TO SLEEP) (Vocal: Ramona Davies) / YOU'RE TELLING ME (Vocals: The Rhythm Boys)................ *Victor 24140* 3-5 32

LIVING IN THE SUNLIGHT, LOVING IN THE MOONLIGHT / YOU BROUGHT A NEW KIND OF LOVE TO ME .... *Columbia 2171-D* 8-10 30
(Vocals: Bing Crosby)
(This release has a picture label featuring the head of Paul Whiteman in caricature form, commonly called the "potato head" label.)

LONELY EYES (Vocal: Wilbur Hall) / WISTFUL AND BLUE (Vocals: Bing Crosby & Al Rinker) ..... *Victor 20418* 5-8 27

LONELY LITTLE MELODY / SOMEONE LOVES ME............... *Victor 19414* 2-4 24

LOOK WHAT I'VE GOT (Vocal: Peggy Healey) / IN THE PARK IN PAREE (Vocal: June Vance)....................... *Victor 24285* 3-5 33

LOVABLE / I'M AFRAID OF YOU........ *Victor 27685* 5-8 41
(Vocals: Bing Crosby.)
(This is a 1928 recording first released in 1941.)

LOVE AND KISSES / MAGNOLIA (Vocals: Bing Crosby, Al Rinker, & Harry Barris) .... *Victor 20679* 5-8 27

LOVE HAS A WAY / THERE'S YES! YES! IN YOUR EYES .... *Victor 19309* 2-4 24

MANHATTAN MARY (Vocals: Jack Fulton, Charles Gaylord, & Austin Young) / BROADWAY (Vocal: Austin Young)................. *Victor 20874* 3-5 27

MISSISSIPPI MUD (Vocals: Irene Taylor, Bing Crosby, Al Rinker, Harry Barris, & trio) / FROM MONDAY ON (Vocals: Bing Crosby, Al Rinker, Jack Fulton, Charles Gaylord, & Austin Young) .... *Victor 21274* 8-10 28

MOTHER GOOSE PARADE / FELIX THE CAT .... *Columbia 1478-D* 12-15 28
(Vocals: Austin Young)
(This release has a picture label featuring the head of Paul Whiteman in caricature form, commonly called the "potato head" label.)

MR. RADIO MAN (TELL MY MAMMY TO COME BACK) / SPAIN............ *Victor 19330* 2-4 24

MUDDY WATER (Vocal: Bing Crosby) / AIN'T SHE SWEET? (by Nat Shilkret & The Victor Orchestra; Vocal: Franklyn Baur)........... *Victor 20508* 5-8 27

MY HEART STOOD STILL (Vocals: Al Rinker, Jack Fulton, Charles Gaylord & Austin Young) / TOGETHER (Vocal: Jack Fulton).......... *Victor 35883* 5-8 28
(This is an oversize 12-inch 78 rpm.)

MY MELANCHOLY BABY (Vocal: Austin Young) / THE MAN I LOVE (Vocal: Vaughn de Leath)............ *Columbia 50068-D* 10-12 28
(This release has a picture label featuring the head of Paul Whiteman in caricature form, commonly called the "potato head" label.)
(This is an oversize 12-inch 78 rpm.)

MY PET (Vocals: Bing Crosby, Al Rinker, Charles Gaylord, & Austin Young) / FORGET-ME-NOT (Vocals: Jack Fulton)........................ *Victor 27686* 8-10 41
(This release was recorded in April 1928 when Bix Beiderbecke was with the Paul Whiteman Orchestra. An alternate take of the first side was issued June 8, 1928, but this recording was first released December 12, 1941.)

NIGHT AND DAY (Vocals: The Pickens Sisters & Phil Dewey) / COLE PORTER MEDLEY (Vocals: Ramona Davies & The Rollickers)........................... *Victor 36085* 3-5 33
(This is an oversize 12-inch 78 rpm.)

NIGHTFALL / SOMETHING IN THE NIGHT...................... *Victor 24096* 3-5 32
(Vocals: Jack Fulton)

NOBODY'S SWEETHEART / AFTER YOU'VE GONE (Vocal: Bing Crosby) .... *Columbia 2098-D* 8-10 29
(This release has a picture label featuring the head of Paul Whiteman in caricature form, commonly called the "potato head" label.)

NOBODY'S SWEETHEART NOW (Vocal: Jack Teagarden) / STOP, LOOK & LISTEN .... *Victor 25319* 4-6 35

NOLA / THE NEW TIGER RAG ..... *Columbia 2277-D* 5-8 30
(This release has a picture label featuring the head of Paul Whiteman in caricature form, commonly called the "potato head" label.)

NO MORE WORRYIN' (Vocals: Jack Fulton, Charles Gaylord, & Austin Young) / VALENCIA (Vocal: Franklyn Baur)........ *Victor 20007* 3-5 26

OH! YOU HAVE NO IDEA / GEORGIE PORGIE (Vocals: Bing Crosby, Al Rinker, & Harry Barris)............ *Columbia 1491-D* 12-15 28
(This release has a picture label featuring the head of Paul Whiteman in caricature form, commonly called the "potato head" label.)

OLD MUSIC MASTER, THE (Vocals: Johnny Mercer & Jack Teagarden) / WAITIN' FOR THE EVENIN' MAIL (by Freddie Slack & His Orchestra; Vocal: Johnny Mercer)..................... *Capitol 137* 2-4 42

OL' MAN RIVER / MAKE BELIEVE ..... *Victor 21218* 5-8 28
(Vocals: Bing Crosby)

ON THE 'GIN 'GIN 'GINNY SHORE / MARIE .... *Victor 1859* 2-4 22

OOH! MAYBE IT'S YOU (Vocals: Jack Fulton, Charles Gaylord & Austin Young) / SHAKING THE BLUES AWAY .... *Victor 20885* 4-6 27

PACK UP YOUR SINS / CRINOLINE DAYS .... *Victor 18983* 2-4 22

PARADE OF THE WOODEN SOLDIERS / MR. GALLAGHER AND MR. SHEAN (Vocal: Billy Murray)...................... *Victor 19007* 3-5 23

PARDON MY SOUTHERN ACCENT (Vocals: Peggy Healey & Johnny Mercer) / HERE COME THE BRITISH (Vocals: Peggy Healey, Johnny Mercer & John Hauser)... *Victor 24704* 3-5 34

RAGAMUFFIN ROMEO (Vocal: Jeannie Lang) / I LIKE TO DO THINGS FOR YOU (Vocals: Bing Crosby, Al Rinker, & Harry Barris) .... *Columbia 2170-D* 5-8 30

RAMONA (Vocal: Austin Young) / LONELY MELODY .... *Victor 21214* 5-8 28

RHYTHM RAG / I'M TIRED OF EVERYTHING BUT YOU.............. *Victor 19773* 2-4 25

SAN / I CAN'T GET THE ONE I WANT.................... *Victor 19381* 2-4 24

SAN / POOR BUTTERFLY (Vocals: Bing Crosby, Al Rinker, Charles Gaylord & Austin Young)........... *Victor 24078* 10-12 33
(A 1928 recording first released in 1933)

SERENADE IN BLUE / I'VE GOT A GAL IN KALAMAZOO .... *Capitol 108* 2-4 42

SHAKE YOUR FEET / SWANEE RIVER BLUES............... *Victor 19185* 3-5 23

SHANGHAI LIL (Vocal: Bob Lawrence) / SITTIN' ON A BACKYARD FENCE (Vocals: Red McKenzie & The Rhythm Boys) .... *Victor 24403* 5-8 33

SHANGHAI LULLABY / THE ONE I LOVE BELONGS TO SOMEBODY ELSE ...... *Victor 19245* 2-4 24

SHOULD I? (Vocal: Jack Fulton) / A BUNDLE OF OLD LOVE LETTERS (Vocal: Bing Crosby)... *Columbia 2047-D* 5-8 29
(This release has a picture label featuring the head of Paul Whiteman in caricature form, commonly called the "potato head" label.)

SIDE BY SIDE (Vocals: Bing Crosby, Al Rinker & Harry Barris) / PRETTY LIPS (Vocals: Bing Crosby & Al Rinker) .... *Victor 20627* 5-8 27

SING LOO / FOOTLOOSE (Vocal: Billy Murray) .... *Victor 19720* 3-5 25

SITTING ON A RAINBOW (Vocals: The King's Jesters) / OLD NEW ENGLAND MOON (Vocal: Jack Fulton) .... *Columbia 2224-D* 4-6 30

SMOKE GETS IN YOUR EYES (Vocal: Bob Lawrence) / SOMETHING HAD TO HAPPEN (Vocal: Ramona Davies) .... Victor 24455 3-5 33

SONG OF THE WANDERER / SO BLUE (Vocal: Austin Young).......... Victor 20570 3-5 27

SONYA (YUP, ALAY YUP!) (Vocal: Billy Murray) / GOT NO TIME........................ Victor 19721 3-5 25

SO THIS IS VENICE! (Vocal: Ed Smalle) / LEARN TO DO THE STRUT........... Victor 19252 3-5 24

STEPPING OUT / I'M GOIN' SOUTH ..... Victor 19229 2-4 24

STEPPIN' IN SOCIETY / LET ME LINGER LONGER IN YOUR ARMS (Vocal: Lewis James)........ Victor 19692 2-4 25

STUMBLING / GEORGIA................ Victor 18899 2-4 22

SWEET LADY / SAY IT WITH MUSIC.... Victor 18803 2-4 21

'TAIN'T SO, HONEY, 'TAIN'T SO (Vocal: Bing Crosby) / THAT'S MY WEAKNESS NOW (Vocals: Bing Crosby, Al Rinker & Harry Barris) .... Columbia 1444-D 8-10 28
(This release has a picture label featuring the head of Paul Whiteman in caricature form, commonly called the "potato head" label.)

TELL HER IN THE SPRINGTIME / INDIAN LOVE CALL................. Victor 19517 2-4 25

THAT CERTAIN FEELING / SWEET AND LOW DOWN.......................... Victor 19920 2-4 26

THERE AIN'T NO SWEET MAN THAT'S WORTH THE SALT OF MY TEARS (Vocals: Bing Crosby, Al Rinker, Harry Barris & trio) / SUGAR................. Victor 21464 10-12 28

THERE'S NO PLACE LIKE YOUR ARMS (Vocals: The Four Modernaires) / WHEN I GO A-DREAMING (Vocal: Joan Edwards)..................... Decca 2076 2-4 38

TILL TOMORROW / JUST AN ECHO IN THE VALLEY..................... Victor 24201 3-5 33
(Vocals: Jack Fulton)

TRAV'LIN' LIGHT (Vocal: Billie Holiday as Lady Day) / YOU WERE NEVER LOVELIER............. Capitol 116 5-8 42

TRICKS / COAL BLACK MAMMY........ Victor 18939 2-4 22

UKULELE LADY (Vocals: The Southern Fall Colored Quartet) / PAL OF MY CRADLE DAYS (Vocal: Lewis James)......................... Victor 19690 4-6 25

WAITING AT THE END OF THE ROAD (Vocal: Bing Crosby) / LOVE ME (Vocal: Jack Fulton) .... Columbia 1974-D 8-10 29
(This release has a picture label featuring the head of Paul Whiteman in caricature form, commonly called the "potato head" label.)

WALLA WALLA (Vocal: Billy Murray) / DIXIE'S FAVORITE SON.............. Victor 19489 3-5 24

WALTZ WAS BORN IN VIENNA, A (Vocals: The King's Men) / GLOOMY SUNDAY (Vocal: John Hauser)..................... Victor 25274 3-5 36

WASHBOARD BLUES (Vocal: Hoagy Carmichael) / AMONG MY SOUVENIRS (Vocals: Jack Fulton, Charles Gaylord, & Austin Young)................ Victor 35877 8-10 28
(This is an oversize 12-inch 78 rpm)

WHEEL OF THE WAGON IS BROKEN, THE (Vocal: Bob Lawrence) / SADDLE YOUR BLUES TO A WILD MUSTANG (Vocals: Bob Lawrence & The King's Men) .... Victor 25251 3-5 36

WHEN I GROW TOO OLD TO DREAM (Vocals: The King's Men) / THE NIGHT IS YOUNG (Vocal: Bob Lawrence) .... Victor 24844 3-5 35

WHEN IT'S SLEEPY-TIME DOWN SOUTH (Vocals: Mildred Bailey & The Romancers) / CAN'T YOU SEE? (Vocal: Mildred Bailey).............. Victor 22828 4-6 31

WHEN MY DREAMS COME TRUE (Vocal: Jack Fulton) / REACHING FOR SOMEONE (Vocal: Bing Crosby)................. Columbia 1822-D 10-12 29
(This release has a picture label featuring the head of Paul Whiteman in caricature form, commonly called the "potato head" label.)

WHEN THE ONE YOU LOVE LOVES YOU (Vocal: Franklyn Baur) / I'LL SEE YOU IN MY DREAMS..................... Victor 19553 2-4 25

WHEN YOU'RE IN LOVE / LITTLE LOG CABIN OF DREAMS (Vocal: Jack Fulton)......... Victor 21325 4-6 28

WHILE A CIGARETTE WAS BURNING (Vocal: Joan Edwards) / HEART AND SOUL................... Decca 2083 2-4 38

WHITEMAN STOMP / SENSATION STOMP................. Victor 21119 5-8 27

WILLOW, WEEP FOR ME / SO AT LAST IT'S COME TO THIS .... Victor 24187 3-5 33
(Vocals: Irene Taylor)

ZOOT SUIT, A (Vocals: Dolly Mitchell & Wingy Monone) / WELL-DIGGER'S BREAKDOWN....... Victor 27801 3-5 42

WHITEMAN, Paul, & His Orchestra as The Virginians

Directed by Ross Gorman
also see GORMAN, Ross, & His Earl Carroll Orchestra, see GORMAN, Ross, & His Fire Eaters, and see GORMAN, Ross, as Ross Gorman's Virginians
(Ross Gorman: circa 1890 – 2/28/53)
(The Virginians were a small, more jazz-oriented unit with members from the Paul Whiteman Orchestra)

AGGRAVATIN' PAPA / AUNT HAGAR'S BLUES.............. Victor 19021 3-5 23

BLUE ISLAND BLUES / BLUEBIRD BLUES.................. Victor 19226 2-4 23
(Vocals: Wendell Hall)

BRINGIN' HOME THE BACON (Vocals: Vernon Dalhart & Ed Smalle) / SHINE.................... Victor 19344 3-5 24

CUDDLE UP BLUES / MY HONEY'S LOVIN' ARMS .... Victor 18881 3-5 22

FAREWELL BLUES / APPLE SAUCE.... Victor 19032 3-5 23

I'VE GOT THE YES WE HAVE NO BANANAS BLUES / JUBILEE BLUES........... Victor 19135 3-5 23
(Vocals: Belle Baker)

I WISH I COULD SHIMMY LIKE MY SISTER KATE / GEE! BUT I HATE TO GO HOME ALONE........ Victor 18965 3-5 22

KISS MAMA, KISS PAPA) / CHOO-CHOO BLUES.................. Victor 18978 2-4 22

LONESOME MAMA BLUES / MEMPHIS BLUES.................. Victor 18895 3-5 22

MAMA LOVES PAPA, PAPA LOVES MAMA (Vocal: Jane Green) / MAMA GOES WHERE PAPA GOES................. Victor 19215 3-5 24

MINDIN' MY BUS'NESS / I'VE GOT A CROSS-EYED PAPA (BUT HE LOOKS STRAIGHT TO ME).................. Victor 19269 2-4 24

NOBODY LIED / YANKEE DOODLE BLUES..................... Victor 18913 2-4 22

NO ONE LOVES YOU BETTER THAN YOUR M-A-DOUBLE M-Y (Vocals: Billy Murray & Ed Smalle) / DON'T THINK YOU'LL BE MISSED (Vocal: Aileen Stanley) .... Victor 19039 3-5 23

SHE WOULDN'T DO WHAT I ASKED HER TO (Vocal: Billy Murray) / HURDY-GURDY BLUES .... Victor 19241 3-5 24

STAVIN' CHANGE (Vocal: Vernon Dalhart) / STACK O' LEE BLUES (by Fred Waring & His Pennsylvanians) .... Victor 19189 4-6 23

THAT DA DA STRAIN / HE MAY BE YOUR MAN............. Victor 19018 3-5 23

WHEN YOU AND I WERE YOUNG MAGGIE BLUES (Vocals: Isabella Patricola & Billy Murray) / COME ON HOME (Vocal: Isabella Patricola)... Victor 19010 3-5 23

WHOSE IZZY IS HE? (IS HE YOURS OR IS HE MINE?) (Vocal: Billy Murray) / SCISSOR GRINDER JOE .... Victor 19292 3-5 24

WHY SHOULD I CRY OVER YOU? / BLUE .... Victor 18933 2-4 22

YOU KNOW YOU BELONG TO SOMEBODY ELSE / WHOA, TILLIE! TAKE YOUR TIME.... Victor 19040 2-4 23

YOU MAY BE FAST, BUT MAMA'S GONNA SLOW YOU DOWN / PROMISE ME EVERYTHING, NEVER GET ANYTHING BLUES.................. Victor 19231 3-5 24
(Vocals: Aileen Stanley & Billy Murray)

WHITEMAN, Paul, & His Swing Wing

HOORAY FOR SPINACH / STEP UP AND SHAKE MY HAND.................... Decca 2418 2-4 39
(Vocals: The Four Modernaires)

I'M COMIN', VIRGINIA (Vocals: The Four Modernaires) / AUNT HAGAR'S BLUES (Vocals: Jack Teagarden & The Four Modernaires).................. Decca 2145 3-5 38

I USED TO BE COLOR-BLIND / PEELIN' THE PEACH................. Decca 2073 2-4 38
(Vocals: The Four Modernaires)

JAMBOREE JONES / SING A SONG OF SIXPENCE................ Decca 2074 2-4 38
(Vocals: The Four Modernaires)

THREE LITTLE FISHES (ITTY BITTY POO) / NOW AND THEN...................... Decca 2417 2-4 39
(Vocals: The Modernaires)

WHITEMAN, Paul, as Paul Whiteman's Bouncing Brass

HEAT WAVE / HOME AGAIN BLUES..... Decca 2697 3-5 39

I'VE FOUND A NEW BABY / ROSE ROOM................... Decca 2466 3-5 39

WHITEMAN, Paul, as Paul Whiteman's Sax Soctette

BLUE SKIES / WHAT'LL I DO?........... Decca 2698 3-5 39

I KISS YOUR HAND, MADAME / AFTER YOU'VE GONE................ Decca 2467 3-5 39

WHITNEY, Jack, & His Orchestra:

see SELVIN, Ben, & His Orchestra

WHOOPEE MAKERS, The:

see ELLINGTON, Duke, & His Cotton Club Orchestra see ELLINGTON, Duke, & His Orchestra, and see MILLS, Irving, as Mills' Merry Makers

WIEDOFT, Rudy, as The Palace Trio

(Rudy Wiedoft: 1/3/93 – 2/18/40)

CLOSE TO MY HEART / THE LOVE NEST................. Emerson 10203 2-4 20

DESERT DREAMS / MISSY.......... Brunswick 2034 2-4 20

HOP, SKIP AND JUMP / BEAUTIFUL FACES.............. Vocalion 14126 2-4 20

I KNOW WHY / DO YOU KNOW?................... Emerson 10197 2-4 20

I WANT A DADDY WHO WILL ROCK ME TO SLEEP / I'VE GOT MY CAPTIN WORKING FOR ME NOW............. Pathe 22243 3-5 19

JUST FOR TODAY / YOU'LL BE SORRY .... Pathe 22205 2-4 19

MISSY / LONE STAR.................. Pathe 20459 2-4 20

UNLUCKY BLUES / MISSY........... Vocalion 14053 3-5 20

YOU'LL BE SORRY / WHERE THE LANTERNS GLOW................. Emerson 1062 2-4 19

YOU'RE JUST LIKE A ROSE / TAKE ME....................... Emerson 10260 2-4 20

WIEDOFT, Rudy, as The Palace Trio & Orchestra

STRUT, MISS LIZZIE / SPREAD YO' STUFF................ Olympic 15101 4-6 21

WIEDOFT, Rudy, as Rudy Wiedoft's Californians / Wiedoft's Californians

BEAUTIFUL FACES / SHOW ME HOW... Pathe 22467 2-4 20

HOME AGAIN BLUES / MIDNIGHT MOON................. Olympic 15103 3-5 21

JUNE MOON / WHEN BUDDHA SMILES.......... Vocalion 14251 2-4 21

LONESOME HOURS / OLD-FASHIONED GIRL........... Brunswick 2248 2-4 22
(Vocals: Walter Haenschen)

ROSY POSY / MR. AND MRS.......... Vocalion 14320 2-4 22

SHEIK, THE / BROKEN TOY......... Brunswick 2175 2-4 21

SONG OF INDIA / DEAR OLD SOUTHLAND........... Vocalion 14285 2-4 22

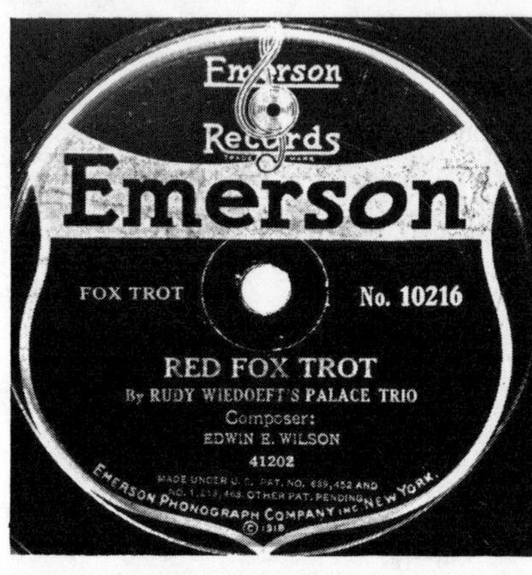

WIEDOEFT, Rudy, as Rudy Wiedoeft's Palace Trio

RED FOX TROT / IN SWEET SEPTEMBER (by Harry Raderman as The Plantation Jazz Orchstra) .... Emerson 10216 2-4 20

WIEDOFT'S CALIFORNIANS:

see WIEDOFT, Rudy, as Rudy Wiedoft's Californians

WILDER, Alec, as The Alec Wilder Octet

(Alec Wilder: 2/17/07 –)

ALL THINGS YOU ARE / BLUE RAIN .... Vocalion 5277 4-6 39
(Vocals: Mildred Bailey)

I'VE GONE OFF THE DEEP END / I SHOULDA STOOD IN BED .... Vocalion 5236 4-6 39

WILLIAMS, Bill, & His Gang:

see HARING, Bob, as Haring's Happy Harmonizers & see McKAY, Marion, & His Orchestra

WILLIAMS, Buddy, & His Golden Echo Music

ON THE MALL / SPRING MADE A FOOL OF ME .... Rainbow 40088 5-8 –
(This record was pressed in red vinyl)

WILLIAMS, Clarence, & His Orchestra / Clarence Williams' Orchestra

(Clarence Williams: 10/8/98 – 11/6/65)

AIN'T GONNA GIVE YOU NONE OF MY JELLY ROLL (Vocals: Clarence Williams) / SUGAR BLUES (Vocal: Chick Bullock).... Vocalion 2805 8-10 34

BEAU-KOO-JACK / SISTER KATE....... QRS R-7044 100-125 29
(QRS records are extremely rare)

BEER GARDEN BLUES / BREEZE (Vocal: Clarence Williams)....... Vocalion 2541 10-12 33

BIMBO / 'WAY DOWN HOME.......... Vocalion 2778 10-12 34

BLACK-EYED SUSAN BROWN / MAMA STAYED OUT ALL NIGHT LONG............... Vocalion 25009 12-15 33
(Vocals: Ed Allen & Floyd Casey)

BLACK GAL / A FOOLISH LITTLE GIRL LIKE YOU (Vocal: Clarence Williams)..... Vocalion 2938 10-12 35

BOZO / BIMBO......................... QRS R-7034 100-125 29
(QRS records are extremely rare)

DISPOSSESSIN' ME / CHOCOLATE AVENUE............... Vocalion 2584 12-15 33
(Some copies credit Clarence Williams as vocalist on the first side, but both are instrumental arrangements.)

HARLEM RHYTHM DANCE / FOR SALE (HANNAH JOHNSON'S BIG JACK ASS) (Vocal: Ed Allen)........... Vocalion 2602 15-20 34

HIGH SOCIETY / I LIKE TO GO BACK IN THE EVENING.......... Vocalion 25010 12-15 33

HOW CAN I GET IT? (Vocal: Ed Allen) / ON THE SUNNY SIDE OF THE STREET (Vocal: Chick Bullock)................. Vocalion 2630 10-15 34
(The label on the first side erroneously credits Henry Allen as vocalist.)

I CAN'T DANCE, I GOT ANTS IN MY PANTS (Vocals: Charlie Gaines, Louis Jordan, & Clarence Williams) / CHRISTMAS NIGHT IN HARLEM (Vocal: Chick Bullock) . . . *Vocalion 2689* 8-10 34

I GOT HORSES AND GOT NUMBERS ON MY MIND / NEW ORLEANS HOP SCOP BLUES . . . *Vocalion 2654* 10-12 34 (Vocals: Clarence Williams)

I'M THROUGH (Vocal: Clarence Williams) / LONGSHOREMAN'S BLUES . . . *QRS R-7040* 100-125 29 (QRS records are extremely rare)

I SAW STARS / RHAPSODY IN LOVE . . . *Vocalion 2899* 5-8 34 (Vocals: Clarence Williams)

JERRY THE JUNKER (Vocals: Clarence Williams & chorus) / CHIZZLIN' SAM (Vocals: Clarence Williams, Eva Taylor, & chorus) . . . *Vocalion 2854* 10-12 34

JUNGLE CRAWL / SAVIN' UP FOR BABY (Vocal: Clarence Williams) . . . *Vocalion 2909* 10-12 35

LAZY MAMA / MOUNTAIN CITY BLUES . . . *Okeh 8592* 35-40 28

LEFT ALL ALONE WITH THE BLUES / I'VE FOUND A NEW BABY . . . *Okeh 8763* 20-25 30

LONG, DEEP AND WIDE / SPEAKEASY . . . *QRS R-7004* 100-125 28 (QRS records are extremely rare)

MILK COW BLUES / THERE'S GONNA BE THE DEVIL TO PAY (Vocal: Clarence Williams) . . . *Vocalion 2927* 10-12 35

PANE IN THE GLASS / SATURDAY NIGHT JAG (Vocal: Laura Bryant) . . . *Paramount 12870* 70-80 29

PANE IN THE GLASS / SATURDAY NIGHT JAG (Vocal: Laura Bryant) . . . *Broadway 5067* 60-70 29 (Simultaneously released on two labels)

PAPA DE-DA-DA (Vocals: Ward Pinkett, Clarence Williams, Eva Taylor & Clarence Todd) / BABY, WON'T YOU PLEASE COME HOME? (Vocals: Clarence Williams, Eva Taylor & Clarence Todd) . . . *Banner 32021* 10-12 30

PAPA DE-DA-DA (Vocals: Ward Pinkett, Clarence Williams, Eva Taylor & Clarence Todd) / BABY, WON'T YOU PLEASE COME HOME? (Vocals: Clarence Williams, Eva Taylor & Clarence Todd) . . . *Domino 4687* 10-12 30

PAPA DE-DA-DA (Vocals: Ward Pinkett, Clarence Williams, Eva Taylor & Clarence Todd) / BABY, WON'T YOU PLEASE COME HOME? (Vocals: Clarence Williams, Eva Taylor & Clarence Todd) . . . *Jewel 6141* 10-12 30

PAPA DE-DA-DA (Vocals: Ward Pinkett, Clarence Williams, Eva Taylor & Clarence Todd) / BABY, WON'T YOU PLEASE COME HOME? (Vocals: Clarence Williams, Eva Taylor & Clarence Todd) . . . *Oriole 2141* 10-12 30

PAPA DE-DA-DA (Vocals: Ward Pinkett, Clarence Williams, Eva Taylor & Clarence Todd) / BABY, WON'T YOU PLEASE COME HOME? (Vocals: Clarence Williams, Eva Taylor & Clarence Todd) . . . *Perfect 15387* 10-12 30

PAPA DE-DA-DA (Vocals: Ward Pinkett, Clarence Williams, Eva Taylor & Clarence Todd) / BABY, WON'T YOU PLEASE COME HOME? (Vocals: Clarence Williams, Eva Taylor & Clarence Todd) . . . *Romeo 1515* 10-12 30 (Simultaneously released on six labels)

RIGHT KEY BUT THE WRONG KEYHOLE, THE / SHE'S JUST GOT A LITTLE BIT LEFT . . . *Vocalion 2563* 12-15 33 (Vocals: Ed Allen)

SHAKE EM UP / JINGLES . . . *Paramount 12587* 25-30 27

SHOOTING THE PISTOL / BOTTOMLAND . . . *Paramount 12517* 25-30 27

SQUEEZE ME / NEW DOWN HOME BLUES . . . *QRS R-7005* 100-125 28 (QRS records are extremely rare)

ST. LOUIS BLUES / MISTER, WILL YOU SERENADE? (Vocal: Clarence Williams) . . . *Vocalion 2676* 10-12 34

SWALLER-TAIL COAT / LOOKA-THERE, AIN'T SHE PRETTY? . . . *Vocalion 2619* 10-12 34 (Vocals: Chick Bullock)

THIS IS MY SUNDAY OFF / LET EVERY DAY BE MOTHER'S DAY . . . *Vocalion 3195* 5-8 35 (On some copies, the label on the second side reads: "Let Every Day Be Sweetheart's Day.")

WATCHIN' THE CLOCK / FREEZE OUT . . . *Okeh 8663* 20-25 29

WILDFLOWER RAG / MIDNIGHT STOMP . . . *QRS R-7033* 100-125 29 (QRS records are extremely rare)

YAMA YAMA BLUES / LADY LUCK BLUES . . . *Vocalion 2991* 10-12 35

WILLIAMS, Clarence, as Clarence Williams' Orchestra:

see WILLIAMS, Clarence, & His Orchestra

WILLIAMS, Cootie, & His Orchestra

(Cootie Williams: 7/24/10 –)

AIN'T MISBEHAVIN' / BLUES IN MY CONDITION . . . *Okeh 6224* 5-8 41

WEST BEND BLUES / G-MEN . . . *Okeh 6370* 5-8 41

WILLIAMS, Griff, & His Orchestra

HAWAIIAN SUNSET / I FORGIVE BUT CAN'T FORGET YOU . . . *Okeh 6433* 3-5 41 (Vocals: Bob Kirk)

HONEY DEAR (Vocal: Dorothy Doe) / WHAT'S COOKIN' COOKIE? (Vocal: Walter King) . . . *Okeh 6510* 3-5 42

I MUST HAVE BEEN BLIND (Vocal: Bob Kirk) / BEAUTIFUL FACES (Vocals: The Williams Warblers) . . . *Okeh 6283* 2-4 41

MAMA'S GONE, GOODBYE (Vocals: The Williams Warblers) / HONOLULU BUNDLE (Vocal: Walter King) . . . *Okeh 6248* 3-5 41

YUM YUM (Vocal: Buddy Moreno) / BIRTH OF PASSION . . . *Varsity 8402* 2-4 40

YUM YUM (Vocal: Buddy Moreno) / YOU'RE THE SUNSHINE OF MY HEART (Vocals: Unknown) . . . *Hit 7052* 2-4 40

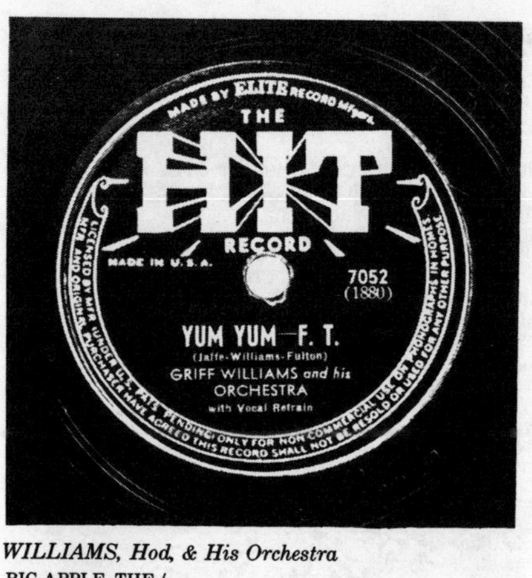

WILLIAMS, Hod, & His Orchestra

BIG APPLE, THE / SHADES OF HADES . . . *Bluebird B-7104* 5-8 37

LADY FROM FIFTH AVENUE, THE / NIGHT OVER SHANGHAI (Vocal: Ralph Fay) . . . *Bluebird B-7106* 4-6 37

LITTLE FRATERNITY PIN (Vocal: Ralph Fay) / MY SECRET LOVE AFFAIR (Vocal: Dorothy Goff) . . . *Bluebird B-7108* 3-5 37

MONOPOLY SWING (WILLIAMS SONG) / OLD KING COLE . . . *Bluebird B-7119* 5-8 37

SOPHISTICATED SWING / SOUTHLAND . . . *Bluebird B-7141* 4-6 37

WILLIAMS, Keith, & His Orchestra

PIXIE FROM DIXIE, THE (Vocals: Keith Williams & Wally Holmes) / COLLEEN (Vocal: Joe McCarthy) . . . *Sunstone 102* 4-6 –

WILLIAMS, Ralph, & His Orchestra

MY DARLING / YOU KNOW I DO (Vocal: Paul Small) . . . *Victor 19957* 3-5 26

WILLIAMS, Ralph, & His Rainbo Orchestra

GET LUCKY / PRINCE OF WALES . . . *Victor 19504* 5-8 25

WILSON, Duke, & His Ten Black Berries:

see HAYMES, Joe, & His Orchestra

WILSON'S NOVELTY TEN:

see LANIN, Sam, & His Orchestra

WILSON, Teddy, & His Orchestra

(Teddy Wilson: 11/24/12 –)

APRIL IN MY HEART / I'LL NEVER FAIL YOU . . . *Brunswick 8265* 5-8 39 (Vocals: Billie Holiday)

BUT NOT FOR ME (Vocal: Helen Ward) / OH! LADY BE GOOD . . . *Columbia 36084* 2-4 41

CARELESSLY / HOW COULD YOU? . . . *Brunswick 7867* 5-8 37 (Vocals: Billie Holiday)

CHRISTOPHER COLUMBUS / ALL MY LIFE (Vocal: Ella Fitzgerald) . . . *Brunswick 7640* 5-8 36

COCOANUT GROOVE / 71 . . . *Columbia 35737* 4-6 40

CRYING MY SOUL OUT FOR YOU (Vocal: Jean Eldridge) / IN THE MOOD . . . *Columbia 35372* 4-6 40

EARLY SESSION HOP / LADY OF MYSTERY . . . *Columbia 35207* 4-6 39

EASY TO LOVE / THE WAY YOU LOOK TONIGHT . . . *Brunswick 7762* 5-8 36 (Vocals: Billie Holiday)

EENY MEENY MINEY MO / IF YOU WERE MINE . . . *Brunswick 7554* 5-8 35 (Vocals: Billie Holiday)

EVERYBODY'S LAUGHING / HERE IT IS TOMORROW AGAIN . . . *Brunswick 8259* 5-8 38 (Vocals: Billie Holiday)

HE AIN'T GOT RHYTHM / THIS YEAR'S KISSES . . . *Brunswick 7824* 8-10 37 (Vocals: Billie Holiday)

HOW AM I TO KNOW? (Vocal: Helen Ward) / I'M COMING, VIRGINIA . . . *Brunswick 7893* 5-8 37

IF I HAD YOU / YOU BROUGHT A NEW KIND OF LOVE TO ME . . . *Brunswick 7960* 4-6 37 (Vocals: Frances Hunt)

IF I WERE YOU (Vocal: Nan Wynn) / JUNGLE LOVE . . . *Brunswick 8150* 5-8 38

I'LL GET BY / MEAN TO ME . . . *Brunswick 7903* 5-8 37 (Vocals: Billie Holiday)

I'LL NEVER BE THE SAME (Vocal: Billie Holiday) / I'VE FOUND A NEW BABY . . . *Brunswick 7926* 5-8 37

I'M PAINTING THE TOWN RED (Vocal: Billie Holiday) / SWEET LORRAINE . . . *Brunswick 7520* 8-10 35

I'M WITH YOU (RIGHT OR WRONG) / WHERE THE LAZY RIVER GOES BY . . . *Brunswick 7797* 5-8 37 (Vocals: Midge Williams)

I NEVER KNEW / EMBRACEABLE YOU (Vocal: Helen Ward) . . . *Columbia 35905* 2-4 41

IT'S LIKE REACHING FOR THE MOON / GUESS WHO . . . *Brunswick 7702* 5-8 36 (Vocals: Billie Holiday)

I WISHED ON THE MOON / MISS BROWN TO YOU . . . *Brunswick 7501* 8-10 35 (Vocals: Billie Holiday)

JUMPIN' FOR JOY / THE MAN I LOVE . . . *Brunswick 8438* 5-8 39

JUMPIN' ON THE BLACKS AND WHITES (theme song) / LITTLE THINGS THAT MEAN SO MUCH (Vocal: Jean Eldridge) . . . *Columbia 35232* 4-6 39

LOVE GROWS ON THE WHITE OAK TREE / THIS IS THE MOMENT . . . *Brunswick 8455* 5-8 39 (Vocals: Thelma Carpenter)

MOANIN' LOW (Vocal: Billie Holiday) / FINE AND DANDY . . . *Brunswick 7877* 8-10 37

MOMENTS LIKE THIS / I CAN'T FACE THE MUSIC . . . *Brunswick 8112* 5-8 38 (Vocals: Nan Wynn)

MORE THAN YOU KNOW / SUGAR . . . *Brunswick 8319* 5-8 39 (Vocals: Billie Holiday)

MY FIRST IMPRESSION OF YOU / IF DREAMS COME TRUE . . . *Brunswick 8053* 5-8 38 (Vocals: Billie Holiday)

MY MAN / CAN'T HELP LOVIN' DAT MAN . . . *Brunswick 8008* 5-8 37 (Vocals: Billie Holiday)

NOW IT CAN BE TOLD / A-TISKET, A-TASKET . . . *Brunswick 8199* 4-6 38 (Vocals: Nan Wynn)

OUT OF NOWHERE (Vocal: Lena Horne) / YOU'RE MY FAVORITE MEMORY (Vocal: Helen Ward) . . . *Columbia 36737* 3-5 42

PENNIES FROM HEAVEN / THAT'S LIFE I GUESS . . . *Brunswick 7789* 5-8 37 (Vocals: Billie Holiday)

SAY IT WITH A KISS / THEY SAY . . . *Brunswick 8270* 5-8 39 (Vocals: Billie Holiday)

SWEET LORRAINE / LIZA . . . *Columbia 35711* 2-4 40

TEA FOR TWO / I'LL SEE YOU IN MY DREAMS . . . *Brunswick 7816* 5-8 37

THESE 'N' THAT 'N' THOSE (Vocal: Billie Holiday) / SUGAR PLUM . . . *Brunswick 7577* 5-8 36

TWENTY-FOUR HOURS A DAY / YANKEE DOODLE NEVER WENT TO TOWN . . . *Brunswick 7550* 5-8 35 (Vocals: Billie Holiday)

WARMIN' UP / BLUES IN C SHARP MINOR . . . *Brunswick 7684* 5-8 36

WHAM (Vocals: J. C. Heard & chorus) / MOON RAY (Vocal: Jean Eldridge) . . . *Columbia 35354* 3-5 40

WHAT A LITTLE MOONLIGHT CAN DO / A SUNBONNET BLUE . . . *Brunswick 7498* 8-10 35 (Vocals: Billie Holiday)

WHAT A NIGHT, WHAT A MOON, WHAT A GIRL / IT'S TOO HOT FOR WORDS . . . *Brunswick 7511* 8-10 35 (Vocals: Billie Holiday)

WHEN YOU'RE SMILING / I CAN'T BELIEVE THAT YOU'RE IN LOVE WITH ME . . . *Brunswick 8070* 5-8 38 (Vocals: Billie Holiday)

WHY WAS I BORN? / I MUST HAVE THAT MAN! . . . *Brunswick 7859* 5-8 37 (Vocals: Billie Holiday)

WITH THEE I SWING / WHO LOVES YOU? . . . *Brunswick 7768* 5-8 36 (Vocals: Billie Holiday)

YOU CAME TO MY RESCUE / HERE'S LOVE IN YOUR EYES . . . *Brunswick 7739* 5-8 36 (Vocals: Helen Ward as Vera Lane)

YOU GO TO MY HEAD / I'LL DREAM TONIGHT . . . *Brunswick 8141* 5-8 38 (Vocals: Nan Wynn)

YOU LET ME DOWN / SPREADIN' RHYTHM AROUND . . . *Brunswick 7581* 5-8 36 (Vocals: Billie Holiday)

YOU'RE GONNA SEE A LOT OF ME / HELLO, MY DARLING . . . *Brunswick 8281* 5-8 39 (Vocals: Billie Holiday)

YOU'RE SO DESIRABLE / LET'S DREAM IN THE MOONLIGHT . . . *Brunswick 8283* 5-8 39 (Vocals: Billie Holiday)

YOU SHOWED ME THE WAY / MY LAST AFFAIR . . . *Brunswick 7840* 5-8 37 (Vocals: Billie Holiday)

WINTER, "Chic", & His Orchestra/ Chic Winter Orchestra

also see ELLINGTON, Duke, & His Orchestra as The Washingtonians

SPRING IS HERE (Vocals: Unknown) / YOU CAN'T BE A GOOD LITTLE FELLOW . . . *Gennett 3294* 4-6 26

TROPICAL PALMS / FOLLOW THE SWALLOW . . . *Puretone 11412* 10-12 24 (This record was pressed in brown shellac)

WINTER, Chic, as Chic Winter's Orchestra:

see ELLINGTON, Duke, & His Orchestra as The Washingtonians and see WINTER, Chic, & His Orchestra

WINTERS, Chuck, & His Boys:

see PALMQUIST, Ernie, & His Carolina Collegians

WISCONSIN ROOF ORCHESTRA, The:

see DEVINE'S WISCONSIN ROOF ORCHESTRA

W. M. C. A. BROADCASTERS, The

AT SUNDOWN (Vocals: Tom & Jerry) / SWANEE RIVER TRAIL (Vocal: Frank Bessinger) . . . *Harmony 354-H* 2-4 27

BREEZIN' ALONG WITH THE BREEZE / LO-DO-DE-O . . . *Harmony 219-H* 2-4 26

KATINKA (Vocal: Irving Kaufman as Ivan Terribilsky) / VALENCIA . . . *Harmony 180-H* 2-4 26

LANTERN OF LOVE / BURGUNDY . . . *Harmony 146-H* 2-4 26

MY IDEA OF HEAVEN / I'LL JUST GO ALONG . . . *Harmony 389-H* 2-4 27 (Vocals: Arthur Fields)

SHADY TREE, A / GOOD NEWS . . . *Harmony 491-H* 2-4 27 (Vocals: Irving Kaufman)

SOMEBODY AND ME! (Vocal: Irving Kaufman) / HERE AM I, BROKEN-HEARTED (Vocal: Charles Hart) . . . *Harmony 461-H* 2-4 27

SOMEDAY / FIRE! (Vocal: The "Old Fireman") . . . *Harmony 293-H* 2-4 26

TAMIAMI TRAIL / NO MORE WORRYIN' .... *Harmony 156-H* 2-4 26

THERE'S A BOATMAN ON THE VOLGA / MOONLIGHT ON THE GANGES.... *Harmony 282-H* 2-4 26

YANKEE ROSE / ALL I WANT IS YOU... *Harmony 339-H* 2-4 27

WOLVERINE ORCHESTRA, The

directed by Dick Voynow
also see ORIGINAL WOLVERINES, The
(Star Performer: Bix Beiderbecke: 3/10/03 – 8/6/31)

FIDGETY FEET / JAZZ ME BLUES...... *Gennett 5408* 40-50 24

I NEED SOME PETTIN' / ROYAL GARDEN BLUES............ *Gennett 20062* 50-60 24

OH BABY / COPENHAGEN............. *Gennett 5453* 40-50 24

RIVERBOAT SHUFFLE / SUSIE .... *Gennett 5454* 50-60 24

SENSATION / LAZY DADDY .... *Gennett 5542* 40-50 24

TIA JUANA / BIG BOY .... *Gennett 5565* 50-60 24

WHEN MY SUGAR WALKS DOWN THE STREET / PRINCE OF WAILS.................. *Gennett 5620* 15-20 25

WOLVERINE ORCHESTRA, The, as The Jazz Harmonists

OH BABY / COPENHAGEN......... *Claxtonola 40336* 40-50 24

RIVERBOAT SHUFFLE / SUSIE..... *Claxtonola 40339* 50-60 24

SENSATION / LAZY DADDY........ *Claxtonola 40375* 40-50 24

WYLIE, Allister, & His Coronado Hotel Orchestra

COME ON, BABY! / SOME OF THESE DAYS .... *Brunswick 4143* 8-10 28
(Vocals: Rich Richards)

LOVE TALE OF ALSACE LORRAINE, A / SOME NIGHTS WHEN YOU'RE LONELY.......... *Brunswick 4144* 4-6 28

WYLIE, Austin, & His Golden Pheasant Orchestra

(Austin Wylie: circa 1893 –)

ALL FOR YOU / RHYTHM OF THE DAY............ *Vocalion 15228* 3-5 26

CHINA GIRL / IF IT WASN'T FOR YOU................. *Vocalion 14975* 3-5 25

COULD I? CERTAINLY COULD (Vocals: Frank Bessinger & Frank Wright) / VALENCIA........... *Vocalion 15332* 2-4 26

HONEY BUNCH / BYE-BYE BLACKBIRD............. *Vocalion 15333* 3-5 26
(Vocals: Frank Bessinger & Frank Wright)

I'M GONNA CHARLESTON BACK TO CHARLESTON / CHARLESTON BABY OF MINE..... *Vocalion 15098* 4-6 25

LOOKING FOR A BOY / THAT CERTAIN FEELING.......... *Vocalion 15225* 3-5 26

MOONLIGHT AND ROSES / WAIT 'TILL THE MORNING AFTER............ *Vocalion 14993* 2-4 25
(Vocals: Irving Kaufman)

MY BEST GIRL / I WANT TO BE HAPPY.................... *Vocalion 14893* 4-6 24
(This record was pressed in brown shellac)

WYNNE, Billy, & His Greenwich Village Inn Orchestra

ALABAMY BOUND / WHAT A SMILE CAN DO............. *Edison 51501* 5-8 25
(Vocals: Ernest Hare)

CHARLESTON BABY OF MINE / SOMEBODY'S CRAZY ABOUT YOU ... *Edison 51606* 10-12 25

I WANT TO BE HAPPY / KEEP ON DANCING.................. *Edison 51432* 8-10 24

NOW NOW, NOT YET, BUT SOON / PETER PAN .... *Edison 51452* 5-8 25

PANGO PANGO MAID / BRIGHTER DAYS .... *Edison 51566* 10-12 25

WHEN MY SUGAR WALKS DOWN THE STREET / LENORE............ *Edison 51549* 10-12 25

WYNNE, Billy, & His Orchestra

DOROTHY / NO FOOLIN' .... *Pathe Actuelle 36431* 4-6 26
(Vocals: Arthur Hall)

DOROTHY / NO FOOLIN'............... *Perfect 14612* 3-5 26
(Vocals: Arthur Hall)
(Simultaneously released on two labels)

DREAMING OF TOMORROW / LET'S WANDER AWAY............ *Harmony 34-H* 4-6 25

FRESHIE / WHY AREN'T YEZ EATIN' MORE ORANGES?..... *Harmony 54-H* 4-6 25
(Vocals: Billy Jones as Billy West)

SWEET SUMMER BREEZE / UNDER THE UKELELE TREE..... *Harmony 135-H* 2-4 26
(Vocals: Irving Kaufman)

YANKEE TEN, The:
see BUFFALODIANS, The

YATES, Danny, & His Orchestra

HE'S MY SECRET PASSION / SHE LOVES ME JUST THE SAME............ *Melotone M-12004* 5-8 30
(Vocals: Smith Ballew)

YERKES, Harry A., as The Happy Six

FIRST, LAST, AND ALWAYS / LOU'SIANA..................... *Columbia A-3948* 2-4 23

GOODBYE, SHANGHAI! / WIMMIN... *Columbia A-3542* 2-4 22

NOBODY LIED / IF I HAD MY WAY, PRETTY BABY............ *Columbia A-3645* 2-4 22

ROCKAWAY BABY / BY THE PYRAMIDS.............. *Columbia A-3314* 2-4 20

SWEET ONE / WHO'S SORRY NOW?............. *Columbia A-3861* 2-4 23

YERKES, Harry A., as Harry A. Yerkes' Dance Orchestra

GRANADA / WOND'RING............ *Vocalion 14107* 2-4 20

SHAKE YOUR LITTLE SHOULDER / OH, BY JINGO!..................... *Vocalion 14041* 3-5 20

MYSTERY / SWANEE................ *Vocalion 14024* 3-5 20

SUNNY TENNESSEE / ROSE OF WASHINGTON SQUARE............ *Vocalion 14060* 2-4 20

YERKES, Harry A., as The Yerkes Jazarimba Band / Orchestra

ALL THE QUAKERS ARE SHOULDER SHAKERS / PATCHES (Vocals: Unknown)........ *Paramount 33039* 4-6 19

ALL THE QUAKERS ARE SHOULDER SHAKERS / PATCHES (Vocals: Unknown)............ *Puritan 9039* 3-5 19
(Simultaneously released on two labels)

CAIRO / SOMEBODY'S SWEETHEART............. *Aeolian Vocalion 12194* 3-5 19

LEFT ALL ALONE AGAIN BLUES / ALEXANDRIA................... *Columbia A-6148* 2-4 20

OLD FASHIONED GARDEN / ROSIE.......................... *Paramount 20043* 3-5 21

ROSIE / YOU OUGHTA SEE MY BABY.................. *Columbia A-3364* 2-4 21

SNAP YOUR FINGERS AT CARE / ANYTIME, ANYDAY, ANYWHERE...... *Lyric 4232* 5-8 20

SYNCOPATED DREAM / DANCE-O-MANIA.................. *Vocalion 14071* 3-5 20

YERKES JAZARIMBA ORCHESTRA, The:
see YERKES, Harry A., as The Harry A. Yerkes Jazarimba Band

YOUNG, Sterling, & His Orchestra

I'M BUBBLING OVER (Vocal: Donna Lee) / NEVER IN A MILLION YEARS
(Vocal: Billy Mozet).................. *Melotone 7-05-21* 3-5 37

NO MORE TEARS (Vocal: Donna Lee) / SWEET HEARTACHE (Vocal: Billy Mozet)..... *Melotone 7-05-01* 4-6 37

ONE IN A MILLION (Vocal: Donna Lee) / WHO'S AFRAID OF LOVE? (Vocal: Billy Mozet)........ *Melotone 7-04-01* 4-6 37

PETER PIPER / NOW THAT SUMMER IS GONE.... *Melotone 7-01-02* 4-6 37
(Vocals: Sterling Young Trio)

ROSES IN DECEMBER / LET'S HAVE ANOTHER CIGARETTE........... *Melotone 7-09-02* 4-6 37
(Vocals: Gil Dagunnis)

SLUMMING ON PARK AVENUE (Vocal: Donna Lee) / I'VE GOT MY LOVE TO KEEP ME WARM
(Vocal: Billy Mozet).................. *Melotone 7-04-04* 4-6 37

SLUMMING ON PARK AVENUE (Vocal: Donna Lee) / I'VE GOT MY LOVE TO KEEP ME WARM
(Vocal: Billy Mozet).................... *Perfect 7-04-04* 4-6 37
(Simultaneously released on two labels)

TOP OF THE TOWN (Vocal: Billy Mozet) / WHERE ARE YOU? (Vocal: Donna Lee)........ *Melotone 7-01-12* 4-6 37

WHISPERS IN THE DARK / STOP! YOU'RE BREAKING MY HEART........... *Melotone 7-08-06* 4-6 37
(Vocals: Donna Lee)

YOUNG, Victor, & The Brunswick Orchestra / & His Orchestra
(Victor Young: 8/8/00 – 11/11/56)

DAY WITHOUT YOU, A (Vocal: Harlan Lattimore) / THIS LITTLE PIGGIE WENT TO MARKET
(Vocal: Jane Vance).................. *Brunswick 6747* 5-8 34

DOWN A CAROLINA LANE / REMEMBER ME.................. *Brunswick 6549* 5-8 33
(Vocals: Smith Ballew)

LADY IN RED / TO CALL YOU MY OWN.......................... *Decca 451* 4-6 35
(Vocals: Milton Watson)

LOVE LETTERS IN THE SAND (Vocal: Scrappy Lambert) / LET'S DRIFT AWAY ON DREAMER'S BAY
(Vocals: The Three Minute Men)......... *Brunswick 6188* 3-5 31

SAY WHEN / WHEN LOVES COMES SWINGIN' ALONG.............. *Decca 278* 5-8 35
(Vocals: Al Bowlly)

SING A LITTLE JINGLE / I FOUND A MILLION DOLLAR BABY........ *Brunswick 6128* 5-8 31
(Vocals: Boswell Sisters)

TWO TICKETS TO GEORGIA / THE GRASS IS GETTING GREENER ALL THE TIME..... *Banner 32731* 5-8 33
(Vocals: Chick Bullock)

TWO TICKETS TO GEORGIA / THE GRASS IS GETTING GREENER ALL THE TIME....... *Oriole 2675* 5-8 33
(Vocals: Chick Bullock)

TWO TICKETS TO GEORGIA / THE GRASS IS GETTING GREENER ALL THE TIME...... *Romeo 2048* 5-8 33
(Vocals: Chick Bullock)
(Simultaneously released on three labels)

WHERE HAVE WE MET BEFORE? (Vocal: Smith Ballew) / YOU'RE AN OLD SMOOTHIE
(Vocals: Lee Wiley & Billy Hughes)...... *Brunswick 6484* 5-8 33

YOURS IS MY HEART ALONE / HAVE YOU FORGOTTEN?......... *Brunswick 6117* 5-8 31
(Vocals: Smith Ballew)

ZOLLO, Leo, & His Orchestra:
see MITCHELL, Al, & His Orchestra

ZURKE, Bob, & His Delta Rhythm Band
(Bob Zurke: 1/17/12 – 2/16/44)

BETWEEN 18TH AND 19TH ON CHESTNUT STREET (Vocal: Sterling Bose) / PINCH ME
(Vocal: Evelyn Poe).......................... *Victor 26450* 4-6 40

BETWEEN THE DEVIL AND THE DEEP BLUE SEA (Vocal: Claire Martin) / I'VE FOUND A NEW BABY........................ *Victor 26355* 4-6 39

COW COW BLUES / RHUMBOOGIE (Vocal: Evelyn Poe)....... *Victor 26646* 4-6 40

CUBAN BOOGIE-WOOGIE / ON A LITTLE STREET IN SINGAPORE (Vocal: Claire Martin)........ *Victor 26411* 4-6 39

EACH TIME YOU SAY GOODBYE (Vocal: Claire Martin) / HOBSON STREET BLUES (theme song) ... *Victor 26317* 5-8 39

FAITHFUL FOREVER / IT'S A HAP-HAP-HAPPY DAY............... *Victor 26395* 3-5 39
(Vocals: Claire Martin)

FIT TO BE TIED (Vocal: Claire Martin) / PEACH TREE STREET
(Vocal: Sterling Bose).................... *Victor 26420* 4-6 39

I'M LOSING MY MIND (BECAUSE OF YOU) / I BOUGHT A WOODEN WHISTLE............... *Victor 26607* 3-5 40
(Vocals: Evelyn Poe)

MELANCHOLY MOOD (Vocal: Claire Martin) / HONKY-TONK TRAIN BLUES......... *Victor 26342* 3-5 39

NICKEL NABBER BLUES / I WANT MY MAMA (Vocal: Evelyn Poe)........... *Victor 26467* 4-6 40

SOMEBODY TOLD ME (Vocal: Evelyn Poe) / HOLY SMOKE (Vocal: Gus Ehrman)....... *Victor 26446* 4-6 40

SOUTHERN EXPOSURE / IT'S ME AGAIN (Vocal: Claire Martin)............. *Victor 26331* 4-6 39

TEA FOR TWO / I LOVE YOU MUCH TOO MUCH (Vocal: Evelyn Poe)........... *Victor 26561* 4-6 40

TOM CAT ON THE KEYS / EVERYBODY STEP.................... *Victor 26526* 5-8 40

YOU HIT MY HEART WITH A BANG / PUT YOUR LITTLE FOOT THERE................ *Victor 26474* 4-6 40
(Vocals: Evelyn Poe)

NOTES

BUYER-SELLER DIRECTORY

The following pages are jam-packed with personal and business ads, certain to be useful and appealing to anyone with an interest in music collecting.

Each of the Osborne publications offer an outstanding opportunity for those in the hobby to cost-effectively spread the word worldwide about their products and services. Equally popular is the ability, particularly through the Directory Mini-Ads, to locate those elusive records for your collection.

Directory Mini-Ads are the absolute best advertising buy available anywhere. The cost is amazingly low and the results have proven to be spectacular.

Call or write the Jellyroll office for complete details on advertising in the upcoming Osborne guides. We'll do for you what we've done for hundreds of others! Also, take a close look at the ads in this edition. We think there's something for everyone. Also, when responding, tell them you saw their ad in Osborne's "DANCE BANDS & BIG BANDS."

Thank you!

AAAA 78 COLLECTOR'S PARADISE! Early 78s OUR SPECIALTY! Get our FREE auction catalogs! We publish: (1)Big Bands/Jazz (2)Personalties/Shows (3)Classical. RARE RECORDS II, 3345 Adams, San Diego, CA 92116.

AARONSON TO ZURKE, All the Bands on PERFECT, BANNER, BRUNSWICK, DOMINO, VICTOR, Edison DDs, HOWs. Early LPs, Send specific wants. Search Service Since 1958. RALPH SIM, 64 RIVERVIEW, CLIFTON PARK, NJ 12065.

ABOUT 135,000 CHOICE RECORDS. All speeds, all styles, VG† to mint. 1900-1980s, books, sheet music, films, etc. LOTS OF BIG BAND from 1918-1970s (Golden era to revival). 24 years collecting. Many oddities! Buy-Sell. Send for lists. Glenn Howard's Musician's Reference Library, P.O. Box 66550, Santa Cruz, CA 95066, 408-335-4356.

BAGATELLE RECORDS BUYS AND SELLS DANCE BANDS & BIG BANDS as well as all other categories of music on 45rpm & 33rpm. Store Hours are 11 to 5:30 Monday thru Saturday. Phone (213)-432-7534. BAGATELLE RECORDS, 140 E. Third Street, Long Beach, CA 90802.

BIG BAND, SWING, JAZZ, BLUES, COUNTRY, ETC. 78s, LPs, 45s from early 1900s on. Old sheet music. Visa/Mastercard. Want lists welcome. CAMPBELL'S RECORDS-CASSETTES, N. 4620 Wall St., Spokane, WA 99205.

BIG BANDS, VOCALIST WITH BIG BANDS, COUNTRY, GOSPEL 1930s-1950s. Many transcriptions! 45s, 78s, LPs. Custom taping, sales. We have your favorite artists & songs. Boyd Robeson, 2425 W. Maple St., Wichita, KS 67213, 316-722- 7765.

BOB'S CUSTOM TAPING SERVICE: Personalized custom cassette taping. 1000s of oldies, most types of music SEND WANT LIST. Write or call for info. 615-352-4667. ROBERT PICKLE, 721 Georgetown Drive., Nashville, TN 37205.

BOXCAR BILL, TEXAS' PREMIER RECORD COLLECTOR since 1935. 1,000,000 records and growing. All kinds of music. Send your lists and best offer. The Record Junction, 9717 Chatfield, Houston, TX 77025, (713) 665-8589.

BRENINGER'S AUDIO ARCHIVES, Box 3052, Grass Valley, CA 95945, (916) 273- 2203. Please send lists. Collect, trade, sell: Radio pgms; personality; documentary audio; cylinder records. 78s: Big Bands, jazz, cowboy, C&W, R&B, BG, R&R.

BRINGIN' BACK THE GOOD TIMES. Oldies DJ with extensive collection specializing in 50s & 60s Rhythm & Blues and Rock & Roll. I'll make your reunion/wedding-/party one you'll remember! Mark Oldies, P.O. Box 729, Santa Rosa, CA 95402, (707) 579-4000.

BUY/SELL/TRADE ALL TYPES OF RECORD & SHEET MUSIC, from before the turn of the century to present. MUSICALLY YOURS, Dick & Jean Tillinghast, 301 S Peru, Walnut, IL 61376. (815) 379-2075.

BUY AND SELL out of print long playing records of all kinds of music. Special information will be sent to those who request it. E.P. Ross, 919 Crosby Street, Savannah, GA 31401.

CLASSICAL RECORD ALBUM COLLECTION. In original boxes and covers. Many are complete operas from the 40s and 50s. Near mint condition. Lee Webster, 5744 Gulf Freeway, Houston, TX 77023, (713) 489-8213.

FLORIDA'S LARGEST SELECTION, Jazz - Big Band - Instrumental - Soundtracks - Original Cast - LPs & 45s. Bananas Records & Tapes, 7210 Central Ave., St. Petersburg, FL 33707, (813) 343-4013. Free search service for any LPs not in stock. We will keep your wants on file until found.

GREAT OLD RECORDS on cassette (Annette Hanshaw, Ted Weems, Hit-of-the- Week, etc.). Just $3.98 each. Send for complete listing. VRCO, Dept. DB, Box 356, St. Johnsbury, VT 05819.

HI! I'VE BEEN BUYING & SELLING COLLECTIBLE RECORDS since 1971. I specialize in R&B and R&R from the 1950s. Write me if you're buying or selling music of this type. Victor Pearlin, Box 199, Greendale Sta., Worcester, MA 01606.

I JUST MIGHT HAVE WHAT YOU'RE LOOKING FOR! Pop, Easy Listening, Big Bands, Jazz, Rock, etc. Want lists welcome. Send SASE. P.D. Hamlin, Box 18443, Reno, NV 89511.

JIVE 78s WANTED! R&B vocal group and small combos circa 1930-52. Top $ for obscure labels & rarities. L.J. Bertelsen, 2210 W. 34th St., San Pedro, CA 90732.

MEMORY LANE. Out-of-print records. 1940 E. University Drive, Tempe, AZ 85281. (602) 968-1512. Tuesday-Wednesday-Saturday (9:00am-6:00pm, Thursday-Friday 11:00am-8:00pm. All catagories of music. Write or call today!

ORIGINAL 78s - BIG BANDS AND BACK. Periodic auctions include bands, novelty, vocals, C&W, one-sided, classical, etc. Send for next list. M. Bryan, 37 Caledonia Street, St. Johnsbury, VT 05819.

RECORDS AND TAPES FOR SALE - Big Bands, Jazz, Personalities, Old Time Radio, C&W. Large tape catalog $3.00. LP catalog $1.00. Seeking transcriptions. Trades considered. NOSTALGIA--JP, Box 82, Redmond, WA 98073- 0082.

REMEMBER BIG-BANDS ON RADIO??? Sample 60-minute audio cassette, plus listings of original music, comedy, drama broadcasts available on cassettes: $5.95. AMERICAN RADIO CASSETTE, Drawer Z, Scottsdale, AZ 85252.

THE VINYL EXCHANGE - Canada's record collectors magazine published monthly. Sample copy $2.00 including postage. U.S. subscription $16.00/year. Unit space ads $20.00 each. Send cheque or money order to #1-12424 118 avenue, edmonton, alberta, canada, T5L 2K4 1,000s OF RARE AND OUT OF PRINT LPs from the 50s, 60s & 70s. Rock, Jazz, Blues, Soul, Country, Soundtracks & Personality. Send specific Wants. Ken Stone, Box 09681, Columbus, OH 43209.

YESTERDAY'S RECORDS, BUY/SELL/TRADE 78s, Big Band, C&W, Jazz & Oldies. Want Lists-Auction-Custom Tapes. P.O. Box 32936, Phoenix, AZ 85064, (602) 279-2642.

Post Office Box 1047, Glen Allen, VA, 23060
(804) 353-0353

Cadence

SPECIAL "DANCE BAND & BIG BAND" PRICE GUIDE PRE-PUBLICATION OFFER!

Order our forthcoming "Big Band" price guide along with any combination of our other new books ("Country Music" & "Elvis - A 30-Year Chronicle") to make a minimum order of just 10 books. . . and take a full 45% discount off the cover price. Mix or match!

ROCKIN' RECORDS
BUYERS-SELLERS REFERENCE BOOK AND PRICE GUIDE

Covering the Entire History of Rock & Roll and Rhythm & Blues Records, from the 1940's ... a Music Lover's Dream Guidebook!

NOW BEING PRINTED!
Call or write us for details ...

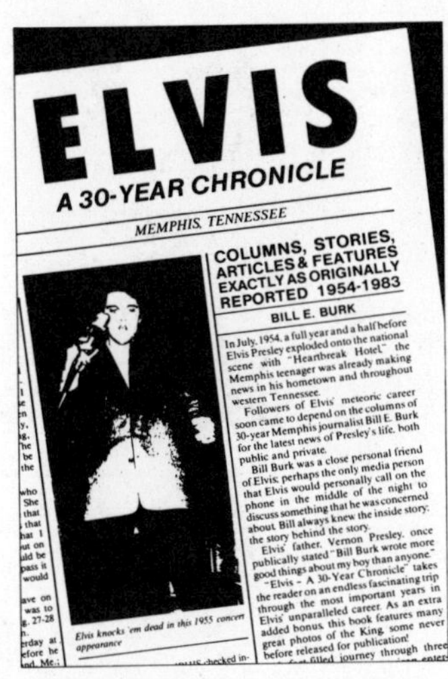

"ELVIS - A 30-YEAR CHRONICLE"
Columns, articles, stories & features exactly as originally reported 1954-1983.

30 years of Elvis history unfolds in this exciting new book that reprints each and every Elvis story from his hometown Memphis newspaper. A deluxe hardbound edition with over 400 pages. Includes several previously unpublished photos of Presley.

NOW AVAILABLE! $14.95

"COUNTRY MUSIC - Buyers/Sellers Reference Book & Price Guide"

From the very first known LPs of the forties to those of the eighties, this huge volume documents and prices nearly 15,000 albums and extended plays. Includes listings by over 4500 artists. 340 pages with over 230 photographs.

NOW AVAILABLE! $14.95

Jellyroll Productions - Box 24092 - Tempe, AZ - (602) 437-3461